Lutheran Churches in the World

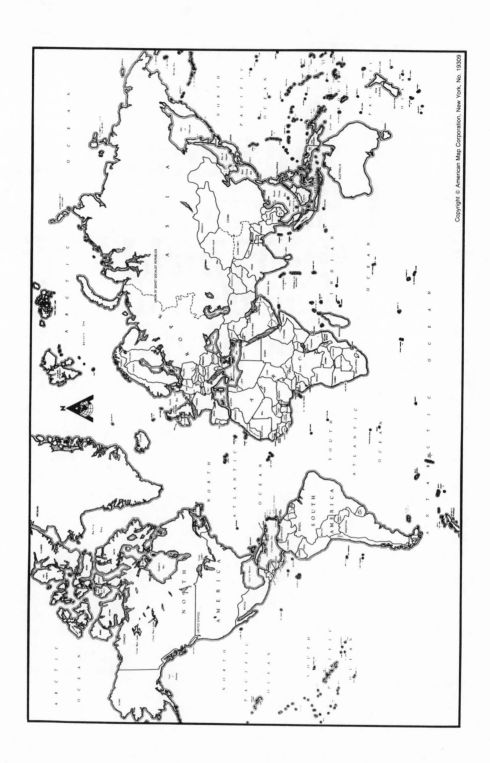

Lutheran Churches in the World

A Handbook

E. Theodore Bachmann and Mercia Brenne Bachmann

Foreword by Gunnar Staalsett

Published in cooperation with
the Lutheran World Federation

Augsburg * Minneapolis

LUTHERAN CHURCHES IN THE WORLD
A Handbook

Map production: Kim Pickering

Library of Congress Cataloging-in-Publication Data

Bachmann, E. Theodore (Ernest Theodore)
    Lutheran churches in the world: a handbook / E. Theodore Bachmann
and Mercia Brenne Bachmann.
      p.   cm.
    Bibliography: p.
    Includes indexes.
    ISBN 0-8066-2371-3
    1. Lutheran Church—History.   2. Lutheran Church—Directories.
I. Bachmann, Mercia Brenne. II. Title.
BX8018.B33   1989
284.1'09—dc19   89-31064
                                                            CIP

Manufactured in the U.S.A.   AF 10-4157

1   2   3   4   5   6   7   8   9   0   1   2   3   4   5   6   7   8   9

CONTENTS_____

GENERAL CONTENTS_____

BIBLE LANDS AND NEIGHBORING COUNTRIES (MIDDLE EAST)   267

GERMANY   336

NORTHERN EUROPE   394

ABBREVIATIONS _____

ECUMENICAL AND LUTHERAN ORGANIZATIONS ON NATIONAL, REGIONAL, OR WORLD LEVELS

AACC	All Africa Conference of Churches
ACKBD	Arbeitsgemeinschaft Christlicher Kirchen in der Bundesrepublik Deutschland und Berlin-West (Association of Christian Churches in the Federal Republic of Germany and West Berlin)
ACK/DDR	Arbeitsgemeinschaft Christlicher Kirchen in der Deutschen Demokratischen Republik (Association of Christian Churches in the German Democratic Republic)
ACKS	Arbeitsgemeinschaft Christlicher Kirchen in der Schweiz (Association of Christian Churches in Switzerland)
AFEC	Argentine Federation of Evangelical Churches (Federación Argentina de Iglesias Evangélicas)
ALC	American Lutheran Church (now part of ELCA)
AK	Arnholdshainer Konferenz (Arnoldshain Conference)
ANDEB	Asociación Nacional de Evangélicos de Bolivia (National Association of Evangelicals of Bolivia)
ANELF	Alliance nationale des églises luthériennes de France (National Alliance of the Lutheran Churches in France)
BCC	Botswana Christian Council
BCC	British Council of Churches
BCC	Burma Council of Churches
BEK/DDR	Bund der Evangelischen Kirchen in der Deutschen Demokratischen Republik (Federation of Evangelical Churches in the German Democratic Republic)
CAN	Christian Association of Nigeria
CCA	Christian Conference of Asia
CCAT	Christian Churches' Association, Taiwan

CCC	Caribbean Conference of Churches
CCEP	Comisión Coordinadora Evangélica de Paraguay (Evangelical Co-ordinating Committee of Paraguay)
CCG	Christian Council of Ghana
CCI	Communion of Churches in Indonesia
CCM	Christian Council of Madagascar
CCM	Christian Council of Malawi
CCM	Council of Churches of Malaysia
CCN	Council of Churches in Namibia
CCN	Council of Churches in the Netherlands (Rad von Kerken in Nederland)
CCN	Christian Council of Nigeria
CCT	Christian Council of Tanzania
CCT	Christian Council of Togo
CCZ	Christian Council of Zambia
CCZ	Christian Council of Zimbabwe
CDS	Community Development Service (of the LWF)
CEB	Confederação Evangélica do Brasil (Evangelical Confederation of Brazil)
CEC	Conference of European Churches
CEDEC	Confederación Evangélica de Colombia (Evangelical Confederation of Colombia)
CEE	Confraternidad Evangélica Ecuatoriana (Ecuador Evangelical Fellowship)
CECH	Concilio Evangélico de Chile (Evangelical Council of Chile)
CECN	Council of Evangelical Churches in Norway
CELFC	Conference of European Lutheran Free Churches
CILCE	Conference of Independent Lutheran Churches in Europe
CILCH	Consejo de las Iglesias Luteranas en Chile (Council of Lutheran Churches in Chile)
CLAI	Consejo Latinoamericano de Iglesias (Latin American Council of Churches)
CLCAT	Chinese Lutheran Churches' Association in Taiwan
CLCHKA	Chinese Lutheran Churches' Hong Kong Association
CONCAP	Consejo de Iglesias Luteranas en Centro América y Panamá (Council of Lutheran Churches in Central America and Panama)
CONIC	Conselho Nacional de Igrejas Cristãs do Brasil (National Council of Christian Churches in Brazil)
CPC	Christian Peace Conference
CSC	Council of Swaziland Churches
DCC	Department of Church Cooperation (of the LWF)
DOC	Department of Communication (of the LWF)
DS	Department of Studies (of the LWF)
ECCA	Ecumenical Council of Churches in Austria (Ökumenischer Rat der Kirchen in Österreich)

ECCC	Ecumenical Council of Churches in Czechoslovakia
ECCH	Ecumenical Council of Churches in Hungary
ECCY	Ecumenical Council of Churches in Yugoslavia
ECD	Ecumenical Council of Denmark (Okumeniske Faellesrad i Danmark)
ECF	Ecumenical Council of Finland (Suomen Ekumeeninen Neuvosto)
ECP	Evangelical Council of Peru (Concilio Evangélico del Perú)
EFM	Evangelical Fellowship of Malawi
EFT	Evangelical Fellowship in Thailand
ELCA	Evangelical Lutheran Church in America
EKD	Evangelische Kirche in Deutschland (Evangelical Church in Germany)
EKU	Evangelische Kirche der Union Bereich Bundesrepublik Deutschland und Berlin-West (Evangelical Church of the Union in the Federal Republic of Germany and West Berlin)
EKU/DDR	Evangelische Kirche der Union im Bereich der Deutschen Demokratischen Republik (Evangelical Church of the Union in the German Democratic Republic)
ELC	European Lutheran Conference
FCCN	Fellowship of Christian Churches in Nigeria
FEET	Fédération des Eglises Evangéliques du Tchad (Federation of Evangelical Churches of Chad)
FELCMS	Federation of Evangelical Lutheran Churches in Malaysia and Singapore
FELCSA	Federation of Evangelical Lutheran Churches in Southern Africa
FEM	Federación Evangélica de México (Evangelical Federation of Mexico)
FEMEC	Fédération des Eglises et Missions Evangéliques du Cameroun (Federation of Evangelical Churches and Missions of Cameroon)
FIEL	Federación de Iglesias Evangélicas Luteranas del Ecuador (Federation of Evangelical Lutheran Churches in Ecuador)
FIEU	Federación de Iglesias Evangélicas del Uruguay (Federation of Evangelical Churches of Uruguay)
FPCI	Federation of Protestant Churches in Italy (Federazione delle Chiese Evangeliche in Italia)
FSPC	Federation of Swiss Protestant Churches
GCC	Guyana Council of Churches
HKCC	Hong Kong Christian Council
ICC	Irish Council of Churches
ILC	International Lutheran Conference
ILLL	International Lutheran Layman's League
KCLA	Korea Christian Leaders' Association
LCA	Lutheran Church in America (now part of ELCA)

LCC	Liberian Council of Churches
LCIC	Lutheran Council in Canada
LCGB	Lutheran Council of Great Britain
LCMS	Lutheran Church–Missouri Synod
LCRP	Lutheran Council of the River Plate
LCUSA	Lutheran Council in the USA
LFC/GB	Lutheran Free Conference of Great Britain
LWF	Lutheran World Federation
LWM	Lutheran World Ministries (USA)
MCC	Melanesian Council of Churches
MECC	Middle East Council of Churches
MELM	Middle East Lutheran Ministry
NCCC/USA	National Council of Churches of Christ in the USA
NCCI	National Christian Council of India
NCCJ	National Christian Council of Japan
NCCK	National Christian Council of Kenya
NCCNZ	National Council of Churches in New Zealand
NCCP	National Council of Churches in the Philippines
NCCS	National Council of Churches of Singapore
NCCSL	National Christian Council of Sri Lanka
NCFB	National Christian Fellowship of Bangladesh
PEC	Polish Ecumenical Council
PCCC	Portuguese Council of Christian Churches (Conselho Português de Igrejas Cristás)
PCFM	Protestant Church Federation of Madagascar
PFF	Protestant Federation of France (Fédération protestante de France)
RBBRD	Reformierter Bund in der Bundesrepublik Deutschland (Reformed Alliance in the Federal Republic of Germany)
SACC	South African Council of Churches
SCC	Sudan Council of Churches
SCCC	Suriname Christian Council of Churches
SEC	Swedish Ecumenical Council
TEE	Theological Education by Extension
UCCI	United Christian Council in Israel
UELCI	United Evangelical Lutheran Churches in India
UELCSA	United Evangelical Lutheran Church in Southern Africa
UELCSWA	United Evangelical Lutheran Church in South-West Africa
UNELAM	Unidad Evangélica Latino Americana (Movement of Evangelical Unity in Latin America)
VELKD	Vereinigte Evangelisch-Lutherische Kirche Deutschlands (United Evangelical Lutheran Church of Germany)

VELK/DDR	Vereinigte Evangelisch-Lutherische Kirche in der Deutschen Demokratischen Republik (United Evangelical Lutheran Church in the German Democratic Republic)
WARC	World Alliance of Reformed Churches
WCC	World Council of Churches
WS	Department of World Service (of the LWF)

• • •

Boldface titles normally indicate church organizations used by Lutherans in countries without a Lutheran church.

An asterisk (*) normally indicates a country, church body, or subject which may be consulted for further reference in this volume.
When a double asterisk (**) occurs after the membership figure of a given church body it denotes non-current data (1988).

(AM) denotes an associate member of the LWF.
(P) indicates a permanent relationship to the LWF, though not a full member.
(R) indicates an LWF recognized congregation.

FOREWORD

Thank God, a seven-year-old child knows what the church is, namely, holy believers and sheep who hear the voice of their Shepherd. So children pray, "I believe in one holy Christian church." Its holiness does not consist of surplices, tonsures, albs, or other ceremonies . . . but it consists of the Word of God and true faith (Martin Luther, The Smalcald Articles, 1537).

The task of discerning "what the church is" is an unending one. It has baffled theologians, caused divisions in the visible structures, and spawned disquiet among faithful believers. Yet, as the seven-year-old child to whom Luther alluded knows, the church is found wherever there is faith based on God's gracious promises.

Lutheran Churches in the World, by Theodore and Mercia Bachmann, is a significant contribution to this unending task of discovering the church. The present volume, a completely new version of the first edition which appeared in 1977, is to be welcomed as a major contribution to our understanding of the church in the world today.

The book stands first as a resource for laity and scholars alike who are eager to know the identity, scope, and character of the many churches throughout the world that adhere to the Lutheran confessions. By clear organization and by a lucid presentation of relevant facts the contours of those churches can now be readily traced in an up-to-date and accurate way.

The volume, moreover, stands as a narrative, a part of the total saga of the life of Christian churches in the world today. The Lutheran churches have their roots in apostolic times, but their particular histories stem from the Reformation of the 16th century. How those stories developed and now face the start of the 21st century is itself a part of the drama of faith in the world. To see how these churches, in weakness and in strength, have faced questions of doctrine, opportunities for global missionary expansion, and challenges of technological, economic, political, and cultural change is to encounter one of the richest elements in the human heritage.

Above all, however, **Lutheran Churches in the World** stands as a testimony to the reality of the communion that holds the people of Christ together in the world. It is no mere coincidence that this volume appears at a time when the Lutheran Federation, a Federation that now numbers 105 member churches throughout the world, is increasingly understanding itself as a communion of churches. A crucial statement adopted by the Federation at its Seventh Assembly in Budapest, 1984, declares:

This Lutheran communion of churches finds its visible expression in pulpit and altar fellowship, in common witness and service, in the joint fulfillment of the missionary task, and in openness to ecumenical cooperation, dialog, and community. The Lutheran churches of the world consider their communion as an expression of the one, holy, catholic, and apostolic church. Thus, they are committed to work for the manifestation of the unity of the church given in Jesus Christ (Statement on the Self-Understanding and Task of the Lutheran World Federation).

The story of much of the life of this communion is found in the pages of this book: fellowship in doctrine and worship, commitment to mission and service, and dedication to move beyond itself to the fullest possible expression of the unity of the whole church of Jesus Christ. This is above all the story of people—women, men, and youth of all races and cultures—who strive to live lives of true faith in obedience to the gracious promises of God. In, with, and behind this story is to be found "what the church is."

GUNNAR STAALSETT
General Secretary

The Lutheran World Federation
Geneva, Switzerland
Easter 1989

PREFACE

The purpose of this second edition of *Lutheran Churches in the World,* like the first (1977), is to foster acquaintance and mutual concern among members of a Christian world communion—and beyond it as well. This aim is further spelled out in the following introduction. But here some added words of explanation as well as the thanks of the authors are in order.

How this book is put together throws light on its purpose. Geography, as an organizing principle, provides the pattern: continents (or regions) and countries are the context of the churches. Like the countries within a region, the churches within a country appear in alphabetical order.

Introductions to continents, regions, and countries include a select amount of basic data and a description of the religious situation in order to locate the Lutheran church or churches in context.

References to specific sources are generally omitted in order to conserve space. Here, however, we hasten to acknowledge our debt to such invaluable works as the *Britannica Book of the Year,* the *New Columbia Encyclopedia,* the *Rand McNally International Atlas,* and particularly the *World Christian Encyclopedia* (Oxford, 1982), edited by David B. Barrett. Other titles are listed in the bibliography at the end of this book.

As agreed for the first edition, a church's account begins with the present before turning to its historical background. This treatment, especially preferred by African and Asian representatives, intends to assert the contemporary partnership of churches young and old. Each church has had the opportunity to check the accuracy of the story we have written of it. Some reviewers have requested that controversial subjects be eliminated, usually on grounds that a wider knowledge of trials or weaknesses would not improve the situation. But the fact remains that in many places churches are having a hard time and are living in Christian hope as well as counting on the concern of partners in the faith.

How to use this book

The table of contents and the indexes provide ready access to a given continent, country, or church. A list of abbreviations spells out the titles of ecumenical and Lutheran organizations on national, regional, or world levels. A short bibliography suggests sources for further reference or reading.

Although many parts of the text have been repeatedly updated, delays have been unavoidable. This book thus reflects the general situation prevailing in the mid-1980s.

The following general introduction supplies a broad overview as well as a brief accounting for how a communion of churches like the Lutheran World Federation (LWF) came about.

May the use of this book open the eyes of its users, as it has opened those of its authors, to marvel at the presence and extent of a worldwide confessional family, and to give thanks. Worldwideness, to be sure, is not a mark of the church. But it is evidence of faithfulness on a grand scale by countless men, women, and children in the still vaster company of God's pilgrim people. Nor should our eyes be blind to the many opportunities lost, or to the struggle and decline continuing in many quarters.

At its best, the LWF exists not for itself but for others, as led by the Spirit of the living God. Toward that end, may this book also prove useful as a guide in the practice of personal and corporate intercession. Two of the Federation's stated functions are:

—To further a united witness before the world to the gospel of Jesus Christ as the power of God for salvation.

—To support Lutheran churches and groups as they endeavor to extend the gospel and carry out the mission given to the church.

● ● ●

Lutheran Churches in the World, first edition, appeared in time for the Sixth Assembly of the LWF (1977) in Dar es Salaam, Tanzania. There it was welcomed as a means of introducing participants to each other's churches, a function it has continued to perform in many places. The first edition was written while one of the present authors was editor of the LWF quarterly *Lutheran World* and its German counterpart *Lutherische Rundschau;* it was published as a 240-page double number of the English edition of that journal, and of the German as well. Much of the research was volunteered by his wife, Mercia, later author and editor of the *Lutheran Mission Directory* (1982, published by the LWF Department of Church Cooperation).

Ecumenically, the first edition may also have had some influence on two subsequent publications of the World Council of Churches: indirectly, on the globe-girdling intercessory volume, *For All God's People: Ecumenical Prayer Cycle* (Geneva, 1978), and more directly on the WCC *Handbook of Member Churches* (1982).

All the greater is the gratitude we, as joint authors, would here express to the Lutheran World Federation for inviting us to undertake this second edition. It has been updated, enlarged, and completely rewritten over the past five years. Our thanks go to the LWF Department of Communication: to its successive directors, Marc Chambron and Norman A. Hjelm, and particularly to Frances Maher and her associates not only for the processing but especially for the contacts with all the churches. Our awareness of input from other LWF staff and of responses from church representatives on every continent mingles collegial joy with our thanks. Nor would much of the contemporary aspect of the church profiles have been possible for us without the steady flow from the editors of *LW Information,* in its German as well as English editions; likewise, from *Asia Lutheran News* (now *Asia Lutheran Press Services*), the WCC *Ecumenical Press Service,* and many other current services as well.

As to the process by which the text was produced, particular recognition goes to Frances Maher, until 1988 staff member of the LWF Department of Communication. To her we sent our manuscript written in the university environs of Princeton,

New Jersey. She then sent carefully edited copies to the respective churches and agencies, soliciting their additions and/or corrections. She and her helpers then sent the word-processed text from Geneva to the USA—one copy to us as authors for final review, the other to the publisher in Minneapolis. The elapsed time proved far longer than anticipated.

We are also very grateful to church leaders, missionaries, and friends in the more than 50 countries who have at one time or another, over past decades, been helpful and hospitable on our journeys, individually or together. Our thanks, not least, go to the editorial staff of Augsburg Fortress, Minneapolis, for seeing this volume through the press. May our gratitude be known to the many others who cannot be specifically named here. But all are included in praise to God, who cares for all the churches and from whom all blessings flow.

E. THEODORE BACHMANN
MERCIA BRENNE BACHMANN

Princeton Junction, New Jersey
Pentecost 1988

THE LUTHERAN WORLD FEDERATION

Within the church universal are Christian world communions (sometimes called world confessional families) like the Lutheran as well as the Roman Catholic, Eastern Orthodox, Anglican, Reformed, Methodist, Baptist, and others. The Lutheran world family is the largest of the Reformation churches and claims approximately 59 million baptized members. Over 90% of this number are in the 105 churches now participating in the Lutheran World Federation (LWF). The prime requirement for membership in this communion is that a church accept the following doctrinal basis:

> The Lutheran World Federation acknowledges the Holy Scriptures of the Old and New Testaments as the only source and the infallible norm of all church doctrine and practice, and sees in the Ecumenical Creeds and in the Confession of the Lutheran Church, especially in the unaltered Augsburg Confession and Luther's Small Catechism, a pure exposition of the Word of God. (Constitution, II.)

This basis, adopted initially and in substantially the same form in 1923 at Eisenach by the Lutheran World Convention (the predecessor of the LWF), has proven acceptable to all but the most conservative Lutherans.

The common ground for Lutheran identity, in legal as well as theological terms, is the *Augsburg Confession* (1530). In contrast to the several nationally oriented Reformed confessions, the *Confessio Augustana* is the one authoritative confession of faith for Lutherans internationally and ecumenically. Equally accepted is Luther's *Small Catechism* (1529), the most widely used guide for Christian instruction among Lutherans in all continents. For these and other reasons, one can speak collectively of the Lutheran church and describe it as a confessional church that is both evangelical and catholic.

Born of struggle, the Lutheran movement reached many lands during the 16th century Reformation. Like Luther himself, the movement survived under political protection and, within the Holy Roman Empire, was guaranteed that right under the terms of the Religious Peace of Augsburg (1555), whereby the religion of the ruler (the territorial prince) determined the religion of his subjects. This laid the basis also for the later Lutheran state churches in Central Europe, as it did in Scandinavia. In Germany itself, the preface to the Book of Concord (1580), signed by the Lutheran rulers, concluded with the express intention "to cooperate with one another . . . in this effort at concord in our lands." This politically conditioned cooperation barely survived the Thirty Years' War (1618–1648) and continued as a Protestant caucus (Corpus Evangelicorum) in the imperial Diet until the dissolution of the Empire (1806).

Initiative for cooperation among Lutherans, meanwhile, sprang from foresighted and resourceful leaders like August Hermann Francke (1663–1727) and others at Halle in the early 1700s (see Germany, Denmark, India, United States). The pattern was thus set for individuals and mission societies in 19th-century Europe to support a twofold outreach: missionaries to people of other religions and pastors to emigrants (see, e.g., Australia, Papua New Guinea, Brazil). The most insistent pleas for pastors came from North America, the major magnet of the European migration. So, for example, in responding to the stirring *Appeal* (1841) of Friedrich C. D. Wyneken (1810–1876), on behalf of the spiritually neglected immigrants in America, an innovative pastor like Wilhelm Loehe (1808–1872) and others in Germany caught the vision of an eventually worldwide Lutheran church.

The larger the vision, the greater the diversity. The common ground of a Lutheran world family was often obscured by the diversity of its ever wider dispersion. Its ways of worship, treasury of hymns, styles of preaching, methods of teaching, modes of mission, forms of administration, sources of support, attitudes toward other believers, concern for justice, and manifold life-styles—these, and much more, flourished eventually in all six continents.

Added to this diversity was the array of languages and dialects used by this confessional family. For the future, as an American (Sigmund Fritschel, 1833–1900, Wartburg Seminary, Dubuque, Iowa) reminded church leaders in Leipzig in 1870, English would soon become a key language for Lutherans internationally. A solid beginning had already been made, and was proceeding in the face of much controversy and numerical loss.

More than a century later, the Lutheran family is regarded by some outside its immediate membership as the most tightly organized of the Christian world communions. Whether viewed as an asset or a liability, this has paralleled the rise of other communions as they have organized worldwide and, as the LWF demonstrates, this Lutheran development has become an inseparable part of the ecumenical movement. Yet the way this has happened is peculiar to Lutheranism and has been profoundly affected by the present century's two world wars. A backward glance is revealing.

• • •

The LWF is often called the youngest of the (organized) Christian world communions, having been constituted in Lund, Sweden, in 1947. But its antecedents go back to the era of the 1860s to 1880s when Anglicans, Reformed, and Methodists laid the basis for their own continuing worldwide associations. Comparable confessional concerns led to the formation of the General Council of the Evangelical Lutheran Church in North America (1867) and the General Evangelical Lutheran Conference (GELC) in Germany (1868). It was at the GELC's first major meeting, at Leipzig in 1870, that Professor Fritschel brought the council's salutations from America. Kindred interest kept the two associations in touch, including a common suspicion of confessional "unionism" as seen in the Evangelical Church of the Old Prussian Union and its alleged curtailment of Reformed as well as Lutheran identity. Scandinavian Lutherans, for other reasons, early showed interest in the GELC. The

General Conference met outside Germany for the first time in 1901, having accepted an invitation from the king of Sweden for a gathering in historic Lund.

Personal friendships strengthened the ties across the Atlantic, not only with Lutherans in Germany but also with those in Scandinavia. Knut H. G. von Scheele, bishop of Visby, and Adolph Spaeth, prominent pastor in Philadelphia, saw the Lund gathering as a stepping stone to meeting in America. However, strife within the GELC blocked an anticipated 1907 meeting in Philadelphia. Even so, the General Conference paved the way in Europe for Lutherans from state churches as well as from free churches and synods to meet on common ground. This was all the more important after World War I, when Germany's state churches became people's (or folk) churches following the revolution of 1918.

A defeated Germany and a liquidated Austro-Hungarian Empire plus a redrawn map of Central Europe shook up the old order also in the Lutheran churches. Responding to widespread need, also in Russia after the 1917 revolution, Swedish, Danish, and Norwegian Lutherans came to the rescue. Surprising even themselves, America's Lutherans reversed the time-honored westward flow from Europe with their unexpected quantities of help rushed eastward (see United States). The times called for a stronger international association than that represented by the German-based GELC. In concert with the GELC, the recently formed National Lutheran Council in America helped organize the Lutheran World Convention (LWC).

Meeting in Eisenach, August 19–24, 1923, the formation of the LWC was seen by the historically minded as the most important event in the Lutheran church since the Reformation. The story of the LWC has been ably researched and published from Swedish, German, and American perspectives. It must not detain us here, other than to note that at Eisenach the conviction became firm that Lutherans of all lands needed to stay together, rendering mutual assistance in matters of theology and education as well as material relief and the resettlement of refugees—like those last ones brought from Harbin, Manchuria, to Brazil (1932) on a daring venture arranged by the LWC's first president, John A. Morehead. The Convention's assemblies in Copenhagen (1929) and Paris (1935) were to have been followed by one in Philadelphia (1941). But again the world was at war, and the three sections of the LWC—German, Scandinavian, American—barely survived. However, after World War II, despite scenes of unparalleled destruction and unspeakable suffering, the basis was laid for a still better structured confessional association, the LWF.

● ● ●

At this point it is necessary to emphasize the ecclesiological and ecumenical transition through which a confessionally committed Lutheran theology passed during the critical years, roughly 1936 to 1946, prior to the formation of the LWF.

In light of the advancing ecumenical movement and the impending world conferences less than a year away, the LWC Executive Committee in 1936 set forth its own policy statement on "Lutherans and Ecumenical Movements." This reaffirmed the "ecumenical character of Lutheranism," as set forth earlier by Saxony's Bishop Ludwig Ihmels at Eisenach (1923), meaning that Lutheran faithfulness to the gospel has significance for the unity of the church of Jesus Christ as a whole, and that true ecumenism means commitment by all communions to the understanding that the true unity of the church is God-given and not a human achievement.

The National Socialist government did not give delegates from Germany permission to attend either Oxford (Life and Work) or Edinburgh (Faith and Order), both in the summer of 1937. But Swedish Lutheran theologians, particularly Yngve Brilioth, Gustav Aulén, and Anders Nygren, made notable contributions. The Nygren-led report on the grace of our Lord Jesus Christ (Section I) was the only one adopted unanimously at Edinburgh.

At the first meeting of the Provisional Committee of the World Council of Churches (WCC) in-process-of-formation (Utrecht 1938), the proposal for proportional confessional, rather than simply national, representation in the WCC assembly and Central Committee was put aside. Frederick H. Knubel (1870-1945), president of the United Lutheran Church in America, had made the proposal not only in light of restrictions that could be imposed by totalitarian governments like Hitler's but also in view of the block of seats already reserved for the Eastern Orthodox churches pending their joining the WCC.

The outbreak of World War II and the ensuing events, also involving the care of "orphaned missions" cut off from their supporting societies in Europe, underscored once again the affirmation of Lutheran ecumenism, as already set forth (1936). In their relations with other churches, according to LWC policy, Lutheran churches of the world were urged "to maintain existing unities among those who hold the Lutheran interpretation of the Christian faith and not to jeopardize the solidarity of ecumenical Lutheranism" ("Lutherans and Ecumenical Movements," LWC Executive Committee, New York, 1936. *Lutheran World Almanac 1934–1937,* pp. 35-38).

Only in June 1946 could this solidarity be reaffirmed. In Uppsala, Scandinavian representatives joined with their American LWC counterparts in support of the request for Lutheran confessional representation in the WCC. In effect, this corroborated developments already under way that related world Lutheranism inextricably to the wider ecumenical movement.

Already in July 1945, Geneva had become the focal point of postwar relief and reconstruction activities under WCC and LWC auspices. Earlier, while the war was still on, the director of the National Lutheran Council (USA), Dr. Ralph H. Long, and others had surveyed the European scene and fixed on Geneva. Two American Lutherans and their spouses began their first terms of service in mid-July: Dr. Sylvester C. Michelfelder (1889–1951), as Special Commissioner of the LWC American Section, and Dr. Stewart W. Herman Jr., as associate director of the WCC Department of Reconstruction and Interchurch Aid.

In the wake of war, self-help in many countries was under way, supplemented increasingly with help from abroad. Nowhere was this more extensively or better organized than in Germany and its Evangelisches Hilfswerk. The Evangelical Church in Germany (EKD) was new, too.

Prerequisite to international and ecumenical assistance across former enemy lines was some tangible sign of reconciliation. Michelfelder's letter (July 27, 1945), "A Message to the Churches of Germany," was the first early word of reconciliation.

In October, he and Stewart Herman were part of a nine-member ecumenical delegation of European and American church leaders under the irenic George K.A. Bell (1881–1958), Anglican bishop of Chichester, and the WCC general secretary, Willem A. Visser't Hooft (1900–1985). The delegation's meeting with the 12-member Council of the Evangelical Church in Germany (EKD) was climaxed by the latter's declaration of guilt. The "Stuttgart Declaration," though challenged by some in Germany itself, opened the way for a resumption of Christian partnership with the churches outside Germany. Years later, Visser't Hooft claimed that without this meeting in Stuttgart, with its confession of guilt and its reconciliation, the first assembly of the World Council of Churches at Amsterdam (1948) would have come much later. The same might have been true for the first assembly of the LWF (1947).

Personal relationships on many sides played roles. One of the most significant, for the long run, was that between Franklin Clark Fry (1900–1968), new (1945) president of the United Lutheran Church in America and the WCC general secretary. As Knubel's successor, Fry explained the concern of the Lutherans in America for the ecumenical movement and their expressed desire that confessional representation become part of WCC policy. Visser't Hooft was open to this challenge to the WCC's ecclesiology. Bearing in mind (as noted above) that Scandinavian and German churches soon joined in this consensus, it meant that the interplay between an incipient LWF and an active yet still officially unborn WCC could prove mutually beneficial. Looking ahead, this seems borne out by the fact that Dr. Fry served three terms on the WCC Central Committee, the first as vice-chair under the bishop of Chichester, the last two (until his death in 1968) as chair (moderator).

A constitution for the LWF was drafted and provisionally approved in the summer of 1946. The work largely of Abdel Ross Wentz, president of Gettysburg Theological Seminary (USA), it grew out of a draft done a decade earlier, much of it the work of Dr. Hanns Lilje (1899–1977), then general secretary of the LWC.

In Geneva and elsewhere, preparations for the first assembly of the LWF laid additional burdens on Michelfelder and his small staff, full as their schedule was with the work of relief, reconstruction, and the resettlement of refugees. Assistance for such help came from many sources and lands. Among the most notable were Sweden's Lutherhjälpen, America's Lutheran World Action, Lutheran World Relief, and others.

• • •

The assembly of the Lutheran World Federation, the first major international church gathering after the war, convened in Lund, June 30 to July 6, 1947. There the Lutheran World Convention officially ended, even as it had supplied the basis for an impressive and extensive unfolding of desperately needed service. By unanimous vote, the proposed constitution was adopted. "At 12:25 after noon on July 1, 1947 . . . 'The Lutheran World Federation' came into official existence," reported Michelfelder with satisfaction.

Today, over four decades later, the history of the LWF still remains to be written. More so even than that of its predecessor agency, the LWF story not only covers the worldwide dispersion of Lutheran churches, as described in this book, but also the ecumenical involvement of most of these churches in the WCC and other aspects of the ever-widening ecumenical movement.

Several historical as well as current observations on the LWF follow:

Why, it is still asked, does the LWF continue to exist? Coming often from other communions (especially in Asia and Africa), or from those who see ecumenical concerns as foremost, the question is legitimate. Yet the LWF sees a working partnership among Lutheran churches as being essentially within the ecumenical movement and, by drawing upon historic confessional forces, a strengthening of that movement. A familiar fourfold reply as to *why* a Lutheran World Federation is this: The member churches desire it; small churches and minority groups are more readily heard in it than in a bigger context; a common spiritual heritage and extensive experience enable swift action; and bilateral dialog with Roman Catholic, Anglican, Orthodox, Reformed, and other Christian world communions advances the concern for unity within a catholic and evangelical context.

When the LWF observed its 40th anniversary in Lund (July 4–5, 1987), there were some present who recalled the Federation's first assembly in the old romanesque cathedral church of St. Lawrence and in the University halls. In the wake of global war and assessing what had survived, the theme of that initial assembly summed up the agenda: "The Lutheran Church in the World Today." The 174 delegates, from churches in 23 countries, plus 320 "visitors," including staff and many special representatives, felt the charge of expectation. Worship was the starting point, and Holy Communion served as an act of repentance and reconciliation. Former enemy lines went into eclipse. The power of God's Spiritus Creator brought renewal and a reaffirmation of durable fellowship in Christ. The tasks at hand focused on Europe and the protracted plight of its uprooted millions. But the lines of imperative action led further: to Africa, Asia, Australasia, and Latin America, as well as to North America, the source of much immediate material aid. And Sweden itself was such a source, also.

In this way, the resettlement of Baltic displaced persons and other refugees into many other parts of the world (see Exile Churches) accentuated the human dimension—a costly one—of the new global interdependence. Lund shaped the pattern and set the pace. The Federation was gifted with strong leadership, dedicated staff, and increasing support. Vision and resourcefulness as well as tireless interpretation were high priorities. Cooperation was the order of the day, coupled with mutual trust; little was routine.

Successive assemblies have met in various parts of the world. Their christocentric themes have been elaborated and their actions world-related. Federation presidents have normally come from the host country of an assembly, but there have been exceptions. The president as well as the members of the Executive Committee are elected by the assembly. The Executive Committee elects the general secretary. Biographical profiles of LWF presidents and general secretaries appear at the end of the book. Organizational highlights fill the following table:

LWF Assemblies, Themes, Leaders

Assembly	President	General Secretary
1947 Lund, Sweden "The Lutheran Church in the World Today"	Erling Eidem (Sweden) Chairman 1945–1947 Anders Nygren (Sweden) 1947–1952	Sylvester C. Michelfelder (USA) 1945–1947, 1947–1951 (dec.)

1952 Hanover, FRG "The Living Word in a Responsible Church" — Hanns Lilje (FRG) 1952–1957 — Carl E. Lund-Quist (USA) 1951-1960

1957 Minneapolis, USA "Christ Frees and Unites" — Franklin Clark Fry (USA) 1957–1963 — Kurt Schmidt-Clausen (FRG) 1960–1965

1963 Helsinki, Finland "Christ Today" — Fredrik A. Schiotz (USA) 1963–1970 — Andre Appel (France) 1965-1974

1970 Evian-les-Bains, France "Sent into the World" — Mikko Juva (Finland) 1970–1977 — Carl H. Mau (USA) 1974–1985

1977 Dar es Salaam, Tanzania "In Christ—A New Community" — Josiah Kibira (Tanzania) 1977–1984

1984 Budapest, Hungary "In Christ—Hope for the World" — Zoltán Káldy (Hungary) 1984–1987 (dec.) — Gunnar Staalsett (Norway) 1985

1987 Viborg, Denmark (Executive Committee) — Johannes Hanselmann (FRG) 1987

1990 Curitiba, Brazil "I have heard the cry of my people"

• • •

Participants in the assemblies have extended Federation horizons ever farther. Among the 174 delegates to the first assembly, only 8% came from the Two-Thirds World of Africa, Asia, and Latin America. Three decades later in Dar es Salaam, 38% of the 250 delegates were from churches in the Two-Thirds World. At the Budapest assembly the proportion was virtually unchanged. Yet among the 312 delegates in 1984, women accounted for 32%; compared with 2.2% in 1947. The assembly does not legislate but sets policy, even as the Federation is not a church but regards itself as a communion of churches.

The LWF Executive Committee's composition reflects this combination of changes. Of its 15 members in 1947, the count was: Europeans 10, North Americans 4, Asian 1. Of the 31 members in 1984, it was: Europeans 15, North Americans 5, Asia-Africa-Latin America 11. Meanwhile, the representation of women on the Executive Committee has jumped from none in 1947 to eight in 1984. Convened annually, the Executive Committee endeavors to meet in representative parts of the world, and on those occasions invites churches in the region to be represented by observers. The Executive Committee acts for the assembly during the normally seven-year interval, and reviews the work of the general secretariat and the several operational departments—Church Cooperation, Communication, Studies, and World Service—each of which is under its own commission. It is the general secretary's task, among others, to keep these and other units working together toward common ends and for the benefit of the member churches. In light of changing conditions, the LWF has periodically been restructured; first in the early 1950s, and most extensively in 1970. Further changes are expected by the 1990 assembly.

These observations on how the newer churches have been gaining representation raise the larger question of change in the global distribution of Lutherans during the 20th century (see Europe Introduction, also Germany). In the 1920s the world total of Lutherans was given at over 80 million. This figure included the estimated number of Lutherans in Germany's major United Church—the Old Prussian Union of the Reformed minority and a Lutheran majority. In 1986, this estimated Lutheran constituency was no longer included in the German reckoning, resulting in a sudden statistical drop of nearly 10 million. As described elsewhere in this book (Eastern Europe, the USSR, etc.), postwar and earlier developments—like the expulsion of ethnic Germans, mostly of Lutheran affiliation—had made drastic incursions which diminished the total figure by another 10 million or so. Meanwhile, the rapid growth of Lutheran-related churches in Africa, Asia, and Australasia as well as in Brazil and North America rearranged the older proportions. The following table makes comparison easy, though the percentages are necessarily approximate:

Region	c. 1928	c. 1986
Europe	91.1%	67.2%
North America	6.1%	15.1%
Africa-Asia Australasia Latin America	2.8%	17.7%

The new churches, members of the LWF, have come mainly from the Two-Thirds World. The LWF began with a charter membership of 49 church bodies. By 1988 the number had grown to 105. But, as noted elsewhere (Africa Introduction; Southern Africa), two of them, in an unprecedented action, were suspended in 1984. This subject will engage us again later. Here it is useful to bear in mind the larger ecclesial scene that unfolded during the decades after World War II, wherein some parallel developments are striking: former colonies become new nations; former mission fields become autonomous churches. How, it is asked, has this array of changes affected a world communion like the Lutheran?

• • •

The ecclesiology wrapped in these developments and others has kept the LWF concerned about its own identity. It started out cautiously, calling itself a "free association of Lutheran churches." But it soon demonstrated that it was also something more than a free association. What really is a "free association of Lutheran churches?" Doctrinally, church bodies holding the same confession and catechism collectively comprise the Lutheran church. Practically, this confessional identity has spread in at least two important ways: as a Lutheran movement within the church universal and as organized Lutheran church bodies. These two aspects of ecclesiology have had a bearing on the action and self-understanding of the LWF. Some examples are illuminating. The Federation early urged that missions and emerging churches in a given country, particularly in new nations, form a single Lutheran church (1947), as in Tanzania. Or, as in the case of the Lutheran movement among the Batak people in *Indonesia, the LWF received into membership (1952) an important church body, the Protestant Christian Batak Church (HKBP), whose constitution did not mention the Lutheran confessions by name but, having been nurtured from the outset on Luther's catechism, spelled out the substance of those confessions. Was the LWF here acting as a church or simply as a free association?

Again, the 1957 assembly adopted a memorable sequence of theses on the theme "Christ Frees and Unites." These pertained to the confessional substance and ecumenical involvement (or obligation) of the Lutheran churches, particularly in light of Article VII of the Augsburg Confession and its reference to what suffices for the true unity of Christ's church. The Federation's quarterly, *Lutheran World* and *Lutherische Rundschau* (1960, 1961), aired further discussions on the nature and ecclesiology of the LWF. The 1963 assembly was reminded that, whether or not there is a Lutheran world church, not all Lutheran churches were in fellowship (pulpit and altar) with each other. Only in 1984, at Budapest, did the assembly state that such fellowship exists among the LWF member churches. Yet church bodies outside the Federation saw the matter differently, believing that the LWF was hereby intervening in the right of Lutheran churches to determine the extent of their fellowship with others, and claiming churchly powers for itself.

A further development in the Federation's ecclesiology surfaced in 1970 with the restructuring of the LWF. The former Commission and Department of World Mission was changed into the present unit on Church Cooperation. Churches in Africa and Asia urged this change in order to overcome the inference that world mission is primarily an activity of the West directed toward the peoples of former colonial territories. Instead, the demand was for full ecclesial equality, regardless of location or age, and for partnership in the missioning task, also among churches in the Two-Thirds World. The accent has since been on a combination of autonomy and interdependence.

In another area, the Federation's former Commission and Department of Theology in 1970 became part of the subsequent Commission on and Department of Studies. The broader focus was intended to facilitate a fuller treatment of the context in which member churches, especially those in Asia, Africa, and Latin America, were having to find their way. Meanwhile, the 1963 assembly, encouraging further interconfessional research, authorized the establishment of the Institute for Ecumenical Research. Opened in Strasbourg (see France) in 1965, the institute has proven immensely helpful in furthering Lutheran participation in the ecumenical movement as enlarged by Roman Catholic participation since Vatican II. The institute has complemented the Federation's Department of Studies in the cultivation of ecumenical relations as well as bilateral and other dialogs.

• • •

Communication, as noted earlier, has been a concern of the Federation from the outset. *Lutheran World Information,* in English and German editions, has provided an indispensable running account of Lutheran churches and their situations in all continents. For years (1948–1977) the Federation's quarterly, first as *Lutheran World Review,* then as the separate language editions, *Lutherische Rundschau* and *Lutheran World,* provided quality theological input for a world confessional body ecumenically engaged and was a ready source of information on Lutheran thought and action. In 1978 the journal was replaced by the series *LWF Report* and *LWF Documentation*. These occasional publications provide information and studies on current concerns of the Federation. Like the former quarterly, they also reach theological and other libraries, Lutheran, ecumenical, and denominational, in all parts of the world. Similarly, the relatively short but highly effective life (1963–1977) of the Federation's powerful shortwave transmitter, Radio Voice of the Gospel (RVOG, see Africa Introduction and Ethiopia), gave rise to many other communication projects in Africa, Asia, and Latin America.

Lutheran World Service, including its related enterprises in refugee resettlement and Community Development Service, stems from the earliest postwar activities, when the LWF was in process of formation. When relief and reconstruction were consolidated as World Service (1950), under Henry Whiting (1910–1977), the complementary service to refugees, led by Stewart W. Herman from Geneva and directed in the field by Howard V. Hong, was already under way. This laid the basis for comparable services in the Holy Land (see Middle East), in Africa (see Tanzania), and elsewhere (see Hong Kong). Community Development, sprung from World Service as an agency to foster long-term projects, shows up in many a country account in the following sections on Asia, Africa, and Latin America.

As might be expected, by the 1970s the question was raised as to how community development projects, although worked out in cooperation with the local churches, relate to the proclamation of the gospel (see Africa Introduction and Ethiopia). As an LWF-sponsored Consultation on Proclamation and Human Development (Nairobi, Kenya, October 1974) confirmed, there appeared to be no easy answer. Nor was it easier years later, when the very idea of development was being questioned in countries heavily in debt to the International Monetary Fund and other banking interests. A Brazilian church leader, addressing the commission meeting (Madras, India, 1988) spoke for many when he challenged: "What will LWS—and the LWF— do to intercede for the peoples it has been helping to 'develop'?" A guiding axiom after World War II seemed poised for broader application: Help peoples, especially the poor, to help themselves.

Human rights and social justice as well as the quest for peace have been major issues on the LWF agenda since 1947. The aftereffects of the Nazi regime's racism, living on in many places, have given the Federation continuing concern. This has involved probing and constructive conversations with representatives of the Jewish people, especially in Budapest in 1984. It has also drawn the Federation into the struggle against apartheid in Southern Africa. From another side, the LWF has endeavored to promote equal opportunity for women in church and society. Work among young people has in recent years regained some of its former farsighted consideration in Christian education and other areas as well.

A transition from mainly doctrinal to ethical concerns became evident during the restless 1960s, replete with warfare in Vietnam, racial conflict in the USA, and student turbulence in many lands. At Helsinki, the 1963 assembly had endeavored, without conclusive success, to explicate the fundamental doctrine of justification by grace through faith, which Lutherans regard as "the article by which the church stands or falls."

• • •

The next assembly was scheduled for Pôrto Alegre, Brazil—after no acceptable meeting place appeared available in Eastern Europe. But the perception of mounting civil rights violations in Brazil raised a chorus of protests from student groups and church leaders in various countries. The LWF, they demanded, should protest against these widespread violations (countenanced by Brazil's military dictatorship) and stand up for human rights by not meeting in Brazil. Six weeks before the July 14 opening, the officers and staff of the LWF determined to relocate the assembly from Brazil to France. Meeting in Evian-les-Bains, on the southern shore of Lake Geneva, the assembly was bestirred like none before it. One of Brazil's leading Pentecostals, Manuel de Mello, pastor of the biggest church in São Paulo, chided the latter day Lutherans for being fainthearted. Luther, he said, had gone to Worms "even if there were as many devils in town as tiles on the roofs." He added that the ordinary folk in Brazil would have welcomed the timely testimony of Lutherans. But many a delegate feared that brave expressions of solidarity would have been curbed by the official media and that the host church itself would have had to bear painful consequences. One sage German bishop, Heinrich Meyer, a longtime missionary in India, believed that the Brazilian church would mature and gain stature if it survived this blow of frustration. In 1987, the Brazilian church invited the LWF to hold its 1990 assembly in that country.

Besides the already-mentioned restructuring of the Federation in 1970, the Evian assembly came out more strongly than any other against racism. It aimed to help abolish the apartheid being condoned by certain white member churches in Southern Africa and to warn against any racial discrimination tolerated by other member bodies. To be sure, assembly policy was cautious: churches but not governments could be criticized. Yet the interlinkage of church and state was implied. Like the Lutheran World Convention before it, the LWF sought to avoid national and international politics and to address root evils, among them the causes of injustice, poverty, and oppression. In doing so, the Federation acted upon the urgent request of its member churches, whether African or any other.

The 1977 assembly in Dar es Salaam intensified the rejection of apartheid. Any condoning of it was both unchristian and a violation of the integrity of a Lutheran confession of faith. The practice of apartheid, it was said, threw out a challenge to confess the truth as it is in Jesus and thus placed conscientious Christians in a state of confessing, a *status confessionis* (like a state of emergency). When even this did not suffice to bring the white and black churches in Southern Africa into full fellowship, the 1984 Pre-Assembly Consultation of Lutheran Churches in Africa (Harare, Zimbabwe) recommended that the unwilling white church bodies (see Southern Africa) be suspended for a time from the LWF. To the 1984 assembly in Budapest this was explained as an African style of discipline as used in an extended family. After prayerful deliberation, the assembly concurred. The action was unprecedented.

Such actions engaged the LWF progressively in the realm of Christian social ethics and had political implications. While such situations lay far from the concentration of Lutherans in Europe, they raised the issue of human rights closer at home. Parallels were drawn between the practice of apartheid and the racism pursued earlier and monstrously in Hitler's Germany and beyond. The failure of the Lutheran World Convention to protest more specifically in the 1930s (had the LWC been as well organized) was seen, a generation later, as sufficient reason to withdraw the holding of its assembly from Brazil. Yet in Evian the 1970 assembly did not single out Brazil specifically by name, lest other countries be also named.

The curbing of civil rights and the restraints upon church activities under Marxian socialism in Eastern Europe or in far-off China evoked no resounding protests, either from the World Council of Churches or from the LWF. This was done lest repressive measures against fellow Christians and member churches in those lands be intensified. For its part, the LWF, after 1970, undertook a perceptive program of studies in Marxism and the Christian faith. Then, as earlier, "quiet diplomacy"— discussion, persuasion, interpretation, and some adaptation—played an important part. An LWF assembly initially planned for Eastern Europe (1970, Weimar) could thus at last be held in Hungary 14 years later.

Indeed, while there was opportunity for delegates and others from abroad at the Budapest assembly to enjoy the hospitality and fellowship of Lutheran congregations in many parts of the country, the assembly activities themselves were pretty well segregated from the Hungarian public. The election of Bishop Zoltán Káldy, presiding head of the Lutheran Church in Hungary, was in line with the generally observed host country motif. His advocacy of a theology of *diakonia*—the church's service to the nation and its people—had its critics as well as supporters. In any case, in the late Zoltán Káldy (see bio appendix) the LWF had its first president from Eastern Europe.

● ● ●

In its first Norse general secretary, Gunnar Staalsett (see bio appendix), the LWF Executive Committee elected a clergyman of political as well as ecclesial experience. His coming in 1985 coincided with a mounting range of problems demanding ever closer involvement with issues of Christian social ethics. The world economy was affecting the Federation's overall budget. It was still around US $19 million in 1986, exclusive of grants for service and community development projects. The Federation's administrative setup, as noted earlier, appeared ready for a restructuring. Relations with the World Council of Churches were marked by a new openness. Continuing dialog with the Vatican and with other Christian world communions called for follow-up. By the same token, approaches to Christian constituencies outside the ecumenical movement—the vast array of Evangelicals, including Pentecostals and many others—were overdue. Besides, given the progressive intermingling of populations and thus also of world religions, the conversations of Lutheran and Jewish representatives as well as Lutheran participation in the dialog with Muslim, Buddhist, Hindu, and other religious representatives, newly undertaken, were awaiting further advancement. The LWF-sponsored Marxist studies in relation to China and other countries have been of proven worth.

In many other areas the Federation strove to carry out tasks entrusted to it by the member churches. How well such tasks are being done, including the basic task to spread the gospel, requires ongoing self-examination. From a practical standpoint, an agency like the LWF was created to serve as a "free association of Lutheran churches." The term stems from an era, the 1920s, when Lutheran churches were in a cautious stage of mutual supportiveness. Years of durable partnership and mutual interdependence have transformed the LWF into a communion of related churches ever more committed to the church universal in its ecumenical reality. As such, it is obligated to be and remain informed about these and other churches in their respective contexts. The current situation and individual histories of these churches comprise a far more important subject than commonly thought. The following chapters may thus help a global family of churches to become better acquainted and, in an ecumenically shared concern for the unity of Christ's church, to continue in mutual intercession and service—*ora et labora.*

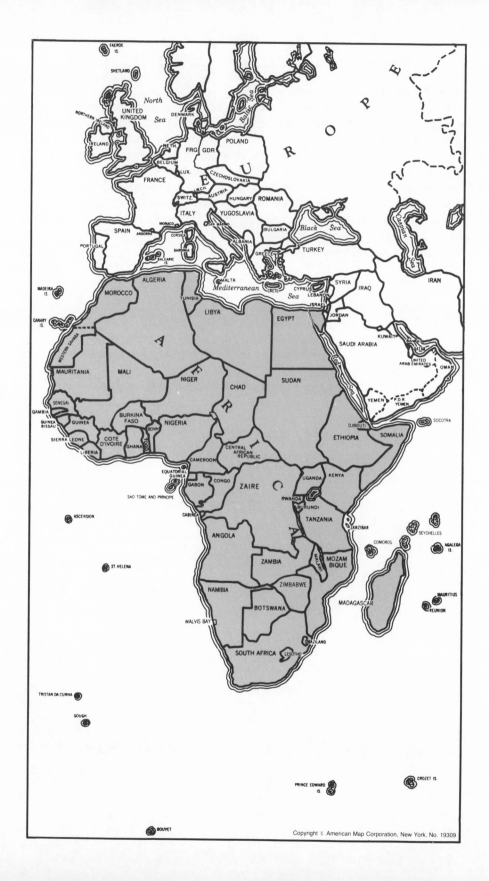

AFRICA_____

About 4.7 million Lutherans live in African lands south of the Sahara and in Madagascar. Although strongly concentrated in certain regions, they are but a small fraction of the rapidly rising total number of Christians in contemporary Africa. The following accounts of the Lutheran churches, as well as of some related enterprises, are here presented geographically by region and alphabetically by country.

I. *Eastern Africa and Madagascar:* Ethiopia, Kenya, Madagascar, Malawi, Mozambique, Sudan, Tanzania, Zambia

II. *Southern Africa:* Botswana, Lesotho, Namibia (South-West Africa), South Africa, Swaziland, Zimbabwe

III. *West-Central Africa:* Angola, Cameroon, Central African Republic, Chad, Zaire

IV. *Western Africa:* Ghana, Liberia, Nigeria, Senegal, Sierra Leone, Togo

Except for a few enterprises undertaken in time of need in Muslim-dominated northern Africa—from Egypt and Sudan to Mauritania—Lutheran involvement has been in regions south of the Sahara. Moreover, the vast majority of the membership in the All Africa Conference of Churches (AACC, below) is in this vast expanse of the continent. The people of the Malagasy Republic wish to be counted as part of the African scene.

Area (including Madagascar): 30,207,913 sq. km. (11,680,700 sq. mi.). *Pop.* (1982 est.): 504,882,000 (cf. slightly under 400 million in 1975). Africa's 10 largest countries, according to population: Nigeria, Egypt, Ethiopia, South Africa, Zaire, Morocco, Algeria, Sudan, Tanzania, Kenya. About 80% of the continent's total population lives south of the Sahara.

History

Of the three continents forming what is sometimes called the "world island," Africa occupies a distinctive place. It has been involved in as well as separated from the main currents of Eurasian history. In the 15th century, its own enormous size launched Europe's discovery of the sea and of the New World. Since then, black Africa has increasingly become part of world history. With millions of its people taken to the Americas, its rich resources supplying the industrialized societies, its own lands dominated by colonial powers, its often painful transition to a composite of independent nations, its costly struggle for survival in the world community, its coping with the rise of population amid the consequences of exploitation and the ravages of nature—all this, and more, invites a closer look at Africa's past as matrix of its present religious life.

Egypt and North Africa are known from ancient times as partners with Greece and Rome and other powers in the rise of western civilization. Knowledge of the history of Africa south of the Sahara continues to enlarge the picture. Traces of cultures from time immemorial emerge. Anthropology—Louis (1903–1972) and Mary (b. 1913) Leakey's discoveries in Tanzania's Olduvai Gorge, for example—may push a horizon of human habitation back two million years. Yet two millennia more than suffice to reveal the often epic dimension of sub-Saharan history.

Today, as some of the following country introductions observe, this earlier history is being recovered. At least in some regions, the pieces of the past hang together, especially as they may be seen from contacts with the outside world. Trade routes, significant also for noting the expansion of Islam or Christianity, trace our access to the past: from Egypt via the Nile; from Asia via the Indian Ocean; from North Africa via the trans-Saharan caravan; from western Europe via the Atlantic caravel.

Specifically, take the great mosque in Mopti, south of Sahara's Timbuktu. This beckoning landmark tells of Arabs plying the gold trade with the storied west African kingdom of *Ghana and also bringing Islam to black Africa long before A.D. 1000. Elsewhere, in the Horn of Africa, note the churches of Lalibela, in modern *Ethiopia, hewn into the massive subsurface rock. In a mountain fastness some 600 kilometers north of Addis Ababa lies this "New Jerusalem." It recalls a king's determination to keep the land Christian despite Muslim advances all around it. And this was in the same century—the 13th—that Europe was raising its Gothic cathedrals.

Again, in the distant southland, a 400-kilometer road led Arab traders from coastal Sofala to the rich gold fields (rivaling those of *Ghana) in the hills where the Great Zimbabwe ("Stone House") gave focus to Shona traditional religion and culture. Such trade, at its height in the 14th century, suggested the wealth of biblical Ophir (1 Kings 10 and 22); yet, in fact, it linked this African kingdom with *India via the coastal commerce of Arab ships blown by seasonal winds.

While the fact of Africa's "being there" challenged Europe to discover the sea, so Europeans, with interests of their own, changed the continent's destiny and, as already mentioned, shaped its people's place in the modern world. The "Dark Continent" was explored; its resources tapped; its best lands taken; its traditions and customs conformed to alien ways. And all this after its living resource—hundreds and thousands of its people—had been taken as slaves to help build yet another civilization. From many "factories" at points between *Angola in the south and *Senegal on the western hump, they were shipped to Brazil, the Caribbean, and North America for tasks requiring endless labor and little reward. In countless ways Africa gave international enterprise a world scale, not least by itself becoming absorbed into the world empires of European nations. This had wide implications for the spread of the Christian faith.

European interests in tropical interior Africa rose rapidly during the mid-19th century, culminating in the Berlin Conference (1884–1885) on colonial questions. Within 30 years, all of Africa had been carved up, with the exception of *Ethiopia and *Liberia. Virtually the whole continent was under some form of European occupation or protection. However, two world wars and their accompanying phenomena—such as the irreversible drive toward freedom, on the one hand, and the economic unprofitability of empire, on the other—brought yet another enormous change.

By 1975, a mere three decades after World War II, practically all of Africa had become a kaleidoscope of independent nations. Their boundaries reflected the arbitrary divisions of colonial times. Their official languages—English, French, Portuguese, Spanish—were useful for international relations and participation in the United Nations but competed with a variety of national tongues. The leadership and officialdom of these new nations, many of them trained in Europe, perpetuated many of the old ways under new auspices. Newly formed universities became centers for a merging of European (Western) and national culture. Development became the motivator. Urbanization advanced, sometimes spectacularly, and usually at the expense of traditional rural life. Population increased rapidly. Young people flocked to the cities. Nationalism—a fostered sense of identity—sought to bridge ethnic differences. Awareness of resources, or the lack of them, determined relations with the outside world. Rising expectations, so strong during the struggle for independence, soon faced serious tests, and often disillusionment.

For the 52 member nations (1983) of the Organization of African Unity (OAU), the future of the continent, as viewed in the mid-1980s, looked far from bright. The struggle for human rights continued, often unpublicized, in many countries. *South Africa's apartheid system—legalized racism—was the prime offender, and the long-sought independence of *Namibia proved chronically elusive. But the wider struggle was not only that of black versus white, but also of black versus black. The near genocide in Burundi (1972) was a terrifying example: the ruling Tutsi minority killed an estimated 100,000 or more Hutus and sent tens of thousands more fleeing to *Tanzania. The dissolution of Portugal's 500-year-old colonial empire in 1975—the liberation of Guinea-Bissau, *Angola, and *Mozambique—climaxed the independence movement among the African states. Yet the victory of black rule in *Zimbabwe (1980) underscored the unfinished business of black *South Africa.

As black African states were thus caught up in power struggles of local intensity and global implications, their problems deepened. Why, for example, should a continent with one-tenth of the world's population have one-fourth of the world's refugees? Recurring droughts in various regions, some of them of unprecedented severity and catastrophic destructiveness, brought famine, set whole populations in search of food, and claimed lives by the hundreds of thousands. From the broad expanses of the Sahel—south of the advancing Sahara—to the Horn of Africa, as well as to *Mozambique and neighboring *Zimbabwe and to over a dozen other countries, the specter of hunger loomed. Assistance from afar, much of it generous, none of it sufficient, was at best a stopgap. The pervasiveness of the people's plight stimulated broad-scale preventive efforts. Belatedly, and counteractive to urban preoccupation, the importance of the rural scene was receiving attention in many places. The potential was there. But so also was the force of circumstances far beyond Africa.

The world situation affected each African country in some particular way. In economic terms, markets fluctuated, trade and industry declined, energy costs staggered. (The enormous rise in oil prices during the later 1970s continues to exact its toll.) National debts have climbed perilously high. In many countries, arms purchases have sold them out to the future. Mounting poverty has widened the gap between rich and poor nations, nowhere more ominously than in Africa.

Yet there is another side. Missiologists and others are saying that by the year 2000, Africa will have more Christians than any other continent. Others say that Islam is advancing even faster, as old connections convey new outreach.

Religion

Traditional religion, Islam, and Christianity continue as the major forces in African religious life.

African Traditional religion's strong sense of community transcends this life and finds tangible expression in the extended family. What it may lack in a developed philosophy and ethical system, it possesses in its will to see life whole—a will important in the modern world and a challenge to both Islam and Christianity. Elements of Traditional religion continue in some independent churches.

Islam's spread across North Africa and its displacement of Christianity in that region is well known. Its penetration of black Africa, to the Sudan, "the land of the black," as Arabs called it, is less well known. Arab traders and migrating peoples have brought Islam to many parts of Africa south of the Sahara. Meetings between Arab and African states, like the Cairo conference in early 1977, have led some observers to see a new Muslim advance at the expense of Traditional religion and Christianity. In some departments of religious studies in the new African universities where Islam, African Traditional religion, and Christianity are taught, it is said that Muslims often show the greater initiative and potential leadership. The leading center of learning in the Muslim world, al-Azhar University, Cairo, observed its 1000th anniversary in 1983. It is called the world's oldest university in continuous operation.

Christianity: The faith of the church forebears, once illuminating Egypt and North Africa, was later eclipsed by Islam. It survived isolated in *Ethiopia and among solitary communities of Copts in the Nile Valley. It was rekindled temporarily in Western Africa during the 16th and 17th centuries. Then, from Moravian beginnings near the Cape of Good Hope in the 1740s and the coming from the Caribbean and North America of Christian freed slaves to Freetown, Sierra Leone, in the 1790s, or to *Liberia in the 1820s, a thousand-fold missionary endeavor eventually spread over the continent. Countless ventures by societies in Europe and North America dotted the continent.

Today Africa counts about one-third of its population Christian. By the year 2000, as noted, some people anticipate that Africa may have more Christians than any other continent. Whatever the case, the church scene in Africa appears more fragmented than in any other continent. For convenience, consider these three groupings, Roman Catholic, Protestant, and Independent.

Roman Catholicism claims over one-half of the Christians south of the Sahara. While its earliest missions go back to the era of Portuguese discovery in the late

15th century, its outreach began in earnest in the 19th. Its varied fields and manifold enterprises remained under mission status until after World War II. Only in the 1950s, the Vatican's "Africa Decade," was a self-governing hierarchy introduced, and "young churches" formed in the rising nations. The changeover was rapid and impressive; so also the rate of growth. An estimated 50 million Roman Catholics were increasing at about 6% annually. In the late 1970s, of the 335 bishops, 237 were African, and the proportion was growing. The greater freedom granted by Vatican II, including mass in the vernacular, also posed certain risks, like the splintering of unity. The first All-Africa Episcopal Symposium (near Kampala, Uganda, 1969) prompted the first of a succession of papal visits to Africa. The aim continues to be that of keeping the church united and on course. Its coping with urban problems has been more successful than that of the Protestants but not of the Independents. Its clashes with Marxist or apartheid governments have been inevitable.

Protestant missioning in Africa dates from 17th-century beginnings in *Ethiopia and 18th-century overtures in *South Africa. But the great advance came in the following century, in some cases, as in *Namibia, preceding a European colonial intrusion. In addition, the missionary role of black Christians—freed slaves—from the Caribbean and North America became important in parts of West Africa, such as modern *Ghana and *Nigeria as well as *Sierra Leone and *Liberia, the countries of black settlement. In time the Anglican and various historic Protestant communions have become well rooted in the African scene. The rise of indigenous leadership and autonomous churches, especially after 1945, drew upon earlier efforts among missionaries to practice comity and to foster Christian unity.

The desire for Christian unity is embodied in the All Africa Conference of Churches (AACC). It was formed in Kampala, Uganda, in 1963, a few years prior to the above-named Roman Catholic symposium. An earlier period of preparation, marked by a widely representative meeting in Ibadan, *Nigeria (1958), had led the way. It had been able to draw upon the experience, among others, of the All-Africa Lutheran Conference in Marangu, *Tanzania (1955). The AACC's aims, functions, and activities focus on mission, evangelism, church unity, and witness to justice and truth. The AACC is concerned for education and development among member churches; for service to refugees; for financial self-reliance; for relationships with ecumenical agencies like the WCC, the Christian Conference of Asia, the Conference of European Churches, the World Association for Christian Communication, the World Student Christian Federation, and others. Its headquarters are in Nairobi, *Kenya (Waiyaki Way, P.O. Box 14205, Westlands). This parklike location is near the edge of the city.

Lutheran churches in the AACC include the *Ethiopian Evangelical Church Mekane Yesus, the *Evangelical Lutheran Church in Tanzania, the *Evangelical Lutheran Church in Southern Africa, the *Malagasy Lutheran Church, and the *Lutheran Church in Liberia. Together these churches account for 86% of the Lutherans in Africa.

African Independent Churches (AICs), so named for their indigenous growth as well as their separation from the Roman Catholic or Protestant churches, are currently estimated to number well over 6500 church bodies and are multiplying. In their profusion, they are best regarded not as separate units but as a movement. The size of the Independents varies from a few hundred to over 50,000. The largest of them all—the Church of Christ on Earth led by the Prophet Simon Kimbangu in *Zaire— claims over five million adherents and is a member of the World Council of Churches. As the AACC is aware, a continent-wide effort on the part of the independents is seeking to bring them together on some ecumenical terms. Their basis is usually scriptural, relying on the vernacular translation, with adapted elements of Traditional religion. A Pentecostal spirit is common, as in the Eden Revival Church in Ghana, often with a deliberate effort to regain certain biblical emphases associated with the first generation of missionaries. Among most of them a strong accent on healing and mutual assistance generates a feeling of hope and expectation. Virtually all of them have sprung up around a strong leader, the earliest of whom appeared in West Africa already in the late 19th century. Much like a tribal chief, the spiritual leader personified the identity of the group. The break was twofold: away from colonial domination and away from the foreign-run churches and missions.

While today the historic (Roman Catholic and Protestant) churches in Africa allow considerable freedom, the independents, taken as a whole, comprise a schismatic movement. A few of their pastors have been trained at recognized theological colleges. Some see this ecclesial development as comparable in significance to the break between Eastern Orthodox and Roman Catholic, or between Catholic and Protestant. The Independent Churches thus embody a significance that is unique as well as challenging to the church catholic and evangelical. Its future bears careful watching.

• • •

Lutherans in Africa trace their beginnings from such scattered starts as the *Strand Street Church in Cape Town, founded in the 1780s among German settlers, and the first missionary efforts among the black people in *South Africa in the 1820s. Other Lutheran missionary efforts began in *Liberia, Eritrea/*Ethiopia, and *Madagascar in the 1860s, and in *Tanzania in the 1880s. These were followed by still others, as in *Nigeria in 1913 and *Cameroon in the 1920s. There were, of course, many other beginnings. In virtually every case, the effects of World Wars I and II altered the missionary situation, drew increased participation from northern Europe and North America (partly as replacement help for the German-sponsored missions) and saw a considerable rise in African initiative in the maintenance of local congregations, educational efforts, and the further spread of the gospel. After 1945, the increase of missionary activity was accompanied by a coordination of effort. Many undertakings in Africa were helped by the USA-based Commission on Younger Churches and Orphaned Missions (CYCOM) and subsequently (1952) by the LWF Commission on World Mission and, since 1970, by the Federation's Department of Church Cooperation.

To Africans especially, the change of name in 1970—to Church Cooperation— was important. First, it recognized the presence of new churches in Africa. By 1970 there were some 14 self-governing Lutheran ecclesial bodies there and in Madagascar that had become member churches of the LWF. Second, it declared that mission is the task of every church. Granted that African, like Asian or Latin

American, churches might still be recipients of outside help, they were eager themselves to engage in mission and thus to emphasize the interdependence of the members in a fellowship of churches like the LWF.

These two developments had been stimulated by the Federation itself as it helped African and Malagasy Lutherans to become acquainted with each other. Responding to a felt need, LWF-sponsored All-Africa Lutheran Conferences had been held in three places prior to 1970: Marangu, *Tanzania (1955); Antsirabé, *Malagasy Republic (1960); Addis Ababa, *Ethiopia (1965). Ecumenically, the Marangu conference encouraged the formation of the All Africa Conference of Churches (above).

Likewise, after 1970, a restructured LWF Department of Studies fostered an inquiry into "the identity of the church and its service to the whole human being." A number of African churches participated in this project and came to a fuller understanding of themselves and others. The results, published in advance of the 1977 assembly, heightened the African input at Dar es Salaam.

Continuing the role of its predecessor (World Mission), LWF's Department of and Commission on Church Cooperation fostered the process of ecclesial nurture. Three regional conferences—Arusha, *Tanzania (1973); Rustenburg, *South Africa (1974); Tananarive, *Madagascar (1975)—treated problems for which the churches desired assistance. Among these were evangelism, self-support, ministerial education, the combating of racism and apartheid, and more. This was input for the fourth All-Africa Lutheran Conference—the first for the Department of Church Cooperation—held in Gaborone, *Botswana, early in 1977.

The impact of continent-wide conferences was cumulative. First, groups of believers long separated discovered each other. Already at Marangu, some representatives called for drawing up a distinctive confession of faith, *confessio Africana*. Although this was not done formally, a sense of solidarity developed. Boundaries of all sorts were to be transcended, and imposed barriers, like apartheid in the church, were to be removed. The spirit of Gaborone prevailed at Dar es Salaam, when the LWF assembly declared the rejection of racism, notably apartheid, an imperative of Christian integrity, a *status confessionis*. At Dar es Salaam, apart from the assembly, an All-Africa Lutheran Churches' Information and Coordination Center (ALICE) was projected. Launched in 1978, it has been operative since then from its base in Arusha, *Tanzania. Despite many obstacles, even a modest performance cast ALICE as keeper and cultivator of a vision.

Second, the African consultations grappled with an inherited Christian theology that has intensified a desire to relate the gospel more effectively to the diverse African scenes. Non-Africans can hardly appreciate the motivation behind this task nor the immensity of it. The All-Africa consultations on theology in the African context—Gaborone (1978), Monrovia, *Liberia (1980)—underscored the change the gospel itself creates when it acts and when its host environment reacts. Although Luther's Catechism is known and used in the churches, Luther himself remains quite foreign to most African Lutherans. Yet this did not prevent them from speaking their mind to other Lutherans at Budapest (1984) on issues that deeply concerned them and other Christians, too.

A third factor, discipline, further demonstrated an African impact on the world communion. This was when the 1984 LWF assembly in Budapest acted upon the recommendation of the All-Africa Lutheran Consultation in Harare, *Zimbabwe (December 1983) and suspended two member churches in Southern Africa for failing to reject "publicly and unequivocally" the existing apartheid system. (See Evangelical Lutheran Church in Southern Africa—Cape Church, and German Evangelical Lutheran Church in South-West Africa/Namibia.) Some saw this action as further evidence of a maturing Federation membership. As in an African family, so it was said, this was not a termination but a suspension—a form of discipline that expected reconciliation and return. Meanwhile, the consequences of suspension were many and the implications for the Federation far-reaching.

African Lutherans sought and found LWF encouragement, meaning the supportiveness of fellow Christians on other continents, in many fields: in upholding human rights; in greater participation in decision making affecting the interdependence among African churches themselves; in church-to-church contacts on a global basis; in greater participation of women and youth in the life and work of the churches; in more effective urban and industrial ministries amid secularized and uprooted populations; in extended community development activity; in a pooling of resources for joint mission activity; in fostering self-reliance for church support; in furthering the study of the church's nature and identity in African society; in continued inquiry into a Christian understanding and treatment of the problem of polygamy, and the like. Concerns like these have led to a greater give-and-take between the African churches and their partners beyond the seas. As the scourge of famine during the 1980s has warned, Africa's problems are world problems, and the role of the churches is at best that of posting signs of hope amid impending or actual catastrophe.

The growing outside involvement in Africa during recent decades is shown by the fact that more than half of all funds from participating western agencies channeled through LWF Community Development Service (CDS) to church-recommended projects in Asia, Africa, and Latin America since 1963 have gone to Africa. Struck by this rising tide of giving, whose sources were mainly European and North American and sometimes only loosely church-related but strongly humanitarian, the *Ethiopian Evangelical Church Mekane Yesus asked the LWF in Geneva a searching question: What is the relation between proclamation of the gospel and human development? An LWF-sponsored consultation in Nairobi, *Kenya (October 1974), wrestled with this question and its implications for churches the world over. There were no easy answers to it, the consultation found, but searching inquiry reaffirmed the profound interrelationship between spreading the gospel and serving people in need, particularly as proclamation and development involved issues of justice, human rights, freedom of religion, and the desire to experience life in its wholeness.

Seldom has proclamation been so daringly undertaken, so widely spread, so filled with promise—and so abruptly terminated—as with RVOG, Radio Voice of the Gospel. Authorized by the 1957 assembly in Minneapolis, located in Addis Ababa, *Ethiopia, RVOG was dedicated in 1963 and remained on the air round the clock for the next 14 years. Its powerful 200,000-watt transmitter, with its directional antennas, beamed programs, most of them prepared in 14 regional studios, via short and medium wave to audiences in Asia, Africa, and the Middle East. The station's motto, "Proclaiming Christ to His World," overarched a wide diversity of programs. About 30% religious, these programs were not only Lutheran but also Orthodox and of other communions. The other 70% included news and many practical projects relevant to a fuller life. In *Japan, *Taiwan, and *Brazil other offices and studios covered interests in East Asia and Latin America, while in Madras, *India, programs were prepared for the subcontinent. In Addis Ababa, a staff of 200, with another 250 in the African feeder studios, prepared programs in 18 languages. Only when government forces seized RVOG early on Saturday, March 12, 1977—and silenced it—did it become evident how widely influential this proclamation had been and how heavily the communication work of the LWF had relied on it.

Since 1977 the LWF electronic media communication program for Africa and Madagascar has become decentralized, with all the new opportunities and frustrations this implies. The most frequently used languages in this outreach include Swahili and Malagasy in the east and Fulfulde and Hausa in the west. Projects of many types have been undertaken in Zaire, southern *Sudan, *Kenya, Rwanda, *Tanzania, *Namibia, and *Liberia, including various types of print media programs such as the *Africa Theological Journal,* an ecumenical semiannual by the Lutheran Theological College, Makumira, Tanzania.

An unexpected sequel to the end of RVOG has been the response of faithful listeners. From West Africa came many requests from the Fulani-speaking people for more of the "good news." The result was the formation in 1980 of the Joint Christian Ministry in West Africa (JCMWA) in Jos, *Nigeria, at a special assembly. The groundwork had been laid a year earlier in Ngaoundéré, *Cameroon, when representatives of over a dozen churches and agencies met with staff of the LWF Department of Church Cooperation. This ecumenical venture, initiated by Lutherans, includes participants from the Church Missionary Society and the Church of Nigeria (both Anglican). The Lutheran churches in *Cameroon, *Chad, the *Central African Republic, *Nigeria, *Liberia, *Namibia, *Senegal, *North America, and the *Federal Republic of Germany as well as mission agencies in *Denmark, *Sweden, and *France are united in this outreach to the Fulani in the dry grazing lands of Western Africa.

Programs in curriculum development for church and public schools in a number of the African countries have long had the service of consultants and other support through LWF channels, all of which has focused on a rising generation of informed and responsible Christians. Equal, if not greater, attention has gone to the development of a well-educated ministry, unordained as well as ordained. In 1982, on the basis of an extensive preliminary study of theological education in Africa, the LWF Departments of Studies and Church Cooperation jointly undertook to assist the churches in developing a comprehensive program for a "spectrum of ministries." This would strengthen such a pivotal school as that at Makumira, *Tanzania, as well as others in *Ethiopia, *Madagascar, *South Africa, *Namibia, *Cameroon, *Liberia, and elsewhere.

The catastrophic drought and famine that ravaged some 20 African countries during the 1980s underscored again the vital role of international assistance, especially through such experienced and widely resourced voluntary agencies as LWF World Service (for the short term) and the LWF Community Development Service (for the long term). The African plight has, as of 1984, brought major church agencies into unprecedented large-scale cooperation. An example is the joint appeal for US $100 million to provide famine relief in *Ethiopia and beyond, as undertaken by Caritas Internationalis, Catholic Relief Services, the Lutheran World Federation, and the World Council of Churches. In the case of *Ethiopia, while governments may appear on the scene later—often too late—with massive help, voluntary agencies not only have greater flexibility of operation but also longer experience in dealing with the people in need. So, for example, the extensive development projects undertaken by LWF/CDS in *Ethiopia have been a basic help. Overcoming the disastrous effects of drought and famine in the early 1970s has kept CDS projects on long-range course ever since. Besides the LWF/WS projects referred to in the accounts below, disaster relief and development projects have been carried on as invited in Mauritania and Uganda where there are no known Lutheran churches. Lutheran World Relief (USA) has projects in Niger, and Norway is active in Mali.

The great expectations of Africa's people extend far beyond the periodic ravages of time. For Africa's Lutherans, having one of their number, Bishop Josiah Kibira of *Tanzania, preside ably over the LWF for seven years, from Dar es Salaam to Budapest, confirmed their place in this worldwide communion (see General Introduction).

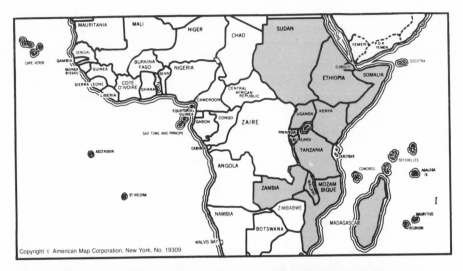

Copyright © American Map Corporation, New York, No. 19309

EASTERN AFRICA AND MADAGASCAR

The countries in this eastern part of the continent are: Ethiopia, Kenya, Malawi, Mozambique, Sudan, Tanzania, and Zambia, as well as Madagascar offshore. For Egypt, see Bible Lands and Neighboring Countries.

In this set of countries, and for Africa as a whole, Ethiopia alone looks back on centuries of independence. Ethiopian Orthodoxy, closely linked with that in Egypt and the Holy Land, provided an initial impulse for the advance of Protestant mission southward while, earlier still, Portuguese navigators launched short-lived Roman Catholic beginnings, especially in Mozambique and Madagascar, in the 16th century. While Arab commerce early planted Islam at various coastal points, it did not penetrate the interior in strength as it did in the inner regions of West Africa via the Sahara trade.

Amid the presently widespread Christian constituencies that have displaced Traditional religion in this eastern region, Lutherans are prominent with more than 750,000 each in Ethiopia and in Madagascar, and about 1.3 million in Tanzania, plus the small groups in Kenya, Zambia, Malawi, and Mozambique. Their estimated total of nearly 3 million accounts for 63.7% of all Lutherans in Africa.

ETHIOPIA

A socialist state in northeastern Africa, mountainous Ethiopia dominates the Horn of the continent and is framed by Somalia, Djibouti, *Kenya, the *Sudan, and the Red Sea. Area: 1,223,600 sq. km. (472,400 sq. mi.). Pop. (1984 est.): 42,019,400. Cap. and largest city: Addis Ababa (pop., 1984 est., 1,412,500). Languages: Amharic (official) and other tongues, Oromo about 40%.

History: Tradition traces this oldest of African states to the founding of the kingdom of Ethiopia by Menilek I, said to be the son of King Solomon and Queen Makeda of Sheba (1 Kings 10:1ff). A varied consolidation of smaller kingdoms owing allegiance to the emperor, Ethiopia maintained ties with the Mediterranean world of Greece and Rome via Egypt over trade routes using the Nile or

53

the Red Sea, and with India as well. Accepting Christianity in the fourth century, the country was subsequently cut off from the rest of the Christian world by the rise of Islam. Sporadic contacts with Rome followed during the Middle Ages. Later these intensified during the age of discovery and Portuguese involvement in Ethiopian affairs.

The 19th century saw Ethiopia struggle with European designs on its control, notably Britain, France, and then Italy. In the process, Menilek, King of Shoa, pursued an expansionist policy and in 1889 claimed the Empire of Ethiopia. As Menilek II (1889–1913), he fostered modernization and (1886) relocated the nation's capital from ancient Aksum to Addis Ababa (New Flower). Although he annexed the provinces of Harer, Sidamo, and Kefa in the south, Italy took Eritrea as a colony and thus controlled the coast, including Ethiopia's two ports, Massawa and Assab. Following the unhappy interlude after Menilek's death, when his successor, a grandson, courted Islam, his daughter, Zauditu, was proclaimed empress (1916–1930) and Tafari Makonnen, regent. A grandnephew of Menilek II, Tafari ruled ably, fostered international ties (League of Nations), and in 1930 was proclaimed emperor. As Haile Selassie I (Power of the Trinity), his rule was interrupted by the Italian war and personal exile (1936–1941) and ended decades later (1974) by a military coup. Devoted to modernization and social reform, he also established a national assembly (1955) and in the 1960s strongly supported the formation of the Organization of African Unity (OAU) whose Africa Hall in Addis Ababa recalls his Pan-Africa concerns.

Changes in Eritrea's status, important for Ethiopia's future, moved Eritrea from an Italian colony (until 1941) to a British-mandated territory (until 1952) to an independent but federated part of Ethiopia (until 1962). Full unification with Ethiopia was voted by the Eritrean assembly in that year.

The Ethiopian revolution in 1974, spawned by general unrest, was occasioned by a serious drought. The emperor was seen as having failed to deal adequately with widespread starvation as well as with the injustices that kept the privileged in power. A policy of economic reorganization and land reform, the Derg, was pursued by the Provisional Military Administrative Council (PMAC). The

National Work Campaign for Development through Cooperation *(Zemecha),* launched in late 1974, mobilized 60,000 students above grade 10 in mainly rural-based projects. The school teachers were included. Literacy work and the organization of peasant associations claimed special attention. The PMAC operated amid a mounting complex of problems, including unrest in Eritrea and tensions within the population and the government itself. Deposed, Haile Selassie died while under detention in Addis Ababa (1975).

Situations on two fronts illustrate Ethiopia's difficulties. To the east, Somalia sought to wrest the Ogaden province from Ethiopia and to reunite it with the nomadic Somalis. Cuban and Soviet support helped Ethiopia defeat Somalia's attempt. In the process at least 300,000 refugee nomads fled to Somalia; thus creating another huge problem for the UN High Commissioner for Refugees and the associated non-governmental organizations engaged in relief work. Meanwhile, to the north, continuous unrest in Eritrea culminated in 1982 in the "Red Star Campaign" against the secessionists and in a diversion of funds to the region for the reconstruction and further development of basic facilities, industry, and social services.

The prolonged drought and great famines of the mid- and late 1980s brought catastrophic consequences especially for the rural population in the regions of Tigray and Eritrea. International relief efforts—the LWF was prominent among the voluntary agencies—proved insufficient to prevent mass starvation. Long-range rehabilitation and development requirements pose a stiff challenge to the people and their government. The Joint Relief Partnership (JRP), formed in 1984 during the grim famine, was an association for the acquisition and distribution of emergency food to the drought-stricken areas of Ethiopia. The partners were the Ethiopian Evangelical Church Mekane Yesus, the Ethiopian Catholic Secretariat, the Catholic Relief Services (USA), the Lutheran World Federation, and, after 1987, the Ethiopian Orthodox Church.

Religion: Christian, about 55%; Muslim, 31%; Traditional, 11%; Jewish, 0.1%.

Islam, probably with more adherents than statistics reveal, is strongest in Eritrea, in the eastern and southeastern parts of the country, as well as in the northwestern part bordering the Sudan. Mohammed is said to have sent a band of his followers to this land prior to the Hegira (A.D. 622). Islam has remained a force to be reckoned with.

Traditional religion remains strongest in the southern and western regions, among the Darasa, Ometo, and Wallega Galla (Oromo) people. Among the latter the ooda tree is the center of village worship. Prayers of thanksgiving and offerings are made to the spirit believed to reside in the tree.

Judaism, in archaic form, continues among the Falashas (Amharic for "stranger"). Known also as Black Jews, their number has declined considerably during this century from perhaps 100,000 at its beginning to about half as many in 1950, to less than 28,000 currently. Inhabiting the region around the city of Gonder, north of Lake Tana, and located also in small communities around Addis Ababa, their forebears are thought to be Ethiopians who resisted Christianization but accepted Judaism from immigrants who came into the country between the first and sixth centuries A.D. Many of them appear to have been assimilated into Amharic culture and become Christian. In the mid-19th century, certain Falashas rendered notable service to the gospel, reaching people both in the Ethiopian Orthodox Church and in the ranks of Traditional religion. The large majority, however, retained their ancestral faith and practices. The rise of the State of *Israel revived latent ties. In 1972 Israel's chief Sephardic rabbi declared the Falashas "undoubtedly of the tribe of Dan." Over the decade since 1975, some 10,000 Falashas have been resettled in the land of their religious roots; about 3000 of them via the devious "Operation Moses" (1984–1985).

Christianity claims over one-half of the population, the vast majority of whom are members of the Ethiopian Orthodox Church (EOC). Largest among the Oriental Orthodox churches, the EOC continues de facto as the country's established church despite its loss of many privileges since the revolution of 1974 and its tenuous relationship to the state. Ecumenically the EOC has been active in the World Council of Churches since 1948 and was host to the WCC Central Committee (1971).

The Ethiopian Orthodox Church has had a venerable and often violent past. The conversion of Ethiopia to Christianity is highlighted by the care r of the young Syrian evangelist Frumentius (ca. 300–380). About the year 340 he was consecrated bishop of Aksum (the ancient royal city) by the famed theologian Athanasius in Alexandria. But the Judeo-Christian antecedents of the EOC run back to Old Testament times (Solomon) and to first-century Christianity (Acts 8:27ff). Christianity became established in its trinitarian form but stopped short of accepting the Council of Chalcedon's dogma on the two natures of Christ (451). It thus became part of the monophysite (single nature) camp, which included also the Coptic Church in Egypt. For some 1500 years thereafter, final ecclesiastical authority in Ethiopia's Orthodox Church lay with the Coptic Patriarch. Coptic bishops and a Coptic metropolitan were gradually replaced by Ethiopian nationals between 1929 and 1951. In the latter year, the EOC became virtually autocephalous, and in 1959 it received its own patriarch, Basilios.

In light of Ethiopia's long isolation as "a Christian island in a Muslim sea," the tie with Alexandria as well as with Jerusalem provided invaluable linkage. (The Ethiopian convents and chapels in Jerusalem have centuries-old roots and today serve an Ethiopian Orthodox community of about 500, including one nun, a former Danish Lutheran, now Sister Abraham.)

Threatened periodically by Muslim advances, the church continued, and tradition became a shield for survival. Already in the fifth century, the Scriptures had been translated into the popular tongue, Ge'ez (Ethiopic). In time Amharic replaced it, and Ge'ez, like Latin in the West, became a church language, unintelligible to ordinary folk. Yet monastic (conventual) life exerted an ongoing influence, helping to keep alive the substance as well as the form of faith.

Among the most enduring symbols of steadfastness are the monolithic churches in Lalibela (see Africa Introduction, above). Cut out of solid rock in the 13th century, this "New Jerusalem" continues to attract the adherents of an ever-resurgent tradition. This quasi-feudal attachment to the past, a lack of trained priests, and the apparent absence of social concern has weakened the position of the EOC, especially in the cities and in the eyes of young people. Groups of clergy and laity have periodically striven to renew the EOC, even as they have received encouragement in more recent times from Anglican and Protestant quarters as well as from the World Council of Churches. The EOC's Holy Trinity Seminary in Addis Ababa is a venture in this direction, as are a number of other schools preparing young persons for various other fields of service under church auspices.

Ethiopia has had the attention of the Roman Catholic Church at various times over the centuries. It began early, then faded out, only to return with growing intensity over the past 150 years. Portuguese, lured to this remote Christian kingdom by the legend of Prester John, sent an embassage to Aksum. Early in the 16th century, having found the sea route around Africa to India, Portuguese naval power dispersed Muslim Arabs invading Ethiopia. Jesuits and others successfully wooed the Ethiopian monarch to the point of submission to Rome. But a popular uprising ended that chapter in 1632. In the 19th century, Roman missionaries (Lazarist, Capuchin, and others) returned, and during the Italian war in the 1930s made important gains, especially in Eritrea. But Roman Catholicism in Ethiopia, aided by the Ethiopian College in Rome (1919), has made comparatively little progress. Impact from the outside came from the Protestants.

• • •

A new kind of contact began with Peter Heyling (1607–1652), the Lutheran layman from Lübeck, Germany, who spent his last 18 years at the royal court in Gonder. A lawyer and physician by training, conversant in theology, and a gifted linguist, he was a favorite in his adopted land. Heyling translated parts of the New Testament into Amarigna (Amharic). Followers of his, never many, but choice, in successive generations caught the vision of Scripture and a faith focused on Christ as calling for a renewal of the church. He was martyred by a Muslim Turk while en route to Egypt.

Two centuries later an Ethiopian monk, Abba Abraham (d.1818), en route to Jerusalem, remained in Cairo, courtesy of the French vice-consul, and completed the translation of the entire Bible into Amarigna. The then-young British and Foreign Bible Society

in London was notified. The translation was a find. The four Gospels were published first. The Anglican Church Missionary Society (CMS), cultivating earlier mission partnership with German Lutherans and others of kindred Pietist leanings, undertook the distribution in Ethiopia of the four Gospels and after 1840 the entire Bible. The Basel Mission supplied the personnel (see Switzerland).

Among the CMS-Basel emissaries, two stand out: the Swiss Reformed Samuel Gobat (1799–1879), ordained in Lutheran orders in Württemberg, Germany, entered Ethiopia in 1830 after several years of preparation in Egypt. He later became the evangelical bishop of Jerusalem, yet he continued his interest in Ethiopia (see Middle East). Johann Ludwig Krapf (1810–1881), a German Lutheran, followed Gobat, entering Ethiopia in 1837. After being forced out of Ethiopia, he resumed work for the CMS near Mombasa, East Africa. Krapf's great concern for the Oromo people influenced the Hermannsburg Mission (1854) and the Swedish Evangelical Mission (1866) to venture into Ethiopia (below). His vision of a line of mission stations spanning across Africa encouraged entries into *Kenya, *Cameroon, and *Nigeria.

The CMS venture, begun in 1826, was already ended by 1843. Nevertheless, its mission was exceedingly fruitful. When the Amarignan translation of the Gospels reached Orthodox priests, spiritual renewal often resulted. The Scriptures revealed to them the centrality of Christ for salvation. These "reformed" priests formed evangelical associations for Bible study, fellowship, and encouragement. Often this had to be carried on in secret due to the objection of, and at times persecution by, the established church.

The Anglican Church Missionary Society, despite frustrations, has continued to work for the spiritual renewal of the Ethiopian Orthodox Church. Pivotal to achieving the desired change was the education of the Orthodox clergy, a sadly neglected field. Only in 1944, under Emperor Haile Selassie, was a beginning made for what, in 1958, became the first university-related theological faculty among the Oriental (Monophysite) Orthodox. Its professors have included Copts from Egypt and Syrian Orthodox from Malabar, *India, as well as Ethiopian scholars. Anglicans have also taken part, teaching as well as offering further study in Britain.

Other communions were likewise active. The United Presbyterian Church in North America began work in Welega in western Ethiopia (1919) as an extension of earlier (1854) activities among the Copts in Egypt. The endeavors among the Galla (Oromo) people took root, expanded, and in 1938 the formation of the Bethel congregation led to the founding of the Ethiopian Evangelical Church-Bethel in 1947. In 1974, Bethel Synod merged with the EECMY (below).

One of the Presbyterian pioneers, Dr. Thomas Lambie, extended the medical mission to Addis Ababa. Lacking the full support of his American board, this step was taken under the Sudan Interior Mission (SIM), which shared his vision of "the importance of Abyssinia." SIM, an interdenominational agency, was predominantly Baptist. During the Italian war, when Protestant missionaries were ordered out of the country, an indigenous Christian movement emerged in the Wallamo region and beyond. After the return of the missionaries in 1945, the movement grew rapidly into the Word of Life Evangelical Church in Ethiopia, one of the largest Protestant churches in the land. A component, the Kambata Evangelical Church, objecting to SIM control, went its own way in 1955. A decade later, it joined the EECMY (below).

Among the other churches entering Ethiopia were the Seventh Day Adventists, the Mennonites, and several Baptist groups. In 1943 the Inter-Missionary Council was formed, which continued until 1978 when the Council for Church Cooperation in Ethiopia was launched. Its ecumenical intent fostered improved relations between its membership and the Ethiopian Orthodox Church. It is not always clear to the EOC that Protestants seek not to proselytize but to cooperate. Nor is it easy for the churches as such to carry on amid the political changes since 1974.

In this setting the rise of Lutheran churches in Ethiopia appears remarkable, and the fact that their growth continues—now approaching 700,000 baptized members—warrants closer examination. Since the *Ethiopian Evangelical Church Mekane Yesus (EECMY) and the *Evangelical Church of Eritrea (ECE) spring from a common origin and share some of the same indigenous leaders, a certain amount of overlap in the following accounts is inevitable. For much of

their history, we are indebted to Gustav Arén's *Evangelical Pioneers in Ethiopia: Origins of the Evangelical Church Mekane Yesus* (Stockholm: EFS Forlaget, 1978) and to Olav Saeveraas, *On Church-Mission Relations in Ethiopia 1944-1969 with special reference to the Evangelical Church Mekane Yesus and the Lutheran Missions* (Studia Missionalia Upsaliensia XXVII, 1974).

ETHIOPIAN EVANGELICAL CHURCH MEKANE YESUS (EECMY)

(Ye Etiopia Wongelawit Bete-Kristian Mekane Yesus)
Member: LWF (1963), WCC, AACC
Membership: 776,673
President: Francis Stephanos
PO Box 2087
Addis Ababa

This autonomous church, constituted in 1959, took the name of its first congregation in Addis Ababa: Mekane Yesus (Jesus' dwelling place). The EECMY was the first church after the ancient Ethiopian Orthodox Church to be recognized by the government (in the 1960s). Beginning with its membership in the LWF, the EECMY has become increasingly active ecumenically in worldwide and continental relationships, as indicated above. Although members have long experienced hardship and persecution, the EECMY remains one of the fastest-growing churches in Africa.

The approximately 2140 EECMY congregations are served by 229 pastors, 530 evangelists, and other workers as well. The congregations are grouped into seven geographic synods, the largest of which are in the western and southern regions. The quadrennial assembly or synodical convention is the EECMY's legislative body. The president, executive committee, and general secretary, as well as a specialized staff, see to the church's governance and various functions. Amharic is the official language, but local tongues have their place.

Education figures prominently in the EECMY. A year after its founding (1960) the EECMY established the Mekane Yesus Seminary in Addis Ababa. From its beginning the institution has maintained a high standard of education, limiting its enrollment to those who qualify for degree or diploma programs. However, the need for pastors has been so great that other avenues of education have been necessary. Between its founding by the Norwegian Lutheran Mission in 1958 and its closing by the government in 1984, the Tabor Seminary near Awasa, south of Addis Ababa, trained both evangelists and pastors, offering courses adapted to the level of education in the area. The same is true of the Onesimos Bible School in the Western Synod. Qualified graduates of these schools, after a year of internship, could continue their education at Mekane Yesus. Tabor and Onesimos, as well as a dozen Bible schools at convenient locations, serve as centers for the theological extension program (TEE) begun in 1971 at Mekane Yesus. By 1984 more than 70 students had graduated from this program and were serving either in paid or volunteer positions, and another 740 students were enrolled. Refresher courses for pastors and evangelists, offered annually, deal with theological and biblical questions and also with the role of the laity as Christians. Voluntary preachers receive instruction at regular times for their vital auxiliary function. Once a year most communicant members attend a spiritual conference for a few days.

The EECMY sees its task as a biblically based endeavor to promote "integrated human development" wherein spiritual and material needs are met as well as seen together. Its inclusive approach to education lays emphasis also on mass projects. Already in 1962, with support from the LWF Community Development Service, this young church launched the Yemissrach Dimts literacy campaign as a five-year project. The 1200 literacy schools begun and operated by the church have made about 100,000 adults literate. The schools are still in operation and receive church support, but they have gradually been transferred to the farmers' associations.

From 1963 until its closing in 1977, the Christian programs of Radio Voice of the Gospel (Addis Ababa) in Amharic, Oromo, and Tigrigna greatly aided the outreach of the EECMY (see Africa Introduction). A limited mass media ministry is now administered by the department of mission and evangelism. Outreach includes extensive use of cassettes (the plan being to record the whole Bible in as many vernaculars as possible) and audiovisual productions on development, education, and evangelism. Production studios are located in Addis Ababa, Awasa, and Hosanna. Solar-powered cassette players are used in remote areas.

The EECMY-sponsored health services have been particularly welcome in rural areas. In recent years some of the church's hospitals have been transferred to the government. In the church's more than 40 clinics, as in its hospitals and mobile health teams, the accent is on preventive care, complete with instruction and vaccination. In light of this concern for the whole person, spiritually and communally, the diversity of church-sponsored projects is shaped by the response to a felt need in a given place, be this for a school or a clinic, an agricultural or a vocational center, a home for the disabled or the aged, a road or a bridge.

Emphasis on development has been balanced in the EECMY by evangelism, which rapid growth confirms. As a church benefiting greatly from the generosity of development projects, the EECMY has reminded the LWF churches of the spiritual hunger of its people. A 1972 letter raised the issue of balance between development and proclamation (see Africa Introduction). Consequently an LWF conference in Nairobi, Kenya, in October 1974 addressed this important question but could find no conclusive answer other than reaffirming the interrelationship between evangelism and development.

Among its own people, too, the leadership of the EECMY has stressed the responsibility of sharing the gospel. The 1976 general assembly decided that henceforth the church members should gradually increase their personal offerings and thereby help the church become independent of foreign aid. To meet this challenge, courses in stewardship have been conducted throughout the church. A five-year (1984–1989) evangelism program has been developed. The seven synods have identified areas within their reach where there has been no proclamation. The churchwide response to these challenges emphasizes the need for thorough education in all aspects of the Christian life, including stewardship. The church anticipates that converts will soon assume their responsibility for the ongoing work and mission.

Rapid church growth—a doubling of membership between 1977 and 1983—necessitated the construction of numerous low-cost chapels. Contributions for these have come from many parts of the world via the LWF Department of Church Cooperation. Some of the giving churches are themselves living under the pressure of poverty. EECMY congregations receiving chapels themselves contribute at least one-half of the costs, much of it in labor or gifts in kind. The support of the EECMY's many institutions is a large order and the need for assistance from cooperating churches and societies overseas continues (see Committee of Mutual Christian Responsibility, CMCR, below).

The EECMY, situated in the midst of war and famine, has drawn upon its resources for help. In April 1973 the church president, Emmanuel Abraham (b.1913), cabled an appeal to the LWF for help in meeting the critical drought situation in the Tigray and Welo provinces. LWF World Service responded and has remained on the scene, meeting subsequent crises and also engaging in long-term development work. All the projects have been in agreement with the EECMY and the government Relief and Rehabilitation Commission. Returning refugees from Somalia have received medical attention, and rehabilitation projects have provided land, oxen, seed, and fertilizer for a new start. During the severe drought (1983–1986), support for vital transport was provided through the EECMY and the ECE (below) to facilitate food deliveries to several affected areas. Since 1986 the EEMCY has assumed more responsibility for the administration of long-term projects. LWF/WS cares for the refugees. Relief is a joint responsibility.

Famine is not the only devastation. After the 1974 revolution, religious freedom became a national priority, and the EECMY was willing to work with the authorities to serve all the people of Ethiopia. Nevertheless, the new regime drastically turned its back on the Christians of Ethiopia. On July 28, 1979, EECMY's general secretary, Gudina Tumsa, (an Oromo), and his wife were kidnapped by armed men. He has not been seen since, and his wife was imprisoned without charges. Since 1980 many church buildings have been taken over by local authorities. Most of them are being used for government offices or community halls. In some areas the church continues to work without incident. In others only a few congregations are allowed to gather for worship. The church headquarters in Addis Ababa were confiscated in 1981.

In spite of persecution the EECMY, with support from Christians in many parts of the world, still continues its famine relief, the building of houses for handicapped factory workers, the resettlement of refugees, and countless other acts of mercy. In face of hunger and persecution, the church continues to grow and serve. This body of Christ in Ethiopia, like St. Paul of old, is saying to the world: "We are afflicted in every way but not crushed . . . ."

• • •

Evangelists have had an important role in EECMY history. The Swedish Evangelical Mission (SEM) arriving in Massawa in 1866, turned their frustration of not being able to proceed to the Oromo into fruitful work in Eritrea by preparing and motivating Ethiopians for the task (see ECE, below). By 1877 two converts were ready and willing to dare the dangerous trip south: Nigusé Tashu, a successful merchant, converted by reading the Amarigna translation of the Bible and by further education at the SEM school; and Amanuel, an Oromo trader, the first Muslim convert of the mission, who, on his way home from Mecca, was befriended and nursed back to health by missionary Lager at Ailet. Nigusé and Amanuel were ordained evangelists and, accompanied by Christian wives, were sent on their way with an Oromo caravan. Yet it was 1884 before they were established in Jima, a Muslim town in the province of Kefa. By becoming secretary to the governor Nigusé was able to acquire land, support the mission, and establish a school. With his own money, he purchased slaves in the market, then freed and educated them in the Christian faith. In time, other children of the area came to the school. Thus the gospel spread.

The next volunteer was Gebre-Ewostateos Ze-Mikael (c.1865–1905), an expelled evangelical Orthodox priest of Tseazega who found refuge and employment with the SEM in Eritrea. Since he was a skillful translator, it was with reluctance that the SEM permitted him to go to the Oromo. Feeling a strong call, Ewostateos left for Jima in February 1897 with his wife, Gumesh, and Daniel Lulu and his wife, Tiru. Although warmly welcomed and urged to stay in Jima by Nigusé, the two families proceeded to Boji in Welega in order to have more freedom to evangelize. There the friendly governor, Dibaba, engaged

Ewostateos as private secretary and chaplain of the Orthodox church next to his home. This enabled Ewostateos to preach evangelical sermons and to read the Scripture in the Oromo language. After the Sunday service, all the worshipers were invited to the Ewostateos' home for coffee, more instruction, and singing. A school was opened with Gumesh, Tiru, and Daniel (until his death in 1904) as teachers. The school became an instrument for recruiting and training evangelists, who in turn opened similar schools in other Welega villages.

Fortunately the governor's chief secretary, Tegenye, was a Bible student and teacher. He was one of the benefactors of the evangelical movement within the Orthodox church that derived its origin from the German Lutheran missionary Peter Heyling more than two centuries earlier (see Ethiopia Introduction). The two men became close friends and colleagues. Tegenye assumed the leadership in Boji after Ewostateos' tragic death while rescuing Daniel's widow and children and Tegenye's wife, children, and animals from fire. His death changed the course of the evangelical enterprise from a reform movement within the Orthodox church to an outreach of lay evangelists.

The work of the evangelists trained by Ewostateos and his colleagues was strengthened by workers in Eritrea. Among them was Onesimos Nesib (c.1856-1931), a freed Oromo slave and the SEM's first convert (see ECE, below). After his SEM schooling and five years of further education in Sweden, Onesimos translated the New Testament (1893), Luther's *Small Catechism,* many hymns, and other Christian literature into the Oromo language. Greatly assisting him were two Oromo women, Aster Ganno (c.1874-1964) and Lidia Dimbo (c.1872-1933). Enslaved as young women, freed by Italians, and entrusted to the SEM for education, they became students of Onesimos in the SEM Imkullu school for girls. Aster's real feel for the Oromo language and her genuine literary gifts enabled her to become Onesimos' assistant in Bible translation. On her own, she composed an Oromo dictionary and, together with Onesimos, produced an *Oromo Reader.* Lidia, Onesimos' wife, greatly encouraged his work. The entire Bible, finished in 1897, was taken to St. Chrischona in Switzerland

by Onesimos, who personally supervised the printing, completed in 1899.

Now Onesimos felt free to return to his people. In 1904, with permission from the archbishop and the emperor to proclaim the gospel (providing he abstain from delicate questions like fasting and the role of the Virgin Mary), Onesimos, accompanied by family and colleagues—including Aster—settled in Nejo, 25 kilometers (16 miles) west of Boji. Here, the governing prince provided tax-free land and built them homes and a school. Within a short time there were 20 students enrolled. Since many more desired to enroll, Onesimos sent an urgent request to Eritrea for more workers.

The promising career of Onesimos, however, was hampered by clerical opposition, reinforced by government officials. He and other evangelists had to stand trial and persecution. The SEM had been of the impression that the people in Welega were animists. However, the Orthodox church had moved into this once independent province and used Orthodoxy as a means of inculcating the Amhara culture and of combating the growing Oromo consciousness, which the evangelical movement strengthened.

The same year that Onesimos settled in Boji, Welega (1904), the first SEM missionary to complete the journey from Eritrea arrived (four previous attempts had failed). Karl Cederqvist (1854–1919), a pastor and close friend of Onesimos from student days in Sweden, was not given permission to evangelize in Welega. Besides, the SEM-trained evangelists did not want a mission established that would stamp their work as "foreign." So Cederqvist settled in Addis Ababa and, like the evangelists, opened a school where a number of later prominent church and government leaders were educated. He also cooperated with the enlightened Christians in the Evangelical Association.

The independent character of the evangelical enterprise on Oromo soil was further strengthened by a conference of evangelists (1907) held in Nak'amet, where Onesimos now lived and was permitted to do limited work. Eight of the 10 evangelists were present. Two of them had been trained in Boji by Ewostateos. Aster, who served as a Bible woman, was included. The participants shared experiences and agreed on a common policy: to continue their schools but in such a way as not to give their critics occasion to complain.

Meanwhile, Cederqvist was able to assist and intercede for the Ethiopian workers in various ways, and in 1916, a time when regent Haile Selassie was introducing modern education, he secured official permission for an evangelical enterprise in Ethiopia. Thus the way was opened to establish schools for girls, to further medical work, and to organize congregations.

The first to be formed was the Mekane Yesus congregation in Addis Ababa in 1921. From the beginning it had indigenous pastors who worked in harmony with the SEM missionaries. The first pastor, Gebre-Sillassé Tesfa-Gabir, was ordained in Asmara in 1920 by the veteran missionary Anders Svensson (1849–1928) and in 1923 was commissioned to serve the capital city congregation. This he did faithfully until his death in 1932. Gebre-Sillassé had come from a family of Orthodox priests (four generations). While a deacon, he experienced spiritual renewal through the Bible reading movement. It was he who answered the call of Onesimos for more workers in Welega, where he served as a teacher and evangelist from 1905 until 1914 (see ECE, below).

As Swedish missionaries arrived and the sacraments were administered, other congregations were formed—Nejo and Nak'amet being the first. However, the reformation of the Orthodox church was not forgotten, and there was great hesitancy to organize congregations in those places where there was an Orthodox church. The missionaries centered their attention on the Oromo who had not heard the gospel.

When the Italians occupied Ethiopia in 1936, all missionaries had to leave and all Protestant schools were closed. Many of the leading evangelical Christians were put in prison and in some cases executed, a fate they shared with other educated Ethiopians. Nevertheless, during this period the number of evangelical Christians increased tremendously—from 1000 in 1935 to 20,000 in 1942. These were also years of intense Ethiopian nationalism, and the Orthodox church became its symbol.

The Ethiopian evangelicals related to the SEM also asserted themselves. For example, the Addis Ababa congregation called Qes Badima Yalew (1885–1973) to be pastor. As a young Orthodox deacon, he served in Boji and was greatly influenced by Gebre-Ewostateos. But as an evangelical priest, he remained faithful to the Orthodox church. Serving with him was Emmanuel Gebre-Sillassé (b.1910), the son of the first pastor. After finishing his studies in Asmara and Addis Ababa, Emmanuel was employed as a teacher by the SEM and later sent to Scotland for further education and to Sweden for a visit. When the missionaries were expelled in 1936, he and Badima were entrusted with the SEM work and property in the capital city. Emmanuel had great gifts as a preacher and administrator. He also kept in touch with the evangelists in Welega and had their confidence. In 1959 he became the EECMY's first president.

When the Italian occupation ended in 1941, the Addis Ababa congregation immediately organized itself as a church independent of the SEM. Without malice, the SEM was notified that its services were no longer needed, that SEM missionaries should be sent to those who had not heard the gospel, and that the congregation would help in this mission outreach. From then on, the evangelical congregation in Addis Ababa became the center for all evangelical Christians in Ethiopia. Here leaders of the various groups met for deliberation and council. When the new church building was dedicated in 1950, the name Mekane Yesus was taken, and other congregations followed suit.

In 1944 the Conference of Ethiopian Evangelical Churches (CEEC) was organized with the express purpose of forming a united evangelical church. Missionaries were not invited to participate. The annual meetings of the CEEC became workshops where the representatives quietly deliberated on everyday problems as well as on basic questions for the new church. The responsibility of representing the CEEC before the government was assigned to the Addis Ababa congregation.

At this time there were only four ordained pastors for the 15 organized congregations. Besides Qes Badima, the Orthodox priest, there were two in Dembi Dolo, Mammo Chorqa and Gidada Solan, who had been ordained by a missionary of the American United Presbyterian Mission (AUPM). The Hermannsburg Mission had also ordained an Ethiopian, Daffa Djammo (b.1912), before the missionaries were forced to leave. Hence it was natural that the CEEC hoped for a united theological training center. In this they were disappointed. The AUPM established a school in Dembi Dolo in 1947, the SEM one in Nejo in 1949, and the Sudan Interior Mission (SIM) gave instruction in various Bible schools. These mission programs, important as they were for church expansion, strengthened denominationalism rather than evangelical unity.

Ordination became a problem to the evangelicals. In the Orthodox as well as the Swedish Lutheran tradition, it was a bishop who ordained pastors. Yet the evangelicals were expected to settle for ordination by a missionary. Baptism and Holy Communion practices in the evangelical congregations were also influenced by those in the Orthodox church, and these did not satisfy the younger men who were being trained and influenced by the postwar missionaries.

To diminish these denominational differences, the CEEC, in 1947, decided that a confessional book of the Ethiopian Evangelical Church should be produced and be a statement of faith based on the Bible alone. This remarkable proposal came from an ordained pastor of the Presbyterian mission, Gidada Solan (1901–1977). Although blind and with little formal education, he was aware of and appreciated the Westminster Confession. A committee was elected to prepare such a book. Unfortunately none of the respected and gifted members had the kind of education necessary for this tremendous undertaking. When no book had been produced by 1954, there was general dissatisfaction. Help and leadership were urgently needed. And, in the wings, there were missionaries waiting to come on stage.

These missionaries represented five Lutheran missions. As already noted, the first SEM missionary, Karl Cederqvist, had come in 1904. Others followed: the Swedish Mission of Bible True Friends (1921), the German Hermannsburg Mission (an unsuccessful attempt in 1854 was renewed in 1927), the Norwegian Lutheran Mission (1948, augmented in 1952 by the Icelandic Mission), and the Danish Ethiopian Mission (1948). Already these five had joined the Inter-Mission Council to deal with comity and other mission relations. But the real initiative for cooperation and consolidation came from the outside.

Since the First Assembly of the Lutheran World Federation (1947) urged the formation of united Lutheran churches in Africa, Asia, and Latin America, the effect was soon felt in Ethiopia. At its 1951 meeting in Germany, the Commission on Younger Churches and Orphaned Missions (CYCOM) designated the Norwegian Lutheran Mission's general secretary, Tormond Vaagen, to investigate the possibilities in Ethiopia. He in turn called together representatives of the five missions working in Ethiopia and initiated the formation of the *Lutheran Missions Committee (LMC)*. As its first task it prepared Christian literature for the congregations—Luther's *Small* and *Large Catechisms*, family sermons, and Galatians. It also promoted higher education by establishing the Ethiopian Evangelical College in Debre Zeyt (1956). Serving as a link with the LWF, the LMC prepared the ground for the Yemissrach Dimts literacy campaign (1962) and the founding of the Mekane Yesus Seminary (1960), both LWF projects (above).

By 1954 the SEM missionary, Manfred Lundgren, was ready to encourage the formation of a confessional church. Until then he had persisted in the original goal of renewing the Orthodox church along evangelical lines. His 1948 proposal of an Ethiopian Christian Council did materialize but with the limited objective of promoting Christian literature. The continuous persecution and de facto excommunication of evangelical Orthodox made clear that there was no room for them within the established EOC. Besides, most of the evangelicals lived in areas that had become a part of the Ethiopian empire very late and therefore they had little or no historic relationship to the Orthodox church. The Presbyterians (see Ethiopia Introduction) had recognized this fact earlier and, in 1947, had encouraged the formation of the Ethiopian Evangelical Church–Bethel in western Welega.

Closer cooperation intensified the confessional issues of the CEEC. At its 1954 meeting, an Ethiopian from Sidamo, an area south of Addis Ababa where the Norwegian Lutheran Mission was working intensively, proposed that missionaries be included in the committee drafting a confessional book or statement of faith. Although the committee comprised two Ethiopians for each expatriate, the missionaries dominated. Instead of a confession statement, they drafted a constitution for a church that would be Lutheran in doctrine but not in name. This was not acceptable to the Presbyterians nor to all the Lutherans. An alternative would be to form a federation of evangelical churches. Although adopted, the plan was never realized. Instead, the energies of the Ethiopians henceforth led toward the formation of a confessionally Lutheran church.

A factor favoring the willingness of Ethiopian evangelicals to be confessionally Lutheran was the participation of Emmanuel Gebre-Sillassé and Emmanuel Abraham in the 1955 All-Africa Lutheran Conference in Marangu, Tanzania. Emmanuel Abraham, son of one of the first believers in Boji, was Ethiopia's ambassador to Great Britain. He was chosen to chair the All-Africa Lutheran Conference and did so admirably. Emmanuel Gebre-Sillassé added a deep spiritual dimension. Both men were greatly appreciated by their fellow Africans. The Ethiopians, in turn, realized for the first time that Lutherans, too, are evangelical. The suggestion that the Mekane Yesus congregation apply for interim membership in the LWF was well received. This necessitated a thorough study of the confessional basis of the LWF, including the *Augsburg Confession*. The congregation expressed its agreement and was received into the LWF at the Minneapolis assembly in 1957. Furthermore, the congregation's representative, Emmanuel Abraham, was elected to the LWF Executive Committee.

Also in 1957, the American Lutheran Church appeared on the scene, beginning its work north of Addis Ababa in a heavily Muslim area. After being accepted into the LMC in September, the ALC's representative, Herbert Schaefer, newly transferred from India, quickly assumed a leadership role. He initiated plans for a joint seminary and a mass literacy program. He also redrafted the constitution. It provided for a church made up of congregations grouped into relatively independent synods. Local heritages could thus be maintained without weakening the central church. The EECMY administration would deal with the government, cultivate international relations, and hold all immovable property.

When the delegates met in convention (January 1959) and the last of the congregations signed the constitution, the Ethiopian Evangelical Church Mekane Yesus (EECMY) was founded. Emmanuel Gebre-Sillassé was elected president; Herbert Schaefer, vice-president; Hagos Legesse, secretary; and Manfred Lundgren, treasurer. The church at large was received into LWF membership in 1963.

The ensuing years were not easy. Relationships had to be worked out with each of the synods and the overseas missions working in their midst. In 1965 the Kambata Evangelical Church applied for membership in the EECMY. After lengthy discussion, it was admitted as a synod. This church was a part of the Word of Life Church until 1955, when it withdrew because of the strong SIM control (see Ethiopia Introduction).

The central administration, hampered by an overworked staff and inadequate facilities, was strengthened in 1966. Gudina Tumsa, of Boji, a man of towering stature, became executive secretary. Earlier, while serving as a dresser in the Nak'amet hospital, he had been chosen for pastoral training. For a number of years he served as pastor in Nak'amet. Through an LWF scholarship he earned his B.D. degree at Luther Seminary, St. Paul, Minnesota. Assisting him was Manfred Lundgren (above), who had first served in Ethiopia as a Red Cross worker during the Italian occupation in the 1930s. He had returned to Ethiopia after three years in Geneva as Africa secretary for the LWF. Working together, Gudina and Lundgren ably guided the relationships between the EECMY and the missions to a satisfactory conclusion in 1969. "Integrated Policy," a document signed by all participating agencies, gave the EECMY full responsibility for all programs and affiliated institutions transferred to it.

Rapid growth and unfolding opportunities moved the EECMY to call on a number of other missions and churches in America and Europe for assistance in personnel and finance. The positive response also complicated administration. Therefore, during the severe Ethiopian famine of 1974, the EECMY called for a consultation with its cooperating agencies. Held the following January, the consultation was presented with EECMY's statement, "Principals for the Relationship between EECMY and the Cooperating Missions/Churches." This landmark in ecclesial growth expedited the streamlining of procedures for better service and closer partnership.

The turbulent political situation of 1977 necessitated another set of consultations. The third of these (with representatives from eight churches, 12 missions, and three LWF offices—DCC, DWS, DOC) convened in Oslo, Norway, in September 1978. The "terms of reference" of the proposed Committee of Mutual Christian Responsibility (CMCR) were drawn, providing for consultations and discussions where all partners would consider all aspects of the relationship. The EECMY was allotted five voting members and all other participants one each. The CMCR, formally organized in Christiansfeld, Denmark (April 1979), included the following members: American Lutheran Church, Berlin Mission, Church of Sweden Mission, Danish Evangelical Mission, Evangelical Lutheran Church of Hanover, Evangelical Church in Berlin-Brandenburg, Evangelical Lutheran Free Church of Norway, Evangelical Lutheran Mission in Lower Saxony, Finnish Lutheran Mission, Finnish Missionary Society, Lutheran Church in America, Norwegian Lutheran Mission, Swedish Evangelical Mission, and the United Presbyterian Church, USA.

The last mentioned supersedes the United Presbyterian Church in North America, supporter of the Ethiopian Evangelical Church–Bethel Synod (EEC-B, 1947), and is an indication of its continued interest and support of Bethel, which merged with EECMY in 1974. At that time its 16,000 members were in 55 organized congregations located in the Kefa, Ilubabor, and Welega provinces near the Sudan border. The EEC-B, as a member of the CEEC, had earlier planned to become a part of an all-Ethiopian evangelical church but withdrew because of a different interpretation of the Lord's Supper. The EEC-B became two synods in the EECMY. The Bethel Evangelical Secondary School (BESS) in Dembi Dolo, owned and operated by the Western Welega Bethel Synod, rates as one of the best schools of its kind in Ethiopia. Founded in 1965 by the UPC-USA, it benefits from well-trained Ethiopian teachers (some of whom have USA university degrees) and from expatriate teachers from the USA and

Finland. Situated in one of the least developed areas of Ethiopia, the school also provides practical training and has been expanding its agricultural department for the benefit of the surrounding region.

The Bethel merger into the EECMY strengthened the Ethiopian evangelicals. They had worked together since the 1940s and early 1950s and had never lost the vision of one Ethiopian evangelical church.

EVANGELICAL CHURCH OF ERITREA (ECE)
(Wenghelawit Bete Kristian Be Ertra)
Member: LWF (1963), WCC
Membership: 7600
President: The Rev. Ogbarebi Hibtes
PO Box 905
Asmara

This church in the province of Eritrea by the Red Sea is the oldest autonomous Lutheran church in Africa and the mother of the large EECMY (above). Self-governing since 1926, it has withstood the effects of foreign invasion, persecution, political strife, civil war, and periodic famine. Today, with countless other northern Ethiopians, its members are suffering intensely. Yet they continue to serve their Lord.

The ECE comprises 35 congregational districts served by only 20 pastors, a number of whom are beyond the retirement age. An annual synod is the ECE's highest authority, with a synodical council acting as an executive body. The present constitution was adopted in 1962. A year later the church was received into the LWF. During the ensuing decade its growth was considerable. A New Life Campaign in the early 1970s was very successful in the highland provinces of Seraye and Hamasen. More recently growth has been hampered by civil strife. Many church buildings have been badly damaged and others completely destroyed.

Under these circumstances and for its size, the ECE has a significant outreach: three elementary schools, three literacy campaign schools (a teaching staff of 25 for 1,350 students), four clinics, a hostel for boys and girls in Asmara, and a domestic school for girls in Adi Ugri. Its school for hearing impaired, in Keren, receives special support from people in Sweden and Finland. Full responsibility was assumed in 1972 for the above institutions, founded by the Swedish Evangelical Mission.

Several attempts have been made by the ECE to meet the great need for pastors. In 1966 and again in 1979, pastoral training courses were offered in Asmara. Due to the economic and political situation and also the decline in the general educational level of candidates, these attempts brought little result. During the 1980s, candidates for the ordained ministry have enrolled in the Lutheran Theological College in Makumira, *Tanzania. The Asmara center is now used mainly for in-service training and shorter courses to meet special needs of clergy and laity.

With assistance from the LWF, the Swedish Evangelical Mission, and the Church of Sweden, the ECE attempts to reconstruct destroyed as well as deteriorating church structures. The Asmara congregation, already founded in 1891, hoped for a much needed church building in 1971, but even in 1985 this had not been accomplished. In the port of Massawa, construction for a church center began in 1985. To meet a variety of needs it contains a community hall and library, guest rooms, a parsonage, and an office for LWF World Service workers. The latter has provided famine relief to Ethiopia, including Eritrea, since 1974 (see EECMY, above) and works with the ECE in giving rehabilitative service to people in need, especially the fishermen and their families in Massawa and on the offshore Dahlak Islands, one of the hottest spots in the world. In 1978–1979, the bitter fighting destroyed all the fish-processing plants, the ice plant, and the Massawa fishing fleet, leaving about 4000 people without their livelihood.

● ● ●

The sturdiness with which the ECE has persevered suggests the forward look that has enlivened it for well over a century. Its historical beginnings go back to Massawa in 1866 and the arrival of the first three emissaries of the Swedish Evangelical Mission (SEM). These pioneers had not intended to commence work in Eritrea but in the distant Galla (Oromo) country. Political tensions with Egypt and other powers, as well as Orthodox pressure, kept the missionaries in Massawa and its deep hinterland.

The missionaries began their work among the Kunama, a large tribe of animists inhabiting the fertile valleys of the Mareb and Tekeze rivers, extending westward to the Sudan border. Missionary Carl Johan Carlsson (1836–1867), in particular, was successful in gaining the confidence of the Kunama people, and for a time he served as a peacemaker between them and the aggressive Muslim Egyptians. His sudden death in October 1867 was a heavy loss to the embryonic work. Although other recruits, including two wives, were sent in by the SEM, tropical disease, death, and the fact that their presence endangered the lives of the Kunama forced the seven missionaries to withdraw to Massawa in February 1870.

In Massawa the missionaries pioneered urban work, attracting a variety of needy people, including Muslim traders and freed slaves. The latter, both male and female, were entrusted to the SEM for education by the French and British consuls. A community developed, including a school for boys and young men. It was known as Bethel congregation in 1872 when the first convert, Nesib (c.1856–1931), was baptized and given the name Onesimos. An Oromo, he had been snatched from his mother, then sold and resold four times. He and two Oromo women became important figures in the spread of Christianity among their people and in the founding of the EECMY (above). In Imkullu, not far from Massawa, a girls' school was established in 1879 on property given by the British Governor-General, Charles G. Gordon. Until 1891 Imkullu served as the mission headquarters, which included a clinic and printing press.

In 1872, while the SEM missionaries were recuperating in the Tigrigna-speaking highlands and also studying the Amarigna language with a Christian Falasha teacher, they were protected by the area chief and befriended by the Orthodox priests at Tseazega. In time the missionaries learned that the priests were studying the Scripture using Amarigna Bibles that had been sent there in 1866 by a colleague of Gobat, J. Martin Flad (1831–1915). A supportive friendship developed between them. Periodically, and especially in the 1870s and 1880s, followers of the Bible movement were persecuted and had to flee for their lives. Some found refuge with the missionaries in Imkullu (Massawa),

Ailet (halfway to the coast), and Geleb (to the north), where SEM stations and schools had been established. A number of these fugitives were employed by the SEM as teachers in village schools; a few volunteered their services as evangelists in southwest Ethiopia. Still others became pastors of evangelical congregations and were an important factor in establishing the Evangelical Church of Eritrea. One pioneer missionary, P. E. Lager (1837–1876), took special interest in the Orthodox priests and in their desire to reform the established church. He became a martyr to the cause in 1876.

Persecution restrained the Bible movement but did not crush it. Rather, the followers urged the SEM to establish work in the highlands. Sites were secured in Asmara and Tseazega, and by 1891 much of the work was transferred there. Through the village schools, education made great strides among adults as well as children. Literacy became a requirement for confirmation.

Adversity also helped to spread the gospel through an innovative relief program. Extended periods of drought in the north beginning in 1888 resulted in a prolonged famine. Great crowds of starving people came to Massawa for food the government had imported from India. Christians in Sweden also responded to the dire situation by collecting 24,000 crowns for famine relief. This enabled the people in Imkullu to provide food twice daily to some 800 refugee families at the nearby camp. Since the recipients came from many different areas of the interior, new doors opened for education and evangelization.

The outreach to the Tigre-speaking people in northern Eritrea, where Islam had made inroads, began slowly. The adults were not interested in literacy or in having their children educated. Yet the young people were eager to have a better life. The first convert was a 15-year-old boy, Dawit Amanuel (1862–1944). He was baptized by missionary Bengt Peter Lundahl (1840–1885) in 1877. Shortly thereafter the mission in Geleb was closed for several years by the authorities, who resented that it was also used as a retreat center for the Bible-reading Orthodox of Hamasen. But Dawit Amanuel was put to work translating the gospel of Mark and then the entire New Testament, which he finished in 1890 with the help of Tewolde-Medhin

Gebre-Medhin (1860–1930). Dawit Amanuel also gathered Tigre ballads, folklore, and lyrics, which the SEM published.

Meanwhile, missionary K. G. Rodén (1860–1943) strove to improve the life of the Tigre-speaking people who were suffering from the prolonged famine. A well-equipped clinic, which included a midwife, attracted many patients. Selected breeding of animals, improved housing construction, and even a 150-kilometer road from the rugged hills to the lowlands and coast below aided the people as well as the government. Due to the semi-nomadic life, boarding schools were established, one for boys (1892) and one for girls (1903). Many of the students experienced conversion. Girls were liberated from bondage, and boys found new purpose in life. A number of the young men took further training to become evangelists and teachers in the surrounding villages. By 1911 the congregation in Geleb had 277 members, most of whom were from Muslim homes.

Work among the Kunama was resumed in 1898 when the Italian conquest of Eritrea made this safe. The first baptism (1910) was the result of the endeavors of a Sudanese couple who had been commissioned missionaries after their training in the school in Imkullu. However, there was no substantial growth until a few girls who had been converted at the mission school established Christian homes. Since the Kunama have a matrilineal social structure, it was necessary for women to lead the way to Christ. World War I, when the missions were closed by the government, caused another setback. Besides, the people were disillusioned by the deaths of members. They had understood eternal life to mean there would be no physical death.

Between 1876 and 1889, five gifted young men, including Onesimos, were sent to the Johannelund Theological Institute in Stockholm for further education. In 1888 two others studied in Florence, Italy, at the Waldensian Seminary. However, the SEM was slow in encouraging the ordination of Ethiopians. And the Ethiopians were not ready to accept a seemingly second-rate ordination. In their minds and tradition, only an archbishop could perform this rite.

In 1888 the SEM authorized two Orthodox priests to perform ministerial acts, and in 1909 two well-prepared men consented to be ordained by the SEM director, Dr. Johannes Kolmodin, from Sweden. One, Tewolde-Medhin, son of the chief priest in Tseazega, served in Geleb. The other, Tekle Tesfa-Kristos (c.1879–1924), trained as an evangelist by missionary Jonas Iwarson (1867–1947), later served the Hembirti congregation.

Already in 1893 the SEM board decided that Eritrea should receive equal consideration with the Galla country, for by that time there had been four unsuccessful attempts to reach the Oromo. It was not until 1904 that missionary Karl Cederqvist made it to Addis Ababa, and only in 1916 were missionaries permitted into Welega, where the Oromo lived.

In the intervening period a score of Ethiopian evangelists had volunteered their services and been sent on their way by the Eritrean churches to do what the missionaries could not do. Young Eritrean congregations also sacrificed financially to support these evangelists in their work (see EECMY, above). One of them, Gebre-Sillassé Tesfa-Gabir (1881–1932), returned to Eritrea for health reasons in 1914. Ordained with a second group of four in 1920, he was sent again in 1923 to be the first pastor of the Mekane Yesus congregation in Addis Ababa (above).

Meanwhile new congregations were being planted and others were growing strong in Eritrea. In spite of differences in religious background—Orthodox, Islam, and Traditional—they joined together to form the Evangelical Church of Eritrea in 1926. Then in 1959, they rejoiced when their daughter church (EECMY) was founded with an Eritrean son as president.

LUTHERAN CHURCH IN ERITREA
(Lutheran Bete-Kristian Be Ertra)
(P)
Membership: 3632
President: The Rev. Temesghen Temnewo
PO Box 1279
Asmara, Eritrea

This church, autonomous since 1957, consists of 12 congregations guided by six pastors as well as assisting elders. An executive committee governs the church. The church dates its beginning to 1911, when several missionaries of the Swedish Evangelical Mission resigned in order to initiate new work under the auspices of the Swedish Mission of Bible True Friends (SMBTF). The early history parallels that of the Evangelical Church of Eritrea (ECE, above). Today, in spite of war and oppression, congregational work continues, but the primary schools, important in mission, have been taken over by the government. The SMBTF personnel were forced to leave in 1975.

LUTHERAN CHURCH IN ETHIOPIA
(P)
Membership: 5000**
General Secretary: Abebe Gashawbeza
PO Box 1002
Addis Ababa

This church, independent since 1959, has a synodical structure with pastors and elders in charge of the 45 congregations, mainly in the area south of Addis Ababa. There are 11 ordained pastors. The school and clinic work of the church continues, but the theological seminary in Asela was closed by the government in 1982. The church has sent pastoral candidates to the Matongo Theological College in *Kenya.

New synods have been formed in the Wollaita area in Sidamo province and in the Kullo area in Kefa province, the most densely populated area in southwest Ethiopia. The great need for pastors and educated church leaders in these areas, where the language is different, prompted the establishment, with LWF help, of the Leadership Training Center and Bible School in Wollaita Awradja.

The Swedish Mission of Bible True Friends began work in Eritrea in 1911 and later (1921) extended into southeastern Ethiopia. During the Italian occupation, the work suffered but amazingly spread to *Kenya. Although the evangelists affiliated with the SMBTF took part in the Conference of Ethiopian Evangelical Churches (1944–1959) (see EECMY, above), they chose not to be part of the EECMY but formed their own small church.

The church is largely self-reliant and has taken over the ongoing educational and medical program of the SMBTF. As the situation permits, the SMBTF continues some financial and personnel support.

KENYA

A republic (1964) and a member of the Commonwealth of Nations. Formerly a British colony and protectorate. Area: 580,367 sq. km. (224,081 sq. mi.). Pop. (1983 est.): 17,850,000, including 2% Asian and European. Cap. and largest city: Nairobi (pop., 1981 est., 919,000). Languages: Swahili (official) and English.

History: In Kenya, as elsewhere in Africa, the people are a spectrum of many ethnic groups. From the pastoral folk, whose traces here run back beyond 1000 B.C., to their continuing counterparts, the Masai (*Tanzania), scores of ethnic groups have enlivened the land. The series of events most prominent in this century has been the struggle for freedom and eventual independence from foreign control. Besides the movement of peoples across the land, from Somalia, *Ethiopia, the *Sudan, and other parts, the access by sea of Arab and then European powers has shaped the country's history.

Already by the eighth century A.D., Arab traders were dealing in ivory and slaves with the island town of Mombasa, the center for coastal shipping on the Indian Ocean. In 1498 the Portuguese came. Seven years later they burned down Mombasa, fortified the town, and for the next two centuries kept the Arabs at bay. When the Arabs regained control, ties were strengthened with Zanzibar (see *Tanzania) and Europeans were admitted only sparingly.

The British, eager to terminate the slave trade in East Africa, progressively extended control along the coast during the 19th century. In 1844 the adventurous Johann Ludwig Krapf (1810–1881), a German Lutheran in the service of the Anglican Church Missionary Society (see also Ethiopia), moved to Mombasa. A gifted linguist, he mastered Swahili (Kiswahili) and a number of other native tongues, explored the interior, and in 1849 was the first white person to see Mount Kenya. The opening of the Suez Canal (1869) speeded up contact with Europe. By the 1890s the British had secured from the Sultan of Zanzibar the right to establish a protectorate along the Kenya coast.

After 1903 British and other white settlers moved into the interior plateau, taking land from the Africans for their own plantations.

Nairobi, a former Masai water hole, became a way station for the newly built Mombasa to Uganda railway. In 1905 Nairobi replaced Mombasa as the capital of the coastal protectorate, and from 1921–1963 it was the capital of the British colony of Kenya. The resistance of the Masai, the Kikuyu, and others mounted, and in the 1950s the Mau Mau movement—including terrorism—hastened the coming of independence. The leader of the movement, Jomo Kenyatta (1893–1978), imprisoned for a time by the British, became the first president of the Republic of Kenya in 1963.

Later in the 1960s, with its newly independent neighbors Uganda and *Tanzania, Kenya led in the formation of the East Africa Community—a common market with emphases also on transportation, higher education, communication, and finance. Differing political directions brought the community to a virtual standstill by 1977, only to be gradually revived in 1985. Following Kenyatta's death, Kenya faced difficulties that the worsening world economic situation intensified. A costly coup (1982) was put down. In the same year Kenya became a one-party state by an act of Parliament amending the constitution.

Nairobi, meanwhile, has established itself as one of Africa's important international cities. From high-rise to shanty, wealth and poverty exist juxtaposed. The Kenyatta Conference Center includes the United Nations Environmental Agency. The University of Nairobi, initially a part of the former University of East Africa with campuses also in Kampala and Dar es Salaam, is a young and vigorous institution. It has had a department of religious studies since the 1970s.

Religion: Christian, 73% (Protestant-Catholic ratio, 3:2); Traditional, 19%; Muslim, 6%; other, 2%. Islam gained a foothold in Malindi and Mombasa after the eighth century and spread inland. Today Islam remains a small but significant minority. Hinduism and other eastern religions have gained converts in recent years through the Indian population. African Traditional religion, a collective term for many variations, is losing numbers even though there have been several strong attempts at revival during the last three decades.

Christianity, brought into Kenya by the Roman Catholic Portuguese in the 16th century, did not endure. It was introduced again in 1844 with the arrival of Johann Ludwig Krapf (above) and the baptism seven years later of a dying cripple by Johann Rebmann, also of the Church Missionary Society.

Krapf's initial vision of a progression of mission centers set south of the Sahara (the Sudan) to West Africa came to him near Mombasa, but it became a partial fact only many years later (*Ethiopia; *Nigeria: Karl Kumm, Sudan Mission). The slow progress in the 19th century finally turned into a massive expansion in the 20th century. What travel by ship had been to the beginning of missions on the coast, access by railway became in the early 1900s for spreading the gospel into the interior regions. The Mombasa-Uganda line, via Nairobi, remains a prime example of this.

Today's inclusive account of the Christian scene, *Kenya Churches Handbook* (1973), is the most exhaustive resource on this subject for any African country. It also set the standard for the *World Christian Encyclopedia* (1982), likewise produced in Nairobi by the same author-editor, David Barrett.

The Roman Catholic Church in Kenya claims over four million members. The hierarchy, in Kenyan hands since 1955, includes the archdiocese of Nairobi and ten dioceses. The Anglican Province of Kenya (1844) claimed over 1.2 million members by the mid-1980s. African Orthodox, Methodist, Presbyterian, Seventh Day Adventists, Friends, and others have constituencies of over 100,000 each. Various groups of Pentecostals have an estimated million adherents. An enormous number of small church bodies account for the rest of the non-Lutheran Christian population. Chief among them are the Independent churches, offshoots of the mission churches. Among the major Independents, the East Africa Revival (1927) has over the decades generated a theologically sound and actively ecumenical spirit among its estimated 300,000 adherents in Kenya, with additional participants in *Tanzania and Uganda.

In effect, Nairobi is one of Africa's prime ecumenical landmarks: here are the headquarters of the All Africa Conference of Churches (1963), of the Association of Evangelicals of Africa and Madagascar (1966), and of the United Bible Societies/Africa Region. The National Christian Council of Kenya (NCCK; so named since 1966, but formed in 1943, and having antecedents to 1918) includes over two dozen church bodies, plus the larger Independent churches. It has maintained over a dozen agencies providing specialized services. With a staff near 100, the NCCK is one of the largest national councils in the world. The Evangelical Lutheran Church in Kenya (below) is active in the NCCK, and the Kenya Synod of the Evangelical Lutheran Church in Tanzania (below) also is a member.

Among the Christian world communions that have met here are the World Alliance of Reformed Churches, the Methodist World Conference, and the Pentecostal World Conference. The World Council of Churches assembly in Nairobi (1975) recognized the deepening partnership between the churches in Africa and in other continents. In 1984 the World Conference of Religion and Peace held its fourth assembly in Nairobi.

EVANGELICAL LUTHERAN CHURCH IN KENYA (ELCK)

(Kanisa la Kiinjili la Kilutheri Katika Kenya)
Member: LWF (1970), NCCK
Membership: 31,000**
Chair: The Rev. Francis Nyamwaro
PO Box 874
Kisii

This young autonomous church in Kenya has quadrupled in size in the last 20 years. Most of its 163 congregations, served by 35 pastors and 79 evangelists, are in the province of Nyanza, a heavily populated area east of Lake Victoria where the Kisii and Luo people live. They are settled agriculturalists. Cotton, millet, sorghum, tea, and coffee are their main crops. Cattle raising and fishing are also important economic assets. The church has extended its work into five provinces, including the capital city of Nairobi where the congregations are strategically located.

The church was organized with an interim constitution in 1958 after nearly 10 years of pioneering by the Swedish Mission of Bible True Friends (SMBTF). In the same year its first candidate for the ministry was ordained after three years of study at Makumira Lutheran Theological College in *Tanzania. In 1963 the constitution was thoroughly revised, and in 1965 the church was registered with the government as an independent church. Authority is exercised by the general assembly, the executive committee, district and parish councils, and congregational meetings. The executive committee oversees the work of the church. Pastoral candidates, called by the executive committee, have four years of theological education and one year of work under an experienced pastor. Evangelists, who assist with pastoral work, have at least two years of training and frequent refresher courses.

In order for pastors as well as evangelists to be educated in Kenya, the church established the Matongo Lutheran Theological College and Bible School in 1978. With help from the LWF Department of Church Cooperation, the Bible school (founded in 1957) was enlarged and the staff increased. Theological education by extension (TEE), part of the school's outreach, has enabled Christians with limited formal education to have training for effective service in their congregations.

The church, with support and personnel from five mission societies (below), sponsors an extensive educational, medical, welfare, and outreach program: 50 primary (two with boarding facilities), six secondary, and five village polytechnic schools; a school for mentally retarded children; four health centers; one maternity ward; and a chaplaincy service to prisoners in Kisii and Nairobi.

Luther's Catechism, translated into both Kisii and Luo, and a hymn book in Kisii have been published. With the Kenya Bible Society, the New Testament in Kisii has been revised and distributed. Programs are prepared for weekly broadcast over the Voice of Kenya in both Kisii and Luo to a listening audience estimated at 200,000. Swahili programs are under way.

Although the church has been autonomous since 1958, the Swedish Mission of Bible True Friends continues its help and financial support. In 1963 the Swedish Lutheran Evangelical Association in Finland joined in the work, followed by the World Mission Prayer League (USA) in 1969 and the Lutheran Evangelical Association of Finland in 1970. All have missionaries in the field who have helped the church to reach out into new areas.

In 1976 the church embarked on a mission to the Pokot tribe, Traditionalists living in the West Pokot district north of Kitale. The work has extended to the Ugandan border. Other missionaries reached out to the Borans living on the northern frontier up to the Ethiopian border, an area of Islamic advance. In 1981 the Samburu, a nomadic Masai-like tribe living northwest of Nairobi, were reached. Like the Samburu themselves, expatriate missionary couples lead a mobile life, setting up camp for periods of two or three weeks and then moving on. Bases have been established in both the northern and southern parts of the tribal area. Recently the ELCK and the Norwegian Lutheran Mission have begun a mission study among the Digo people on the coast below Mombasa.

The ELCK is ecumenically active—a member of the National Christian Council of Kenya, the Christian Churches Educational Association, the Protestant Churches Medical Association, and the Lutheran World Federation.

Historically it was an Ethiopian refugee who first turned the attention of the Swedish Mission of Bible True Friends to Kenya. The mission, having been expelled from *Ethiopia in the mid-1930s by the Italian occupation, was seeking a new field of labor, one that might permit some continued contact with its Ethiopian churches. A protégé of the mission school who had found refuge in Kenya wrote to the board in Sweden telling of the difficulties he and many other Ethiopians were facing. Early in 1939 a board member and a missionary came to Kenya. Through the wise counsel of the Kenyan government and the African Inland Mission, the team was able to help the refugees and also to find a new field of work.

EVANGELICAL LUTHERAN CHURCH IN TANZANIA—KENYA SYNOD
Member: NCCK
Membership: 4500**
Chair: The Rev. Joel Buya
PO Box 54128
Nairobi

The Kenya Synod of the ELCT came into being in 1965 in order to care for the large number of its members who had migrated to the cities of Nairobi and Mombasa. Later the work expanded into two rural areas. The

Ukanbani parish, centered in the village of Mutyambuu, southeast of Nairobi, serves a large area where the Yakamba as well as the nomadic Masai live. The other is along the Tana River, which flows into the Indian Ocean at Kipini north of Malindi. Here, where most of the people are Muslims, eight small congregations have been formed. In order to facilitate and strengthen this outreach, the ELCT plans to construct a church center at Gerzen, a river town of 6000. Assistance for this project is from the LWF Department of Church Cooperation and the Community Development Service.

The synod has the services of 10 pastors—four Kenyan, three Tanzanian, two American, and one German. Like the other synods of the ELCT, this one receives assistance through the Lutheran Coordinating Service. It is a member of the NCCK and cooperates with this council in its missionary outreach and service. The common Swahili language facilitates conversations with the ELCK (above) in discovering possible areas of cooperation.

MADAGASCAR REPUBLIC

The Madagascar Republic, proclaimed in 1958 and fully sovereign in 1960, is a member of the French Community of Nations. It occupies the island of Madagascar and adjacent islands in the Indian Ocean. Area: 587,051 sq. km. (226,662 sq. mi.). Pop. (1984 est.): 9,600,000. Cap. and largest city: Antananarivo (pop., 1982 est., 600,000). Languages: Malagasy and French (official).

History: Although geographically close to Africa, Madagascar's culture and language have pronounced Indonesian elements. Specifics are lacking, but scholars believe that in the distant past Indonesians, following the Arab coastal routes along the Indian Ocean, settled for a while on East African coastal lands. There they mingled with certain African people. Prior to A.D. 1500, there were several crossings of significant numbers to Madagascar. Through the Arab trade, Islamic as well as Swahili ingredients entered the Malagasy scene.

Strategically located, Madagascar was a well-developed kingdom prior to becoming a French overseas territory (1895–1958). A major uprising against the French (1947–1948), put down with great violence, did not prevent subsequent reconciliation. In 1960 the national assembly, elected by universal suffrage, adopted a comprehensive constitution. The republic's first president, Philibert Tsiranana, who favored a centralized government, held office for a dozen years (1960–1972).

In 1972 unrest over economic and other policies caused a change in government, with Colonel Richard Ratsimandrava being given popular support to govern without parliament. Conditions failed to improve, and Ratsimandrava was assassinated. The second Malagasy republic, proclaimed as the Democratic Republic of Madagascar, was launched in early 1975 with Didier Ratsiraka as president. In 1982 his reelection for another seven-year term suggested a general support for the socialist course being followed in seeking to cope with an ailing economy. During the years since 1960, the population had increased by about 80%. While the Madagascar Republic's foreign relations remain closest with France, it also plays an active role in the Organization of African Unity and cultivates connections with the francophone countries in Africa.

Religion: About half the people adhere to Traditional religion, the other half to Christianity. Observance of the Traditional includes following the customs of the ancestors and cultivating a joyously grateful fellowship with the departed. Certain Traditional elements continue among Christians, notably in a vivid sense of the church triumphant.

Roman Catholic Christianity first touched the Great Island in 1540. Missionary efforts began in Tananarive in 1643 and were linked to similar work, under Portuguese auspices, across the channel in Mozambique and across the Indian Ocean in Goa. But in Madagascar there were no lasting results. The 19th century brought renewed Roman Catholic missionary activity and also the unfolding of extensive Protestant work from Britain, Norway, and France. Today more than half of the Malagasy Christians are Roman Catholic. There are 14 dioceses grouped under three archdioceses. The oldest of the three is in the national capital, Antananarivo. The second (1896) is at the island's northern tip, Diégo Suarez; the third (1913), in Fianarantsoa. The heaviest concentration of Roman Catholic as well as Protestant Christians is in the central and southern regions of the island.

The London Missionary Society (1818) opened the way for Protestants. In 1820 its first schools opened under the royal favor of King Radama I. After his early death in 1835, Queen Ranovalona I reestablished Traditional religion, persecuted the Christians, and expelled the missionaries. Upon the queen's death 25 years later, the returning missionaries found a strong indigenous church of 5000 and some 30,000 people who had learned to read. The entire Bible had been printed in Malagasy.

Today the largest Protestant church, situated mainly in the northern half of the island, is the Church of Jesus Christ in Madagascar. It is a union (1968) of churches formed by the London Missionary Society (above), the British Friends, and the Paris Mission (1897). The predecessor bodies of this union church, together with the Anglicans and Lutherans, formed the Christian Council of Madagascar in 1958. It was reorganized in 1979 to include the Roman Catholics, and in early 1985 it was officially recognized by the government. The council's recent activities include efforts to have common scriptural terms, to study interdenominational marriage practices, supervision of a chaplaincy program at the university, and the coordination of religious education in the schools. Not included in the council are the Adventists, Pentecostals, and a number of other small bodies.

MALAGASY LUTHERAN CHURCH (MLC)

(Fiangonana Loterana Malagasy)
Member: LWF (1950), WCC, AACC, CCM, PCFM
Membership: 840,000**
President: The Rev. Benjamin Rabenorolahy
PO Box 1741
Tananarive

Situated mainly in the southern half of Madagascar, this autonomous church consists of 10 regional synods within a unifying general synod. The latter meets every three years and is the chief authority in matters of doctrine, discipline, institutions, and evangelization.

A president and executive committee, assisted by a general secretary, have charge of administration. The same pattern holds for the regional level. Although Fianarantsoa is closer to the geographic center of the MLC membership, a 1975 decision placed a new church headquarters some 400 kilometers (250 miles) to the north, in the nation's capital, Antananarivo. In fact, the church is expanding northward.

The MLC, nearly 90% rural, has 4500 congregations served by 550 pastors. Most of them have been trained at the United Lutheran Theological Seminary (Seminary Teolojika Loterana) in Ivory, a suburb of Fianarantsoa. This school has been training pastors since 1871 and was instrumental in uniting the work of the three pioneering mission boards. The church's continued growth and new opportunities for ministry have stimulated an increase in the number of theological students.

This situation led to a bold decision in 1980 not to enlarge the old seminary but to open five regional ones for the first two years of academic work plus a year of internship closer to a student's home base. Opened in 1983, they follow a common core curriculum. The faculty in each of the regional seminaries thus prepares students for a concluding two-year program in Fianarantsoa/Ivory. Facilitating this change has been the nationwide educational system, the improvement of which has also raised the intellectual level of theological students.

Meanwhile, this deployed plan of seminary education is augmenting the usefulness of some of the MLC's regional Bible schools as well as of certain former boarding schools of the church. It is also anticipated that in due course the original seminary in Fianarantsoa will become a full-fledged theological faculty. Complementing these developments are the church's seven Bible schools. These are enabling many lay people to become well-informed Christians.

The continuing outreach of the MLC, recalling its rootage in mission, occurs through evangelization, education, medical and social work, and development. Traditional parish programs in Sunday schools, among young people, and in women's work are supplemented innovatively. The use of the media—print and electronic—provide examples. The Lutheran Printing Press, one of the oldest and largest in the country, is a joint project of the MLC, the American Lutheran Mission, and the Norwegian Missionary Society. Its publication list includes Bibles, hymnals, texts, catechisms, devotional books, and a gamut of materials in Christian education, as well as the regular church papers and other items.

On the electronic side, programs produced by the church's studio—Radio Feon'Ny Filazantsara in Antsirabé—are beamed to the entire island of Madagascar from the Seychelles via the Far East Broadcasting Association (FEBA). These daily half-hour programs take the place of those formerly beamed from Addis Ababa, Ethiopia (see Africa Introduction). Some notion of the impact via radio derives from the fact that in the 10-year period prior to 1976, 8000 listeners were enrolled in Bible correspondence courses. In 1986 the radio studio was transformed into a Lutheran Center for Communication, which interacts with the other service departments of the MLC and has direct contact with the local people.

The MLC's educational involvement, from another angle, reaches some 60,000 students enrolled in its 90 primary and 35 secondary schools. Ten of the latter include teacher training programs, and five prepare students for university exams. In addition, the school for the blind in Antsirabé (since the 1920s) and a companion school for the deaf and dumb (since 1953) are not only up-to-date institutions but also the only ones of their kind in the country. A special chaplaincy program, including Bible study and discussions, is based in Antsirabé and, through periodic visitations, reaches young people in the secondary schools of southern Madagascar.

In its medical services the MLC was considerably limited during the French period, but following World War II the church's first hospital, now a medical center, was opened in Manambaro, 27 kilometers inland from Fort Dauphin, in the south. Then another hospital, in Ejeda, in the southwest, became the base for a network of childcare clinics with emphasis on preventive medicine. A third hospital, in Antsirabé, the stopover city between Fianarantsoa and the national capital in the center of the island, has links to two dispensaries and five first-aid stations. Two leprosaria, in Morondova and Antsirabé, have long records of service. Their modern methods of treatment and educational programs for adults and children have turned these places into productive villages. An extensive primary health care program, which emphasizes the importance of prevention rather than care, was started a few years ago.

A healing ministry, distinctive to the MLC, was initiated already in 1894. It is associated with the work of the catechist Rainisoalambo who had the gift of healing along with that of evangelism. A revival began from his work and has since become a churchwide movement in the MLC. Accents fall on healing and diaconal care. In camps or Christian community centers volunteers called *mpiandry* ("shepherds") are trained to care for the sick and handicapped. Others are trained to be "apostles," to be sent forth as messengers for a period of two years or more into areas where the gospel has not been preached. Today this form of outreach is recognized as a beneficial influence not only in the MLC but in other Malagasy communions as well. The government itself has approved of this manifestly valued service. Meanwhile, with assistance through the LWF Community Development Service, the MLC arranges training courses under experienced medical staff so as to maintain or increase the effectiveness of the *mpiandry*. Shelters are provided for the patients, especially for those requiring prolonged physical, mental, or spiritual care.

The MLC's expansion northward is an advance into a large region where the proportion of Christians is very low, often only 2% or 5% of the population. Since 1975 the church's evangelism department has been concentrating on three geographic areas mainly along the coast. Together they form a triangle, Toamasina (on the east coast, northeast of the national capital), Antsiranana (near the northern tip, formerly called Diégo Suarez), and Mahajanga (Majunga, in the west, on the Mozambique Channel). In 10 years, 150 congregations have been created and are served by 20 pastors and 15 evangelists. In 1985 two new regional synods, comprising seven districts, were inaugurated at Antsiranana and Mahajanga. A seminary for this region, the MLC's sixth, is in Marovoay, near Mahajanga.

In the field of church and society, Madagascar's independence in 1960 ushered in an era of community development. Via LWF channels, numerous development projects have been succeeding through MLC planning and sponsorship. Some samples: a farm school at Tombontsoa (1960), an agricultural extension program at Manakara (1974), and several smaller rural development projects. Plans projected earlier are now materializing in most of the 10 regional synods. Health and medical programs, assistance to the handicapped, training for technicians, teachers, and others, have all received attention and are seen as benefiting the community at large.

Ecumenically the MLC has become an active participant in the Christian Council of Madagascar (CCM). Mutual trust has grown between the MLC and its considerably larger neighbor, the 1,250,000-member Church of Jesus Christ in Madagascar (above), and there has been talk of an eventual merger of these bodies. Malagasy Lutherans have received encouragement to proceed along these lines from various quarters, including their participation in the World Council of Churches (since 1966) as well as the All-Africa Conference of Churches. In addition, the MLC membership in the LWF already in 1950 set the stage a decade later for the second All-Africa Lutheran Conference in Antsirabé (see Africa Introduction). In 1973 the LWF-related Strasbourg Institute for Ecumenical Research conducted one of its traveling seminars in Madagascar. This seminar focused on the continuing education of pastors and also demonstrated how Vatican II was opening the way for closer relations between Roman Catholics and Lutherans, as well as other Protestants, in the Madagascar Republic.

● ● ●

In 1966, when the Malagasy Lutherans celebrated their 100th anniversary, they were reminded of a long history and of their partnership with Norwegians and Americans. The Norwegian Missionary Society began its work in southern Madagascar in 1866. The field was ripe. As noted above, the Bible had been translated into Malagasy and the Christians who had endured the period of persecution were spreading the good news throughout the island. A new queen was friendly. Thus, within five years, the Norwegians were able to establish a strong network of missions and schools, including a seminary in the Fianarantsoa area, undergirded by a considerable amount of Christian literature translated into Malagasy. In 1888 a Norwegian-American missionary couple arrived in Fort Dauphin and were welcomed by government officials as the first Protestant missionaries to the southern tip of the country. Here, too, the Malagasy catechists had prepared the way among the Tanosy people. Within six months, seven boys were ready for baptism. In 1889 another Norwegian-American couple started work around Manasoa on the west coast. These fields were developed by two American churches that later became part of the American Lutheran Church.

Inter-Protestant and intra-Lutheran cooperation made possible an orderly development of mission activity. The seminary at Fianarantsoa gradually became an institution for all Lutherans and prepared the way for the formation of one national Lutheran church. Events of World War II accelerated the process, as hopes for independence increased. In 1950 the church was organized and became a member of the LWF. In 1961, a year after national independence, the first Malagasy church president, the Rev. Rakoto Andrianarijaona, was elected.

A much-needed updating of the church/mission relationship was consummated in 1975 when the church assembly approved an agreement suggested by and worked out with the supporting Norwegian Missionary Society and the Division of World Mission of the American Lutheran Church (now ELCA). This agreement recognized fully the oneness of the Malagasy Lutheran Church and provided for the total integration within the church of the missionaries and their activities. It withdrew the right of the missions to be represented at all levels of the church structure, provided for a direct relationship of the church with the two supporting missions, and recognized the freedom of the church to relate to other churches or missions. The two supporting missions pledged increased assistance in the ongoing mission of the MLC. In 1978 the Danish Missionary Society became a partner in mission.

MALAWI

A republic (1966) and a member of the Commonwealth of Nations in East Central Africa.

Area: 118,484 sq. km. (45,747 sq. mi.). Pop. (1984 est.): 5,547,400. Cap.: Lilongwe (pop., 1981, 120,000). Largest city: Blantyre (pop., 1981, 230,000). Language: English (official) and Nyanja (Chichewa).

History: The Bantu-speaking Malawi kingdom of the Shire River valley, emerging in the 15th century, conquered present-day *Zimbabwe and *Mozambique during the 18th century. Soon thereafter the kingdom was weakened by internal conflicts as well as by Arab slave traders and the arrival of the predatory Ngoni from *South Africa. David Livingstone explored the country (1858–1864) and rallied European opposition to this slave trade. Britain declared the land a protectorate (1889), ruling it until it became a part of the Federation of Rhodesia and Nyasaland in 1953. Freedom revolts, begun as early as 1915 under a Yao Christian, culminated in 1964 when Nyasaland became independent and took the name Malawi. Two years later the country was declared a republic with the leader of the Malawi Congress Party, Dr. Hastings Kamzu Banda, elected president for life.

Religion: Traditional religion (19%) exists among all tribes. Islam (16.5%) is strongest among the Yao in eastern Malawi. Christianity (64%): Of the estimated four million 27% are Roman Catholic. Introduced in the 16th century from Mozambique, Roman Catholicism has grown greatly since 1950. Encouraged by David Livingstone, Scottish Presbyterian missionaries arrived first in 1875 and were joined by Dutch Reformed in 1888. These groups merged in 1926 to form the Central African Presbyterian Church, which today has more than 2000 congregations and shows steady growth. Seventh Day Adventists and Disciples are also strong.

The Malawi constitution affirms human rights and freedom of conscience. The state accepts the churches as partners in development. Religious instruction being required in the primary grades, provision is made for the training of teachers of religion. The national network, Radio Malawi, gives over three hours a week for religious programs.

The Christian Council of Malawi (1939) was built on earlier foundations. Its membership includes a wide spectrum of church traditions: Anglican, Methodist, Baptist, Seventh Day Adventist, and various evangelical bodies as well as African Traditional churches. Lutherans were latecomers to this region.

EVANGELICAL LUTHERAN CHURCH OF MALAWI (ELCM)

Member: LWF (1988) FELCSA, EFM
Membership: 4860**
General Secretary: The Rev. Joseph Paul Bvumbwe
PO Box 650
Lilongwe 3

This indigenous and fast-growing church was started by a Lutheran layman, Gilbert Msuku, upon his return to Malawi after 17 years of residence in Tanzania. There he had been active in the *Evangelical Lutheran Church in Tanzania (ELCT). By personal evangelism, he was able to gather a congregation in Lilongwe, the capital of Malawi. The church received government recognition in 1982.

Encouragement came from LWF staff and member churches in neighboring Tanzania and Zimbabwe. In 1983, first the *Evangelical Lutheran Church in Zimbabwe (ELCZ) and then the ELCT sent pastoral teams to survey the situation in light of already existing Christian churches. Their reports indicated the need for pastors, leadership training, and the construction of permanent church buildings. The prime responsibility for nurturing the embryonic church body was given to the ELCT (see Tanzania, below) with supportive cooperation from the ELCZ and the LWF. In 1988 the ELCM was received into membership by the LWF Executive Committee. It also has a link with the Federation of Lutheran Churches in Southern Africa.

LUTHERAN CHURCH OF CENTRAL AFRICA (LCCA)

Membership in Malawi: 9500
Mission Coordinator: The Rev. Raymond G. Cox
PO Box 120
Blantyre

This church of 19,000 members was first planted in Zambia in 1953 by the *Wisconsin Evangelical Lutheran Church (USA) and then extended into Malawi in 1963. A year later a synod was formed, uniting the congregations in both countries. The synod became autonomous in 1972 under its own constitution, but has chosen to elect expatriate pastors as coordinators.

The main administrative office is in Blantyre, the chief commercial and industrial city in the far south. A Bible school, opened in 1981 in the capital city, Lilongwe, central Malawi, trains evangelists in a two year course. Of the LCCA's 116 congregations, 54 are in Malawi, served by three national pastors, 20 evangelists, and seven expatriate pastors. The language is Chichewa (see Zambia, below).

MOZAMBIQUE

Mozambique (People's Republic, 1975) is bordered by the Indian Ocean, Tanzania, Malawi, Zambia, Zimbabwe, Swaziland, and South Africa. Area: 799,300 sq. km. (308,642 sq. mi.). Pop. (1982 est.): 12,615,200. Cap. and largest city: Maputo. Language: Portuguese (official) and local tongues.

History: Africans moved into this area about A.D. 500. Persian and Arab traders arrived about A.D. 1000 and took control of the coast. Beginning with the explorations of Vasco da Gama (1498), Mozambique increasingly came under Portuguese control and exploitation, including forced labor on feudal estates and extensive slave trade in the 18th century. By 1926, Portugal had direct control and forced Mozambicans to work in South African mines. In resistance, the Mozambique Liberation Front (Frelimo) began guerrilla warfare in 1964. During the struggle, some 100,000 nationals sought asylum in neighboring Tanzania and Zambia. After the military coup in Portugal (1974), Mozambique gained independence in 1975. Samora Machel, leader of Frelimo, became the first president of a Marxist regime. At first land was collectivized and most whites fled. Later, however, in 1983, Frelimo opted for a mixed scheme of private agriculture, state farms and cooperatives. Since independence, the Mozambique National Resistance (MNR) or Renamo, supported by South Africa, has

destabilized the country and brought widespread destruction of cropland, forcing thousands to flee. An estimated 200,000 are in Malawi and about an equal number may be in Transvaal, South Africa. The war between MNR and the Frelimo army is the main reason for the present devastating famine and chaos.

Religion: Traditional, 48.8%; Muslim, 16.5%, mainly among the Yao people east of Lake Malawi; Christian, 16.5%, of which Roman Catholics are the majority; others, 18.2%.

Protestant work begun in 1879 by the American Board was soon turned over to the Methodists. Following World War I, Scandinavian Baptists, Seventh Day Adventists, Nazarenes, and Pentecostal groups arrived. Anglicans missioned among the Muslims. African Traditional religious groups have remained small due to government opposition. Although President Machel had a Free Methodist background, his Marxist sentiments discouraged religion. He blamed the churches, especially the Roman Catholics, for prolonging subjugation. However, freedom of or from religion is assured, and the government established good relations with most religious groups in 1982.

The Christian Council of Mozambique, organized in 1944, has a membership of eight churches. Carrying forward the work of the Evangelical Missionary Association (1923), it sponsors a paper, audiovisual programs, and a youth hostel and carries on evangelistic and diaconic work.

EVANGELICAL LUTHERAN CHURCH IN MOZAMBIQUE (ELCM; in process of formation)
Contact person: Mr. Kenny E. Nyati
Lutheran Church Working Committee
PO Box 1133
Maputo

The still new and struggling ELCM took shape in 1988. A Lutheran consultation in Maputo, opened by the Mozambican Minister of Justice, resulted in a joint project aimed to give the new body a good start. Staff houses and initial running costs would be provided by six outside partners: the Church of Sweden Mission, the *Evangelical Church in Germany, the *Evangelical Lutheran Church in

America, and the LWF member churches in *Brazil, *Tanzania, and *Zimbabwe.

Portuguese-language literature and education materials came from the Evangelical Church of the Lutheran Confession in Brazil. Germany's EKD would coordinate the assistance, while LWF World Service as well as Church Cooperation would play a facilitating part.

The story behind the ELCM begins during the Mozambican struggle for liberation from Portugal. During the 1970s Mozambicans by the thousands sought asylum in Tanzania, Swaziland, and Zambia. Many of them received humanitarian assistance through programs operated by LWF World Service (*Tanzania). Assistance continued as refugees were resettled in their own country. In 1977 LWS set up a permanent office in Maputo, doing so in cooperation with the UN High Commissioner for Refugees (UNHCR). In cooperation with other agencies LWS provided various forms of assistance in such areas as community development, vocational training, adult literacy, and health work. In 1987, when famine struck and anti-government attacks on population centers intensified, the LWF launched a US $2,000,000 appeal to aid the victims of famine and terror—a number estimated at 3,500,000 people.

At the same time, the Lutheran churches in Tanzania and Zimbabwe joined in providing, respectively, a pastor-missioner and an evangelist. The already mentioned 1988 consultation took the first steps toward a projected multipurpose Lutheran center with church hall, offices, bookstore, and other facilities.

SUDAN

A republic of North Africa, with a coastline on the Red Sea. Area: 2,503,890 sq. km. (966,757 sq. mi.). Pop. (1985 est.): 23,645,000. Cap.: Khartoum (pop., 1985 est., 476,218). Languages: Arabic (official) and others.

History: The "Land of the Blacks," as the Arabic *Bilad as Sudan* denotes, is the largest in area of all African countries. It embraces the reaches of the Upper Nile and other vast territories as well. Northeast Sudan, the Nubia of ancient times, was colonized by Egypt

(ca. 2000 B.C.), later ruled by the Cush Kingdom (c.800 B.C. to A.D. 350), then again by Egypt into modern times. Khartoum (founded 1823) became a trading center for ivory and slaves. British intervention, allied with Egyptian, destroyed the Sudanese Mahdist power. The Agreement of 1899 was reaffirmed by the Anglo-Egyptian treaty of 1936 governing the Sudan, as Britain divided the Muslim northern part from the mainly Traditional southern part. Independent nationhood, achieved in 1956, led swiftly to civil war, the southerners fearing domination from the north.

The 17 years of civil war ended in 1972. An estimated 500,000 southerners had died of war, disease, or starvation. The peace terms, signed in Addis Ababa in 1972, granted considerable autonomy to the southern part of the struggling democratic republic. However, in 1983, the longtime president of the Sudan, Muhammad Gaafur al-Nimeiry (b.1930), declared the country an Islamic republic, much to the alarm of the non-Muslim southerners. Then, a year later, he decreed *Sharia* (Islamic law) the law of the land. Unrest and violence in the south made life hazardous for expatriates as well as others.

Meanwhile, the severe drought of the mid-1980s and the calamitous famine that scourged neighboring *Ethiopia did not spare the Sudan. Refugees by the thousands poured across borders and sought relief. Although a coup overthrew the Nimeiry regime in April 1985, an earlier division of the south into three regions, a dispute over the utilization of newly discovered oil and a planned pipeline, the implementation of the *Sharia* on the entire country, and the construction of the Jonglei Canal promised no speedy return to quieter times. In 1986 the *Sharia* was repealed, with conditions.

Religion: Nearly 75% of the people are Muslim. Most of these live in the northern part of the country and are of Sudanic-Arab stock. Followers of African Traditional religion account for another 15%. The nearly two million Christians are largely in the southern regions. Although Christianity spread early into the Sudan, it later gave way to Islam. Mainly as the result of missionary efforts from abroad, unfolding since the 19th century, the Christian community is today about 50% Roman Catholic, 25% Episcopal

(Anglican), 8% Coptic Orthodox, plus a diversity of smaller Protestant bodies.

The Sudan Council of Churches (SCC), established in 1967, replaced the Northern Sudan Christian Council. Membership includes 12 churches with a wide spectrum: Catholic, Orthodox, Anglican, and Protestant. Lutherans have no organized churches in Sudan but have responded to the acute needs of people, often at the request of and in cooperation with the SCC.

Lutheran World Service (LWS), in cooperation with the United Nations High Commissioner for Refugees and on invitation of the Sudanese government, was one of several nongovernmental organizations brought on the scene following the civil war. In 1973 reconstruction activities began in the Upper Nile Province and were led by an international LWS staff working in consultation with the Sudanese and in accordance with the people's desires.

Following the LWS program evaluations in 1978 and 1982, in which the SCC participated, the orientation of the LWS program changed from reconstruction and rehabilitation to a more community development-oriented approach. The major emphases have been on increasing agricultural production, supporting the government's primary health care program, initiating community development projects, and training the necessary local staff to carry them out. A more concentrated effort has been undertaken by limiting the operational area. The LWS program operation was scaled down considerably following the severe unrest in the area in 1984. Escalation of civil war in southern Sudan greatly restricted relief. In 1987, LWS was asked to leave the country.

Meanwhile, the Swedish Evangelical Mission supported and provided personnel for the SCC's Eastern Sudan Relief Program, aiding the waves of refugees from Ethiopia and, at times, also from Uganda. Complementing these many relief and development activities are the SCC's programs in evangelism, education, and leadership training. Since 1975, the LWF Department of Communication (DOC) has assisted the SCC's radio studio in Juba in producing programs in local Arabic and in English for broadcasting over Radio Juba. The studio has now also initiated the production of cassette programs in seven languages. In cooperation with Norwegian Church Aid (below) and the SCC, the LWF/DOC has also conducted the Communication for Development Project (CDP) in the Eastern Equatoria region. Its research, begun in 1980, studied ways in which both traditional and modern communication efforts could further development. The project was completed in 1986 and evaluated at a consultation of African churches held in Limuru, Kenya, in late 1986. A number of specific recommendations were formulated to assist the churches in planning their communication and development activities. The services rendered to the cooperating agencies are being run by the Norwegian Church Aid Sudan program.

Norwegian Church Aid (NCA) came to southern Sudan with relief supplies in 1972. Its Sudan project developed into a long-term program based on agreements with government. Because of the tremendous need of a very isolated people, the Norwegian government consented to pay 80% of the cost, with the understanding that the church agency would provide the personnel and program planning. After the establishment of a basic infrastructure, efforts have been centered on assisting the local people by means of rural councils to organize their skills and resources in such a way that production of food and other commodities would increase. For some time the area was peaceful, and the people attributed this to the presence of the NCA's staff and their supportive assistance. This, the largest of the NCA development projects, was painfully disrupted early in 1985 by the unrest and violence caused by the *Sharia* decree (above), when most Norwegian staff members and their families had to be evacuated to Kenya. Later in the same year, it was able to start operating again, though with a reduced program.

TANZANIA

The United Republic (1964), a member of the Commonwealth of Nations, consists of two parts: Tanganyika, a republic since 1961, and the islands of Zanzibar and Pemba, independent since 1963. Total area: 945,050 sq. km. (364,886 sq. mi.). Total population (1984 est.): 21,202,000, including 98.9%

Africans, 0.7% Asians, 0.4% Arabs, Europeans, etc. Cap.: Dodoma. Largest city and former capital: Dar es Salaam (pop., 1978 prelim., 769,400). Languages: Swahili and English. Education: Public but not yet nationwide. Literacy: Concerted effort being made to include everyone; currently over 50% in Swahili.

History: The people of this land are a composite of scores of ethnic groups, none of which has dominated the rest and each of which has its own distinctive history. Present boundaries, set in the late 19th century, tend to obscure the migration and mingling in earlier times.

Antecedent as well as more recent ties extend across the border, whether to *Kenya in the north, to *Mozambique in the south, or to the arc of neighbors—*Malawi, *Zambia, *Zaire, Rwanda, Burundi, and Uganda—set from southwest to northwest. This is the scene of Tanzania's internal history, some of whose roots extend eastward to the Congo basin, or northward beyond *Kenya into *Sudan and *Ethiopia. From the latter area came the Masai, a pastoral people whose Nilo-Hamitic language links them with the regions of the Upper Nile. Cattle herding differentiates them from the subsistence farming common to the other ethnic groups. To cite but a few: the Chagga and the Pare in the region of Mount Kilimanjaro (Africa's highest peak); the Haya on the western shore of Lake Victoria and the Sukuma (the largest ethnic group, 13%) southeast of the lake; the Hehe, the Bena, and others in the Rufiji River basin; and clusters of kindred peoples in the southern highlands.

Along the coast the Makonde in the south, the Zaramo around Dar es Salaam, and the peoples of the Usambara Valley in the north were among those making contact with the Arab traders already in the eighth century. Not only did this coastal trade have links to India, and even to China, but it also penetrated ever deeper into the Tanzanian interior. Via what is now the town of Tabora, the route westward reached Lake Tanganyika at Kigoma-Ujiji.

The trade in ivory and slaves had its offshore base on the Arab-held island of Zanzibar, home also of a growing concentration of clove plantations. With the Arabs came also the mixed race of coastal people, the Swahili, as well as the language of that name.

A blend of Bantu and Arabic, Swahili became the language of commerce, spoken from the coastland westward to the Congo basin and providing a means of inter-ethnic communication. Eventually its Arabic cursive was changed to Latin letters (by 19th-century missionaries), giving Swahili fresh viability in connection with the ever-further encroaching European world.

The arrival of the first Portuguese traders (1498) opened a succession of widening contacts with the West. For a time it extended the slave trade even to *Brazil (prior to its independence from Portugal). In the late 19th century, Zanzibar became a British protectorate, while the Tanganyikan mainland in 1886 came increasingly under colonial rule as German East Africa. Submission to a foreign government and conformity to unaccustomed schemes of agricultural production as well as other impositions created smoldering resentments and a passion for freedom. Especially in the southern part of the country, and later elsewhere, the hitherto separate groups and Traditional religions became united. The Maji Maji rebellion (1905–1907) was the explosive outburst. Although it was crushed by the German forces with great loss of life, it gave the colony as a whole a sense of unity.

In its own way the German presence helped set the course for future development. Not only had the Conference of Berlin (1884–1885) set boundaries, but the emphasis on education set objectives, and the work of missionaries (Lutheran and Roman Catholic) gave new scope to religion. While the German period lasted a little over three decades, the 42 ensuing years (1919–1961) under British governance—first as a mandated territory and then, after World War II, as a British-administered trust territory—prepared Tanganyika for internal autonomy (1960) and full independence as a republic (1961).

An immemorial sense of oneness found expression in the country's African socialism which, unlike Marxism, included the Deity. Whatever the flaws and failings in application, *ujamaa* accentuated extended familyhood and the exercise of mutual concern. The egalitarian Arusha Declaration (1967), coming four years after consolidation with Zanzibar and Pemba, spelled out *ujamaa* as the guide for Tanzanian living and laid stress on self-reliance as well as on a full development of resources provided by nature or inherited from a distant Bantu past.

As the nation's two official languages, Swahili helped unify the people at home and English facilitated communication abroad. Politically the one-party principle was embodied in the Tanganyika African National Union (TANU) already in 1929. In Zanzibar and Pemba, the Afro-Shiraz Party (ASP) shaped political power. In 1977, TANU and ASP consolidated, forming the Chama Cha Mapinduzi (CCM) party. A common will, cultivated as an educational process, has been personified in the born teacher *(Mwalimu)* and political leader, Julius Nyerere. President from 1962–1985, his period in office gave the nation remarkable stability, though not immunity from serious problems.

From 1960–1985, the country's population more than doubled. The overwhelmingly agricultural economy is mainly subsistence farming. Major crops include cassava, rice, millet, corn, sorghum, and yams. Among the chief cash crops are sisal, cotton, coffee, cashew nuts, tea, tobacco, and pyrethrum. Important parts of the country are subject to drought. Expansion in agriculture as well as industry has been slowed by problems of transportation and inflation, the latter speeded by the oil price explosion and the worldwide economic recession. In southwestern Tanzania, near Lake Malawi, are said to be large deposits of coal and iron. The country's modest export in minerals includes gold, tin, salt, and mica. In diamonds Tanzania ranks among the world's top 10 producers. The Chinese-built Tanzam Railway (1976), paralleling an American-built highway, connects the huge Zambian copper belt with Dar es Salaam as an important point of export.

Foremost in the field of foreign relations has been the disruption of the East Africa Community (see Kenya). The war precipitated by Idi Amin of Uganda, overrunning northwestern Tanzania at Lake Victoria in late 1978, drew a heavy reaction. Tanzanian forces, supplemented by disaffected Ugandan troops, invaded Uganda early in 1979 and by April captured Kampala and ended the ruthless Amin regime. Tanzanian intervention required a prolonged follow-up until acceptable order could be restored. After the withdrawal of its major forces, it was estimated that the war had cost Tanzania about US $500 million; an enormous sum for one of the world's poor countries.

Tanzania is heavily dependent on foreign aid of various types: from the East (China), the West (Federal Republic of Germany, United Kingdom), also from the UN (especially for its resettlement of refugees from oppressive regimes in neighboring countries, see below).

Religion (1980 est.): Traditional (23%), most numerous among the Sukuma, are declining at a rate of 1% per year; Muslim (33%) are strongest along the coast and the old caravan route through Tabora to Ujiji on Lake Tanganyika; Christian (44%). The Roman Catholic Church is the largest, with its estimated five million adherents divided into two provinces. It has national leadership and a large number of Tanzanian priests, brothers, sisters, and catechists. Of the two million Protestants, about half are in the Evangelical Lutheran Church in Tanzania (ELCT, below). The Anglicans come next, followed by the approximately 100,000 Moravians. The latter are divided into two bodies, one in the west and one in the southwest. Together they form the largest Moravian community in the world.

The three Protestant denominations, together with smaller bodies—African Brotherhood Church (Independent), African Inland Mission, Baptist, Friends, Mennonite, Presbyterian, Salvation Army—in 1975 formed the Christian Council of Tanzania (CCT), replacing the Tanganyika Missionary Council of 1936. The YMCA, YWCA, the Bible Society, and the East African Venture Society are associate members, and the Adventists and Pentecostals have a consultative relationship. Thus strong support is given to an expansive program of development, education, mass communication, and much more. Relations with the Roman Catholics are cordial.

In 1964, at the request of the churches now in the CCT, the Tanganyika Christian Refugee Service (TCRS) was formed to meet the needs of refugees from the neighboring countries. Operated by the LWF Department of World Service on behalf of the World Council of Churches and in consultation with the CCT, the TCRS works in cooperation with the government of the United Republic of Tanzania and the United Nations High Commissioner for Refugees.

Since 1964 TCRS has developed nine settlements and assisted over 200,000 refugees. One of the Burundi settlements, in Ulyankulu west of Tabora, became the third largest concentration of population in the country. Since the soil and water supplies at Ulyankulu did not suffice for 50,000 people, half of them were moved to Mishamo in 1978 and 1979. Mishamo, with 34,000 people, the last of the nine settlements, was turned over to the government administration in 1985 after achieving self-reliance.

In August 1985 TCRS occupied its new office and warehouse complex, complete with two houses for expatriate staff, in Dar es Salaam. The building was done by TCRS staff, and the structures are now the property of the ELCT. The location and the large storage facilities are expected to speed the shipment of supplies to the interior settlements.

EVANGELICAL LUTHERAN CHURCH IN TANZANIA (ELCT)

(Kanisa la Kiinjili la Kilutheri Tanzania)
Member: LWF (1964), WCC, AACC, CCT
Membership: 1,301,013
Presiding Bishop (Mkuu): The Rt. Rev. Sebastian Kolowa
PO Box 3033
Arusha

As Africa's largest Lutheran church body, the ELCT claims over one million adherents. Its 17 judicatories—five synods led by presidents and 12 dioceses led by bishops—cover most of the country and are aided by a central administration headed by a presiding bishop (from one of the judicatories) and an executive secretary. Its 2350 congregations and preaching places are served by 640 ordained pastors plus a large number of evangelists, teachers, and other workers in related ministries. A significant number of expatriates from Europe and America, most of them non-ordained, render special services on request of the church.

In effect the ELCT is a close federation of formerly separate church bodies and has been self-governing since 1963. Its wide-ranging ties to other bodies in Africa and the rest of the world made this church a fitting host to the LWF Sixth Assembly in Dar es Salaam (1977). The election of one of its bishops, Josiah Kibira, as president made history, since no one from Africa or elsewhere in the Two-Thirds World had held this position before.

Forces holding the ELCT together include: a common faith; a biblical basis; a confessional legacy, capsuled in Luther's Catechism and caught in indigenous worship; a unifying theological college (Makumira); a firm but adaptable ecclesial organization that allows dioceses and synods to coexist; substantial and coordinated overhead support from abroad; and the momentum of continuing growth. These and other forces find expression through a national consciousness in which the common language and social mobility respect but transcend local tongues and folkways. Divisive forces are inevitable but have thus far posed no serious threat to the ELCT's unity.

Following a survey of the ELCT's present situation, a review of the church's past makes clear how a diversity of forces have been channeled into an inclusive model of interchurch cooperation.

Today the church language is that of the nation, Swahili, but local dialects are also used. Continuing growth since World War II has brought an eightfold increase in membership in four decades, from about 130,000 in 1946 to the present over one million. The ELCT is particularly strong in the northern and southern parts of the country, with the eastern coastal region (Dar es Salaam and inland) connecting them. The church's members are mainly engaged in subsistence farming, yet they are also numerous in towns and cities, employed in trades, business, education, the professions, and civil service. Some have become prominent in public life.

The largest Protestant church in the country, the ELCT operates in an ecumenical context that extends from the Christian Council of Tanzania to the international scene of the All Africa Conference of Churches, the LWF, and the World Council of Churches.

The ELCT consists of 12 dioceses and five synods; designations are equivalent and reflect the preference of a given region. Proceeding clockwise from Tanzania's extreme northwest, the regional bodies follow roughly in this order (location of headquarters in parentheses): Karagwe Diocese (Karagwe); Northwestern Diocese (Bukoba); Lake Victoria East Diocese (Mwanza); Central Synod (Singida); Mbulu Synod (Mbulu); Arusha Region Synod (Arusha); Northern Diocese

(Moshi); Pare Diocese (Same); Northeastern Diocese (Lushoto); Dodoma Diocese (Dodoma); Eastern Coastal Diocese (Dar es Salaam); Ulanga Kilombero Synod (Ifakara); Iringa Diocese (Iringa); Southern Diocese (Njombe); South Central Diocese (Bulongwa); Konde Diocese (Tukuyu); Kenya Synod (Nairobi).

The ELCT general assembly meets every two years and is the church's highest legislative authority. Its chief officer, the presiding bishop (president), is elected for a four-year term. This position was given stature and steadiness by the late Stefano R. Moshi, bishop of the Northern Diocese and head of the ELCT from 1963 to 1976. The executive council carries out the functions assigned to the general church body. Its full-time officer is the executive secretary, stationed at ELCT headquarters in the northern city of Arusha. Various ministries of the church are planned and organized by boards: communication, congregational life, parish education, health services, theological education, and church unity.

Pastors are educated at Makumira Lutheran Theological College in Usa River, some 19 kilometers (12 miles) east of Arusha. Founded in 1954, it has helped to advance church unity. Recently its program and facilities have had LWF assistance for expansion. Among the 150 students are also some from *Angola, *Ethiopia, *Kenya, *Mozambique, and *Zaire. There is an increasing number of women and a few students from other denominations than Lutheran. Spouses of students are enrolled in special courses. The faculty comprises mainly Tanzanians with a few expatriates from Europe and North America. Practical off-campus training includes work in pastoral care at the Kilimanjaro Christian Medical Center and in supervised duties in congregations.

In Morogoro, about 200 kilometers inland from Dar es Salaam, is the church's junior seminary (1976), a secondary school for young people looking forward to church careers. Other departments of the institution provide training for Christian education teachers, women and youth leaders, and language instruction for expatriate missionaries.

Education for church service is also carried on at the synod/diocese level. The Arusha Synod has a program of theological education by extension (TEE) with headquarters at Oldonyo-Sambu, a few miles west of Arusha. Ordainable persons, already active in other careers, are chosen for the courses.

Five synodical Bible schools—Mwika in the Northern Diocese, Kidugala in the Southern Synod, Ruhija in the Northwestern Diocese, Kiomboi in the Central Synod, and Waama in the Mbulu Synod—train evangelists, deacons, and parish workers as well as other church members. The graduates of these schools are responsible for much of the missionary outreach of the ELCT. The general course is two years after primary school. Evangelists are required to take one more year of training, parish workers two. Capable and respected evangelists with a number of years of experience are selected for two more years at the Bible schools, whereupon they are ordained as deacons, assigned to congregations, and authorized to administer the sacraments.

The nationalization of education in 1969 integrated the numerous formerly church-operated elementary schools into the public system. Many communities unable to provide adequate school facilities have been helped to do so by "Operation Bootstrap," a private enterprise founded and administered by an American Lutheran missionary pastor. The church's former teacher-training colleges were also nationalized. One of the best known, now the Marangu College of National Education in the Kilimanjaro region, was host in 1955 to the first All-Africa Lutheran Conference (see Africa Introduction).

Religious education is part of the public school curriculum, and the church is encouraged to provide good teachers for this enormous task. The Morogoro Junior Seminary, mentioned above, trains both primary and secondary Christian education teachers. The only school of its kind in the country, it is also used by other denominations. Interdenominationally, the Christian Council of Tanzania, in which the ELCT is an active member, has prepared a curriculum helpful to teachers in all parts of the country. A board of parish education, serving all 17 dioceses and synods, provides curriculum and visual aids for Christian education and nurture on the congregational level.

The basic task of evangelism has been advanced by the congregations and the many anonymous but committed Christians. Yet with 56% of Tanzanians outside the Christian fold, organized evangelism is a heavy responsibility, which the ELCT shares with partner churches. The synods and dioceses, aware of the opportunity for outreach in their areas, submit projects needing help. For example, the Southern Diocese, challenged by the huge paper mill being built by the government in Mgololo, planned accordingly and requested LWF assistance in building a church center. In time some 5000 to 10,000 people will be employed at this mill coming from all parts of Tanzania and also a few from Europe. The staff at the church center will be ready to receive and nurture the Christians and to reach out to the non-Christians. Chapels and staff are also needed for the new villages being built along the Tzara and Tanzam railroad.

In the far north, on the east side of Lake Victoria, the Mbulu Synod, with assistance from the Norwegian Lutheran Mission, is continuing the ELCT work begun by the Northwestern Diocese in 1965 to the unevangelized Mara people. There is a continuing need here for evangelists, pastors, and other workers as well as for chapels, housing and transportation. The Karagwe diocese has special needs. Situated on the boundary of Rwanda and Uganda, its people suffered most from the devastation of the recent war. The Northwestern Diocese, which first evangelized the Karagwe, receives help to build village churches and to provide other rehabilitative services for the people of this area. Lake Victoria East is the newest diocese.

Evangelism outreach, supported by all the synods and dioceses as well as partners, is provided by the Sauti Ya Injili radio studio in Moshi and the audiovisual department of the ELCT in Arusha. These units prepare evangelistic and development-oriented programs that are broadcast daily from TWR in Swaziland and reach Tanzania and surrounding Kiswahili-speaking areas at prime time for 75 minutes. A cassette program is also a ready tool for evangelism.

The outreach of the ELCT goes beyond national borders. The Kenya Synod was formed to care for Tanzanians migrating northward. The young Lutheran churches in eastern *Zaire and *Malawi look to the ELCT for pastors and assistance in the training of pastoral candidates and other workers. Since 1977 pastors of the ELCT have also been active in Burundi and *Mozambique. In 1987, in collaboration with the Evangelical Lutheran Church in Zimbabwe, more extensive missioning began in Maputo, the capital of Mozambique. Burundi work also expanded. (See Mozambique, above.)

The medical program of ELCT includes 14 hospitals and 60 dispensaries as well as numerous mobile medical units, some of which are under diocese or synod management. The government now shares in the cost and control of certain institutions that were built by partner churches or missions. The church provides chaplaincy service to the Kilimanjaro Christian Medical Center, a referral and teaching hospital in Moshi that was built with funds secured through the LWF (CDS). It is operated by the Good Samaritan Foundation in collaboration with the Tanzanian Ministry of Health.

The ELCT, in line with the government's policy of self-reliance, has done its part in planning projects that strengthen the economic status of its people. Most of the funds for the various projects have come through the LWF/CDS. The projects emphasize education, primary health care, and agricultural and technical know-how. To strengthen local involvement, the ELCT established its own department of development in 1982. Through education the department seeks to stimulate the dioceses, synods, and local congregations to foster activities that alleviate poverty, disease, and hunger and advance social justice.

The role of women in the faith and life of the ELCT has developed significantly over the years. When the Northern Diocese, for example, came under indigenous leadership in 1959, women as well as men were named to the council. Today, in congregations, women are organized for study, prayer, Christian service, and evangelizing outreach. The synods and dioceses have secretaries to encourage women's work regionally and locally, and a national secretary coordinates the total program.

With uncommon resourcefulness women in the Northern Diocese in 1974 launched their "Safari Project" for building simple chapels. It has caught on and is now an annual venture in other synods and dioceses. Each year some outlying village—whose people are very poor and have no place of worship but would like one—is chosen. A group of Safari women go there with provisions for a week to help the local people put up a chapel. For the visitors and the local women, this is a time to share the faith by joining in hard work, Bible study, testimonies, and song.

A growing number of women with higher education are providing service and leadership within the church. Their importance as teachers, nurses, and other careerists can hardly be overstated. In 1979 the first woman to earn a theological degree at Makumira was graduated. Subsequently there have been others. Pressure for the ordination of women is mounting.

In another area, the nation's burden of poverty and the dislocation of traditional social ways has given rise to a growing number of women seeking not marriage but a career of service. In Moshi something akin to a deaconess community emerged in 1980. Sisters from the deaconess house in Augsburg, Federal Republic of Germany, aided by an ELCT pastor and other helpers, set up a service-oriented program for girls and interpreted it to the congregations.

The South Central Diocese (Bulongwa) elected a woman as its general secretary in 1982, the first time the ELCT has had a woman in a key post for regional church administration. Experienced as administrative head of the church women's work, she manifested the qualifications for her new task.

• • •

Behind the present church scene lies a story of missionary beginnings and wartime interruptions that make the rise of this large and unified Lutheran church all the more remarkable. In 1987, the centennial of these beginnings was observed in Dar es Salaam and beyond, and the Coastal Synod thereafter bore the title of diocese.

The 73 years between the coming of the first missionaries and the formation of the ELCT saw recurring change combined with continuing growth. Three German mission societies led the way: the Berlin Mission to the southern highlands (1890), location of today's Southern Diocese; the Bethel Mission to the picturesque Usambara valley (1891), the present Northeastern Diocese; and the Leipzig Mission, inland to the Kilimanjaro region (1893), now the Northern Diocese. Beginnings were slow, but the groundwork thorough. An outstanding and not unchallenged missionary-theorist, Bruno Gutmann

(1876–1966), a Leipzig man among the Chaggas, sought to engraft the gospel by working through African institutions, redirecting rather than destroying them—a policy that gained the support of the chiefs. World War I interrupted this promising work. German missionaries were repatriated. British mission agencies served as trustees. American and Scandinavian participation began in the 1920s and spread in the 1930s. In 1922, the Augustana Synod (Swedish by descent and an antecedent of the Lutheran Church in America), responding to an appeal from the Leipzig Mission, came to northern Tanganyika. Its interim assistance turned into ongoing partnership. When the Leipzig missionaries returned, the Augustana staff revived an earlier Leipzig work in Iramba (1927) and laid the foundation of today's Central Synod. In 1938 the Swedish Evangelical Mission, already active in Ethiopia, undertook work in the southern highlands, in cooperation with the Berlin Mission.

World War II removed the Germans once again, and the British authorities entrusted the work of the Berlin, Bethel, and Leipzig missions to Augustana. Requisitioned Swedish colleagues, Professor Bengt Sundkler from South Africa among them, helped to sustain the work. The small missionary staff included a lone Leipzig person, Richard Reusch (1891–1975), a Russian-born ethnic German who headed the Mission Churches Federation (MCF), which already in 1940 envisioned a united Lutheran church in Tanganyika. The people themselves responded to the situation, and evangelization continued. By the end of this wartime moratorium, the number of Lutherans in Tanganyika had jumped from about 80,000 in 1939 to 130,000 in 1946.

Events following World War II not only brought back missionaries from Germany but greatly increased Nordic and North American participation. The Church of Sweden Mission assumed special concern for the Bukoba region (now the Northwestern Diocese). The Finnish Missionary Society, barred from Angola, helped in the southern highlands. Some Danish and Norwegian Lutheran mission work, excluded from China, was rerouted to Tanganyika—the Danes going to the southern highlands and elsewhere, the Norwegian Lutheran Mission taking up the work that has become the Mbulu Synod. The Augustana work in the Central Synod was strengthened. In the Dar es Salaam area, the Eastern Coastal Synod, the point of entry was prepared by a unified aid program directed by the USA National Lutheran Council Commission on Younger Churches and Orphaned Missions (CYCOM) and its successor, the Department of World Mission Cooperation, a service that was extended also to other parts of Tanganyika. Later (1952–1961) this coordinating work was carried forward by the LWF Division of World Mission until it was turned over to the Lutheran Coordinating Service (below).

Aware that the powerful forces for independence and nationhood active in Asia and Africa were also affecting Christian constituencies, the First LWF assembly (Lund 1947) had the Tanganyikan as well as Southern African situations especially in mind when it resolved "to encourage the formation, as soon as practicable, of united Lutheran churches in the various mission fields." The advance was by stages. In Tanganyika, regional churches began to be formed in 1948. The same year the Evangelical Lutheran Church of Northern Tanganyika became the first of a succession of indigenous churches. Within a decade the Federation of Lutheran Churches of Tanganyika (1958) was organized.

It soon included all seven regional churches: Southern Tanganyika, Usambara-Digo, Uzaramo-Uluguru, Northern Tanganyika, Northwestern Tanganyika, Central Tanganyika, and the Iraqw (Mbulu). The northern church and Usambara-Digo became members of the LWF in 1961. By 1963, when the Tanganyika Federation was dissolved and the ELCT formed, all the others had either joined the LWF or were closely related to it. But the period thereafter has seen the ELCT and the LWF as one entity.

A tiny fragment of this larger story has been told autobiographically by one of the early Tanganyikan pastors. Andrea Kajarero, a Haya, wrote not about his own ministry but about the Lord's doing among the Haya people. Before writing, he had retraced his steps to all the people among whom he had served. In 1983 this man, a lad when the first missionaries arrived, died at the age of 105.

Also in 1983 Max Paetzig, oldest of the German East African missionaries, died at 97. Seven years earlier he had returned to

Tanzania to visit the nomadic Masai, among whom he had baptized the first convert in 1934.

One of the dilemmas of a church comprising units with different histories and supporting partners is to treat them all fairly. In order to confront this problem, the Lutheran Coordinating Service (LCS) was formed in 1973. It includes in its membership representatives of all supporting churches and missions of the ELCT except the Norwegian Lutheran Mission. The LCS was a merger of cooperative efforts beginning as early as 1961. Currently the office of the LCS general secretary is in Helsinki.

Although LCS is a means of sharing gifts and resources, it does not offer unsolicited assistance. All requests for help are prepared by units within the ELCT and are presented to the LCS by the executive council of the ELCT. Final allocation of expatriate personnel, of scholarship and training programs, and of capital subsidies are made with ELCT representatives at the annual meeting, which is always held in Tanzania. In 1983 the European and North American partners (14 in all) were able to provide all but 65 of the 211 missionaries requested by the ELCT. In 1984 the LCS participants agreed to contribute a total of US $11 million to the Tanzanian church.

A reverse evangelism exercise has in recent years brought Tanzanians, mainly pastors and teachers, to Europe and North America. In parishes, student centers, and elsewhere, they have become de facto missionaries to their secularized fellow Christians in Europe and North America. They have been used by the Spirit in unexpected ways to relate the gospel to daily life. The experience of the parishioners in Anderstorp, Sweden, was perhaps typical. For nearly a year they sponsored a Tanzanian teacher, Nathanael Byashara, to live among them. Dismayed at first, they soon began to learn from him and, when he left, thanked him for being "the living gospel in our midst."

In a related way, the ELCT has provided leading personalities who have left their mark in many lands. Stefano R. Moshi (1906–1976), the first presiding bishop of the ELCT, was a second generation Christian and a member of a leading Chagga family. A gifted and popular teacher, he later took up theology, was ordained at 43, studied further in

America, and, when elected to lead his Chagga church, brought skill and vision to his administration. A member of the presidium of the All Africa Conference of Churches, he was also for a time president of the national YMCA as well as a member of the governing board of the world YMCA. Elected a vice-president of the LWF in 1963, his seven-year term included frequent travel to Europe and other parts of the world. He and his wife made the church in Africa a living reality to many people.

Even more so is the case of Josiah Kibira of Bukoba (1925–1988), the first person from the Two-Thirds World to be elected president of the LWF. He was a second-generation Christian and the son of Haya parents who had joined the Anglican mission. Growing up in a town just south of the Ugandan border and west of Lake Victoria, his education led him into a teaching career and then into theology. Marked by gifts of leadership, he was sent to the Federal Republic of Germany, the United States, and Sweden for further study. Elected in 1961 as the first African bishop of the Northwestern Diocese, he was consecrated by his predecessor, Bishop Bengt Sundkler, the noted missiologist, with two other Swedish and two Anglican bishops assisting. Kibira and his wife, Martha, continued to be active in the ecumenically significant East Africa revival movement. At the New Delhi assembly of the World Council of Churches (1961) he became a member of the Commission on Faith and Order and, seven years later, at the Uppsala assembly, was elected to the WCC Central Committee, on which he continued until 1983.

Meanwhile, in 1970, Kibira chaired the newly formed LWF Commission on Church Cooperation (formerly World Mission), and in 1977 the Dar es Salaam assembly elected him president of the LWF. Despite a progressive illness, he filled his duties ably, traveling worldwide when needed, raising crucial issues fearlessly, and, as one who knew him well reflected, acting as the "hard-hitting conscience" of the LWF. At the end of 1984, at age 59, he took early retirement. The real significance of Kibira's career, like that of his African church, is emerging with the passing years.

ZAMBIA

A republic (1964) and a member of the Commonwealth of Nations. Area: 752,614 sq. km. (290,586 sq. mi.). Pop. (1984 est.): 5,679,808, about 99% of whom are Africans. Cap. and largest city: Lusaka (pop., 1980 prelim. est., 538,500). Language: English, Bantu, and over 30 local dialects.

History: Most of the present-day Zambians trace their origin to migrants from *Angola and Zaire arriving between the 16th and 18th centuries. In the late 18th century, traders (Arabs, Swahili, and black Africans) penetrated their region, exporting from it copper, wax, and slaves. In the early 19th century, the Ngoni, a warrior group from South Africa, invaded. David Livingstone, the famed Scottish missionary-explorer, in 1855 came upon the great falls he named after Victoria, the British Queen. He died near Lake Bangweulu in 1873. Later named Northern Rhodesia, the area was administered by the South Africa Company from 1889 until 1924. Then, as a British protectorate, it became part of the Federation of Rhodesia and Nyasaland until gaining full independence in 1964.

Religion: Nearly 30% of Zambians are adherents of Traditional religion, still strong in rural areas. Muslims are less than 1%. Christians are the majority (70%). Protestants of all types about equal the number of Roman Catholics. A number of agencies promote interdenominational cooperation. The Evangelical Fellowship of Zambia has 15 members; the Association of Independent Churches, about 10; and the Christian Council of Zambia (CCZ; 1945), 13.

Affiliated with the CCZ is the Mindolo Ecumenical Foundation begun as a Pan-African lay training center in 1958. It is located in Kitwe, the chief commercial and industrial center of the copper belt in north central Zambia near *Zaire. This foundation has wide support both from within and without Zambia, including some from Lutheran sources. The board of directors is augmented by Roman Catholics and government officials. Programs emphasize group encounters, action training, and worship. Courses are offered for women, youth workers, and industrial and commercial managers. Mindolo is a place for conferences and research projects. For experienced pastors, it coordinates an advanced theological training program.

The Zambian Christian Refugee Service (ZCRS), organized in 1967 to aid some 10,000 refugees from *Mozambique, *Angola, and other bordering countries, is operated by Lutheran World Service on behalf of the World Council of Churches and in consultation with the Christian Council of Zambia. It also works with the UN High Commissioner for Refugees.

During the struggle for Zimbabwean independence, neighboring Zambia was a temporary home to numerous refugees who fled Rhodesia. The ZCRS assisted in meeting their daily needs and, when independence came (1979), repatriated some 21,000 by October 1980. In cooperation with the All-Africa Conference of Churches, the ZCRS gives support to drought-affected inhabitants of *Angola and provides extensive assistance to the Namibian refugees in that country. Through recognized liberation movements, the ZCRS is able to provide material, educational, and spiritual assistance that helps the refugees to become self-sufficient in their countries of asylum and better-equipped citizens when they return to their own country.

LUTHERAN CHURCH OF CENTRAL AFRICA (LCCA)
Membership in Zambia: 9500
Mission Coordinator: The Rev. Mark Krueger
PO Box 71424
Ndola

This church, as its title indicates, is not limited to a single country. Zambia was the entrance point of the missionaries of the *Wisconsin Evangelical Lutheran Synod in 1953.

Growth in the southern and eastern part of Zambia opened the way for congregations in neighboring *Malawi, where the main headquarters are now located.

At present 62 of the 116 congregations are in Zambia. They are served by four national pastors, 11 evangelists, and nine expatriate pastors. Bantu and other local languages are used. Village medical work, begun in Zambia and extended into Malawi, has high priority. The work is strengthened by expatriate nurses, two in each country. The annual patient total is over 60,000.

Chelston, 16 kilometers from Lusaka, the capital, is where the church's first Bible Institute (1964) trains Zambian evangelists and their spouses. Since 1969 the school includes a seminary. Here pastoral candidates from both countries receive a five-year course that includes the study of Greek. In 1986 there were nine students. Teachers from this institution as well as the one in Malawi have assisted the *Lutheran Church in Cameroon in the training of its workers (see Malawi, above).

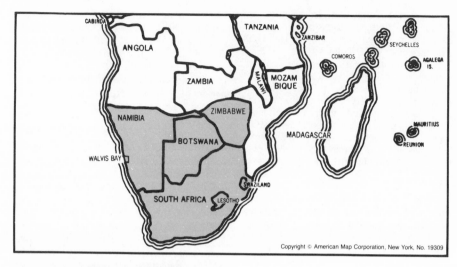

Copyright © American Map Corporation, New York, No. 19309

SOUTHERN AFRICA

Adherents of the Lutheran churches in this region number over 1.3 million, which is slightly less than one-third of the total for the continent. The vast majority of them (95%) live in South Africa and Namibia. The rest are in Zimbabwe and Botswana, plus a few enclaves in Lesotho and Swaziland.

The region is huge. Two former Portuguese domains, *Angola in the northwest and *Mozambique in the northeast, set its outer bounds, while *Zambia (formerly Northern Rhodesia) borders it in the north. Its area of 3.5 million sq. km. (nearly 1.5 million sq. mi.) includes much arid as well as productive land and a wealth of natural resources. Its combined population of about 45 million is overwhelmingly black. White minorities as well as colored and Asian constituencies reflect the region's history as a way station between Europe and Asia. White settlers and native blacks have fought and coexisted here since the first Dutch came to stay (1652). More Europeans settled in this region than elsewhere in sub-Saharan Africa, but their numbers have remained dwarfed by the black population. This fact contrasts sharply with the European settlement of North America or Australia and in part helps to account for the Afrikaner-devised system of separate development. Begun in *South Africa and extended to *Namibia, the injustices of apartheid cast their ominous shadow across the rest of the region and the whole of black Africa as well as other parts of the world.

This southern region, long a sphere of British influence, retains English as its lingua franca. Likewise, the region's economic interdependence continues. But the long-term tensions between Afrikaners and the British, as well as the black people's deep-seated demand for independence, has kept the region in various stages of turmoil. After some 150 years of British involvement in one form or another, the 1960s saw the rise of new national entities.

The map of the region bore new names. The Union of South Africa became the Republic of *South Africa (1961) and left the Commonwealth of Nations. Rhodesia

unilaterally declared independence from Britain (1965) only to see its white su-
premacy defeated by black power and become the nation of *Zimbabwe (1980).
*Botswana, the former British Bechuanaland, gained independence quietly (1966),
as did the two small kingdoms of *Lesotho (1966) and *Swaziland (1968), located
virtually inside South Africa. Only *Namibia remained unfree as South Africa
refused to relinquish its mandate, assigned after World War I, over the former
German colony, which it still calls South-West Africa.

Religion in this southern region has long played a highly important role. This
fact becomes apparent in the following write-ups of the several countries, also with
respect to the Traditional African religion. From the Christian side, at least two
generalizations—one ecumenical, the other confessional—speak for the region.

Ecumenically, the national councils of churches that have been formed in *Botswana, Zimbabwe, Namibia, and South Africa usually include the major communions and find Anglicans and Protestants cooperating and Roman Catholics
participating as observers. (In Namibia the Roman Catholics are full members.)
Generally Lutherans are active participants, especially in South Africa and Namibia
where their numbers are strong. Yet Lutherans, like the Reformed, live with the
internal problem of tense relations between the settler (white) and mission (black
or colored) churches in their respective communions (see South Africa, Namibia).
If we call this the failure of success, then a reminder of missionary beginnings is
helpful.

Because of its location and early settlement, the southern tip of the continent
became the point of entry for many a subsequent missionary advance northward.
Moravian efforts early (1737–1744) demonstrated the evangelizing intention, but
white hostility cut it short. In the 19th century, British efforts unfolded, drawing
in German, French, Scandinavian, Swiss, Dutch, and American ventures. An example was John Philip, the London Missionary Society's (LMS) pioneer in the Cape
(1819), who helped other societies select their fields, among them the Rhenish
Mission's entry into *Namibia in 1842, over 40 years before it became a German
colony. Similarly, the work of Robert Moffat (1795–1883), also for the LMS, was
early (1821) based in Kuruman, *Botswana. From there he launched David Livingstone in his career, as the missionary-explorer pressed ever further northward
into the interior. In many other ways the ecumenical outlines of today could be
traced to the interplay, internationally and interconfessionally, of distant beginnings.
Missionaries often served white settlers as well; until the latter grew in number and
required their own pastors. Then, as with the Dutch and the Lutherans, interracial
church unity tended to fall apart.

Confessionally, for the Lutherans, the vision of unity was not lost, but it has
been at times severely tested. For them an instructive precedent for unity within a
kindred communion was the formation of the Church of the Province of South
Africa (Anglican) in 1870. Its name was changed to Southern instead of South
(1982), giving recognition to its work in Namibia as well as in Lesotho and Swaziland
and the several designated "independent homelands." Meanwhile, in 1955 an offshoot became the Church of the Province of Central Africa, which included
Botswana, Zambia, and Zimbabwe. In both church provinces, black, white, colored,

and Asian are united. For the Lutherans, a similar integration has proven elusive despite its being the announced goal.

One problem has been the diversity of background marking the Lutheran missionaries as well as settlers who came to Southern Africa. Even so, already in 1912 a circle of Berlin, Norwegian, and Swedish representatives formed the "Cooperating Lutheran Missions in Natal-Zululand" (CLM). It soon attracted other partners from the Hermannsburg and American (Norse) missions (see South Africa, ELCSA-Southeastern Diocese). The church body formed from these efforts joined the LWF in 1961. That same year the much larger Ovambokavango Church (see ELCIN, Namibia) was also received. And a year prior to this, the *German Evangelical Lutheran Church in South-West Africa (GELCSWA), a small body, had become the first LWF member church from this Southern Africa region. Behind these actions lay developments pertaining to the region as a whole. Successive stages outline the story.

First, during World War II the severe curtailment of customary assistance from Europe put the work in this region into the category of "orphaned missions and younger churches." Swedish and American help came to the rescue. Second, the First Assembly of the Lutheran World Federation (Lund, Sweden, 1947) encouraged the formation of a single, national church in each country or region. Third, the Council of Churches on Lutheran Foundation in Southern Africa (CCLFSA), formed in 1953, determined to unite Lutherans and Moravians (they used Luther's Catechism) in the region so far as humanly possible. But here vision and reality began to clash.

The vision of an eventually united church had to cope with the rise of self-governing black, colored, and white churches. In *Namibia the first of the "young churches" emerged: the Ovambokavango (see Namibia, ELCIN; 1954), of Finnish connection; and the *Evangelical Lutheran Church in South-West Africa (1957), of Rhenish/German mission connection. With the situation in Namibia becoming more tense under the imposition of apartheid by South Africa, such ecclesial formation carried urgency. It also breathed a spirit of independence. Not to be left out, the small German church (*GELCSWA) became self-governing in 1960 and qualified as a white partner with the other two, which were black and colored.

For the CCLFSA a policy decision was in order. Under circumstances then prevailing, it was a question of how the LWF-proposed policy of one Lutheran church be carried out in this southern region. Was it better to wait until all the would-be components could be consolidated into an inclusive church? Or should the proliferation of separate self-governing churches continue? Already in 1958 the CCLFSA decided in favor of the latter. Some have called this a fateful decision. For it "actually cemented the divisions of the Lutherans according to ethnic and racial groupings."

The FEDERATION OF EVANGELICAL LUTHERAN CHURCHES IN SOUTHERN AFRICA (FELCSA) in 1966 succeeded the CCLFSA. This regionally inclusive body of 10 churches, promising in its affirmations of unity, was handicapped before it started. In the year prior to its formation, three white German churches, one in *Namibia and the other two in *South Africa, had organized their own bloc. Called the *United Evangelical Lutheran Church in Southern Africa (UELCSA), its title corresponded to the vision of confessional unity, but its agenda (including an equiv-ocal attitude toward apartheid prompted by the stand of most of the white laity) tended to deflect FELCSA from its agreed course.

Even so, as a service agency FELCSA filled many an urgent need. Theological education, urban and rural mission, evangelism, religious literature, church school curricula, social work, resettlement, development projects, and the like comprised its functions. FELCSA convened conferences on church unity and other theological issues. These, as well as church-state relations, had their ethical side; and always the ugly fact of apartheid intruded.

Impatient of the others, the two nonwhite churches in *Namibia in 1971 drafted their appeal for human rights and an end to apartheid. The two church leaders personally presented this open letter to South Africa's Prime Minister John Vorster. In and beyond the FELCSA membership the feeling was electric. Yet the situation remained unchanged.

The LWF itself had meanwhile thrown its influence on the side of combating racism. The 1970 assembly in Evian-les-Bains, France, came out bluntly in favor of a public rejection of apartheid. Unbarred pulpit and altar fellowship—integrated black and white reception of the Lord's Supper—was the standard. Churches failing this test, it was voted, should receive no further LWF aid. Southern Africa's white churches claimed that this, too, was their position, only there were local problems in the congregations. In fact, those familiar with the situation from the inside were struck by two things: one was the often racist (ethnic) stance expressed in the constitution of a given congregation; the other was that Lutherans of German descent or recent arrival regarded themselves as guests in South Africa and felt obliged to do as their hosts, the white Dutch Reformed, were accustomed to do—at times even exceeding them. All of which was part of what has been called the South African church struggle, reminiscent of the German church struggle under the Nazis.

The vision of Lutheran union persisted, and the frustration mounted. In 1975, before Christmas, the black churches in South Africa went it alone and constituted the *Evangelical Lutheran Church in Southern Africa (ELCSA). They left intact a badly strained FELCSA, which nevertheless continued its functions. To these had been added (1970) the role of LWF national committee for Southern Africa, a name that in other parts of the region seemed progressively inappropriate in light of a rising national consciousness in the newly independent countries.

FELCSA's hosting of the 1976 All-Africa Lutheran Conference found other black churches sharing *ELCSA's stand. This meeting in Gaborone, *Botswana, wrote the script for the still sharper action by the 1977 LWF assembly in the Tanzanian capital, Dar es Salaam. In no uncertain terms apartheid was to be "unequivocally and publicly rejected" by the LWF member churches, including the white member churches in Southern Africa. To reject apartheid was to affirm the integrity of the Christian faith. The duty to do so involved an act of confessing, placing also a church in a *status confessionis*.

FELCSA continued, but with waning powers. Its white member churches pro-fessed again and again the duty of rejecting apartheid, as their clerical leaders affirmed. But other things were happening, including the merger (1981) of two white churches into the present Natal-Transvaal church (see South Africa). One of them, of Hermannsburg origin, had been a member of the LWF since 1963. The other, of Berlin Mission antecedents and a church since 1955, had a so-called permanent connection with the LWF. In late 1983 the Pre-Assembly Consultation of Lutheran Churches in Africa (Harare, Zimbabwe) followed the demand of *ELCSA and recommended that the remaining white member church in South Africa, along with the white member church in Namibia, be suspended from the LWF. Early in 1984, while visiting in Germany, Bishop Rapoo, the presiding head of FELCSA, claimed that there were still grounds for hope and that a public rejection of apartheid would be forthcoming from the white churches. This hope was in vain. Meanwhile, the council of ELCSA voted to withdraw from FELCSA, pending further developments. The LWF assembly in Budapest, confronted by a decision without precedent, made no hasty decision. The LWF constitution provided for a suspension of membership but not for termination. As the South Africans explained, the situation was like a family relationship, which cannot be terminated. To suspend was to admonish in hope of eventual reconciliation and reunion. The assembly agreed.

Late in 1984 the ELCSA assembly, confirming the church council's earlier action, voted to withdraw from FELCSA, the decision to become final in six months. However the FELCSA assembly, meeting in September 1986, refused to accept the withdrawal of ELCSA on the grounds that it had not "fulfilled its constitutional obligation to the federation." The assembly also pledged that its member churches would work together more closely and elected the Rev. Martin Wessels of the Moravian church as president to lead in this endeavor.

Before detailing the various individual churches, a further word of caution is in order. The nomenclature can be confusing. Many of the church bodies use the same major designation in their title: Evangelical Lutheran Church in Southern Africa (ELCSA), and then modify it front or aft. So, then, the federation of these churches becomes FELCSA. The bloc of German-speaking churches becomes *UELCSA. The smaller churches add their telltale: *ELCSA/Cape Church, or *ELCSA/Natal-Transvaal. But the biggest one of all, the black church formed out of four merging synods in 1975, is simply *ELCSA. This applies mainly to *South Africa, but some of this same problem spills over into *Namibia and *Botswana.

UNITED EVANGELICAL LUTHERAN CHURCH IN SOUTHERN AFRICA (UELCSA)

(Verenigde Evangelies-Lutherse Kerk in Suider Afrika)
Chair of the Church Council: The Rt. Rev. Lothar T.K. Müller-Nedebock
16 Eighth Avenue
PO Box 873
1610 Edenvale, Transvaal

Constituted in 1965 in connection with efforts to promote church unity in Southern Africa,

UELCSA began as a federal union of four white church bodies in two countries. A merger in 1981 left the following three: ELCSA/Natal-Transvaal, ELCSA/Cape Church, and the *German Evangelical Lutheran Church in South-West Africa (see Namibia). Some independent congregations have affiliated with the UELCSA, among them the Strand Street Church in Cape Town (*South Africa).

The three bodies comprising the UELCSA retain their autonomy in worship, constitution, legislation, and administration, while together they encourage cooperation and unity among different churches and racial groups. For those in positions of leadership, the fostering of church unity on a larger scale is complicated by the fact that the local congregations, most of them far older than the general bodies of which they are members, have their own constitutions and customs as well as attitudes.

Most of the pastors of the member churches are from the *Federal Republic of Germany, serving the congregations for longer or shorter periods. The *Evangelical Church in Germany (EKD) has subsidized pastors' salaries and other UELCSA expenses.

In an effort to develop a core of indigenous pastors who could meet the needs and challenges of the white churches in South Africa, a theological training program was initiated in 1973. The department of divinity at the University of Natal in Pietermaritzburg provided the main curriculum and institutional privileges. Students lived together near the campus where they had additional lectures by Lutheran tutors. A sense of community developed through group living and a disciplined devotional life. For a year of inter-ethnic encounter and an introduction to systematic theology, students attended the Lutheran Theological College, Umpumulo, a seminary of *ELCSA. Living and studying together proved to be a valuable experience for all.

In order to further understanding and integration among South African Lutherans and to give the opportunity for theological education at a respected university to all ethnic groups, UELCSA proposed that the Lutheran Theological Training Center in Pietermaritzburg be a shared project with *ELCSA. With help and encouragement from the LWF, many years were spent working out an arrangement that the South African government would approve and that would be acceptable to ELCSA. This was accomplished in 1984. Ironically, this same year two members of the UELCSA were suspended from the LWF on the strong recommendation of the black churches of Africa, who claimed that the larger challenge—the public rejection of apartheid on the part of the white churches—remained unmet.

BOTSWANA

An independent republic since 1966, Botswana (formerly Bechuanaland) is a member of the Commonwealth of Nations. Area: 581,700 sq. km. (224,600 sq. mi.). Pop. (1981 prelim.): 936,600, almost 99% African. Cap. and largest city: Gaborone (pop., 1981 prelim., 59,700). Language: English (official) and Setswana.

History: The Tswana people have occupied this land since the 18th century when they overpowered the San (Bushmen). Khama, the chief of the largest Tswana tribe, established a fairly unified state. In the 19th century, when Boers from South Africa encroached on this territory, the British, with the sanction of Khama, set up a protectorate known as Bechuanaland (1885). Without much pressure from the people, Britain granted self-government in internal affairs in 1965 and full independence a year later. Khama's grandson, Sir Seretse Khama, became Botswana's first president in 1966.

Landlocked and sparsely settled, Botswana is dependent on *South Africa for port facilities, and *Zimbabwe controls the railroad passing through the country. A water shortage over vast areas makes sheep and cattle raising the main occupations. Since independence, mineral deposits—including diamonds and coal—have been found, thus improving the country's economic outlook.

Botswana was a refuge for Zimbabweans during their political strife. LWF World Service began relief operations in 1977 with national headquarters in Gaborone. This was in close consultation and coordination with the government authorities, the United Nations High Commissioner for Refugees, the Botswana Christian Council, the Botswana Council for Refugees, and the Red Cross. LWF World Service has operated a refugee settlement at Dukwi since 1978.

Religion: Traditional about 50%; among the Bushmen about 90%. Roman Catholics (15%) have grown rapidly since 1959. Protestants (27%) have exerted a significant influence on the country since the early 19th century when the London Missionary Society (LMS) began work. Lutheran missionaries from Hermannsburg instructed and in 1862 baptized Khama, the chief of a major tribe in Bechuanaland. His encouragement to LMS missionaries helped make the United Congregational Church the major church body in the country. The United Congregational Church of Southern Africa is the largest denomination, followed by the Seventh Day

Adventists. Traditional churches, though small, are exerting an increasing influence.

The Botswana Christian Council (BCC), formed in 1966, has seven members—including the Roman Catholic Church—and four observers. The BCC's main work is in urban and rural development. Since Botswana has no theological seminary and it is increasingly difficult to send students out of the country, six denominations, including the Lutherans, formed the Botswana Theological Training Program in 1975. A five-year extension course at mid-secondary level provides an opportunity for mature men and women, involved in secular jobs, to prepare for ministry. Many of them are ordained by their respective churches. In addition, the University of Botswana (see Lesotho) has an undergraduate and graduate department of religion. Here students prepare for teaching religion in the public schools. Extension courses (of three-year duration) are offered to students who meet the university entrance requirements and who are able to do independent work toward a diploma in theology.

EVANGELICAL LUTHERAN CHURCH IN BOTSWANA (ELCB)

Member: LWF (1986), BCC
Membership: 14,407**
Bishop: Philip Jeremiah Robinson
PO Box 1976
Gaborone

This church declared its autonomy in 1978. The congregations had been a part of the Botswana Circuit of the Western Diocese of the *ELCSA. They withdrew in order to identify with and better serve their members and others living in the independent nation of Botswana. In 1983 the *Evangelical Lutheran Church in South-West Africa/Rhenish Mission (ELCSWA) willingly released to the ELCB its several small congregations, centers, and clinics in western Botswana. Located in Sehithwa near Lake Ngami on the edge of the Okavango swamp area and in Hukuntsi in the Kalahari desert, these congregations were the result of work by the ELCSWA and the United Evangelical Mission (FRG).

The 59 congregations of this young church are divided into three circuits: northern, central, and southwestern. They are served by 18 pastors (four being expatriates), six evangelists, and 10 parish assistants. Languages used are Setswana, English, Herero, and Afrikaans. An annual assembly, known as the synod, elects the officers. The northern and central circuits each have a diaconal worker; the youth department has a staff of four; and the church office a secretarial force of two. As the staff indicates, the church has great concern for its young people and has initiated programs to combat illiteracy, poverty, hunger, and ignorance. An adult literacy program is doing well.

The training of indigenous pastors is another priority of this young church. Since Botswana has no seminary and the cost of establishing one is prohibitive, other means of education must be used (see above). At its formation, the ELCB had only three pastors, none of whom were native to Botswana. To meet the emergency, a crash program was conducted by the dean of the department of religion at the University of Botswana, a Lutheran from Zimbabwe. Chosen for the four-month course were mature and tested people who had already received two years of evangelist training by the mother church. Ordained as pastors, they continue their education through extension courses.

In 1983, due to severe drought in the Kgalagadi, Ghanzi, and Ngamiland districts, the church called upon LWF World Service (above) for assistance in transporting their aid of food, blankets, and clothing to these areas. This emergency relief initiated an ongoing welfare program by the ELCB, including the care and rehabilitation of disabled persons.

By 1987 the ELCB responded to the BCC's initiated reconciliation with the Botswana Diocese of the ELCSA. Cooperation will take the form of pulpit exchange, common programs for youth and women, united seminars, and worship services.

EVANGELICAL LUTHERAN CHURCH IN SOUTHERN AFRICA (ELCSA) / BOTSWANA DIOCESE (*South Africa)

Membership: 5500**
Bishop: The Rt. Rev. Michael Nthuping
PO Box 400
Gaborone

This diocese of ELCSA was established in 1981 to gather and nurture the 22 congregations that did not withdraw and join the

ELCB (above). The congregations are divided into 11 parishes and are served by eight pastors, one evangelist, and one missionary. They include Tswana-speaking people formerly served by the Western Diocese and also Kalahari Bushmen who had been reached by the Cape Orange Diocese.

LUTHERAN CHURCH IN SOUTHERN AFRICA (*South Africa)
Membership: 1600**
Dean: The Rev. F.A. Haefner
PO Box 31
Kanye

In eastern Botswana there are 21 congregations and several preaching points that are a part of the Lutheran Church in Southern Africa. To strengthen the work in this area as well as to pioneer in the Khakea area of the Kalahari desert, two missionaries of the *Lutheran Church–Missouri Synod (USA) are working under the direction of the Bleckmar Mission of the *Independent Evangelical Lutheran Church (FRG), a partner of the Lutheran Church in Southern Africa.

LESOTHO

A constitutional monarchy (1959), independent since 1966, and a member of the Commonwealth of Nations, Lesotho is entirely surrounded and largely controlled by the Republic of *South Africa. Area: 30,355 sq. km. (11,720 sq. mi.). Pop. (1983 est.): 1,438,000. Cap. and largest city: Maseru (pop., 1980 prelim. est., 30,000). Languages: English and Sesotho (official).

History: Moshoeshoe I, paramount chief of the Lesotho people, unified the Basotho clans during the 1820s, defended (mainly by conciliatory means) his mountainous kingdom against the encroaching white (Boer) settlers, and was hospitable to Christian missionaries, especially French Protestants and the members of the Paris Evangelical Missionary Society (PEMS). Later he requested the British to make his country a protectorate (1868), which it remained until independence. The public school system culminates in the University of Botswana, Lesotho, and

Swaziland. Situated in Roma, east of the capital, it has a fully ecumenical department of theology.

Religion: An estimated 83% of the population are Christian (Roman Catholic 44%; Protestant 39%); Traditional 6.2%; other 1%. The Christian Council of Lesotho (1964) includes the 206,000-member Lesotho Evangelical Church (result of the PEMS), as well as Anglican, Methodist, Assemblies of God, and Roman Catholic churches. The Lutheran connection with Lesotho, originally through the Paris Evangelical Mission Society, continues today through the Evangelical Community for Apostolic Action (CEVAA), in which the two Lutheran churches in *France participate. Also, the South-Eastern Diocese of the *Evangelical Lutheran Church in Southern Africa (ELCSA) includes Lesotho congregations.

NAMIBIA

A United Nations territory since 1966 when the General Assembly took action to terminate South Africa's mandate over South-West Africa; renamed Namibia (1968) by the UN for the Namib Coast by which the land was originally known. South Africa considered the UN resolution invalid and determined to continue the jurisdiction it exercised over South-West Africa since the end of World War I as a League of Nations mandate. Namibia gained independence in 1989.

Area: 824,292 sq. km. (318,261 sq. mi.). Bordered by the Atlantic Ocean on the west, *Angola on the north, *Zambia at the extreme northeast (off the Caprivi Strip), and *Botswana on the east, Namibia's major neighbor is *South Africa, across the Orange River to the south. The topography is of four types: the narrow Namib Desert along the entire coast backed by a range of mountains; the central plateau (averaging about 1100 meters or 3600 feet above sea level); the fringes of the Kalahari Desert in the east; and the alluvial plain in the north (mainly beyond the huge salt basin, the Etosha Pan).

Population (1982 est.): 1,050,600 (black 93%, white 7%). Cap. and largest city: Windhoek (pop., 1978 est., 75,100). Summer cap.: Swakopmund (pop., 1978 est., 16,800). Ports: Walvis Bay (pop. 25,000), a

South Africa enclave but administered for half a century as part of South-West Africa; Lüderitz (pop. 4200).

Major ethnic groups: Ovambos (half of Namibia's population) in the north, with Kavangos to their east; Damaras and Hereros in the central plateau; Namas in the south; Basters (European, African, and some Asian mix) in urban areas; San (Hottentots or Bushmen are European designations) dispersed around the fringes; and others. The European minority perpetuates Afrikaner, German, English, and other antecedents and has shaped the country's modern history.

Language: Afrikaans and English (official); various African (Bantu and Khoikhoi family) tongues; some German.

History: The early story of the San and others among Namibia's original nomadic inhabitants is veiled in lore and in legend. Like the pastoral Namas, the Hereros were a people on the move, coming with their cattle into the Namibian central plateau in the 18th century after a generation-long trek from the region around Tanganyika. Conflicts over grazing land made for often tense relations between Namas and Hereros until the German colonial rule. In the north, the Ovambos, an agricultural society, kept largely to themselves, their kin being in neighboring Angola.

Contacts with Europe remained slight until the 19th century. During the wars of Napoleon, the Namib coast gained new importance, especially for the British. The Germans acquired South-West Africa (Namibia) as a colony in 1884.

During 40 precolonial years, missionaries unfolded their work. Traders also came, offering easy credit for the manufactures they sold. Collectors followed up, demanding payment, and by default acquiring the people's land and other possessions. Europeans (mostly Germans) moved onto the land, opening ranches and planting farms. Alarmed over what was happening, the Hereros fought the Namas for more land. Failing in this, both tribes finally rebelled against the Germans (1904–1908). Defeated by military superiority, their populations were decimated, the Hereros cut brutally from some 70,000 to 16,000, the Namas from 50,000 to 20,000. Their tribal structures were almost destroyed. The church, in part, substituted for the vanquished order.

Seized by South Africa during World War I (1915), South-West Africa was in 1919 mandated to South Africa by the new League of Nations. The German minority settlers were offered, and in large part accepted, South African citizenship. Later, during the 1930s, National Socialist influence was strong among ethnic Germans. After World War II, South Africa clung to its mandate over South-West Africa. Although declared illegal by United Nations action, this mandate continued through 1988.

The country's abounding mineral and natural resources have been progressively exploited during the present century. Its diamonds, uranium, copper, lead, and other products have flowed into the international market, due to modern technology and especially to an indigenous labor force. Mining camps and company towns annually house close to 50,000 contract laborers, most of them from Ovamboland. Away from family for about a year at a time and living in barracks, these men and women serve as contract labor. Wages are low. Cash flows home, but the social fabric suffers, and the burden of injustice grows heavier.

Since World War II, mounting protests by blacks and various measures by others have created patterns of frustration. Key developments on the black side (especially Ovambo) included: creation of the South-West Africa People's Organization (SWAPO) in Cape Town, 1958; protests against the imposition of a tribal "homelands" policy (the Odendaal plan, 1964); the launching by SWAPO of a guerrilla war for independence (1966); and South Africa's subsequent adoption of the Terrorism Act (1967), which provided for detention without trial. These and other grievances were summed up in the "Open Letter" presented to Prime Minister B. J. Vorster in 1971 by black Lutheran church leaders.

The United Nations, meanwhile, created a Council on South-West Africa (1966); later, an opinion (1971) of the International Court of Justice called South Africa's continued presence in Namibia illegal. This stimulated plans for Namibia's independence. A constitutional convention set for Windhoek (1975) was backed by the country's Democratic Turnhalle Alliance (DTA). A mixed black and white political organization, it was welcomed by some blacks but rejected by most others. Especially in Ovamboland the DTA was seen as a puppet of South Africa. The assassination (1975) of the Ovambo chief, Filemon Elifas, the territorial officer representing South African policy, and the ensuing prolonged trial of suspects (in Swakopmund) fed tensions. UN Security Council Resolution 435 (1978) mapped out plans for free elections and independence. These began to be implemented 10 years later.

A major excuse for delay was South Africa's fear that its two recently independent coastal neighbors—*Angola to the west and *Mozambique to the east—could become bases for a Communist advance. With kinfolk across the border in southern Angola, the people of Ovamboland came progressively under South African police surveillance. Periodic military action, spilling over into Angola, cost many lives.

As South Africa continued its support of the DTA for an independent Namibia, confusion grew. The UN recognized SWAPO, not the DTA, as the leader of independence. South Africa's repressive measures are said to have caused some 70,000 Ovambos, most of them young people, to seek refuge in Angola, Zambia, or elsewhere. The visit of UN Secretary General Pérez de Cuéllar to South Africa and Namibia (1983) failed to break the deadlock. South Africa's precondition to Namibian independence, backed by the USA, called for prior withdrawal of Cuban troops from Angola, which began in January 1989.

For the Ovambo people, and others, their land was a war zone. Informers divide families. Interrogation, search, threats, violence, as well as arrests, imprisonment, and death have taken a costly toll. To the extent permitted, official encouragement and support from churches overseas (below) have helped to ease the burden.

Religion: The population is estimated to be about 95% Christian—Lutherans claim about 58%, Roman Catholics 17%, Dutch Reformed 9.5%, Anglicans 8.5%. Traditional religions account for less than 5%.

The Council of Churches in Namibia (CCN), formed in 1978, includes all major denominations (except the white Dutch Reformed churches): Lutheran, Roman Catholic, Anglican, African Methodist Episcopal, Methodist, and Congregational. The first objective of the CCN is to promote Christian unity and to bring justice to the Namibian people. It also fosters self-help projects, training and educational programs, and a communication system. The latter exchanges information at home and keeps churches abroad informed.

The CCN's first general secretary was Albertus Maasdorp, previously the LWF's associate general secretary. After three years in Windhoek, he was called to the Lutheran congregation in The Hague (Netherlands). Another Lutheran, Abisai Shejavali, was elected general secretary in 1983. Dr. Shejavali, until then president of the Paulinum Seminary (below), completed advanced theological education in Finland and the United States.

In 1983 the CCN appealed to the UN Secretary General to help "prevent the escalation of war" and its attendant suffering in northern Namibia and Angola and to speed the process of independence. In August, as already mentioned, Secretary General Javier Pérez de Cuéllar responded.

Among the communions in Namibia, the Lutherans, being the far largest, present a special case.

The UNITED EVANGELICAL LUTHERAN CHURCH IN SOUTH-WEST AFRICA is a federation of Namibia's three Lutheran churches (below)—two black and one white. UELCSWA has served as the LWF national committee for Namibia as well as the agency for a number of common projects in theological education, social action, and diaconal service. Its periodic conventions, like that in 1983, committed the participating bodies to form one Lutheran church, hopefully by 1992. Its board of directors, elected by the conventions, guides the work, strengthened now by a general secretary, the Rev. Iipinge Kristof Shuuya of the *ELCIN. Heads of the three church bodies have served as officers.

Like the other churches in Southern Africa, those in Namibia have been members of *FELCSA and partners in its strivings for unity and justice. In that context, the *Evangelical Lutheran Church in South-West Africa (Rhenish Mission) (ELCSWA) and the Evangelical Lutheran Ovambokavango Church (ELOC, now *ELCIN) in 1972 formed a federal union. The bold protest the preceding year, delivered in person by the presidents of the two churches to South Africa's Prime Minister Vorster (above), stimulated the will to oneness. The new general body, with the hope of union, took the name UELCSWA. This allowed each church to retain its own identity while cooperating in matters done better together than separately, such as theological education.

Five years later (1977) the *German Evangelical Lutheran Church (GELCSWA), much smaller than either of the other two, joined them. A uniting project for the three of them was the pastoral care of the approximately 50,000 contract laborers (above), most of whom were from the Ovambo and Kavango regions but worked, removed from their families, in the central and southern parts of the country.

The persistent challenge to combat racism and apartheid often provoked internal crises that proved hard on this black-white partnership. For a time its importance seemed to fade and its future to be in doubt. Particularly so when the alleged failure of GELCSWA and *ELCSA/Cape Church (see South Africa) to oppose apartheid caused the Pre-Assembly Consultation of Lutheran Churches in Africa (Harare, Zimbabwe, December 1983) to recommend suspension of the two from LWF membership.

When the 1984 Budapest assembly acted accordingly, the three Namibian churches, and the LWF itself, were put to the test. As noted elsewhere (see Southern Africa Introduction), suspension was not termination but discipline. This required continued effort, painful and profound, from which a new beginning might arise and full partnership be restored. The ensuing October meeting of the UELCSWA board, in Windhoek, was intensive and crucial, an experience of confession and reconciliation "in the presence of our Lord." The board's three-part resolution, sent to the congregations, called for: (1) continued joint action against racism and apartheid; (2) a reaffirmed commitment (in line with the 1983 UELCSWA action) to forming one Lutheran church; and (3) a speeding of the process toward unity in the spirit of the 1984 assembly's challenge to confessional integrity. The road ahead would be hard. UELCSWA seemed on course until 1987 when relationships again faltered. As a federation it is now on hold. However, for the two black churches a new educational project shows promise.

The plight of Namibians has moved fellow Lutherans throughout the world. Efforts continue to meet needs and to foster liberation.

The new ELCA (see USA) pursues the program initiated by the ALC and LCA in 1986. It provides higher education for Namibian Lutherans who, upon finishing a college degree in the USA, will return to Namibia to provide leadership in areas of education and public service. (No system of higher education exists in Namibia and Namibians are given no opportunity to study in South Africa.) By 1987, 30 students were enrolled in ELCA colleges and universities where tuition, room, and board are donated by the institutions. Travel and other costs have come from a variety of individuals and congregations. Through the LWF, funds also come from the West German development agency, Evangelische Zentralstelle für Entwicklungshilfe. The goal is to continue until 100 students have finished their work.

EVANGELICAL LUTHERAN CHURCH IN NAMIBIA (ELCIN)

(Evangeliese Lutherse Kerk in Namibia)
Member: LWF (1961), FELCSA, UELCSWA, CCN
Membership: 372,154
Bishop: The Rt. Rev. Kleopas Dumeni, D.D.
Oniipa, Private Bag 2018
Ondangwa 9000

Among Namibia's churches, the Evangelical Lutheran Church in Namibia (ELCIN) is by far the largest. Located in the far north in a militarily restricted area bordering southern *Angola, this large body comes close to being a folk church of the Ovambo and Kavango people. The Ovambos alone account for a good half of Namibia's population.

For three decades after becoming autonomous (1954), this body was known as the Evangelical Lutheran Ovambokavango Church (ELOC). Practical considerations, including progress toward church unity, underlay the change of name. (See UELCSWA, above.)

The many congregations of this Finnish-initiated church body are grouped into about 71 parishes and served by some 130 ordained pastors as well as a large number of teachers, church workers, and other helpers. The Ovamboland parishes are in the central part of this northern region, Kavango in the eastern.

The more recent San (Bushmen) parishes lie south of the Kavango. They speak Khoisan.

Organizationally the church has a bishop, a legislative body (the biennial synod), and a governing executive board. Four regional districts care for the more immediate needs of the parishes and congregations. The church installed its first indigenous president in 1960. Three years later he received the title of bishop. Leonard Auala (1908–1983), the initial incumbent, filled this top office with distinction for virtually two decades (1960–1979). During this time he was a courageous champion of human rights and an ecumenically recognized church leader. His successor has followed ably on this difficult course.

Church headquarters are in the village of Oniipa, 49 kilometers (31 miles) south of the Angolan border. The location is quite central because historically the Ovambo people have lived on both sides of the later-drawn river boundary between Namibia and Angola. Oniipa is the vibrant center of a vigorous church. As in many other comparable regions, daily radio communication maintains contact with 10 outlying centers. Telephone and telex link church headquarters with the outside world. Likewise in Oniipa is Onandjokwe Hospital, whose generator provides power and light—including nighttime protection from prowling terrorists—for the offices, staff homes, and church press. The latter, founded in 1901 by Finnish missionaries, was twice destroyed by terrorists (1973, 1980) and rebuilt each time with help from overseas as well as from the church members. The Oniipa press publishes a fortnightly church paper in three languages (Ndonga, Kwanyama, and Rukwangahi) with a circulation of 8000. Other publications provide for the worship, educational, and evangelistic needs of the members. The technical department of ELCIN is also centered here in Oniipa. Its task includes the construction and maintenance of church buildings, vehicles, machinery, and equipment. Since many of the buildings are old and the war has caused much destruction, the cost of this work is great and has required the help of the LWF Community Development Service and partner support.

Most of the ELCIN's members are subsistence farmers. Usually, however, one member of every family works in the central or southern part of the country, mainly in the diamond, uranium, and copper mines, but also on commercial farms and in domestic service. They account for 20% of the church's membership. Another 10% have fled to neighboring countries such as *Angola and *Zambia for safety. Some of the members have been drafted by the South African defense force. Others have joined SWAPO. To meet the physical and spiritual needs of this diverse membership requires patience and ingenuity. One ELCIN pastor drove 112,000 kilometers (70,000 miles) in a year to reach his 30,000 labor camp parishioners with Word, sacrament, and encouragement. As indicated in the introduction, the two other Namibian Lutheran church bodies share in this pastoral service.

Heir to the many educational and medical institutions founded by the Finnish Missionary Society (FMS, now Finnish Evangelical Lutheran Mission), ELCIN endeavors to maintain them, with partner assistance. An extensive primary school system was taken over by the government already in 1960. However, since secondary education for blacks is extremely limited and inferior, the church tenaciously holds on to its first class Oshigambo High School. Here an equal number of boys and girls are prepared for matriculation, national leadership, and Christian service. Five of the 10 teachers are expatriates. The Namibian teacher of religion is a graduate of the Paulinum Theological Seminary where ELCIN's pastors are trained (see ELCSWA, below). This teacher has continued her theological education by correspondence and earned the bachelor of theology degree from the University of South Africa.

One training center for church workers is the Engela Parish and Adult Education Center. Combining education with diaconal service, it has been instrumental in bringing about better care for the handicapped. Another, the Kavango Education Center in Nkurenkuru, brings educational and development opportunities to people in an isolated region where school facilities are at a minimum. Bible schools and hostels for school children are also a part of the educational enterprise.

Although the government runs a few central hospitals and gives some subsidy, most rural medical care falls to ELCIN and the Roman Catholic Church. The Lutheran Medical Mission of ELCIN has 24 hospitals, health centers, and dispensaries. Its strong mobile health unit was discontinued due to the danger of land mines on the roads. Less preventive care has increased the workload of the hospitals. The death toll has increased because patients, no matter how ill, cannot get medical care during the dusk to dawn curfew.

ELCIN, in cooperation with the Finnish Evangelical Lutheran Mission, has two missions beyond Namibia. It supports five pastors and 10 evangelists in *Angola as well as two missionary families in *Senegal. ELCIN is also a charter member of the Joint Christian Ministry in West Africa (JCMWA), an outreach to the Fulani (see Africa Introduction).

• • •

The Epiphany 1983 centennial of the first baptisms in Ovamboland was a joyous, popular outpouring and also a reminder of the difficult missionary beginnings. On the site of the original event, marked by a simple cross and the grave of the first missionary, about 1200 people gathered under the hot sun for worship, Bible study, sermons, and greetings. Church leaders from Finland, Germany, and North America had come for the occasion. The South African military checkpoint and the curfew were reminders of the perennial struggle of the gospel in the world. Five old-timers, children of the first baptized, were honored at the celebration and personified the hundred-year span of time. The text of the 1883 founding event underlay the main sermon, "as for me and my house, we will serve the Lord" (Josh. 24:15).

In 1857 Carl Hugo Hahn, the Rhenish Mission's pioneer among the Hereros (see ELCSWA, below), and a colleague made the first of two exploratory treks northward. After an almost disastrous rebuff, the way opened. Rhenish resources, however, were already fully extended. A rumored Roman Catholic design on the Ovambos in southern Portuguese Angola (the international boundary was yet undrawn) aroused Rhenish anxieties. Hahn, a native of Riga and of German Baltic stock, happily secured help from Finland. With continued Rhenish assistance, Ovamboland in 1870 became the young Finnish Missionary Society's (1859) first field of endeavor. Evangelization proved an uphill struggle. Finally, after nearly 13 years in Omulonga, six Ovambo men received baptism on January 6 (Epiphany Day), 1883, at the hand of Tobias Reijonen of the FMS.

Although the Rhenish Mission undertook its own work in Ovamboland a little later, it was of short duration and in an unfavorable location. When the boundary between Angola and German South-West Africa was officially drawn (1891), the Rhenish venture had to be relocated southward. During World War I, the Rhenish work was turned over completely to the FMS, and so it remained.

The remarkable rapport between the persons sent by the FMS and the people of northern Namibia has marked the history of this church. By the centennial of the Ovamboland venture in 1970, the FMS had sent 200 ordained pastors and other workers. Memorable among the pioneers was Martin Rautanen, a missionary among the Ovambos for 50 years. His translation of the New Testament into the Ndonga dialect of the people was published in 1903. The complete Bible became available in 1954, the year when the Ovambo-kavango church became an autonomous body.

Already in 1901 a printing press began turning out helps for spreading the gospel. This shared gospel touched many areas of life. The first medical doctor arrived in 1906. Five years later the first hospital was opened. In 1913 the first teacher training school led the way for a later extensive educational system. As an indigenous church was taking shape, 1925 saw the first ordination of Ovambo pastors. This growth came to a climax with the statement of self-government in 1954.

From Ovamboland an eastward movement reached the Kavangos in 1928. Later on, still other ventures reached the San. Language difficulties and conflicting tribal allegiances increased the work's complexity. Nevertheless, the forward movement has continued to this day, also in spite of the already-mentioned burdens of injustice and of harassment by the military. Living near an international border, with Ovambo and Kavango kinfolk for generations also on the Angolan side, has widened the horizon of these Christians. They have also experienced the supportiveness of fellow believers in distant lands as well as in their own country. The policy of Christian nonviolence in the struggle for justice, having been firmly established during the two decades of Bishop Auala's leadership, has been bravely continued by his successor.

EVANGELICAL LUTHERAN CHURCH IN SOUTH-WEST AFRICA— RHENISH MISSION (ELCSWA)

(Evangeliese Lutherse Kerk in Suidwes-Afrika—Rynse Sending)
Member: LWF (1970), FELCSA, UELCSWA, CCN
Membership: 193,000**
President: The Rt. Rev. Hendrik Frederik
PO Box 5069
Windhoek 9000

This church, constituted in 1957, an offspring of the missionary endeavors of the Rhenish Mission of Germany, became fully autonomous in 1972 when it elected its first black president.

ELCSWA's nearly 200,000 members, including several ethnic groups in central Namibia, are gathered into 45 congregations and served by 60 pastors. The congregations are grouped into six circuits each headed by a moderator. The biennial synod is the top decision-making body. A church board meets every two months to ensure that the synod's decisions are duly executed by the management committee of the president, vice-president, general secretary, secretary, and treasurer. The church languages are Herero, Nama, Afrikaans, and English. Its members are engaged in a variety of occupations— subsistence farming, education, civil service, trade and business.

ELCSWA recognizes its women members as the most vital and active. Every congregation has an organized group for Bible study and prayer, visitation of the sick and aged, as well as for choral performance. The youth, too, enliven the congregations, especially in performing and composing songs and church music of Namibian character. An office in Okahandja, north of Windhoek, coordinates this work as well as that of the women. Men retain their governing and decision-making role in most congregations. Male choirs also add vitality to the worship services.

ELCSWA lays stress on education at various levels. It manages 20 hostels or boarding schools and conducts 20 kindergartens. For these schools, young women receive teacher training at the Heinz-Stöver Seminary in Karibib. For Sunday school and evangelistic volunteer workers, the George-Krönlein Center at Berseba provides courses, often over weekends.

The Martin Luther High School, established in 1962 in the town of Karibib, was pressured by the government to move from this advantageous "white area" to Okombahe in an arid region near the Namib desert, 112 kilometers (70 miles) from the nearest town and railway station. Presently some 160 students (one-third girls) are here being educated in the English language, using a British syllabus, which prepares them for 0-level matriculation. Since Namibia has no university, and the South African institutions do not accept the 0-level, very few Martin Luther graduates have a chance for higher education. But a fair number of them go on into nursing and teacher training schools.

ELCSWA's pastoral candidates are educated with their counterparts from the ELCIN (above) at the Paulinum Theological Seminary, a school jointly owned and operated by the two churches. Situated in Otjimbingwe, where the first Christian colony of the Rhenish Mission stood, the school is halfway between Swakopmund (on the coast) and Windhoek. Its remoteness as well as its hot and dry climate have adversely affected the recruitment of professors as well as students. Relocation is being considered. An average of 30 students enrolled in the four-year course are taught by four professors.

Diaconal service, evangelism, and mission outreach are important aspects of ELCSWA life. A diaconal committee is entrusted with the responsibility of working among the sick, aged, and destitute. A printing and editorial office aids the proclamation of the gospel. A mission outreach to western Botswana, in cooperation with the United Evangelical Mission, was begun in 1960. After some 20 years, several small congregations had been formed. These and an active medical service were then turned over to the newly formed *Evangelical Lutheran Church in Botswana in 1983.

Since its independence, ELCSWA has striven for financial independence. But oppression and poverty have deferred this goal. The church remains heavily dependent on foreign aid. Most of it still comes from its founder, the United Evangelical Mission, known earlier as the Rhenish Mission.

The Rhenish Mission began its work at the urging of the London Missionary Society, which had surveyed the area in 1814. The first Rhenish missionaries arrived in 1842. Outstanding among them was the Latvian-born Carl Hugo Hahn (1818–1895). Working among the Hereros, he reduced their language to writing and won their confidence but waited nearly 20 years for the first converts. With them, at Otjimbingwe, he founded a Christian colony (1863) for the preparation of lay workers. Next he opened a theological seminary (1866), admitting only the most talented young men (usually the sons of chiefs). Hahn and others trained them as evangelists and teachers and sent them forth as a missionary task force.

As the work expanded northward, and when Rhenish Mission resources proved inadequate, Hahn appealed to the Finnish Missionary Society (now FELM) to work among the Ovambo tribes where he had prospected (see ELCIN, above). Hahn himself became more Lutheran and persuaded the Rhenish Mission, which included both Lutheran and Reformed elements, to permit the work in South-West Africa to develop a broadly Lutheran character. In the process, Luther's *Small Catechism* imparted confessional identity.

Times of severe testing have faced this church as noted above. Prolonged unrest saw the breaking away of various groups from the mission. To counteract this trend, a basically African ELCSWA was formed in 1957. As the political and social pressures of apartheid built up, the unity of the church tended to grow stronger.

GERMAN EVANGELICAL LUTHERAN CHURCH IN SOUTH-WEST AFRICA (GELCSWA)

(Duitse Evangelies-Lutherse Kerk in Suidwes-Afrika)
Member: LWF (1963), FELCSA, UELCSA, CCN, UELCSWA
Membership: 12,000**
Landespropst: (A new LP to be elected in 1989) Acting as representative: The Rev. Karl Sundermeier
PO Box 233
Windhoek 9000

The 17 congregations of this German-speaking church, an autonomous body since 1960, are served by eight ordained pastors. It is an all-white church body, most of its members being descendants of immigrants who arrived after South-West Africa became a German colony in 1884. They are mainly engaged in farming and ranching; some, including more recent arrivals, in business, industry, mining, and the professions. As part of their own indigenization, spurred on by two world wars, they have tended to adopt the attitudes and outlook of most Afrikaner whites. Constituted similarly to churches in Germany, the GELCSWA has a synodical form of polity. The *Landespropst,* or general dean, is the chief spiritual and administrative officer. The synod, comprising representatives of all congregations, has a lay president. Through its council, each congregation elects and calls its own pastor, accepting or rejecting a candidate proposed by the Foreign Office of the Evangelical Church in Germany. This arrangement, in effect since 1950, also includes financial grants from overseas.

The church administration in Windhoek cannot escape the influence of the laity and of the surrounding society. The lack of an indigenous ministry in this church derives from the fact that the earliest German congregations were gathered and served, on the side, by pastors of the Rhenish Mission. Dependency on such service has survived two world wars. In 1912 the first pastoral conference took place, and in 1926 the first synod. The position of the pastors vis-à-vis the resident laity has from time to time been problematic. Already in colonial times (to 1915), many of the Rhenish missionaries serving German congregations tended to side with the Africans. This created opposition in white congregations. In recent years white pastors have often spoken up for unity among all Lutheran churches in Namibia—white, black, colored. This has on occasion led to government refusal to renew their residence permits, or, in more extreme cases, to congregations seeking their pastor's resignation.

Noting the periodic lack of pastors in the German church as well as the favorable attitude toward wider unity on the part of some of its congregations, the *ELCSWA (Rhenish Mission) offered to supply the white church with pastors. Although declining this offer, GELCSWA leaders expressed willingness to join the two black churches—ELCSWA and ELCIN—in a united church.

The blacks were willing to accept, provided the white church joined with them in the continuing struggle for human rights and the abolition of apartheid. A crisscross of earlier developments had already placed GELCSWA in a dilemma. In 1965 it had joined with the other German-speaking churches in South Africa forming the *United Evangelical Lutheran Church in Southern Africa (UELCSA). A year later it also joined the *Federation of Evangelical Lutheran Churches in Southern Africa (FELCSA, above). In these two organizations, one representing separateness, one unity, lay a practical contradiction. This surfaced in Namibia where relations between GELCSWA and the two other churches became periodically deadlocked. Yet, in March 1977, the German-speaking church joined the other two in the aforementioned Namibian federal union, UELCSWA.

For the German church the demands of partnership were intensified by pressures following the 1977 LWF assembly, which called for a public and unequivocal rejection of apartheid. As noted earlier (see Southern Africa Introduction), GELCSWA's intentions were good—as expressed repeatedly by its leaders in consultation—but were not backed by public action; i.e., no synodical decision by the congregations was forthcoming. As already described, the way led inexorably to this church's eventual suspension from the LWF. Nevertheless, significance and hope seemed to lie in the reaffirmation of fellowship made by the three churches of *UELCSWA in October 1984. However, when this white church withdrew unexpectedly from the Council of Churches in Namibia in 1987, its two partners suspended their activities in the Lutheran federation (see UELCSWA, above). As of 1988 the German church stood alone.

Meanwhile, a new Social Educational Institute (1985) was launched. Located in Windhoek, the institute's program includes social studies, domestic science, and counseling. This undertaking is in response to the need for workers in school hostels and kindergartens as well as in youth activities and old-age care. The language of instruction is mainly German and the services rendered are

to the German-speaking community of Namibia, which numbers more than the GELCSWA membership.

SOUTH AFRICA

A republic (1961) occupying the southern tip of Africa. Area (excluding the Walvis Bay enclave in *Namibia, but including the four so-called independent homelands): 1,221,037 sq. km. (471,320 sq. mi.). Population (1985 est.): 27,424,100 (black 72%, white 16%, colored 9%, Asian 3%). Executive cap.: Pretoria (pop., 1985, 711,500); judicial cap.: Bloemfontein (pop., 1980, 230,700); legislative cap.: Cape Town (pop., 1985, 942,851). Largest city: Johannesburg (pop., 1985, 1,666,085. Including its black township of Soweto, Johannesburg's actual population may be significantly higher). Language: Afrikaans and English (official); ethnic (African) languages.

History: The earliest known inhabitants are the Khoikhoi (Hottentots) and the San (Bushmen), who were also in *Namibia. Their presence antedates the year 1500. From central East Africa (*Tanzania), the southward migration of Bantu-speaking peoples, the Xhosa in particula¯, changed the course of developments after about 1500. Many settled, for example, between Great Kei and the Great Fish, two rivers flowing into the Indian Ocean and draining a region at whose coastal center is modern East London.

Further north along the coast, adjoining *Mozambique and *Swaziland, the Zulu established themselves in the late 17th century. Extending their realm southward, they constituted a powerful kingdom under their king, Shaka (d. 1828), and subdued other tribes.

The earliest contact with Europeans began in 1488 when Bartholomeu Dias rounded what was soon named the Cape of Good Hope by the Portuguese. It remained for the Dutch to found the first permanent European settlement (1652). French Huguenot refugees joined them (1688), as well as Germans and others. Slaves from West and East Africa and from distant Dutch holdings in Malaya were early brought in to augment the labor supply. The white settlements grew. So did the new category of colored. The eastward movement of white farmers (Boers) led to frontier wars

(1779–1877) against the Xhosa, who sought to retain their land.

During the Napoleonic wars which pitted Britain against France at sea, the British gained the Cape (1806) and in time turned the province into their colony. Boers, seeking to escape British rule, culminated their expansion of the white frontier with their Great Trek (1835–1837), breaking the bitter resistance of the Zulus at great cost. The modern names of Natal, Transvaal, and Orange Free State are reminders of this period when the Boers (Afrikaners) founded their own republics.

The discovery of diamonds (1870) and gold (1886) attracted outsiders to the Orange Free State and the Transvaal. Afrikaner-British tensions erupted in the Boer War. After the British victory (1902) came the Union of South Africa (1910), incorporating the British colonies of the Cape, Natal, the Transvaal, and the Orange Free State, and providing dominion status in the British Commonwealth. Following two world wars and a rising tide of Afrikaner consciousness, a popular referendum took the Union out of the Commonwealth and created the present Republic of South Africa (1961).

Separate development of the races—apartheid—had already been declared official in 1948. The white-operated government, in 1959, legislated the eventual creation of 10 or more "Bantu" nations (Bantustans), or partially self-governing black "homelands," intended as major habitations for the nation's black population. Four of these have been granted "independence" (below) yet are without international recognition. The other six are in various stages of autonomous rule. Forced resettlement into these territories is a continuing process of huge proportions, creating profound injustice as well as suffering. Blacks are thus deprived of South African citizenship in exchange for that in their respective Bantustans.

Meanwhile, for the colored and Asian peoples in South Africa itself, the new constitution (1983) provides for a single Parliament with a white House of Assembly (178 members, like the former Parliament), a colored House of Representatives (85), and an Asian House of Deputies (45). Passed by the white electorate by a large majority, the new constitution nevertheless created much opposition and continues to build up volcanic unrest in the immense and unrepresented black majority.

BANTUSTANS OR "HOMELANDS" WITHIN SOUTH AFRICA

Created to segregate blacks according to tribe and language, these concentration states are all on less desirable land and account for only some 13% of the entire area. By granting a few of them "independence" the South African government hopes to relieve itself of social or political responsibility for the citizens of these states, many of whom are there against their will.

Transkei: ("independent" 1976) comprises three discontinuous geographic areas, with the largest on the Indian Ocean coast northeast of East London. Area: 41,002 sq. km. (15,831 sq. mi.). Pop. (1982 est.): 2.4 million, of whom 95% are Xhosa. The majority are Christians, with Methodist being predominant.

Bophuthatswana: ("independent" 1977) comprises six discontinuous landlocked geographic units, one bordering *Botswana. Area: 40,430 sq. km. (15,610 sq. mi.). Pop. (1983 est.): 1,395,000, including 69% Tswana and 7.5% Sotho. It is predominantly Christian, including many Lutherans who are members of the Western Diocese of ELCSA.

Venda: ("independent" 1979) comprises two geographic units in extreme northeastern South Africa, separated by a narrow corridor from the Gazankulu homeland. Area: 7184 sq. km. (2488 sq. mi.). Pop. (1982 est.): 374,000, including 90% Venda, 6% Shangaan, and 3% Northern Sotho. Traditional religions predominate. Lutherans form the largest Christian minority.

Ciskei: ("independent" 1981) borders the Indian Ocean and is surrounded on land by South Africa. It is separated by a narrow corridor from Transkei. Area: 5386 sq. km. (2080 sq. mi.). Pop. (1983 est.): 690,000, including 97% Xhosa. It is predominantly Christian (Methodist, Lutheran, Anglican, and independent Christian churches).

The other homelands, with their populations, are: Gazankulu (519,280); KaNgwane (160,160); KwaNdebele (156,380); KwaZulu (3,442,140); Lebowa (1,746,500); Qwaqwa (157,620).

Religion: Christian, nearly 80%; Traditional under 18%; Jews, about 0.05% (some

3% of the white population); Hindu and Muslim minorities among the Asian (mainly Indian) population.

Roman Catholicism comprises the largest of South Africa's communions. Its nearly three million adherents are distributed among four archdioceses and 17 dioceses. In the 1950s, the Vatican's "Africa Decade," the church here received its own hierarchy and thus moved from missionary to indigenous status. Extensive undertakings in the fields of education, health, and welfare, linked with social action on behalf of justice, are bearers of continuing outreach and evangelism. Since Vatican II, and in the face of apartheid, Roman Catholic relations with other Christians have become closer.

Protestantism, including Anglicanism, comprises the largest grouping of Christians and represents the missionary outreach of churches in Europe and North America. But it has been badly divided by the effect of apartheid as well as by denominational proliferation. This is true quite apart from the African Independent Churches (AICs, see Africa Introduction). The Federal Council of Dutch Reformed Churches in South Africa is prominent. The Dutch Reformed Church (DRC) is the country's largest Protestant body and a champion of apartheid. Yet nearly 30% of its claimed 2.3 million membership is colored. Nearly as large is the Church of the Province of South Africa (Anglican), which opposes apartheid. The Presbyterian Church of Africa, with about two million adherents, is the largest exclusively black church. The Methodist Church of Southern Africa and its related bodies place Methodism close to the DRC in size. Among the other Protestants, Lutherans, Baptists, Moravians, Congregationalists, and others are well represented in the colored as well as in the black population. From here on diversity explodes in profusion.

African Independent Churches (AICs) in this country, mainly congregational in format, are part of a continent-wide movement of secession, first from the white mission churches—Roman Catholic as well as Protestant—and then from already formed AICs. Efforts to bring them together have so far failed, but collectively they represent an indigenous third force in religion. The country's several thousand AICs are thought to have between six and eight million adherents.

Swedish missiologist Bengt Sundkler has discerned two family types among a large number of AICs. The one is *Ethiopian,* retaining forms of worship, hymns, and catechism from the European or American church, but laying major emphasis on what is African. Leadership, customs, the vision of a free Africa, latch on to the long-free *Ethiopia; so, too, does the sense of authentic religion that associates itself with the references to Ethiopia in the Bible. "Africa for the Africans" is often the prevailing mood. The other family type is that of *Zion.* Its thrust is apocalyptic, millenarian, charismatic, Pentecostal. Prophecy, healing, and speaking in tongues may be prominent. The accent on a given location brings Zion into the here and now. This highly proliferated "Zionism" in South Africa traces its roots to John Alexander Dowie's utopian community, the Christian Catholic Apostolic Church in Zion near Chicago, whose missioners came to South Africa early in this century. As elsewhere in the world, the Zion motif extols the unfolding of God's purpose in a specific place, as the Bible attests.

Church cooperation is best represented in the South African Council of Churches (SACC, 1936). Its antecedents, through missionary comity, go back to 1904. Its doctrinal basis is the same as that of the World Council of Churches. In recent years, SACC's firm opposition to apartheid has impressed some member churches—the Baptist Union, the Salvation Army, and others—as too radical, and they have left it. Much earlier some of the Dutch Reformed Synods had helped found SACC, but they withdrew by 1941 when the Council's English-language orientation made the Afrikaner participation seem superfluous. Likewise, the DRC had been a charter member of the World Council of Churches but withdrew in 1960 over the apartheid issue. Gradually SACC gained strength as the religious voice against apartheid. Its Anglican and varied Protestant composition included a mix of white, colored, and black. SACC leaders in recent years have included Lutheran Bishop Manas Buthelezi (ELCSA—Central Diocese) as president; Archbishop Desmond Tutu (Anglican —Johannesburg) as general secretary; and, more recently, Dr. Beyers Naudé (a former moderator of the DRC Transvaal Synod), successor to Tutu as general secretary. In addition, Naudé's founding of the Christian

Institute of Southern Africa (banned by the government in 1977) had been to bridge the language barrier between Afrikaans- and English-speaking church constituencies and thus to foster common effort on behalf of racial justice. Meanwhile, Lutherans, like Roman Catholics, have been latecomers to the English-speaking side. Yet the Lutherans as members of SACC (through FELCSA, above) and the Roman Catholics as observers have strengthened the council's position.

SACC concerns have included functions aimed to advance Christian unity such as communication (including EcuNews), interchurch aid, justice and reconciliation, mission and evangelism, theological education, women's work, and resettlement. Support for this work comes in large part from outside the country.

SACC has been especially helpful in advancing theological education on an interracial basis. In 1973 a generous gift from the Theological Education Fund made possible the appointment of a director in this field for SACC. This director also served as executive secretary for the Association of Southern African Theological Institutions (ASATI) and of the National Committee on Theological Education (NCTE). The latter, organized by SACC, strengthened the relationships of theological institutions to the churches they served.

Lutherans supplied the director: Dr. Axel-Ivar Berglund, a Swedish lecturer at the Lutheran Theological College Umpumulo and secretary of the FELCSA committee on theological education. His leadership established standards of excellence. The ASATI diploma course, with a prescribed syllabus and a common examination, raised the quality of many institutions. Continuing education for pastors, clinical pastoral education, internship training, and theological education by extension (TEE) were part of the new approach. A theological college was also established for the African Independent Churches, most of whose pastors did not have opportunities for formal education. This also enhanced the relationship of the independent churches to those in SACC. Some of these programs are now operating on their own.

For more than a decade the modern and sturdily built Khotso (Peace) House, in its urban location, lodged not only the SACC headquarters but also those of the (Anglican)

Church of South Africa, the ELCSA (below), and others as well. On August 31, 1988, the building was severely bombed. The police declared it unsafe for further use. The loss was costly and painful.

EVANGELICAL LUTHERAN CHURCH IN SOUTHERN AFRICA (ELCSA)
(Evangelies-Lutherse Kerk in Suider Afrika)
Member: LWF (1976), WCC, AACC, SACC
Membership: 552,000**
Presiding Bishop: The Rt. Rev. Solomon E. Serote
Head Office: Central House
70 Central Avenue, Mayfair
Johannesburg 2092

In December 1975 the Evangelical Lutheran Church in Southern Africa was constituted by the merger of four autonomous regional churches. It created an ecclesial unity binding together in faith and service people of many groups and languages living in all parts of South Africa and beyond. The four churches became the four dioceses of the new church. Since then two other dioceses have been formed: the Central, covering the Johannesburg and Pretoria areas, and, across the border, the *Botswana.

ELCSA has an episcopal form of church polity. Its church assembly meets every two years, serves as the legislative and decision-making body, transacts business concerning the church as a whole, and elects the presiding bishop. The church council, as an executive committee, oversees the church's general work. An episcopal council deals with special concerns. Each diocese reflects the setup of the ELCSA at the regional level.

Today the church is a body of over a half million baptized members. Its 1617 congregations are grouped into 326 parishes. They are served by six bishops, 450 pastors, 190 evangelists, and 579 lay workers.

In January 1984 five Indian congregations were received into ELCSA at a festive communion service in Chatsworth, an Indian suburb of Durban. This was the culmination of a decade of work by three agencies (Hermannsburg Mission, Norwegian Missionary

Society, and Church of Sweden). Their adoption of Indian work as a new challenge balanced the efforts of the South-Eastern Diocese to bring about cross-cultural understanding through Christian faith and acceptance. In 1985 also the newly formed white St. Michael's congregation was received into membership. (See St. Olav Lutheran Church, below.)

Most of ELCSA's pastors have been educated at one of the church's two seminaries: Lutheran Theological College Umpumulo at Mapumulo, Natal (north of Durban), and Marang Theological Seminary in Tlhabane, Bophuthatswana, near Rustenburg (northwest of Johannesburg). Since the early 1970s these two institutions have been under a single governing board. While the Marang school had long fostered the more practical side of ministerial training, the entrance requirements and academic standards of the two schools are now the same.

Early in 1984 the ELCSA church council agreed to participate in the proposed interracial theological program at the University of Natal in Pietermaritzburg, a project initiated by UELCSA (above). Approval came after obstacles to multiracial training were overcome. The government waived the individual permit requirement for black students at the university. Likewise, the "quota system," limiting the number of black students at a white university, was removed. As academic qualifications became the sole criteria, the way opened to the earning of recognized academic degrees in a white residential university. A site near the university now houses black and white theological students. In light of these concessions, the LWF advisory committee on theological education in Africa approved the project (1984) and sought funds for the two teaching positions that the Lutherans are to provide for the university's department of divinity.

Except for this accomplishment at Pietermaritzburg, ELCSA's work continues to be thwarted by apartheid. Whites, blacks, colored, and Indians continue to be separated. Even more painful at times is the separation of blacks according to tribe and language. This tears congregations and even families apart. It also means that the church's resources are stretched to the limit as it strives to establish new congregations in the "homelands" and to provide educational opportunities and social services for the people living there against their wishes. Therefore the church continues to need and receive the support of partners: the *American Lutheran Church (now a part of the *Evangelical Lutheran Church in America); Church of Sweden Mission; Division of World Mission of the Evangelical Church in Berlin-Brandenburg (West); Evangelical Lutheran Mission (Hermannsburg), FRG; Norwegian Missionary Society; United Evangelical Mission, FRG. They help support the work in the following six dioceses:

ELCSA—Botswana Diocese (see Botswana, above)

ELCSA—Cape/Orange Diocese is spread out over the Cape Province and the Orange Free State. Its members in Cape Town are 1760 kilometers (1100 miles) from those in Port Elizabeth to the east, and 1120 kilometers (700 miles) from those northwestward near the Namibia border. They are even farther from their bishop, the Rt. Rev. D.S. Hart, in Kimberley. A large portion of the members (70%) are colored. Many are subsistence farmers; others work in the Kimberley diamond mines; still others in urban occupations. Most of them live in designated townships or "homelands." The "independent" state of Ciskei, west of Transkei near the coast, is within the diocesan region and has one congregation.

One of the many difficulties this diocese faces is the South African policy of keeping coloreds and blacks separate. In the Southern and Eastern Cape, the congregations are mainly colored with a few black congregations in Cape Town and Port Elizabeth, plus the one in Ciskei. In the Orange Free State, the congregations are mainly black except for colored congregations in Bloemfontein and Adamshoop.

In the Kimberley area of northern Cape, the parishes are half colored and half black. This is also an area of tremendous growth as both coloreds and blacks stream into the cities seeking work. The diocese has three parishes in Kimberley itself, two in the black township and one in the colored township. Between the two townships there is a narrow strip, a no-man's-land. After long negotiations with local authorities and with financial help from the LWF Community Development Service, a multipurpose church center was built in this buffer zone. It serves all three parishes as well as being the diocesan headquarters.

This center has given the diocese new opportunities for serving the numerous needs of its members as well as the general community. The social worker now has a suitable center from which to organize relief: soup and milk for the many undernourished school children; assistance for the aged in collecting their meager pension; and a chance to get together for fellowship. The youth have a place to listen to music and to discuss their common problems. Out of such discussions come urgent requests for equal opportunities for higher education; also ministerial candidates. Over the weekend, the center is used as a gathering place for religious activities.

In the segregated areas of the city of Oudtshoorn, where extreme poverty and tuberculosis exist, the church provides day care for 100 small children of working parents. The facilities are also used for adult education and recreation as well as Christian instruction and fellowship. Other centers of this kind relieve the intense privation of people who have been forced out of their homes and relocated. As church buildings, too, have been demolished, these centers become places of worship. One of them in Bellville, near Cape Town, also serves as a hostel for students attending the University of Western Cape, an ethnic institution designated for colored.

This diocese traces its history to 1834 when the first Berlin missionaries entered this area. However it was not until 1911 that the Orange Free State and Cape Synods were formed. They merged into an autonomous regional church in 1963 and joined the LWF four years later. When ELCSA was formed in 1975, this church became the Cape/Orange Diocese.

ELCSA—Central Diocese has its headquarters in the new center in Jabavu, Soweto, which was dedicated on May Day 1983. Led by their bishop, Manas Buthelezi, members and guests came by the busload to celebrate the occasion in worship and fellowship. This place serves not only as the administrative offices of the diocese but also as a much-needed community center. Although partner churches contributed funds, South Africans did their share; and the furnishings were provided by the congregations and women's league groups of the Central Diocese.

This newest of ELCSA's six dioceses is predominantly urban. It includes metropolitan Johannesburg and Pretoria, the country's executive capital, as well as the massed suburban domiciles for blacks. Of these, Soweto (meaning South-West Township), situated over 19 kilometers (12 miles) outside Johannesburg with a population of over one million, is the best known. Many Lutherans reside in this and other black townships and have their churches there. They have come from different places to find work in the cities. The new Central Diocese thus has a greater mixture of African types than the other five. In 1983 Bishop Buthelezi was elected president of the South African Council of Churches (above).

The racism the bishop and his people experience is fed by the life-style of the black township. As they experience it, separate development makes the rich richer, the poor poorer. A black township parish comprises members living, like the rest of the population, in "matchbox" houses they do not own. It means schools, cinemas, bars, small shops with high prices, police, and some hospitals, but no parks, playgrounds, or supermarkets. It means commuting a long way to work or to shop; mingling with whites during the day in the big city but returning to the township by curfew at 2100 hours. It means facing the challenge of young people impatient for change and eager for a taste of human rights. In many ways this Central Diocese is the focal point of ELCSA's quest for full partnership in the gospel among blacks, whites, and coloreds. And its members are wondering if there is still time.

ELCSA—Northern Diocese headquarters are in a township outside South Africa's most northern large city, Pietersburg. Led by Bishop Solomon E. Serote (also presiding bishop of ELCSA), the diocese faces awesome obstacles to its work in the large province of Transvaal. Most of its members live either in the suburban townships for blacks or in "homelands." Still others live in Venda, the "independent" state for the Venda people. It has a population of about half a million, the majority of whom are not Christians. Of the Christians, most are Lutherans. The 102 congregations of Venda are included in the Devhula Circuit served by a dean, eight other pastors, and 33 trained lay workers.

Besides the normal congregational work and the care of its many church-operated institutions and programs, the diocese tries to make the life "in captivity" more tolerable. This may mean providing nursery care for the children left to fend for themselves while both parents work in the white city or in the mines and factories. It may mean providing a center where church activities can be conducted. One such center is at Lobethal in a "homeland" near the city of Middelburg. The Berlin Mission's property, surrounded by the "homeland," was considered a "white spot." This was transferred to the church, and with LWF help a conference center was constructed. The facilities are also used for adult education classes, youth activities, and as a focus for the cultural, social, and religious activities of a large area. It has been a great encouragement to the church and has provided partner churches with an opportunity to share in the burdens.

In Pietersburg, the central city for all of eastern and northern Transvaal, the church lends support to an ecumenical group of professional blacks (lawyers, university professors, social workers, church leaders) who, in 1983, established a community counseling office to help the countless laborers bewildered by the many restrictions facing them.

International attention was attracted to this diocese in November 1981 by a tragic event. The territory of the diocese borders *Mozambique and *Zimbabwe, countries friendly to the African National Congress struggling against apartheid. The Venda part of the diocese is in a particularly vulnerable position, and when South African officials react, the wrong people are often made to suffer. Following an attack on a police station in Sibasa in which two Venda policemen were killed, a number of persons were held in detention without trial. Among them were the dean of the Devhula Circuit, three other pastors, and 10 lay workers. One lay preacher, Tshifhiwa Muofhe, died as the result of his treatment. His bishop was not allowed to conduct the funeral nor to visit the bereaved. Dean T. A. Farisani, after being tortured, had to be hospitalized for months. Convalesced sufficiently, he bravely returned to Venda, seeking to live out a ministry of forgiveness and service. In 1986, he was again jailed. When released, he and his family found refuge and healing in the USA.

Historically, this is frontier country with an intertwined story leading to the present Northern Diocese. Hermannsburg missionaries, diverted from their beginning in *Ethiopia, came to the Transvaal some time after 1854 and subsequently pressed westward into Bechuanaland (*Botswana). Berlin missionaries arrived in northeast Transvaal in 1858, working first among the Bakoba people; later, to the north, among the Basotho, Bavenda (Venda), Ama Ndebele, and the detribalized Oorlams. During the 20th century, two world wars were hard on German-sponsored mission work. After World War II aid via the LWF and other ecumenical agencies rendered timely help. Finally, over a century after the Berlin Mission's entry here, the Evangelical Lutheran Church/Transvaal Region was constituted in 1962. Three years later it joined the LWF. In 1975 it became the Transvaal Diocese of the newly formed ELCSA; and when the Central Diocese was created around Johannesburg, the Transvaal Region was renamed the Northern Diocese.

ELCSA—South-Eastern Diocese, with headquarters in Mapumulo, Natal, is led by Bishop L.E. Dlamini. Most of its members are Zulu living in rural areas throughout Natal, but in recent years many have migrated to the cities, especially Johannesburg and Durban. The diocese also extends into *Swaziland. In Durban there is a more diversified membership, including an increasing number of Indians and coloreds. Working together on joint projects strengthens their relationship. The diocese has a strong educational program: Sunday schools, farm schools, hostels, youth groups. Its publishing house provides books on many aspects of Christian teaching and living. These materials are used by all the dioceses of ELCSA.

Until recently the Lutheran Medical Foundation of this diocese supervised the work in 13 hospitals and provided many preventive medical programs. When the government took them over, this greatly reduced the church's influence in the medical field, one that was pioneered by the mission agencies and carried forward by the church. There is still great need. Infant mortality is high. Malnutrition and tuberculosis continue to be threats to life.

Kwazulu, the designated "homeland" for the Zulu, is in this diocese's area. It covers

31,440 sq. km. (12,140 sq. mi.), comprising isolated tracts of land, only some of which were a part of historic Zululand. The church has a special responsibility for the people gathered here, often against their wishes.

The Kwazamokuhle Diaconal Center, located on the former Hermannsburg Mission compound, is the church's attempt to meet some of the basic needs of the people in this vicinity. Designed as a community self-help program, its clinic gives curative and preventive health services; a demonstration farm supplies food for the staff and patients; and a handicraft unit offers rehabilitation to the handicapped and keeps alive traditional South African craft skills. This is but one of eight centers of service the diocese maintains.

The ELCSA Art and Craft Center in Rorke's Drift is a unique and successful cross-cultural venture. It is the only fine arts school for blacks in all of Southern Africa. It is also a place where skilled craftsmen and women live and work in a Christian atmosphere and produce art pieces with potential influence in a changing society. Situated on the premises of a one-time Swedish mission station, it fulfills the dream of a Swedish artist and a South-Eastern bishop. The newest workshop trains young women in the art of tapestry making. Recently a large tapestry was made for the Anglican Cathedral in Pietermaritzburg. The school's art objects have been exhibited in Europe and America, and every year thousands of visitors find this remote little village where artists flourish.

The South-Eastern Diocese traces its history to the pioneer work of five mission agencies. The Norwegian Missionary Society began medical work in Natal in 1844. The Berlin Missionary Society opened its first center in 1847 at Emmaus, the location of a Lutheran Evangelist school. The work expanded into *Swaziland, and, in 1911, the Zulu-Xhosa-Swazi Synod was formed. The Hermannsburg Missionary Society entered Natal in 1857, naming its first center Hermannsburg. A folk school, after the Danish pattern, early trained parish workers. American missionaries of Norse descent came to Natal in 1870; and the Church of Sweden Mission began work in interior Natal in 1876. Their pastoral training school in Oscarsburg later moved to Umpumulo, where the Norwegians once had a teachers' training school

until it was closed by the Bantu Education Act.

The contrary forces of Christian unity and of racist oppression have accelerated the process of confessional unification. Already in 1912 the mission agencies turned their comity toward unity and formed the "Cooperating Lutheran Missions in Natal-Zululand." Further developments led to the formation of the Evangelical Lutheran Church in Southern Africa/South-Eastern Region in 1960. As such, it became active ecumenically, joining not only the South African Council of Churches but also the LWF and the World Council of Churches. Its first bishop was the Swedish missionary statesman Helge Fosseus. In 1975 this region became the South-Eastern Diocese of ELCSA.

ELCSA—Western Diocese, in Transvaal, has its headquarters in a township outside Rustenburg. Its first bishop, the Rt. Rev. Daniel Porogo Rapoo, was formerly presiding bishop of ELCSA. The membership of this diocese comprises mainly Tswana-speaking blacks. Congregations in the Republic of Botswana (above) were until recently part of the Western Diocese.

One of the ELCSA theological schools, Marang, in Rustenburg, has traditionally trained both evangelists and pastors. But since 1981 the governing board of the church's theological schools has limited enrollment to applicants who have completed high school. Evangelists have played a vital part in the growth of the Lutheran church in this region. Supervised by ordained pastors, they did much of the congregational work, except for administering the sacraments and confirming new communicants. In the long run, a well-trained clergy promises to strengthen the work of congregations, both rural and urban. However, during a time of transition, this diocese, like the others, continues to seek ways of supplementing the pastor's work with a well-trained laity.

Within the area of the Western Diocese are "homelands," one of which is in the independent state of Bophuthatswana. It consists of six discontinuous pieces of land, one bordering Botswana. The people transplanted here are mainly Tswana, with a small minority of Sotho. They are predominantly Christian with many Lutherans among them.

Bophuthatswana is reputed to be the best-governed of the black states that South Africa has spawned. A development corporation is making efforts to improve and expand the economy. However, poverty is oppressive, as manifested by a cholera epidemic in 1981-1982.

The Western Diocese has indigenous roots. Years before the coming of the first Hermannsburg missionaries from Germany, a first generation Tswana Christian, David Modipane, converted by his master while serving as a war prisoner, returned to his people and, in the 1840s, preached the gospel and won many to Christianity. He did not baptize but told the people that others would soon be coming with authority to do so. In 1857 Hermannsburg missionaries found the field remarkably prepared. Land was bought by the Tswanas and Christian villages were formed. This gave the Tswana congregations a stronger sense of independence than was felt in most other missions.

The Boer War and two world wars disrupted life, the growth of the gold mining industry dominated the economy, and the imposition of apartheid become an immense burden. In 1955 steps were taken that led to the constituting of an autonomous church of some 100,000 members in 1959. Named initially the Lutheran Botswana Church, in 1963 it became the Evangelical Lutheran Church in Southern Africa/Tswana Region. As such, it joined the LWF that same year. A dozen years later, with the formation of ELCSA, this body became the Western Diocese.

EVANGELICAL LUTHERAN CHURCH IN SOUTHERN AFRICA/CAPE CHURCH (ELCSA/CC)

(Evangelies-Lutherse Kerk in Suider Afrika/Kaapse Kerk)
Member: LWF (1963), FELCSA, UELCSA
Membership: 6394**
President: The Rev. Nils Rohwer
240 Long Street
Cape Town 8001

The Cape Church is the oldest among the four church bodies of German descent that, in 1964, formed the United Evangelical Lutheran Church in Southern Africa (see Southern Africa Introduction). Of immigrant origin, its 23 congregations are served by 18 ordained pastors, some of whom come via the Foreign Office of the Evangelical Church in Germany, with which ELCSA/CC has had a formal relationship since 1961. ELCSA/CC is a union of congregations administered by a church council and led by a president. The Cape Church is trilingual, using German, Afrikaans, and English as required. Many of its members are engaged in farming. Others, having moved to the cities, are employed in a variety of occupations and professions.

The strong individualism and distinctive character of each congregation give some indication of their diversified heritage. In addition, this small church extends over a vast geographic territory—from its origins in the Cape Town area eastward beyond Port Elizabeth and East London; northeastward to Bloemfontein and Orange Free State; and northward to other parts of Cape Province.

For the mid-19th-century newcomers from Germany, the Strand Street Church (1780, below) was neither German enough nor Lutheran enough. Their answer was the St. Martini Church (1861), which became the real mother of the Cape Church. Pastors from Germany served the growing number of congregations. Among them was Carl Hugo Hahn, pioneer missionary among the Hereros in what is now *Namibia, who left the Rhenish Mission in 1873 and took a pastorate in Cape Town.

Various mission societies sought to help the congregations, as they did other German churches being formed in South Africa. It was easy for black people, on the one hand, and the immigrants and their descendants, on the other, to develop separately. In 1895 the congregations in Cape Province formed the German Evangelical Synod of South Africa (Cape Synod), for which the Evangelical Lutheran Church of Hanover assumed supervision. When World War I caused a closing of the German schools, the Cape Synod churches were forced to adapt to the dominant culture. In the congregations, the use of Afrikaans or English came to parallel that of German.

After World War II and further losses in membership to other communions because of the German question, the synod in 1961 constituted itself a church and assumed its present name. Its struggle to adapt to changing situations continues. Its membership is stationary or even decreasing. Indigenous leadership has been hard to develop and dependency on pastors from abroad continues. The will to preserve an identity cultivated over generations struggles with the will to foster fellowship with the 100-times larger black church (ELCSA) and others in FELCSA. The 1984 Budapest assembly action to suspend the Cape Church from LWF membership for not "publicly and unequivocally" rejecting apartheid has been a severe blow. Rejection of it in principle has been expressed through FELCSA pronouncements for some years. But Cape Church leaders and many members hope they can find a way out of the present agonizing dilemma that catches them between history and hope.

EVANGELICAL LUTHERAN CHURCH IN SOUTHERN AFRICA/NATAL-TRANSVAAL (ELCSA/N-T)

(Evangeliese Lutherse Kerk in Suider Afrika/Natal-Transvaal)
Member: (P), FELCSA, UELCSA
Membership: 15,500**
President: The Rt. Rev. Lothar T.K. Müller-Nedebock
PO Box 873, 16 Eighth Avenue
Edenvale 1610, Transvaal

This church was constituted on March 3, 1981, by a merger of the Evangelical Lutheran Church in Southern Africa/Hermannsburg and the Evangelical Lutheran Church in Southern Africa/Transvaal. Both churches were founding members of FELCSA and components of the UELCSA. The smaller of the two, ELCSA/H, was a member of the LWF from 1965 to 1981.

ELCSA/N-T has 34 pastors serving 43 congregations, both rural and urban, in the large provinces of Natal and Transvaal. They are divided into four districts. A governing board and executive council supervise the administration of the church.

The majority of the church's members are descendants of early German settlers and missionaries. Recent arrivals from Germany,

Norway, and Sweden, as well as accessions with South African background, have added variety. Numerically, however, the membership has been declining.

The church's work in diaconia and mission gives priority to German immigrants and transient laborers for whose spiritual well-being the local congregations are open. The ELCSA/N-T church maintains a church school in Hermannsburg, Natal, as well as two homes for the aged. Several congregations have day schools. The mission work of other Lutheran churches also receives contributions from ELCSA/N-T.

The origins of this united church are the work of two German mission agencies. The Hermannsburg Mission entered Natal in 1857 and named its first center Hermannsburg. The early missionaries to the Zulu also served as pastors to the German settlers. In 1887 separate congregations emerged, but the white members retained an active interest in their black brothers and sisters. In 1911 the Hermannsburg German Evangelical Synod was organized and later became the Evangelical Lutheran Church in Southern Africa/Hermannsburg (1963). Two years later it joined the LWF.

The Berlin Mission opened its center at Emmaus in 1847. As German farmers settled in the Transvaal area, Berlin missionaries ministered to them as well as to the Zulu and stood by them during hard times. Periodic drought, grasshopper plagues, cattle disease, tribal wars, and the Boer War (1899–1902) made life difficult for both the Africans and the European settlers. Nevertheless, by World War I, German congregations had been formed, still with Berlin Mission assistance. A school system was developed that still continues. Two world wars were hard on this German church. However, some strong congregations developed, also in Pretoria and Johannesburg. In 1955 they joined to form a self-governing synod and later the Evangelical Lutheran Church in Southern Africa/Transvaal.

Today the merged ELCSA/N-T continues to face a serious dilemma in relation to the black Lutheran church (ELCSA) on the one hand and the white establishment on the other. In light of the suspension of two other white Southern Africa churches by action of the 1984 Budapest assembly, this church has deferred its application for membership in the

LWF. It meanwhile cooperates with its partner churches in *UELCSA and also with ELCSA.

Healing and change require endless steps, as in the case of an ELCSA/N-T congregation near Rustenburg (Transvaal). The guest preacher was a black man from a black congregation not far away. Earlier he had served four years in a parish in Germany. His preaching of the gospel pure and simple, "without politics," said the people afterward, had opened the way afresh for mutual acceptance.

FREE EVANGELICAL LUTHERAN SYNOD IN SOUTH AFRICA

(Freie Evangelisch-Lutherische Synode in Südafrika)
Membership: 3034**
President: The Rev. Günther F. Scharlach
3183 Lüneburg, Natal

The 12 congregations of this independent church, located mainly in the rural areas of Natal and Transvaal, are served by 14 pastors. Most of its members are descendants of German immigrants to South Africa in the latter half of the 19th century.

The Synod supports the Lutheran Hour (ILLL/USA) based in Johannesburg. Its programs are aired weekly on three stations, one in *Lesotho and two in *Swaziland. Its Bible courses enroll over 300 people. The church has close ties with the *Independent Evangelical Lutheran Church (IELC) in the Federal Republic of Germany and a working relationship with its partner, the Lutheran Church in Southern Africa (below). In 1981 the Synod established a seminary in Pretoria with two professors, one sent by the IELC.

The pioneer congregations of this Synod were served by Hermannsburg missionaries to the Zulu. A separation occurring in the Evangelical Lutheran Church of Hanover in 1878 was followed in 1892 by the same action in South Africa.

LUTHERAN CHURCH IN SOUTHERN AFRICA

(Lutherische Kirche im Südlichen Afrika)
Member: ILC
Membership: 32,100**
Bishop: The Rt. Rev. George Schulz
PO Box 11
Pomeroy, Natal 3020

Formed in 1956, this church became autonomous in 1967. It is the black counterpart to the Free Evangelical Lutheran Synod (above) and receives support from the Mission of the Independent Evangelical Lutheran Church (FRG) and the *Lutheran Church–Missouri Synod (LCMS, USA, see Botswana). The 148 congregations, served by 50 pastors, are spread over a large territory, including Natal, Transvaal, and the neighboring countries of *Botswana and *Swaziland. Local languages are used. An outreach to Indian communities includes scattered settlements around Glencoe, Wasbank, and Dannhauser in northern Natal and the urban areas of Goldfield and Durban. Pastors are trained at the Enhlanhleni Theological Seminary in Pomeroy. The LCMS provides one of the professors.

The church's story begins in 1892, when the Mission of the Evangelical Lutheran Church of Hanover, a breakaway from the Hermannsburg Mission, began work in South Africa. The supporting agency in Germany today is called Mission of the Independent Evangelical Lutheran Church; its headquarters are in Bleckmar.

MORAVIAN CHURCH IN SOUTHERN AFRICA (MCSA)

(Evangeliese Broederkerk in Suider-Afrika)
Member: LWF (1975), WCC, AACC, SACC, FELCSA
Membership: 102,132
Western Region:
The Rev. Martin J.R. Wessels
PO Box 24111, Lansdowne 7780, Cape Province
Eastern Region:
The Rev. M.B. Muimbi
Moravian Church, Mvenyane
PO Box 524, Cedarville 4720

The MCSA was formed in 1973 when two Moravian churches in widely separated areas of Cape Province merged. Its constitution provides for two regional synods with superintendents who take turns presiding over the provincial board. Some 200 congregations are grouped into 74 parishes and served by 60 pastors.

The church's ministerial education is based in the Moravian Theological Center in Heideveld. Completed in 1979, the center provides permanence for an educational institution long accommodated in temporary quarters as it was moved between Cape Town and Port Elizabeth. Of the 22 students enrolled in 1982, 12 were part-time. The program retains the Moravian tradition of combining work and study.

Since the 1960s these Moravians have emphasized social work: child care centers, health clinics, hostels, and a home for mentally retarded children. Piety and practical service—true diaconia—have long marked the Moravian presence in this country.

Indeed, Moravian brethren were the first Protestant missionaries to the indigenous people of Southern Africa. Georg Schmidt, an emissary of Zinzendorf, came to the western Cape Province in 1737. His work was cut short in 1744 by the hostility of the European settlers. Others came in 1792 and reestablished mission stations in the Cape Town region and later (1828) in the eastern Xhosa region. These grew to sizable settlements of indigenous people—Afrikaans-speaking in the west and Xhosa-speaking in the east. The number of adherents increased considerably when the slaves in the Cape Province were liberated in 1838. In the Moravian settlements, spiritual and material life centers characteristically around Christ and his example of service.

In 1834 a training school was founded at Gnadendal near Cape Town. The first of its kind in the country, it has supplied the church with generations of able teachers and pastors who have helped to establish a self-supporting South African church. The first indigenous ministers were ordained in 1882. In 1869 the church was divided because the main centers of their growing work were too far apart (some 1600 kilometers or 1000 miles) for effective administration. In the decades that followed the mission expanded its work and membership increased. In the west congregations were established in the cities for those who migrated there. In the

east the work extended into the interior where a whole district became Christian. Gradually the churches became financially and otherwise independent. The Western Cape Province was fully autonomous by 1960; the Eastern Province by 1967. With so many members of both church provinces moving to the cities and with faster transportation, it seemed wise by 1973 to combine resources and meet problems together.

In South Africa, as in Denmark, Moravians considered themselves missionary enablers within the Lutheran fold. Early they participated in unity conferences and became charter members of the FELCSA. After the merger in 1973, the MCSA applied for membership in the LWF. Like all applicants, the Moravians presented proof of their Lutheran doctrinal basis. They were received into full membership in 1975. In 1986 the Moravians took a lead in revitalizing FELCSA.

INDEPENDENT LUTHERAN CONGREGATIONS

Evangelical Lutheran Church— Strand Street
Membership: 693**
Pastor: The Rev. A. A. Brandt
19 Buitengracht
Cape Town 8001

Strand Street Church, as it is known, is an independent self-supporting congregation affiliated with the United Evangelical Lutheran Church in Southern Africa. Strand's membership conforms to the prevailing cultural and thought patterns of South Africa. Both Afrikaans and English are used. Pastors, once supplied by the Evangelical Lutheran Church of Hanover, are now recruited through UELCSA. A long history gives special significance to this church. As early as 1660, the first Lutherans settled in the Cape area. The Dutch East India Company, which governed the Cape, sanctioned only the Reformed Church. Eventually Lutherans were tolerated, and in 1780 they erected their house of worship on Strand Street. It was made to look like a warehouse so as not to compete with the Reformed establishment. The present remodeled church edifice has been declared a national monument.

St. Johannes Church
Fairway, Kelwin
Sandton, Johannesburg
Membership: 100**
Pastor: The Rev. Nils Skold

This congregation, organized in the 1920s, has an affiliation with the Church of Sweden. It ministers to all Scandinavians in the Transvaal region.

St. Olav Lutheran Church
Membership: 620**
Acting Pastor: The Rev. Carl Cronje
214 St. Thomas Road
Durban 4001

St. Olav congregation was founded in 1879 by Norwegian settlers and descendants of Norwegian missionaries who had remained in South Africa. They were engaged in farming, exporting/importing, and other business enterprises. The congregation was linked to the Church of Norway through the Bishop of Oslo. In time its services were extended to all Scandinavians in the area, and more recently also to other nationalities and races.

In the early 1970s St. Olav initiated closer working relationships with the black, Indian, and colored congregations in the Durban area. This led to a desire for closer organizational unity. Discussions began with the then South-Eastern Regional Church regarding membership. Before this was consummated, ELCSA was formed (see above). Negotiations shifted to the South-Eastern Diocese and then the Central Council of ELCSA. By May 1977 ELCSA had drafted bylaws that would apply to St. Olav, allowing for some independence and property ownership. However, constitutional conflicts, legalities, as well as some inertia on ELCSA's part delayed St. Olav's quest for membership.

The decision of the LWF assembly in August 1984 to suspend the two white Southern African member churches brought pressure, also from the Bishop of Oslo, for St. Olav to unite with ELCSA. A vote taken in April 1985 resulted in a split. The majority of the 620 members indicated their intention to remain an independent congregation, open to all. Some 20 families, mainly the church

leadership, withdrew and formed St. Michael's congregation with the intention of affiliating with ELCSA. The new congregation worships in the chapel of the Norwegian Seamen's Mission. (See ELCSA, above.)

St. Peter's by the Lake Lutheran Church
Membership: 90**
Pastor: The Rev. Andreas Johannes Wernecke
43 Lower Park Drive
Park View 2193, Johannesburg

St. Peter's is at present an independent congregation with a loose affiliation to ELCSA/N-T. Founded under the auspices of the Lutheran World Federation in 1961, it was meant to serve English-speaking Lutherans in the Johannesburg metropolitan area. After a slow start, the congregation has grown and reflects a strongly cosmopolitan membership. Members are from America, Sweden, Norway, Germany, and Australia in addition to a few South Africans.

SWAZILAND

A landlocked monarchy in Southern Africa and a member of the Commonwealth, Swaziland is bounded by *South Africa and *Mozambique. Area: 17,364 sq. km. (6704 sq. mi.). Pop. (1982 est.): 585,200. Cap. and largest city: Mbabane (pop., 1982 est., 33,000). Language: English and siSwati, a Nguni language (official).

History: The royal house of Swazi goes back 400 years. Early in the 19th century, fleeing the attacks of the Zulu, the Swazis moved into a mountainous region, today's Swaziland. By mid-century, Europeans arrived seeking concessions. The Swazi king granted them self-government. But soon Swaziland became a High Commission Territory under British protection. In 1963 the Swazis regained limited self-government, then full independence in 1968. King Sobhuza II (1899–1982) was the world's longest reigning monarch (61 years). He had led his nation to independence, abandoned the British-designed constitution, and reverted to a form of government in which the king and his personal advisers exercised power. Queen Ntombi now reigns. Racial tension in Swaziland is lower than elsewhere in Southern Africa. The country's combination of natural resources, agricultural productivity, and good climate are prime assets. Traditional cultural patterns and modern technology have combined constructively. The country also attracts tourists.

Religion: Traditional: 23%. Although decreasing in numbers, the influence and practice of Traditional religion remains strong. Christian: 77%. At the invitation of the Swazi king, Methodist missionaries came from South Africa as early as 1825, and Methodism is one of the larger Protestant churches. About 40 churches grew out of the work of overseas missions. Some of them have changed their name, for example, the British South Africa General Mission is now incorporated into the African Evangelical Church. Indigenous African churches are an important factor in Swazi church life. Today about 40% of the population are members of some 200 independent churches, the largest of which is the Christian Catholic Apostolic Holy Spirit Church in Zion (see *South Africa). An association, the League of African Churches in Swaziland (1937), serves these independent churches.

In 1976, the unmet ecumenical and refugee needs brought about the formation of a Council of Swaziland Churches (CSC). Its membership includes the African Methodist, Episcopal, Anglican, Lutheran, Mennonite, Roman Catholic, and the United Christian Church of Africa. The latter church is the result of the king's attempt, begun in 1939, to unite the country's small independent churches into one national Swazi church. The CSC's original concern for the refugees coming into Swaziland from *South Africa, *Mozambique, and *Zimbabwe has been supplemented by work in the fields of communication, child care, theological education by extension (TEE), development and welfare, family life and women's work, youth activities, worship, and evangelism. The CSC's headquarters were built on land belonging to the Lutheran church.

SWAZILAND CIRCUIT, SOUTH EASTERN DIOCESE, ELCSA (*South Africa)
Membership: 3000**
Dean: The Rev. R. Schiele
PO Box 278
Manzini

The 29 Lutheran congregations in Swaziland, with approximately 3000 members, form part of a circuit of the South-Eastern Diocese of ELCSA. A few schools supplement the congregational activities. The circuit is a member and active participant in the work of the CSC (above). The TEE program helps to prepare workers for the increasing demands on this small portion of ELCSA.

In 1980, at the request of ELCSA and the Swaziland government and with UNHCR support, LWF World Service helped resettle several thousand rural refugees from *South Africa in the Lubombo district of Swaziland at Ndzevane. By 1982 the new settlers had already harvested a cotton crop worth $100,000. Scholarship and vocational training have also been provided for youthful refugees. In 1985 the Swazi government asked LWF World Service to assist them with a second refugee settlement, this time to meet the needs of several thousand Mozambican refugees who had fled famine and civil disruption in their home country. For some time these refugees had been temporarily accommodated at Ndzevane, but as the number increased plans were made to create a new settlement for them. The LWF Community Development Service's first project in Swaziland was a farmers' training center at Piggs Peak, begun in 1966. Since 1973 this project has been run with some subsidies from the government.

A current CDS project in the Manzini parish has combined teacher training with the production of toys (using local materials) and with a garden project. It offers facilities for vocational training to the national organization Lutsango la Kangwane. This has raised the standard of preschool education in the area and given mothers some supplementary income.

ZIMBABWE

A republic in Eastern Africa and a member of the Commonwealth, Zimbabwe, called

Rhodesia until 1979, is bounded by four nations—*Zambia, *Mozambique, *South Africa, *Botswana—and has no access to the sea. Area: 390,759 sq. km. (150,873 sq. mi.). Pop. (1982 est.): 7,730,000, of whom 96% are African and 4% white. Cap. and largest city: Harare (formerly Salisbury; urban area pop., 1981 est., 686,000). Language: English (official) and various Bantu languages (1969 census, Shona 71%, Ndebele 15%).

History: This nation, with pride, takes its name from the Zimbabwe ruins of an early and highly developed civilization that climaxed in the 11th century. Zimbabwe is the African word for "Stone Houses." In the 16th century the Portuguese found the Shona occupying this territory and developed a trade with them in gold and other items. The Shona were invaded and forced to pay tribute to the Ndebele in the 1830s. They had come from Zululand in South Africa. Fleeing from the Zulu King Shaka, they pushed northward, destroying or absorbing the tribes on their way through Transvaal to the area now known as Matabeleland where they settled as herdsmen and farmers. Close behind came the British hunters and traders. In 1889 the British South Africa Company, organized by Cecil Rhodes (1853–1902), began promoting commerce and colonization in the region. Both the Shona and the Ndebele staged unsuccessful revolts against the British.

Ostensibly the British move was to prevent Portugal from linking Angola and Mozambique by a land bridge, while Rhodes dreamed of a continuous occupation from South Africa northward to Egypt. From Rhodes' efforts came the vast landlocked colony of Rhodesia. The northern part became the Republic of *Zambia in 1964. Southern Rhodesia remained a British colony until declaring itself independent in 1965 under white minority rule (Ian Smith). The prolonged struggle by blacks finally won majority rule in 1979. Its president from 1980-1987 was (the Rev.) Canaan Banana, who once served a term on the World Council of Churches staff in Geneva; its present executive president is Robert Mugabe, a practicing Roman Catholic and a declared Marxist.

Religion: Traditional African religion claims nearly one-half of the population. Among the Christians, Roman Catholicism comprises the largest church body, numbering nearly 600,000 baptized members. Methodism (with British and American ties) leads the Protestants, and Anglicanism is strong among the older denominations. Pentecostalism is in the forefront of the newer movements. Independent churches of indigenous impulses are growing rapidly. Black churches played a key role in the struggle for majority rule. The Christian Council of Zimbabwe, formed in 1964, was actively in support of the black struggle and included Anglican as well as other mainline denominations. But in size it is second to the Zimbabwean Christian Conference, a conservative and evangelical association, akin in position to the original missionary conference in 1903. In 1905 Swedish missionaries came on the scene.

EVANGELICAL LUTHERAN CHURCH IN ZIMBABWE (ELCZ)

(Kereke yeEvangeri yamaLutera muZimbabwe)
Member: LWF (1963), FELCSA, CCZ
Membership: 44,613**
Bishop: The Rt. Rev. Jonas Chiwariro Shiri
PO Box 2175
Bulawayo

Since the coming of black majority rule in 1980, this small but active church body has played an increasingly significant role ecumenically and in the life of the nation.

Although most of the ELCZ members are rural folk living in and around Mberengwa, Beitbridge, and Gwanda in the Matabeleland region of southeastern and southwestern Zimbabwe, growing numbers are being drawn to the urban centers, chiefly to Bulawayo and the national capital, Harare. Besides Shona and Ndebele, the use of Sotho, Venda, and Shangani dialects among the members suggests the multilingual challenge to which the ELCZ has responded resourcefully.

Autonomous since 1962, the ELCZ fell heir to developments two decades earlier, during World War II. A constitution, adopted already in 1941 to fix the sharing of responsibility between the Church of Sweden Mission and the people, was revised and provided continuity. The church's 227 congregations are grouped into 29 parishes. These, in turn, form two districts or deaneries. Since 1959, a bishop has headed the church. Between the biennial assemblies, attended by all parish pastors and their lay delegates, a church council governs.

Candidates for the ordained ministry who were formerly trained at the Lutheran Theological College Umpumulo, in Mapumulo, Natal, *South Africa, presently attend the United Theological College (UTC) in Harare, the national capital, some 440 kilometers (275 miles) northeast of Bulawayo. The UTC, established in 1954 by the Methodists, is now jointly governed and supported by five Protestant churches including the Lutheran. The ELCZ's 32 pastors are assisted by well over 100 evangelists, trained mainly at the church's two Bible schools. A large number of teachers, elders, and other lay workers carry on an extensive ministry.

Women comprise the majority of active members. Ever since the 1930s their volunteer organization, Vashandiri, has influenced the church's life and work. Wives of pastors and evangelists organized and led this movement and now continue to serve as advisers to the elected officers on the local and district levels. Nationally the bishop's wife has been able to inspire and lead the women to ever new heights of service. Vashandiri women are prepared to lead Bible studies, visit the sick in hospitals and homes, give courses on child and home care, and organize ways of supporting and building up the church. In 1983, with help from Finnchurchaid, a women's center was completed in Gweru (Gwelo), a town of 64,000 people situated halfway between Harare and Bulawayo. These headquarters also provide short courses, enabling women—especially those with little formal education—to develop their talents and to learn new skills. The accommodations for 40 are also used for retreats, church meetings, weddings, and numerous other occasions.

Before the liberation struggle peaked in the 1970s, a youth center was erected at Njube, near Bulawayo, with assistance from the Church of Sweden Mission and Lutherhjälpen. In its own way the Njube center brings into focus the ELCZ's interest and concern for its youth and also for its young adults, many of whom have returned to their homes after bitter experiences as refugees or soldiers. Work in the cities or mines has been

drawing them away from their rural families. Therefore the church faces the enormous task of providing more congregations and pastoral care in the cities. Over 23 have already been established. Harare leads with seven; Bulawayo has six; Kadoma five; Gweru three; Zvishavane two.

Education in general has high priority for the church as well as the government. The ELCZ operates six secondary schools. Providing mature and competent teachers for so many classes stretches the resources to the limit. Expatriate volunteers during this "catch up" period of the 1980s are appreciated. Medical work has played an important role since 1915. Aided by partner churches, the ELCZ operates and staffs four hospitals.

In the wake of the bitter struggle for liberation, this ELCZ region, with its distinctive tribal identity, has experienced not only the homecoming of soldiers, the disarming of factions, the tasks of reconstruction, the testings of drought, and the challenge of agricultural productivity, but also the call to nation building, and the role of the church in it.

In 1980 LWF World Service (LWS) facilitated the return to Zimbabwe of more than 41,000 refugees. At ELCZ's request, LWS then opened an office in Harare to assist with their resettlement through major reconstruction projects. Technical assistance was also provided through LWF Community Development Service (CDS) projects. One of the first, initiated and largely carried out by the women, was the repair and reequipping of village water supplies in southern Matabeleland. The repaired schools and hospitals were also supplied with clean water. In 1984, through a CDS rural development project, ELCZ, in cooperation with Roman Catholics, reached out to the more depressed areas in northern Matabeleland.

Following a major drought response effort in 1984-1986 (village grain storage, drought preparedness through training, and a development project in lower Guruve district), the LWS program has recently emphasized a more training-oriented and less technically oriented program. Among the new projects have been a cattle improvement program for communal areas, a cooperative development and settlement program in Masvingo province, cooperative development and education nationwide, rural market gardening, rehabilitation and training for South African and Namibian refugees, community motivation activities, and assistance to displaced Mozambicans in Chipinge district.

An international consultation on the role of the churches in national building convened in the Njube youth center in September 1982. With LWF assistance, representatives had come from a dozen countries in four continents. The accent was on the gospel in its bearing on justice, human rights, peace, and reconciliation. The intention was to learn from one another. For the ELCZ, the host church, high on the agenda was the reconciling of lingering tensions between the government and the party in power, on the one hand, and the somewhat differently oriented people in Matabeleland. Here the ELCZ, striving to mediate, found it an immensely maturing process—helpful also to the nation's future. Shared experiences from India, Indonesia, Namibia, Brazil, East and West Germany, Sweden, the United States, Liberia, Tanzania, Madagascar, and Canada supportively underscored the ELCZ's task.

Likewise the December 1983 Pre-Assembly Consultation of Lutheran Churches in Africa (see Africa Introduction), held in Harare, acquainted representatives from many churches across the continent with the ELCZ and updated the acquaintance of all the churches with each other as they faced profound concerns together.

Meanwhile, from outside the continent, via CDS and other channels, persons from Europe and America, often experts in their fields, have volunteered their services in schools and elsewhere. Representatives of church women in Sweden, the United States, and other countries have come to Zimbabwe for short periods of orientation and fellowship with their counterparts in Vashandiri groups. A team from North America found the venture inspiring, revealing the life and work of the ELCZ and its women in fuller perspective. In 1983 ELCZ sent a delegation to visit the new Lutheran church in *Malawi. As a result, missionaries have been sent to assist this church in its outreach and leadership training.

The beginnings of this church date from 1903 when missionaries from Sweden, then serving in Natal, *South Africa, followed the northward course of white settlement into what was then southern Rhodesia. This brought them again in contact with Zulu-related people, the Ndebele (see Zimbabwe Introduction). Other communions had come into southern Rhodesia earlier. As early as 1861 the London Missionary Society had established a mission to the Ndebele. A comity agreement assigned the Church of Sweden Mission a territory in the country's southwest. There in Matabeleland, where the chief city is Bulawayo and the main language Ndebele, the work unfolded.

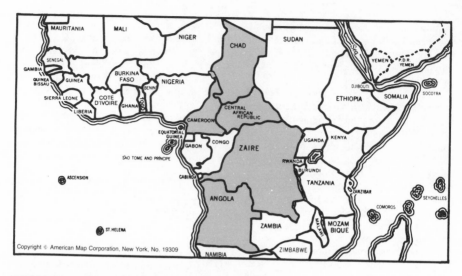

Copyright © American Map Corporation, New York, No. 19309

WEST-CENTRAL AFRICA

The countries of this contiguous grouping span the vastness from the Sahara to Southern Africa. They are Angola, Cameroon, the Central African Republic, Chad, and Zaire. French is the official language in all of them except Angola, where it is Portuguese. In Cameroon, English is also official. The total number of Christians in these countries is large, but the number of Lutherans is very small (some 235,000) and of these about 51% are in Cameroon.

ANGOLA

The People's Republic of Angola, situated on the southwest coast of Africa between *Namibia and *Zaire, achieved independence in 1975 after five centuries of Portuguese rule. In 1976 it was admitted to membership in the United Nations. Area: 1,246,700 sq. km. (481,353 sq. mi.). Pop. (1985 est.): 8,573,000 (Ovimbundu 35.7%, Mbundu 22.3%). Cap. and largest city: Luanda (pop., 1985 est., 960,000). Language: Bantu languages (predominant), Portuguese (official), and some Khoisan dialects.

History: The Mbundu, a large ethnic group closely related to the Ovambo in *Namibia and southern Angola, had an established dynasty in central Angola in the 16th century, when the Portuguese began colonization. By this time there was a widespread Roman Catholic Church as the result of missions by the Franciscans (1491) followed by the Dominicans and Canons of St. John the

Evangelist. Their work was encouraged by a remarkable Christian king, Afonso I. His son, Henrique, became the first black African bishop. This promising beginning was followed by the disintegration of both the kingdom and the church due to the slave trade. The Portuguese captured thousands for slavery in Brazil. However the Mbundu were not completely subjugated until 1902.

The independence gained in 1975 has been complicated by civil conflict, which continues unabated between several liberation parties, and also by outside forces. A treaty with the USSR has influenced the Marxist socialist government, which rules most of the country. Cuban troops have been stationed mainly in southern Angola as a peacekeeping force. Here, too, large numbers of people from northern *Namibia, most of them connected in some way with SWAPO, the South-West Africa People's Organization, have sought refuge. Even so, the South African military, seeking to curb SWAPO activities in Namibia, have not hesitated to cross the border into

Angola in hot pursuit or in temporary occupation. Loss of life has at times been high as unrest and violence continue. Economically the nation as a whole has been experiencing hard times, which recession in other lands has only intensified.

Religion: Traditional (9.5%) has been in decline since World War II. Roman Catholicism (from 50% to 70%), once favored, has in recent years been handicapped by its identification with the former Portuguese colonialism. Protestantism (ca. 20%) has been on the increase. Already in 1922 the Evangelical Alliance of Angola, comprising Baptists, Evangelicals, Methodists, and others, worked out comity agreements. In consequence there has been little overlapping in mission activities, even in the cities. Southern Angola, where the Lutherans are now, was closed to Protestant activity from 1914 to 1960. The Angolan Council of Evangelical Churches (1977), based in Luanda, is a partnership of six denominations sharing mutual efforts in evangelism, theological education, social service, church support, and information. This council has connections with the World Council of Churches, but none of its partners are members of the WCC.

EVANGELICAL LUTHERAN CHURCH OF SOUTH ANGOLA
Membership: 11,900
President: The Rev. Noa Ndeutapo
PO Box 42, 985 Lubango
Xangonga

This church was organized in 1979, four years after the closing of the border between Angola and *Namibia cut the ties with the Evangelical Lutheran Ovambokavango Church (now renamed Evangelical Lutheran Church in Namibia, ELCIN). Even so, the ELCIN constitution and traditions set the pattern for this new church. Its activities and most of its congregations are in the southern border province of Cunene, where living conditions have been especially difficult. The church's 65 congregations are served by 16 pastors, 14 evangelists, and 12 congregational workers. Prolonged violence has scattered the church's members and many of them have been killed. In Shangalala, where much of its work is centered, the church maintains a Bible school and a clinic.

The roots of this church go back to 1891, when the Rhenish Mission Society (1828) of Germany began work among the Kwanyama-speaking people in southern Angola. At a time when the boundary line between German South-West Africa and Portuguese Angola was still somewhat flexible, it made sense for the German missionaries to work among a people on the northern banks of the Cunene River who were kin to the Ovambos on the southern banks. In agreement with the Rhenish Mission, the Finnish Missionary Society (now FELM) became involved (see Namibia).

Although a few small congregations had been formed among the Kwanyama-speaking people, the German missionaries had to give up their work not long after the outbreak of World War I and the fall of German South-West Africa (1916). It was then that most of these new Christians, also under Portuguese Roman Catholic pressures in Angola, crossed over into the land of their kindred Ovambo and joined the Lutheran congregation there. Years later, upon returning to their own country, these Angolans maintained their ties with the Ovambokavango parishes.

Responding to this situation, the Finnish Missionary Society sent two missionary families to southern Angola in 1939. With the outbreak of World War II that same year, Angolan governmental regulations required the removal of the missionaries from the south to the central part of the country. Until 1946 the Finns teamed up with the Swiss Alliance Missionnaire Evangélique, from Francophone Switzerland. For various reasons, restraints continued to be placed on Protestant work.

Early in the 1960s the church in Ovamboland (ELCIN) sent a pastor into southern Angola. In 1973–1974, when the movement for independence from Portugal was then nearing its climax, ELCIN and the Finnish society, again in cooperation with the Swiss, were able to send several pastors and other missionary workers into this region. Due to the civil war, in 1975 the Finnish missionaries returned to Finland. Soon they were back but in 1980 had to leave the region again. Since 1981 the Cunene province has repeatedly suffered from inroads by South African forces and felt the brunt of violent encounters. In this time of trial and loss, also for the Lutheran congregations, outside contacts have been minimal and communication difficult. Yet the church lives.

In November 1986, at the initiative of the ELCIN and with the endorsement of the Angolan Council of Evangelical Churches, Lutheran World Service (LWF) and the government of Angola concluded a bipartite agreement. The immediate concern is to provide assistance to the internally displaced nationals and to assist exiled Namibians and South Africans.

CAMEROON

The United Republic of Cameroon (1960) on the Gulf of Guinea is bordered by *Nigeria, *Chad, the *Central African Republic, the Congo, Gabon, and Equatorial Guinea. Area: 465,458 sq. km. (179,714 sq. mi.). Pop. (1983 est.): 9,065,000, made up of 200 tribes. Cap.: Yaoundé (pop., 1981 est., 435,900), on a low plateau 264 kilometers (165 miles) inland from Douala (pop., 1981 est., 637,000), the country's main port and largest city. Language: English and French (official); Fulani is the major trade language.

History: The Cameroon region has experienced numerous invasions and migrations, especially by Fulani, Hausa, Fang, and Kanuri. Contact with Europe began in 1472 when the Portuguese arrived looking for gold. This was followed by a large-scale slave trade by Portuguese, Spanish, Dutch, French, and English traders. In the 19th century palm oil and ivory became the main items of commerce. The English were in control until 1884 when the Germans took over, forming the colony of Kamerun. Captured by the British and French in 1914, the region was divided between them (1919) and made Trust Territories by the League of Nations. The United Nation's reaffirmed these trusts in 1946. French Cameroon to the east was much the larger. Britain administered western Cameroon as part of eastern Nigeria. When independence was achieved in 1960, the people in the southern region of the British Trust, including the Bamenda Highlands and Cameroon Mountain, voted to be a part of the United Republic of Cameroon. Ethnically they are closer to their neighbors to the east. However, administration by different countries and the use of different languages and

monetary systems for some 40 years, created problems.

Cameroon has been relatively stable in contrast to the political and militaristic conflict generally prevalent in Africa. Ahmadou Ahidjo, who had served as president since independence resigned in 1982. A Muslim, he was respected by both Muslims and Christians. The prime minister, Paul Biya, a Christian, succeeded him. Cameroon has often had to provide temporary accommodation to refugees from neighboring Chad.

Religion: African Traditional (25%); Muslim (22%); Christian (53%). Of the nearly four million Christians, about half are Roman Catholics. A self-governing hierarchy has an archbishop in Yaoundé. A Federation of Evangelical Churches and Missions of Cameroon (Fédération des Eglises et Missions Evangéliques du Cameroun, FEMEC, 1970) includes Baptist, Presbyterian, Reformed, and various evangelical groups as well as two Lutheran bodies. In 1979 the FEMEC launched a national campaign for evangelism—"New Life for All"—that has become an ongoing movement. The United Theological Seminary in Yaoundé, aided initially by the former Theological Education Fund (TEF), is intended to serve the needs of all Francophone Protestant churches in Africa.

CHURCH OF THE LUTHERAN BRETHREN OF CAMEROON (CLBC)
(Eglise fraternelle luthérienne du Cameroun)
Member: FEMEC
Membership: 39,097
President: The Rev. Jacques Hoursang
PO Box 30
Yagoua

This church, autonomous since 1964, is situated in the northern triangular point of Cameroon. The 324 organized congregations and the 297 newly formed groups of believers are served by 55 ordained and 25 unordained pastors plus 57 catechists. The annual general assembly, with representatives from the congregations and groups, is presided over by a president, elected biennially, who oversees the ongoing work. Church members are mainly subsistence farmers.

Great emphasis is placed on evangelism and Bible study. On an average Sunday, some 53,000 people gather for worship throughout the church's region. District Bible schools enroll some 1900 students, and the advanced regional Bible schools almost 200. A pastoral training school in Kaélé provides a six-year program for about 30 students.

The church is strongly committed to Bible translation and literature production. The entire Bible has been translated into Fulani, the prevailing trade language, and was published recently in cooperation with the ELCC (below). The New Testament is now in five other languages of the people served: Mundang, Masana, Musgum, Fali, and Giddar. Progress continues on five more. These translation projects are encouraged and assisted by the Bible Society of Cameroon. To serve the literature needs of the Brethren in both Cameroon and *Chad, the church maintains a publishing house and a wholesale book outlet in Garoua.

The CLBC shares in the ownership and outreach of the Sawtu Linjiila Radio Studio in Ngaoundéré (below); provides modern treatment for lepers; participates in the "New Life for All" evangelistic outreach; is a charter member of the Joint Christian Ministry in West Africa; and belongs to FEMEC.

The CLBC began as a mission of the *Church of the Lutheran Brethren/USA (CLB/USA). In 1920 Pastor and Mrs. B. Revne opened a station in Yagoua, a town on the Logone River (and Chad border). The CLB/USA continues to provide personnel and financial aid for the various programs and outreach. This has not been done without sacrifice, as the death of two veteran missionaries (May 1978) attests. Victims of an apparently ritual murder, Ernest and Miriam Erickson had served in the country for 34 years. They were widely mourned in the civic as well as the Christian community.

EVANGELICAL LUTHERAN CHURCH OF CAMEROON (ELCC)
(Eglise évangélique luthérienne du Cameroun)
Member: LWF (1971), FEMEC
Membership: 78,229
President: The Rev. Pierre Amtsé Songsaré
PO Box 6
Ngaoundéré

This church, established in 1960 by its founding missions, became fully autonomous in 1974 when the mission integrated with the local church. Its members are mainly subsistence farmers widely scattered throughout a heavily Muslim population.

The 685 congregations are served by 36 indigenous pastors, 71 evangelists, and 449 catechists. The general synod, the highest authority, convenes biennially to review the work, determine policy, and elect its president for four years and an administrative council for two years.

Ngaoundéré, the headquarters city, is situated on the main highway midway between Yaoundé and the northern border. Here, with help from the LWF Department of Church Cooperation, offices were recently built for the president and the various church departments. They are centrally located for the work that extends into the six regional synods headquartered in Meiganga (southwest); Garoua Boulai (east); Tibati (southwest); Poli (northwest); Tcholliré (northeast); and Ngaoundéré (central). The synods function independently in their tasks of evangelization and development.

The ELCC pastors have had their training at the mission-founded seminary in Meiganga. Its recent enlargement, both physical and academic, has made it possible to double the enrollment, now about 40 students. Since the need for a well-trained indigenous leadership is urgent, several pastors have had advanced theological education in *Nigeria. On the recommendation of an LWF committee that studied the overall needs in theological education in Africa, the ELCC has resumed its relationship with the United Theological Seminary in Yaoundé. Gifted students may thus study at an accredited, French-speaking school within Cameroon. Lutherans provide a professor. Such opportunities have alerted the church to its responsibility for the spiritual welfare of the many young people who have migrated to the cities. Hence a diaspora ministry in the big towns and the city of Yaoundé receives top priority.

Similarly the great need to increase the dignity and productivity of the farm families has been obvious for some time. Beginning in 1965, with the help of the LWF Community Development Service (CDS), a churchwide agricultural program has been under way and is bearing fruit. Villagers in remote areas also benefit from other CDS projects such as those related to clean water systems, bridges, and ferries.

The church's outreach is complicated by language problems. Although 65-70% of the younger people can communicate in French, the older generation and up-country folk have difficulty. Of necessity the church newspaper is printed in six languages. Language centers are translating the Bible into 10 tribal languages: Fulani, Mbum, Gbaya, Baboute, Tikar, Mambila, Duru, Kutin (Péré), Karang, and Kondja.

Since 1970 the ELCC has actively participated in the national campaign for evangelism "New Life for All" launched by the FEMEC. Besides awakening congregations to their local mission opportunities, teams of evangelists go into remote villages among the Traditionalists and the Islamized Fulani. Some of these people had heard the gospel over the powerful Radio Voice of the Gospel (RVOG) and remain eager for the good news. Others have never heard it. Pictures, films, cassettes, and friendly care help to convey the gospel. While individual conversion usually results in isolation, efforts are made to await group decisions. Already in 1966 the general synod resolved to accept converted polygamists into the church through baptism.

The importance of radio in these remote areas of high illiteracy prompted the Lutheran churches of Cameroon, *Chad, and the *Central African Republic (with LWF help) to open the Sawtu Linjiila radio studio in Ngaoundéré in 1966. From there programs in the Fulani language were broadcast over RVOG (*Ethiopia). Since RVOG's silencing in 1977, the ELCC and its neighboring partner churches have continued to carry out multimedia projects (LWF/DOC). Programs for the national radio station in Bertoua are produced in the Gbaya language, and Fulani programs are broadcast over Radio Garoua.

The women's movement in the church, Femmes pour Christ, has grown remarkably since its organization in 1975. With active groups in almost every congregation and a membership between six and seven thousand, it is possible to speak of a real awakening among the women as to their potential and also to their responsibilities as Christians. This success can be attributed in part to work begun in 1972 by four women missionaries assigned to the four districts as well as to the continued interest of partner churches.

A Sunday school program throughout the church and Christian education in the primary schools receive mounting emphasis. These educational endeavors are supplemented by a youth program, JECA. Efforts to organize it also on the secondary level continue.

The church faces ever new responsibilities in operating the mission-founded institutions: three hospitals, eight major dispensaries, two leprosaria, two orphanages, 52 primary schools, and one boarding school with both primary and secondary classes. Most of the evangelists and catechists are trained in the ELCC's four Bible schools located at Meng, Poli, Tchollire, and Garoua Boulai. The latter also serves as a base for theological education by extension. Some 250 people are enrolled in the nine TEE courses offered in their villages.

Although efforts toward self-sufficiency are being made, the ELCC still has need of assistance from its partners. In 1983, 57 expatriates served in various capacities within the church.

The ELCC owes it earliest roots to a Norwegian-American layman, A. L. Gundersen. Feeling called to mission, he prepared himself in Bible school and seminary and then spent four years in West Africa surveying possible fields and another two arousing interest and selecting staff in the USA. When his church body was unable to sponsor the work, he organized the Sudan Mission. In 1923 he arrived in Douala with his wife, Deaconess Olette Bertsen, and Anne Olsen. They trekked 375 kilometers north to where no missionaries had ventured. The first station was opened in Mboula, southeast of Ngaoundéré, among the Gbaya. The friendliness of the chief in Meiganga, the second station, kept the missionaries safe during a Muslim-inspired antiwhite insurrection. New recruits in 1928—Pastor and Mrs. Ernest R. Weinhardt and Andrew Okland—extended the work into the present *Central African Republic. Further north the Muslim king, Rei Bouba, was friendly; but the area remained closed to missionary work until he died. Then his son donated the land necessary for a mission station in Tchollire (1953).

Two years after Gundersen's arrival the Norwegian Missionary Society began work in neighboring Ngaoundéré (1925). Early work was among the Muslims, whose slaves at times found refuge at the mission station.

Later the Norwegians turned their main attention to the Duru and Tikar people. Solid education and medical work laid the basis for further outreach.

After World War II, when the Evangelical Lutheran Church in the USA (later the *ALC, now the *ELCA) assumed the work of the Sudan Mission, the two enterprises combined. In recent years the *Evangelical Lutheran Church in Canada and the two French churches have added support and personnel.

In return Cameroon Lutherans have been able to give encouragement and assistance to the *Evangelical Lutheran Church of the Central African Republic; to provide theological education to students from the Evangelical Lutheran Community in Zaire-West; and to be supportive of the ALC (now ELCA) missionaries in Senegal. The ELCC is a member of the All-Africa Lutheran Information and Coordination Center (ALICE); a charter member of the Joint Christian Ministry in West Africa—a united mission to the Fulani; and a member of the FEMEC.

LUTHERAN CHURCH OF CAMEROON (LCC)

Member: FEMEC
Membership: 4285**
Executive President: The Rt. Rev.
Bruno Njume Njume
PO Box 103
Kumba, Meme Division
Southwest Province

Situated in the English-speaking southwest and northwest provinces of Cameroon, this church is one of several offshoots of the *Lutheran Church of Nigeria. The founding members were largely Nigerians who settled in west Cameroon while it was a British Trust Territory (see Cameroon Introduction). During the Biafra crisis (1967–1971), other Nigerians also found refuge here, and for a time the young church had over 6000 members. Many of these have now returned to *Nigeria. The reduced membership is divided into 52 congregations. These and a number of preaching places are served by eight ordained pastors who also supervise the evangelists and vicars.

Already in 1970 the LCC appealed to the *Wisconsin Evangelical Lutheran Synod

(WELS, USA) for spiritual counsel and financial aid. Instructional material and some aid were given. In 1975 the WELS voted to adopt the church as a mission, but since the LCC has not achieved national registration, no missionaries have been sent. WELS church officials have made regular visits, and an African partner, the *Evangelical Lutheran Church of the Central African Republic, has sent teachers to conduct in-service seminars for pastors and lay workers as well as to help the church's ongoing program of theological education by extension.

The church has permission to work in the two provinces mentioned above. As the church grows, the need for more regular aid mounts. Other independent Lutheran groups in the Kumba area are also striving for recognition and aid. Two LWF members—the *Lutheran Church of Nigeria (the mother church) and the ELCC (the Cameroon member, above)—consider the LCC the most stable of these groups. At LWF request, these member churches are encouraging the LCC's growth and outreach.

CENTRAL AFRICAN REPUBLIC (CAR)

An independent nation since 1960. Landlocked, it is surrounded by *Cameroon, *Chad, *Sudan, *Zaire, and the Congo. Area: 622,436 sq. km. (240,324 sq. mi.). Pop. (1984 est.): 2,658,000. Cap. and largest city: Bangui (pop., 1984 est., 473,800). Language: French (official); Sangho is the common language of the four major ethnic groups: Banda, Mbaka, Azande, Mandja-Baya. The Gbaya are a smaller ethnic group that has moved eastward from *Cameroon into the western region of the Central African Republic as far as the town of Bouar.

History: This land, heavily raided for slaves from the 16th to the 19th centuries, was occupied by the French in 1887 and organized (1894) as the colony of Ubangi-Shari—named for the two rivers flowing through the vast interior. In 1910 this became part of French Equatorial Africa. Forced labor and other abuses sparked rebellions in 1928, 1935, and 1946. Full independence with a parliamentary government was attained in 1960. In 1965 a coup was followed by 14 years of tyranny under Jean-Bédel Bokassa. For two years (1977–1979) he changed the country's designation from republic to empire, with himself as emperor. He was overthrown by the French. The discovery of diamonds, the processing of other minerals, and the government's drive to develop the agricultural resources, especially cotton, has somewhat improved the economy. However, CAR remains one of the poorest countries in Africa, unable to provide for the educational, medical, and development needs of a complex people. It is heavily dependent on foreign aid, especially from France. Only in 1970 was a university established in Bangui.

Religion: Traditional religion (12%) is practiced by a diminishing minority of the main tribes but by virtually all of the Binga Pygmies. Islam (3%) is strongest among the non-African population and in the cities. Christianity: Protestant (50%); Roman Catholic (33%). The mass conversion of the Central African people is one of the most dramatic stories in Africa. Baptist and Brethren churches are the largest. There is no Christian council, but most Protestants cooperate in the Association of Central African Evangelical Churches (1974). The Roman Catholic Church, here since 1894, is organized into five dioceses under an African archbishop.

EVANGELICAL LUTHERAN CHURCH OF THE CENTRAL AFRICAN REPUBLIC (ELC-CAR)

(Eglise évangélique luthérienne de la République Centrafricaine)
Member: LWF (1974)
Membership: 22,000
President: The Rev. Paul Denou
PO Box 100
Baboua via Bouar

This church became autonomous in 1974 when it separated from the *Evangelical Lutheran Church of Cameroon (ELCC). It did so in order to identify more fully with the Central African Republic and thereby be more involved in its evangelization. During its early independence the church grew rapidly in the villages on the western *Cameroon border. From there the work extended eastward some 150 kilometers to Bouar, a city

connected with the national capital (450 kilometers farther east) by an improved road.

The present 250 congregations are grouped into parishes and divided into 15 districts and five regions. A general synod, the administrative authority, meets every two years and elects the president and other officers who make up the executive committee. The church is served by 26 pastors and numerous lay catechists and evangelists, most of whom have had their training in Baboua, a small town at the Cameroon border where the church headquarters, a Bible school, and a seminary are located.

The Bible school, established already in 1952, has recently been updated with help from partners. It meets the needs of a mixed student body. A three-year course trains catechists and evangelists. Almost all the graduates, numbering hundreds, serve the church either as full-time workers or as self-supporting ministers. Since educational opportunities in rural CAR are extremely limited, the school has a literacy department. This is especially useful to student wives and their families. The school also provides practical training in agriculture and other skills to improve the life of villagers. Recently these have been linked to a demonstration farm in Gallo (between Baboua and Bouar). Here an LWF Community Development Service project provides training in the construction of stronger mud houses, the production of more food, the securing of clean water and sanitary facilities, and other development skills.

The seminary, staffed by ALC (now ELCA) missionaries, began preparing pastors for ordination in 1976. A two-year theological extension course for evangelists was followed by two years of residential work. The staff has been augmented by a professor from the Hermannsburg Mission (FRG) who is supported by the *Evangelical Lutheran Church of France. Several classes of about 10 candidates each have been graduated and ordained. This has more than tripled the pastoral force, which in 1976 was only seven. Nevertheless the church is still greatly dependent upon evangelists and catechists to guide the spiritual life of the congregations and to work among the young people.

The youth work of the church is in special need of encouragement and organization to attain its promising potential. Life in the rural villages centers around the church, and there is little else to stimulate the growth and ambition of the young. Many of them seek their future in Bouar, a city of over 30,000. The youth work begun here by an ALC missionary in 1972 has grown. Young leadership has strengthened the new congregations of the city. A youth center not only accommodates the normal activities of a church program but also the release-time religious education classes of the public school. Teachers from Baptist, Roman Catholic, and Lutheran churches reach 350 students each week.

Although the main mission of the ELC-CAR has been to the Gbaya villagers, the more migrant Fulani (*Nigeria, *Cameroon) have been moving down from the north and settling among them. The Fulani are mainly Muslim, and the church is eager to share the gospel with them. A pastor has been assigned to this work, and in each district an evangelist assists him. Medical work (staffed by expatriates) is another service. Better acquaintance with the life and culture of these nomadic herders has been helpful to the Joint Christian Ministry in West Africa (JCMWA, see Africa Introduction). ELC-CAR is a charter member of the JCMWA and has contributed one of its ALC pastors to serve as director.

Besides the history it shares with the *Evangelical Lutheran Church of Cameroon, the ELC-CAR has a story of its own. In 1929 mission explorers Okland and Weinhardt (see Cameroon, ELCC) from the then American Sudan Mission penetrated the west boundary of the Ubangi-Shari region of French Equatorial Africa. In a land hostile to the French, it was not easy for the exploring missionaries to convince the people of their good intention. But in the town of Abba, some distance southeast of Baboua, they were met by a crowd called together with the words, "Come and hear the white men of God." Three years later the first baptism, that of Joseph Garga, took place. He became a chief and later a district judge over the Gbayas. This witness, like that of the early Christians, bore fruit. Chains of chapels were built and staffed by the Gbaya. In 1951 a mud-brick Bible school was built in Baboua so they could have training.

Today, as an independent church, the ELC-CAR also strives for economic independence and has accomplished this on the congregational level. Assistance is still necessary in education and outreach. Thus expatriate pastors and others are called for specialized ministries in such areas as literacy, youth, Sunday school, distribution of literature, teaching, and medical work. Most of them have been supplied by the American Lutheran Church (now a part of the Evangelical Lutheran Church in America). Recently the Sudan United Mission of Denmark has become a partner in the endeavors. In theological education, as noted, help has also come from Germany and France. In addition, the Evangelical Lutheran Church of Cameroon continues its interest and concern. Several pastors have furthered their theological education in the ELCC's seminary in Meiganga. A past relationship thus continues as both churches share the gospel with the Gbaya and Fulani.

CHAD

A landlocked republic (1960) of central Africa, bounded by *Cameroon, Lake Chad, Niger, Libya, *Sudan, and the *Central African Republic. Area 1,284,000 sq. km. (495,755 sq. mi.). Pop. (1983 est.): 4,990,000, including Africans (Saras, Tubu, Tama, Masalit) and Arabs. Cap. and largest city: N'Djaména (pop., 1983 est., 225,000), formerly known as Fort-Lamy. Language: French (official).

History: Chad has been a focal point for trans-Saharan trade since at least the 7th century. Shortly thereafter nomads from the north moved down and established the kingdom of Kanem, which reached its zenith in the 13th century. Other kingdoms followed, with the kings converting to Islam. In 1891 French expeditions moved in. Chad became the northernmost territory of French Equatorial Africa (1910). A territorial legislature in 1946 and autonomy within the French Community in 1958 was followed by full independence in 1960. By 1965 a one-party government took control. A year later discontented northern Muslim tribes began a full-scale guerrilla war against the southern one-party power. After an uneasy respite in 1982, the war took on new international dimensions.

Chad's economy, based on sedentary agriculture in the south and nomadic herding in the north, has suffered greatly from the war, drought, and diseased animals. The people, encouraged by the government to plant cash crops such as cotton, have been caught short of food in times of drought.

Religion (1980): Islam (44%), introduced in the 11th century, spread rapidly during the 16th and 17th centuries. Its influence on the Chadian black people has been a 20th century phenomenon. Traditional (23%) is most prevalent among the population living by agriculture and fishing. Christian (33%). Roman Catholics, numbering about a million, are grouped into four dioceses. An intensive and organized outreach since 1947 has been most successful among young people. Protestants as a whole number over 500,000. The Evangelical Church of Chad (Eglise évangélique du Tchad) is the largest and combines the work of the Sudan United Mission, the French Mennonites, and the World Evangelical Crusade. Its youth movement, Flambeau (Little Flame), is especially effective in evangelistic outreach. One of the 10 largest missions is the Lutheran Brethren (below). The Federation of Evangelical Churches of Chad (FEET) is a loose grouping of missions and some national churches.

CHURCH OF THE LUTHERAN BRETHREN OF CHAD (CLBC)

(Eglise fraternelle luthérienne au Tchad)
Membership: 38,036
President: Pasteur Jean Maloum
Fadanne
PO Box 11
Léré

This church, autonomous since 1964 and recognized by the government since 1970, is situated in the Mayo Kebbi and Tandjili prefectures in southwestern Chad. Only the border separates the CLBC from the Brethren in *Cameroon. Léré, where the Church of the Lutheran Brethren (*USA) began work in 1920, is midway between Kaélé and Garoua, important centers of the church in *Cameroon.

Their common heritage and mission partner and the physical proximity enable the Brethren in Chad to work cooperatively with the Brethren in *Cameroon in many areas, especially in translation, production, and distribution of literature (*Cameroon). The first

whole vernacular Bible in Chad (Moundang) and the New Testament in Masana, Musgum, and Pévé are the result of this partnership and Bible Society assistance. Translation into four other Chad languages is in progress. The diversity of tongues illustrates the complexity of working with so many different groups. Most of them are subsistence farmers. However, the church has been very successful in reaching the Fulani, Muslim herders who migrate into this area from the north.

The people in this area have been responsive to the church's evangelism. The 47 ordained, 12 unordained, and 530 catechists minister to an average Sunday audience of 48,000, of whom 16,500 are communicant members. Christian instruction in district Bible schools enrolls close to 3000. The advanced regional Bible schools have about 150 students. The pastoral training school in Gouana Gaya, a small town between Fianga (on the border) and Kélo, has about 30 students in a six-year course.

Aided by strong support from the Lutheran Brethren (USA), the CLBC developed a pilot project in community health and by 1985 had trained some 75 village health workers. This project is designed for replication elsewhere in Chad. The founder and faithful partner, CLBC/USA has six missionaries in Chad (1985).

The CLBC participates with neighboring Lutheran churches in *Cameroon and the *Central African Republic in the Sawtu Linjiila radio ministry in *Cameroon. It is also a charter member of the Joint Christian Ministry in West Africa (see Africa Introduction) and participates in FEET (above).

ZAIRE

A republic of equatorial Africa earlier known as the Democratic Republic of the Congo (1960), the country adopted its present name, Republic of Zaire, in 1971. Zaire, meaning "big river," broadly denotes the Congo basin. Area: 2,344,885 sq. km. (905,365 sq. mi.). Pop. (1985 est.): 33,052,000. Cap. and largest city: Kinshasa (pop., 1980 est., 3,000,000). Language: French, Swahili, Lingala, Kikongo, and other regional languages.

History: African scholars attribute the development of the Bantu languages to migrants from present-day *Cameroon and *Nigeria who settled most of what is now Zaire around 1000 B.C. These people, advanced in iron technology and agriculture, forced the native pygmies into small scattered areas. The Bantu in time coalesced into states, some of which governed large areas with complex administrative structures.

The arrival of the Portuguese explorer Diogo Cão at the mouth of the Congo in 1482 initiated ties with Europe. During the last third of the 19th century, the colonial ambitions of Belgium's King Leopold II focused on the Congo. Using the explorer-journalist Henry M. Stanley (the rescuer of David Livingstone) to lay the groundwork, Leopold set up the International Association of the Congo. At the subsequent Conference of Berlin (1884–1885), the European powers recognized the association's claim to the Congo Basin. Leopold declared himself head of the new Congo Free State, annexed additional lands, and ruthlessly exploited the natural resources as well as the people. This scandal ended his personal rule.

In 1908 the Belgian Parliament annexed the Congo. Although conditions improved, exploitation continued. Copper mining in the Katanga province was a law unto itself. A flow of population to the cities created new problems. Religious freedom was overshadowed by the privileges of the Roman Catholic Church. For the most part schools and hospitals—the country's education and health concerns—lay under church missions. Only in 1955, amid an awakened national consciousness, were two universities opened.

When plans for self-government proceeded too slowly, riots broke out in 1959. Belgium lost control. The Congo became independent June 30, 1960. The new republic threatened to fall apart, as the copper-rich Katanga province declared its independence. As unrest continued, United Nations forces intervened. UN General Secretary Dag Hammarskjöld, on an inspection tour in 1961, lost his life in an airplane crash. Internal conflicts continued until the late 1960s. From 1970 onward, the government, under the firm hand of Mobutu Sese Seko, has had a single political party— the Popular Movement of the Revolution— with a policy of centralized control, foreign economic participation, and an openness to the West.

Religion: African Traditional, about 50%; Christian, about 43%, of whom a small majority are Roman Catholic; the other 7% are of Muslim and other adherence. On government initiative in 1972, Protestant churches were united in the Church of Christ in Zaire (CCZ), a federation of government-recognized Christian communities.

The CCZ today embodies 60 confessional groups, including the Lutheran (below). Five of these communities—Presbyterian, Evangelical, Mennonite, Disciples, and Light— are members of the World Council of Churches. The 14,000 parishes of the CCZ have a total membership of eight to ten million. With assistance from the LWF and the WACC, a study completed in late 1984 showed the means of communication at a still early stage. A pooling of resources, at home and from abroad, is enabling development. Music is the prime communicator. Each congregation has from four to eight singing groups. The future may see distinctive African liturgies. Joyfully the gospel message resounds to the Zaire version of black spirituals.

Paralleling the CCZ is the five million-member Church of Christ on Earth by the Prophet Simon Kimbangu. Beginning in 1921 as an Independent church, the CCE/PSK claims to have drawn 87% of its present membership from the mainline mission churches. Its prophetic founder, Simon Kimbangu, feared by the authorities and jailed for life, died after 30 years in prison (1951). The CCE/PSK adheres to the Scriptures, confesses the Nicene Creed, and maintains extensive programs in education and social services. It has adherents in Zaire's neighboring countries and in Europe and since 1969 has been a member of the World Council of Churches. The CCE/PSK is perhaps the best-known example of indigenous African Christianity and is of significance for the church worldwide.

EVANGELICAL LUTHERAN COMMUNITY IN ZAIRE EAST (ELCZE)

(Communauté évangélique luthérienne du Zaire Est)
Member: LWF (1986)
Membership: 24,630**
Legal Representative: Ngoy Lusanga Mwanana
Main Pastor: The Rev. Ngoy Kasukuti
PO Box 259
Kalémié, Shaba

In the southeastern state of Shaba a group of Christians were strengthened in their faith by the programs of Radio Voice of the Gospel (see Africa Introduction) and desired Lutheran affiliation. Subsequent contacts with representatives of the *Evangelical Lutheran Church in Tanzania (ELCT) and the Lutheran World Federation led to scholarships in ELCT institutions for prospective church leaders. Swahili, the language of the Tanzanian schools, is understood by the Shabas.

The first pastoral candidate graduated from Makumira Theological College in 1975. He was ordained in *Tanzania by the ELCT's Bishop Moshi in the presence of 10 members of the congregation he would serve in Kalémié, Zaire. In 1976 a church body of several small congregations was received as a community within the Church of Christ in Zaire (see Zaire Introduction). Four years later the Lutheran community obtained official government recognition. A general assembly elects the legal adviser and spiritual leader, and an executive council coordinates the work.

The ELCZE has eight pastors: six Zairian and two Tanzanian. All were educated at Makumira, and five have been ordained in Zaire by Tanzanian bishops. The main work is in Kalémié, a commercial center on the west bank of Lake Tanganyika that handles the trade moving between Tanzania and Zaire. Here, with help from the LWF and a grant of land from the government, a church was built with facilities for worship, education, pastors' residences, and the church's diaconal service to the handicapped. The latter benefits from the service of women trained in the Kijota Women's Seminary of the Central Synod of the ELCT. Evangelists, graduates of three-year Bible schools in *Tanzania, are stationed in Lubumbashi (the

Shaba state capital and copper center) and in Kamina (an administrative and commercial center some distance northwest of the capital). Rented halls are used for worship. In the villages adjacent to these cities, homes become worship centers. Between the visits of the pastors, who alone administer the sacraments, elders lead the services of worship.

Encouragement for the church's development continues to come from the ELCT and its partners. A joint board meets annually in the ELCZE headquarters to discuss the needs of mission. Several visits and seminars led by Tanzanians as well as scholarship grants continue to develop leadership.

EVANGELICAL LUTHERAN COMMUNITY IN ZAIRE WEST (ELCZW)

(Communauté évangélique luthérienne du Zaire Ouest)
Membership: 17,200**
President and Legal Representative: The Rev. Kulungu-di-Kayidi
PO Box 70
Limété, Kinshasa

This church of 35 congregations, served by 30 ordained pastors and 22 assistants, has been seeking government recognition and Lutheran acceptance since 1968. Toward this end the LWF Department of Church Cooperation has provided counsel and leadership training grants. LWF scholarships have drawn students to the School of Theology at Meiganga, an institution of the *Evangelical Lutheran Church of Cameroon. A friendly and helpful relationship has thus been established between these two churches in this Francophone region of Africa.

Kinshasa, the country's capital and educational and cultural center, is the hub of the church's work. Centered in the far northwest near the Congo border, the breadth of Zaire lies between it and the Evangelical Lutheran Community in Zaire East. Nevertheless, the LWF has facilitated meetings between the leaders of the two churches so that the legal recognition of the ELCZ East can be extended to the ELCZ West and that a friendly working relationship will develop into a united church.

The church's theological institute in Kinshasa provides in-service courses for pastors.

The Bible institute in Tschela has three unordained teachers serving the needs of young people and mothers. The Congo congregation has a primary school with 250 students. The ELCZW also runs dispensaries in almost all of its eight districts. As in the other Zairian churches, choruses and choir singing are an important part of worship.

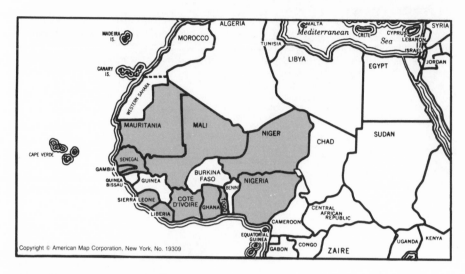

Copyright © American Map Corporation, New York, No. 19309

WESTERN AFRICA

West African countries here treated (situated east to west) are Nigeria, Togo, Ghana, Liberia, Sierra Leone, and Senegal. All but the latter three front on the Gulf of Guinea. English is the official language in three of them; French in the other three. These countries, and others in the region, have a proud early history. Their long connection with Europe and the Americas, including colonial rule, slave trade, etc., precedes their modern role as independent nations. Nigeria is the continent's most populous nation.

Lutherans in these lands are few, totaling under 185,000 baptized—about the same as in West-Central Africa (above). The oldest Lutheran work is in Liberia (1860); the newest, a Norwegian Lutheran Mission undertaking in Ivory Coast (1984). For the Joint Christian Ministry in West Africa (JCMWA), based in Nigeria, see Africa Introduction. A northern tier of nations—Mauritania, Mali, Niger—have been host to development projects under Lutheran auspices.

GHANA

A republic of West Africa on the Gulf of Guinea, Ghana is bordered by the Ivory Coast, Upper Volta, and *Togo. It is a member of the Commonwealth of Nations. Area: 238,533 sq. km. (92,098 sq. mi.). Pop. (1984 est.): 12,206,000. Cap. and largest city: Accra (pop., 1982 est., 1,045,400). Language: English (official); regional Sudanic dialects.

History: Modern Ghana (the former Gold Coast) bears the name of a medieval West African empire that attained its zenith about A.D. 1000. More recently the area comprised

the independent kingdoms of Gonja and Dagomba in the north, Ashanti in the center, and the Fanti states along the coast. Late in the 15th century the caravels of the Portuguese explorers arrived. The fortified trading base at Elmina (1482) was soon noted for its access to gold from mines in the interior. The exact whereabouts were also kept secret from the trans-Saharan caravans under Berber monopoly coming from the north. Elmina still stands, marking not only this region's first permanent contact with Europe but also the point from which the "factories" of the slave trade multiplied.

In time the Portuguese traders faced stiff competition from the Dutch, French, British, and Danish slavers as the demand for plantation labor in the Caribbean and the Americas remained high. Untold suffering burdened the generations before the slave trade was finally abolished during the 19th century. Thereafter most Europeans withdrew, but the British remained. They allied themselves with the Fanti, the commercial middlemen along the coast. Making common cause against the Ashanti further inland, the British eventually controlled both them and the Fanti. Known as the Gold Coast, the colony was enlarged when Britain was assigned the mandate over a part of *Togoland (1919).

Nationalist activity, begun in the interwar period, intensified after World War II. On March 6, 1957, Ghana became an independent country within the Commonwealth. In 1960 Premier Kwame Nkrumah, a Christian of Basel Mission antecedents, transformed Ghana into a republic with himself as president for life. Failing to meet the economic and democratic needs of his country, he was overthrown by a military coup in 1966. A tempestuous period followed, its repeated coups intensified by tribal rivalry and economic difficulties. In 1970 Ghana expelled most of its two million aliens, mainly Nigerians, who had, as laborers, failed to secure resident permits. In 1983 Nigeria returned the disfavor by expelling about a million Ghanians working in Nigeria. Since 1982 a Provisional National Defense Council (PNDC) has been the governing power in Ghana.

Religion (1980 est.): Traditional religions 21%, mainly in northern interior; Muslim 16%, mostly Malikite rite (Wala people are nearly all Muslim); Christian 63%. The Christians, comprising some 500 separate bodies, fall into three main categories: Roman Catholic, Anglican-Protestant, and Independent.

The Roman Catholics, gathered under the Cape Coast Archdiocese (1878) and seven other dioceses, account for some 40% of Ghana's Christians. At times growth has spurted. The Wa Diocese (interior northwest) numbered 50,000 in 1965; a decade later it was nearly six times that size.

On the Anglican and Protestant side, exemplifying the missionary efforts from abroad, are the Anglican, Methodist, Presbyterian, and Evangelical Presbyterian churches. The latter two bodies have both

Reformed and Lutheran heritage (see history, below). Together these four churches account for an estimated one million members. In Ghana they are termed "orthodox" churches. They are the mainstay of the Christian Council of Ghana (CCG; founded in 1929 as the Christian Council of the Gold Coast), and it is their common voice and agency.

A 1982 memorandum from the CCG to the government deplored the deterioration of the economy and the social and political injustices certain policies had caused. Through the CCG, the WCC has helped alleviate hunger and homelessness among the returning citizens from *Nigeria (1983). Continuing concern for the uprooted is monitored through the WCC Refugee Service and the CCG. Meanwhile, negotiations for an organic union of Protestant churches, begun in 1957 under the Ghana Church Union Committee, was greatly weakened by the withdrawal of the Anglican, the Presbyterian (1983), and most small church bodies, including the Lutheran (1977).

The newer indigenous independent church bodies, numbering over 400, emerged often as the result of disputes with the "orthodox" churches. For their emphasis on the Holy Spirit, prayer, and healing, they are called "spiritual" churches. Since many of their leaders are not well grounded in Christianity, their influence can be precarious. To meet the need for basic Christian teaching, the Mennonites in 1969 began informal Bible classes in certain spiritual churches. The enthusiastic reception as well as the support that came from the CCG's member churches resulted in the establishment of the Good News Training Center in Accra. For a time the Evangelical Lutheran Church of Ghana was a leading participant in this movement. When it withdrew (below), the opportunity to provide a teacher for independent pastors and laity was assumed by the *Lutheran Church in America (now *ELCA) in 1975.

Historically the first Protestant mission on the Gold Coast began in the 18th century when German Moravians, encouraged by the Danish coastal trading center, began to send missionaries. The first team, in 1737, included a mulatto. The climate was deadly. Thirty years later a larger team was sent. Still no advance—only graves. In 1828 the Evangelical (Basel) Missionary Society gave it a try. The missionaries sent were sturdy Pietists, mainly Lutherans from Württemberg. Gradually the work took hold, especially after Moravian converts from Jamaica arrived in 1843. By the end of the century the Twi language had been reduced to writing and a seminary established. Economically the people were helped by the introduction of cocoa from Cameroon by the Basel missionary, Mohr, in the 1880s. This laid the basis for an economic revolution.

During World War I, deprived of German staff, the Basel Mission had to withdraw, and the church became autonomous. Help came from the United Free Church of Scotland and the Netherlands Reformed Church. Today, as the Presbyterian Church of Ghana, with headquarters in Accra, it has a membership of over 261,000. After World War II the Evangelical Lutheran Church in Württemberg reestablished partnership with the Ghanian church it had helped to found.

The Evangelical Presbyterian Church in Ghana (EPC), with headquarters in Ho, in the Volta region, is the Ghanian branch of the Ewe Evangelical Church begun in Togoland in 1847 by the North German Mission Society, Bremen (see Togo). Despite the internment of the North German missionaries during World War I and the change of imperial rule, the church prospered under the leadership of well-trained indigenous teachers and pastors, a number of whom had been sent to Germany for higher education. At the request of the British government, Scottish missionaries assisted the church after both world wars. Later help came also from the Evangelical and Reformed Church in America, and assistance continues to come from its successor, the United Church of Christ. However the EPC again receives support from its founder, the North German Mission Society, which in turn links it with the *Evangelical Lutheran Church in Oldenburg (FRG).

Ghanian church leaders have contributed significantly to the ecumenical movement since World War II. Best known is the EPC's *Togo-born Christian Baeta (b. 1908), whose background and education combines the North German and Basel legacy. As a student in Basel (1930–1935), he mingled with peers of various continents and confessions—Lutheran, Reformed, United, Free Church. Later, as professor of theology at Trinity College, Legon, he contributed a clear African

voice in the International Missionary Council (IMC). He chaired this body (1959–1961) prior to its merger with the World Council of Churches. As to the significance of ecumenical meetings in Accra, the 1957 IMC there voted to merge with the WCC; and the 1974 Faith and Order meeting opened a next phase in church unity.

EVANGELICAL LUTHERAN CHURCH OF GHANA (ELCG)
Member: (P), CCG
Membership: 8000**
President: The Rev. Paul Kofi Fynn
PO Box 197
Kaneshie, Accra

This young church of some 32 congregations and stations in five of the nine regions of Ghana has six pastors and 53 trainees and lay leaders. Work began in 1960 when the *Lutheran Church–Missouri Synod (USA) sent its first missionary following an initial survey by the Evangelical Lutheran Synodical Conference. The venture began in the newly built government housing in suburban Accra, Kumasi, and the port cities of Tema and Takoradi, areas neglected by other churches. Although 40% of the residents claimed to be Christians, only a few were attending church or instructing their children. Some were from Nigeria and knew about the Lutheran church there. By 1966 four congregations had been formed and joined together to create the Evangelical Lutheran Church of Ghana. In 1971 the LCMS officially accepted the ELCG as a partner.

Church growth was handicapped by political strife and a lack of trained leaders. In 1964 two pastoral candidates were sent to the Lutheran Seminary in Obot Idim, *Nigeria. One was ordained in 1969; the other, a Nigerian, remained in his country. In 1970, when the government of Ghana ordered most Nigerians to leave, some of the congregations lost over half of their communicants in just a few weeks.

The exclusion of missionaries, the depressed world economy, and social changes going on throughout the country forced the church to decide on its future direction in ministry and mission. Work begun among the

Bimbos in 1969 was strengthened by a theological extension program for village evangelists (1971) and an agricultural project. The latter was aided by Lutheran World Relief (USA) and other agencies.

For a time the ELCG participated in the Ghana Church Union Committee, sent students to Trinity College (an interdenominational theological school), and, as already noted, cooperated with the Moravians in opening the Good News Training Center (GNTC) in Accra. These ecumenical activities, however, caused controversy within the ELCG, which it resolved by withdrawing from them in 1977. However the ELCG president maintains a relationship with the GNTC by serving on its board and teaching part time as a volunteer.

The ELCG continues in the Christian Council of Ghana and also participates in conferences and projects sponsored by the Lutheran World Federation in western Africa. The seminar on "Women and Development in Church and Society" (*Liberia, 1978) benefited from the participation of Ghanian women. The LWF Community Development Service assisted the congregation in Kumasi in establishing a center for child care and social services. World Service aided the ELCG during crisis when Ghanians were being deported from *Nigeria.

In spite of conflicts and reverses, the church found new avenues for mission in the late 1970s. The congregation in Tema sponsored a literacy program. Work among Muslims began in a village near Kumasi. An outreach to Ghanian seamen and their families was based in the port city of Takoradi. The first ordained pastor returned from overseas with training in communication to strengthen the church's radio and TV ministry. Further survey work in the Western, Brong-Ahafo, and Northern regions helped the ELCG to adopt an aggressive 12-year plan intended to guide its ministry and mission through 1990.

LIBERIA

A republic (1847) on the west coast of Africa bordered by *Sierra Leone, Guinea, and Ivory Coast. Area: 99,067 sq. km. (38,250 sq. mi.). Pop. (1984 est.): 2,160,000. Cap. and largest city: Monrovia (pop., 1980 est.,

243,000). Language: English (official) and tribal dialects.

History: The oldest African republic, Liberia was founded by the American Colonization Society (1821) for the purpose of resettling freed slaves in the continent of their forebears. Its territory was a grant from the local chiefs. The first of eventually 15,000 settlers arrived in 1822. Amid French and British colonial rivalry, Britain took the lead in declaring Liberia independent (1847). Domestically, friction between the native and the Americo-Liberian population continued into the 20th century, with the latter becoming the ruling class as well as an elite in education and wealth. The country's economy, tied to fluctuating export markets, faced periodic fiscal crises requiring outside aid. Its constitution modeled on that of the USA, the country was governed by the True Whig Party for nearly a century.

The military coup of April 12, 1980, marked the end of an era. The former president, William R. Tolbert, and other leaders were executed. Led by Samuel K. Doe, a 28-year-old enlisted sergeant, the new government professed high aims. Under the People's Redemption Council, corruption was proscribed and injustices combated. Measures were taken to strengthen the economy and to join all classes and peoples into a united Liberia. Civilian rule was promised for 1985, and attained.

Religion: Traditional (43.5%), especially among the inland people. Muslim (21%), strongest among the Vai tribe, with missionaries (Ahmadiya) from Egypt and Pakistan active since 1956. Christian, 35%.

Unlike some other countries south of the Sahara, Liberia has no really large church bodies, but the Liberian Baptist Convention and the United Methodist Church are the two largest. Both have their origins in America and trace their beginnings from the time of the early settlers. Baptists consider theirs an indigenous development, while Methodists advanced upon the arrival of the first missionaries (1833). Successively, other communions entered: Episcopal, Presbyterian, Lutheran, African Methodist Episcopal and AME Zion, Roman Catholic, as well as the Pentecostal movement and many smaller groups.

In 1982 most of the mainline Protestant communions and the Roman Catholics together formed the Liberian Council of

Churches (LCC). Behind it is an impressive legacy. Protestant ministers also contributed much to nation making. Four of the country's presidents were ordained clergy, including William Tolbert (above), who also headed the Baptist World Alliance (1967–1970). The formation of the LCC reflects the will to national unity as well as the spirit of ecumenism. As yet only the Lutheran and Presbyterian churches are members of the World Council of Churches.

Currently the Pentecostal movement is showing the most rapid growth. The older denominations, through their institutions and programs in health, education, and various other services, help undergird the social order, as exemplified in Cuttington College (Bong county) of the Episcopal Church. A telling force in spreading the gospel is radio station ELWA (Eternal Love Winning Africa), the Sudan Interior Mission's station near Monrovia. Its programs, produced locally, go out in English, French, Arabic, and 30 vernacular languages. Its Bible correspondence courses have enrolled a total of over 10,000 listeners.

LUTHERAN CHURCH IN LIBERIA (LCL)
Member: LWF (1966), WCC, AACC, LCC
Membership: 25,650**
Bishop: The Rt. Rev. Ronald J. Diggs
PO Box 1046
Monrovia

Organized in 1947, after 87 years in mission status, this church became fully autonomous in 1965 and elected one of its pastors, Roland J. Payne, bishop. The LCL joined the LWF the following year. Currently the church's 150 congregations and a similar number of preaching points, all grouped into 20 parishes, are served by 25 ordained pastors as well as by ordained deacons. Numerous other workers, including expatriates, are in health, education, and other services. The church structure combines congregational and synodical elements, providing for a balance between local responsibility and common action. Church headquarters in Monrovia include conference and transient facilities.

The members are mainly Kpelle and Loma people who speak these languages. The Kpelle live in the interior region drained by the St. Paul River; the Loma still deeper inland, near the Guinea border. They are mostly in subsistence farming, but over the years many young people have found employment in industry in the Monrovia area and elsewhere.

The LCL maintains a number of elementary and junior high schools as well as language centers in the Kpelle and in the Loma regions. The New Testament and parts of the Old are available in both these languages. Since 1946 the church's literacy work has contributed significantly to a population still predominantly illiterate. Literacy in English, a lesser part of the program, remains important for inter-tribal and international communication.

Beginning in 1976, LCL pastoral candidates received their education at the Gbarnga School of Theology, 220 kilometers inland from Monrovia. This initially Methodist institution is interdenominational, with professors and support being supplied also from Episcopalian and Lutheran sources. Since 1982 the LCL ordains women. Deacons prepare in a two-year course at the LCL Lay Training Center (1968) in Salayea (Loffa county). When ordained, they are authorized to administer the sacraments in the absence of a pastor. Also in Salayea is the high school for Christian workers (1947), with a student body of 250.

Christian education at the congregational level has been strenthened by a long-term curriculum project begun by the LWF Department of Studies. In cooperation with the Liberian and Sierra Leone United Methodists, materials have been produced that are now used in all the public schools of Liberia.

In health work, Curran Hospital in Zorzor (Loffa) includes a school for practical nursing and midwifery and serves as base for mobile medical services to villages in the region. The Phoebe Hospital and Nurses' Training School, founded in 1921 by Lutherans from America, became interdenominational in 1965 with Methodist and Presbyterian participation. Relocated at that time to Suakoko (Bong county), near Gbarnga, its contribution to the country's health services has been significant. Since 1970 Phoebe has been a government-sponsored hospital, but the *Lutheran Church in America (now a part of the *Evangelical Lutheran Church in America) still contributes one-sixth of the operating costs in addition to providing a physician, two nursing instructors, a pastor, and an engineer. The registered nurse degree program is run jointly by Phoebe and nearby Cuttington College, the Episcopal-related institution. Today 95% of the hospital personnel are Liberian.

The LCL's use of the electronic media ties in with Radio ELWA (above). It includes LCL worship services, preaching, and the singing of indigenous hymns. Over the national TV station, and with LWF help, the LCL has been involved since the mid-1960s in an hour-long program each week. Called "Concern," the program treats social, ethical, and spiritual issues. Its outspoken stand on moral values has made it a popular ecumenical venture backed by the Liberian Council of Churches.

An example of media effectiveness is the response of the Gbandi, jungle-bound people in Loffa county. LCL programs via ELWA drew enthusiastic pleas from the people for a local church. In 1972 villagers completed two chapels, having carried the building materials—cement blocks and corrugated roofing—on their heads over bush trails in a 48-hour hike. They also cleared landing strips to enable LCL's Cessna plane to bring medical aid or to transport seriously ill patients to a hospital.

Also from the Pallipo people in remote eastern Liberia came repeated requests for the services of the church. Barriers of language and finance were finally overcome in the late 1970s when a cooperative project was worked out that included the Pallipo people, LCL, LWF/CDS, the Liberian government, and three LWF member churches—the *Church of Sweden, the *Evangelical Lutheran Church in Bavaria, and the *Lutheran Church in America. Interest and assistance also came from the Christian Medical Commission (WCC), Canadian Lutheran World Relief, and the Churches' Development Service (FRG). Thus, evangelism, education, medical services, and agricultural improvement were introduced. Progress, slower than anticipated, continues. In 1980 a Pallipo student graduated from the Gbarnga School of Theology and was ordained to become a pastor to his own people.

In helping to discover and support new avenues of service and mission, women, individually and collectively, play an important role. In a Muslim area where a new palm plantation was drawing workers from Bong and Loffa counties, a Christian woman called her neighbors together to express her faith and her desire to have a church. A house congregation was formed; later a church was built and dedicated by the bishop. A Muslim husband converted to the Christian faith—the first in LCL's history. This was an inspiration to the entire church and revealed the importance of Christian/Muslim dialog.

Lutheran Church Women of Liberia (LCWL), a churchwide organization, gives women an opportunity for education, fellowship, service, and influence. Drawn into a wider African fellowship through the LWF, already in 1978, Liberian, Nigerian, and Ghanian women, meeting in Liberia, requested the LWF to give more support to African women desiring to study theology. In 1982 the LCL convention voted almost unanimously to admit qualified women to the church's ordained ministry.

● ● ●

The LCL is the product of work begun in 1860 by Morris Officer and other missionaries sent from North America by antecedent bodies of the *Lutheran Church in America. David A. Day, a physician and pastor who served from 1874 to 1897, was the first to survive the difficult climate for any length of time. The mission itself advanced only slowly. Leading Protestant denominations, as noted above, were already active in the Monrovia area when Officer arrived. Therefore, he set up his station, Muhlenberg (popularly, Millsburg), 40 kilometers inland from the city, on the St. Paul River. Officer learned the ways of the people, opened a school for boys, and began to evangelize. A school for girls came in 1898. It was 1908 before the next station was opened, up river at Kpolopelle in the Kpelle county. Then followed Sonoyea, east of the river. In the 1920s the Zorzor station, in the Loma county, reached the farthest into the country's interior.

Developments were similar in these and other places: evangelism, education, health services, and the forming of congregations with outlying preaching and visitation points. Among the missionaries long remembered is Esther Bacon. Her midwifery and concern for the Kpelle and Loma women were said to have destroyed the traditional hold of medicine men.

Gradually indigenous leaders emerged who were given opportunities for education in American theological seminaries. Among them was Roland J. Payne, the son of a chief. In 1965, when the *Lutheran Church in America agreed that the LCL was ready for autonomous status, Payne was elected bishop. He served in this capacity through a period of rapid church growth as well as a period of national unrest and economic difficulties. He retired in 1984.

Since 1972 the LCL has been striving for economic self-sufficiency. This was encouraged by a planned reduction of funds from the Lutheran Church in America and aided by an LWF program of church economy and stewardship. Progress has been made, especially in the cities where members have cash-producing jobs. The church encourages members who fled their farms during the coup to return to the land and produce food for themselves. It also expects congregations to provide additional food and wood for the market from farms set aside for this purpose.

LCL, long left to the care of its American parent body, now has the added interest and support of a number of European churches. Besides those supporting the Pallipo project (above), the Danish Evangelical Mission (Dansk Ethioper Mission) began in 1980 to assist the church with personnel. The Church of Sweden Mission provides a pastor in Yekepa, where many Swedish workers are employed in the iron mining industry. LCL, in turn, has provided staff for LWF mission in Africa. LCL is also a charter member of the Joint Christian Ministry in West Africa.

EVANGELICAL LUTHERAN MISSION, MISSOURI SYNOD
Membership: 350**
Manager: Roland Newton
PO Box 3577
Monrovia

Situated in the Guma district of Upper Loffa county, this is an embryonic church among the Mende people. The mission was begun in 1978 by the *Lutheran Church–Missouri Synod after two exploratory surveys showed that only about 10% of the population is Christian. Most of the people are animists (African Traditional) and Islam is making

inroads. Outreach of the mission extends to the neighboring Kisi people among whom Lutheran Bible Translators (an LCMS affiliate) has a team at work. Besides its manager, the mission is served by two expatriate missionaries, four lay preachers, and others.

NIGERIA

A federal republic (1960) of 21 states plus the federal capital district, Nigeria is a member of the Commonwealth. Located on the Gulf of Guinea, its neighbors are (from west to east) Benin, Niger, *Chad, and *Cameroon. Area: 923,768 sq. km. (356,669 sq. mi.). Pop. (1984 est.): 94,502,000, comprising (1978 est.) Hausa 21.5%; Yoruba 21%; Ibo 18.4%; Fulani 11.1%; other 28%. Cap. and largest city: Lagos (pop., 1982 est., 1,404,000). Ibadan (pop., 1982 est., 1,009,000) is the largest purely black African city anywhere. Language: English (official), Hausa, Yoruba, Ibo, local dialects.

History: Antecedents of modern Africa's most populous nation are diverse and emerge at various times from at least 700 B.C., as archaeological finds reveal and later records enlarge.

In the vast northern plateau east of the Niger, today's Fulani and Hausa people have their roots in distinctive cultures. The Fulani, a mixture of black and Berber (aboriginal Caucasoid people of North Africa) heritage, were herders who spread over large areas of northwest Nigeria. Their outside contacts were with Arab world. The steady trans-Sahara trade (a Berber monopoly) brought foreign products in exchange for gold and slaves, thus supplying the commercial world's need for coinage and labor. Meanwhile the black Hausa developed a more agricultural life. Yet, in time, their language became the lingua franca in much of West Africa. By the 11th century most of the Fulani had become Muslim. Organized political power developed in the Lake Chad region and spread southwestward. The kingdom of Bornu endured some five centuries, until its collapse about 1850.

In the coastal region west of the Niger, the Yoruba created an early and extensive urbanized culture. The oldest city, Ife, dates from before A.D. 1300. Other old cities are

Lagos and Ibadan. The traditional artwork of Ife and other centers ranks high in today's western world. The Yoruban kingdom of Oyo prospered as one of the largest states in West Africa but went into decline after 1700 under the impact of Fulani invasions and European interventions through the slave trade.

East of the Niger the Ibo people developed a sense of unity that overarched their predominantly village culture. In the modern period their capacity to govern, along with their position on Christianity and education, made them prominent in the struggle for independence after World War II.

As in *Ghana and elsewhere, the slave trade with the Caribbean and the Americas was a prolonged torment in which various European nations took part. After its abolition in the 19th century, the British stayed on as competitors with the French. The latter eventually settled for modern Niger and Chad, in the interior, while the British, in their antislavery drive, first seized Lagos (1861) and gradually turned the rest of the country into a colony, holding it until independence in 1960.

Since then this nation, rich in resources and well-educated leaders, has moved from crisis to crisis. Two military coups in 1966 were followed by civil war when the Ibo people in the eastern region seceded and formed the short-lived Republic of Biafra (1967–1970). The consequent suffering aroused the conscience of people from many lands, bringing aid from governments as well as from nongovernmental agencies. The LWF World Service won high credibility with the Nigerian government for its rehabilitation and relief work following the war. However, the nation's almost total dependence on petroleum exports resulted in economic reverses. Attempts to increase agricultural production and stem the drift of people into the cities have had limited success. In January 1983 Nigeria expelled two million illegal immigrants, about half of them Ghanians (see Ghana).

Religion: Muslims and Christians are about evenly divided in numbers. Islam is strongest in the northern states. Traditional religion, now a small segment, is most prevalent in the central plateau. Protestants are slightly more numerous than Roman Catholics. Wesleyan Methodists from Britain, Southern Baptists from USA, and Jamaican

Presbyterians all began work here before the middle of the 19th century. In 1893 the Sudan Interior Mission, a Canadian agency, planted what is now the Evangelical Churches of West Africa, one of the largest denominations in Nigeria.

The Fellowship of Christian Churches in Nigeria (FCCN, 1955) is a loose federation of eight separate church bodies. Four of the members, one being the Lutheran Church of Christ (below), owe their beginning to the Sudan United Mission, an international agency founded in Britain in 1904. Its dynamic pioneer, Dr. Karl Kumm, a German by birth and education, had hoped to place missions all across Africa in the Muslim-dominated lands south of the Sahara in the broad Sahel zone. The word *Sudan,* a term used long ago by Muslim Arabs, denotes the black people of Africa.

Pentecostals, Apostolics, and Assemblies of God are more recent. Independent spiritual churches have found fertile ground in Nigeria. They number in the hundreds and increase every year. The Nigerian Association of Aladura (praying) Churches (1960), about a hundred bodies strong, claims a total membership of over a million people. This is but one of several councils linking independent churches. The Nigerian Evangelical Fellowship has 10 member bodies.

Founded in 1930, the Christian Council of Nigeria (CCN), with nine member bodies, includes the large Anglican, Methodist, Baptist, Presbyterian, Lutheran Church of Christ (below), and Qua Ibo churches. It has established a number of programs and institutions, including the Institute of Church and Society (1964) in Ibadan. In 1976 the CCN joined with the Roman Catholics to form the Christian Association of Nigeria (CAN). The secretary of the CCN serves as the executive secretary of this association.

LUTHERAN CHURCH OF CHRIST IN NIGERIA (LCCN)

(Ekklesiyar Kristi Ta Lutheran A Nigeria)
Member: LWF (1961), CCN, CAN, FCCN
Membership: 88,779
Bishop: The Rt. Rev. David Windibiziri
PO Box 21
Numan, Gongola State

Situated in Gongola State in northeastern Nigeria near the Cameroon border, this church of 1092 congregations and about 100 pastors brings together people speaking about 50 different languages and dialects. Since becoming autonomous in 1954, its growth and influence in a strongly Muslim area has been phenomenal. This can be attributed in part to the emphasis the founding mission placed on lay training and participation. The bulk of the congregational work is carried on by unordained evangelists and catechists. A group of congregations form a district in charge of a pastor who administers the sacraments. Several districts comprise a division with a dean at the head. A general church council meets twice a year to decide on essential matters concerning the life of the church. Since 1973 a bishop, elected for five years, has led the church, and, with the help of an executive committee, directs the work, including that of the mission-founded institutions.

The people served by the LCCN are mainly poor subsistence farmers and cattle herders living on dry savannah land. In an attempt to strengthen farm life, the church, with help from the LWF Community Development Service, established the Mbamba Christian Rural Center in 1971. Here, three miles south of Yola, 500 acres of savannah land were cleared and facilities built to enable 48 families at a time to have intensive agricultural training, Bible instruction, and other practical education for a two-year period. About 500 families have had this experience; some move to new areas as volunteer evangelists. The center also provides short courses.

For a rural-oriented church, the movement to the towns of many members has increased its responsibilities and also its mission. Yola, the state capital, and Numan, the church headquarters, now have English worship services and special programs for young people.

The need for a well-trained ministry is urgent. The sharp decrease in missionary personnel has forced the church to raise its own professional standards at the three Bible schools where evangelists, catechists, and other workers are trained and to expand this program by establishing local Bible schools. Theological education by extension (TEE), begun in 1975 by a Danish missionary, is now carried on by one Nigerian and two Danish theologians. The materials produced for this program are reaching about a thousand students in their villages.

LCCN's pastors are educated at the Theological College of Northern Nigeria near Bukuru, an institution of the Fellowship of Christian Churches in Nigeria, of which the LCCN is a founding member. With the help of partner churches, the LCCN helps the school meet many needs, including higher standards and concern for the education of pastors' wives and women candidates.

The Theological College also trains qualified teachers of religion in the public schools. This provides the churches with continued influence in the community schools they once owned and operated. The two high schools and a teachers' college of the church were taken over by the government in 1973. A new institution, the Brønnum Lutheran Seminary, was opened in Dashen in 1986 with an enrollment of 28 students.

Dispensaries, maternity wards, child welfare programs, and a leprosarium are other avenues of mission. These institutions as well as the schools require continued overseas support. However, at the parish level, self-support is generally in effect.

The Muryar Bishara Communication Center in Jos, owned and operated by the LCCN, produces programs in Hausa that are broadcast over local stations in the north of Nigeria. Prior to 1977 the programs were broadcast by Radio Voice of the Gospel in *Ethiopia, and from September 1982 to May 1985 over Africa No. 1 in Gabon. This introduced the Christian faith to countless Hausa-speaking people. Radio proclamation is supplemented by a cassette ministry (on such subjects as health, development, evangelism, and music) as well as Christian literature preparation and translation. A chain of bookstores in the main towns and villages disseminate this literature.

Through evangelism the church continues to grow in numbers and zeal. The method is to send lay evangelists and their families into new territories. There they settle, farm to support themselves, and share the gospel with their neighbors. In 1983 six evangelist families moved into the Atlantica mountains, southeast of Yola, among the Kuma people. By 1987 there were 30 evangelists living among these primitive mountaineers. About 1000 were attending worship services, 10 had been baptized, another 60 were completing their instruction, and 300 were in an introductory baptismal class. A Bible school has been established. A new project in the federal capital district of Abuja, surveyed by the pastor who was elected bishop in 1987, shows similar promise.

The LCCN continues its partnership with the Danish branch of the Sudan United Mission. Work began in 1913 with the arrival of Dr. Niels Brønnum, his Scottish bride, Margaret C. Young, also a medical doctor, and Dagmar Rose, a nurse from Copenhagen. The Province of Yola, Gongola State today, had been assigned to the newly formed independent (Danish) Sudan Mission (1911) by the Sudan United Mission (above). During the war years the Danish-derived United Evangelical Lutheran Church in the United States came to its assistance and continued the relationship through the merged body, the *American Lutheran Church, now *ELCA. Until 1960, when the first indigenous pastor was elected president, administration was in the hands of the missionaries.

The LCCN is a member of the Council of Evangelical Churches of Northern Nigeria. It has also joined with other churches and the LWF in forming the Joint Christian Ministry in West Africa, an outreach and concern for the Fulani-speaking people (see Africa Introduction). Headquarters in Jos are on LCCN territory.

LUTHERAN CHURCH OF NIGERIA (LCN)

Member: LWF (1973), ILC
Membership: 60,000**
President: The Rev. Dr. Nelson Udo
Unwene
Obot Idim Ibesikpo
Uyo, Akwa Ibom State

The 248 congregations of this autonomous church (1963) are coordinated and advised by a synod composed of the ordained pastors and two elected delegates from each congregation. The LCN is served by 42 pastors, 31 evangelists, and more than 100 lay preachers.

The church has its headquarters in Obot Idim, Uyo, in a densely populated rural area. The people are mainly Ibibios, a tribe that shares many of the characteristics of the Ibos, who are traditionally ultrademocratic, energetic, and individualistic. Most of the members are small farmers. However, because of the overpopulation and the impoverished soil,

some are leaving the area for other rural districts or the cities. Congregations have been established in Calabar, Port Harcourt, Lagos, Ibadan, Sapele, Oshogbo, Uyo, Ikot Ekpene, Ogaje, and other cities. There, too, land is scarce, and it is difficult to obtain building sites.

The history of the Lutheran Church of Nigeria has several unique features. The Ibesikpo people, living inland from Calabar along the Qua Ibo River, had been reached by three conservative mission groups from Britain. An indigenous United Ibesikpo Church was formed. However, confusion developed when the Qua Ibo Faith Mission refused to baptize infants as had been the practice of the original Free Scottish Presbyterian Mission and later of the Primitive Methodist Mission. The Ibesikpo congregations, numbering about 60, were therefore determined to conduct their own schools and to train their own pastors. They gathered money and in 1928 sent one of their own evangelists, Jonathan Ekong, to the United States for pastoral education. There he learned that the Lutheran Synodical Conference, led by the Missouri Synod, was seeking an African field of work in response to a strong movement, backed by sacrificial giving, of its black members in the south. Jonathan appealed to the conference for help.

After a field survey by a commission of the conference and another by Nigerian church leaders, an agreement was reached. Dr. and Mrs. Henry Nau, former missionaries to India, were sent in 1936 to begin a ministry to the 16 waiting congregations and to prepare the way for the corps of workers who followed. When the news of the Lutherans' arrival spread, delegations came from other clans and villages requesting services. The work moved forward. Outstations developed into districts. Schools—primary, secondary, adult, vocational, teachers' training—plus a hospital, seminary, radio station, printing press, and bookstore were all established before the mid-1950s. During World War II and the civil war, missionaries had to leave the country. This prepared the church for greater independence. In 1963 one of its own pastors was elected president.

The civil war caused great hardship but also broadened the outlook of the church and the scope of its evangelism efforts. During this same period of political unrest and hoped-for independence, there were pastors who left the LCN, taking their congregations with them to form church bodies of their own. These sought and often found encouragement and financial aid among ultraconservative Lutheran groups in the USA.

Discouragements and losses were balanced by new areas of growth. The church applied for and was received into LWF membership (1973). The radio studio at Uyo embarked on new programs for rural development and health education using Efik as well as English. The seminary at Obot Idim expanded its facilities to include concern for students' wives. Theological education by extension began training lay preachers in "tentmaking ministry." After 20 years of hard work among the Ukelle, Bokyi, Yala, and Yachi people in the dry savannah area around Ogoja came encouraging signs of hope. With help from the LWF Community Development Service, a well-digging project brought clear water to 20 villages. Several of the chief citizens of these villages accepted Christ. This had an influence on many others. New requests for preachers of the Word continue from all sides. In April 1976 the church celebrated 40 years of fruitful relationship with the Lutheran Church–Missouri Synod. On that occasion the mission work was completely integrated into the life of the church.

Present efforts for renewal and restructuring focus on ministry at the congregational, parish, and circuit levels. After an intensive study of the problem of polygamy, the LCN's ministerial conference voted unanimously for a new attitude toward polygamists who have sincerely converted to the Christian faith.

More encouragement came to the LCN in 1982. The largest defecting group of the 1970s returned to the fold, and discussions began with two other groups. Meanwhile, work among the Khana, Eleme, Izon, and Ekajuk people was getting under way. Dialog also began with the Lutheran Church of Christ in Nigeria (above) regarding possible areas of cooperation, such as ministry to the Fulani and to urban areas. And, finally, the long-awaited construction of a church and community center for the Resurrection congregation in Lagos began. A swampy piece of land—allotted the LCN in 1979, 10 years after the downpayment—increased the cost

of construction. However, sacrificial stewardship on the part of the 250 baptized members and aid from the Lutheran Church–Missouri Synod have made possible a project that will serve the surrounding community as well as Lutherans from both church bodies moving into this most densely populated city in all Africa. The LWF Department of Church Cooperation has also given construction aid for this significantly located congregation.

SENEGAL

Senegal, a West African republic within the French Community (1958). Area: 196,722 sq. km. (75,955 sq. mi.). Pop. (1984 est.): 6,352,000. Cap. and largest city: Dakar (pop., 1979 est., 978,500). Language: French (official), Fulani, Dyola, Malinke, and other tribal dialects.

History: Archaeological and other evidence reveals Wolof and Serer people migrating into this area from the northeast around the sixth century A.D. and the Tukolor around the ninth. The Tukolor dominated from the 10th to the 14th centuries and accepted Islam during the 11th. This precipitated the Morocco-based Almoravid state that included Ghana. During the 15th century the Wolofs gained power, and the first Europeans, the Portuguese, entered the scene, followed by Dutch and French (1638). As French influence extended farther inland, so did the slave trade. Britain took over in 1763, establishing Senegambia, its first African colony. In 1815 France regained its holdings and by a policy of assimilation gradually drew the country into the francophone orbit with Dakar the administrative base of French West Africa. By 1946 French citizenship was extended to all Senegalese. Subsequently Senegal became an autonomous republic (1958) within the French Community. Democratic institutions and a multi-party system thrive. In February 1982 Gambia, the independent enclave in the southwest, joined Senegal in forming the Senegambia Confederation. Retaining individual sovereignty, they have joint defense, foreign, and monetary policies. Since the early 1970s Senegal has been seriously affected by the African drought.

Religion: Muslim 91%; Christian 6%, Traditional 3%. Roman Catholic missions began in the 15th century, and today all but a small fraction of the Christians are Roman Catholics. In 1862 the Paris Mission began Protestant work. Since World War II a number of small conservative missions, mainly from the USA, have taken up work. They are joined in the Evangelical Fellowship of Senegal. The government encourages the various religious groups, without discrimination, to be involved in development and to manifest the importance of a spiritual dimension to life.

Lutherans are newcomers to the Senegalese scene. The Finnish Evangelical Lutheran Mission (FELM, formerly Finnish Missionary Society) began work among the Serere-speaking people in 1974. A decade later there were 28 small congregations, with a total membership of 1400, forming eight parishes in southwestern Senegal. Most of the members come from a group that dissociated itself from the Assemblies of God and sought acceptance by the FELM. Their repeated requests received serious attention, and an extended period of instruction followed. The leading evangelists were further instructed by Finnish missionaries. One of them was ordained in 1984 along with two other Senegalese who had attended the FELM Bible school in Fatick, some distance southeast of Dakar. Here, as well as in two coastal cities—M'bour, to the south of Dakar, and St. Louis, to the north—FELM urban work centers on students and other young people, and on women and children. High priority goes to Bible translation, literacy work, and the training of nationals as teachers.

The FELM is not the only Lutheran contingent in Senegal. In 1975 the FELM and the Evangelical Lutheran Church in *Namibia (ELOC, now ELCIN) worked out an agreement to share this mission advance. For a number of years this complex partnership was tested, and the lessons learned are reflected in a revised agreement.

The *American Lutheran Church (now *ELCA), in consultation with partner churches in *Cameroon, the *Central African Republic, and *Nigeria, began work among the Fulani-speaking people in 1979. Although the mission is recognized as the Evangelical Lutheran Church of Senegal (Eglise évangélique luthérienne du Sénégal), no congregations have as yet been formed. The Département de promotion humaine has granted permission for service projects in central and northern Senegal around the towns of Linguére, Tiel, and Ndioum. At present they include primary health care units and small garden projects. The ELCA and the FELM are beginning a joint missionary action in Ndioum, and two missionaries have already been sent to the area. An Urban Ministry Center in Yeumbeul, a Pulaar-speaking suburb of Dakar, is the latest project. It provides a library and literacy classes. In 1986, 24 students were enrolled. Drought relief programs have been subsidized by Lutheran World Relief (USA).

All the missions and churches mentioned above are members of the Joint Christian Ministry in West Africa (JCMWA), an agency with special concern for strengthening mission among the Fulani-speaking people, including those in Senegal (see Africa Introduction).

SIERRA LEONE

Sierra Leone, a West African republic (1961), member of the Commonwealth of Nations, is situated adjacent to Liberia. Area: 71,740 sq. km. (27,699 sq. mi.). Pop. (1987 est.): 3,823,100. Cap. and largest city: Freetown (pop. 464,776). Language: English (official); native tongues.

History: The original inhabitants, the Temne, saw the arrival of Portuguese navigators (1460), who named the region "Lion Mountains." European trade developed, but proportionately few slaves were taken. Arab traders and Fulani-speaking people from present Guinea won many Temne for Islam. British interests prevailed when the Sierra Leone Company was formed and in 1792 resettled 1100 freed slaves from Nova Scotia and founded Freetown. Others came from Jamaica. By 1864 some 50,000 freed slaves had come. Connections with the Gold Coast (today's *Ghana) were close until Sierra Leone became a separate British colony (1896) and the interior a British protectorate. White settlers plied commerce and agriculture and staffed the government. The colony had strategic value during two world wars, but in 1961 gained independence.

Religion: Traditional, 51%; Muslim, 39%; Christian, 10%—Protestant and Anglicans,

6%; Roman Catholic, 4%. Among the non-Roman, 12 denominations are full members of the United Christian Council of Sierra Leone (UCCSL, 1924). There is also an SL Evangelical Fellowship. Methodists, first on the scene, far outnumber other Protestants, but are divided into several church bodies. Baptists, Pentecostals, and many other groups are active, as well as the Sierra Leone Church (Anglican).

Lutherans are among the newcomers, and an organized church body is in process. Grace (Lutheran) Church, on Campbell Street, Freetown, is served by the Rev. J. E. Max Brown. Persons returning from study in Europe and North America in the early 1980s gave the initial impulse. The membership, numbering about 700, has a high proportion of young people. Assisting Pastor Brown are four evangelists, active in various parts of town. The background of some members is United Brethren, a North American church body of Methodist affinity and German antecedents that had begun mission work in Sierra Leone in 1855. These new Lutherans, dynamic and enterprising—they have bought a former Brethren church—are being encouraged locally and internationally, especially from the Lutheran Church in *Liberia, and from the LWF Department of Church Cooperation in Geneva.

• • •

Lutheran Bible Translators (Private Mail Bag 139, Freetown), a recognized service organization of the Lutheran Church–Missouri Synod and also affiliated with Wycliffe Bible Translators, has been active in Sierra Leone for some years. Its linguistic staff, composed of about 10 persons, has been translating the Scriptures into four of the nation's ethnic languages: Krio (a form of English-African Creole which serves in parts of the country as a lingua franca, like Swahili in East Africa), as well as Limba, Loko, and Kono. The exacting task of translating, often done in more remote parts of the country, expresses the prefix of the LBT official title: Messengers of Christ.

TOGO

Togo, a West African republic situated between Ghana on the west and Benin on the east. Area: 56,785 sq. km. (21,925 sq. mi.). Pop. (1984 est.): 2,947,000. Cap. and largest city: Lomé (pop., 1980 est., 283,000). Language: French (official), Ewe, Kabye, and over 40 tribal languages.

History: Present-day Togo, the eastern part of what was Togoland, is an area consisting principally of Ewe people in the south and Voltaic-speaking ethnic groups in the north. During the 17th and 18th centuries, the Ewe were raided by the Ashanti (from present-day *Ghana), who took captives and sold them as slaves to European traders penetrating the area. In 1884 Gustav Nachtigal, a German explorer, signed treaties with several coastal rulers. Soon thereafter a German protectorate over south Togoland was recognized at the Conference of Berlin. By 1890 German military expeditions had also gained control of north Togoland. Germans fostered the development of agriculture, trade, and communication, but they also aroused resentment by levying direct taxes and forcing labor. In 1914 the British and French easily captured the land.

The League of Nations in 1922 divided the region into two mandates, one French and one British. After World War II, in 1946, they became trust territories of the United Nations. British Togoland, in 1956, joined independent *Ghana; and on April 27, 1960, French Togoland became the independent Republic of Togo. Its first years of independence were stormy, but since 1967 it has had a fairly stable military government under President Eyadéma. Togo maintains ties with both France and the Federal Republic of Germany, which provide it with economic aid. Relations with Ghana are strained, due in part to old tribal antagonism. In 1983 Togo was deluged by a huge influx of Togolese and Ghanian nationals who had been expelled from Nigeria in the wake of rising unemployment in that country.

Religion: Traditional religions are strong, in some areas as high as 70%, with an overall average of 46%. Islam (17%), introduced in the 18th century and later aided by German colonial policy, is strongest in the north (where missionaries were not permitted until 1913) and in the cities. Mosques are being built throughout the country.

Christianity (37%), strongest in the south among the Ewe people, is 25% Roman Catholic. The earliest Protestants were immigrants from the Gold Coast or local people trained in Christian schools there. By 1870 British Methodists were working in the coastal Anécho area.

German missionary work preceded German control. The Bremen Mission, now part of the North German Mission Society (NMG), began work as early as 1847 among the Ewe. The expulsion of the German missionaries at the beginning of World War I encouraged self-reliance in the congregations. This remained strong even when help came from the Paris Mission and the United Church Board for World Mission. Andreas Aku (1863–1931), educated in mission schools and also in Germany, personified brilliantly an indigenous leadership and the striving of Ewe Christians for unity above political boundaries. Aku became the first president of the autonomous Ewe Evangelical Church (1922). Divided later, it continues as the Evangelical Presbyterian Church (see Ghana Introduction) and the Evangelical Church in Togo, the largest Protestant church in the country. It carries on extensive educational and social work aided also by the founding mission, the NMG, the agency through which

the *Evangelical Lutheran Church in Oldenburg, FRG, does its overseas work.

According to the Togo constitution, all religions are "respected." However in 1978 the People's Party of Togo banned 20 religious bodies, including Jehovah's Witnesses and various indigenous Pentecostal groups, on the grounds that sects were multiplying at an alarming rate and were not contributing to the social development of the country.

LUTHERAN CHURCH IN TOGO
(Eglise luthérienne au Togo)
Member: CCT
Membership: 1343**
Pastor: The Rev. Walter L. De Moss
PO Box 53
Dapaon

This new church is served by two missionary pastors of the *Lutheran Church–Missouri Synod (USA). Since work began in 1980, six congregations have been formed in the vicinity of Lokpano among the Moba people. A clinic, built by the LCMS, is maintained by the government.

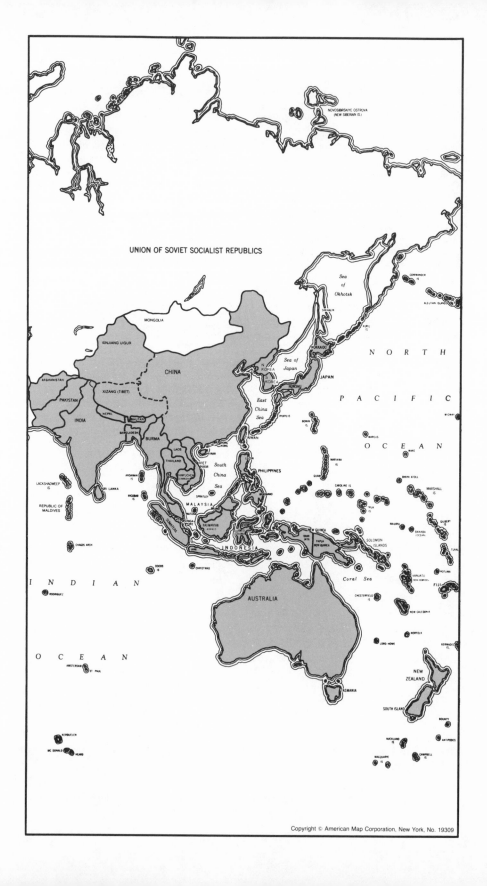

UNION OF SOVIET SOCIALIST REPUBLICS

Copyright © American Map Corporation, New York, No. 19309

ASIA/PACIFIC————————————

The proportionately few Christians in this vast geographic expanse (minus the Middle East and Asian *USSR, which are described elsewhere) and the concentration of nearly two-thirds of the human family within its borders make it desirable to approach the continents of Asia and Australia and the adjacent islands together. Organizations in this area—the Christian Conference of Asia (CCA), for example— prefer this inclusive view. Lutheran church or mission enterprises in the following countries, by the most recent figures (1988), claim about 4,800,000 adherents. Limitation of space and lack of information on minor mission undertakings account for their omission here. For our purposes, this vast area—stretching from Pakistan to New Zealand and from India to Japan—is subdivided as follows:

I. Asia

China Area—People's Republic of China, Hong Kong, Taiwan
East Asia—Japan, Korea, Philippines
Indian Subcontinent—Bangladesh, Bhutan, Burma, India, Nepal, Pakistan, Sri Lanka
Southeast Asia—Indonesia, Malaysia/Singapore, Thailand

II. Pacific

Australasia—Australia, New Zealand, Papua New Guinea

Area: Asia (omitting the *Middle East and Asian *USSR), 38,559,673 sq. km. (15,023,547 sq. mi.). Pop. (1984 est.): 3,027,662,000. Six of the world's most heavily populated nations —the People's Republic of China, India, Japan, Indonesia, Pakistan, Bangladesh—are located in this area and account for about one-half of the world's entire population today. The Pacific of our concern covers an area of 8,413,844 sq. km. (3,248,651 sq. mi.) and has a population of 22,173,000 (1985 est.).

History

Asia and the Pacific together reveal the widest spread in racial and cultural diversity; from the aborigines in the heart of Australia to the countless descendants of those ancient civilizations arising in the valleys of the Indus and Ganges in India and the Yellow River in China. To these the periodic thrusts from the Middle East must be added. Millennia of intermingling, intensified by a European admixture after the 16th century, have culminated in a new era of Asian nationhood. The problems of a colonial past (some Asians have called it the Vasco da Gama era [1498–1945], after the Portuguese navigator) have been replaced by new ones. The

147

politics of living together as neighboring and interdependent nations in a progressively technological age are seen as being equally important alongside the economics of supporting life. The complications of poverty and huge population increases have mounted immensely over the past four decades. The Bandung Conference (Indonesia) in 1955 remains a landmark in the determination of the then 29 recently independent Asian (and African) nations to cooperate in economic and cultural affairs and to oppose colonialism.

Religion

Of the three religions of monotheism cradled in the Middle East—Judaism, Christianity, and Islam—the latter has made the most massive impact on Asia. It is important to bear in mind the region of origin and the eastward thrust of all three of these faiths, each surpassing the previous one in numbers and present extent. From the Arab and Persian Middle East, Islam extended through modern *Pakistan, *India, *Bangladesh, and *Malaysia, onward to *Indonesia and out to the southern Philippines.

Not without clashes, this Islamic monotheism was accommodated in various contexts; in India by Hinduism, the country's majority and most characteristic religion. Buddhism (its founder, Siddhartha Gautama [d.483 B.C.], called Buddha, the Enlightened One, was from south *Nepal) was exported from India. In its Theravada or Hinayana (more doctrinal) form it claims *Sri Lanka, *Burma, *Thailand; in its Mahayana (more adaptable) form it is found in *China, Tibet, *Korea, *Japan, and parts of Southeast Asia. Traditional Confucianism and Taoism have in recent times had difficulty in coping with change in mainland China. State Shinto was officially abolished in *Japan after World War II, but sectarian Shinto continues strong and diversified. Scattered in Asia are Parsee (Zoroastrian, from Persia), Jain (of Hindu origin), Sikh (monotheist opponents to Hinduism and Islam), as well as Jewish and Christian minorities.

Among the latter is the Mar Thoma Church in *India, probably the oldest church outside the Middle East. While tradition claims the Apostle Thomas as its founder, this church has a verifiable history at least to the fourth century, and ties that have thereafter linked it to the great missioning outreach of the Nestorians (see Iraq). Traditional religion, animism for the most part, continues not only among isolated hill tribes but also in the midst of higher religions.

Like Christianity, major Asian religions like Islam, Hinduism, and Buddhism, as well as the still young Bahaism, have developed ever new forms of missionary advance. These have been making a progressive impact upon people in other parts of the world. Contacts among the adherents of these and other religions are manifold. In consequence, every religion is going through test and change as together the adherents of all religions are being permeated by secularism in this technologically oriented age. Discourse among the religions—dialog in human community—is seen as a basic necessity in a world in transition. Christians have increasingly taken initiative in this boundless field, whether under ecumenical auspices such as the World Council of Churches (WCC) or the Roman Catholic Church, or under the broader aegis of the World Council on Religion and Peace (now Geneva-based).

Lutheran participation in such dialog, as alert Asian leaders have affirmed repeatedly, is urgent.

Asia is the least Christian continent in terms of numbers, the most magnetic in terms of its power to attract, and the most difficult in terms of its firmly-rooted religions. Here, except for work among peoples of Traditional religion, Christianity has succeeded in winning individuals but not in transforming a whole people or religion from within. Even so the missiologist Walbert Bühlmann sees the present as a time of fresh opportunity in Asia, for his own Roman Catholic Church as well as for Protestants and the Orthodox. Others share this view, fully recognizing that, with exceptions like the Philippines, Papua New Guinea, and parts of Indonesia, the Christian church is dispersed into often isolated minorities, dependent on various forms of outside assistance and limited in the exercise of the freedom of religion as expressed in Article 18 of the United Nations Universal Declaration of Human Rights (1948). In Asia as a whole, Roman Catholics, even without their 30 million adherents in the Philippines, outnumber Protestants by a ratio of 3:2.

Christianity's successive venturings eastward have followed trade routes, gathered adherents, benefited from political favor, spread widely, and later succumbed to hostile forces—and to the forgetfulness of Christians in the West. In terms of time, the dozen or more centuries spanning the earliest coming of Christians to India's west coast (above) and the arrival of the Portuguese in 1498 directly from Europe—both of which events have living descendants—easily obscure Asian developments elsewhere. So, for example, the Nestorian (Assyrian) Christian advance into central Asia moved from Merv (Mary; Central Asian USSR) over the ancient silk route to Changan (Sian), the western capital of *China. The famous monument there (the Sigan-Fu Stone, erected in A.D. 781 and discovered in 1625) commemorates a still earlier Christian community. For years Changan was known for the missioning activities of three foreign religions: Buddhism from *India, Christianity and Islam from the Middle East. Further west, the Turks, prior to their entry into Asia Minor and their conversion to Islam, had in large part accepted Christianity. But this overland Christian presence suffered heavily from the destructiveness of the Mongol invasions as well as from other forces.

The 16th century changed the Christian approach as Europeans came via the high seas and latched on to the existing coastal routes of Arab, Chinese, and other traders. The Roman Catholic entry onto this scene was exemplified by the remarkable career of Francis Xavier (1506–1552), which ranged widely and included India, Ceylon, the East Indies, Japan, and almost China—he died offshore, on the island of Chang-Chuen-Shan, while awaiting entry. Other Jesuits enlarged on his beginnings, as did other Roman Catholic orders. Xavier's contribution to Christian missioning was to challenge the prevailing European notion that "heathen" ideas must first be exterminated in order to provide a blank slate for the sowing of the gospel.

When Protestant overseas mission work began in Asia in 1706, Bartholomew Ziegenbalg (1683–1719), in Tranquebar, *India, became its prototype. In order to find room for the gospel, this Lutheran pioneer was careful to become as fully acquainted as possible with the prevailing religious context, in this case that of Hinduism.

By the year 1900 the missionary outreach of Roman Catholics and Protestants had touched most accessible areas of Asia. As schools, the printing press, medical, agricultural, and other services complemented the planting of Christian congregations, the spread of the gospel was hastened by still other means. In the words of a prominent missionary journal, many welcomed the 20th century as the time when, in Asia as elsewhere, the railway would greatly facilitate the spread of the gospel to new localities. Soon highways and the automobile would mean an even greater step ahead. Few persons would readily admit that these and other gains were but the convenient tools of a Western-based colonial power, the emblems of empire on its utilitarian side. Nor was it until after World War II, and the rise of independent nations, that in retrospect it became evident how much the spread of Christianity had depended on the intervention of foreign governmental power for its freedom to advance the cause of Christ. In that context, communication across international lines as well as within nations—by radio especially, and by satellite eventually— became a most effective tool for relaying the ancient gospel.

Hidden behind these developments, yet essential for the survival of any new and authentic church, was the threefold missionary objective: self-propagation, self-governance, self-support. Advanced almost simultaneously by two of the 19th century's leading missionary thinkers—Henry Venn (*UK, Church Missionary Society) and Rufus Anderson (*USA, American Board of Commissioners for Foreign Missions, Congregational, the well-known ABCFM)—this three-pronged policy was not easily applied. Later the era of "orphaned mission," during and shortly after World War II, proved that churches grew, often impressively, during the absence of missionaries (see Indonesia, for example). Nor did most Western Christians recognize that the advocacy of the Three-Self Movement in the *People's Republic of China was in fact an application of a policy that was born in the West but was too long put off. Today this is the goal of churches not only in Asia but also in *Africa and *Latin America, and it is also an essential element in an enduring ecumenical movement.

The Christian Conference of Asia (CCA) is a ready reference to the Protestant, Anglican, and Orthodox elements in the Asian and Pacific scene. It includes 15 national councils of churches and over 100 member churches in its fellowship. Based in *Singapore until 1987, the CCA was evicted from there by the government which charged the conference with political interference—a charge which the conference's parent body, the WCC, rejected outright. Since 1988 the CCA general secretariat is in Japan (Tokyo); communications in Hong Kong; development services, mission, evangelism, and theology, in Thailand (Bangkok); education, women's concerns, and youth, in the Philippines (Manila).

Prior to its present name, adopted in 1973, it was the East Asia Christian Conference, and its antecedents go back still further. Already in the 1920s, agencies like the World Student Christian Federation and the growing number of national Christian councils had laid the groundwork. Following World War II, the rise of newly independent nations and the worldwide ecumenical movement accentuated the felt need for a regional expression of Christian unity. The WCC and the International Missionary Council (IMC) therefore jointly supported an East Asia secretaryship. Its first incumbent (1951–1956) was Rajah B. Manikam (later bishop of the *Tamil Evangelical Lutheran Church, India). He was surprised to learn how little the Asian churches, and those in Australia and New Zealand, knew of each other. They were also generally in the dark about Christianity in Europe and America, except for their links with supporting churches. The 1950s were thus a time of discovery for Christians in the Asian and Australasian region. When a planning meeting was held in Parapat, *Indonesia, in 1957, and the East Asia Christian Conference was formally organized two years later in Kuala Lumpur, Malaysia, Lutheran churches were among the early members, although a fuller Lutheran participation is still awaited.

With the same credal basis as the WCC, the CCA aims to advance the spread of the gospel through study, witness, and service, and in the process to make an Asian contribution to Christian thought, worship, and action worldwide. Its program committees deal with message and communication, life and action, and justice and service. CCA assemblies, hereafter to be held every five years instead of every four, have highlighted the problems—even of survival—that the churches face in their respective countries. Issues such as the exploitation of women, the deprivation of civil rights, and the burden of poverty have come before the CCA with hopes for a common Christian course of action. But the 1985 assembly in Seoul, *Korea, made it clear that contrasting conditions in different countries apparently prevent the CCA members from taking a common stand. In that connection, the Indonesian participants—objecting to certain procedures, including political statements by certain action groups mainly against Indonesia's seizure of Timor Island and treatment of its people—declared that they would not take part in CCA decision making for the next five years, although they would retain their membership. Christian communities in Asia remain under constant pressure either to conform to dominant ideologies or to escape into private piety.

The CCA is headed by a four-member presidium. Its support comes from member churches and councils, mission societies, and the WCC. Its general secretaries have been from Sri Lanka (D.T. Niles), Burma (U Kyaw Than), Malaysia (Yap Kim Hao), and, as of 1985, from Korea.

It should surprise no one that Lutheranism in Asia/Pacific, when seen as a whole, is an extraordinary agglomeration of over 50 ecclesial bodies whose combined total exceeds 4.8 million adherents. The surprising fact is that 93.7% of the Lutherans, organized into 21 church bodies, dwell in three countries: *India, *Indonesia, and *Papua New Guinea. The other 6.3%—around 305,700—are dispersed among 15 other countries and gathered into some 30 church bodies. Not only is the linguistic and cultural diversity of this array very great, and a valid reflection of this part of the world, but it is also compounded by antecedent ties and contemporary links with other parts of the world. Besides the Bible, the common confessional denominator is Luther's *Small Catechism*. For most of the church bodies, membership in the LWF has become part of their life. Generally, the larger Lutheran churches are also the most active ecumenically. Even so, the complaint continues from various quarters that Lutherans in Asia and Australasia remain too much to themselves.

In this area the 32 LWF member churches, plus the four with some permanent relation to the Federation, account for 96% of the 4.8 million Lutheran total. In size, the two-million member *HKBP church in Indonesia is far in the lead. At the other end of the scale are 9 member churches with under 10,000 adherents. From the smallest to the largest, as the following accounts bring out, each ecclesial body has a story to tell and a context to be taken into account.

The LWF has sought to assist the Asian churches, as it has those in *Africa and *Latin America, in planning and carrying out programs that would enhance their autonomy, self-reliance, and witness, as well as strengthen their activities in evangelism, education, communication, health services, and community-related development programs. In the latter field, for example, LWF Community Development Service (CDS), in response to projects proposed by, and worked out in consultation with Asian churches, resulted in grants averaging over US $1,000,000 annually during the two decades from 1963 to 1983. In another category, the LWF service to refugees in the *Middle East and to Chinese refugees in *Hong Kong, launched in 1949, provided an Asian-based lesson that led Lutherans to render prolonged service—solely on the basis of need and regardless of religious adherence—to people made homeless in other parts of the world.

Conditions in Asia have indeed challenged Lutherans to draw together their dispersed and divided forces. Occasions to do so multiplied after World War II. The Commission on Younger Churches and Orphaned Missions (CYCOM), formed by the USA National Lutheran Council in 1945, was an exercise in trusteeship on behalf of German and other mission agencies. Embodied into the LWF in 1949, the CYCOM function became the Federation's Commission on World Mission (CWM; renamed Commission on Church Cooperation in 1970). Over the decades this unit's operational department has been a clearinghouse for concerns in many lands and provided a variety of invaluable services.

In fostering the fellowship of faith across domestic and national lines, conferences of many kinds have helped to consolidate and coordinate efforts in Asia. Australian Lutherans, along with Europeans and Americans, have worked effectively with their Asian partners. The learning experience has been mutually profitable as well as progressively inclusive, as illustrated in the rise of All-Asia conferences. In 1952, at Pinang, *Malaysia, a Southeast Asia Lutheran Consultative Conference set the lines for a unified policy and procedure on the Malay peninsula. In 1956, at Madras, *India—the 250th anniversary year of protestant missionary beginnings in Tranquebar—the first All-Asia Lutheran conference drew representatives of churches from Pakistan to Japan. In 1964, at Ranchi, *India, the second All-Asia conference included representatives also from the Philippines, New Guinea, and Australia.

A change in 1971, in Tokyo—the first meeting of the new LWF Department of Church Cooperation—widened horizons still further, and the work of the Asian churches appeared in a new global perspective. This meeting accentuated the importance of partnership and interdependence as well as mutual responsibility for mission. In 1976, at *Singapore, the largest All-Asia conference thus far dealt with challenges and needs faced by Asian Lutheran churches, and thus also provided input for the LWF Sixth Assembly, soon to meet in Dar es Salaam, *Tanzania.

Similarly, in 1983, meeting on Samosir Island in Lake Toba, North Sumatra, the fourth All-Asia conference had the forthcoming Seventh Assembly in mind, while at the same time treating Asian needs. The paramount task of evangelism (mission) at all levels was, individual to churchwide; the rising role of women as theologically trained and ordained pastors; the exchange of young persons—potential leaders—and visitation programs between churches in the region; the promotion of dialog with people of other religions; the concern for peace and the nuclear threat, and for justice and human rights, especially for those of women, youth, and children; the development of Asian cultural forms of language, song, and liturgy as essential for a more effective Asian involvement in mission—these and other issues reflected the concerns of the churches. Structurally the conferences sought a "closer physical presence of the LWF in the Asian region," possibly through a regional liaison office. Finally they resolved to invite the LWF to hold its Eighth Assembly in Asia, thus "reflecting the coming of age of the Asian Lutheran churches."

Although there was no specific reference at these All-Asia conferences to efforts toward manifesting Christian unity ecumenically—especially through the World Council of Churches—it would be misleading to assume that such a concern was missing. The churches described below list their various confessional and ecumenical memberships. Besides, the more than 30 conferences, consultations, and workshops facilitated by the LWF on the Asian scene between 1977 and 1984 drew inevitably on more than Lutheran resources. From the ecumenical *China studies or the place of the church in the Muslim world to the meaning of the *Augsburg Confession* in an Asian setting or the theology of Luther and Asian thought, the subjects were such as would widen the ecclesial horizon. So, likewise, were the conferences for regional church leaders, for youth leadership, and for women in various occupations (ordained ministry included). Similarly there were intensive sessions on mission, central Christian doctrines, ethical issues, local ecumenism, root causes of social and economic injustice, communication and use of the media. In sum, the LWF units in the fields of studies, church cooperation, communication, and world service—and also the Strasbourg Institute for Ecumenical Research (*France)—have endeavored to help the Asian churches do together what they could not do separately and, in the process, to become increasingly indigenous, self-reliant, and mutually helpful.

As an example, the Asia Program for the Advancement of Training and Studies (APATS), initially proposed by a pastor/scholar in *Korea, supports the specific needs of Lutheran churches in the areas of theological research, study, and training. The particular religious, cultural, and sociological environment of the churches, say its participants, is the context for treating issues bearing on witness and service. The programs are related to theological seminaries in nine areas, including one in the Middle East. The areas are: Hong Kong/Taiwan, India, Indonesia, Japan, Korea, Malaysia/Singapore, Papua New Guinea, the Philippines, and West Bank (*Jordan). Periodically APATS has sponsored pan-Asian workshops or symposia, as in the field of Luther studies during the 500th anniversary year of the Reformer. For the individual participants, APATS is an enabler of a more excellent ministry. Collectively the APATS program is demanding and uneven in its accomplishments, but it is also beneficial beyond immediate assessment.

Communications—alerting and feeding the minds of Christians and others—remains an unending challenge to the Lutheran churches in the Asia/Pacific area. Radio programs—the Lutheran Hour and more—as well as the publications accompanying interpretively the basic work of the Bible and literature societies, are part of an ever-unfinished agenda. Usually undersupported, this part of the churches' outreach also shows some exciting developments, as in *Hong Kong, *Indonesia, *Japan, *Korea, and *Taiwan. Anniversaries, too, have stimulated fresh efforts in publication, like the 450th of the *Catechism* and the *Augsburg Confession* and the 500th of Luther's birth. From 1977–1985, *Asia Lutheran News* kept a scattered fellowship mutually informed and concerned. Authorized by the All-Asia conference in 1976, and aided by an LWF grant, the *ALN* service was sent monthly or bimonthly to about 1700 recipients. During this time the editorship was mainly based in Hong Kong, with brief interludes in Sri Lanka and Tokyo/Taipei. At the beginning of 1986, the name of this news service was changed to *Asia Lutheran Press Services* (ALPS) and the main emphasis is now on serving about 200 church/secular media agencies/newspapers through news releases. In addition, the *ALPS* editor, David Lin, initiated a quarterly news roundup that goes to about 1200 individual receivers. Since 1984 the service has had an international board, appointed by the Asia Lutheran Church Leaders' Conference.

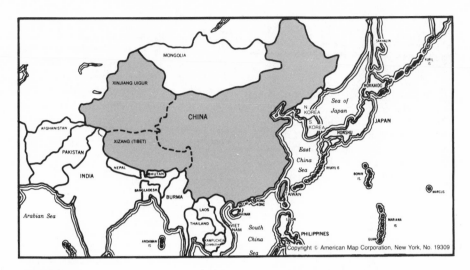

ASIA

The Asia area covered here under four sub-headings—China Area, East Asia, Indian Subcontinent, and Southeast Asia—has a total of about four million Lutherans. Over half of them are in Southeast Asia. Lutheran mission work began in this area (*India) in 1706.

CHINA AREA

Included in this area are Lutheran connections in the People's Republic of China, Hong Kong, and Taiwan. In the latter two there are at least 52,000 members in the several Lutheran church bodies. These church bodies cannot be understood apart from the movement of thousands of Lutherans who joined the two million or more refugees fleeing the mainland at the end of the 1940s, nor apart from the amazing story of the *Lutheran Church of China (below). Some 4000 people of Chinese origin are now members of the Lutheran churches in *Malaysia and Singapore and are dealt with in the Southeast Asia section. Thousands of others are gathered in Chinese-speaking congregations in many parts of the world or have been absorbed into churches using other languages or into other denominations or, sadly, perhaps lost to the Christian church. By contrast the *Lutheran Church of China, during its brief rally after World War II, had a membership of about 100,000.

CHINA, PEOPLE'S REPUBLIC OF

The world's most populous and, in area, third largest country, the People's Republic of China (Communist, 1949) is bounded by the Yellow Sea, the East and South China Sea, and 11 neighboring states: the *USSR, Mongolia, North Korea, Vietnam, Laos, *Burma, *India, *Bhutan, *Nepal, *Pakistan, and Afghanistan. On its southern coast, near Kwangchow (Canton), lies *Hong Kong. Offshore, *Taiwan Province is under Kuomintang (Nationalist) control.

Area of the People's Republic: 9,561,000 sq. km. (3,691,521 sq. mi.). Pop. (1985): 1,043,100,000. Cap.: Beijing (Peking), pop. (1982) 9,230,700. Largest city: Shanghai, pop. (1982) 11,859,700. Language: Chinese (the Mandarin dialect is now taught everywhere).

Note on spelling: *Pinyin,* the new Chinese romanization, endeavors to transliterate sounds in a way more true to Mandarin Chinese, the standard dialect, than older systems. Thus Peking becomes Beijing. But a southern city name can become virtually obscured, as when Canton becomes Guangzhou. When the new spelling is used in the following text, the familiar is in parenthesis.

History: China's documented history covers 35 centuries. It is highlighted by a sequence of dynasties from the beginning of the Shang, in 1523 B.C. to the fall of the Ch'ing, in A.D. 1911. There followed the revolutionary period in the present century: Led by Sun Yat-sen (1866–1925) from Canton, it began in 1911 and culminated on October 1, 1949 with the proclamation of the People's Republic by Mao Zedong (Tse-tung; 1893–1976) in Beijing (Peking).

The legacy of China's culture and civilization is immense and varied. At times the broad indigenous base, held together by an inclusive ethic (Confucius, 551-479 B.C.), assimilated outside influences. From India, for example, came Buddhism in the first century B.C. The Chinese classics in literature left an abiding legacy; and the civil service examination system, based on those classics, endured over a millennium, to the beginning of the present century. Printing, silk, metal casting, the compass, and gunpowder were all first used in China. Best known of the invasions of China is that of the Mongols under Jenghiz Khan (1167–1227) and the ensuing rule of Kublai Khan (1215–1294), made known to Europeans by Marco Polo (1254–1324). His following of ancient overland trade routes to China anticipated by two centuries the circumnavigation of the globe and the linking of China—reluctantly, to be sure—into the world of ocean trade and competing empires. Arab merchants were the first sea traders.

Western intervention by sea unfolded slowly but surely. Vasco da Gama (1469–1524) continued his exploratory voyage from India and reached Canton in 1497. Sixty years later Macao, on the Pearl River's estuary, became a Portuguese trading base and the first European settlement in China. As Canton long remained the only port in the Middle Kingdom open to foreign trade, it attracted shipping from other European nations and, after 1784, from the newly independent United States of America. British efforts to expand its trade with China led to the introduction of opium from *India, the ensuing Opium War (1839–1842), and Britain's acquisition of *Hong Kong (1842). (A treaty for the return of Hong Kong to China in 1997 was signed in December 1984.)

China was forced to grant equal and free access to the major trading nations. It complemented China's concession of extraterritoriality, whereby legal cases involving foreigners could be tried in foreign courts on Chinese territory. Granted first to the British, the same privilege was soon extended to other nations. In major treaty ports like Shanghai, Canton, and Tsingtao, specific territory was ceded to foreign governments for commercial and residential purposes. In effect, China was not master of its own affairs internationally. Yet it had much to offer. Protests against foreign intervention flared periodically, for example, the Boxer Rebellion (1900).

The demand for labor in other countries enlarged an already centuries-old Chinese dispersion. Railroad building in the western United States and Canada, rubber plantations in Southeast Asia, and similar ventures in Indonesia and elsewhere drew Chinese into lands far away as well as closer to home—especially to Manchuria, whither millions moved. This was all part of a worldwide migration of peoples marking the 19th and early 20th centuries.

China became a republic on January 1, 1912, following the revolution inspired by Sun Yat-sen. The revolutionary party, the Kuomintang, based in Canton, had little power; for a generation the country was held by warlords. Failing to find help in Western Europe and America, Sun found it in the USSR. The Chinese Communist party was organized in 1921, and the Kuomintang allied itself with it. In 1927 the new leader of the Kuomintang, Chiang Kai-shek, repudiated this alliance, actively opposed the Communists, and set up a national government in Nanking. Forced out of the southeast (Jiangxi [Kiangsi] Province), the Communists retreated via the famed Long March (1934–1935) to the northwest (Shensi Province), there to await their opportunity years later.

The Japanese, meanwhile, having designs on the whole of China, occupied Manchuria in 1931 and attacked China proper in 1937. All of which set the Asian stage for World War II and the involvement of the United Kingdom and the United States against Japan and on the side of China. With the surrender of Japan in 1945, China's liberation was largely accomplished. After a period of readjustment, the Communist forces made their relentless advance. On October 1, 1949, the People's Republic of China was proclaimed. Mao announced: "China has stood up." Chiang Kai-shek retreated to offshore *Taiwan, there to perpetuate the Republic of China, originally launched on January 1, 1912.

A drastic reordering of society followed. Assistance from the USSR was prominent. In the Korean War (1950–1953), China intervened on the side of North Korea. Western ties and influence were condemned. Great alienation set in against the past as all energy went into self-help. Mao Tse-tung, as party chairman, and Chou En-lai (1898–1976), as prime minister, provided firm and astute leadership. But in 1958 the People's Republic undertook its industry-oriented "Great Leap Forward" (1958–1960). By 1960 disagreement resulted in the withdrawal of Soviet aid. Military clashes with India (1962) involved border disputes. By development aid to countries in Latin America, Asia, and Africa, such as the construction of the Tanzam railway

line (giving *Zambia a new coastal outlet via *Tanzania for its copper ore), the People's Republic of China declared itself champion of the peoples of the Third World. Its successful explosion of its first atomic bomb (1964), a hydrogen bomb (1967), as well as the launching of its first satellite (1970) affirmed China as an international power. The time had come for the People's Republic of China to take its place in the United Nations (1971); much to the displeasure of Nationalist China (*Taiwan), which it displaced.

Meanwhile, China was experiencing the domestic crisis of the harsh Cultural Revolution and its aftermath (1966–1976). Added to this was the bitter warfare next door—the *United States against Communist North Vietnam supported by China. Thus, the state visit of USA President Richard Nixon to China in 1972 was surprising. However, the trial of the Gang of Four (including the late Chairman Mao's widow) in 1980 tended to confirm the new disposition of openness to the West. Modifications in the economy and other areas of national life also indicated a turning away from doctrinaire Marxism. Thousands of students in specialized fields were sent to Canada, the USA, and Europe; teachers as well as experts in many fields of science and industry were brought in from the West, in contrast to the postwar years when they had come in from the USSR. The change was not all at once, and some of China's new takeover generation has benefited from advanced training in Eastern and Western Europe.

Japan, meanwhile, is China's chief trading partner, and the bitter memory of Japanese aggression during the 1930s and World War II has been allayed in large part by treaties normalizing the relationships between the two countries.

Deng Xiaoping (b. 1904), the nation's top political leader, replaced the old guard leaders in government and the military. By 1985 many of the younger generation were coming into key positions. Where Deng's pragmatic modernization would lead remained the great question. In 20th-century China, changes have been frequent. The student unrest in late 1986 appeared symptomatic of this complex, ongoing process.

Religion: Atheism and agnosticism have taken a strong hold in modern China. Yet Chinese folk religion lives on. It combines elements of Confucian ancestor worship and ethics, Taoist mysticism and Buddhist (Mahayana) eschatology. Folk religion enables all these elements to coexist in a Chinese cultural context. As to the number of adherents of a specific religion, there are no figures except for Islam and Christianity. Muslims are said to exceed 30 million, and that may come close to fact. Christians, divided into two camps, were in 1985 said to number at least three million Roman Catholics and another three million or more Protestants. Many claimed the total Christian community to be far greater in number by the late 1980s.

"We have no scientific basis for foretelling the future of religion in China . . . It may last forever, or it may disappear." So Premier Chou En-lai concluded his conversation in 1956 with Bishop Rajah B. Manikam of India's *Tamil Evangelical Lutheran Church and at that time East Asia secretary for the World Council of Churches and the International Missionary Council.

Leaving for later a summation of the Christian movement in China prior to the revolution of 1949, it suffices here to assess some of the developments since then. In 1951 the Chinese Christian Three-Self Patriotic Movement took up an old issue and began to attack the foreign influence in the churches, sparing neither missionaries nor church-related institutions such as hospitals, schools, colleges, universities, and seminaries. The Three-Self Movement bypassed denominational differences and displaced the National Christian Council, dating from 1922. Some churches remained open for worship, but in 1966 the Cultural Revolution closed them all. Also closed was the one remaining theological seminary, in Nanjing (Nanking), which itself had been a last consolidation of several others. Even earlier the government had taken over the church-related institutions. Religious instruction was banned. But Christianity did not die; it went underground.

During the 1970s reaction against the Cultural Revolution and its excesses set in. By 1978 government policy toward religion grew less rigid. Blame for the nation's misguidance fell on the Gang of Four (above). Visitors from the West were welcomed. Before the end of the decade, mosques and temples were being refurbished at government expense. Christian churches, many of them having been used for other purposes, were readied

for worship. In Shanghai the nondenominational Mo-en ("bathed in grace") Church drew crowds as Christians surfaced and others satisfied their curiosity.

As China's Christian community emerged, more and more former churches were reopened. Tales of suffering, survival, and outreach were endless. By 1985 over 2000 churches were reportedly again in use. House congregations gathered in homes and apartments. Theological education, urgently required for a new generation of ministers, was by 1985 being offered in nine reopened seminaries. Some 32,000 lay members were said to be enrolled in training by extension (TEE).

Under these circumstances structure and unity posed enormous problems. For Roman Catholics, leadership was in the hands of the College of Bishops, in association with the Commission on Church Affairs (government) and the Patriotic Association. For the Protestants, there is the National Three-Self Movement, which relates to public policy; the China Christian Council (CCC); and the Amity Foundation (AF), an agency formed in 1985 to receive foreign support for approved welfare, educational, and social projects and to facilitate and oversee the placement of teachers and other personnel from abroad. The AF's most ambitious project is Amity Press, built in cooperation with United Bible Societies and the Jiangning Industrial Corporation. It produces 25,000 Bibles and 500,000 New Testaments annually, besides hymnals, journals, and theological texts. Chairing these three structures is Bishop K. H. Ting (Anglican). Among its tasks the CCC has also published a catechism (1984). Denominational structures have not been revived.

On the human side, many a personal tie, severed in 1949, has been restored by visits in recent years. After 30 years, Andrew Hsiao (head of the Lutheran Seminary in *Hong Kong, and a former vice-president of the LWF) was enabled to see his aged mother and other relatives and friends in the People's Republic. Others who served in China during the war years and thereafter are impressed by what has changed and what has survived—especially the curiosity and the spiritual hunger, marked by tales of steadfastness under trial. These tiny events of restoration and renewal, multiplied by the thousands, are the stuff of a new sense of oneness in Christ.

The CCC has been watchful that foreign contacts, through churches and agencies, respect what the Three-Self Movement has achieved over the past decades. The Christianity that survives and is growing is indeed diversified, but it is not denominational in the former sense. The 1960s and 1970s were the heyday of China watchers, outsiders eager to learn what was happening. The 1980s are the time of the China communicators and interpreters, like Bishop Ting. Outside help is now welcome, but within limits. A condition is that requests for assistance originate with the Christians in China and that these requests be coordinated, cleared, and conveyed through the CCC and the Amity Foundation. The procedure is not unlike that of *Germany's Evangelisches Hilfswerk after World War II.

In recent years the LWF has maintained a coordinating office in *Hong Kong so as to give some order to Lutheran approaches to China. But by 1985 contacts from abroad were being made directly with CCC offices in Shanghai. The question remains: How can Christianity in China, having rid itself of foreign dominance and become recognized as indigenous, retain this gain and, at the same time, reenter the worldwide *oikumene?*

• • •

For Christians in China the period that ended in 1949 brought an abrupt halt to a vast array of missionary endeavors built up over generations. Before focusing on the Lutheran enterprise, an awareness of the larger context is essential.

China's earliest known contact with Christianity was in A.D. 635 when Nestorian missionaries from the Middle East founded a Christian community in Xi-an (Sian), capital of the T'ang dynasty (618–906), in Shensi Province (over 12,890 kilometers, or 800 miles, due west of Shanghai). A monument from the year 781 tells the community's story. Six centuries later, also by the ancient silk route, came the Italian Franciscan John of Montecorvino and others. Initial opposition from the almost extinct Nestorian community did not prevent the gathering of a Catholic following early in the 14th century. A generation later the records stop (1353). Christianity was replanted in China when the Jesuit Mattheo Ricci (1552–1610) gained a remarkable response in Beijing (Peking). Having sailed as far as Macao with the Portuguese

(1582), he and his colleagues adopted Chinese customs, became fluent in Mandarin, and—what was later censured in Rome— adapted the Christian faith enough to allow for a continued veneration of ancestors and other traditional practices. From its beginnings during Ricci's time, today's Roman Catholic Church in China possesses a rich and varied history of over four centuries. But that is another story.

The earliest Russian Orthodox entry came after the Treaty of Nerchinsk (1689), the first one signed by China and a modern power. In the later 19th century, Beijing became the seat of a Russian Orthodox archbishop. Shanghai received its own bishop and cathedral. (The latter was converted into a machine shop in the 1950s, with the figure of Christ, the Pantocrator, gazing from above upon the workers below.)

Protestant contacts with China, first made by the Dutch Reformed in 1624, were limited to the island called Formosa (*Taiwan) by the Portuguese. The latter had a base in Macao, on the mainland, from about 1560. Not far eastward, at the mouth of the Pearl River, the port of Canton was opened to British, then also to Dutch, French, and American shipping. The first Protestant missionary, Robert Morrison (1782–1834), sent by the London Missionary Society in 1807, completed a translation of the Bible by 1818. At personal risk of life, two Chinese friends taught him their language (the law said that it was to be kept unintelligible to foreigners). An earlier Roman Catholic translation of the New Testament was a timely help. Morrison supported himself as a translator for the East India Company.

It was Morrison's translation of the Bible that Karl Gützlaff (1805–1851) carried with him when sailing along the coast of China as the first Protestant missionary among the people beginning in 1833. Gützlaff was a German Lutheran who had been trained in Berlin and was then sent out by a Dutch society to the East Indies. Moving to Bangkok, he, with local assistance, translated most of the Bible into Siamese (Thai). In China he learned the language fluently and approached the people with high expectations. His travel reports— widely published in the UK, the USA, and Germany—awakened great interest. "China," he claimed, "is not open to commerce but to the gospel."

Soon thereafter, the Opium War, Britain's acquisition of Hong Kong (above), and the influx of commerce from the West brought also the rising flow of missionaries—including Congregational, Presbyterian, Methodist, Anglican, and Baptist. Roman Catholic missionaries and converts, favored with French protection, enjoyed certain advantages. Among the Protestants, comity avoided an overlapping of effort. Evangelism was the prime activity, but Protestants more than Roman Catholics fostered education, including secondary schools, colleges, and seminaries.

Medical work and hospitals as well as the production of Christian literature were early on the agenda. Under the unequal treaties forced on the weak Manchu dynasty, missionaries as well as merchants were especially privileged. Reaction among the Chinese flared up at times, but did so most violently during the Boxer Rebellion, a movement of protest during which some 200 Protestant missionaries, women and children, and many more Chinese Christians died. Even so, by the time of the missionary centennial (1907), about 4000 Protestant missionary personnel were active in China. By 1925 this number had more than doubled, declining gradually thereafter.

American Protestant participation in the challenge of China was especially strong, with that from Britain not far behind. Christian associations (YMCA, YWCA) for the laity became prominent and multiplied international contacts widely. The 1922 Peking conference of the World Student Christian Federation was the second of its kind in Asia (the first having been held in Tokyo in 1907). It stimulated the further rise of Christian leaders in all walks of life, as well as anti-Christian activity. A product of the Peking conference was the organization of the National Christian Council, with a Chinese majority from the outset. The very presence of this kind of a coordinating service agency would have great significance during the trying times not far distant.

While most of the Protestant work was in the hands of English-speaking churches and societies, Lutherans—like the Roman Catholics—had a multilingual foreign support system. In this context it becomes all the more useful to trace, briefly, the rise of the *Lutheran Church of China (1917), for there remain significant Lutheran elements also in

today's nondenominational Protestant church (above).

LUTHERAN CHURCH OF CHINA (LCC; 1920–1958)

The LCC, formed in 1917 and constituted in 1920, was actually a loose federation of synods, each located in a given territory and each the result of activity by some German, American, or Scandinavian missionary society or church board. By 1948 reportedly all Lutheran synods in China had become members of the LCC except the work sponsored by the *Lutheran Church–Missouri Synod.

Lutheran involvement in the China mission developed in two stages, and mainly in two regions of the vast nation. First came a succession of missionaries from *Germany to Canton and the Province of Kwangtung. Pioneers (1846) of the Basel and Rhenish societies were followed by those from Berlin (1850). In 1898 Berlin began work also in the northeast port city of Ch'ing-tao (Tsingtao) but transferred this undertaking to the (United) Lutheran Church in America in 1925. Second in point of time (1890–1920) came an influx of missionaries from Scandinavian and North American societies and churches. These found opportunities mainly in China's central provinces where as yet few other missionary groups were active. American Lutherans of Norwegian descent (later the ALC) led the way in 1890. Daniel Nelson, a perceptive farmer, was the first, and went out on his own, entering Honan Province and later Hupeh. By 1920 a dozen Lutheran groups—Americans of Scandinavian descent, Norwegians, Swedes, Finns, and Danes—were busy in the above-mentioned provinces as well as farther south in Hunan and west in Shensi, and in China's northeast, Manchuria, where the Danes had gone.

Some 600 missionaries of many nationalities were stationed in China during the height of Lutheran activity in the 1920s and 1930s. The pattern of activity in most places included person-to-person evangelism, elementary schools in villages, secondary schools in some cities, Bible schools for evangelists and church workers, health services and hospitals at key points, and translation and publication of Christian tracts and books. Bibles and portions of the Scriptures were widely distributed and places of worship erected in hundreds of locations.

Common concern for an indigenous leadership led in 1913 to the founding of the Union Lutheran Theological Seminary in Shekow, near the centrally-located metropolis of Hankow on the Yangtze River. By 1948 this seminary had graduated 287 students, and these opened the way to a common Lutheran ministry in China.

A Lutheran Board of Publication (1924) produced a large amount of Christian materials. A weekly newspaper, *Hsin Yi Pao* (1913–1952), had a churchwide circulation. A youth program was developed. A revival movement animated the churches across the land in the 1930s, as Bible women, evangelists, and teachers found that ordinary folk showed fresh receptivity to renewal of life in Jesus Christ.

There were, however, also ominous signs. Antiforeign uprisings, especially in central China, during the years 1925–1928, created difficulties for the LCC and its mission. Already in 1929 Karl Ludwig Reichelt (1877–1952), the imaginative Norwegian missionary to Chinese Buddhists, relocated his center from Nanking to the New Territories of *Hong Kong. Looking back, Reichelt's timing was perceptive, and his move would later prove beneficial to China's Lutherans.

A difficult period followed. Periodic open conflicts between the Kuomintang and the Communists in the 1930s disrupted the work and endangered lives. Japan's invasion (1937) of the coastal region as well as the lower Yangtze River valley determined a move westward. Missionaries relocated their endeavors. Their children in the American School (at Kikungshan, 160 kilometers south of Shekow) were led to safety by the principal, Joseph Aalbue, to an island in Hong Kong bay (1938).

With the outbreak of World War II in the Pacific and the deepening Japanese advance into China, the struggle for the various missions to survive became ever more intense. In 1944 the American Section of the Lutheran World Convention set up its memorable center for assistance and coordination in Chungking, the new capital. Its director was Daniel Nelson Jr., son of the pioneer (above). At his side was Dr. Peng Fu, president of the LCC, as well as a number of other highly competent Westerners and Chinese. The seminary in Shekow (above), which had been forced to close, was reopened in 1944 in Chungking. A Lutheran Service Center for military personnel (American, Canadian, and others) became a welcome rendezvous.

The assistance of the American and other embassies in the capital greatly facilitated Nelson's task of coordination, which involved the evacuation of many missionaries (including some 150 Norwegian Lutherans) to India by military air transport. When the war ceased (1945) and the problem of transportation within China itself was acute, Nelson acquired a DC-3 airplane from surplus US military stock—and also a second one for spare parts. Named the "St. Paul," the plane and its crew rendered invaluable service not only to Lutherans but also to others.

War's end brought other immense problems to the Lutheran Church of China, first among them being the rebuilding of war-destroyed properties and the reorganization of the church and its work. German Lutheran missionary forces, free to operate under the Japanese occupation, were interned or at least cut off from support. Under these circumstances, the Lutheran World Convention and its successor, the LWF, stepped in as trustee of the mission properties, as helper of the stranded personnel, as well as supporter of the Chinese members. Meanwhile, by plane, LCC headquarters were returned to Hankow (after 1950 part of Wu-han, an expanded metropolis), and the theological seminary was back in Shekow. But this was only a respite. China, released from the Japanese scourge, fell back into its own unfinished struggle between the Communists and the nationalist Kuomintang.

Nevertheless, the Lutheran Church of China sent five delegates to the First Assembly of the LWF in Lund, *Sweden (1947). Leading them was the LCC President, Dr. Peng Fu, who made a deep impression on the assembly. He pleaded for a stronger missionary effort in Asia at a critical time when new nations were being born and the prospect of revolution was creating anxiety in many places, including his own land. On behalf of the hungry, he appealed: "Share your food with the world of Asia . . . as well as the 'bread of life!' "

In China, meanwhile, the Communist advance was accelerating. In late 1948 the Lutheran Theological Seminary was relocated from Hankow to *Hong Kong, finding lodging in the center built by Reichelt for his mission to Buddhist monks, named Tao Fong Shan, "the mountain from which the Christ-spirit blows." By 1949 the flight of many from mainland China was in full surge. The LCC's Peng Fu was among the hundreds of Lutherans in those countless thousands seeking a new start elsewhere. By 1955 he had been elected president of the new *Evangelical Lutheran Church of Hong Kong. Slightly earlier, in 1954, the Lutherans in *Taiwan, of whom a number were old Lutherans from the mainland, had organized the *Lutheran Church of Taiwan.

Only a few Lutherans left their country. In 1951, when the last expatriate missionaries left the People's Republic and contacts with the LWF were cut off, LCC reported a baptized membership of 100,000. The 1250 congregations were still located in the dozen areas where Lutheran missionaries had worked in south, central, and north China. Most of the work was being carried forward by 1000 lay workers and 180 Chinese pastors. The Lutheran Theological Seminary, where most of the pastors had been trained, was closed. The remaining students and professors become part of the Union Theological Seminary in Nanking, a consolidation of 11 denominational schools. Bishop Manikam (above) visited this institution in 1956.

Reports on the course of events in the LCC itself after 1951 are few. That year it was reported that a Three-Self Movement-related leadership had taken office in the Justification-by-Faith Church of Christ, as the LCC was called; declared it liberated from the missions that had brought it into being; and vowed to build an independent church. The denomination declined in importance but existed formally, presumably, until 1966.

HONG KONG

Crown Colony of Britain, adjoining the southeast coast of *China, 130 km. (80 mi.) southeast of Guangzhou (Canton), 60 km. (37 mi.) east of Macao. Area: 1060 sq. km. (400 sq. mi.). Pop. (1985 est.): 5,415,000. Cap.: Victoria (pop., 1981 est., 590,770). Language: English, Mandarin Chinese, Cantonese. Ethnic composition: Chinese (97%), Europeans, and others.

History: The Crown Colony grew to its present size by stages. Hong Kong Island (91 sq. km. or 35 sq. mi.), on which the capital, Victoria, is situated, was ceded to Britain by China at the end of the Opium War (1842). Kowloon Peninsula (ca. 8 sq. km.), across the harbor, was added in 1860. The New Territories (946 sq. km. or 365 sq. mi.) on the mainland, plus numerous adjacent small islands, were in 1898 leased to Britain by China for 99 years. The provisions for the return of all Hong Kong from Britain to China were signed in Beijing (Peking) in December 1984. In 1997 Hong Kong will become the Hong Kong Special Administrative Region of China, with a high degree of autonomy except in foreign affairs. The social and economic systems and life-style are to remain unchanged for 50 years. Freedom of speech, press, assembly, association, travel, right to strike, and religious belief, among others, will be assured by law.

Like Singapore, Hong Kong was long a British naval base. Taken by Japan in late 1941, it was reoccupied by Britain in September 1945. The metropolis remains one of the world's great trans-shipment ports and financial and communication centers. Its textile, electronic, and other industries became highly developed, particularly after the Western embargo on Chinese goods in 1950.

Between 1949 and 1962 Hong Kong absorbed over a million refugees from the mainland. The flow continued at a lessened and irregular rate thereafter, augmented in the mid-1970s by Vietnamese refugees. Forests of high-rise, low-cost buildings are the hallmark of this scenic metropolis. The extreme population density, the highest in the world, is relieved by the open spaces of the bay. The University of Hong Kong (1912), on the British model, and the Chinese University of Hong Kong (1964) are atop an educational ladder whose elementary and secondary schools are in part government-run and in part privately run under public control and subsidy.

Hong Kong's number one medical problem—drug addiction—is largely due to Europe's greed. Britain led the way in breaking China's closed door policy of centuries by pushing opium from India to pay for tea and silk. When, in the 18th century, China's emperor issued an edict against the importation of opium, smuggling began. A century later, when Chinese officials burned 20,000 chests of contraband opium, the Opium War (1839–1842) cost China Hong Kong. Imports continued. Among the many Chinese immigrants to Hong Kong were opium addicts. Thus British Hong Kongers became heirs to Britain's investment. In 1946 the British colonial government outlawed opium, and addiction went underground. The government's facilities for dealing with the problem of addiction are limited, but it supports various private programs. In the follow-up service by church and private agencies, Lutherans have been active (below).

The colonial government has a British-appointed governor, an executive council, and an administration capable of maintaining order in an amazingly complex metropolis. Many services, particularly in the field of health and welfare, depend on a high degree of responsibility and support shared by government and voluntary organizations.

Religion: The religious practices of Buddhism and Taoism continue to thrive in Hong Kong. Among the believers, almost every household has its ancestral shrine. Religious studies are conducted in monasteries, convents, and hermitages, the best known of these being in the remote and unspoiled parts of the New Territories. The 30,000 followers of Islam are mainly recent immigrants from China as well as from Pakistan, India, Malaysia, Indonesia, and the Middle East. The Heavenly Virtue Holy Church, a widespread religious movement claiming 100,000 or more in Hong Kong, is an attempt to combine Confucianism, Buddhism, Taoism, Islam, and Christianity.

The Christian community, Catholic and Protestant, is estimated at about 10% of the population. Roman Catholicism was introduced in 1841 when Pope Gregory XVI established the Apostolic Prefecture of Hong Kong. Today, about 275,000 adherents are grouped into 54 parishes and are served by 332 priests, 111 brothers, and 781 sisters. In recent years there has been increased involvement of the laity, organized under the Central Council of the Catholic Laity. The Catholic Youth Council oversees extensive activities.

The Protestant community comprises over 50 denominations and independent groups, the largest being the Baptists and the Church of Christ in China (Presbyterian and Congregational traditions). Others include the Adventist, Anglican, Alliance, Lutheran, Methodist, Salvation Army, and Pentecostal. Protestant missions began after 1842 when Hong Kong was ceded to Great Britain. The London Missionary Society, the American Board, and German mission agencies (Basel and Rhenish) were on the scene before 1850. The largest influx of missionaries came after 1949. Their efforts, principally among the refugees, greatly increased church membership during the 1950s and early 1960s. This has now leveled off. Independent Chinese churches have developed since the 1930s. The Church Assemblies (begun in *China in 1926) are also active in Hong Kong.

The Hong Kong Christian Council (HKCC; 1954) includes major denominations, the YMCA and YWCA, the Bible Society, and the Chinese Christian Literature Council. The HKCC is committed to building closer relationships among churches in Hong Kong as well as overseas. This is achieved through operational bodies including the Hong Kong Christian Service, the Communication Department, the Industrial Committee, and the United Christian Medical Service.

In 1975 the HKCC's Hong Kong Christian Service incorporated the work and staff of the LWF World Service program for refugees. This far-reaching work had begun during the period when mainland Chinese were pouring into Hong Kong. Between 1952 and 1954 LWS worked in concert with the World Council of Churches. Directed by Karl Ludwig Stumpf, a German Lutheran businessman and later pastor in Shanghai, the service reached people far beyond confessional and Christian frontiers. Support came from Lutheran churches as well as from other sources.

Follow-up programs for the refugees who stayed in Hong Kong as residents included a vocational training school, which provided career opportunities for 1000 unemployed people at a time; a rehabilitation project for victims of drug addiction; and eight new villages on nearby small islands or reclaimed land. In 1968 a nine-story building replaced the original headquarters and grouped hitherto scattered services. Foster care for children and school social work as a preventive measure were among other services set up by Stumpf and his colleagues and made possible by LWF World Service aid.

These programs and all the accumulated assets of the Hong Kong Lutheran World Service project, including the headquarters building, were turned over to the Hong Kong Christian Service (HKCS) at the end of 1975. Dr. Stumpf became the first director of the HKCS and continued to add much-needed programs, including training courses for social workers, until his death in 1987. In addition to assisting Hong Kong's needy, the HKCS was in the forefront in caring for the thousands of Indochinese boat refugees. At present the programs are almost totally financed from sources within Hong Kong.

The *Evangelical Lutheran Church of Hong Kong, the German-speaking Evangelical Congregation in Hong Kong, and the *Tsung Tsin Mission are the Lutheran members of the HKCC.

Closely related to the HKCC and of special interest to Lutherans is the Tao Fong Shan Ecumenical Center, a merger (1980) of the Tao Fong Shan Christian Institute and the WCC-related Christian Study Center on Chinese Religion and Culture (1950). For some time the two groups had been sharing the Chinese-style facilities of Tao Fong Shan in Shatin, New Territories. Situated on a hilltop with a magnificent view, the place was built in 1929 by the Norwegian Lutheran Karl Ludwig Reichelt (1877–1952) for work among Buddhist monks (above). A local board is responsible for the continuation of both programs.

The long-time concerns of Tao Fong Shan, "the mountain from which the Christ-spirit blows," continue. These include: dialog with people of the traditional Chinese religions; an understanding of the cultural heritage as well as the contemporary setting of the Chinese people; a porcelain workshop producing Chinese-style art with Christian motifs; the House of Friendship where people of various faiths can meet; the Ai Tao Yuan home for elderly women patterned after the Buddhist vegetarian halls; and a Lutheran congregation using the beautiful chapel (subsidized by the Scandinavian East Asia Mission [SEAM] and affiliated with the ELCH, below). The relocated Lutheran Theological Seminary adjoins it (see ELCHK, below).

The Chinese Lutheran Churches' Hong Kong Association, consisting of the five largest churches described below (i.e., CRC, ELCHK, HKMLC, LCHKS, and TTM), is

a means of strengthening and coordinating their efforts in theological education, evangelism, Christian education, and the mass media. In 1986 this association assumed responsibility for the distribution and rental of the films of the former Joint Lutheran Communication Committee (JLCC). These films, meant for the general public and geared to evoking discussion, were produced by competent personnel in mass electronic media during the 1970s when LWF/DOC and partner churches provided liberal grants. The JLCC's radio program, especially geared to youth, was turned over to the Lutheran Hour.

For almost two decades (until 1985) the Hong Kong churches took part in an LWF/DS sponsored Lutheran Southeast Asia Christian Education Curriculum Project. Initially work centered on producing Sunday school and youth curricula, a new life catechism, daily devotional materials, and basic teacher-training courses for Chinese-speaking churches. Efforts also concentrated on training Christian education leaders. Now several of the churches are able to produce their own materials.

Some Hong Kong churches are united in supporting the Hong Kong Lutheran College, a university-level school opened in 1978 by the Southeast Asia Lutheran Association for Higher Education. Since enrollment in the two Hong Kong universities is very limited, the school provides a much-needed educational opportunity.

Strengthening the working relationship of the churches is the Hong Kong Lutheran Women's Fellowship Association. Its aim is to advance the full participation of women in the life and work of the churches and to foster understanding among diversified groups. The five elected officers are divided between the five church bodies.

Hong Kong has several foreign language congregations. The German-speaking Evangelical Congregation (Lutheran and Reformed), founded in 1965 by businessmen stationed in Hong Kong, now has a membership of about 250. It receives financial and personal support from the *Evangelical Church in Germany (EKD). As a member of the Hong Kong Christian Council, the church participates in its service to the blind, handicapped children, and Vietnamese refugees. The *LCMS-related Church of All Nations provides a church home for English-speaking

Lutherans of all branches. The adjoining Hong Kong International School provides quality education through high school. Members of the faculty, students, and congregational members are actively engaged in service and support of the refugees in Hong Kong. The Norwegian Seamen's Church ministers to seamen and their families.

CHINESE RHENISH CHURCH, HONG KONG SYNOD (CRC)

Member: LWF (1974), CLCHKA
Membership: 10,470**
President: Elder Lee Ge Keen
7-9 Ferry Street, 2/F
Yan Yin Mansion
Kowloon

This Cantonese-speaking church comprises 20 congregations (including those in *Taiwan, the *USA, *Canada, and the *UK, below). They are served by 14 pastors, 10 unordained preachers, 10 parish workers, and other staff. Dating back to 1847, its presence in Hong Kong antedates by far the great influx of refugees from mainland China after 1949. With the rise of the *People's Republic, this Hong Kong district was separated from its four sister districts in Canton and the Kwangtung Province. It then became a self-governing church.

Offerings of members continue to be the main source of funds, and in recent years this was supplemented by rental income from its 20-story Rhenish building. Thus, in partnership with the United Evangelical Mission (Rhenish) and with some government subsidy, the CRC has been enabled to provided much-needed schools in the Hong Kong area and beyond—seven kindergartens, four primary schools, two evening schools, and three secondary schools. One of these, the Rhenish Church College, built in the 1970s, provides secondary education for over 1000 students. Other programs for children and young people include camps, conferences, and vacation Bible schools, reaching about 2000 with Christian instruction and wholesome recreation.

The church's welfare program—also receiving some government subsidy—includes recreation centers for the elderly and children, hostels for the aged, nurseries, and medical clinics. CRC's work among Vietnamese refugees, supplementing that of the Red Cross, is a spiritual ministry plus educational and recreational programs.

Since 1977 the CRC has supported and used the Lutheran Theological Seminary (LTS) in Shatin, New Territories. Here some of the candidates for the ordained ministry receive their training. Others study overseas. The LTS and CRC have jointly sponsored a laity program in theological education. One 10-session summer evening course brought a daily attendance of over 100. CRC also arranges summer trips for its members, mainly to visit *Taiwan, but also to *Malaysia, *Singapore, and *Thailand. While enjoying splendid scenery and Christian fellowship, the participants visit churches and gain an appreciation of the problems and opportunities for mission.

Five of the CRC congregations are overseas. In *Taiwan CRC missionaries reach out to the Cantonese-speaking people, especially to students. Hostels are provided for them and also for the elderly. In England a graduate student in theology began working among Chinese students and restaurant people in 1979. Today this is a flourishing program. In Toronto, *Canada, with its more than 200,000 Chinese-speaking residents, CRC members have not only gathered a church but in 1981 also opened a high school. Another congregation in Oakland, California, was formed in 1981. Its bilingual program serves CRC immigrants, Vietnamese refugees, Chinese students, and other people living in the San Francisco Bay area who desire a Chinese-speaking ministry.

Since 1974 the CRC has been a member of the LWF and participates in the Federation's work, especially in projects involving Chinese-speaking churches. Like the Batak churches in *Indonesia, the CRC admits to a long preponderance of Lutheran influence, despite the basically united (Lutheran and Reformed) composition of the Rhenish Mission. One of the decisive factors shaping the spiritual life of this church has been the consistent use of Luther's *Small Catechism*. This has now been supplemented by the recently published *New Life Catechism*. Its worship employs the liturgy and hymnal developed by missionaries on the basis of Lutheran usage in parts of the *Evangelical Church in the Rhineland. Its membership in the LWF is consistent with a long-held position.

The Chinese Rhenish Church, Hong Kong Synod, remembered its heritage by a year-long celebration of the 130th anniversary of its founding in 1847. In that year two missionaries—Heinrich Koster and Ferdinand Genähr—began work in Hong Kong.

Appropriately the celebration was in three parts and in three different locations. The first (September 24, 1977) was one of worship and commemoration. A throng of 1700, including many honored guests, filled the auditorium of Hong Kong's City Hall. They heard Dr. Fredrik A. Schiotz—a former LWF president and first director of the LWF service to orphaned missions and younger churches—speak from experience on the "Significance of Thanksgiving." A representative of the United Evangelical Mission (Rhenish) expressed a deep appreciation for the CRC's gift of DM 10,000, a Chinese gesture of "gratefulness to parents from the younger generation." A festive meal followed.

The second celebration, in November, was a two-day Youth Evangelism Rally at the Urban Stadium in Kowloon. The event, shared with the Chinese Christian Church Union as well as with other Lutheran churches, drew an attendance of 23,000. Special arrangements in assigned zones anticipated the needs of the blind, deaf, lame, and other handicapped. Choirs and bands set a tone of joy.

The third celebration was set in *Taiwan in February (1978). At Chung Ho, near Taipei, a new outpatient clinic was dedicated. Given the name "Pu-tse," it honors the memory of the first CRC hospital opened in the city of Tung Kwun, Kwantung Province, China, in 1888. It had grown out of the medical work the early missionaries had initiated a dozen years earlier. A former nurse of Putse, Mrs. Chen Hwang Tzu-lien, presented a large picture of the hospital, which in 1902 had become the first medical institution in China to provide beds for women patients.

Five years later (1982) the CRC celebrated again by raising funds for an extension of its ministry.

EVANGELICAL LUTHERAN CHURCH OF HONG KONG (ELCHK)
(Hsiang Ka Hsin Yi Hui)
Member: LWF (1957), HKCC, CLCHKA
Membership: 12,400**
President: The Rev. John C. M. Tse
50A Waterloo Road
Kowloon

The 53 congregations of this church are served by 30 pastors as well as a large staff of other workers, full-time and voluntary, in various fields of service. Both Mandarin and Cantonese languages are used, with interpretation of sermons to accommodate older members from central *China as well as the increasing number of indigenous Hong Kongers and Cantonese. In 1981 a Cantonese-speaking pastor was elected president of the church body. Since its organization in 1954, the church has had a polity combining congregational and synodical elements. The highest authority is the synodical convention, with the president and executive council serving as the administrative body.

Almost all of the pastors have been educated at its Lutheran Theological Seminary, Shatin, New Territories, which was relocated from Shekow in central *China in 1948. The accredited seminary offers a variety of programs for theological students, parish workers, and lay leaders. Since 1977 other Hong Kong churches—the *Chinese Rhenish Church and the *Hong Kong and Macao Lutheran Church—and the *Taiwan Lutheran Church have joined in the use and support of this institution. This partnership was reaffirmed in 1982 by a long-term cooperative agreement. At present its enrollment includes about 64 full-time students and 200 in evening extension classes. The seminary's immediate concern is the relocation made necessary by the construction of a major highway through its property. The nearby Tao Fong Shan Ecumenical Center (above) has agreed to share its hilltop property for a new campus. Construction costs are to be borne by the supporting churches and their overseas partners.

Additional educational service agencies of the church include three middle (secondary) schools, 13 primary schools, 14 kindergartens, six nurseries, a halfway house (for the rehabilitation of ex-drug addicts), and seven youth community centers. The Shatin Youth Center, opened in 1976, was the ELCHK's first structured social service project. Its programs, planned by three seminary graduate students, reach about 13,500 individuals between the ages of seven and 25.

From the early 1950s the ELCHK had been a partner of the *Taiwan Lutheran Church in maintaining the Taosheng Publishing House. Operated by the Lutheran Literature Society, it had production facilities and bookstores in both countries. In 1982 the assets and board were divided, creating two financially independent Taosheng Publishing Houses, both of which trace their roots to the Lutheran Board of Publication (LBP) of the former *Lutheran Church of China. Beginning in 1924 it published liturgies, hymnals, and theological textbooks. When the members of the LBP board came to Hong Kong in 1949, they reorganized under the name Lutheran Missions Literature Society. With the formation of the ELCHK and the TLC, another reorganization omitted "Missions" from the name.

Although the Taosheng Publishing House in Hong Kong is an enterprise of the ELCHK, other Chinese-reading churches profit from its many publications. The Everyman Reader service has some 60 titles; children's books about 30; and others totaling over 500. Ten volumes of *Luther's Works* are on sale. In 1987 a revised hymnal for use in Lutheran churches appeared. Since 1979 supplies of literature have been going to mainland *China.

Most of the older members of ELCHK are from mainland China and represent a variety of backgrounds and activities. Some still recall that in 1953 the Hong Kong Lutheran Mission, comprised of representatives of the various missions that had supported the *Lutheran Church of China (LCC), laid the basis for a provisional organization of the church. A permanent body was formed in 1955 and elected Dr. Peng Fu president, the position he had held in the *LCC before coming to Hong Kong.

The churches and missions formerly supporting the church in China have continued to support the ELCHK. Since 1960 they have been organized into a China Area Coordinating Committee (CACC). Membership includes the Danish, Finnish, Norwegian, and Swedish Missionary Societies, the ELCA

(former *American Lutheran Church and *Lutheran Church in America) as well as the ELCHK. Initially the CACC confined itself to considering projects sponsored solely by the ELCHK and the *Taiwan Lutheran Church. Later projects supported in cooperation with other churches were added. Now the annual meetings are more like forums at which all the local Lutheran churches and their partners plan for the overall good.

In 1984 the ELCHK worked out a relationship with the Finnish Evangelical Lutheran Mission and Norwegian Missionary Society whereby the church gained both title and administrative responsibility for several schools, study centers, and youth and elderly centers. Congregations formed by these societies had already become part of the ELCHK.

The ELCHK supports the *Lutheran Mission in Thailand (with the Norwegian Missionary Society and the Finnish Evangelical Lutheran Mission) and a Chinese language congregation in Toronto, *Canada, in cooperation with the ELCA.

HONG KONG AND MACAO LUTHERAN CHURCH (HKMLC)

Member: CLCHKA
Membership: 1966**
President: The Rev. Tsang Ming Sun
Shek On Building
8 Chun Yan Street
Wong Tai Sin, Kowloon

This church, founded in 1978, is the result of a long-time ministry of the Norwegian Lutheran Mission (NLM) to refugees from mainland China now living in crowded areas of Kowloon. Since 1978 the work has been extended to new immigrants from China living in Macao. From 1979–1984 the church also worked among Vietnamese refugees in Hong Kong and Macao.

In the seven congregations, six preaching places, three nurseries, six kindergartens, an old people's home, and two government-subsidized schools, HKMLC evangelistic, educational, and social service is carried on by five Chinese pastors, six evangelists, and several women parish workers and missionaries. A pattern of church organization is still in flux. About one-third of the church's budget is supplied by the Norwegian Lutheran

Mission. The church is known for its care and concern for drug addicts and for its efforts in the prevention of addiction. This work started in 1956 and a new rehabilitation center was built in 1985. These endeavors were greatly influenced by a lifelong missionary, Pastor Agnar Espegren (d.1982), who became the church's first president.

The HKMLC traces its roots to the work of the Norwegian Lutheran Mission in the mainland provinces of Honan, Hupeh, and Shensi, one of the largest Lutheran missions in *China. Deprived of Norwegian support during World War II when *Norway was occupied, the missionaries and the Chinese workers were helped through US Lutheran "orphaned mission" aid. Most of the missionaries were flown to *India during the crises of 1944 and 1945.

During the Japanese invasion, Espegren's life had been saved by a Chinese friend who later died of heroin addiction. Espegren determined then to do what he could to help other addicts. Coming to Hong Kong, he was one of the first Lutherans to enter this type of work. He moved freely among addicts in the "underground." In 1956 he started a withdrawal center for relapsed addicts—men in their 30s and 40s. Although only a few—about 11%—remained free of addiction, and fewer still became Christian, Espegren continued this program until his death.

The NLM has run schools in Hong Kong since 1950. Between 1956 and 1961 there was a strong expansion in the educational work, and by 1975 eight primary schools and one middle school with more than 6000 students were operating. Due to redevelopment in Hong Kong, the educational work has now been reduced. An evening Bible school was started in 1974, and since 1984 the HKMLC and the NLM have run a Bible institute for lay people. The HKMLC uses and supports the Lutheran Theological Seminary in Shatin (see ELCHK, above).

LUTHERAN CHURCH, HONG KONG SYNOD (LCHKS)

Member: LWF (1979), ILC, CLCHKA
Membership: 6580**
President: The Rev. Benjamin Bun-Wing Chung
68 Begonia Road
Yau Yat Chuen, Kowloon

This church body of 24 congregations and three mission stations, mainly in Kowloon

and the New Territories, is served by 34 national pastors, six expatriate missionaries, many teachers, and other lay workers. Until 1976 LCHKS was a mission of the *Lutheran Church–Missouri Synod (LCMS), USA. As an autonomous church, it requested and received the status of a "sister church" in 1977. The church has a congregational polity, but a synod coordinates the overall work.

The LCMS mission began in 1950 when an ordained missionary and three women workers leaving *China were in Hong Kong temporarily on their way home. The need for teachers and social service was so great that they stayed. Work in the Rennie's Mill refugee camp, where 22,000 mainlanders were huddled, was strengthened by a Bible school that trained new workers. Rented quarters in Kowloon were soon outgrown. Thus the mission started.

Beginning in 1952 the work was greatly strengthened by the International Lutheran Hour and its correspondence courses. Since the Lutheran Hour reaches out to non-Christians and Christians not strong in faith, it is a helpful opening for personal evangelism. The Sparkle Drama Society presents evangelistic dramas, Christian folk hymns, and variety shows to large audiences in churches, schools, and factories. The Lutheran Hour has been broadcast from Macao since 1957 and is heard as far as the *People's Republic. The tapes are prepared in Hong Kong. Many of the producers have other jobs during the day and contribute their time in the evenings.

The LCHKS's extensive educational program enrolls some 2600 children in kindergarten, over 10,000 in primary, and 6500 in secondary schools; employs 1011 national teachers; and includes a school for deaf children. Clubs and vacation Bible schools supplement the regular school work. The Hong Kong Lutheran College (above), initiated by people from this church, continues to receive their encouragement and support.

Concordia Seminary in Kowloon trains future pastors, offering both day and evening courses. In 1986 its social service department enrolled 38 students. The faculty consists of seven full-time professors and 12 part-time instructors.

The Martha Boss Community Center in Kowloon is the place where the LCHKS's department of social services coordinates its various social ministries: children's clubs, clinics, centers for the elderly, and, in co-operation with the government, the construction and administration of hostels for the aged. The late Martha Boss, for whom the center was named, served as a missionary of the LCMS in the Far East for almost three decades. The building was dedicated in 1981.

As a member of the LWF and the Chinese Lutheran Churches' Hong Kong Association, the LCHKS works in close harmony with others. LCHKS pastors have taken the lead in the Southeast Association for Higher Education and the formation of the Hong Kong Lutheran College.

The 1985 China visit of a 12-member delegation—including LCMS and LCHKS representatives—opened a new range of relationships with governmental, academic, and religious affairs agencies.

As indicated above, the Hong Kong Synod traces its roots to the work of the LCMS in *China. In 1917 LCMS accepted the responsibility for the mission begun in 1913 by the Rev. E. L. Arndt. At the age of 49 Arndt left his teaching post in St. Paul, Minnesota, and, with support from some 20 midwestern congregations, began work in the Hankow area. The work continued in spite of wars and hardships until 1949, when the Communist wave engulfed the Hankow area. Members as well as missionaries met again in Hong Kong.

SOUTH ASIAN LUTHERAN EVANGELICAL MISSION (SALEM)
Membership: 121**
Counselor: The Rev. Gary Schroeder
4 Broadcast Drive
1/F Kowloontong
Kowloon

The South Asian Lutheran Evangelical Mission (SALEM, incorporated 1977) works in cooperation with the *Wisconsin Evangelical Lutheran Synod (WELS), USA. Mediums for SALEM ministries include three congregations, a Bible institute, a seminary, a middle school, and two study centers. SALEM is served by four pastors and two evangelists. Cantonese is the primary language used.

A Chinese pastor, a graduate of Bethany Lutheran Seminary of the small Evangelical Lutheran Synod of Norse origin began a ministry that led to the formation of the Chinese Evangelical Lutheran Church (CELC) in 1965. In response to a request for assistance in achieving indigeneity, WELS subsidized the ministries of the CELC and the salaries of its workers until 1977. In that year the work was restructured, renamed, and continued under SALEM, with an emphasis on lay ministry.

TSUNG TSIN MISSION, HONG KONG (TTM)
Member: LWF (1974), HKCC, CLCHKA
Membership: 8000**
President: Poon Ki Simon Sit
144 G Boundary Street, 2/F
Kowloon

Autonomous since 1929, the 14 Tsung Tsin congregations are served by 24 ordained pastors and eight preachers, as well as by a staff of teachers and others in related ministries. Originally Hakka-speaking, some of the congregations also use Cantonese and Mandarin. The church members are scattered in Hong Kong Island, Kowloon, and the New Territories. The TTM form of organization combines congregational and synodical features. The church is governed by a board of directors representing the several congregations. A lay president heads the church. (The term *mission* in the title recalls the old connection with the Basel Mission Society.)

The TTM conducts three secondary schools, nine primary schools, and seven kindergartens. In the field of welfare it runs three nurseries and six clinics and operates a (revolving) assistance fund for people in need. The church's seven departments operate in the fields of youth, evangelism, women, Sunday school, education, welfare, and publications. Each department is headed by voluntary church workers elected at the TTM general meeting. Pastors were educated at the church's Lok-Yuk Theological College until 1967 when the school was merged with the theological department of Chung-Chi College, Chinese University of Hong Kong.

TTM history begins with the Basel Mission work launched in Hong Kong and in the Kwangtung Province of mainland *China in 1847. After the Communist revolution, the church was formed from those congregations of the Tsung Tsin Church that were cut off from the main body. Like the Chinese Rhenish Church (above), the TTM is of united Protestant origin, the Swiss-German Basel Mission Society being supported by Lutheran and Reformed constituencies. Here, too, Lutheran influence eventually became preponderant. During the time of readjustment after World War II, services rendered to refugees and others in Hong Kong by the LWF, as well as an intensification of missionary activity by Scandinavian and North American agencies, tended to make the TTM receptive to wider partnership, including membership in the LWF. The TTM also had old ties in Hong Kong that proved very helpful in time of need. It accepts the *Augsburg Confession* and uses Luther's *Small Catechism* for confirmation instruction.

The TTM is active in the Chinese Lutheran Churches' Hong Kong Association, the Hong Kong Christian Council, and the Hong Kong Christian Service.

TAIWAN

The Republic of China, situated some 160 kilometers (100 miles) east of the southern coastland of mainland *China, consists of the island of Taiwan (Formosa) and its 77 outlying islands (14 in the Taiwan group and 63 in the Pescadores group). Area: 36,002 sq. km. (13,900 sq. mi.). Not included in this area are the disputed and heavily defended Quemoy and Matsu islands, just off Fukien Province of the mainland, which have been Nationalist outposts since 1949. Pop.: (1985) 19,135,000. Cap. and largest city: Taipei (pop., 1984, 2,388,374). Language: Mandarin Chinese (official).

History: Presumably the first Taiwanese came from the Malayo-Polynesian islands about 2000 years ago. In the seventh century the first mainland Chinese came to Taiwan. Europeans—Portuguese (who named the island Formosa, "beautiful"), Spanish, and then Dutch—briefly claimed the island during the 17th century. In 1662 a Chinese sealord, Koxinga, ousted the Dutch and established an independent kingdom. Two decades later, when the Manchus gained control,

Chinese immigration increased and the aboriginal Taiwanese were pushed into the interior. Following the first Sino-Japanese war, Japan annexed Taiwan (1895). Development, industrialization, and the exploitation of resources followed. Japanese-held Taiwan was heavily bombed by USA planes during World War II. In 1945 Taiwan was returned to China as a province.

With Chinese Communists in control of the mainland (1949), the Nationalist government of Chiang Kai-shek, the remnant of his army, and about two million civilians fled to Taiwan. Here Chiang took firm command. With USA aid he reorganized his military forces and in time instituted limited democratic reforms, including an elected national assembly. Taiwan's international position was weakened in 1971 when the China seat in the United Nations was given to the *People's Republic of China and Taiwan withdrew. Chiang Kai-shek's death in 1975 caused little disruption, for his son, Chiang Ching-Kuo, who was already influencing the ruling party, was elected president. A second major setback for Taiwan was the USA's recognition of mainland China in 1978.

Serious tension between the 85% majority of long-time Taiwanese and the powerful minority of recent Chinese immigrants has decreased. Taiwan has remained politically and economically viable, defying pressures to consolidate with the Communist government of the mainland. It follows Japan, Hong Kong, and Singapore in its per capita income.

Religion: Traditional religion (48.5%), whose adherents are mainly the descendants of the prewar Chinese settlers, combines magic, ancestor veneration, and devotion to divinities with influence from Taoism, Buddhism, and Confucianism, as well as animism. Buddhism (43%) is strong but is strictly practiced by only a few. The small number of Muslims (0.5%) are mainly recent immigrants from *China. Tribal religions are fast disappearing as conversions to Christianity take place.

Christianity came to Taiwan in 1621 through Roman Catholic Dominicans from the Philippines. Three years later, when the Dutch gained control, their work was suppressed. Roman Catholic efforts resumed in the 19th century, counting 8000 members by 1945 and 40 years later 275,000. The Roman

Catholic Church has a committee for Christian unity within its Episcopal Commission for Social Action and the Lay Apostolate.

Protestantism entered during the Dutch occupation (1624–1662), but tragically all 6000 of the tribal converts as well as the missionaries were killed when the Chinese took the island in 1662. Two centuries later Presbyterians (British in 1865; Canadian in 1872) came and founded what is now a strong and growing indigenous church. The Presbyterian Church in Taiwan joined the World Council of Churches in 1951 (Taiwan's only member body), but for political reasons it has not been active in the WCC. This church doubled in size between 1955 and 1965. Its membership is over 160,000.

After the influx of Chinese from the mainland in 1949, other Protestant denominations, related mainly to America, regrouped their membership and evangelized among the non-Christians. The Taiwan Missionary Fellowship fostered intermission cooperation. Although the new churches grew rapidly during the 1950s, the majority have remained small fragments of the Christian church. The Chinese indigenous churches seem to have greater vitality. The largest of these, the Church Assemblies (also known as the "Little Flock"), ranks third in size after the Roman Catholic and Presbyterian churches. Under Watchman Nee, it began on the mainland in 1926 and came to Taiwan in 1948. It is congregational, anticlerical, antiliturgical, fundamentalistic, and enthusiastically evangelistic.

Taiwan has no council of churches related to the WCC. A general fear tends to equate the Christians who live in Communist countries with Communism itself, preventing the development of certain ecumenical relationships. The Association of Christian Churches of the Republic of China, organized in 1966, is open to all denominations, local churches, and individuals. It serves mainly as a link between the churches and government.

Mass media—radio and television—as used by many of the churches, have fostered some cooperation. Lutherans in 1975 led in a nationwide evangelistic effort, "His Wounds—Our Healing." This multimedia project published a book, produced three television and 14 radio programs, printed 10,000 posters, distributed 100,000 tracts, and was widely reported in the secular newspapers

and on radio and television news. Follow-up programs in 1976–1977 and again in 1980 were well received. Since then, rising costs and some restraints on religious broadcasts have diminished such mass projects. Besides, the Taiwanese people in general, experiencing prosperity and security, are less open to the gospel than earlier. This is of great concern to the churches of all denominations.

The total number of Lutheran adherents may exceed that reported by the five small church bodies. Several active Lutheran missions have not as yet formed autonomous church bodies. The Norwegian Lutheran Mission (NLM), in the Changhua area since 1953, has established 14 or more congregations with a membership of 1000. It supports the "Voice of Salvation," an evangelistic radio project. Bible correspondence courses for young people and adults have nearly 3000 students. A vigorous follow-up campaign encourages listeners to attend church and to decide for Christ. The NLM also supports the China Lutheran Seminary in Hsin-Chu and is a member of the Chinese Lutheran Churches' Association in Taiwan (CLCAT, below).

The *Chinese Rhenish Church, Hong Kong Synod ministers to the Cantonese-speaking people and provides hostels for students. Its youth and women's work emphasizes music in the spread of the gospel. The USA *Wisconsin Evangelical Lutheran Synod, as the result of contacts made through the "Voice of Salvation" of the NLM, began work in Taiwan in 1968. One national pastor and three Wisconsin missionaries serve small congregations in the Chung Hua and Taipei areas. With a membership of 130 baptized, they are known as the Christian Lutheran Evangelical Church. The Scandinavian East Asia Mission, with a local board of both Lutherans and Anglicans, maintains the House of Friendship in Taipei, a dialog center for Christians and Buddhists similar to the Tao Fong Shan Ecumenical Center in *Hong Kong.

The Chinese Lutheran Churches' Association in Taiwan (CLCAT), organized in 1979, is the means of enabling the five churches (below) as well as the Norwegian Lutheran Mission, the Finnish Evangelical Lutheran Mission, and the Chinese Rhenish Church to cooperate more effectively in their evangelism and service. Two of the churches are

members of the Lutheran World Federation—
the Taiwan Lutheran Church (since 1960),
and the Lutheran Church of Taiwan (since
the 1984 assembly in Budapest). Four of the
members cooperate in the maintenance of the
China Lutheran Seminary in Hsin-Chu, a city
on the Formosa Strait, southwest of Taipei.
All CLCAT members agree on the need for
stronger Lutheran theological education
within their country.

Other cooperative efforts are in publications and broadcasting, generously aided by
the LWF. The Taosheng Publishing House
(TPH), founded by the Lutheran Literature
Society in 1959, was a joint project of the
*Taiwan Lutheran Church and the *Evan-
gelical Lutheran Church of Hong Kong until
1982. Now it has the support of all the Taiwan
Lutherans. The separation was initiated by
the Taiwan Lutheran Church. For some time
the main office had been in Taipei and the
director was a TLC pastor. Since 1972 the
locally published Lily books have been best-
sellers in 400 secular bookstores across the
land. Now numbering 126 titles, they include
religious books for Christians, evangelistic
books for non-Christians, as well as other
literature for young and old. TPH is the first
self-supporting Christian publisher in Taiwan.

CHINA EVANGELICAL LUTHERAN CHURCH (CELC)
Member: (P), CLCAT
Membership: 2621**
President: The Rev. Jen Chih-Ping
4th Floor, No. 127
Section 1, Fu Hsing South Road
Taipei

An autonomous church since 1966, the CELC
is related to the *Lutheran Church–Missouri
Synod. Its 23 congregations, mainly in the
Taipei area and the region around Chiayi on
the western plain, are served by 24 ordained
pastors. Evangelists, teachers, and others are
active in related ministries. The Chinese
workers have the assistance of two LCMS
missionaries. The church combines congregational and synodical elements in its polity.
Its first general conference in 1966 led to the
adoption of a constitution in 1968.

The "China Lutheran Hour," established
in 1953, was the first religious broadcast on
the island. Important in the mission of the
CELC, it has an office at the church headquarters and a studio in the center of the city.
In 1981 the high cost of broadcasting terminated the sacred music program. In its
place, one-hour cassettes of sacred music are
sent weekly to all former listeners known to
the station and to others on request. Its flexibility and popularity has led to the greater
use of cassettes in meeting other needs such
as Christian instruction material for adults as
well as children. These tapes are now sent
to Mandarin-speaking Chinese in other countries. Tapes in other Taiwanese languages are
also being prepared. "Evening Prayer,"
"Everybody Sing Along," and the "Lutheran
Hour" continue to be broadcast. Supplementing the radio ministry is the Bible correspondence school, also located at the
church headquarters. The "China Lutheran
Hour" is supported by the International Lutheran Laymen's League of the USA, although a considerable amount is raised locally.

The CELC, a partner with the Taiwan Lutheran Church (below) in the Joint Lutheran
Television project, also cooperates with other
Lutheran Chinese-speaking churches in the
production of Christian literature through the
Taipei-based Taosheng Publishing House
and, until 1985, with the Lutheran Southeast
Asia Christian Education Curricula Committee in *Hong Kong.

Concordia Seminary for the training of
pastors and the Concordia Middle School are
both located in Chiayi. The latter's enrollment
of more than 1600 includes 900 vocational
students. As a community service the school
runs a kindergarten for 200. A teaching staff
of 50, under a Taiwanese principal, serves
this large educational complex.

The USA-based Voluntary Youth Ministry
(VYM) program brings two or more LCMS
young people to the CELC each autumn for
a 30-month term. After six months of intensive Mandarin study, they are assigned to a
congregation to work with the young and with
church leaders in evangelism. Their partial
support comes from teaching English in
schools, youth centers, or private classes.

The origins of the CELC are in the missions
west of Hankow, *China, where the Lutheran
Church–Missouri Synod began its work in
1913. Following the rise of the People's Republic of China and paralleling the formation

of the *Lutheran Church—Hong Kong Synod, emigrés in Taiwan formed their separate church. The first missionary to arrive in 1951 was Olive Gruen, who had 30 years experience in China. Together with a Chinese lay assistant, she prepared candidates for baptism and confirmation. She also taught Bible classes at Taiwan University and the University Hospital in Taipei, initiated a Bible correspondence course, and followed up on Lutheran emigrés in the outlying towns of Hualien, Huwei, and Chiayi. In 1952 Pastor Roy Suelflow arrived and opened a seminary in his Taipei home. With an enrollment of 25, the seminary was moved to Chiayi in 1954. Evangelism, strengthened by the "Lutheran Hour," was reinforced by solid education—the strength of LCMS mission. Outstanding among the Chinese leaders was the Rev. Winston S. Chu (d. 1988), former CELC president and media promoter.

CHINA LUTHERAN GOSPEL CHURCH (CLGC)
Member: CLCAT
Membership: 150**
President: The Rev. Ming-Hsiang Hsing
PO Box 12
Tung Chi Street 387
Tungshih 423

Organized in 1973, the CLGC membership is located in and around Taichung, a city southwest of Taipei noted for its educational and cultural activities. Of the eight congregations, six are Mandarin-speaking, one is Taiwanese, and one Hakka. Five pastors and two evangelists serve the church.

Under its synodical polity, the church elects a president for a two-year term. Although ineligible to be president, expatriate missionaries otherwise have the same status as the Chinese workers. The pastoral candidates are trained at the China Lutheran Seminary in Hsin-Hsu, which the church supports in cooperation with three other small churches and their related mission agencies. The CLGC provides one teacher. It also runs four kindergartens.

The CLGC is the fruit of the *Evangelical Lutheran Free Church of Norway (ELFCN), which began the work in 1961. The ELFCN maintains responsibility for the Lutheran

Gospel Center (a Bible camp in Kukuan) and also for a clinic in Tungshih.

CHINESE LUTHERAN BRETHREN CHURCH (CLBC)
Member: (P), CLCAT
Membership: 1600**
President: Bishop Su Fu-Li
No. 127, Section 1, Fu Hsing South Road
Taipei

This autonomous church, formed in 1957, is composed of 16 congregations served by 11 ordained pastors. Its members, former refugees from mainland *China and later adherents, live mainly around Hsin-Chu, southwest of Taipei in the coastal area. The language used is Chinese—Mandarin and Amoy. This church combines congregational and presbyterian forms of polity in its organization.

Pastoral candidates are educated mainly in the China Lutheran Seminary, established in 1966 in Hsin-Chu by several Lutheran missions, including the Brethren. The school has a Chinese president, the Rev. Hsin-Min Hsu—a member of the CLBC—devoted to strengthening Lutheran theological education in Taiwan. Students and faculty of the small school visit congregations to elicit interest and support. At present there are more women than men enrolled.

Historically this church continues the work begun in 1902 by the *Church of the Lutheran Brethren, a USA body of Norse descent, in the mainland provinces of Honan and Hupeh. There the intensely evangelistic and pietistic mission experienced occasional revivals. Periods of great hardship culminated with Japan's war on China (1937–1945). After the war, the Brethren resumed their mission briefly until the proclamation of the People's Republic (1949). That year some Brethren missionaries prospected in *Japan for alternative work. Meanwhile, a few members had fled to Taiwan. In 1952 they were joined by missionary Arthur E. Nyhus from Japan. The Brethren cooperated in efforts leading to the formation of the Taiwan Lutheran Church (below). However, in 1957, believing it important to preserve their own distinctive ways, they withdrew from the TLC and formed their own church.

LUTHERAN CHURCH OF TAIWAN (LCT)

Member: LWF (1984), CLCAT
Membership: 1300**
President: The Rev. Tsai Ho-Hsing
Nan Chin Road, Lane 2, No. 18
Chaochou 92006

The Lutheran Church of Taiwan (LCT), founded in 1977, comprises 21 congregations and chapels (organized groups of at least eight adult members). Although the baptized membership is small, the church activities encompass many more, both native Taiwanese and mainlanders, and growth is steady.

In 1956 the Finnish Evangelical Lutheran Mission (FELM) began its work in and around the towns of Hengchun and Chaochou in southern Taiwan where there were few Christian workers. Although the missionaries served the numerous Chinese refugees, they also ministered to the Taiwanese. Using the language of the various people, Taiwanese, Mandarin, Hakka, and Paiwan (tribal), the work flourished. However, when a big migration, especially of the refugees, to the large, developing cities began, the church redirected its outreach. Now the main work of the LCT is in the growing suburbs of Taipei, Taoyuan, Kaohsiung, and Pingtung, neighborhoods with few if any Christian congregations. The church aims to start one new congregation each year in addition to its present nine urban ones.

The general assembly, which meets twice a year, elects the nine-member church council (five clergy and four lay) and from this group selects the president and vice-president. The FELM elects two observers to the assembly. They have voice but no vote. The joint committee of the LCT and FELM discusses all cooperative efforts. The church has 13 ordained pastors and 16 evangelists (both men and women). On the local level, Chinese and Finnish pastors work side by side sharing all the tasks. The church invites expatriate missionaries as needed.

At the church headquarters in Chaochou there is also the Hsin-yi Broadcasting Center, a cooperative project of the LCT and FELM. Twelve qualified nationals prepare half-hour programs in Mandarin, Taiwanese, and Hakka for broadcast over local stations in southern Taiwan. This venture includes a Bible correspondence school whose annual enrollment ranges between 5000 and 8000 students.

The Hsin-yi Literature Center (1966), also in Chaochou, is another cooperative project. Over each of these two centers is a governing board of six members, three from the LCT.

The LCT cooperates with the FELM in maintaining the China Lutheran Seminary in Hsin-Hsu together with three other small Lutheran churches. Some of the pastors and most of the church workers have had their training in seminaries of other denominations. More adequate preparation for both clergy and laity is considered the foremost need of the LCT. Through its membership in the LWF, received at the 1984 Budapest assembly, the LCT hopes to strengthen its relationship with other churches and to advance a stronger theological program in Taiwan.

TAIWAN LUTHERAN CHURCH (TLC)

Member: LWF (1960), CLCAT, CCAT
Membership: 6909**
President: The Rev. Stanley Tung
15 Hang Chow South Road, Section 2
Taipei 10608

The TLC, founded in 1954, is presently the largest of the Lutheran churches in Taiwan. Its 43 congregations, served by 34 pastors, divide into four districts centered in the cities of Taipei, Taichung, Tainan, and Kaohsiung. A federated synodical polity with biennial conventions reflects the international mission cooperation that the TLC has experienced since its formation. Post-1948 immigrants from mainland *China and their descendants make up the bulk of the membership, but Taiwanese are joining in increasing numbers.

Besides its congregational work, the TLC conducts one of the strongest denominational student programs in Taiwan. The Taipei Truth Church student center, opened in 1954, is strategically located across from the National Taiwan University, the country's largest. An active program for students and other young adults reaches hundreds. Since 1980 two hostels have provided housing for 130 students as well as some income for the program. This dormitory ministry has increased the number of students requesting baptism. On one day there were 26 who took this courageous step.

Two smaller student centers, also with dormitory facilities, are located in Taichung and Tainan, cities farther south.

The TLC maintains two hospitals. The one in Chiayi, in west central Taiwan, which opened in 1958, continues to provide service as well as spiritual care to the surrounding rural community. In 1985 a new five-story wing was opened and facilities expanded. In the southern city of Kaohsiung, TLC converted a closed Bible school into a useful hospital. This was enlarged in 1980 by a six-story addition dedicated to those unable to afford more costly medical care.

Since the late 1960s the TLC has cooperated with the China Evangelical Lutheran Church (above) in the Joint Lutheran Television project. "Week End Theater" replaced the popular "Sunday Theater" that ran for 14 years and received the Golden Bell award. Because of rising costs and lack of support, these broadcasts were stopped in 1980. Attempts have been made to relaunch an ecumenical TV program, but so far this has not been possible.

The TLC is served by the Taosheng Publishing House (see Taiwan Introduction) and the Lutheran Theological Seminary in Shatin, *Hong Kong. However in recent years the church has depended more on the interdenominational China Evangelical Seminary (CES) in Taipei for the education of its ordained ministry.

In November 1984 the TLC celebrated its 30th anniversary with a thanksgiving service in Taipei, its headquarters. A two-day retreat for all church workers reviewed the church's past history and made plans for the future. A few of those present had been among the mainlanders who had come to Taiwan in 1949. They recalled how small groups of Christians had met in homes for Bible study and prayer. A gifted leader among them, C. A. Chin, a medical doctor, had been an active lay preacher in mainland China. In Taiwan he continued, gathering factory workers into his home in Kaohsiung for Bible study. From him came the plea to fellow Lutherans in Hong Kong for pastoral care. Others recalled the two Norwegian nurses who came in 1950 to Taipei, served in a Presbyterian hospital, conducted Bible classes in English for women, and supported the plea for church workers.

When two American missionaries arrived in June 1951 to survey the situation, they found 37 people ready for baptism and many others eager to form the first Lutheran congregation in Kaohsiung. Dr. Chin was licensed to serve as pastor and was later ordained.

Soon thereafter eight American and Scandinavian Lutheran mission boards began sending missionaries to work in various cities among the emigré mainlanders. These incoming expatriates formed the Taiwan Lutheran Mission (TLM) in order to coordinate the various efforts. A Bible school was opened in Kaohsiung (1952). To strengthen the core of Chinese workers, the Lutheran Theological Seminary in *Hong Kong sent several of its graduates to Taiwan, and congregations grew rapidly. In 1954 an autonomous Taiwan Lutheran Church was organized with Chinese leadership and a membership of over 1000. A seminary, opened in Taipei and later moved to Taichung, graduated nine in its first class. The young church was received into the LWF in 1960. By 1963 the TLC membership exceeded 5000.

About this time the expatriate TLM turned over all its duties in administration as well as its responsibility for evangelism to the TLC. Henceforth the missionaries, reorganized as the Taiwan Lutheran Missionary Association and still supported by their various boards, served under the TLC.

The following years were difficult ones for the TLC. Like many other churches in Taiwan, it suffered from a decline in interest and support. Several of the overseas mission boards withdrew their support and began work of their own. Besides, the general atmosphere of economic prosperity that prevailed in Taiwan seemed to suppress the desire for spiritual nurture. With few candidates for the ordained ministry, the seminary was closed (1966), and the *Hong Kong-based Lutheran Theological Seminary became the official school for training pastors. Since leaving the island was not always practicable for students, other denominational schools were used, especially the Presbyterian seminary in Tainan. For a church seeking unity of spirit, this was not the best solution. Growth was almost at a standstill. A low point had been reached.

During the 1970s the TLC determined to become self-supporting and succeeded. Nevertheless, personnel and funds for special projects continued to come from most of the original supporting partners: The American Lutheran Church, the Danish Missionary Society, the Lutheran Church in America (a merger of the Augustana and United Lutheran churches), and the Norwegian Missionary Society.

New life came to the TLC when its long-time student work eventually brought a harvest of committed young and well-educated men and women into the church, giving rise to a new generation of leaders, both lay and clergy. Having grown up in Taiwan, they are more comfortable in its highly industrialized and secularized milieu than the older pastors and laity who live in the hope of returning to the land of their birth. A number of the young pastors have chosen the gospel ministry, which in Taiwan has little status and economic security, over against opportunities for successful careers in business or the professions. Thus the TLC lives with hope and confidence.

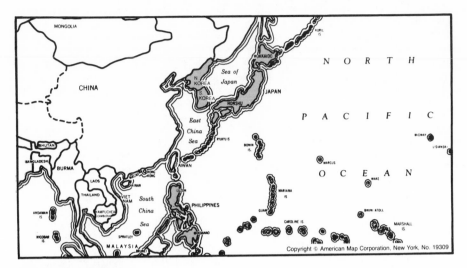

Copyright © American Map Corporation, New York, No. 19309

EAST ASIA

East Asian Lutherans account for only 1.3% of the Lutheran total for Asia. Lutheran work began in Japan (1892), extended to the Philippines (1946), and to Korea (1958). The churches in this region cultivate active relations with those elsewhere in Asia as well as those in America and Europe. Despite their small membership, these churches have made effective use of electronic and print media and of educational programs. Thus they have exercised an influence beyond their modest numbers.

JAPAN

A representative parliamentary democracy with the emperor as symbol of the state (present form since 1947). Nihon (or Nippon) occupies an archipelago off the northeast Asian mainland. Its four main islands are Honshū (largest, location of capital), Shikoku, Kyūshū, and Hokkaidō. Far to the south lies Okinawa, part of the Ryukyu chain. Area: 377,765 sq. km. (145,866 sq. mi.). Pop. (1985): 120,760,000. Cap. and largest city: Tokyo (pop., 1984 est., 8,389,758). Language: Japanese.

History: According to legend, the empire was founded in 660 B.C. Political power was exercised by successive families of shoguns (military dictators over many centuries— 1192–1867), until the "restoration" of imperial power by Emperor Meiji (1852–1912) in 1868. Tokyo became the capital city, as successor to Kyōto. American initiative

(1854) led to the opening of contacts with the outside world, from which emerged Western-style industry, technology, and education. Contacts with the *China mainland and its civilization had been many; and also with *Korea. War with China (1894–1895), and with Russia (1904–1905), as well as the annexation of Korea (1910) marked Japan's rise as a major power. Participation in World War I and an ensuing preeminence internationally spawned the crowning Japanese idea for developing a "Greater East Asia Co-Sphere." Inroads on the mainland led to war with China (1937) and to opposition from the United States. The conflict in the Pacific (1941–1945), culminating in the nuclear bombing of Hiroshima and Nagasaki, was the other major scene of World War II. Occupied until 1952, Japan's sovereignty was then restored. Despite terrible wartime destruction, the nation rallied for a new beginning. Phenomenal growth in industry and technology, led by farsighted planning and resourcefulness, have turned Japan into a producer with few, if any, peers. In 1985 the 40th anniversary of the atomic age made the Japanese people existential proponents of peace and justice among the nations. The accession of Emperor Akihito in 1989 was seen as marking a new era.

Religion: Shinto, the ancestral religion, and Buddhism, the 6th-century arrival from *China, have dominated the religious scene for most of Japan's history. Christianity in modern times has been reckoned a *third* religion in Japan, but at best a foreign entity and ever a small minority. Since World War II the number of nonreligionists has been growing (now about 10%). But religious statistics as such are elusive, particularly because of the common distinction between family religion, to which many adhere (perhaps over 70%), and personal religion, to which relatively few admit—notably because of an advancing secularism. A clue as to the family religion was the actual count of persons visiting Shinto shrines and Buddhist temples at New Year 1976—over 60% of the population.

When, at war's end, on New Year's Day 1946, Emperor Hirohito (1901–1989) declared that the previous religious doctrines of the state were myths, Shinto became a purely private religion. For Christianity, despite its Japanese leadership and the huge missionary efforts in the postwar period—favors were granted to Protestant and Catholic enterprises by the American occupation—the advance was relatively modest. The real growth appeared to be in the upsurging new religions.

The multiplication of sects among all Japan's religions, and especially during the postwar period, has been described as "the rush hour of the gods." Among the new religions, largely sprung from the old as adaptations to changing conditions, there has been much borrowing. In some of them elements of Buddhism, Shinto, Christianity, Confucianism, and the like have been combined. Among the five leading new religions, the number of adherents ranges between more than two million to more than 15 million. The leader, Soka Gakkai (Value Creation Society), emerged in the mid-1930s as a strongly nationalist Buddhism of the laity; its phenomenal growth (after 1951) being accompanied by political aims and an intolerance of other religions, an attitude that growth

and time have somewhat mellowed. Reiyukai (Association of Friends of the Spirit) sprang from Buddhist roots in 1923 but began to flourish only after the war. Today it is the second largest among the new religions. An offshoot from it in 1938, Rissho-koseikai (Society for the Establishment of Righteousness), treasures the ancestral legacy while cultivating fairer family and interpersonal relations. "Hoza" (group counseling) is seen as the secret of its Buddha-oriented success. While the new religions have many local meeting places, each has some large center for worship, assemblies, and conferences, such as Rissho-koseikai's impressive complex in Tokyo, with its 5000-seat Fumon Hall and other facilities, or the 60,000-seat Soka Gakkai temple that draws the faithful to the foothills of Mount Fuji.

Japan's 150 new religions give some indication of the competitive field in which a vastly proliferated Christianity operates and today claims about 1% of the population. Its 125 separately identifiable ecclesial bodies range in size from the approximately 400,000-member Roman Catholic Church and the more than 200,000-member Kyodan (United Church of Christ) to splinter groups of under 100 members. Even so, Christians in Japan have exercised an influence far beyond their numerical strength, even as the main denominational bodies have long cooperated in common tasks.

The National Christian Council of Japan (NCCJ), formed in 1948, enlarged upon the work of the earlier (1920) National Christian Conference. Japanese leadership figured prominently already in the 1920s and 1930s, and thus, in the period of mounting national crisis, helped to obtain legal recognition (1939) for Christianity from the Imperial Diet, thus placing it on a par with Buddhism and Shinto. A further step was the movement toward unity that, in 1941, brought 41 Protestant denominations into the Kyodan. After the war, Baptist, Anglican, and Lutheran bodies withdrew. The largest of these, the Anglican, is now known as the Japan Holy Catholic Church.

Since Vatican II relations between the major communions have improved to the point of an interconfessional translation of the Bible published by the Japan Bible Society. A special edition of this Bible in large type was financed by a gift of a precious family jewel to the society. When appraised and sold, the jewel brought Y 10,000,000 (US $62,500). Dr. Chitose Kishi, long active in the society and chairman of its board in recent years, supervised the translation until its official publication in 1987. He is himself a first generation Christian and a past president of the Japan Lutheran Theological College and Seminary.

The Roman Catholic presence in Japan goes back to 1549 when Francis Xavier (1506–1552), the great Jesuit missionary, spent a couple of years there. The ensuing Christian advance, aided and abetted by internal strife among the Japanese, eventually spread to various parts of the country. The line of communication for the Christian missionaries with the outside world was via the Portuguese in Macao, on the China coast, and in Goa, on the shores of western India. Already on Xavier's departure, about 1000 converts were claimed. In time their number grew, despite official resistance, to perhaps 650,000. Well-rooted in such centers as Kyō-to, Nagasaki, and Osaka, some overzealous converts even destroyed Shinto shrines and Buddhist temples. The first expulsion order (1587) was directed against the Jesuits. Yet they had been joined on the scene by Spanish Franciscans, archrivals of the Jesuits up from the *Philippines. Bitter strife between the Catholic orders aided the resolve to rid Japan of all Christians. Martyrdoms followed; even a massacre of a claimed 30,000 converts. By 1650 a "Christian century in Japan" (the title of C. R. Boxer's brilliant account) came to an end. Catholicism went underground, surviving among the Hanare Kirishitan (Separated Christians) to this day in small groups totalling 30,000 that have not rejoined the Roman Catholic Church. One result of Japan's earlier experience with Christians is that after 1650 it cut itself off from outside powers, except those of China and the Netherlands. Two centuries of near isolation from the European world changed Japan's history—and more.

In the 1860s Roman Catholic missionaries joined the influx of Protestants and began almost afresh. Evangelism, education, and health and welfare work became part of a multi-pronged advance. Centerpiece of the Roman educational venture was Sophia University (1911) in Tokyo. While Protestants moved much more quickly in developing an indigenous leadership and ministry, Catholics relied on the various orders from Europe and America. During World War II this reliance on German, Italian, and other personnel spared the church much of the painful internment of American and Allied missionary staff. After 1937 the Japanization of the Roman church moved more rapidly. The controversy over Japanese rites (homage to the Emperor, who is claimed divine; is this a religious or a civic act?) was settled in favor of a nonreligious, patriotic interpretation, even as it was for most Protestants. During the war the Roman foreign bishops resigned, thus opening the way to Japanese leadership.

The first Protestant missionaries—Episcopalian and Reformed—arrived from America in 1859. Others soon joined them. Progress was slow, given the generations of antichurch agitation led by the rulers. But a persuasive emphasis on education at all levels proved effective. In Kyōto, the nation's cultural center, the Doshisha University—which grew out of efforts initiated in the 1870s by Jo Niijima, a Japanese educated in America—continues as a reminder among the numerous subsequent Protestant institutions of higher education. Besides, a meaningful line connects Doshisha with the International Christian University (1953) in Mitaka, a Tokyo suburb. It was founded on American initiative and Japanese supportiveness as a sign of postwar reconciliation.

From across the Sea of Japan came Russian Orthodox missionaries already in 1861. The venture grew slowly, but in 1970 the Patriarch of Moscow granted autonomy to the Japan Orthodox Church.

The several Lutheran church bodies described below reported a combined membership of nearly 30,000 in 1984. This is a modest number, considering that over nine decades have passed since the first Lutheran missionaries arrived from America (JELC, below). Compared with the other major Protestant communions, the Lutherans were latecomers. They have set up schools and health facilities and welfare programs; also Bible schools and theological seminaries and conference centers. But they have not entered the field of higher education as such, relying rather on work among students in colleges and universities. Evangelism and the gathering and nurture of congregations has been their main task.

Lutheran work in Japan received a major impetus in 1948 when the revolution in *China redirected many mission efforts to Japan. Happily, the already established LWF policy of fostering Lutheran unity in a given country also had some effect in Japan. For over three decades there has been the kind of cooperation among Lutherans in Japan from which other church bodies could also benefit. There follow two examples, one from the electronic and the other from the print media.

The "Japan Lutheran Hour," introduced in 1951, refers listener inquiries for follow-up by the several churches participating in its support. It has helped pastors and laity become better aware of the role of the media in their own outreach. Rising costs have curbed but not stopped successful Lutheran programs on television. A Lutheran Office of Communication now coordinates the various offerings in radio and TV. Its director is secretary for the regional forum, Lutheran Communications in Asia (LUCIA), the latter being a reminder of the 1960s and 1970s when an LWF-related enterprise linked the offices in *Hong Kong and Tokyo to the pivotal station, RVOG, in *Ethiopia. Now the communications office in Tokyo is part of Seibunsha's media research center.

Seibunsha, organized in 1951 as the Lutheran Literature Society, is an independent, inter-Lutheran organization. Its work includes communication and other enterprises as well as the production of a wide variety of Christian literature. Its initial commitment was to undertake the translation and publication of a Japanese edition of *Luther's Works.* The first series of 12 volumes was completed in 1983. An additional 24 volumes will complete the set. Living up to its name— Sacred Publishing House—Seibunsha has in recent years produced a Japanese edition of the Lutheran *Book of Concord;* an illustrated biography of Luther; an *Old Testament Hebrew-Japanese Lexicon* for biblical study; and (1985) a five-volume translation of the *Interpreter's Dictionary of the Bible,* a resource widely used in the English-speaking world. Its imaginative and enterprising director, Masaru Mori, and his colleagues have developed the art of encouraging many others in advancing the Lutheran Literature Society, which is the other name for Seibunsha.

A third field of inter-Lutheran cooperation is in Christian education and the development of a common curriculum for instruction in the congregations and schools. Begun in the late 1960s, and with LWF consultation, a three-year curriculum was completed in 1981. A comprehensive lifelong sequence was undertaken.

Finally, cooperation in theological education links the preparatory and ongoing education of pastors to the serving task of the church in communication, publication, and the congregation's teaching ministry. The two major theological schools are each supported by two church bodies; the one in Tokyo by the *JELC and the *JLC, the one in Kobe by the *Kinki and the *West Japan. The role of the faculties includes participation in the research, writing, and translating vital to the aims and outreach of the church. In both seminaries the usual theological curriculum includes clinical pastoral education and counseling, the latter also as an ongoing offering to pastors.

In Japan's Lutheran churches, the nationwide protest against nuclear weapons—particularly in 1985, 40th anniversary of the bombing of Hiroshima and Nagasaki— evoked moving responses. A book of *Testimonies,* written by Lutheran survivors of the bombing (they are called Hibaskusha), commemorated the occasion. "As Jesus took the sin of man and died on the cross," said one resident of Hiroshima, who was 26 at the time, "I must, having been a victim of the bomb, carry the terrible experience of others. . . . God has given me the mission to shout 'Peace!' " Numerous delegations and individuals from Japan have visited their fellow Lutherans in the *USA and elsewhere in recent years. In Tokyo, meanwhile, St. Paul International Lutheran Church has, since 1965, been carrying on its ministry to English-speaking residents there.

JAPAN EVANGELICAL LUTHERAN CHURCH (JELC)
(Nihon Fukuin Ruuteru Kyookai)
Member: LWF (1952), NCCJ
Membership: 20,576**
President: The Rev. Teiichi Maeda
Lutheran Ichigaya Center
1-1, Ichigaya Sadohara Cho
Shinjuku Ku, Tokyo 162

This church, the largest Lutheran body in Japan, has been autonomous since 1922 and was enlarged by merger in 1962. There are 137 congregations served by 145 ordained Japanese pastors. A large corps of workers is active in evangelism, education, communication, social welfare, and other services. External ties are maintained with churches within the Lutheran fellowship in North and South America and Europe, as well as with other churches in Japan and East Asia. Congregations are located on all four major islands of Japan from Hokkaidō in the north to Kyūshū in the south, including the metropolitan areas of Tokyo and Osaka, and other urban and some rural areas. The membership represents a variety of occupations and backgrounds.

JELC headquarters, located near the center of Tokyo, stands on the site of an earlier Lutheran student center. The large, multipurpose church center includes administrative and publication offices, meeting rooms, and a hospice for visitors, as well as a spacious sanctuary for the Ichigaya congregation.

The church has a synodical form of polity. Each of its five districts—Eastern (Tokyo), Tokai (northeast), West (Kobe, etc.), Kyūshū (Kumamoto, etc.), Hokkaidō (Sapporo, etc.) —carries out its constitutionally designated responsibilities under its own elected president and executive and other committees. District conventions are held annually. The biennial national convention, a representative body of clergy and laity, decides major policy and elects the president, members of the executive committee, and other main boards.

Most pastors are educated in the Japan Lutheran Theological College and Seminary (JLTC/S) in Mitaka, a western suburb of Tokyo, adjacent to the Tokyo Union Theological Seminary and the International Christian University. Pastors of the Japan Lutheran Church (below) are also educated here. By government recognition (1964), JLTC/S became a degree-granting college. A site acquired in Mitaka, on the campus of the International Christian University, in 1965 enabled the seminary to relocate. Its architecturally distinctive main building has become the base for learning theology and linking the gospel to contemporary life. The social welfare course added in 1976 helps to provide Christian workers in this important field of service. A strong, supervised internship program is proving its worth. A personal growth and counseling center (1982) emphasizes the school's role in the church's healing ministry, aiding pastors in their continuing education and students in their preparation for ministry. Work with the media opens ever new ways of communication. None of this is to the neglect of the school's reputation in biblical studies or in Reformation-guided theology. There the 12 volumes of *Luther's Works* in the new Japanese edition (above), edited by Professor Yoshika Tokuzen, play a pivotal part. Besides, the successful campaign for an endowment fund—the initial goal of Y 100 million was oversubscribed—has stimulated the laity's commitment to sound theological education.

The JELC's many undertakings include a wide range of educational programs from the parish to the university level. The Kyūshū Jogakuin (School for Girls) was founded in 1926 and a junior college was opened in 1974. This serves as a center for training daycare and kindergarten teachers.

On the frontiers of life, the JELC is variously involved. The Kamagasaki Diaconia Center in the slums of Osaka is a remarkable venture initiated in 1964 by Elzbeth Strohm from Germany. Its fourfold services include child care, mutual learning, problem study, and community projects. Situated in a notorious quarter in Osaka, Kamagasaki attracts homeless people—mostly men—from many parts of the country. Diaconia Center gives a second chance. It has new facilities and enjoys interdenominational support, even as it thereby recalls another woman's pioneering in Kumamoto decades earlier (below).

JELC has radio programs in cooperation with the "Japan Lutheran Hour" and provides financial and other support for the latter's overall work. There is a close cooperative relationship with Seibunsha (Lutheran

Literature Society) in the production of Christian books and other materials.

A specialized mission, the Kyōto Christian Institute, in 1985 became an integral part of the JELC, although it retains its identifying name and function. The institute is a center for religious studies founded by the Scandinavian East Asia Mission (SEAM) in 1959. The work originated early in this century in *China as the Christian Mission to Buddhists. In 1929, owing to the troubled conditions in *China, the work was transferred to the New Territories of *Hong Kong and in 1953 entered Japan. The SEAM also operates a Christian agricultural center in Shizuoka prefecture, midway between Kyōto and Tokyo, on the south coast of Honshū island. This center functions basically as an outreach to the farming communities in that area.

● ● ●

Lutheran work in Japan began during the 1890s, three decades after the first Protestant missions. For the Lutherans it was, characteristically, a mixed ethnic beginning: American, Danish, Finnish. Two Americans, sent by the United Synod of the South (an antecedent of the *Lutheran Church in America, now part of the ELCA), came in 1892. After language study in Tokyo, they went south to Kyūshū—today the most densely populated island—making their debut in 1893 in the small city of Saga and knowing that evangelism would be difficult. They were James A. B. Scherer, who arrived first, and Rufus Benton Peery. These two had an indispensable Japanese partner, Ryohei Yamanuchi. Scholars aided them with an early translation of Luther's *Small Catechism* and the Common Service, the historic order of Lutheran worship.

While en route to China in 1898 on behalf of the West Schleswig Missionary Society of Denmark, Dr. J.M.T. Winther (d.1970) visited these two in Saga to size up their situation. He did so at the request of Danish Lutherans in America, and he remained a missionary in Japan for the rest of his 95 years. In 1900 the first emissaries of the Lutheran Evangelical Association of Finland arrived: Pastor Wellvoos and his wife and another woman worker, Esteri Kurvinen. (Finland at the time was a Grand Duchy of Russia, and, as noted above, the Russian Orthodox had begun to mission in northern Japan in 1861.) The Finns began in the Tokyo

area remote from Kyūshū, and their work remained separate until 1940. The work in Saga, early in this century, expanded to the more promising city of Kumamoto. Schools were opened for boys and girls. Here, too, the training of a Japanese ministry began in 1909, and this led to the opening of a seminary. This was moved to Tokyo in 1925.

Evangelism, education, and service went hand in hand. The founding of Jiai-En, the Colony of Mercy (1921), in Kumamoto underscored the church's concern for people. Here an amazing story of loving care unfolded under the imaginative and resourceful diaconia of Maud Powlas. The institution, which introduced modern social work into Japan, has grown into one of the largest and most respected in the country. In 1949 Ms. Powlas and Jiai-En were honored by a visit of the emperor.

In 1920 an embryo church was organized with a Japanese as president, and in 1931 the church reorganized under a new constitution that separated the overseas church mission organization and the national church and provided for the achievement of greater autonomy. World War II brought severe setbacks. The church was compelled by the government to enter the United Church of Christ (Kyodan) along with all other Japanese Protestants. Missionaries were expelled and pastors forced into war employment. There was loss of life and property. The first postwar figures listed 2050 baptized Lutherans (JELC), a loss of over 60% from the prewar membership. In 1947 the JELC withdrew from the Kyodan and was once again officially established. United Lutheran Church in America and Lutheran Evangelical Association of Finland supporters once again joined their Japanese fellow believers, and together they undertook the task of reconstruction and new outreach.

In the late 1940s and 1950s, 12 additional churches and mission societies began work in Japan. Of these, two—the Augustana Lutheran Church (1950) and the Suomi Synod (1950), later part of the *Lutheran Church in America—from the beginning cooperated with, and let their work become a part of, the JELC. Another two—the Evangelical Lutheran Church (1949) and the Lutheran Free Church (1951), later part of the *American Lutheran Church (now ELCA)—formed the Tokai Lutheran Church, which merged with the JELC in 1964. In 1957 the Danish Missionary Society joined the JELC mission effort, and in 1969 the *United Evangelical Lutheran Church of Germany began cooperation.

In a bold decision in 1968, the JELC determined to become self-supporting. By 1975 this had been accomplished, not only in the congregations, but also to a large extent in the administrative costs at the district as well as the national level. Assistance from overseas has continued for certain specialized functions such as pioneer evangelism, the "Lutheran Hour," and certain new undertakings in theological education at the JLTC/S.

To coordinate outside assistance, the Japan Lutheran Committee for Cooperative Mission (JCM) was set up in 1965. The various supportive agencies in Europe and America could thus coordinate their responses to requests coming from the JELC. A basic change occurred in 1972. The progress toward self-support had been so gratifying that the JELC could no longer be seen as a beneficiary but as a full partner, also in a missionary outreach of its own. The ensuing reorganization—dropping the word Japan — created the present Lutheran Committee for Cooperative Mission (LCM), which meets annually. Its reports reveal difficulties and tough problems as well as bold projects and show how the JELC is becoming a versatile partner in church cooperation and mission at home and abroad.

The first JELC missionary to go abroad was commissioned in 1964 at the biennial convention of the church. Since that time, three consecutive missionaries have been sent to serve a congregation in São Paulo that is a part of the *Evangelical Church of the Lutheran Confession in Brazil. In 1975 the first exchange pastor to go abroad to serve on a long-term basis went to the Federal Republic of Germany. He has been followed by another to the FRG and two to the USA. As these service placements overseas have multiplied, they have also enabled the church at home to provide care for Japanese Christian communities in Europe, the Americas, and elsewhere in Asia.

In the LWF itself it is noteworthy that since 1977 two members of the JELC have served in top staff positions in Geneva: Dr. Yoshiro Ishida, directing the Department of Studies

(until 1986), and the Rev. Satoru Kishii, serving as Asia secretary for the Department of Church Cooperation.

JAPAN LUTHERAN BRETHREN CHURCH (JLBC)
Membership: 904**
President: The Rev. Masami Satake
12-38 Tegata Tanaka
Akita Shi 010

The 17 congregations and several preaching places of the JLBC are served by 16 ordained pastors, an expatriate staff of three, and other workers. The congregations are mainly in northern Honshū, reaching from Akita and Morioka southward to Sendai, and on to Tokyo and Yokohama. A mission of the *Church of the Lutheran Brethren (USA), the JLBC has passed its first decade as an autonomous church body. Expatriates serve under JLCB boards.

In Akita the church's seminary and Bible school, an institution aided by the Lutheran Brethren World Mission of America, prepares pastors and other workers. The president of the school, Tsugio Kosukegawa, is a pastor, author of several books, and active in several national associations. The church's radio program, "Dial of Hope," is broadcast weekly from Akita and is complemented by correspondence courses. A bookstore in Akita meets a felt need.

The mission began in Akita in 1949. Four of the earlier Brethren missionaries had previously worked in mainland *China. This enterprise in Japan shows slow but steady growth.

JAPAN LUTHERAN CHURCH (JLC)
(Nihon Ruteru Kyodan)
Member: (P), NCCJ
Membership: 3088**
President: The Rev. Yoichi Imanari
1-2-32, Fujimi
Chiyoda-ku, Tokyo 102

The church, closely related to the *Lutheran Church–Missouri Synod (USA), was constituted a self-governing body in 1968 and became self-supporting in 1976. Its 33 congregations are served by 33 ordained Japanese pastors, one evangelist, and one missionary from the LCMS. Other workers are employed for administrative, office, communication, and educational programs.

JLC's members come from a variety of occupations and social backgrounds. Many of them responded originally to radio evangelism programs sponsored by the JLC (e.g., the "Lutheran Hour" since 1951) and the follow-up Bible correspondence courses. Two high schools were established by the JLC and are recognized by the government. JLC pastors serve as chaplains. Students total about 1700. English-language programs are run by the JLC as effective evangelism tools and are served by members of the Volunteer Youth Ministry (VYM) program of the *LCMS.

The church is organized on a congregational basis, akin to that of the LCMS. It has three districts: Kanto, Niigata, and Hokkaidō. Okinawa is also its field. In 1970 a sister-church relationship was concluded with the LCMS. Already in 1968 the JLC and the larger JELC (above) had officially declared pulpit and altar fellowship.

JLC headquarters are in the central part of metropolitan Tokyo. Here are the Tokyo Lutheran Language Institute and offices for the telephone counseling service (TELL) and other programs. JLC pastors are educated under the church's own program offered in association with that of the Japan Lutheran Theological College in Tokyo (JELC, above).

The first missionary of the LCMS arrived in Japan in 1948. Developments in mainland China (the revolution of 1949) made Japan a ready alternative, and within three years 30 LCMS missionaries had arrived, coming from North America as well as China. A theological training program was begun in 1952. Regular meetings of Japanese and expatriates, first held in 1957, led to the adoption of an operational constitution in 1962 and to the formal constituting of the JLC six years later at its first national convention. The JLC has several joint projects with the LCMS in which five missionaries and VYM people are engaged.

KINKI EVANGELICAL LUTHERAN CHURCH (KELC)
(Kinki Fukuin Ruteru Kyokai)
Member: LWF (1976)
Membership: 2340**
President: The Rev. Kohji Sugioka
2-2-18, Isoji, Minato-ku
PO Box 32
Osaka 552

This autonomous church (1961), located largely in urban areas around Osaka, Kobe, Nara, Tsu, and Wakayama, comprises 30 congregations and preaching places served by 34 pastors (22 Japanese and 12 Norwegian expatriates). The members are from a variety of occupations and social backgrounds. Organizationally the KELC combines congregational and synodical features. In 1965 it elected its first Japanese president. Church headquarters in Osaka are not far from Kobe.

Since 1971 the KELC and the Norwegian Missionary Society have cooperated with the *West Japan Evangelical Lutheran Church (WJELC) and its partner, the Norwegian Lutheran Mission, in maintaining the Kobe Lutheran Theological Seminary and the Kobe Lutheran Bible Institute. Candidates for the ordained ministry spend at least one year in the institute before entering the seminary. The seminary has recently started M. Div. and Th. M. programs accepted by the Asia Theological Association. The seminary is also the base for the Kansai Mission Research Center, founded in 1980 by groups and individuals of the Kansai area belonging to several denominations. Its purpose is to gather and share mission-related information including studies in comparative religion, anthropology, and church growth. The Kansai Pastoral Counseling Center, initiated by the WJELC, enlarges the scope of the seminary (below).

The church cooperates in various undertakings not only with the *WJELC but also with the *Japan Lutheran Church and the *Japan Evangelical Lutheran Church. These include mass communication (radio and television) programs, publication, and evangelism. The presidents of the four churches have their own official consultations twice a year.

The Kinki church began as an alternative to Norse mission work terminated by the rise of the People's Republic of China. The Norwegian Missionary Society and the *Evangelical Lutheran Free Church of Norway both started work in Japan in 1950. They joined forces and in 1961 their eight congregations were constituted a church and took the present name, which denotes the Kinki area in west Japan.

WEST JAPAN EVANGELICAL LUTHERAN CHURCH (WJELC)
(Nishi Nihon Fukuin Ruteru Kyokai)
Member: (P), NCCJ
Membership: 2453
President: The Rev. Yoshiaki Hirono
2-2-11 Nakajimadori, Chuo-Ku
Kobe 651

This autonomous church (1962) comprises 22 congregations situated mainly in and around the city of Kobe in western Honshū. Its members are mainly urban people. Organizationally the church combines congregational and synodical features. Its diversified ministry is served by 33 pastors and many lay workers. They are trained at the Kobe Lutheran Theological Seminary and/or the Kobe Lutheran Bible Institute, both maintained in cooperation with the *Kinki Evangelical Lutheran Church and the two supporting Norwegian mission societies.

With the support of the Norwegian Lutheran Mission, the WJELC is extending its work at home and abroad. A goal of 50 congregations by the year 2000 has been set. Already work among youth in Tokyo, in an apartment complex in Osaka, and in a rural agricultural mission have been ventured. This outreach is aided by the Kobe Lutheran Hour, "Light to the Heart." Since 1968 daily 10-minute preaching programs by the church's evangelist have been broadcast from Kobe, Okayama, and Yonago. The evangelist also visits listeners and conducts camps and rallies. To reach the numerous Japanese living in South America, recorded programs are sent to the "Voice of the Andes" in Quito, *Ecuador. In 1976 the church's president was a visiting professor at the Lutheran Theological Seminary in Baguio, *Philippines. Since 1980 two missionaries have worked with Lutheran churches in *Indonesia.

As indicated above (KELC), the WJELC was the initiator of the Kansai Pastoral Counseling Center (1973) based at the seminary. Its program, open to pastors, medical doctors, psychiatrists, nurses, counselors, and teachers from many denominations, works in close cooperation with the Yodogana Christian Hospital in Osaka. The executive director conceived the plan while doing graduate work in the USA.

The Norwegian Lutheran Mission (NLM) began work in Japan in 1949, the year its activities were terminated in mainland China. In 1950 the NLM opened the Kobe Lutheran Bible Institute, which rendered a unique contribution also to interdenominational lay training in Japan.

KOREA

This 1056-kilometer (660-mile) peninsula, jutting out from the *China mainland and facing *Japan, has the Sea of Japan to the east, the Yellow Sea to the west, and the 192-kilometer (120-mile) wide Korea Strait separating it from the main Japanese island of Honshū. Because of its strategic location between these two major powers and the USSR, the peninsula has historically been a corridor of imperial rivalry and frequent invasion. In 1945, following World War II, the country was partitioned at the 38th parallel by action of the USSR and the United States. This terminated a period of annexation to Japan that had started around 1905 and been formalized in 1910. Already in 1882 Korea offset its near neighbor's influence by making trade agreements with the United States and various European countries. All of which brought to an end the seclusion, from all contacts except those with China, that had earned Korea the title of the Hermit Kingdom.

Today the most widespread reminder of this distant past is in the traditional or folk religion, Shamanism, led by the numerous local shamans. A shaman is "he who knows" and who, like a Traditional Indian medicine man, mediates between the seen and the unseen world.

While the northern part of Korea now claims two-thirds of its population to be without religion, or atheist, the southern part is alive with religions, including Shamanism, Buddhism, Confucianism, new religions, and a rapidly growing Christianity. The contrast between the religious climates of the northern and southern regions accentuates the continuing alienation between them, a condition profoundly deepened by the costly Korean War (1950–1953). Signs of reconciliation have begun to appear and, it is hoped, may promise a new day.

NORTH KOREA

Democratic People's Republic of Korea, 1948. Area: 121,929 sq. km. (47,007 sq. mi.). Pop. (1985): 20,082,000. Cap.: Pyongyang (pop., 1981 est., 1,283,000).

Religion: With about two-thirds of the population said to be non-religious or atheist, most of the remaining one-third are either Shamanist or Chondogyo (Religion of the Heavenly Way), an indigenous religion arising in 1860. Christian pioneers began work in the north. The number of Christians, once much larger but reduced sharply by the flight southward, is variously estimated, ranging from a high of 150,000 *(World Christian Encyclopedia)* to a low of perhaps one-tenth that figure. Presbyterians are by far the most numerous, followed by Roman Catholics, Methodists, Seventh Day Adventists, and others. The freedom of religion guaranteed in the country's constitution has not prevented periods of suppression when church activity was drastically curtailed. Today the Korean Christian Federation appears to unite the various Protestant communions and claims some 5000 members. According to a federation representative, there are a "great many more."

The first American delegation of church visitors spent two weeks in North Korea in July 1984. Its four members included a Presbyterian, a United Church of Christ pastor, and two Lutherans. Dr. Paul Wee, then general secretary of Lutheran World Ministries (the former *USA national committee of the LWF), later related how active this little Christian community was in its worship life, its quiet outreach, and in its preparation of new pastors. The construction of church facilities is permitted, and the presently 15 ordained pastors are shouldering heavy responsibilities. Specific knowledge of the outside world and the church in other lands is very sketchy, but in this lack the North Korean Christians are not alone. They are aware of a caring, global community in Christ, and they seek the reconciling power that will one day also reunite their divided country.

SOUTH KOREA

Republic of Korea (1948). Area: 98,992 sq. km. (38,221 sq. mi.). Pop. (1985): 41,215,000. Cap.: Seoul (pop., 1983 est., 9,204,000). Language: Korean.

History: The Potsdam conference of July-August 1945 set the 38th parallel as the dividing line between the Soviet occupation in the north and the American in the south. Displacing the Japanese, US forces entered South Korea in mid-August and remained until withdrawn four years later. The ensuing invasion from the north precipitated the devastating Korean War (1950–1953). US forces were the mainstay of a concerted United Nations action to restore the agreed partition. The heavily-guarded neutral zone is comparable to the barrier between East and West Germany and has kept the two Koreas severely separated. Meanwhile, foreign aid has helped a rapidly growing and industrious people to develop a vigorous economy. Talk of reunification was long taboo. In recent years, however, Christian leaders and others have repeatedly raised the subject. A thaw in cold relations has appeared occasionally (above). Domestic protest against injustices suffered by migrants and the poor have flared up repeatedly, with prominent Christians often in the lead.

Religion: Shamanism (above) still claims about 25% of the population but appears to be decreasing. Mahayana Buddhism continues active (about 15%). Confucianism, a code of ethics more than a religion, retains significant numbers (13%). One of the earliest of the new religions (there are over 250 non-Christian sects in the land) is Chondogyo. This indigenous Religion of the Heavenly Way, emerging about 1860, combines elements of Shamanism, Buddhism, Confucianism, and Roman Catholicism, and bears a spirit of nationalism. About 14% of the population adhere to this religion.

Christianity, by recent estimates, claims between 20 and 25% of the population. Up from one-half of 1% of the nation in 1900, developments in South Korea have been phenomenal. After the *Philippines, South Korea has now proportionately the second largest Christian community in Asia. Its church gained heavily by the accession of tens of thousands of Christian refugees fleeing south during the Korean War.

The first Christian contact in Korea came briefly via a Jesuit from *Japan in 1592, and thereafter periodically when French and Chinese missionaries crossed the Yalu River border—only to risk martyrdom for themselves and their converts. Christianity's rejection of traditional ancestor worship, a major tenet of the Confucian-based state religion, caused intense opposition. Nevertheless, a small Christian community survived into the 19th century, when the Hermit Kingdom finally opened to the outside world; which is a paradoxical statement inasmuch as Korean history itself is a long sequence of invading powers moving to and fro between Japan and the China mainland (above).

The first Protestant feeler was in 1832 when Karl Gützlaff (1805–1851), the German Lutheran pioneer missionary to *China, tried in vain to deliver a Bible to the Korean royal court. Fifty years later Korea's trade treaties with America and various European nations opened the door for the first permanent Protestant work. In 1884, the Presbyterian and Methodist vanguard arrived from America, as did an Anglican from Britain. Soon others joined them from Canada and Australia. Korea soon became known as the country in Asia most receptive to Christianity. The practice of lay evangelism carried the gospel also into China, and a policy of self-support was pursued early. Methodist endeavors attracted many adherents, but Presbyterian gains moved about three times as fast. Both communions were innovative in educational and medical work, winning approval in high places as well as receiving influential converts with the humble folk.

Today Presbyterians (3–4 million) remain the far largest ecclesial family in South Korea, but their division into four major bodies and numerous splinter groups frustrates the proponents of Christian unity. Roman Catholics (about 2 million) are the second largest

constituency, having grown more than fourfold during the 15 years after 1953, when thousands of Catholic refugees from the north were resettled and a burst of evangelizing spirit animated many church programs in relief and reconstruction. Methodists occupy a strong third place among the communions from abroad. Scores of smaller churches and groups from afar round out the scene.

Indigenous pseudo-Christian movements are also present, among them these two: the Holy Spirit Association for the Unification of World Christianity, (the well-known Unification Church, 1954) led by its founder, the Rev. Sun-Myung Moon, whom his followers regard as the final messiah; and, second, the Olive Tree Church (1955) whose founder, Pak T'ae-son, healer and oracle of God, considers himself the immortal olive tree (Rev. 11:4).

Church and state relations in this crisscrossed scene rest on religious liberty. The constitution rules out the establishment of a state religion. All religious bodies, before being authorized to hold public meetings or worship, must register with the Ministry of Culture and Information. The state has the power to tax church property, but so far it has not done so. Practices that offend against patriotism are forbidden. Religious instruction in the schools during normal class hours is not allowed. Since World War II Protestants have been prominent in government. Opposition to social injustice and to the violation of human rights has been sparked by various Roman Catholic and Protestant groups, and, on occasion, articulated by prominent personalities.

Interdenominational organizations include the National Council of Churches. Organized in 1946, its antecedent structures go back to 1919. Today its six participating bodies include one-third of the country's church membership. On the more fundamentalist side is the National Association of Evangelicals, which includes over a dozen church bodies. The Roman Catholic Committee on Justice and Peace cooperates with Protestant counterparts in development projects and other activities. A more recent gathering point is the Korea Christian Leaders' Association (KCLA), which makes it possible for the heads of church bodies to become acquainted and keep in touch on matters of common concern.

Lutherans are still newcomers and their numbers few, but through the mass media their contacts have been many and their potential contribution great. Their observance of the 25th anniversary of the "Korean Lutheran Hour" in 1984 coincided with the centennial celebration of the coming of the first Protestant missionaries. It was also 200 years since Christianity began a continuing life in Korea through Roman Catholic efforts from China (Peking). The "Lutheran Hour" radio drama programs depicting the advance of the gospel over these two centuries drew special recognition for its interpretive skill from the Cardinal Archbishop of Seoul.

LUTHERAN CHURCH IN KOREA (LCK)

(Kidokyo Hankuk Lutuhoi)
Member: LWF (1972), KCLA, ILC
Membership: 2611**
President: The Rev. Dr. Won Sang Ji
CPO Box 1239
Seoul 100

An autonomous church since 1971, the LCK is small in numbers but significant in outreach. From small beginnings in 1958, it today comprises some 18 congregations and about 17 ordained Korean pastors, as well as a large number of workers—full-time and volunteer—in supporting ministries. Four expatriate pastors and one teacher, members of the *Lutheran Church–Missouri Synod, fill special functions.

Its membership, having more than doubled since 1976, resides mainly in metropolitan Seoul and Pusan and represents a variety of backgrounds. Besides personal contact, much of the response has been to evangelism through the mass media, in which innovative radio and television programs as well as publications prove attractive. The monthly magazine, *New Life,* appeared regularly for two decades (1961–1980). Newsletters and other periodic publications now take its place. Various types of extension courses have met a felt need. Since the program began in 1960, more than 675,000 respondents from all over the country have enrolled in one or more of these courses. As other denominations began to offer similar types of work, the LCK adapted its programs. It has placed particular emphasis on the Bethel Series of Bible study.

Initiated in 1974, this Bethel offering continues to expand and reaches across denominational lines. Evangelism by radio has featured the "Lutheran Hour" since 1959. From the outset it aimed to engraft the gospel into life situations using a Korean drama format. Listener response to individual programs has at times exceeded 400,000 pieces of mail. At its height the program was carried by 26 radio stations.

The LCK's extensive Braille literature program has been welcomed by Korea's blind. Likewise, the church's concern for the poor, the handicapped, and the disadvantaged has been expressed through its diaconia program of Christian service. Pioneering it until 1973 was a veteran Norwegian couple whose long experience in China set these services in a rewarding direction.

The LCK polity combines congregational and synodical elements. The annual assembly reviews the work of the church and sets policies. Among the officers it elects is the president, whose term of office is four years. The present president, Dr. Won Sang Ji (brother of Dr. Won Yong Ji, below), has been re-elected to this office regularly since the LCK was organized in 1971. Church headquarters are in downtown Seoul. A staff of about 25 maintains the LCK programs in education, communication, and stewardship as well as the ongoing business of the church.

The growing need for qualified pastors made the LCK plan ahead. There was also the government requirement (1980) for all theological schools to meet licensing standards. For years LCK pastors had been trained at the small Lutheran Theological Academy, operated as a "house of studies" in association with degree-granting Yonsei University in Seoul, an interdenominational Christian institution. Steps toward accreditation included transforming the academy into the more inclusive Luther Seminary (1981). Open to various types of church workers, the seminary's main purpose is ministerial education. For this newly licensed school the authorized enrollment is 160. The seven-year curriculum begins with four preparatory years, followed by three in theology. The sixth year is for supervised parish practice (vicarage). The 10-hectare (25-acre) seminary campus, acquired in 1982, is about 32 kilometers (20 miles) south of Seoul near the city of Suwon. The main building was ready in 1984, and housing for students and faculty followed. The cost of over US $2.2 million was met mainly by the LCMS with contributions from the LCK membership as well as from Canada, Germany (Bavaria), and the LWF. Luther Seminary, though still growing into its full academic program, is the visible sign of a worldwide communion as it takes its place among the country's many theological schools, one of which is the world's largest Presbyterian seminary.

The LCK occupies a distinctive position at home and abroad. In Korea, it aims to be of service to all Christian communions. It seeks the good will of the National Council of Churches and of the National Association of Evangelicals but is a member of neither. LCK President Won Sang Ji, however, was a founder of and is active in the Korean Christian Leaders' Association and has taken his turn as chairman. Overseas the LCK appears as an embodiment of confessional unity, being a member both of the LWF and of the *LCMS-led International Lutheran Conference. Although the LCK is not a member of the Christian Conference of Asia, the 1985 CCA meeting in Seoul reaffirmed the importance of churches like the LCK being ready to fill an ecumenically mediating role as expressed in a Lutheran understanding of the gospel and Christian unity.

Toward that end another look at the LCK's beginnings and theological task is instructive. As in the case of Lutheran work in the *Philippines and *Lebanon, that in Korea sprang from the presence of a student from abroad attending Concordia Seminary, St. Louis. Brought to America initially on a government scholarship, Won Yong Ji entered Concordia in 1949 and within eight years had earned his master's and doctor's degrees. His Presbyterian background in Korea had helped, and so did his year (1957–1958) in a Lutheran parish in St. Paul, Minnesota.

Accompanying the first three-man team of LCMS missionaries to Korea in 1958, Dr. Ji gathered and soon became pastor of Immanuel Lutheran Church, Seoul. The following year he received the first class of adult catechumens, for whom he translated Luther's catechism and other documents. This led him, in 1967, to project a Korean edition of *Luther's Works*. In preparation for this he prepared a lengthy lexicon (multilingual) of equivalent terms. Behind it lay the shared concern for a clearer grasp of the Asian mind and of the importance of dialog among Christians themselves as well as with people of other religions.

In order to respond to the ecumenical and interreligious challenges of the vaster scene, Ji, like others of kindred mind, sought to relate Asian Lutherans more closely to each other, particularly in the area of ongoing theological education.

During his term of service in Geneva as the Asia secretary in the LWF Department of Church Cooperation (1968–1975), plans for the still operative Asia Program for the Advancement of Training and Studies (APATS) were adopted in 1975. APATS has since provided linkage among and beyond the Lutheran seminaries in Asia and *Australia (see Asia Introduction). As Ji is currently dividing his time between St. Louis and Seoul in teaching, the lessons of interlinkage are being passed on. When the seventh volume of *Luther's Works* appeared in 1984, the publication was lauded by Presbyterians, Methodists, and others. More volumes continue to come. Dr. Ji is general editor and chief translator. As in *Japan, the availability of a growing selection of Luther's writings in an Asian language has transconfessional significance.

THE PHILIPPINES

A republic (1946) off the southeast coast of Asia, the nation comprises about 7100 islands. Area: 300,000 sq. km. (115,800 sq. mi.). Pop. (1985): 54,669,000. Cap. and largest city: Manila (pop., metro area, 1980, 5,925,900). Language: Pilipino (based on Tagalog) and English, official; also Spanish and many local dialects.

History: Negritos, a Far Eastern pygmy people, are the first known settlers in the Philippines, arriving there an estimated 30,000 years ago. Others followed, bearing a primitive Malayan culture. Descendants of these early dwellers survive today among certain mountain people such as the Igorot in North Luzon. The majority of Filipinos are descendants of later waves of Malayan migration. Mountainous islands, some of them volcanic, fostered the perpetuation of independent communities.

Contact with Europe began in 1521 with the arrival of the globe-girdling ships of Ferdinand Magellan (c.1480–1521). By 1542 the island realm was taken by Spain and named for Philip II, heir to Emperor Charles V. Spanish rule was firmly established in most places by the end of the 16th century. Contact with China proved profitable for trade and also as a source of laborers, and even Japan entered the picture. Like the Chinese, Arab traders had plied the sea lanes to the Philippines for centuries, and in the 13th century introduced Islam in Mindanao and other southern islands. There the Moros (a term they dislike) resisted Spanish rule with Muslim zeal from the 16th century onward; even as the region today continues to struggle for independence.

The encomienda system of tributary labor, introduced by the Spaniards also in the Americas among the Indians, turned owners into tenants and spawned chronic rebellion. Manila, meanwhile, rose to prominence as a great trading port of Southeast Asia. Likewise, the vast property ownership by Roman Catholic orders, coupled with the decline of Spanish imperial power, made the 19th century progressively ripe for Filipinos to rebel successfully. Emilio Aguinaldo (1869–1964), their leader, accepted the offered U.S. military aid. Admiral George Dewey (1837–1917) entered Manila Bay in May 1898 and carried out the Pacific phase of the Spanish-American war. He encouraged Aguinaldo's forces to defeat the Spaniards. This they did, but their briefly won independence with a democratic constitution, the first in Asia, was a lost cause. The subsequent Treaty of Paris (December 1898) did not recognize the Philippines as independent but assigned them to the United States. In the ensuing struggle for independence from the new occupier, Aguinaldo and his forces were defeated at a great cost of lives.

Americans themselves were divided over the future of the Philippines, as in their hands lay but the latest chapter in the long Filipino struggle for justice. In 1934 the American Congress voted independence for the Philippines, to be effective after still another decade of foreign tutelage. World War II delayed matters. The Japanese invasion and subsequent occupation of the Philippines created a new sense of comradeship between Americans and Filipinos as together they experienced brutality and suffering. Less than one year after the ending of war in the Pacific, the USA granted independence to the Philippines. As of that day—July 4, 1946—the new Philippine government gave the USA a 99-year lease for military bases, a term later reduced to 25 years with provision for extension.

Nation building was complicated by postwar reconstruction and political unrest. Communist guerrillas in central Luzon and Muslim secessionists in Mindanao intensified the problem. Government policy to resettle people from the overcrowded northern islands to the opener south, mainly Mindanao, drew mounting Muslim reaction, particularly since land long in Muslim hands was thus opened to Christian newcomers. The Philippines also had troubled relations with equally new neighboring nations, especially *Malaysia (claiming Sabah, the former North Borneo).

By a narrow margin Ferdinand Marcos (b.1917) and his Nationalist Party took over in 1965. Despite the promise of a "New Society," unrest continued and so did the use of military measures. Martial law remained in effect from 1972 until 1981. Though the Muslim threat lessened, Communist forces (the New People's Army—NPA) grew larger. Local elections (1983) eased some pressures, but the airport assassination of Benigno Aquino, the leader of the nonviolent opposition, strengthened the people's struggle for human rights and democratic rule. National Assembly elections (1984) only strengthened popular opposition to the entrenched New Society Movement of President Marcos. Corazón Aquino, widow of Benigno, defeated Marcos impressively in the 1986 election. Marcos and his entourage found refuge in Hawaii, while Aquino—new to the role of political leader—met a succession of crises skillfully, even to the passage of a new constitution in 1987. Nevertheless, crises continue.

Religion: Roman Catholic, over 80%; Muslim, over 4%; indigenous (Aglipayan), 4%; Protestant, over 5%; and others.

The Philippines have the largest percentage of Christians in all of Asia. Christianity came with the arrival of Magellan's party in 1521 and the priests accompanying the expedition. Mission work in the manner then being followed in Spanish America got under way after 1550 and made steady progress over the next three centuries as Franciscans, Dominicans, Jesuits, Augustinians, and other orders pursued their aims. The conversion of the Philippines, half a world away from *Spain, remains the more remarkable because the way of access—as determined early by the papal line of demarcation—lay via Mexico westward; while Portugal's routing lay eastward to Macao, on the South China coast. Besides, conflict between Roman Catholic orders eventually proved detrimental to the spread of Christianity in parts of the Far East like *Japan. Even so, the colleges and universities (like Santo Tomas, 1611) over the generations aided not only the Filipinos but also the Catholic missionary advance into Southeast Asia (Indochina—Vietnam and Kampuchea) and China.

With the arrival of the Americans in 1898, 500 expatriate priests were expelled, and the church lost its favored position. A change in tactics followed. The first Filipino bishop was consecrated in 1905. A reorganized hierarchy ensued, and new mission orders arrived to work in the mountain areas. By 1934 a Filipino archbishop had been appointed, and in 1960 the first cardinal. The numerous Chinese Catholics in 1955 were grouped under a National Office for Chinese Missions in the Philippines. The John XXIII Ecumenical Center, founded in 1968, functions as the permanent secretariat of the Roman Catholic bishops' Committee for Promoting Christian Unity. It deals directly with the National Council of Churches in the Philippines (NCCP) in all joint ecumenical endeavors.

Since 1965 numerous priests, sisters, and lay people have become very involved in social action. President Marcos accused them of fomenting unrest, and a number were imprisoned. Concern for the poor and oppressed by a few has not changed the fact that there is a serious shortage of priests and other workers to serve the masses. Only 13% of the villages have resident priests. Many receive but one visit a year, and still others none at all. Some city parishes have as many as 55,000 members to one priest. Thus the Roman Catholic Church continues to be confronted with its longtime problems of a vast nominal membership and an understaffed paternalistic clergy.

Nevertheless, the enthusiastic welcome accorded Pope Paul VI in Manila (1970) could be seen not only as hailing a historical "first"

but also as displaying the people's hope in the church as a champion of social justice and human rights. Meanwhile, Radio Veritas (1969) in Manila has increasingly become the voice of a missionary thrust to the Asian mainland as well as to far-flung Oceania.

Islam gained strength in Mindanao and the other southern islands during the great Muslim missionary extension from *India in the 15th and 16th centuries. Fiercely independent, they have fought Roman Catholic domination. Since the 1930s this has been aggravated by a government policy of relocating people from overcrowded northern islands to the south. Although the Muslims have lived on the land for centuries, they often do not have papers to prove their ownership. Being displaced by Christians increases their longheld hatred and desire for revenge. This has made for constant unrest and at times civil war.

Besides being a political force, Islam is taking on new vitality as a religion. This seems to be the result of a cultural awakening among the elite. Muslims are now receiving more thorough training from their religious leaders, some of whom have studied in *Egypt and other countries. The number of Quranic schools and Muslim religious associations has increased. An East Asia regional office of the World Muslim Congress (headquarters in Karachi, *Pakistan), is located in Manila.

The Philippine Independent Church (PIC), known as Aglipayan, is the largest of the many indigenous churches that broke away from the Roman Catholic Church. In 1902 it was founded by a priest, Gregorio Aglipay, and a nationalist leader, Isabelo de Los Reyes, who were among those who had joined the revolutionary forces of Emilio Aguinaldo. Over 1.5 million Filipinos soon joined this new church, which retained most of the beliefs of the Roman Catholic Church but discarded confession and celibacy for priests. In 1906, when the Supreme Court ordered the return of all Roman Catholic Church property, the Aglipayans went through a period of decline. For a time they were attracted to Unitarianism and rationalism. But after the death of the founders in the 1930s, firm relations developed with the Philippine Episcopal Church. Today the two churches are in full communion, and the PIC priests are trained at the St. Andrew's Episcopal Seminary in Quezon City. The Aglipayans are experiencing rapid growth and vitality. St. Andrew's is the setting for the Asian Institute for Liturgy and Music, an autonomous regional center for research, training, and the spread of worship materials. The *Lutheran Church in America (now part of the *ELCA) supplied a staff member in musicology.

Protestant churches entered the Philippines after its annexation by the USA in 1898. Presbyterians were the first, followed by American Methodists, Congregationalists, Baptists, Disciples of Christ, Christian Missionary Alliance, and Seventh Day Adventists. These churches stressed education, social service, and cooperation. Presbyterians joined with Congregationalists to form the United Evangelical Church in 1929, which in turn became part of the United Church of Christ in the Philippines in 1948. The latter was a reorganization of a union church created during the Japanese occupation. The other participants were the independent Philippine Methodists and the Evangelical Church (a union of Disciples and United Brethren in 1943).

Since World War II an influx of nonecumenical churches has broken down the former comity agreements. However these new groups, now numbering over 400, have contributed to the rapid aggregate growth of Protestantism.

Among the Protestant missionaries, Frank Laubach (1884–1970) rates special recognition, for he has had a great influence also on many a Lutheran mission. As Congregationalists recruited by the Student Volunteer Movement, Laubach and his wife, Effa, arrived in the Philippines in 1915 to work among the Muslims in the southern island of Mindanao. However warfare between the Muslims and the government forces delayed their beginning until 1929. Laubach, meanwhile, had immersed himself in the local language, put it into writing, and taught the people to read. This work was so successful that other tribes requested his services, and soon 21 other languages were reduced to writing. When hard times prevented the missions from paying literacy teachers, a Maranao chief ordered everyone who had learned to read to teach another. Laubach spread this method, "Each one teach one," worldwide.

The Protestant concern for an indigenous ministry led early to the founding of seminaries. The most important of these is the Manila-based Union Theological Seminary (UTS, 1907), a merger of a Presbyterian and a Methodist school. UTS soon attracted the participation of other denominations as well. Its special relations with Union Theological Seminary, New York, have been advantageous. In recent years its role among the associated theological schools of the Pacific Basin has benefited from its favorable location as well as from the Geneva-based (WCC) Program on Theological Education.

The National Council of Churches in the Philippines (NCCP), organized in 1963, has a history of united efforts going back to 1901. Today it has a membership of 10 churches and four associate organizations. The Lutheran Church in the Philippines (below) is a member, but at times disagrees with the tactics of protest against injustice. The NCCP has a threefold social program: resettlement; Muslim-Christian reconciliation; and a ministry to political detainees and their families. The NCCP's work is carried out by the following commissions: theology and Christian education; evangelism and ecumenical relations; community development; health and healing; and youth work.

LUTHERAN CHURCH IN THE PHILIPPINES (LCP)

Member: LWF (1973), NCCP, ILC
Membership: 20,245**
President: The Rev. Dr. Thomas P. Batong
PO Box 507
Manila

The LCP, organized in 1957, became an autonomous church in 1967. Currently its 141 congregations and a number of mission stations are served by 47 pastors, 45 lay ministers (including teachers), and six expatriate American missionaries. The church's membership is mainly rural, and about 70% live in the highland region of North Luzon. Congregations are also located in and around Manila as well as on the Visayan (central) islands and on the large southern island of Mindanao. The members represent a variety of backgrounds: from urban metropolitan to tribal interior; from various social strata and occupations; and from nonpracticing Roman Catholic to traditional animist. In its worship and work, the LCP employs nine different Filipino languages.

The synodical-congregational church polity is similar to that of other churches founded by the *Lutheran Church–Missouri Synod (USA). The church convention, meeting every four years, elects the president and board of directors, who are responsible for the conduct of church affairs between conventions. A similar pattern obtains regionally. The congregations are grouped into four districts—North Luzon, North Luzon Lowland, South Luzon, and Mindanao—each with its president and board. The church's major functions and specific ministries are guided by their respective boards and committees.

While the LCP maintains offices in Manila, the center of its work and the residence of its president are in Baguio City, the nation's summer capital. This modern city, first settled by the Spaniards but laid out as a city by the Americans, is known for its gold and copper mining. The region is also noted for its woodcarvings by the Igorot aborigines.

While the education of pastors is the prime concern of the Lutheran Theological Seminary, now located in Baguio City, it also provides for the education of deaconesses and teachers of religion for the public schools. The seminary's extension program (TEE) reaches into the four districts of the LCP and assists in preparing evangelists, deacons, and lay ministers. The dean of the seminary, José Fuliga, has a doctorate in theology from Concordia Seminary, St. Louis.

The LCP's major emphasis is on evangelism. Three new tribes have been reached since 1980. Use of the mass media has greatly strengthened personal work and congregational activities, as church-sponsored radio and television programs reach into homes hitherto unknown to church workers. The Lutheran Hour (aided by the International Lutheran Laymen's League in St. Louis, Missouri, USA) prepares weekly broadcasts in four languages, including English. Private church-related as well as government stations carry these programs. Roman Catholic stations, too, have given them free air time. As a result, thousands of listeners have completed the radio Bible courses. The LCP's

mass media department also produces radio dramas in Pilipino and four major dialects.

The LCP's use of the print media, also in several languages, is diversified. "New Life in Christ," a curriculum for confirmation instruction, was prepared by the LCP's department of parish education with guidance from the LWF Department of Studies. Illustrated and produced in six languages, it relates to the Filipino context. The LCP continues to develop hymnals and modes of worship using native forms of music and indigenous styles as vehicles of the liturgy. Youth camps, where this music can be introduced, are proving attractive in all four districts.

The organization of women's leagues on local and district levels has given the LCP women an opportunity for Christian nurture as well as for self-development and service to others. For example, the North Luzon District, many of whose members are illiterate and live in remote villages, introduced a small-scale weaving center in 1981. This has given encouragement, instruction, and income to many rural back-strap weavers and pleasure to the purchasers of the products—everything from dress material to pastors' stoles. In 1984 LWF/CDS made funds available for a women's weaving center in Baguio.

In health and community service, the LCP's chief problem is to keep up with the ever-growing opportunities. The Lutheran hospital (35 beds) in Abatan Buguias (Benguet Province) responds to the needs of the mountain people. An additional annex building was dedicated in September 1985. Some of the congregations operate medical clinics. The general health of the tribal people has been improved with the growing of more protein-rich foods that have been introduced by the church's experimental farm. Another farm assists fishermen to acquire technical knowhow in fish stocking and prawn culture. These farm projects have had assistance from LWF/CDS.

For students and others the LCP maintains Hope Lutheran Dormitory in Baguio City. Funded mainly through the LWF/CDS and the LCMS, this hostel helps many indigent young people from the villages to further their education. The Bible classes and worship at the hostel complement the variety of opportunities offered by Baguio's four major universities and its vocational schools. In Manila, an LCMS pastor serves the LCP in its ministry to overseas Lutherans.

These signs of encouragement stand out against the chronic problems of fear, hardship, and uncertainty caused by the general economic depression and the gnawing political unrest of the Marcos years. Unemployment in the cities and harassment in the countryside forced many an LCP family to move elsewhere.

• • •

Lutheran work in the Philippines began officially on July 6, 1946, two days after national independence. Although Lutherans were latecomers among the Protestants entering the land, the origin of their venture lies in the late 1920s. Alvaro A. Carino, in 1927, went to the United States with a prosperous American family and served in their home in St. Louis, Missouri. Over the simple crystal set given him by friends, he tuned into programs broadcast by the Concordia Seminary radio station. Eventually Carino entered the seminary. Graduating in 1937, he resolved to become a missionary pastor in his native Philippines. In 1940 Carino accompanied the *LCMS mission executive to the islands for a survey, but this could not be followed up until after World War II. When the time came to act, Carino's knowledge and feel for the Filipino people not only guided the LCMS missionary beginnings but also helped subsequently to shape the emerging church. Nevertheless, in postwar Philippines, the missionary struggle was uphill.

Among the tribes in North Luzon's hill country came the readiest response. One of the early converts in the Igorot tribe (see Introduction) was a young man named Thomas. Over the centuries his people had been pushed ever deeper into the mountains. Living in thatched bamboo dwellings, the people survived on local rice and sweet potatoes. Unreached by earlier missions, Igorot animism kept them in fear of the spirits lurking in rivers, trees, and rocks, ready to take revenge if taboos were broken. Sacrifices of pigs, chickens, or dogs might ward off sickness or trouble. Thomas had known and believed all this, his two grandfathers being priests of this traditional religion. The change

came for him while serving as interpreter for two missionaries learning the Kankanaey dialect. As Thomas presented the gospel message for the missionaries to the villagers, he himself was changed. Baptized Thomas Batong, he followed the missionaries' counsel, studied theology, and was ordained in 1961. His pastoral ministry disclosed a deep understanding of the people he served. After gathering and serving five congregations, he was sent to the United States in 1972 for further study. Returning to Baguio City, he taught at the Lutheran Seminary and later became its dean. A second stay in America (1980) earned him a doctorate. His dissertation sketched a model for theological education in the Philippines, some of which has subsequently been put into practice.

Since late 1980 Batong has also been president of the LCP. His emphasis on mission, education, and stewardship endeavors to engage all church members as active participants at their respective stations in life. To help people confronted by change, pastoral counseling also plays a vital part.

In this context, the seminary continues its crucial function. The controversy over inspiration versus revelation that rocked its early years until 1959 was not without its maturing impact. In effect, when the seminary was relocated from Manila to Baguio City in 1961, a new era began; and when the LCP in 1971 was received as a full partner church by the LCMS convention (Milwaukee), the effects of the storm then raging over Concordia Seminary, St. Louis, were felt in the Philippines also. As if to assure itself of a continuing wider view of the church, the LCP, like its counterparts in *India and *Nigeria, went a step beyond the mother synod and joined the Lutheran World Federation.

Confident of its confessional heritage, the LCP has not hesitated in becoming ecumenically involved. It has been active in the National Council of Churches in the Philippines, and a past president of the LCP served his turn as NCCP president. In another area, a series of bilateral dialogs led to the signing of a "baptismal agreement" whereby baptism in the LCP and in the Roman Catholic Church in the Philippines was mutually recognized.

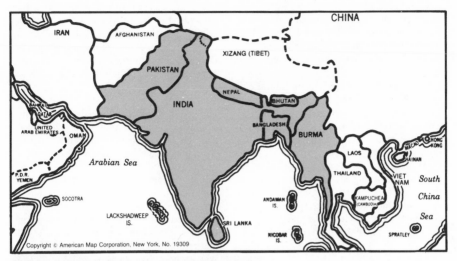

Copyright © American Map Corporation, New York, No. 19309

INDIAN SUBCONTINENT

Over one out of four (27.8%) of Asia's nearly 4 million Lutherans lives in India, where Protestant missions, under Lutheran auspices, began in 1706. Small groups, nearly all of them relating in some way to developments in India during this century of independence and nation making, are in Bangladesh, Burma, Nepal, Pakistan, and Sri Lanka. Whether large or small, they are all minorities within a Christian minority. Their service, oriented to the larger environing community, gives ever-fresh import to ecclesial and ecumenical interdependence.

BANGLADESH

An independent republic (1971) and a member of the Commonwealth of Nations. Area: 143,998 sq. km. (55,598 sq. mi.). Pop. (1985): 98,699,000. Cap. and largest city: Dacca (1981 prelim., city pop. 2,244,000; metro. pop. 3,459,000). Location: combined, low-lying delta of the Ganges, Brahmaputra, and Meghna rivers. Language: Bengali.

History: Originally larger than the present country, Bengal included a mountainous region and a fairly homogeneous population. About A.D. 1200, Muslim invaders took over. By 1500, first Portuguese, then Dutch traders arrived, but were ousted by the English after 1642; the Danes came on the scene. By 1757 British rule over Bengal began and so continued for the next 190 years. In 1947, when India and Pakistan gained independence, a reduced Bengal became East Pakistan. With an expanse of India separating them, relations between East and West Pakistan became polarized: the central government in the West, and 56% of the population in the East.

Demands of East Pakistan for greater economic benefits and political reform led to riots (1968–1969) and civil war (1971), involving India also, and finally to independence. After more than a decade of relative stability, a change of government (1982) endeavored to brace the nation for harder times ahead.

Bangladesh is one of the world's most densely populated and poorest countries, a ready symbol of world hunger, yet not beyond self-help. Recurring natural disasters—cyclone, flood, drought—intensify the chronic problems of poverty, disease, and an economy hard hit by a worldwide recession. Today's rural poor crowding the cities for relief seem like a modern counterpart to the refugees created by the struggle for independence as the Bengal nation.

195

Religion (1984): Muslim, 86.9%, mainly Sunni; Hindu, 12.1%, a moderating influence; remaining 1% divided between Buddhist, Christian, and Traditional. The latter includes Garo, Santal, and Chittagong Hill tribes.

Christians, about one-half million, are divided. Roman Catholic beginnings are traced from 16th-century Portuguese trading posts and missioning orders. Today church membership is mainly urban with elements of Portuguese descent. Church growth is slower than population increase. Among Protestants, Baptists are strongest, with work begun by William Carey (1816) in Chittagong Hills. Anglicans and Presbyterians (joined in 1970) constitute the Church of Bangladesh.

Lutherans have been in this area since 1867, working among Santals. Partitioning of India and Pakistan (1947) left a remnant of the *Northern Evangelical Lutheran Church of India in Bengal (later Bangladesh). From this base outreach continues to Santal and Bengali people.

Partnership in service with the two churches (below) has been steadily fostered by the Bangladesh Lutheran Mission of the Northern Churches. Its four supporting members—the Danish and Norwegian Santal Missions, the Finnish Lutheran Overseas Mission and the World Mission Prayer League (*USA)—also have projects of their own. Village health work, clinics and small hospitals, and treatment of leprosy are the main services. LWF/CDS has supported these projects. Cooperation with the United Bible Societies facilitates the distribution of the New Testament and Scripture cassettes. The latter are most welcome in a society still 80% illiterate.

Community projects, cleared by the government and encouraged by the two Lutheran churches, receive aid from LWF sources. The Rangpur Dinajpur Rural (formerly Rehabilitation) Service (RDRS), largest and best-known among these projects (1972), is a long-range development program. Planned by the people themselves, it operates in partnership with a multinational staff. Diversified in its work, RDRS grew out of emergency services rendered in the wake of the Bangladesh struggle for independence. Aid to refugees fleeing the country—especially into India's Cooch Behar District, north of the Tista and Brahmaputra rivers and opposite the Bangladesh districts of Rangpur and Dinajpur — was the start of more to follow.

As refugees returned to northwestern Bangladesh, LWF emergency aid, coordinated with the Office of the UN High Commissioner for Refugees, became a long-range development program. Dwellings were reconstructed, schools rebuilt, medical services organized, agricultural methods improved, vocational training provided, women instructed in small-scale industry and self-help projects, sanitation improved, clean water supplies tapped (bamboo pumps). These all were part of the inclusive RDRS venture.

At its height, it was a model of international partnership. Scandinavians, North Americans, plus Bengali foremen, interpreters, technicians, special assistants, and others numbered nearly 700. Its initiator and former director, Dr. Olav Hodne, a pastor-scholar and veteran of the Norwegian Santal Mission, was awarded the Nansen Medal in 1976 by the United Nations High Commissioner for Refugees, Geneva. LWF World Service continues to maintain a resident staff member in Bangladesh.

The frequently catastrophic floods inundating huge areas—the worst to date was that of 1988—far exceed the capabilities of self-help and emergency aid from abroad. Heavy monsoons locally, when augmented by run-offs from a progressively deforested Nepal and the swollen Ganges and Jamuna Rivers (two of India's largest) that converge near Dacca, give the problem an awesome international aspect. Bangladesh and its struggling millions cannot cope with this problem alone—as the valiant LWF operation, employing some 2000 Bangladeshians, testifies.

BANGLADESH LUTHERAN CHURCH (BLC)

Member: LWF (1986), NCFB
Membership: 2900**
Synod Chair: The Rev. Thoronikanto Roy
BLC Center, Village Jogdal
PO Birganj, Dinajpur

This church was launched in November 1979 when Bengali-speaking members of the *Bangladesh Northern Evangelical Lutheran Church met in Saraswatipur. Since their numbers were increasing and their culture and language were quite different from the Santals, the Bengali desired a church of their own. In 1981, when officially organized, the BLC had 70 members of whom 28 had Hindu background. It was and continues to be largely a lay movement. By 1987 there were 2500 members in 110 congregations, grouped into seven circuits, all in the northwestern part of the country.

The BLC is governed by a representative synod. A pastoral committee chooses capable leaders for ordination. Each congregation has a lay leader and each circuit a pastor or catechist. The latter watch over the congregations and also serve as liaison between the circuit executive committee and the synod. A deacon's training center in Nilphamari provides a nine-month course of Bible instruction and practical courses—health, agriculture, leadership training, English, music, bookkeeping. As of 1987, 25 people had finished the course and are now serving in their home localities as church leaders, five of them as ordained pastors. The church also has ties with the Christian College of Theology in Dacca where five BLC students were enrolled in 1987. The TEE program reaches other young people.

Lutheran Social Service is an arm of the BLC. Leaders of local congregations serve on the LSS Committee. With support and assistance from the Danish Santal Mission, LSS operates a village primary school program. This includes 20 primary and two teacher-training schools. In the latter, 50 to 100 students are regularly enrolled. Funds obtained via LWF/CDS are used to support vocational training and adult leadership programs. Scholarships are also provided, enabling 90 students to attend high school.

The Danish Santal Mission (DSM), one component of the Bangladesh Lutheran Mission of the Northern Churches, has been the counselor to and supporter of the BLC since its inception. The DSM has transferred some of its property to the church but on BLC's request continues its supervision. The DSM also operates the Danish Bangladesh Leprosy Mission in one of the worst leprosy areas in the country. A 60-bed hospital for inpatients in Nilphamari is its base, with a number of subclinics. Thousands of patients are treated each year. Preventive work has high priority. The project has had LWF/CDS support. In all its work, including some water projects, the DSM consults with BLC leaders. The church's autonomy is respected.

The LWF accepted the BLC into membership in 1986. This strengthens ties already established by WS, CDS, and DCC. The latter is encouraging and assisting construction of straw or mud chapels by providing the roofing. Already 35 of the 110 congregations have completed their chapels. In August 1987 the LWF/DCC Asia secretary spent some time with the church leaders, surveying the work in order to give encouragement and assistance to a people struggling to spread the gospel and to meet the needs of an impoverished membership.

BANGLADESH NORTHERN EVANGELICAL LUTHERAN CHURCH (BNELC)
Member: NCFB
Membership: 6500**
General Superintendent: The Rev. Ismail Hembrom
Amnura Mission, PO Amnura
District Nawabganj

Organized in 1959, this church was formerly part of the *Northern Evangelical Lutheran Church of India. A constitution, called the Memorandum and Articles of Association, was adopted in 1968. The church now has 165 congregations and 11 pastors. Its members are mainly Santals, India's largest and most widely scattered tribal group, of whom over 100,000 reside in Bangladesh among the Bengali. The church members are mostly small farmers and day laborers. Amnura, seat of the church's headquarters, is a city north of the Ganges in the Rajshahi District and about 30 kilometers from the Indian border.

Ministerial education is provided in the church's Bible Seminary. A boys' Hostel/Christian Leadership Training School, set up by the church with help from the LWF and other agencies, encourages education and the use of public schools. At present the church has 39 primary schools using the Santal language and a curriculum approved by the government. They serve 2400 pupils. Several students are in vocational training, 300 in high school, 50 in college, and three in a university. An ongoing literacy program in the congregations, aided by LWF, responds to the desire of villagers, including nonmembers, to learn to read and write.

The eagerness of the BNELC to respond to other community needs as well, such as health, education, agricultural, and other services, stimulates further assistance also from outside the country. Its main support and assistance comes from the Norwegian Santal Mission. When the Bengali members left to form a new church in the Rangpur District (above), the BNELC sent a pastor to help during the first year. (See India, Northern Evangelical Lutheran Church, for early history.)

BHUTAN

A kingdom situated between *India and the Tibet region of *China. Area: 40,000 sq. km. (15,444 sq. mi.). Pop. (1985 est.): 1,423,000. Cap. and largest city: Thimbu (pop., 1982 est., 12,000). Administrative cap.: Paro (pop., 1984 est., 3000). Language (official): Dzongkha Bhutanese.

History: Native tribes were conquered by closely related Tibetans in the 16th century. Britain's interest and eventual limited control dates from 1774, with the arrival of a trade mission. It continued through 1949, when independent *India assumed Britain's role of directing Bhutan's foreign affairs. When Communist *China occupied Tibet in 1950, the border was closed.

Religion: Tantrayana (Tibetan or Tantric) Buddhism (official), 69.3%; Hinduism, 24.8%; Islam, 5%; other 0.9%. Most of the estimated 1000 Christians in Bhutan are expatriates, mainly Indians. Evangelistic activity and proselytism are strictly forbidden. Yet the government invites medical and educational services. The Roman Catholics have had several schools since the 1960s, and the Church of North India (CNI) operates several village schools in the western region. The Lutheran work appears to be one of the largest church endeavors in Bhutan.

Bhutan, one of the poorest and most isolated countries of the world, has been the concern of the Norwegian Santal Mission (NSM) since the early 1960s. Bhutanese with leprosy and others seeking medical care crossed the border into *India and came to the Parkijuli Hospital in Assam, conducted by the Santal Mission and India's *Northern Evangelical Lutheran Church. In time the NSM was granted permission to conduct a clinic for leprosy patients in Riserboo, 95 kilometers (60 miles) north of the Indian border. Weekly clinics were started in 1966, and a year later the construction of a hospital began. Today this is a 100-bed hospital with wards for leprosy, tuberculosis, and other diseases, and five basic health units in outlying areas.

The government of Bhutan soon gave the NSM responsibility for all health work in the area around the hospital and also the care of leprosy and tuberculosis patients in an even larger territory, the Tashi Gang District. Here there are about 2000 patients with leprosy and another 500 with tuberculosis. Treating the afflicted means extensive walking for the doctors and paramedics into areas where there are no roads or bridges.

Although public preaching is strictly forbidden in Bhutan, the NSM was granted permission in 1978 to employ an Indian pastor of the *Northern Evangelical Lutheran Church to minister to the needs of the Indian Christians working at the hospital and clinics. Gradually young Bhutanese, the majority of whom are Buddhists, have been trained for all levels of medical work. Concern for the education of the children of staff members prompted the NSM, in 1981, to request aid from the LWF Community Development Service to enlarge the nearby government Wamrong Junior High School. The government will assume operating costs but cannot afford the capital expense. This is one of several LWF/CDS subsidies. Projects for the enlargement and improvement of the hospital and clinics have been funded by Canadian Lutheran World Relief, Norwegian Church Aid, and Swedish Church Aid.

In 1984 Bhutan government officials visited *Norway bringing a request for even more extensive health work in the eastern part of the country. In response the NSM intends to step up activity to the amount of US $3.5 million, part of which will be paid by NORAD, Norway's agency for international development.

Complementing the work of the NSM is that of the Women's Mission Society of Sweden. Since 1972 it has provided a school in Khaling, East Bhutan, for children and young people who are blind or have impaired eyesight. They are given basic instruction in braille and are also taught to weave products for sale in the local markets. The NSM has on occasion seconded staff to the school, and the German Christoffel Mission to the Blind has assisted financially.

BURMA

A republic (1948) of Southeast Asia. Area: 676,577 sq. km. (261,228 sq. mi.). Pop. (1985): 37,686,000 Cap. and largest city: Rangoon (metro. pop., 1983 est., 2,458,712). Language: Burmese.

History: A succession of small kingdoms and dynasties attempted for centuries to establish control over this country. Of the many constituent ethnolinguistic groups, Burmese comprise 75%; Shan, nearly 9%; and Karen, 6.6%. In 1866 the British annexed the kingdom of Burma, and later also Upper Burma with its non-Burmese tribes. Movements for Burmese independence gained strength during the 1930s. During World War II, with Japanese forces occupying most of the country, the daringly engineered "Burma Road" became famous as the overland supply line to southwestern free China. After the war came Burmese independence and the creation of a new, politically Socialist nation outside the Commonwealth. In the 1960s stiff regulations forced most Indians of non-Burmese citizenship to leave the country. All foreign personnel had to choose to remain permanently or to leave. Most left. Non-Burmese citizens are called Burmans. Internationally Burma stands among the nonaligned nations, and it maintains close relations with the People's Republic of China, among others.

Religion: Buddhism of the Theravada type (i.e., Hinayana, or more conservative, as in *Sri Lanka) is the dominant religion and claims about 88% of the population, including the Burmese, the Shans, and some of the Karens. A revived Buddhism has stimulated Burmese nationalism. The Kaba Aye (World Peace) Pagoda (completed in 1952) near Rangoon was the site of the noted Sixth Buddhist Council (1954–1956). Its purpose was to provide for the world Buddhist community an official edition of the Dhamma, the teachings of Gautama Buddha.

Traditional religion still prevails among about 80% of the Karens, yet it is from these and other tribal groups that the Christian churches have grown. Baptists comprise the far largest of the Christian communions. The inclusive Baptist community is estimated at about one million and traces its beginnings to 1813, when a young American, Adoniram Judson, and his wife arrived in Rangoon. Judson, a Congregationalist under appointment for India by the London Missionary Society and prepared to confront Baptist missionary William Carey (1761–1834) on the scriptural grounds of infant baptism, was himself converted by Carey and rebaptized in Serampore (Calcutta). The change took him to Burma and also challenged support from Baptists in America, whose own diverse community was united by this new responsibility overseas. The Burma Baptist Convention dates from 1865. It combines the Karen, Kachin, and Chin conventions.

Roman Catholicism made its first contact with Burma in 1544, but little resulted until the 19th century. Today this is the second largest Christian communion in the land, yet less than one-half the size of the Baptist. Anglicans, likewise, became active after the first missionaries arrived in 1859. Other communions have also entered Burma.

After World War II only missions operating in Burma prior to 1945 were allowed reentry. In 1966 the government asked the last missionaries to leave the country. Given the prevailing pressures, a strong sense of unity exists in the Christian community. Its numerical strength was (1985) estimated at about two million, approximately 5% of the population. The early Christian emphasis on a trained leadership, lay and ordained, as well as on an educated laity generally, has proved an invaluable asset to the churches.

The Burma Council of Churches (BCC, 1975), begun as the Burma Christian Council in 1949, includes Baptist, Anglican, Methodist, Presbyterian, Salvation Army, Lutheran, and other participants. Given the circumstances, cooperation is close. Since 1978 the BCC has conducted a Bible correspondence course called "Ways of Love." At present it is directed by one of the Lutheran Bethlehem Church's lay preachers (see below), and about 1800 are said to be taking the course. The BCC participates in the Christian Conference of Asia (CCA) and has links to the World Council of Churches. Ministerial education is provided at Burma Divinity School (Baptist and Methodist) in Insein, northwest of the capital, and at Holy Cross College (Anglican) in Rangoon. An unusual interfaith feature is the annual prize for Old Testament knowledge offered by the Israeli embassy. The reward is a trip to Israel. The winner is regularly a Protestant, there being few Jews in Burma.

LUTHERAN BETHLEHEM CHURCH
Member: BCC
Membership: 718**
Head pastor: The Rev. Joseph John Andrews
181-183 Theinbyu Street
Kandawgalay PO 11221
Rangoon
Postal Address: PO Box 773, Rangoon

Bethlehem Church, in the heart of the capital, is the Evangelical Lutheran Church in Burma. Its membership of over 700 embraces two former Indian congregations (Tamil and Telugu) plus Burmese- and English-speaking members. Its head pastor has an able staff, including an ordained associate pastor; three theologically trained but unordained associates; four lay evangelists; three youth evangelists; and three Bible women, whose special duties include home visitation as well as leading in Bible study. Worship at Bethlehem Church includes services in Burmese, Tamil, and Telugu.

An active youth group serves this church as it grows and strives to be self-reliant under many handicaps. Its evangelists reach out to Burmese as well as to Indo-Burmans. Chapels are being set up in order to serve better the members in this sprawling metropolis. One in the Thamaing district ministers to a Karen ethnic group. From Upper Burma calls continue to come from Tamil- and Telugu-speaking groups requesting a Christian ministry. These Indo-Burmans, now citizens of the country, are periodically visited by the pastors and others of Bethlehem Church. Alive to its evangelizing potential, this church is grateful for material help and spiritual encouragement, within existing limits, from partner churches in India, Sweden, Germany, and the United States as well as from the LWF. These connections lie in its diverse background.

When Lutheran Bethlehem Church celebrated its centennial in 1978, Bishop Jacob Jayasalan, of India's *Tamil Evangelical Lutheran Church (TELC), area secretaries from the *Church of Sweden Mission and the *Lutheran Church in America, (now part of the ELCA), and other foreign guests joined in the festivities. Prominent throughout was the head pastor, Joseph John Andrews, as he encouraged a sharing of memories. Members recalled how parents or grandparents, Christians from Tamil Nadu, had been brought from *India by the British for special tasks in Burma. Among them were accountants, clerks, administrative officers, and others. In Christian lineage they were descended from the first Protestant mission in India (1706). Others, on the Telugu side, recalled how, at a later date, poor folk were brought over from India's Andhra Pradesh to work on the docks in Rangoon. For them it was not the centennial but the 60th year since the formation (1918) of Rangoon's Telugu-speaking Lutheran congregation. Pastors and assistance of various kinds have been supplied for decades by India's *Andhra Evangelical Lutheran Church.

For the Tamil and Telugu congregations, the fact of being united gave fresh meaning to the founding year 1878. It was the German Leipzig Mission that had followed its people from the Tamil country to Rangoon. With the outbreak of World War I, the Church of Sweden Mission stepped in where the Leipzig Mission had to let go and included Rangoon among its Tamil outposts on the eastern coast of the Bay of Bengal.

In the 1960s, when (as noted) government pressure required most Indians of non-Burmese citizenship to leave the country, the Tamil and Telugu pastors also departed. Severely depleted, the Telugu congregation was forced to close. Its few remaining members then affiliated with the Tamil congregation as a linguistic chapter. Only in 1978 did the formerly two quite separate groups become officially one.

At the time of the centenary, Bethlehem Church became the designated Lutheran church in Burma. It declared itself autonomous, being no longer a diaspora congregation of the TELC. Self-reliance was henceforth the watchword.

Seldom has a church been served by a pastor of as varied accomplishments as Joseph John Andrews. Tamil by birth and long a Burmese citizen, his acquired Christian name (not uncommon among Asians) reflected his commitment as an active layman. His business career had led him to the position of general manager of Burma's largest construction company when, in the 1960s, the pastors from India found it necessary to leave the country. Andrews stepped in. Duly ordained, he served as pastor and church administrator while continuing with his construction firm. Upon retirement, Andrews became a full-time pastor. One of his sons, a graduate from Rangoon's Holy Cross College (Anglican) and *Tamil Nadu Theological Seminary Madurai (India) was commissioned for the holy ministry by the TELC bishop, and became his successor. A son-in-law is one of the unordained associates. Like many of his people, Andrews knows sorrow and suffering, even as in recent years death has taken one of his other sons, his daughter, and his wife.

Pastor Andrews—U Ba Thein to his people—and Bethlehem Church have a federated relationship with the Anglican Church in Burma in order to facilitate theological training and the receipt of support. Bethlehem Church sponsors a United Christian Fellowship for social, cultural, and welfare purposes, basing these in the church's parish hall. It is also active in the Burma Council of Churches. The church's engagement in social services reveals the plight of many an Indo-Burman, especially of those who have failed to secure citizenship.

INDIA

A federal republic (1950) and a member of the Commonwealth of Nations. Area: 3,287,782 sq. km. (1,269,420 sq. mi.), including the Pakistani-controlled section of Jammu, Kashmir, and Sikkim. Pop. (1984 est.): 746,000,000; Indo-Arayans and Dravidians are dominant, with other admixtures. Cap.: New Delhi (metro pop., 5,729,283). Largest cities: Calcutta (1981 prelim., 9,165,700) and Greater Bombay (1981 prelim., 8,243,405). Language: Though Hindi and English are the official national languages, regional languages (such as Tamil, Telugu, Bengali, Malayalam) are dominant in the 22 states.

History: The Indus Valley, from which the country's name derives, was for about 1000 years the place of India's early civilization. After 1500 B.C. the Indo-Arayan era took over, bringing with its Brahmanic civilization the caste system as well as Hinduism (below). The empire of Alexander the Great, in the fourth century B.C., linked the Indus Valley to the Hellenistic world of the West. And, in later centuries, trade routes by land and coastal waters established ties with the Roman Empire. By the 10th century A.D., the southward and eastward thrust into India by Islamic forces developed. From the Delhi Sultanate (1206) there evolved the Mogul Empire (1526–1857) which, at its height, stretched from Afghanistan to the Bay of Bengal and southward into the Deccan region. The strong influence of Persian art and architecture is still evident in such masterpieces as the Taj Mahal, not far from Delhi.

India's numerous links with the rest of Asia and the islands to the southeast are recalled today by the continuance of Hinduism on the island of Bali, where, as in Java and elsewhere, it had come in the seventh century. The advance of Islam into Southeast Asia and the East Indies had displaced Hinduism everywhere except in Bali. Buddhism, which originated in India, is strong in the rest of Asia (below).

India's direct involvement with Europe began in 1498 with the Portuguese. Vasco da Gama's voyage to Calicut and Portugal's taking of Goa (1510) marked the beginning of India's central role in the modern world. East India Companies—the British (1600), the Dutch (1602), the French (1664), and even the Danish (1620)—led from trade to colonial conquest. In the course of this, Britain defeated France and also the Dutch during a prolonged contest. The victory of Robert Clive's forces in Plassey (West Bengal) over Indian resistance in 1757 is seen as the beginning of the British Empire in India. That era ended 190 years later with Indian independence.

In the meantime, Britain's pervasive presence drew India increasingly into the orbit of European civilization. India became the major bridge between Europe and Asia, yet not without struggle. As British power expanded, it also faced mutiny in the Indian army (1857). Nearly 20 years later Queen Victoria was crowned Empress of India (1876). Less than a decade later the Indian National Congress (1885) was organized to secure greater rights for the people. The widespread educational system, with study in Britain's Oxford and Cambridge and other universities as a lure for the "brightest and best," in time gave India an indigenous leadership that could meet British governance on its own terms. Yet its most successful weapon for securing independence proved to be nonviolence, as led by Mohandas K. Gandhi (1869–1948). Violence, however, flared in the process of separating Pakistan from India in 1947.

The governing of India, enormously complex yet remarkably cohesive, has been according to a constitution reflecting Anglo-Saxon elements of democracy. Equally remarkable has been the continuity of one family in particular. Pundit Motilal Nehru (1861–1931) was a leading Indian nationalist. His son, Jawaharlal Nehru (1889–1964), was independent India's first prime minister (1947–1964). Jawaharlal's daughter, Indira Gandhi (1917–1984), first became prime minister in 1966. When she was assassinated, her son, Rajiv Gandhi, became prime minister. Except for two brief intervals, 1964–1966 and 1977–1980, India's electorate has counted on members of this family for its parliamentary leadership.

Internationally India has endeavored to steer a middle course and, supportive of the United Nations, to remain among the non-aligned countries. Economically, too, it has become increasingly self-reliant.

Religion (1985 est.): Hindu, 82.6%; Muslim, 11%; Christian, 2.4%; Sikh, 2%; Tribal, 2%; Buddhist, Jain, and others, under 2%.

Understood to be a secular state in its constitution (1947), India is a multi-religious nation. Reflecting the United Nations Universal Declaration of Human Rights (1948), India affirms that "everyone has the right to freedom of thought, conscience, and religion" (Article 18). For millenia, India has been hospitable and creative in the realm of religion, giving and receiving in its own syncretic way.

Emancipation from a long colonial era has given fresh purpose to the quest for identity in India. The Hindu majority as well as its reforming offshoots of Buddhist, Sikh, or Jain tradition have been stirred to reappraise their identity. Most dramatic of all was the Muslim resolve to create not another secular but a specifically religious state, *Pakistan.

Meanwhile, the continuing presence of a large Muslim minority and of a much smaller Christian minority assure India's involvement in the religious give and take of the modern world.

Known for its religious syncretism, India's early landmark in this field is represented by Akbar (1542–1605), grandson of the founder of the Mogul Empire. Going beyond guaranteeing freedom of religion, he encouraged major religions to consolidate into one, with the sun symbolizing one God. Open also to Christianity, as presented by Jesuits, he stopped short of becoming a Christian himself since his own Muslim faith rejected the Trinity and the Incarnation. The coexistence of Hinduism and Islam was fostered by Akbar's espousal of the Jain principle of nonviolence (later so important for Mahatma Gandhi) and his own chosen motto: "Peace to all."

India has been an exporter of religions. Just as under Emperor Asoka (d.232 B.C.) Buddhism was sent to neighboring lands, thus starting it on the way to becoming a major world religion, so in modern times religious movements of Indian origin have become firmly attached to the Western world. It suffices merely to mention two Hindu-derived new religions: Transcendental Meditation (TM) and Hare Krishna.

India's impact on Christian unity makes it an early contributor to the modern ecumenical movement. The words of Jesus' prayer called for obedience: "That they may all be one."

The Christian presence in India was traced to the tradition of St. Thomas, the apostle. (Near Madras, in 1972, the 1900-year anniversary of his supposed death in India was celebrated.) On the southwest coast the Syrian Orthodox Church of the East claims its beginnings in the year A.D. 180, with a continuing community since then. Equal antiquity is claimed by the Mar Thoma Syrian Church of Malabar (today a member of the WCC). Roman Catholic contacts are traced to the year 1319, marked by the visit of Franciscan missionaries. A continuous presence began in 1533 with the Portuguese mission that became the Patriarchate of Goa (1558). Only in 1950 was the Portuguese right to name the top church people (ordinaries) in India returned to the Vatican. Thus the way was open to the complete indigenization of the Roman Catholic Church in India, whose inclusive membership by the mid-1980s was estimated at about nine million, about one million more than the Protestant. The Catholic Bishops' Conference in India (1944), which includes certain bishops of Eastern rite, in 1950 assembled for the first time in plenary council and thus demonstrated the unity of their church and their loyalty to the new, independent India. Today the church has some 85 dioceses. The Eucharistic Congress in Bombay (1964) and Pope Paul VI's visit gave India worldwide publicity.

On the Protestant side, the very profusion of missionary enterprises in a vast country (under a favorable British rule) stimulated steps toward Christian unity. The 255 years between the arrival of Bartholomew Ziegenbalg (1706; see Tamil Evangelical Lutheran Church, below) and the New Delhi assembly of the World Council of Churches (1961) saw developments in India that became models elsewhere. City-wide interdenominational (Anglo-Saxon) missionary consultations (1825) led to regional conferences (1855) and then to a succession of all India decennial conferences (1872–1912). The last—following up on the World Missionary Conference at Edinburgh, 1910—became the Missionary Council of India. Eleven years later (1921) this turned into the National Christian Council of India, Burma, and Ceylon. The present National Christian Council of India (NCCI), which built on all these foundations, was founded in 1953.

Amid events foreshadowing World War II, when Japan had already invaded China, the worldwide conference of the International Missionary Council, formed in 1921, gathered on the campus of Madras Christian College in Tambaram and affirmed the unity, especially of Asian Christians (1938). After the war one of the early meetings of the WCC Central Committee met in Lucknow (1952/1953). Significantly, the 1961 New Delhi assembly became a double landmark. It consummated the consolidation of the WCC and the International Missionary Council, and it saw the admission of most of the world's Eastern Orthodox Churches into WCC membership. It also welcomed Roman Catholic observers for the first time.

Among Protestants and Anglicans (long a privileged communion) the most durable and widely known achievement in unity has been the Church of South India (CSI; 1947) and its smaller counterpart, the Church of North India (CNI; 1970). After 30 years of negotiation, initially inspired by the bicentennial of the first mission in Tranquebar (1706; *Tamil Evangelical Lutheran Church), major differences separating Protestants since the Reformation were resolved. The CSI, which included Methodist but not Baptist or Lutheran constituencies, was constituted in Madras in the year of India's independence. The message of this accomplishment made a strong impact throughout the ecumenical movement, coming as it did during the year prior to the constituting assembly of the WCC in Amsterdam (1948). As the scene of Protestantism's oldest and largest mission enterprise, India thus demonstrated its role as a proving ground for Christian unity. In numbers, today's total membership of the CSI and the CNI remains smaller than the combined total of the Baptist and Lutheran bodies and the still-unmerged Methodist conferences.

Conversations between the then Federation of Evangelical Lutheran Churches in India (UELCI, below) and the CSI advanced after 1947 and eventually led to doctrinal agreement. But organic union, while advocated by some Lutheran churches, is still for the future. Significantly, there is joint theological education and ministerial preparation for Lutherans, members of the CSI, and others in various seminaries and theological colleges, as in Bangalore, Secunderabad, or Madurai.

Lutherans, the first Protestant Christians in India (1706), are today gathered into 10 autonomous bodies with a combined baptized membership of over one million. Established by German, Danish, Norwegian, Swedish, American, and Latvian societies and boards, they extend from the southern tip along the eastern part of the country to the far north. Diverse in language and culture, nevertheless already in 1926 nine of them formed the Federation of Evangelical Lutheran Churches in India. This has become the United Evangelical Lutheran Churches in India (UELCI). An account of its development and present responsibilities follows that of the description of the 10 churches below. The Latvian church, not in the union, is one of several small Lutheran groups founded in recent years.

Lutheran World Service–India, since the early 1970s, has aided community development in areas of pronounced need, including

West Bengal. LWS–I projects have been requested in such fields as education, health, water supply, sanitation, light industry, resettlement. Since 1978 a PREM unit (planning, research, evaluation, monitoring) has reviewed the manifold LWS–I program.

ANDHRA EVANGELICAL LUTHERAN CHURCH (AELC)
(Andhra Suvesesha Lutheran Sangham)
Member: LWF (1950), NCCI, UELCI
Membership: 400,000**
President: The Rev. Kaki Nathaniel,
PO Box 203
Guntur 522 002
Andhra Pradesh

The 2500 congregations of this church, the second largest Lutheran enterprise in India and the third largest Lutheran church in Asia, are served by 250 ordained pastors plus a large number of workers in evangelism, education, health, and other ministries. The church is located north of Madras in the large state of Andhra Pradesh, most of whose 45.32 million inhabitants are of Dravidian descent and speak Telugu. The AELC was constituted in 1927. Prior to this it was a mission of the United Lutheran Church in America (now part of the ELCA).

The AELC is active in urban centers like Guntur and Rajahmundry, places remembered for their role in the era of missionary beginnings. Not a few of its members have achieved well in various occupations and professions, and a growing proportion have caste background. Yet the large majority of AELC members are rural villagers and are mostly employed as laborers. A great number of them know the burden of poverty and unemployment. Industrialization, for instance, has been a blow to the economy of many villages. Weavers—called Harijan by Gandhi, and scheduled caste (by the British) instead of outcaste—have been forced to migrate to cities in large numbers. This, in turn, has affected the support of the local congregations, not to mention that of the church at large.

The AELC has a synodical form of church organization. It comprises five regional synods, each with its own president, within the general church body whose several functional units and president serve the church as a whole. The first Indian president was the Rev. E. Prakasam, elected in 1944, the year the church was reorganized. Headquarters are in Guntur, a city of 500,000, about 368 kilometers (230 miles) due north of Madras and 208 kilometers (130 miles) southeast of Hyderabad, the Andhra Pradesh capital.

Church outreach follows new as well as old ways. Evangelism via film and electronic media (radio especially) supplements much personal work. Some 200 Bible women are effective in gaining access to Hindu and Muslim homes. About 500 Sunday schools, with 610 teachers, bolster the teaching ministry to children. Similarly, there are 200 youth fellowships with about 6500 young men and women members. Women of the church are organized into 800 samajams (sections) with some 30,000 women studying and promoting the Christian faith. A special project of theirs is a home for retired Bible women.

Women of the AELC have also found new and innovative ways of spreading the gospel. Teams of women—each consisting of a Bible woman, a public health nurse, an adult educator, and a social worker—have established centers of service with outreach into the surrounding villages. With initiative and persistence, women have also established five AELC ashrams. Here people of various castes and races live together for a time in search of truth. In uniquely Indian ways of communication and expression, the gospel becomes real to many people, including those of caste. A number of AELC women, like Dr. Bathincui V. Subbamma, have had theological education equal to that of the pastors. They have been urging the church to consider the ordination of women and also to provide other opportunities to employ their education and gifts more fully. One AELC woman has served on the WCC Central Committee and another on the LWF Executive Committee.

The AELC's educational program is farreaching—from 20 student hostels to institutions of higher learning. Besides Andhra Christian College (originally Lutheran but now interdenominationally supported) the church operates a college of education, a law school, and 19 secondary schools (one for blind students). For vocational training it maintains an agricultural school, a sewing school, two industrial schools for boys, and one for women. Its Bible school and a Leadership Training School in Rajahmundry prepare Christian workers. Together with Anglicans, Baptists, Methodists, the Church of South India, and other Lutherans, the AELC supports the Andhra Christian Theological College in Secunderabad, near Hyderabad (see below). Here, as formerly in Rajahmundry, most AELC pastors have their training. Many lay men and women are studying theology and earning degrees in the college's external studies program. The church also uses the Ramapatnam Baptist Theological Seminary and the United Theological College, Bangalore.

AELC health services today include nine hospitals (over 1000 beds), a public health center, and other village services. All of these have sprung from the work of the pioneer medical missionary Dr. Anna S. Kugler of Philadelphia, USA. Beginning in 1883, her work attracted a growing number of influential Indian women and men as coworkers. In 1983 the Kugler hospital celebrated its centennial by installing an intensive care unit. Catherine Fahs, an associate of Dr. Kugler, was also gratefully remembered as the one who established a nursing school, the first of its kind in India and among the best today.

The AELC's varied and extensive community services and social programs have been aided greatly by projects of the LWF Community Development Service: aiding the destitute poor to build fire- and flood-proof houses and helping them—through dialog, literacy, and action—to gain their own liberation. These programs, and many others, include Christian instruction and development in responsibility. Some projects require the maintenance of hostels for children and young people; others set up accommodations that serve as models for better living conditions in the villages.

The many-sidedness of the AELC undertaking accentuates the urgent need for qualified workers, wise leadership, and indigenous support—ingredients ever in short supply. The church's goal of self-support has been difficult to attain due to devastating cyclones and massive unemployment. A strong sustaining relationship with the *Lutheran Church in America (now *ELCA) continues, although grants from that body are being diminished every year.

All of which recalls the time of simple beginning when, in 1842, "Father" C.F. Heyer arrived in Guntur via Madras. He was the first foreign missionary sent out by Lutherans in America. His sending agency was a missionary society related to the then Ministerium of Pennsylvania, the oldest synod in North America. Beginnings by the North German Missionary Society (Bremen) in 1845 were turned over to the American Lutherans already in 1850. As the work spread, Guntur became the base for general and higher education, and Rajahmundry, an old Telugu center of learning and culture, became the theological center. The Bible training school set up there in 1885 became Luthergiri (Luther Hill) Seminary 30 years later. In 1947 Luthergiri affiliated with Serampore University, India's theological degree-granting institution, near Calcutta. In the 1960s Luthergiri became host to the interdenominational Andhra Christian Theological College until its relocation in 1973 (above) to Secunderabad.

Like India's other Lutheran churches, the AELC is a part of the United Evangelical Lutheran Churches in India and is extensively involved ecumenically. It now has pulpit and altar fellowship with the Church of South India and with Baptist, Methodist, and Roman Catholic churches.

ARCOT LUTHERAN CHURCH (ALC)

Member: LWF (1961), CCA, NCCI, UELCI
Membership: 30,000**
Bishop: The Rt. Rev. Moses Samuel
ALC Campus
Cuddalore 607 001
Tamil Nadu

The 388 congregations of this Tamil-speaking church are grouped into 25 parishes. They are located southwest of Madras in the districts of North and South Arcot, Salem, and Darmapuji. The church is served by 26 ordained pastors, along with numerous associates in a diversified ministry.

Organized in 1913, 50 years after the Danish Missionary Society began work in North Arcot, the ALC has periodically revised its constitution to meet the needs of an indigenous church. The first Indian president, the

Rev. Dorairaj Peter, was elected in 1960 and consecrated bishop in 1981. The general assembly is the legislative body of the church, also electing the church board and administrative officers. Headquarters are in the coastal city of Cuddalore some 160 kilometers (100 miles) south of Madras. Pastors are educated jointly with those of other Lutheran churches and of the Church of South India at the Tamil Nadu Theological College in Madurai.

The church is strong on education, conducting 85 elementary schools and three secondary schools. In September 1983 permission was granted by the government to establish two teacher-training schools. These are expected to strengthen the educational system. Other institutions of the church include three orphanages, a home for unmarried mothers, two hostels, and two hospitals. The church aims to involve each of its members in Christian witness, and for this purpose offers training courses for adults and young people. Many of its youth, having received higher education, have found employment with the church or the government. Members are also encouraged to participate in the country's community development programs.

In recent years the ALC has found new frontiers of service. An aid in this process was the participation in the self-identity study of the LWF Department of Studies. This involved taking a serious look at the church's theological foundation as well as its work and structure. Courage to reach out into new fields was strengthened by support from faithful partners.

Since 1977 a new area of mission is in the Kalvarayan Hills, about 300 kilometers (187 miles) southwest of Madras. Here some 60,000 tribespeople live in remote villages that can only be reached on footpaths through thick jungles. Until 1976, when the government intervened, they were ruled and taxed by three Jagidars—local landlords. There was no opportunity for education or development. Although the government built one all-weather road into the hills and surveyed the needs, most of the work of bringing new life to these people was left to the churches. The ALC, helped by the Danish Missionary Society, the LWF Community Development Service, and Danchurchaid concentrated its work in the Kariyalur area where missionaries had attempted work almost a half century earlier.

Here evangelism and congregational work for 25 villages is supplemented by education. The primary school teachers also conduct adult classes. Already some 3000 persons have become literate. A hospital in Kumankurchi and an administrative base in Kariyalur serve as centers for an extensive health program serving 50 villages. Emphasis is on training village health workers who are selected by the villagers. Consequently, traditional medicine men have disappeared, malaria has been eradicated, and people are working to provide clean water. A demonstration farm, bringing new methods and crops to the area, has improved the diet of the people. New converts are strengthened by instruction from students of the Madurai seminary.

Cross-community centers have also been established in other poor areas, such as Tholudur and Thiagadorgam. Near Tiruvannanalai a gypsy tribe, the Narikurava, has been approached for the first time. Among these and other poorest of the poor there have been spiritual awakenings. Many Harijan (see AELC, above) and other deprived people have requested baptism despite the loss of economic privileges when they convert to Christianity.

A mission to children is another area of growth. The present bishop, impressed with the junior ministry of the *Evangelical Lutheran Church in Malaysia and Singapore, began a similar program in Arcot. A cassette ministry has also helped to revitalize the church members.

The ALC dates its history from 1863 when the Danish Missionary Society sent its first emissaries to Tiruvannanalai. They picked up and organized the work begun by a lone Leipzig missionary who had left his mission post due to disagreement over the caste problem. From the outset, the Danes sought to cooperate with other Protestant groups. Evangelism, backed by education, was its main thrust. One of the early missionaries, Lars Peter Larsen (1862–1940), became an outstanding professor of Old Testament and the history of religion at the United Theological College in Bangalore. He was also a forerunner of the modern phase of ecumenical dialog.

EVANGELICAL LUTHERAN CHURCH IN MADHYA PRADESH (ELCMP)

(Madhya Pradesh Evangelical Lutheran Kalisiya)
Member: LWF (1950), CCA, UELCI
Membership: 11,000
Bishop: The Rt. Rev. S. Ahlad
Luther Bhawan
PO Box 30
Chhindwara 480 001
Madhya Pradesh

This church, with its 43 congregations, is served by 37 ordained pastors plus a staff of workers in diversified ministries. It is located among Hindi-speaking people in towns and villages along the southern border of India's elevated central state, Madhya Pradesh. Recently it has extended its work into the neighboring states of Orissa, Maharashtra, and Delhi. Its early adherents were from a tribal people, the Gonds. Later caste Hindus, Uraons, Panka, Kewat, Pabhiyas, and Baris also joined.

The annual synod, representing all congregations and church organizations, is the policy-making body. Its decisions are carried out by a 12-member council. The bishop (in his absence the archdeacon) presides over synod and council.

The church was pioneered in 1877 by the Swedish Evangelical Mission (Evangeliska Fosterlands-Stiftelsen). The first conversion came after five years. The parallel mission and church structures set up in 1923 were replaced in 1949 by a single Indian church body. Its present name (in place of the former ELC in the Central Provinces) and an episcopal form of church government were adopted at that time but fully applied only in 1968.

The church's diversified ministry includes 20 elementary, three middle, and five higher secondary schools, besides eight hostels and an industrial shop. The Danielson Higher Secondary School, located in Chhindwara with a student body of 1500, shares its building with the Danielson Degree College. The latter was started in this tribal district in 1970 by public demand. (Tribal people receive special consideration and aid from the several states.) The college has an affiliation with the University of Sangar, has government recognition, and receives some maintenance grants. The ELCMP has special responsibilities for student work in Delhi (UELCI, below).

The church maintains five hospitals, all contributing valuable service to the rural poor. The Padhar Hospital, Betul district, has a community health and development department serving 30 villages. It is also preventing deforestation, a serious problem in this area, by the invention and distribution of solar cookers and gobar (cow dung) gas plants. The Swedish Mission Hospital situated in the village of Rethore near Khurai in the Sagar district has a mobile unit that serves the surrounding villages where tuberculosis, leprosy, and blindness are extremely prevalent.

Other community development projects have also been undertaken with LWF assistance. Some of this work is self-supporting, but grants are still needed and continue to come from the Swedish Evangelical Mission and also from the Church of Sweden Mission and Swedish Lutheran Relief.

GOSSNER EVANGELICAL LUTHERAN CHURCH IN CHOTANAGPUR AND ASSAM (GELC)

Member: LWF (1947), NCCI, UELCI
Membership: 340,325**
President: The Rev. Martin Tete
GEL Church, Main Road
Ranchi
Bihar 834 001

This is the largest and most widespread Lutheran church in India. Its 1387 congregations are served by some 2500 catechists who are supervised by the 157 ordained pastors. The church is divided into five regional and internally self-governing units, each with its synod. A president heads the church.

The congregations are located in the states of Assam, Bihar, Madhya Pradesh, West Bengal, and Orissa, and include the Indian islands of Andaman and Nicobar in the Gulf of Bengal. The main concentrations are in Chotanagpur (the hilly plateau area surrounding the city of Ranchi, Bihar), in Assam, northeast of Calcutta, and in Bangladesh, where India borders Bhutan. Church headquarters are in Ranchi, an industrial city of about 450,000 some 320 kilometers (200 miles) west of Calcutta. Many of the members live here, but the majority are subsistence farmers living in rural villages. Hindi is the language most commonly used, but local tongues are also employed.

Since 1921 pastors have had their training at the Gossner Theological College (GTC) in Ranchi. Originally it was a Bible school for teachers, founded in 1864. The GTC, in 1949, became affiliated with Serampore University, the institution that grants theological degrees in India. GTC also serves other Hindi-speaking churches in northern India. In 1971, the campus of the theological college and the church headquarters in Ranchi became host to Gossner College. It offers courses related to church and community that strengthen lay leadership. The same is true of the Pracharak (Bible) Training School in Govindpur, some 64 kilometers (40 miles) south of Ranchi. With the establishment of the New Life Light Center here (January 1985) for Bible and agronomy training, a new dimension to religio-socio-economic training has been added to public schooling.

The GELC also maintains 19 secondary schools and eight boarding homes where young people can stay while attending public schools. The GELC's continued contribution in the field of education in the country is evidenced by the establishment of three colleges: Gossner College (above), with nearly 4000 students, is the second largest institution in the region; Bethesda Women's College (1979) and the Bethesda Women's Primary Teachers' Training College are also quality institutions.

The GELC, begun by laymen, continues to rely heavily on lay workers. Much of the parish work as well as evangelism and mission outreach is carried on by the catechists and women parish workers. The Board of Evangelism and Literature provides refresher courses in the various regions of the church for the members serving as missionaries in new villages. The Gossner Mission of the Federal Republic of Germany pays the salary of a missionary until the offerings come nearly to this amount. The congregation is then considered "established" and a new one is started. Thus the church continues to grow.

Since its beginning, the GELC has ministered mainly to the poor and downtrodden people of rural northeast India. The farmers who own land often cannot produce enough food for the entire year. They must supplement their income by working as day laborers. The scheduled caste people who have no land may have skills in traditional vocations like bamboo work or weaving, but they may not have enough money to buy materials or a market for selling their products. To meet these needs requires initiative and planning. In recent years, the church has requested and received help from the LWF Community Development Service. One project is in Sarnatoli near the town of Khunti. Here, the church owns a 32-acre farm which, since 1964, has been the base of a number of projects—including those of Lutheran World Service—designed to help the people of the surrounding villages. At present, it serves as a demonstration farm, a training center for cottage industries, and headquarters for cooperative buying and selling.

The GELC has two hospitals and many other avenues for serving its members as well as those it would reach with the gospel. The founding Gossner Mission in Germany continues its partner relationship.

The beginnings of this church go back to 1844 when four missionaries, themselves basically farmers and artisans, were sent from Berlin, Germany, by Johannes Evangelista Gossner (1773–1858), an ex-Roman Catholic Bavarian deeply committed to the Lutheran understanding of the gospel. In Calcutta, the new missionaries were attracted to some street laborers—aboriginal "Kols"—who were actually farmers from the Ranchi region. The Gossner people followed the laborers to their rural homeland. There the missionaries supported themselves by farming. A few converts at first, eventually a mass movement—and the mission was under way.

On the initiative of the members, this church was restructured during the period after World War I, when no German missionaries were permitted and when other communions were ready to receive them. The autonomous Gossner Evangelical Church (1919) became India's first fully self-governing and property-owning Protestant church. Its constitution has been periodically revised to adapt to changing situations. Rich in achievement, the church has also had its periods of ecclesial "storm and stress."

INDIA EVANGELICAL LUTHERAN CHURCH (IELC)

Member: LWF (1970), NCCI, UELCI
Membership: 56,493**
President: The Rev. D. John Hus
Lutheran House, Concordia
UPS Compound
Perukada
Trivandrum 695 005
Kerala

Fifth in size among India's 10 Lutheran churches, the IELC has 450 congregations grouped into 150 pastorates, 15 circuits, and three districts. In polity it combines congregational and synodical features. The church is served by 205 ordained pastors, 40 catechists, 30 women workers, and a core of teachers, plus expatriates (three pastors and one teacher). The IELC covers a large area in South India in the states of Tamil Nadu, Kerala, and Karnataka. Diaspora congregations are located farther north in the city of Bombay and in some parts of Andhra Pradesh. The city of Nagercoil on the southern tip is an important church center and the location of Concordia Theological Seminary, where the pastors have been trained since 1924. Headquarters are in Trivandrum, around the tip to the west. Tamil is the main language, but Malayalam, Kannada, Marathi, and English are also used. The members are urban as well as rural, generally of modest to low income and engaged in various occupations.

The church maintains a large institutional ministry: 102 elementary, 16 secondary, and 2 teacher-training schools; special schools for the blind, deaf, and mentally retarded; and six boarding homes and hostels for students. These are under the supervision of a board for education. A board for healing ministry oversees three hospitals and two mobile clinics. Another board has responsibility for pastoral lay training and a fourth for missions.

The IELC engages in innovative programs of church renewal and mission outreach. For over 25 years, a great asset in this work was the Christian Arts and Communication Service (CACS), an Indian agency with headquarters in Madras. Traveling CACS troupes reached people of all social levels through religious drama, music, and dance. Until the end of 1983, CACS was supported by the International Lutheran Laymen's League (ILLL) of the LCMS and LWF grants. The main activity of CACS—the production of radio programs (in Tamil, Malayalam, Kanarese, and English) for broadcast over the "Lutheran Hour" from the FEBA station in the Seychelles and from Radio Sri Lanka—has now been taken over by the ILLL-supported Christian Media Center, also based in Madras. CACS now uses its well-equipped studio and sophisticated recording facilities to develop educational cassette packages for the purpose of lay training on local parish levels. The cassettes contain educational programs on the Christian understanding of evangelism, stewardship, and community development, and also include material to motivate pastors and catechists on how to initiate discussions for group participation among lay people. The LWF Commission on Communication has approved funds for this project.

Other forms of Christian outreach include three of special note. In the Dharavi slums of Bombay a young pastor, encouraged and helped by his church, is seeking ways of bringing new life and hope to some of the desperately poor people living in one of India's most depressing places. The IELC retains an interest and supplies an occasional pastor for the *Lanka Lutheran Church, at one time part of the Indian church. Sri Lankan pastoral candidates are trained at Nagercoil. Also at the seminary, IELC women are trained as deaconesses. Requested to postpone marriage for five years, they take two years of training and then give several additional years of service to the church. This program was introduced by two members of the Lutheran Deaconess Association in Valparaiso, Indiana, USA.

The church emerged from the mission activities of the *Lutheran Church–Missouri Synod (USA). This pioneer overseas venture of 1895, aided by Leipzig and other missionaries, was a realization of a long-felt need of the Missourians to undertake "foreign" missions. Although the IELC continues to maintain a strong partnership with LCMS, receiving grants and personnel, a working relationship has also been established with the other Lutheran churches in India. It is a member, exerting influence and leadership, in the United Evangelical Lutheran Churches in India. In 1970 it became a member of the Lutheran World Federation.

JEYPORE EVANGELICAL LUTHERAN CHURCH (JELC)

Member: LWF (1950), CCA, NCCI, UELCI
Membership: 88,000**
Bishop:
JELC Central Office
Jeypore 764 001, Koraput District
Orissa

The 460 congregations of this multilingual church are served by 82 ordained pastors and a staff of coworkers in evangelism, education, and health services. This includes 450 catechists and evangelists. The church is located mainly in the southeastern part of the state of Orissa—the former Jeypore Kingdom—in the district of Koraput. This is some 1000 kilometers (619 miles) southwest of Calcutta in the Eastern Ghats hill country. The members comprise several distinct groups: the scheduled caste Harijan; some higher caste people, the Karna and Rana; the Adivasis; and other tribal groups. The languages used are Oriya, Kuvi, Gadaba, Bonda, Bhotra, Dedei, and Koya. Jeypore, the church's headquarters, is a town rich in history and well located for the church's work.

In 1982 the JELC celebrated the 100th anniversary of the arrival of the first Christian missionaries to the Koraput district. These had come from the Schleswig-Holstein Evangelical Lutheran Mission (SHELM) in Breklum, North *Germany, founded by Christian Jensen (1839–1900) in 1876. The original intention was to work among the Adivasis, a tribal group akin to those served by the Gossner Mission. However, for various reasons the Adivasis did not respond to the gospel at that time, and the work shifted to the Harijans, depressed people of the community. Within a few years this work resulted in a mass movement among the Harijans to Christianity. In order to prepare the converts for baptism, evangelists and catechists were needed. For their training, a seminary was opened in 1897. Today this institution, the Jensen Theological College and Bible School in Kotpad, is still the main training center for the church's pastors and other workers. Gurukul, Bangalore, and Serampore theological colleges are also used.

The congregations formed by the mission were organized into a church when the first synod met in 1928. The constitution provided a synodical form of polity that federated the various language groups. In 1954 a new constitution transferred the management of church affairs to Indian personnel, and the mission became an advisory body. At that time the Rev. Abinash Chandra Kondpan was elected president, and in 1962 he was succeeded by the Rev. Jacob Nag. In 1966 the church adopted episcopacy, and Jacob Nag was elected the first bishop of the church. The church is divided into 14 districts (deaneries), six of which are mission areas.

After World War II, with encouragement from returning missionaries, the JELC went on record as favoring another attempt among the tribal Adivasis. At present work continues among 14 tribal groups, each with its own language, in the districts of Koraput and Kalahandi to the north, in Orissa; and also in the Bastar district of Madhya Pradesh, west of Koraput. These districts have a population of two million; 90% of them agriculturalists; 87% live below the poverty line; and 95% are illiterate. To oversee this intensive work, the Adivasi Mission Board was formed in 1973 (renamed Adivasi Christiya Samaj in 1985). Tribal leadership is encouraged and used to promote the work. Since 1975, with support from the LWF Community Development Service and the participation of the United Evangelical Lutheran Churches in India, development has supplemented evangelism.

To help the poorest of the poor, an Integrated Rural Development Center of Weaker Sections (scheduled caste and scheduled tribes) was established in Semiliguda, Koraput (an LWF/CDS project). The program, covering 56 villages with a total population of 20,000, attempts through development enablers to graft these groups into the production system of the region, allowing people to become aware of their rights as full members of their society. The Jensen Theological College provides workshops to prepare the enablers for their tasks and to give them theological understanding for their work. Village health workers supplement the educators. This project has functioned well since 1981.

The church's general educational work and theological education by extension (TEE) has had some assistance from the LWF Department of Church Cooperation. The JELC maintains 34 elementary and nursery schools, five secondary schools, one English middle school, 22 boarding homes and hostels, and one technical training school. In addition, it conducts a mobile clinic and two hospitals, one in Nowrangapur, the other in Bissamcuttack. The latter is situated in a very sparsely populated and underdeveloped region of tribal people. Founded in 1954 on the verandah of the local church, by popular demand it gradually became a 60-bed hospital. It is now being extended to serve a larger area and accommodate more than 150 patients. To increase the medical personnel in this remote area, the hospital has added a training program for nurses and midwives. The JELC now shares the management with the Medical Association of India and the Danish Missionary Society.

The JELC, now experiencing new life and mission zeal, has known difficult years. Its main membership has come from the poorest of India's poor. They sometimes lacked confidence and were painfully aware of the struggle of the few elites for control. Providing for pastors and institutions has not been easy, but in recent years the JELC has been self-supporting on the congregational level. The church suffered reverses during the two world wars when the missionaries from Europe were forced to leave. On both occasions temporary help for this "orphaned mission" was extended by the United Lutheran Church in America (later LCA, now ELCA) and after 1955 by the LWF Commission on World Mission.

Today the church has the continued interest of the North Elbian Center for World Mission and Church World Service (NMZ, the former Schleswig-Holstein Evangelical Lutheran Mission), which is the authorized mission agency for the North Elbian Evangelical Lutheran Church, a partner of the JELC. The Danish Missionary Society also renders assistance.

LATVIAN EVANGELICAL LUTHERAN CHURCH IN TAMIL NADU (LELCT)
Membership: 5200
President (Dean): The Rev. G. Stephen
1-B Benwells Road
Tiruchchirappalli - 1
Tamil Nadu 620 001

Formally organized as a church in December 1981, the LELCT comprises 14 congregations and is served by two pastors and a number of other church workers. The dean is a man of experience and a former pastor in the TELC (below).

From the church's administrative base in Tiruchi (this shorter form is commonly used to denote the city of Tiruchchirappalli, long known for its significance in government, education, commerce, and crafts) the work of the LELCT extends northeastward toward Madras and deals mainly with disadvantaged minorities like the Harijans. The work is co-ordinated with that of the *Tamil Evangelical Lutheran Church (TELC), which early gave encouragement to this Latvian-supported enterprise.

When *Latvia became an independent republic after World War I, Sweden's Archbishop of Uppsala, Nathan Söderblom, consecrated Karlis Irbe, the first bishop of the newly structured Evangelical Lutheran Church of Latvia. As chairman of the Church of Sweden Mission (CSM), Söderblom could also encourage the Latvian church to engage in mission work overseas. A most opportune place seemed India, where the *Sweden-related TELC had just become autonomous.

The work in India began in 1924 when Anna Irbe, daughter of the Latvian (now) archbishop, arrived in the Tiruchchirappalli district. For nearly a decade she served under the general oversight of the TELC before setting out on an independent course. She and her Tamil coworkers counted on support from Latvia but contributions from the Baltic were modest.

In Tamil Nadu, meanwhile, a growing concern for the disadvantaged induced Anna Irbe and others to organize two complementary agencies: the Progressive Charity Board, for service, and the Karuniepuri, for funding. During World War II, the loss of support from afar almost terminated the work. But a major change was in the making.

A Latvian pastor, resettled in *Australia, traveled to India in 1968 at the request of the Canadian Latvians. There he persuaded Anna Irbe to come out of retirement and reactivate the work. Hereafter support came from Latvian churches composed of resettled displaced persons in the USA, Canada, Australia, Sweden, Germany, and elsewhere. In effect the support system for the India mission had become worldwide.

This partnership enabled the establishment of a charity center 24 kilometers northeast of Tiruchi along the main highway to Madras.

By 1972 this included an orphanage for boys and a rehabilitation home for destitute women. They were dedicated by the Latvian dean from Australia. Other work includes a primary school and six adult literacy centers.

Time finally came to transform the work in Tamil Nadu into a church. The two agencies, Progressive Charity Board and Karuniepuri Foundation, were merged, a constitution adopted, and the LELCT organized. Small as it is, the service of this church in India also provides a common tie for its Latvian partners in many parts of the world (see Latvian Evangelical Lutheran Church in Exile).

NORTHERN EVANGELICAL LUTHERAN CHURCH (NELC)
Member: LWF (1950), CCA, NCCI, UELCI
Membership: 56,029**
Moderator: The Rt. Rev. Sagenen Kisku
Church Office, NELC
Bandorjuri Mission
Dumka PO 814 101
Santal Parganas, Bihar

This religious body designated itself a church from the time of the first baptism of members in 1869 and thus bypassed the long period of "mission status" through which most other churches in Asia and Africa have gone. The 383 parishes are served by 58 ordained pastors with an associated corps of workers in various allied fields including 529 catechists and 242 Bible women. The languages used are Santali, Boroni, Bengali, and Hindi. The congregations are located in three states of North India—Bihar, West Bengal, and Assam—and extend into the Morang and Jhapa districts of *Nepal. Headquarters, about 320 kilometers (200 miles) northeast of Calcutta, are in Dumka, a growing educational center for the surrounding agricultural area. The chief bishop (formerly president) is moderator, a title used since 1984 when five heads of NELC judicatories were made bishops.

The church's membership is diversified. Santals, one of India's aboriginal tribes, form the majority. Of their two main groups, one is west of the Ganges River in Bihar, and the other in northeast Assam. A smaller Santal group lives between them on the plains of northwest Bengal. The Boros, originally a Mongolian tribe but long in Assam, comprise a second distinct linguistic group. A third group is the Bengali members. Scattered in numerous small congregations, they have been a part of this church from its early years. Most of the Santals, Boros, and Bengals have been kept poor by the successive ravagings of hurricane, flood, drought, and famine. A fourth group, of Hindu and Muslim origin, is the fruit of the Swedish Mission in Cooch Behar and the Norwegian Mission among Muslims. No other Lutheran church in India has such a richly mixed membership, nor has any other followed the leading of the Spirit with such apparent spontaneity as has the NELC.

The church structure, according to its 1950 constitution, is pragmatic. Its congregations form circles (under a president); the circles, dioceses (each under a bishop); the dioceses, a synod. The church thus gathered was led by a bishop (until 1973 called a general superintendent). Since November 1984, it is led by a moderator. Of the five dioceses, three are Santali, one Boroni, and one Bengali. This structure accommodates diversity within unity and allows for flexibility.

The NELC's name is like a theme with variations. Its present name stems from 1958. Before that it was Ebenezer Evangelical Lutheran Church (1950–1958). Originally it was the Indian Home Mission to the Santals, expressing the founders' envisioned self-support from Indian resources. When such support proved insufficient, help was organized in Great Britain among Anglicans and Presbyterians and in Scandinavia and North America among Lutherans. Today the Danish and Norwegian Santal Missions and the U.S. World Mission Prayer League continue their support. They work cooperatively, and in India they are known as the Santal Mission of the Northern Churches. In 1968 Santal Mission property was turned over to the NELC. Some support also comes from Sweden. The American Lutheran Church (now *ELCA) and the *Evangelical Lutheran Church in Canada are partner churches. In 1976 all these partners met with NELC representatives in India and worked out separate agreements (since twice revised and renewed) for the support of theological education and other projects. Most of the NELC congregations are self-supporting.

For the NELC's other work, outside support is essential. The financial help from the partners has made possible the establishment and maintenance of 86 elementary, 25 secondary, and six Bible training schools; seven boarding homes and hostels, one built in 1984 to accommodate students and guests in Dumka; five mobile clinics, three general hospitals, and two leprosy homes and hospitals. The latter, originally providing only segregation and care, now serve large rural areas with preventive and outpatient care as well. The Saldoha Leprosy Home and Hospital (founded in 1922 by the Danish Santal Mission) is using part of its campus as a training farm for leprosy patients (a project of the LWF Community Development Service).

• • •

Although the first two Santal pastors were ordained as early as 1876, it was not until 1916 that the Danish Santal Mission established the Santal Theological Seminary. Located in Benagaria, Santal Parganas, Bihar, it is the only theological school in India giving instruction in the Santali language. Consequently it is used by other denominations of India and by the *Bangladesh Northern Evangelical Lutheran Church. Since 1974, theological education by extension (TEE) has found increasing favor. It aims to provide local leaders with training for teaching, pastoral, and sacramental ministry as well as a means of offering continuing education to pastors.

The two founders of this church were Hans Peter Boerresen (1825–1901), a Dane, and Lars Olsen Skrefsrud (1840–1910), a Norwegian. Initially both men had been with the German Gossner Society. In 1867, however, they went on their own and began work among the Santals. Boerresen became the promotor and skilled beggar for support. Skrefsrud gave the mission its dynamic character and resolute sense of purpose.

In recent years, in the spirit of Skrefsrud, the NELC has benefited from the services of a unique Norwegian couple, Olav and Britt Waagbo Hodne (see Bangladesh). They were sent to the newly independent India in 1948 by the Norwegian Santal Mission after Olav had finished his theological education. In 1956, the then Ebenezer Evangelical Lutheran Church commissioned him district missionary in Cooch Behar, West Bengal, the

low, poorly drained area north of today's *Bangladesh. In this unpromising district the population doubled in a few years. Following India's and *Pakistan's independence from Britain in 1947, Hindu East Pakistan began a struggle for its separation from Muslim West Pakistan. To escape death, thousands of Bengalis crossed over to Cooch Behar, India.

In response to the needs of these people, Hodne entered a new field of work, first with the Bengal Refugee Service, and then with the LWF Department of World Service, which in 1965 founded the Cooch Behar Refugee Service. Hodne, as director, provided for the unending stream of refugees from East Pakistan into India. After East Pakistan's independence as Bangladesh in 1971, Hodne became director of the LWF Rangpur Dinajpur Rehabilitation Service (RDRS) in *Bangladesh, assisting these same erstwhile refugees to return to their former homes and villages. In late 1974 the Cooch Behar Refugee Service expanded its work to other districts and states in India under the name Lutheran World Service–India. Hodne became its director and supervised effective Christian service in the states of Orissa and Bihar from the organization's headquarters in Calcutta. For this imaginative resourceful service, in 1976 he was awarded the Nansen Medal by the United Nations High Commissioner for Refugees. Hodne also worked out arrangements with the United Evangelical Lutheran Churches in India and the LWF Department of World Service for a closer working relationship (see UELCI).

Britt Waagbo Hodne, Olav's wife, founded a school for blind children in Cooch Behar in 1965 and was its principal for a number of years. With degrees in both special and Christian education, she provided the NELC with advanced methods of work among blind children and wrote an instruction book for confirmation, *This I Believe,* published both in the Santali and Bengali languages.

Many other missionaries, unsung but faithful expatriates, have served this church as it seeks valiantly to help the poorest to help themselves. But most of the NELC work is carried forward by those who themselves have known both suffering and the Good News. In all of this they are not alone.

Their church has been participating ecumenically, yet not without problems, in the

Christian Conference of Asia, the National Christian Council of India, the Bengal Christian Council, the Bihar Christian Council, the Santalia Christian Council, and the Christian Council in North East India.

The retired moderator, the Rev. Munshi M. Tudu, ably led the NELC for nearly three decades (1958–1987). A second generation Christian, Tudu cultivated wide ecclesial contacts in Europe and North America as well as in Asia. His late wife, Elbina (d.1984), daughter of a lay preacher, was a tutor in theological education by extension (TEE). A delegate to the Vancouver assembly (1983), she was there elected to the WCC Central Committee.

SOUTH ANDHRA LUTHERAN CHURCH (SALC)

(Dakshana Andhra Lutheran Sangham)
Member: LWF (1952), NCCI, UELCI
Membership: 22,500
President: The Rev. Thurimerla Anantham
East Mission Compound
Tirupati 517 507
Chittoor District
Andhra Pradesh

This Telugu-speaking church comprises 186 congregations divided into 39 parishes. Some 33 ordained pastors, nine pastors-to-be, and an assisting contingent of workers in related ministries serve the SALC, as do 10 evangelists and 10 Bible women. The field of service is mainly in the Nellore, Cuddapah, and Chittoor districts of Andhra Pradesh, a large coastal area north of Madras. Most of the members are rural villagers, but there are also city congregations, including some in Madras.

Organized in 1945, the SALC's revised constitution of 1962 unites the parishes, grouped into eight zones, under a synodical form of polity. The annual convention is the legislative body, which also elects the church officers. The first Indian president, the Rev. A. D. Benjamin, was elected in 1954. Most of the SALC pastors have been educated at the Andhra Christian Theological College in Secunderabad or at its predecessor, Luthergiri. Some have attended the United Theological College in Bangalore. Both institutions are ecumenical and include Lutheran faculty members.

Financial support from the SALC membership is extremely limited. An estimated 95% of them are of Harijan background and are low on the economic scale. The SALC area is heavily rural, but most of the people are landless. Many are unemployed or poorly paid. Even so, since 1958 the church has been striving toward self-sufficiency. Parishes in each of the eight zones continue to encourage each other to be self-supporting. Sunday schools and youth and women's groups aid this effort. Since 1977 SALC has been converting some of its property into income-producing investments that can be used for the budgetary support of the church.

In education, high on the church's agenda, the SALC maintains 10 elementary, five secondary, and one industrial school. Church hostels also help young people from rural areas to continue their education. Two of these, one for men and the other for women, are situated near the university colleges in Tirupati. A student center also serves their needs. A reward for faithfulness in education came to the church in 1955 when the Tirupati Lutheran High School (now in Renigunta) celebrated its 75th anniversary. Among the grateful graduates, one in particular returned to say thank you with a speech and a gift. He was the noted scholar, and later (1962–1967) president of India, Sarvepalli Radhakrishnan (1888–1975).

Since 1975 the SALC has been a partner in the Telugu Indigenous Curriculum Project, which brings the church into a working relationship with other Telugu-speaking churches—the *Andhra Evangelical Lutheran Church, five dioceses of the Church of South India, and the Methodist Church in South Asia. The project was initiated by the then education secretary (Herbert Schaefer) of the Lutheran World Federation. Son of an SALC missionary, he also had served earlier as a pastor in the church. The resulting curriculum promotes Christian education in homes as well as churches in the context of the social, religious, and economic life of India. This educational effort includes the use of festivals, songs, dramas, and traditional Indian forms of communication. New lyrics that teach the Christian faith are also circulated through cassettes and records to the general public as well as to the churches.

The social service department of the church (1970) is based in Tirupati, Chittoor

District. With assistance from the LWF Community Development Service, it has aided the very poor by specializing in water problems (well-drilling), well-revitalization, food for work, agricultural development, the resettlement of landless Indians in new farming communities, and other projects. The 120-bed Katherine Lehman Christian Hospital in Renigunta has served a rural area for over 50 years. It not only provides care for the sick but also water for the surrounding villages in time of drought. A boarding school in Nayudapeta provides care for some 100 retarded, handicapped, and orphaned children.

In July 1978 the SALC began a ministry to the unchurched Christians living in the oil center, Dubai, in the United Arab Emirates on the Persian Gulf. The spiritual needs of Indians, Pakistanis, Sri Lankans, British, and Americans living in Dubai came to the attention of the SALC by a member, a lawyer who had been a lay preacher and evangelist for 20 years in his home church before being transferred to Dubai. Without any financial commitment, the SALC commissioned him to be its emissary. Although his language is Telugu, he has been able to serve also the Tamil-speaking Indians. In 1984 Victor Balamukunda Doss was ordained a pastor. While observing government restrictions in the field of religion, the congregation continues to care for the unchurched Christians irrespective of their denomination or race.

The SALC is the result of work begun in 1865 by the German Lutheran Hermannsburg Mission. In 1923 the Joint Synod of Ohio (oldest predecessor body of the American Lutheran Church, now *ELCA) began to assist in the work. Due to impoverished conditions in Germany after World War I, the Hermannsburg Mission agreed to turn over its work in India to the Americans. However, in February 1985 the Evangelical Lutheran Mission (the present name of the founder) agreed to be a partner in the ongoing programs of the SALC. The present *ELCA continues to aid its South Andhra partner with funds and counsel, especially in its institutional and missionary endeavors. This relationship has benefited from numerous exchange visitations at levels ranging from students to bishops. A New Life Retreat Center, headed by an ELCA missionary, has strengthened the spiritual life of the church.

Membership in the United Evangelical Lutheran Churches in India as well as in the LWF has proven supportive, particularly during times of inner tension. The SALC is now an active member of the National Christian Council of India at the national level and the Andhra Pradesh Christian Council at the state level.

TAMIL EVANGELICAL LUTHERAN CHURCH (TELC)
(Thamil Suvesesha Lutheran Thiruchabai)
Member: LWF (1947), NCCI, UELCI
Membership: 88,250**
President: The Rt. Rev. Jacob Jayaseelan
Tranquebar House
Tiruchchirappalli 620 001
Tamil Nadu

This oldest Protestant church in India is third largest among the Lutheran bodies. It is at home in Tamil Nadu (the former Madras state) and its congregations extend from the city of Madras to the subcontinent's southernmost tip, reaching also into the neighboring states of Karnataka, Andhra Pradesh, Kerala, and the Pondicherry enclave of former French India. Some 102 ordained Tamil pastors serve in the TELC and are aided by over 60 catechists and evangelists. The Tamil language prevails, being the mother tongue of most people of Dravidian (oldest Indian) descent.

Constituted in 1919, the church adopted an episcopal form of organization expressive of the Swedish part of its heritage. A synod, convened every three years, is the legislative body whose duties include electing the members of the church council (the executive unit) and the bishop, who is also president of the church. Boards and departments supervise the extensive work. Headquarters are in Tiruchchirappalli, a city in the heart of Tamil Nadu on the Cauvery River.

The church's pastors are primarily educated at Tamil Nadu Theological Seminary in Madurai. This school, supported jointly by the TELC, the Church of South India, and others, offers one of the most forward-looking ministerial programs in India. Theological education is combined with development training in nearby villages supervised by the Rural Theological Institute, a department of the seminary. Thus pastors are prepared for constructive work among the very poor. A growing number of women are enrolled. Another institution of the church, the TELC Spiritual Center in Tranquebar, is meant especially for the renewal and continuing education of pastors and other church workers. Bethania in Tanjore is the headquarters for the TELC deaconesses, a select number of dedicated women who have been prepared for lifelong service in the church. The directing sister is aided in administration by a deaconess from Sweden. Tranquebar Bishop Manikam Lutheran (TBML) College, a secular school run by the church, helps to prepare the church's many lay workers as well as to provide Christian participation in civic undertakings.

In evangelization, education, health, and welfare services, as well as in the utilization of print and electronic media, the TELC's activities are comparable to those of other medium-sized churches. A department of education supervises 10 pre-primary and nursery, 139 elementary, 28 middle, four high, seven higher secondary, one technical, and two teacher-training schools, plus 30 boarding homes and hostels. Integrated education for the visually handicapped and blind is provided.

Christian education on the congregational level is assisted by a children's department, a youth board, and a secretary for junior work. The latter, an outreach to young people between the ages of 10 and 15, was given impetus by a visiting group of young people from the Evangelical Lutheran Church in *Malaysia and Singapore. A special mission to children is conducted in the city of Kallakurchi and in the rural area of Tholudur. The church is using its well-educated but unemployed young people to serve in needy rural areas.

The TELC participates with the IELC and the ALC in developing and publishing curricula in the Tamil language and materials for religious instruction in the primary and secondary schools as well as in Sunday schools. These are based on an intensive study of the characteristics of children at various age levels. A new program for baptism and confirmation has been introduced. Teacher training receives fitting emphasis.

This church also (see IELC) encourages the use of music and other forms of Indian art to propagate the gospel. A recently formed band plays typical South Indian music. A congregation in Madras, celebrating the Augsburg Confession and Luther anniversary years, installed an organ and introduced Kathakaleshebam, an Indian way of telling stories with music, which is becoming a new form of liturgical communication.

The TELC's medical board oversees three hospitals. One of these, the Joseph Eye Hospital, has been accredited (1983) by the Bharathidasan University as a postgraduate study center for opthalmology. The staff of this hospital has performed more than 20,000 operations. A socioeconomic development board of the church works in close cooperation with the Division of Social Action of the UELCI (below) to build social awareness. Women's work has the leadership of the bishop's wife and a full-time secretary.

The TELC'S 275th anniversary (July 1981) recalled the event at Tranquebar when Bartholomew Ziegenbalg (1683–1719) and Heinrich Plütschau initiated the work of the Danish-Halle Mission. Amid the mingled joy and solemnity of the occasion, a statue of Ziegenbalg was unveiled, a new history of the church presented, felicitations delivered—including those by representatives from *Denmark, *Sweden, and the *Federal Republic of Germany—and seminars held for Christian poets and scholars. The occasion was reminiscent of similar events at Tranquebar in 1906, for the bicentennial, and then again in 1956, when Dr. Rajah Manikam, on the 250th anniversary, was consecrated the first Tamil Lutheran bishop.

Within this span of history unequaled anywhere else in Protestant missions lies an instructive sequence of events. Ziegenbalg produced numerous writings on the Tamil language, Indian religion, and other topics, and gave India its first printing press. He translated the New Testament and much of the Old into Tamil, a process completed by successors, especially J.P. Fabricius in the 18th century. The newest 20th-century version by Tamil scholars was completed in the mid-1970s under the direction of Devanesan Rajarigam and sponsored by the Bible Society of India.

During the 18th century, Christian Frederick Schwartz and others continued the Danish-Halle venture with Anglican help and developed a considerable Christian community. With the rise of rationalism in Europe during the later 18th century, support for the India mission fell off, and the work was reduced to the area around Tranquebar. The Church Missionary Society (Anglican) picked up the rest, employing largely German Lutherans as missionaries until the 1830s, when Church of England personnel took over.

In 1840 the new Evangelical Lutheran Mission of Leipzig (Leipzig Mission) entered the Tamil scene. Its missionaries eventually restored many of the Tamil Christians to their former Lutheran allegiance. Swedish Lutherans began to assist the Leipzig undertaking in 1849, and 25 years later the newly formed Church of Sweden Mission assumed responsibility for a share of the enlarged field, establishing it as a separate Swedish diocese in 1901. During World Wars I and II, when Leipzig personnel were removed from their work for prolonged periods, Swedish Lutherans kept things going. As already noted, this entire enterprise was constituted a church in 1919.

Meanwhile, already during World War I, J. D. Asirvadam (below, UELCI), as a member of the Tamil church, strove with others to advance cooperation among Lutherans in India. When the Federation of Evangelical Lutheran Churches in India (the present UELCI) was formed in 1926, Madurai-born Swedish churchman Johannes Sandegren became its first president. He was instrumental in relocating the Tranquebar seminary to the centrally located Gurukul campus, in Madras, in 1927. He also introduced the deaconess work by sending the late Deaconess Mother, Sister Lydia Vedanayakam, to Sweden and Germany for training.

On Leipzig nomination, Sandegren was elected bishop of the TELC, a position he filled until retirement in 1955. His successor, Rajah Bushanam Manikam, born in Cuddalore, Tamil Nadu, was widely experienced in education and ecumenism, having served as general secretary of the National Christian Council and then as the first Joint East Asia secretary (1951–1956) for the then still separate International Missionary Council and the World Council of Churches. One of Asia's best known churchmen, Manikam held episcopal office until he retired in 1967.

During earlier decades of this century, TELC connections had been cultivated also outside India, notably with Tamil Christians in *Malaya and *Burma, and, during the years immediately after World War II, with the Batak Christians in *Indonesia. These connections, fostered by Bishop Sandegren and others, linked various missionary heritages and created a triangular relationship— Tamil, Batak, Malayan—that has been helpful in furthering a Christian witness in Southeast Asia.

UNITED EVANGELICAL LUTHERAN CHURCHES IN INDIA (UELCI)

President: The Rev. Jacob Jayaseelan (TELC)
Executive Secretary: Dr. Kunchala Rajaratnam
1 First Street
Haddows Road
Madras 600 006
Tamil Nadu

The UELCI was formed in 1975 when the constitution of the former Federation of Evangelical Lutheran Churches (1926) was changed. It brings together nine Indian Lutheran churches, all members of the Lutheran World Federation, in annual executive and enlarged executive committee meetings and a triennial convention. It is the body through which the members participate collectively in the Christian Conference of Asia and the World Council of Churches. It serves as the India national committee of the LWF and conducts programs and projects that benefit all the churches, the combined membership of which is over one million.

The UELCI's foremost project is the Gurukul Theological College and Research Institute in Madras. Since 1971 Gurukul has been an institution for the extension of theological education through seminars, workshops, pastor's in-service training programs, dialogs, and theological courses for the laity. Its publications include a quarterly bulletin, *Gurukul Perspectives,* and books on various issues of church and mission. Indigenous Christian art is also promoted.

Gurukul is governed by a council of representatives from all nine churches plus the moderators of the Churches of South India and North India. Support comes from the member churches and from world Lutherans through the LWF. The programs are ecumenical.

Although the present program is fairly new, Gurukul has a long history. The land on which the college stands was purchased in 1859 by the Leipzig Mission. In 1927 the Tamil Evangelical Lutheran Church moved its seminary, then located in Tranquebar, to the Gurukul location. In 1953, under the auspices of the Federation of Evangelical Lutheran Churches in India, Gurukul became an advanced Theological College and Research Institute serving all Indian Lutheran churches and missions. Later, in 1971, the B.D. program of Gurukul was transferred to the ecumenical schools now in Secunderabad and Bangalore (see India Introduction).

However, convinced that most Indian pastors required still more training for their work, and especially for effectiveness in ecumenical circles, Gurukul again introduced B.D. courses in late 1985. Within the framework of the Serampore University, the degree-granting institution for theological schools in India, the new program requires a yearlong pre-B.D. course for university graduates. The subjects include Sanskrit, problems of society, social dynamics, and higher level English. The nonformal and ecumenical programs continue. Gurukul also seeks to restore the vision of its founders—that it be a theological resource center for all of Asia.

The Division for Social Action (DSA) was embodied in the UELCI in 1979. This followed a development workshop held earlier in Madras that was sponsored by the UELCI and the LWF Community Development Service (CDS). The DSA mandate is to give leadership and support to the development programs of the nine member churches. A committee of nine—one from each church plus a chair appointed by the UELCI executive committee—oversees the work. The executive secretary of the UELCI has led the DSA with vision and determination. Most of the participating churches now have their own development units, thus providing local initiative and follow-through on LWF-aided programs and projects.

As the screening committee for all Indian LWF/CDS projects, the DSA has increased their number and quality. It has also kept the CDS governing committee abreast of the current needs of the Lutheran churches: the upgrading of old schools and hospitals; provision of clean water and sanitation in the villages; and the training of development workers at all levels.

The DSA, through its director, has a close relationship to the Center for Research on the New International Economic Order, an institution affiliated with the University of Madras. Ph.D. studies in economics and the preparation and evaluation of development projects are its chief concerns.

The UELCI also assists the member churches in youth and women's work. Full-time secretaries in both areas promote these undertakings. Youth conferences and workshops on regional and national levels include Bible studies and mission and evangelism training. Women's work, traditionally limited to congregational groups led by Bible-trained women, is now slowly adding a new dimension. Encouraged also by the women's desk in the LWF, women are awakening to their potential. Those who have had the fortune of an education have found new ways of helping their less fortunate sisters. The UELCI women's desk works with Lutheran World Service-India to train a group of unemployed, educated women in vocational skills so that they in turn can open workshops and train other women. The ashram movement (see AELC, above) is also being introduced in other churches. This ancient Indian institution was revived and adapted by Dr. Bathineni Subbamma as a channel for preaching the gospel. Headquarters for the movement have been established on the Gurukul campus and several ashrams are under way in the Madras area.

At present the UELCI provides campus ministry in Madras and Delhi. Besides serving Indian students, special concern is shown for foreign students from Africa, of whom there are a large number. Often exposed to spiritual apathy, financial hardship, social and cultural problems, and even harassment, they welcome Christian fellowship and the concern of a pastor. Work among them was pioneered by a group of Lutheran lay people working in Delhi in government or business (for a time known as the Delhi Lutheran

Church). This endeavor now has the support of the UELCI, especially the *Evangelical Lutheran Church in Madhya Pradesh, as well as of the North Elbian Center for World Mission (NMZ, FRG). The Madras unit of UELCI's campus ministry also shows this concern for African students. The UELCI expects to expand this work to other universities (LWF/DCC project).

UELCI Mission works in the Bhind and Morena districts of Madhya Pradesh. This replaces the historic Rewa Mission, the fruits of which are now a part of the *Evangelical Lutheran Church in Madhya Pradesh. The Rewa Mission was an indigenous Lutheran venture formed in 1916 when German work was curtailed. It soon became part of the Lutheran National Missionary Society led by the Rev. J. D. Asirvadam, a Tamil pastor (TELC, above). At that time Rewa was a princely state in North India not friendly to Christian work. The pioneer missionary was the Rev. Gnana Bharanam. Later many equally dedicated workers from South India joined the field. Notable among them was a woman medical graduate, Dr. Ramabai Gopal. In 1923, at the founding of the Lutheran World Convention in Eisenach, *Germany, the mission's promoter, J. D. Asirvadam, captured the imagination of the gathering with his vivid account of Indian resourcefulness in evangelization. The only nonwhite person at this historic gathering, he challenged the Christians from other parts of the world with his message. When the Rewa Mission celebrated its golden anniversary in 1966, the work had grown to include six parishes, four schools, and one hospital—all having the services of 18 missionaries from the supporting nine churches.

Other pioneers of Lutheran unity efforts were Bishop Sandegren (Sweden), the Rev. S. W. Savarimuthu of the *Tamil Evangelical Lutheran Church, and the Rev. Joel Lakra of the *Gossner Evangelical Lutheran Church in Bihar, North India. One outcome of their efforts was the formation of the Federation of Evangelical Lutheran Churches in India (FELCI) in 1926.

Meanwhile, under the enthusiastic leadership of missionaries like Dr. Heinrich Meyer of the *Jeypore Evangelical Lutheran Church and Drs. Carl Oberdorfer and Henry W. Mayer of the *South Andhra Lutheran Church, Lutherans came close to establishing an Evangelical Lutheran Church in India comprising all the Lutheran churches. But the vision faded. The FELCI, however, was strengthened by a plan for the All-India Lutheran Theological College and Research Institute, with potential development into an All-Asia Lutheran Institute. Thus the Gurukul Theological College was founded in 1953, and, together with the FELCI's official organ, became a symbol and instrument of Lutheran unity in India.

Another leader was Dr. Rajah B. Manikam, first Indian bishop (1956) of the *Tamil Evangelical Lutheran Church. An able administrator, he fostered the fellowship of the Lutheran churches through FELCI council meetings and conventions. When he retired from the TELC, he became the first promotional director of FELCI, just at the time when the question of Lutheran union with the Church of South India was coming strongly to the fore. The first important move was the merger of Gurukul's academic programs with those of the United Theological College, Bangalore, and the Theological College of Serampore University near Calcutta.

With the prospects of Gurukul Theological College's disestablishment, the question of Lutheran identity was revived more fervently than before. Amid the debates and negotiations Bishop Manikam died (1972). His successor, Dr. Kunchala Rajaratnam, led the FELCI into new dimensions of ecumenical cooperation and participation. Meanwhile, the already mentioned "New Gurukul" was strengthened.

At present a further step toward Lutheran unity is in progress. In 1983 an enlarged executive committee of the UELCI, composed of its officers and those of the member churches, endorsed constitutional changes that would strengthen the UELCI if approved by the churches and the triennial conference of the UELCI. There would be a name change to the collective singular: United Evangelical Lutheran Church of India. In addition, there would be a reordering of the common statement of faith; a development of a common liturgy, lectionary, and hymnal; and a provision for an appellate (judicial) facility to deal with disputes within member churches. This would reduce the many cases now being taken to civil courts by congregation and church bodies—long a cause for pain and ill repute. Were these constitutional changes to pass, a synod could be formed and the nine member churches could become dioceses of the inclusive body.

NEPAL

A constitutional monarchy (1951) situated in the Himalayas between India and the Tibetan Autonomous Region of China. Area: 145,391 sq. km. (56,136 sq. mi.). Pop. (1985 est.): 16,525,000. Cap. and largest city: Katmandu (pop., 1981 census, 235,200). Language: Nepali (official) and other Indo-Aryan and Tibet-Burman languages.

History: The Nepalese represent a long intermingling of Mongolians and Indo-Aryans. By the fourth century the Newars of the central Katmandu valley had a flourishing Hindu-Buddhist culture. The Newars were conquered by warrior Hindus, the Gurkhas, who continued their expansion, also into North India, until defeated by the British in 1816. Internal power struggles led in 1846 to the dominance of the Rana family, who controlled the country until 1951. During this period Nepal was deliberately isolated from foreign influences. This helped to maintain its independence during the colonial period, but it also prevented economic and social modernization. Relations with Britain remained friendly, and in 1923 a British-Nepalese treaty affirmed Nepal's full sovereignty.

Indian independence (1947) stimulated democratic sentiments in Nepal. A revolt in 1951 forced the Ranas to share their power and open the country to the outside world. In the 1960s King Mahendra introduced land reforms, but he also dissolved parliament and introduced a controlled "basic democracy." Political parties were banned. Nepal is one of the poorest countries in the world. Economic assistance has come from the USA, USSR, and China. Agriculture is the main occupation.

Religion: Nepal is the world's only Hindu kingdom, and about 90% of the inhabitants adhere to this faith. As the state religion, Hinduism is protected by laws that prohibit conversion to another religion. Buddhists (6%) have their main following in the northern region bordering Tibet. The founder of Buddhism, Gautama Buddha, was born about

567 B.C. in the Tarai district of Nepal. Muslims make up about 3% of the population.

Christians have freedom to worship and profess as long as they do not evangelize. Indian Christians were the first to organize after the 1951 change. As early as 1952 the Mar Thoma Indian Christians formed the Peace of Christ Brotherhood. More recently the *Northern Evangelical Lutheran Church in India has established several congregations of Santals in the Morang and Jhapa districts of Nepal. These churches are expected to confine their activities to the Indians.

In 1954 the first opportunity for a visible Christian presence opened. In that year the United Mission to Nepal (UMN) was formed by 10 mission agencies working in nearby *India. This breakthrough came via a Methodist, Robert Fleming. An ornithologist collecting birds in Nepal for Chicago's Natural History Museum, he was at times accompanied by medical missionaries who used their skills to help the sick. A grateful government asked the doctors to continue their work and establish a medical program for the country. The first hospital in Katmandu was established in an old palace that once belonged to the powerful Ranas. In 1982 this was replaced by a modern hospital in Patan, south of Katmandu. Geared to serve the 170,000 people in the rural Lalitpur district, it is also a referral hospital.

Over the years the government has requested other services to help in the development and well-being of the country. These include schools and literacy work as well as agricultural and technical projects such as hydroelectric plants. UMN trains nurses, paramedical workers, teachers, and technical craftsmen. It helps students to obtain higher education through its scholarship program and promotes the use of literature and related aids.

As the work expanded, so has the UMN. At present almost 40 churches and agencies from all continents, including seven Lutheran churches or mission agencies, are members of this enterprise. They supply about 40 staff members in various fields of service and also contribute funds for the projects.

The UMN had adhered strictly to its promise not to evangelize nor to form congregations, nevertheless the number of Christians in Nepal has grown significantly since 1954. Some estimate their number as high as

10,000. Besides the expatriate Christians, the Nepalese Christians include soldiers who served in the British army and were introduced to Christianity in, for example, *Malaysia and *Singapore. When they returned to Nepal as Christians, they often moved into remote places. One army officer, Prem Pradhan, converted to Christianity in India. In 1959 he returned to Nepal and began evangelistic activity, which led to eight conversions. All nine then paid for it with five years in prison, but since his release Pradhan has continued to preach. In 1966 the Church of Christ in Nepal was organized as an indigenous body, entirely separate from any mission. The Nepal Christian Fellowship, not formally organized or recognized, embraces both expatriate and Nepalese Christians and conducts an annual Bible conference. The Bible Society in Nepal serves the whole Christian community and sponsors a bookshop as a legitimate outlet for the distribution of Scripture. This was made possible by the 1980 Freedom of the Press Act.

LWF World Service, upon invitation of the Nepal government, in 1984 began a development program. The interest of the government was largely due to the success of the LWS–*India program, which was known to several Nepalese government officials. The LWS consulted with and received endorsement from the UMN (above). Since the government was not then ready for an integrated rural development scheme, less complicated projects were started. In the Baglung district west of Katmandu, for example, a clean drinking water project was begun.

About 3000 people benefited from the first year's work and another 3000 from the work in 1985. The present project is carried out in close collaboration with the district council (panchayat) and the village leaders. The government's recent Decentralization Act encourages local decision making and participation in development. The Red Cross shares some responsibility with the LWS and the government. Plans are under way for more water projects throughout the district.

A project in silk culture began in 1984 in the eastern district of Ilam in cooperation with the Women's Development Coordination Committee and with the assistance of technical staff from the India program.

PAKISTAN

A federal republic (independent 1947; a republic 1956); a single territorial state since the separation of Bangladesh (East Pakistan) after the civil war in 1971. Area: 796,095 sq. km. (307,374 sq. mi.), excluding Pakistan-controlled section of Jammu and Kashmir. Pop. (1985): 100,356,000. Cap.: Islamabad (pop., 1981, 204,364). Largest city: Karachi (metro. area pop., 1981 prelim., 5,103,000). Language: Urdu (official), English (lingua franca), Punjabi, Sindhi, and Pashto.

History: The creation of Pakistan as an independent Muslim state accompanied the achievement of Indian independence in 1947. Two geographically separated parts of Pakistan, East and West, combined a mixture of many different peoples whose common bond, however, was Islam. Already in 1906 the newly-formed Muslim League aimed to safeguard the rights of India's large Muslim minority as well as to work together with the Hindus in the Indian National Congress (organized in 1885) for eventual independence from Britain. Swayed by a philosopher-poet, Muhammad Iqbal (1873–1938), and led politically by Muhammad Ali Jinnah (1876–1948), the Muslim League demanded an independent Islamic state, to which the Indian National Congress agreed reluctantly in 1946.

Today Pakistan occupies a complex position internationally and on its borders. Bangladesh, though separated, recalls the bitter civil war (1971). India still has a Muslim minority nearly as numerous as the population of Pakistan itself. Turbulent Afghanistan has forced refugees by the hundreds of thousands into Pakistan. Kashmir territory, long disputed with India, is mainly Muslim.

Religion: Muslim 97%; Hindu 1.6%; Christian 1.4%. Over one-half of the Christians are Protestant. Although Roman Catholic missionaries worked in Sind and Lahore in the 16th century, no trace of their work remained. American Presbyterians (1833), Anglicans, Scottish Presbyterians, Methodists, and others undertook mission among Hindus, Sikhs, and Muslims. Mass movements, especially among the casteless aboriginal people in Punjab, highlighted Christian missionary work in the early 20th century. Education—from elementary school through college—accompanied the missionary enterprise.

In 1970 Lutherans in Pakistan joined with Anglicans, Methodists, and Scottish Presbyterians to form the Church of Pakistan. Its membership accounts for one-third of the Christians in the land. Organizationally the church is divided into eight dioceses with a bishop presiding over each. It has 600 pastors. Its institutions include Forman Christian College, Murray College, United Christian Hospital, Gujranwala and Karachi theological seminaries. The church also has a broad program of Christian education and social development programs to meet the needs of the poorest of the poor. The church holds membership in the World Council of Churches (1971), the National Council of Churches in Pakistan, the Christian Conference of Asia, the World Alliance of Reformed Churches, and the World Methodist Council.

The Lutheran element goes back to 1903 when Maria Holst, a medical doctor of the Danish Pathan Mission (DPM) began working near Peshawar among Pathan women. A pastor of the DPM, Jens Christensen, laid the basis (1926) for an indigenous Christian literature and an outreach among Muslim Pathan tribesmen. The first Pathan Lutheran pastor was ordained in 1937. A small church was in the making. The (then) Norwegian Mohammedan Mission (NMM, 1940) joined forces with the Pathan Mission; and in 1946 they were joined by the World Mission Prayer League (WMPL), an independent association in *North America comprising Lutherans of mainly Nordic descent. Lutherans combined in 1955 to form the Pakistani Lutheran Church (PLC) with Jens Christensen as its first bishop. In 1961 the Finnish Missionary Society (FMS; now Finnish Evangelical Lutheran Mission) came on the scene and centered its work in Dera Ismail Khan, a town on the Indus River in the North West Frontier Province. Soon thereafter it had a Bible school, three Pakistani pastors, five congregations, over 1000 members, and an expatriate staff that at its peak numbered 25.

Unhappily, in 1962, disputes over authority in internal affairs moved the three mission societies (NMM, WMPL, FMS) to part company with the Pakistani Lutheran Church. In 1966 a Norwegian, Arne Rudvin, became the second bishop. Under his leadership the PLC

joined with other Christians to form a united Church of Pakistan. Rudvin then became bishop of the Lahore Diocese of the new church, a position he held with respect and influence for over a decade. He was the first chairman of the Inter-Aid Committee (see below). In 1988, 25,000 of the 950,000 members of the Church of Pakistan were Lutherans.

Today the World Mission Prayer League is a cooperating agency in the Church of Pakistan, participating in the work of two of the church's schools. Its workers associate with congregations in places where they live. WMPL also has projects of its own: a 100-bed hospital in the frontier town of Tank; a village health care program in the surrounding area (LWF/CDS); a Bible institute and day dispensary in a neighboring town. In these places it also assists in relief work among the Afghan refugees in cooperation with Inter-Aid. Some of these projects, including the medical work, are in cooperation with the Finnish Evangelical Lutheran Mission. FELM continues its emphasis on Christian education. Since the Church of Pakistan was formed, the FELM has cooperated with this church in the fields of literacy and education, especially among Christians. The FELM has also participated in research work at the Christian Study Center in Rawalpindi and has seconded missionary personnel to various other projects.

The Danish Missionary Society, the Norwegian Christian Muslim Mission, the Society for the Support of the Church of Pakistan (*Denmark) give support directly to the Church of Pakistan.

The National Council of Churches in Pakistan (1949) includes Presbyterians, the Church of Pakistan, and other bodies, among them the FELM.

Since 1979 more than 2.5 million refugees have fled Afghanistan and found refuge in Pakistan. The majority are Muslim. The churches, including the Roman Catholic, have formed the Inter-Aid Committee to supplement the work of the United Nations High Commissioner for Refugees in receiving and channeling aid to the refugees.

SRI LANKA

An island in the Indian Ocean, officially the Democratic Socialist Republic of Sri Lanka, and a member of the Commonwealth. Area: 65,510 sq. km. (25,332 sq. mi.). Pop. (1985 est.): 16,109,000, including Sinhalese, 74%; Tamil, 18.2%; Sri Lankan Moor, 7.1%. Capital and largest city: Colombo (pop., 1981, ca. 585,776). Language: Sinhalese (official), Tamil, English.

History: The island was settled by Indians from the Ganges region in the sixth century B.C., and their descendants still comprise most of the population. The first Tamils came from southern India to northern Ceylon about 300 B.C. A succession of outsiders laid claim to the island: the Portuguese (1505); then the Dutch (1658); and later the British (1796–1948). During the British rule, Tamils were brought in as laborers on the tea plantations, and they make up one-fifth of the population. Ceylon, independent since 1948, changed its name in 1972 to Sri Lanka. This young nation has been challenged by rapid population growth, economic difficulties, and separatist demands by the Tamil minority. Hostility on an unprecedented scale broke out in July 1983 and again in 1984. Tamils continue their demands for an independent state, and the president's efforts to resolve the ethnic divisions have met with little success. As many as 40,000 Tamil refugees left Sri Lanka for India during this period.

Religion: (1981 est.): Buddhist 69.3%; Hindu 15.5%; Muslim 7.6%; Christian 7.5%.

Sri Lanka is the world center for Hinayana Buddhism (the Lesser Vehicle), on the island since the third century B.C. Although Sri Lanka guarantees religious freedom, it favors Buddhism. Religious instruction is mandatory and must be that of the parents. Hinduism is the religion of most of the Tamils; Islam, of the country's Moors and Malays.

According to tradition, Christianity was introduced by St. Thomas. A Nestorian visitor of the sixth century reported the presence of many converts and churches. In more recent times, the Portuguese introduced Catholicism; the Dutch, the Reformed tradition; and the British, Anglicanism. Today these churches are holding their own, showing little if any growth by evangelism. The same is true of the National Christian Council of Sri Lanka (NCCSL), formed already in 1923. A high point in the life of the NCCSL was during the leadership of D. T. Niles (1908–1970). A Tamil Methodist, he was an evangelist and churchman of wide influence. A leader in the ecumenical movement, he participated actively in the World Council of Churches (WCC) from the time of its formation (1948) and also in the Christian Conference of Asia.

Yet the churches were quick to identify with the victims of the uprisings of 1983 and 1984. Catholic and Protestant churches alike opened their schools to the homeless and supplemented the efforts of the government to care for the afflicted. The NCCSL set aside a considerable sum for relief work, and the WCC, expressing the concern of churches worldwide, sent an ecumenical delegation and timely assistance. During the crises the recently formed United Religious Organization, comprising the clergy of the main religions—Buddhism, Hinduism, Islam, and Christianity—observed a period of reconciliation and harmony, including a planned island-wide peace march. In this complex situation, Lutherans have a stake.

LANKA LUTHERAN CHURCH (LLC)
Membership: 685**
President: The Rev. M. Sathiyanathan
31 Haddon Hill Road
Nuwara Eliya

The seven small congregations of this Tamil-speaking church are located mainly in the highlands of south central Sri Lanka. In general its members are workers in the tea plantations. LLC is served by two Sri Lankan pastors and three missionaries from the *Lutheran Church–Missouri Synod (LCMS).

The church began as part of the LCMS mission in South India. When members of these congregations moved to Ceylon for employment, Indian pastors followed them, beginning in 1927. The work was strengthened in 1952 by the arrival of the first missionaries from America. The Ceylon congregations were counted among those forming the *India Evangelical Lutheran Church (IELC) in 1963. Pastoral candidates in Ceylon trained at the Concordia Seminary in Nagercoil, India. As the congregations grew more indigenous, outreach to Sinhalese-speaking people increased, especially around Colombo, the capital, on the southwestern coast. Nuwara Eliya, south of Kandy, in the highlands, is the main center.

LLC is actually a mission of the LCMS, but its ties with the IELC remain strong and helpful.

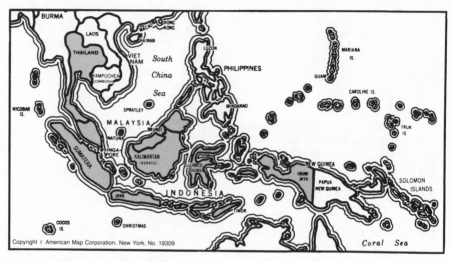

Copyright © American Map Corporation, New York, No. 19309

SOUTHEAST ASIA

Astride the equator is the immense, elongated, island world of Indonesia. Opposite Sumatra lies the southernmost extension of the Asian mainland—from Thailand to Malaysia and Singapore. Of the more than 2.8 million baptized members of Lutheran-related churches, only 1.8% are outside Indonesia. Of the more than 2.7 million in Indonesia, the vast majority live in Sumatra.

INDONESIA

A republic, proclaimed in 1945, with full sovereignty achieved in 1949. It is the world's largest archipelago with over 3000 islands, the major ones being Sumatra, Java, Kalimantan (Indonesian Borneo), and Irian Jaya (West New Guinea). Area: 1,919,443 sq. km. (741,101 sq. mi.). Pop. (1985): 167,550,000. Cap. and largest city: Jakarta (pop., 1981 est., 6,556,000). Language: Bahasa Indonesian (official), Javanese, Sudanese, Madurese, Batak, etc.

History: Indonesia came under the influence of India through Indian traders and Buddhist and Hindu monks. By the seventh and eighth centuries A.D., kingdoms closely connected with India had developed in Sumatra and Java. Sumatra was the seat of the important Buddhist kingdom of Srivijaya (11th to 13th centuries). In the late 13th century the center of power shifted to Java, where the fabulous kingdom of Madjapahit had arisen. For over two centuries (1293–1518) it held sway over Indonesia and large areas of the Malay Peninsula. This was the "golden age" of Indonesian history. With the arrival of Arab traders in the 14th and 15th centuries came a gradual infiltration of Islam. By the end of the 16th century, Islam had replaced Buddhism and Hinduism as the dominant religion. The island of Bali became the refuge of Hinduism and has remained Hindu ever since. The once-powerful kingdoms broke into smaller states that quarreled among themselves and fell easy prey to European imperialism.

Portuguese trading ties of the 16th century were displaced by the Dutch East India Company (1602–1798). In 1799 the Netherlands assumed direct control. Then came the British interlude (1811–1816) until the East Indies became a Dutch crown colony (1816–1942). The outer islands were not finally subdued until the early 20th century when the full area of present-day Indonesia was united under one rule for the first time in history. The Japanese occupation during World War II (1942–1945) spurred the Indonesian will to independence. Nationalists, led by Sukarno and Mohammad Hatta, proclaimed a republic. After four years of fighting, the Netherlands ceded sovereignty on December 27, 1949.

With its wealth of natural resources, Indonesia nevertheless passed through difficult times in finding its way internationally as well as domestically. It gained stature as host to the 1955 Bandung Conference, the meeting of diplomats from 29 African and Asian countries that promoted economic and cultural cooperation and opposed colonialism. In rounding out its island domain, Indonesia in 1963 acquired Netherlands New Guinea (now Irian Jaya) and in 1975 formally incorporated the Portuguese island of Timor. Domestically, President Sukarno's policy of guided democracy encountered an impasse in 1965, when the anti-Communist coup installed General Suharto. Local retaliation resulted in a great loss of life. Over the years the Indonesian economy has grown increasingly self-sufficient.

Religion: Indonesia is neither a religious nor a secular state. Its state philosophy is based on the Five Principles: belief in unitary deity; nationalism; democracy; humanitarianism; and social justice. On this basis the great religions are recognized by the government and given equal status and rights in practicing and propagating their faith. However, the Department of Religion is always led by a Muslim. Tribal religions still claim 4.7% of Indonesians, mainly those living on small islands or in isolated regions—Bataks in North Sumatra, Nias and Mentawai islanders, Dayaks of Kalimantan, and Irian Jayas of West New Guinea.

Islam, according to some statistics, claims 83.6% of the population. However, about half of these are followers of new religions—syncretizations of Islam, Hinduism, and Buddhism. In purer form, Hindu and Buddhist minorities have been growing since Indonesian independence. Hindus (2%) are mainly on the island of Bali; Buddhists (1%), mainly among the Chinese in the large cities.

Christianity accounts for about 11% of the population. Roman Catholics have been in Indonesia since the 16th century. However, during Dutch control, expatriate missionaries were expelled and replaced by Dutch Reformed chaplains supported by the Dutch East India Company. When the Company was disbanded (1798), a nonconfessional East India State Church was formed (1816). The political and religious climate of the 19th century also allowed for other missionary ventures. Rhenish, Basel, and Netherlands societies laid the basis for churches in every major area of the country. Roman Catholic missions resumed their work in 1807.

Of the 17 million Christians in Indonesia today, Roman Catholics number over four million. Catholic educational and social service agencies excel in numbers and quality. The Protestant Church in Indonesia—the former state church enlarged by a number of mergers over the years—is 2.25 million strong. Other large Protestant churches, stemming from Rhenish Mission work begun in 1861, are located mainly in North Sumatra and on the island of Nias. Those declaring themselves Lutheran are described below. Small but active church groups include Pentecostals, Adventists, Southern Baptists (USA), Christian and Missionary Alliance, and many indigenous bodies.

The Communion of Churches in Indonesia (CCI, 1950) includes some 50 Protestant churches (several Pentecostal) and represents a Christian community of about eight million. LWF member churches are active participants. Dr. Soritua Nababan, long general secretary and then CCI president, is now bishop of the HKBP (below). The CCI has service programs, but its main objective is "to establish one Christian Church in Indonesia." The CCI has a wide range of service activities strengthened by 14 affiliated regional councils. The main objective is to strengthen Christian unity.

In 1977 the CCI published an 800-page report on its eight-year study of the church in Indonesia. The need for such a study became evident to the Christian community after the coup of 1965, when they realized that they did not have sufficient knowledge of their faith, polity, and historical background, nor of their political, social, and cultural environment. This study involved securing a comprehensive picture of each member church, the church in each region, and the church throughout Indonesia. Structure, leadership, nurture, proclamation, service, ecumenical relations, and church-world relations were all a part of the study. The cumulative result of these self-studies gave the CCI and each church body's participant a better understanding of the problems and opportunities of the Christian church in Indonesia.

An Association of Evangelical Churches of Indonesia unites most of the Christian groups that are not affiliated with the CCI, about 10% of the Christian population. Many of these churches stem from recent American missions and stress evangelism rather than education and social service. Pentecostals have flourished most among the Indonesians of Chinese descent in Java and in North Sumatra and North Sulawesi.

Several ecumenical educational institutions have strengthened unity and Indonesian identity within the one Christian church. The Jakarta Theological Seminary, the oldest union seminary at university level in Indonesia, was founded through the efforts of the Dutch Reformed Church, the Rhenish Mission, and the (then established) Protestant Church of the Netherlands East Indies. In 1954, when it took its present name, administrative authority was transferred to the CCI. It continues to be an institution of high standards, attracting students from all areas of Indonesia.

The Jogjakarta Theological School in central Java is making a special contribution to Indonesian churches through its center for research and education in basic communication. Here students learn to describe their Christian faith in terms of local culture—music, art, puppetry. These two institutions have been used by the Indonesian Association of Theological Schools to prepare qualified teachers for the growing number of theological institutions. They are also used by a few students of the LWF-related churches (below). The Jogjakarta school has received considerable subsidy from the Lutheran Church in America (now *ELCA). It has also provided a professor and support for the Satya Wacana University in Salitaga, north of Jogjakarta. This school, supported by 13 Indonesian churches, has a department of religion where special emphasis is given to pastoral counseling. The school also trains teachers of religion for the public schools.

● ● ●

Background of the LWF member churches: The churches described below have a common history stemming from their Batak ancestry, their Sumatra island home, and the Christian heritage brought to them by the German Rhenish Mission.

The Bataks are an ancient people whose ancestors came from the Asian mainland long before the birth of Christ. They settled in the hill country in north-central Sumatra. There they developed a culture of their own, including a comprehensive legal system (Adat), a wide knowledge of mathematics, astronomy, and medicine, and a written language. Eventually six related tribal groups were formed, each with a distinctive dialect: Toba, Karo, Simalungun, Angkola, Mandailing, and Pakpak. Animism was their religion. Islam did not take hold in North Sumatra as it had further south. However, local animism was influenced by Islam, as it had been earlier by Hinduism from mainland Asia. Christianity was introduced into Sumatra in the 19th century (see below).

Today the largest group are the Toba Bataks living around Lake Toba. Some 90% of them are Christians, members of the *Protestant Christian Batak Church (HKBP). The Karo Bataks, north of the lake, were evangelized by the Netherlands Missionary Society. They formed the Karo Batak Protestant Church (Reformed), which is rapidly evangelizing this area. To the east of the lake are the Simalungun Bataks, approximately 50% of whom are in the *Simalungun Protestant Christian Church (GKPS). Farther south and to the west of the Tobas are the Angkola Bataks with a smaller church *Protestant Christian Church—Angkola (GKPA), amidst a Muslim majority. The nearby Mandailing are also strongly Muslim. The Pakpak Bataks to the west of the lake are largely animists.

Batak Christians have had a great impact upon the Indonesian society. Because of their concern for nation building, they hold a very influential position, especially in North Sumatra. Many Christians hold high positions in the government and society; many are thriving in business; and many more are employed in education, the armed forces, and other fields. Christians form the majority in some towns and villages. Pematangsiantar, the second largest city in North Sumatra, is over 50% Christian. Tarutung, the center for HKBP, is nearly 90% Christian.

Sumatra is a large and economically rich island. The Bataks occupy the north-central part, much of which is hilly country surrounding Lake Toba. Some mountains rise to over 2000 meters (7000 feet). In the early 19th century, the British in Singapore regarded Sumatra as important for their control of the Strait of Malacca, but in 1825 they withdrew and the Dutch took over. However, Batakland was off limits to the Dutch colonial government and also to the Muslims, for the Bataks jealously guarded their freedom and their traditional tribal religion.

Today, due to the overpopulation of Java, Sumatra is the chief recipient of the relocated Javanese. During 1983, 2.5 million people were lured to Sumatra, Kalimantan, and Irian Jaya by offers of a parcel of land, a wooden shanty, food for a year, seeds for two years, and an assemblage of garden tools. Although the transmigrants are "volunteers," pressure has often been exerted. Some are experiencing a new hopeful life, but most of them face vast problems: crop failures, drought, no means of marketing crops, etc. Nevertheless, plans to resettle another four million Javanese are being carried out.

Christian heritage: In April 1984, 400 Batak Christians gathered 40 kilometers north of the port city of Sibolga to remember with thanksgiving the lives of two American missionaries, Samuel Munson and Henry Lyman. On this site the two men, who had struggled through the pathless jungle for five days, were killed by hostile Bataks in 1834. Since the missionaries did not know the Batak language, they could not convey their peaceful intentions.

The Dutch Bible Society in 1849 sent an expert in linguistics, Dr. Neubronner van der Tuuk, to the coastal village of Barus, near Sibolga, where he studied the Batak language, compiled a dictionary, gathered local legends, and began to translate parts of the Old Testament. These developments formed the invaluable prelude to the subsequent work of the Rhenish missionaries.

October 7, 1861, is remembered by many Bataks as the day the Christian church began in their midst. The first emissaries of the Rhenish Mission (Barmen), ousted from Borneo (Kalimantan), came to the edge of the Batak country (HKBP, below). In 1884 Ludwig Ingwer Nommensen (1834–1918) penetrated to the hallowed heart of their tribal land. He survived initial threats to his life, gained the goodwill of the people, opened the way for many missionary colleagues, and pursued a strategy of tribal conversion. Complete with village churches, schools, and economic improvements—advanced in large part by an indigenous leadership of pastors, catechists, teachers, and many other workers—mission stations extended to the borders of the Muslim territory by the time of his death.

Animating Nommensen's consuming vision of the "kingdoms of this world becoming the kingdom of God" was a keen sense of urgency, shared by leaders of the Rhenish Mission. Dr. Friedrich Fabri, its director, sensed the time—the 1860s—as the *kairos* to bring the gospel to the Bataks, who otherwise would be left to Islam. They became the Rhenish Mission's major concern, and a Batak folk church arose. With decisions made collectively rather than individually, many of the Batak folkways (*Adat*) came into the church. In 1899 a Batak mission society (*Zending*) was initiated by indigenous pastors to spread the gospel in and beyond Sumatra. Meanwhile in 1889 the first woman missionary arrived from Germany, and in 1891 the first two deaconesses came from Kaiserswerth (see Germany Introduction).

In the 1920s a "big road" linked for the first time Medan on the north coast and Padang on the south, passing Lake Toba on the way. A spirit of independence stirred people here and in many other parts of the country, including Jakarta. From this ardently Batak dispersion, influences flowed back to the people at home. Self-assertion against the Dutch government appeared futile, but against the Rhenish Mission it succeeded. The role of the missionaries was diminished, the self-government of the church affirmed.

Two separate movements, in Jakarta (Java) and Pematangsiantar (Sumatra), already in 1927 had expressed this spirit of independence (see HKI and GPKB, below). Then, in 1930, the big "mother church" went independent and took the name Huria Kristen Batak Protestan (HKBP). Other churches were to draw their varied stories from the same origins (see GKPI, GKPS, GKPA, and GKPM). But first, several common concerns should be mentioned.

The Batak churches face a language problem. What the HKBP says about its own situation applies largely to the other churches too. The church language is old Batak, which is very dear to the older generation. Many younger members know only Bahasa Indonesian. Others prefer still a third language, new Batak, a mixture of Batak and Indonesian. Add to this the persistence of local dialects and the problem deepens. Moreover, Batak culture clings to the authority of the spoken word. It is therefore important for the churches to use several languages during this period of transition. Some city congregations worship in Indonesian on Sunday afternoons. But regardless of language, music remains a powerful conveyer of the gospel message. Bataks young and old are famed for their singing.

At present there is no common agency in Indonesia through which the LWF member churches can cooperate. However, several undertakings promote their working together. Joint efforts in women's work, encouraged by LWF programs, are a step in this direction. In 1981 over 400 women from all of the then six member churches considered the theme: "Behold, I make all things new." They left with a renewed will to participate in the development of their church and society, a desire for church unity, and an increasing awareness of the importance of their primary task—the care of the family.

Theological education is increasingly becoming a joint responsibility. The Faculty of Theology at Nommensen University (1954), in Pematangsiantar, was separated from that institution in 1978 by HKBP in order to give the church more control over the training of its pastors. Since then other churches using this school have been granted seats on the governing board. Theological education by extension (TEE), begun by the *Indonesian Christian Church (HKI), has developed into a system benefiting most of the churches in North Sumatra. With the exception of HKBP, all churches follow one lectionary and publish one book of sermons every three months—a great help to the numerous lay preachers. The LWF-sponsored Asia Program for the Advancement of Training and Studies (APATS) focuses largely on common problems facing churches at the congregational level.

In electronic and print media, various projects have fostered cooperation. A venture in the writing of contemporary Christian literature, sponsored by *Indonesian Christian Church (HKI) in the 1970s, was open to all the churches. Aided by the *Lutheran Church of Australia and the International Lutheran Laymen's League (*LCMS/USA), the Sumatra Lutheran Hour and Lutheran Literature Team were formed in 1977. They merged in 1982 and took the name Society for the Communication of Spiritual Blessings (SCSB). This agency's governing board includes representatives from six participating churches. Its programs are carried by 14 radio stations as well as distributed on cassettes to hospitals and prisons. For Luther's 500th anniversary (1983), SCSB published a short life story of the reformer. The agency's most ambitious project is publishing a first-time rendition of the Lutheran Confessions into Bahasa Indonesian. Luther's *Small* and *Large Catechism* and the *Apology* to the *Augsburg Confession*, all in the *Book of Concord*, have already appeared. After long preparation, *Key-Words* for the understanding of Lutheran theology appeared in 1983. The Christian Publishing House in Jakarta, developed by HKBP members in cooperation with others, serves all Indonesian churches.

Joint biennial pastoral conferences have furthered mutual understanding, cooperation, and the movement toward a united church. To follow historical developments it is best to turn first to the Protestant Christian Batak Church (HKBP), below.

BATAK CHRISTIAN COMMUNITY CHURCH (GPKB)
(Gereja Punguan Kristen Batak)
Member: LWF (1972), WCC, CCA, CCI
Membership: 16,000**
Ephorus/Bishop: The Rt. Rev. M.P. Lumbantoruan
Jalan HOS, Cokroaminoto 96
PO Box 96/MT
Jakarta 10310

The 35 congregations of the GPKB are served by 15 ordained pastors (one of whom is a woman), five evangelists, and other church leaders. The church was established in 1927 after the congregations broke with the mother church on organizational grounds. The new church, acknowledged by the government in 1933, adopted a presbyterial-synodal polity. In 1975 the church's chair was made bishop and given the title of ephorus.

The central synod, the governing body of the church, calls the pastors, sends them to the congregations, and pays their salaries. All congregations, most of which are in the Jakarta area, are visited at least annually by members of the central synod who survey their progress and provide guidelines. The ephorus himself visits the Sumatra congregations at least twice a year. The congregations are divided into six districts. The majority of members are engaged in business or governmental work.

Most of the pastors have had their training at the Jakarta Theological Seminary, an ecumenical institution; others have attended the Theological Faculty in Pematangsiantar (Sumatra) or the Jogjakarta Theological School. The evangelists are trained at the church's two Bible schools: Batu Malang and Tanjungenim. Two of the present five evangelists are women.

Mission outreach has been to the Maya-Maya, a fishing people around Tebingtinggi in North Sumatra, many of whom have requested baptism. In South Sumatra the mission is to the transmigrants from Java, in Banyulincir near Palembang. Here, too, the response to the Christian message has been positive.

Although aware of the opportunities for mission both in cities and on the frontier, the church is handicapped by a lack of pastors, evangelists, and funds. GPKB welcomes its partnership with the United Evangelical Mission (VEM) of *FRG and also with the *Lutheran Church of Australia.

CHRISTIAN PROTESTANT CHURCH IN INDONESIA (GKPI)
(Gereja Kristen Protestan Indonesia)
Member: LWF (1975), WCC, CCA, CCI
Membership: 219,134
Bishop: The Rev. Ruben M.G. Marbun
Jalan Kapten M.H. Sitorus No. 13
Pematangsiantar, North Sumatra

The 701 congregations of this church are spread over the island of Sumatra as well as in central and western Java. They are served by 107 pastors and sufficient lay teacher-preachers for every congregation. The latter have been trained for three years in a special school for teachers of religion or have been selected by the local elders and appointed by the bishop.

Each congregation has a council consisting of elders, evangelists, heads of sections, and advisers. The teacher-preacher serves as chair. Several congregations led by a pastor form a circuit called "Pendeta Resort." The 80 circuits are organized into 11 districts headed by superintendents who have been chosen by the pastors and appointed by the bishop for a five-year period. Pastors are educated at the Theological Faculty in Pematangsiantar (see Indonesia Introduction).

The general synod, meeting every five years, is the highest legislative body. The synod ratifies the election of the bishop and general secretary, who are chosen by the pastors. It also elects an executive committee, which serves as a legislative body between synods. In addition to the bishop and general secretary, this consists of five ordained pastors, seven teacher-preachers, three elders, two representatives of youth, two representatives of women, and 10 people recruited from among scholars and prominent leaders in society—a total of 31.

The GKPI has a mission outreach. One-third of its pastors are evangelists in rural areas of Sumatra and in towns and factories of western and central Java. They reach transmigrated Javanese in North Sumatra as well as primitive tribes—the Sakai near Pekanbaru in the southern part of North Sumatra and the nomadic Kubu near Jambi in the Central Sumatran jungles. In the fanatically Muslim area near Palembang there have been many converts to Christianity. The evangelists visit the people in their homes, at work, and in hospitals. They give out tracts and explain the role of Jesus Christ for all humankind. They also share practical knowledge, helping the people make better use of their land and time. The evangelists give monthly reports to the bishop and director of missions. This mission outreach has the support of the LWF Department of Church Cooperation, through which Lutherans in Denmark, Germany, Norway, Sweden, and the United States participate.

Besides its school for the training of teachers in religion, the GKPI maintains an orphanage and supports social programs and relief work as well as a fund for education. It participates with five other Lutheran churches in maintaining the Society for the Communication of Spiritual Blessings, a media mission (above), and since 1981 has joined in the theological education by extension program of the HKI and GKPS.

GKPI emerged out of several renewal and reform movements within the HKBP in the early 1960s. When these efforts failed, several of the reform movements united, creating the Coordinating Body for Reformation within the HKBP. Soon thereafter, on August 30, 1964, an independent church emerged, taking the name Gereja Kristen Protestan Indonesia (GKPI). It was registered and recognized by the Indonesian government in November 1966. After more than 10 years of tension with the "mother church" came reconciliation. Then, in 1975, the GKPI was accepted into LWF membership, and partnership with the United Evangelical Mission (VEM) in the FRG was restored. Ecumenical relationships were also established: CCI (1976); WCC (1977); Regional Council of Churches in North Sumatra (1978); and the CCA (1981).

INDONESIAN CHRISTIAN CHURCH (HKI)
(Huria Kristen Indonesia)
Member: LWF (1970), WCC, CCA, CCI
Membership: 329,641**
President: The Rev. Wilmar J. Sirait
Jalan Marihat 111
Pematangsiantar 21128
North Sumatra

The HKI is one of the first independent, self-supporting churches in Indonesia. It was formed in 1927, when three congregations withdrew from the Batak church then operated and controlled by the founding Rhenish Mission. At issue were the ordination of Batak ministers, the place of the indigenous in regional and local affairs, and the Batak role in national identity. Soon after the Indonesian proclamation of independence in 1946, the church changed its original name, "Huria Kristen Batak," to "Huria Kristen Indonesia." The HKI adopted a synodal form of polity, headed by a president.

Today the church has 548 congregations, an increase of about a hundred for each decade of its life. They are located mostly in North Sumatra where the language is Toba Batak. The majority of members live in rural areas, working small farms and raising cattle, water buffalo, pigs, and chickens. Others live in towns and cities, also in Java, working as civil servants, policemen, soldiers, retailers, etc.

The congregations are served by 74 pastors, most of whom have had their training at the Theological Faculty of Nommensen University (since 1978 independent of the university). They are assisted by 561 teacher-preachers as well as many volunteer workers.

Since the church has always been economically independent (even though most of its members are poor), HKI does not have as large an institutional ministry as do its sister churches, who receive overseas help. However, it manages 35 primary and secondary schools as well as a technical one and operates an orphanage and a health center. HKI is also involved in development projects. In 1976 a small holders' rice-growing project was initiated with outside aid. As the investment money is repaid, the revolving fund will help launch new projects for more people. In 1982 a CDS project enabled the church to bring clean mountain water to the villages surrounding Tigalingga in the Tapanuli district.

During the 1970s, in partnership with the *Simalungun Protestant Christian Church (GKPS) and with personnel and financial assistance from the Lutheran Church in America (now *ELCA), the HKI embarked on a leadership training program. The primary objective of the program was to provide educational opportunities on a regular basis for preacher-teachers and elders. The two churches at that time had 900 lay preachers and about 4000 elders. However, the 90 pastors were given the first attention so they in turn would be prepared to help the teacher-preachers deal with new situations in their local congregations.

Since the pastors all had full-time responsibilities, the curriculum had to deal with specific concerns of their work. These concerns included the relationship of Christian teaching to the rules and customs set down by the ancestors (Adat); the distance between the pastors and the members of their congregations; and much more. Goals and priorities were set and materials and experiences provided that would help the pastors achieve what was important in their ministry. People of experience shared with the younger pastors. The former included the late ephorus of *HKBP, then 87 years of age; the retired president of HKI, who was a first generation

Christian; a Roman Catholic professor whose field is church and society, and a *GKPS layman who had spent many years relating Christian faith to the tradition of his people.

The pastors-in-training were expected to relay what they learned to their congregational leaders and get their reactions. This helped to bring both clergy and laity into the educational process. It also became clear that although outsiders may be good catalysts, it is very difficult for them to present material as effectively as those from the local culture. The courses were finally prepared and led by six Indonesians.

By 1981 the pastors were ready to turn their attention to the teacher-preachers and elders. Once again, their needs had to be identified before adequate courses could be prepared. Meanwhile the shortage of pastors was acute. Therefore, in 1982, 20 capable teacher-preachers were chosen for a three-year theological course that would prepare them for ordination. Some of the newly trained workers were sent to the frontiers as evangelists. Others strengthened the already-established congregations and reached out to the Muslims and animists in their midst.

Beginning in 1980 the teaching staff and materials of this project were shared with the Nias Protestant Christian Church on the offshore island of Nias. This church of 250,000 members, affiliated with the Reformed churches, also stems from the early work of the Rhenish Mission. In 1982 the same service was extended to the Karo Batak Protestant Church (135,000) founded by the Netherlands Missionary Society in 1890. Now these two Reformed churches manage their own programs. The Christian Protestant Church in Indonesia (GKPI, above) in 1982 joined with HKI and *GKPS in this training program. Thus a large portion of the churches in North Sumatra benefit from the initiative of HKI. A further ecumenical step has been taken by HKI in establishing a working relationship with the church in the city of Hamm, a part of the *Evangelical Church of Westphalia in the FRG.

INDONESIAN CHRISTIAN LUTHERAN CHURCH (GKLI)
(Gereja Kristen Luther Indonesia)
Membership: 14,534**
Ephorus: The Rt. Rev. Dr. J. Sinaga
Kantor Pusat
Lumban Siagian Tarutung
North Sumatra

Most of the congregations of this church were part of the HKBP (below) until 1965 when they declared themselves to be HKBP–Luther. Ten years later, in order to avoid confusion, they changed the name to Indonesian Christian Lutheran Church (GKLI). The 59 congregations are served by 17 pastors, 51 teacher-preachers, and 365 elders. In matters of organization, GKLI gives broad autonomy to local congregations and districts. The majority of the congregations are located south of Lake Toba. The members are mainly poor subsistence farmers.

Spiritual renewal is the main thrust of this church. Christian nurture is strengthened by four elementary schools, a Bible school training religious teachers for government schools, and a theological school for teacher-preachers (also for pastors until 1983). A health center, with government technical assistance, serves a rural area.

Since 1982 the GKLI has had an agreement of cooperation with the Norwegian Lutheran Mission (NLM). After two years of waiting, six NLM missionaries were permitted to enter Indonesia. This agreement led to a relationship with the interdenominational Indonesian Missionary Fellowship located in Batu near Malang, in eastern Java. Here the NLM is assisting with theological education and mass media projects. Through the fellowship and the NLM, GKLI is establishing congregations in Java, reaching Chinese, Javanese, and others. The same is taking place in the plantation and industrial areas of North Sumatra. In 1983 the fellowship and the NLM helped with the founding of Luther Theological Seminary in Siborongborong in North Sumatra (between Tarutung and Lake Toba). The school, intended to prepare missionaries as well as pastors, opened with a student body of 58.

According to the present ephorus, the founders of this church had no intention of leaving *HKBP. Rather, they hoped for spiritual renewal within the mother church. To foster this, in 1963 they formed the "Committee for Reformation" and promoted an emphasis on the Lutheran Confession. When the government, at the request of HKBP, banned the committee's activities, the HKBP–Luther was organized. By a study of Luther, the members are strengthened in faith and are better able to cope with Catholicism and Pentecostalism, two churches that have been gaining members at the expense of the HKBP and other churches of the area. In 1966 HKBP–Luther sponsored the translation, printing, and distribution of the *Augsburg Confession* in Batak and Indonesian. Today the GKLI supports the work of the Society for the Communication of Spiritual Blessings (see Introduction).

The GKLI has repeatedly applied for membership in the LWF in order to be restored to fellowship with Indonesian LWF member churches and also to take part in the wider LWF programs. According to LWF membership policy, HKBP must first give its approval. This has been withheld because GKLI occupies one of HKBP's church buildings.

PROTESTANT CHRISTIAN BATAK CHURCH (HKBP)

(Huria Kristen Batak Protestan)
Member: LWF (1952), WCC, CCA, CCI
Membership: 2,000,000**
Ephorus: The Rt. Rev. Dr. Soritua A. E. Nababan
Pearaja Tarutung, Sumatra

This folk church, active in the Christian Conference of Asia as well as the Communion of Churches in Indonesia, is a religious phenomenon in East Asia. Mainly a regional body in northern Sumatra, the HKBP, as it is commonly called, has a dispersion of its own with congregations and missions in various parts of Indonesia as well as in *Singapore and *Malaysia. In size it is second only to the Protestant Church in Indonesia, the former Indonesian State Church (Reformed).

HKBP comprises 2200 congregations grouped into 228 parishes. Several parishes form a resort, and the resorts are united into 16 districts. Each parish is led by a teacher-preacher, each resort by a pastor, and each

district by a superintendent. The church is served by 413 pastors, 259 teacher-preachers, 94 Bible women, and 30 deaconesses. Since 1982, women who have completed the subscribed course for pastoral training are eligible for ordination. Bible women have the same status as the teacher-preachers and may preach and pronounce the benediction. Administration of the sacraments is limited to the ordained pastors. Many other workers in education, youth, health, and community services round out the broad range of ministries.

Headed by an ephorus (presiding bishop) and a general secretary, the HKBP (formed in 1930) was the first major independent and self-governing church body in the then Dutch East Indies. For the affairs of the church as a whole, the biennial synodical convention, a representative body of pastors and parish churches, hears reports on the life and work of the church, debates issues, authorizes programs, makes decisions, enforces discipline, and elects officers. To organize and administer its extensive work, HKBP has nine departments and six bureaus. Headquarters in Tarutung, southeast of Lake Toba in the north central part of the island, are near where the mission began.

The majority of the members are rural people, engaged in small farming and living in villages, some of which still preserve the traditional multipurpose houses with characteristically pitched protruding roofs. Many of the members are city dwellers, with large numbers in Pematangsiantar, as well as in Jakarta, other parts of Java, and various places in Kalimantan (Borneo). Many are engaged in education, business, civil service, the armed forces, and various crafts and professions. As Christians and as Bataks, they are making a positive impact on Indonesian national life. The church language is Toba Batak, but the church faces a language problem (see Introduction).

Most HKBP congregations are self-supporting. The members give in kind or in money. Two offerings are customarily received at each service of worship. Since 1970 the second offering has gone to the church headquarters to be used for the salaries of the ephorus, the presidents of the church's 16 districts, the executives of the nine departments of work, the staff at the school for preachers and teachers in Sipoholon (near

Tarutung), the Laguboti Bible School for Women, the Deaconess Training School at Balige, the 46 parishes classified as "poor areas," and other general work and obligations. On the occasion of the mission society's (Batak Zending) 75th anniversary (1974), the week's festivities brought in 57.5 million rupiahs.

Pastors of HKBP are educated by a theological faculty that, until 1978, was a department of Nommensen University in Pematangsiantar (history, below). After several years of tension between the elected officers of the church and those who were running the university, HKBP took firm steps to resolve the crisis. It formed a theological college separate from the university and responsible directly to the church. In 1981 HKBP gave one-third of the board member seats to the other North Sumatran churches using this school. Government requirements may in the future reunite these schools, but the church will retain control and responsibility for the training of its pastors. The theological college has links with Luther Seminary in South *Australia and plays an important role in APATS, the LWF-initiated Asia Program for the Advancement of Training and Studies (see below).

Most of the 160 students at this institution support themselves. A few receive small scholarships from the sponsoring churches or from the college itself. In order to meet the acute shortage of well-trained ordained pastors, the church is now choosing experienced teacher-preachers for additional education at the Sipoholon Seminary near Tarutung. When they are ordained as pastors, they are expected to strengthen the work of the church, especially in the rural areas where 80% of the membership live and where growth is fastest.

Women have an important role in the life of HKBP. Choirs, study and prayer groups, as well as service projects engage women of all ages. An increasing number are gaining leadership roles, not only as ordained ministers but also as Bible women. To encourage and assist in these developments, the HKBP women's department publishes a monthly magazine.

The youth department focuses attention on HKBP's 400,000 young people. It maintains a youth center in Jetun Silangit, Siborongborong, a barber shop in Tarutung, and a farming project near Lake Toba. A magazine, "Lam magadang dibagasan Kristus" (Be mature in Christ), is published. The Sunday school department provides teaching aids and publishes a quarterly guidebook for Sunday school teachers.

The department of social service maintains an orphanage in Pematangsiantar, a training center for the blind and crippled in Hephata-Laguboti, a workshop for dropouts in Sei Loba, and a home for retired pastors in Patmos. The school department supervises four kindergartens and 19 elementary, three junior high, and eight senior high schools. Four of the latter also train teachers. A training center for women in Doloksanggul and one for young men dropouts in Parparean-Porsea are part of the school system.

Another emphasis of the HKBP today is development. Since most of its members are subsistence farmers, efforts are made to increase productivity and improve nutrition. Demonstration farms and agricultural counselors are increasing in numbers. Community development centers are located in Butar, near Siborongborong, and in Jetun Silangit. In Pematangsiantar the church maintains a technical school that greatly benefits young people from the numerous surrounding villages. Here, they learn vocational skills, including auto mechanics and printing, that prepare them for work much needed in a developing society.

The church's involvement in health and community services includes the hospital in Balige, near Lake Toba, with its deaconess center and training program. A growing number of Batak deaconesses serve as nurses and community workers. The initial group of sisters (as noted earlier) were from Kaiserswerth, Federal Republic of Germany. HKBP's health department also maintains four public health centers, including one on the underdeveloped island of Rupat in the Strait of Malacca.

As already mentioned, the Batak Christians early became a missioning people. HKBP's "Zending" for years bolstered the work of VEM on the Mentawai islands (see GKPM, below). At present the outreach is to the nearby city of Medan among the Japanese and Tamils; to the eastern Sumatra Riau area among the primitive Sakai tribes; to South Tapanuli among the transmigrants; to

*Malaysia among the Senoi; and to *Singapore among the Bataks (see LCMS).

Although the church became independent in 1930, the German missionaries retained leadership until May 1940, when they were interned by the Dutch government after Hitler's attack on the Netherlands. This left the church with neither money nor leadership. In July of the same year, an extraordinary synodical convention met and elected one of its own pastors, the Rev. K. Sirait, ephorus. Presumably to be helpful to the churches, the Dutch government created the Batak Nias Zending (BNZ), but HKBP experienced this agency as a hindrance to its work. Teacher-preachers and nurses were asked to leave their church posts and work for government subsidized schools and hospitals; the church was not permitted to use the houses and offices of the interned missionaries. The situation worsened during the Japanese occupation (1942–1945) when the members were forced to conform to Shinto and work on Sunday. Religion in the schools was prohibited, church meetings were controlled, and houses of worship often used as stables.

Despite those trying years, the membership grew, as mission-mindedness and self-discipline kept the church on course. Toughened by its members' participation in the struggle for independence and the task of nation making, the HKBP entered the confessional and ecumenical scene with a clear sense of purpose as to its faith, its fellowship, and its educational task.

A confession of faith was adopted by the HKBP synod in November 1951. This was seen as of "utmost necessity for establishing our faith and opposing heresy." The ecumenical creeds, the Reformation-era confession (not individually named), and more recent ones like the Barmen Theological Declaration (1934) provided foundations on which to build for confessing Jesus Christ today. Until recently animism and Islam, threats from within and without, were the main temptations. New ones came, and the church's confession of faith named them— e.g., Adventists, Pentecostals, nationalistic Christianity, and syncretism. The Confession draws its basic content from the Bible, Luther's *Catechism,* and the *Augsburg Confession.* The result is a statement, by Ephorus Justin Sihombing and HKBP theologians, transcending traditional Western confessional

positions—the first to be drawn up by an autonomous church that originated in the modern missionary movement. Other Batak churches have either adopted this Confession or tried to produce an equivalent. It is said to qualify equally well for reception by Lutherans and Reformed and was accepted by the LWF in lieu of the *Augsburg Confession* when the HKBP applied for membership in 1952, a precedent that made history and the consequences of which are yet to be fully fathomed even after decades of membership.

This LWF membership was sought only after long deliberation and with the full knowledge and consent of the Rhenish Mission. As early as 1947, the *Tamil Evangelical Lutheran Church had sent a fraternal worker from South India. A Tamil physician, Rajah Williams, was sent by Bishop Sandegren to offer his service to the Bataks in the struggle for independence. The need for relief, rehabilitation, and reconstruction was great, and Lutheran experience in this field was well known. So was the confessional kinship: Dutch and Reformed associations seemed alien to the Batak experience. Immediate and large-scale assistance from the Rhenish Mission and Germany generally was not possible, but through the LWF new sources of support were opened up.

The HKBP Nommensen University, opened in 1954, was created in response to the felt need for higher education in the new nation. Help from many sides—churches, individuals, the LWF, the Ford Foundation, and others—joined with the Bataks' ability and will to make the university possible. Its main campus in Pematangsiantar has a school of education and a theological faculty (until 1978, see above); its second campus in Medan, the agriculture and economics departments and the schools of technology and business administration; and more recently a department of language and art, including music. The university currently has a student body of 10,000.

Like all churches, this one is not above criticism. At times the perennial struggle for renewal has led to tension and schism, but also to helpful self-criticism. Anyone who visits Sumatra's Batak country and attends Sunday worship can sense in the singing of the many choirs a vibrant expression of spiritual life and an invitation to the common praise of God.

In Pematangsiantar a massive week-long celebration in 1986 observed the 125th anniversary—October 7—of missionary beginnings in the heart of the Batak country. The festivities included a visit by Indonesia's President Suharto. In recalling the great evangelizing pioneer Ludwig Nommensen, the church set new goals for its striving. In his later years, Nommensen bore the title of overseer—*ephorus*—of the church. The latest person to fill this office (1987) is the recent president of the Communion of Churches in Indonesia, Dr. Soritua Nababan—a vice-president of the LWF and active also in the WCC.

In April 1987 a strong earthquake struck Tarutung, seat of HKBP headquarters, causing death, injuries, and much destruction. LWF World Service quickly responded to Bishop Nababan's request for emergency aid.

PROTESTANT CHRISTIAN CHURCH—ANGKOLA (GKPA)
(Gereja Kristen Protestan Angkola)
Member: LWF (1977), CCI
Membership: 17,850**
Ephorus: The Rev. Ginda P. Harahap
Jalan Teuku Umar No. 60C
Padang Sidempuan 22722
South Tapanuli
North Sumatra

The members of this church are grouped into 105 parishes served by 20 pastors, 380 assistants, and two Bible women. One woman pastor serves as an evangelist. The parishes are divided into 12 districts, all in northern Sumatra except for the one in the capital, Jakarta. The major concentration is in the hill country south of Lake Toba in the strongly Muslim Angkola region.

The Angkola language, one of the Batak tongues, is the main reason these congregations could amicably separate from the *HKBP in 1974. Since then the spiritual life of the congregations has been strengthened by the translation of the New and then the Old Testament into Angkola. This serves as common ground for Christian-Muslim conversation as well as a means of enhancing the Christian education programs of the congregations.

At its second synod meeting in 1976, GKPA voted to apply for LWF membership, having affirmed the Federation's doctrinal basis. The following year the church was accepted into LWF membership, and it also became a member of the (present) Communion of Churches in Indonesia.

The GKPA pursues an ambitious program of community development. A skilled team, including a physician, an engineer, and an economist who were in consultation with colleagues at the Christian University in Indonesia (Jakarta), directed a training center for villagers to promote self-help and interdependence. All the villages and homes within villages where the church is located were classified according to their development: good, moderate, and poor. The goal was a practical application of the Christian faith. GKPA's history coincides with that of the mother church, *HKBP. It is noteworthy that the small town of Sipirok, where the church at first had its headquarters, is the place where the Rhenish Mission originally began its work on October 7, 1861 (above).

PROTESTANT CHRISTIAN CHURCH IN MENTAWAI (GKPM)
(Gereja Kristen Protestan di Mentawai)
Member: LWF (1984)
Membership: 22,325
President: The Rev. M. Tatubeket
Nemnemleleu, Sikakap
Sumatra Barat

Upon the recommendation of the Indonesian member churches, GKPM was received into membership of the LWF at the Seventh Assembly in 1984. The congregations that form the GKPM are located on the four largest of the small Mentawai islands, 150 kilometers (94 miles) west of Padang, Sumatra. These volcanic islands are surrounded by sunken coral reefs, which make approach difficult. Transportation within each island is also difficult due to the heavily forested mountains. Small boats are the usual means of getting from one part of an island to another.

The Mentawai people, numbering about 35,000, have a language and culture resembling that of the Karo Bataks, Celebes, and Filipinos. Family structure is patriarchal with strict moral codes that exclude polygamy.

Fishing and subsistence farming are the main occupations. In general they have had very little opportunity for education and development. Most of the Mentawai accepted Christianity during the Dutch period, when both Protestant and Roman Catholic missionaries worked among them. An increasing number of islanders are the Muslim Pedangs who have moved in from Western Sumatra. They dominate in the government and also in the timber industry, which is advancing without regard to reforestation. Javanese are also being placed here by the government's resettlement program.

In this setting the 113 congregations of the GKPM are in need of the solidarity that a church body supplies, yet not all the congregations comprehend this. Of necessity, their isolation fostered self-sufficiency. Local elders carry on the congregational work, including preaching, between pastoral visits. The congregations are grouped into 10 parishes or resorts and are served by 14 pastors, six evangelists, and 19 teacher-preachers. A synod meets every three years to assess the work and needs as well as to elect officers. The church headquarters are in Nemnemleleu on the southern tip of North Pagai. The GKPM is the only indigenous church on the islands.

The Mentawai schools, established by Christian missions, are now almost entirely in government hands and are staffed by Muslim teachers. This increases the importance of the GKPM's several primary schools and the secondary school in Nemnemleleu. The latter has recently been updated with help from the Protestant Central Agency for Development Aid (EZE) in the FRG. It is this school, with students coming from all four islands, that has given the church its leadership since 1957. For further education students must go to Sumatra, where Muslim influence is even stronger. GKPM would like to open a vocational school that would give students the kind of training that is needed in developing the islands. Scholarships to schools in North Sumatra have been a great help to young church members. Candidates for the ordained ministry are in training at the HKBP Theological Faculty in Pematangsiantar. GKPS has been sending several pastors to meet the immediate need.

Since governmental health services do not reach the remote area of the islands, the church has four subclinics with nine health attendants. In Siberut, the least-developed northern island, two nurses from the (Rhenish) Evangelical Mission (VEM) provide care and consultation. Since nurses are rare in the islands, the church would like to provide two for each parish. Development of all kinds is needed, especially motivators to increase the interest of the parishioners. The islands have wide areas of uncultivated fertile land, that, if not used wisely, will be taken by the newcomers. In 1982 the general synod decided to open an agricultural training center, and 30 hectares of land have been prepared for this purpose. Several of the parishes have done likewise.

The GKPM has a remarkable as well as a depressing history, summarized as follows: A pious Muslim, a harbormaster, at Padang on the west coast of Sumatra, opened the way for Christian missions on the Mentawai islands. When he heard that a Mentawai had killed a Chinese sailor, he felt sorry for the murderer. He sent a letter to the Rhenish Mission in North Sumatra on a spear: "When can the Mentawai hear the gospel of love?" The Rhenish Mission received the letter as a call and sent an experienced pastor, August Lett, to the island in 1901. Tragically, Lett was killed by a Mentawai in 1909 while mediating between the Dutch and the Mentawai. Other missionaries carried on, but not until 1916 were people ready to be baptized.

Christianity prospered under the Dutch, who assigned educational responsibilities for the Mentawai to the Rhenish Mission. Primary schools were established and capable students chosen for further education, including theological education for a select few. During World War II, Rhenish missionaries had to leave. Pastors came from *HKBP until they, too, were forced out. To meet the emergency a few Mentawai were ordained after a short training course. The church was on its own until 1954.

When the Rhenish and HKBP missionaries returned, they focused attention on the church's need for indigenous leadership. Pastoral candidates were sent to HKBP's seminary, then to Sipoholon near Tarutung. Primary schools were upgraded and a secondary school established in Nemnemleleu. The first general assembly (1962) adopted a temporary constitution and elected the Rev. I. Sakerebau president. GKPM expected independence from HKBP, but this was not granted until 1973. Upon HKBP recommendation the church was received into the (present) Communion of Churches in Indonesia in 1976 and recognized by the government the same year.

By invitation of the LWF member churches in North Sumatra, GKPM pastors attended a seminar on Luther's *Large Catechism* in 1980. This fellowship and educational opportunity created a desire for more. The church applied for membership in the LWF and was accepted in 1984. In July 1985 the LWF/DCC Asia secretary, accompanied by the ephorus of the *Simalungun Protestant Christian Church, made the arduous trip to the Mentawai islands to express the good wishes of the other LWF churches and to discuss future cooperation and mutual concerns.

SIMALUNGUN PROTESTANT CHRISTIAN CHURCH (GKPS)
(Gereja Kristen Protestan Simalungun)
Member: LWF (1967), WCC, CCA, CCI
Membership: 161,098**
Ephorous: The Rev. Armencius Munthe
Jalan Jenderal Sudirman 14
PO Box 2
Pematangsiantar, North Sumatra

This church became autonomous in 1963, when Simalungun congregations were amicably released from the HKBP to form their own church in order to serve the Simalungun-speaking people (about 300,000). The language has some similarities with other Batak dialects, but it also has affinity with Sanskrit, the ancient language of the Hindus in India.

GKPS now comprises 439 congregations that are grouped into 44 parishes, forming three districts. About 70% of the members live on small farms in the mountain region northeast of Lake Toba. The rest are engaged in various occupations in urban centers to which they have migrated: Pematangsiantar, Medan, Tebingtinggi, and the nation's capital, Jakarta. The congregations are served by 78 pastors and an almost equal number of evangelists. Most of the latter are women who have graduated from a special training school. They usually serve full time among the women and youth of the parishes and are authorized to preach. Theological study is

coeducational in the seminaries where this church trains its pastors: Jakarta, Jogjakarta, and Pematangsiantar. The first two women were ordained in 1988, 19 years after GKPS authorized women's ordination.The church also participates in the theological extension program in cooperation with *HKI and *GKPI (see above).

Church organization combines congregational and synodical features similar to those of the "mother church." All elected officials (except elders) are chosen for a five-year period. The great synod, which meets in the second, fourth, and fifth year of each five-year period, comprises all pastors, heads of departments, selected evangelists, and parish representatives. Between synod meetings an executive council—consisting of the chair plus four other pastors, the presidents of the three districts, and 11 lay members—carries out the synodical policies and decisions. The elected ephorus and general secretary are responsible for the execution of the decisions as well as for the placement of pastors, evangelists, and vicars (probationers).

Locally each congregation elects its elders and deacons from the confirmed adult membership. Elders, who normally serve for life, are chosen from among those who have completed at least one five-year term as deacon. Both elders and deacons are authorized to preach. This gives the GKPS some 7000 lay preachers—men and women—who are a strong force in the life of the church and community.

Although GKPS stems from HKBP and shares much of its heritage, it has a history of its own as well. This history was written and published for its 80th anniversary celebration. It began on Sunday, September 6, 1903, when evangelist Theophilus Pasaribu preached the first Christian message on Simalungun soil. Theophilus was one of two Toba evangelists who accompanied missionary August Theis of the Rhenish Missionary Society to a territory that had been carefully surveyed by Ludwig Nommensen and colleagues working among the Toba Bataks. A few months later missionary G.K. Simon, two Batak pastors, and several evangelists were sent to the eastern Simalungun area where a number of Toba Bataks had migrated. Simon, realizing the importance of using the local language, began to teach Simalungun to the Tobas so they could transmit the gospel to their Simalungun neighbors. He also translated parts of the New Testament and Luther's *Small Catechism*. Unfortunately, for health reasons, he had to leave in 1906. The work in Simalungun progressed very slowly even though schools were soon established and the people's health needs given care. Growth was also impeded by the rugged terrain and the negative example of the Rajas. Although these clan leaders had agreed to having missionaries on their territories and were friendly as well as often helpful to them, they themselves were not open to the gospel. Besides, a spirit of nationalism was growing. In the eyes of some the missionaries were identified with the colonial power, the Dutch.

With the 25th jubilee in 1928 a change began. The realization dawned that proclamation was the task and responsibility of the Simalungun people as a whole. A threefold program developed. A "committee" was formed to promote the use of the Simalungun language in church, school, and community. Led by J. Wismar Saragih, the first ordained (1929) Simalungun pastor, the committee translated Bible stories, Luther's *Small Catechism*, the hymnal and liturgy, a book of daily prayers, and a grammar. The committee also prepared educational materials and published *Sinalsal*, the only magazine in the Simalungun language. It was read avidly by both Christians and non-Christians. By 1936 Saragih had also finished a Simalungun dictionary.

A "Let's Go Society" was formed in 1931. Its aim was to activate Simalungun Christians to become witnesses to their faith. Its members agreed that into every conversation that lasted five minutes, they would bring some form of testimonial. For this purpose they went regularly into non-Christian villages. A "fund" was also established by persons in salaried positions who agreed to give 1% of their income for Christian schools and teachers.

During World War II, under foreign occupation, this Christian work was interrupted. Missionaries had to leave, and schools were taken over by the Japanese. Yet the Simalungun Christians did not despair. They formed an organization, Parguru Sakse ni Kristus (PSK), to educate a large number of lay workers willing to do evangelistic work during their free time. When more than 70 men joined the first PSK in Pematang Raya,

the Japanese became suspicious, but when it was explained in terms of Dr. Toyohiko Kagawa's Christian program in Japan, they were permitted to continue. By 1943 some 300 persons had enrolled in courses established in various places. Men and women, young and old, joined this movement to spread the gospel of Jesus Christ.

The postwar period, too, was difficult, but freedom of religion, as guaranteed by an independent Indonesia, favored those ready to accept the Christian faith. Besides, *HKBP, now under indigenous leadership, was also more ready to grant ecclesial independence. In 1940 the Simalungun district was formed. A special school for training Simalungun pastors was established in 1950 at Pematang Raya. Most of the cost was borne by the local people. Two years later, when seven candidates were ready for ordination, there was great rejoicing. However, when HKBP assigned only three of them to work in the Simalungun area, the frustrated district declared its independence. A meeting with HKBP followed and resulted in Simalungun remaining in the mother church, but with far-reaching independence. The seven candidates were now permitted to remain in the HKBP–Simalungun. In addition, a returned missionary, Vollmer from *Germany, and the medical doctor Williams from India (see Introduction) were assigned to the area. Joyfully the church's 50th anniversary was celebrated, as well as the completion of the New Testament translation by Saragih. Ten years later (1963) the church was granted full independence.

Since then GKPS has joined the Communion of Churches in Indonesia (1961), the Lutheran World Federation (1967), the World Council of Churches (1973). It also established fraternal relations with the *Lutheran Church in America (now ELCA) and the *Lutheran Church of Australia. Through these bilateral relations the church has received help in erecting the Bethesda hospital at Saribu Dolok, the educational center at Sondi Raya, and the church headquarters at Pematangsiantar. Expatriate personnel from the Federal Republic of Germany, Australia, and Japan have aided the work.

With assistance from the LWF Community Development Service, the church has for years been conducting an agricultural training center near Pematangsiantar. Here short courses are offered in rice growing, poultry raising, cattle breeding, and other aspects of rural economy. In 1983 a CDS project installed 19 hydraulic ram pumps to benefit at least 9000 farmers in 23 villages in the high mountains of Upper Simalungun. The medical clinic at Bethesda concentrates on development projects such as clinics for expectant mothers, child immunization programs, and nutrition classes. In 1981 GKPS was honored and rewarded by the president of Indonesia for its "contribution to society."

In the field of education the church is still active, even though many of the schools have been taken over or subsidized by the government. In cooperation with other church bodies GKPS has established a training school for evangelists and teachers of Christian religion.

Although GKPS's main concern is for the Muslims and animists in its midst, its mission zeal reaches beyond the Simalunguns. In cooperation with the Karo Batak Protestant Church (Reformed), work has begun in Gunung, Karoland. Here, in 1983, 322 persons were received into the Christian church through a mass baptism. Pastors have also been sent to GKPA (above) and to the parish of Solingen in the Federal Republic of Germany. The latter is by way of thanking the Rhenish Mission for bringing the gospel to the Simalunguns in 1903.

MALAYSIA

Malaysia, earlier Malaya, is a federation (1963) of 13 states under a constitutional monarch elected every five years by a council of nine hereditary rulers. It is a member of the Commonwealth. The 11 states of West Malaysia comprise the southern tip of the Malay Peninsula (excluding Singapore). The two states in East Malaysia—Sabah and Sarawak—are the northern part of Borneo, the larger section of the island (Kalimantan) being part of *Indonesia. East and West Malaysia are separated by the South China Sea. Area: 329,747 sq. km. (127,316 sq. mi.). Pop. (1985) 15,676,700, including (1980 est.) Malays, 47%; Chinese, 32.7%; Indians, 9.6%; Dayaks, 3.7%; and other, 7%. Cap. and largest city: Kuala Lumpur (pop., 1985 est., 1,103,228). Language: Malay (official).

History: The Malays, historically the dominant cultural group on the peninsula, probably came originally from South China about 200 B.C. Intermarriage has modified their ethnic characteristics. Over the centuries they have been dominated by many intruders: Indian, Sumatran, Javanese, Portuguese, Dutch, Siamese (Thai). Beginning with the settlement of the island of Pinang (1786), the British gradually gained control over all of present-day Malaysia. By World War II Chinese immigrants almost equaled the Malays in number. During the Japanese invasion, the Chinese received particularly harsh treatment, and the Malays were encouraged in their resentment of them. Some Chinese, facing massacre, escaped to the jungle highlands of central Malaya. There they formed a guerrilla army to oppose the Japanese and to work against all imperialism, including the British. Others left their villages and became "squatters" on the fringe of the jungles. The guerrillas secured food and supplies from them.

When the British returned in 1946, they arranged a centralized colony called the Union of Malaya. This was opposed by influential Malays who feared the granting of citizenship to the Chinese and Indians. Britain rescinded and formed the Federation of Malaya (1948) with a British high commissioner. There was no common citizenship, and more privileges were restored to the Malays.

When the guerrillas rebelled openly against the Malayan government (1948), "The Emergency" was declared. Squatters then became prey to both the guerrillas and the antiterrorist police. Forced to provide the terrorists with food and supplies, they were punished by the police for doing so. Therefore, in 1950, the British began to resettle the half-million squatters into "New Villages" under the so-called Briggs plan. It was difficult to convince the transplanted people that curfews and barbed wire fences were for their protection, not for their imprisonment. On the whole the 342 "New Villages" provided facilities and opportunities that improved the lives of the squatters. Thousands of other workers in the tin mines and rubber estates were also regrouped for safety.

"The Emergency," so-called during the entire 12 years of civil war, had the positive effect of spurring Malayan independence.

This was achieved in 1957. In 1963 Singapore, Sabah, and Sarawak were added to the federated states, creating the Federation of Malaysia. Two years later Singapore withdrew amicably.

Within the Federation the Malays and other indigenous people—known as Bumiputra (sons of the soil)—are given certain rights and privileges such as special land reserves, business licenses, university education, scholarships, and jobs. The Chinese, Indians, and other non-Bumiputra people have rights of citizenship guaranteed without these privileges. Today Malaysia's New Economic Policy (NEP) is attempting to eliminate poverty and eventually to eliminate the identification of race. All economic, educational, social, and developmental plans are geared toward national unity. In recent years Malaysia has received thousands of Vietnamese refugees.

Religion: Islam is the state religion and claims about half the population. By law this includes most of the Bumiputra. Almost all of the Pakistani, some of the Indians, and a third of the aboriginal population in East Malaysia are also adherents of Islam. The Islamic legal code (Sharia) does not apply to non-Muslims. Chinese folk religions account for another fourth. Hindus, Buddhists, and Christians make up the rest.

The first Christian church in the area was the Roman Catholic, introduced by the Portuguese. Today Roman Catholics are twice as numerous as Protestants and include Indians, Chinese, and Eurasians in West Malaysia and aboriginals and Chinese in East Malaysia. Among Protestants there is a great diversity, especially since World War II when many missionaries, forced out of China, found new opportunities here. The Methodists are the largest group, followed by the Anglicans. The third is the Evangelical Church of Borneo, the fruit of a mission to the East Malaysian tribespeople by Australians.

The Council of Churches of Malaya and Singapore (CCMS, 1948) was divided in 1965 when the two countries separated. Today, as the Council of Churches of Malaysia, it has its headquarters in Petaling Jaya in the state of Selangor. Due to the large number of national and ethnic churches, the CCM has had difficulty in breaking through denominational self-sufficiency.

The National Christian Conference of Malaysia, a free association, met for the third time in 1987. It was organized by the Christian Federation of Malaysia, which includes representatives of the CCM, the Roman Catholic Church, and the Evangelical Fellowship. Meeting with government officials and others, the agenda has dealt mainly with common concerns such as the rights of Christians or the fostering of good relations among the religious communities: Muslim, Buddhist, Chinese folk, Hindu, and Christian.

SINGAPORE

Independent since 1965, Singapore, a republic, occupies a group of islands, the largest of which is Singapore, at the southern extremity of the Malay Peninsula. Area: 618 sq. km. (239 sq. mi.). Pop. (1982 est.): 2,472,000, including (1981 est.): 76.8% Chinese, 14.6% Malays, 6.4% Indians, and 2.2% other. Official languages: English, Malay, Mandarin Chinese, and Tamil.

History: Founded in 1819 by Sir Thomas Raffles, Singapore remained a British colony until 1959 when it became autonomous within the Commonwealth. In 1963 it joined with the Federation of Malaysia. Tensions between the Malayans, dominant in the Federation, and ethnic Chinese, dominant in Singapore, led to a peaceful separation in 1965.

Religion: Approximately 54% are adherents of Chinese folk religions; 17% of Islam; 9% of Buddhism; 6% of Hinduism; 9% of Christianity; 5% of other faiths. About half of the Christians are Roman Catholic, and of these 70% are Chinese. Singapore is the headquarters for the Roman Catholic Chinese Diaspora. The Apostolic Visitor, with the rank of bishop, has responsibility for all Chinese communities throughout the world with the exception of Hong Kong, Macao, and Taiwan. Of the Protestants, the Methodist Church is the strongest, followed by Anglicans, Presbyterians, Southern Baptists (USA), Lutherans, and several conservative groups. Differences in language, race, and varying interpretations of the gospel create difficulties for the churches and the efforts toward unity.

The National Council of Churches of Singapore (NCCS)—a part of the CCMS (above) until 1965—includes nine churches and four agencies, 23% of Singapore's Christians. Affiliated with the NCCS is the Singapore Urban Industrial Mission Board. It was formed in 1969 to pioneer community work in two of the large housing projects and a satellite town built by the government to accommodate immigrants.

Singapore was until 1988 headquarters of the Christian Conference of Asia (CCA) founded in 1959 (see Asia Introduction). Trinity Theological College (1948) is an ecumenical venture that represents the will to rise above differences and to serve all of Southeast Asia. Besides pastors, Trinity educates a large corps of teachers of biblical knowledge, a subject recently included as an elective in the secondary schools of Singapore.

Malaya and Singapore received special consideration at the 1952 Southeast Asia Lutheran Consultative Conference held in George Town on the island of Pinang off the northwest coast of the Malaya Peninsula. Sponsored by the Lutheran World Federation and the USA-based Commission on Younger Churches and Orphaned Missions (CYCOM), it brought together participants from Lutheran churches in Hong Kong (*ELCHK), India (*TELC), Indonesia (*HKBP), the diaspora congregations in Malaya and Singapore, and mission leaders from Europe, North America, and the LWF. The purpose of the conference was to review the church situation in the different countries of the vast Southeast Asia area and to survey the possibilities of expanding the Lutheran work in Malaya/Singapore to include an outreach to the Chinese.

The conference recognized the fact that the People's Republic of China was closed to Christian mission. Yet, a dispersion of 20 to 30 million Chinese of recent migration were living in various countries of Southeast Asia. Of these nearly 3,000,000 were living in Malaya and Singapore and, due to "The Emergency," a half-million in the "New Villages." Of the 342 "New Villages," less than half were being reached by Christian work. The Council of Churches of Malaya and Singapore had set up a Coordination Committee of Resettlement Work, and the director had urged that Lutherans share responsibility with the already active Methodists, Presbyterians, Anglicans, and the China Inland Mission.

Although the Malayan government strictly forbade evangelization among the Malay people, it encouraged the churches to work among the Chinese and even gave financial assistance for their schools.

The conference also assessed the Lutheran resources. Since China had been a major Lutheran mission field, there were sufficient well-trained Chinese-speaking missionaries as well as funds for reassignment. Malaya and Singapore already had some Lutheran work. The *Tamil Evangelical Lutheran Church had two congregations served by two pastors. Their members—1000 strong—were located in 78 places on the Peninsula and in Singapore. The Tamils had expressed willingness to transform their church into a Malaya Evangelical Lutheran Church that would include all races and languages. Its Zion Church compound in Kuala Lumpur had sufficient space for a missionary residence. The HKBP had one congregation in Singapore, but no building; the members were served by a part-time pastor. In Sabah, on the island of Borneo, there was the Basel Self-Established Church, a group of Chinese Christians of an earlier migration who had been helped by the LWF after World War II (see Basel Christian Church, below). The Evangelical Missionary Society (Basel) was beginning work among the Rungus people on the Kudat Peninsula (see Protestant Church in Sabah, below).

In spite of the variations in ethnic culture and language, the Pinang conference expressed the hope that the Lutheran venture in Malaya and Singapore would be a united one. Responsibility for coordinating this effort was given to the United Lutheran Church in America (ULCA), later part of the *Lutheran Church in America (now ELCA).

The ULCA lost no time. By 1953 a corps of international missionaries under the direction of an experienced China missionary began work in the "New Villages." From the beginning efforts were made to incorporate and coordinate the work with the Tamil and Batak congregations. To further this effort a Lutheran Conference was formed with representatives of all three groups.

Nevertheless, after 10 years of missioning, two church bodies were constituted in 1963: the Evangelical Lutheran Church in Malaysia and Singapore (below), predominantly Tamil, with headquarters in Kuala Lumpur; and the Lutheran Church in Malaysia and Singapore, mainly Chinese, with headquarters in nearby Petaling Jaya (below). In 1965 a major attempt to merge these two churches failed, largely because of racial, cultural, and language differences but also due to disparity in church polity. Both churches applied and were accepted into LWF membership. Relationships continued, strengthened and enriched by contacts with the *Basel Christian Church of Malaysia and the *Protestant Church in Sabah. In 1977 these four churches organized the Federation of Evangelical Lutheran Churches in Malaysia and Singapore with the stated purpose that they would in time become a united church. The first project of the federation was a training course for the staff of the member churches. Retreats and camps have furthered understanding and friendship. Leadership training for the women of these churches was introduced in 1981 under the auspices of the Women's Desk of the LWF. Together the four churches have a membership of nearly 51,000.

BASEL CHRISTIAN CHURCH OF MALAYSIA (BCCM)

(Gereja Basel Malaysia)
Member: LWF (1979), CCA, CCM, FELCMS
Membership: 19,500**
Bishop: The Rt. Rev. Thu En Yu
PO Box 11516
88816 Kota Kinabalu, Sabah

This church is located in the East Malaysian state of Sabah in the northern part of the island of Borneo. Its 74 congregations are in all the main cities and towns accessible by road and/or plane and in the villages on the banks of two great rivers that provide transportation by boat. Members of 42 congregations are of Chinese descent, members of the other 42 are Bumiputra (a racial-political designation for aborigines and Malayan citizens). The languages used are Chinese (Hakka and Mandarin), Bahasa Malaysian, Kadazan, and other aboriginal tongues. The congregations are served by 35 Chinese-Malaysian and 21 Bumiputra pastors plus a large team of associates in evangelism, education, community service, and other types of ministry. Since 1983 the chief pastor has had the title of bishop.

The pioneer members of the BCCM were a group of Hakka people from China's Kwangtung Province. They had responded to an official invitation to settle and "open up" the island. Via the port city of Canton they arrived in Borneo in the 1880s. Many of the settlers had become Christians through the work in South China of the Swiss-German Basel Mission and the Berlin Mission. In their new home they held family worship, organized a congregation, and by 1886 had built their first chapel. Not until 1902 did Basel missionaries arrive to assist them. World War I interrupted the missionaries' work. When they returned they encouraged the formation of the Basel Self-Established Church of Borneo in 1925.

World War II dealt other heavy blows to the church—loss of life, property, and the aid of the Basel Mission. After the war, emergency help came from the LWF. This opened the way for new assistance from the Augustana Lutheran Church, USA (later *LCA, now ELCA). The continuing independence and self-government of the Basel church were guaranteed, and a warm partnership developed after 1949 with the arrival of the first Augustana missionaries and continued until the last American teacher withdrew in 1973. During this 24-year period, the church was assisted in rebuilding its demolished primary and secondary schools. With additional help from the Sabah government and the LWF/CDS, new high schools were built in Sandakan, a city on the northeast coast, and in Jesselton on the west coast. Teachers arrived from the USA. Scholarships were also provided so that Sabah teachers and administrators were able to study overseas. The strong academic records of these schools attest to the value of this assistance. In the mid-1950s, the Sung View Secondary School in Sandakan was rated the top school in Sabah.

In 1963 the church took its present name. A few years later it launched its own mission outreach, first, to the Murok aborigines in the east coast hill country (1967). Seven years later the first Murok catechist was ordained. Next came the approach to the Kadazan tribe on the west coast (1975); then, to the Kuala Penyu Peninsula and to the Murut tribe in the interior Sapulut-Pensiangan area. To strengthen this mission a Bible Training Center was founded in Kota Kinabalu in 1980.

This school provides the aborigines with basic training so that they, too, are prepared to extend the mission further inland and deeper into the aboriginal society.

The enforced curtailment of expatriate missionaries in the early 1970s has encouraged this traditionally self-reliant church to even greater self-sufficiency in leadership and support. A 1983 decision of the BCCM permits women to be ordained as pastors. Since the church has no theological school of its own, it sends candidates to various schools: the Chinese University of Hong Kong, the Lutheran Theological Seminary in Hong Kong, Trinity Theological College in Singapore, the Singapore Bible College, and the South East Asia Bible Seminary (Seminary Alkitab Asia Tenggara) in Malang, Indonesia. Stewardship and development are high on the church's agenda. Offerings of members are augmented by various projects.

In 1982, while celebrating the centennial of its first congregation, a decision was made to build a much-needed church complex that would also generate funds (through rental of its facilities) to sustain church extension and self-reliance (LWF/CCC project). By 1988 an enlarged Bible Training Center (above) had become the Sabah Bible College/Theology and Leadership Training College, offering a four-year diploma course and receiving interdenominational support.

The Basel Mission, the church's longtime and faithful partner, continues to provide grants to BCCM. Together they encourage and support the Protestant Church in Sabah (below). In 1984 BCCM provided two pastors for the Evangelical Church in Polynesia, a Basel Mission related body, 94% of whose members are Hakka Chinese.

The church is broadly Lutheran. In 1977 it joined with three other churches to form the Federation of Evangelical Lutheran Churches in Malaysia and Singapore, and two years later it was received into the membership of the Lutheran World Federation. BCCM is open to worldwide Christian fellowship. It has a relationship with the Chinese Coordinating Center on World Evangelism (an outgrowth of the Lausanne Covenant), is a member of the Council of Churches of Malaysia, and was one of the founders of the Sabah Council of Churches. It is now considering membership in the World Council of Churches.

EVANGELICAL LUTHERAN CHURCH IN MALAYSIA AND SINGAPORE (ELCMS)

(Gereja Evangelical Lutheran di Malaysia dan Singapura)
Member: LWF (1968), CCA, CCM, NCCS, FELCMS
Membership: 2458**
Bishop: The Rt. Rev. Julius Paul
21, Jalan Sultan Abdul Samad
Kuala Lumpur 50470

The 14 congregations, 10 church groups (potential congregations), and other members living in outposts are located in both West Malaysia and the Republic of Singapore. Most of the members are descendants of immigrants—laborers and artisans—from Tamil Nadu in South India, who arrived in the latter part of the 19th century. They are served by 19 pastors and 13 church workers. The latter include deacons, deaconesses, congregational assistants, and 14 worship leaders—male and female—selected from local congregations and trained as volunteers to assist in conducting worship services, Bible studies, etc. Two of the pastors are *Church of Sweden missionaries. Three are on loan from the *Tamil Evangelical Lutheran Church in India. One serves the ELCMS as a theological professor at Trinity Theological College in Singapore, where a number of pastors have had their training. Other pastors have attended the Tamil Nadu Theological Seminary in Madurai, South *India.

Today the church has four districts, each under the supervision of a district pastor. Mission outreach is extended to most major towns, the rubber plantations, and the rural areas of the west coast. Nurseries for small children, Sunday schools, junior ministry, youth and women's work are all ways of serving. In Singapore the work is stimulated by the Singapore Tamil Evangelical Committee. The church has shared its new hymnal with Tamil Christians in *Burma and other diaspora churches and its English hymnal with a congregation in *South Africa.

In 1974 the ELCMS joined with the Anglican and Methodist churches of Malaysia to form a training center for theological students in Kuala Lumpur. By 1979 the school had become the Malaysian Theological Seminary. It has outgrown its original location on the Zion Lutheran compound and is located at a former Methodist high school in Kuala Lumpur, which is likely to become its permanent location. This ecumenical institution serves both East and West Malaysian students and churches. Trinity Theological College (Singapore) in 1983 agreed to give it academic standing. In October 1984 it received accreditation from the Association for Theological Education in South East Asia.

Other training programs for church workers, members of congregational councils, and youth in various types of related work play an important part in the life of this church. Deacons and deaconesses take a three-year course followed by a year of field work in a parish. They then render community service. This is coordinated by a secretary of the diocesan diakonia department who has had specialized training in this field. This service includes the Bethany Home in Simpang Ampat, an institution that cares for 28 epileptic children. It has had high commendation from the Malaysian government.

The Lutheran Institute of Vocational Training (LIVE) for underprivileged youth, established by the church with LWF/CDS assistance in the late 1970s, is now the Negeri Agro-Industrial Training Complex. It is jointly administered by the ELCMS, the state government of Negeri Sembilan, and the National Union of Plantation Workers. The trainees, both Christian and non-Christian, find ready employment.

It was in the late 19th century that Tamil Indians migrated to the Malay Peninsula. Many were Lutherans, and their spiritual care became the concern of the Tamil Evangelical Lutheran Mission. The first diaspora congregation was formed in 1907, but it was not until 1924 that the Zion Lutheran Church building was constructed in the Brickfields section of Kuala Lumpur. Pastors were provided by TELC. As members were scattered throughout the country—in 78 different locations by 1952—there was a need for more congregations and pastoral care. In 1961 the Church of Sweden Mission responded to the ELCMS's request for missionaries. Two years later the congregations formed an autonomous church with an episcopal form of government. The first Malaysian bishop was consecrated in 1976.

In 1977 the ELCMS joined with the other three Lutheran churches in Malaysia to form the Federation of Evangelical Lutheran Churches in Malaysia and Singapore. The ELCMS is active in the National Council of Churches of Singapore as well as the Council of Churches of Malaysia and holds membership in the Christian Conference of Asia.

LUTHERAN CHURCH IN MALAYSIA AND SINGAPORE (LCMS)

(Gereja Lutheran di Malaysia dan Singapura)
Member: LWF (1971), CCM, NCCS, FELCMS
Membership: 4427**
Bishop: The Rt. Rev. Daniel Chong Hoi Khen
PO Box 1068, Jalan Semangat
46870 Petaling Jaya, Selangor

In 1983 this church celebrated the 20th anniversary of its founding and admitted two new congregations, increasing the number to 34. Four unorganized worship centers are on the growing edge. The congregations, whose members are mainly Chinese immigrants, are divided into three districts. The Northern District congregations center around the city of Ipoh, 240 kilometers north of Kuala Lumpur, and in the large village area of Grik near the Thailand border. The congregations of the Selangor District are in and around the capital city, Kuala Lumpur, and in the fast-growing suburban area of Petaling Jaya. Here the church has its headquarters in a new (1981) three-story building that also accommodates a large, active congregation. For the most part the congregations in the Singapore District are located in housing areas built by the government to care for the rapidly expanding population in the 1960s.

When the church was organized in 1963, it had one indigenous pastor. Today there are 14. Their work is augmented by 13 full-time theologically trained workers, seven expatriate ordained pastors, and a corps of volunteers in various fields of service. Most of the pastors have had their training at the interdenominational Trinity Theological College in Singapore. Here the students participate fully in the life and work of the school and have special instruction in systematic theology to prepare them for the Lutheran ministry. In 1983 the secretary of the LCMS, a

New Testament scholar of repute, became principal of the college. The church also officially recognizes and uses the Singapore Bible College.

The LCMS, constituted in convention in 1963, became an official body on January 1, 1964. A synodical form of government has been largely maintained. For the first 14 years leadership was provided by American missionaries. The Rev. Carl M. Fisher, the third president, in 1972 became the first with the title of bishop. During these early years, leadership developed in both clergy and lay ranks. The latter, men and women, played a significant role in evangelism and social services.

As indicated above (see Introduction), the Lutheran Church of Malaysia and Singapore is the result of concerted efforts following the Pinang conference of 1952. Coordinated and largely supported by the (U)LCA (now ELCA), a corps of international workers, mainly former missionaries to *China, began work in the "New Villages" of western Malaya already in 1953.

The villagers, mainly Chinese who had been uprooted from their homes near the jungle and transplanted to a semiconfined life, were in need of understanding and assistance. Medical care and educational opportunities were especially needed. Church centers, residences for the staff, chapels, and clinics were quickly built. Doctors and nurses were employed. Literacy classes for children as well as adults were organized and staffed. Vacation Bible schools and evangelistic services were other means of reaching the people with the gospel. By 1955 the first congregation was formed comprised mainly of English-speaking young people who came from Christian families in China. In 1959 a Bible Institute opened in Petaling Jaya with a student body of nine. This enabled the embryo church to train villagers as evangelists, Bible teachers, and social workers. When the terrorist "Emergency" ended officially in 1960, the "New Villages" had either been merged with neighboring towns or had themselves become townships. Many of the young people moved to the cities to find employment and educational opportunities. It was time to give special attention to the cities: Ipoh, Petaling Jaya, Pinang, Kuala Lumpur, and Singapore.

Already in 1954 work had begun among the Chinese, Tamil, Batak, and English-speaking Christians in Singapore. By 1960 Redeemer Lutheran Church had been built and had become a center for worship, service, and fellowship for all. With continuous financial support from the LCA and LWF, the newly constituted church embarked on a major thrust in the housing projects that the Singapore government was erecting to accommodate the multitude of new immigrants as well as the thousands of young people streaming into the cities from the "New Villages."

In 1966 the Queenstown Lutheran Center was completed in the midst of 11 eight-story apartment buildings housing some 30,000 people. The occupants had other needs that the church attempted to meet with the help of an international staff. Late in 1965 beginnings were made for an industrial evangelism program in Jurong, a 9000-acre government-developed industrial suburb of Singapore that had 47 completed factories with 16 more under construction. Three residential communities would provide housing for an estimated 25,000 workers. The LCMS secured land between two of the communities and built facilities that became a model for urban industrial evangelism. They combined in one project an ecumenical locus for evangelism, worship, instruction, community involvement, industrial encounter, and relaxation. The largest of the housing estates in Singapore was Bedok New Town on the east side. Sixteen families from Redeemer, Queenstown, and Jurong congregations had moved there and became the basis of a new congregation formed in November 1978. In 1985, in cooperation with the Anglicans, a new church building was undertaken in Yishun, Singapore.

Meanwhile, in Malaysia, other projects met the needs of the developing congregations. In 1964, under the able guidance of Sister Gladys Rydenour, an LCA deaconess from the USA, nursery schools were established by congregations to provide care and training for young children whose parents were employed. This program developed an important corps of capable Christian women who found self-esteem as they learned skills and attitudes that benefited not only Chinese children and their parents, but also Malayans and Eurasians.

By 1973, 10 years after its organization, the LCMS was self-supporting except for theological education and special projects. In cooperation with two other churches it began work among the Senoi, the largest group of aborigines in Malaysia. This work prospered, and membership in the church grew rapidly. "Glad Sounds," a media agency, was founded in 1974. It now operates four city bookstores and a van that serves outlying areas with books, cassettes, and Christian movies. It also assists the congregations in training Sunday school teachers to use audiovisual techniques in teaching and in developing church libraries.

In 1977 a national pastor was elected bishop. The same year the LCMS joined with the other three Lutheran churches serving in Malaysia to form the Federation of Evangelical Lutheran Churches in Malaysia and Singapore. Membership is held in the National Council of Churches of Singapore as well as the Council of Churches of Malaysia. LCMS was received into the Lutheran World Federation already in 1971 and is an active participant in its projects and programs. In 1987 the church convention received two new congregations, one from the Northern District and one from Singapore (Yishun). It also voted to join in the support of the *Lutheran Mission in Thailand.

PROTESTANT CHURCH IN SABAH (PCS)

(Gereja Protestan di Sabah)
Member: WCC, CCM, FELCMS
Membership: 24,600
President: The Rev. Masandoh K.K. Majupi
Peti Purat 69
89057 Kudat, Sabah

The Kudat and Bengkoka peninsulas of Sabah (former North Borneo) jut out into the Balabac Strait with the South China Sea on the west and the Sulu Sea and the Philippines to the northeast. Here the Protestant Church in Sabah is at home. Organized in 1966, it now has a membership of over 20,000 Momogun-speaking people, the largest ethnic group in the state of Sabah. The church comprises 220 small congregations grouped into 14 parishes and four districts. The highest decision-making body, which meets every two years, is called a synod. In alternate years the districts meet.

The PCS supports three primary schools with some 700 pupils, one home science school, and six hostels. Located in the neighborhoods of public secondary schools, the hostels provide living accommodations for more than 500 young people who would otherwise not have an opportunity for secondary education. The church has an extensive youth program as well as a growing outreach to neighboring tribes beyond the Kudat District. In 1981 a translation of the New Testament into Momogun became available. The translation of the Old Testament is nearly complete.

A Bible school, with a two-year course, trains men and women for service. They return to their home communities, earn their living by farming or a trade, and serve in the local congregations as parish helpers without pay. Some of the Bible school graduates are ordained and work in teams, often on a voluntary basis. Pastors from the *Basel Christian Church of Malaysia (BCCM) have helped to train an indigenous leadership. Very few candidates have had the opportunity for additional education.

Although the work among the Momogun was started by the Basel Mission in partnership with the BCCM in 1953, it has not been easy to maintain this working relationship. Sabah is officially a Muslim state, even though the majority of the people are animist or followers of ancient Chinese religions. Between 1969 and 1975 all foreign missionaries were expelled by the pro-Muslim government. Church activities were limited (the Bible school was closed), and favor was shown to those who converted to Islam. Nevertheless, the church has not only survived but also learned to live without much outside help, even during periods of great hardship. For example, in 1983, after a long drought, plentiful rain produced a good crop, but it was devoured by locusts. The Basel Christian Church of Malaysia was the first to send relief. With the BCCM, the PCS has a joint committee for mutual assistance in witnessing to Christ among the Sabah people.

The Protestant Church in Sabah is a member of the Kudat Christian Council, the Sabah Christian Council, and the Council of

Churches of Malaysia. In 1975 it joined the World Council of Churches and has been a member of the Federation of Evangelical Lutheran Churches in Malaysia and Singapore since its formation in 1977. Its relation to the LWF is informal.

THAILAND

A constitutional monarchy in Southeast Asia, Thailand is bordered by Burma, Laos, Kampuchea, Malaysia, the Andaman Sea, and the Gulf of Thailand. Area: 513,115 sq. km. (198,115 sq. mi.). Pop. (1985): 51,301,000. Cap. and largest city: Bangkok (pop., 1985 est., 5,175,000). Language: Thai.

History: Legend has it that Thai nomads trekked from central Asia into southern China about 2000 B.C. Pressed from the north, they pushed south, and by the middle of the 14th century had established a kingdom in present-day Thailand and had a written language. When Portuguese traders and missionaries arrived in the 16th century, Siam (as it was then called) was able to resist Western civilization and dominance by adroit diplomacy. The country was closed to most foreigners for a period of time. In 1782 the founder of the present dynasty, Rama I, moved the capital to Bangkok and resumed relations with the Western world. Surrounded by the British in Burma and Malaya and by the French in Indochina, Siam strengthened its central administration and played the British against the French. Becoming a constitutional monarchy in 1932, Siam soon (1939) changed its name to Thailand (Land of the Free). Japan seized the country in 1941 and a year later, under duress, Thailand declared war on Great Britain and the USA. Since World War II Thailand has had a strong military control. In 1979 it received some 150,000 Kampuchean refugees awaiting resettlement after fleeing the disastrous strife in their own country. Rich in resources and human enterprise, Thailand continues to have one of the highest standards of living in Southeast Asia.

Religion: Theravada Buddhism is the state religion. Law requires the king to profess and defend it; yet he must also allow citizens the freedom to profess another faith. Most of Thailand's population on the Malay peninsula (nearly 4% of the country's total) are Muslim.

An estimated 0.5% are Christian. About half of these are crypto-Christians—secret believers affiliated with churches or isolated radio-and-Bible-correspondence-course believers. Most commercial stations broadcast Protestant programs daily—about 75 hours per week. Catholics have a weekly 15-minute news program. Christian programs from Manila can also be heard easily. Christianity is strongest among the citizens of Chinese and Vietnamese origin. Although few in numbers, Christians have made major contributions in areas of education and health.

Roman Catholicism, introduced in the 16th century by the Portuguese and later advanced by the French, was severely persecuted in the 18th century but is now a growing church. Its membership of nearly 200,000 is twice that of Protestants. The first Thai bishop was consecrated in 1945. Protestant missionaries were sent by the Netherlands and London missionary societies already in 1828. Congregationalists, Baptists, and Presbyterians from North America followed. In 1934 the Presbyterians (the largest) and Baptists merged with two younger churches, the United Church of Christ and the Lutherans of the German Marburger Mission, to form the Church of Christ in Thailand (CCT). Since World War II several other groups have been growing, often at the expense of the older churches. The largest of these is the United Pentecostal Church.

The Church of Christ in Thailand, consisting of Thai, Chinese, Karen (Tobeto Burmese), and English-speaking congregations, remains the largest and strongest among the Protestant bodies. The merger was later followed by the integration of all missions into the CCT. The church now receives missionaries from India, Japan, Korea, Indonesia, and the Philippines, as well as from Europe and North America. Most of its supporting churches and the CCT itself are members of the World Council of Churches. Since the earlier Siam National Christian Council (1930) became the CCT, there is now a Council of the Church of Christ and Affiliated Missions in Thailand. Most of the newer churches and missions, including the Lutheran Mission in Thailand (below), are related to the Evangelical Fellowship in Thailand. The combined membership of the churches related to the EFT is estimated to be about half of the Protestant community.

Since 1974 the Lutheran Church in America (now *ELCA) has added support to the CCT, including missionaries serving as teachers at the Payap University in the northern and second largest city, Chiang Mai. Founded in 1974 by the CCT, Payap is the only private degree-granting four-year liberal arts college in the country. Its departments include the humanities, social sciences (including business), theology, and nursing. Its McGilvary Faculty of Theology was the former Thailand Theological Seminary. Since 1984, on invitation, the ELCA has supplied two professors in religious studies to Mahidol University, a government institution, in Bangkok.

LUTHERAN MISSION IN THAILAND
Member: EFT
Membership: 349
Chairman: The Rev. Christopher Woie
1869-1875 Soi Saen Tai (Uthaifarm)
Rama 4, Klong Toey Bangkok 10110
Postal Address: PO Box 11-1173,
Bangkok 10112

This mission operates eight church centers and a bookstore in metropolitan Bangkok. A day nursery cares for 90 children, some of them from the slum areas. A media office provides programs for "Lutheran Hour" broadcasts in cooperation with the Far East Broadcasting Company. Emphasis is on church planting and training national co-workers, the aim being to establish an indigenous Lutheran church. Work in northeastern Thailand began in 1985. The newest thrust is among the Thai-speaking people of Singapore. In 1987 six students were enrolled in the mission's institute for theological education; four were ordained in 1988 by the ELCHK bishop.

The mission, organized in 1980, is the result of work begun in 1976 by the Norwegian Missionary Society. It was later (1978) joined by the Finnish Evangelical Lutheran Mission, the *Evangelical Lutheran Church of Hong Kong (1982) and the *Lutheran Church in Malaysia and Singapore (1987). The mission is a member of the Evangelical Fellowship in Thailand, the Asian Christian Communication Fellowship, and Lutheran Communications in Asia (LUCIA).

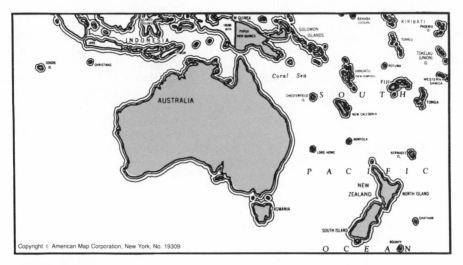

Copyright © American Map Corporation, New York, No. 19309

PACIFIC

South of the equator, off Asia and farthest from Europe, lies Australasia: Australia, New Zealand, and Papua New Guinea. Geography relates them physically, the Christian faith spiritually. Among their combined population of 22 million are about 755,000 Lutherans. Of these, more than four out of five are Papua New Guineans. Most of the others are of European origin, along with a fair number of Australian aborigines and some New Zealand Maoris. How churches emerged among them and what they mean today in a worldwide confessional family is part of the epic spread of the gospel as recounted here.

AUSTRALIA

A federal parliamentary state (1901) and member of the Commonwealth of Nations. Its landmass dominating the South Pacific quadrant of the globe, Australia occupies the world's smallest continent but, including the island state of Tasmania, is geographically the world's sixth largest country. Area: 7,682,300 sq. km. (2,966,200 sq. mi.). Pop. (1985 est.): 15,749,000. Cap.: Canberra (metro. pop., 1983 est., 255,900). Largest city: Sydney (metro. pop., 1983 est., 3,335,000). Language: English.

History: Australia's aboriginal population, thought to have entered from Southeast Asia about 20,000 years ago, links the present with prehistoric times. A seminomadic people, they moved about most parts of the continent and may have numbered about 300,000

when the first white settlers came. Earlier in the present century their number had been reduced by about two-thirds but is again on the rise. Many have been assimilated into the white society, others live in their own communities near urban centers, and still others—as in central Australia—maintain a vivid semblance of their traditional life. Beneath their distinctive simplicity in appearance dwells an immemorial sophistication of which few whites are aware.

Portuguese and Dutch contacts in the 17th century took only fleeting note of this vast obstruction lying south of Java. From the Indies, under primitive sail, came native adventurers searching Australian waters for sea slugs, a delicacy. On May 6, 1770, the explorer James Cook (1728–1779), sailing into Botany Bay and making contact with the aborigines just south of present Sydney, claimed the land for Britain. Settlement began in 1788

249

near this point, ironically as a penal colony. Although the records are silent, the strategy was imperial. The prisoners rendered an involuntary public service by providing Britain with a way station for its rapidly growing trade with China and the Pacific. Safely off the more direct routes, Sydney became a source of naval supplies as well as a vantage point from which to curb the rivalry of Spanish, French, Dutch, or American interests. The subsequently growing settlement locked the continent ever more firmly into the world scene.

The settlement of Australia belongs to that enormous and prolonged egress that brought Europeans to less settled parts of the world such as the Americas, Southern Africa, and New Zealand.

Australia's heavily British immigration gave it a particular homogeneity. This, however, was gradually modified during the present century, especially by collaboration with the USA and Canada during World War II and then by a huge postwar immigration. During the 30 years after 1945, about three million newcomers arrived. Only half of them were from Britain, the rest from the European continent—displaced persons from the Baltic states (most of them Lutheran) and far larger numbers from Greece, Italy, and elsewhere. Local color has also been added. As government policy changed, Asians were at last permitted entry. In 1979, for the first time, refugees from Indochina were the largest single group of immigrants.

Looking back, two stages of early settlement were formative. The first, 1788-1840, saw a total of 162,000 convicts—men and women—brought out and settled for life at government expense. Present also were government officials, guards, and enterprising businessmen promoting agriculture (wheat), cattle and sheep raising, as well as shipbuilding and trades to create a viable economy. The second stage, beginning in the 1830s, put the land under the crown. No longer granted free, the land was sold to immigrants by the government. By their labor the newcomers paid the government, which, in turn, repaid the shipping company for passage from Britain. The new colony of South Australia (1834), permitting no convicts, represented this new departure. Its first settlers (1836) were followed two years later by a large contingent, not from Britain but from

*Germany, thanks to a wealthy (Baptist) benefactor in London and partner in the South Australia Company in London who made this resettlement of freedom-seeking Lutherans possible (below).

Religion (1981): Anglican, 26.1%; Roman Catholic, 26%; Uniting Church of Australia, 15%; Orthodox, 2.9%; Baptist, Lutheran, Presbyterian (Continuing) all under 2%. Numerous smaller groups. Jews under 1%. Buddhism, Islam, and other religions under 0.5%.

The Church of England (Anglican) was first on the scene, having sent chaplains to accompany the "First Fleet" in 1788. Anglican affairs were under the Bishop of Calcutta (India) until 1836, when the first bishop was appointed for Australia. Today there are 24 dioceses and about 3,750,000 members. The Archbishop of Sydney is Primate. The church has been active in education, health, and welfare services and has taken a leading role in work among the aborigines.

The Roman Catholic Church reckons its beginnings from 1803, when the first priest was appointed. For over a century the constituency was almost completely Irish. At two points in time, church growth has been rapid: after 1852, following the potato famine in Ireland, and in the present century, especially with the large influx of Italian and Polish and other Catholics. The ecclesial structure introduced in 1920 continues to prove viable. The Australian Episcopal Conference, comprising the heads of 19 dioceses and seven archdioceses, operating on its own since 1976, oversees the church's work among the aborigines, about one-third of whom are Roman Catholic. This church has experienced an amazing growth, contributes to the common good in many fields, has fully overcome its earlier ghetto mentality, makes effective use of the mass media, and has engaged in ecumenical undertakings, including a bilateral dialog with the Lutheran Church of Australia (LCA) since 1976 (below).

The 40th World Eucharistic Congress (1973) in Melbourne focused wide attention on Australia and was perceived as a turning point toward a fuller acceptance of Roman Catholicism in this country.

The Uniting Church in Australia (1977) claims some two million members of Presbyterian, Methodist, and Congregational background. A substantial number of Presbyterians declined to go along, as have some Methodists and Congregationalists, wherefore the original denominational name of each body now adds the word "Continuing." These respective communions have been on the Australian scene since early in the 19th century, and their influence has been extensive. The Uniting Church, today third largest among Australia's church bodies, is but the latest addition to a growing number of United Churches, such as in *Canada, *India, *Germany, and elsewhere. The Australian use of "Uniting" was chosen to indicate an outreach to still other communions, including Anglicans, Lutherans, and Baptists.

The Australian Council of Churches (ACC) was begun in 1946. It consists of 12 member churches and four observer churches. The Lutheran church does not participate. Prominent among its concerns is working for the rights of the aborigines (below, LCA). Toward that end the ACC invited an ecumenical commission, under WCC auspices, to survey the situation. The undertaking, and its report, revealed considerable public opposition.

In Australia as in *Canada, there is a large number of persons—an estimated 80,000—who have indicated Lutheran preference or background but are not church members.

A few Lutheran congregations outside the LCA serve ethnic groups: German congregations in Sydney and Melbourne; Scandinavian in the Sydney area and beyond (see below). Finns and Latvians have their own conferences of congregations within the LCA (below). Also within that body is a scattering of Estonian, Hungarian, Polish, Slovak, and additional German congregations.

DANISH CHURCH IN SYDNEY (DCS)
Membership: 200**
Pastor: To be appointed
52 Anthony Road
West Ryde
NSW 2114

This church, formerly known as the Scandinavian Evangelical Lutheran Church in Sydney and later the Scandinavian Lutheran Church in Australia, was formed in 1978 in response to the need for Scandinavian language worship services. Until 1977 these had been provided by the Norwegian Seamen's Mission. The Sydney congregation forms the core of the new church, and its outreach is to the approximately 4200 Scandinavians, 50% of Danish birth, living in the area. However, the constitution of 1982 (amended 1983) seeks to proclaim the gospel among Scandinavians in all Australia. Although sponsored by the Danish Church Abroad of the *Evangelical Lutheran Church in Denmark, there are ties to the Norwegian and Swedish churches and close cooperation with the Lutheran Church of Australia. The Swedish Church Abroad has a congregation in Melbourne. Four times a year its pastor exchanges pulpits with the Danish pastor in Sydney. Besides the spiritual ministry, the DCS provides help and counsel in personal and social matters in cooperation with the local authorities and the Scandinavian diplomatic offices.

LUTHERAN CHURCH OF AUSTRALIA (LCA)
Membership: 111,415**
President: The Rev. Lance G. Steicke
Lutheran Church House
58 O'Connell Street
North Adelaide
South Australia 5006

This church body, the product of a 1966 consolidation, includes the majority of the nation's Lutherans. Its 575 congregations and many additional preaching places cover the country. By states, the largest number of congregations is in South Australia (Adelaide), followed by Queensland (Brisbane), Victoria (Melbourne), and New South Wales (Sydney), with a scattering in Western Australia (Perth), Northern Territory (Darwin, Alice Springs), and Tasmania (Hobart). The *New Zealand congregations form a separate district of the LCA but are in effect an autonomous church body. The polity combines synodical and congregational elements.

The LCA's 418 pastors have nearly all been trained in Australia, as have also the large number of other workers in the congregations, schools, homes, youth work, welfare programs, publication, and, above all, mission enterprises of the church. The diversity of these and other activities has its counterpart in the composition of the LCA itself.

Basically it is of German descent, but since the end of World War I the language of worship has become English. The massive immigration after World War II brought the linguistic spectrum of European Lutheranism also into the worship life of a growing church. Added to the several aboriginal tongues, nearly a dozen European languages besides English are perpetuated in the worship life of ethnic congregations. All of which is seen as an asset as well as a transitional phenomenon, akin to that in the *UK, yet with promise as in *Canada. One of the larger groups, the Finns, has a Suomi Conference within the LCA. Although Finnish congregations exist in all the major cities, efforts are being made to create English-Finnish parishes to ease the transition to an Australian-oriented church without losing valued customs, culture, and language.

With the decline of Lutheran immigration during the 1960s, growth in the number of church members slowed down to 3.5% by the mid-1970s. Since 1975 it has remained relatively constant.

The LCA, meanwhile, has been adapting to changing conditions, from a mainly rural body to a more urbanized one, and from a constituency seen as alien by the Anglo-Saxon majority to one essentially part of the ethnically more diversified Australian scene. In contrast to the nation's leap in population by 40% between 1964 and 1984, the LCA's only modest growth nevertheless shows up favorably over against the decline in Anglican membership and the lack of increase among the mainline denominations comprising the Uniting Church (above). It may even be that the rapid advance of the Roman Catholic constituency may preview something similar for the Lutherans.

Since 1966 the LCA has been sorting out its relationships and responsibilities. A precondition of merger was that both church bodies would terminate their existing international ties. The United Evangelical Lutheran Church in Australia (UELCA), a charter member of the old Lutheran World Convention (1923), gave up its membership in the Lutheran World Federation. But substantial contributions to human needs on the part of the LCA have continued through a field office of LWF/World Service in Albury, between Sydney and Melbourne. Correspondingly, the Evangelical Lutheran Church

of Australia (ELCA) ended its official link with the *Lutheran Church–Missouri Synod in America. However, LCA representatives attend the Missouri-influenced International Lutheran Conference as observers. At home the LCA is friendly toward Christians of other communions but is not a member of the Australian Council of Churches. The LCA continues the caution of its predecessor bodies against doctrinal compromise (unionism), but in the post-Vatican II era has since 1975 engaged in bilateral dialog with the Roman Catholics, notably on the subject of the eucharist.

The LCA continues to serve as well as to include the aboriginal Australians of the two predecessor bodies—the Dieri in northeastern South Australia, the Aranda and Loritja in Central Australia, and the nomads on the Cape York Peninsula of Queensland. From among them there are at present 14 ordained pastors on the LCA rolls, most of whom are serving in Central Australia. Here the LCA is encouraging self-reliance of the congregations under indigenous leadership. Former missionaries, stationed in Alice Springs, serve as resource personnel—ready to help when needed and requested.

This relationship was tested when the government implemented the return of mission land to the aborigines. This policy was strongly protested by those living on the LCA Hermannsburg Mission tract of 2330 sq. km. (900 sq. mi.). The aborigines claimed that the land had always been their sacred property and that the government and mission had never been anything more than uninvited tenants. All they needed was proof of their ownership. The Hermannsburg Mission staff supported the aborigines in their protest and spent months in mapping out individual claims. When the government finally agreed in 1982, the claimants received their titles.

The LCA has also shown concern for the numerous aborigines who moved into the urban areas beginning in the 1960s, when the national policy emphasized assimilation. Although the city churches attempted to assimilate them, only a small percentage of the more sophisticated felt at home. The rest sorely missed their communal life. With LCA encouragement and help and some government financial assistance, an all Aboriginal Lutheran Fellowship of Greater Adelaide was formed in 1970 to meet this need for community. In 1979 the South Australia District of the LCA assisted the fellowship in its purchase of an adequate and well-furnished church plant (made available by the merger of two congregations). Now a flourishing congregation with indigenous leadership serves a growing community, meeting the physical, educational, social, and spiritual needs of displaced people.

Further afield, the LCA's early involvement in mission among the aborigines and then among the people in New Guinea (below) led to a deepening relationship with the strong Lutheran churches in *Indonesia, especially in the fields of publication and broadcasting. Representative of this outreach is the LCA's Luther Seminary in North Adelaide. It, too, is a consolidation of two former seminaries and the point where the forces of change and continuity converge. Luther Seminary is the southern anchor of the church-and-community-oriented Asia Program for the Advancement of Training and Studies (APATS). (See Asia Introduction and *Korea.) Through APATS, Luther Seminary keeps in touch with such kindred schools as that of the *HKBP in Indonesia and Martin Luther Seminary in Lae, *Papua New Guinea, as well as those in *Hong Kong, the *Philippines, *Japan, and *Korea.

The LCA gives Christian education at all levels top rating. Besides its theological seminary and its Lutheran Teachers College in Highgate (adjoining Adelaide), the larger districts maintain preparatory schools and colleges (the equivalent of the American high school), some of which have boarding facilities for country students. There are six colleges in Queensland, three in South Australia, two in Victoria, and one in New South Wales. The LCA's accent on sound education makes it a productive church, with an ever-larger number of solid citizens in Australian society. It was this type of person that the initial proponent (below) of sending pious Germans to a struggling British penal colony had hoped for back in the 1830s.

Through the Lutheran Publishing House and its outlet chain, The Open Book, have come hymnals, yearbooks, church papers, many printed materials for congregations and schools, as well as works of regional church history. The centennial history of the Hermannsburg Mission (1977) and of the Evangelical Lutheran Church in *Papua New Guinea (1986)—in German and English editions for international distribution—are recent examples of an active print media program of the LCA.

● ● ●

The tale of settlers and synods, of spiritual leaders and schisms, not uncommon in the global expansion of Christianity, is particularly poignant in Australian Lutheranism. In a setting of religious freedom and remote location, small membership magnified personal differences. To say this is to welcome all the more the creation of the Lutheran Church of Australia in 1966. The event recalled the initial separation 120 years earlier, when dissident Lutherans from the same family tree followed two strong leaders who disagreed.

In summary, the year 1838 harbored three events marking Lutheran beginnings in Australia. In March a party of pastors and lay folk, including a variety of artisans, commenced missionary endeavors as a colony of settlers among the aborigines not far from modern Brisbane, in Queensland. The party was the first group sent out by the rising mission leader Johannes Evangelista Gossner (1773–1858) from Berlin (*Germany). Gossner was responding to a plea by the Presbyterian leader Dr. J. D. Lang (1799–1878) in Sydney. As a missionary move, the venture was short-lived, but as a forerunner to later Lutheran synodical developments from Queensland to Victoria it played a part.

In October of the same year two outspoken confessional missionaries from Saxony arrived in Adelaide, South Australia. The first to be sent overseas by the Dresden (later Leipzig) Missionary Society in anticipation of the coming settlers, they too were to work among the aborigines. This they did for a time, but then they became pastors among the settlers.

Sunday, November 25, 1838, according to the Australian church historian, Th. Hebart, ranks as "the day of the founding of the Lutheran Church in Australia." On that day the first contingent of some 600 Lutherans, dissenters from the Church of the Old Prussian Union, worshiped with thanksgiving in Port Adelaide. Their original plan to emigrate to the USA had failed. After two years of frustration, their passage to Australia was made possible by an affluent and devout Baptist merchant in London. George Fife Angas, a director of the recently formed South Australia Company, while not initially looking for Germans, readily supported the coming of solid Christian settlers to the new colony, for he had gained full confidence in their leader, Pastor August Ludwig Christian Kavel (1798–1860) visiting London.

Coming into a setting of religious liberty, in sharp contrast to the duress under which the Prussian state had required conformity to the Church Union (*Germany), Kavel seized the opportunity to set up an apostolic type of church order as he derived it from the New Testament. He shared its governance with elders. Three little settlements around Adelaide from the outset formed their own congregations, complete with local church and school. In May 1839 representatives of the three congregations were convened by Kavel in the first of many annual synod meetings.

In 1841 the second group of Prussian Lutheran dissidents arrived, led by their pastor, Gotthard Daniel Fritzsche (1797–1863). They, too, formed their own settlement and church. The harmony marking the early years in time gave way to discord, as Fritzsche took exception to Kavel's apostolic church order and soon also accused him of chiliasm. The belief in a thousand-year rule of the church on earth, whether before or after the return of Christ, had remained undefined in the Lutheran Confessions, but Fritzsche saw Kavel as interpreting it to support his own position. The power struggle between them came to a head in 1846, and schism ensued.

From here on, two lines pursued parallel and at times converging courses: the Kavel line (eventually the United Evangelical Lutheran Church in Australia, UELCA, 1921), and the Fritzsche line (eventually the Evangelical Lutheran Church of Australia, ELCA, 1944). Both lines were conservative.

As immigration, mainly from Germany, increased the number of Lutherans, the Kavel line recruited its pastors and missionaries from Hermannsburg and Neuendettelsau as well as from the less confessional Swiss-German Basel Mission. New synods, extending from Victoria to Queensland, took up fellowship with the Kavel line, which from 1874 called itself the Immanuel Synod. Fellowship led to federation and later to consolidation in 1921.

The ELCA, or Fritzsche line, maintained itself and spread with help from Hermannsburg also. However, after 1881, it began to receive pastors and teachers from the Missouri Synod as well (*USA). The Fritzsche line's concern for an Australian-trained ministry was intensified by its break in 1892 with Hermannsburg over the latter's alleged "unionism" with the state church of Hanover. (A similar break occurred at that time in *South Africa, forming the Free Evangelical Lutheran Synod.) Concordia Seminary, opened in 1893 in Murtoa, Victoria, was subsequently located in Adelaide. Teacher training, undertaken at various intervals before becoming firmly established, also maintained close ties with the LCMS (USA).

A reconciliation in 1864, soon after the death of both Kavel and Frizsche, led the two synods (soon called Immanuel and South Australia respectively) to form a confessional union and to venture at last a joint mission to the Dieri, aborigines in the far northeast corner of South Australia. By 1867 the project was under way, with support from the congregations and missionaries from Hermannsburg, *Germany. For those at the mission station, Bethesda, the Dieri, like the aborigines generally, proved hard to reach because of their nomadic ways. The partnership between the two synods was fragile. In less than a decade the then Immanuel Synod was bearing the burden alone while the now Australia Synod made larger plans— again with the Hermannsburg society of Germany. Out of these grew the Finke River Mission (1877) in the vast Aranda country west of Alice Springs, the halfway station of the trans-Australian telegraph (1872).

Europeans were introduced to the aborigines also through the scholarly works of missionary Karl Strehlow (1871–1922). After some years with the Dieri, he spent the rest of his career (1894–1922) serving the Finke River Mission. His weighty volumes on the Aranda and Loritja people amazed the learned world of Europe, while his school primer, dictionary, hymnal, and translation of Luther's *Small Catechism* as well as of the New Testament introduced literacy among these people. Years later his son, Theodore, who had grown up among the Aranda, brought out a revised version of the New Testament (published by the Australian Bible Society, 1944). Later still his *Song of Central Australia* was published (Sydney, 1971), complete with music and interpretation.

The talents of the Aranda, products of mission schools, have also amazed white Australians and others. The watercolors of Albert Namatjira depict familiar landscapes with a beauty his fellow Aranda had not noticed before and with a sensitivity that awakened interest among art critics of many lands. The caring engagement of missionaries among the aborigines—accepting them with mutual respect and understanding—is in sharp contrast to the often violent and degrading treatment by which the first Australians were deprived of land and life. The Finke River Mission and others, including those of the Anglican, Methodist, Presbyterian, Roman Catholic, and more, are said to have kept the aborigines from extinction.

It was at Bethesda that Johannes Flierl (1858–1947), one of the first Neuendettelsau missionaries, estimated that work among the relatively few and ever-moving Dieri had little prospect for growth. Already in 1878 his interest had been drawn to the more settled situation in far distant New Guinea. On his way there in 1885 he made a stopover in Queensland and initiated work among the aborigines on the Cape York Peninsula. The Immanuel Synod responded to this field, which developed into the Hope Valley Mission (1886) near Cooktown north of Cairns. Immanuel also followed with interest the work of Flierl and the Neuendettelsau mission in New Guinea. After World War I, when German missionaries were excluded from New Guinea, Australian as well as American Lutherans filled in the gap.

In Australia, too, World War I affected the churches. The government curb on the use of the German language accelerated the indigenization of both churches culturally. However, it did not overcome their separation. In 1921, when Immanuel and other cooperative synods joined to form the United Evangelical Lutheran Church in Australia (UELCA), Wartburg Seminary was opened in Tanunda, South Australia. When the seminary was transferred to Adelaide in 1923, it assumed the name "Immanuel." Ties with the Iowa Synod (ALC), also Neuendettelsau-related, supplemented those with Germany. In 1923 the UELCA joined the Lutheran World Convention. At much sacrifice it maintained its mission among the Aranda in Central Australia (Finke River) and continued its

participation in New Guinea. Despite its conservative doctrine and prudent practice, the competitive ELCA charged it with "unionism."

World War II and its aftermath brought both churches new responsibilities and made them fully indigenous in Australian life, a process aided by greater contact with Lutheran churches in North America. In 1945 the ELCA introduced the Lutheran Hour and began sending theological students to the Missouri Lutheran Seminary in St. Louis. The UELCA, in 1947, became a charter member of the LWF. It was soon a major partner, along with Lutheran churches in *Canada, the *USA, *Brazil, *Venezuela, and elsewhere, in the resettlement of immigrants from Europe via the extensive program of LWF Service to Refugees. Soon both churches were overtaxed. Some 100,000 Lutherans were among the two million Europeans entering Australia during the two decades 1946–1966. Church membership grew considerably, but the number of immigrants outside the church remained almost as high as those in membership. The UELCA augmented its ministry by the use of Latvian, Estonian, Hungarian, Polish, and Finnish in order to serve better the new Lutheran Australians.

The unity question was resumed and reinforced in 1949 when Professor Hermann Sasse (1895–1976) from Erlangen University in *Germany moved to North Adelaide to teach at the Immanuel Seminary. Sasse had formerly been a member of the Evangelical Church of the Old Prussian Union and was ecumenically active in the Faith and Order movement. A theological giant and more positive toward Missouri than other major American Lutheran bodies, he was heard by both the ELCA and the UELCA. His role as mentor to theologians in both churches encouraged unity talks. Beginning in 1952, these finally bore fruit in the Document of Union that both churches adopted in 1965.

Even so the charge of unionism continued to be heard, because the UELCA remained an active member of the LWF. The Federation, it was charged, had not made clear whether it was a church or a federation. The only way out of the deadlock was for both of the merging churches to terminate their international church ties. The ELCA separated formally from the Lutheran Church–

Missouri Synod, a step that was not easy to take, particularly at a time when Missouri's relations with other Lutherans appeared to have entered a new era of openness (*USA). Similarly, the UELCA dropped its link with the *American Lutheran Church (ALC) and quit the LWF. Dr. Fredrik A. Schiotz, president at that time of the ALC and of the LWF, spoke for many when addressing the UELCA's final convention (1966) in Horsham, Victoria. He agreed that this plan of union could be "accepted with the heart but not the head." However, the mission ties of both merging bodies with Papua New Guinea remained intact. The union was completed at the constituting convention in Tanunda in 1966, where the first separation had occurred 120 years earlier. There was now the Lutheran Church of Australia—the LCA.

The possible resumption of the LWF connection remained under discussion during the ensuing years. Other relations, like those with the Indonesian Lutherans (above), proved stimulating. Meanwhile, LCA presidents attended LWF assemblies as observers—Max Lohe in Evian, 1970; Leslie Grope in Dar es Salaam, 1977. At Budapest (1984) the LCA was represented by Dr. Ronald W. Gerhardy, who was invited to attend the assembly as an advisor in view of his position as Director of the LCA Board of Overseas Mission and Church Cooperation.

Advance notice that the agenda of the Seventh Assembly would include a proposed amendment to the constitution that pulpit and altar fellowship was understood to exist among the LWF member churches raised serious questions in Australia. Among other things, the LCA theologians believed that by this amendment the LWF would be claiming churchly powers for itself and diminishing the right of a church body like the LCA to determine its own standards of fellowship in the pulpit and around the altar.

Significantly, Australia has given leading staff members to LWF World Service, notably Bruno Muetzelfeldt, long-time head of the department, and Brian Neldner, expert in resettlement. Australians have also contributed generously to World Service over the decades. The office of this department's Australian representative, Sidney K. Bartsch, in Albury, New South Wales, has been an indispensable link for a long time and bodes well for the future.

NEW ZEALAND

An independent parliamentary state (1947) and a member of the Commonwealth of Nations consisting of North and South Islands, Stewart, Chatham, and other minor islands. Area: 268,704 sq. km. (103,747 sq. mi.). Pop. (1985), 3,291,300; over 90% British stock; over 8% Maoris; some Polynesians. Cap.: Wellington (North Island; pop., 1984 est., 133,700). Largest city: Christchurch, South Island; (pop., 1984 est., 162,100). Largest urban area: Auckland (North Island; pop., 1984 est., 778,000).

History: Polynesian Maoris settled early in this picturesque land, preferring North Island with its hot springs. A fleeting contact with Europeans occurred in 1642 when the Dutch captain Abel Janszoon Tasman (1603–1659), on his circuitous voyage from Java, sailed past the archipelago. During the 18th century the famed explorer of the Pacific, James Cook (1728–1779) repeatedly visited the islands and claimed the whole for Britain. In 1814 the Anglican missionary Samuel Marsden made the first of seven voyages from Australia (1920 kilometers, or 1200 miles, from Sydney) and conducted the first Christian service in New Zealand on Christmas Day. Impressed with the Maoris, he was respected by them. At times he could pacify their tribal feuding. His method of missioning, common at the time, linked conversion and civilization, largely by means of missionary artisans living among the people. The method failed, although it drew in the first European settlers and—in contrast to Australia—saved the country from becoming a penal colony.

The New Zealand Company, in Britain, promoted settlement. In 1840 British sovereignty was proclaimed. The colony had representative government from 1853 and became a dominion in 1907. Wool and gold were the making of the colony's economy. But politics among the resident newcomers and Maori resistance against the white advance brought recurring unrest and a decade of Maori wars (1861–1870). New Zealand's participation in this century's two world wars has drawn it ever deeper into world affairs. The effect of the European Common Market in curtailing New Zealand imports has been to link the country more closely to Asia, to the people of Oceania, and to the Americas. By accepting a proportionately significant percentage of Europeans and other refugees after 1945, the heavily British culture has been enriched, and New Zealand's policy of admitting refugees with handicaps, long before the International Year of the Handicapped, became a model for others. Meanwhile, the Maori population has increased, and a culture that was at one time threatened with extinction has become an important element in New Zealand life.

New Zealand's prime minister David Lange (elected 1984), an active Methodist of German descent, became internationally known for his strong convictions about nuclear arms reduction.

Religion: Traditional religion survives among some Maori, but the majority are now Christian. The pioneering work of Samuel Marsden (above) was much expanded by the Anglican Church Missionary Society. Other communions entered the field. Today about one-third of the Maori are Anglican, and almost as many are Roman Catholic. Presbyterian and Methodist work began early and have grown. In recent decades Latter Day Saints (Mormons) have made impressive gains, accounting now for nearly 10% of the Maoris.

The white population shows a Christian preference of over 90%. Anglicans retain a shrinking lead (26%), followed by Presbyterians, Roman Catholics, Methodists, Baptists, and many others in descending order. As in Australia, the Roman Catholic Church has shown remarkable growth in the latter decades of this century. Its hierarchy includes the archdiocese of Auckland and three dioceses.

Efforts to unite the main communions of British background began in 1964 and came close to success before foundering on a proposal for the unification of ministries (1982). Of the five bodies involved—Anglican, Congregational, Disciples, Methodist, and Presbyterian—all but the Disciples are members of the World Council of Churches and have been so from its beginning in 1948. Along with this recognition of the importance of a worldwide Christian community, New Zealand churches have also developed a closeness with their partners in the distant Cook Islands and in other island nations of Oceania.

The National Council of Churches in New Zealand (NCCNZ) includes in its membership the five above-mentioned churches as well as the Baptist Union, the Greek Orthodox, the Religious Society of Friends, the Salvation Army, the Cook Islands Christian Church, and the Liberal Catholic Church. Its agenda includes interchurch aid, united witness, race relations, ecumenism, and joint study with Roman Catholics. The Lutheran Church of New Zealand has observer status with the NCCNZ and is participating with other churches in discussions with a view to the possible formation of a new ecumenical body, the Conference of Churches of Aotearoa (New Zealand), which may include also the Roman Catholic Church. Lutherans, according to census figures, are more numerous than church membership confirms.

LUTHERAN CHURCH OF NEW ZEALAND (LCNZ)

Membership: 2563**
President: The Rev. Rodney H. Beh
38, Somerset Crescent
Palmerston North

Most of the 21 congregations of this small but energetic body, a district of the *Lutheran Church of Australia (LCA), are in North Island. The LCNZ membership represents a variety of backgrounds and ethnic groups. Of the currently 14 active pastors, most are graduates of the seminary in Adelaide. Family and other ties, also in parish ministry, link many of them to Australia.

In the making of basic decisions this body is like other districts of the Lutheran Church of Australia, but in dealing with the government and other national matters affecting it, the LCNZ is on its own. Authority resides in the annual synod of the church, which comprises the pastors and lay delegates representing the congregations. In the first year of their eligibility (1982), women formed 20% of the delegates. The synod elects the 10-member church council, which includes the president, to govern its affairs between meetings. The church offices, in Palmerston North, are in a city known for its industry and farm marketing as well as for its young (1964) Massey University. Among the LCNZ activities, evangelism, stewardship, development, education, and communication have long been prominent, as well as special activities for men, women, and young people. The *New Zealand Lutheran* has appeared regularly for years.

With LCA approval, the LCNZ officially launched a Christian literature department in 1982. Its agency, Lutheran Publications, located on Auckland's North Shore, operates a retail shop under the name The Open Book in Takapuna. On a larger scale this continues the distinctive ministry carried on for 18 years by a local couple from their own home. The Lutheran Publishing House (LPH) in Adelaide, Australia, subsidized the operation for the first few years, and the associate manager of LPH is a member of Lutheran Publications Board of Management. The New Zealand "Lutheran Hour" endeavors to reach people of non-European origin, especially the Maori.

Although not a member of the LWF, the LCNZ—like other LCA districts—is a generous contributor to the development, relief, and refugee programs of Lutheran World Service (see Australia). This was the major theme of the 1984 synodical convention in Christchurch, South Island. Of the US $450,000 contributed by New Zealand and Australian Lutherans in 1983, some went for special assistance to *Papua New Guinea after the devastating flood of 1982.

All of New Zealand's Lutheran congregations became a district in the Lutheran Church of Australia at the time of the 1966 merger. A precedent for this was set in 1914 when those New Zealand congregations related to the USA Lutheran Church–Missouri Synod joined the Evangelical Lutheran Synod (later Church) in Australia (ELCA), which was also Missouri-related.

Steps in this direction had begun soon after the coming of Missouri Synod pastors to Australia in the 1890s and the consultative visit (1902) of Augustus L. Graebner, a leading professor on the Concordia Seminary faculty in St. Louis. The time he spent in New Zealand helped to overcome the sense of isolation long experienced by the German Lutherans, some of whose forebears had come as early as 1843. The support that had come from Germany and America up to 1914 (as noted) was provided thereafter by the Missouri-related Australians.

Similarly, around the turn of the century, an influx of Scandinavians, especially from Denmark, led to the formation of eight Scandinavian congregations. The other Australians, the later United Evangelical Lutherans (UELCA), lent a hand to them because one of their own synods included Scandinavian antecedents. In 1958 the last remaining congregations of Scandinavian background joined the then Evangelical Lutheran Church of New Zealand, which in turn became the LCNZ.

Among the Maoris, Lutherans built on 19th-century initiatives from Germany (Hermannsburg). Subsequent work by Missouri Synod missionaries achieved modest gains. Hamuera Te Punga, a native Maori, received his ministerial preparation at Concordia Seminary, Springfield, Illinois. Upon graduating in 1912, he worked among his people for a decade, but with little response. Thereafter he continued his long ministry among Maoris in other parts of the country. Members of his family and other Maoris continue active in the LCNZ, one of them serving on the church council.

Following World War II a fairly large number of immigrants—displaced persons—from the Baltic countries settled here. They added to the Lutheran constituency, as, for example, the Latvian congregation in Christchurch (see Australia). During the two decades from 1962–1982 the nation's population increased by 31% while the Lutheran church membership remained virtually unchanged. Reaching a peak of slightly over 3000 in 1975, the present figure of about 2600 is practically the same as in 1962. However, a comparable number of nonmembers receive the care and ministry of the church.

PAPUA NEW GUINEA

Papua New Guinea (PNG) has been an independent parliamentary state and a member of the Commonwealth of Nations since September 16, 1975. Situated in the southwest Pacific, it comprises the eastern half of the island of New Guinea (the other half is Indonesia's Irian Jaya); the Bismarck Archipelago with the larger islands of New Britain, New Ireland, New Hanover, and Manus; the Louisiade Archipelago and the D'Entrecasteaux islands off the tip of Papua; the northern

Solomon Islands; and smaller islands or island groups such as Woodlark, Trobriand, Rooke, Karkar, and Manam.

Area: 462,840 sq. km. (178,704 sq. mi.). Pop. (1985): 3,345,000. Cap. and largest city: Port Moresby (pop., 1984 est., 144,300). Language: English, Hiri-Motu, and Pidgin English are official. The latter, also called Neo-Melanesian, is widely spoken. Local languages number about 520.

History: Archaeology and folklore claim evidence of human life on this awesome island as much as 50 millennia ago. Regard for this venerable past is awakened in ever-new ways as PNG students probe their own history prior to the advent of the first Europeans. Antonio d'Abreu, the Portuguese navigator, sighted the island in 1511, calling it New Guinea for the resemblance of its coast to African Guinea. Contacts with the Western world remained sporadic over the next centuries, while relations with seafaring Pacific islanders—from the Solomons and beyond—appear to have been from time immemorial, and suggest a Melanesian world whose scope and significance continues to unfold today.

The island of New Guinea was divided in the 19th century between the Dutch (now Irian Jaya), the British (Papua, closest to eastern Australia), and the Germans (Kaiser-Wilhelm-Land or German New Guinea, the northeast quarter of the island and region). Australia governed Papua (1905–1975) and from World War I also governed German New Guinea under mandate (1914–1975). Japanese occupation of the coastland, except southern Papua, during World War II exacted its toll of suffering and privation. With the gradual relaxation of intertribal tensions that had kept them mutually suspicious, Papua and the Territory of New Guinea (as the northern portion was known) became a self-governing country in 1973. Australia's supervision of defense and foreign relations continued until full independence was achieved in 1975. Years before this event Australian aid in education and economic development had helped prepare the way. To this day, neighborly assistance continues.

During the past decade PNG has taken its place in the United Nations and has followed a cautious course in world affairs. At home, problems of communication, transportation, and association have been compounded by the extremely rugged terrain of highland and coastland but also eased by the use of radio and airplanes. The quest for balance between agriculture and rising industry has often been difficult to achieve, especially in face of foreign designs or accelerated exploitation of the country's natural resources, especially minerals and timber. Worldwide phenomena such as the dislocation of traditional family life and the trek of young people from the country to the city are much in evidence. The rapid growth of Port Moresby (35% in seven years) has its parallels in Lae, Madang, and elsewhere. Beyond the visible lies the moral and spiritual challenge of rapid change and culture shock.

Religion: Traditional religion, outwardly at least, has receded rapidly in recent years to the point where today over 90% of the people claim to be Christian, an elusive figure at best. One-third of the Christians are Roman Catholic. The Roman Catholic ecclesial structure, going back to 1885, includes four archdioceses—Port Moresby, Rabaul, Madang, and Mt. Hagen. Its greatest growth came in the 1960s, but indigenous priests are still few in number. Among Protestants, Lutherans comprise by far the largest single communion and are mainly in the former Territory of New Guinea. Next in number are the United Church people (London Missionary Society—1871—and Methodist antecedents) in Papua and the Bismarck Archipelago. Other large groups—Anglicans (1891), Seventh Day Adventists, Baptists, Pentecostals, and a wide variety of fringe groups—bring the number of religious groups to about 100. The United Church of PNG and the Solomon Islands (1968) comprises a number of earlier churches.

Ecumenically PNG has been making history. The Melanesian Council of Churches (MCC, 1965) includes those of the Solomon Islands. It brings into working relationship Anglican, Baptist, Lutheran, Salvation Army, and United Church bodies as well as Roman Catholic (since 1971). Local ecumenical councils function in Lae and other centers. The MCC, related to the World Council of Churches, has an even closer affinity with the Evangelical Alliance of the South Pacific, to which nearly a score of Christian bodies not participating in the MCC belong. Since 1961 PNG communions have been partners in the far-flung Pacific Conference of Churches. The Melanesian Association of Theological Schools (1969) includes Anglican, Lutheran, Roman Catholic, United Church, and Evangelical institutions and is a result of the former Fund for Theological Education (1959), now the WCC Program on Theological Education. The Melanesian Institute for Pastoral and Socioeconomic Service (1965), located in Goroka in the highlands, provides new missionaries with knowledge and understanding of the people, their culture, and their tradition and also holds special seminars for and among the native people. Founded by the Association of Clerical Religious Superiors of the Roman Catholic Church, this institute has drawn Anglican, Lutheran, and United churches into its work. More recently these denominations have provided staff, financial support, and representatives on the governing council.

Media efforts—publications and radio—are means of uniting the churches in response to common needs. Word Publishing, founded by a Roman Catholic missionary and linguist in 1970, is now an ecumenical organization with Lutheran, Anglican, and United Church representatives on the board of directors. Kristen Radio, established in the highlands in 1966 and now located on the campus of Martin Luther Seminary, Lae, has the support of 21 Protestant churches. With literacy about 33%, transistor radios and cassette players have become important means of communication. The weekly five hours of programs by Kristen Radio, aired by the 18 provincial stations, can reach 95% of the population.

At the same time a new rivalry has come on the PNG scene. Numerous Christian sects and denominations have entered the country, causing confusion. Their apparent threat to the unity of the established religious and social groups has made the government step up its search for ways to curb their influx. Sectarian proliferation has been paralleled by reawakened aspects of traditional religion—ancestral veneration and belief in the magical powers of good and evil spirits. A resurgence of cargo cults is a manifestation. They first arose with the impact of Western civilization in the late 19th century and were most prevalent after World War II. People had seen the bountiful supplies received by the military on both sides, supposedly from their ancestors.

They also witnessed American troops dump supplies—trucks, jeeps, and bulldozers—into the sea after the war. This completely confused the people so that their suspicions were confirmed that the white people were lying as to the origin of the goods. Christians were not free from this confusion. Were not the missionaries themselves sustained by cargoes sent by benevolent forces far away?

Against this background, Christian beginnings in PNG gain perspective. The first successful pioneer missionaries came to Papua from the London Missionary Society in the 1870s. Their work was strengthened by national workers from the Loyalty, Cook, and Fiji Islands. In (German) New Guinea, Roman Catholics (1882) were followed by Lutherans (1886). As already noted, it appears that the very diversity of tongues and tribes has given the churches in PNG strong impulses to strive for Christian unity.

EVANGELICAL LUTHERAN CHURCH OF PAPUA NEW GUINEA (ELC/PNG)

Member: LWF (1976), MCC
Membership: 545,500
Bishop: The Rt. Rev. Getake S. Gam
PO Box 80
Lae

This large church of more than 2000 congregations is served by 524 ordained Papua New Guinean pastors plus a number of evangelists, pastors' assistants, teachers, and other workers in associated ministries. Some 50 expatriate ordained missionaries work in rural areas assisting the indigenous staff. About 100 other expatriates aid the church in various aspects of its extensive program. The languages used are Pidgin, various local languages, and some English. In 1986 the ELC/PNG observed the centennial of its beginnings (below).

The members live in many parts of the country: coastlands, highlands, and offshore islands. Most of them are engaged in subsistence farming or other forms of agriculture. Increasing numbers are moving to the cities where they are employed in trades, business, education, civil service, and other occupations. Unemployment is on the rise and social uprooting poses problems.

Organized in 1956 as the Evangelical Lutheran Church of New Guinea, 70 years after the arrival of the first Lutheran missionary, the church's name was changed to the present title with the formation of the nation in 1975. In the late 1960s the church began to take over many of the responsibilities of the Lutheran Mission New Guinea (LMNG), an agency that in 1953 had combined the efforts of the Australian, German, and American missions. On the 90th anniversary of the missionary beginnings (1976), the governmentally incorporated LMNG turned over all its property and responsibilities to the church and requested a repeal of the incorporation. Having become fully autonomous, the ELC/PNG applied for and was received into LWF membership. Nevertheless, the church continues to rely on overseas personnel and grants for certain programs and for its central administration.

Church headquarters are in Lae, a busy trading center and also the home of the PNG University of Technology. Church organization combines congregational and synodical features. The basic unit, the congregation, usually consists of several local centers forming a parish. Neighboring parishes form circuits and geographically close circuits become districts. One of the present eight districts is the former Siassi Lutheran Church, which in 1976 merged with the ELC/PNG (see history, below). Another is the Papua district formed in 1981. The 1984 biennial convention voted to form three new districts: the New Guinea Islands, Wahgi, and the Southern Highlands.

Churchwide functions—evangelism, education, ministerial training, medical services, finance, and the economics of self-support—are governed by boards and full-time staff. Outside assistance to the church continues, as noted. In the dozen years prior to its full autonomy (1976), the ELC/PNG received grants via LWF channels totaling over US $2,300,000 for community development projects in agriculture, education, and health services.

From its inception the church has been headed by a bishop, the first being the veteran American missionary Dr. John Kuder. In 1973 he was succeeded by the Rev. Zurewe K. Zurenuo, a national of broad experience as teacher, district secretary, and then church secretary—all of this before receiving ordination. As bishop his aim was to foster a truly indigenous church, hospitable to the traditions of Melanesian culture as long as they harmonized with the Word of God. Already in 1971 the government had honored Zurenuo for his services to church and community by awarding him the Order of the British Empire. In 1981, the year of his retirement as bishop of the ELC/PNG, he was knighted by Queen Elizabeth II. The present bishop previously served as parish pastor, evangelism secretary, and part-time teacher of church music at the Martin Luther Seminary, his alma mater. He sees his task as fourfold: to lead the church to evangelize unreached areas of his country and beyond: to prepare local leadership for the church's higher educational institutions; to work for concord and communication within the ELC/PNG; and, together with other churches, to strive for world peace.

The church's three seminaries prepare candidates for the ordained ministry: for the coastland, Senior Flierl Seminary, Logaweng, Finschhafen; for the interior, Lutheran Highland Seminary, Ogelbeng, Mt. Hagen; and for more advanced pastoral education, Martin Luther Seminary, Lae. With renewed fervor, and also under government pressure, the church is preparing Papua New Guineans for the teaching positions at these seminaries. High on the agenda is the training of pastors able to deal with the problems born of rapid cultural, social, and economic change. A number of women study at Martin Luther Seminary, mainly in preparation for parish work and specialized services. A department of pastoral training seeks to identify and meet the ministerial needs of the church. Due to a serious pastoral shortage, a series of crash courses prepare some older, more experienced church workers for ordination. In-service education for pastors, pastors' assistants, and workers among women and youth is also provided.

Education using local languages was launched by the first missionaries and has been vital in the church's ongoing mission. Only in the 1950s, when the government entered the field of education, was English instruction introduced. Since 1970 the ELC/PNG has been a full member of the National Educational System. In cooperation with the government, the church conducts (in English) 150 primary schools, four high schools, and the Balob Teachers' College in Lae. The latter, a long-time ELC institution, now also receives some use and support from the Gutnius Lutheran Church (below) and the Anglicans. Besides the above-mentioned, the church still maintains many community schools with instruction in Pidgin, as this proves a better way of communicating with the vast number of rural children who seldom hear English. A number of small technical, commercial, and agricultural schools are a part of the ELC/PNG school system, which includes over 1000 indigenous teachers.

The central place of the Scripture in the church's teaching ministry has been much strengthened by the translation of the New Testament into Pidgin. A translation of the Old Testament is in progress. Much earlier and still today various parts of the Bible have been rendered into hundreds of local languages. But the Scripture in Pidgin, the lingua franca of the new nation, is especially significant. In the ever-widening application of Christian nurture from infancy to old age, further materials, also in Pidgin, are in the making for Sunday schools, confirmation instruction, youth work, and other areas. The writing is being done by about 100 talented ELC/PNG members. Working in groups, they represent a wide variety of backgrounds and parts of the country. The project has LWF support.

For a number of years the ELC/PNG has worked with the Gutnius Lutheran Church (below) and the LWF's education secretary in developing the Paradise Series, a Christian education program in English. Complete with teachers' guides and pupils' books, the series is designed for use in the public schools. A number of other denominations also make use of these materials. Books and printed matter are published by Kristen Press at Nagada, near Madang. Antecedents go back to 1909 when the first printery was set up.

The impact of the Christian faith on daily living has substantially reduced tribal violence. Even so, "payback" killing—the traditional form of justice by retaliation—remains a problem. Local tragedies as well as memories of World War II keep prodding the church to educate for peace—at home as well as internationally.

Work with youth receives special attention. Besides formal education, a church-wide Five-Star program—emphasizing worship,

study, community work, sports, and mission—follows through on baptism and confirmation instruction. For rural youth this is supplemented by the Yangpela Didiman (Young Farmers), a program to develop skills and motivation for an improved rural life. In 1984 the synod voted to expand the evangelism department to include a national youth coordinator's office.

Women, vital and respected members of the ELC/PNG, bear the main task of creating and fostering Christian homes. They are aided at the local level by study material, biblical and practical, provided by the districts. In each local congregation a chosen leader organizes activities to support the work of the church. Twice a year representatives from the districts meet nationally to coordinate concerns and plans. Every other year 20 women from each district gather for a week-long seminar on a current subject. In 1982 attention focused on the problems confronting young people migrating to the cities and the church's responsibility in meeting these needs.

In evangelism the ELC/PNG continues the early mission policy (see below) of a community approach. When a new area is chosen, the village leadership is first consulted. If positive, evangelists move in with their families and engage in a prolonged period of instruction. Baptisms are often delayed until there is a group of individuals or even an entire village ready to accept Jesus Christ as Savior. Thus new congregations can be formed without abandoning the support of a community, which is of extreme importance in Melanesian culture. An example: until 1950 the Australian government did not consider the Southern Highlands (Papua) safe for outsiders due to violent aspects of Stone Age culture such as tribal wars, ritual murder, and cannibalism. Yet, in 1958, the newly formed church stationed 50 New Guinean families over a 600-square-mile (1550-sq.-km.) area. By 1970 these evangelists, teachers, and pastors had prepared 1100 people for baptism, and by 1984 the church in this area was sufficiently large and strong to form the Southern Highland District. The ELC/PNG has also begun and intends to increase overseas missions. In 1979 its first missionary was sent to work among the Australian aborigines, a people with whom the Papua New Guineans feel a special kinship.

With continued support and personnel from partner churches, the ELC/PNG took over the Lutheran Medical Service of the LMNG. By 1969 this included 15 hospitals (one a former U.S. Army hospital purchased by the American Lutheran Church after World War II), in addition to school dispensaries, numerous rural aid posts, and health centers. The Lutheran School of Nursing in Madang has helped to supply the country's medical personnel. In 1972 the Christian Medical Commission of the World Council of Churches surveyed the entire program and, in cooperation with the government, helped the church to set up the National Health Care Delivery System. Although today the government assumes more of the health responsibility, the Lutheran Medical Service continues to promote health care, especially in the rural areas.

Since 1973 the church's social concerns office in Lae has wrestled with problems of "hunger, disease, insecurity, poverty, industrial conflict, juvenile delinquency, drug addiction, marital strife." LWF Community Development has assisted with this program and in 1983 approved funds for a "walk-in center." Social centers have also been opened in Mt. Hagen, Finschhafen, and Kundiawa. Lutheran Economic Service (LES), an affiliate of the church, organizes small aid and development projects in areas of greatest need. Numerous LWF/CDS projects are initiated and supervised through this agency. A holding company (Kambang) coordinates the various business enterprises: shipping, coconut plantations, farms, etc. These economic ventures—begun early in the life of the church to foster self-support—contribute 56% of the church's administrative budget; 2% comes from the member congregations, and the remainder from overseas partners. Established congregations are self-supporting. Pastors' salaries may be low, but they are usually supplemented by agricultural produce. Some congregations have found other means of increasing their income such as a community store or a truck or boat for transport. Nevertheless, the temptation remains for pastors and other church workers to leave their church, calling for more remunerative work with government or business. Even so there are ever-new ministerial recruits.

Partner churches—*Lutheran Church of Australia, *American Lutheran Church (now ELCA), *Evangelical Lutheran Church in Bavaria, *Evangelical Lutheran Church in Canada, and the *North Elbian Evangelical Lutheran Church—continue to send missionaries and other personnel as requested. These churches have written agreements with the ELC/PNG for continued cooperation in matters of personnel and finance. The Papua New Guinea Coordinating Committee, made up of representatives from each of the partner churches, facilitates ongoing assistance.

• • •

The historical background, prior to the organization of the church in 1956, falls into two periods. The first, 1886-1918, includes the beginnings made by two mission societies in *Germany: the Neuendettelsau (since 1886) and the Rhenish (1887–1932). The pioneer missionary Johannes Flierl (1858–1947) at first was assigned to work among Australia's aborigines but then moved on to New Guinea (a new German colony), initiating work near Finschhafen. He was active in the land, except for the interruption of World War I, from 1886 to 1930. Progress was slow for Flierl and his colleagues until a change of method was introduced. Tribal conversion, as developed by Christian Keyszer, sought the consent of an entire tribe, or village, to accept the gospel of Jesus Christ before proceeding with individual baptisms. (This method was not unlike that of Nommensen and his colleagues among the Bataks in *Indonesia.)

In 1908 the first native New Guinea evangelists were sent out. This set the pattern of every congregation having its own mission field. The two leading regional languages, Katé and Yabem, were reduced to writing. Dictionaries were prepared, translation of the Scriptures begun, and wider communication made possible. The Rhenish missionaries followed these methods in their area around Madang. Their staff was supplemented by six Samoan pastors loaned by the London Missionary Society. World War I severely restricted the work, but firm foundations and sound methods paid off as New Guineans themselves were ready to advance the mission.

The second period, 1919–1956, includes fresh starts after two world wars. Hard lessons in self-reliance and partnership were learned and the way opened to indigenous growth. Following World War I, German missionaries were excluded until 1927. Meanwhile, personnel and aid from the United Evangelical Lutheran Church in Australia and the *USA Iowa Synod (later ALC) filled the gap.

Pioneering in the Eastern Highlands was begun by Stephen Lehner in 1919. Others followed, and in 1921 Leonhard Flierl began annual visits. The first permanent Neuendettelsau missionary in this area, Wilhelm Bergmann, settled in Kambaidam in 1931. Bergmann, together with Henry Foege of the ALC (USA), also made exploratory flights by chartered plane to survey possible openings to the west. In 1934 they led parties of missionaries to begin work in Ega, Kerowagi, and Ogelbeng.

In 1936 the Neuendettelsau Mission turned over its work on the offshore Rooke and Siassi Islands to the Evangelical Lutheran Church of Australia (now part of the LCA). The Siassi Lutheran Church sprang from work begun in 1911 by a Neuendettelsau missionary, Georg Bamler, who had been in contact with the Siassi people for 20 years. The ELCA, using New Guinea pastors and evangelists, also developed work among the Kukukuku people at Menyamya and Aseki west of the Huon Gulf on mainland New Guinea. These people left the Siassi church and joined the ELC/PNG before the Siassi Lutheran Church merged with the ELC/PNG in 1976. This merger had been contemplated as early as 1963 when the Australian Lutherans appealed to the ELC/PNG for the creation of a united church "in view of the possible short time left for mission work in New Guinea, and the uncertain and difficult future facing the Lutheran church in New Guinea."

The growth of the New Guinea activities as a whole accelerated until halted by war in the Pacific and the Japanese occupation (1942–1944). German missionaries were interned in Australia once again. Casualties occurred. Twelve missionaries and two New Guinea church workers were killed while being held prisoners. A beautiful memorial church to their memory was dedicated near the lagoon in Madang in 1964.

The closing decade of this period, 1945–1956, saw postwar reconstruction and mission activity boom. An initial survey of the spiritual situation in the congregations and of the condition of church properties (1945) revealed a continuing spread of the gospel in some areas. In others apostasy had set in, and so-called cargo cults were flourishing. The accent of the latter on material gain via corrected relations with ancestors had been stimulated by the huge quantities of abandoned American military material. Missionaries began returning in late 1945 and early 1946. Youthful "mission builders," as they were called, came from North America and Australia to help reconstruct destroyed facilities and build new ones in advance positions. Later the Neuendettelsau and Leipzig Missions were again able to participate, the Leipzig entry being made possible by the relocation of much of its work to Bavaria (see Europe—the German Democratic Republic).

The entire effort was coordinated by the aforementioned Lutheran Mission New Guinea (1953). Three unifying languages received enlarged usage: Yabem in the Lae area, Katé in the Finschhafen area, and Bel in Madang. Pidgin, a true lingua franca, spread despite much mission and government opposition in all areas. Ministerial training was resumed and expanded. A publications program was set up. Evangelism was extended through tribal conversion, with strong participation by local congregations. Village schools and teacher training were extended into the Central Highlands. The leadership role of New Guineans was encouraged and their exceptional gifts given opportunity to unfold. From the time of its organization in 1953, the LMNG was headed by the recognized leader John Kuder. By 1956 the time had come for the organization of this entire undertaking as a New Guinea church.

Thirty years later impressive observances around July 12, 1986, celebrated the first hundred years of the Lutheran church in Papua New Guinea. The comprehensive centennial history—a 677-page volume (Lutheran Publishing House, Adelaide, Australia) in English and German editions—is a feat of international collaboration and painstaking research as guided by the editors, Herwig Wagner and Hermann Reiner, and prefaced by Bishop Gam.

GUTNIUS LUTHERAN CHURCH— PAPUA NEW GUINEA (GLC)
Member: LWF (1979), MCC
Membership: 95,000**
Bishop: The Rt. Rev. David Piso
Irelya, Enga Province
PO Box 111
Wabag

The Gutnius (Good News) Lutheran Church, formerly known as the Wabag Lutheran Church, was organized in 1961. Its 325 congregations are served by 124 national pastors and 114 teachers. Besides the bishop, there are five assistant bishops, one for each region. The synod elects a church council of 32 members that meets three times a year. The largest part of the church is in the Enga Province of the Central Highlands and extends into the Southern Highlands. The languages used are Enga, Pidgin, Hewa, and some English.

Most of the Gutnius pastors have been trained at Timothy Lutheran Seminary in Wapenamanda, which opened in 1960. Instruction is in Enga. In 1984 the school had 39 students. Theological education by extension is carried on, and pastors as well as students receive clinical training in a hospital. Some of the pastors and the present bishop have had their training in English at the Martin Luther Seminary in Lae. The GLC partner, the *Lutheran Church–Missouri Synod, provides both theological schools with two professors. It does the same for the Balob Teachers' College of the ELC/PNG, a school that trains many of the teachers of the Gutnius schools: the Highland Lutheran School (international), the St. Paul Lutheran High School, 31 primary schools, and the Muka Farming Training Center.

Situated in the highlands, the GLC encounters many hardships. Killing frosts and inflation have caused the GLC's business enterprise, WASO, to fail. Work at the Immanuel Lutheran Health Center has been curtailed for lack of funds. The current high cost of expatriate work permits is a burden. However, in the long run it may be helpful, for this money is used to train nationals to do comparable work. Meanwhile, the old custom of "payback" fosters continuing tribal fighting in the Enga Province and causes tragic deaths and loss of property over even small thefts. Christian instruction seeks with some success to convince the members not to retaliate, a difficult restraint for first generation Christians.

Nevertheless, the church continues its mission. A communications department publishes a monthly magazine in Pidgin and prepares 60-minute religious programs for the national broadcasting company. A film library is being augmented by a cassette ministry. The Bible in Enga is being published by the Bible Society of Papua New Guinea.

The GLC has also reached out to the Hewa people living in remote forest areas of the highlands. The work goes well despite the extremely rugged terrain and scattered small settlements. To reach some of them requires many hours of tramping after leaving the mission plane. Other churches have started work here but given up. About 2000 people are being reached along the Lagaip River. Other groups have asked for evangelists, but few workers are willing to go into this primitive area. As elsewhere in New Guinea, group baptism is usual. To strengthen this work a school for evangelists was opened in Porgera and the Bible is being translated into the Hewa language. An improved edition of the Ipili catechism, with Scripture for memorization, is an aid in Christian nurture.

It was not until 1949 that the Lutheran Church–Missouri Synod, celebrating its own centennial, resolved to begin work in Papua New Guinea. Encouraged by a sister church, the Evangelical Lutheran Church of Australia (now a part of the LCA), work began as agreed in the Central Highlands, a good deal west of Mt. Hagen and the work of the ELC/PNG. Today, however, the work overlaps in some areas where the Gutnius church has mission programs in Port Moresby, Mt. Hagen, Lae, and the mining camp communities of Bougainville. The two churches cooperate (see Christian education project in ELC/PNG), and signs are hopeful for an ultimately single Lutheran church in Papua New Guinea. In 1979 GLC was received into LWF membership.

Ecumenically the GLC is active in the Melanesian Council of Churches, the Enga Christian Council, the Churches' Council for Media Coordination, Kristen Radio, Melanesian Association of Theological Schools, and Wantok Publications.

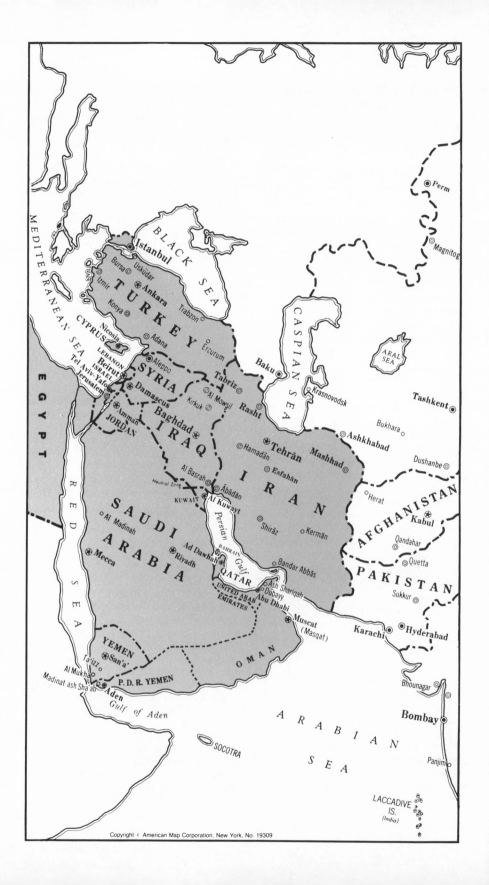

BIBLE LANDS AND NEIGHBORING COUNTRIES (MIDDLE EAST)_____

Lutheran work in this historic crossroads of continents and birthplace of the Christian faith, though numerically small, is nevertheless significant. It bears on the relationship between the legacies of Christianity, Judaism, and Islam.

Geographically, Middle East is the term designating the countries of Southwest Asia and Northeast Africa. On the Asian side, this includes Iran and Turkey, forming an upper tier from east to west. Below them, in a central cluster, are Iraq, Syria, Lebanon, Jordan, and Israel. On the Arabian Peninsula, huge Saudi Arabia is fringed on the east and south by Kuwait, Bahrain, Qatar, United Arab Emirates, Oman, Yemen (Aden), and Yemen (Arab Republic). On the African side the countries are Egypt, Sudan, and Libya. Contracted, Middle East may imply the older term, *Near East* (or the French term, *Levant*) which denotes the lands bordering the eastern Mediterranean: Turkey, Syria, Lebanon, Palestine (now, in part, Israel, the West Bank), Jordan, and Egypt. The island of Cyprus (80% Greek, 19% Turkish) plays an invaluable mediating role. For our purpose, the region is divided into two parts:

Bible Lands: Israel, Jerusalem and West Bank, Jordan, and Lebanon—where there are organized Lutheran entities.

Neighboring Countries: Arabian Peninsula, Cyprus, Egypt, Iran, Iraq, Syria, and Turkey—where Lutherans have minor service projects.

Area: c.8.8. million sq. km. (c.4 million sq. mi.). Pop. (1985 est): ca. 190 million.

History

Distant are the days when the once powerful Ottoman Empire of the Turks, with the Sultan in Constantinople, held sway over most of this region as well as Southeastern Europe as far as Hungary. Today, Europe's once burning Eastern question—What to do about the Turkish occupation?—has become the world's Middle East question.

Religion colored the scene then, and it does so now—only more so. Political power struggles have obscured the basic kinship between Jews, Christians, and Muslims and impeded the path to justice and coexistence. Judaism prevails in Israel (below). Islam is the dominant religion in other countries. The call of the minaret proclaims daily: "There is no God but God (Allah), and Mohammed is his Prophet." The 99 names of Allah mark his attributes, and on a string of as many beads the faithful recite them. Allah is the God of the covenant with Abraham, Moses, and the prophets—including Jesus. Through His Prophet, Mohammed, God has given the revelation essential to submitting to him and discerning as well as doing his will. Through the Angel Gabriel, this revelation was given to Mohammed who dictated it to those who wrote it down in the Book—the Quran. Muslims believe that the Quran, as the latest and ultimate revelation, corrects errors in the Hebrew and Christian Scriptures. The Quran honors Jesus, even as Messiah, but not as Son of God—for Allah is ever above his creation. The Quran implies that Christians worship three Gods: God, Jesus, and Mary. Muslims attribute the major errors to Paul and his Christology.

Beginning his ministry in Mecca (in present day Saudi Arabia), Mohammed's message was at first rejected. Fleeing to Medina, he found his first community of believers. This flight—the Hegira (A.D. 622)—marks the beginning of the Muslim calendar. The phenomenal spread of Islam (submission) among the Arabian desert dwellers and then across vast reaches west and east remains unique in the history of religions. Among its many variants, two main branches stand out: the Sunni (traditional) are the large majority; the Shiite (sectarian) are in various places a vigorous minority. The two branches differed over the line of Caliph succession immediately after the Prophet's death. Disputes among Muslims can be intense.

Christians in the Middle East—numbering about 12,000,000 in spite of significant losses in recent decades—are mainly members of the various Eastern and Oriental Orthodox churches that trace their rise to the early Christian era. Protestantism entered in the 19th century, with the purpose of strengthening these churches. Their efforts grew in response to suffering, including the massacre of Christians in Lebanon in 1860 and the wiping out of thousands of Armenian (Turkey) Christians in 1915. Evangelical churches resulted. Among these are the Lutherans, a tiny fraction. Yet their history and presence are significant for Lutherans the world over.

Today, 70% of the Christian population is affiliated with churches that comprise the *Middle East Council of Churches* (MECC), with headquarters in Lebanon. These churches include four Eastern Orthodox, three Oriental Orthodox, and 10 Protestant church bodies. By country these are: the Greek Orthodox Church of Cyprus; the Coptic Evangelical Church, the Coptic Orthodox Church of Alexandria, and the Greek Orthodox Church of Alexandria and All Africa (Egypt); the Evangelical Presbyterian Church in Iran; the Episcopal Church in Jerusalem and the Middle East, the Greek Orthodox Church of Jerusalem, and the Evangelical Lutheran Church in Jordan (below, *West Bank and East Jerusalem); the Armenian Church of Cilicia, the Armenian Evangelical Union, and the National Evangelical Union of Lebanon; the Greek Orthodox Church of Antioch, the National Evangelical Synod of Syria and Lebanon, and the Syrian Church of Antioch and All East; the Evangelical Church of Sudan and the Presbyterian Church–Sudan; and the Ecumenical Patriarchate of Constantinople (Istanbul), Turkey.

Organized in Nicosia, Cyprus in 1974, the MECC has a long history. In 1927 the Protestant churches took the lead in forming the Council of Western Asia and Northern Africa, which in 1964 became the Near East Council of Churches. It accomplished a great deal in bringing the separate traditions together. It also endeavored to overcome the worst effects of proselytism which had led to the growth of Western churches—Roman Catholic as well as Protestant. The modern ecumenical movement has helped immensely to acquaint not only the old churches with the new, but also the old with each other.

The MECC constitution provides for a three-member presidium of regional church leaders (as in the World Council), an executive committee, and a general secretariat. The range of the MECC program includes: dialog and witness (interconfessional and interreligious); literature publication and distribution; interchurch aid and community development; youth and student service; theological education; and service to Palestinian refugees. The latter service, based in Nicosia, Cyprus, reaches out to five area offices: East Jordan, Gaza, Israel, Lebanon, and West Bank.

To foster mutual acquaintance the MECC maintains an Ecumenical Travel Office. It endeavors to help Christians visiting the Holy Land and Middle East to acquaint themselves with the local churches, with Islam and Judaism, and with the issues of justice and peace in this explosive crossroads of the world. Such assistance is intended also for Middle East Christians when traveling in their own region so that they may share in each other's spiritual and cultural heritage.

Preceding the MECC assembly in February 1985 came an unprecedented consultation on unity that included representatives of the six Catholic churches in communion with Rome (the Melkite, Armenian, Coptic, Latin, Maronite, and Syrian) as well as of the Assyrian Church of the East. (The Council expects that before long a number of these church bodies will associate with it.) According to this consultation, the worldwide theological dialog—bilateral and others—are stimulating further efforts toward Christian unity in the Middle East. So also are the dialogs-in-community, which involve relations between Christians and Muslims as well as Christians and Jews. This Nicosia meeting, gathered in the headquarters of the Church of Cyprus, was marked by the presence of the president of the Vatican's Secretariat for Promoting Christian Unity, Cardinal Johannes Willebrands. He called for "a greater advance in our communion of love . . . between our churches."

The consultation expressed a determination to strive for the kind of Christian unity that will bridge the separation of the centuries. It also sent a challenge to the churches of the world pleading for a better understanding of the situation of Christians in the Middle East, for whom diminishing numbers as well as mounting responsibilities are testing their spiritual resources.

Lutheran involvement in this region is of long standing (below). Furthermore the trusteeship of German mission properties and the continuing work among Palestinian Christians was first assumed by the American Section of the Lutheran World Convention and then (1948) by the LWF itself. Dr. Edwin A. Moll (1892–1961), the Australian-American churchman, came on the scene in 1946. Following the proclamation of the state of Israel (May 14, 1948), the plight of the 500,000 Palestinian refugees demanded immediate action. The LWF response was swift and ecumenical as well as interfaith. The Federation's Department of World Service worked in cooperation with the United Nations Relief and Works Agency for Palestinian Refugees in the Near East (UNRWA). It complemented the help rendered Israel by many Jewish and other agencies. And it set an LWF policy of rendering assistance to people in need regardless of race, religion, or politics, and of working with the UN in aiding refugees in other parts of the world as well. For decades after 1948, the LWF program in the Near East was the largest single voluntary endeavor in the area (see Bible Lands, below).

However, Lutheran undertakings in the Middle East have not been limited to work with refugees. Service agencies, hospitals, schools, congregations, study programs, and a variety of other activities are supported by churches and groups in Europe and North America. They give expression to the attachment felt for the people in these lands and for the geographical context of the biblical legacy.

The need to bring this variety of enterprises into closer partnership was underscored by the LWF-sponsored consultation on Lutheran involvement in the Holy Land and its broader context. In 1975 representatives from 28 organizations and agencies gathered in Geneva to seek ways of carrying out more effectively a faithful witness in word and deed. A similarly inclusive consultation, held in Cyprus in 1982, reviewed the current situation as well as the historical background and spelled out requirements for the future. Approved by the LWF Executive Committee, the report of the consultation called for closer coordination of Lutheran efforts in the Holy Land, greater ecumenical involvement, continuing social services, support of church-related education, increased striving for peace and justice, improved assistance to Holy Land visitors and persons engaged in study, and a sustained Christian witness in its manifold forms and opportunities.

In taking this stand, the Lutheran consultation affirmed that of the MECC's general secretary, Gabriel Habib, who in 1985 pleaded for a "new understanding of the Middle East as a whole, and particularly of the Middle East churches."

BIBLE LANDS

This area includes Israel, Jordan, and Lebanon, as well as the disputed area of East Jerusalem and West Bank. Here Lutherans have organized church entities—a tiny fraction of the Christian minority.

Bible Lands or the Holy Land are also known as Palestine. Although Palestine as a political entity no longer exists, its history and significance serves as an introduction to this section in order to give background for the present situation.

History: The boundaries of Palestine, though never constant, have always included the land between the Mediterranean Sea and the Jordan River. In Old Testament times, this was Canaan, so named for Cana the son of Ham, who was the son of Noah. To Abraham and then to the Israelites, liberated from Egypt, this was the promised land. In the 13th century B.C., under Joshua, successor to Moses, the Israelites began their conquest of it. The process was a gradual one.

Around 1200 B.C., the Philistines—a nonsemitic people from Crete in the Aegean Sea—took the southern coastland of the Mediterranean and established the powerful kingdom of Philistia, with Gaza, Ashqelon, Ashdod, Ekron, and Goth its main cities. Located on the great commercial route from Egypt to Syria, these cities formed a confederacy. The names of the great Hebrew heroes—Samson, Saul, and David—live in biblical history, but the Philistines were never really conquered. The name of their land lives on as "Palestine."

Under Solomon, the Hebrews had an expanded kingdom (950 B.C.). It later broke into two kingdoms, Israel and Judah (Judea). Israel fell to the Assyrians (721 B.C.) and Judah to the Babylonians (586 B.C.). The Persian conquest of Babylon in 538 B.C. fostered Jewish autonomy and facilitated the rebuilding of the temple in Jerusalem. Later, Alexander the Great conquered the entire area in 333 B.C. (Hebrews as well as Philistines) and they remained under Greek control—except for the period of the Maccabees—until Pompey took the region for Rome in 63 B.C.

At the time of Jesus, the Romans were using the Idumaean Herods as puppet kings to maintain control. The double destruction of Jerusalem—A.D. 70 and 135—

271

added greatly to the number of Jews living in the dispersion. Centuries later, after the Muslim conquest (A.D. 638), Jerusalem became a holy city of Islam—the third after Mecca and Medina. From the 11th century, the Fatimid dynasty from its newly founded capital, Cairo, harshly oppressed both Christians and Jews. Western Europe's crusades captured parts of Palestine, and in 1099 established the Latin Kingdom of Jerusalem. In 1291, the last crusaders were driven out of Palestine by the Seljuk Turks and the Egyptian Mamelukes. Palestine subsequently came under the long rule of the Ottoman Turks. In the 1830s, Muhammad Ali (c.1769–1849), an aggressive subject of the Ottoman Sultan and founder of modern Egypt, opened the region of Palestine to European influence and settlement.

Russian Jews were the first to come. In the 1890s, the newly founded Zionist movement (Theodor Herzl, 1860–1904) encouraged the settlement of Jewish colonies within Palestine. Somewhat earlier, Arab nationalism—fanned by Christian and then Muslim Arabs in Beirut, *Lebanon—was developing in opposition to Turkish rule. After World War I, with Arab aid, Britain gained control of Palestine. Britain's Balfour Declaration (1917) supported Zionist aspirations to establish a Jewish national home in Palestine, but with due regard for the rights of non-Jewish Palestinians. Britain (through T. E. Lawrence, 1888–1935) promised the Arab leaders support in creating independent Arab states. The Arabs believed that Palestine would be one of them.

Palestine presently became the scene of conflicting aims. After the first Arab anti-Zionist riots (1920), the League of Nations approved the British mandate (1922) that would foster a Jewish homeland by aiding Jewish immigration. Although a limited immigration was urged after the Arab-Jewish clashes of 1929, the rise of Nazism soon accelerated immigration: 5000 in 1932, 65,000 in 1935. The Peel Commission recommended the partitioning of Palestine into Jewish, Arab, and British states. The Zionists approved the plan, reluctantly; but the Arabs rejected it. Unrest continued. The White Paper of 1939, limiting immigration and the purchase of Arab land by Jews, was shelved by the outbreak of World War II.

The horrible plight of European Jews—the Holocaust revealed by Hitler's concentration camps—led influential forces in the USA to support an independent Jewish state. Despite the continuing British ban on it, large-scale illegal immigration followed. The independent Arab states organized the Arab League to exert international pressure against Zionism. When a conference in 1947 between the British, Arabs, and Zionists brought no agreement, Britain turned the Palestinian problem over to the United Nations. At that time there were in Palestine 1,091,000 Muslim Arabs, 614,000 Jews, and 146,000 Christians (mostly Arabs). In May 1948, the State of Israel was created without a provision for the other Palestinians. At once, Arab countries declared war on Israel.

Religion: Today, this land retains a holy meaning for the followers of the three monotheistic faiths descended from Abraham: to Jews because of their centuries of habitation there as chosen people. To Christians, this is the Holy Land because of the ministry of Jesus, his redemptive death and triumphant resurrection, and because from Jerusalem the church—the new people of God—went forth to all the world. To Muslims, their derivation from Abraham recognizes Mount Moriah—the rock where tradition says Abraham was ready to sacrifice Isaac (today Dome of the Rock

Mosque in the Temple area). It is from this rock that Mohammed, the Prophet, dreamed he ascended to heaven to meet with Allah and receive the authentication for the revelation in the Quran. The modern secular mind has often overlooked, and thus not reckoned with, the enduring power of this triple legacy of the spirit.

Over the centuries, pilgrims have flocked to the Holy Land. For Christians, the pace was set by St. Helena, the mother of Emperor Constantine. Her visit to Jerusalem and Bethlehem resulted in the construction of churches and monuments to commemorate, as holy places, events in the life of Christ and in the Judeo-Christian tradition. The pilgrim traffic rehabilitated much of the land, even as the holy places provided focal points for pondering the historic faith. As late as the 18th century, maps showed Jerusalem at the center—the navel—of the world, the location mentioned by the 6th-century (B.C.) prophet, Ezekiel: "Thus says the Lord God: This is Jerusalem; I have set it in the center of the nations" (5:5).

During the four centuries of Ottoman imperial rule (1517–1917) Palestine remained fairly accessible. Conflict was more likely to arise between the various Christian factions than from other quarters. Roman Catholics had felt free to proselytize among the Eastern and other Orthodox churches ever since the Great Schism of 1054. When, in 1847, the Greek Patriarch reestablished his domicile in Jerusalem, Rome responded by reactivating its Latin Patriarchate of Jerusalem. The lesser oriental Orthodox like the Copts, Ethiopians, Armenians, Syrians, and others all maintained a base in the Holy City. For good reason, the chief Muslim in Jerusalem, the Mufti, held the keys to the Church of the Resurrection (Holy Sepulcher), as he does to this day.

As the 19th century opened, Protestants and Anglicans became increasingly attracted to the Holy Land generally, and to Jerusalem in particular. This West-East relationship stimulated Protestants—as in the British and Foreign Bible Society (1805)—to trust that the Scriptures in the vernacular would both evangelize the Eastern churches and move them to share the gospel with the Muslims. Their interest turned to Jews as well as Muslims, and soon the Church Ministry among Jews (CMJ) was active. Although success was slight, the implications of these beginnings were far-reaching.

By 1841, Anglicans and Prussian Evangelicals (mainly Lutheran) had launched an Evangelical Bishopric in Jerusalem. The plan was simple. The Bishop of Jerusalem would ordain German clergy on their subscription to the *Augsburg Confession,* and Anglican clergy on their subscription to the *Thirty-nine Articles.* Politically, moreover, the presence of this bishopric was not to detract from the already existing ecclesiastical dignitaries in Jerusalem, but rather to express an Anglo-German protectorate over Protestants in the Near East as a counterweight to an already considerable French Roman Catholic influence in the region.

Reflecting the aims of the CMJ, a former Jew became the first Bishop of Jerusalem. Solomon Alexander was consecrated to this position in London (1841). Himself a native German and a rabbi's son, he had served briefly in England as a rabbi before converting to Anglicanism. His brief career in Jerusalem—he died in 1845—gave the project a promising beginning. Next, upon German nomination, came Samuel Gobat (1799–1879). A Swiss, he had been trained in the Basel Mission and had already served with the Church Missionary Society (CMS) in *Ethiopia. He served

39 years (1846–1885) as Bishop of Jerusalem. After him, the joint bishopric was dissolved and became Anglican.

German mission beginnings in Jerusalem and the Near East merit special attention, particularly as they related to Samuel Gobat. First, in 1846 a company of six South German artisans arrived in Jerusalem and opened their Brother House. By their skills and an exemplary Christian life, they hoped to open doors for the gospel among Jews and Muslims as well as to be of service to the community, including the growing colony of Europeans and Americans in the Holy City. The idea as such was not new, but Gobat had come to favor it while in *Ethiopia, and his friend, Christian Frederick Spittler (1782–1867) had picked it up. A visionary Lutheran layman, Spittler had moved from his former post in the Basel Mission and was now heading his own, less academically oriented school, St. Chrischona, near Basel, Switzerland. Eventually, Gobat and Spittler agreed that Jerusalem would be the first in a line of mission stations extending like an apostles' highway all the way to Ethiopia. The project was never completed, but the team in Jerusalem foreshadowed other developments.

Next, also in 1846, while in London awaiting his consecration as bishop, Gobat met Theodor Fliedner (1800–1864), founder of the deaconess movement in *Germany. Gobat apprised Fliedner of the need for Christian hospitals in many cities of the Near East, not only for the care of Westerners but also for the needy native population. The idea caught on. Two years after bringing four deaconesses to Pittsburgh—to run the first Protestant hospital in the *USA—Fliedner, in 1851, came with four deaconesses to Jerusalem. Welcomed by Bishop Gobat and his wife and aided by British, German, and other friends (including Jews, Muslims, and Arab Christians), the deaconess hospital was dedicated on the second Sunday after Easter. An English physician served as medical staff. Besides their work as nurses, the deaconesses also organized a school and orphanage for Palestinian girls, the later famous Talitha Kumi institution (see Jerusalem and West Bank, below).

This Jerusalem venture encouraged Fliedner and the deaconesses to set up similar institutions in Constantinople (1852), Smyrna (1854), Alexandria (1857; later Cairo), and Beirut (1860). This unsung chapter of the creative and courageous work of women in the Near East should be highlighted (see Egypt, Turkey, below).

Interest and support came mainly from Germany. With encouragement from the King of Prussia, Frederick William IV, the Jerusalem Society was formed in 1852 and became a valued support system for work in the Holy Land. (Since 1973 the Jerusalem Society has been part of the Division of World Mission of the *Evangelical Church in Berlin-Brandenburg, known as the Berlin Mission.)

Back in Jerusalem, a third step came in 1856 with the arrival of the missionary couple, Johann Ludwig Schneller (1820–1896) and his wife, Magdalene. Lutherans from Württemberg, they were associated with Spittler in "Chrischona," but had broken with their mentor's ideal of celibacy and were determined to serve as a married couple in the Holy Land. The decisive moment came in 1860, with the terrible massacre of Christians by the Druses in *Lebanon. Spittler urged Schneller to offer his services in Lebanon. On November 10 Schneller returned to Jerusalem with nine orphaned boys, entrusted to him through the intervention of American

Presbyterian missionaries. The enlarged Schneller family home on the edge of Jerusalem became the later famous Syrian Orphanage.

Meanwhile, during the 39-year incumbency of Bishop Gobat, the English and German Protestants in Jerusalem had a visible symbol of unity, and a general spirit of helpfulness prevailed. By 1871 the German colony (so-called) numbered about 200 and had built its own chapel, on a site near the Church of the Holy Sepulcher given by the Turkish Sultan to the King of Prussia. The chapel was later replaced by the present Church of the Redeemer (1898) and dedicated by the German emperor.

The Schnellers' goal was to educate and provide Christian instruction for the boys in the orphanage. Bible study, daily worship, and Luther's *Small Catechism* shaped the spiritual life, while the teaching of trades in the institution's shops provided the community at large with skilled workers. Besides the institution becoming a congregation of its own, new congregations were gathered in Bethlehem, Beit Jala, Beit Sahour, and elsewhere. These, with Redeemer Church as the center, became the basic constituency of today's Evangelical Lutheran Church in Jordan (see Jerusalem and West Bank).

A global missionary outlook—from the German side—found expression in the Augusta Victoria Foundation, adjacent to the Mount of Olives on Mount Scopus. Overlooking the city from across the Kidron Valley, this massive structure—named in honor of the German empress—was to serve furloughed and retired missionaries and to be a study center. Dedicated in 1911, it never could be put to its intended use. After World War I its chief claim to fame was as host to the first—the Jerusalem meeting—of the International Missionary Council (1928). Greater service lay ahead (see below, West Bank).

The Swedish Jerusalem Society, founded in 1900, opened a school in Jerusalem in 1902. It developed into a school with a student body of some 280—both Arabs and Jews—and a program that included kindergarten and primary schooling as well as vocational courses. It was completely demolished in the Arab-Israeli War of 1948. The society's 80-bed hospital in Beit Jala, near Bethlehem, was opened in 1904, but closed in 1925.

Following World War I and the coming of the British mandate over Palestine as well as Jordan and Iraq, the German institutions were temporarily under the international Near East Relief Agency before being returned. The Syrian Orphanage, the Deaconess Hospital, Talitha Kumi, Redeemer Church, and several other installations, like the Christmas Church in Bethlehem, were once again supported mainly from Germany. The support system, however, counted increasingly on supplemental help from Christians also in other countries, especially from Switzerland, the USA, and Canada. Title to much of the mission property was in the hands of the Jerusalem Society in Berlin.

With the rise of the Hitler era in Germany, the flow of support was further curtailed. During World War II all these properties came under the category of Orphaned Missions. During the remaining time of the British mandate after 1945, the American Section of the Lutheran World Convention—later the LWF—was officially granted trusteeship (as it had already been given that ecclesially by the Germans). In more ways than could be anticipated, Lutherans the world over were being drawn ever more deeply into the rapidly changing destiny of Palestine.

ISRAEL

A parliamentary republic (1948) in the Middle East, bounded by the Mediterranean Sea, Lebanon, Syria, Jordan, the Gulf of Aqaba, and Egypt. Area (not including territory—*West Bank and East Jerusalem—occupied in the June 1967 war): 20,700 sq. km. (7992 sq. mi.). Pop. (1986 est.): 4,381,000. Cap. (proclaimed, 1950, but pending international recognition) and largest city: Jerusalem (pop., 1983 census, 428,668). Language: Hebrew and Arabic.

History: On May 14, 1948, the state of Israel was formally proclaimed. Behind this act lay a long and painful process. It culminated in the plan of the United Nations Special Commission on Palestine (UNSCOP), adopted by the General Assembly in November 1947. Britain abstained, and the Arab nations walked out before the vote. Unrest prior to the partitioning was rife in the land. The departure of the British High Commissioner on May 14 was the signal for Israel's emergence as a nation. It was also the moment for its attack by Arab nations: Lebanon, Syria, Iraq, Jordan, Egypt. East Jerusalem (the Old City)—part of a proposed international zone—was surrendered by the Israelis to Jordan's Arab Legion. For nearly two decades (until 1967) Jerusalem was to remain a divided city. Meanwhile, Israel's occupation of its allotted territory concluded only with the armistice of 1949. By then, about 600,000 Palestinian Arabs had fled the country, leaving less than that number to remain in Israel. For most of them, the *West Bank—taken by Jordan—was their place of refuge and resettlement.

Nation making proceeded in Israel with energy and innovation unparalleled in the region. A city like Tel Aviv, begun in 1909 as a Jewish suburb of Arab Jaffa, burgeoned into a modern urban center. Many a kibbutz became a new-style community. Behind the struggle for survival lay recent memories of the Holocaust, while ahead loomed mingled promise and foreboding.

The first prime minister, David Ben-Gurion (1886–1973), in and out of office four times between 1948 and 1963, personified the tenacity of Zionist leadership. In 1949 Israel gained admission to the UN and also relocated its capital from Tel Aviv to Jerusalem (West). With outside help (Europe and the USA), Israel withstood the Arab economic boycott. In the Arab-Israeli wars of 1956, 1967, and 1973–1974, Israel's position became more firmly entrenched. The Six-Day War, in June 1967, saw Israel expand far beyond its original borders. It annexed the Old City of Jerusalem—with the places holy to Islam and Christianity as well as Judaism—and took the *West Bank from Jordan, as well as the Golan Heights from Syria, and the Sinai Peninsula from Egypt. But the Yom Kippur War of 1973–1974 saw the economic side of the Arab-Israeli conflict expand to global proportion. In the subsequently Arab-led Organization of Petroleum Exporting Countries (OPEC) oil prices skyrocketed.

The Camp David Accords of 1979, including Egypt, Israel, and the USA, became a landmark for Israel. Egypt's recognition of Israel was the first such act by an Arab country, but it cost Egypt broken diplomatic ties with most other Arab countries. It resulted, however, in the return of the Sinai Peninsula to Egypt. Meanwhile, the unresolved question of the Palestinian people—those outside Israel as refugees and those under its governance—bred chronic outbursts of violence. The Palestine Liberation Organization (PLO)—the self-help agency of the Palestinians—having been ousted from *Jordan and relocated to *Lebanon posed a chronic threat. Israel's longest war, 1982–1985, was its invasion and occupation of southern Lebanon and, for a time, of Beirut. To many an Israeli this "preventive aggression," and ensuing devastation, loomed as a turning point in the young nation's history and as a loss of moral authority. To other Israelis it hardened their reliance on force.

Israel became the point of return for many a cultural, intellectual, scientific, and technological achievement of the Jewish dispersion worldwide. A symbol of this return is the Hebrew University in Jerusalem, whose initial campus on Mount Scopus (1925), and another one in the New City, combine the world of learning in science and the arts. While modernization changed Jerusalem greatly after World War I under the British mandate, this was modest when compared to the transformation through which it has passed since becoming the capital of Israel. The bearers of change have been the people: Ashkenazic (Yiddish-speaking) Jews from Eastern and Central Europe; Sephardic Jews from Spain and Portugal and Northern Africa; and Oriental Jews from Arab lands of the Middle East and elsewhere. During the early decades, the Ashkenazim predominated, but in recent years the Sephardim have rapidly grown in number. In politics, they are nearly a majority, while in religion they oppose secularism and side with Jewish orthodoxy.

Religion: About 88% of the population are Jewish; 8% Muslim; and less than 2% Christian. As in many a European country, a Ministry of Religion oversees religious affairs—in this case the affairs of the three Abrahamic religions.

Among the more than 6000 synagogues, the Ashkenazic and Sephardic are given to preserving the traditions of their members' origin. All, however, are accountable in matters of religion to the Chief Rabbinate of Israel (comprising one Ashkenazic and one Sephardic rabbi). The Supreme Rabbinical Council is the country's highest religious authority. Of the three major branches of Judaism—Orthodox, Conservative, Reformed—the Orthodox are in control. Even so, most Israelis claim a secular outlook as their own.

Islam continues among the sharply diminished Muslim Arab population. Like the rabbis, the imams (leaders) of the mosques are paid by the state. The chief mosques—Al Aksa and Dome of the Rock—are in East Jerusalem (see West Bank). There is freedom of worship, and Muslims keep to themselves. Centuries have passed since Muslims have been a minority and Friday has since been overshadowed by Saturday as the day of rest. In many different ways Muslims, like the Christians, inevitably come to feel the pressures of the dominant majority.

Christianity has long been a small minority, and in recent years its numbers have been diminishing more rapidly than earlier. Of the estimated 65,000 Christians in Israel, nearly two-thirds are Roman Catholic; about 25% are Greek Orthodox and Oriental Orthodox of various traditions; and about 9% are Protestant. The latter include the Episcopalians (Anglicans) as well as the Lutherans and numerous other groups.

The Roman Catholic communion in Israel divides into the Latin Patriarchate of Jerusalem (reestablished in 1847, and including Maronite Christians) and the Archdiocese of Acre (including Melkite Christians of the Greek rite). The Roman Catholic is the one church with more of its membership in Israel than in the West Bank. Less than half of the Greek Orthodox Patriarchate of Jerusalem's members live in Israel. Here, too, are small groups of Armenian, Coptic, Russian, Syrian, and Ethiopian Orthodox.

The United Christian Council in Israel (UCCI)—including the West Bank—in 1980 reported 19 member bodies, including Episcopalian, Lutheran, Baptist, and Nazarene among the participating Protestant groups. A concern of the UCCI has been the government's curb on the change of religion (1977).

The Bible Society, early active in the Holy Land, opened a national office in 1966. During the period between 1950–1982, more than 1,000,000 Bibles, or portions of it, were distributed. Present work is being done on readers' helps for the recently published New Testament in modern Hebrew.

Among the many study centers in Jerusalem (New City) is the Swedish Theological Institute. Opened in 1951, it has gained distinction from its researches in Jewish-Christian origins and relations. The Danish Israel Mission features Christian–Muslim–Jewish dialog and provides pastoral care for Danes living in Jerusalem and for Danish young people active in kibbutzim. It relates to the Lutheran Church in Israel (below).

LUTHERAN CHURCH IN ISRAEL (LCI; in process of formation)
(Haknesia Haluteranit)
Member: (P), UCCI
Membership: 275**
Superintendent: The Rev. Helge Høyland
43 Meir Street
PO Box 525
31004 Haifa

This embryonic church body brings together in a working relationship the congregations in Haifa and Tel Aviv, formed by the Norwegian Mission to Israel (NMI) and the one in Jerusalem, formed by the Finnish Missionary Society—now known as the Finnish Evangelical Lutheran Mission (FELM). A constitution having been adopted, and an agreement of cooperation signed, formal recognition by the government is pending.

The NMI congregations in Tel Aviv and Haifa as well as smaller groups in the southern and northern part of the country have for some time been a *de facto* church body. This status goes back to Turkish times when no Protestant church was legally recognized. The membership—including East European Hebrew Christians as well as those of Oriental and Israeli background—has produced leadership, including one pastor, who supplements the work of the missionaries sent by the NMI.

The church buildings of both congregations are located on former German church property, confiscated during World War II and then turned over to the Lutheran World Federation in 1951. The LWF made these properties available to the needs of the NMI, an agency founded in 1844 "to awaken interest in the people of Israel among Christians and to further knowledge of Christianity among the Jews." In 1891, the NMI began work among the Jewish people in Eastern Europe. During the Nazi period, the NMI helped many Jews to escape the Holocaust, and among them were Christians who relocated to Israel. The NMI then sent workers—ousted from *Romania in 1948 and from Hungary in 1950—to minister to their needs. Thus, building on foundations laid by the NMI during the 1920s, small congregations were formed, augmented over the years by other immigrants as well as by Israelis who have come to a Christian faith through the ministry of the congregations.

With help from the NMI, the LWF, and other sources, the small congregations have acquired adequate facilities for worship and community service. In Haifa, the new Elias Church and Community Center was dedicated in 1970, and six years later the Ebenezer Home for the Aged. The latter is a charitable institution "open to all regardless of race, nationality, or religion." The NMI retains title but has support from the three congregations, the residents, and also from the *Evangelical Lutheran Church in Bavaria (FRG), the International Hebrew Christian Alliance, the Evangelical Mission in South-West Germany, the Finnish Evangelical Lutheran Mission, and the Danish Israel Mission.

The Tel Aviv Immanuel congregation has over the years modernized the old German church. Besides its worship services, using Hebrew, Hungarian, and English, the church is used for Saturday evening concerts of choral singing and organ recitals. These attract an average of 160 people. The Bible shop in the center of Tel Aviv provides information about the work of the congregation.

The Jerusalem congregation worships in the Shalhevetyah Christian Center at 25 Shivtei Israel Street, where the Finnish Evangelical Lutheran Mission (FELM) has carried on work since 1925. Over the years, the needs and the programs have changed: a refuge for Jews—including a children's home and school until 1968; a care center for Arab children until 1976; and now an accommodation for two kindergartens—one using Hebrew and English, the other Arabic—as well as retreats for various groups including those of the Danish Israel Mission. The congregation is a bridge, for its membership includes Arabs and Hebrews. Besides supporting the Ebenezer Home with interest, staff, and funds, the congregation and its partner, the FELM, contribute to the Evangelical Lutheran Church in Jordan and the Arabic Episcopalian Church. The LCI congregations have actively supported the Bible Society in Israel (above).

According to reports of the leading pastor, the work of these congregations is not easy. Jews in general are said to look upon Christians as persecutors of the Jewish people and upon Jesus as a blasphemer. However, today there seems to be an openness and growing interest in the person of Jesus, in the New Testament, and in the Christian faith and life. In part, he attributes this to the fact that the Jewish people have gained an independent national life in the land of Jesus as well as to the growing concern of Christians throughout the world for the well-being of the Jewish people.

In order to prepare indigenous leadership for the LCI as well as to educate and train other Christians in the art of conversing with Jewish people, the NMI in 1983 opened the Caspari Center for Biblical and Jewish Studies. Located since early 1986 in the Shalhevetyah Center, theological education courses by extension (TEE) are being developed for about 10 Israeli students. Seminars are also conducted for foreign pastors and church workers. The first of these was for Norwegian pastors on the "Jewish background of the New Testament and its significance for the proclamation of the gospel today." In 1987, the Norwegian Mission to

Israel, founded in 1844, changed its official English name to Norwegian Church Ministry to Israel (NCMI).

JERUSALEM (OLD CITY) AND WEST BANK

West Bank is a collective term for a Palestinian area of 5600 sq. km. (2165 sq. mi.) west of the Jordan River and the Dead Sea that is claimed by both Israel and Jordan. Occupied and controlled by Israel since 1967, it includes the Old City of Jerusalem as well as the cities to the north (Jenin, Nablus, and Ramallah), to the south (Bethlehem and Hebron), and to the east (Jericho). The Israelis call this entire area by the biblical names, Samaria and Judea. Over 60,000 of the population of about 810,000 are Jewish settlers living in high rise apartments on land appropriated from the Palestinians.

History: After the Israeli-Arab War of 1948, an armistice granted the West Bank to *Jordan. At that time, the population of the area was about 450,000, many of whom were homeless refugees from Palestine. This annexation by Jordan was not favored by many Palestinians, who expected the establishment of an independent Palestinian state. There were at this time some 1,800,000 registered Palestinian refugees and their offspring. Those registered were persons who had lived in Palestine for at least two years before Israel's creation in 1948 and who had by this action lost a home and all means of livelihood.

As a result of the Six-Day War of 1967, Israel occupied this territory even though the Security Council of the United Nations adopted Resolution 242 (November 1967) calling for withdrawal of Israeli forces from this Arab territory. The resolution was ignored by Israel. Instead, Jewish settlements on Arab soil have been encouraged by successive Israeli governments, and the basic rights of Palestinians disregarded. (Palestinians leaving the country temporarily, for study or other purposes, may not be permitted to return to their homes. West Bank students often find it difficult to obtain a sustained education. Birzeit University, near Ramallah, has been closed many times since 1973 for various reasons and lengths of time. Even some duly elected Arab city mayors have been dismissed or deported by the Israelis.)

With little or no hope of a solution to their problems, two-thirds of the Palestinians, especially the well-educated and young, have fled to other countries. The Palestine Liberation Organization (PLO), which claims to be the legitimate representative of the Palestinians, has been banned from the West Bank and also from neighboring countries. Thus, the Palestinian problem remains a matter of great urgency.

Religion: With the constant emigration of Christians and the encroaching settlements of Jews, religious statistics for the West Bank are elusive. The majority of Palestinians are followers of Islam and the Dome of the Rock in the Old City is for them very holy. About 8% of the population is Christian, with a heritage that goes back to the late fourth century—a fact seldom recognized by the rest of Christendom. Small in number as they are, Christian churches are further weakened by their divisions. The most numerous are the Eastern Orthodox. The Greek Melkites, whose patriarch lives in Damascus, are in communion with Rome and have a Byzantine rite much like that of Constantinople but in the Arabic language. The Latin Patriarch of Jerusalem also oversees the churches in Jordan, Cyprus, and Gaza. The Maronites, also in communion with Rome, come under the archbishop of Tyre in Lebanon. Franciscans are the traditional custodians of the Holy Places. Among the newest and most vital Roman Catholic-owned enterprises is the Ecumenical Institute for Advanced Theological Study, Tantur, between the Old City and Bethlehem. In Tantur's creation after Vatican II as well as among its visiting scholars and staff, Lutherans have been prominent. The Anglicans are part of the Episcopal Church in Jerusalem and the Middle East. Their bishop lives in East Jerusalem. Protestant churches of the West Bank are included in the United Christian Council in Israel (1957).

In this setting, the Evangelical Lutheran Church in Jordan (below) is indeed a tiny minority but its influence, and that of its confessional partners, far exceeds small numbers.

Lutheran World Federation Department of World Service (LWS) continues the assistance begun in 1948 to the Palestinian refugees in partnership with the United Nations Relief and Works Agency for Palestinian Refugees in the Near East (UNRWA). LWS also has an agreement with the Hashemite Kingdom of Jordan and with the Israeli Ministry of Labor and Social Affairs to provide services to needy persons, both refugees and non-refugees.

The Augusta Victoria Hospital (AVH) and eight related village health clinics throughout the West Bank provide medical care to the 340,000 UNRWA-registered refugees and other Palestinians in the area. The Vocational Training Center (VTC) accommodates up to 150 young men of secondary school age and offers a three-year course in auto mechanics, carpentry, and metal work. Like other schools in the West Bank, the school follows the Jordanian curriculum, and the diplomas of the graduating students are certified by the Jordan government. LWS also continues the scholarship program launched in 1960. Annually about 60 young men and women benefit from higher education in Middle East colleges and universities. Presently, scholarships are 50% grant and 50% loan. Gaza Strip students are also eligible. In late 1986, the Lutheran churches in the Federal Republic of Germany, through their Protestant Central Agency for Development (EZE), agreed to meet 50% of the cost of redeveloping AVH. That year the number of patients served reached 39,500. UNRWA has also requested AVH to reserve beds for seriously ill patients from Gaza Strip.

The Swedish Jerusalem Society (see Holy Land introduction, above) continues its educational work at the Good Shepherd Swedish School, located near Bethlehem. Here about 300 Arab children—90% Christian and 10% Muslim—receive education from kindergarten through college preparaton. Fees of the students cover part of the cost, and the rest comes from Sweden.

CHURCH OF THE REDEEMER
(Erlöserkirche)
Membership: 175**
Pastor: The Rev. Tilman F. Bergman
Propst (of the German-speaking congregation): Dr. Johannes Friedrich
PO Box 14076
Jerusalem—Old City

The Church of the Redeemer, an inspiring structure situated in the middle of the Old City of Jerusalem, is itself a proclamation of hope. A gift of the German government and dedicated by Kaiser Wilhelm in 1898, it replaced a restored Crusaders' chapel where a German congregation worshiped. It was also meant to serve German Protestant pilgrims and visitors to the Holy Land. Redeemer's commanding tower affords the Old City's best view of sacred places including the nearby Church of the Resurrection (Holy Sepulcher). Recent restoration work on both the 19th- and 12th-century structures of Redeemer has brought praise from architects and archaeologists alike.

Today, Redeemer is an international church. It brings into a working relationship several congregations using different languages. The German-speaking congregation formed in 1868 was once the largest. It has an extensive outreach to German-speaking Protestants (Lutheran, Reformed, United) in Jerusalem, Israel, West Bank, and Jordan, whether they be residents, visitors, or pilgrims. This includes a full program of worship, fellowship, and educational activities for a broad constituency of some 500 people. About 300 have regular contact with the church and 80% of these attend church regularly. Weekly Bible studies attract 40 to 50 people. An annual series of concerts has made the church well-known in musical circles. The work is subsidized, and pastors are supplied by the *Evangelical Church in Germany (EKD).

Redeemer also serves as the headquarters for the Evangelical Lutheran Church in Jordan and the worship place for its Jerusalem congregation. Until 1978, the dean of Redeemer served as the spiritual leader of the ELCJ.

An independent English-speaking congregation, with pastors supplied by the Lutheran Church in America (now *ELCA), is the third group using Redeemer for worship and other congregational activities. The pastor heads the ELCA's Middle East program, which includes service to pilgrims, tourists, students, and residents of the area and which provides a professor for the Birzeit University.

The pastor of the Danish Israel Mission (located in Jerusalem, Israel) conducts services twice a month in Redeemer's restored Crusaders' chapel (see above, Israel).

EVANGELICAL LUTHERAN CHURCH IN JORDAN (ELCJ)

Member: LWF (1974), MECC
Membership: 1650**
Bishop: The Very Rev. Naim Moussa Nassar
PO Box 14076
Jerusalem—Old City

The ELCJ, constituted in 1959, consists of six congregations. Located in East Jerusalem—the Old City—and in nearby Bethlehem, Beit Jala, Beit Sahour, and Ramallah in the West Bank, and also in Amman in *Jordan, they are served by five pastors and one evangelist. In 1978, a Palestinian, the Rev. David Haddad, was consecrated bishop. He was succeeded by the present bishop in 1986. The bishop chairs the church council and, with the assistance of the synod president, supervises administration. The pastors of the ELCJ have had their education in Europe or North America or, more recently, in the Near East School of Theology, Beirut, *Lebanon—an institution that partners of the ELCJ help to support.

The wars and unrest of recent years in this area have taken a heavy toll: During the last 30 years, almost 60% of the ELCJ membership—especially the young—have emigrated to other Arab countries, but also and especially to the USA. Some of the remaining members lost their homes without compensation. The church feels a responsibility for its members living in other countries. In Amman, *Jordan, a young congregation is endeavoring to draw the scattered members together and to strengthen the Christian presence there. On the home front, members are strengthened in their spiritual life by Bible studies, churchwide family retreats, youth conferences, and seminars in leadership.

The congregations comprising the ELCJ are the fruit of German mission agencies that had founded homes and schools for children during the second half of the 19th and the early 20th century while the Ottoman Empire controlled the land. Many of the graduates of these schools have been loyal members of the church and strong advocates of the importance of Christian schools in a Muslim-dominated country. With a public educational curriculum that promotes Islam, the church has no other alternative for survival. Muslim children attending Christian schools seldom convert to Christianity. However, their acquired understanding of and tolerance toward Christians and the Christian faith are important by-products.

The ELCJ's extensive educational system has an enrollment of about 2200. The decreasing ELCJ membership has lowered the number of Lutheran children from 18% in 1977 to 10% in 1983. Muslims have remained constant at 18%. The rest are mainly Orthodox.

Beit Sahour school, founded in 1901, now serves 10% of the town's children and is the only school that managed to stay open during World War II. The Bethlehem school has grown dramatically since 1980, and there is strong community pressure to keep it open in spite of financial difficulties. The Beit Jala congregation has no school but provides a boarding house for boys who are either orphans or come from needy Christian homes or areas that are overwhelmingly Muslim. Some of the boys are Muslim. This boarding house is a link with the former Schneller school in Jerusalem that had to leave this area in 1948 (above). The boys attend the nearby Bethlehem school or the equally nearby Talitha Kumi secondary school (below). When the Jerusalem congregation was formed in 1909, a mission school was already serving the children. Closed during World War II, it was reopened in 1948. All three of these schools—Beit Sahour, Bethlehem, and Jerusalem—have kindergartens as well as the nine grades required by Jordan. The Jordanian curriculum—still in effect in Arab communities in the West Bank—helps children maintain their identity.

The Ramallah congregation developed its own school, largely through the efforts of Pastor Nijim, who died suddenly in 1984. Beginning in 1965 with a kindergarten in the new church basement, the school grew—a grade at a time—to be a secondary school with high standards, with an adequate building (made possible by the Church of Sweden), and with an active parent council.

Another secondary school, Talitha Kumi, is a part of the ELCJ school system but is supported and administered by the Berlin Mission. Founded in 1855 by German deaconesses who came to Jerusalem with Theodor Fliedner, Talitha Kumi has been for girls what the Schneller school has been for boys.

Talitha Kumi (meaning: "Young maiden, I say arise.") has helped to raise the status of women in Palestine. Today, on a spacious campus in Beit Jala—east of Jerusalem—it accommodates both boys and girls in modern classrooms and dormitories built recently by German contributors according to their specifications.

Understandably, the ELCJ cannot on its own support such a large inherited educational program. Partner churches as well as the LWF have been deeply concerned over rising prices and diminishing income. Efforts have and will continue to be made for a more equitable sharing of the costs between the ELCJ, the parents of the children, and the partner churches. Already in 1977, the latter formed the Coordination Committee of Overseas Partners of the ELCJ (COCOP) in an effort to be more helpful to the ELCJ. COCOP includes the Church of Sweden Mission, the Finnish Evangelical Lutheran Mission, the Division of World Mission of the Evangelical Church in Germany (EKD), and the United Evangelical Lutheran Church of Germany. The Division for World Mission and Ecumenism of the Lutheran Church in America (now ELCA) and the Norwegian Church Ministry to Israel (formerly Norwegian Mission to Israel) are affiliated members with voice but no vote. COCOP symbolizes the shared concern of Lutherans worldwide for the followers of Jesus Christ in the land of his earthly ministry.

Aida Haddad, Jerusalem, was elected an LWF vice-president in July 1987 by the Federation's Executive Committee (Viborg, Denmark). She is librarian at Birzeit University, Ramallah, and wife of emeritus Bishop Haddad. She filled the vacancy created by the interim election of Bishop Hanselmann to the LWF presidency as successor to the late Bishop Káldy. Ms. Haddad's presence gives voice to the concerns of Christians in Asia and especially in the Bible Lands.

JORDAN

A constitutional monarchy, bounded by Syria, Iraq, Saudi Arabia, and Israel. Area (including some 5440 sq. km.—2100 sq. mi.—occupied by Israel in the June 1967 war): 94,946 sq. km. (36,659 sq. mi.). Pop. (excluding Israeli-occupied West Bank, 1986 est.): 2,749,000. Cap. and largest city: Amman (pop., 1979 census, 648,587). Language: Arabic.

History: The story of Jordan west of the Jordan River—today's *Jerusalem (Old City) and West Bank—is part of the history of Palestine (above). The region to the east, known in Bible times as Amman, Bashan, Edom, and Moab, is mostly on the Arabian plateau. From the Syrian Desert in the northeast to the Gulf of Aqaba in the south, this land of stony beauty is sparsely populated.

In the eras of Greece and Rome, the region came successively under Seleucid (Greco-Syrian), Nabatean (Petra-based), and Roman (Province of Arabia) rule. Cities like Jerash and Amman (Philadelphia) recall the Greek era in their ancient ruins. Petra, the capital of the Nabatean trading empire that linked the Persian Gulf to the Mediterranean, early had a Christian community. The larger story behind its rock-hewn monuments has been devulged only in modern times. As Jordan lay exposed to change, so the Muslim Arab conquest in the seventh century swept the country into the world of Islam. There it has remained, except for the interval under the European Crusaders' Kingdom of Jerusalem (12th and 13th centuries). The Muslim hold continued under Turkish rule (1516–1918), when the region was part of the Ottoman empire. The British mandate over Palestine (1919–1946), included a separately administered region known as Transjordan, and its strategic value emerged in a new context.

Independence, coming in the wake of World War II, made it the Hashemite Kingdom of Jordan (1946) and simply Jordan (1949) after its acquisition of the West Bank and East Jerusalem. This occurred according to the approved partitioning of Palestine by which, under United Nations vote, the state of Israel was recognized. Yet the outcome was at the cost of the first Arab-Israeli war. While Palestine ceased as a geographic term, it continued to denote the Palestinian people, some 400,000 of whom were refugees in Jordan.

Jordan's relations with its Arab neighbors were complicated by the presence of the new state of Israel. Jordan's northern border was troubled by Syrian designs, particularly after Syria and Egypt formed the United Arab Republic (1958–1961). The second Arab-Israeli war (June 1967) lost Jordan the West Bank and East Jerusalem. Along with the wave of refugees into Jordan came also political forces, most prominent of which was the Palestine Liberation Organization (PLO). Ousted from Jordan after a brief but bloody civil war (1970), the PLO and related factions moved to *Lebanon.

Under King Hussein I (1953–) Jordan has followed a cautious middle course. It remained relatively apart from the third Arab-Israeli war of 1973–1974. Jordan's periodic peace proposals have raised hopes but found little success. In 1984, Jordan was the first among Arab nations to restore official ties with Egypt, and a year later professed readiness to negotiate—in company with other concerned nations—over the future of the West Bank.

Jordan's economy, never strong, had to cope with two basic handicaps. One was water; the other was oil. Jordan is not an oil-producing country. Yet, by the early 1980s, an estimated 320,000 Jordanians were employed in oil-rich countries. But as the oil boom kept on receding in 1985 remittances from Jordanians abroad were falling off, leaving the country ill-prepared for a return of large numbers of its own people.

Religion: The great majority of Jordan's 93% Muslim population are traditional Sunnis, with some fundamentalist Shiites residing near the Syrian border. In that region are also the country's Circassian and Kurd minority.

Among the estimated 100,000 Christians, the Greek and other Orthodox number about 43%; Roman Catholics 39%; Protestants 6%; and Anglicans 4%. Formerly, these constituencies depended administratively and otherwise on Jerusalem, but difficulties in travel have thrown Jordanian Christians largely on their own. Interdenominational and ecumenical concerns and services are entrusted to the Middle East Council of Churches (MECC).

Among the communions, the Greek Orthodox Diocese of Amman is over 90% Palestinian Arab. The Roman Catholic adherents are divided between the Archdiocese of Petra and Philadelphia (Amman) for the Melkite followers of the Eastern Rite and the Roman Patriarch of Jerusalem for the Palestinians. The Anglicans are part of the Episcopal Diocese of Jerusalem. Like the Orthodox and Roman Catholic, the Episcopal church has its own system of canon law and ecclesiastical courts. In this capacity, it is the one church body recognized by the Jordanian government to act in legal matters also in behalf of other Protestants.

Today, the Greek, Syrian, and Armenian Orthodox, as well as the Episcopalians (Anglicans) and the Lutherans are members of the Middle East Council of Churches (above).

Lutheran involvement in Jordan, while slight in numbers, has been significant in service. Three areas deserve attention.

The LWF World Service program among the Palestinian Arab refugees in Jordan proper was an early extension of the service begun on the *West Bank in 1948. Among the several non-governmental organizations (NGOs) operating under the auspices of UNRWA (United Nations Relief and Works Agency for Palestinian Refugees in the Near East), the LWF program in the Near East soon became the largest single program in that area. From Jordan, it extended into Syria. Ably led by the American Joseph Thompson (ALC), it became a model of humanitarian service and demonstrated an authentic partnership between Christians and Muslims as well as between Christians of various communions.

When the tide of refugees rose sharply after the Arab-Israeli war of June 1967, the LWF program in Jordan expanded rapidly. With the West Bank placed under Israeli governance, a separate structure for the LWF setup in Jordan became necessary. Of the six quickly organized refugee camps, the Bakaa camp was the largest (c.40,000). Besides the basic needs supplied by UNRWA, the LWF work included clinics and health care as well as agricultural projects and various other community services. An LWF-aided village development program included irrigation, road building, and training in trades and crafts.

As on the West Bank cooperation between governmental and voluntary programs was essential. The government of Jordan, faced with this vast influx, granted citizenship to the Palestinian Arabs. A university was founded in Amman (1967), and some years later another was opened at Zarqa. The University Hospital in Amman soon set standards for medical and health care. LWF work carried through until 1977.

The Theodor Schneller School in Jordan—like its counterpart in *Lebanon—is a continuation of the Schneller-founded Syrian Orphanage in Jerusalem (*Palestine). Located in Marka—five kilometers beyond the airport on the highway between Amman and Zarqa, Jordan's second largest city—the school was dedicated in November 1966. The presence of King Hussein on that occasion affirmed the old friendship between the royal house and the Schnellers. The two grandsons of the founder, Hermann and Ernst, were leading the work in Lebanon and Jordan.

The venture in Amman originated with former students at "Schnellers" in Jerusalem, some of whom had been living in Jordan since the 1920s. The dispossession of the Schneller institutions in the new state of Israel gave the matter urgency. Not only should the new project continue the trade school tradition but also the presence of a Christian congregation. Besides local support, most of the funding came from friends of the Schneller mission in Germany, Switzerland, America, and elsewhere.

The 56 hectare (140 acre) campus comprises a complex of native stone structures. The massive main building, with its lofty Christ Church, houses classrooms, offices, dining hall, and recreation rooms as well as living quarters for some 200 students. Adjoining are the workshops and other facilities, including those for the agricultural program. Also on campus are staff residences and dwellings for a limited number of families from town who wish to be part of the institutional congregation.

Ironically, in an expanse north of the Schneller campus is the former Marka refugee camp of 20,000. LWF services were extended to Marka's people also. Now the camp is a permanent settlement.

Until recently, the director of the Schneller School has been Lutheran, but an Arab Episcopalian was elected to this position in 1984. Relations with the Episcopalians have long been close, if not always clear. The fact that the Episcopal Diocese of Jerusalem holds title to Schnellers in Amman is a case in point. Through that church body's ecclesial court (above) the Schneller school could be incorporated as a "Waqf," a perpetual charitable foundation. The Evangelical Lutheran Church in Jordan, having been constituted only in 1959 and lacking a comparable legal capability, nevertheless serves the spiritual needs of the Schneller institutional congregation.

EVANGELICAL LUTHERAN CONGREGATIONS IN AMMAN

(ELCJ; above)
Amman Congregation
Pastor: The Rev. Numan Smir
PO Box 950 370
Amman

In response to persistent requests for pastoral care from Lutherans living in Jordan, the ELCJ sent a pastor and his family to Amman in 1979. Together, they gathered some 40 families from many walks in life and organized a congregation. Most of the participants—professional and business people and their families—had been active members of ELCJ congregations in Jerusalem and the neighboring cities until the 1967 Arab-Israeli war forced them to leave their homes and begin a new life in Amman. Rented quarters served as a parsonage with a large room for worship and congregational activities.

The congregation's outreach is threefold. Its basic concern is for the Christian Arabs of Lutheran connection—Palestinians as well as Jordanians. It shares its pastor with the Schneller School congregation for regular Sunday services and for membership on the school's local board. It also serves the expatriate community, providing English and German worship services on festive occasions.

Fellowship with other evangelical churches is strengthened by monthly pastoral conferences, joint youth meetings, and evangelistic programs. Opportunities for Christian–Muslim dialog occur especially at times of bereavement—when Christians can share the consolation of the gospel with their sorrowing Muslim friends. From the time of LWF service among refugees, Muslim esteem for Lutherans has grown. One Muslim, for example, recently donated a piece of land in the Jordan valley for the work of the congregation in Amman.

The congregation's members and pastor are aware of the many opportunities for Christian service in Amman. Although there is a high percentage of young people, including

14,000 university students, there is no Christian center for them. A constant flow of uprooted Palestinians in and out of Amman are in need of understanding and assistance. The fast growing western section of the city, which embraces the university and the Hussein Medical Center, is without a Christian church. In view of these factors, the ELCJ, on behalf of the Amman congregation, requested the LWF Department of Church Cooperation for funds to help in the purchase of land for a church center.

Before making a decision on this request, the LWF/DCC held a workshop (1983) in Amman to assess the situation from the ecumenical as well as the Lutheran point of view. The LWF workshop participants confirmed the strategic importance and urgency of the Amman proposal. With the help of the Church of Sweden Mission and the Finnish Evangelical Lutheran Mission, and with the local congregation's promise to contribute J.D. 10,000 (US $27,000), a piece of property was purchased and building plans made. In August 1987, the new church was dedicated. Thus, this Amman congregation may be a great help in preventing the constant loss of members who must leave their homes in East Jerusalem or the West Bank for a fresh start in Amman.

LEBANON

A republic (1944) in the Middle East fronting on the Mediterranean. Syria borders it on the north and east, and Israel on the south. Area: 10,230 sq. km. (3950 sq. mi.). Pop. (1986 est.): 2,707,000. Cap. and largest city: Beirut (metro. pop., 1986 est., 1,500,000). Language: Arabic.

Political and religious history: Over 3500 years ago, this coastal region was home to the Phoenicians, a Canaanite people who founded the storied Tyre and Sidon, who provided the precious cedar and minerals for neighboring lands, and who established a commercial maritime empire. These resources were the envy of successive dominant powers: Persian, Greek, and Roman (64 B.C.). Here, Christianity early took root. In the wake of subsequent theological controversy, the Lebanese became Maronites—a version of Christianity that arose in Syria in

the 5th century and adhered to monothelitism (that Christ had but one will, yet two natures). The monks leading this movement and their followers withstood the expansion of Islam in the seventh century by withdrawing into mountainous Lebanon. There the movement grew. As a surviving Christian community, they linked up with the 12th-century Crusaders, and in 1182, some 40,000 of them submitted to the Bishop of Rome. About the same time, Arab Druses were settling in the southern mountains. An offshoot of Islam, they followed Hakim, the sixth Fatimite caliph who in the 11th century declared himself God. Although small in number, this secretive sect remained cohesive by insisting on its distinctiveness.

After a period under the Mamelukes of Egypt and an invasion by the Mongols, the Lebanese came under Turkish rule in 1516 and remained part of the Empire's province of Syria until 1917. During this period, the Lebanese had considerable autonomy and powerful families ruled the country. Both Maronites and Druses were granted virtual self-government. This attracted a variety of Eastern Christians, including the Armenians and 19th-century Protestant missionaries, to Lebanon. Americans were among the early arrivals. Congregationalists, finding little promise in Jerusalem, moved to Beirut (1823). Presbyterians soon followed. They founded the American University in Beirut, a continuing influence.

The scene changed drastically in 1860. With Turkish authorities looking on, the Druses—resenting Christian growth and power—murdered many thousands of Maronites. This led to the intervention of the French, and the Ottoman Sultan was forced to appoint a Christian governor for Lebanon. Following the massacre, British, German, and American relief efforts developed into permanent work, including the Syrian Orphanage in Jerusalem, Palestine. French influence continued to grow, and Lebanon and Syria became known as the Levant States.

After the Turkish defeat in World War I, the mandate to govern them was awarded to France by the League of Nations and the area was called Greater Lebanon. In 1920, the predominantly Christian Lebanon was enlarged by the surrounding Muslim areas. Since these communities were internally autonomous, the prevailing system continued.

The structure of a national government was based on religion not geography. The constitution of 1943 provided that the president be a Christian, the prime minister a Muslim, and the head of the military a Druse. The national parliament and government offices were divided according to the relative strength of the religious groups. This gave the Christians six seats in parliament to every five assigned to Muslims and Druses. Independence, in 1943, favored the Christians.

By the early 1970s, there was considerable dissatisfaction with this balance of power—not unrelated to the rise of *Israel. Beginning during the first Arab-Israeli War in 1948, thousands of Palestinians—mainly Muslims—emigrated to Lebanon. Some were integrated into Lebanese society, but the majority gathered in refugee camps administered by the United Nations Relief and Works Agency for Palestinian Refugees in the Near East (UNRWA). By 1968, there were 15 of these camps, most of them near the coastal cities of Tripoli, Beirut, Sidon, and Tyre. Here discontent grew, fostered by the Palestine Liberation Organization (PLO) driven here from *Jordan.

Civil war broke out in 1975. Syria entered the war on the side of the Christians, and Israel supported a Christian faction known as the Phalange. In an attempt to stop the fighting, the Arab League established an international Arab Deterrent Force with Syria as the major partner. Syria thus shifted sides. The Civil War triggered a large scale emigration of Christians—some 500,000 in the next five years. After the war, a strong central government did not emerge. Rather, the power was in the hands of local political leaders and their militia, the Syrians, and the Palestinians. In the south, former Lebanese army major, Saad Haddad, established a zone of control with Israel's support. A United Nations peacekeeping force was set up to separate the Palestinians and Israelis in southern Lebanon. Israel's invasion in 1982 was followed by a series of tragedies: the assassination of president-elect Bashir Gemayel; the massacre of 2000 Palestinians of all ages by the Phalange; continuous fighting between Lebanese; and terrorist attacks on peacekeeping forces. Despite thousands of dead and wounded, a devastated country, and the departure of foreign troops—there was still no peace.

During this period, the resources of UNRWA were strained, and the assistance of nongovernmental organizations (NGOs) was necessary. Among these NGOs was the World Council of Churches, and for a time also the LWF. During the past dozen years, the civil conflict and then the prolonged Israeli occupation have drawn a new combination of relief agencies into the picture. Among them is the Middle East Council of Churches (above). Through it, as the on-site coordinating agency, assistance has come through various European and North American channels—which also conveyed substantial Lutheran contributions.

Although there is no separately organized Lutheran church in Lebanon, five different ventures are noteworthy:

The *Near East School of Theology* (NEST) in Beirut is the official training center for the Evangelical Lutheran Church in *Jordan and is supported by its partners in COCOP (Coordination Committee of Overseas Partners of the ELCJ). Founded in 1873 as a seminary of the American Board (Congregational), NEST has gone through several consolidations. Now owned by the Union of Armenian Evangelical Churches and supported also by various church agencies abroad, NEST is a noteworthy cooperative effort. There is Lutheran representation on the board, the faculty, and the student body.

The German-speaking *Evangelical Congregation in Beirut* (PO Box 4018, Ras-Beirut) traces its beginnings to 1860 and the relief and medical work carried out among victims of the massacre of Christians in the interior (above).

The *Middle East Lutheran Ministry* (MELM; PO Box 2496, Beirut), is a branch of the Lutheran Hour and draws support from the International Lutheran Laymen's League of the Lutheran Church–Missouri Synod. Begun in 1950, MELM continues to prepare weekly programs in Arabic. They are carried over the local government station but are also beamed to a far wider audience via Radio Monte Carlo (TWR) and Radio Cyprus. Bible study courses via correspondence (in Arabic) have been popular and have drawn response even from North Africa. MELM is now staffed totally by Lebanese.

The *Contact and Resource Center* (CRC; PO Box 113-5216, Beirut) was formed in 1977 to help meet the needs of victims of

Lebanon's ongoing violence. Reconciliation dialogs, sponsored by CRC, have brought Muslims and Christians—disabled and able-bodied—together to share their hopes for themselves and their country's future. CRC's services include: therapy for the handicapped, drug rehabilitation, career guidance and counseling, a telephone ministry for those in crisis. Director Dennis Hilgendorf, a pastor of the Association of Evangelical Lutheran Churches (now ELCA, *USA), has served in Lebanon for over 20 years and was formerly director of MELM. The staff of more than a dozen nationals is assisted by many volunteers and is fully interconfessional.

The *Johann-Ludwig Schneller School* in Khirbet Kanafar, Bekaa Valley, Lebanon, is one of the institutions that continues the work of the former Syrian Orphanage (Schneller School) in Jerusalem and its extension in Nazareth (*Jordan). The relocation took place in 1948 under the continuing direction of Hermann Schneller, a grandson of the founder.

The modern campus is near Khirbet, a small and mainly Christian village, about 50 kilometers (30 miles) north of the Lebanon-Israel border, and about the same distance south of old Zahle, the Bekaa Valley's main city and way station on the Beirut-Damascus highway. Relocation in this valley has placed the school in the region from which—after the great massacre of 1860—came the orphan boys for whom Johann-Ludwig Schneller had opened his home in Jerusalem (above).

The program of the school in Khirbet continues the time-tested combination of curricular study, vocational training, and Christian instruction and worship. Despite the years of civil strife and Israeli invasion, the school has managed to carry on with a limited program due to the loyal supporters in various parts of the country. In April 1985, the Israeli forces withdrew from this region. For some years, they had also occupied the Schneller School campus. Support for the school continues from Germany and America, but the situation remains precarious.

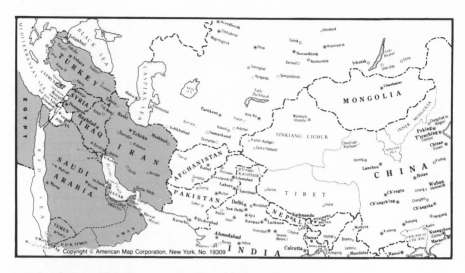

Copyright © American Map Corporation, New York, No. 19309

NEIGHBORING COUNTRIES

The countries included below round out the greater Middle East except for Sudan (see Africa). In none of them are there organized church bodies. However, in outreach and service Lutherans have touched most areas. Besides, a number of these countries have biblical and early church history of significance.

ARABIAN PENINSULA

Saudi Arabia and the seven other Muslim states of the Arabian Peninsula forbid Christian evangelization. Expatriate Christians may form their congregation within limits. Oil interests have brought to these lands many Westerners and Asians, some of whom are Lutheran. Usually they have joined with other Christians to form international congregations. One such in Saudi Arabia grew to a worshiping group of about 600. This was too large. Members divided into groups and continued to worship in their homes.

In Dubai of the United Arab Emirates, a Lutheran congregation of diaspora Christians, mainly from India but also including Sri Lankans, Pakistani, British, and Americans was formed in 1978. This is the result of the work of a concerned member of the *South Andhra Lutheran Church (SALC) in India, a lawyer and lay evangelist, who was stationed in Dubai. Responding to his concerns, the SALC commissioned him—Victor Balamukunda Doss—to be the volunteer lay

pastor. He has since been ordained and continues as part-time pastor of a church that must limit its outreach to unchurched Christians, irrespective of denomination or race.

The Danish Missionary Society (DMS) has successfully established a low-profile outreach that is acceptable to the governments. This includes medical, educational, and literature work. Eight bookshops, registered by the various governments, have been organized into a chain, the Family Bookshop Group (FBG), thus benefiting economically and from shared experiences as well. The FBG is now owned and administered by the Middle East Council of Churches. It is carried on by trained bookdealers who provide friendly shops in the market place. The first DMS Bible reading room was opened in Aden, South Yemen in 1903 at the suggestion of Dr. Samuel Zwemer, the noted American Reformed missionary to the Muslims.

CYPRUS

This country, uneasily independent since 1960, is a strategic island and a vital meeting point of Christians in the Middle East. Of the 658,000 Cypriots, nearly four out of five are Greek Orthodox and speak Greek. Most of the others are Muslim and speak Turkish.

Christianity came to Cyprus during the missionary journeys of Paul and Barnabas; the church became self-governing (autocephalous), with its own patriarch, in the later fifth century. This continuity of Christianity is all the more remarkable in light of the succession of foreign powers occupying Cyprus, including Egypt, Greece, Rome, Byzantium, the Crusaders, France, and Venice. Liberated from the Latin West in 1571, Cyprus remained under Turkish rule until assigned to Britain in 1878 and made a British colony from the 1920s until independence. Torn between forces seeking union (Enosis) with Greece versus others coveting control by Turkey, the federated state—voted by the Turkish minority in 1974—maintains an uneasy calm. A UN peacekeeping force practices a low profile across the divided island.

Ecumenically, early contacts with Anglicans helped bring the Orthodox Church of Cyprus into the Faith and Order movement and then into the World Council of Churches (1948). The (Roman) Catholic Church of Cyprus, linked to the Latin Patriarchate of Jerusalem, includes the island's old Maronite constituency. Similarly, the Anglican Diocese of Cyprus (mainly of British subjects) is part of the Episcopal Church in Jerusalem and the Middle East. A fair number of Armenian Christians began coming to Cyprus in the 12th century and today continue their own diocese. The prolonged strife in *Lebanon as well as tensions in *Israel and the *West Bank have brought growing numbers of Christians as refugees.

For the Middle East Council of Churches (introduction, above), the opportunity to relocate some of its operations from Beirut to Cyprus has been advantageous. In times of limited access to various parts of the Middle East, Cyprus has offered unmatched opportunities for interconnected travel, such as the MECC work requires.

EGYPT

This republic (1953) of the Nile Valley, in Northeast Africa is the largest of the Arab-speaking countries. Its capital, Cairo (pop.,

1983 est., 5,881,000) is the largest city in the Mediterranean region. The country's inhabitants include those descended from ancient Egyptians, as well as Berbers, Bedouins, Arabs, Greeks, Turks, Black Africans, and others. Since the 10th century, Arabic is the common language.

Historically, Egypt is heir to one of the world's great civilizations whose antecedents are traced back over some 7000 years. Besides its own polytheism, Egypt is today best known for its role in the rise and extension of the world's three great religions of monotheism.

For Judaism, the bondage of the children of Israel and their exodus (about the mid-13th century B.C.) makes this experience of deliverance the creative center of the Old Testament. In Alexandria, 1000 years later—during the 3rd century B.C.—the Septuagint translation of the Old Testament into Greek was undertaken for the benefit of Jews living in the diaspora.

For Christianity and the early church, Egypt—and especially Alexandria—remains enormously significant (see Africa Introduction). A direct line leads from that distant day into the present, even though the number of Christians dropped drastically and has remained a minority since the coming of Islam.

For Islam itself, Egypt is the recognized center for Quranic studies and, in the eyes of many, the foremost intellectual center of the Muslim world. At least 80% of the population are Muslim, mainly of the Sunni tradition.

The Christian community, estimated at 7.5 million, is the biggest of any country in the Middle East. Over 90% of the Christians are Coptic Orthodox. Coptic is not an ethnic type but a designation of those descended from Egypt's early Christians in a line unbroken despite 14 centuries of Islam. The Coptic language, although replaced by Arabic long ago as the language of the land, remains the liturgical tongue in the churches and recalls the common speech of pre-Arabic Egypt. Headed by a pope, the church comprises many self-governing dioceses and maintains a theological seminary in Alexandria. Theologically, it is monophysite (one nature) in its Christology. The Coptic Orthodox Church is a charter member of the World Council of Churches and also participates in the Middle East Council of Churches (MECC).

Among the other Christian groups in Egypt are the Greek Orthodox Patriarchate of Alexandria and All Africa whose antecedents (like those of the Copts) go back to New Testament times; the Catholic Church of Egypt; the Episcopal Church (Anglican); and the Coptic Evangelical Church (Presbyterian). Of these bodies, all but the Roman Catholic are members of the MECC and the WCC.

Although there is no separately organized Lutheran church in Egypt, there has long been a German-speaking Evangelical congregation in Cairo and a Swedish Seamen's Mission in Alexandria. The Protestant hospital founded by Theodor Fliedner and the deaconesses in Alexandria in 1858 (*Palestine) has its successor in Cairo, whose Victoria Hospital (1885) has served a widely ranging international clientele.

In recent years, a shared ministry of Lutheran pastors from the *USA (one former ALC and one former LCA) has been serving in two community churches in the national capital: St. Andrew's (Church of Scotland) in Cairo, and the Heliopolis Community Church of St. Michael and All Angels (Episcopal) in Heliopolis. This involvement also links into the programs of the Coptic Evangelical Organization for Social Services. The LCA (now ELCA) cultivates ties with the Coptic Orthodox Church as well as with the Coptic Evangelical Seminary, and—through the LWF—with the MECC.

The Lutheran Orient Mission (USA), once active among the Kurds in *Iran and *Iraq, now maintains a small station in Cairo.

For the Christian community as a whole, it is a great benefit to have the American University in Cairo. Like its counterpart in Beirut, *Lebanon, this university—of Presbyterian origin—has been prominent in fostering understanding between the several religious constituencies in Egypt. The same must be said for the long-established YMCA and YWCA as well as other institutions.

IRAN

This Islamic republic, heir to the Persia of old, is about twice the size of its western neighbor, Turkey. Iran's 43,000,000 inhabitants are mainly Persian, but include Turk, Kurd, Arab, Armenian, and Assyrian minorities. Iran is integral to the Middle East and is part of the Muslim but not of the Arab world. Its official language is Farsi. The discovery of Iran's vast oil resources early in the present century and their subsequent development has drawn the country deeply into the modern world economy. By way of reaction, a resurgent Islam—Shiite fundamentalist in character—has sought to reverse the tide of Westernization. In the pivotal year 1979, the Shah was forced out and the Ayatollah Ruholla Khomeini took over. The full-scale war that erupted between Iran and *Iraq in 1980—over the long-disputed access waterway to the Persian Gulf—continued into 1988.

The three largest Christian communities total about 250,000, of whom about 80% are Armenian. The rest divide almost equally between the Assyrian or Ancient Church of the East (Nestorian) and the Catholic Church in Iran (a combination of mainly Nestorian and some Armenian Christians). The Nestorian (Chaldean) Church—with a missionary outreach that in the distant past had reached even to *China—had initially attracted American Congregationalists and Presbyterians (1834). They anticipated that a revitalized Nestorian Church would help to effect the evangelization of all Asia. Anglicans, too, sought to enliven the Chaldean household of faith. But these efforts succeeded mainly in forming separate entities. Three of these churches, with a combined membership of less than 10,000, formed the Iran Council of Churches in 1951. The largest Protestant church, the Evangelical (Presbyterian) Church in Iran, is a member of the MECC.

For Lutherans, Iran is a largely obscure yet pointed example of Christian service to expatriates as well as to a minority group, the Kurds. The German congregation in Tehran has been serving German-speaking expatriates of various backgrounds since 1930. An American Lutheran congregation (1970–1979) did the same for English-speaking expatriates.

The Lutheran Orient Mission (LOM) began work among the Kurds in Iran in September 1911 with a staff of three: Ludvig Olsen Fossum (1879–1920), pastor in the then Norwegian Lutheran Church in America; and a medical doctor, E. Edmund, and his wife. In 1906, Fossum, responding to the pleas of an Armenian pastor soliciting support among Norse Americans, began his service of three years as educational missionary within the somnolent Nestorian Church. Yet his judgment, corroborated by visiting mission professor, M. O. Wee, was that the real challenge in Iran lay with the Kurds. This was reinforced when the World Missionary Conference, meeting in Edinburgh in 1910, challenged American Lutherans to undertake hitherto delayed work among the Kurds. With Fossum as the chief promotor, Norwegian Americans formed the LOM the same year.

By comity agreement, the LOM located in Soujbulak, a town south of Urmia (today Rezaiyeh, capital of Iran's West Azerbaijan province), where there were also some Nestorian Christians.

While Dr. Edmund set up a health clinic, Fossum perfected his command of Kurdish. To the north lay the mountainous reaches of Kurdistan, a land of fiercely independent yet periodically conquered and politically separated people. Their Islam, in the Sunni tradition, seemed impervious to change. As one who sensed that time was short, Fossum compiled an English-Kurdish grammar that would help his coworkers and others. For literate Kurds, he translated the gospels, scores of hymns, and Luther's Catechism. He also wrote religious tracts. By 1916, at the age of 37, he had laid significant groundwork.

During World War I, the plight of the Armenians fleeing Turkish retaliation for their alleged pro-Western position, drew Fossum into the American Red Cross in Armenia (1916–1919), and then into the post of district commander of the massive Near East Relief Program (1919–1920). His efforts to mediate a dispute between rival factions—at a point high in the slopes of Mount Ararat—proved physically exhausting. He died in Erivan (Yerevan) in October 1920 and lies buried in the capital city of Soviet Armenia, USSR.

The LOM sent out new staff in 1921 but soon lost its director, a victim of mistaken identity in the fighting between Muslim Kurds and Nestorian Christians. In 1924, an LOM staff of five missionaries resumed work in Soujbulak. The All-Persia Intermission Conference in 1926 emphasized the importance of the LOM work; and the centennial (1934) account of Protestantism in Iran commended the LOM's presence. However, on government request, the LOM pulled out of Soujbulak (in 1938) and moved to *Iraq.

After World War II, the LOM again undertook to serve in Iran while still maintaining its work in Iraq. Its medical services in Ghorveh, Kurdistan, begun there in 1962, grew into a 46-bed hospital with three physician-surgeons on the staff. During the 1960s and 1970s, the Kurdish struggle for freedom placed the LOM work in jeopardy, and it was pressured to withdraw from Iran in 1980. The work was left in local hands, but without the needed indigenous support. (See Egypt and Iraq.)

IRAQ

A Socialist republic since 1958, this Arab country, rich in oil, is the storied Mesopotamia of antiquity and the seat of Assyrian, Babylonian, and earlier civilizations. Embracing the Tigris and Euphrates valleys northward into Kurdistan, its area is less than one-third that of neighboring *Iran, while its population of 15,000,000 is just over one-third that of Iran. From 1980–1988 Iraq was in a bitter war against Iran.

Historically, religion has given Mesopotamia peculiar significance since Bible times. Abraham was called by God from the city of Ur on the Euphrates and (via Egypt) his descendants entered the Promised Land (*Palestine). Seven centuries later (586–538 B.C.), the Babylonian captivity cut deeply into Israel's life and also hastened the dispersion of Jews throughout the East. Christianity was to benefit from this dispersion, even as it took root early in Mesopotamian cities. These and other places became centers of a strong Nestorian Church whose missionary thrusts spread the faith as far as *China and as relatively near as the Malabar Coast of *India. The near fatal blow to Nestorian Christianity (Chaldean, when related to Rome) came not with the Muslim advance in the seventh century, but with the ruthless Mongol invasions of the 13th. For Islam, Baghdad was for five centuries (from its founding in A.D. 762 to its destruction by the Mongols in 1258), the base of the Abbasid caliphate and one of the great cities of the Muslim world. For good reason, then, Iraq is important today for what it was as well as for what it is.

Over 95% of Iraq's population is Muslim, with about two-thirds of them Shiite. Christianity accounts for a little over 3% of the total. Nearly three-quarters of the Christians are in the Catholic Church of Iraq, and are of Chaldean (Nestorian) background. The affiliation with Rome developed in the 16th century. Among the other bodies, the Apostolic Catholic Assyrian Church of the East (its adherents are spread in several countries, including the USA) is in communion with the Anglican Church and is also a member of the World Council of Churches (since 1948).

There is no longer a Lutheran presence in Iraq, but the Lutheran Orient Mission (LOM) carried on its modest work in Arbil (also Irbil, the ancient Arbela) and other places in Kurdistan for two decades. Having to close its work among the Kurds in *Iran in 1938, the LOM moved westward into Iraq. In Arbil, due east from Mosul (close to ancient Nineveh) and the oil fields, the LOM opened a reading room and then gradually extended its work. From 1953 to 1958, the LOM was actively represented by four missionary families. When unrest began brewing again among the Kurds, expatriate missionaries were required to leave Iraq in 1958. The LOM program was left in the care of Sadiq Shammi, an Arab evangelist, and his wife, both first generation Christians. They continued this work until 1977 when the LOM resumed its ministry of healing in Iran (above).

SYRIA

In this mostly Muslim country, Christians number less than 10% of Syria's approximately 10,000,000 inhabitants. Located over an area of 185,000 sq. km. (71,498 sq. mi.) that touches the northeast Mediterranean between *Lebanon and *Turkey, modern Syria became a fully independent republic in 1944. On its territory are many sites recalling the early spread of Christianity, notably Antioch (now Antakya) where "the disciples were for the first time called Christians" (Acts 11:26). For the church worldwide, the role of Syria, as one of the Bible Lands, retains great importance for Jews and Christians as well as for Muslims.

Four major churches in Syria account for most of the nation's Christians. The two oldest—the Greek Orthodox Patriarchate of Antioch and All the East, and the Syrian Orthodox Patriarchate of Antioch—claim ca.

A.D. 30 for their founding. The Catholic Church in Syria (A.D. 295) and the Armenian Apostolic Church (Cilicia; 1440) preserve their respective traditions. The Greek and the Syrian Orthodox, along with four smaller church bodies (Episcopal and Evangelical) are members of the Middle East Council of Churches (MECC) and most of them are also in the WCC. The Greek Orthodox Patriarch, Ignatios IV, was elected to the WCC presidium in 1983.

With no separately organized church of their own in Syria, Lutherans nevertheless have at least three noteworthy links with this land. On the academic side, the first and long standard work on the history of Antioch was published in 1839 by the Göttingen orientalist, Karl Otfried Müller (1797–1840). Other Lutheran scholars have contributed further. In recent years, the recognized authority on the Syriac New Testament and on the role of Syrian Christianity was Arthur Vööbus (d. 1988), Lutheran School of Theology at Chicago (*Turkey).

On the evangelizing side, the Danish Mission to the Orient (DMO; see also Pakistan, as well as the Arabian Peninsula, above) came to Syria in 1898. Unable to work in Damascus, the DMO unfolded its work in an area some 80 kilometers (50 miles) northeast of the city. At the peak of its work in the 1930s, the DMO had a staff of 17 in the field, some of whom had been there for three decades. The German occupation of Denmark during World War II deprived the Syrian work of outside support. Developments on the scene led to a consolidation of the Lutheran, Reformed, and Presbyterian constituencies into today's National Evangelical Synod of Syria and Lebanon (NES/SL). The NES/SL is active in the MECC and, since 1948, in the WCC. Emigration has reduced its membership.

On the humanitarian side, the LWF World Service assistance to Palestinian refugees (*West Bank, *Jordan) was invited to follow the large numbers who had fled as far as Syria after 1949. For a time, some of the largest refugee camps were in Syria. The "Luthery" program, in local parlance, was based in Damascus. It operated under UN auspices and with Syrian government sanction. An international and Syrian staff of Christians and Muslims provided health services, community development in the camps, feeding programs in the schools, and eventually also scholarship grants. An already existing nurses' training school in Homs took on new character. The nurses from Finland proved especially durable under difficult circumstances, and the Arab doctors and other staff members showed exceptional resourcefulness. The first LWF director of the overall refugee program, Chris Christiansen of Denmark, received a high award from the Syrian government. The Syrian program director, Victor Bannayan, was the deputy to Amman-based Joseph Thompson (*Jordan), who brought it to a conclusion in 1977. For some years thereafter, it is said, Syrian co-workers continued to meet and recall their "Luthery" experience.

TURKEY

A republic since 1923 and heir of the once vast Ottoman Empire, Turkey occupies historic Asia Minor and a patch of Southeastern Europe, where Istanbul (the former Constantinople) stands at the crossroads of forces ancient and modern. On its territory (779,452 sq. km. or about 300,000 sq. mi.) live nearly 49,000,000 people. Of these about 99% are said to be Muslim, although the modernization espoused in the 1920s has advanced secularism perhaps further than elsewhere in Islam. Besides, the Christian minority was drastically reduced in 1923 by the relocation of 1,500,000 Greeks to Greece, while some 800,000 Turks were repatriated from Bulgaria, Greece, and elsewhere.

Today's tiny Christian remnants total less than 1% of the population: 0.3% Greek Orthodox, 0.1% Roman Catholic, 0.4% various Protestants and others. The Ecumenical Patriarchate of Constantinople, begun in A.D. 330 by the Emperor Constantine, claims some 65,000 members within Turkey, of whom about 30,000 are in Istanbul. Headquarters are in the Fener (Greek district), just south of the Golden Horn. Besides the archdiocese, the patriarchate includes three dioceses in the western region.

The importance of the patriarchate for the rise of the ecumenical movement, for the participation of the Greek Orthodox Churches in the World Council of Churches, and for the advancement of bilateral dialogs—not least between Lutherans and Orthodox—is

not to be overlooked. From overtures by *Sweden's Archbishop Nathan Söderblom to the Patriarch during World War I to the repeated visits by Lutheran church leaders in recent years, the concern for sharing more fully in a common legacy of faith has been growing.

The Roman Catholic constituency in Turkey, though small, is a reminder of the centuries-long efforts to bring scattered Eastern and Oriental churches under one allegiance. Armenian Christians, however, still maintain their own patriarchate in Istanbul. There are also several Bulgarian, Serbian, and other small Orthodox groups. Among the Protestants, the Congregationalists (American Board) are the most numerous, reminiscent of the Ottoman days when Robert College, the Girls (Kudz) College, and other schools played a part in ushering in a new era.

Today, the Evangelical (Lutheran) German Church in Istanbul also recalls a pioneering past. Formed in 1843 by traveling apprentices and others working in Constantinople, they saw their congregation also as an aid station for itinerant workers. In 1850, a school was opened, and 11 years later a church building was erected. Located in a modest part of the once New City, between the Golden Horn and the Bosporus, the congregation has a membership of about 200 families. Yet that number includes members also in other parts of the country. The pastor—recently Heinz Klautke—has an extensive itinerary that includes Ankara, the capital, as well as other cities. He is also the resident representative of the Evangelical Church in *Germany (EKD) to the ecumenical patriarch in the Fener. Several German schools, maintained for children of Germans resident in the country as well as for Turkish children seeking to learn German, are also on the pastor's beat. Besides, not very far from the church lies the Goethe Institute as well as the German Deaconess Hospital founded by Fliedner (see Bible Lands Introduction) in 1852.

In the region of Mardin, north of the Syrian border among the Syrian Christians, a fund of ancient texts, biblical and other, have unfolded the long forgotten history of ancient Syriac Christianity and its thrust still farther east. They were discovered by the late Arthur Vööbus, an Estonian transplant to the Lutheran School of Theology at Chicago (above, Syria). Akin to the spectacular ruins of the ancient Hittite capital city in Bogazköy, east of Ankara, or the scattered remains of the Seven Churches addressed in the Book of Revelation, Vööbus's finds are moving reminders of historic Asia Minor's muted message of faith to successive generations.

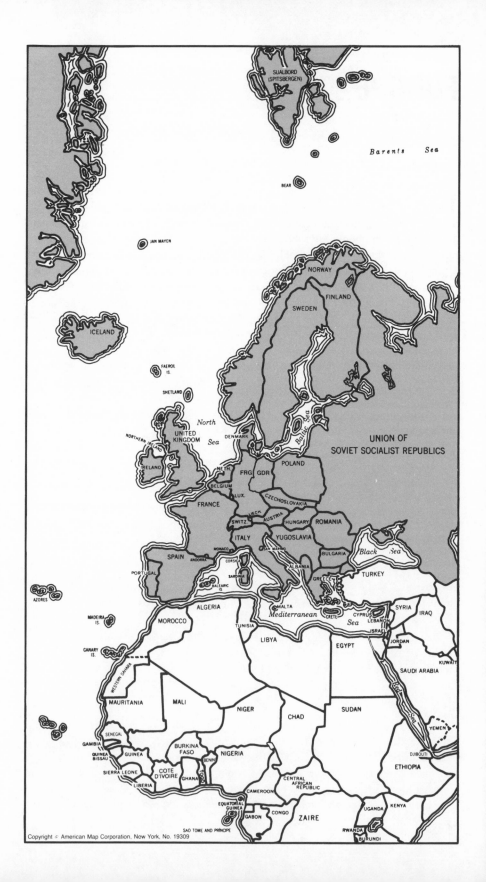

SUALBORD
(SPITSBERGEN)

Barents   Sea

BEAR

JAN MAYEN

ICELAND

FAEROE
IS.

NORWAY

FINLAND

SWEDEN

SHETLAND

*North
Sea*

Baltic Sea

UNION OF
SOVIET SOCIALIST REPUBLICS

NORTHERN IRELAND

UNITED
KINGDOM

DENMARK

IRELAND

NETH.

FRG GDR

POLAND

BELGIUM

LUX.

CZECHOSLOVAKIA

FRANCE

LIECH.

SWITZ.

AUSTRIA

HUNGARY

ROMANIA

ITALY

YUGOSLAVIA

MONACO

SAN MARINO

BULGARIA

Black   Sea

SPAIN

ANDORRA

CORSICA

PORTUGAL

SARDINIA

ALBANIA

GREECE

TURKEY

BALEARIC
IS.

AZORES

MADEIRA
IS.

MOROCCO

ALGERIA

TUNISIA

MALTA

Mediterranean

CRETE

CYPRUS

Sea

LEBANON

SYRIA

IRAQ

ISRAEL

CANARY
IS.

WESTERN SAHARA

LIBYA

EGYPT

JORDAN

KUWAIT

SAUDI ARABIA

MAURITANIA

MALI

NIGER

CHAD

SUDAN

Red Sea

YEMEN

SENEGAL

DJIBOUTI

GAMBIA

BURKINA
FASO

NIGERIA

ETHIOPIA

GUINEA
BISSAU

GUINEA

BENIN

SIERRA LEONE

COTE
D'IVOIRE

GHANA

LIBERIA

CENTRAL
AFRICAN
REPUBLIC

CAMEROON

UGANDA

KENYA

EQUATORIAL
GUINEA

GABON

CONGO

ZAIRE

RWANDA

SAO TOME AND PRINCIPE

BURUNDI

EUROPE_____

Two out of three of the world's approximately 59 million Lutherans are in Europe—the home base of the 16th-century Reformation. Europe's Lutherans, still close to 40 million on the books in 1986, were nearly 10 million fewer than reported the previous year, due to a changed policy in compiling statistics (see Germany). Today's 59-million world total must be a sobering figure when recalling that about 70 years earlier, in 1917, amid wartime conditions, observers of the Reformation's 400th anniversary claimed a total of over 82 million Lutherans worldwide. The stories behind this prolonged decline in membership are many, and are wrapped up in the epic history of this continent during the present century. Confessionally and ecumenically, European Lutheranism—as a map of the continent suggests—is itself amazingly diversified while, at the same time, remarkably at one in its adherence to a spiritual legacy in the gospel. To trace historical developments, read Germany first.

For our purposes this European section falls into four regional groupings, listed alphabetically:

Eastern Europe—Czechoslovakia, Hungary, Poland, Romania, Union of Soviet Socialist Republics, Yugoslavia

Germany—Federal Republic of Germany (West), German Democratic Republic (East)

Northern Europe—Denmark, Faeroe Islands, Finland, Greenland, Iceland, Norway, Sweden

Western and Middle Europe—Austria, Belgium, France, Ireland, Italy, Liechtenstein, the Netherlands, Portugal, Spain, Switzerland, United Kingdom

Area (including European USSR): 10,504,263 sq. km. (4,055,700 sq. mi.). Pop. (1982 est.): 689,500,000. Of Europe's 38 countries, the top 10—USSR, West Germany, United Kingdom, Italy, France, Spain, Poland, Yugoslavia, Romania, East Germany—account for over 60% of the continent's total population.

History

The smallest of the continents (after Australia), yet in population second only to Asia, Europe is paradoxically a world apart and a worldwide influence. Heir to the spiritual legacy of the Bible lands and to the ancient civilizations of Greece and Rome, Europe's diverse peoples have for nearly two millennia brought thought and life, faith and works, and subsequently science, technology, and industry as well as the arts into ever-changing combinations of creativity—and periodic outbreaks of conflict—that have variously benefited and blighted their native lands and the rest of the world.

Descended from westward moving ancestors and inhabiting the western tip of the Eurasian-African "world island," Europe's people have remained on the move. Exploring and circumnavigating the globe, relentless in trade, given to colonization, and tempted to dominate peoples in other continents even as they have dominated each other in national and imperial rivalries, Europeans have shown up everywhere in the human family—white cousins to people of color. Leaving their native lands—in recent centuries by the millions—emigrants have planted adaptations of European civilization especially in the Americas, Australasia, and Southern Africa. From the Arabs, Europeans picked up the slave trade and spun human ties between the Americas and Africa as well as between those continents and their own.

The two world wars of the present century convulsed the continent's old order. With World War I (1914–1918), empires fell. Germany, of the Hohenzollerns, went democratic. Russia, of the Romanovs, went Communist. Austria-Hungary, of the Hapsburgs, broke up into self-determining new nations: Czechoslovakia, Poland, Yugoslavia. Austria was diminished and a truncated Hungary surrendered Transylvania to Romania. The fragmentation did not bode well for the future. The old Ottoman Empire of the Turks had been pushed out of Europe—except for Istanbul and environs—with British and French mandates replacing Turkey's sway over the Middle East (*Bible Lands and Neighboring Countries). International relations entered a new era.

World War II (1939–1945) brought terror and destruction to the home front as perhaps never before, with enormous cost of human life. Mixed motives played in the uprooting of populations. Such, for example, was the harsh resettlement of ethnic Germans (Soviet citizens) in 1941 from the Ukraine to new land east of the Urals. Or, as the war was ending, the headlong expulsion of some 12 million Germans from their generations-old homelands in Eastern Europe and their crowding into a shattered Third Reich. Tens of thousands of refugees from the Baltic countries, "Displaced Persons" by designation, likewise fled to Sweden as well as Germany (see Exile Churches).

Worst of all was the Nazi exploitation of slave labor and network of concentration camps, the context within which the anti-Semitism of the Hitler regime carried out the "Final Solution," the extermination of the Jews. The terrible inhumanity toward fellow humans, rehearsed in the Russian pogroms in the later 19th and early 20th century, reached its horrifying climax in the Holocaust of the war years (see Germany).

As European domination over much of the world showed signs of breaking up after World War I, it went into rapid decline, at least in terms of political empire, after World War II. To some observers the new, nuclear age appeared not only as post-European but also as post-Christian; as a time when secularism had taken over and when, religiously speaking, life was ordered as if God did not exist. Yet a profound quest for community continued.

To its inhabitants, Europe became a divided continent: its Eastern countries under USSR-directed Communism, its Western countries drawn into a prospering European

Economic Community (1958)—counterbalancing the USA, in effect Europe's alter-ego across the Atlantic. Given the alienations of the Cold War and the accelerating race in nuclear and other arms between the two superpowers, European strivings for disarmament and peace gained renewed momentum in the 1980s—particularly in light of the Helsinki Final Act (1975), a product of the Conference on Security and Cooperation in Europe.

Religion

Christianity and the rise of European civilization are inseparable. But the Christian faith, when seen from other parts of the world, is more than Europe's churches have made it. Europe's diversified confessional composition is estimated numerically: Roman Catholic 264 million (40% of the continent's population); Eastern Orthodox 75 million (11.4%); Lutheran 54.6 million (pre-1986 reckoning, 8.3%); Anglican 27 million (4.1%); Reformed/Presbyterian 16 million (2.4%); plus a spectrum of smaller communions. Jews 4.25 million (0.6%). Muslims 2.4 million (0.36%). Europeans claiming no church connection number about 222 million.

A Europeanization of Christianity accompanied the prolonged process of conversion, from the Greeks and Romans in the first century to the Baltic peoples in the 13th. The process firmed the role of the churches (collectively the church) in terms of worship, mission, education, governance, and unity—a divinely entrusted task ever subject to human corruption and distortion.

Given the legacy of close relations between church and state, given fresh application during the 16th-century rise of Protestantism, the religious map of Europe remained remarkably constant until the present century. Today, however, in many cities, majestic cathedrals and impressive churches tend more to be monuments to earlier ages of faith than lively centers of Christian worship. Besides, the established churches of the Reformation era—Lutheran, Reformed/Presbyterian, Anglican—have for generations faced a challenge from Free Churches. Baptist and Methodist developments, especially in Britain, were accelerated, beginning in the 19th century, by missionaries coming from the USA to the European continent and thus laying the basis for a progressive religious pluralism in many parts of Europe.

Accentuating this diversity are the striking changes in Europe's Jewish and Muslim communities. The number of Jews, said to have numbered over 10 million in the year 1900, had fallen to 4.25 million by the mid-1970s, showing the effects of the terrible Holocaust. Yet of the present number, some three million are said to be in European USSR. Conversely, Muslim numbers in the 1980s have been estimated as high as seven million (exclusive of the USSR). Historic territories of Muslim population—Yugoslavia, Bulgaria, Albania, Romania—have been joined by some 2.2 million newcomers to Germany (Turks), France (Northern Africans), United Kingdom (Pakistanis, etc.), the Netherlands (Indonesians, etc.), and elsewhere. A renewed concern for the Jews and the new presence of Muslims challenge the major Christian communions to foster constructive relations with these historic religions of the Book in their own midst.

Church unity under these changing circumstances is fostered, in quite general terms, by several inclusive agencies. Roman Catholics are represented in the Council of European Bishops' Conference (CCEE). The Anglican, Orthodox, and various

Protestant communions participate in the Conference of European Churches (CEC; 1959), headquartered in Geneva. The CEC's credal basis is the same as that of the World Council of Churches (they "confess the Lord Jesus Christ as God and Savior according to the Scriptures"). The CEC includes 118 church bodies, plus one observer church, representing 15 communions (confessions) in 26 countries and four international areas. It seeks to foster church cooperation through assemblies (Nybørg Strand, Denmark, was the first), working groups, study commissions, and publications. The CEC acts as a bridge, 45% of its member churches are in Eastern Europe, 55% in Western Europe. Among its successive presidents, Dr. André Appel (*Church of the Augsburg Confession in Alsace and Lorraine, France) served longest (until 1987), over a decade. CEC concerns include the furtherance of peace and justice (in line with the Helsinki Final Act, above), dialog between the churches, cooperation, and reciprocal relations with churches in other parts of the world. The CEC, as the World Council's largest grouping of churches, thus seeks to complement the aims and tasks of the Council.

Lutheran unity in Europe presupposes the given unity of the church in Jesus Christ. It affirms a faithful adherence to the Word and a proper administration of the sacraments (*Augsburg Confession,* Article VII). This confession—as the 450th anniversary of its signing recalled in 1980—continues to serve as the legal basis of churches, and in many countries the Augsburg designation instead of Lutheran is used to identify a church body. Luther's *Small Catechism* (1529) continues to serve, in scores of European languages and dialects, as a classic explication of the Christian faith. Applied with evangelical freedom, this common confessional basis has produced a richly diversified unity. From the Church of Sweden's High Mass to the simpler ways of worship in many other places, the liturgical forms may vary, but the substance is the same, retaining the basic elements of the Catholic Mass. Mode of church administration may also vary. Most Lutheran churches have bishops, but the apostolic succession of those in Sweden and Finland carries no priority of rank. Not the historic episcopate but a faithful succession in the Word is seen as foremost. Likewise, relations with the state vary. They are closer, for example, in *Denmark than in *Finland; and freer in the filling of church positions in *East Germany than in *Norway, so it is claimed. The voluntary support of the churches— as in the Americas, Africa, and Asia—has still to be worked out in most of Europe, though *East Germany has been obliged to set the example.

Here it suffices to note that unity among Lutherans in Europe has often grown out of the desire to help minorities in need—the scattered islands of fellow believers in the "diaspora," whether on the continent or far away. The story is an old one. Mission societies sent their emissaries not only to peoples in distant continents and of other religions but also to neglected kindred in the faith who had emigrated to North America, Latin America, South Africa, Australasia. Nor did they overlook the needy at home as they founded hospitals and homes, health and welfare services, later taken over or at least partly supported by the government. Church personnel engaged in such services—deaconesses, deacons, pastors, lay workers—repeatedly blazed the trail toward cooperation among the churches on an international and confessional as well as ecumenical basis. Europe's experience with two world wars in this century intensified recourse to and appreciation of such services, not least in the helping of hundreds of thousands of refugees and displaced persons and in finding new homes for them either in Europe itself or in lands overseas.

As the social and material needs of people in most European states have come to be met increasingly by government programs, the desire of Christians to help their fellows has had to be innovative, lest there be a lapse into quietism or passivity. A stimulus to service, as the General Introduction to this volume has noted, has found readiest expression in the free association of churches in the LWF.

More recently, at three points the unitive role of the LWF in the life of European Lutheran churches has come out clearly. The first is that of service to others. Here it helps to see synoptically what recurs in separate accounts below. Danchurchaid in *Denmark, Finnchurchaid in *Finland, Kirkens Nødhjelp in *Norway, and Luth- erhjälpen in *Sweden have shaped the ordinary person's understanding of the LWF and of help going to others, cooperatively, in far places. The same is true of the half-dozen specialized agencies described in the Federal Republic of Germany, below.

The second point is that of study. Europe's Lutheran churches, in recent decades, have learned to look at themselves critically from new angles. They have done so in concert with churches in other continents and thereby have learned more about themselves and their obligations of concern for justice, human rights, and the dynamic role of the gospel in service to the whole person amid change.

The third point is that of church cooperation. Especially those churches that are small and dispersed—say, in a traditionally dominant Roman Catholic, Orthodox, or Socialist context—have longed for the reassurances of partnership and shared concern. Responding to this need, the Conference of Lutheran Churches in Europe held its first meeting in 1956, in Semmering, Austria. The ninth such gathering (Liebfrauenberg, near Strasbourg, France, in 1976) and the tenth (Tallinn, Estonia, USSR, in 1980), revealed the realities of life in dispersion and the costliness as well as the compensation of faithfulness to the gospel (below, USSR). In this respect, the plight of the Saxon Lutherans in *Romania illuminates a current problem with a perspective of centuries.

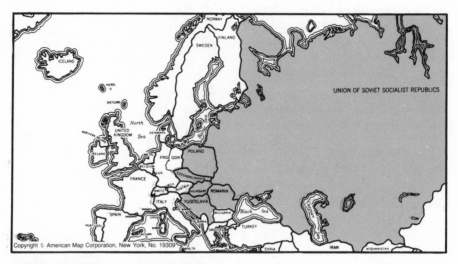

Copyright © American Map Corporation, New York, No. 19309

EASTERN EUROPE

The countries here included are Czechoslovakia, Hungary, Poland, Romania, the Soviet Union, and Yugoslavia. The total population of this enormous expanse well exceeds 300 million. Of this number, Lutherans comprise about five persons among every 1000. Besides, in relation to the nearly 40 million Lutherans in Europe, those in these eastern countries account for 3.8% of the whole. In some of these places, Lutherans have been present since the time of the 16th century Reformation. In others, they were more recent arrivals. But in all their overall number has gone down, often drastically, during the 20th century and in the wake of two world wars. Here are small churches with unsung but often epic histories.

Present Eastern Europe is a region of unstable political boundaries and of periodically restless peoples. In geopolitics, this region has been called the "crash zone" of the Eurasian continent and, more than that, the "heartland" of the Eurasian-African world island. In the two world wars of the present century, the struggle has been enormous for the control of this heartland, and the casualties have been staggering—also on the religious scene.

In Eastern Europe, on the Protestant side, at least, the Lutheran church has been collectively the conspicuous loser. At the time of the Reformation's 400th (1917) the total number of Lutherans living in these lands was estimated at about 6.5 million. Seventy years later (with presumably greater accuracy) the number had shrunk to 2,041,947 baptized members in this Lutheran dispersion.

As the following accounts suggest, each of the two world wars and the ensuing aftermaths disrupted an existing order, destroyed possessions, took lives, displaced church leadership, and impoverished the people, and—especially in the wake of World War II—expelled most of the ethnic Germans from their eastern homelands.

With the ending of World War I came the collapse of four empires: the Russian (Romanov), the Turkish (Ottoman), the Austro-Hungarian (Hapsburg), and the German (Hohenzollern). The map of Eastern Europe was redrawn on the basis of the right of "self-determination of peoples." While Austria and Hungary were sharply reduced in size, and Russia as well as Turkey rolled back, three new countries appeared on the map: Czechoslovakia, Yugoslavia, and Poland (restored from its 18th-century partitioning). At Hungary's expense, Romania was awarded Transylvania (a stronghold of Hungarian Reformed and German Lutheran stock; see below).

These dislocations and new national entities affected all the churches, but some more than others. Roman Catholic majorities, present everywhere but in Romania and the Soviet Union, took advantage of the new freedom. Lutheran minorities, collectively the largest Protestant confession, often lacked leadership and organizational know-how as well as financial and other resources to assert themselves. For these and other reasons churches in the dispersion were among the earliest and strongest supporters for the creation of a free association of churches that included confessional solidarity as well as mutual assistance on its agenda. The Lutheran World Convention (1923, see General Introduction) was prefigured by visits from American commissioners, like John A. Morehead, as early as 1919. By 1920, the newly formed United Lutheran Church in America had formed a mutual recognition agreement with the Hungarian Lutheran church, and a similar one with the Lutherans in Slovakia. A little later, a theological seminary was opened in Leningrad — supported largely by contributions from North America—for the training of pastors in the widely dispersed Evangelical Lutheran Church of Russia (*USSR). Similar supportiveness was shown the Lutherans in Poland, divided as they were. Timely responses to the needs in Yugoslavia helped to sustain the members amid a multiethnic situation. Nowhere was the postwar experience more traumatic than in Romania, greatly enlarged by the accession of Transylvania and a population—Magyars and Germans—lamenting the breaking of centuries-old ties with Hungary. This litany could go on.

Eventually, far more painful and convulsive for hundreds of thousands were the closing stages of World War II. Except for the majority of the Saxon Germans (Siebenbürgener Sachsen), in Transylvania since the 12th and 13th centuries as frontier folk against the Turks, most of the subsequently settled Germans (mainly agricultural) were expelled and sent fleeing back to Germany. Ethnic Germans (Volksdeutsche) as well as German nationals (Reichsdeutsche) living in East Prussia, Silesia, and other parts of German lands assigned in 1945 to Poland (whose boundaries were moved westward) are estimated to have numbered some 12 million. Most of them were women and children, augmented later by returned prisoners of war. This flood tide of humanity moved through East Germany and, for the most part, found resettlement in West Germany. Meanwhile, in the Soviet Union (below) the relocation of ethnic Germans (Russian citizens) to the east of the Urals had commenced already in October 1941. Here again, it was mainly the mothers who kept the faith, who taught the children hymns, Bible verses, the catechism, and thus laid the groundwork for today's many congregations in Kazakhstan and beyond (below).

The countenance of the expellees, moving in its muted message, has disappeared from refugee camps in the West, and the memories of the human cost have dimmed. Details, here and there, illumine the violent past. Church buildings, some half-filled, others destroyed, are reminders of earlier bodies of believers. Their total number has been reduced by over two-thirds, but those remaining are the indigenous Lutherans, of many nationalities and, most often, of a lineage going back to the Reformation. The description of their churches as well as of their countries follows here in alphabetical order.

CZECHOSLOVAKIA

The Czechoslovak Socialist Republic (CSSR, 1948), a federal entity comprising the Czech Socialist Republic and the Slovak Socialist Republic, lies in Central Europe and is bordered by six countries: East and West Germany, Austria, Hungary, the Soviet Union, and Poland. Area: 127,889 sq. km. (49,378 sq. mi.). Pop. (1985 est.): 15,509,000, including (1980) Czech 64.1%, Slovak 30.6%, Hungarian and other 5.3%. Cap. and largest city: Prague (pop., 1984 est., 1,186,200). Language: Czech and Slovak (official).

History: The problem of nationality in Central Europe is summed up in the story of Czechoslovakia. Bohemia, Moravia, Slovakia, and some of Silesia were part of the great Moravian empire when it was overrun by the Magyars in A.D. 906. Slovakia remained under mainly Magyar (Hungarian) rule for the ensuing thousand years (until 1918). Bohemia and Moravia in time became part of the Holy Roman Empire of the German Nation. In this context, under Bohemia's kings, 14th-century Prague became Central Europe's cultural capital and host to the first university (1348) in the empire. In 1526, the Austrian Hapsburg, Ferdinand I—younger brother of Emperor Charles V—became king of Bohemia and Hungary. Later, the lands were absorbed into the larger realm of Austria-Hungary. During most of the 16th and 17th centuries, the Turkish presence in the Danube valley posed a threat. The much older Czech nationalism asserted a will to independence that never died. Jan Hus (c.1369–1415) and the ensuing Hussite wars were a pre-Reformation manifestation.

Especially after 1848, the year of revolution in Europe, a national spirit revived among the Czechs, Slovaks, and others, as the various nationalities craved the right of self-determination. A rising Germany—progressively unified—caused frustration in Austria. Austria's own grip on power was challenged by Hungary. The *Ausgleich,* or compromise, of 1867 established a dual monarchy. The Austro-Hungarian combination became an ever more ready target for Slavic protest—whether Czech, Slovak, Serbian, or other.

As World War I was ending the republic of Czechoslovakia was proclaimed—provisionally in Britain and the United States of America (the Pittsburgh Declaration of Czech and Slovak patriots in May) and officially in Prague, October 28, 1918. Combining Bohemia, Moravia, and Slovakia, the new country inherited the most industrialized part of the Hapsburg legacy. Later (1938), Nazi Germany took the German-inhabited border region, Sudetenland, occupied the Czech part of the country, and agreed on the establishment of the Slovak state (a satellite state of Nazi Germany).

Following World War II the country was restored. Communism emerged as the strongest political force in 1946, and in 1948 the country became a socialist republic. In 1968 Czechoslovakia became a federal state. Henceforth the Czech lands (Bohemia and Moravia and Silesia) and Slovakia would have their respective regional governments and legislatures. The powers of the federal government remained pivotal in foreign affairs and various areas of national life. The long history of this part of Central Europe gives Czechoslovakia a specially noteworthy place among its neighboring nations.

Religion: An estimated 80% of the population claim some Christian connection. Roman Catholic 65%; Protestant 8.5%; Czechoslovak Hussite Church 4.4%; Orthodox 1.4%. Lutherans account for about one-half of the Protestant total. Over the centuries, a highly significant Jewish community resided in these lands (over 300,000 in 1900). Decimated during the Nazi-run Holocaust, their number today is said to be under 5000.

The Federal Office of State for Ecclesiastical Affairs (under the vice prime minister of the federal government) is authorized to handle all religious questions. Created by parliament in 1949, this office watches over religious and ecclesial life so that all things in this realm develop in harmony with the constitution and principles of the regime.

The conversion of the Moravian empire's people to Christianity began about A.D. 860 under the Eastern (Byzantine) missionaries, Cyril and Methodius. They were apostles to the Slavs also in other lands and keepers of the liturgical church language, Old Slavonic. Their work found favor also in Rome. Eventually brought under the papacy, the church in these countries generated periodic movements of renewal, including those of the Moravian (Czech) Brethren (in the 15th century) and of Jan Hus, whose contribution Luther esteemed. The Roman Catholic Counter-Reformation of the later 16th century drove Protestantism underground in Moravia and Bohemia—under Hapsburg rule—but was somewhat less oppressive in Hungarian-ruled Slovakia. Roman Catholicism, long the established religion, wielded wide influence and continued to do so, particularly in Slovakia, until the end of World War II. Today's hierarchy comprises three archdioceses, of which Prague (973) is the oldest, and 10 dioceses. Relations with the state have been strained. The government for some time refused to endorse Vatican nomination of bishops.

The Czechoslovak Hussite Church, Catholic but not in communion with Rome, is the largest of the country's six member bodies in the World Council of Churches. The celebration of the mass in the vernacular in 1919 led not only to the formation of a new church body the following year but also to greater prominence being given to some of the teachings of Jan Hus. Headed by its own patriarch, the church maintains the Hus Theological Faculty in Prague and an ecumenical institute.

The Eastern Orthodox Church, autocephalous and a member of the WCC, has about 80% of its 150,000 members in Slovakia. In that same region the Reformed Christian Church in Slovakia (130,000), uses mostly Magyar and, until 1918, was part of the large Reformed Church in Hungary.

Among the Czech Protestants, the largest is the Evangelical Church of Czech Brethren (240,000). The result of a merger of Lutheran and Reformed churches (1919), its origins go back to the 14-century religious awakening through the work of Jan Hus and the Unitas

Fratrum (Unity of Brethren). Its theological faculty is named after John Amos Comenius (1592–1670), last bishop of the Unitas and noted educator, exiled with many other Protestants from Moravia and Bohemia early in the Thirty Years' War (1618–1648). It is ecumenically active and widely known. A member of the World Alliance of Reformed Churches, this church also continues to express interest in some Lutheran congregations in Silesia, former German parishes.

The Ecumenical Council of Churches in the Czech Socialist Republic (1970) included Baptist, Czech Brethren, Hussite, Old Catholic, Orthodox, Methodist, Silesian Lutheran, and Unity of Brethren churches. 1985 saw the establishment of the Ecumenical Council of Churches in Czechoslovakia, in which the Slovak Lutheran church in the CSSR and the Reformed church are also members. The initiative of the Lutheran theological faculty in Bratislava and the support of the Comenius faculty in Prague led to the formation of the Christian Peace Conference (1958). It soon became international as well as ecumenical. Its main following is in Eastern Europe, but its ties run also to Western Europe and North America, membership being on an individual basis.

Lutheran churches have been at home in this land since the time of the Reformation, when they latched onto the movement of Jan Hus begun a century earlier. German farmers, miners, and crafts people, drawn earlier to Slovakia, became adherents of the Lutheran movement and spread it among the Slovaks as well as among Hungarians—although for them Calvinism eventually proved more attractive. Meanwhile the Turkish victory over the Hungarians at Mohács (1526)—the danger continued for generations—gave special importance to the more secure Slovakia, called also Upper Hungary.

By 1570, there were said to be about 2000 Evangelical (Lutheran) congregations in Slovakia. Soon thereafter, the Counter-Reformation set in. The hierarchy and the Jesuits, working freely under successive Hapsburg monarchs, recatholicized most of the nobility and the people on their lands. The period of the Thirty Years' War was difficult, but the second half of the 17th century was worse. Seizure of churches and the imprisonment or exile of pastors—and martyrdom for some—was part of the price of a Protestantism driven underground. Relief came gradually. The Edict of Toleration (*Toleranzpatent,* 1781) promulgated by Emperor Joseph II of Austria, became effective also in lands governed by the associated monarchy of Hungary, which included Slovakia. The way to full ecclesial equality opened only with the law of 1848, which removed Roman Catholicism's status of "principle religion."

An example of the resurgence of Lutheranism in Slovakia is that almost half of today's parishes were either founded or revived during the decade 1791–1800. During the two decades after 1781, over 130 new church buildings were erected by the Lutherans. Behind this upsurge was a confessional commitment made already in 1610 at the memorable synod in Žilina, south of Teschen on the Polish border. Through the imperial officer, Count Juraj Sturzo, the legal status of the Lutherans was confirmed; while the leading superintendent (bishop), Eliaš Láni, made his district a model of church organization and set the direction in the nurture of faith and practice. His translation of Luther's Catechism (1612) became standard. Underlying these developments was Luther's reform of worship, the "Wittenberg Agenda." The first centennial of the Reformation (1617) was observed with exultation in Bytča near Žilina. The following year, in Prague, the fateful Thirty Years' War broke out, and the brilliant Láni died in the prime of life (at 48).

The Kralice (Kralitz) Bible—a Czech translation (1577)—became standard among the Slovaks in shaping a liturgical language as well as providing a basic resource of public instruction. The hymnal of Juraj Tranovský (1592–1637)—Wittenberg-educated and a pastor of great poetic gifts—included the contributions of many others. The 1636 "Cithara Sanctorum" (Saints' Harp), popularly known as "Tranoscius"—in attractive poetic form—became an enduring standby of evangelical teaching and counsel. In the 18th century, the prayerbook of Paul Jakobei, pastor of Modra, not far from Bratislava, became a favorite.

Three things, among others, mark Slovak Lutheranism in the 19th century. One was the continuing good relations with Czech Protestants as well as with the Germans in their midst and in Germany itself. Another was their remarkable role in the rise and fostering of the Slovak idea of nationality, an idea that recognized a cultural indebtedness to the Czechs—as in the Kralice Bible—while at the same time asserting the distinctiveness of the Slovak language as the vehicle of a people's identity and literature. Although employed initially by Jesuits to recatholicize the predominantly rural Slovak people more effectively, it was Lutheran pastors and theological students (Jan Kollár, 1793–1852, pastor of the Lutheran congregation in Budapest, is one of the best known) who not only pursued their idea of nationality with all the fervor of a Slovak minority (over against a Slovak Roman Catholic majority) but who also affirmed the kinship they saw between their own language and other Slavic tongues. This accent found support elsewhere—among Serbs, Poles, Russians, and others—as Pan-Slavism.

Thirdly, the mounting Magyarization fostered by a Hungarian aristocracy and others in Slovakia caused chronic frustration. An example was the reorganization of the Lutheran church into four districts in a manner that gave Hungarians the majority in each one—at least when supported by the Germans who were also members of this inclusive Lutheran church.

In the present century, Lutherans have contributed leadership to the Protestant churches, notably to the Evangelical Church of Czech Brethren (above). After World War II, Germans in the Sudetenland and in Slovakia were relocated to Germany, and a German-language Lutheran church of about 120,000 members disappeared from the Czechoslovakian scene. Similarly, an exchange of people brought many Slovaks from Hungary into Slovakia and Hungarians from Slovakia into Hungary. The two Lutheran church bodies in the CSSR today—located in Slovakia, Moravia, and Silesia in regions mainly northeast of the former imperial capital, Vienna—hold an important place in the ongoing Christian life in Eastern Europe.

SILESIAN EVANGELICAL CHURCH OF THE AUGSBURG CONFESSION IN THE CSSR

(Slezská církev evangelická a.v. v ČSSR)
Member: LWF (1956), WCC, CEC, CPC, ECCC
Membership: 44,800**
Bishop: The Rt. Rev. Dr. Vladislav Kiedron
Na Nivach 7
CS—737 01 Český Těšín

This church (earlier it extended into *Poland) currently comprises 19 congregations that are served by 22 pastors and over 50 lay preachers. The ecclesiastical structure, according to the constitution, provides for self-government at the congregational level, and decision making by a synod and governing council at the church level. The bishop is the ecclesial head. Here is a church body linked historically with Poland. The little Olsa River separates Český Těšín from Cieszyn. The worship languages are Czech and Polish, reminders of the storms of political and religious change which this ecclesial body has endured since its Lutheran beginning in the 1520s.

With the coming of the Counter-Reformation, flourishing years gave way to generations of religious repression. Yet to this predominantly Protestant principality of Teschen (Czech: *Těšín*)—under Austrian Hapsburg rule 1625-1918—toleration came earlier than elsewhere in the realm (see Poland).

Even in modern times, true religious liberty was slow in coming to this church. During the 20th century, it passed through five stages of identity: up to 1918 it was part of the *Evangelical Church of the Augsburg Confession in Austria; 1918–1920 part of the Lutheran church in the new Poland; 1920–1938 autonomous within the new Czechoslovakian republic; 1939 again under the Lutheran church in Poland; 1940–1945 part of the Evangelical Union Church in Breslau. Amid postwar changes, it finally became officially recognized in 1948 as an equal among the other churches in the CSSR. Overarching these changes is Europe's political history and its impact upon church life.

Nevertheless, in the local congregations, the practice of Christian faith has persisted, as worship, preaching, religious instruction, confirmation, and a motivation for mission have been cultivated. In recent years, future pastors have been educated in Slovak-speaking Bratislava on Czechoslovakia's southern border. Old ties have found new form. Fellowship with Lutheran brethren in Slovakia (see SECAC below), Poland, Hungary, Yugoslavia, the German Democratic Republic, and elsewhere, including visits and assistance from the LWF, have helped to give this church a new lease on life, as has also its membership in the WCC.

Contrary to those Lutheran elements joining the Czech Brethren (above), this church with a contrasting history has clung to its confessional identity. Yet its East Silesian location and use of the Czech as well as the Polish tongue have facilitated its taking part in the Ecumenical Council of Churches in Czechoslovakia.

SLOVAK EVANGELICAL CHURCH OF THE AUGSBURG CONFESSION IN THE CSSR (SECAC)

(Slovenská evangelická a.v. církev v. ČSSR)
Member: LWF (1947), WCC, CEC, CPC
Membership: 369,000**
Bishop-General: The Rt. Rev. D. Dr. Ján Michalko
Palisady 46
CS—811 06 Bratislava

With its members gathered into 328 parishes, mostly in reasonable proximity to each other, the SECAC is served by 263 pastors as well as other workers. It includes about 10% of the nation's Slovak population and in certain districts has features of a folk church. Its 14 districts are grouped in two dioceses, East and West, each with a bishop. The congregations have their local presbytery (council of elders). The church at large is governed by a general convention and headed by a presidium, its executive unit led by the bishop-general and a lay inspector.

Church headquarters are in Bratislava (German: Pressburg; Hungarian: Pozsony), capital of Slovakia and a picturesquely situated control point on the Danube which served as Hungary's capital (1541–1784) during the era of Turkish invasions. Here is the Slovak Evangelical Theological Faculty (1934), which prepares future ministers of the SECAC as well as those of its sister Silesian church (above) and of the Slovak and Slovene churches in *Yugoslavia. Students from other Protestant churches in Slovakia also attend it. With a program of graduate study leading to the theological doctorate, the faculty maintains contacts with kindred academic institutions. Ecumenically oriented exchanges and conferences give the faculty as well as the church an international dimension.

This church's confessional fidelity and ecumenical openness has been aided by a distinctive brand of Slovak mobility. Pressures of a growing population, reaction against "Hungarianization," and inducements of a fresh start somewhere else played their part in bygone generations. Once it was the beckoning farmlands in what is now *Yugoslavia. Later, it was the lure of the Americas. Those on the move were mainly Roman Catholic, but there were also many Lutherans among them. Slovak congregations in *Canada and the *USA upheld cherished traditions, even while being drawn into larger church bodies. The Slovak Synod (1902) later became part of the *Lutheran Church–Missouri Synod. The Slovak Zion Synod (1919) was the one nongeographic component of the *Lutheran Church in America (now ELCA). Both American synods shared ways of self-reliance with the mother church when the SECAC set forth on its own in the new Czechoslovakia after World War I.

Formally organized in 1921, the emergence of this independent Slovak church is most appreciated when seen against the long historic background already described. Initial steps taken in October 1918 led to the landmark conference in historic Žilina that set the direction from early 1919 onward (see introduction). Like its larger Hungarian-led predecessor body, its name—omitting the word Slovak—indicated that German and Hungarian Lutherans on the territory would be welcome as full partners in the Evangelical Church of the Augsburg Confession in Slovakia. For the first time there existed a preponderantly Slovak church on its own. Then, as now, the situation drew upon a legacy of confessional firmness and theological clarity.

Appropriate ways—at times hard to find and harder to follow—were sought to foster the faith individually and in common. Today, as then, the rich worship life of the congregation stands at the forefront of evangelical commitment.

The liturgy, scriptural preaching, and Christian nurture are components of an ingrained tradition. Attesting to this are the more than 1600 hymns in a hymnal that in 1984 reached its 150th edition—a record among hymnals. A long-established emphasis on quality education was seen as no less essential and beneficial to the broader community and nation than in earlier times. An example of new directions was the admission of women to the ordained ministry. In the early 1920s, women were admitted to the study of theology. In 1951 the first woman was ordained (as vicar or pastor's assistant). By 1964, there were 15 ordained women, and since then their number has exceeded 30. In 1971, the first woman was assigned to a full pastorate.

Over the years the church has had to work out its relations with the government, upholding the place of the gospel in a society led by a Marxist ideology. It has promoted movements for international peace. The same spirit initially moved it to become a charter member of the WCC, the LWF, and later also the Conference of European Churches and the Christian Peace Conference. The latter, as noted above, was launched from Bratislava.

With its sister Silesian church, the SECAC in 1965 hosted the fifth Conference of Lutheran Churches in Europe (convened in Sliač by the LWF) and a consultation in 1979, in Bratislava, on theological education for service in a secular society. Assistance from the LWF has fostered a give-and-take, including the construction or restoration of church facilities and aid to such church-operated enterprises as the Tranoscius Publishing House. The latter bears the Latinized name of Juraj Tranovský (1592–1637), the Teschen-born son of a blacksmith who became a leading Lutheran churchman and hymn writer. Coming to Slovakia with many Czech exiles during the Thirty Years' War, he brought many books written in the spirit of the Reformation. These included the Kralice translation of the Bible, which made also the Czech language at home among the Slovak people.

During one busy biennium (1967–1969), the Tranoscius house published 90,000 hymnals, 15,000 copies of Luther's *Small Catechism,* 50,000 copies of several other books on Christian nurture and related fields, and 30,000 copies of the New Testament in a new translation. In 1978, a new translation of the entire Bible in Slovak was published. Done with help from the United Bible Societies, this version parallels but may not easily replace the liturgically familiar and long treasured Kralice Bible.

Undertakings such as these have been possible because the authorities, on occasion, could be convinced that a church adhering to the gospel is not a threat to the Socialist system but a true servant of the people as well as of God.

HUNGARY

A people's republic (1949) in Central Europe's Danube valley, bounded by Austria, Yugoslavia, Romania, the Soviet Union, and Czechoslovakia. Area: 93,036 sq. km. (35,921 sq. mi.). Pop. (1984 est.): 10,679,000, of whom over 96% are Magyar. Cap. and largest city: Budapest (pop., 1985 est., 2,071,000). Language: Magyar (Hungarian).

History: Between a ninth-century Magyar invasion and a 20th-century Hungarian people's republic lies an epitome of much European history. A Finno-Ugrian people, originally from east of the Urals, displacing Slavic and Germanic settlers; an acceptance of Western (Latin) rather than Eastern (Greek) Christianity, and the crowning—with a crown sent by the pope—of Stephen I (975–1038) in the year 1001; a time of testing under Mongol (Tartar) occupation (1241), followed by a cultural flowering under Matthias Corvinus (1458–1490); renewed testing under Turkish invasion (battle of Mohács, 1526) and occupation (1541–1686); ties with Austria's Hapsburgs, leading to the creation of the Austro-Hungarian Empire; an *Ausgleich* (compromise; pushed by Ferenc Deák) achieving the dual monarchy in 1867 that recognized the Hapsburg Franz Josef I (1830–1916) as emperor of Austria and king of a quasi-independent Hungary; independence (1918) at a cost of two-thirds of the

former Hungarian lands (parts going to *Romania [Transylvania], *Czechoslovakia, *Yugoslavia, and *Austria); allied with Germany in World War II, and brought under Russian occupation; a coalition government (1947) leading to a people's republic (1949); a major uprising (1956); two movements of refugees (1945, 1956); and in recent decades an evenhanded government and a productive economy—these data are but pieces of the imposing Magyar epic.

The focus today is on Budapest, where 20% of the nation's population live. Buda (west bank) and Pest (east bank) were united in 1872. Astride the Danube (here flowing north to south) the capital's bridges are themselves showpieces as they link the landmarks of government in Buda with the centers of commerce and industry in Pest. The neo-Gothic parliament building (1885–1906) is the symbol of the city and the nation. During World War II, about three-fourths of the city was badly damaged and much of it destroyed. A sustained building program has carried the city far beyond its former makeup, but the new is made compatible with the old. Besides, a religious dimension remains.

Religion: About 54% of the population are Roman Catholic. The hierarchy is led by the archbishop of Esztergom, primate of Hungary. The church structure includes three archdioceses and eight dioceses, plus other judicatories. Following drastic readjustments after World War I, the church experienced renewal and regained much of its former influence, a course not repeated after World War II. The state's 1948 agreement with the Lutheran and Reformed churches and 1950 agreement with the Roman Catholic Church brought them all under the prevailing system.

Of the remaining population the Reformed account for about 19%, and the Lutherans 4%. There are also Orthodox, Baptists, Methodists, and other Christian groups. Jews comprise under 1% of the population. Those professedly nonreligious or atheist are said to total about 20%.

The Reformed Church in Hungary, slightly younger than the Lutheran, also has its roots in the Reformation era and today numbers nearly two million adherents. While its headquarters are in Budapest, its history center and Theological Academy are in Debrecen, the nation's third largest city—located in the east, near the Romanian border. Relations between the Reformed and Evangelical (Lutheran) confessions have long been good.

The State Office of Ecclesiastical Affairs, created in 1951, continues a similar prewar office but with a different orientation. It maintains close supervision of the churches and their activities. Pastors take an oath of loyalty to the constitution. The state, in turn, provides a subsidy for clergy salaries as well as for voluntary religious instruction in the public schools.

Despite the salutary effects of Vatican II, relations between Roman Catholics and other Christians still reflect certain alienations born of earlier times. The Ecumenical Council of Churches in Hungary (ECCH, 1948) includes the Reformed, Lutheran, Baptist, Methodist, and Orthodox bodies, as well as the Council of Free Churches, which has seven members. The ECCH's participation in Faith and Order studies and other affairs of the World Council of Churches, as well as in the Conference of European Churches and the Christian Peace Conference is significant. These activities and those of the several ECCH member churches—including involvement in their respective world confessional organizations, like the LWF and the World Alliance of Reformed Churches—are reported regularly in the fortnightly *Hungarian Church Press*. The English and German editions of this news service have been appearing since 1948. The current general secretary of the ECCH is an ecumenically recognized Lutheran theologian, Ernö Ottlyk.

Good relations between the Lutheran church and the Jewish community have been made noteworthy in various ways. For instance, the golden communion chalice presented to the Deák church in 1839 came from members of the Budapest synagogue in thanks for aid received during a devastating flood. In education—for generations prior to World War II—Jewish families preferred to send their children to the Lutheran high school (below) because of its fairness as well as its academic quality. Several of its Jewish graduates have become world famous (Nobel laureates) in science.

LUTHERAN CHURCH IN HUNGARY

(Magyarországi Evangélikus Egyház)
Member: LWF (1947), WCC, CEC, CPC, ECCH
Membership: 430,000**
Presiding Bishop: The Rt. Rev. Dr. Gyula Nagy
Üllöi út 24
H—1085 Budapest

In the Lutheran "dispersion" in Eastern Europe, the Magyar (Hungarian) Evangelical church is one of the largest bodies. Its long history reflects endurance and vision. Its present membership resides mainly in the country's northwest, north, and southeast. The 276 parishes are served by 277 pastors and comprise two dioceses (districts), northern and southern. Each diocese is headed by a bishop and a lay president. The senior bishop is the presiding bishop. Every parish has its own governing council. The entire church is governed by an assembly (convention), which is chaired jointly by a general inspector (lay) and the presiding bishop. The synod is convened only upon special request of the assembly and is the legislative body of the church. The capital has six Lutheran congregations in Buda and 17 in Pest, with a total membership of about 80,000.

Relations with the Socialist government are termed good. Several church people have been elected to public office and to parliament. Though the postwar years were a difficult time of adjustment, they also brought Lutherans and other religious bodies equality of recognition along with Roman Catholics, an advantage they were not accorded earlier. Following the secularization of several hundred church-operated schools in 1948, the ensuing agreement with the government (above) has given the church freedom within recognized limits.

The church constitution of 1966 and its accompanying regulations mark the centrality of the gospel in the life of Christians and of the church. In recent years, Hungarian Lutherans have developed a "theology of diaconia," which accentuates service and lays emphasis on the necessity of confessing Christ not only by words but also by deeds of Christian love. This is part of a daily witness in a Marxist society. Proclamation of the gospel is seen as inseparable from the Christians' practice of love for all people and for their common life.

The congregations' source of strength lies in worship. A rich legacy of hymnody and church music finds ready expression, also through such contemporary works as the two cantatas by Sándor Szokolay, observing the 450th anniversary of the *Augsburg Confession* (1980) and the 500th of Luther's birth (1983). The cultivation of a Lutheran type of Christian identity has long been fostered through church-sponsored education. This honored heritage has enabled Lutherans to produce leaders active in church and society in proportionately greater numbers than other communions. After 1945 "Fasor," the former Lutheran high school in Budapest, was run by the state. In 1983 it observed its 425th anniversary with special recognition to its confessional past. The return of this school to Lutheran administration was begun in 1988 (see introduction).

The Lutheran Theological Academy in Budapest (formerly in Sopron), newly housed in 1974 and enlarged in 1987, heads the church's educational program. It has seven professors, five lecturers, and a student body ranging between 40 and 50, women as well as men. Theological education by extension is also under way, the first graduates in this three-year course having completed their work in 1983. Likewise in that year, a long-awaited large statue of Luther was completed and placed prominently in the academy court-yard.

Some 18 diaconic institutions for the elderly and for handicapped children are supported by voluntary contributions, as are most congregational expenses. The church has an educational program for workers in these institutions. It also has its own publication department. A new hymnal has found wide welcome. A completely new translation of the Bible into modern Hungarian—the work of two decades of shared scholarship—was published in 1976. Regular publications include the weekly, *Evangélikus Elet,* as well as a monthly journal for pastors and church workers, and the semi-annual *Diakonia,* a cultural, social, and theological review. Commentaries on books of the Bible, devotional works, materials for religious instruction, theological and other books are also published.

In the late 1970s a Lutheran museum was opened in Budapest on the premises of the downtown church on Deák square. Choice reminders of the past tell how Lutheranism arrived and developed in Hungary after 1518. The Reformation spread rapidly (see Romania). Turkish victories (above, introduction) and prolonged occupation of the land made Lutheranism a more radical popular movement than in Germany. From 1522 until the time of Luther's death (1546), 148 students from Hungary attended Wittenberg University. A leader among them, Mátyás Dévai (d. 1545), was later called the "Hungarian Luther." The first complete Magyar translation of the New Testament (1541) and of Luther's *Small Catechism* (1550) stimulated the rise of numerous Lutheran printing houses, also in Magyar Transylvania (*Romania). Some time after 1550, the Reformed faith supplanted Lutheranism in many places. As Turkish pressures relaxed, a resurgent Roman Catholicism menaced Protestantism during most of the 17th century. Both Lutherans and Reformed lost much ground during this belated Counter-Reformation. Its severity was most intense during the 1670s, the "tragic decade." Many Evangelical pastors were banished from their parishes, and a considerable number sold into slavery, working in Italian ships. The situation improved slowly during the 18th century, but scars have remained to this day.

Full toleration for Hungary's Protestants—the Reformed and the Evangelical (as the Lutherans were often called)—came only with the Edict of Tolerance of Austria's Hapsburg emperor, Joseph II, in 1781. Legal equality of the confessions was recognized in 1848 and constitutionally granted in the *Ausgleich* (compromise) year inaugurating the dual monarchy, 1867—also the 350th anniversary of the Reformation. Even so, Protestants remained disadvantaged. Little over half a century later, with the dissolution of the Austro-Hungarian Empire and the drastic reduction of Hungarian territory (Transylvania was awarded to Romania by the Trianon Treaty in 1920), the size of the Lutheran church fell sharply and the problems confronting it revealed the plight as well as the resourcefulness of a minority.

Hungarians have also been a people on the move. Among the nearly half-million who had emigrated to North America prior to 1914 were also a fair number of Lutherans. A Hungarian Conference with the then United Lutheran Church in America was the bridgehead for an official relationship formed between that body and the Lutheran Church in Hungary (1922). Elsewhere, ethnic affinity and a common faith relate Lutherans in Hungary to those in *Finland. There are Hungarian Lutherans in many other parts of the world, including *Romania, *Yugoslavia, the *Federal Republic of Germany, *Austria, *Czechoslovakia, *Scandinavia, *Latin America, and *Australia. They have given an international dimension to the church of their forebears by ad hoc conferences of Hungarians abroad.

Little known but ecumenically significant is the role of Hungary's Lutherans in speeding the formation of the Lutheran World Convention (1923). Soon after 1919 Bishop Sándor Raffay (1866–1947) saw the need for Europe's minority Lutheran churches to work together across the newly created national boundaries. In this he had the encouragement of Sweden's archbishop, Nathan Söderblom (1866–1931), the ecumenical pioneer. Although Raffay's plan for an all-Lutheran conference in Budapest—set for 1923—did not materialize, his shared vision helped to form the Lutheran World Convention. Besides, the ties between Lutherans in Sweden and Hungary became an asset for the Hungarians.

The church situation since 1945 has evoked a variety of leaders. Among them was the valiant Bishop Lajos Ordass (1901–1978), successor to Raffay, who also studied in Sweden and who became well known in the World Council of Churches as well as in the LWF, wherein he served two separate terms as vice-president (1947–1952, 1957–1963). From 1959 to 1987 Bishop Zoltán Káldy headed the Hungarian church. Others could be cited who are even now contributing significantly to Hungarian Lutheran participation in the LWF and the WCC as well as in other ecumenical work.

The holding of the LWF's Seventh Assembly in Budapest (above, General Introduction) widened horizons all around and fostered the rise of a new generation of partners in faith and service. For many, 1984 remains a memorable year of bridge building locally. Assembly delegates and others found the generous hospitality of the host church deeply moving. This was especially so on the Sunday (the last in July) midway through the assembly when participants were deployed to congregations across the Hungarian land. In at least one instance this dispersal extended to Bratislava (*Czechoslovakia). For over two centuries (1541–1784) this Slovakian stronghold on the Danube, also known as Pressburg, was the Hungarian capital (Pozsony) during and beyond the era of Turkish occupation.

"In Christ—Hope for the World," the assembly theme, gave pointed significance to this manifold exercise in local ecumenism. Bishop Káldy's election as president of the LWF until the next assembly assured that in member churches there would be a continued awareness and appreciation of the church in Hungary as well as of the other Lutheran churches in Eastern Europe. His lamented death in May 1987 (see below, LWF presidents) ended a dynamic ministry. Among the 6000 attending his funeral were numerous ecumenical leaders. His successor, Bishop Gyula Nagy (a professor of theology), is widely experienced, including terms of service in Geneva with the LWF and the Conference of European Churches. While Nagy is now the presiding bishop, Káldy's successor as bishop of the southern diocese is Dr. Béla Harmati, who has also served the LWF in Geneva.

POLAND

A people's republic (1947), Poland's neighbors include the Soviet Union, Czechoslovakia, and East Germany, while to the north it borders the Baltic Sea. Area: 312,683 sq. km. (120,727 sq. mi.). Pop. (1984 est.): 36,745,000. Cap. and largest city: Warsaw (pop., 1983 est., 1,641,300). Language: Polish.

History: Poland's varied past includes its role as a great power (14th to 17th centuries); its political disappearance through partitioning between Austria, Prussia, and Russia (1795–1918); its return to independence as a republic (1918–1939); its occupation by Nazi Germany (1939–1945) and the USSR (1939–1941) during World War II; its return as a nation and its relocation westward as a result of its being awarded German lands east of the Oder-Neisse (rivers) line in place of the

Polish territory retained by the USSR. The abrupt removal of most of the German population immediately after the war, and the eventual emigration of nearly all the rest over the years since then, involved many millions of people—a migration that ranks as one of the most precipitous anywhere. The present government was set up in 1945. A treaty normalizing relations between the Federal Republic of Germany—recipient of most of the refugees—and Poland was signed in 1970.

Religion: Polish and Roman Catholic are said to be synonymous terms largely because the continuity of national consciousness has been fostered by the church amid the changing fortunes of the state. Statistically, about four out of five Poles are church members. In 1978, Karol Cardinal Wojtyla, archbishop of Kraków, became Pope John Paul II, the first non-Italian in four centuries and the first Pole ever elevated to that position. His subsequent visits (1979, 1983) reaffirmed the powerful hold of the traditional religion in Europe's easternmost bastion of Roman Catholicism. Poland has an official representative at the Vatican with the status of minister, and there are conversations between the state and the Roman Catholic Church about the relationship to the Vatican. Joszef Cardinal Glemp, succeeding the late Stefan Cardinal Wyszynski in 1981 as head of the Polish hierarchy, has pursued a firm but mediating policy. Ecumenically, he has been more open than his predecessors.

Of the less than one million non-Roman Catholics—under 2% of the population—the Polish Orthodox Church accounts for over one-half this number. The Lutherans, themselves a million-strong prior to World War II and then minus the Germans, come in a distant second. Smaller are the Polish National Catholic, the Mariavite, the United Evangelical (Pentecostal in part), the Reformed, and other churches.

The Polish Ecumenical Council (PEC; 1945) includes the 10 largest of these bodies. As a precedent for cooperation, the council recalls the Consensus of Sandomir (1570) that provided for Lutherans, Reformed, and Bohemian Brethren to work together. A joint commission of the PEC and the Catholic Episcopal Commission for Ecumenism, formed in 1974, has become more active in recent years. Despite a first-ever meeting of

the Ecumenical Council with the pope (1983), and the presence of its members at the mass rally addressed by John Paul II, his silence toward the invited guests perpetuated the popular impression that Poland is monolithically Roman Catholic. Although tensions persist, relations between the majority church and the minority groups are expected to improve. The Ecumenical Council is a sign of this expectation.

During the time of martial law and acute need early in the 1980s, the Polish Ecumenical Council channeled Protestant aid from abroad to the neediest. These efforts were coordinated with the larger activities on the Roman Catholic side, and furthered ecumenical understanding between the minority churches and the majority.

The interconfessional and university-related Christian Theological Academy (CTA) educates pastors and other workers for service in Lutheran, Reformed, Old Catholic, Polish Orthodox, and other churches. The CTA has government recognition and financial support.

Similarly, the continuing distribution of the Scriptures—complete Bibles, New Testaments, portions—has been deepening common bonds among Christians of whatever affiliation. Backing this is the British and Foreign Bible Society in Poland, its Warsaw base headed by Barbara Enholc-Narzynska (a graduate of the CTA [above] and wife of the present Lutheran bishop). The 350th anniversary of the oldest Polish Bible—the Gdańsk (Danzig) Bible—in 1982 was a tribute to a version in continuous use until recent years. Of the modern revised translation, completed in 1975, 200,000 copies were printed in 1982. The illustrated New Testament, out in 1978, has found wide favor.

EVANGELICAL CHURCH OF THE AUGSBURG CONFESSION IN THE PEOPLE'S REPUBLIC OF POLAND (ECAC/PRP)

(Kosciól Ewangelicko-Augsburski w PRL)
Member: LWF (1947), WCC, CEC, CPC, PEC
Membership: 91,000
Bishop: The Rt. Rev. Janusz Narzynski
ul. Miodowa 21
PL—00-246 Warsaw

This church, the largest Protestant body in Poland, is rooted in the Reformation and active in today's strivings for Christian unity.

Gathered in 120 congregations and over 200 preaching places, its spiritual needs are served by 107 pastors and other church workers. The ECAC'S six dioceses form a wide swath from north to south down the middle of Poland—from the Masurian Lakes and Gdańsk region in the north, near the Baltic, to the region west and southwest of Kraków in the south, toward the Czech border. The southernmost diocese includes over half the entire ECAC membership. There, around Cieszyn (Teschen), live the direct descendants of Reformation forebears. "Tough as a Tessian in faith," is the saying. In the nation's midsection lie the two other dioceses, one to the west, around Wroclaw (Breslau), and the other in the capital city, Warsaw.

The ECAC headquarters are in the national capital, an easy walk from the restored Old City and near the residence and chancery of the Roman Catholic Primate of Poland. The Lutheran center, attractive in its functional modern design, is a postwar structure housing several allied activities. Among these is the Christian Theological Academy (above). Closer to the main business section of Warsaw stands Trinity Church, called the Lutheran cathedral. Rebuilt in the mid-1950s with help from abroad, Trinity's drum-and-dome construction makes it a landmark, set off by Victory Park.

Organizationally the ECAC's congregations are self-governing, each with its own presbytery or parish council. Each of the six dioceses is headed by an experienced pastor, called a senior, who attends to common regional concerns. For the ECAC as a whole, the synod is the decision-making body. It legislates and also elects the governing consistory or executive board. The president of the synod, according to Lutheran practice on the continent, is a layman. The bishop presides over the governing consistory as chief spiritual officer of the church, an office that also requires considerable visitation throughout the ECAC and includes ecumenical relations at home and abroad. The late Bishop Andrzej Wantula, a theologian and church historian, for example, served as a vice-president of the LWF (1963–1970). The present bishop, Janusz Narzynski, is prominent in the Polish Ecumenical Council, a task that, on occasion, brings him together with Poland's primate, Cardinal Glemp, as well as with government officials. At the installation of Pope John Paul II, in 1978, Narzynski represented Eastern European Lutherans in the LWF delegation's audience with the pope.

For the ECAC, the pressures of coexisting with a massive popular Catholicism, on the one hand, and a Marxist official ideology, on the other, intensify the continuing need for resourcefulness in keeping the Evangelical faith. This is especially evident in the challenge of Christian education at various levels, whether in Sunday schools, catechetical instruction, or in connection with the public schools. (At Roman Catholic insistence religion has remained in the curriculum; Poland is alone in this among Eastern European countries.) Pastors and church-trained teachers share the responsibility. Youth work, likewise, has its special programs, including larger gatherings in summer. In many a congregation, church music has its honored place, as in Bielsko-Biala, whose Redeemer Church choir sings old chorales and contemporary compositions and goes on tour. A recovered 16th-century hymn has become a favorite, praying: "As night descends / may God preserve and keep us / in his gracious care / against all evil / and against our own despair."

Other facets suggest the ongoing course of church life. Women play an important part as teachers and in other forms of service as well. The lone deaconess motherhouse, Ebenezer, in the southern village, Dziegielow, continues a strong tradition of service in parishes and other places also. There the recently dedicated retirement center for pastors and other church workers fills an urgent and otherwise unmet need. So, too, does the church's modest conference center, Bethany, near Bielsko-Biala. Meanwhile, in the parishes many a pastor experiences the burden of diverse demands as well as the challenge to be innovative. One example is the young pastor in the Masurian Lake region whose resident congregation numbers about 150, but whose nine preaching points keep him on the move. When summer brings the vacationers, also from outside the country, the tiny little church doubles as a music center. Elsewhere, as in Wroclaw or the nation's capital, specialized ministries, such as that to students, play a vital part. In still other places, impressively large church edifices serve but a fraction of the congregation's former membership. Even so, the ECAC is in need of more pastors.

The 1983 observance of Luther's 500th anniversary gave the ECAC a new self-awareness. Tours to historic Luther sites in East Germany drew many participants. The jubilee was also celebrated in the still thriving "mother church" in Cieszyn (Teschen). The building itself is a reminder of the time when, after more than a century (the 17th) of oppressive intolerance, Lutheranism surfaced from "underground." Guests and participants were on hand from neighboring *Czechoslovakia, the *German Democratic Republic, the *Federal Republic of Germany, and elsewhere to swell the overflow crowd marking this 1983 event. Bishop Narzynski reminded the people of the way Luther's teaching had originally swept Poland, and Barbara Enholc-Narzynska accentuated the Reformer's influence on the widespread use of the Bible.

The ECAC maintains contacts with churches abroad, especially with the Evangelical churches in the *Federal Republic of Germany. It participates in the Conference of European Churches (CEC) and is a charter member of the WCC (1948) as well as of the LWF. The 1974 LWF-sponsored conference of Lutheran (minority) churches in Europe gave much encouragement to the ECAC, host to the event in Warsaw. Politically and ecclesiastically, the Polish Lutherans support a policy of reconciliation amid the tensions troubling their own society and that of the world at large, believing that this is a way more viable for a dedicated minority than for many others.

● ● ●

The antecedents of the present ECAC in 1939 numbered around 500,000 members in a total Evangelical population of approximately one million. After World War II, as noted above, the number dropped to 270,000; by 1963 to 120,000. During the early 1970s attrition continued, reducing the ECAC membership to about 91,000. This church shows vividly the effect of harsh forces creating a dispersed denomination as well as the determination of its remaining members to be steadfast. In fact, since 1981, its membership has shown an increase. During the early postwar years the ECAC lost a staggering number of places of worship and other church properties—about 2000, it is said—taken over for other purposes. In various localities where Lutherans are sparse, Roman Catholic "squatters" have moved into Lutheran churches.

The Polish Ecumenical Council retains this tense issue on its agenda, while the Lutherans are learning to live with it. They know the cost of being different and also faithful.

The boundaries of present-day Poland approximate those of a distant past when the country was a kingdom and the eastern outpost of a missioning Roman Catholicism. Here, the Lutheran Reformation made early gains so that by the mid-16th century two-thirds of the population were said to adhere to the Evangelical faith. The point of entry was East Prussia and—in the south—West Poland (the Teschen region). In the city of Königsberg, East Prussia, Germans and Poles lived in friendly coexistence. The Lutheran church in East Prussia continued to use Polish as well as German until well into the 19th century. Here, too, the first translation of the New Testament into Polish, and of Luther's writings, originated. Yet the aggressive Counter-Reformation erased most of these gains.

Poland's strongest concentration of Lutherans, near the southern border in the environs of Cieszyn (Teschen), was once a principality under Austrian rule but then divided in 1920 between Poland and *Czechoslovakia (Silesian Evangelical Church of the Augsburg Confession). The first Evangelical (Lutheran) service of worship was held near the present city of Cieszyn in 1523. Despite the prolonged and repressive Counter-Reformation, the Lutheran constituency in these parts has been continuous for over 450 years. Intervention by Sweden's King Charles XII secured religious toleration for Teschen and parts of Silesia from the Hapsburg Emperor, Joseph I, in 1707.

Pastors and teachers provided through August Hermann Francke, in Halle—the dynamic center of Lutheran Pietism—plus strong local support by the laity led to the opening in Cieszyn of the first Evangelical school on Hapsburg lands. The school later also trained pastors before this task was relocated to Vienna. Jesus Church, in Cieszyn, is a massive three-balcony baroque structure seating originally 5000. It was built over the years 1720 and 1750 by special dispensation (as a *Gnadenkirche*) in anticipation of the official Edict of Toleration (1781, *Austria). It stands as an exultant reminder of religious liberty granted long ago. A lofty tower (72 meters, or 234 feet) marks this forebear of many Lutheran churches in Southeastern Europe. Even today the Cieszyn parish has 8000 members, served by a team of pastors. On festive occasions Jesus Church is filled—as on Reformation Sunday—while the liturgy, the chorales, and the proclaimed Word bear resounding witness to the Lord of the Church. This is among people who have known suffering and national tragedy.

During the last three decades of the 18th century Poland was progressively partitioned until in 1795 it disappeared completely into its three neighboring nations: Prussia, Austria, and Russia. This opened a new phase of religious history for the Polish people, and for Protestants the freedom guaranteed by Prussia was balanced by the religious toleration granted in 1781 by Joseph II in the Austro-Hungarian realm. Likewise, in Russia's portion, called Congress Poland (as ratified by the Congress of Vienna, 1815), Protestantism spread, as colonists from Silesia, Bohemia, and various parts of Germany responded to the opportunity to settle and cultivate the land. In the cities of Warsaw, Łódź, and Kraków, large Lutheran congregations were gathered. In Prussia's part of Poland, strong parishes developed in a much enlarged Silesia.

When in 1919 the new Poland emerged as an independent republic there were five Evangelical church bodies, of which two large ones were Lutheran, the others United (Lutheran and Reformed). In general, this situation remained until World War II. During the occupation, Polish members of the Lutheran church fared badly. Their own pastors, teachers, and church leadership were severely diminished by persecution, imprisonment, and death. At war's end, the Potsdam Agreement (1945) relocated the boundaries of Poland westward, the Oder-Neisse Rivers forming the present frontier with the German Democratic Republic. The accompanying expulsion of most of the ethnic Germans resulted in the already mentioned drastic loss in church membership. By slow and painful steps, the ECAC was reshaped into the present active body.

ROMANIA

This Socialist republic (1947) in Southeastern Europe is bordered by the Soviet Union, the Black Sea, Bulgaria, Yugoslavia, and Hungary. Area: 237,500 sq. km. (91,700 sq. mi.). Pop. (1985 est.): 22,924,500 including (1977) Romanian 88.1%, Hungarian 7.9%, German 1.6%. Cap. and largest city: Bucharest (pop., 1985 est., 1,975,800). Language: Romanian, some Magyar and German.

History: Modern Romania is heir to the Dacian kingdom occupied by Rome A.D. 107–270, when the people and their language were Romanized. Periodic invasions by various peoples spanned centuries and culminated in a long Turkish domination of much of the country (1391–1877). The principalities of Walachia and Moldavia, united in 1858, became Romania in 1861. Declaring its independence from Turkey (1878), Romania became a kingdom in 1881 and a constitutional monarchy five years later. The royal line was German: Carol (Karl) of Hohenzollern (a Roman Catholic who became Orthodox) and Elizabeth, an Evangelical princess and poetess under the name of Carmen Sylva.

After World War I, Romania, continuing as a monarchy, was awarded additional lands, including Transylvania, which until then had been part of Hungary and which was known in Magyar as Erdély and in German as Siebenbürgen—Land of the Seven Fortified Cities. On the side of Germany early in World War II, Romania later (1944) joined the Allies.

The ensuing Communist people's republic (1947) was upgraded to a Socialist republic in 1965. Among the Warsaw Pact nations, Romania has been the most independent of the Soviet Union, and the only one to maintain diplomatic relations with Israel. Domestically, the policy to create a balanced economy has drawn a considerable part of the population from agriculture to the developing centers of industry in the cities, a move affecting also the churches.

Today, Transylvania requires further notice. A region half again the size of Switzerland, it lies eastward of Hungary and "across the forests": a high plateau, virtually surrounded by mountains, entered by passes, and crossed by medieval trade routes. The one from Constantinople to Leipzig, for example, went via Sibiu (Hermannstadt). Much earlier, Transylvania was the heart of the Roman province of Dacia.

Transylvania stands out in the Romanian economy for its natural resources, its productive agriculture, and its developing industry. Here, perhaps more than elsewhere in Europe, fortified churches—mainly from the pre-Reformation era—stand as mute reminders of a turbulent past. Already in the year 1003, St. (King) Stephen brought Transylvania under the Hungarian crown. Later, about 1140, on royal invitation, the first Germans—from Luxembourg and the Rhineland—arrived as settlers of the frontier and as defenders of it against incursions by Turks, Mongols, and others. Even today the massive fortified churches are awesome landmarks in many a strategic location. From the watchtowers, with characteristically angled roofs, the countryside could be kept under surveillance. Behind the ramparts and encircling wall were the storage bins for grain and other foods, the cellars for wine and beer, and enclosures for cattle, fowl, and sheep. Meats were smoked and hung in the spaciously built watchtower. For the villagers and their families, in time of danger, motel-like rooms stretched along the inside wall. The water supply, crucial in time of siege, was a well or spring, heavily protected.

In the center of the enclosure stood the church, the product of local labor as well as of Bohemian and other traveling craftsmen in stone, glass, and metals. Today, many of the encircling walls have provided stone for other buildings in the environing towns. But the rugged churches remain. They are Europe's farthest east buildings of Gothic architecture, and are also designated as national monuments. The government pays the cost of restoration. However, the task of restoring the old Reformation-era paintings on the triptychs over the altars requires voluntary contributions and skilled artists. Noteworthy churches are in Brashov (Kronstadt), Sibiu (Hermannstadt), Sebes (Mühlbach), Cisnadie (Heltau), Codlea (Zeiden), Medias—to name but a few.

Religion: Romanian Orthodox 70%; Greek Orthodox 10%; Roman Catholic 6%; Reformed 3.3%; Pentecostal 1%; Lutheran under 1%; Unitarians 0.2%; atheist 7%; and others. There is no national council of churches, but since about 1965 relations between the several communions have improved. This was due to several factors. The Romanian Orthodox Church joined the WCC (1961), a membership in which Romania's Hungarian Reformed and Hungarian Lutheran bodies had preceded it (1948), and with Romania's Saxon Lutherans following (1964). Romanian Orthodox Patriarch Justinian (d.1977), earlier having experienced the prolonged postwar pressures of the state upon the churches, became ecumenically outgoing. Relations between the government and the churches improved for a time, beginning with the presidency (1965) of Nicolae Ceauşescu. A state department of cults oversees religious affairs.

In Romania, as in much of Eastern Europe, ethnic origin and a specific church tradition go hand in hand. In effect, what Roman Catholicism is to the Poles, Romanian Orthodoxy is to Romanians—an ethnic identity in ecclesial terms. The Day of St. Demetrius (October 26), when crowds throng the churches and honor the nation's fourth-century saint, recalls a long past. From conversions in A.D. 864 under the influence of Boris, King of the Bulgars, the people have remained traditionally Christian over centuries of change. Ties with Constantinople—the Ecumenical Patriarchate—were loosened when the Romanian Orthodox Church was recognized as autocephalous (1885). Later, it had its own patriarch (1925). After World War II the 1.6-million-member Uniate Catholic Church (Eastern Rite with papal allegiance), comprised of people residing chiefly in Transylvania, was declared dissolved by government decree (1948) and merged with the Romanian Orthodox Church (ROC). Based in Bucharest, the ROC is divided into five metropolitanates. For its 11,000 priests, the major theological seminaries are in Bucharest and Sibiu. Lutheran pastors are also educated in Sibiu (below).

Romanians of Hungarian (Magyar) origin or language, are a seeming exception to the ethnic-confessional overlap mentioned above. During and following the 16th century they split four ways: Roman Catholic (the majority); Reformed (the 700,000-member leading Protestant group); Unitarian (a 32,000-member group of 16th-century beginnings and Christian humanist orientation); and the Hungarian Lutherans (below). When Transylvania was still part of Hungary, pastors of the latter three confessions were educated in that country or elsewhere; the Roman Catholics likewise. After World War II this was no longer possible.

The United Protestant Theological Institute, formed in 1949, is based in Cluj-Napoca (in German Klausenburg) and educates pastors and other workers for the Reformed, Unitarian, and Lutheran churches. Baptists, Evangelicals, Adventists, and others are also accommodated. In impressive old buildings, which also house the headquarters of the Reformed Church, the institute has extensive facilities on a centrally located campus. All instruction is in Magyar (Hungarian). The institute's German-language section is 170 kilometers (102 miles) to the south, in Sibiu (below). The government subsidies for higher education include the salaries of theological professors. Because of this and other reasons, the drastic reduction in allowed quotas of theological students (1983)—seemingly an economy move by the government—was viewed with apprehensiveness. The quota was subsequently raised. The theological institute, being government-authorized, has the right to confer academic degrees.

Romania has two Lutheran church bodies, the larger of German descent, the smaller of Hungarian origin and language. The ethnic-confessional overlap keeps them one in faith but separate in organization. There are few Lutherans of Romanian stock. Each of the two Lutheran churches has a congregation in Bucharest and at various points in old Romania. Only in Bucharest is Lutheran worship in the Romanian language. The major concentrations are in specific parts of the country, especially in Transylvania. For both Lutheran bodies the ecumenical movement has strengthened their associations with other Christians.

The severe flooding of 1975 and the disastrous earthquake of 1977—the one more intense in agricultural lands in the Danube basin, the other widely destructive in Bucharest—found the Lutheran churches generous in aiding self-help as well as resourceful in channeling aid from LWF-related agencies. In these and other ways, the Lutheran churches have been contributing their diaconia to the common life of the nation.

While the number of Reformed in Romania has remained fairly constant since the end of World War II, the Lutheran constituency of German origin has declined by more than one half. In 1940, the Lutherans numbered 435,000, compared with over 700,000 Reformed (Hungarians). By 1984, the Hungarian and Saxon Lutherans had decreased to

165,000. This nearly 60% loss is borne almost entirely by the Saxons (below). The loss has been by stages. It began with the postwar rush of folk or ethnic Germans back to Germany from the farmlands of Bukovina, Dobruja, and Moldavia where their forebears had settled during the 19th century. Gone is their church, which once counted over 100,000 members. So, too, others from northern Transylvania were "resettled" by the Nazis already during the war; still others became refugees after 1945. Lutheranism in Romania prior to 1940 never achieved a real unity; connections with various parts of Germany took precedence. For those who remained, the traumatic experience of loss—akin to that among Lutherans in *Poland—has reaffirmed an age-old ruggedness and deepened the sense of belonging to a worldwide confessional family. For the Saxons, however, the westward drain continues, as the following account attests.

EVANGELICAL CHURCH OF THE AUGSBURG CONFESSION IN THE SOCIALIST REPUBLIC OF ROMANIA (ECAC-SRR)

(Biserica Evanghelică C.A. din RSR)
Member: LWF (1964), WCC, CEC, CPC
Membership: 115,000
Bishop: The Rt. Rev. D. Albert Klein
Strada General Magheru 4
R—2400 Sibiu

The Evangelical Church of the Augsburg Confession in the Socialist Republic of Romania (ECAC-SRR) derives from the pre-Reformation antecedents of its Transylvanian-Saxon congregations. At present, the ECAC comprises 174 congregations (parishes served by one or more pastors) and 75 affiliates, or diaspora congregations, with a total membership of some 115,000 baptized. These are served by a rapidly declining number of pastors (140 in 1986, 115 in 1988), due to emigration to West Germany. The top decision-making body is the territorial church assembly or synod. Its actions are carried out by the territorial consistory—the executive committee of the synod—over which the bishop presides.

Each of the five church districts has its own consistory, chaired by a dean, for dealing with local matters. Similarly, each parish presbytery is led by the local pastor. Church support is raised locally from voluntary offerings. The salaries of pastors and church officials are supplemented by grants from the state.

Church headquarters are located in Sibiu, still known among the Saxons as Hermann-stadt. A large, modernized building, near the center of town, houses the church's administration offices, the bishop's residence, and the school of theology—complete with student living quarters. The courtyard captures the charm of this compact multipurpose center whose remodeling was aided by gifts from sister churches abroad.

Future pastors of this church are educated here in Sibiu. The school of theology, or the theological faculty, is the German-language section of the United Protestant Theological Institute, whose main base is in Cluj (above), where Hungarian (Magyar) is the language of instruction. The Sibiu faculty of six (some of them part–time) provides quality instruction over a four-year curriculum. Contacts with Cluj are augmented by those with the Orthodox institutes in Sibiu and Bucharest. The ecumenical dimension of these arrangements has become increasingly fruitful, notably during the Luther anniversary year (1983). In that year, however, the allowed quota of entering theological students was drastically reduced; for the Saxon Lutherans, only two new students per year. This stands in sharp contrast to a student body of 42 in the Sibiu section in 1978. Later the quota was slightly increased. As yet there have been no women theological students. But women are prominent in the church music school in Sibiu, whose demanding routine prepares choir directors and organists for the congregations.

Sunday worship remains central in the life of the congregation. Toward this end, the liturgy has been newly shaped and a new hymnal prepared. Supplementing the main service of worship are Bible studies as well as special devotional services during Advent and Lent. Besides these, the ecumenical Week of Prayer for Christian Unity (January), and the women's World Day of Prayer have increasingly been observed. For the young, Christian nurture in the Scriptures and instruction in Luther's *Small Catechism* are provided in every congregation. The ECAC's official paper is the monthly *Kirchliche Blätter.*

The relations of the ECAC to the state have been governed since 1948 by the law for religious bodies (*Kulturgesetz*). Within the body of state law, this one guarantees the churches self-government, the freedom to fashion ways of worship, the conduct of religious education and pastoral care, and the training of worship leaders.

The ECAC holds membership in the LWF, the World Council of Churches, the Conference of European Churches, and the Christian Peace Conference. Material aid received in recent years from the LWF, the Gustav-Adolf-Werk, the Martin-Luther-Bund, and from individual churches has been used especially for theological literature, scholarship grants, and the restoration of churches and parsonages.

● ● ●

It was in the mid-16th century that the Reformation drew the Transylvanian Germans together into the Church of God of the Saxon Nation (Ecclesia Dei nationis saxonicae). In 1572, this church obligated its pastors to the *Augsburg Confession.* As such, it was recognized as an Independent church in the principality of Transylvania. Governance was entrusted to a synod of the church, which was headed by a superintendent elected for life and soon referred to as bishop. As in pre-Reformation times, the center of church life continued to be in the local congregations. These were self-governing and elected their own pastors.

After the incorporation of Transylvania into the Hapsburg Empire (1691), the congregations—sorely tested during the preceding Turkish occupation—proved themselves able to resist the efforts of a (belated) Counter-Reformation. They were even able to provide for the resettlement, about the mid-18th century, of large numbers of fellow Evangelical believers fleeing their ancestral homes in the original Hapsburg realms.

About the middle of the 19th century, the church was able to secure a new constitution, approved by the (Vienna) government and patterned according to a synodical-presbyterial model that preserved the traditional self-government of the congregations. In updated form, this constitution still serves as the basis of the "Evangelical-Saxon" church life and governance.

During the era of Rationalism and cultural Protestantism, the church was sound enough to outlast these leveling influences. This was in itself a noteworthy achievement, for the church carried the entire educational system of the Transylvanian Saxons. This soundness stemmed from a vital worship life and a neighborly concern fostered by influence from spiritual awakenings, evangelization (Inner Mission), and theological reassessment.

Since the end of World War II, the church has been confronted by new tasks arising from the radical change of living conditions in a Socialist state. Also, the drop in Romania's rural population from 90% to 30% has taken its toll among the Saxon Lutherans and their predominantly rural parishes. Migration of members to the industrial centers has required special assistance for them: seeking them out, counseling them, and developing a congregational diaconia capable of matching the needs.

Annually (since 1978), about 5000 Saxon Lutherans have left their native land and resettled in the *Federal Republic of Germany. They have been encouraged to emigrate by organized groups of their fellow countrypeople in West Germany as well as by the generous terms granted by the FRG to ethnic Germans in Eastern Europe adversely affected by World War II.

Most disconcerting for the parishioners of the Saxon church has been the emigration of pastors. Of the 131 who have left during recent years, 104 had been educated in Sibiu. The egress of pastors goes on. They have found placement either in *West Germany, *Austria, *Switzerland, or in German congregations farther away, even in the Lutheran congregation in Rome. For rural parishes, the loss of pastoral leadership has been an especially hard blow. Lay helpers have been pressed into service. Sibiu's city parish, for example, enlisted some 230 volunteers for various tasks, especially in the field of visitation and stewardship.

In face of these changes, the church has not tried to block emigration but has urged the pastors to faithfulness. "The church does not emigrate," Bishop Klein reminded the people. Yet, if recent trends continue, he warned (1984) that in three decades there might no longer be a Saxon Lutheran church in Romania. The Saxon attachment to the Transylvanian homeland has a way of reasserting itself. Many who have resettled have found life in West Germany disillusioning. An adventurous few have returned. Noteworthy among them is the Heidelberg theologian, Paul Philippi. In place of his professorship in church and society and his heading of the Diaconic Institute in Heidelburg, he made ready to join (1985) the theological faculty in Sibiu. The tide may turn. Despite being of retirement age (1987) Bishop Klein continues to provide strong leadership.

SYNODAL EVANGELICAL PRESBYTERIAL LUTHERAN CHURCH OF THE AUGSBURG CONFESSION IN THE SOCIALIST REPUBLIC OF ROMANIA (SEPLC)

(Biserica Evanghelică Lutherana Sinodo-Presbiteriala de Confesiune Augustană din RSR)
Member: LWF (1964), WCC, CEC
Membership: 29,000**
Bishop: The Rt. Rev. D. Paul Szedressy
Bvd. Lenin 1
R—3400 Cluj-Napoca

In Cluj-Napoca (Klausenburg), the nation's second city—where almost half of the nearly 250,000 inhabitants are of Hungarian origin—this modest body of Magyar-speaking Lutherans has its headquarters and educates its ministers. Its 36 congregations, served by 33 pastors, are dispersed over a broad area: some 660 kilometers (400 miles) east–west and about 460 kilometers (280 miles) north–south. The smaller of its two districts, Timisoara, touches the Hungarian and Yugoslavian borders and also includes five Slovak congregations. The larger district, Brashov (Kronstadt), embraces 20 parishes. Its congregation in Bucharest is one of the few Lutheran ones where Romanian is used each Sunday. Among its members are former Jews who have joined under the influence of the long-established Norwegian Mission to Israel (*Israel).

Recognized by the state in 1948, the SEPLC governs its affairs at the district and congregational levels through presbyteries, and at the national level through a general assembly or synod, the highest decision-making body. A bishop (also called superintendent) heads the church, aided by a lay president. The two co-chair the general assembly.

As with its counterpart in Hungary, the roots of this church body go back to the time of the Reformation. Only in 1975 did a Bible translation in modern Hungarian replace the one from the 16th century. That same year the fourth edition of a new hymnal (1948) was a boon to the worship life of the congregations. Having a fairly high proportion of communing members, a careful preparation of young people for confirmation, and an accent on the ongoing education of pastors through conferences and self-directed study, this church is fully aware of its minority status and is striving to retain its identity as a loyal partner with other churches in the land. One evidence of this is the SEPLC participation in the United Protestant Theological Institute in Cluj (above). In 1978, the institute, the largest of its kind in Eastern Europe, enrolled 122 Reformed, 20 Unitarian, and seven SEPLC students. Five years later, with the imposition of a drastically reduced quota for students in theology and certain other subjects, the SEPLC was limited to one new theological student every two years. Efforts continue to raise the quota.

The church's edifices in Cluj and elsewhere—many of them dating from the decades after the granting of religious toleration by the Hapsburgs (1781)—suggest its spiritual powers of endurance. Various aspects of the SEPLC's ecumenical ties offer encouragement. An example was the ecumenical observance of Luther's 500th anniversary. Besides, the increased intermingling of Lutherans—whether of Magyar or Saxon stock—with the Romanian Orthodox majority presents an ecumenical challenge close at hand. A new translation, for example, of Luther's *Catechism* into Romanian—the previous one was made in the 16th century—is seen as but one urgently needed aid toward a mutual understanding in matters of faith as well as life. The new edition of the hymnal includes the catechism as well as an order of worship and 438 hymns. Meanwhile, the outreach of this church to the Magyar dispersion is proceeding, especially through its urban congregations.

UNION OF SOVIET SOCIALIST REPUBLICS

The USSR is a federal state (1917). Its 15 republics cover much of Eastern and Middle-Eastern Europe as well as Northern and Central Asia. Between its border with northernmost Norway in the west and its island proximity to Japan in the east, its neighbors include 11 other countries plus its long coast on the forbidding Arctic Ocean. Area: 22,402,200 sq. km. (8,649,500 sq. mi.). Pop. (1987 est.): 281,700,000 including (1979) Russians 52%; Ukranians 16%; Belorussians (bordering Poland) 4%; Kazakhs 3%; Uzbeks 5%. Cap. and largest city: Moscow (pop., 1985 est., 8,275,000). Language: Russian (official); in the republics the language of the ethnic majority (official), but many others are spoken.

History: From the ninth century A.D. to the revolution of 1917, Russia went through a long process of development and expansion, culminating in the creation of the Union of Soviet Socialist Republics (Soviet: an elected governmental council). Each of the now 15 republics is inhabited by a variety of peoples. In contrast to the Armenian SSR (the smallest of the 15) in the south, and the also small Estonian SSR in the northwest, the Russian SSR is the giant that claims half of the Union's population and covers three-quarters of its territory.

Over the centuries, an originally landlocked Russia won its "window to the west" (the Baltic Sea), and to the south (the Black Sea). Likewise, after more than two centuries of occupation, the Russians overcame the Mongols (Tatars), and from the 16th century onward pressed their conquest across Siberia to the Pacific—reaching the Far East already in 1640 and then consolidating their eastward movement by trade and colonization. Forts held the ground and later became cities. Momentum of this advance carried to Alaska (Kodiak Island, 1784; Sitka, 1799) and to northern California (1812). Vladivostok (1860) became the chief Asian base for Russian expansion in the Far East. In czarist Russia, the Romanov Dynasty (1613–1917) steered a cautious course between the more conservative Slavophile and the more progressive Westernizing forces. Among the latter, Peter I (Peter the Great, czar 1682–1725) early set a Westernizing course, including a relocation of the capital from Moscow to St. Petersburg (Leningrad), on the Gulf of Finland. Eventually, this became Russia's second largest city. Defeated by Germany in World War I, the Russian revolution later in 1917 ushered in the era of Communism. Of the lands on the Baltic Sea that Russia lost in 1918-1920, Finland has remained independent; but during World War II Estonia, Latvia, and Lithuania came once again under Russian rule.

Religion: The USSR is not officially atheist, but education and laws favor atheism. Most people claim to be nonreligious. Yet, an estimated 15% to nearly 40% of the population are said to adhere to some form of Traditional religion: 70 to 96 million Christians, 30 million Muslims, and 3.1 million Jews, with Buddhist, Shamanist (tribal), and other groups adding diversity. Among the Christians, the Russian Orthodox Church— it celebrated its 1000-year history in 1988— claims about 50 million adherents; the Georgian Orthodox-Apostolic Church, five million; the Armenian Apostolic Church, two million; the Union of Evangelical Christian Baptists, 1.1 million; Mennonites, about 75,000; the several Lutheran churches (below), about 700,000. Most of these bodies have ecumenical ties, including the World Council of Churches. The Roman Catholic Church claims over four million adherents, notably in Lithuania, White Russia, and the former parts of Poland. There are also unnumbered other Christians. The Council for Religious Affairs (a 1966 consolidation of government offices) exercises oversight for the Soviet Union as a whole, being aided by regional and local counterparts. Laws of 1975 and the following years, based on the decree of 1929, set limits to the activities of the churches and communities, requiring the registration of religious groups.

Today, the Soviet Union's territory encompasses some of the grandest, saddest, and least known aspects of Christian history. From mountainous Armenia in the Caucasus to the Baltic "window to the west," and across Siberia to the Far East, the Orthodox as well as other communions are set in a vast context. Russian Orthodoxy's beginnings (A.D. 988) center in Kiev on the Dnieper. A medieval state of eastern Slavs, Kiev, in the Ukraine, is the predecessor of the modern USSR. The conversion of Grand Duke Vladimir (d.1015) and his ties with the Eastern (Byzantine) church set the course for Orthodoxy's greatest expansion. Succeeding Kiev as the seat of government, Moscow eventually became a patriarchate (1589). It was often called the Third Rome, especially in light of the fall of Constantinople—the second Rome—to the Turks in 1453. Under Peter the Great, a Holy Governing Synod, based on Anglican and German Evangelical (Lutheran) precedent, replaced the patriarch (1721–1917). Restored in 1918, the Moscow Patriarchate has since then been the seat of Russian Orthodoxy, though with reduced powers and scope. Today, this church of about 50 million members in 20,000 parishes is served by some 30,000 priests. Its 76 dioceses span the country. When it joined the World Council of Churches in 1961, it led the way for the Armenian, the Georgian, the Baptist, and two Lutheran churches—the Latvian and Estonian—to do the same. Later, the small Lithuanian church followed suit. In this ecumenical context, as evidenced at the 1983 WCC assembly in Vancouver, Canada, interest continues to grow as to how Christianity has fared in the world's most immense country.

Among the other churches already mentioned, the Armenian Apostolic, with its patriarch in ancient Echmiadzin (Etchmiadzin, Ejmiadzin), traces its roots to A.D. 301, the year the king proclaimed Christianity the official religion of Armenia, making it the first Christian kingdom. Not long thereafter, in A.D. 330, the royal house of Iberia (later Georgia), in the Caucasus, accepted Christianity, thus giving rise to the Georgian Orthodox-Apostolic Church. In the 19th century, the Russian Baptist Union (1884) resulted from work begun by German Baptist pioneers, like Johann Gerhard Oncken and Martin Kalweit. Far earlier, the effects of the 16th century Reformation increasingly made themselves evident.

Peter the Great allowed the Lutheran church in Livonia (Latvia) and Estonia to keep their rights. He failed in his attempt to unite the Lutheran congregations in the interior of Russia under a superintendent, Barthold Vagetius. The congregations remained under the jurisdiction of the empire. At the beginning of the 19th century, new efforts were made to bring together Lutheranism in the Russian Empire. In 1832, these efforts led to a church law for Lutherans, including those in the Baltic provinces. The result of this was that the church administration of these provinces received a lower legal status than that which had existed up to that time.

At first came eight consistorial districts, six of which were in the Baltic provinces. The smaller districts of Riga, Reval, and Oesel were later abolished. The remaining Baltic provinces were Courland (including Byelorussia and the two Lithuanian governments), Livonia, and Estonia. The headquarters of the two other, considerably larger, consistorial districts were in St. Petersburg (for western Russia from the north to the Black Sea) and in Moscow (for the interior of Russia, Siberia, and Central Asia as far as the Pacific Ocean). The headquarters of the general consistory for the entire church was in St. Petersburg. There was only one theological faculty, in Dorpat (Tartu; see EELC, below).

After World War I and the creation of independent Baltic states, the unity of the church was broken. Even with the new changes that came about after World War II, the former unity was not reestablished. Each of the three Baltic churches has its own constitution and church order. The German congregations in Central Asia hope to be united into one church.

Lutheranism in the Soviet Union is of mixed composition: A church body of Reformation era rootage in each of the three Baltic Soviet Socialist Republics—Estonia, Latvia, and Lithuania; two registered congregations of Finnish-speaking Lutherans, in Pushkin near Leningrad and Petrozavodsk/Karelia; and nearly 500 German-speaking, mostly registered congregations in regions east of the Urals (see below). Periodic visits by Lutheran church representatives to Estonia and Latvia—and in 1980 also to Lithuania—have been on invitation of the Baltic churches and have disclosed a durable spiritual vitality. A similar spirit was evident in a decidedly different situation, when in 1976 the Europe secretary of the LWF Department of Church Cooperation was able for the first time to visit German congregations in Central Asia. There is more to the present Lutheran scene in the USSR than anyone knows, just as there was once much more of a Lutheran presence than now remains. In 1905, Lutherans within the boundaries of the present USSR (including the Baltic provinces but excluding Finland) numbered 3,440,000; today there are only one-fifth as many.

To sum up the course of Baltic history: Conversion to Christianity in the 12th and 13th centuries came comparatively late and much of it by force. Response to the Reformation accentuated worship and the Scriptures in the language of the people. Most Lithuanians, under Polish rule, returned to Roman Catholicism. But Estonians and most Letts (Livonia), under Swedish rule, remained Lutheran. Then, 1721–1917, two centuries under the Russian czars and a Baltic German ruling class made many Estonians and Letts archly Lutheran. Between the two world wars (1918–1940), Estonia, Latvia, and Lithuania were independent nations. Their folk-type churches, having been reconstituted, became a mark of ethnic identity. World War II ended this episode. The churches sustained heavy losses—not for the first time—in members, pastoral leadership, life, and property. Thousands, fearing the future, fled with the retreating Germans, became displaced persons, and eventually found homes in other lands where they formed exile churches (see below). The majority who remained faced the hard task of reconstruction and adaptation also of their church life. In a sense, their modern history has come full circle—but with a difference.

In September 1980, the Conference of Lutheran Churches in Europe (above, Europe Introduction) met in Tallinn, Estonia. With the Estonian Lutherans as hosts, this tenth gathering of the conference was its first in the USSR. Worship, deliberation, and fellowship became memorable in this historic place, not only by confessional ties but also by ecumenical evidence of Christian hope. Subsequent to the gathering, brief visitations included parishes in the three Baltic churches as well as the Finnish congregations in Pushkin. In contact with the Riga-based superintendent, Harald Kalnins—he was made bishop in 1988—LWF officials were permitted to visit German-speaking congregations east of the Urals (below).

ESTONIAN EVANGELICAL LUTHERAN CHURCH

(Eesti Evangeelne Luterlik Kirik)
Member: LWF (1963), WCC, CEC, CPC
Membership: 175,000
Archbishop: The Most Rev. Kuno Pajula
Raamatukogu tän. 8
UdSSR—ESSR—200103 Tallinn

This church of 145 congregations (including one in Petsevi, in the Russian Soviet Federated Socialist Republic, and the two Finnish congregations in Pushkin) and 88 pastors has its headquarters in the city of Tallinn (Reval) on the southern coast of the Gulf of Finland. The Lutheran Theological Institute (1946) is at the same address. Here a small, select faculty seeks to maintain the high standard of its predecessor, the theological faculty at the University of Tartu (Dorpat). (The University—founded by Sweden's Gustavus Adolphus in 1632 and closed in 1710 when Russia took Estonia—was reopened in 1802.) Recently, the student body has numbered over 50. The church's legislative body is the synod; its executive unit, the consistory; and its ecclesial head, the archbishop.

The history of Lutheranism in Estonia parallels that in Latvia: Christianization and subjection, first to the Danes and then to the Teutonic Knights. Later, Estonia was held by Sweden (from 1561, the northern part of Estonian territory; from 1620 also the south of Estonia). After the Northern War (1700–1721), it came under Russian rule (1721–1918). After a brief period of independence following World War I—the nation's "golden era," as many called it—the Estonian Soviet Socialist Republic was proclaimed (1940) and became part of the USSR.

The forced Christianization of so-called Livonia in the 13th century was followed by a gradual building up of the church. Early in the Reformation era, the Estonian towns of Tallinn and Tartu, along with the chief Latvian city, Riga, formed an Evangelical alliance (1524). Gradually, the Reformation spread among the rural people. The Counter-Reformation and periodic wars (1558–1629) were a time of widespread suffering for the young Lutheran church—especially in southern Estonia (Livonia, with a great number of Estonians), which was occupied by Poland.

During the Swedish era, the church was reorganized along episcopal lines, corresponding to the Swedish church. From 1846, about 18% of the Estonians converted to the Orthodox church.

With the creation of the Estonian Republic (1918), the church was once again reorganized with first a bishop and later an archbishop at its head. The archbishop elected after the war, Jan Kiivit (1949–1967), played a decisive role in launching the participation of this church in the WCC (1962), the Conference of European Churches, and subsequently the LWF. His successors were Alfred Tooming (1967–1977) and Edgar Hark (1978–1986). At a special session in June 1987, the church council elected the late Dr. Hark's successor. The new archbishop, Kuno Pajula, had long served as parish pastor in the capital, Tallinn.

For many years after 1945, the repair or reconstruction of churches damaged or destroyed by the war occupied its members and put heavy demands on their giving. As elsewhere in the USSR, church property is state owned, with the congregation paying rent for its use (see also EELC in Exile).

EVANGELICAL LUTHERAN CHURCH OF LATVIA

(Latvijas Evangeliska Luteriska Baznica)
Member: LWF (1963), WCC, CEC, CPC
Membership: 120,000**
Archbishop: The Most Rev. Karlis Gailitis
Lacplesa iela 4, Quartier 4
LetSSr—226010 Riga 10

This church comprises 206 congregations served by 98 pastors. Its headquarters are in the republic's capital, which is situated at the southeastern end of the Gulf of Riga. Education for the ordained ministry and for diversified ministerial functions takes place in the Evangelical Lutheran Theological Institute, also located in Riga. As in neighboring Estonia, the ecclesial head is the archbishop, assisted by a consistory with executive power. The synod is the church's legislative and decision-making authority, while each congregation has its own three-member council for dealing with local matters.

The Latvian people, inhabiting what was long called Livonia (since the Reformation era, Livonia and Kuronia), were converted mainly during the period 1180–1230 and largely by force. In 1522, during the Reformation era, the city of Riga turned Lutheran, with St. James Church becoming the first parish. The further spread of the Reformation was slow. The Counter-Reformation, under the Polish kings and the Jesuits, offered stern opposition. The German-ruled part of the country remained Lutheran, and under Swedish rule the rest fell into line. The first Lettish pastor was not ordained until 1648. The complete Bible in the Latvian language appeared in 1689, and the Lutheran hymnal in 1685. When Russian rule replaced the Swedish (1721), Peter the Great determined that the country would remain Lutheran.

The people's struggle for freedom culminated in the creation of a Latvian republic in 1918. Of its two million inhabitants, 74% were Letts. The religious distribution was: Lutheran 56%; Roman Catholic 24%; Russian Orthodox 14%; Jews 5%; others 1%. The Lutheran church was reconstituted, first by government action (1922) and further by a synod (1928). The consistory, an executive unit, included six Lettish and three German members. In 1922, Sweden's archbishop, Nathan Söderblom (1866–1931) consecrated the church's new bishop, Karlis Irbe (1861–1934), and Peter Harald Poelchau (1880–1945), bishop of the German congregations that were autonomous within the church. Prompted by Söderblom, Irbe encouraged mission work in *India. In 1932, Irbe's successor, Teodor Grünbergs (1870–1962), became archbishop, as provided in the constitution. After the war, he continued as archbishop, heading the Latvian *exile church. In 1940, first the Russians occupied Latvia, then the Germans. More than 200,000 Latvians fled as the war was ending and ultimately were resettled elsewhere. The Lutheran church recovered only with great difficulty from the heavy human and material losses it had sustained. In 1948, Gustav Turs was elected resident archbishop, serving until

his retirement in 1968. In that year, the designated successors, Peter Kleper and Albert Freijs, died. Janis Matulis held office from 1969 until his death in 1985. Erik Mesters was archbishop 1986–1989.

EVANGELICAL LUTHERAN CHURCH OF LITHUANIA
(Lietuvos Evangeliku Liuteronu Baznycia)
Member: LWF (1967), CEC
Membership: 25,000**
Bishop: The Rt. Rev. Jonas Kalvanas Gagarino 68
LitSSR—235900 Taurage

This small church—one tenth its former size—comprises 27 congregations and is served by 12 pastors and some lay assistants. Its headquarters are in Taurage (German: Tauroggen), an agricultural and industrial town of medieval origin in the country's southwest and some 220 kilometers (140 miles)—by road or rail—from Riga (Latvia), where its future pastors are educated. The church's decision-making body is the synod, which convened four times between 1955 and 1983. Major responsibility for the ongoing direction of the church is left to the bishop (called senior pastor until the mid-1970s) and an assisting executive unit, the consistory. The congregations have their own local councils. Besides the modest hymnal and prayer book (editions 1957 and 1982) and Luther's *Small Catechism*, the church publishes a small yearbook for the Lutheran and Reformed congregations.

Lithuania's forced conversion in the late 14th century was superficial, and the people remained largely pagan until the Reformation. In 1550, Kaunas (Kovno), one of the larger towns of Lithuania, accepted the *Augsburg Confession*. The Lithuanian language was reduced to writing, and Luther's *Small Catechism* was printed in 1547, the first hymnal in 1560, readings of Scripture for the Sundays in the church year in 1591, and the entire Bible in 1701. The Reformation spread quickly over the entire country except for seven parishes. But later, under Jesuit leadership, most of these Lutherans were obliterated and only Taurage (Tauroggen) and the environs remained Lutheran.

During the period of independence in this century, the Lithuanian church's pastors were educated in the theological faculty of the University of Kaunas, until it closed in 1936. Prior to World War II, according to the present bishop, the church had some 120,000 members. Today, most of its remaining 27 congregations are in towns and villages in the western part; others are in the northern part with Lettish population. The proportion of baptisms and confirmations among Lutherans in Lithuania is said to be higher than in Latvia and Estonia.

This church has good working arrangements with its counterpart in Latvia and cultivates ecumenical relations with Orthodox and Roman Catholics. A particularly close relationship exists with the small Reformed constituency in the northeast. Bereft of a pastor of their own communion, the Reformed have for years been served by a Lutheran pastor and also aided in other ways. In 1982 the Lutheran bishop represented this Lithuanian group at the assembly of the World Alliance of Reformed Churches in Ottawa, Canada. In fact, long before the 1973 Leuenberg Agreement (*Germany), Lithuania's Lutherans and Reformed had been in full pulpit and altar fellowship.

In a joint effort, Lutheran and Roman Catholic scholars in 1972 published a long overdue translation of the New Testament in modern Lithuanian. A new edition, marking the 600th anniversary of the Christianization of Lithuania, and an ecumenical translation of the entire Bible are also on the way.

Until 1949, when he was arrested, the senior of the church, the leading pastor, was Erik Leijeris. Ansas Baltris (1950–1954) was succeeded by Vilhelmas Burkevicius (1955–1970), and then by Jonas Kalvanas. Since the 1976 synod, the title of senior has been replaced by that of bishop.

In light of the extreme dearth of pastors, there was particular rejoicing after Easter 1984 when the son of the present bishop—a practicing physician—was ordained as an assistant pastor. Later that year, two delegates and two advisers represented the ELCL at the LWF assembly in Budapest.

INDEPENDENT CONGREGATIONS IN USSR—MAINLY GERMAN-SPEAKING

Bishop: The Rt. Rev. Harald Kalnins
Maskavas 427-120
Latvian SSR—Riga 65

Of the reportedly almost 500 Lutheran congregations and circles—a number of them pending registration—outside the three Baltic republics (above) a few are Finnish-speaking and some retain the language of their Estonian and Latvian forebears. Most, however, are German-speaking. The majority are in sprawling Kazakhstan, on its distant southern border, touching Afghanistan and China. Other Lutheran congregations are in adjacent republics, notably the Tadzhik, Kirgiz, and Uzbek; as well as in several of the administrative districts (oblasts) of the Siberian part of the Russian Soviet Federated Socialist Republic (RSFSR). A number of congregations are also in the northern Caucasus region and in the Volga expanse in and near Kotovo. Still others of Finnish origin are in European Russia's northeast, in and around Syktyvkar, capital of the Komi Autonomous SSR.

While most of the congregations are in towns or rural communities, many are in important cities like Omsk, Novosibirsk, and Tomsk, capitals of Siberian oblasts. Others are in Frunze, capital of the Kirgiz SSR; in Dushanbe, capital of the Tadzhik SSR; in Tashkent, capital of the Uzbek SSR, and in neighboring regions. Most of them, however, are in south-central Kazakhstan: in Alma-Ata, the bustling capital city; in Karaganda, capital of the oblast by that name; in Tselinograd (Celinograd), formerly Akmolinsk, as well as in many other places.

Into this vast expanse east of the Urals most of the ethnic Germans (Soviet citizens) were relocated from the Ukraine and Volga regions in late 1941 as Germany's military invasion was advancing. According to the 1979 census, there are more than 1,950,000 ethnic Germans of Soviet citizenship. An estimated 55-65% of them still use German among themselves but Russian at work. In many places their labor is sought after, in trades and construction as well as in agriculture. After the lifting of government restrictions in 1955, their rehabilitation revealed a latent religious dimension.

Most of the Soviet Union's ethnic Germans have had Lutheran forebears. About one-third have Roman Catholic forebears; others Reformed and/or Mennonite. The Protestant side of this background gave rise to certain movements that have left their mark on present-day Russian religious life, particularly among the Stundists (today: Evangelical Christians/Baptists)—so named for their appropriating into Russian Orthodoxy a Bible-study-oriented Christianity that was common among Pietists from Württemberg in the 19th century. For those who clung to their Lutheran heritage, the developments were quite different, manifested particularly by their adherence to the German language.

Women played a central part in the resurgence of Lutheran congregations. In the absence of fathers and sons, some never to return, mothers taught children the rudiments of Evangelical faith. Without Bibles, hymnals, or devotional books—only a few such items had survived the hasty relocation in 1941—memory was the priceless spiritual treasury. Family devotions attracted others and made for little house congregations. Only gradually did these widely scattered Germans learn of each other's whereabouts. Sundays and festivals were "rediscovered" on the work-a-day calendar. Here and there, a pastor who had survived the closing of congregations in the late 1930s showed up among the workers. Of the three such pastors, two lived to enjoy the retirement offered to them in the Federal Republic of Germany. Congregations like the one in Tselinograd (formed in 1953 by lay folk and served until 1972 by Eugen Bachmann) became an encouragement to the formation of still others. Dedicated and qualified lay persons received basic training in various ways and have been ordained by local elders.

The worship life of these congregations, their scriptural orientation, and their intense commitment have impressed the visitors as suggesting the character of the early church. Congregations of 600 or more members are now not unusual. A diversity of style and theological position among them is to be expected: elements of formal Lutheran worship; Pietist Bible study; the practice of the priesthood of all believers persist.

Two objectives of special importance—achieved much earlier by Baptists, for example—are gradually being attained: the creation of an association of registered congregations with a recognized and functioning

Lutheran church body like those in the Baltic republics; and education by extension, from the Riga or Tallinn Lutheran theological academy, for the pastors of these congregations.

In addition to the registered congregations, there are apparently many informal ones now seeking registration. Most of them have in recent years been free to gather for worship and to provide their members with spiritual care. This is in keeping with the USSR constitution, which allows freedom of religious worship—and also freedom of antireligious propaganda. Permission was granted the LWF in 1978 to send Bibles, and eventually also hymnals, orders of worship, and other materials. Initial shipments from Geneva, like the 5000 German Bibles, brought overwhelming joy, as did other publications as well. Slowly other essentials have been allowed in as gifts, such as communion vessels, small organs, and the like. By 1984, the Russian Orthodox publishing house in Moscow was printing a Lutheran worship book in German, which the LWF gave to the congregations. At the same time, the LWF was cleared to send an additional book shipment from Stuttgart (FRG), including 3000 Bibles, 5000 hymnals, and 3000 catechisms (with German and Russian texts).

Although these items only begin to meet the demand, they are signs of a caring fellowship of faith. Visitors from the LWF, as well as from churches in Germany, Scandinavia, and elsewhere have been permitted brief visits. Usually this has been in company with the Latvian pastor from Riga, Harald Kalnins, whose own tireless and pioneering visitation of these congregations has earned him the amply deserved title of superintendent and then bishop. In mid-November 1988 the 77-year-old Kalnins was consecrated in Riga by Archbishop Erik Mesters. Other visits have included the representatives of the Moscow patriarchate and the theological seminary in Zagorsk, as well as the government office of the Council for Religious Affairs.

Today's registered congregations and other worshiping groups are but a fraction of what was earlier in this century the Evangelical Lutheran Church of Russia. Its history spans more than four centuries, from the erection of the first simple church building in Moscow in 1576—by ex-war prisoners and other Livonians from Dorpat (Tartu)—to the re-emergence of Lutheran congregations east of the Urals. Already in 1523, Luther had written his first letter to the Christians at Riga, Reval, and Dorpat in Livonia. Later on, the Northern War (1700–1721) between Sweden and Russia over these eastern Baltic territories—as well as the continuing presence of Germans from the time of the Teutonic Knights—made Livonia a staging area for East-West interchange. Periodically, on invitation of the czars, people of German and north German nationality came to help settle frontier rural lands to the south and east as well as to participate in the trades, business, and professions essential to the development of a nation of enormous potential.

The influx of newcomers extended from the 17th into the 19th century, not evenly but in periodic advances eastward and with occasional reverses, paralleling in many respects the westward movement of people of these same stocks to North America and in a lesser degree to South America and Australia. Those coming to Russia were for the most part Lutherans. The organizational development of an Evangelical Lutheran Church of Russia began with the enactment of the church law of 1832 (above), and its demise came with the intensification of antireligious policies a century later.

As the law of 1832 provided, Lutherans of all kinds were included in one church organization. By the end of the 19th century, it had been divided into two geographic areas or ecclesiastical provinces. St. Petersburg (Leningrad), then the capital, was the base from which fellowship was cultivated with congregations in western Russia, from Murmansk on the Arctic Ocean to Bessarabia and Crimea on the Black Sea. Moscow was the base for contact with congregations in middle and eastern Russia and across Siberia to Vladivostok, and with a congregation (up to 1867) in Russian Alaska. The last reliable statistics (1905) for the inclusive Lutheran church, excluding Finland and the Baltic provinces then under Russian rule, give the St. Petersburg geographic area 702,000 members; the Moscow area 546,000. The ethnic composition of this 1,248,000-member church included: Germans, 905,000; Estonians, 119,000; Finns, 148,000, concentrated in Ingermanland; Latvians, 67,000; Swedes, 7000; Armenians, 1000; others, 1000. Although this church was heavily rural, it also had some large urban concentrations.

St. Petersburg counted 89,950 Lutherans, the biggest parish being that of the Estonians with 17,000 members. In Moscow, a large German parish also had 17,000 members. Pastors for the churches came from the University of Helsinki for the Finns outside Finland. For the other nationalities, pastors came from the Baltic region; to a growing extent also from the rural congregations in Inner Russia. They were educated in Dorpat (Tartu).

A succession of setbacks began to diminish the church. During World War I, the Germans were suspected of being Germanophile, and many of those living near the western border were relocated to Siberia. With the revolution of 1917, hard times began not only for the established Russian Orthodox Church but also for the officially sanctioned Lutheran church. Lutheran unity was jeopardized from within by tensions between the German majority and the other minorities. The great famine of 1920–1922—the worst among such periodic occurrences—sent many Germans, Estonians, Latvians, Finns, and others emigrating, largely to the Baltic states and North America, but also to South America (*Argentina). Among the churches prominent in famine relief were those recently banded into the National Lutheran Council (NLC) in the *USA. Contacts of NLC commissioners on relief service, especially John A. Morehead (1867–1936), the council's top man, with their Russian brethren in the faith contributed strongly toward the formation and development of the Lutheran World Convention (LWC; 1923), predecessor to the LWF. Prominent among the LWC's long-term projects was the theological seminary organized by the Evangelical Lutheran Church of Russia in Leningrad in 1925. This was to replace the no longer accessible theological faculty in Tartu.

In Moscow (1924), the first general synod since 1832 provided the church with a constitution. Its opening lines indicated that the Evangelical Lutheran Church of Russia considered itself part of a worldwide Lutheran church. All ethnic groups worked together. Administratively, the top church person for the Leningrad geographical region, Bishop Arthur Malmgren (1860–1947), was given responsibility for relations with Lutheran churches outside the USSR. The head of the Moscow region, Bishop Theophil Meyer (1865–1934), covered the far-flung domestic front. The accounts of his extended tours of inspection in the 1920s are not only classics in ecclesial necrology but also bear the marks of great faith and devotion. *Nach Sibirien* tells of his visitation beyond the Urals (1925) to secure the participation of the congregations in the reconstituted Evangelical Lutheran Church of Russia.

As the new Soviet society struggled forward and asserted its will to change, Lutherans were particularly vulnerable on two counts: The public policy against organized religion made rapid inroads on an already depleted church leadership (an insufficiency of pastors); the collectivization of farms broke up the economic base of the rural congregations and of the Lutheran church as a whole. By the early 1930s, the seminary in Leningrad was closed. Not many years thereafter, the church as a whole practically ceased to function, and in 1938 the last church, in Moscow, was closed. Here and there, islands of faith remained. World War II gave the Lutheran church in the USSR a virtually mortal blow. But the faith has continued, and after much hardship, new congregations in the Lutheran tradition are carrying on east of the Urals.

YUGOSLAVIA

A federal Socialist republic (1946) along the eastern Adriatic Sea, the country is bordered by seven others—ltaly, Austria, Hungary, Romania, Bulgaria, Greece, Albania—and comprises six republics: Serbia, Croatia, Slovenia, Montenegro, Bosnia-Herzegovina, Macedonia. Area: 255,804 sq. km. (98,766 sq. mi.). Pop. (1985 est.): 22,236,000; of these, Serbs 36.3%; Croats 19.7%; Bosnian-Muslims 8.9%; Slovenes 7.8%; Albanians 7.7%; Macedonians 6%; Montenegrins 2.6%; others 11%. Cap. and largest city: Belgrade (pop., 1981 prelim., 1,470,100). Language: Serbo-Croatian, Slovenian, Macedonian, Albanian; also some German, Hungarian, and Slovak.

History: Formed after World War I out of pieces of the former Austro-Hungarian (Hapsburg) Empire, Yugoslavia is a remarkable patchwork of Balkan diversity in terms of topography as well as people. From the picturesque Dalmatian coast, across the often awesome mountainous interior (glimpsed by TV viewers of the 1984 Winter Olympics at Sarajevo), north and northeast to the fertile Danubian basin, the country has its own way of keeping historic forces alive and mutually supportive. Rooted in the Roman Empire, poised between Latin and Byzantine cultures, host to Serbian, Croatian, and other monarchies, held long under Turkish occupation, then liberated and absorbed into the Austro-Hungarian realm, this land of the south Slavs, by its extraordinary complexity, has played a distinctive part in European history. A German element was added when, in the 18th century and on Hapsburg invitation, south German farmers and others began to resettle and build up the country vacated by the Turks. During the 19th century, thousands more Germans arrived, settling among the Slavs and, more often, founding their own communities. (By ca. 1930, the Germans numbered about 700,000, of whom the vast majority were Roman Catholics. The Protestants, mainly Lutherans, accounted for nearly 100,000 of the total.) Early in the present century, strivings for independence were frequent in certain quarters, especially among the Serbs. The assassination of the Austrian Archduke Franz Ferdinand and his wife on June 28, 1914 (in Sarajevo, seat of the "Greater Serbia" movement) became the occasion—not the cause—for the outbreak of World War I. The breakup of the Austro-Hungarian Empire ensued. So far as possible, the map of Europe was redrawn on a basic principle: the right of self-determination of nations.

Emerging after the war as the Kingdom of Serbs, Croats, and Slovenes, this largest and most complex of the Balkan lands slowly achieved nationhood and in 1929 changed the official name of the country to Yugoslavia. As the land of the south Slavs, it fared poorly during World War II, being torn between compliance with the Axis powers (notably Nazi Germany), on the one hand, and a Communist-oriented indigenous liberation movement on the other. Under Josip Broz—the later Marshal Tito (1892–1980)—a new Yugoslavia entered the international scene after 1945. Rejecting absorption into the status of a USSR satellite, the nation under Tito adapted Marxian Socialism to its own needs. In the process, Yugoslavia achieved standing among the world's leading nonaligned nations. Tito's death in 1980 removed the last of the World War II leaders. Since then, under a rotating presidency (the president of each of the six republics takes his turn a year at a time), the nation has been weathering hard times relatively well.

Religion: Orthodox (large Serbian majority, but also Macedonian and others) over 40% of the population; Roman Catholic (Croats, Slovenes, and others) about 32%; Muslims 12%; Protestant (mainly Lutheran, some Reformed—about 22,000—and various other groups, including Adventist, Pentecostal) 1%. Jews, about 8000, down from 72,000 before the Holocaust; many others to Israel after 1945. The remaining 14% of the population claim no religious connection. Since the end of World War II, all religious bodies have benefited from a separation of church and state, which allows the churches more freedom than in most of Eastern Europe's Socialist countries. It is a freedom within limits. Each commune, each republic, and the federal government has a commission on relations with religious bodies at a given level. Church support is all voluntary, a policy contrasting with that of Yugoslavia's neighbors, where the state grants subsidies. Besides, two principles have guided church–state relations in Yugoslavia. The one has been to depoliticize the relationship between church and state so that each goes its proper way. The other has been to politicize the relationship between the individual church member and the state, seeking in him or her the exercise of responsible citizenship.

Church–state relations in Yugoslavia have long been affected also by the relations between the major churches themselves. Nowhere else in Europe are the forces of Eastern Orthodoxy and Roman Catholicism so nearly balanced. When, for example, the Roman Church, via the Vatican, had virtually arranged a concordat with the Yugoslav government in 1937, the powerful Serbian Orthodox Church blocked its passage. Interfaith tensions continued. After the war, the new government was determined to be free from any kind of church interference; even as the Yugoslavs determined to be rid of any ethnic Germans living among them (below, Lutherans). Looking back, certain stages in the church-state relationship become evident: 1945–1950, confrontation; the 1950s, adaptation in face of continued antireligious campaigns; the 1960s, improved relations, especially with the Roman Catholic Church (1966 agreement between the Vatican and the government, guaranteeing Roman Catholic loyalty to the Yugoslav state). Meanwhile, in 1965, the Serbian Orthodox Church (it claims 8 million members) joined the World Council of Churches. The 1970s saw a hardening of positions against the church. This, in turn, was followed by a new stage of mutual recognition. Meanwhile, the issue of a Uniate (Byzantine Rite) constituency in Roman Catholic ranks continues to bloc closer accord with the Orthodox.

The Ecumenical Council of Churches in Yugoslavia (1968) includes the three bodies in the WCC—Serbian Orthodox, Reformed, Slovak Lutheran—as well as the Slovene Lutheran and two other churches. The rapport developed over the years between Lutherans and Orthodox is evident from the fact that a number of Lutheran pastors—the present Slovak Lutheran bishop is one of them—have received part of their education at the Serbian Orthodox Theological Academy in Belgrade.

Experimentally, in 1976, a small interdenominational theological seminary was opened in Zagreb (Agram), capital of Croatia and Yugoslavia's second largest city. Located in a Lutheran parish house, this was a joint venture of Baptists, Methodists, Lutherans, and several other groups.

The principal Protestant tradition in Yugoslavia is Lutheran. Its story is heavy with hardship and steadfastness under great trial. The combined membership of the three Lutheran bodies is over 75,000. During the 1920s and 1930s, efforts to draw all the various constituencies into one Lutheran church failed. However, the formation of an Evangelical Church of the Augsburg Confession (Novi Sad—Neusatz; 1923) included the German and Hungarian Lutherans. It continued after 1931 as the German Evangelical Church in Yugoslavia until most of its 100,000 members were relocated to West Germany and Austria at the close of World War II, along with the far larger number of Roman Catholic ethnic Germans. The Slovak Lutherans, having been part of the Hungarian Evangelical (Lutheran) Church prior to World War I, chose to form their own church body (below).

Outside encouragement and aid have from time to time highlighted the Lutheran scene.

Already in 1919, the National Lutheran Council in the USA initiated interchurch help from abroad. Since World War II, the LWF has mediated much of the aid from abroad, making possible the rebuilding of churches and parsonages; the rendering of a variety of urgently needed services; and the distribution of Bibles, hymnals, catechisms, and other publications. A new church center (1965) in Novi Sad, adjacent to the former German Evangelical (Lutheran) edifice, provides for conferences and the training of workers. Likewise, over the past two decades the Gustav-Adolf-Werk in the *Federal Republic of Germany has been able to resume its traditional role of assisting minority churches.

The Reformation early found response among the Slavic peoples, and students from this south Slav region became known to Luther in Wittenberg. Among them was Primus Trubar (below), the "Slovenian Luther." Another, Matthias Flacius (1520–1575), from near Trieste, became well known as a theologian and reformer in Germany. In Magdeburg, he initiated a Lutheran-oriented writing of church history known as the *Magdeburg Centuries*. To be from the Slavic lands was quite different than surviving there, as the Lutheran epic in this part of Europe proves.

The *Yugoslavian national committee* of the LWF comprises representatives of the three churches described below. It is headquartered in Novi Sad. For years, it was chaired by Bishop Struharik. As in many other countries, this committee deals with problems and needs of the three participating churches, especially as these needs may relate to the churches' partnership in the LWF. The committee's annual meeting is frequently an extended gathering where all pastors in the country can meet together and deal with present-day theological issues as well as with new methods of fostering understanding and cooperation.

EVANGELICAL CHURCH IN THE SOCIALIST REPUBLICS OF CROATIA, BOSNIA, AND HERZEGOVINA AND THE AUTONOMOUS PROVINCE OF VOJVODINA

(Ev. Crkva u SR Hrvatskoj, SR Bosni i Hercegovini i SAP Vojvodini)
Member: LWF (1951), CEC
Membership: 4950**
Senior Pastor: The Rev. Dr. Vlado Ladislav Deutsch
Gunduliceva 28
YU—41000 Zagreb

This church has its headquarters in Zagreb, capital city of the Croatian republic, and its congregations scattered in the eastward-lying Vojvodina (the southern part of the fertile "Hungarian Plains") and in the Bosnia-Herzegovina republic to the south. It comprises the non-German remnant of what was until 1944 the 130,000-member and largely rural German Evangelical Church in Yugoslavia (see above). Its church languages today include Serbo-Croatian, Hungarian, and German. With its internal diversity and diminutive size—and with 480 kilometers separating its most remote congregations east and west—it is an extreme example of a dispersed church. It also serves as a striking reminder of the agonizing relocations of peoples after World War II. And losses have continued. The migration of additional ethnic Germans back to the land of their forebears, the aggressiveness of Roman Catholics in the region, and the growth of sectarian movements and other factors have contributed to reducing this church to half the size it was in the mid-1960s. Nevertheless, its story also carries signs of hope.

In 1966, the LWF Executive Committee meeting in Belgrade gave evidence of an ongoing supportive fellowship for this and the other host churches comprising the Federation's national committee in Yugoslavia. Encouragement came from another quarter on Reformation Day 1976, when 51 students enrolled in the newly opened interdenominational theological seminary located in the parish house of the Zagreb Lutheran church (see introduction).

EVANGELICAL CHURCH OF THE AUGSBURG CONFESSION IN THE SOCIALIST REPUBLIC OF SLOVENIA, YUGOSLAVIA

(Evangeličanska cerkev A.V. v. SR Sloveniji, Jugoslavija)
Member: LWF (1952), ECCY
Membership: 19,020**
Senior Pastor: The Rev. Ludvik Novak
Titova c. 9
YU—69000 Murska Sobota

The congregations of this Slovenian-speaking church are located in mountainous country which forms the northernmost tip of Yugoslavia in the republic of Slovenia. Prior to World War I, this so-called Prekmurje district was part of Hungary. The senior pastor, who presides over the church, has his residence in Murska Sobota, east of the Austrian border. Each congregation has its presbytery, and an annual synod is the church's governing body. Its future pastors are educated at the Evangelical Theological Faculty in Bratislava, *Czechoslovakia, and elsewhere. Membership in the LWF has built upon a longtime reliance on fellowship beyond periodically changing frontiers.

During the 1920s and 1930s, this church was part of the then big (130,000-member) German Lutheran Church in Yugoslavia (see above). It became autonomous after 1945. Before 1918, it was a member of the *Evangelical (Lutheran) Church in Hungary. Its history goes back to the time of the Reformation when, as early as 1527, Protestants in the Slovenian mountains were subjected to persecution. Primus Trubar (1508–1586), the "Slovenian Luther," translated the Scriptures for his people and thus created the Slovenian literary language. Other printed works followed, as German Protestant princes and townspeople provided assistance. Initial contacts with Turkish Muslims presented a missionary challenge. The Counter-Reformation and Hapsburg power virtually exterminated this church outwardly, although it continued a precarious life underground. After the Edict of Toleration of Emperor Joseph II (1781), the church surfaced and regained much of the ground it had lost.

SLOVAK EVANGELICAL CHRISTIAN CHURCH OF THE AUGSBURG CONFESSION IN YUGOSLAVIA (SECCAC)

(Slovenská ev.-kr. a.v. cirkev v SFR Juhoslávii)
Member: LWF (1952), WCC, CEC, CPC, ECCY
Membership: 51,276**
Bishop: The Rt. Rev. Andrej Beredi
Karadziceva 2
YU—21000 Novi Sad

In the autonomous province of Vojvodina—east of the Danube River and outward from Belgrade to the great plains on the Hungarian and Romanian border—lie most of the 30 parishes and 13 affiliates of this Slovak-speaking church (SECCAC). They are served by 25 pastors plus preaching assistants. The chief cultural center of Slovak Lutheranism in Yugoslavia is Petrovac, three-fourths of whose 8000 inhabitants are members of the SECCAC. However, the church headquarters and residence of the bishop are in Novi Sad, a city of 260,000, whose Lutherans number about 1500.

Of Yugoslavia's three Lutheran church bodies, the SECCAC is by far the largest. Each parish is governed by its own local council, and the church as a whole by a synod. The bishop, as spiritual head, and a lay president are the church's chief officers. Earlier, the SECCAC constituency was part of the Evangelical (Lutheran) Church in *Hungary, but upon the creation of Yugoslavia, it became autonomous. Its future pastors are educated at the Evangelical Theological Faculty in Bratislava along with those of the *Slovak Evangelical Church of the Augsburg Confession in Czechoslovakia.

In 1967, the SECCAC added the then 7000-member Evangelical Church in the Peoples Republic of Serbia, a Lutheran body of Hungarian descent. Prior to 1918, that small church also had been part of the Evangelical (Lutheran) Church in *Hungary. Then from 1918 to World War II it was part of the German Evangelical (Lutheran) Church in Yugoslavia (above), remaining alone for the next 22 years.

A challenge to Slovak identity is gathering force as the Serbian language gains wider usage. Meanwhile, a Slovak translation of the Bible, completed in the 1970s in Czechoslovakia, is widely used and also enjoys Roman Catholic approval. A variety of books and tracts as well as a new hymnal express the vitality of this church.

The kinship between the SECCAC and its much larger counterpart in *Czechoslovakia continues to be cultivated as conditions permit, *Austria and *Hungary lying between the two. A special event like the retirement of Bishop Juro Struharic (after 26 years of noteworthy service) and the installation of his successor (November 1983) transcends the routine and links local recognition with the wider fellowship. The general bishop from Slovakia (*Czechoslovakia) installed the new bishop. Assisting was the bishop of the Slovak-Zion (*LCA) in North America. Others, too, were present representing the LWF, the Gustav-Adolf-Werk (FRG), the WCC, and other churches and agencies: the Serbian Orthodox bishop of Novi Sad, clergy of the Byzantine Rite (Uniate) and Roman Catholic dioceses, and the bishop of the Reformed Church, as well as the senior (dean) of the Slovenian Lutheran, and all active pastors of the SECCAC were on hand. So also were representatives of the government. Laud was ample for this forthright and faithful churchman. Support was promised his successor. Under the baroque tower of this sturdy church in Novi Sad, many changes have occurred over the generations. With quiet trust the assembled throng went forth in hope.

EXILE CHURCHES

As Estonian, Latvian, and Lithuanian Lutheran churches in exile—a designation of their own choice—the following churches represent the native lands they fled in 1944 and the continued feeling of attachment to the ancestral home. Their long histories speak of Baltic lands subject to powerful neighbors and alive with ethnic identities going back to pre-Christian times. *Denmark, *Sweden, *Germany, *Poland, and *Russia have all played some part in this region over the past many centuries. Through German settlers and landowners, Lutheranism rooted here already in the 16th century.

With the Russian Revolution (1917), the Baltic peoples struggled bitterly and successfully for independence. Estonia, Latvia, and Lithuania were free nations for about two decades (1918–1939). With the outbreak of World War II, Soviet forces moved in (1939–1941). Then came the German occupation (1941–1944), whereafter the lands were retaken and embodied into the USSR. The human cost of this political and cultural as well as military storm was enormous. Many of the inhabitants remained. But others, by the thousands, fled westward by land, with the retreating German forces, or by sea to Sweden. For the survivors of this epic of agony and faith, the church remained the keeper of their identity and of their fractured heritage.

The refugees from the three Baltic republics became internationally recognized as Displaced Persons. Many Estonians were received by Sweden; the others joined the Latvians and Lithuanians in West Germany, where the UN International Refugee Organization (IRO) cared for them in DP camps. Except for the Lithuanians, the large majority of the Balts were Lutheran. The three exile churches, formed under many difficulties and scattered in many locations, nevertheless proved indispensable as mediating agencies working in concert with Lutheran World Service to Refugees (LWSR), an arm of the LWF. One of the noteworthy features of the resettlement program in its early stages in Germany was its youthful staff. Under the initiating direction of Dr. Howard V. Hong (St. Olaf College, Northfield, Minnesota), most of the field workers serving the DP camps were older college and seminary students whose dedication, resourcefulness, and energy were exemplary.

In time it became possible for LWSR—directed in Geneva by Dr. Stewart W. Herman (1948–1952)—in cooperation with a corresponding unit in the World Council of Churches and with other agencies, to resettle well over 100,000 Baltic DPs. Besides those who had already made it to Sweden or other countries of Northern Europe on their own, the comprehensive resettlement program, as facilitated by IRO and the churches, counted heavily on receiving countries in various parts of the world. Outside Europe, the major receivers were *Canada, the *USA, *Australia, *New Zealand, *Brazil, and other Latin American countries. Lutheran churches and agencies in many parts of the world, with the help of local congregations and voluntary sponsors, took active part in an enormous operation described as a "chain of hands." Wherever they have resettled, most of the Baltic DPs and their descendants have become active members of their communities.

Given the problems of living in dispersion, the task of organizing churches drew heavily on the faith, stamina, and ethnic loyalty of the people. The formation, administration, and maintenance of a far-flung ecclesial body was something new; so also the task of exile church leaders and pastors relating to churches in whatever the host country. Most difficult and delicate was the effort to retain and foster ties with what remained of the churches in the homeland.

On occasion, the exile churches have been of timely assistance to the home churches. For example, the Estonians abroad have over the intervening years produced a theological literature that includes substantial portions of a new translation of the Bible into modern Estonian, a revision of the hymnal, and an array of scholarly works. Foremost among scholars and researchers has been Dr. Arthur Vööbus (1909–1988), an Estonian, long professor at the Lutheran School of Theology at Chicago (see *USA and *Turkey). A basic problem for the exile churches continues to be the provision of pastoral care for the laity, and it appears to grow more intense. Besides, the question of retaining identity has led the exile churches in the *USA and *Canada to reaffirm their separate organizations, while also fostering close cooperation with the larger Lutheran church bodies.

ESTONIAN EVANGELICAL LUTHERAN CHURCH IN EXILE (EELCE)

(Eesti Evangeeliumi Luteri Usu Kirik)
Member: LWF (1947), WCC, CEC
Membership: 50,000**
Archbishop: The Most Rev. Konrad Veem
Wallingatan 32-2
PO Box 45074
104 30 Stockholm 45
Sweden

This is a fellowship of 65 congregations served by 52 pastors. The membership is scattered in many countries, chiefly *Sweden, the *Federal Republic of Germany, *Canada, the *USA, and *Australia. Its archepiscopal seat in Stockholm provides for a general secretariat, which administers the concerns of this dispersed church. Its future pastors are educated in theological schools of the host countries. The magazine, *Eesti Kirik* (Estonian Church), which was founded in Estonia in 1924, resumed publication in exile in 1959 and has appeared ever since.

This church in exile arose out of a mass exodus of about 80,000 fleeing their homeland in the autumn of 1944—about 30,000 going to *Sweden and 50,000 to *Germany. About 65,000 of these claimed to be Lutheran. Pastors accompanying the refugees included Archbishop Johan Köpp, who went to Sweden. The order prevailing there was conducive to a fairly rapid organization of a church in exile. In war-torn Germany, the situation was much more difficult. Eventually, the refugees found a place in camps in the British and American zones of occupation. When opportunity came to emigrate, all but about 4000 left Germany. In their new countries of resettlement, they formed congregations. They also have contributed significantly to the professions as well as to the life of church and society. The present archbishop once served on the staff of Lutheran World Service to Refugees. His travels keep him in touch with the EELCE's dispersed constituency.

LATVIAN EVANGELICAL LUTHERAN CHURCH IN EXILE (LELCE)

(Latvijas Evangeliski Luteriska Baznica Eksila)
Member: LWF (1947), WCC
Membership: 50,000**
Archbishop: The Most Rev. Arnold Lusis
5 Valleymede Road
Toronto, Ontario M6S 1G8
Canada

This fellowship of 138 congregations is served by 134 pastors and extends into 14 countries. Its chief concentrations are in *Canada, the *USA, and *Australia. A 21-member church council, with executive powers, assists the archbishop, who is its president elected for life. LELCE headquarters have been in Canada since the late 1960s.

For the first two decades, the headquarters were in Esslingen, not far from Stuttgart, *FRG. Here sagacious Archbishop Teodor Grünbergs—once expelled from Latvia by the Germans—joined the 120,000 Lutheran Latvians who had fled to Germany and with the help of able colleagues organized them into the LELCE. Grünbergs, an influential member of the first LWF Executive Committee (1947–1952), summed up his people's situation: "Our enemies want to destroy us; our friends want to assimilate us; but we want to live." He added: "Our home in exile is our church."

Since the late 1950s, 50 churches have been built or rebuilt in the various countries; a new hymnal and many theological books have also been published. Inevitably, a second generation—now at home in their adopted countries—faces a mounting language problem.

However, the international Latvian folk festival—music, drama, the arts and crafts, ecumenical worship, and more—continue to celebrate a people's heritage. The 1988 event (Indianapolis, USA) drew about 8000, including many from Europe, Australia, Canada, the USA, and other parts of the world, as well as from Latvia itself. This cultural and spiritual event has been held every few years since the 1830s. Its initiator, Juris Neikens, was a Lutheran pastor and acknowledged literary figure serving the Dikli, some 80 miles (120 kilometers) from Riga. His successor in Dikli, many years later, was Zanis Krisbergs, who—with his wife Tekla—found a new beginning in the USA and a compelling reason, shared with many others, for continuing the festival tradition (see Latvian Evangelical Lutheran Church in America).

LITHUANIAN EVANGELICAL LUTHERAN CHURCH IN EXILE (LELCE)

(Lietuviu Evangeliku Liuteronu Baznycia)
Member: LWF (1947), CEC
Membership: 10,000**
President: The Rev. John Juozupaitis
9000 South Menard Avenue
Oak Lawn, Illinois 60453, USA

The 19 congregations comprising this dispersed fellowship are served by 12 pastors. Headquarters, recently moved from Germany to suburban Chicago, are now more central to the majority of dispersed congregations. Like the other exile churches, the Lithuanians face an aging membership and a language problem for the rising generation. Yet, a sense of identity is kept alive through mutual assistance, pastoral care, publications, and worship.

This exile church took shape slowly. When the Lithuanians of German stock were ordered to leave the country, many others decided to flee with them. By 1941, some 20,000 had emigrated back to Germany. By 1946, the number of refugee Lutherans alone had risen to 26,000. Of these refugees, 12,000 were in Displaced Persons camps and 14,000 were privately lodged. A church paper helped pastors and people to remain in contact. Bible story books, Luther's catechism, and a small hymnal provided substance for congregational gatherings. A constituting synod in 1946 formed the LELCE. Adolf Keleris became the first president and senior pastor. Two years later, the provisional leadership was strengthened by a three-member presidium.

In 1949, opportunities opened for emigration to *Canada, the *USA, and *Australia, thus dispersing the hitherto reasonably accessible Lithuanian Lutheran communities. By 1957, many still living in Lithuania were receiving permission to join their families. The LWF provided assistance both to congregations already settled and to those formed by later emigrants to distant places.

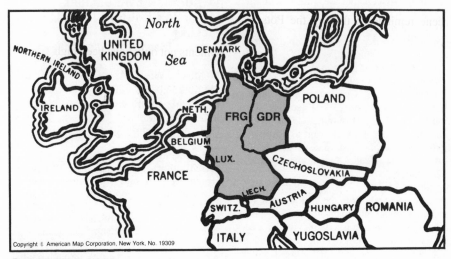

Copyright © American Map Corporation, New York, No. 19309

GERMANY

Some 30% of the Lutherans in LWF member churches live in Germany, and of them the proportion of those in the Federal Republic to those in the Democratic Republic is 3:1. Some have formed Independent Lutheran churches. In addition, there are other Germans of Lutheran heritage in the several Union churches.

History: Germany's epic, in briefest summary, enters the concert of Europe under Roman occupation. Place names like Augsburg (for Emperor Augustus) and Cologne (Colonia) recall that much of today's West Germany was once part of the Roman Empire. Later, Germanic and other peoples toppled Rome. In its place, under Charlemagne, king of the Franks, and based at Aachen, came the grandly named Holy Roman Empire (HRE) of the German Nation. The coronation of Charlemagne in Rome by the Pope (A.D. 800) set the stage for a power struggle extending over centuries. It pitted pope against emperor, church against state, spiritual power versus temporal power—on such issues as the emperor's rights and the pope's rights to name bishops or other high clergy and to invest them with the insignia of office. The struggle also involved church reform, the responsibility finally being left to the emperor or the territorial prince; a situation that made the Reformation possible. That was also the time when Emperor Charles V, a Hapsburg, having extended his rule worldwide, sacked Rome (1527). But as other nations arose, the HRE declined. Napoleon, master of Europe, finally dissolved the HRE in 1806, after a 1000-year history.

Accompanying Germany's achievements in education and culture, science and industry were the contrary phenomena of large-scale emigration and national unification. The latter, led by Bismarck, the "Iron Chancellor," culminated in the Second Reich (proclaimed in Versailles after the Franco-Prussian War, 1871). It endured until 1918, the defeat of Germany in World War I. The failed experiment with democracy opened the way to National Socialism and Hitler's proclamation of the Third Reich in 1933. With the defeat of Nazi totalitarianism in World War II came the partitioning of Germany into the two separate countries described below.

But here an overview of the combined scene reminds us that by the Potsdam Agreement (August 1945) West Germany and West Berlin (these are popular designations) came under British, French, and American zones of occupation. East Germany and East Berlin came under Russian (USSR) occupation. Besides, Poland's relocation westward to the Oder-Neisse (River) line reduced the overall size of Germany by nearly one-fourth, placing East Prussia, most of Silesia, and Pomerania under Soviet or Polish rule.

The westward rush of German refugees during the closing stages of the war continued at a steady pace for years thereafter, necessitating the resettlement of millions. Their coming provided labor for the enormous tasks of reconstruction, and it also changed the religious map of Germany. Many Protestants wound up in predominantly Roman Catholic regions, and vice versa. Confessional coexistence entered a new era. The flow of refugees from the East Zone westward was viewed with alarm by the authorities there, to whom the reconstruction of this geographically and numerically smaller part of Germany was of first importance. Berlin was the focal point of East-West tension. During 1948–1949 the Soviet blockade of West Berlin; the declaration of East Berlin as the capital of the German Democratic Republic (1951); the rioting of East Berlin workers (1953); and finally the building of the Berlin Wall (1961), recall the painful steps toward a fully divided Germany. Certain details of this story show up in the following accounts of the several church bodies.

Religion: An understanding of Lutheranism in the Federal Republic of Germany and the German Democratic Republic requires some familiarity with their common rootage in the Lutheran

Reformation of 1517 and with confessional developments in Germany over the centuries since then. These developments not only have been highly complex, but also have affected Lutheranism virtually worldwide.

Confession and territory. The issues raised by Martin Luther—particularly a right understanding of the gospel in terms of justification by God's grace through faith and the removal of abuses from the organized church—presupposed then, as they do now, the catholicity of the church and the given unity of that church in Jesus Christ. The movement began in Wittenberg. It took tangible form in Augsburg, where, in 1530, certain territorial princes and representatives of free cities signed a confession of faith. The *Augsburg Confession* (unaltered from its original test), along with Luther's *Small Catechism* (1529), has since then been the distinguishing theological and legal document of Lutheran churches everywhere.

From 1530 until 1806—the year when, under pressure from Napoleon, the Holy Roman Empire ceased to exist and many petty principalities were merged into larger political units—two criteria determined a Lutheran church: territory and confession. In 1530, each signer of the *Augsburg Confession* had accepted responsibility for reforming the church in his territory. This so-called *ius reformandi* made the Protestant ruler, as the executor of reform, the chief overseer and temporal head of the church in his territory—a function that Roman Catholic rulers had already exercised prior to the Reformation. Although Luther and his coworkers considered this a temporary expedient, it endured, with modifications, until church and state were separated at the end of World War I by the German revolution of 1918. However, ambiguities in this arrangement soon became evident already in the 16th century.

The Religious Peace of Augsburg in 1555, ending the war between the Lutheran princes and the Roman Catholic forces of the emperor, gave Lutheran territories the right to coexist with Catholic territories within the German empire. The principle was that the religion of the territorial ruler determined the religion of his subjects (*cuius regio eius religio*). In the Protestant territories, the authority of bishop was accordingly given to the respective princes, who became *summi episcopi*. Over 90 years later, the Peace of Westphalia (1648, ending the costly Thirty Years' War) confirmed the earlier divisions. The same legal rights as already enjoyed by the Lutherans were given belatedly to the Reformed princes as relatives in the Protestant faith.

In the interval, much had happened to complicate German Protestantism. As Calvinism surfaced in Germany, especially in the Rhine valley regions, during the second half of the 16th century, some princes began changing from Lutheran to Reformed, either secretly or openly. Theologians spoke of a "crypto" or secret Calvinism being present in certain Lutheran churches and among theological teachers. The *Formula of Concord* (1577) was intended to clarify the Lutheran position and to screen out Calvinistic discrepancies. On the 50th anniversary of the *Augsburg Confession,* the *Book of Concord* (1580), containing the three ancient Ecumenical Creeds and the Lutheran confessional writings, was published. A Lutheran orthodoxy then developed in an age when the Roman Catholic Counter-Reformation was in progress and when Reformed teaching was vigorously asserting its own orthodoxy.

Mission afar, union at home.   The nearly 170 years from the Peace of Westphalia to the formation of the Evangelical Church of the Old Prussion Union (1817) saw far-reaching changes in German Lutheranism. Orthodoxy had lost favor. Pietism emerged as a new force, readily crossing the lines of territorial churches. The new University of Halle and the Pietist leader, August Hermann Francke (1663–1727), gave German Lutheranism a new kind of international and interconfessional (Anglican, etc.) involvement through mission in *India and *North America, and aid, for example, to Swedish prisoners of war in *Russia. As Pietism was a reaction against an overly rigid orthodoxy, so Rationalism (Deism) endeavored to replace Pietism and also the traditional forms of Lutheran worship. During the wars following the French Revolution, the early 19th century ushered in a time of religious awakenings and also an ensuing era of Romanticism.

In Prussia, already in 1613, under the Elector Sigismund, the house of Hohenzollern changed from Lutheran to Reformed and held sway over a predominantly Lutheran population. The Reformed elite were later (from 1685) augmented by refugee French Huguenots who resettled in Prussia. In observing the 300th anniversary of the Reformation, King Frederick William III (1795–1861) of Prussia caused Lutherans and Reformed to combine in one Evangelical church, an administrative union of the Prussian territorial churches.

Other union churches of different character were created in other territories. Their official statements of faith either included both the *Augsburg Confession* and the *Helvetic Confession,* or as in the case of Prussia, left it to the congregation to remain either Lutheran or Reformed. Luther's *Small Catechism* and the *Heidelberg Catechism* (1562) were equally authorized for catechetical instruction, the choice being left to the local parish and pastor. But in so-called consensus unions, where Lutherans and Reformed were also doctrinally consolidated, as in Baden and the Palatinate, new common catechisms were introduced. For their worship life, the congregations (in Prussia) were provided with a common liturgy based on that of the Lutheran churches in the 16th century. The ordination vow in Prussia was either on the Lutheran or the Reformed confessions. As to designation, the names Lutheran and Reformed were replaced by "Evangelical," the common denominator for Lutheran and Reformed Christians together. All actions to create unions for the sake of uniformity in the territorial churches were aimed by each respective prince, as *summus episcopus*, to settle the problem of Lutheran and Reformed co-existence in his territory. For Lutheranism, especially, such action was to have far-reaching effects (below, Evangelical churches).

Creativity   and   complications.
Politically, the high point between 1817 and 1918 was the unification of Germany and the creation of a new (Second) German Reich under Bismarck in 1871. Relations between state and church entered a new phase. Roman Catholicism's international character (allegedly this was a threat to the quest for national unity) made it the target of repressive measures and engaged it in a bitter *Kulturkampf*. Protestantism's territorial character, seen as a weakness to be overcome, made it subject to unitive efforts within the new Reich. Difficulties stood in the way. One was the structure

of the Protestant (Evangelical) churches as state and territorial churches. The other was the presence of a trifurcation of Germany's Reformation legacy. Lutherans, United, and Reformed represented three different degrees of attachment to the Lutheran confessions, although all of them considered Martin Luther a German national church father.

"Confessional" or pure Lutheranism arose in autonomous German states like Saxony and Bavaria, with their respective universities in Leipzig and Erlangen, as well as among various anti-Union groups in Prussia itself. Protests against "Unionism"—and against an accompanying theological liberalism in the university faculties where future pastors were being educated—filled the ecclesial air with debate and also prompted many confessionally bound pastors and their people to emigrate. So, for example, emigrants from Silesian Prussia pioneered new Lutheran churches in the *USA and *Australia, while Saxon emigrants, fearing Rationalism, settled in the *USA and became progenitors of "Missouri" Lutheranism. In Bavaria's Neuendettelsau, Wilhelm Löhe (1808–1872) trained a new type of pastors and teachers for service among spiritually neglected Germans in North America, and allied himself temporarily with the Saxons there.

Meanwhile, mission societies were formed, drawing adherents selectively. Confessionally Lutheran societies included the Leipzig, the Gossner, the Hermannsburg, the Neuendettelsau, and the North German. United yet predominately Lutheran mission societies included the Rhenish, the Berlin, the Bethel, and even the Swiss-German Basel, whose main support came from broadly Lutheran, non-Union Württemberg (see Switzerland). The work of these societies carried the designations "confessionalism" and "unionism" overseas, not only to North America but also to Latin America, Africa, Asia, and Australia.

Within Germany itself, the Inner Mission was launched in 1848 (Johann Hinrich Wichern, 1808–1881, of Hamburg) and rallied various persuasions of Protestants to respond to the challenges of evangelism, welfare services, and social action as posed by the rapidly growing cities and by railway, canal, and other supra-territorial development projects. Personnel, such as deaconesses (Fliedner, Lohe) and deacons (Wichern), and practical training for theological students (Bodelschwingh) activated a wide range of services through church-related institutions. Inner Mission congresses, especially after 1871, promoted a nationwide outlook among church people as well as a service-oriented concern for church unity. The spiritual care of German Protestants outside Germany, in such diverse places as Eastern Europe, Brazil, and South Africa, fell to the Union-oriented Gustav-Adolf-Werk (1832) and to the confessionally Lutheran *Gotteskasten* ("Lord's Treasury") movement (1853).

Evangelical and/or Lutheran? Against this background, one can trace the rise of two comparable developments pointing toward the eventual unification of Germany's divided Protestant churches. On the *Evangelical* (United) side in 1846, Prussia took the lead in gathering representatives of church governments in 26 German states for exploratory discussions on confessional and constitutional matters. This was followed in 1848 by the Evangelical Kirchentag (Church Congress), the first of a sequence of "grassroots" gatherings inspired by leading lay people and theologians, a counterweight to the meeting of church officials and the setting in

which the Inner Mission (above) found its initial support. By 1852, the Eisenach Conference of Church Administrations was giving organizational form to the exploratory meetings begun in 1846. In 1903, the German Evangelical Church Committee became the successor to the Eisenach conference and tried to accelerate the movement toward Protestant church unity. In 1917, despite the limitations imposed by World War I, the 400th anniversary of the Reformation was celebrated as a pan-German Protestant event, even the Reformed seeing in Luther a leader who had helped shape their own Calvinist tradition.

On the *Lutheran* (confessional) side in 1841, an appeal issuing from a German-American pastor, Friedrich C.D. Wyneken (1810–1876), awakened responses in Germany, especially among the confessional Lutherans. Wilhelm Löhe, in Neuendettelsau, became their chief protagonist. In 1844, he envisioned an eventually worldwide Lutheran church, seeing Europe, North America, and Asia (India) as places of its coming strength. In the early 1860s, Prussia's annexation of Schleswig-Holstein, Hanover, and other states of Lutheran confession aroused reaction. In 1868, the General Evangelical Lutheran Conference (GELC) was organized (Hanover, Saxony, Bavaria, etc.) and the *Evangelisch-lutherische Kirchenzeitung* begun. This paper soon became the very influential voice of the Lutheran conference. International ties early found a welcome in the conference. In 1901, in Lund, *Sweden, for the first time, it ventured outside Germany. The plans of the conference to meet in the *USA in 1914 did not materialize, due to war. For the GELC membership, too, the Reformation festival of 1917 was a stirring, though subdued, event, celebrated in Wittenberg and elsewhere.

The separation of church and state, brought about by the German revolution of 1918, created a new situation for the churches. The princes—*summi episcopi,* or heads of their respective territorial churches—abdicated, and the Protestant churches had to fill their place. This was not difficult, however, because between 1817 and 1918 these churches had developed synodical structures. Synods with duly elected members from the clergy and laity had come into being, and these proved ready-made instruments for the church self-government.

Developing new structures.   The 30 years between 1918 and 1948—from the separation of church and state to the constituting of the Evangelical Church in Germany (EKD)—were a time of intensive and manifold testing for Lutheran and other churches in Germany. The bankrupting inflation of the early 1920s; the groping adventure with democracy under the Weimar Republic; the takeover by National Socialism in 1933; the perilous struggle against Nazism within the ranks of the churches and repressive measures by the state against the church; rampant anti-Semitism culminating in the Jewish Holocaust; the catastrophic World War II; the agonizing era of relief, resettlement, reconstruction, and partitioning under allied occupation—these and many other forces determined the setting in which the churches had to find their way.

During the three postwar years 1919–1922, all the territorial churches provided themselves with new constitutions. The church retained its right to receive taxes. This gradually led to the common practice of the churches continuing to be supported by the help of the respective (regional) state governments. The income tax system was used as a means of collecting the people's basic financial contribution to the church, and the church paid the state governments for this service.

In the new situation, the churches moved closer together in order to create firm interchurch structures essential for carrying on their spiritual and practical functions. In 1922, significantly in Wittenberg, the German Evangelical Church Federation (DEKB) was formed. It stood upon the basis laid earlier by the work of the Eisenach conference (1852) and the German Evangelical Church Committee (1903). The new church federation aimed to safeguard the interests of the several member churches, to foster an awareness of German Protestantism, and to advance the religious and moral worldview of the German Reformation.

The General Evangelical Lutheran Conference, meanwhile, sought to supplement the functions of the church federation by assisting its member churches in every way possible. The new and most exciting dimension of such assistance was made possible by help from North America. At Eisenach in 1923, the GELC and the then recently created National Lutheran Council (*USA) jointly sponsored the formation of the Lutheran World Convention (LWC). This extension of confessional awareness on a global basis ushered in a new era for Lutherans in many lands, not least in Germany. The so-called Luther Renaissance, shaped by scholars like Karl Holl (1866–1926) in Berlin; Nathan Söderblom (1866–1931) in Uppsala; Ludwig Ihmels (1858–1933) in Leipzig; and many others, had begun earlier in the century and now served to enrich as well as balance the interests expressed by the new LWC.

The church struggle. When the National Socialist Party took over the government in 1933, relations between state and church entered a new period of tension and open conflict. The party platform professed to espouse a "positive Christianity." Yet in the same sentence it removed the Jews from the right of citizenship. Most church people seemed little troubled by this thought. Only later some of them—Berlin's Dean Heinrich Grüber (1891–1975) and his service bureau are best remembered—risked their lives to help Jews escape the Nazi dragnet (below, *FRG). Concern for what happened to the Jews was overshadowed by fears of the Bolshevist danger, against which Nazism was seen as a bulwark.

Roman Catholics and Protestants reacted variously to this challenge. The Vatican negotiated a concordat (July 1933) with the Third Reich. Even so, this did not prevent subsequently bitter conflict, with strong measures taken against Catholic schools, orders, and organizations. The Protestant response was divided. This division lay at the root of the church conflict. On the one side, the so-called German Christians—many of them were of liberal and cultural Protestant persuasion—promoted the formation of a unified national church to serve the aims of the state. Their optimism seemed typically expressed by Fritz Engelke, of Hamburg, head of the Rauhe Haus (birthplace of the Inner Mission) and designated Reich Vikar, who claimed that the German people had entered upon a "new age of mysticism." The state would henceforth accomplish a mission among the people that the church over previous generations had failed to do. (Told to the author personally in 1934.)

On the other side, opposition had been building up against such ideology-prone German Christians. Already in the 1920s, the rise of a dialectical theology was challenging the views of liberal Protestantism. Karl Barth (1886–1968)—the Swiss Reformed theologian who taught at the universities of Münster and Bonn before being ousted by the Nazis and returned to his native Basel—became the leading spokesman of dialectical theology. This Bible- and Reformation-oriented theology, sometimes called neo-orthodoxy, rejected the premises of liberal Protestantism as well as the pagan ideology of the Nazi state. Others, too—notably Hans Asmussen (1898–1968), pastor in Altona near Hamburg and later first chancellor of the Evangelical Church in Germany (EKD), and Hermann Sasse (1895–1974; see Australia), both of them Lutherans—spoke out early against the impending Nazi threat to the church.

The gathering conflict broke out over the leadership of the German Evangelical Church (DEK). Constituted in July 1933, it was voted into existence by Nazi-influenced elections. The new structure proved incapable of becoming the national church it had been intended to be. Instead, it became the battleground for opposing forces in and among the churches.

The Barmen Theological Declaration (1934), largely the work of Karl Barth and Hans Asmussen, became the best-known expression of the resistance against the political intentions of the Nazi-oriented German Christians. The movement of the Confessing Church—so-called for its firm stand on the confessions of the Reformation era—took different forms in the individual churches. In some parts of Germany, it organized itself as a Confessing Church, i.e., as a structural alternative to the "legal" but Nazi-corrupted church structures.

The Reformation confessions and a revived active confessing gave rise to an inner renewal of the churches. Best known as tactical leader in the Confessing Church was Martin Niemöller (1892–1984), pastor in Berlin/Dahlem and subsequently held in Nazi concentration camps, 1937–1945.

By 1936, the ranks of the resistance were divided. After the Confessing Church synod at Bad Oyenhausen, those in the United churches (mainly in Prussia, where German Christians controlled church affairs) went one way, keeping the name Confessing Church, and those of the confessional Lutheran churches (called "intact" because they were in charge of their own affairs) went another. The latter, comprising Hanover, Bavaria, and Württemberg, in 1936 formed the Council of Evangelical Lutheran Churches, known simply as the Lutheran Council and its churches as confessional churches. Whether confessing or confessional, resistance to the German Christians and to the tactics and ideology of the government continued through World War II.

Women achieved a significant role in the Confessing Church. At times they filled the gap left by imprisoned pastors or by pastors drafted for military service. According to a provision of 1927, they received the equivalent of ordination, theirs being called consecration—like that accorded deaconesses since the mid-19th century. A woman in this pastoral role was a vicar *(Vikarin)*. Not until 1943 did the Confessing Church undertake the first full-fledged ordination of women. During World War II, the spontaneous service of women, ordained and otherwise, held many a parish together. Meanwhile, deaconesses—some 50,000 of them members of motherhouses all over the country—and countless other women rendered indispensable service in hospitals, communities, and church-related institutions.

Beginning again. War's end, with its enormous destruction and multiplied misery, also brought a drastic alteration of Germany's religious map, especially in the zones of British, French, and American occupation. The influx of nearly 12 million expellees—about half of them Protestant—from the former eastern parts of Germany and from German enclaves in Eastern Europe made the difference. In the absence of an overall plan of resettlement, the headlong rush often brought large numbers of Protestants into hitherto traditionally Catholic territory, and vice versa. Yet the prolonged church struggle during the 1930s had, in many instances, drawn Catholics and Protestants together. Across parish lines, in prisons or concentration camps, lay people as well as pastors of the two confessions had learned to understand each other better. Very soon after military action ceased—and even before that—Catholics and Protestants shared each other's church buildings and distributed material aid without regard for credal distinction. Personifying this mutuality in an exemplary way was the Roman Catholic-Lutheran dialog as initiated in 1945 by the Cardinal Archbishop of Paderborn, Lorenz Jäger (1892–1975), and the Lutheran bishop of Oldenburg, Wilhelm Stählin (1883–1975). Comprising theologians of rank in each of the two communions, the study group has met annually for some 40 years. Its ecumenical contribution, also to Vatican II, has been significant.

The end of the war also brought the possibility of a new beginning for Protestant church unity. The German Evangelical Church, shaken by the serious *Kirchenkampf,* had lasted 12 years. It still existed legally, but it required a successor. Resistance and renewal during those years had deepened the fellowship in the Confessing Church, represented by the Council of Brethren, and in the confessional Lutheran churches, represented by the Lutheran Council. Württemberg's Bishop Theophil Wurm (1868–1953) had emerged as a mediator between these two constituencies. At Treysa, north of Frankfurt, in August 1945, representatives from the Confessing Church in all territorial churches convened and laid the basis for a new, inclusive body: The Evangelical Church in Germany (EKD).

Prior to the Treysa meeting, key representatives of the nationwide Council of Brethren had met with Karl Barth in Frankfurt, and the leaders of the several Lutheran territorial churches had also met. As to the future, these two groups had different visions. The old dichotomy between Evangelical (United) and Lutheran (confessional) was quick to reassert itself, particularly with respect to the importance of the Lutheran confessions in or for the new church body. The opportunity to create what some had hoped for—a unified Evangelical Church of the Augsburg Confession—was lost (see below, Oldenburg). However, the Evangelical Church in Germany (EKD) was organized in Treysa in July 1945. Representatives from the several territorial churches adopted a preliminary constitution and elected a 12-member council.

Later, the new EKD council invited representatives from the churches outside Germany and from the World Council of Churches, then in process of formation, to its meeting in Stuttgart. There, in October 1945, the council presented a Declaration of Guilt, expressing the solidarity of the churches with the German people in the wrongs that had been committed during the Nazi era. This was a moment of confession on which the future turned. Reconciliation with the ecumenical brethren followed. The way was opened to an era of growing partnership with churches and Christians abroad such as the churches in Germany had never experienced before.

The relief and reconstruction activities of the churches—led by Eugen Gerstenmaier (1906–1986), and aided by many talented men and women drawn from various fields—organized and utilized the available resources at home and coordinated the assistance channeled from aboard. The *Hilfswerk der Evangelischen Kirchen in Deutschland* was speedily formed at war's end in 1945. It included the free churches and cooperated with the Roman Catholic *Caritas*. As a new structure, it complemented the well-established and institution-orientated Inner Mission (1848, above). In 1952, Hilfswerk and Inner Mission were consolidated. Known thereafter as the *Diakonisches Werk* of the EKD, this comprehensive diaconic agency maintains its central administration in Stuttgart as well as regional branches elsewhere. (Its counterpart in East Germany continues active; below, German Democratic Republic.)

The role of the laity in the life of the church has become prominent in the decades since 1945, especially through the Evangelical Academies. The one at Bad Boll (below, Württemberg), the oldest and largest of these conference centers, today has a dozen counterparts in the other West German territorial churches, and equivalents in the GDR as well.

So, too, the Evangelischer Kirchentag—its antecedents go back to 1848— is an immense assembly, mainly of laity, on a national or regional basis in East as well as West Germany. Initiated by Reinold von Thadden-Trieglaff (1891–1976), a former head of the Student Christian Movement in Germany, the Kirchentag was launched in Hanover in 1949. It returned there in 1983. Accent is on worship, Bible study, Christian unity, peace, and living the Christian life amid changing times. The Kirchentag influence is ecumenical. In its evangelical way, it parallels and keeps in touch with the older Katholikentag, long popular with Roman Catholics. Like the Evangelical Academies, the Kirchentag has been emulated in other countries. Many people feel that it has been responding to a deep spiritual hunger as its offerings seek to link faith and life to personal problems as well as to major issues of our time.

Leipzig 1954, under the theme "Rejoice in Hope," was the most heavily attended Kirchentag, with 650,000 at the closing rally. Over three decades later, the 21st Kirchentag—noting also the 40 years since the end of World War II—proclaimed "The Earth is the Lord's." The average attendance at this gathering in Düsseldorf (1985) was 135,000 on each of the four regular days. Half the attendants were said to be under 18 years of age. For them especially, the Bible study, lectures, forums, discussion groups, and career guidance made the Kirchentag a true "opportunity fair" of the Spirit, as one of its most popular sections—*Markt der Möglichkeiten*—has been called for many years. The concluding eucharist, in the Düsseldorf stadium, drew about 80,000 communicants. The 1987 Kirchentag was held in Frankfurt.

Global fellowship and restructuring. Again it was initiative from the outside, especially from the USA and Sweden, that led to the formation of a successor to the Lutheran World Convention. In Lund, *Sweden, in late June and early July 1947, the Lutheran World Federation was organized. In a preliminary way, the LWF, prior to being officially constituted, had been actively serving the needs of war victims in Germany and other countries. German Lutheran churches found themselves part of a reconciling fellowship of faith and service, an experience that would later be extended as Germany gave aid to peoples in other countries (see General Introduction).

Ecclesiastical restructuring, meanwhile, had been in progress. Two historic meetings took place successively in Eisenach in July 1948: The first formed the United Evangelical Lutheran Church of Germany (VELKD); the second formally adopted the EKD preliminary (1945) constitution. Ten Lutheran territorial churches had achieved a long-sought goal in organizing the United Lutheran Church in Germany (VELKD), although minus the Lutheran churches of Oldenburg and Württemberg. Care was taken to make the VELKD part of the larger and inclusive body, the EKD, comprising all of Germany's territorial churches (*Landeskirchen*). Although clarified, the relation of VELKD and EKD remained complex, not only inside Germany but also with respect to relations outside. As to the VELKD, each of its member churches had already in 1947 become a member of the LWF. But all German territorial churches together became members of the WCC, whose initial assembly was held in Amsterdam in August 1948. They were represented in the World Council by a single body, the EKD. Due consideration was given to a proportional allocation of delegates from Lutheran, Evangelical (United), and Reformed bodies.

For two decades, 1948–1968, organized Protestantism was a symbol and expression of German unity. Both the EKD and the VELKD spanned the four zones of allied occupation. They continued to do so after 1949, the year when the Federal Republic of Germany (comprising the British, French, and American zones) and the German Democratic Republic (the Russian zone) were proclaimed. As postwar reconstruction created productive economies—first in the FRG (aided by the Marshall Plan) and then also in the GDR (by dint of self-help)—the political situations in the two German states followed two different courses. Amid the persistence of tension between the two constrasting life-styles of the FRG and the GDR, it became increasingly difficult for two overall church bodies like the EKD and the VELKD to maintain their overarching unity. When the 450th anniversary of the Reformation in 1967 focused attention on Martin Luther's Wittenberg, in the GDR, only a few church people from the FRG were granted permits to enter. Attempts to hold simultaneous but geographically separate sessions of EKD and VELKD meetings proved unsatisfying. (For the EKD and VELKD in West Germany today, see below.)

By 1968, this divided condition became too much for the churches. In that year the EKD split in two, and the VELKD followed suit in 1969. The names of the general bodies and the majority of the member churches remained in the Federal Republic. In the Democratic Republic, the former EKD constituency became the Federation of Evangelical Churches in the GDR (BEK/DDR); the former VELKD constituency became the United Evangelical Lutheran Church in the GDR, until dissolved in 1988 (VELK/DDR, below).

A new phase in the complicated life of German Protestantism had begun. The separate courses taken during the ensuing years are evident below. Yet signs of a shared spiritual concern transcend political as well as confessional boundaries. Even before 1980, for instance, EKD and BEK/GDR representatives held consultations on peace; and young people, especially, have demonstrated for peace. Supportive ties between specific churches in the West with others in the East continue. Luther observances in 1983 crossed frontiers by television as well as by tourism. The Sixth International Luther Research Congress, held in Erfurt during August of that year, accentuated how worldwide and ecumenical the interest in this "Doctor of Faith" had become in the half-millennium since his birth.

In observing the 40th anniversary of the ending of World War II, the EKD in West Germany and the BEK in East Germany jointly issued a statement of thanksgiving for what God has done over the past four decades. "He has made new fellowship grow between Christians and between Christian churches as a result of our confession of guilt" (at Stuttgart, October 1945). Among the signs of reconciliation, the statement noted "a new relationship with the neighboring peoples." "As churches in the two German states we both declare that a war must never start from German soil again. . . . We both advocate a European order of peace. We both remind the industrialized countries of their responsibility for creating a life worth living for the peoples of the Third World."

A Luther-awareness persists variously in Germany's churches. Today, Lutheran, Reformed, and United churches are linked in eucharistic fellowship as affirmed in the Leuenberg Agreement of

1973—a kind of revisitation of Marburg (1529) with a positive outcome. Although Germany's Evangelical (United or Union) and Reformed churches are not to be counted as Lutheran, they are included here for ecumenical reasons. Without them the story of Germany's Lutheran legacy would remain incomplete. They are treated as "Evangelical Churches" in separate sections appended, respectively, to the following accounts of Lutheran churches in the *Federal Republic of Germany and in the *German Democratic Republic.

FEDERAL REPUBLIC OF GERMANY

A country of Central Europe, the FRG (*Bundesrepublik Deutschland*; West Germany), following the partitioning of Germany after World War II, was proclaimed a republic on May 23, 1949. Area: 248,687 sq. km (96,010 sq. mi.). Pop. 1985 est., including West Berlin, an enclave within East Germany 60,940,000. Provisional cap.: Bonn (pop., 1982 est., 291,500). Largest city: Hamburg (pop., 1984 est., 1,609,500). West Berlin (pop., 1985 est., 1,851,800—a 9% decline over the past ten years). Language: German.

History (see also Germany, History): In the wake of "the Catastrophe"—the German version of "Unconditional Surrender"—two complementary attitudes seemed to prevail: a profound sense of loss and disillusionment, and a determined will to self-help and reconstruction. By late 1948, the USA-sponsored Marshall Plan was helping to revive the economy. Attempts at a "reorientation of the German people"—the aim of the occupation was accompanied by a widespread legal process of denazification—were accompanied by a thorough overhaul of the political system and the rise of two major parties: the Social Democrats (SD) and the Christian Democratic Union (CDU).

The Federal Republic of Germany (FRG) was proclaimed in May 1949, its capital located in Bonn (near Cologne on the Rhine), and its first chancellor, or prime minister,

given the reigns of government. Konrad Adenauer, founder of the CDU party, remained chancellor for 14 years. "Der Alte," as he came to be known, guided the new nation through a period of remarkable recovery. People spoke of West Germany as the "economic miracle" *(Wirtschaftswunder)*, led by Ludwig Erhard, later chancellor. An unprecedented accord with France—the "traditional enemy"—became basic to West Germany's reacceptance in the European community. Because of the Cold War and the creation of the North Atlantic Treaty Organization (NATO), the Federal Republic continued to be occupied. The USA was in the lead role in the West vis-à-vis the other superpower in the East. Much like Japan, West Germany's energies could be concentrated on the productivity of a peacetime economy. Later, under Chancellor Willy Brandt (1969–1974), a new *Ostpolitik* created improved relations with the USSR, Poland, Czechoslovakia, and East Germany. Ties with the USA continued strong.

Religion (1982): Roman Catholic 43%; Protestant 42%; Orthodox 1%; Jews 0.05%; Muslims 2.2%. Other, affiliated or of no religion, 11.7%.

Roman Catholicism—far stronger in the FRG than in the neighboring GDR—some time during the late 1970s edged slightly ahead of Protestantism in numbers. Its hierarchy in the FRG comprises five archdioceses and 17 dioceses. Some ancient ecclesial boundaries, like that of archdiocesan Paderborn, extend into East Germany and remain a continuing political problem. Age plays a part. Cologne (Köln)—the old Roman Colonia—traces its antecedents to A.D. ca.150 and is the oldest as well as the largest of the archdioceses. The National Conference of Bishops—commonly called the Fulda Bishops' Conference, for the location from where St. Boniface advanced his mission among the Germans in the 8th century—has been active for decades but was formally organized only in 1967. It serves as the common meeting ground for the leaders of the church. The *Katholikentag*—now a biennial mass rallying of the laity—was begun during the stirring events of 1848, the year of revolution. Its importance has grown since World War II and the ensuing drastic alteration of West Germany's religious map (above).

While at great price expellees changed the religious map, church leaders and laity changed the climate of interconfessional relations. The effect was cumulative. Since 1973, there has been Roman Catholic participation in the common association Arbeitsgemeinschaft Christlicher Kirchen (below). On the occasion of the visit of Pope John Paul II to Germany in November 1980, the ecumenical rapprochement received further impetus. Through the quality of its theologians, the caliber of its church leaders, the extensiveness of its educational system, and the inclusiveness of its welfare services (Caritas), West German Catholicism has been widely influential in the Roman Catholic Church as a whole. A prime example of this is the work of Augustin Cardinal Bea (1881–1968), pioneer of the Vatican Secretariat for Promoting Christian Unity. A south German by birth and education, a Jesuit by training, and an Old Testament scholar by specialization, Bea early embraced a vision that included the two confessions, Catholic and Protestant. In the Scriptures, in Christ, in baptism, he saw the already given unity of the church and strove lifelong for a fuller manifestation of it. His great opportunity came when Pope John XXIII welcomed Bea's plan for promoting Christian unity as part of the preparation for non-Roman Catholics to participate as observers at—and indirectly as contributors to—Vatican II. In the process the West German ecumenical experience fell into place.

Protestants, in almost equal numbers with Roman Catholics, are mainly in the folk churches of Reformation origin described below. In addition to these are some nine Free churches (Methodists, Baptists, Moravians, and others) as well as 21 so-called sects (Latter Day Saints, Swedenborgians, Jehovah's Witnesses, and others) and a half-dozen special fellowships (Catholic Apostolic Church, the Philadelphia Movement, and more). The Greek Orthodox Metropolitanate of Germany embraces nearly half a million adherents. This church along with the small Russian Orthodox and others of Eastern rite were strengthened by the influx of migrant workers after World War II, as mentioned above.

Ecumenically, the Association of Christian Churches (Arbeitsgemeinschaft Christlicher Kirchen in der Bundesrepublik Deutschland und Berlin-West, ACKBD) begun in 1948 and based in Frankfurt, provides opportunity for sharing the concerns of the so-called Free churches (those that have grown up outside the traditional territorial and formerly established churches) as well as of the Roman Catholic Church with the churches comprising the EKD. In conjunction with this association, the German Ecumenical Study Committee was formed in 1950. It publishes the *Ökumenische Rundschau,* the quarterly counterpart to the WCC's *Ecumenical Review.*

Jews in the Federal Republic represent a venerable history. The vast majority remained committed to Judaism despite their espousal of German culture and the conversion of many to Christianity. The anti-Semitism of the Nazi era re-awakened Jewish identity, but at a terrible price. Since the end of World War II, the number of Jews in the FRG has hovered around 30,000, a small fraction of their strength a half-century earlier. A larger than average number of those in the FRG today are in the older age brackets. Those who could do so emigrated to *Israel and other countries. In the FRG as well as in the GDR and *Poland, monuments to the Jews annihilated during the Hitler era are former concentration camps, like the infamous Dachau (near Munich) or Bergen-Belsen (near Hanover). The 40th anniversary (1985) of the liberation of these extermination centers—which also included many non-Jews—recalled the enormity and horror of the Holocaust.

As President Richard von Weizsäcker on that occasion reminded his fellow Germans, "We seek reconciliation. . . . If we for our part sought to forget what had occurred instead of remembering it, we would also impinge upon the faith of the Jews who survived and destroy the basis of reconciliation."

Efforts of Christians and Jews to uphold each other in mutual trust thus have an importance far beyond their modest pursuit over the years. Already in the mid-1930s the Confessing Church (above) spoke out clearly against Nazi anti-Semitism, while Catholics and Protestants cooperated in assisting Jewish refugees. Yet such help, often heroic, was woefully insufficient. The "final solution" became a grizzly reality, and the near genocide of a people remains a trauma for the survivors as well as for Jews generally. For Christians themselves the Holocaust remains an ineradicable fact of radical evil gone rampant, and its memory is kept alive in order that reconciliation and mutual supportiveness may be an ongoing obligation. In the FRG, conferences of Christians and Jews have taken up this task, pursuing it in various ways since the late 1940s. With little publicity, countless conversations and personal associations as well as the West German government's compensation to survivors and former refugees—and also its assistance to Israel—are among the signs of a new day.

For Lutherans in the FRG, the problem of coming to terms with what was done to the Jews has been mitigated by the often heroic efforts of Swedish, Danish, and Norwegian Lutherans during and after the Nazi era. Those efforts revealed a faith active in love. A succession of conferences, under LWF sponsorship, on the Church and the Jewish People were held over a period of years in the FRG and elsewhere. In Bossey, near Geneva (1979), Copenhagen (1981), and Stockholm (1983), a way was cleared for mutual trust and understanding. Luther's defamation of Jews late in his career was rejected, but his biblical stance on human responsibility *coram Deo* (in the presence of God) and on the centrality of the Word of God were seen as very near to Jewish sources. Lutherans and Jews rejected any organized proselytizing of each other, leaving their abiding differences in God's keeping.

Islam underscores the changes in the West German religious scene. Its approximately 1.5 million adherents have poured in since the 1950s. Most of them are Turks, prominent among the foreign laborers recruited to speed postwar reconstruction and spur the *Wirtschaftswunder*. As Muslims, they are demanding the same kind of consideration shown by the government to Christians. These demands reflect those of the "guest worker" community as a whole, which, by the mid-1970s, numbered 2.5 million people. In recent years, the debate has intensified over repatriating at least some of them. Meanwhile, Catholic and Protestant agencies—drawing upon postwar experience with German refugees—have aimed to help the migrants to receive fair treatment and, as in the case of the Turks, to become citizens (EKD, below).

For traditional Protestantism, the relative homogeneity of a given territory is long past. For pastors and church members various kinds of guides and handbooks have been produced to shed light on the new situation and to promote understanding. A leading example is the 760-page *Handbuch Religiöser Gemeinschaften* (1978; new and enlarged edition, 1985), whose penetrating accounts range from the long-present Free churches to the more recently arrived exotic sects derived from Asia and the Americas, such as Brazilian Spiritism, American Scientology, or Indian Hare Krishna.

In this setting, the former Protestant establishment, in important ways more united than formerly, strives to adapt to the times.

Interchurch Relations in the FRG

1. Association of Christian Churches in the FRG and in Berlin (West), Friedrichstr. 2-4, D-6 Frankfurt/Main (ACKBD = Arbeitsgemeinschaft Christlicher Kirchen in der Bundesrepublik Deutschland und Berlin-West)

I. *Territorial†* *Churches*	II. *Free Churches*	III. *Roman Catholic and Orthodox*
Evangelical Church in Germany (EKD) (see below, 2)	Free Evangelical congregations in Germany Evangelical Methodist Old Catholic Mennonites Moravians Salvation Army Guests: Federation of Free Evangelical congregations Society of Friends (Quakers) Independent Evangel- ical Lutheran Pentecostals	Greek Orthodox Roman Catholic

2. Evangelical Church in Germany (EKD), Herrenhäuser Strasse 12, Postfach 210220, 3 Hanover 21

   Comprises the 17 territorial churches (above I) in three combinations:

(a) *Lutheran*	(b) *United*	(c) *Reformed*
United Evangelical Lutheran Church of Germany (VELKD)— members of LWF: Bavaria Brunswick Hanover North Elbian (former Eutin, Hamburg, Lübeck, Schleswig- Holstein) Schaumburg-Lippe Other Lutheran churches— members of LWF: Oldenburg Württemberg	Evangelical Church of the Union: Berlin/Brandenburg (West) Rhineland Westphalia Other Union churches: Baden Bremen Hesse and Nassau Kurhessen-Waldeck Palatinate The United and Re- formed churches comprise the Arnoldshain Confer- ence	Lippe Reformed Church of NW Germany

3. LWF National Committee in the FRG, Postfach 510409, 3 Hanover 1. Chairperson: The Rt. Rev. D. Karlheinz Stoll, Schleswig; Executive Secretary: The Rev. Käte Mahn, Hanover.

   Comprises representatives of the eight LWF member churches:
   the five in the VELKD
   the two other Lutheran territorial churches
   the (free) Evangelical Lutheran Church in Baden

   † A territorial church is an autonomous church within a given geographical area.

EVANGELICAL CHURCH IN GERMANY (EKD)

(Evangelische Kirche in Deutschland)
Member: WCC, CEC, ACKBD
President of the Church Office:
Baron Otto von Campenhausen
Herrenhäuser Strasse 12
PO Box 210220
D--3000 Hanover 21

This account continues the EKD story in West Germany since the separation of 1968. A parallel treatment is in the section on the *German Democratic Republic, below. Without the caveats of bilateral considerations the situation in each of the two Germanies becomes clearer.

The EKD in the Federal Republic is a federation of 17 self-governing territorial churches (described individually below) and the Evangelical Church of the Union (EKU), which is a special combination of EKD members—United churches—formerly part of the Old Prussian Union. Affiliated to the EKD are the Continental European Unity of Brethren (Moravian) Fellowship and the Federation of Evangelical-Reformed Churches in Germany.

As noted earlier, the United Evangelical Lutheran Church of Germany (VELKD) is made up of most of the country's territorial Lutheran churches, with the exception of Oldenburg and Württemberg. The VELKD is fully within the structures and purpose of EKD and is in full communion with the other EKD member churches—an openness affirmed by the Leuenberg Agreement (above), now part of the EKD constitution. An estimated 80% of the entire EKD membership retains some form of Lutheran legacy. But the position of the EKD is ecumenical. The preamble to its constitution declares:

> The foundation of the Evangelical Church in Germany is the gospel of Jesus Christ as given us in the Holy Scriptures of the Old and New Testaments. In recognizing this foundation, the Evangelical Church in Germany confesses the one Lord of the one, holy, catholic and apostolic church. In common with the ancient church, the Evangelical Church in Germany affirms the creeds of the ancient church. For their

understanding of the Holy Scriptures as well as of the ancient creeds the Lutheran, Reformed, and United member churches and congregations, the confessions of the Reformation pertaining to them are standard.

By its historical and other variations, the EKD is both a church and a federation of territorial churches. Each of its approximately 10,600 parishes is incorporated and has no overlapping boundaries. For local matters, each congregation has its own governing council in which the lay (elected) members and pastor(s) work together. The individual church member, whether active or inactive, is at least indirectly involved in the diaconic service and missioning (outreach) tasks of the church by means of being a contributing member of the church through the supporting church tax structure. In contrast to East Germany, this traditional system is a holdover from state church days. By prior arrangement with the respective territorial churches, the respective state governments in the Federal Republic collect a given surcharge (normally 8% to 9%) for the church (Roman Catholic as well as Protestant) on each income tax return. In recent years, a decline in income has faced the EKD member churches with critical problems. Meanwhile, the raising of special offerings for diaconia and mission purposes continues as a long-established practice.

In the several EKD member churches the structures are the same. Parishes form districts, headed by a superintendent (dean or provost) and an administrative committee (Kreissynodal-/Dekanats-/Propsteivorstand) elected by the district synod. The larger territorial churches are usually subdivided into regions, or districts, over which a regional superintendent (prelate) presides, dealing exclusively with clergy matters. The territorial church itself—the Landeskirche—has its distinctive history and confessional imprint, mainly Lutheran or United, and in a few instances Reformed. The elected head of a territorial church—a bishop in most Lutheran and United churches, in others a Präses or church president— presides over the church council and its administrative officers. The synod of the territorial church normally meets twice a year and deals with matters of church policy and practice as well as with special problems and issues. The synod has a lay president and a lay majority among its elected representatives. The synod is the territorial church's legislative body and elects the clerical president or bishop.

The leadership and governance of the EKD is threefold: 1. The *synod* of 120 members deals with issues affecting the EKD as a whole, whether in relation to society, the government, or the ecclesial realm. Its lay president serves a six-year term. 2. The *church conference,* a gathering of the heads of the member churches, advises on the sharing of responsibility between the EKD and its partners. 3. The *council* comprises 15 clerical and lay members. The synod's president is an ex officio member. The other 14 are elected by the synod with due regard being given to geographical and confessional considerations. The chair of the council is elected from among its members by the synod in concert with the church conference. The council deals with subjects not specifically assigned to the synod or the conference. It bears particular responsibility for the ongoing cooperation of the several agencies and associations within the EKD.

The administrative work of the EKD is carried out by a church office, which has three divisions: one for juridical and administrative questions; one for theology and public responsibility; and one for ecumenics and foreign relations. Since mid-1986, all of them are located in Hanover (until then, the Division for Ecumenics and Foreign Relations, formerly known as the Kirchliches Aussenamt, or Foreign Office, was in Frankfurt).

The church office deals with all relevant legal matters, government agencies, public issues, legislation affecting the churches, public relations, and the media, as well as with relations to other churches, the World Council of Churches, Christian world communions, and other worldwide church organizations. It also promotes dialog with some of the Orthodox churches and carries responsibility for the spiritual welfare of Protestant and Orthodox migrant workers in the Federal Republic. Roughly 190 EKD pastors are regularly sent to German-speaking congregations and churches in other countries (some of which are affiliated with the LWF). Through the Division for Foreign Relations, there are ties with more than 500 pastors of

churches or congregations serving German-speaking emigrants or temporary residents in other countries, most of them serving under the jurisdiction of other churches.

The agencies and associations whose cooperation the EKD Council oversees represent a remarkable array of activity at home and abroad. Foremost among them is the *Diakonisches Werk* (DW) of the EKD (Germany, above). This immense enterprise, including that of its more recent related agencies, has been set forth in a seven-volume series of handbooks (*Handbücher für Zeugnis und Dienst der Kirche*) completed in 1983. The concluding volume depicts the ecumenical outreach and international scope of this inclusive endeavor. The newer donor agencies were active already prior to the 1968 split of the EKD. As the responsibility of West German Protestants, they express the concern of Christians on both sides of the border. Their outreach is to countries and churches in Asia, Africa, and Latin America. They were formed during the decade after 1959, when the West German economy was booming and when it seemed right for Germans to help others even as they themselves had been helped earlier (see ELCO below).

Prominent among these new agencies are *Brot für die Welt* (Bread for the World), 1959; *Dienste in Übersee* (Services Overseas), 1960; *Evangelische Zentralstelle für Entwicklungshilfe* (Protestant Central Agency for Development Aid), 1963; and *Kirchlicher Entwicklungsdienst* (Church Development Service), 1968. Similarly, the program called *Kirchen helfen Kirchen* (Churches Help Churches) comprises projects of European and overseas churches supported by the Diaconic Agency of the EKD. The whole complex enterprise receives information and guidance from the Association of the Churches' Development Services (*Arbeitsgemeinschaft Kirchlicher Entwicklungsdienst*), 1970, an exchange agency which, like most of the others, is located in Stuttgart. All these undertakings feel the effects of today's worldwide economic problems, abroad as well as at home.

A leading challenge at home, as already noted, is the high number of migrant workers and their families. The Federal Republic has more than any other country in Western Europe. EKD policy—like that of the Roman

Catholic Church—drew on postwar experience with German refugees and aims to help migrants become citizens, easier done with Orthodox and Roman Catholics than with the large Turkish majority who are Muslim. Guided by the *Diakonisches Werk*, the several regional churches have endeavored to implement EKD policy and accommodate the new Muslim presence.

Mission work overseas, traditionally done by large societies, experienced structural modifications as policy changes were applied by the churches in the 1970s. The societies ceased to be fully independent and were consolidated into regional church structures. Names of societies, long familiar, were subsumed under new titles. The Evangelical Churches in Rhineland and Westphalia led the way when, in 1970, the Rhenish (1828) and Bethel (1886) mission societies became the United Evangelical Mission (VEM, Wuppertal). There followed these further changes: the Schleswig-Holstein Evangelical Lutheran Mission (1876) became in 1971 the North Elbian Center for World Mission and Church World Service (NMZ, Hamburg); the German branch of the Basel Mission (1815) and 17 smaller societies joined in 1972 in the Association of Churches and Missions in Southwestern Germany (EMS, Stuttgart); the Leipzig Mission in the GDR (1836), in part, shared its West German constituency with that based in Neuendettelsau (1841), becoming in 1972 the Bavarian Mission Work; the Berlin (1824), the Jerusalem (1852), and the East Asia (1884) societies are since 1975 the Mission Work of the Evangelical Church in Berlin-Brandenburg (Berlin West); and the Hermannsburg (1849), Hildesheim, and another part of the Leipzig constituency became in 1977 the Evangelical Lutheran Mission in Lower Saxony (ELM, Hermannsburg). Associating and assisting the above-mentioned mission agencies is the *Evangelisches Missionswerk im Bereich der Bundesrepublik Deutschland und Berlin-West* (EMW; Protestant Association for World Mission in the FRG and West Berlin). Founded in 1975, it replaces the *Deutscher Evangelischer Missionsrat* and the *Deutscher Evangelischer Missionsbund*.

The underlying policy in these changes is that mission, abroad as well as at home, is a task of the whole church; a task in which societies have long led the way and in which

they continue to play a vital part today through closer ties with the churches. Correspondingly, this arrangement expresses the newfound partnership with churches overseas. Asian or African church leaders, for instance, when visiting Germany, no longer find their contacts confined to the mission societies but now extended also to their personal counterparts in ecclesial office as well as in the parishes.

EVANGELICAL LUTHERAN CHURCH IN BADEN

(Evangelisch-Lutherische Kirche in Baden)
Member: LWF (1968)
Membership: 4400
Superintendent: The Rev. Gottfried Daub
Ludwig-Wilhelm-Strasse 9
D—7570 Baden-Baden

This church body of seven congregations and six pastors is a living reminder of the struggle for confessional identity that arose during the 19th century in southwestern Germany. Although it is an independent religious body, it considers itself to be in fellowship with all churches and congregations of the Evangelical Lutheran confession, especially those in Germany. It has contractual relationships with the Independent Evangelical Lutheran Church and with the United Evangelical Lutheran Church of Germany (VELKD), and, since 1968, has been a member of the LWF. The church has cooperated in the Association of Christian Churches in Baden-Württemberg (ACKBW) since the association was founded in 1973.

History: Baden came into early contact with the Reformation, not least because of the University of Heidelberg (1386), from which emerged Luther's Heidelberg Disputation of 1518. The political fragmentation resulted in strong confessional divisions. In some areas, the Lutheran type of Reformation was carried through; others turned to the Reformed doctrine (*Heidelberg Catechism*, 1563); and still others remained with the Roman Catholic Church. When, in the era of Napoleon, the various areas were brought together in the Grand Duchy of Baden, the situation of the churches also had to be changed. The archbishopric of Freiburg was formed out of those parts of the bishoprics of Constance, Strasbourg, and Speyer that were situated to the east of the Rhine. At first, the Lutheran and Reformed churches were brought together in an administrative church union. In 1821, with the consent of a general synod, this arrangement became a consensus union. In 1851, the first congregation of an opposing minority of confessional Lutherans was formed in Baden. Others followed, yet not many. Internal differences prevented any greater growth. New congregations were formed after 1945 with the settlement in Baden of Lutherans from other areas.

EVANGELICAL LUTHERAN CHURCH IN BAVARIA (ELCB)

(Evangelisch-Lutherische Kirche in Bayern)
Member: LWF (1947), WCC, CEC, EKD, ACKBD, VELKD
Membership: 2,561,000**
Bishop: The Rt. Rev. Dr. Johannes Hanselmann
Meiserstrasse 13
D—8000 Munich 2

A stronghold of confessional Lutheranism in a predominantly Roman Catholic state, this church comprises 1515 parishes, grouped into 73 deaneries, which are served by 2077 pastors and many other workers in related fields. About 23% of Bavaria's population is Lutheran, and about 60% of Bavaria's Lutherans reside in the northern part, Franconia—in rural villages as well as in the Nuremburg and other urban areas. Bavarian Lutheranism has its own diaspora, or dispersion, including people in cities like Munich and Augsburg. This combination of being at once concentrated and deployed has given the ELCB its characteristic concern for confessional unity near and far. Its understanding of unity is not monolithic, however, for Bavarian Lutheranism has a record of internal diversity, accentuated by the large influx of other Lutherans from East Germany and elsewhere in Europe after World War II.

The church's four governing authorities—all holding equal rank—are the bishop, the church council, the synod, and the synod executive committee. The synod elects the bishop (called president prior to 1933). The church is divided into six districts (Ansbach, Augsburg, Bayreuth, Munich, Nuremberg, Regensburg), each headed by a district bishop. As with other churches in the Federal Republic, support is gathered for the church by the government's fiscal office as a surcharge on the income tax. Voluntary offerings for special purposes, notably for mission, theological education, etc., are received in the congregations.

Most of the pastors are educated in the two Bavarian university faculties of theology, Erlangen and Munich, and in the church's Augustana Hochschule, Neuendettelsau, near Nuremberg, operating on a university academic level. The church maintains other teaching institutions, notably those clustered in Neuendettelsau for deaconess work and other activities. Still others include the Mothers' Service Institute in Stein and the training center for deacons in Rummelsberg, both places near Nuremberg, and the Evangelical Academy in Tutzing and the general theological school for the United Evangelical Lutheran Church of Germany in Pullach, both places near Munich.

Worship in Bavarian Lutheran churches has long valued the liturgy and hymns as integral to preaching the Word and administering the sacraments. In education, a strong accent remains on confirmation instruction, religious education in the public schools, and work among young people. The practice of a diaconal year of service by young women, introduced in the 1950s, has spread to other churches. Church attendance among Bavarian Lutherans is said to be above the average for the country.

● ● ●

History: The part played by Bavarian, especially Franconian, Lutherans in the emergence of a confessionally united worldwide Lutheranism is noteworthy. The present state of Bavaria, early settled by three tribes—Bavarians, Swabians, and Franconians—began to be Christianized by Boniface, the missionary bishop, and others in the eighth century. Slowly the faith took root, and the church and its institutions became firmly implanted. In the Franconian area, Nuremberg became a commercial crossroads during the Middle Ages and a free imperial city.

The Lutheran Reformation became fully established in Nuremberg by 1524. In 1530, the city of Augsburg gave its name to the major Lutheran confession. The Religious Peace of Augsburg (1555)—fixing on the old principle that the religion of the ruler determines the religion of his subjects (*cuius regio, eius religio*)—and the rising Counter-Reformation effectively returned to the Roman Catholic Church over one-half of the Protestant gains made in Bavaria. The host of small self-governing political units made Bavaria a religious patchwork of Roman Catholics and Lutherans. The *Formula of Concord* (1577) became a unifying force among most Lutherans; in Nuremberg, however, it was not officially adopted.

Seventeenth-century theological orthodoxy, the Thirty Years' War (1618–1648), Pietism, and the Napoleonic era left their various marks on Lutheranism. So did the asylum granted in Erlangen to Huguenot refugees from France and the subsequent founding of a Franconian university in Erlangen in 1743. The modern state of Bavaria was formed in 1806. Some 90 political units were merged, under Napoleon's directive, into the kingdom of Bavaria. The Roman Catholic king, by the old principle that the political ruler is also head of the Protestant church (*summus episcopus*), thus became nominal head of the Lutherans in Bavaria. The church constitution of 1818 laid the basis for a Protestant community under a governing consistory. In the process, a Lutheran confessional emphasis developed. In time, this found expression in the "Erlangen theology." Adolf von Harless (1806–1879) and others with and after him saw the *Book of Concord* (1580) as the confessional basis of the Lutheran church. The confessions themselves were understood historically; the Scriptures were interpreted as *Heilsgeschichte*, not as prooftexts but as the living account of God's redemptive activity in history. Justification by faith, experienced as new life in Christ, is operative as a controlling principle in systematic theology.

An outstanding proponent of a renewed Lutheranism was Wilhelm Löhe (1808–1872) of Neuendettelsau, whose vision of a worldwide Lutheran church (above, Germany Introduction) was stimulated by a missionary fervor and a response to Friedrich C. D. Wyneken's appeal (1841) on behalf of the thousands of spiritually neglected German immigrants in *North America. In the 20th century, others have carried forward this Bavarian contribution. Among them was Hans Meiser (1881–1956), who served as bishop of the ELCB 1933–1955, stood firmly on the side of the resistance during the German church struggle, and energetically supported the formation of the United Evangelical Lutheran Church of Germany (1948). An active participant in the Executive Committee of the Lutheran World Convention, he became one of the founders of the LWF. His successor, Hermann Dietzfelbinger (1908–1984), ELCB bishop 1955–1975, was instrumental in the founding of the LWF-related Institute for Ecumenical Research (Strasbourg, France) and in the promotion of Lutheran unity through the Federation. His successor as bishop, Johannes Hanselmann, had been an LWF vice-president since the 1977 assembly. Hanselmann became president in 1987 upon the death of Bishop Káldy (see Hungary). Good relations between Lutherans and Roman Catholics in Bavaria began during the church struggle and the postwar years and improved further after Vatican II.

EVANGELICAL LUTHERAN CHURCH IN BRUNSWICK

(Evangelisch-Lutherische Landeskirche in Braunschweig)
Member: LWF (1947), WCC, CEC, EKD, ACKBD, VELKD
Membership: 505,000**
Bishop: The Rt. Rev. Prof. Dr. Gerhard Müller D.D.
Neuer Weg 88-90
PO Box 1664
D—3340 Wolfenbüttel

Located east of the Hanoverian church and adjacent to the German Democratic Republic, this church of 398 parishes is served by 302 pastors as well as by other staff. Its headquarters are not far from the famous Wolfenbüttel library of medieval manuscripts and books. On the basis of its constitution of 1922 (most recently amended in 1970), the church has an episcopal-synodical form of polity. The bishop, elected for life by the synod, presides over the church's administration. The church is divided into 13 conferences, each headed by a dean. Each conference has its own synod and executive committee to deal with local concerns.

The church's pastors are educated at various universities—especially Göttingen—and receive further training at the theological seminary in Brunswick and in the congregations. The deaconess houses in the city of Brunswick, Bad Gandersheim, and Bad Harzburg and their related institutions testify to the church's longtime diaconal and social concern. This commitment also extends overseas. Through the Evangelical Lutheran Mission in Lower Saxony, there are close connections with churches in *Africa, *Asia, and *Latin America. The church also has a working relationship with the *Japan Evangelical Lutheran Church.

History: Following a period of centuries when the Roman Catholic Church, with monastic properties as well as churches, had become firmly established, the Reformation made gains slowly. The city of Brunswick accepted Lutheranism in 1528, the duchy of Brunswick-Wolfenbüttel only in 1568. Duke Julius led the change, assisted by Martin Chemnitz (1522–1586). The latter, called the "second Martin" after Luther, was a leader in the second generation of Reformers. The documents he gathered in the *Brunswick Confession* of 1569 anticipated much of the content of the Lutheran *Book of Concord* (1580) and have continued as the basic confession of the Evangelical Lutheran Church in Brunswick to this day.

Encouraged by Duke Julius, Chemnitz collaborated with the Württemberg theologian, Jakob Andreä (1528–1590), and others in drafting the *Formula of Concord* (1577), which was designed to settle theological controversy and bring peace to the various Lutheran factions. However, when it failed to bring concord on the Evangelical side, Chemnitz withdrew his support of the *Formula* and it was not adopted in Brunswick.

Earlier (1572), Chemnitz had produced a comprehensive analysis of the Roman Catholic Council of Trent. In 1576, he participated in founding the University of Helmstedt. Among the university's later theologians was Georg Calixt (1586–1656), irenic yet controversial advocate of church unity. His long career at Helmstedt (1614–1656) exerted a moderating influence on the Lutheranism of the church in neighboring Hanover. The Helmstedt church historian, Johann Lorenz von Mosheim (1694–1755), imbued with the spirit of Calixt, earned the title of "father of modern church history writing" by his fairness and scholarly method. In 1747, Mosheim became a professor and chancellor of the new University of Göttingen. In 1809, Brunswick's Helmstedt University was closed. During the 19th century, a revived Lutheranism slowly superseded Rationalism, and the church benefited from its new forms of government and its rising diaconal institutions and mission endeavors.

EVANGELICAL LUTHERAN CHURCH IN OLDENBURG (ELCO)
(Evangelisch-Lutherische Kirche in Oldenburg)
Member: LWF (1957), WCC, CEC, EKD, ACKBD
Membership: 502,000**
Bishop: The Rt. Rev. Dr. Wilhelm Sievers
Philosophenweg 1
PO Box 1709
D—2900 Oldenburg

West of the River Weser and the city of Bremen, this church of 119 parishes and 223 pastors lies like a confessional buffer between the big Evangelical Lutheran Church of Hanover to the east and the Reformed churches in the Netherlands to the west. Oldenburg is an administrative district of the state of Lower Saxony, and Plattdeutsch is still spoken in some country areas. Formerly, the inhabitants in the north were of Frisian descent and those in the south of Saxon descent. Nearly seven out of every 10 people are said to be members of the Lutheran church. The others, in the southern part, are mainly Roman Catholics. The city of Oldenburg itself, seat of a former grand duchy (to 1918), is the location of the church administration.

The church is headed by a bishop (the title since 1934) and a superior church council (Oberkirchenrat). The synod is the church's legislative body and elects the bishop and council members. The pastors are educated at various universities and theological schools. With its diversified staff, the church maintains a variety of institutions and services in the fields of Christian education, health, and welfare. Like the other Evangelical churches in Lower Saxony, Oldenburg, too, has a working agreement with the state of Lower Saxony, which guarantees good cooperation between church and state (Loccumer Vertrag 1955).

The Christianization of this *Confinium Saxoniae et Frisae* began in 780. By about the year 1000, part of the organized church came under the archdiocese of Hamburg-Bremen and part under the diocese of Osnabrück. After 1050 the Duchy of Oldenburg was formed. During the ensuing era, some large and attractive church edifices—like the one in Wiefelstede—were built and still draw admiration today.

The Reformation era found Oldenburg opening slowly to Lutheran, then to Calvinist, and—via the city of Münster—also to Anabaptist influences. The Lutheran forces won out. In 1573, the first Lutheran church order (constitution, liturgy, doctrinal guidelines, etc.) was introduced, to the exclusion of Calvinists and Anabaptists from freedom of worship. Orthodox Lutheranism, however, generated no great response in the relatively passive parishes. When the duchies of Oldenburg and Delmenhorst came under Danish rule (1667–1773), King Frederick IV, with the help of Pietist influence, tried to stimulate church life and introduced a new church order. In 1773 Oldenburg again became independent. During the Enlightenment and under a change of political rule, still another church order was enacted. Heavily influenced by Rationalism, it completely bypassed the Lutheran confessions. The 19th-century awakening brought renewal in the church and—through the church orders of 1849 and 1853—a restoration of confessional emphasis. Similarly, the church constitution of 1920 reaffirmed the confessions of the Reformation. A specifically Lutheran commitment reasserted itself during the church struggle of the 1930s and early 1940s when a scripturally founded confession of faith was of vital importance. This kind of emphasis underlay the subsequent church constitution of 1950—still in effect—which is itself a confessionally based and ecumenically oriented document.

Under the leadership of Wilhelm Stählin, the church's first postwar bishop (1945–1952), a renewal of the church took place, especially in worship (liturgy) and preaching. Veterans of the church struggle like Hermann Ehlers, Heinz Kloppenburg, and Edo Osterloh, as members of the superior council, added to the stature and spirit marking the church. With Stählin, the church favored the unification of all German territorial churches into an Evangelical Church of the Augsburg Confession. That this did not happen when the Evangelical Church in Germany (EKD) was formed, Stählin and others considered a lost opportunity (see above, Germany Introduction). Had it succeeded, it would have meant a broadly Lutheran (grosslutherisch) solution to the age-old problem of church unity among Germany's territorial Protestant churches. When the United Evangelical Lutheran Church of Germany (VELKD) was organized in 1948, Oldenburg did not join.

Some saw the nourishing of a more inclusive vision of unity by a church near the Dutch border as an expression of the creativity encouraged by a buffer or marginal location in an ecumenical era. In 1957, the Oldenburg church, then under Bishop Gerhard Jacobi, joined the LWF. Its recent bishop, Hans Heinrich Harms, fostered the emphasis on unity as chair of the German Evangelical Missionary Council and as member of the World Council of Churches' Central Committee. In 1971, the ELCO joined the Confederation of Evangelical Churches in Lower Saxony (KEKN).

EVANGELICAL LUTHERAN CHURCH IN WÜRTTEMBERG (ELCW)

(Evangelische Landeskirche in Württemberg)
Member: LWF (1947), WCC, CEC, EKD, ACKBD
Membership: 2,392,000**
Bishop: The Rt. Rev. Theo Sorg
Gänsheidestrasse 2-4
PO Box 92
D—7000 Stuttgart 1

This church—which celebrated its 450th anniversary in 1984—lies in the state of Baden-Württemberg in southwest Germany, within the bounds of the earlier kingdom (1806–1918) and former state of Württemberg. Its membership is about the same as that of the Roman Catholic on this territory, with Methodist, Greek Orthodox, and other small minorities giving color to the religious scene.

A Muslim community, mainly Turkish workers and their families, appeared in the 1960s and has stayed.

The 1391 parishes of the ELCW cover a region whose metropolis is Stuttgart, whose towns and villages are set amid hills, fields, and forests, and whose agriculture and industry have struck a fair balance. With 1850 pastors and 441 vicars, as well as many others in careers of Christian service, the ELCW maintains a venerable spiritual legacy amid the renewing forces of diversity within unity.

In common parlance, the Württembergers are "Schwaben" (Swabians). Their distant origins go back to the Germanic tribes, to the Alemani and the Suevi, so known in imperial Roman times. Since 1945, Württemberg has welcomed a great many refugees, mainly from the Old Prussian Union. In recent centuries, Swabians have exercised their propensity to reach out, emigrating to beckoning lands in Eastern Europe, especially Russia, to North America, and to other parts of the world, or going forth as missionaries of the gospel to Asia, Africa, and the Americas. They have contributed many leaders in the arts and sciences, in trade and industry, and in the church. When the single state of Baden-Württemberg was formed in 1952, the ELCW and the Evangelical Church in Baden (below) remained separate.

Confessionally, since 1534, the Württemberg church has been Lutheran, moderately so and on its own terms. When the LWF was formed in 1947, the ELCW became a charter member. The following year, when the several member bodies adopted the constitution of the Evangelical Church in Germany (EKD), the Württembergers could be thankful that their bishop, Theophil Wurm (1868–1953), courageous throughout the long church struggle against Nazi ideology, had during the war years led the movement to unify the Protestant territorial churches in the spirit of a confessing church. The first to chair the EKD council (1945–1949), Wurm's hope for a Germany-wide church, instead of only a federation called a church, remained unrealized. Likewise the desire for eucharistic fellowship among all the EKD member churches came fully only in 1973 with the adoption by them individually of the Leuenberg Agreement (see Germany Introduction). Holding this inclusive view of Protestant unity, the Württemberg church declined to join the United Evangelical Lutheran Church of Germany.

In another way, however, the inclusiveness of Wurm's vision lives on as the city of Stuttgart is host to a concentration of church agencies serving in and beyond the EKD. These include the headquarters of the Diakonisches Werk (1957), the diaconal agency of EKD that combines the long-established Inner Mission (1848; see Germany Introduction) and its many health and welfare institutions with the Evangelical Hilfswerk (1945) and its array of postwar churchwide programs. In Stuttgart, too, are the main offices of most of the agencies participating in overseas work (above), and of the Association of Churches and Missions in Southwestern Germany (EMS). Here also are the national headquarters of the church's work among youth, university students, and professionals in higher education (above).

Organizationally, the ELCW structure is synodical, with its clerical head a bishop. The title was introduced in 1933, on the eve of the church struggle. It replaced the title of church president, an interim designation after the separation of church and state in 1918. The legislative functions of the synod, the governing role of the executive committee, the administrative task of the superior church council, and the duties of the Landesbischof are all interdependent. In practice, congregations expect this structure to allow them a maximum of freedom, and the many voluntary associations of Pietist-oriented laity count on it to safeguard their time-honored practice of criticizing (constructively) any suspected aberrations from the Scriptures by pastors, theologians, administrators, and others.

The ELCW parishes are grouped into 51 church districts, each led by a dean, who also carries out the official visitation of the parishes. Each district—27 parishes on average—governs its local affairs through its own synod and executive committee. The districts, in turn, comprise four conferences (Sprengel)—Stuttgart, Heilbronn, Reutlingen, and Ulm—each of them graced by a prelate whose functions are those of a regional bishop.

Most of the Württemberg clergy have been educated at the University of Tübingen (1477) with its famed theological institute (*Stift*), which has counted among its residents such people as Johann Kepler (1571–1630) and Georg F. W. Hegel (1770–1831). In the ELCW, as in other churches, provision is made for the continuing education of pastors. Increasing numbers of women are being ordained. For generations, women have outnumbered men among those being trained for specialized forms of church work. For the many active laity, Württemberg pioneered the first Evangelical Academy (1945)—under Eberhard Müller (d.1989)—in Bad Boll, earlier famed as a place of Christian healing (by Johann Christoph Blumhardt, 1805–1880, and his son, Christoph Friedrich Blumhardt, 1842–1919). Citywide spiritual emphasis weeks and many other lay-directed means of renewal had their beginning in the Württemberg setting, and in recent years have given rise to forces of evangelical conservatism.

History: From the sixth century onward, missionaries from Ireland and France succeeded in Christianizing the country. In the high Middle Ages, Piety—developed through such leaders as Johann Tauler (d.1361) and Meister Eckehart (d.1321)—exercised a strong influence, which has been reflected in Württemberg Pietism ever since. The separate churches (under local patrons) and various monastic institutions were gradually consolidated, many of them under the protection of the dukes of Württemberg. The creation of the university in Tübingen furthered the influence of humanistic theology. In effect, all these developments prepared the ground for a change of emphasis in the Christian faith.

The Reformation made its influence felt as early as 1517. Its advance, however, was slowed by the Austrian Hapsburgs, overlords in Württemberg and archly Roman Catholic. Besides, the country lay in the path of two competing Protestant forces: the Zwinglian reform from Zurich and the Lutheran from Wittenberg. Württemberg, led by Johannes Brenz (1499–1570), decided for the Lutheran. An initial agreement (1525) was followed by the Stuttgart Concord (1534) which, with Luther's consent, abolished the Mass and made the medieval preaching service central. This determined the kind of low-church pulpit-oriented worship that marks the Sunday service in Württemberg to this day, an order that also utilizes the altar for Holy Communion and prayer.

Württemberg's church history has run through a sequence of stages, each of which has left some residue in those following. The confessional stage included the *Württemberg Confession* (1551), equivalent to the *Augsburg Confession;* the *Great Church Order* (1559), spelling out the ways of parish life and the relation between church and state, which in actual practice made Württemberg, in the eyes of some, a model Lutheran territory; and the *Formula of Concord* (1577), drafted by Württemberg's Jacob Andreä (1528–1590), aided by Brunswick's Martin Chemnitz (1522–1586) and others, seeking to achieve unity among adherents of the *Augsburg Confession.*

The stage of Lutheran orthodoxy included proponents like Matthias Hafenreffer (1561–1619). His *Loci theoligici* (1600) gave precise formulations to Lutheranism and found many readers, even in distant Sweden.

The stage of Pietism, which was to mark Württemberg's Lutheranism until today, was led by Johann Albrecht Bengel (1687–1752). His strong emphasis on Scripture and Christian experience found wide acceptance among the Swabians.

Other stages followed, including the Enlightenment (Rationalism) and the rebuttal to it (scriptural supernaturalism) by the first "Tübingen school" of theologians. The awakenings of the early 19th century drew strong Swabian responses, such as the formation of the Württemberg Bible Society (1812); the heavy participation in the Basel Mission Society (1815) and its eventually global outreach; the founding of many kinds of institutions for aiding the young, the old, and the ill; and the gathering of the like-minded into groups for Bible study and into associations for all sorts of service. The motivating power was Piety, and its bearers, encouraged by many influential preachers, were the laity.

Various theological currents flowed through the university in Tübingen during successive generations, from the interpretation of the history of Christian thought in dialectical terms by Ferdinand Christian Baur (1792–1860) to the relating of scientific thought to Christian theology by Karl Heim (1874–1958). During the church struggle in the 1930s, the Tübingen theological faculty, like that in Erlangen, resisted Nazi influences. In the church, as noted above, the efforts of Bishop Theophil Wurm, on behalf of a confessing Christian unity, typified the ecumenical and evangelical role of Württemberg's Lutherans.

EVANGELICAL LUTHERAN CHURCH OF HANOVER (ELCH)

(Evangelisch-Lutherische Landeskirche Hannovers)
Member: LWF (1947), WCC, CEC, EKD, ACKBD, VELKD
Membership: 3,453,000**
Bishop: The Rt. Rev. D. Horst Hirschler
Haarstrasse 6
D—3000 Hanover 1
Church Administration:
Rote Reihe 6, PO Box 3726
D—3000 Hanover 1

This biggest of the German territorial churches is in the state of Lower Saxony. Its 1550 parishes are currently served by 1884 pastors, besides a large number of deaconesses, deacons, teachers, musicians, and specialists in various fields. About 52% of the people on its territory are included in the church's membership. Among the population, 30% are employed in agriculture and 52% in industry. Politically and otherwise, the people are mildly conservative, open to realism but not to radicalism. The urban population has grown rapidly in recent decades, and the city of Hanover—the largest (c.517,000) on the church territory—ranks eighth among the cities of the Federal Republic. Its location makes Hanover a crossroad of church activities. Here are not only the territorial church headquarters but also the general secretariat of the Evangelical Church in Germany (EKD), the Foreign Relations Office of the EKD (from Frankfurt-am-Main after mid-1986), the offices of the United Evangelical Lutheran Church of Germany (VELKD), and the base of the LWF German national committee. Here, too, the Second Assembly of the LWF took place in 1952; also the 1988 meeting of the WCC Central Committee.

The Evangelical Lutheran Church of Hanover (ELCH) combines episcopal, synodical, and other elements in its organization. The constitution (first adopted in 1922 and most recently amended in 1965) provides for the following central church organs: the territorial synod and its standing executive committee for the legislative functions; the church senate and upper chamber for exercising the right formerly (to 1918) held by the sovereign; and the central church council on administration, comprising theologians and lawyers, for policy and operational concerns. The bishop is the spiritual (clerical) head of the church and chairs the senate, the church council, and the bishop's council, which is made up of the district superintendents of the church's eight districts. Since the office of bishop was introduced in 1925, it has had but four occupants: August Marahrens (1925–1947), who also served as president of the Lutheran World Convention (1936–1946); Hanns Lilje (1947–1971), who was president of the LWF (1952–1957) and also in the presidium of the World Council of Churches (1968–1975); Eduard Lohse, who chaired the council of the EKD until November 1985 and retired as bishop in 1988; then Horst Hirschler.

The Hanoverian church's several districts, each headed by a district superintendent, are made up of circuits. Each circuit includes 20 to 30 pastorates and has its own superintendent. Pastors of the ELCH receive their education at Göttingen and in other universities. Additional training is provided by the church's four seminaries for preachers, which prepare theological students for the parish ministry, and by other centers, including the venerable abbey of Loccum, with its special programs. Increasing numbers of women have become vicars and pastors in recent years.

The bishop of Hanover is also abbot of Loccum, the medieval and now Lutheran monastery (honorary membership). He assumes this office on the death of his predecessor. The church's Evangelical Academy is also in Loccum. The academy was initially opened in Hermannsburg in 1947 and has been widely influential in activating the faith and life of the laity. Many other schools, institutions, and agencies are maintained by the church, including centers for deaconesses and others (Henriettenstift, 1860) and for deacons (Stephansstift, 1869). Religious instruction continues in the public schools, complemented by two-year preparatory courses for confirmation and by extensive youth programs.

An agreement with the state of Lower Saxony regularizes cooperation between the church and the government (1955). Although church and state have been separated since the revolution of 1918, support for this church, as for others in the Federal Republic, is still gathered by the public fiscal office as a voluntary surcharge on the individual income tax. Stewardship, the voluntary support of church programs, has received increasing emphasis since the early 1950s, when it was modeled on North American practice.

History: During the reign of Charlemagne (768–814), Anglo-Saxon missionaries assisted in the conversion of the people of Lower Saxony. The incorporation of this Saxon country into the Frankish empire led to the formation of a network of parishes exerting considerable influence on common life. Many of today's parish boundaries are from medieval times. Loccum cloister (1163), with a continuous history through the Reformation, has been a training center for future clergy since 1677, and daily vespers have continued unbroken as a moving reminder of an abiding Christian presence.

The introduction of the Reformation into many smaller territories comprising the present Lower Saxony began in 1527. Political rulers promoted it more readily than the bishops. The hardships of Antonius Corvinus (1501–1553) reveal the difficulties faced by the Reformers in engrafting the Evangelical faith. In a later generation, Johann Arndt (1555–1621), general superintendent in Celle, became widely read for his four books on *True Christianity*. They are among the most important Lutheran devotional books for use in the home and have been translated into most European and some Asian and African languages.

Moderating influences, like those of Georg Calixt (1586–1656) in neighboring Helmstedt (Brunswick, above), guarded Hanoverians from excessive Lutheran orthodoxy. Pietism gained little following. The Enlightenment proved more popular, but eventually yielded to the religious awakenings of the 19th century. The latter asserted the Lutheran character of the church and fostered the founding of many institutions of social service.

In 1814, as the Napoleonic era ended, the kingdom of Hanover emerged, a consolidation of several smaller territories joined to Electoral Hanover under its ruling House of Guelph. The merger of the Lutheran churches on this territory (1864–1866) marks the beginning of the present ELCH. It united 17 hitherto separate territorial churches and laid the basis for an influential unity, including impulses for the creation of the General Evangelical Lutheran Conference (1868), a forerunner of the LWF.

The five Hanoverian British monarchs, beginning with George I (1714–1727), placed Hanover in a mediating role between the German- and English-speaking world (see below, United Kingdom; also Canada and the USA). Illustrative of this is the founding of Göttingen University (1737) by George II, as well as the office of Lutheran chaplain at the royal court in London.

The Hanover church territory has contributed to Lutheranism internationally. Examples: Henry Melchior Muhlenberg (1711–1787) of Einbeck—a Göttingen graduate—went to Pennsylvania in 1742 and organized the first permanent Lutheran church body in North America. Friedrich C.D. Wyneken (1810–1876) of Verden went to the USA in 1838; issued his stirring appeal concerning the spiritual needs of the Germans in North America; gained the support of Hanover's Ludwig Adolf Petri (1803–1873) and Bavaria's Wilhelm Löhe (1808–1872); and became a pioneer in the *Lutheran Church–Missouri Synod. Wilhelm Rotermund of Hanover went to Brazil in 1834, and in 1886 organized the first church body of what is now the *Evangelical Church of the Lutheran Confession in Brazil. The outreach from Hanover also included the work of Ludwig Harms (1808–1865), founder of the Hermannsburg Mission (1849), a rallying point for Hanoverians and a missionary force in *Africa and *Australia.

Hanover's contemporary contribution to world Lutheranism and to the modern ecumenical movement is best summed up in the dynamic career of Hanns Lilje (1899–1977). His grasp of the unity of faith and life, of the local and the global, led many to a new experience of the majesty and mercy of God in Jesus Christ.

EVANGELICAL LUTHERAN CHURCH OF SCHAUMBURG-LIPPE

(Evangelisch-Lutherische Landeskirche Schaumburg-Lippe)
Member: LWF (1947), WCC, CEC, EKD, ACKBD, VELKD
Membership: 69,000**
Bishop: The Rt. Rev. Dr. Joachim Heubach
Herderstrasse 27
PO Box 1307
D—3062 Bückeburg

Schaumburg-Lippe, a part of the old duchy of Schaumburg and since 1946 a county in Lower Saxony some 56 kilometers (35 miles) west of the city of Hanover, contains one of Germany's smallest autonomous territorial churches. Its 23 congregations are currently served by 37 pastors. About 85% of the mainly rural population are members of the Lutheran church. Besides agriculture, there is some mining and light industry in the area. Traditional folk costumes are worn on occasion.

The polity of the church has episcopal and synodical elements, with the bishop presiding over the church council. Church headquarters are in the historic house of Johann Gottfried von Herder (1744–1803), the churchman, author, and friend of the German poet Johann Wolfgang von Goethe.

History: In the period from the introduction of Christianity during the time of Charlemagne until the 16th century, Roman Catholicism became firmly established in this region. Despite the resistance of the ruling Catholic bishops, the Reformation took hold. By 1559, the entire duchy had become Lutheran, and the sovereign was declared temporal head of the church. In 1614, a new church order replaced the one adapted from that of Mecklenburg. New schools, including the University of Rinteln (1620–1809), advanced education at all levels. Protestantism weathered the storm of the Thirty Years' War. Lutheran orthodoxy was mellowed in the 18th century through the Pietism fostered by followers of Count Nikolaus Ludwig von Zinzendorf (1700–1760). Among the superintendents of this church, Johann Gottfried Herder, serving in Bückeburg 1771–1776, is the best known. Although the Enlightenment

also made its impact here, a renewal of Lutheranism swept through the church during the 19th century. The marks of this renewal included the formation of a mission society (1840), a new evangelically oriented order of worship, and an awakened Christian concern among the people.

In religious terms, Schaumburg-Lippe is a world in miniature. Besides its few Roman Catholic and Reformed congregations, it is also experiencing the impact of various sectarian groups, including Jehovah's Witnesses, Latter Day Saints (Mormons), and others. In 1976 and 1982, the church was host to the synod of the United Evangelical Lutheran Church of Germany. Indeed, it was the first church to join the VELKD. It is also a charter member of the LWF.

INDEPENDENT EVANGELICAL LUTHERAN CHURCH (IELC)

(Selbständige Evangelisch-Lutherische Kirche)
Member: ILC
Membership: 37,000**
Bishop: The Rt. Rev. Dr. Jobst Schöne
Schopenhauerstrasse 7
D—3000 Hanover 61

Constituted in 1972, this general body comprises four former Lutheran free churches in West Germany, each with its own distinctive history. Its 150 congregations, served by 115 pastors, are self-supporting and are scattered in various parts of the country, including West Berlin, Bavaria, Hesse, the Rhineland, Westphalia, and Lower Saxony. The IELC has no direct fellowship with member bodies of the United Evangelical Lutheran Church of Germany and no relations with the LWF. Internationally, it has ties with its counterpart in the *German Democratic Republic; with the Lutheran Church of *Australia; with the Lutheran Church–Missouri Synod (*USA); with "Missouri"-related churches in the *United Kingdom and other European countries as well as in *Latin America, Africa, and Asia. It also has some connection with the *Wisconsin Synod (USA).

The IELC combines episcopal, synodical, and congregational elements in its organization. It is headed by a bishop, who presides over the nine-member church council. The church's legislative organ is the synod, which also elects the bishop and the council members. Each of the church's three districts is supervised by a dean; the several circuits within a district by a superintendent. The pastors are educated in the church's preparatory school and theological seminary (1948) in Oberursel, near Frankfurt. The IELC supports the "Lutherische Stunde" broadcasts, the German version of the Lutheran Hour, and publishes the monthly *Lutherische Kirche* and the quarterly *Lutherische Theologie und Kirche* (successor to the *Lutherische Rundblick,* 1953–1976).

Separate development, periodic internal strife, heavy wartime and postwar losses (particularly with the redrawing of East Germany's eastern boundary), and the effects of a partitioned Germany (*German Democratic Republic) have been hard on the Lutheran free churches. Steps to unite them in West Germany began in 1948. The IELC is the outcome of a painstaking process. Its antecedents must be noted.

The *Evangelical Lutheran (Old Lutheran) Church* (ELC) grew out of opposition to the creation of the Evangelical Church of the Old Prussian Union (1817) and to the ensuing unionism of Lutherans and Reformed (see above, Germany Introduction). In Silesia and elsewhere, congregations determined to remain confessionally Lutheran formed the Evangelical Lutheran Church in Prussia (1830), also known as the Breslau Synod. Repressive measures by the government of King Frederick William III made many so-called Old Lutherans ready to emigrate. Some went to *Australia (1838), becoming the pioneers of the present *Lutheran Church of Australia. Others emigrated to *North America (1839), forming the Buffalo Synod, an antecedent body of the American Lutheran Church (now *ELCA) and an early contributor of part of its membership to the *Lutheran Church–Missouri Synod. Under Frederick William IV, relations with the Prussian government improved and toleration was granted the Old Lutherans. By 1860, the ELC membership numbered about 50,000. Its headquarters were in Breslau and also its theological seminary. In the wake of World War II and the setting of the Oder-Neisse boundary, nearly half the ELC congregations—those east of the new line—were lost

to this church and their members made refugees. In the process of resettlement, considerable help came from the Missouri Synod. In 1948, the seminary lost in Breslau was replaced by a new one in Oberursel.

The *Evangelical Lutheran Free Church* (1846) was formed by opponents of the Union as introduced in the territory of Hesse. Their numbers were reinforced by those of like mind in Saxony, where relations between Lutherans and Reformed had been relaxed by the removal of confessional subscription (as a legal requirement for the holding of certain offices) and the introduction of open communion (see below, Kurhessen-Waldeck).

The *Independent Evangelical Lutheran Church* (1945) emerged in West Germany when a number of Free churches in Hesse, Lower Saxony, Baden, and Hamburg joined forces. Under a federated structure, chaired by a church superintendent, the concerns of this body were governed by a college of five superintendents.

The *Confessional Evangelical Lutheran Church* (in the diaspora) was organized in 1946. Known initially as the Evangelical Lutheran Refugee Mission Church (1946–1951), its members were mainly from the former Evangelical Lutheran Free Church of Poland (Lodz). The smallest of the Lutheran "Frees," this church body had ties with the Wisconsin Synod (USA) and rejected church fellowship involving any semblance of unionism. As of January 1, 1976, this church joined the aforementioned three churches which, as noted at the outset, in 1972 had formed the Independent Evangelical Lutheran Church.

NORTH ELBIAN EVANGELICAL LUTHERAN CHURCH (NEELC)

(Nordelbische Evangelisch-Lutherische Kirche)
Member: LWF (1977), WCC, CEC, EKD, ACKBD, VELKD
Membership: 2,656,000**
Chair of the Church Council
and Bishop for Holstein-Lübeck:
The Rt. Rev. Dr. Ulrich Wilckens
North Elbian Church Administration:
Dänische Strasse 21-35
D—2300 Kiel

On January 9, 1977, the constituting convention of this church took place in the picturesque Hanseatic city of Lübeck. The North

Elbian Evangelical Lutheran Church (NEELC) unites the former churches of Eutin, Hamburg, Lübeck, and Schleswig-Holstein, each described separately below, and Harburg, formerly a district of the church of Hanover. Those who have striven long for this consolidation hope that a pooling of resources and a coordinating of functions will give the new church a creative combination of rural and urban elements. Its name is derived from the River Elbe, near whose mouth Hamburg—West Germany's largest city and major port—is situated. In this region where Central and Northern Europe meet, lines of travel and trade have for centuries forged ties also with Britain and from there with North America and many other parts of the world. In this setting, the bodies comprising the North Elbian church have had a record of innovativeness and missionary fervor that has periodically benefited the Christian enterprise at home and abroad.

The NEELC's nearly three million baptized members are gathered into 673 parishes and are served by 1415 ordained pastors, as well as by a large staff in associated ministries. The new constitution provides for the following church structure and administrative setup. The church is divided into three districts: Hamburg, Holstein-Lübeck, and Schleswig. The first two are nearly equal in size; Schleswig is the smallest district, numerically about half the size of either of the other two. Each district is headed by a bishop: Peter Krusche, Hamburg; Ulrich Wilckens, Holstein-Lübeck; Karlheinz Stoll, Schleswig. The general secretariat of the NEELC is in Kiel.

On the church's territory are two theological faculties—at the universities in Hamburg and Kiel; the Evangelical Academies in Hamburg and Bad Segeberg, Schleswig-Holstein; and the offices of four church-related publishing houses and of the *Deutsches Allgemeines Sonntagsblatt*, the widely read and influential church weekly, of which the late Bishop Hanns Lilje was publisher from its inception in 1946 until his death in 1977. The Protestant Association for World Mission— the former German Evangelical Missionary Council—and the university-related mission academy, with students from many countries, are both located in Hamburg. The Lutheran Coordinating Service, which keeps channels open between the Evangelical Lutheran

Church in Tanzania and the helping agencies in Europe and North America, was in Hamburg for nearly a decade before its relocation to Helsinki in 1982. Many other undertakings affecting the local situation as well as the German scene as a whole are suggested in the separate accounts that follow.

The formation of the NEELC reduced the number of church bodies in the United Evangelical Lutheran Church of Germany (VELKD) from eight to five and removed the names of three churches—Hamburg, Lübeck, and Schleswig-Holstein—that were LWF charter members. The logic of the change, as some have noted, is evident; that it did not happen sooner attests to the persistence of historic forces which, in churches with centuries of tradition, are not readily redirected. That not everything has gone smoothly in the merged church is not surprising. Here is the story of the four merging churches in retrospect.

The *Evangelical Lutheran Church in the State of Hamburg* (ELCSH; Evangelisch-Lutherische Kirche im Hamburgischen Staate), held within the ancient boundaries of a strategically located city-state, tells a capsuled story of how the gospel has fared over more than 11 centuries. At the end of 1976, the Hamburg church, with about 480,000 members, comprised some 80 congregations and was served by about 200 ordained pastors as well as by others in supporting ministries. From a reported baptized membership in the early 1960s of about 800,000, the number declined steadily. Territorially, though not numerically, the smallest of Germany's historic churches, the ELCSH occupied an area of only 42 square kilometers (16 square miles)—the old city of Hamburg.

For years, the growing suburbs of Hamburg have been annexed to the city, but until 1977 places east of the Elbe like Altona remained part of the Schleswig-Holstein church, and Harburg, across the river, remained a circuit of the church of Hanover. In light of the larger North Elbian unity, some elements of the Hamburg church's past are instructive. An early trading center, Hamburg (with Bremen) became a missionary archdiocese in the ninth century. Ansgar used it as a base for advancing the faith into Scandinavia. By 1300 Hamburg had become a virtually independent Hanseatic commercial center and ecclesiastical stronghold. The 16th-century Lutheran Reformation was backed by the middle class. By 1526, virtually all pulpits were filled by Lutheran preachers, and in 1529, under the guidance of the ubiquitous organizer of northern churches, Johann Bugenhagen (1485–1558), Hamburg received its church constitution. The city subscribed to the *Augsburg Confession*. Its Lutheran leadership held out against lapsing back into old ways and in 1580 adopted the *Book of Concord* as its confessional basis. Until 1860, the same parish boundaries marked the civil and ecclesiastical units of the city.

Controversy was not absent from church life and flared up in conflicts with incipient or crypto-Calvinism, with Pietism, and with the Enlightenment. Successive generations of pastors took an active part in education, welfare, and other aspects of community life. The laity backed projects for appropriate church buildings, including the erection of a new St. Michael's Church (in the 1750s). "Der grosse Michael" was the largest baroque-style church in German Protestantism. The 19th century brought economic recession during the Napoleonic years to 1814; a decline of church income; a destructive fire (1842); and the beginning of an influx of people from the country seeking work and of the departure of emigrants looking for a fresh start in the Americas and Australia. Meanwhile, the spiritual awakening in Britain and North America was also stirring in Hamburg. The British innovation of Sunday schools was applied in Hamburg, as were Scottish developments in dealing with the needs of the poor. No German exceeded Johann Hinrich Wichern (1808–1881) in Christian social enterprise. His program for dealing with homeless youth and for training deacons and their wives as houseparents for the homeless boys gathered in the Rauhe Haus became the starting point for Germany's inclusive Inner Mission movement (above, Germany Introduction).

In 1860, Hamburg's new constitution ended the union of church and state, and new school laws in 1870 separated church and school. From 1860 to 1918, while the city population increased sixfold, the number of congregations only doubled. In 1923, a new church constitution gave the congregations virtual autonomy. In 1933, the title of the senior pastor was changed to bishop. During the Nazi era, however, the church council and synod were prevented from functioning.

After World War II, in face of enormous destruction and loss of life, the Hamburg church made valiant efforts at recovery. In 1951, the church set up its own divinity school, which later became the theological faculty of the University of Hamburg. A new church constitution (1959) pulled the congregation and diversified ecclesial functions together and gave fuller responsibility to the leadership of the church. In the succession of bishops since 1945, Volkmar Herntrich (1908–1958) was outstanding in his farsighted activity in reconstruction work at home and—in the spirit of a Wichern—in the advancement of church-sponsored diaconal activities throughout the member churches of the Evangelical Church in Germany. He was also a member (1952–1957) of the LWF Commission on World Service.

Evangelical Lutheran Church of Eutin (Evangelisch-Lutherische Landeskirche Eutin): This 570-square-kilometer (220-square-mile) enclave in Schleswig-Holstein is centered around the ancient commercial town of Eutin. In 1976, its approximately 92,000 members were in 20 parishes served by 26 pastors. Some of the church edifices date from the 12th and 13th centuries, near the time when this territory was given (1136) by the duke of Saxony and Bavaria to the bishop of Lübeck. Subsequent bishops retained Eutin as their official residence. In 1535, the Reformation was introduced. In 1937, Eutin was embodied into Schleswig-Holstein, but the church territory remained an entity in its own right. After World War II, the influx of refugees from East Germany doubled the population of Eutin and the church became active in resettlement work. Confessionally Lutheran, the Eutin church joined the United Evangelical Lutheran Church of Germany in 1967. It became a member of the LWF in 1963.

Evangelical Lutheran Church in Lübeck (Evangelisch-Lutherische Kirche in Lübeck): This church of about 215,000 members and 31 congregations, with 86 pastors, along with others in allied ministries, for centuries occupied the territory of the once flourishing Hanseatic commercial center, the Free City of Lübeck. As early as 1163, it became an episcopal see and an important base for the eastward spread of the Christian faith. As in Hamburg, the Reformation was introduced by the lay middle class, against the will of the cathedral chapter and the Roman Catholic city council. Lutheran services were begun in 1530, and a church constitution, drawn up with the help of Johann Bugenhagen (1485–1558), was adopted the following year. Over the generations, the church in Lübeck had strong leaders. Its churches, notably St. Mary's, the cathedral, and St. Peter's (both badly damaged during World War II) remain noteworthy examples of northern brick Gothic architecture, and in their time have been outstanding centers of music (Dietrich Buxtehude, 1637–1707, and others) and church art. During the 19th and 20th centuries, Lübeck church members have taken an active part in missionary outreach. Heinrich Meyer (1904–1978), bishop of the Lübeck church (1955–1972), a former missionary in India and a leading missiologist, was chairman of the LWF Commission on World Mission during the period of its most intensive development of fellowship among the churches worldwide.

During the Third Reich, the church struggle was especially intense in Lübeck. After the war, the Lübeck church received many refugees from East Germany and gave assistance to the Evangelical Church of Pomerania (today *Greifswald) in the GDR.

The *Evangelical Lutheran Church of Schleswig-Holstein* (Evangelisch-Lutherische Landeskirche Schleswig-Holsteins) brought into the new North Elbian Evangelical Lutheran Church some 2,300,000 members, 509 parishes, 937 pastors, and an extensive staff engaged in supportive services and institutions, as well as a rich spiritual heritage. As the northernmost of the Federal Republic's 10 states, Schleswig-Holstein forms a corridor between Germany and Scandinavia. For centuries the church of Schleswig-Holstein was under Danish rule. By conquest in 1864, it came under Prussia, and in 1920 the northern part of Schleswig was ceded to Denmark. Relations between the Danish and Schleswig-Holstein churches have been cooperative, notably in dealing with language minorities in their respective territories. Following World War II, many East German refugees were resettled in Schleswig. Today, as earlier, the population is overwhelmingly Lutheran (about 87%).

Christianity was brought to this region in the ninth century by Ansgar, the "Apostle to the North," and many others, including various monastic communities. A suffragan bishopric was set up in Schleswig in A.D. 948. In face of Norse and Slavic opposition, the missionary advance was slow but eventually complete.

The Reformation in Schleswig-Holstein was promoted by the kings of *Denmark, Frederick I and Christian III. The *Articles of Haderslev* (1528) anticipated the *Augsburg Confession* (1530) as a statement of faith and church reform. The 1537 *Ecclesiastical Order of the Realms of Denmark, Norway, and the Duchy of Schleswig-Holstein* was followed by a church constitution for the duchy in 1542, a document prepared with the help of Johann Bugenhagen (1485–1558). Although the *Formula of Concord* (1577) was not adopted, Lutheran orthodoxy in Schleswig-Holstein, as in Scandinavia generally, was in line with the theology of the *Formula*. This was long the position of the University of Kiel (1665), although modified in time by the influence of Pietism.

In the later 17th century, the duchy offered asylum to Reformed, Roman Catholic, Quaker, Mennonite, Jewish, and other refugees. The Enlightenment's influence was overshadowed by religious revival. The *95 Theses* as updated by Claus Harms of Kiel (1817), in observance of the Reformation tercentenary, also rallied people in many places beyond Schleswig-Holstein to promote a scripturally oriented renewal of the church. A sustained missionary impulse expressed itself at home and abroad. Deaconess houses were founded in Altona (1867), a suburb of Hamburg, and Flensburg (1874). These prepared women for nursing, educational, and parish services. The Schleswig-Holstein Evangelical Lutheran Mission (1876), often called the Breklum Mission for the village of its location, was founded by Christian Jensen (1839–1900) and undertook work in *India (Jeypore Evangelical Lutheran Church), in northern *Tanzania, and for a time in *China. It drew support also from Hamburg, Lübeck, and parts of *Denmark. To help provide pastors for German immigrants in North America, two programs were developed in Schleswig-Holstein, one in Kropp (1882), the other in Breklum (1883); the two were consolidated in 1920, then discontinued in 1930 when the need for such assistance was no longer felt. Together, these two programs provided some 340 pastors for North American Lutheran congregations.

During the Third Reich, the *Confession of Altona* (1933), prepared by Hans Asmussen (1898–1968) and other Schleswig-Holstein pastors and lay leaders, was in effect the opening statement by the resistance in the German church struggle (Germany Introduction, above). In the postwar era, the church in Schleswig-Holstein took an active part in the newly formed United Evangelical Lutheran Church of Germany (VELKD) and in the LWF.

UNITED EVANGELICAL LUTHERAN CHURCH OF GERMANY (VELKD)
(Vereinigte Evangelisch-Lutherische Kirche Deutschlands)
(P)
Presiding Bishop:
The Rt. Rev. D. Karlheinz Stoll
(North Elbian Evangelical Lutheran Church)
Plessenstrasse 5a
D—2380 Schleswig
Lutheran Church Office:
President: The Rev. Friedrich-Otto Scharbau
Richard-Wagner-Strasse 26
D—3000 Hanover 1

As already noted (introduction), after spanning the whole of Germany, the VELKD was divided into two parts in 1969. The eastern part, in the GDR, is treated below. The western part today comprises five member churches described above: Bavaria, Brunswick, Hanover, North Elbian, and Schaumburg-Lippe. Together these land churches include about 9.2 million baptized members in some 4160 parishes (congregations) and are served by about 5680 pastors and many other workers.

The VELKD considers itself a church even though its member bodies remain independent churches in terms of administration, finance, and decision making. Forms of worship, certain legal regulations, and other matters are decided by the VELKD as a whole, the general synod being its legislative

organ. A high degree of cooperation exists within and through the services of the VELKD in matters of theology, liturgy, spiritual life, ecumenical questions, relations to Lutheran churches in other lands and to the LWF, as well as in publications and other matters.

The governance of the VELKD lies in the general synod, the bishops' conference, the presiding bishop, and the church council. Some 20 commissions and working groups take up the various tasks and projects of the VELKD. The church office is in Hanover.

The widely read VELKD monthly magazine, *Lutherische Monatshefte* (Editorial Office: Knochenhauerstrasse 38-40, D—3000 Hanover 1), treats contemporary issues in theological perspective and ecumenical breadth. Beyond the FRG it has readers in many lands and all continents.

The VELKD is a partner to the *Japan Evangelical Lutheran Church through its membership in the Lutheran Committee for Cooperative Mission in Japan, to the Evangelical Lutheran Church in *Tanzania through its membership in the Lutheran Coordination Service—East Africa (Helsinki), and to the Lutheran Church in *Liberia (above). The VELKD represents its member bodies on the Coordination Committee of Overseas Partners of the Evangelical Lutheran Church in *Jordan (COCOP) and in relations with joint ecclesial bodies such as the *United Evangelical Lutheran Churches in India, the Federation of Evangelical Lutheran Churches in *Southern Africa, the Joint Christian Ministry in West Africa, based in *Nigeria, and in other relations as well.

Ecumenically, in October 1986, the VELKD member churches declared full pulpit and altar fellowship with the Evangelical Methodist Church in Germany. The theological dialog preceding this action paralleled the continuing bilateral sponsored by the LWF and the World Methodist Conference. A greater kinship between the two communions exists in Germany than in most other countries.

EVANGELICAL CHURCHES OF REFORMATION ANTECEDENTS

As heirs of the Reformation, Germany's Evangelical folk churches combine Lutheran and Reformed (Calvinist) elements in varying degrees. As United churches they are ecumenically significant and justifiably do not wish to be known as purely Lutheran. Yet they are included in this handbook because without them the story of the several confessional Lutheran churches would be incomplete. Not only are Lutheran, Reformed, and United churches the partners that comprise the Evangelical Church in Germany (above), but since their mutual acceptance of the Leuenberg Agreement during the mid-1970s they all practice pulpit and altar fellowship.

Before turning to these Evangelical churches individually—in the Federal Republic of Germany here and in the German Democratic Republic (below)—an overall backward glance suggests what might have been. Very soon after World War II, when the churches in Germany had been shaken profoundly and were facing the immense task of reconstruction, some farsighted church leaders—veterans of the *Kirchenkampf* (church struggle, above) under the Nazis—proposed the formation of a single, unified Evangelical Church of the Augsburg Confession (above, Oldenburg: W. Stählin). This was not to be. Instead, there was formed the Evangelical Church in Germany (EKD), a federation of Lutheran, Reformed, and United churches. Most of the Lutheran churches, as we have seen, formed their United Evangelical Lutheran Church of Germany (VELKD) within the EKD (1948). Meanwhile, with renewed resolve, those churches formerly part of the Evangelical Church of the Old Prussian Union in 1950 achieved a partial restoration of that body, calling it the Evangelical Church of the Union (EKU). Besides these developments there are also other Evangelical churches in the Federal Republic of Germany whose individual accounts are here included. They are loosely joined in the Arnoldshain Conference (AK), so named for the Evangelical Academy near Frankfurt where the association was formed.

EVANGELICAL CHURCH OF THE UNION (EKU) IN THE FEDERAL REPUBLIC OF GERMANY AND WEST BERLIN

(Evangelische Kirche der Union— Bereich Bundesrepublik Deutschland und Berlin-West)
Church Secretariat:
Jebensstrasse 3
D—1000 Berlin 12

This church includes the components of the former Evangelical Church of the Old Prussian Union in both East and West Germany, although in 1972 it was divided into two regions with relatively independent structures. In West Germany, the EKU today comprises the two large churches in the Rhineland and Westphalia as well as the church in West Berlin (below). Most of its parishes have Lutheran roots and orientation and Luther's catechism remains widely influential.

The EKU maintains its character as a church in that its representative synod acts as a legislative body for the member churches, doing so by mutual trust and prior consultation. In this manner, uniform practice in the member bodies has been won in such areas as liturgy, the pastoral ministry, the ordination of women, parish administration, church finance, and the like. Theologically, the EKU bodies occupy common ground in their focus on the centrality of Jesus Christ, the basic authority of Scripture, and the guiding function of the Reformation-era confessions and the *Barmen Theological Declaration* (1934; Germany Introduction, above). Thus, the historic position of Lutheran, Reformed, and United legacies, as represented in parishes within the several member churches is respected. Not only so, but this multiple heritage is seen as a unitive force, contributory to the advance of the ecumenical movement in our time. With its respect for the Reformation confessions, the EKU rejects any facile or homogenizing "unionism." Ecumenism and the visible unity of the church remain a first concern of the EKU. Perceptively, some have called this the "larger Lutheran" (grosslutherisch) response to the ecumenical challenge, open to other church bodies not historically part of the Old Prussian Union. The deletion of "Prussian" from the name facilitates accession. For example, in 1960 the Evangelical Church of Anhalt (below, German Democratic Republic) joined the EKU.

Outside the German scene, the EKU finds itself in company with other United churches such as those of *Canada, *India, *Japan, and the *United States; an association in which the Continental Reformation heritage often appears in marked contrast to heritages of Anglo-Saxon derivation. However, the presence in the United Church of Christ/USA of the former Evangelical (Prussian Union) and German Reformed church elements has encouraged continuing exchanges between the American United Church of Christ and the EKU. A brief account of the three EKU component bodies in West Germany follows.

EVANGELICAL CHURCH IN BERLIN-BRANDENBURG (BERLIN WEST)
(Evangelische Kirche in Berlin-Brandenburg—Berlin/West)
Member: WCC, CEC, EKD, EKU, ACKBD, AK
Membership: 866,000**
Bishop: The Rt. Rev. Dr. Martin Kruse
Bachstrasse 1-2
D—1000 Berlin 21

Of West Berlin's almost 1,900,000 inhabitants about 58% rate as members of the Evangelical church. Other Protestant groups account for a further 3%. The western part of the city also has 276,000 Roman Catholics. The now settled Turkish "guest" workers and their families make up most of the 100,000 Muslim constituency.

The Evangelical Church in Berlin-Brandenburg (Berlin West) comprises 167 parishes, grouped into 12 districts and served by 501 pastors. Aside from two groups of Reformed—of French Huguenot and Dutch as well as German origin—the church is virtually all Lutheran.

The church's future pastors may receive at least part of their theological education in one of the West German universities and the rest, if not all, in the Kirchliche Hochschule (the "Ki-Ho" to its friends) in West Berlin.

For many years after World War II, LWF World Service maintained a representative in

Berlin, a practice continued from the early 1970s up to 1984 by the Department of Church Cooperation. The local mission societies (EKD, above), the Berlin, Gossner, Jerusalem, and others formed the Berliner Missionswerk (BMW) in 1972 and continue their cooperative relationship with the LWF, while the churches overseas—sprung from their missionary activities—are themselves members of the LWF.

Berlin as a whole was long a capital where Protestant history was in the making. It went Lutheran by popular demand (1539). Its ruler switched from Lutheran to Reformed (1613), but the people remained Lutheran. Thousands of French Huguenot refugees, granted asylum in 1685 by the Great Elector, Frederick William, deeply affected cultural and economic life and enhanced the role of the Reformed. As capital of an expanding Prussia in the 18th and 19th centuries, Berlin's new university (1810) included a strong theological faculty and became the center of ecclesiastical and cultural influence. The creation (1817) of a church uniting Lutherans and Reformed, at least administratively, gave Berlin a supra-confessional character—assailed elsewhere (by Lutherans) as the promoter of "unionism."

Until the revolution of 1918, moreover, Berlin was the seat of a conservative church establishment loyal to throne and altar. In 1933, the national capital became the main stage of church conflict (above, Niemöller, Germany Introduction). A dozen years later, under occupation by the four allied powers after World War II, it became increasingly the symbol of a divided world wherein the church, at least, sought to demonstrate unity. But in 1969, as we have seen, even that effort had to end. Inclusive synods of the Evangelical Church in Berlin-Brandenburg were convened no more, and even the semblance of a common church administration—personified by Otto Dibelius, the first bishop of Berlin (1945–1966)—gave way to a church organized in two provinces within one Evangelical Church in Berlin-Brandenburg. Each province maintains its own administrative and synodical institutions but entertains deep and constant fellowship with the other province.

EVANGELICAL CHURCH IN THE RHINELAND (ECR)

(Evangelische Kirche im Rheinland)
Member: WCC, CEC, EKD, EKU, ACKBD, AK
Membership: 3,194,000**
President: The Rt. Rev. D. Gerhard Brandt
Hans-Böckler-Strasse 7
PO Box 320340
D—4000 Düsseldorf 30

The ECR—next after Hanover—is West Germany's largest Evangelical church. Covering the territory of the former Prussian province of the Rhineland, the ECR is spread out among the governmental districts of Aachen, Cologne, Düsseldorf, Koblenz, and Trier, including part of the Saar and the Hessian county of Wetzlar. In many parts, the region is heavily Roman Catholic. Organized on a presbyterial-synodal basis, the ECR's 828 parishes form 46 synods and are served by some 2089 pastors as well as deaconesses, deacons, and other workers.

Church headquarters are in Düsseldorf, capital of the postwar state of North-Rhine-Westphalia (see below, Westphalia). Many ECR pastors have been educated at Bonn, made famous in the early 1930s by Karl Barth; others in Westphalian and other theological faculties. The Evangelical Academies in Mühlheim/Ruhr and Iserlohn are run jointly with the Westphalian church. So, too, is the United Evangelical Mission (VEM), a 1970 consolidation of the Bethel Mission (1886; Westphalia) and the venerable Rhenish Mission (1828), which pioneered work in *Namibia (already before it became German West Africa) and in *Indonesia (when it was the Dutch East Indies). The churches arising from these labors are today partners in the Lutheran World Federation.

In Kaiserswerth, a suburb north of Düsseldorf, is the famous Deaconess Motherhouse and training center, complete with hospitals and schools, where in 1836 Theodor Fliedner (1800–1864) opened new avenues of service for women in the church. From here, it has spread across confessional lines and into all continents. The Kaiserswerth

Conference of Deaconess Houses is the forerunner of today's worldwide association, *Diakonia*.

Historically, the Rhineland was a patchwork of counties and fiefs of all sizes before Napoleon consolidated it early in the 19th century. In 1815, the Congress of Vienna awarded it to Prussia, whose big western province it became. Here, political antecedents went back to Roman times, and episcopal structures to the era of Charlemagne—and earlier, as in the case of Trier or Cologne or Aachen. With the Reformation, Lutheranism gained an initial footing, subsequently yielding ground to the Counter-Reformation or to Calvinism, particularly as it was strengthened by the influx of Dutch Reformed refugees fleeing the harsh Roman Catholic rule of Spain over the Netherlands. The city of Wesel, on the Rhine, is an example of a massive resettlement of refugees turning a once strongly Lutheran center into an even stronger Calvinist one.

In this Rhine region generally the relations between Lutherans and Reformed were shaped by a Calvinist type of Pietism. Adherence to Lutheranism thus tended to become less doctrinal and more liturgical, with the confessional contrasts being brought out in ways of worship. So things continued through the generations after 1817 under the Prussian Union. Unlike the sharp reaction in Silesia (below), which gave rise to the "Old Lutherans" and to emigration to *Australia (above), and to *North America (below), the Rhineland situation remained more calm. To this day, even Lutheran congregations that rejected the Union did not leave it. Among them is the largest Lutheran parish in all of Germany. Situated near Wuppertal, it comprises a membership of over 70,000 and is served by nearly a score of pastors.

The years of the church struggle under the Nazis were indeed difficult ones. But the platform of steadfastness was the *Barmen Theological Declaration* (Germany Introduction, above). At Barmen, a component of Wuppertal, in May 1934, a national synod challenged the churches to uphold the lordship of Christ and to oppose the neo-pagan ideology wherever espoused in their own infiltrated ranks. Karl Barth was the declaration's chief author. For perhaps most of Germany's Lutherans as well as for the Reformed and

United in the Confessing Church, this Barmen declaration was common ground.

After the war, with the Prussian Union broken up, no one worked more effectively than the Rhinelanders to create its successor, the Evangelical Church of the Union. Besides, the Evangelical Church in the Rhineland was the first in the EKD to make overseas mission a recognized task of the church as a whole and not only of a mission society (Germany Introduction, above).

As to the social concern of this church, the first full-scale Evangelical *Kirchentag*—that massive rallying of the church's laity on a nationwide scale—was held in Essen in 1950. An initial test run in Hanover the previous year (above, Germany Introduction) had signaled promise. Meanwhile, for the instruction of the young, Luther's *Small Catechism*—used by itself or supplemented with questions from the *Heidelberg Catechism*—is apparently still used in most of the Rhineland parishes; for reasons not confessional but pedagogical.

EVANGELICAL CHURCH OF WESTPHALIA (ECW)

(Evangelische Kirche von Westfalen)
Member: WCC, CEC, EKD, EKU, ACKBD, AK
Membership: 2,914,000**
President: Dr. Hans-Martin Linnemann
Altstädter Kirchenplatz 5
PO Box 2740
D—4800 Bielefeld 1

Like other parts of the former Old Prussian Union, the Westphalian church became independent in 1945. A province of Prussia from 1815 until the end of World War II, Westphalia was merged politically with its western neighbor to form the present federal land of North-Rhine-Westphalia. However, the churches of Rhineland (Rhenish) and Westphalia remained separate, retaining the political boundaries of these two former Prussian provinces. Roman Catholicism is strong in parts of Westphalia, but Protestantism claims a majority of the inhabitants.

The 642 congregations of the ECW are served by 1641 pastors, and by many deacons, deaconesses, and other church workers.

The church order is presbyterial-synodal. Church headquarters in Bielefeld keep track of the manifold challenges to the church in a highly diversified industrial society. Pastors are educated at Münster, whose theological faculty was begun in 1914, and at Bochum, the new (1964) University of the Ruhr, as well as at the Bethel theological school in Bielefeld. In the manner of an Evangelical Academy, the Social Service Center in Villigst pursues concerns in such areas as church and society, labor and management, and the professions. With its Rhenish partner, the ECW maintains the Evangelical Academies in Iserlohn and Mühlheim/Ruhr (above).

For generations, the social concern of Christian faith has been exemplified by Bethel (1867), the extensive complex of institutions adjacent to Bielefeld. From 1872 until after World War II, it was led by the Bodelschwinghs, father and son. Friedrich von Bodelschwingh the elder (1831–1910) gave the place its innovative character as a "Colony of Mercy"; Friedrich the younger (1877–1946) extended its outreach. Bethel proper cared for epileptics. "Sarepta" became the motherhouse and training center for deaconesses. "Nazareth" trained deacons who donned the blue apron of service. Bethel Theological School was the first such school independent of the state. It complemented university study and provided the practical experience in service not otherwise present in ministerial preparation. In the 1970s, Bethel became a leader in clinical pastoral education—an import from America via the Netherlands.

Outreach overseas through the United Evangelical Mission (combining the Bethel and Rhenish mission societies in 1970) has important Westphalian as well as Rhenish antecedents (EKD, above). The Bethel Mission, a relative latecomer, was launched in 1886 and undertook work in *South Africa and then in *Tanzania.

Relations between Roman Catholics and Protestants, positive since the church struggle of the Nazi era, have been ecumenically noteworthy; particularly through the Lutheran-Roman Catholic dialog initiated in 1945 by Wilhelm Stählin (bishop of Oldenburg, above) and Lorenz Jäger (cardinal archbishop of Paderborn). Stählin's 20 years on the Evangelical faculty at Münster University had opened the way. Jäger's Lutheran-Roman

Catholic openness is today furthered by the Johann Adam Möller Institute for Confessional and Diaspora Studies, named for the 19th-century pioneer of an ecumenism exemplified by Vatican II.

The long perspectives in Westphalian church history enter the Reformation era through Augustinian monks. Communities of them in Lippstadt, Herford, and Osnabrück were attracted by developments at Wittenberg. After a brisk beginning, the Lutheran Reformation was curbed by the large influx of Anabaptists from the lower (mainly Dutch) Rhineland. Aroused by the fiery Thomas Müntzer (c.1490–1525) and other leaders of the radical Reformation, they made the city of Münster their fateful stronghold. The awaited apocalyptic return of Christ turned, instead, into a bloody catastrophe (1534–1535). Its aftermath proved a serious setback to the Reformation. The Roman Catholic Reformation recovered the bishoprics of Münster and Paderborn—today leading centers of confessional rapprochement.

Westphalian absorption into the Evangelical Church of the Old Prussian Union did not dilute the Lutheranism to which most of the land's Protestant population adhered, and of which the Bodelschwinghs were leading representatives. This cultivation of a confessional legacy was broad-gauge: enlivened by unassuming Piety; strengthened by purposeful tenacity; and gifted by ecumenical openness. So, for example, at the outset of the notorious church struggle (1933) and in opposition to Nazi manipulation of a newly constituted German Evangelical Church, the Confessing Church—albeit unsuccessfully but significantly—championed Friedrich von Bodelschwingh, the younger, as Reichsbishop. Later, during the war, when the Nazis practiced euthanasia on "worthless lives" like epileptics, Bethel, it was said, was protected by a "wall of prayer."

In a Union church like the ECW, confessional identity surfaces through individuals. So it was in the case of Wilhelm Zöllner (1860–1937), able superintendent of the church for nearly the first three decades of this century (1905–1931). With a clear confessional emphasis, his Lutheranism also enabled him to become an early champion of the ecumenical movement in Germany. A generation later, Edmund Schlink's academic career began in the Bethel theological school

in Bielefeld. There he wrote his classic work, *The Theology of the Lutheran Confessions* (first published after the war), before embarking on his significant career at Heidelberg as an ecumenical theologian of the first rank. A Westphalian Lutheran at heart, Martin Niemöller administered an Inner Mission agency in this church prior to his call to Berlin in 1930 and his subsequent leading role in the church struggle (above, Germany Introduction). His brother, Wilhelm Niemöller became the widely read historian of that struggle as waged by the Confessing Church. Last but not least, Karl Barth's early academic career at Münster (1925–1930)—and later his few years at Bonn—prepared the way for many a pastor and lay person, regardless of confessional background, to become a confessing Christian when the test came.

OTHER EVANGELICAL CHURCHES OF REFORMATION ORIGIN

Lutheranism, Calvinism, and Roman Catholicism intertwine remarkably in the long Rhine valley and adjacent regions. The Evangelical churches of this region do not consider themselves Lutheran, but in each of them a measure of Lutheran Reformation legacy endures. Their involvement is such that no overview of Lutheranism in Germany would be complete without reference to them. "Evangelisch" here is often—certainly not always—equivalent to "Lutherisch" elsewhere and stands in convenient contrast to "Reformiert."

The Rhine valley or vaster Rhine basin has been a major region of Roman Catholic strength for many centuries. Its key cities—Cologne, Mainz, Worms, Speyer, Strasbourg—boast political as well as religious importance.

As a famed commercial artery, the Rhine valley linked the Swiss and the Dutch, and both peoples ardently promoted the Reformed faith. Attempts to bring Evangelical Lutherans and south German and Swiss Reformed together—as Margrave Philip of Hesse did at Marburg in 1529—succeeded only in part. Yet in this long north-south corridor and adjacent lands, Lutheran and Reformed coexistence produced a distinctive type of both—

an Evangelical Christianity, both Lutheran and Reformed, which continues to this day.

The politics of church-state relations tended to homogenize the Lutheran and Reformed traditions. The Religious Peace of Augsburg (1555) for the first time officially tolerated Lutheran as well as Roman Catholic territories within the Holy Roman Empire of the German Nation. The principle—tribal in origin—was that of uniformity: the territorial ruler's religion determines that of his subjects. In 1648, the Peace of Westphalia granted the Reformed confession equality with the Lutheran. Until that time, the *Augsburg Confession* provided the umbrella under which Calvinism spread—among rulers, to be sure, more so than among their subjects. In the Rhine valley and neighboring lands, this confessional agglomeration was compounded by a patchwork of territories great and small.

Encouraged by the Reformation tercentenary and by the example of the Evangelical Church of the Old Prussian Union in 1817 (above, Germany Introduction), United Evangelical churches in various parts of the Rhine and neighboring regions emerged (below). These unions, unlike the Prussian, were not administrative ones in which Lutherans and Reformed were separately recognized. Instead, they were, or came close to being, consensus unions in which Lutheran and Reformed elements were blended. In most cases, the *Augsburg Confession* (Variata version) remained the legal basis and was subscribed by pastors at the time of ordination. Locally, too, the option of using Luther's *Small Catechism* or the *Heidelberg Catechism* continued; although non-confessional versions were sometimes sanctioned as alternatives.

The separation of church and state after World War I gave the churches a freer hand, making self-government the mode of operation. However, with the political takeover by National Socialism and the unleashing of ideological forces among pastors and people, the *Kirchenkampf* became especially bitter in many parts of Germany here under survey. Only after World War II could the churches really exercise their freedom; but then only under the most trying conditions of rehabilitation and reconstruction. In the process, however, their ecumenical interest and participation gathered newfound strength. The

Evangelical Academy, for example, at Arnoldshain, near Frankfurt, became the frequented place where—for all Germany—Lutherans, Reformed, and Evangelicals converged on agreement. The focal point, as always, was the Lord's Supper, and the aim was altar fellowship. At last, in the Swiss conference center of Leuenberg, near Basel, agreement was achieved (1973). Its great significance internationally as well as ecumenically and confessionally—the Leuenberg Agreement was before long accepted by all the member churches of the EKD—underscores the welcome place in this handbook of the Evangelical churches whose brief descriptions follow.

CHURCH OF LIPPE (CL)

(Lippische Landeskirche)
Member: WCC, WARC, CEC, EKD, ACKBD, RBBRD, AK
Membership: 230,000** (including 42,000 in Lutheran Section)
Landessuperintendent:
The Rt. Rev. Dr. Ako Haarbeck
Leopoldstrasse 27, PO Box 132
D—4930 Detmold
(AM) *Lutheran Section:*
Superintendent: The Rev. Dieter Lorenz
Martin-Luther-Strasse 91
D—4902 Bad Salzuflen

Lippe-Detmold, the small territory covered by this Reformed church, lies between the Weser River in the east and the Teutoburg Forest in the west. To the north of Lippe-Detmold lies Schaumburg-Lippe, now in the Land of Lower Saxony and home of the Lutheran territorial church by that name (above). The division of Lippe into two parts goes back to 1613, following some years after its count had switched from Lutheran to Reformed.

The Church of Lippe (Detmold) comprises 63 parishes (10 Lutheran and 52 Reformed). They are grouped into half a dozen circuits, one of which is Lutheran and largely self-governing. The service of 133 pastors is augmented by that of many others. Church headquarters are in Detmold, home also of the

Deaconess Motherhouse and training center—a place of refuge and hospitality during the *Kirchenkampf* years under the Nazis. In recent years, the church has had more theological students and prospective ministers than it has places available.

The CL shares with the Evangelical Reformed Church in Northwest Germany (below) a leading role in the Reformed Alliance in the FRG (RBBRD). It maintains ties with the Evangelical Church of Anhalt (below, GDR) as well as with the Reformed Church in *Hungary. It supports interests of the World Alliance of Reformed Churches. Having readily accepted the *Leuenberg Agreement* (1973), it is in eucharistic fellowship with all the member churches of the EKD. Through the North German Mission Society this church is in a supporting relationship with the Evangelical Church of Togo and the Presbyterian Church of Ghana.

The Lutheran section of the Church of Lippe, composed of 10 large parishes, has grown considerably since the end of World War II because of large influx of Lutheran refugees from the East. Numerically, Lutherans account for one-fifth of the CL membership. Today, the Lutheran section, or classis, is related to the United Evangelical Lutheran Church of Germany (VELKD). Internationally, this section is also represented at LWF assemblies. In 1987, at Viborg, Denmark, this Lutheran section was received as an associate member by the LWF Executive Committee. Behind this phenomenon lie some interesting historical developments.

Originally, this land was under the jurisdiction of the archbishop of Paderborn. In Lemgo, the first Lutheran voice was raised in 1525 and a new church order (constitution) fashioned (1533). The Lutheran position was reaffirmed in 1556, after the Religious Peace of Augsburg. Later, the *Formula of Concord* was turned down (1579). In 1600, Lippe's Count Simon VI, dissatisfied with difficulties into which Lutheranism had run, turned Reformed. The *Heidelberg Catechism* was subsequently introduced in 1618, the year the Thirty Years' War began. In Lemgo, two parishes remained Lutheran. A Reformed church constitution, introduced in 1684, took the rights of the Lutheran minority into account and remained substantially in force until 1931.

Lippe-Detmold has often been regarded as a lively corner in the Lutheran diaspora. Here, Lutherans learned the principle of voluntarism: if they desired a church of their own confession, they would have to pay for it—while still being required to pay the church tax supporting the Reformed church. In 1721, a Lutheran congregation was reestablished in Lemgo, and today it claims some 15,000 members. In Bergkirchen, Salzuflen, and elsewhere Lutheran congregations emerged, on the same voluntarist principle. In 1854, Lutheran and Roman Catholic parishes were granted equality with the Reformed. In 1877, a new synodical constitution gave limited representation to the Lutherans; which they also had in the church consistory. After the separation of church and state in 1918, the synod executive committee and the consistory comprised the new church council.

Tensions between the Lutheran and Reformed were inevitable, and for a time the Lutherans threatened to join the church of Hanover. But the church struggle in the later 1930s brought the two groups together as active participants in the Confessing Church. Since 1945, Lutherans as well as Reformed have made the Church of Lippe ecumenically active.

EVANGELICAL CHURCH IN BADEN (ECB)

(Evangelische Landeskirche in Baden)
Member: WCC, CEC, EKD, ACKBD, AK
Membership: 1,332,000**
Bishop: Professor Dr. Klaus Engelhardt
Blumenstrasse 1
PO Box 2269
D—7500 Karlsruhe 1

The ECB, since 1821 a consensus union of Lutheran and Reformed antecedents, is situated in the western part of the federal state of Baden-Württemberg in a region about half Roman Catholic. Its 712 parishes, in 30 districts, are served by 1079 pastors (290 of whom are full-time religious instruction teachers in public schools) as well as other workers. ECB headquarters are in Karlsruhe, a city known for its culture, industry, and technical university as well as for the location of the West German Supreme Court. Until the consolidation of Baden-Württemberg in 1952, Karlsruhe was the capital of Baden. Pastors of this church are, for the most part, educated at Heidelberg, Germany's oldest university (1386). Since the end of World War II, the university's theological faculty has been regarded as having one of the strongest combinations of Lutheran scholars in Germany and as being ecumenically very influential.

Heidelberg, as capital of the Palatinate (below) until the time of Napoleon, shares the complexity of Baden's church history. When the consensus union was formed in 1821, Lutherans outnumbered Reformed by about three to one. A union catechism, introduced in 1834, replaced the Luther and Heidelberg catechisms in most places. Reaction in Lutheran ranks was not strong enough to overcome these steps, but some of those breaking away formed the present Evangelical Lutheran Church in Baden (above).

The ECB's Evangelical Academy at Herrenalb helps to apply the Christian faith to life in industry, agriculture, and the professions. Through the Association of Churches and Missions in Southwestern Germany and other channels, the church maintains overseas ties especially with the Church of South India, the Communion of Churches in Indonesia, the National Council of Churches in South Korea, the United Church of Christ (Kyodan) in Japan, the Evangelical (Presbyterian) churches in Ghana, Cameroon, and Portugal and also with the Waldensians in *Italy and the Moravians *South Africa (above).

EVANGELICAL CHURCH IN HESSE AND NASSAU (ECHN)

(Evangelische Kirche in Hessen und Nassau)
Member: WCC, CEC, EKD, ACKBD, AK
Membership: 2,045,000**
President: The Rt. Rev. Helmut Spengler
Paulusplatz 1
PO Box 4447
D—6100 Darmstadt

This church of Lutheran and Reformed antecedents comprises 1166 parishes in seven districts, and is served by 1255 pastors plus other workers. Its membership accounts for about 55% of the population in the federal Land of Hesse, most of the other inhabitants being Roman Catholic. Organized in its present form in 1945, the ECHN combined the already confessionally consolidated churches of Nassau, Hesse-Darmstadt, and Frankfurt. Its headquarters are in the old Hessian capital, Darmstadt, south of Frankfurt; but under its first president, Martin Niemöller, in Wiesbaden, capital of Hesse.

Pastors of the ECHN have usually been educated at one of the German universities, such as Marburg, Mainz, or Heidelberg. Their practical preparation is in the preachers' seminaries: Friedberg and Herborn. Provision is also made for their continuing education. The church maintains the Evangelical Academy Arnoldshain, in Schmitten, northwest of Frankfurt, a conference center for the laity especially. The place has also given its name to ecumenically important documents, like the Arnoldshain Theses on altar fellowship between Lutherans and Reformed in the EKD—in advance of the *Leuenberg Agreement* (above)—as well as to the Arnoldshain Conference of Evangelical churches within the EKD, a counterweight to the United Evangelical Lutheran Church, also within the EKD (see Federal Republic of Germany Introduction).

Frankfurt has been the focus of ecumenical activities since the end of World War II, being the site (until 1986) of the EKD Foreign Office (Aussenamt) as well as of the Association of Christian Churches in the FRG (ACKBD, above). The EKD Aussenamt, with its ties in every continent, works in close cooperation with the Geneva-based WCC and LWF. In 1983, its president, Dr. Heinz Joachim Held, was elected moderator of the WCC Central Committee. (In 1986 the Aussenamt moved to Hanover, adjacent to EKD headquarters.) Frankfurt's ecumenical importance shows also in its mammoth annual Book Fair, an opportune meeting place for publishers also of religious and theological works in translation. The Book Fair's antecedents go back to the invention of printing in the 15th century by John Gutenberg at Mainz, where the Main River joins the Rhine.

About the confessional past of this region as a whole (above), here are a few additions on the background of the ECHN. The first

Lutheran sermon was preached in Frankfurt in 1522, but the city was slow in accepting the Reformation. When it did so, it absorbed the influence of Martin Bucer (Strasbourg) as much as that of Luther. This mediating position between Wittenberg and the south Germans was evident also in the role of Philip, Landgrave of Hesse, who ruled over a territory roughly that of today's ECHN. The famed Marburg Colloquy (1529), as already noted, fully attained its goal only in today's ecumenical era. But Frankfurt's role as a host to Dutch, Scottish, and other refugees during the Reformation era was complemented by the asylum granted in Hessian lands to Waldensian refugees from Italy. John à Lasco— the Polish Evangelical "Father of the Reformed Church" and, second only to Calvin, a shaper of the Reformed local church constitution—found refuge in Frankfurt for some years before going to Emden (below). In the late 17th century, Hessian and other German Protestant lands welcomed Waldensian refugees from religious intolerance in Italy and France, and the city of Frankfurt became a prime reception center for Huguenots fleeing by the thousands from France.

Shortly before this time a quest for church renewal had been launched in Frankfurt by its head pastor, Philipp Jakob Spener (1635–1705). His *Pia Desideria,* setting forth a composite of devout desires, appeared in time for the 1685 Frankfurt Book Fair and soon made him the leading figure of the new movement which its opponents called Pietism.

While Pietism smoothed the edges of Lutheran and Reformed orthodoxy, Rationalism dismissed the importance of confessional differences. The example of the Evangelical Church of the Old Prussian Union found varied response on this territory, and also stubborn reaction from the Lutherans.

Almost until the creation of the Second Reich, under Bismarck in 1871, Frankfurt was the base of the German Confederation— the forerunner to unification. In 1866, the city was taken by Prussia and lost its ancient status as one of Germany's four Free Cities (along with Hamburg, Bremen, and Lübeck).

Protests against the union of confessions were vigorous in parts of Hesse and Frankfurt; more so than in Nassau. There the Reformed were the dominant Evangelical constituency and—next to Geneva and Leiden—Herborn had been an influential center

of Calvinism. On the present ECHN territory were men and women who helped found the Evangelical Lutheran (then Old Lutheran) Church, whose theological seminary is in Oberursel (above; Independent Evangelical Lutheran Church). Driving these protests against union was the awareness of a rich Lutheran heritage. It turned some to separatism, others not.

In more recent times a Lutheran strain in Evangelical Hesse has given the church at large such noted theologians as Edmund Schlink (1903–1984) and Peter Brunner (1899–1982), both professors at Heidelberg (above, Baden).

In its missionary outreach to churches in Asia, Africa, and Latin America the ECHN participates in the Association of Churches and Missions in Southwestern Germany. Besides, it fosters close ties with the Presbyterian (former Evangelical) Church of Ghana; and, honoring the memory of John à Lasco, keeps in touch with the Polish Ecumenical Council. Connections with the Waldensian Church in *Italy likewise remain lively expressions of ecumenism.

EVANGELICAL CHURCH OF BREMEN (ECB)

(Bremische Evangelische Kirche)
Member: WCC, CEC, EKD, ACKBD, AK
Membership: 333,000**
President: Eckart Ranft
Franziuseck 2-4
PO Box 106929
D—2800 Bremen 1

The 69 congregations of Bremen Land are variously Lutheran, Reformed, or United and are served by 139 pastors as well as other church workers. The ECB's membership represents about two-thirds of the population of this smallest of West Germany's federal states. Roman Catholics account for about 10%. Methodists, Baptists, and other religious adherents are small in number but not in influence. The Ecumenical Working Group in Bremen acts as a council of churches and includes Roman Catholic participation. ECB headquarters easily keep in touch with a territory of under 400 square kilometers (160 square miles), yet nowhere in Germany is congregational autonomy more jealously guarded than here.

After Hamburg, Bremen (with Bremerhafen) is Germany's largest port. Situated at the mouth of the Weser river, Bremen's location was early recognized as significant for the expansion of Christianity. Scandinavia, Iceland, and Greenland were initially under the jurisdiction of the archbishop of Bremen. The statue of Roland the Giant (1404) still stands as the symbol of Bremen's freedom as a Hanseatic city. Initially Lutheran and then Reformed influences gave Bremen confessional attachment, but looser than in Hamburg, where Lutheranism became established. In Bremen, ecclesiastical commitments were more diffuse, yet in part also deep. The deaconess community in Bremen, active in hospital and welfare services, is part of the former Inner Mission and now Diakonisches Werk in this state. Outreach overseas, begun in 1836, continues through the North German Mission Society (NMG; known as Bremen Mission).

The NMG is the agency through which the Evangelical Lutheran Church in Oldenburg (above) does its work overseas in partnership with the ECB as well as with the Church of Lippe and the Evangelical Reformed Church in Northwest Germany (below), particularly in *Togo (Evangelical Church) and in *Ghana (Presbyterian Church).

Bremen's church connections with other parts of the world grew out of its major role in the 19th century as a port of embarkation for emigrants from Germany. Among them were some from the city of Bremen itself, like Johann Diederich Lankenau (1817–1901). A young businessman with good connections, he settled in Philadelphia, built up the German Hospital (renamed Lankenau in 1917). In 1884, he established the widely influential Lutheran Deaconess House—a model followed elsewhere in the USA.

The young University of Bremen (founded in 1974), a point of entry for certain American and other ways of higher education, has no theological faculty. As before, ECB pastors are educated in various universities and theological schools in Germany. Significantly, the ECB is one of the few German churches with Lutheran, Reformed, and United types of congregations. In 1952, after some delays, this church joined the EKD. Two years later, by special arrangement with the church in Hanover, six Lutheran congregations joined the ECB with the right to retain their confessional status and to elect one of their pastors as their spiritual leader ("Senior"). The Reformed have the same right.

EVANGELICAL CHURCH OF KURHESSEN-WALDECK (ECKW)
(Evangelische Kirche von Kurhessen-Waldeck)
Member: WCC, CEC, EKD, ACKBD, AK
Membership 1,033,000**
Bishop: The Rt. Rev. Dr. Hans-Gernot Jung
Haus der Kirche
Wilhelmshöher Allee 330
PO Box 410260
D—3500 Kassel-Wilhelmshöhe

The ECKW covers the former electorate of Hesse. In 1934, Waldeck (once part of the principality of Waldeck-Pyrmont) was added. The ECKW comprises parishes with Lutheran, United, and Reformed tradition. The statutes laid down by the synod in 1967 stipulate that the ECKW is primarily influenced by the *Augsburg Confession* and the symbols of the ancient church adopted by it. Within the diversity of confessional traditions of the Reformation, it has grown together to form one church. Since Reformation times, the ECKW has been characterized by its endeavor to overcome differences that cause church division (1529 religious discussions in Marburg between Luther, Zwingli, and other Reformers on the initiative of Landgrave Philipp).

The church's 949 parishes, in four districts and 27 circuits, are served by about 750 pastors as well as other workers. Its headquarters are in Kassel, prominent already in medieval times as a trade route crossroads. Its future pastors are trained at historic Marburg and other universities and in the church's own seminary in Hofgeismar. Hofgeismar is also the location of the Evangelical Academy, which is especially concerned with problems of health, education, and welfare.

The ecumenical stance of the ECKW is nothing recent. Waldensian and Huguenot refugees found asylum here (above, Hesse-Nassau). In the mid-1970s, this church was the second to sign the Leuenberg Agreement, which underscored an already prevailing practice of altar fellowship between Lutheran, Reformed, and United traditions. Through the United Evangelical Mission (VEM), the ECKW maintains supportive relations with the Evangelical Lutheran Church in *Southern Africa/Western Diocese, the ELCSWA in *Namibia, and the Church of South India/North Karnataka Diocese. The church also has an affiliated relationship with the Evangelical Lutheran Mission in Lower Saxony (ELM) and thus contributes to its work in *Ethiopia, *Brazil, *Southern Africa and *India. Closer at hand are its relations with the Reformed Churches in the Netherlands/Brabant Synod, and the continuing dialog with the neighboring Roman Catholic bishopric of Fulda—historic eighth-century base of the pioneer mission of Boniface to the Germans and today seat of the Fulda Conference of Catholic Bishops in Germany. In Fulda, too, are the headquarters of the Evangelical Kirchentag (above). In Kassel are the headquarters of the YMCA and the Gustav-Adolf-Werk.

On the ECKW turf, as in other parts of Hesse and Nassau—absorbed politically into Prussia in 1866—the issue of church union turned into a bitterly opposed contest, resulting in the emergence of the small but bold Evangelical Lutheran Free Church (above). Called the Renitent (Refractory) Lutheran Church, with August Vilmar (1800–1868), it resisted the imposition of a Prussian Union-style ecclesiastical consistory and protested the abolition of Hessian church constitution of 1657. The latter had already allowed for Lutheran and Reformed coexistence. In 1950, the Renitent Church amalgamated with the *Independent Evangelical Lutheran Church.

EVANGELICAL CHURCH OF THE PALATINATE (ECP)—PROTESTANT CHURCH

(Evangelische Kirche der Pfalz—Protestantische Landeskirche)
Member: WCC, CEC, EKD, ACKBD, AK
Membership: 633,000**
President: Oberkirchenrat Werner Schramm
Domplatz 5
PO Box 829
D—6720 Speyer/Rhein

A consensus union of Lutheran and Reformed confessions, this church was formed in 1818 in the wake of enthusiasm generated by the Reformation tercentenary. Alone among the EKD member churches, the ECP retains the name "Protestant," recalling the protest of the Lutheran princes at the imperial diet of Speyer in 1529 (above). The Palatinate today is a part of the West German state of Rhineland-Pfalz, extending westward from the Rhine to the French border and having a slightly larger Protestant than Roman Catholic population. The church's 428 parishes—158 of them are without a resident clergy—are grouped into 20 districts and served by 469 pastors and a considerable number of other workers. Most of its pastors are educated in Heidelberg, capital of the once greater Palatinate in the post-Reformation era; the seminary for preachers is in Landau. Church headquarters are in Speyer, seat of various church agencies, including the Evangelical Academy and the well-known deaconess community with its extensive health and welfare services.

Called a "church of the people," the ECP is a ready exponent of ecumenism. External ties run to the Evangelical Church of Anhalt (below, GDR); the United Reformed Church in the United Kingdom; the Reformed Church of France; the Reformed Church in Yugoslavia; the United Church of Christ in the USA; and the United Church of Canada. Through the Association of Churches and Missions in Southwestern Germany it is linked to churches of various communions—including the Lutheran—in *Asia, *Africa, and *Latin America.

Spurred on by crop failures and war devastation, large migration from this area in the early 18th century to the American colonies made the name "Palatinate" almost synonymous with German in New York, Pennsylvania, and elsewhere (Lutheran Church in *America, now ELCA). A century later, many emigrated from the Palatinate to southern *Brazil. Customary Union churches of Lutheran and Reformed in the Palatinate became reminders in the Americas of the homogenizing character of the Palatine church history.

Receptive to Lutheran and then Reformed influences, jolted by the effects of local rulers changing confessional sides, mauled by forces of the Counter-Reformation, and exposed to periodic invasions from France, the Palatinate suffered not only from the Thirty Years' War but from subsequent violence as well. During the French Revolution and the era of Napoleon, drastic action included the separation of Heidelberg from the Palatinate, the reduction of its territory, and the placing of its governance under the greatly enlarged new kingdom of Bavaria. In the process, the Evangelical and originally partly Lutheran church came under the Lutheran church in Bavaria, itself a minority under a Roman Catholic monarch. The Palatinate's own "Thirty Years' War" against this confessional situation ended in 1848 with separation from Bavaria. After prolonged internal tension, the church reached a state of confessional equilibrium in which the *Variata* version of the *Augsburg Confession* (1540)—friendly to Calvinism—was recognized, and a mutually acceptable catechism, order of worship, and other changes were introduced. After World War I, a new constitution set the course for a church now separated from the state.

For the Palatinate, a sense of history pervades the church: Luther at Worms (1521), the protesting Lutheran princes at Speyer eight years later, and the presence there of the superb Romanesque cathedral (11th century)—burial place of eight emperors and site of an episcopacy going back to the seventh century—all have something to say about the continuity and unity of the church despite change. This fact was amply reaffirmed during the bitter years of the *Kirchenkampf*, the Nazi era, and the postwar rise of ecumenism.

EVANGELICAL REFORMED CHURCH IN NORTHWEST GERMANY (ERCNG)

(Evangelisch-Reformierte Kirche in Nordwestdeutschland)
Member: WCC, WARC, CEC, EKD, ACKBD, RBBRD, AK
Membership: 195,000
President: The Rev. Hinnerk Schröder
Saarstrasse 6
D—2950 Leer

This church, a member of the EKD, is one of West Germany's two Reformed churches, the Church of Lippe (above) being the other. It is a partner in the North German Mission Society along with the *Evangelical Lutheran Church in Oldenburg, the *Evangelical Church of Bremen, and the *Church of Lippe. It maintains a good working relationship with the neighboring *Evangelical Lutheran Church of Hanover. On the basis of the *Leuenberg Agreement*, this Reformed church is in eucharistic fellowship with all the EKD member churches.

GERMAN DEMOCRATIC REPUBLIC

A country of Central Europe, the GDR (*Deutsche Demokratische Republik* or DDR; also East Germany), following the partitioning of Germany after World War II, was proclaimed a republic on October 7, 1949. A UN member since 1973. Area: 108,333 sq. km. (41,827 sq. mi.). Pop. (1985 est.): 16,703,000. Cap. and largest city: East Berlin (pop., 1985 est., 1,185,533). Language: German.

History (see also Germany above; and Federal Republic): The German Democratic Republic (GDR) is the westernmost of the nations forming the Soviet bloc. The GDR has Czechoslovakia to the south, the Federal Republic to the west, the Baltic Sea to the north, and Poland to the east. Since the end of World War II, East Germany is under special obligation to the USSR, a fact that requires the country to practice its Marxian Socialism often with rigidity, particularly in order to distinguish itself from the much bigger West Germany. The nub of these intra-German relations is the former chief city, Berlin. East Berlin, now the GDR capital, abuts West Berlin, the Federal Republic's enclave 160 kilometers inside the GDR. This geographic proximity provides access especially for TV from the West and thus complicates the nurture of an East German identity. The great strides toward a maturing nationhood—accentuated in the popular mind by the East German prowess in sports—make it easy to forget the rubble and poverty of 40 or more years ago.

For the first decade after the war's end, much of the industrial equipment in the Soviet Zone of occupation was delivered to the USSR as reparations. With nothing equivalent to Marshall Plan aid (as available to West Germany, above), economic recovery was slower, but it gained momentum by dint of a people's creativity and hard work. Today, East Germany's manufactured output is second only to that of the Soviet Union among the Warsaw Treaty countries and places the GDR among the first 10 industrial nations in the world. This advance weathered hard times as different as the workers' uprising in Berlin (1953) or the chronic drain of refugees to West Germany. To block this loss, a heavily guarded 5-kilometers-wide "no man's land" marked the border with West Germany (1952). Nine years later the 47-kilometer Berlin Wall sealed off the last exit.

Politically, the party running the country is the Socialist Unity Party of Germany (SED). Among its leaders, Otto Grotewohl was the first prime minister; Walter Ulbricht, the strategist and reorganizer; and Erich Honecker (since 1971), under whose general secretaryship conditions became somewhat more relaxed. The small Christian Democratic Union (CDU) recalls the reinstatement of the German party system after 1945, and the effort of a Christian laity to assume their share of political responsibility. But in East Germany this intention faced handicaps. An initial postwar friendliness between Communists and Christians who had opposed Nazism gradually yielded to the demands of political realism under the shadow of the occupying power.

Religion (1986 est.): Protestant (predominantly Lutheran) 40%; Roman Catholic 7%; unaffiliated and other 53%.

The three Lutheran and five Evangelical (United) folk churches claim a total baptized membership of about 5,800,000. These include some 21,000 Reformed, whose 20 parishes form a separate conference within the *Bund der Evangelischen Kirchen* (BEK, Federation of Evangelical Churches) in which the eight folk churches are closely joined. The combined membership of the six Roman Catholic dioceses comes to 1,200,000. Among the various small constituencies, Methodists count 28,000; Seventh Day Adventists 25,000; Baptists 23,000; Lutheran Free 10,500; Moravians 3000; Old Catholics 1200; and others (see chart below). The loosely linked *Arbeitsgemeinschaft Christlicher Kirchen* (Association of Christian Churches) in the GDR includes Roman Catholic and Russian Orthodox observers (see chart below). At its 1988 ecumenical conference (Dresden), the ACK tackled issues of justice, peace, and the care of God's creation, and attempted to show how Christians together, in the GDR, were eager to "teach a hope to walk."

East Germany's geography embraces the beginnings of Luther's Reformation. Countless tourists (and pilgrims, too) have been drawn to Wittenberg (now Lutherstadt Wittenberg), home base of Luther and Melanchthon, to Erfurt (where Luther studied), and to Eisleben (where he was born in 1483 and died in 1546)—these three places are in today's Church Province of Saxony (below). In Thuringia, the Lutherhaus at Eisenach and the lofty Wartburg overlooking the fabled Thuringian Forest never cease to attract visitors. In Leipzig, where Luther debated Eck (1519), the greater attraction is St. Thomas Church, where Johann Sebastian Bach's career flowered and—as some contend—set Luther's spiritual legacy to music. Here in East Germany, the 450th anniversary of the Reformation (1967), the 300th of the birth of Bach (1980), and the 500th of Luther (1983) were observed grandly on an international and ecumenical scale.

From East Germany—as the course may be followed in this book—the Reformation spread westward to what is now the *Federal

Republic of Germany, and on to *France, the *Netherlands, the *United Kingdom (Britain); northward to *Denmark, *Sweden, *Finland, *Norway, and *Iceland; eastward to *Poland, the Baltic lands in the modern *USSR; southeastward to *Austria, *Czechoslovakia, *Hungary, *Romania, and *Yugoslavia. Fittingly, East Germany today retains the largest Protestant constituency in Eastern Europe. But this is at a price of so-called "minorization"—of declining numbers and changing circumstances.

• • •

"The church in Socialism" is how the Lutheran and Evangelical churches describe themselves with respect to their context. There was a time—roughly for about the first two decades after the war—when the East German Protestant churches saw themselves, over against the state, in a relationship of confrontation. Gradually, after severing their ties with EKD—the one Evangelical Church spanning the two Germanies until 1968—the East German churches considered themselves alongside the state, in a relationship of co-existence. At three points one could discern a change in progress: (1) the *Leuenberg Agreement* (1973; above, FRG Introduction) corroborated the already long-established pulpit and altar fellowship among the Lutheran and Evangelical and Reformed churches in East Germany. (2) A "book of faith," entitled *Aufschlüsse* (1977), was produced jointly by the eight churches in the BEK and informed Christians on how to live positively in a society whose ideology was negative toward the Word of God and the church. The book gained acceptance in many quarters, especially among young people. (3) The meeting on March 6, 1978—when two chairmen, Albrecht Schoenherr, of the BEK, and Erich Honecker, of the government council, engaged in a protracted dialog—came to be regarded as a turning point for better relations between church and state. Nothing at that time was pinned down on the government's side. Ironically, the tensions in 1988—the 10th anniversary year of the "turning point"—were accompanied by the oft-repeated censorship of the church press. Such matters as concern for the environment were ruled as being off-limits for the church to discuss; so, too, was the ruling out of references to greater freedom for the church in

the Soviet Union at the time of Russian Orthodoxy's celebration of its millennium. This tension, attributed by some to indefiniteness or a noncommital attitude by those in power, did not imply a return to square one. Rather, it was seen as an opportunity to reaffirm the article on religion in the GDR constitution: "Every citizen of the German Democratic Republic has the right to acknowledge a religious faith and to engage in religious practices."

• • •

For the churches, the era since the war has been enlivened by the spiritual legacy of the Confessing Church as well as by the challenge to adapt. Three stages are discernible: 1945–1957, the struggle for survival; 1948–1968, partnership with the West German churches in the EKD and, for the three Lutheran bodies, membership in the VELKD as well; since 1969, separation and the formation of two East German equivalents—the BEK/DDR and the VELK/DDR. The Lutheran bodies decided in 1988 to discontinue their parallel VELK and to merge their projects with those of the BEK. Representatives of the three Lutheran churches and the Evangelical Church of Greifswald continue to compose the LWF national committee in the GDR (see chart below). The long-held hope for a single body to include the eight now federated in the BEK appears nearer realization. Some have seen these developments as contributing to a "coming of age" in a Marxian Socialist state. The real challenge, they add, is in the practice of Christian faith and service.

Religious activities are limited to private homes and church premises. Special dispensation has been available for youth and other gatherings. The big assemblies for church members—the popular *Kirchentage*—attracted an estimated 100,000 participants in 1988. The one in Halle, claiming that the time had come for the church to break its silence, spoke out for citizens supporting social reform and challenged the dominant political party to relax its claimed monopoly of the truth.

Unlike the West German arrangement, the churches in the GDR are dependent on voluntary contributions entirely. Likewise, there is no religious instruction in the public schools and all of it is confined to church facilities. Christian nurture has been recast in mode and substance to meet the needs of children and young people; a precedent for this approach has been Luther's Catechism. In its institutes for catechists and other programs the churches train voluntary and full-time workers.

For the education of ministers, state universities—Berlin, Leipzig, Halle, Jena, Rostock—maintain departments of theology as successors to the long-established theological faculties. Church-supported schools of theology, on a parallel track, provide ministerial education in Leipzig and East Berlin. In the seven Predigerseminare maintained by the churches, the academically qualified receive practical training for the parish ministry.

For Christian service in the community at large, the *Diakonisches Werk* is an inclusive association, uniting the efforts of the eight territorial churches in the BEK and the Free Churches. *Diakonia*—serving love—has a long multiform tradition here. In principle, Marxian ideology includes the care of all people, regardless of their need. Yet in practice the GDR sanctions a curtailed range of church-related health and welfare services not only among the elderly but also among the mentally ill and the handicapped. In the latter category are some 400,000 children, an easily overlooked mass in a society world-famous for its athletes. Despite its "minorization"— the vogue term for declining membership— the church's role on life's frontiers remains significant. An Evangelical (Protestant) hospital—there are 45 of them—is known as a "House of the Church." Pastoral care is a vital part of the healing team's ministry. A limited number of training schools for nurses and others are permitted. Likewise, solicitation for the support of these church-related services is permitted annually in the streets. Some of the staff in these institutions are provided and paid by the government; the others, by the church—and at a necessarily lower scale.

Traditionally, the church has staffed much of its diaconal (Inner Mission) outreach with nonsalaried but lifetime-supported deaconesses and deacons (see Germany Introduction, above). A few centers for deacons continue in East Germany. On a far larger, yet proportionately much reduced scale, the 12 deaconess communities (motherhouses) contribute to the ranks of nurses, parish workers,

teachers of volunteers, and the like. An example is the deaconess community in Dresden (1842), the oldest in the GDR. Its adjunct hospital, not yet fully reconstructed since the catastrophic bombing of Dresden (1945), retains a high reputation. Internationally, assistance from abroad continues modestly. Between Coventry (UK) and Dresden, the Fellowship of the Cross of Nails marks the bond of Christian reconciliation, linking Coventry cathedral and the deaconess community as symbolic of two destroyed and restored cities.

Communication, as already indicated, has at times been a problem for the church press. A limited number of TV programs are allowed the church over the government network, and likewise over the radio. Publication of books and journals, limited in quantity, accents quality. Illustrative is the handbook, *Orientierung Ökumene* (1979), a product of the BEK department of theological study. Among the periodicals, *Die Zeichen der Zeit* is a sophisticated monthly for the church's coworkers. Two successive numbers in 1984, for instance, brought further materials from the WCC assembly (Vancouver 1983) on peace, justice, and human rights; and then a penetrating 50th anniversary account of the noted Barmen Theological Declaration of May 1934 which gave direction to the church struggle during the Nazi era. The weeklies and fortnightlies published by the several territorial (folk) churches make maximum use of available space and rationed paper to focus church members' attention on issues of an active faith.

Overseas Christian missions in the customary manner have been ruled out for the church, but participation in "Bread for the World" and various humanitarian programs has been possible. Nor is that all. In Leipzig, the former and long widely active Lutheran Mission continues its interest, and indirectly its contacts, with churches in Asia and Africa. But already in 1939 it received government authorization to use its facilities for the training of pastors serving in Germany. Since the late 1940s its Mission Seminary parallels and complements the Leipzig University Department of Theology and serves the Lutheran churches of the GDR. Meanwhile, the venerable Gossner Mission has a curtailed program in the GDR and, like the Leipzig and Berlin agencies, has relocated its overseas commitments to West Germany (see above). In East Berlin, the imposing building of the former Berlin Mission is now the Ecumenical Mission Center. Within the established guidelines the EMC maintains projects in such diverse places as India, Tanzania, Hungary, Cuba, and Japan. The EMC may also invite nationals from various lands to visit in Berlin. It also conducts a seminary for "second career" persons, late vocationers for the ordained ministry or other church work. For the church at large these new directions are proving their worth.

Ecumenical relations at home and abroad are a vital element in the life of the churches in East Germany. Aid from their counterparts in West Germany, and exchanges with those in Eastern Europe are indicative of the still wider connections through the World Council of Churches, the Lutheran World Federation, and other supranational agencies of the church universal. The meeting in Dresden (1981) of the WCC Central Committee laid emphasis on this sustaining interrelatedness.

Interchurch Relations in the GDR

The Lutheran (§) and other Evangelical churches are described below.

1. Association of Christian Churches in the GDR (ACK/DDR) Auguststr. 80, DDR-104 Berlin

(Roman Catholic Dioceses in the GDR)

I. *Territorial†* churches:	II. *Free churches:*	Berlin
§Mecklenburg	Baptist	Erfurt
§Saxony	Free Congregations	Magdeburg
§Thuringia	§Lutheran,	Dresden-Meissen
Anhalt	Independent	(immediately
Berlin—	Mennonite	subject to Rome)
Brandenburg	Methodist	Schwerin
Görlitz region	Moravian	Görlitz
§Greifswald (see	Old Catholic	(Russian Orthodox
description of	Reformed	Exarchate for Middle
church)		Europe)
Saxony Province		

This is the counterpart of the ACK in the Federal Republic of Germany, where Roman Catholic participation, contrary to here, is incomplete.

(Roman Catholics and Russian Orthodox take part as observers in the ACK/DDR)

2. Federation of Evangelical Churches in the GDR (BEK/DDR), Auguststrasse 80, DDR-104 Berlin. Presiding bishop: The Rt. Rev. Werner Leich (Thuringia)

Comprises the eight territorial churches (above, I).

a) *Lutheran:*	b) *United:*	c) *Associated:*
Mecklenburg	Anhalt	Moravian
Saxony	Berlin-Brandenburg	
Thuringia	Görlitz Region	
	Greifswald	
	Saxony Province	

---

†A territorial church is an autonomous church within a given geographical area.

3. United Evangelical Lutheran Church in the GDR (VELK/DDR), Auguststrasse 80, DDR-1040 Berlin. Presiding Bishop: Dr. Christoph Stier (Mecklenburg)

   Comprised the three Lutheran territorial churches (above, a) to 1988.

4. Evangelical Church of the Union in the GDR (EKU/DDR), Auguststrasse 80, DDR-1040 Berlin. Chair: The Rt. Rev. Gottfried Forck

   Comprises the five United territorial churches (above, b) and is the EKU counterpart in the realm of the GDR.

5. LWF national committee in the GDR. Chair: The Rev. Folkert Ihmels (Saxony). General Secretary: The Rev. Helmut Tschoerner, Auguststrasse 80, DDR-1040 Berlin.

   Comprises the three Lutheran territorial churches (above, a) plus one United church—Greifswald (above, b).

EVANGELICAL LUTHERAN CHURCH IN THURINGIA (ELCT)

(Evangelisch-Lutherische Kirche in Thüringen)
Member: LWF (1947), WCC, CEC, ACK/ DDR, BEK/DDR
Membership: 1,000,000**
Bishop: The Rt. Rev. Dr. Werner Leich
Dr.-Moritz-Mitzenheim-Strasse 2a
PO Box 139
DDR—5900 Eisenach

Picturesque Thuringia has a folk church of roughly a million members. Some 700 pastors, 11% of whom are women, serve the 1500 congregations. These are organized into 40 superintendencies plus the Smalkald district, which is attached to this territorial church. These districts are further organized into four visitation areas, each presided over by a member of the provincial church council.

Ministers and church workers are trained in the theology departments of the state universities, in church seminaries, and in the church college in Hainstein and the Deaconess Training College (Johannes-Falk-House) in Eisenach.

Among the many well-run service institutions, the two largest are the Sophia Hospital in Weimar and the Deaconess Hospital in Eisenach. Both are affiliated to training centers for nurses and nursing staff, with courses leading to professional qualifications. Paralleling the work in institutions is a parish service diaconal ministry supported by district diaconal centers.

Conference work in the Thuringian region also embraces parts of the neighboring church province of Saxony (below). Of the regular church conferences, the most important is held every four to five years in Erfurt, attracting from twenty to thirty thousand participants, most of them young people. Provincial youth Sundays in Eisenach every three or four years, in cooperation with the Saxony church province, draw as many as 10,000 young people.

Naturally, in the native land of Johann Sebastian Bach (born in Eisenach) and Heinrich Schütz (born in Köstritz near Gera), music is very much to the fore. There are countless church choirs and trombone bands.

In publications, in addition to an official paper, the Evangelical Weekly Journal for Thuringia, *Glaube und Heimat (Faith and Home*, 35,000 copies), has appeared since 1924. In cooperation with central GDR publishers, the publishing house (formerly the Wartburg Verlag) in Jena and the Bible Institute in Altenburg publish every year about 30 titles of biblical and parish literature.

The ELCT arose from Luther's Reformation, for which Thuringia early formed part of the stage. In Eisenach the Luther House (now a museum) recalls Luther's days as a schoolboy. Overlooking the city is the Wartburg—made famous in medieval times by St. Elizabeth—where Luther translated the New Testament (1521–1522) and set the direction of the German language. In nearby Weimar, the standard critical edition of Luther's works—now totaling over 100 volumes—has been published over the years since 1883. In Eisenach many important events have taken place, none more so than the one in 1923 which saw the founding of the Lutheran World Convention (see General Introduction), the forerunner of the present Lutheran World Federation.

EVANGELICAL LUTHERAN CHURCH OF MECKLENBURG

(Evangelisch-Lutherische Landeskirche Mecklenburgs)
Member: LWF (1947), WCC, CEC, ACK/ DDR, BEK/DDR
Membership: 700,000**
Bishop: The Rt. Rev. Christoph Stier
Münzstrasse 8
DDR—2751 Schwerin

The approximately 400 parishes of this church are served by about 340 pastors and, like GDR churches generally, also by a goodly number of nonordained full-time workers and lay volunteers. After World War I, an episcopal form of church polity was introduced. In 1922, the church was reorganized on a synodal-episcopal basis. It was recently divided into eight districts. Church headquarters are in the attractively situated city of Schwerin, former seat of the duke of Mecklenburg. Eastward lies the cathedral city of Güstrow, home in the earlier part of this century of the sculptor Ernst Barlach. Along the Baltic coast, the industrialized port cities of Wismar and Rostock show how the new era is overlaying the old. Mecklenburg pastors are educated in Rostock and elsewhere in the GDR.

After World War II many people left the country for the West, and church membership declined. The sturdiness in matters of faith, developed during the 1930s by those in the Confessing Church, continues to animate many members of the Mecklenburg church, including its retired bishop and historian, Niklot Beste. His membership on the first Executive Committee of the LWF (1947–1952) reminded the Federation of the special needs of the church in the GDR. His account (1975) of the intense church conflict in Mecklenburg (1933–1945) provides insight also into the ongoing task of the church in a changing world.

Like Beste, his successors—Heinrich Rathke and, since 1984, Christoph Stier— have continued to be supportive of the congregations and their outreach in the community. Prior to his election, the present bishop had served over a decade as a pastor of a virtually new parish on the outskirts of Rostock—a venture undertaken in close partnership with the Roman Catholic minority. The church edifice—in sight of high-rise apartments—is an old one, dating from the 14th century. Its interior renovated, it now beckons an industrial society.

Relatively isolated, Mecklenburg was the last of the north German areas to be Christianized. But already in 1419, the University of Rostock was founded, the first institution of higher learning for northern Germany and the Scandinavian countries. By 1557, the introduction of the Reformation had been completed. The Thirty Years' War (1618–1648) brought terrible devastation. Later, in eastern Mecklenburg, the spiritual forces of Pietism found a welcome among the people and motivated the processes of reconstruction and development. Despite influences of the Enlightenment (Rationalism), the ensuing religious awakening led to an eventual firming of confessional Lutheranism, notably through the theologian and churchman, Theodor Kliefoth (1810–1895). A rejection of ecclesiastical "Unionism" and a renewal of the Mecklenburg church marked a new day. Kliefoth was a leader in the General Evangelical Lutheran Conference (above, Germany).

EVANGELICAL LUTHERAN CHURCH OF SAXONY (ELCS)

(Evangelisch-Lutherische Landeskirche Sachsens)

Member: LWF (1947), WCC, CEC, ACK/DDR, BEK/DDR

Membership: 1,800,000**

Bishop: The Rt. Rev. Dr. Johannes Hempel

Tauscherstrasse 44

DDR—8021 Dresden

With its almost two million church members and over 1150 congregations, the Evangelical Lutheran Church of Saxony is the largest of the eight Evangelical territorial churches of the GDR. It covers the districts of Dresden, Leipzig, and Karl-Marx-Stadt (the former Chemnitz). Its boundaries correspond to those of the former kingdom of Saxony after 1815. In accordance with the 1555 Religious Peace of Augsburg, the religion of this territory was determined by that of the prince (see history below).

The characteristic features of the ELCS derive from the diversity of its countryside and its religious customs, as well as from its pattern of leadership and its history. The intensity of spiritual life in the ELCS varies with the territorial region.

In the mineral-rich, mountainous Erzgebirge, it has revealed an encouraging constancy—a tradition of Piety has been sustained from the time before the region became industrialized and densely populated. Here are congregations of a churchly tradition, firm in faith, personally committed, and known for their sacrificial giving. Their offerings and the willingness of their young people to enter the service of the church lend stability to the church at large.

The expansive Leipzig plain, by contrast, has been much more secularized. Here the centuries-old Leipzig Fair accentuated the importance of the trade routes crossing Europe, and commercial centers familiarized the people with a variety of intellectual currents as well. Besides, this area has rich deposits of lignite (brown coal) exploited by strip mining, as well as heavy buildup of chemical industry. Here are the extensive settlements of workers and their families to whom a middle-class church has had little access.

Again, by way of contrast, in the east-central hills of Saxony, in the Oberlausitz, there is an austere spirituality with a character all its own. Here, new forms of worship and church assemblies are tested, and attempts are made to translate Christian insights into terms understandable to a secular society.

In another district, around the city of Bautzen (not far from Dresden), there are still many of Wendish stock—the Sorbs, an ethnic minority descended from the original Slavic inhabitants—but very few of them are Protestant.

In terms of structure, it was mainly during the previous century that the congregations, or parishes, of the territorial church were given their pattern of organization. Regionally, they are grouped into ecclesial districts. These are self-governing to a large extent and have their own agencies: the district synod and the district church executive—the superintendent. The office of superintendent is the oldest in Saxony and continues the function of ordination, parish visitation, and other duties.

For the ELCS as a whole, the territorial synod represents all the congregations and is the top decision-making body. The ELCS administration (*Landeskirchenamt*) is a collegial executive combination entrusted with overseeing and guiding the church's manifold ministry. The synod and the church administration thus complement each other. The synod has a lay president, while the spiritual leadership of the ELCS resides in the bishop. The bishop presides over the church's executive council, which includes the presidents of the district synods, members of the territorial church administration, a corresponding number of synod members, and others. The office of bishop, introduced in 1922, was given distinction by its first incumbent, Ludwig Ihmels—one of the cofounders of the Lutheran World Convention (see General Introduction). The present bishop, continuing the confessional and ecumenical role of the ELCS, is a member of the presidium of the World Council of Churches.

The ELCS is today in a transitional stage between its former status as a folk church and its present position as a virtual minority church. (By way of comparison: While the number of congregations today is nearly the same as about 1950, the number of baptized church members is less than half of what it

was then.) The ELCS sees itself increasingly as a community of fellow-workers in which the priesthood of all believers assumes contemporary form. In contrast to earlier times, church support is now entirely on a voluntary basis. The effort to live the gospel in a secular environment and in a Socialist society finds characteristic expression in such activities as house visits, group work, and family retreats. Practical service—diakonia—in various institutions and agencies linked to the church continues to have a very important place.

Future pastors are still educated at the University of Leipzig (1409; now renamed Karl Marx University), which played a creative role in shaping Lutheran theology from the 16th to the 20th century. Students from the three Lutheran churches also study at the theological seminary in Leipzig. In addition, the ELCS runs training institutes for deacons, laywomen assisting with catechism and youth work, cantors, and organists.

Historically, Saxony has played an important role in the political as well as the religious past of Germany. In the late Middle Ages, Saxon lands were ruled by the house of Wettin, whose head was one of the seven princes electing the Holy Roman Emperor. In 1485, the territory was divided between two brothers, Ernest and Albert, and remained so divided. To Ernest went the office of elector; and electoral Saxony, under the Ernestine line, included Wittenberg. To Albert went the title of duke, and ducal Saxony included the urban centers—Leipzig, Dresden, Chemnitz.

The Reformation led by Luther in Wittenberg thus placed electoral Saxony in the forefront of the Protestant movement. Elector Frederick III (1463–1525), called the Wise, had earlier founded the University of Wittenberg and became Luther's protector. The opposite occurred in ducal Saxony. Duke George, the Bearded, remained a life-long opponent of Luther, saw himself as a reforming Catholic, and prevented the introduction of the Reformation down to his death in 1539. Yet the Evangelical movement had been gaining ground among the people, and in 1539—after Duke George's death—Luther conducted the first Protestant worship service in Leipzig, the city where he had debated John Eck 20 years earlier.

Complications developed. Maurice (Moritz), duke of Saxony (1541–1547) and then also elector (1547–1553), wavered between

Lutheran and Roman Catholic; but in 1551 declared himself a Lutheran. Under the terms of the Religious Peace of Augsburg, with Augustus I the Elector, all Saxony (united since 1547) became officially Lutheran. Later, during the Thirty Years' War, the ecclesiastically independent Lusatians (Wends living on lands extending northward from Bohemia) came under Saxony by terms of the Peace of Prague (1635). Most Lusatians remained Roman Catholic (above). Yet, even when the prince (August II, the Strong) in 1697 turned Roman Catholic in order to qualify as king of Poland, the Saxon people remained steadfastly Lutheran.

Amid changing political fortunes—the era of Napoleon and the dissolution of the Holy Roman Empire (1806)—Saxony was again divided and its present ecclesial identity fixed. The Treaty of Vienna (1815) reaffirmed an earlier settlement that awarded the traditional electoral Saxony to Prussia, thereafter called the province of Saxony (see below, Evangelical Church of the Province of Saxony). Traditional ducal Saxony (after 1815 called the kingdom of Saxony) retained its independence and also its confessional Lutheran identity (see above).

The musical heritage of Saxony's Lutheranism has become world-famous through Johann Sebastian Bach, organist and cantor at St. Thomas Church, Leipzig, and through Heinrich Schütz in Dresden. The tradition of the boys' choirs at St. Thomas and at the Church of the Cross (*Kreuzkirche*) in Dresden extends over 750 years.

Saxony's role in the mission and migration of Lutherans is noteworthy. On its territory the Leipzig Evangelical Lutheran Mission (1836) was for decades the most important Lutheran mission society in Europe. Support came from Germany, Russia, Poland, Hungary, Alsace, and the Scandinavian countries. Missions extended to *India, *Papua New Guinea, and *Tanzania. Today, most operational aspects of these missions are carried on by agencies in the Federal Republic. However, mission interest and support continue through prayer, interpretation, and, recently, limited sending.

Among the best known emigrant groups from Saxony was that led initially by Martin Stephan in 1839 and then by C. F. W. Walther, founder of the present Lutheran Church–Missouri Synod in America (see USA).

ADDITIONAL EVANGELICAL CHURCHES IN THE GERMAN DEMOCRATIC REPUBLIC

The Federation of Evangelical Churches in the GDR, as shown on the chart above, comprises three Lutheran territorial churches and five United churches. In many respects the United are as much imbued by a Lutheran heritage as the others. The fact is that, at the formation of the Evangelical Church of the Old Prussian Union in 1817, all but an elite and influential Reformed minority were confessionally Lutheran. Union under those circumstances generated opposition and caused the rise of an "Old Lutheran" movement. Basically—for the Protestant majority— these Prussian churches were churches of the *Augsburg Confession*. They used Luther's *Small Catechism* as well as Lutheran liturgical practices. To be sure, the royal family of Hohenzollern was Reformed; so, too, were many of Huguenot and Dutch descent, Berliners especially. The abolition of the names, Lutheran and Reformed, and the substitution of Evangelical (Evangelisch), gave status to the new designation and seemed to attach a certain obscurantism to the name Lutheran.

The following brief accounts of the five Evangelical churches in the GDR provide not only a close-up of the East German counterpart of the West German EKU but also complete the story of historic Lutheranism. This is especially true of the church province of Saxony (Provinz Sachsen), the heart of the "Luther country."

EVANGELICAL CHURCH IN BERLIN-BRANDENBURG (ECB-B)

(Evangelische Kirche in Berlin-Brandenburg)
Member: WCC, CEC, ACK/DDR, BEK/DDR, EKU/DDR
Membership: 865,000**
Bishop: The Rt. Rev. Dr. Gottfried Forck
Neue Grünstrasse 19-22
DDR—1020 Berlin

The Evangelical Church in Berlin-Brandenburg is one of the eight regionally organized

Evangelical churches in the German Democratic Republic which make up the Federation of Evangelical Churches in the GDR. The territory in which the ECB-B has jurisdiction includes, in addition to East Berlin (GDR), the part of the former province of Brandenburg to the west of the rivers Oder and Neisse. Geographically, therefore, the church lives on the frontier between the two main social systems of the contemporary world. It tries to maintain unity with the Evangelical Church in Berlin-Brandenburg (Berlin West) across this frontier ever since the two regions of the church—each of which now has its own synod, its own executive, and its own bishop—mutually agreed to go their separate ways to the extent that this was mandatory. Its ecclesial landmarks include the medieval Church of St. Mary (Marienkirche) and the prominent Cathedral (Dom)—still in process of restoration.

The confessional tradition of both regions of the Evangelical Church in Berlin-Brandenburg is that of a United church predominantly Lutheran in orientation. This common tradition is a bond of unity given expression in the official preamble on "Scripture and Confession," which forms part of the constitution of each church: "In accord with the Reformation fathers, it confesses that Jesus Christ alone, revealed only in the Holy Scriptures of the Old and New Testaments, given only by grace and received only by faith, is our salvation. It is a church of the Lutheran Reformation in which the Lutheran confessional statements are the main authoritative doctrinal standards. Its distinctiveness lies in its fellowship of church life with the Reformed congregations belonging to it, among whom the Reformed confessional documents are the doctrinal standards."

The Union of the Lutheran majority and the Reformed minority dates back to 1817 and the celebration of the 300th anniversary of the Reformation. It was encouraged and given royal assent by King Friedrich Wilhelm III with the highest of hopes. The controversies to which the Union gave rise—fierce controversies in some cases—are today a thing of the past. The congregations of the ECB-B now think of themselves simply as Evangelical. Both regions of the Evangelical Church in Berlin-Brandenburg form part of the Evangelical Church of the Union, to which four other regional churches in the

GDR and two West German provincial churches also belong.

Along with the other Christian churches in the GDR, the ECB-B had to pass through a radical period of rethinking in the years following World War II. It had to learn what it to do within a new social system whose leaders were committed to an atheistic ideology but whose social aims nevertheless represented a challenge to Christian witness and service.

In the space of a single generation, church membership declined from 90% of the population to about 30%, so that today only about a million inhabitants of the region served by the ECB-B claim to be Evangelical. A network of parishes has nevertheless been maintained, embracing every locality, however small. In the 1600 or so church parishes, arranged into 48 dioceses, there are 770 pastors (including 120 women) at work, assisted by 1800 other full-time colleagues.

Candidates for the ministry study in the theology departments of the state universities or church seminaries. The ECB-B has two such institutions: the so-called language school (Sprachkonvikt), a theological college originally founded as a seminary for ancient languages, and the Paulinum Theological College (for students who have completed their secular professional training but have no degree). One-third of all the church diaconal institutions in the GDR are located within the ECB-B—hospitals and nursing schools, institutions for the mentally or physically handicapped, retirement homes and nursing homes, etc.—with a total full-time staff of about 4000 workers.

In their witness and service, the congregations of the ECB-B confront a great diversity of social situations. In addition to Berlin, there are three other large industrial concentrations within the territory served by the church, as well as recently developed centers of industry along the border with Poland. But the territory served by the church also includes extensive and thinly-populated rural areas in the north and northwest. The new housing estates that already exist or are being built in the large cities and industrial centers present a considerable missionary challenge and an opportunity to develop new communities. In the rural areas, the service of the church seeks to cope effectively with the new working and living conditions of an agricultural economy using industrial methods of production. The Cottbus district, with its extensive opencast brown-coal mining works, represents a special challenge. The clearing and stripping of large stretches of the countryside for the purpose of mining this important raw material of the GDR necessitates the evacuation of the people living in the areas concerned and confronts the congregations with difficult tasks of pastoral care.

Membership in the World Council of Churches and ecumenical solidarity with other communions are highly important to the life of the ECB-B. The church constitution reminds the local parish of its task "to establish contacts with local congregations of other confessions" and to foster "relationships with other ecumenical communions." (Art. 4,2)

Toward neighboring Roman Catholic or Evangelical Free Churches (Baptist or Methodist), good contacts are being cultivated. Toward congregations farther away, in various neighboring countries, ecumenical partnerships are increasingly being developed. These connections make it easier for ECB-B members, at the local level, to have a sense of belonging to a worldwide family wherein the faithful mutually enrich, encourage, and correct one another.

The ECB-B enjoys close partnership relations with two overseas churches that are the fruit of the work of missionaries which it sent out from its territory in the 19th century: the Gossner Evangelical Lutheran Church in Chotanagpur and Assam, Ranchi (*India), and the Evangelical Lutheran Church in *Southern Africa/Southeast Diocese, contacts with which are maintained via church groups in the kingdom of *Swaziland. The most important element in this partnership is the regular exchange of themes for intercession, making it easier to pray together for one another on an agreed Sunday in all church services.

Both the above partner churches are members of the Lutheran World Federation, whereas the ECB-B regards itself as equally close to both the Lutheran World Federation and the World Alliance of Reformed Churches and has therefore refrained from joining either world body.

EVANGELICAL CHURCH OF ANHALT (ECA)
(Evangelische Landeskirche Anhalts)
Member: WCC, CEC, ACK/DDR, BEK/DDR, EKU/DDR
Membership: 150,000**
President: The Rev. Eberhard Natho
Otto-Grotewohl-Strasse 22
DDR—4500 Dessau

Although the Evangelical Church of Anhalt joined the EKU/DDR in 1960 and cultivates close ties with the Church of Lippe and the Evangelical Reformed Church of Northwest Germany, it is a United church of Lutheran character. Historically, it subscribes to the *Augsburg Confession,* is liturgically in a Lutheran tradition, and makes wide use of Luther's Catechism. Refugees from further east swelled the Lutheran ranks after 1945. Yet there, as elsewhere in the GDR, the decline in church membership has been pronounced: from about 400,000 in the late 1950s to about 150,000 in the early 1980s. Pastors of the ECA receive their theological education at the University of Halle and at various other places, including church-supported seminaries in East Berlin or Leipzig.

The 210 congregations of this church form five circuits and comprise 90 pastorates. A synodical church government guides the affairs of this United church. Once a duchy surrounded by the former Prussian provinces of Brandenburg and Saxony, and situated along the Elbe and Saale Rivers, Anhalt presents a miniature of Protestant church politics from the Reformation onward, though its Christian beginnings go back to the 10th century. In 1522, its then still independent Zerbst portion joined the Lutheran Reformation. By the end of the century, however, its prince had turned Calvinist. Repeated changes of political boundaries and confessional position ensued. The impact of Halle Pietism was strong for a time as was Rationalism later on. All political divisions were united under one administration in 1863, and church policy was committed to the same principles as those of the Prussian Union.

Anhalt continued as a duchy until 1918, when it ceased to be governed by a ruling house descended from Albert the Bear, a prince of 12th-century fame. After 1945, this long independent territory became consolidated into the East German state of Saxony-Anhalt (below). Its chief cities, Dessau and Köthen, are industrial centers. Their history goes back over 800 years. The church in Dessau has a Lucas Cranach altarpiece from Reformation times; and at Köthen's main church J.S. Bach was organist and concertmaster (1717–1723) before moving on to Leipzig. Sophie, of Anhalt-Zerbst, married a Romanov and, upon her husband's death, became Catherine II (the Great), Empress of Russia (1762–1796).

EVANGELICAL CHURCH OF GREIFSWALD

(Evangelische Landeskirche Greifswald)
Member: LWF (1956), WCC, CEC, ACK/
DDR, BEK/DDR, EKU/DDR
Membership: 450,000**
Bishop: The Rt. Rev. Dr. Horst Gienke
Rudolf-Petershagen-Allee 3
DDR—2200 Greifswald

With its 362 parishes and 220 pastors, this small church is in the northeast corner of the GDR, bounded by the Baltic Sea and the Oder River, the new western border of Poland. Known until 1968 as the Evangelical Church of Pomerania, it occupies the only remaining German part of the once expansive Pomeranian grainbelt. Its headquarters are in the city perpetuating the name of the native princely family of Greifen, rulers of the duchy until the 17th century.

Prior to 1945, the Pomeranian church comprised 53 districts with a total of 785 pastors. It was reorganized, headed by a bishop, in 1946. Its constitution, adopted in 1950, declares: "The Pomeranian Evangelical Church is a church of the Lutheran Confession," adding that "as a result of its history, it is a member church of the Evangelical Church of the Union." On these grounds, the renamed Greifswald church joined the LWF and was first represented by its bishop and other delegates at the Minneapolis assembly in 1957. This church has a history of lay activity, influenced by Pietism and strengthened by such witness during the hard years of the Kirchenkampf. Leading the confessing thrust

was Reinold von Thadden-Trieglaff, then president of the Student Christian Movement in Germany and later founder of the Evangelischer Kirchentag (above, Germany). The church actively cultivates confessional and ecumenical ties and continues to draw upon a rich legacy in the new situation.

The entire region of Pomerania went Lutheran in 1535. Luther's close co-worker, Johann Bugenhagen (1485–1558), himself a Pomeranian, provided the land with a model "Church Order" in 1535. As Otto of Bamberg (c.1062-1139) earned the name of "Apostle to the Pomeranians" for leading their conversion to Christianity, so Bugenhagen, who introduced Lutheran church orders in many parts of Northern Europe, including Denmark, is remembered best as the "Reformer of Pomerania." Strong emphasis was laid on Christian instruction in biblical content and on Luther's *Catechism*. The University of Greifswald's theological faculty became in time a stronghold of Lutheran orthodoxy. Under Prussian rule and with the introduction of the Union church (1817), the Lutheran solidarity was broken, although a firm confessional consciousness continued. This found expression in the formation of Old Lutheran congregations (countering the Old Prussian Union, above, Germany), and also in the emigration of many Pomeranians to North America and Australia, where they became active church members.

EVANGELICAL CHURCH OF THE GÖRLITZ REGION

(Evangelische Kirche des Görlitzer Kirchengebietes)
Member: WCC, CEC, ACK/DDR, BEK/
DDR, EKU/DDR
Membership: 105,000**
Bishop: The Rt. Rev. Dr. Joachim Rogge
Berliner Strasse 62
DDR—8900 Görlitz

This church body of 78 congregations—one of them Reformed, the others Lutheran since the Reformation—is located in and around the border city of Görlitz in southeastern GDR. A United church, it is served by 81 pastors as well as other workers. Its membership in the EKU/DDR recalls the time when the Evangelical Church in the province of Silesia was part of the Old Prussian Union. Today, the Görlitz region is but a tenth of the former Silesia. The other nine-tenths, east of the Neisse River, were awarded to Poland in 1945. The expulsion of the large German population in the postwar months swelled the westward fleeing tide of refugees. Retaining some of the earlier mixture of Evangelical and Roman Catholic inhabitants, the Görlitz region—politically the eastern part of the Dresden district—suggests a long history, politically as well as religiously.

According to the constitution of 1951, the Evangelical Church of the Görlitz Region is "a church of the Lutheran Reformation and has the distinction of being in church fellowship with the Reformed congregations in its area." This position was reaffirmed in 1974 by the church's adoption of the *Leuenberg Agreement.* Preaching and catechetical instruction are the main vehicles of outreach. Luther's *Catechism,* with its scriptural basis, underlies all religious instruction.

Despite all efforts to the contrary, church membership during the past decades has been almost halved, falling from a claimed 250,000 in the late 1950s. But church-state relations have improved.

From medieval times to 1526, Silesia was part of the kingdom of Poland; then, until 1742, part of the Hapsburg kingdom of Bohemia; and for the next two centuries part of Prussia, and then of modern unified Germany. The Lutheran Reformation took hold in Breslau in the 1520s. Its rapid spread, also into Poland, was reversed by the Roman Catholic Counter-Reform in most places, but not as much in Silesia. There, Lutheranism developed a characteristic firmness. When, after 1817, the Evangelical Church of the Old Prussian Union was introduced, opposition to it arose among certain Lutherans, especially in the Breslau region. Reminders of this old Lutheran protest remain in West as well as East Germany—the Evangelical Lutheran (Old Lutheran) Church, the Union of Independent Evangelical Lutheran Churches in the GDR; and also overseas, through emigration, in *Australia and in *North America (in the *Lutheran Church–Missouri Synod as well as in the *American Lutheran Church,

now ELCA). Lutheranism in Silesia produced a considerable number of leading theologians active in various parts of Germany. The proximity in Silesia to Roman Catholicism strengthened Lutheran conviction and also cultivated a spirit of tolerance. It further deepened a Lutheran commitment to sound education.

EVANGELICAL CHURCH OF THE PROVINCE OF SAXONY (ECPS)
(Evangelische Kirche der Kirchenprovinz Sachsens)
Member: WCC, CEC, ACK/DDR, BEK/DDR, EKU/DDR
Membership: 750,000
Bishop: The Rt. Rev. Dr. Christoph Demke
Am Dom 2
DDR—3010 Magdeburg

The territory covered by this church unites several regions that were formerly parts of the kingdom of Prussia. After the wars of Napoleon, an important part of the kingdom of Saxony was added to the new province. Hence the retention today in the name "Church Province of Saxony"—a major component of the Evangelical Church of the Old Prussian Union. After 1945, this territory merged with the old duchy of Anhalt and was called the political state of Saxony-Anhalt in the GDR. Since 1952, the church has relations to many regional administrations (districts), especially in Magdeburg, Halle, Erfurt, Leipzig, Cottbus, and Suhl.

The 2200 parishes of the ECPS, grouped in 49 districts, are overseen by eight general superintendents (having the title *Probst,* or dean) and served by about 850 pastors as well as duly called and prepared pastors' helpers, deaconesses, deacons, catechists, welfare workers, and others. The bishop chairs the church administration, giving overall guidance to ecclesial affairs on the territory and representing the ECPS in its relations with the government as well as with other church bodies. The regularly convened synod of the church exercises the necessary legislative functions as set forth in the church constitution (as adopted in 1950, and most recently amended in 1980).

Most of the pastors of this church have studied theology at the University of Halle, an institution founded in 1694 and made famous in its early years through the teaching of August Hermann Francke, the Lutheran Pietist leader. In 1817, under Prussian rule, the then quite run-down University of Wittenberg was relocated to Halle and merged with the flourishing younger university, today known as the Martin Luther University Halle-Wittenberg. After 1945, a practical seminary was established at Wittenberg (relocated to Erfurt in 1960) for the ministerial training of late vocationers: men—subsequently also women—from various occupations who, as active members in their home congregations, are prepared as preachers. University graduates in theology receive their practical training in Wittenberg.

Current church statistics, as noted above, stand in sharp contrast to those of about 1960. At that time, pastorates numbered 1750, of which only 1150 were filled. By comparison, today's 850 pastors indicate a shrinkage of about 15%. Far more revealing is the sharp drop in claimed church membership: from 3.5 million to about 750,000 today. Drastic changes of this kind make East Germans speak of a "minorization," a diminution of the church which, on its positive side, can—and does—call forth forces of renewal.

The observance of the 500th anniversary of Luther's birth culminated in Wittenberg in October 1983 with a *Kirchentag*. The last of seven such rallies of the laity drew some 12,000 people. Bishop emeritus Werner Krusche challenged the people to a dynamic Evangelical faith and to end the pseudo-security of cryptic Christianity and cautious indecision. His challenge was cheered. Upon leaving the castle church, where Luther lies buried, the crowd moved through the streets of Wittenberg, and people from the windows joined in singing "A Mighty Fortress."

The Church Province of Saxony has the richest Reformation lore. Already during the time of Charlemagne, the first bishopric was established in Halberstadt (before 814). By 968, Magdeburg became an archdiocese, as this fortified "City of the Maid" served as the base of the Germanic eastward movement—also of Christianity—into the lands of the Wends and other Slavs, and provided the

model for future cities. Southward lies Eisleben, Luther's birthplace and the town in which he died (1546), as well as Mansfeld, the place of his early schooling, completed at Magdeburg.

Beginning his university studies at Erfurt in 1501, Luther spent the better part of the decade there, switching from law to theology, joining the Augustinian monastic order, being ordained priest, earning his doctorate "in biblia," and then being transferred from there permanently to Wittenberg. Founded in 1502, the new university in the city of the "White Hill" on the Elbe, Wittenberg, became the birthplace of Luther's Reformation. Developments after 1517 are, of course, interwoven into the larger history of the church.

Besides many other places of significance in this land of Luther, the territory covered by the present ECPS includes a sizable Roman Catholic element. Besides, one of the ECPS districts has six Reformed congregations, which are represented in the church council by their senior pastor. A number of Free Churches, Methodist, and others, as well as Lutheran, are also present.

Although limited today in missionary outreach, Halle remains the historic center from which Lutheranism spread to *India and *North America during the 18th century. There, in the Francke tradition, the subsequent work of Gustav Warneck (1834–1910) is still honored. At Halle, Warneck pioneered the scientific study of mission, a discipline further developed by his son, Johannes, in Indonesia and later in the Rhineland as director of the Rhenish Mission (above, Evangelical Church in the Rhineland). The elder Warneck, a proponent of united effort, in 1878 founded the Halle Mission Conference. This conference—encouraged after World War II by the noted missiologist, Arno Lehmann—continues to be supported by the ECPS, and in 1978 observed its centennial, featuring a Latin American theme. Relations with the WCC are sturdy and—indirectly—with the LWF and worldwide Lutheranism as well, a fact borne out by the observance of the Reformation's 450th anniversary in Wittenberg in 1967 as well as by Luther's 500th. The ECPS, in the role of host church, is thus best known for its abiding connection with Luther.

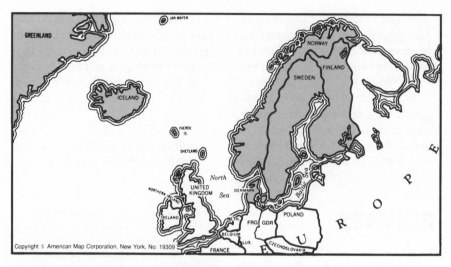

Copyright © American Map Corporation, New York, No. 19309

NORTHERN EUROPE

From the Finno-Soviet border westward to the vicinity of North America lie the northern countries—Finland, Sweden, Denmark, Norway, Iceland, Greenland— whose combined population is near 23 million. Since the 16th-century Reformation era these lands have been officially Lutheran. Today, they account for over 35% of the world's Lutherans. Their established churches are loosely joined in a Nordic Conference of Churches.

Although richly diversified, the Lutheranism of these northern countries collectively stands in contrast to that of the German scene, on the one hand, and to that of the North American, on the other. A confessionally homogeneous situation has, on the whole, kept Evangelical and Catholic emphases in perspective and given the northern churches a distinctive role in the modern ecumenical movement (*Sweden) as well as in the formation of a world Lutheran communion such as the LWF and its predecessor, the Lutheran World Convention. This outreach of the Nordic churches became evident early in the present century, for instance, in the peace efforts led by Archbishop Nathan Söderblom (1866–1931) during World War I and his subsequent leadership in launching the universal Christian Conference on Life and Work (Stockholm, 1925).

Similarly, the stalwart resistance to the Nazi German occupation of Norway, as personified by Eivind Berggrav (1884–1959), bishop of Oslo, revealed a Lutheranism different from the submissiveness often ascribed to it. Likewise, the Danish bishop and church historian, Valdemar Ammundsen (1875–1936) of Haderslev, already in 1934 was instrumental in bringing ecumenical recognition to the Confessing Church in Germany, when the Life and Work council held its decisive meeting on the island of Fanø, Denmark.

In Finland, Aleksi Emanuel Lehtonen (1891–1951)—theologian and bishop of Turku and archbishop of Finland (1945–1951)—was a steadying influence during the turbulent 1930s and 1940s and also prominent in the World Conference on Faith and Order. In the global confessional family, the Lutheran World Convention benefited greatly from the statesmanlike participation of Denmark's Alfred Theodor Jørgensen; and the Lutheran World Federation was led on a confident course by its first president, Anders Nygren (1890–1978), noted theologian and then bishop of Lund. Figures like these should not obscure the fact that countless others from the northern countries have served with great effect overseas as well as at home in making the gospel a mediating power among peoples in many lands. This has been exemplified in an ongoing Nordic concern for the Jewish people (cf. *Germany, Federal Republic), for world peace and nuclear disarmament (the Uppsala Conference, 1983), for improved understanding between East and West, and for more just relations between North and South.

DENMARK

A constitutional monarchy (1849) with a unicameral parliament (1953). Area, including the Jutland Peninsula and some 100 inhabited islands (excluding the Faeroe Islands and Greenland): 43,080 sq. km. (16,633 sq. mi.). Pop. (1984): 5,109,000. Cap. and largest city: Copenhagen (pop., 1984, 482,900). Language: Danish.

History: Copenhagen—the fishing *havn* or port—dates from ancient Viking times and became the region's trading center. Bishop Axel Absalon (1128–1201) is considered the city's actual founder and its defender against pirating Wends. Danish power extended to *Sweden and *Norway, to *England, *Iceland, and *Greenland. The Christianization of Denmark, begun in the 9th century, was completed in the 11th. The country early had close ties with England, has been a bridge between Central and Northern Europe, and during the 17th and 18th centuries participated in Europe's commercial and colonial expansion. During the 19th century, it sustained numerous reverses, including the loss of Schleswig to Prussia. In 1917, it sold the Danish West Indies (Virgin Islands) to the USA. During World War II, like Norway, Denmark was under German occupation. The country has contributed many participants to peace movements.

Religion: Christian 95.9% (Lutheran official); nonreligious 2.4%; atheists 1.2%; Muslim 0.2%; Jews 0.1%.

Christianity in Denmark has a long and rich history. There is a span of 11 centuries between the activities of St. Ansgar, "Apostle to the North" (d.865) and the appointment of a government commission in 1965 to study and recommend structural changes to improve the service of the national church. Ansgar, archbishop of Hamburg, periodically visited Ribe, and even went as far as Sweden, but it was only in the 11th century that the Danish Vikings converted to Christianity. Their outreach included southern Sweden and thus also the diocese of Lund. Most of today's stone village churches in Denmark were built in the 13th century. Danish kings, like the church, had ties with Rome, but the king controlled the bishops.

The Reformation came to Denmark already in the 1520s and by 1569 all Roman Catholic activity was forbidden. In 1849, when the democratic constitution proclaimed freedom of religion, Roman Catholicism was reintroduced into Denmark, mainly by immigrants. During and after World War II, the presence of some 250,000 refugees, including 24,000 Catholics, gave an impetus to religious diversity and to charity. In keeping with the favorable developments of the postwar years, Pius XII in 1953 made Copenhagen a diocese and placed it directly under the Holy See. Since then, Danish Catholicism has displayed a vigorous activity. Its membership is about 30,000.

The Ecumenical Council of Denmark (1939), reorganized in 1947, 1954, and 1971, includes the established Evangelical Lutheran Church, plus smaller religious bodies: the Roman Catholic Church, Baptist Union, Salvation Army, Mission Covenant, Apostolic Church (Pentecostal), Methodist Church, Reformed Synod, Anglican Congregation, and Russian Orthodox Congregation, and also 26 church organizations. The council's credal basis corresponds to that of the WCC.

The Danish Missionary Council (1912) is an ecumenical consultative body whose purpose is to promote mission interest and support. It provides services that no single agency could afford; and when necessary negotiates with the government in matters pertaining to missions. It is associated with the WCC.

EVANGELICAL LUTHERAN CHURCH IN DENMARK (ELCD)

(Den evangelisk-lutherske Folkekirke i Danmark)
Member: LWF (1947), WCC, CEC, ECD
Membership: 4,624,000
Bishop of Copenhagen and Primate:
The Rt. Rev. Ole Bertelsen
Nørregade 11
DK—1165 Copenhagen K

This national church—by law Evangelical Lutheran—comprises 1368 congregations, which are served by 1813 ordained pastors, of whom some 300 are women. The ordination of women was legislated by parliament—as part of equal employment opportunity—and approved by the crown in 1947. The many others in church work include deaconesses, deacons, teachers, missionaries, parish workers, and those in specialized ministries among students, in folk high schools, in hospitals, and in penal and other institutions. The Danish language is used everywhere except in a few German-speaking congregations near the country's southern border. About 93% of the people are members of the church. Accepting its status as a national institution, the folk church tries to serve people who range from cultural humanists to ardent Pietists, plus a large array of youth, often seeking spiritual fulfillment beyond acculturated Christianity or in other religions (below).

Church attendance is generally low (about 5% of the people attend once a month, it is said), but church buildings and premises are known for their attractive appearance. Religious freedom was granted by stages after the constitution of 1849. In addition to baptisms and confirmations, most weddings and burials are under local church auspices. Religious instruction in the public schools retains something of the long Christian legacy

and is part of the standard curriculum. Folk high schools, introduced in the 19th century, are both state- and voluntarily-supported centers for ongoing lay education in many fields, from arts and crafts to social issues and spiritual matters.

Organizationally, this national church is episcopal. Of its 10 dioceses, five—Roskilde, Odense, Ribe, Aarhus, and Viborg—were formed in the 11th century. Five others came later: Copenhagen, Aalborg, Haderslev, Helsingør, and Lolland-Falster. Outside Denmark proper, the approximately 40,000 Lutherans on the *Faeroe Islands comprise a vice-diocese within the diocese of Copenhagen under a vice-bishop. The nearly 50,000 Inuit (Eskimo) in *Greenland—virtually all Lutherans, except for some Roman Catholics—comprise another vice-diocese within the diocese of Copenhagen (see below).

Bishops are elected by all pastors and congregational council members in the diocese and appointed by the crown on the nomination of the minister of church affairs. The bishop of Copenhagen is "first among equals." However, Danish bishops have little power. They have no legal authority to speak for the church. The highest administrative authority is with the ministry of church affairs, which is advised by the bishops, who meet semiannually. Parliament legislates for the church, and determines the size of church support from the state on the general budget. Most church expenses are covered through church taxation paid only by church members.

The church is also congregationally organized. Since 1903, elected congregational councils have managed the affairs of the local churches. When a pastor is to be called, the church council submits a list of three candidates to the ministry of church affairs, and the candidate to whom the church has given the most votes is usually chosen. In cases of unanimity, the candidate must be appointed.

Administratively, the ELCD is, in the words of a Nordic scholar, an agency of the state rather than a church in the institutional sense. The law obliges the church to hold to the *Augsburg Confession*. Yet the church has no official body that can foster conformity to this confession or debate contemporary issues concerning the faith.

The church's pastors are educated by the theological faculties at the universities of Copenhagen and Aarhus. Continuing education is provided by the School for Pastors at Lø-gumkloster, near Denmark's southern border. A variety of schools educate other types of church workers, e.g., the two deaconess houses in Copenhagen and institutes for deacons in Aarhus and in Filadelfia, Dianalund.

Given this kind of national church, much is left to free association and voluntary action. Church renewal at home has a legacy of Inner Mission as well as other activities (below).

Outreach overseas includes the work of a number of independent missionary agencies. Eleven are united in the Church of Denmark Missionary Council, which interprets their work to the congregations. The Danish Missionary Society has been an instrument for mission work on behalf of the church since 1821. Today, it is a partner with Lutheran churches in *Hong Kong, *India, *Japan, *Madagascar, *Taiwan, and *Tanzania. It has low-profile projects in the Middle East and a concern for migrants (mainly Muslims) within Denmark. The Danish Society for Moravian Mission has served the church since 1773, when missionaries were sent to Danish outposts in the West Indies (*Virgin Islands, see Caribbean), Greenland, the Gold Coast of Africa, and Tranquebar, India. Today, it serves in Tanzania and in Labrador, Canada. Its historic Mission House in Christiansfeld also provides headquarters for the Danish Evangelical Mission (1948) working in *Ethiopia and *Liberia; the Danish Israel Mission (1885); and the Sudan United Mission—Danish Branch (1911), working in Nigeria with the *Lutheran Church of Christ. The Danish Santal Mission (1878) supports the *Northern Evangelical Lutheran Church in India, which it founded, and the two Lutheran churches in Bangladesh. The Church of Denmark Missionary Council and its members are a part of the larger ecumenical Danish Missionary Council (1912; above).

Danchurchaid (1922), which works for interchurch aid, development, and other forms of assistance overseas, is one of the oldest church agencies of its kind. Among its pioneers was Alfred Theodor Jørgensen, one of the founders of the Lutheran World Convention (1923). The agency has been active in the wake of two world wars, and today cooperates with the LWF and the WCC on projects in the Middle East and other troubled parts of the world. Its board includes representatives from the Ecumenical Council of Denmark, the Danish Missionary Council, and others.

The church's Council of Interchurch Relations, comparable to that of the Church of Norway, serves as the Danish national committee of the LWF.

● ● ●

As already indicated, the 1520s brought the Lutheran Reformation to Denmark. Hans Tausen (1494–1561), "Denmark's Martin Luther," after studying in Germany, became court chaplain and promoted the new teaching in Copenhagen. He later became bishop of Ribe. Johann Bugenhagen (1485–1558) prepared the new order (constitution, liturgy, and regulations) for the Danish church. In 1537, the year after the official reception of the Reformation, Bugenhagen crowned the new king and consecrated the seven new superintendents who replaced the former bishops and—in contrast to Sweden—broke the apostolic succession.

Lutheran orthodoxy in the 17th century included the Danish chorale and the development of the melodious "hymn mass." Poets like Thomas Kingo (1634–1703), and later Hans Adolf Brorson (1694–1764), enriched the treasury of song. Pietism, from Halle in Germany, made an early impact in the royal court. With the help of August Hermann Francke (1663–1727), King Fredrick IV in 1705 sent out the first Protestant missionaries of the modern era to Tranquebar, the Danish colony in *India. With royal Danish help, the Norwegian, Hans Egede (1686–1758), began mission work among the Eskimo in Greenland in 1721, a task completed by the Moravians.

Erik Pontoppidan (1698–1764), the Danish-Norwegian bishop, produced for the laity a classic exposition of Luther's *Small Catechism* (*Norway). Renewal came to the Danish church in various ways: through the stern orthodox churchman, Jakob Peter Mynster (1775–1854), bishop of Copenhagen; through the biting critic and profound existentialist theologian, Søren Kierkegaard (1813–1855); through the gifted champion of the laity, Nikolai Frederik Severin Grundtvig (1783–1872), with his accent on the church's continuity in the words used in baptism and the eucharist and his promotion of folk high schools; through Vilhelm Beck (1829–1901), pious proponent of evangelization through

Inner Mission as a means of renewing the national church; and from many other sources, such as the Copenhagen Church Fund, by which the people rallied to build churches (40 between 1911 and 1934) with voluntary contributions when the capital city was growing and the government had other priorities.

With its rich legacy, the Danish church, as a folk church, has tended to experience renewal on an individual basis. Pietism, like liberalism, accentuated religious freedom. It created religious societies and appropriated certain activities for itself. This left the local congregation with few tasks in relation to outward-directed activity. But during recent decades, the voluntary organizations have increasingly come to recognize themselves as instruments of the church, and at the same time the congregations have engaged more actively in the work of these organizations. It remained for the critical period of German occupation (1940–1945) to reveal the closeness of church and people, especially in resistance. But since that time, less obvious crises have been shaping Danish church history.

One of these has been the influx of cults and new religions into many a local parish. This process has been going on for years. It is subtle and seemingly unnoticed by the official church and most pastors. Buddhist and Muslim influences are being felt, but most of the new religions appear to have roots in Hinduism. Young people especially, seeking spiritual satisfaction in a foreboding and pluralistic age, have been susceptible to these substitutes for a traditionalized Christianity. Numbers of them have traveled to India and become adherents of gurus. Many have become stranded and disillusioned.

To counteract this trend, a Dialogue Center (established in connection with the Institute for Missionary and Ecumenical Theology at the University of Aarhus) has exposed the problems and offered assistance to young people both in Denmark and in India. The church has also published a new catechism to anticipate the problems confronting today's baptized children and young people. Congregations, likewise, are being helped to serve the social and pastoral needs of youth more effectively.

(See also FAEROE ISLANDS and GREENLAND)

EVANGELICAL LUTHERAN FREE CHURCH IN DENMARK

(Den evangelisk-lutherske Frikirke i Danmark)
Member: ILC, CELFC
Membership: 155**
President: The Rev. Leif G. Jensen
Ewaldsvej 9
DK—8723 Losning

This church comprises seven congregations and is served by three pastors. It represents a will to independence from state control of church life. It has connections with the *USA Lutheran Church–Missouri Synod, the International Lutheran Conference, and the Conference of European Lutheran Free Churches.

FAEROE ISLANDS
(see also Denmark)

An integral yet remote part of the Danish realm, the Faeroes have been self-governing since 1948. Location: North Atlantic, about midway between Norway (Trondheim) and Iceland. Area: 1399 sq. km. (540 sq. mi.), comprising a cluster of 18 mountainous islands (one uninhabited). Pop. (1985 est.): 45,000, of Norse ancestry. Cap. and largest town: Thorshavn (pop., 1984 est., 14,443), on Strømø, largest of the islands. Language: Faeroese (akin to Icelandic), Danish, and some English. Industry: fishing, limited agriculture (sheep, some cattle, a little farming), chartered shipping, and trade.

History: Celts, earliest known inhabitants were displaced by Vikings from Norway in the 9th century. The Faeroese Løgting (parliament) with 32 members has about 1000 years of history. In 1380, both Norway and the Faeroes came under Danish rule. For the Faeroes this status has continued except for a brief interruption. While Denmark came under German occupation during World War II, the Faeroes became a British protectorate. The islanders achieved home rule in 1948 and have two representatives in the Danish parliament. The independent spirit of the islanders is attested in their folklore and modern literature, of which there is a growing body. Faeroese became a written language after the mid-19th century.

Religion (est.): 85% Lutheran; 12% Christian Brethren (Plymouth). Tiny groups of Roman Catholics, Salvation Army, Jehovah's Witnesses, Seventh Day Adventists. The Brethren (entered in 1865) remain aloof from the established church, and do not recognize Lutheran baptism. Roman Catholics arrived in 1857, were dismissed from the islands in 1870, and returned in 1931 when their worship was legally permitted. The annually observed Week of Prayer for Christian Unity has improved relations between Lutherans and Roman Catholics. The first-ever visit in 1982 by a World Council of Churches team made local ecumenical history.

FAEROE ISLANDS VICE-DIOCESE EVANGELICAL LUTHERAN CHURCH IN DENMARK

Vice-Bishop: The Rt. Rev. Eivind Pauli Vilhelm
J. Paturssonargøta 20
3800 Thorshavn

With their wooden churches prominent in a treeless land, the 60 parishes are clustered into 11 districts and together form a vice-diocese of distant Copenhagen. With few exceptions, the 20 pastors and vicars are native to the islands but have been theologically educated in Denmark. An arrangement akin to that in Greenland (below) gives the vice-bishop oversight in church affairs and provides for cooperation with the civil government in such matters as Christian instruction in the public schools.

Each parish church has its clerk (klokker) who assists the pastor in various tasks. He opens the worship service and, on occasion, may conduct all of it, including the reading of a sermon. The sermons of Jakob Dahl (1878–1944), one of five collections available in Faeroese, contain many favorites. Dahl was the first to translate the New Testament into the islanders' language. By 1961, the entire Bible was published in Faeroese. The previous year the first hymnal in the native tongue had appeared.

The transition from Danish to Faeroese is but one sign of change in church and spiritual life. People speak of a generation gap between old timers who still consider Danish to be the language of worship, and the younger generation who resonate to Faeroese. In any case, religious life here on the islands is said to be livelier than in Denmark. Outside influences, borne by the electronic age, are mounting, as illustrated by weekly broadcasts in Faeroese from Trans World Radio (Monaco). The people here know themselves as isolated and as virtually living "in the sea." But with daily plane connections, lively navigation, radio and television, the sense of isolation is lessened. Through the Danish Seamen's Church in Foreign Ports and the Danish Church Abroad, there has developed a lively ecumenical connection with Christians in other countries. As the presence of the ecumenical visitors made clear (above), the Faeroese know themselves to be a part of the worldwide church of Jesus Christ.

FINLAND

An independent nation since 1917, and a republic since 1919. Area: 337,032 sq. km. (130,129 sq. mi.). Pop. (1984 est.): 4,875,800. Cap. and largest city: Helsinki (pop., 1985 est., 484,410). Language: Finnish and Swedish.

History: Finns probably migrated from the Ural area in the early centuries A.D. Swedish settlers brought the country into the kingdom of Sweden (1154–1809). Upon Sweden's defeat by Russia (1808–1809), Finland became an autonomous grand duchy under the czars. A strong nationalist spirit (expressed, for example, through the revived ancient epic, *Kalevala*) and a sense of Finnish identity developed in the 19th century and culminated in independence after the revolution in Russia (1917). Invaded by the USSR in 1939 and defeated in the ensuing Winter War, Finland ceded its eastern borderlands in 1940.

During the next phase of World War II, Finland became involved in Germany's eastern campaign. The scorched earth retreat of the Germans from northern Finland left widespread destruction. An armistice with the USSR (1944) reconfirmed the country's eastern boundary as of 1940, and subsequently imposed heavy reparations on the Finns. A treaty of mutual assistance and friendship with the USSR has stabilized relations between the two countries since 1948. Finland's position has facilitated East–West mediation in political, commercial, and cultural affairs.

The Helsinki name remains associated with the 35-nation Conference on Security and Co-operation in Europe (1975), with its accord bearing also on human rights and religion.

Religion (1983): Christian 94.4% (Lutheran 90.3%, Orthodox 1.2%); nonreligious 4%; atheist 1.5%; Bahai is 0.1%; a few Jews and Muslims.

Finland's location has long made it the meeting place in Northern Europe between Western and Eastern Christianity. Mission from the West began in the 11th century. In 1155, the English-born Bishop Henry of Uppsala came to the Turku area and was martyred there a year later. Early in the 13th century, another English-born churchman, Bishop Thomas, established the diocese of Turku. Before the end of the century, Finland's first medieval cathedral was completed in Turku, a place of pilgrimage honoring the memory of the by-then canonized Bishop Henry, the patron saint of Finland. More students from Finland than from other northern dioceses attended Europe's rising universities, especially the one in Paris, which for a time had a Finnish rector. In the 16th century, *Sweden's break with Rome and the introduction of the Lutheran Reformation affected Finland as well. Finland's coming under Russian sovereignty in the 19th century was accompanied by a modest influx of settlers from the East and an advance of Russian Orthodoxy under protection of the czar, a development that laid the basis for today's Finnish Orthodox Church.

The Orthodox Church of Finland (c.57,000) comprises two dioceses (Helsinki and Karelia, both formed in 1925), but its beginnings in this country date back to the 12th century. Pentecostals (c.40,000) came to Finland in 1911; the Salvation Army (c.30,000), in 1889. Among the small constituencies are the Seventh Day Adventists (5000); the Baptists (c.3000); the Methodists (c.2000); the Roman Catholics (c.3000), and others. All of these small groups came on the scene after 1860. The Ecumenical Council of Finland (1920), whose constitution of 1950 was amended in 1958 and 1968, has the same credal basis as the World Council of Churches.

Except for very small and diminishing conservative groups, Finnish Lutherans present a unified pattern which, however, is far from monolithic.

CONFESSIONAL LUTHERAN CHURCH OF FINLAND

(Suomen Tunnustuksellinen Luterilainen Kirkko)
Member: ILC, CILCE
Membership: 353**
President: The Rev. Markku Särelä
Kaukapellonkatu 9
SF—33710 Tampere 71

This body was organized in 1928 in an effort to promote conservative Lutheranism. Its relations with the *Lutheran Church–Missouri Synod (USA), begun in 1928, were terminated in 1970, because of the latter's alleged liberalism, and reestablished in 1982.

EVANGELICAL LUTHERAN CHURCH OF FINLAND (ELCF)

(Suomen Evankelis-Luterilainen Kirkko)
Member: LWF (1947), WCC, CEC, ECF
Membership: 4,616,691
Archbishop of Turku and Finland:
The Most Rev. Dr. John Vikström
Office of the Archbishop:
PO Box 60
SF—20500 Turku 50
Office for Foreign Affairs:
Satamakatu 11
PO Box 185
SF—00160 Helsinki 16

The 595 parishes of this church are served by about 1500 ordained pastors plus many other church workers: c.300 lectors, nonordained theologically trained women; 700 church musicians; c.1000 deacons and deaconesses in nursing and community service; c.1000 youth workers, besides other staff in specialized ministries to various groups, including Finns emigrated to such other countries as Sweden, West Germany, and Canada.

After discussion lasting nearly 30 years, the ELCF church assembly on November 6, 1986, passed an amendment to its constitution allowing women to be ordained. Thereupon, the country's Ecclesiastical Act, as amended in 1987 by parliament, opened the way for the first women to be ordained in 1988. More than 100 women with the necessary qualifications were soon applying for ordination. Until recently, theologically trained women have been permitted to preach in Finnish churches with permission of the parish pastor, but not to conduct baptisms, weddings, or funerals.

Most church members are of Finnish origin, but 6% speak Swedish. Lapps comprise a small number, as they do also in churches in northern Sweden and Norway.

The church is organized on an episcopal-synodical basis, and through Sweden its clergy have apostolic succession. Its eight dioceses bear the names of the cities of episcopal residence: Turku (Swedish, Åbo), a bishop's seat since 1300 and an archdiocese since 1817; the other seven in order of their founding, are Tampere, Oulu, Mikkeli, Porvoo, Kuopio, Lapua, and Helsinki. The Swedish-speaking diocese spreads over coastal Finland, and its seat, Porvoo, lies east of Helsinki. The dioceses are subdivided into deaneries (districts), and these into parishes. The diocese is governed by a chapter, or executive committee, with the bishop presiding and a dean as vice-president. The church assembly (1876), which meets semiannually, is the legislative body of the church; its laws require the approval of the national parliament, but the latter can make no changes in them. The ecclesiastical board (1944) oversees administrative and financial matters. In the 1950s and 1960s, several committees were established to assist the work in the parishes, as well as to care for foreign contacts. These committees have taken over many of the activities formerly carried on by the Central Association of the Church of Finland for Parish Work (1919). The committees are under the general supervision of the assembly.

Liturgically like the Church of Sweden, the ELCF in its public worship accentuates the preached word. A modest use of Christian art punctuates the basic simplicity of the average house of worship. On a given Sunday, it is said, more people worship at home (by radio) or, during the week, in small groups (engaged in Bible study, discussion, and prayer) than attend church. This reflects the strong tradition of Piety generated in the 19th century. In summer, gatherings of people of all ages may bring together up to 100,000 for a single long weekend. There keynote speakers relate Bible teachings to daily life; the assembled join in much singing, praying,

intercession—and socializing. Motivations generated there find expression in missionary outreach at home and overseas.

Lay leadership in the church is strong. The church's pastors are educated in the country's two theological faculties, in the University of Helsinki and the Swedish University in Turku. There is currently no lack of students. Deaconess centers in Helsinki, Lahti, Oulu, Pieksámáki, and Pori advance in new ways the well-established role of trained women in the life of the local church and community. Schools for teachers, youth workers, and many other forms of service are located in various parts of the country.

Basic to all this activity is a sound relationship between church and state. The historian and previous archbishop, Mikko Juva, put it this way: "Of decisive importance for the development of the Finnish church was a new church law which came into force as early as 1896, i.e., at a time when it was still possible to achieve democratic renewal of church administration on the basis of a clear confessional Christianity. The new church law granted the Evangelical Lutheran Church of Finland almost complete autonomy from the State."

Eventually the church took the lead in granting full religious liberty, abolishing compulsory participation in the Lord's Supper, allowing civil marriage, and otherwise recognizing an Evangelically oriented freedom of conscience. Religious instruction—at times a debated subject—continues in the public schools.

The ELCF, meanwhile, has been gaining a new understanding of mission. It has set up its own church committee for mission to serve as a formal link between the ELCF and the six mission organizations recognized by the church as its agencies for world mission. Its duties are not operational but coordinative—to promote, inform, and help train mission personnel (see below).

Its Council for Foreign Affairs continues the ELCF's early receptivity toward ecumenism. Like its Swedish counterpart, the ELCF is in communion with the Church of England. As the major partner in the country's Ecumenical Council, this church has pursued unity at home and abroad. Cordial relations with the Finnish Orthodox have encouraged the talks (since 1970) with the Russian Orthodox, which has also benefited the

LWF-sponsored dialog with Eastern Orthodoxy as a whole. In 1983, the Finnish Free Church (12,000 members) for the first time joined in conversation with the ELCF, seeking to work out some long-standing issues.

Behind all these developments lies a chronicle of centuries.

● ● ●

Michael Agricola (d.1557), once a student in Wittenberg and in his last years bishop of Turku, promoted the Reformation in Finland tactfully. The transition proved peaceful. Agricola's works, including a prayerbook, a worship manual, an "ABC-book," plus his translation of the New Testament and parts of the Old, laid the groundwork for a Finnish national literature. The decision of Sweden's Council of Uppsala (1593) established the Bible and the unaltered *Augsburg Confession* as the basis of public religion also in Finland. Luther's *Small Catechism* became the basis of popular instruction, and a growing treasury of hymns strengthened the life of devotion in the age of Lutheran orthodoxy. The entire Bible was published in 1642; the translation has been periodically revised since then. In 1640, the University of Turku was founded (after the disastrous fire in 1827 the university was relocated to Helsinki).

Late in the 17th century, Pietism entered the scene. At first a radical challenge, it became during the 18th century a strengthening force in the church. A resurgent Pietism flowed in five main currents, each bearing the name of a spiritual leader.

Foremost was that of Paavo Ruotsalainen (1777–1852), a peasant whose spiritual experiences, said to be similar to those of Luther, and powerful personality drew a large following and generated influences still active in Finnish Christianity today. Almost equally influential was Lars Levi Laestadius (1800–1861), a Swedish pastor among the Lapps and Finns. He was called the "reviver of the North," including the Lapp country in Sweden and Norway. In dealing with private confession and publicly pronounced absolution, he emphasized the forgiveness of sin and a fresh start in life. Via emigration, his influence extended overseas where it led to the formation of the Finnish Apostolic Church (*ALCA, USA).

A third movement, led by F.G. Hedberg (1811–1893), accentuated the certainty of salvation based on the objective word of the gospel rather than on subjective feelings. He and his followers formed the Finnish Lutheran Gospel Association and stimulated the translation of Luther's works, the Lutheran Confessions, and related writings. A fourth movement was led by Henrik Renqvist (1789–1866) whose own conversion experience led him to advocate a stern moral life as the fruit of faith. Changing his name from Kukkonen to the Swedish Renqvist (meaning a pure branch of Christ's vine), he led the life of an ascetic.

A fifth movement arose after World War II around the Pietist leader, Urho Muroma (1890–1966). It absorbed a number of Anglo-Saxon influences and today includes several subgroups of a strong missionary thrust.

The 19th century saw the formation of many associations among students and other concerned people. Among the most durable has been the Finnish Missionary Society (1859), whose work extended to *Southwest Africa (Namibia, 1870); *China (1901); *Tanzania (1946); *Taiwan (1956); *Thailand (1976); and to other countries as well including *Israel, *Bangladesh, *Angola, *Kenya, *Ethiopia, and *Senegal. In 1985, the Finnish Missionary Society changed its name (only in English) to the Finnish Evangelical Lutheran Mission (FELM). The Lutheran Evangelical Association of Finland (1873) undertook evangelistic work at home and began work in *Japan (1900). As mentioned above, four other small mission agencies have also been endorsed by the church.

Conversely, Finland has periodically been a focus of attention for Lutherans in many lands. In North America—not to overlook Swedish help—the Winter War (above) gave rise to Finnish Relief, the forerunner to Lutheran World Action (*USA). Following World War II, American and Canadian Lutherans in 1946 coordinated their assistance, via Geneva, in an intensive relief and reconstruction program in northern Finland, a program paralleled by American Friends (Quakers). By 1952, Finland had become a strong and well-known partner in the LWF as well as in the ecumenical movement.

In 1963 the ELCF was host to the LWF Fourth Assembly in Helsinki. Over the years it has contributed strong staff members to Federation work in Geneva and beyond. The

Fifth Assembly (Evian) in 1970 elected Professor (later Archbishop) Mikko Juva president.

FREE ASSOCIATION OF EVANGELICAL LUTHERAN CONGREGATIONS IN FINLAND
(Suomen vapaa Evankelis-Luterilainen seurakuntaliitto)
Membership: 628**
Chairman: Eero Savola
Tesomajärvenk 10F 84
SF—33310 Tampere 31

This also is a conservative religious body, in character comparable to the Confessional Lutheran Church of Finland.

GREENLAND (KALÂTDLIT-NUNÂT)
(see also Denmark)

In 1979, Greenland achieved home rule, but it remains part of the Danish realm. The world's largest island (exclusive of Australia), lies mostly within the Arctic Circle. Area: 2,175,600 sq. km. (840,000 sq. mi.) 84% under ice cap. Pop. (1985 est.) 53,000, of whom about 80% are Inuit (Eskimo) and 20% Danes. Cap. and largest city: Nuuk (Godthaab) (pop., 1983 est., 10,559). Language: Inuit (Greenlandic) and Danish.

History: Native Greenlanders are regarded as of ancient Asian origin. By about the year A.D. 1000, their ancestors had moved across upper North America to the west coast of Greenland. Norwegian (Viking) settlements in southwestern Greenland begun during Europe's Middle Ages—Leif Ericson reached "Vineland," North America, about the year 1000—had become extinct by the early 15th century. The remains of Norse churches and houses are archaeological monuments. They are mute testimony to the effect of climatic and other—possibly epidemic—changes. Danish interests, moving via the Faeroe Islands and Iceland in quest of a northwest passage to fabled China, explored Hudson Bay in northern Canada, but established themselves permanently in Greenland. While the first census in 1865 showed a population of 6046 and that in 1925 only 13,600, the increase was fourfold during the next five decades. World War II and subsequent developments demonstrated the strategic significance of Greenland, and air travel made it accessible. Sealing, fishing, and some cattle and sheep raising, balanced since the 1950s by limited mining ventures, sustain the economy. Greenlanders guard this jealously, as their exercise of home rule indicates. Objecting to fishing curbs applied from the outside, in 1982 they voted to seek withdrawal from the European Community.

In various ways, Greenland is a developing country. Towns have attracted Greenlanders from their isolated habitations and introduced them to the ways of a technological age and to modern dwellings. Public education, as well as instruction in the vocational schools and folk high schools, is in Greenlandic. Increasing emphasis has been placed on the Inuit or native Greenlanders' culture and history. Health and welfare services are helping the "people" (*inuit*, as the Eskimo call themselves collectively) adapt to new conditions.

Religion: Lutheran (about 95%), plus a scattering of other Christian groups gaining converts since World War II. Some entered via the Faeroes, others through the presence of U.S. military bases. These include Pentecostals (came c.1952), Jehovah's Witnesses (1950), Seventh Day Adventists (1953), and others. Roman Catholicism—present from the time of Christianization until the 15th century—returned in 1960. Its one congregation is under the Roman Catholic Bishop of Copenhagen and, like most of the others, its base is in Nuuk (Godthaab). There is no ecumenical organization, but the good relations between Lutherans and Roman Catholics in Denmark is reflected here, too.

GREENLAND VICE-DIOCESE EVANGELICAL LUTHERAN CHURCH IN DENMARK
Membership: 50,000
Vice-Bishop: The Rt. Rev. Kristian Morch
PO Box 90
39000 Nuuk

Organizationally the church in Greenland is part of the Evangelical Lutheran Church in

Denmark. Its 82 congregations, grouped into 18 deaneries (circuits), constitute a vice-diocese—akin to that in the Faeroes—of the Copenhagen diocese. The church is enormously spread out along an often forbidding coastal region. Its bounds run from Julianehaab at the southern tip to Thule in the far northwest. Thirty-four pastors are currently serving.

An ecclesiastical commission (*Kirkenaeum*) governs church affairs. Its membership includes the governor, the vice-bishop, and others. A major concern is the supply of pastors. The average age of those serving in 1983 was 52. Before the end of the decade it is estimated that some 26 pastors will be needed. To meet this challenge the home-rule government in 1982 approved the curriculum and funding for a theological training program new to Greenland. The new school's five-year program requires that four be spent in Greenland. The fifth year provides for study abroad in another Nordic country, North America, or a seminary in Asia, Africa, or Latin America. Formerly, pastors were trained in Copenhagen and its supplemental Greenland seminary. Theological studies in Godthaab include strong emphasis on Greenland and its people. For years, catechists have enjoyed such contextual training. As assistants to the pastors, especially in Christian education, their own teaching task is coordinated with the public school curriculum. The Bible and Luther's *Catechism* have long been available in Inuit (Greenlandic), the language of the church.

The conversion of the people was initiated by the Norwegian missionary pioneer, Hans Egede (1686–1758). He arrived in 1721, seeking the descendants of earlier Norse settlers, but found only Eskimo. The missionary task he and others began was taken over by the Moravians. They turned over the fruits of their efforts to the church of Denmark in 1901. From then until 1953, when Danish law extended religious freedom to Greenland, the church there was exclusively Lutheran.

ICELAND

A republic in the North Atlantic. Area: 103,000 sq. km. (39,769 sq. mi.). Pop. (1985 est.): 243,000. Cap. and largest city: Reykjavík (pop., 1985 est., 87,309). Language: Icelandic.

History: Iceland was first settled in 874 by the Norse. It was an independent republic A.D. 930-1362, and then joined with *Norway. Both countries came under Danish rule in 1380. *Denmark recognized Iceland as a sovereign state in 1918, but the latter acknowledged the Danish crown until 1944 (German occupation), and then dissolved the 567-year ties. The republic was proclaimed in 1944, without bitterness toward Denmark. King Christian X overcame his initial protest and sent a goodwill message to the people of Iceland, 97% of whom had voted for independence. Today, Iceland is fully respected as one of the five northern nations.

While traditionally some Icelanders have emigrated to Denmark and Norway, the later 19th century saw a veritable exodus to North America. Of the 15,000 leaving during the years 1870-1900 (about 20% of the total population), about two-thirds of them settled in *Canada.

When Vigdis Finnbogadóttir was chosen president of Iceland in 1980, she became the world's first elected woman head of state. Re-elected unopposed to a second term in 1984, she remained highly popular despite the difficulties of changing times.

Religion: Lutheranism is the official religion of the republic. Some 92% are baptized members of the national church; another 5% are members of free or independent Lutheran congregations. Roman Catholics, Seventh Day Adventists, and other groups account for another 2%. The remainder are without affiliation.

Iceland's Christian beginnings are traditionally dated from the year 1000, when the Althing (parliament) of the republic voted the acceptance of Christianity. Missionary work by Irish monks antedated this peaceful event. Highlights during the ensuing 10 centuries include the establishment of two dioceses, Skálholt (near Reykjavík) for the south, Holar for the north; the founding of monasteries as seats of culture, where the ancient Eddas and Sagas were reduced to writing; and the voting of the kinship union with Norway, which in 1380 brought Iceland, together with Norway, under the Danish crown. The union subsequently affected the course of church life as it resulted in the bringing in of foreign bishops and other officials who tended to neglect the needs of the people. The introduction of the Reformation brought no immediate benefits.

EVANGELICAL LUTHERAN CHURCH —THE NATIONAL CHURCH OF ICELAND

(Thjodkirkja Islands)
Member: LWF (1947), WCC, CEC
Membership: 227,018**
Bishop of Reykjavík and Primate:
The Rt. Rev. Pétur Sigurgeirsson
Sudurgata 22
IS—101 Reykjavík

The national church in the island of ancient Eddas and Sagas comprises 296 congregations, grouped into 110 parishes and served by some 127 ordained pastors plus 13 pastors in specialized ministries. Most of the members are employed in the fishing industry, others in farming, light industry, business, and the professions. Their participation in the life of the church is routine, beginning with baptism for most children, and confirmation for 97% of them. Marriages and funerals are almost always conducted under church auspices. Church attendance is moderate but growing. Religious instruction is part of the public school curriculum. The general attitude toward the church has been described as passive goodwill toward an institution most people take for granted. Daily religious broadcasts over radio and television, as well as Sunday services, presumably reach a large audience, but the mass media are said to have hastened the decline of daily family devotions, which were customary for generations. However, the work of the church in peace movements and development/emergency aid has created new expectations and a growing dialog.

Relations between church and state are facilitated by a ministry of church affairs. The Althing (parliament) legislates for the church in nondoctrinal matters. The church organization is episcopal. Since 1801, the entire island has been a single diocese. The bishop is elected by the pastors, the theological professors in the university, and some lay delegates from each deanery. Two "consecrating pastors"—actually suffragan bishops without other episcopal duties, from the seats of the two former dioceses of Skálholt (1056) and Holar (1105)—install the bishop. As in Denmark, however, there is no apostolic succession. The bishop and clergy meet annually in synod and deal with the church's concerns. Also meeting annually is the church assembly, consisting of 11 clerical and 11 lay members.

Parishes are grouped into 15 deaneries or districts, each headed by a dean. The deans meet annually with the pastors and councils—from three to five lay persons from each congregation—in their districts. Pastors are educated in the theological faculty of the University of Reykjavík (1911), and when possible do additional study in Europe and North America. Continuing education for pastors has recently been introduced. Prior to 1843, when a theological college was opened, most Icelandic pastors were trained in Denmark. Visiting scholars stimulate Icelandic theological education with international and ecumenical input.

Youth work, often on the conservative side, is promoted widely by the YMCA and YWCA, whose roots are in the pioneering work begun in 1898 by Fridrik Fridriksson, a pastor. The Christian Student Association (1936) in 1974 received its first full-time pastor to assist in the work among some 4000 students in higher education. In 1975, Icelandic students were host to the Nordic Christian Student Conference. The participation of nearly 1200 students from Norway, Denmark, Sweden, and Finland made this the biggest international gathering ever held in Iceland.

Missionary activity includes evangelization (Inner Mission) at home and outreach (overseas mission) abroad. For a while, Icelanders participated with Norwegians in work in China; since the end of World War II, they have assumed responsibility for work in a particular area of *Ethiopia, among the Konso people, and in northwest *Kenya in the Pokot area. They have also responded generously to development projects on other continents.

During the last few years, the Icelandic church has experienced increasing financial problems due in large part to the movement of people into the capital city, Reykjavík. This necessitates the construction of new facilities for growing urban congregations and the continuous costly care of the scattered rural members, many of whom are in congregations too small to support a pastor.

An encouraging sign of new life in the church has been demonstrated in Skálholt, the seat of the southern bishop in the 18th century and the center for Icelandic culture. Here, in the 1960s, a church and a church camp for youth and children were built. In 1972, a folk high school, the only one in Iceland, was started and the interest has been so great that in 1974 three times as many students applied as could be accepted. The buildings are also used for various kinds of courses for lay men and women, pastors, and theological students, and for conferences and group meetings.

The meeting of the LWF Executive Committee in Reykjavík (1964) underscored for the Icelandic church the importance of its membership in the Federation as well as in the WCC and the Conference of European Churches. The church is also a full partner in the Conference of Northern Churches and benefits from the work of the Nordic Ecumenical Institute in Sigtuna, Sweden. Close, informal ties with North American Lutherans continue.

● ● ●

The Lutheran Reformation did not come to Iceland without some violence, and Danish pressure accompanied the Althing's adoption of the new church order (1541). Skálholt (1541) and Holar (1552) received Lutheran bishops. Oddur Gottskalksson's translation of the New Testament (1533–1540)—he had studied in Germany—became a landmark publication, saving the Icelandic language from becoming a Danish dialect. From Gudbrandur Thorlaksson, longtime bishop of Holar (1570–1627), came the completed Bible (1584), translations of Luther's *Large* and *Small Catechisms*, a hymnal (1589) which was standard for 200 years, an order of worship (1594), and books of sermons and devotional materials. The Passion Hymns by Hallgrimur Pétursson (1616–1674) revealed an Icelandic genius for interpreting the theology of the cross in ways that have made them popular classics to this day, with translations into many languages. The book of sermons by Jon Vidalin (1666–1720), bishop of Skálholt from 1698–1720, was regularly used for family devotions, and even today some Icelanders can recite portions of it. Indeed, in a land of periodic volcanic eruptions,

earthquakes, isolation, famine, and plague, a stronghold on the spiritual foundations of life was essential.

During the 19th century, the effects of Rationalism were widely felt. Many saw the merging of Skálholt and Holar into the single diocese of Reykjavik as a surrender of Iceland's equivalent of Oxford and Canterbury.

Other religious currents—spiritism, theosophy, liberal theology—gained a hold in the later 19th and during the first half of the 20th century, but are losing ground. Growing international and ecumenical relations have diminished the isolation of the island. However, isolation—both geographical and cultural—can be an enemy of the islanders and must be fought. The National Church of Iceland regards itself as a full member of the church catholic and evangelical. A visible affirmation of this is the now-dedicated (1986) and virtually completed Hallgrim's church in Reykjavík. It does not replace the much more modest cathedral, but this imposing structure of modern design was undertaken as a national project in the later 1940s, when Sigurgeir Sigurdsson (father of the present incumbent) was bishop and primate. The impressive structure's name honors the memory of Hallgrimur Pétursson, while its upward sweeping spire lifts high the cross.

NORWAY

A constitutional monarchy with a unicameral parliament (*Storting*). Area: 323,895 sq. km. (125,057 sq. mi.), excluding the Svalbard Archipelago (Spitzbergen) and Jan Mayen Island in the Arctic Ocean. Pop. (1983 est.): 4,157,000. Cap. and largest city Oslo (pop., 1985 est., 447,400). Language: Norwegian.

History: From Viking raids of long ago to oil rigs poised in the ocean, a millennium of sagas of the sea have linked Norway ever wider to a changing world. Under Harald the Fairhaired (872–930) a patchwork of little kingdoms began to be unified, and, presumably, seaborne adventures achieved conquests in the *Faeroes, *Iceland, Scotland, *Ireland, and elsewhere. By A.D. 1000 Norsemen had plundered and occupied important parts of coastal Europe, especially the duchy of Normandy (991) in northwest France; from whence came Duke William's Norman conquest of England (1066). Earlier, however, English missionaries had initiated the Christianization of Norway—an epic in its own right (below).

Norway's role in the Scandinavian north was determined by its neighbors and its unrivaled exposure to the West. The country was united with Denmark under one monarch for over four centuries (1381–1814). For a while, the Kalmar Union (1397–1483) included Sweden as well as Denmark and Norway under the same crown. Remaining in Danish partnership, Norway's political and ecclesial directions were set in Copenhagen (below). Economically, fishing became a flourishing industry in the 17th century, and lumbering in the 18th. Paralleling the rise of a commercial middle class was the country's growing merchant fleet. By British intervention late in the era of Napoleon, Denmark was forced to cede Norway (Treaty of Kiel). On "seventeenth May" 1814, Norway became a constitutional monarchy under personal union with the Swedish crown. Full independence came in 1905. A Danish prince became King Haakon VII of Norway. Meanwhile, a growing population and periods of economic stagnation resulted in heavy emigration, to North America especially. Except for *Ireland, no other country contributed so high a percentage of its population to the settlement of North America as did Norway. Most of the migration took place between 1840 and 1915. But the total number (1820–1975) was 885,000, equalling the entire population of Norway in 1820.

During the present century, Norway's course has been marked by such developments as a strong merchant marine and a significant shift in its economy (from the 1970s) by its North Sea oil operations. Politically, it gained wide recognition for its resistance under Nazi occupation during World War II. With the creation of the United Nations, Norway's statesman, Trygve Halvdan Lie (1896–1968) became that body's first secretary general. The ancient westward orientation of Norway continues.

Religion: Christian 97.5% (Evangelical Lutheran official); nonreligious 1.2%; atheist 0.5%; Muslim 0.4%; small numbers of Jews, Roman Catholics, and Buddhists.

Norway's Christian beginnings are related to missionary activities emanating from the British Isles. Pre-Christian Norse mythology, preserved in ancient sagas and runic monuments that have been restudied in recent years, fostered a quest for power, security, and protection against evils. Paganism yielded in the 11th century. Christianity was finally accepted under King Olav Haraldson, who died in battle in 1030. Though the conflict was politically based, he was soon honored as a martyr, was canonized by the local bishop, and became Norway's patron St. Olav. His grave in Nidaros (Trondheim) was long a place of pilgrimages.

The king was *de facto* head of the Norwegian church, the bishops were his officers, and the local clergy were often appointees of patrons, the church owners (local nobility). After 1104, the Norwegian church was included in the province of Lund (at that time part of Denmark). But in 1152, the archdiocese of Nidaros (Trondheim) was established, responsible directly to Rome. As the capital of medieval Norway, Nidaros saw its lines of political and ecclesiastical authority extend also across the sea to the *Faeroes (Denmark) as well as to *Iceland and *Greenland. In many places during the 12th century, distinctive wooden stave-churches (*stavkirker*) were erected, of which some 25 are still standing.

The Reformation came to Norway via *Denmark. The Danish Church Ordinance of 1537 was accepted by the diets in Oslo and Bergen in 1539. The archbishop of Trondheim fled the country and the bishops were deposed. The Evangelical Lutheran Church was established (see Church of Norway, below).

Not until 1842, after the liberalization of church-state relations, was the Roman Catholic Church reintroduced into Norway. During the latter half of the 19th century, different orders of sisters, mainly from Germany and Holland, established numerous hospitals, often the first in their areas. A reduction in the number of sisters has caused some of them to be taken over by the state hospital system. In 1956, Norway abolished the prohibition of Jesuits, which had been incorporated into the constitution of 1814. In recent years, the Roman Catholic Church has gained members both by conversion and immigration. Prejudice against them is decreasing, and the number of Norwegian-born priests is increasing. Today, Roman Catholics number well over 10,000.

During the second half of the 19th century, a number of Protestant groups entered Norway from Britain and America, including the Baptists in 1850 and the Methodists in 1853. The Evangelical Lutheran Free Church (below) and the Mission Covenant (1856) grew out of the renewal movement within the Lutheran church. The Salvation Army (1888) and the Pentecostals (1906) are the two largest non-Lutheran churches. Methodists are third with some 30,000 members.

These and the other small churches are mainly conservative and nonecumenical. Thus there is no council of churches. The Church of Norway Council on Foreign Relations is responsible for carrying on dialogs with Roman Catholics, Methodists, and Baptists. The Center for Ecumenical Theology (1967) provides theologians of different denominations an opportunity to study together. The University of Oslo has an Ecumenical Institute. Another avenue for ecumenical understanding is provided by the Egede Institute of Missionary Study and Research. Its staff is largely Lutheran, but it has an ecumenical board and character.

Besides the national Church of Norway and the Evangelical Free Church of Norway (described below), Oslo has several expatriate congregations: the American Lutheran Church (Fritznersgate 15, Oslo; Pastor: The Rev. Harry T. Cleven), founded in 1958 by the *American Lutheran Church, USA, has a close relationship with the Church of Norway. The German Evangelical Church (Eil, Sundsgate 37, Oslo; Pastor: The Rev. Gerhard Heilman) has served German-speaking people—Lutherans and others—since 1908. Occasional services are held in five other cities. Sponsored by the *Evangelical Church in Germany, the congregation also receives financial subsidy from the Norwegian government. The *Church of Sweden maintains the Swedish Church Abroad (Margaretarkyrkan, Hammarsborg Torg 8, Oslo) and the Swedish Seamen's Church (8501 Narvick).

CHURCH OF NORWAY
(Den Norske Kirke)
Member: LWF (1947), WCC, CEC, CECN
Membership: 3,800,000
Bishop of Oslo and Primate: The Rt. Rev. Dr. Andreas Aarflot
Church of Norway Council on Foreign Relations
PO Box 5816, Hegdehaugen
N—0308 Oslo 3

The 616 parishes (comprising some 1340 congregations) of this folk church are served by 1162 ordained pastors, as well as many other church workers in related ministries. Over 90% of the country's population are baptized members of the national church. The vast majority use the services of the church for the confirmation of the young, for weddings, and for funerals. Frequent participation in Holy Communion is for most people the exception rather than the rule. Religious instruction (confessionally based) is part of the public school curriculum.

The Church of Norway comprises 11 dioceses. Three of the five oldest were founded before the year 1100: Trondheim/Nidaros (an archdiocese by 1152), Bergen, and Oslo. These were followed by Stavanger (Norway's modern North Sea oil city) and Hamar (north of Oslo). Six other dioceses have been added over the centuries: Kristiansand (at the country's southern tip), Tönsberg (west of Oslo), Borg/Fredrikstad (east of Oslo), Möre/Molde (southwest of Trondheim/Nidaros), and the two northernmost dioceses, South and North Helgeland (Tromsø), reaching far beyond the Arctic Circle.

Each diocese has a bishop and a seven-member diocesan council. For some years, the several dioceses have held synod meetings every fourth year, but only in 1984 were these given legal status when parliament passed legislation providing the church more autonomy than it has had in the past. These synods now meet biennially and each consists of the bishop, the diocesan council, one lay delegate from each parish, two pastors and one church worker from each deanery, and the deans of the dioceses. The diocesan councils now have the authority to appoint parish pastors and catechists. This was formerly done by the government or the ministry of church and education.

The 11 dioceses are subdivided into some 90 deaneries (districts), and these deaneries into parishes. Chief pastor of a parish is the *søgneprest,* who takes part in the parish council. The council is composed of four to 10 members elected every fourth year in elections open to each baptized church member. The *søgneprest* is assisted by other pastors and church workers.

At the other end of the scale are the bishops' conference, chaired by the bishop of Oslo (primate) and the national church council. The latter includes five clergy and eight laity, representatives of the diocesan councils, supplemented by three additional members elected by the church's general synod. In 1984, parliament authorized the establishment of a national church synod. It consists of 80 members, of whom 77 are the members of the 11 diocesan councils. The other three are the members of the national church council (mentioned above) and must represent the clergy, the nonclerical church workers, and the laity. The country's three theological faculties each have a nonvoting delegate. The church council serves as the national synod's executive body and has the services of a general synodical consultant. On behalf of the synod, the Church of Norway Council on Foreign Relations (below) takes care of ecumenical relationships.

This new structure resulted from a prolonged debate over state-church relationships. The majority of a politically appointed commission in 1975 advocated the disestablishment of the church. That seemed too drastic a step to most interested parties. The present structure is a compromise and shows similarities with the Finnish and Anglican models. The first national synod was held in November 1984.

The Church of Norway's pastors are educated at three recognized theological faculties. The oldest is that of the University of Oslo (1811). The Free (Independent) Theological Faculty (Menighetsfakultetet) was formed in 1907 in protest against the theological liberalism in the university at that time. Long supported by voluntary contributions, it has since 1972 also received subsidies from the state (recently about 40% of its annual budget). Today, some 80% of the church's pastors are graduates of the Menighetsfakultetet. A third faculty at the School of Mission and Theology of the Norwegian Missionary Society in Stavanger has recently been upgraded to university level. Here, missionary pastors, as well as lay workers, are trained.

Pastors have had their own association since 1900; it is part of the national society of academically educated professions. Continuing education of pastors is one of the association's concerns. Deaconesses (training centers in Oslo and Bergen), deacons (college in Oslo), and church workers of many kinds, as well as lay preachers, are trained in various parts of the country.

The Church of Norway Council on Foreign Relations (1971) relates the Church of Norway to the World Council of Churches, the Conference of European Churches, the Nordic Ecumenical Institute (Sigtuna, Sweden), and other international undertakings. It also serves as the Norwegian national committee of the LWF. Its two subunits are a theological commission and a committee on international affairs. Various study groups deal with matters of concern to the council and engage as many as 80 co-opted participants who serve without pay. In recent years, the Council on Foreign Relations has dealt also with ecumenical questions on the national level (above). It is or has been responsible for carrying out dialogs with Roman Catholics, Methodists, and Baptists. Though the Church of Norway is a charter member of the WCC, the powerful missionary societies, which are within the church but are organizationally independent, were critical of the merging of the International Missionary Council into the WCC (1961) and are still cool toward the world body.

Kirkens Nødhjelp (Norwegian Church Aid), the church's emergency aid program based in Oslo, raises large sums through its nationwide appeals. It engages in relief work and development projects in Africa, Asia, and Latin America, and by its instructive interpretation of human need in many lands has helped to develop a keen sense of stewardship among Norway's people.

These outward signs of a Christian legacy, it is said, are accompanied by a widespread attitude of secularism, triggered also by such gifted critics of the church as the authors Henrik Ibsen (1828–1906) and Bjørnstjerne

Bjørnson (1832–1910). But the spiritual dynamism of Norway's Lutheranism is evident in the strong Pietist lay movements that have long pervaded the church. Perhaps one Norwegian in 10 is affiliated with some such movement. The largest is the Inner Mission. Attendance at its prayer houses, often located near the local church, is more often than not a supplement to, but may also serve as a substitute for, churchgoing. With its own extensive organization, the Inner Mission, along with other societies for world mission (below) or domestic needs, has been called a "church within the church." Through these movements, lay people have been able to express and activate their faith without disrupting the unity of the nationwide church, even in periods of conflict.

• • •

As indicated above (Religion), with the acceptance of the Danish Church Ordinance of 1537, the church in Norway continued as Evangelical Lutheran. The new evangelical superintendents, who replaced the Roman Catholic bishops were soon called bishops, but the continuous line of apostolic succession had been broken. Hymnals, orders of worship, church order, catechism, and ecclesiastical law were the same in Norway as in Denmark. Danish Bibles were still in use after 1814, as Danish was the church language. The Norwegian Bible Society was founded in 1816. (A complete translation of the Bible into Norwegian came late: the Old Testament in 1891, the New in 1904, and a totally revised edition in 1978.

The Evangelical faith, maintained during the Lutheran orthodoxy of the 17th century, became engrafted into the life of the people only with the coming of Pietism. Erik Pontoppidan's explanation of Luther's *Small Cathechism* (1737)—see Denmark—became a major force in shaping the people's understanding of Christianity and continued in use for some 150 years. The spiritual father of today's lay Christianity in Norway was Hans Nielsen Hauge (1771–1824), a tireless lay preacher who combined warm piety with a concern for the people's economic development. Repeatedly imprisoned, he became a forerunner of later champions of religious liberty.

Norway's constitution (May 17, 1814) named "the Evangelical Lutheran religion"

as "the public religion of the state." The state church system was retained, with the parliament functioning as the church's legislative body. Ecclesiastical appointments, the promulgation of church legislation, and other functional matters remained the privilege of the king with his government (after 1905, Norway's own King Haakon VII and his successors).

The religious liberty introduced in 1845 gave the lay movements and Christian dissenting societies full freedom to develop. The former remained within the Lutheran church. The Inner Mission movement (above) was shaped as an organization in 1855 by the Oslo professor, Gisle Johnson (1822–1894), who also gave it theological standing and literary expression. Missionary motivation extended overseas as well. The Norwegian Missionary Society (1842), based in Stavanger, launched work in *South Africa, *Madagascar, *China, *Cameroon, *Japan, *Ethiopia, *Taiwan, *Hong Kong, *Tanzania, *Thailand (1974), and *Brazil (1975). The Norwegian Mission to Israel (1844; now renamed Nowegian Church Ministry to Israel) had the double purpose of awakening interest in the people of Israel and of furthering knowledge of the Christian faith among them. Until 1950, its main work was in Hungary and Romania. When the Hebrew congregations there migrated to *Israel, they were followed by the interest and support of the Norwegians. The Norwegian Seamen's Mission (1864) today operates in ports of 19 different countries and also provides spiritual care for students and other Scandinavians living abroad. The Norwegian Santal Mission began work in *India in 1867—a joint endeavor of Lars Olsen Skrefsrud (1840–1910) from Norway and Hans Peter Borresen from Denmark. This work continues there and in Bangladesh in the Santal Mission of Northern Churches. Santal staff are also in *Bhutan and *Ecuador.

The more low church and lay-oriented Oslo-based Norwegian Lutheran Mission (1891) first undertook work in *China, then in *Ethiopia, *Tanzania, *Japan, *Hong Kong, and more recently in *Kenya, *Indonesia, Peru, and *Bolivia. Other agencies include those of the Christian Mission to Buddhists (1922)—pioneered in China by Karl Ludwig Reichelt and relocated to *Hong Kong with an extension in *Japan. Now an ecumenical outreach with headquarters in

*Sweden, it is known as the Scandinavian East Asian Mission. The Norwegian Christian Mission (to Muslims; 1940) first began work in *India and then spread to *Pakistan and more recently to *Indonesia, as well as to the increasing number of Muslims in Norway itself.

Today, many in Norway still consider overseas mission as the proper concern not of the organized church but of the voluntary society. But few churches have within their membership a deeper commitment to mission than does the Church of Norway. By 1985, some 1500 Lutheran missionaries (including spouses) were serving overseas as coworkers in national churches of Asia, Africa, and Latin America.

EVANGELICAL LUTHERAN FREE CHURCH OF NORWAY (ELFC)

(Den Evangelisk Lutherske Frikirke i Norge)
Membership: 19,700**
President: The Rev. Sverre Joelstad
St. Olavsplass, PO Box 6787
N—0130 Oslo 1

This church body, with its 69 congregations, 60 pastors, and generally active membership, is an alternative to the Church of Norway and an old model for separation of church and state. Firmly committed to the Lutheran confessions, the church's doctrinal concern is paralleled by a synodical-presbyterial form of organization.

The synod, which meets biennially, is the legislative authority and elects the church's officers. Congregations have considerable freedom and elect their own pastors under supervision of the district board. Each of the four districts is led by a president who has visitational functions. Some of the pastors are educated at the Free (Independent) Theological Faculty with students from the Church of Norway. Others are trained at the church's own Bible and Theological Seminary, situated in the church headquarters building. It also has a department where lay people are prepared for different types of service.

A number of ELFC evangelists are gathering new congregations in Norway, while more than 30 missionaries extend the outreach to churches in *Japan, *Ethiopia, *Taiwan, and *Cameroon. A good relationship exists between the ELFC and the Church of Norway. The ELFC has no ties with other free churches, but sends observers to the Conference of Lutheran Free Churches in Europe and maintains friendly relations with the *Church of the Lutheran Brethren in North America (USA). Although not a member, this church cooperates with the LWF and has at times provided staff members.

The history of the ELFC goes back to 1877. At that time Paul Peter Wettergren (1835–1889), an ordained pastor in the Church of Norway and a missionary in South Africa, became a leader in the struggle of the Lutheran state church for independence from the state. Wettergren and others with him insisted that Jesus Christ must be freely recognized as head of the church and as the determiner of its affairs without the interposition of a temporal political ruler like the sovereign of a state. Objection was also raised against the frequent lack of church discipline, against doctrinal aberrations, and against the accepted moral standards. For that reason congregations demanded the right to choose their own pastors and to exercise some degree of autonomy. When these demands were not granted, a number of pastors and congregations seceded from the Church of Norway.

The ELFC thus represents an old yet not outdated model of separation of church and state. The debates and minor changes of the past few years have convinced the ELFC that parliament and the people of Norway overwhelmingly want a continuation of the "old system." At the same time, the ELFC sees a Norwegian people, especially suburbanites, becoming more secularized and even looking upon themselves as nonchristian. The great challenge for the ELFC is therefore to develop an effective strategy for evangelism.

SWEDEN

A constitutional monarchy governed as a parliamentary democracy with a king as titular head of state (1975). Area: 449,793 sq. km. (173,654 sq. mi.). Pop. (1985 est.): 8,330,600. Cap. and largest city: Stockholm (pop., 1985 est., 1,409,000). Language: Swedish, with some Finnish and Saamish ("Lappish") in the north.

History: Distant ancestors of modern Swedes were mentioned by the historian,

Tacitus (*Germania,* ch. 44) in the late first century A.D. The Suiones, or Svear, were a people living beyond the northern limits of the Roman Empire. Except for minor trade activities in Roman times, Sweden entered European history with far-flung trading ex-peditions during the seventh and eighth cen-turies. Not long thereafter, these voyages turned into warlike incursions, with Nordic Vikings ravaging Western Europe's coast-lands as far away as the Mediterranean. East-ward, Swedish Vikings (Varangians) traveled Russia's rivers from the Baltic to the Black and Caspian Seas.

Under Olaf Skotkonung (993–1024), who accepted Christianity, Sweden gradually be-came a unified kingdom. Yet the northern scene was alive with contending forces. Vis-by, on Gotland—the island noted for its 13th-century Gothic churches—was for genera-tions the coveted center of a brisk Baltic com-merce run by the Hanseatic League of Ger-man cities. Later, Sweden, *Norway, and *Denmark joined in the Union of Kalmar (1397) until the Danish-perpetrated "Stock-holm Bloodbath" ended it in 1520. With Gustavus Vasa (ruled 1523–1560), Sweden established a strong royal line, sided with the Lutheran Reformation (below), and for a time became the leading power of Northern Eu-rope.

Most Swedish wars have been with Den-mark over control of what is now southern Sweden. For six centuries until 1809, Finland was part of Sweden; the aim was to control the Baltic Sea. This was also one reason for Sweden's participation in the Thirty Years' War. Since 1815, it has avoided war, re-maining neutral in World Wars I and II. Throughout its history, Sweden has been a free nation, with the people being represented in parliament since the 15th century. Until the industrial revolution around 1870, the Swedes were mainly freehold farmers. With the increase in population in the 19th century and before industrialization, tens of thou-sands emigrated, most of them to North America. Industrialization made the country one of the richest in the world. It is also well-endowed with natural resources, such as for-ests and iron ore. Social changes have never come through revolution, but in an evolu-tionary manner. Since World War II, Sweden has received more migrants and refugees than any other country of Northern Europe—large

groups of Estonians, Finns, Yugoslavs, Danes, Greeks, Turks, Iranians, Africans, and Latin Americans. Today, every eighth person is either a migrant or the child of migrants. The largest group are the Finns. Sweden is known for its liberal immigration policy, which, in 1975, was formulated in terms of three principles: equality, freedom of choice, and cooperation. These imply that migrants have a right to preserve their identity and culture. To implement the policy, chil-dren of migrants may have education in their own language, and workers may have time off to study Swedish. Furthermore, immi-grants have the right to vote in local elections.

Religion: Lutherans 92%. The long con-formity to Lutheran tradition began to be re-laxed in 1860, and the trend continued until full religious freedom was legislated in 1951. The Swedish Ecumenical Council was formed in 1932, its present constitution dat-ing from 1970. Its membership, besides the Church of Sweden, includes the Mission Covenant Church of Sweden, the Baptist Union of Sweden, the Methodist Church, the Salvation Army, the Roman Catholic Church, the Swedish Evangelical Mission, and as-sociations like the Student Christian Move-ment and the YMCA/YWCA. Its associate members include the Swedish Alliance Mis-sion, the Pentecostal Movement, the French Reformed Church, the Örebro Mission, and several Orthodox and Oriental churches.

After a lapse of over 450 years, Sweden and the Vatican have resumed diplomatic re-lations. A papal pronuncio presented his cre-dentials in Stockholm in October 1982, and a Swedish ambassador presented his in the Vatican in April 1983.

With the extensive immigration after World War II, especially in the 1960s, the scope of religious life was notably enlarged. Between 1960 and 1980, the number of Ro-man Catholics increased from 29,000 to 102,000. By 1985, there were 130,000 Ro-man Catholics in Sweden. The Freedom of Religion Act (1951) gave the Roman Catholic Church the right to establish monasteries and convents in Sweden. A number of religious orders are active in the country and staff mi-nor institutions.

The Orthodox immigrants generally live over more scattered areas than the Roman Catholic and now number 66,000 (as com-pared to 10,000 in 1960). The predominant national groups are Greeks, Yugoslavs, Estonians, Finns, and Orthodox from the Middle East. The Orthodox make great use of the established church's places of religious assembly.

There are also some purely exile churches, for example the Estonian Orthodox and Estonian Lutheran. Not least noteworthy within the immigrant religious communities are the large number of Pentecostal congregations, especially among the Finns.

Judaism has eight congregations in Sweden, with some 15,000 members. Three of these congregations have their own rabbis. There are about 2000 Buddhists and perhaps 30,000 Muslims. The latter are mainly immigrants from Turkey, North Africa, and the Middle East. Finally, the proliferation of imported and domestic sects is making rapid inroads on the traditional religious situation.

Nonmembers of the Church of Sweden are required to pay one-third of the church tax to cover the vital statistics service (which keeps records on all Swedish nationals) as well as the upkeep of all cemeteries. At the same time, each church with a membership of 3000 receives a state subsidy toward their activities, church buildings, and pastors' salaries. In 1985, government grants, totaling SEK 35 million, were divided among the Free churches, and the immigrant churches.

CHURCH OF SWEDEN

(Svenska Kyrkan)
Member: LWF (1947), WCC, CEC, SEC
Membership: 7,700,000
Archbishop of Uppsala and Primate:
The Most Rev. Dr. Bertil Werkström
PO Box 640
S—751 27 Uppsala 1

This largest of all Lutheran churches comprises 1384 parishes (2566 congregations) served by 4827 ordained pastors, a growing number of whom are women. The many others in church work include deaconesses, deacons, teachers, missionaries, parish workers, youth workers, and those in specialized ministries.

The Church of Sweden has been intimately linked with the state since the Lutheran Reformation was formally accepted in 1527. Today, Sweden has a dual image. On the one

hand, about 95% of the total population—including many active Pentecostals, Baptists, and others—are still members of the Church of Sweden; 82% of the newborn are baptized; 74% of the youth are confirmed in church; 65% of all weddings take place in church, and 96% of all funerals. Since the 17th century, the pastors have doubled as registrars of the nation's vital statistics in their keeping of parish records. Their involvement in rites of passage is not only a heavy responsibility but also a mark of continuing ties between the church and the people. This folk church sees itself as entrusted with a message for the population as a whole. On the other hand, actual church attendance averages only about 5% of the population per Sunday. No one knows how many more people participate in public worship via radio and television in the privacy of their homes. Nor is it easy to assess the indifference to the church—or the rejection of it—manifest in many parts of society. Yet, it is estimated that nearly 500,000 church members are unbaptized, and the number is increasing. Some of these may have dual membership in Baptist or Pentecostal churches practicing adult baptism.

The Church of Sweden has an episcopal polity, including apostolic succession. The archbishop, first among equals in episcopal office, is the church's presiding officer and represents the church ecumenically. He chairs the newly formed (below) Commission on International and Ecumenical Affairs. Organizationally, the Church of Sweden comprises 13 dioceses. The oldest ones—Skara, Linköping, Strängnäs, and Västerås—were established around 1100, the newest—Stockholm—in 1942. In between come the others, each with its own features and named for an historic city—Uppsala, Visby, Växjö, Lund, Göteborg, Karlstad, Härnösand, and Luleå. The dioceses comprise deaneries (districts) and the deaneries, parishes. For their self-government, parishes have elected councils. Dioceses have chapters with executive functions, as well as biennial diocesan conventions of clergy and laity and diocesan synods, normally every six years, for the clergy.

Until 1985, the central administration of the church was carried on by five official boards. Then—with a major restructuring of internal affairs—the church created nine commissions to supervise work in various fields under a Central Board: Worship and

Evangelism, Diaconia and Social Responsibility, Education, Parish Administration, Communication and Media, International and Ecumenical Affairs, Church of Sweden Abroad, Church of Sweden Mission, and Church of Sweden Aid/Lutherhjälpen. In 1988, the first four were concentrated into a Commission for Congregational Work.

Modern organizational structures facilitate the functioning of the church and are fostering closer cooperation locally, among the parishes. The Swedish Parish Association renders administrative counseling to parishes, some of which were formed prior to 1300. The Union of Church Personnel strengthens it members in their professional role.

The government, generally speaking, is the highest authority in the administration of the church. The king and the government's minister for civil affairs must be members of the Church of Sweden. Under Sweden's new constitution (1975), the king is regarded as the first member of the Church of Sweden. The government appoints bishops and cathedral deans.

Church reforms were instituted in 1982, when the national parliament and the old church assembly adopted legislation that reformed structural and functional aspects of the ongoing church/state relationship. Henceforth, the church has independent rights of decision making in areas of doctrine, sacraments and worship, books of worship, special offerings, evangelism, social services, and world mission. For its part, the government retains the above-mentioned right of appointment to top ecclesial offices as well as the control of local municipal laws affecting church/parish management.

For the church at large the big change lies in the realms of self-government, notably in the general assembly. Formerly this 96-member body met every five years, or more often when needed. Now the general assembly meets annually, its 251 members being elected for a three-year term. The church assembly is not a legislative body in the full sense—parliament alone has that right—but from the government it has delegated authority to decide certain questions, such as those bearing on worship, doctrine, and practice in the church. Being preponderantly lay in composition, many different parts of the country as well as categories of laity are represented. The church assembly reflects on a national

scale the sociopolitical patterns of democracy in Sweden—patterns already prevailing in local parish councils. Of the 90 clergy elected to the first enlarged assembly, only three were bishops. The remaining bishops, however, attend the assembly, having voice but not vote. Efforts succeeded (1985) to give all bishops a vote as well as voice, regardless of whether or not they had stood for election to the assembly.

In theological matters the assembly is advised by a newly created confessional council, comprising all the bishops plus eight others. Likewise, a new executive council of 15, headed by the archbishop, carries out the decisions and policies determined by the assembly, and prepares that body's agenda. These changes reflect the outcome of decades of debate and are intended to facilitate the church's proper task in the realm of faith and life.

Thorny issues confront the assembly, among them the nature of membership in the Church of Sweden. Shall it be by baptism? Or simply, as customary, by birthright, through one baptized parent? Another is the confessional character of the Church of Sweden. An assembly-sponsored study of the Church of Sweden's status as an "Evangelical Lutheran denomination" is due in time for the 400th anniversary of the Council of Uppsala of 1593, the year the country became officially Lutheran. The outcome of this study promises to be significant ecumenically as well as confessionally for many other Lutheran churches.

The assembly's power has not gone unchallenged. Its declaration (1984) that no pastor be ordained who is unwilling to work with female clergy led to the formation of a free synod within the Church of Sweden. This synod is determined to oppose the further ordination of women. However, 12 of the 13 bishops do ordain women and the church has 550 women pastors.

The church, meanwhile, has helped the Swedish people to develop a stronger sense of interrelatedness among themselves and with people in other countries and continents. Many Swedes, who live in one of the most affluent societies in the world, have become conscious both of the needs of the exploited people in Africa, Asia, and Latin America, and of the bad consequences of the consumer attitude at home. Agencies within the church—voluntarily supported—have transformed this frustration into a sense of responsibility and into positive action.

Church of Sweden Aid (Lutherhjälpen)—a department of the Church of Sweden's LWF national committee until 1985, when it was restructured under a commission of its own—has for years raised about U.S. $11 million for development aid overseas, largely through a campaign during Lent. Lutherhjälpen has become the biggest voluntary donor agency in the country and has personified the LWF. (The Commission on International and Ecumenical Affairs now serves as the LWF national committee.) The Ecumenical Development Week, which was initiated in 1972, continues to play a very important role for church and society in Sweden. Since 1985, this campaign week is organized under the name of Development Forum of the Swedish Churches, in order to underline the year-round engagement for peace, justice, and global sharing of resources.

These accents on development are complemented by others on the proclamation of the gospel. The Church of Sweden Mission (1874) remains active in *South Africa, *Zimbabwe, *Tanzania, *Liberia, *Ethiopia, *India, and *Malaysia. Each year it raises US $7 million for its far-flung work. The Swedish Evangelical Mission (1856) is active in *Ethiopia, *Tanzania, and *India. It fosters evangelism at home and renders services to seamen. The Swedish Mission of Bible True Friends (1911), a protest against liberalism, is active in Sweden as well as *Kenya and *Ethiopia. The Swedish Jerusalem Society (1900) works in *Israel.

To help meet the needs of migrant workers and their families the Church of Sweden Central Board for Evangelism and Parish Work set up a special committee in 1979. The task among the Finns, most of whom are Lutherans and members of the Church of Sweden, was relatively clear. But ways are still being sought to help the various types of Eastern Orthodox as well as other groups, without causing fears of proselytism, especially such as practiced by a number of free churches. In 1985, the Church of Sweden's parish work among Finnish people in Sweden became a part of the Commission on International and Ecumenical Affairs. The work is carried out in cooperation with the National Association for Parish Work among Finnish-Speaking People.

• • •

Christianity in Sweden traces its beginnings to the missionary endeavors of St. Ansgar (801-865), the first archbishop of Hamburg and "Apostle of Scandinavia." Pagan resistance finally yielded in the 11th century to German and English missionaries. The archdiocese of Uppsala, economic and legal privileges, an influential order founded by St. Bridget (at Vadstena) and the University of Uppsala (1477) were signs of the church's growing strength during the centuries before 1500. The introduction of the Reformation (1527) under King Gustavus Vasa was led by the brothers Olavus and Laurentius Petri (both of whom had studied at Wittenberg under Luther) and others. Olavus Petri led in producing sermon books, handbooks on revised church practice, a simplification of the Mass in Swedish, a translation of Luther's *Small Catechism* (1537) and of the entire Bible (1541), a hymnbook, and more besides. Laurentius Petri became the first Lutheran archbishop of Uppsala (1531), and was consecrated in that position by Petrus Magnus. Magnus had himself consecrated bishop of Strängnäs in 1525 while in Rome. Through Magnus, apostolic succession was continued in the Church of Sweden. In 1593, the convocation of clergy in Uppsala firmed the position of the Church of Sweden as Lutheran. The *Unaltered* (official designation 1530 version) *Augsburg Confession* was adopted as the doctrinal norm. Adherents of foreign religions were not tolerated. (A new confession of faith, more directed to the present day, is in preparation and scheduled to appear in 1993—the 400th anniversary of the Uppsala convocation.)

King Gustavus Adolphus (1594–1632) advanced the Lutheran commitment. As the most powerful northern monarch, he intervened in the Thirty Years' War in Germany and died in battle. Later, the founding of the University of Lund (1668) on land wrested from Danish occupation was a further sign of the Church of Sweden's extension into the southern part of the land. In the 18th century, the Edict of Toleration (1781) granted religious liberty to Christians of other confessions seeking to establish residence in Sweden. The same privilege was granted to Jews

(1782). Pietism had also been introduced through Swedes who had visited Halle and Moravian Herrnhut in Germany.

The 19th century brought upheavals in economic, cultural, political, and religious life. While the economy remained largely rural, cities grew, industrialization began, and emigration, especially to North America, promised a fresh start for many. This time of unrest greatly affected the Church of Sweden. Its earlier complete identification with the community began to dissolve. This is seen in the changing relations between church and state, on the one hand, and the Pietist-led struggle for church renewal, on the other. Mikko Juva (above, Finland) makes this serious situation clear:

First, parliamentary reform in 1866 abolished the "spiritual estate." Until that time, the church as a whole had a representative body in the diet. In its place, a church synod was established as the supreme legislative organ of the church. It consisted of pastors and laymen, with the latter a majority. Its task was to take part in the shaping of church law, although the final right of decision lay with parliament. The Church of Sweden thus possessed an instrument both to defend the confession of the church and to adopt positions on contemporary questions on the basis of that confession.

Second, religious and nonreligious critics brought the Church of Sweden under heavy fire. In the latter part of the 19th and early in the 20th century, most of the movements of religious renewal separated from the established church. This was contrary to developments in other Nordic countries. In Sweden, many rejected the national church as unchristian. Revival movements contended that the real community of God is a free fellowship of believers, joined by individuals on the basis of a personal decision of faith. The state church was seen as a danger because, in offering baptism and the Lord's Supper to all, it appeared to ally believers and unbelievers. The Church of Sweden, shaken by the attack, lost its best members in tens of thousands.

Third, in reply, leaders like Einar Billing (1871–1939), bishop of Västerås, envisioned a "religiously motivated national church." When the visible historical Swedish church adopts a person into its fellowship, it is an expression of the anticipating (prevenient) grace of God. The outward form of the national church from which no one is excluded is the "forgiveness of sins accorded to the Swedish people." Without testing who is fit or unfit, as the separated free churches do, the Church of Sweden calls all human beings to participate in the sacraments and in the hearing of God's Word. This church adheres to the Evangelical Lutheran confession of faith but does not examine its members with confessional documents in its hands.

Fourth, the "Young Church Movement" led by Billing and others has marked the Swedish church to this day. It has provided leaders with a basis on which to act. However, the problem now lies at the local level. Many people who have joined the separatist free churches remain nominal members of the Church of Sweden, a membership which is a civil matter.

In this century, the ecumenical pioneer, Nathan Söderblom (1866–1931), gave new stature and direction to the office of archbishop. His sustained efforts toward peace— from Sweden's neutral ground during World War I—and his initiatives leading to the Stockholm Conference on Life and Work (1925) attest to this change. The role of the archbishop of Uppsala continues significant as the Church of Sweden pursues its ecumenical involvement and international concern.

A noteworthy instance of this was the Swedish initiative in the April 1983 ecumenical conference on "Life and Peace." Held in Uppsala under joint sponsorship of the northern churches, it drew some 160 leading representatives from Orthodox, Roman Catholic, Anglican, and Protestant communions in all continents. Appealing to the superpowers and to the UN for the advancement of justice and an end to the nuclear arms race, the conference strengthened the witness of others as well, including the WCC and the USA Roman Catholic bishops, at this awesomely foreboding time in history.

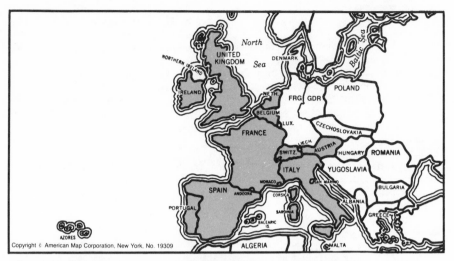

Copyright © American Map Corporation, New York, No. 19309

WESTERN AND MIDDLE EUROPE

The 11 countries treated here follow in alphabetical order: Austria, Belgium, France, Ireland, Italy, Liechtenstein, the Netherlands, Portugal, Spain, Switzerland, and the United Kingdom. Their combined Lutheran constituencies do not exceed 700,000, less than 2% of Europe's inclusive Lutheran total. But their dispersed presence is significant and their varied histories form an instructive collage.

To be attentive to the Lutheran minorities in Western and Middle Europe is to learn something about a confession in dispersion. In these countries Lutherans are at times struggling minorities, seeking ways to maintain themselves purposefully—often on minimal resources. A sign of the times is that even churches with long histories, like those in France and the Netherlands, show a declining membership.

Yet the focus is here not only on components of a confession but also on the ecclesial and ecumenical context of these Lutheran churches as well as their countries. In fact, among these countries are those which over centuries have represented the worldwide expansion of Europe and thus have facilitated settlement in the Americas and other continents as well as the spread of the gospel. Especially Britain (the United Kingdom) has played a vital part in the deployment of Lutheran emigrants from Germany and Scandinavia to other parts of the world, even as during and after World War II it was host to Lutheran and other refugees from the continent.

The Lutheran minorities in these lands are today's living reminders of the need for Lutherans everywhere to be and remain ecumenically alive, employing their identity to enrich the give-and-take between people of different confessional backgrounds. They also remind the LWF family, although collectively large, that it, too, is a minority in the church universal.

AUSTRIA

A republic (1919), the remaining centerpiece of the former Austro-Hungarian Empire. Area: 83,853 sq. km. (32,376 sq. mi.). Pop. (1985 est.): 7,552,000. Cap. and largest city: Vienna (pop., 1985, 1,531,346). Language: German.

History: Austria's past is the saga of East meeting West. From imperial Rome's first-century A.D. occupation of Vindobona (Vienna) as a strategic frontier settlement on the Danube to the location of several United Nations agencies in 20th-century Vienna, Austria's history illuminates the emergence of modern Europe. In A.D. 811, this land became the Ostmark—the eastern frontier—of Charlemagne's Frankish empire. In 1273, Rudolf of Hapsburg, a small duchy between the present sites of Zurich and Basel, was crowned king of the Germans. He established himself in Austria and became the first in the succession of Hapsburg rulers, a line from which came the emperors of the Holy Roman Empire of the German Nation, 1440–1806.

As Austria expanded—Tyrol was added in 1363, Bohemia (*Czechoslovakia) and *Hungary in 1526—its domination of many German lands was successfully challenged by Prussia. In 1867, the Austro-Hungarian Empire was formed, and the emperor of Austria, Franz Josef I, became king of Hungary. The dual monarchy had a common foreign policy. With the dissolution of the empire in 1918, Austria was reduced to a republic composed of nine small states. The turbulent years between the two world wars included the *Anschluss,* or union with Nazi Germany in 1938. After 1945, Austria reemerged as a republic. Following a period of four-power military occupation by Russian, French, British, and American forces, it resumed its role as a free East/West meeting point. At last Austria saw itself as a nation and not simply as a remnant of the Hapsburg empire.

Religion: 84.3% (est.) of the population are Roman Catholic. The Roman Church, with two archdioceses—Vienna and Salzburg—and seven dioceses, has a long history that is bound up with that of the state. Toleration was granted religious minorities in 1781 (under Emperor Joseph II). Today, Lutherans comprise 5.2% of the population and are by far the largest non-Roman communion. A Jewish community has regained something of its traditional place (1981: 7127). The last census (1981) showed that 76,932 people were followers of Islam. There has been a high increase in the number of people belonging to no religious denomination. The Ecumenical Council of Churches in Austria (ECCA; 1958) includes Reformed, Orthodox, Old Catholic, Methodist, and Anglican as well as Lutheran bodies in its membership.

EVANGELICAL CHURCH OF THE AUGSBURG CONFESSION IN AUSTRIA (ECACA)

(Evangelische Kirche Augsburgischen Bekenntnisses in Österreich
Member: LWF (1947), WCC, CEC, ECCA
Membership: 357,620
Bishop: The Rt. Rev. Dieter Knall
Severin Schreiber-Gasse 3
A—1180 Vienna

Members of this church are gathered in 181 congregations served by 300 pastors. There are also over 80 filial or branch congregations too small to support a pastor of their own and nearly 800 preaching stations. The church is divided into seven geographic districts, each under a superintendent. Although church members are scattered across the country, there are several pockets of concentration, around Villach in Kärnten, and in certain mountain valleys. A good quarter of the church's total membership resides in Vienna.

The church's polity, reaffirmed by its constitution of 1949, provides for self-government at the congregational level through local church councils, and the treatment of regional concerns at the district level. The legislative body of the whole church is the synod, which appoints the synodical executive board and the administrative board (superior church council), and elects the bishop. Pastors of congregations, superintendents, and the bishop are elected for life, i.e., from the time they take up office until they reach the age of 68.

For purpose of legal recognition by the government, the Lutheran majority and the small Reformed minority comprise an ecclesiastical entity named the Evangelical Church of the Augsburg and the Helvetic Confessions

(ECAHC), a designation that provides for cooperation in certain areas but leaves the two groups fully independent as to confessional identity and administration. The ECAHC dual legal entity is the basis of Austrian Lutheran and Reformed participation in the WCC, an arrangement akin to that of Germany's Lutherans participating under the Evangelical Church in Germany (EKD). Austrian Lutherans are LWF members through their own ecclesiastical body, the ECACA, just as the Reformed are members of the World Alliance of Reformed Churches (WARC) through their own Reformed Church of Austria.

Worship has remained the central reality and source of power in the life of the church, and Christian education for school children and young people is a task of prime importance. Pastors and lay workers give religious instruction to about 45,000 children in nearly 4000 places.

Various types of ongoing education and missionary outreach are provided for pastors and laity. Problems, to be sure, have persisted, notably those springing from indifference. Since 1961, the edict regarding the legal rights of the Evangelical Church has provided public support for the Evangelical Theological Faculty in the University of Vienna, for the religious instruction given by the church, and for military chaplaincies and church-related welfare services.

The ordination of women, authorized already in the mid-1960s, filled a definite need of the ECACA. Since 1980, there has been full equality between women and men in the ministry of the church.

Jointly with the Reformed, the ECACA has an active communications program, including radio and television as well as publications. The *Evangelischer Pressedienst fur Österreich* (epd-Ö) is a news service with an ecumenical horizon. Overseas, the church works through the Association of Churches and Missions in Southwestern *Germany (EMS), supporting work in *Ghana, *Cameroon, *India, *Papua New Guinea, and *Chile.

Over many years, the Gustav-Adolf-Werk and the Martin-Luther-Bund in Germany have assisted the Austrian church to meet its building needs. LWF help in postwar church reconstruction and service to refugees—a Federation field office, 1950–1966, and a

program to help integrate some 4000 "forgotten" refugees into Austrian life—have served to reaffirm that Austrian Lutheranism is significant far beyond its relatively small numbers.

• • •

The Lutheran Reformation came early to Austria and made rapid initial gains. Unlike Hungary, Austria has only a few Reformed. The Turkish threat may have helped to make the Hapsburgs temporarily more lenient toward Lutherans in Austria than elsewhere. In the 1570s, church orders (liturgy, constitution, guidelines) on the Saxony model were provided for Lutheran parishes in Lower Austria, Styria, and Carinthia. During the 17th century, however, the Counter-Reformation began to make headway, and Lutheranism in effect went underground for six generations. The driving into exile of 20,694 Lutherans from the archdiocese of Salzburg on Reformation Day 1731 drew wide attention to their plight. Most of them were resettled in East Prussia (*Poland); others, via England, in the North American colony of Georgia (LCA, *USA; now ELCA).

Emperor Joseph II's Edict of Toleration (1781) signaled a reappearance of Lutheranism and the formation of congregations on a self-supporting basis. These developments began (1707) in Teschen (*Poland), at that time an Austrian principality. During the 19th century, the situation improved. In 1821, the theological school was authorized, which in 1922 became the Evangelical Faculty in the University of Vienna. In 1861, a Lutheran church government, initially in Teschen, was set up by the imperial court in Vienna; its structure underlies the present one.

The "Free from Rome" movement in the late 19th and early 20th century increased the numerical strength of Lutheranism considerably. Accessions through mixed marriages and conversions from Roman Catholicism, and also through Lutheran refugees from Southeastern Europe (*Yugoslavia, *Hungary, *Romania), particularly between the end of World War II and the Hungarian uprising of 1956, also swelled the Lutheran ranks. During the tempestuous years of this century, the Lutheran congregations have found their faith tested (under Nazi occupation), their spiritual life deepened, their assistance to others enlarged, and their partnership with churches at home and abroad strengthened ecumenically as well as confessionally.

Postwar leadership over the past four decades has seen three able bishops. To Gerhard May went the task of pulling things together and, over a period of more than two decades, helping the church to achieve a fresh sense of unity. With others, he worked hard for the passage of the *Protestantengesetz,* the 1961 law that at last accorded Protestant individuals and churches the same rights as those enjoyed by the Roman Catholic Church and its members.

Bishop May's successor, Oskar Sakrausky, saw the church in distinctly Austrian terms and not as an extension of the Evangelical Church in Germany. He spoke his mind on such debated issues as abortion, opposing it publicly also against Chancellor Bruno Kreisky. Besides, Sakrausky's was a strong voice favoring the already-mentioned sense of nationhood that marks the new Austria. The present bishop, in office since 1982, has brought a welcome ecumenical vision to his task. A native of *Romania, he is a Transylvanian Saxon who knows the Eastern European situation well. in fact, Austrian Lutherans have a readier access than most others to those in the East. When, for example, the East Germans received permission to build 10 churches in new housing areas in the *Democratic Republic, they came to Austria to find out how a small body like the ECACA managed something similar on very limited funds. And the Austrians, in turn, would not have been able to do so well—as a minority— without themselves being helped by others. The ECACA is thus a lively example of interdependence.

BELGIUM

A constitutional monarchy (1830), one of the Benelux countries. Area: 30,519 sq. km. (11,783 sq. mi.). Pop. (1985 est.): 9,859,000. Cap. and largest urban area: Brussels (pop., 1985 est., metro. area 989,877, commune 138,910). Language: Dutch (Flemish), French, and German.

History: The land of the Belgae was conquered by Julius Caesar and for 1800 years was ruled by others, including Rome, the Franks, Burgundy, Spain, Austria, and France. After Napoleon's defeat at Waterloo (1815) near Brussels, this region, inhabited by Flemings in the north and Walloons in the south, became part of the Netherlands. In 1830, an independent Belgium emerged. Its inviolability was guaranteed in 1839 by the Treaty of London. Nevertheless, it was occupied by Germany during both world wars and twice sustained heavy losses. Yet the nation has endured and retained international significance. In 1960, it granted independence to *Zaire (the former Belgian Congo). At home, the old controversy between French-speaking Walloons and Dutch-speaking Flemings has continued to the present.

Religion: Predominantly (98%) Roman Catholic. Belgian Roman Catholics have a long record of ecumenical activity (e.g., Cardinal Mercier in the 1920s, Cardinal Suenens in the 1960s).

The archdiocese of Malines-Bruxelles (1559) and six other dioceses comprise the Belgian hierarchy. Three ecumenical centers deserve special notice: the Benedictine Monastery at Chèvetogne (1926) fosters Roman Catholic-Eastern Orthodox rapprochement. The Ecumenical Center for Church and Society, Brussels (1965), is in touch with various international agencies while guided and supported by the Churches' Commission to the European Communities (the Common Market nations and others). The Foyer Oriental Chrétien "Pro Russia," Brussels (1954), promotes the study of Russian Orthodoxy.

The various Eastern Orthodox groups (mainly Greek and Russian) number over 60,000.

The major Protestant body—United Protestant Church of Belgium (UPCB)—is a product of earlier unions, including Methodists, and of still earlier mission efforts by Swiss, French, and Dutch Reformed. Its organization in 1979 brought to an end the Federation of Protestant Churches in Belgium (1922) and the Protestant Missionary Department in Belgium. The UPCB counts over 35,000 members. Jehovah's Witnesses, having entered Belgium in 1901, claim nearly as many.

Lutherans in Belgium are mainly expatriates whose congregations are supported in part by home churches or agencies. The **Norwegian Seamen's Church,** having ministered in Antwerp since 1865, also reaches out to Norwegian communities in Brussels and Mons, in Belgium, as well as to others in Luxembourg and northern France. The **Danish seamen's churches** are in Antwerp and Ghent and another congregation is in Brussels. Also in Antwerp are the **Finnish Seamen's Mission** and a congregation maintained by the Church of Sweden.

The **German-speaking Evangelical Congregation in Belgium** has a church building in Brussels (Avenue Salome 7, Woluwe St. Pierre). It deploys its three pastors to various parts of the country. With assistance from the Foreign Office of the Evangelical Church in Germany (EKD), it serves some 5000 members—Lutheran, Reformed, and United.

The Germans share their facilities with the **American Lutheran Church of Brussels** (ALCB). This independent congregation serves not only Lutherans but also other English-speaking Protestants. Since its organization in 1979, the Lutheran Church in America (now ELCA) has supplied pastors, who also serve a satellite congregation at the SHAPE (military) headquarters in Mons. The ALCB supports projects of the LWF and also those of the UPCB (above). It is an active member of the Association of International Churches in Europe and the Middle East.

The only indigenous Lutheran church body is the very small one listed below. An effort to gather the diverse congregations into a federation that might strengthen their combined efforts seems lacking.

Although Lutherans today are a tiny minority, Lutheranism had an early and dramatic beginning in Belgium. The Reformation was eagerly welcomed as early as 1518, when the gospel was proclaimed in the Augustinian church in Antwerp. The monks of the local Augustinian monastery had been profoundly influenced by their German brother-member, Martin Luther. In 1523, two of them, Hendrik Vos and Jans van Essen, were burned at the stake in Brussels for being his followers. Antwerp also attracted merchants from the northern countries of Europe, many of whom were Lutherans. Finally, Antwerp Marranos (Jews from Spain and Portugal who had been converted to Christianity by force) took an interest in the new movement.

An important Lutheran congregation, combining these three elements, came into being in 1566. Under the leadership of German clergy, among them Flacius Illyricus

(1520–1575), a confession of faith and a church order were composed. The latter gave the congregation an ecclesiastical administration independent of the government. For a short time, it seemed as though the whole region would become Protestant. However, Emperor Charles V (1500–1558) and his son, Philip II (1527–1598), used all their power to exterminate the movement. Thousands of Lutherans and other Protestants paid for their faith with their lives, and hundreds of thousands left their home country. The Antwerp congregation fled to Amsterdam and reorganized in 1588 (see Netherlands).

BELGIAN EVANGELICAL LUTHERAN CHURCH OF THE AUGSBURG CONFESSION (BELCAC)—PARISH OF THE HOLY TRINITY

(Eglise évangélique luthérienne belge de la confession d'Augsbourg—Paroisse de la Sainte Trinité)
(R)
Membership: 614**
Chair: The Rev. Corneil J. Hobus
26 rue du Major René Dubreucq
B—1050 Brussels

In 1950, the Parish of the Holy Trinity in Brussels withdrew from the Evangelical Lutheran Church—Synod of France and Belgium (*France) and formed the BELCAC. The intention was to have an indigenous Belgian church open to fellowship with other Lutheran churches and to a relationship with the LWF. The government authorization entitled the new church, as others in Belgium, to state support for its pastors. The LWF recognizes Holy Trinity parish, and its chief pastor has participated in European conferences. Although the relationship with the *Lutheran Church–Missouri Synod was broken, the church still benefits from the "Lutheran Hour" radio ministry broadcast from Luxembourg. At present, the BELCAC has two pastors, one serving outposts in the Flanders and Walloon areas. Membership has been declining during the last decade.

EVANGELICAL LUTHERAN CHURCH—SYNOD OF FRANCE AND BELGIUM (see France)

FRANCE

A republic (First Republic, 1792; Fifth, 1958). Area: 544,000 sq. km. (210,040 sq. mi.), including Corsica. Pop. (1984): 54,879,000. Cap. and largest city: Paris (pop., 1982, 2,176,200). Language: French, plus local languages like Basque or Alsatian in a half-dozen border regions.

History: As Gaul in the ancient Roman empire, as a place of transit or settlement for invading tribes from Eastern Europe, as the main part of the Frankish empire of Charlemagne, and as one of the early nations (13th century) of modern Europe, France has played a leading role in shaping and spreading European civilization. This process was hastened by the French Revolution (1789–1793), the First Republic (1792–1804), and the First Empire under Napoleon (1804–1814). The rivalry of France with neighboring lands—notably Spain, Italy, Britain, and Germany—has affected the course of European and world history in recent centuries. It also had its effect on the course of church history.

Religion: Roman Catholic (1980 est.) 81%; Protestant 2%; Orthodox 0.5%, and various other religious groups, including two million Moslems. As in many other countries, figures do not reflect accurately a situation in which secularism has progressively replaced Christianity and made the work of the churches difficult but, at times, also creative. Christian beginnings in France go back at least to the second century. Since that time, French Christians have repeatedly given new impulses to the unity and mission of the church. Toward that end, the first (314) of a long succession of synods at Arles, on the Rhone, decided against the divisive teaching of Donatism. It declared that the efficacy of a sacrament does not depend on the character of the officiating priest, a decision that holds to this day. In the early Middle Ages, the monastery at Cluny—north of Lyons—became the starting point (910) of church renewal in many parts of Western Europe, a process that has repeated itself in various

ways ever since. Visible reminders of the so-called Age of Faith in France are its unsurpassed array of 13th-century Gothic cathedrals, churches, and chapels; while the seven decades of papal captivity at Avignon, on the Rhone, recall the rise of French nationhood and royal power over the church during the 14th century.

The Protestant Reformation, when Lutheran overtures were followed by the far more French-oriented Calvinism, for a time gained an impressive following, only to be blocked by the rigorous Roman Counter-Reformation. The fierce massacre of St. Bartholomew's Day (1572), the limited toleration, and then its revocation (1685) sent Huguenot refugees en masse (300,000) to Holland and Germany, to Switzerland and Britain, and overseas to North America and South Africa—much to the benefit of the host countries. The recent tricentennial commemoration made many French people discover the horrors and mistakes of the Counter-Reformation. After the French Revolution, Roman Catholicism faced a new situation. Religious toleration curbed old powers and fostered new ones—especially in the changing relations between church and society, the challenges of worldwide mission, and the deepening of attachment to Rome (Ultramontanism).

Today's French Roman Catholicism, influenced by Vatican II as well as influencing it, is holding its own in a secularized nation. Among the notable changes in recent decades is the structuring of the hierarchy into nine *régions apostoliques* (1961). Together they embrace the 17 archdioceses and over 70 dioceses, and enable each district to develop and administer appropriate pastoral programs. In liturgy, theology, and ecumenical dialog, the French church has produced leaders; even as it has also had to contend with reaction against change within its ranks. The bishops' conference has tried to take a stand in a number of current problems, the private school issue remaining particularly sensitive. Meanwhile, French Roman Catholicism has, until recently, exercised undisputed leadership in this century in Catholic action and theological thought. French remains the leading language in international gatherings of the Roman Church. Besides, there are more French-using Roman Catholics in other lands (Africa, Madagascar, Canada, etc.) than in

France itself. The same is true of Protestants; those in Francophone lands outnumber those in France.

From the 19th century onward, Protestants have likewise unfolded new enterprise, yet always with modest means. Although the Reformed Church of France continues as the nation's main Protestant body, it admittedly suffers from a chronic malaise. Internal conflict in the last century between liberal and conservative forces dissipated its energies, while social mobility in more recent times has dispersed its membership. This new diaspora at least stimulates new resourcefulness.

Amid turbulent modern times a renewal venture was launched in Taizé, near Cluny (1947), after a preparatory stage in Switzerland (1940). Begun by Swiss and French Protestants as a Protestant monastic community, it has attracted adherents from many other countries and confessions. Taizé's major concern is the unity of the church. Its vibrant outreach to young people in every continent has few equals and is creatively ecumenical.

Despite its modest material resources, French Protestantism—mainly Reformed but with Lutheran participation—has developed new ways of working with fellow Christians nearby as well as far away in fostering the gospel outreach. In 1971, the historic Paris Evangelical Missionary Society (PEMS) of 1822 was dissolved. In its place, the five major Protestant bodies, including the two Lutheran churches, formed the French Protestant Department of Apostolic Action, which is a branch of the Evangelical Community for Apostolic Action (*Communauté Evangélique d'Action Apostolique—CEVAA*) formed by 27 French-speaking churches in Europe, Africa, the Pacific Islands, and now even Argentina. Respecting diversity, CEVAA encourages its members to question those traditions and religious practices that sometimes paralyze action. CEVAA members relate to each other. Resources of both money and personnel are pooled and distributed according to the needs of each church.

Protestants have long lived with this reputation: To be French is to be Catholic; to be Protestant is to have a history of persecution. This aspect is now past. It is overshadowed by such events as the formal acceptance of the joint Roman Catholic-Protestant translation of the Bible in the Cathedral of Notre Dame, Paris, with a Lutheran church president, André Appel, as one of the main speakers (1975). Recently, documents against the sale of arms and on building peace have been issued jointly by the Protestant Commission on International Affairs and the Catholic Commission "Justitia."

The *Protestant Federation of France* (PFF; 1913) includes the major non-Roman and non-Orthodox communions, among them the Reformed, Lutheran, Baptist, and Pentecostals. The PFF works closely with lay movements and diaconic institutions. Its departments, services, and study commissions assist the member churches in the fields of study and research, youth work, government and public relations, communications, interchurch aid activities, ecumenical and international questions. Reformed and Lutherans engage jointly in several projects (pastoral training, cooperation with the Roman Catholic Church). Being in their country the only members of the World Council of Churches, they constitute in France a permanent Lutheran-Reformed Council to deal with their common call and with ecumenical affairs.

A particularly urgent ecumenical project—done in cooperation with the World Council of Churches—is that of service to migrant workers from abroad. As one of the largest recipients of them, France in 1985 had more than two million migrants—most of them from Spain, Portugal, Algiers, and other parts of Africa. French Lutherans and Reformed continue to tackle this problem, mainly through a common agency, the CIMADE, in order to help solve the many issues arising over it and to react against public apathy or criticisms.

The various Eastern Orthodox groups have been ecumenically involved here in distinctive ways. Paris has long been a center of Russian Orthodoxy, and its cultural strength—particularly among the emigrés from the 1917 revolution. It has the only Russian Orthodox theological school in Western Europe. At the other end of the denominational spectrum are Jehovah's Witnesses, largest (about 100,000) of the fringe groups.

Lutheran background: Lutherans in other continents are greatly indebted to those in France. It was contacts with French Lutherans during the closing stages of World War

I that made American Lutherans aware of the partnership in service awaiting the churches. In meeting with French leaders, representatives of the then newly formed National Lutheran Council (*USA and *Canada) became oriented to the European scene. These contacts contributed significantly to the subsequent creation of the Lutheran World Convention (LWC; 1923), predecessor of the LWF. In 1935, Lutherans in France were hosts in Paris to the third international meeting of the LWC. Thirty-five years later, French Lutherans became hosts to the LWF Fifth Assembly, when it was relocated on short notice from Brazil to Evian-les-Bains on the shores of Lac Léman.

In 1964, the Lutheran World Federation located its newly created Institute for Ecumenical Research in Strasbourg due to the favorable ecumenical climate in Alsace. The task of the institute is to assist the Lutheran churches of the world in fulfilling their theological responsibility in the area of ecumenism. The institute can also act as a pioneer in areas where Lutheran churches have not yet become engaged. Besides those in Strasbourg, consultations and seminars have been held in Africa, Asia, Latin America, and North America.

Still another aspect of international Lutheranism became visible in the commemoration of the 350th anniversary of the beginning of the Swedish church in Paris (1976), where Nathan Söderblom (1866–1931), later archbishop of Uppsala and ecumenical leader, once served as pastor. Observances of the Reformation era have also given fresh visibility to Lutheranism. A new translation of the *Augsburg Confession* as well as ecumenical dialog on the significance of that document for the unity of the church helped mark the 450th anniversary of the Augustana in 1980. In this connection, the Institute for Ecumenical Research played a leading part. Similarly, the 500th anniversary of Luther's birth (1983) was marked by various special publications, including the translation into French of Luther's Lectures on Romans— Volume XI of the growing Luther edition in French. *Positions Luthériennes,* a quarterly, also noted the Reformer's significance. The national postal service printed a Luther commemorative stamp not only for France but also for French Polynesia in the distant Pacific.

At this point, clarity requires some explanation for the two major Lutheran churches in France. Both have histories that go back to the Reformation era. Both have ties with the Reformed that antedate the modern ecumenical movement. And at one time there was no division.

It was in 1802 that Napoleon placed the three recognized confessions—Roman Catholic, Reformed, and Lutheran—under government supervision. The 1801 concordat with Rome had its Protestant counterparts. The terms of the Lutheran concordat included government subsidy of clergy's salaries. Fifty years later (1852), this arrangement was updated. The Lutheran church was united and administratively subdivided into eight inspectorates (districts). Six of these were in Alsace and Lorraine. The other two were based in Montbéliard and Paris. Lutheran outreach in the national capital, which developed in the 19th century, received substantial help from Alsace.

Then came the Franco-Prussian War (1870–1871). The sudden transfer of Alsace and Lorraine to Germany's Second Reich (proclaimed in Versailles, 1871) was a profound blow to the future of Lutheranism in France. The Lutheran remnant voted to retain its confessional identity, reaffirming adherence to the *Augsburg Confession*. But it also entered into closer cooperation with the Reformed. Together, Lutherans and Reformed set up the Free Protestant Faculty of Theology in Paris (1877), inasmuch as the one in Strasbourg was now on the German side.

A further and far-reaching change came in 1905 with the separation of church and state in France. Therewith government subsidies to the churches were discontinued. Church support now being on a voluntary basis, the Paris and Montbéliard inspectorates adapted their constitution and took the name Evangelical Lutheran Church of France (ELCF).

Late in 1918, after an absence of 47 years under German rule, Alsace and Lorraine returned to France. For the churches—Roman Catholic and Reformed as well as Lutheran— the terms of the concordats of 1801/1802 continued; meaning government subsidy and religious instruction in school, but also state appointment of clergy.

While the inequality in church support continues, the Church of the Augsburg Confession of Alsace and Lorraine and the Evangelical Lutheran Church of France find unity in the National Alliance of the Lutheran Churches in France (*Alliance nationale des églises luthériennes de France*—ANELF). It fosters the spiritual unity that arose out of the Lutheran Reformation, shares material and personnel resources, and seeks a common stance on matters affecting French Protestantism. To realize these aims, the ANELF has a theological commission and a Commission on Relations with Overseas Churches. The former prepared a common Lutheran statement on the WCC Faith and Order document "Baptism, Eucharist, and Ministry" (BEM). The latter serves as the mission agency for the two churches, sending missionaries to *Cameroon and *Madagascar and giving assistance to other French-speaking churches in the Two-Thirds World. ANELF also serves as the national committee of the LWF.

CHURCH OF THE AUGSBURG CONFESSION OF ALSACE AND LORRAINE (CACAL)

(Eglise de la Confession d'Augsbourg d'Alsace et de Lorraine)
Member: LWF (1947), WCC, CEC, PFF, ANELF, CPC
Membership: 220,000**
President: The Rev. Michel Hoeffel
1 A quai Saint-Thomas
F—67081 Strasbourg-Cedex

This historic church body retains the names of two ancient provinces—Alsace and Lorraine—which today constitute the territorial departments of Rhin, Bas-Rhin, and Moselle, where most of the Lutherans live. Protestants even in this region are a minority, but Lutherans outnumber Reformed by five to one—the only such instance in France. On the west of this most eastern part of France is the Montbéliard region, which is also largely Lutheran. To the south is Switzerland, with Basel at the border, and across the Rhine to the east is the Federal Republic of Germany. The more than 200 parishes of the church are served by about 250 pastors—both women and men—and by other lay ministries. French is the church language, but German is also used.

The church members are employed in agriculture, industry, business, and other professions and live in both rural villages and urban centers. Recently, the movement to the cities has accelerated, especially around Strasbourg, requiring the construction of new church centers and the training of lay workers for new mission responsibilities.

The church's organization still reflects features of the Napoleonic concordat relating it to the state (above), although recent restructuring is endeavoring to adapt ecclesial administration and programs to shifts in population and other changes. The central authority of the church is the supreme council, a 25-member body to which some are appointed and others elected. The council's executive committee of five consists of three members appointed by the French government and two elected by the supreme council. The church president, normally a layperson, is president of both the council and the executive committee, and is appointed by the government. A recent incumbent, Dr. André Appel, appointed in 1974, was the first theologian in this position. He also chaired the Conference of European Churches for over a decade (see Europe Introduction).

The church comprises seven inspectorates. An inspectorate is comparable to a diocese or district and consists of a number of consistories or circuits, each of which, in turn, is made up of a number of parishes. The head of an inspectorate exercises the powers of a bishop or synod president, including ordination. In 1975, the supreme council elected the first woman inspector, to the St. Thomas inspectorate, Strasbourg. In her seven years of office, Marie Louise Caron ordained a number of men—the first time, so far as is known, that this has occurred in a Lutheran church.

Church headquarters in Strasbourg are not far from the university where the theological faculty prepares most of the church's future pastors. Others are educated at the Lutheran and Reformed faculty in Paris, or abroad. The church assures the professional training of its pastors. For diaconic services to the young, the ill, and the elderly, the CACAL maintains a number of institutions. These range from deaconess houses of 19th-century origin to the modern conference center, Liebfrauenberg, north of the city of Haguenau. Many training programs, such as those among youth and in education and communication, as well as common services for society, are carried on jointly with the Reformed, with whom there is pulpit and altar fellowship.

• • •

Evangelical preaching was authorized through a city council vote in Strasbourg in 1521. The Reformation subsequently covered a third of the Alsatian country. Martin Bucer (1491–1551), early a friend of Luther and then also of Calvin, led in these developments and later on sought to mediate between the Wittenberg and Geneva forces of reform. Later still, when exiled to England, Bucer brought his Strasbourg position to bear on the Church of England through his lectures at Cambridge. Until Napoleon's unifying decisions, the political fragmentation of Alsace led to the rise of independent churches in various areas. Strasbourg remained the religious center. The Counter-Reformation prompted many to return to the Roman church, and the Thirty Years' War (1618–1648) brought destruction and suffering.

Persistence and vitality have marked this church. Its location made it a bridge between German Lutheran and French Reformed developments. Among those personifying this was Philipp Jakob Spener (1635–1705), the Strasbourg pastor, later serving in Frankfurt/Main and Berlin, and famed as the founder of Pietism. Jean Frédéric Oberlin (1740–1825), renewer of his impoverished "Stone Valley" community, became well known among Protestants also in Britain and America. Franz-Heinrich Haerter (1797–1874), the Alsatian evangelist and leader in Christian service, founded the deaconess motherhouse in Strasbourg (1842) only six years after Fliedner's pathbreaking venture for women's service in the church had begun in Kaiserswerth (*Germany). From Strasbourg, too, came ready help for the neglected German Lutheran migrant workers in Paris.

During the Franco-Prussian War (1870–1871), the siege of Strasbourg took a heavy toll. Although Alsace and Lorraine were embodied into the Second German Reich for the next decades (1871–1918), the church situation remained relatively unchanged. Earlier patterns of structure and support, as set by the French government (1801, 1852, above) continued; doing so—in the case of the CACAL, the Reformed, and the Roman Catholic churches—even after the return of these churches to France following World War I (above). Between the two world wars, the personality of Albert Schweitzer (1875–

1965) underscored the contribution of Alsatian Protestantism: theological insight and concrete application of faith.

World War II brought severe destruction and hardship to the church and its people. The spiritual and cultural heritage, however, persisted; and the editing of the works of Martin Bucer, the theological mediator, was symptomatic of a church opposed to isolation and given to partnership confessionally in the LWF and ecumenically in the WCC.

With Strasbourg a focal point of converging interests—in 1949 the city became the seat of the Council of Europe—the CACAL itself has assumed new bridging functions. The Conference of Churches Along the Rhine (CCR), in which the CACAL participates, gathers church bodies from *Austria, *Switzerland, the *Federal Republic of Germany, France, and the *Netherlands in a common effort to overcome old territorial and folk church patterns wherever these impede a response to the new missionary challenges brought by secularism and closer European cooperation.

EVANGELICAL LUTHERAN CHURCH OF FRANCE (ELCF)

(Eglise évangélique luthérienne de France)
Member: LWF (1947), WCC, CEC, PFF, ANELF
Membership: 40,000**
President: The Rev. Jean-Michel Sturm
13 rue Godefroy
75013 Paris

This church, made up of two inspectorates or districts, has about 50 parishes and an equal number of pastors and assisting staff. The smaller and widely scattered Paris inspectorate includes the congregations in the metropolitan Paris area as well as those in the cites of Lyons and Nice. The Montbéliard inspectorate centers in the industrial town of Montbéliard situated on the Rhone-Rhine canal almost directly west of Basel, Switzerland. The organization of the ELCF is synodical. The two districts have two regional conventions per year and come together in a general synodical meeting.

Like other French churches (the CACAL, above, being an exception) the ELCF is entirely dependent on voluntary contributions (above). This is especially difficult for a small church with a declining membership. In a day of increasing costs, contributions have not kept pace with obligations. After the devastating World War II, new church buildings were necessary. Debts were incurred. The shortage of pastors to serve and expand the congregations is due in part to the very low salaries. Their salary increase has been only half of that made by the state in the low-salaried category. This situation in both districts has necessitated the training and use of lay assistants in the teaching and preaching task of the church.

In the environs of Montbéliard, for example, extensive industrialization (including the Peugeot automobile works founded years ago by a Lutheran entrepreneur) has changed the social composition drastically. Some 150 years ago, this rural region between Basel and Besançon was almost entirely Protestant. Today, the proportion is one in six, and there is a definite anti-church atmosphere. Thus, the ELCF finds itself challenged to train new kinds of leaders for Bible study, counseling, and practical services to meet the problems of an industrialized society. Helpful in this endeavor is the district's conference center in nearby Glay for workshops, retreats, seminars. The facilities are also used for family retreats and special programs for the aging.

The Montbéliard inspectorate—its finances strained to the limit to provide church centers in the industrial areas—now faces a reverse situation. Many of the people are moving back to their home villages and commuting to work. Meanwhile, many old churches, some dating back to the 16th and 17th centuries, have been in disuse or neglected. They now need costly renovation for modern use. A group of volunteers have offered to help with the restorations. Nevertheless, the cost is beyond the resources of the local congregations and synod, and financial assistance comes from other churches through the LWF Department of Church Cooperation (DCC).

In the Paris area, movement is also away from the center of the city—where many of the churches are located—to the rapidly expanding suburbs where two-thirds of the members now live. New church centers, especially in the eastern and northern suburbs, have also been financed in part through the LWF/DCC. Although a tiny dispersed minority, the Paris inspectorate has undertaken new approaches for evangelization among its own members as well as to the countless unchurched. The projects of a special organization called the "Mission Intérieure" include: the broadcasting of programs over the new private radio stations; increased work among students of many nationalities and religious backgrounds; a center for Africans coming to Paris; a cassette program for evangelization; and summer work among tourists.

The Paris district works closely with the Reformed Church of France with whom there has been altar and pulpit fellowship for a long time. Besides some joint congregational activities, this includes pastoral care to military personnel, prisoners, and students; radio and TV projects; and the support of the Protestant Theological Institute where most ELCF pastors are trained.

The monthly paper, *Fraternité Evangélique*, is published by the ELCF congregations in the Paris district. Its 1400 subscribers are mainly in the Paris area but include many others, also from Francophone Africa and Madagascar. Besides biblical studies, the content features articles and news items bearing on the ecumenical and missionary task of the church locally and worldwide. Founded in 1941, while Paris was under German occupation, the paper is a continuation of the century-old *Le Témoignage* (The Witness), which the Nazis had shut down. Produced by a staff of volunteers—the current editor has combined this work with his duties as parish pastor for over a decade—*Fraternité Evangélique* receives modest subsidies from the ANELF and the LWF to defray its cost of publication.

Historically, the two geographic parts of the ELCF have sprung from different constituencies that were first brought together during the time of Napoleon in 1802 (above). During the 16th century, the Montbéliard region—then part of the duchy of Württemberg (Germany)—accepted the Reformation under the initial leadership of Guillaume Farel (1489–1565), who later became Calvin's forerunner in Geneva. The Lutheran church order of 1560 introduced compulsory education and urged that book learning be undergirded with genuine piety. Developments in Montbéliard generally paralleled those in Strasbourg and the surrounding Alsace.

These included periodic waves of evangelical renewal—stimulated by Oberlin (above) and others—that extended also to the Paris area.

In Paris, the early influence of Lutheran teaching during the 1520s and 1530s was absorbed into Calvinism. A century elapsed before the first permanent Lutheran congregation was formed in 1626 by Swedes who met in the chapel of the Swedish embassy. Subsequently, another met in the Danish embassy. Only in 1809 was the first really indigenous congregation formed, and early it received support from fellow Lutherans in Alsace. This kind of exchange was facilitated by a unified Church of the Augsburg Confession (1802–1870), as noted above. The number of congregations in the Paris area increased. A missioning outreach to the thousands of German laborers developed ties also with Germany. Through the leading Lutheran pastor, Louis Meyer, Friedrich von Bodelschwingh (1831–1910) began his ministerial career among the destitute and also the successful Germans in Paris. He later became the influential developer of the Bethel institutions in Bielefeld, *Germany.

Today, the ELCF sees its problem not only as one of survival but also of avoiding retreat. Threatened isolation has been met in part by an ever fresh and imaginative concern for others.

EVANGELICAL LUTHERAN CHURCH—SYNOD OF FRANCE AND BELGIUM

(Eglise évangélique luthérienne— Synode de France et de Belgique)
Membership: 865**
President: The Rev. Frédéric Bohy
21 chemin des Ardennes
F—68100 Mulhouse

This church has 14 congregations, mainly in Alsace but also in other parts of France, including the Paris area, and in Belgium. It is served by nine pastors and by others in supporting ministries. It is basically congregational in polity, with the synod serving in an advisory capacity. The church president is the executive officer of the synod.

The church maintains the Lutheran Theological Study Center in Chatenay Malabry, near Paris, and also the Sanatorium Bethel

in Aubure, near Colmar, in Alsace. Mission work is conducted in France. Work in Belgium, undertaken in 1934, was disrupted during World War II but was resumed after 1945 (see Belgium).

In partnership with the *Lutheran Church– Missouri Synod (USA), the church has sponsored the French "Lutheran Hour" since 1949. At present, 30-second spots are aired several times weekly at prime time over Radio Europe No.1; Radio Monte Carlo; Radio Haiti in the Caribbean; and Radio Zaire in Africa. Three stations in Quebec, Canada, air a 15-minute program. About 1500 people are enrolled in the Bible correspondence course.

The beginnings of this church lie in the latter half of the 19th century when a number of congregations withdrew from the Church of the Augsburg Confession in protest against the influx of theological liberalism and became upholders of confessional Lutheranism. Later, some of the congregations returned to the Alsatian church, but others in 1927 organized this free church.

IRELAND (EIRE)

A sovereign, democratic state (1937), Eire became a republic and withdrew from the Commonwealth (1948). The six northeastern counties, Northern Ireland, remain in the *United Kingdom, but this British claim has not been recognized by Eire. Area of the 26 counties comprising Eire: 70,285 sq. km. (27,137 sq. mi.) or 83% of the island. Pop. (1985 est.): 3,614,000. Cap. and largest city: Dublin (pop., 1985, 525,900). Language: Mostly English (72%); Irish (28%).

History: Celtic tribes settled Eire in the fourth century B.C., and by the fifth century A.D. their flourishing Gaelic culture and Christian faith—brought by St. Patrick—began spreading to Scotland and England. Danes, then Norwegians, invaded Eire. English invasions began in the 12th century, ushering in a struggle that continues to this day in Northern Ireland. There was extensive emigration from Northern Ireland (Scottish-Irish Presbyterians) to the North American colonies in the 18th century and from the present Eire (Roman Catholic Ulster Irish) in the 19th.

The refusal of Eire to recognize the six northern counties—Northern Ireland—as a continuing part of the United Kingdom has led to the prolonged and tragic civil war in the north. The question of a united Ireland is basically political. But from the outset of the struggle for Irish independence from Britain, the question has been viewed in terms of religious factions: the Roman Catholic minority in Northern Ireland pitted against a Protestant majority.

The Protestants are mainly Presbyterian descendants of 17th century settlers. They were brought from Scotland by James VI of Scotland (James I of England) to pacify and develop the land; and they cling tenaciously to their United Kingdom legacy. The unofficial Irish Republican Army (IRA) for years has fought for a politically united Ireland. Despite considerable underground assistance to the IRA from Irish people in the USA and elsewhere, the aims of a united Eire have not been realized. In place of violence that begets more violence—and keeps a standing British army in Northern Ireland—cooler and courageous Roman Catholics and Protestants have continued to strive for a reconciliation of differences.

Religion: Roman Catholic (est.) 94%. Head of the hierarchy is the archbishop of Armagh (located in Northern Ireland). Animated by missionary zeal, the Celtic (Irish) church extended its influence from the fourth to the ninth century to Britain and many parts of Europe—as far as Austria and Switzerland. Flourishing in culture and spiritual life, it long held a position independent of Rome and the papacy. With the Reformation in Britain, the Anglican Church became established in Ireland, a superimposition that stirred Irish reaction and strengthened Roman Catholicism.

The Irish Council of Churches (1922) comprises eight non-Roman Catholic churches: Anglican, Lutheran, Methodist, Moravian, Presbyterian (two), Friends (Quakers), and Salvation Army. The council meets twice yearly, alternately in Dublin (Eire) and Belfast (capital of Northern Ireland).

LUTHERAN CHURCH IN IRELAND (LCI)

Member: (R), ICC
Membership: 800**
Pastor: The Rev. Paul Gerhard Fritz
21 Merlyn Park, Ballsbridge
IRL—Dublin 4

This church, recognized by the LWF and officially connected with the *Evangelical Church in Germany (EKD) as well as with the *United Evangelical Lutheran Church of Germany (VELKD) is based in Dublin. Preaching points are in Wexford, Cork, Killarney, Limerick, and Galway. Since 1983, it has been augmented by the Evangelical Lutheran Church of Belfast and Northern Ireland, formerly a congregation of the German-speaking Evangelical Lutheran Synod in Great Britain. Thus this small but significant Lutheran church transcends the Emerald Isle's political borders. It also maintains a relationship with the *Lutheran Council of Great Britain (LCGB).

The entire island has but one pastor for the approximately 800 Lutherans. About 90% of them are Germans, the others Scandinavians and Americans. The Dublin congregation has weekly German services and on the last Sunday of the month one in English. Since 1961, worship is held in St. Finian's church, made available to the Lutherans on a 99-year lease by the Church of Ireland (Anglican). The Belfast congregation has monthly services in a Moravian church.

Besides the usual congregational duties, the pastor provides religious instruction in Dublin's German school, attends to the services of the seamen's mission in the Irish ports, and joins in the ecumenical activities of the Irish Council of Churches (ICC). These include a striving for peace and reconciliation in a Northern Ireland torn by civil war since 1970. The LCI provides periodic service to women and children who, worn down by the prolonged civil strife, are sent to the Federal Republic of Germany for recuperation. These and other efforts, such as providing information and interpretation, retain their importance in face of the terrorism that has claimed an average of 200 lives per year since the early 1970s.

The LCI is a postwar creation. From 1952 to 1955, Lutherans in both parts of Ireland were served by the pastor stationed in Bristol, England. Receiving a pastor of their own in 1955 helped recall the fact that a Lutheran congregation serving Germans and Scandinavians had existed in Dublin from 1697 to 1850. Then, as in recent decades, the periodic need to resettle refugees gave added life and purpose to a Lutheran presence in Ireland.

ITALY

A republic (1946) occupying the Apennine Peninsula, Sicily, Sardinia, and a number of smaller islands. Area: 301,245 sq. km. (116,320 sq. mi.). Pop. (1985 est.): 57,079,000. Cap. and largest city: Rome (pop., 1985 prelim., 2,830,600). Language: Italian.

History: Base of the Roman empire and, with Greece, a forebear of European civilization, Italy succumbed to barbarian invasions and Rome fell in A.D. 410. Over ensuing centuries, the land was divided by competing forces that prized its resources. Best known and longest was the struggle between the papacy and the Holy Roman Empire of the German Nation, a conflict between spiritual and temporal power (church and state). France, too, was a strong competitor. Commercially and culturally, Italy sustained the Renaissance, returning to prominence the culture of classical antiquity and also playing a role in the rise of the 16th-century Reformation as well as of the ensuing Counter-Reformation.

Italy was comparatively late in becoming a modern European nation. By 1859, its process of unification was under way, and two years later the first Italian parliament declared Victor Emmanuel II of Sardinia the nation's king. The ancient Papal States were taken in 1870—just prior to the First Vatican Council of the Roman Catholic Church—only to be returned to the papacy, in diminished form, in 1929. Fascism arose in the wake of World War I (1919) and continued until 1943 under the dictatorship of Benito Mussolini (1883–1945). Italy's political partnership with Nazi Germany and Japan (the Axis powers) ended with the overthrow of Fascism and Italy's joining the Allied side (1943). After the war, Victor Emmanuel III abdicated (1946), and the nation became a republic. The Christian

Democrats remained the largest of Italy's political parties, governing by coalition with certain other parties—excepting the Communist, the largest Communist party in Western Europe. Italy's boundaries were stabilized in 1975 when Trieste, earlier Austrian and, after 1919, claimed by Yugoslavia, became permanently Italian.

Religion: Roman Catholicism claims about 84% of the population, yet it is no longer the state religion. In 1977, a renegotiated treaty with the Vatican reduced its influence by reaffirming freedom of religion and by curtailing the influence of the church in education and marital questions (divorce).

Vatican City (108 acres; 44 hectares) was established as a separate state in 1929 by the Lateran Treaty. It is indirectly a successor to the former, sometimes very extensive, Papal States that existed for over 11 centuries (745–1870). It is on the Vatican City's status as a nation state that papal diplomatic ties are maintained with other nations as well as with the United Nations. Thus the Vatican serves the Roman Catholic Church as a whole.

Italy's exceptionally high number of dioceses—of the 283 there are 55 archdioceses—suggests the incomparably complex character of a church history that began in Rome during the lifetimes of Saints Peter and Paul. Since Vatican II (1961–1965), the number of dioceses has been in process of reduction. For greater effectiveness, they have been grouped into 18 conciliar regions. The diocese of Rome includes and extends far beyond Vatican City.

Rome itself, as the geographic base for a global church, presents an unrivaled array of ecclesial enterprises, both ancient and modern. Among them are 17 pontifical universities, institutes, and faculties of theology; 89 educational and other institutes; and the headquarters of major orders like the Dominican, Franciscan, and Jesuit. The pope, as bishop of Rome, administers the diocese through a cardinal-vicar. The chief papal involvement is with the Curia, the time-honored vast bureaucracy of the Vatican.

Ecumenism, as a subject and a commitment to church unity, was affirmed in distinctively Roman Catholic terms by Vatican II (Decree on Ecumenism, 1964). Opening the way to this new departure was the establishment of the Secretariat for Promoting Christian Unity (1961). Authorized by Pope

John XXIII, it had been proposed and initially headed by Augustin Cardinal Bea (d. 1968; *Federal Republic of Germany). The secretariat has direct access to the pope, but any actions it proposes must be cleared through the Curia. Jan Cardinal Willebrands, until 1983 archbishop of Utrecht (*Netherlands), has long presided over the secretariat and kept it a leading center for tracking the numerous bilateral dialogs and other ecumenical ventures in which the Church of Rome is engaged. As in other countries, the Italian Conference of Bishops has its own Commission on Ecumenism.

For the church at large, and for the Italian scene particularly, the 1978 election of a non-Italian pope departed from a 455-year-old practice. As John Paul II, Poland's Karol Wojtyla (b. 1929) has made full use of the electronic media and of jet air travel to give the Roman Catholic Church an unprecedented visibility and sense of presence on all the continents. With a native conservatism he has fostered Roman Catholic aims as well as Christian unity.

Protestantism in Italy is both old and new, with the Waldensians (27,500) going back in time to the 12th century and with the Pentecostals (300,000) making long strides in the 20th. The Federation of Protestant Churches in Italy (FPCI; 1967) includes the Waldensian, Baptist, Methodist, and Lutheran. The Evangelical Baptist Union and the Waldensian Church are members of the World Council of Churches.

Although recently merged, the Waldensians and Methodists retain their separate identities. The Waldensian theological faculty in Rome has been of help to other Protestants in and beyond Italy. Especially since Vatican II, it has been a resource to Italian Roman Catholics in furthering an understanding of evangelical Christianity. With Waldensian settlements historically in the valleys of northern Italy as well as in the regions around Naples and in Sicily, ties with their own emigrant groups in Uruguay, Argentina, and North America give this small communion international significance (see also Spain). Today, practical programs of cooperation with the Roman Catholic Church include an ecumenical translation of the Bible into contemporary Italian.

During this century, the Eternal City has seen the construction of a number of impressively attractive non-Roman Catholic church buildings, notable among them being the Anglican, the American Protestant, and the (German) Lutheran.

EVANGELICAL LUTHERAN CHURCH IN ITALY (ELCI)

(Chiesa Evangelica Luterana in Italia)
Member: LWF (1949), CEC, FPCI, special contract with EKD
Membership: 7000
Dean: The Very Rev. Joachim Mietz
Via Palestrina 14
I—20124 Milan

The church consists of 11 congregations and 46 preaching stations scattered throughout Italy from north to south. Criterion for recognition of a congregation is the existence of a working church executive body. At present, there are three Italian and six German pastors in full-time service.

The official authority of this self-governing church is the synod. The president is a lay person and, since 1983, a woman, Hanna Franzoi. The synod consists of representatives of the congregations, members appointed directly by the synod itself, and the pastors' association. Its executive body is the consistory, composed of three lay persons (legal adviser, treasurer, president) and two ministers (dean and deputy-dean). The latter are appointed for five years, the former for three. Between annual meetings of the synod, a minimum of internal contact and information is maintained by circulating the minutes of consistory meetings and the church news *Miteinander* ("Together," edited in Bozen). Wider communication is ensured by the press service (NEV—Notizie Evangelice) in Rome.

The majority of the members are German, Italian of German heritage, or people from countries where German is spoken. Thus the German language has been a unifying factor. Many of the members are in Italy on temporary assignment and are accustomed to a national church with its system of support. Others are from long-established German-speaking settlements and are used to voluntarily supporting their churches, as in Bozen and Trieste. An increasing number are Italians who have intermarried with German-speaking members. These include Italian guest workers who have returned to Italy with German or Scandinavian wives and children. Other members are the result of evangelism, mainly those in the Italian-speaking congregations in the Naples region (see below).

The ELCI has a close working relationship with the *Evangelical Church in Germany (EKD). Through its Division for Foreign Relations, the EKD assists the German-speaking congregations with stipends for their pastors' salaries. Most pastors are on a fixed-term contract with the EKD or are German-educated Italian nationals. The ELCI in turn provides pastoral care for EKD members holidaying in Italy or in temporary residence there. It also represents EKD's ecumenical interests in Italy. Protestant religious instruction is provided in the German schools in Rome, Milan, and Genoa.

The ELCI helps maintain two Protestant hospitals, one in Naples and the other in Genoa. It benefits from the services of deaconesses from Germany, Austria, and Switzerland who serve in the old people's homes and hostels in Rome and Milan. The ELCI also provides a pastor for the ecumenical congregation of Ispra-Varese.

Places of worship are in most cases modest buildings dating back to the 19th century, the exceptions being those in Trieste, Venice, and Rome. Christus church in Rome, a monument to German Protestantism, is a chaste Romanesque structure at the corner of Sicilia and Toscana. It was built during the final decade of Hohenzollern rule in Prussia and dedicated in 1915 after World War I had begun. It ranks in beauty with other non-Roman Catholic church buildings in Rome. The Escuola dell'Angelo Custode church in Venice was built in 1715 and became Protestant in 1812.

After the devastating earthquake that destroyed many small towns of Friaul in northeast Italy (1976), the ELCI, especially the Trieste congregation, pledged practical aid and requested the LWF, via the Italian government, to promote a project in the mountain villages where the destruction was worst and assistance minimal. Encouraged and supported by the diaconic agency of the EKD (Diakonisches Werk, Stuttgart), gifts from the churches of *Sweden and the *United States, and generous labor and contributions by the ELCI itself, it was possible to erect over 100 prefabricated houses on foundations prepared by the local communities. After the earthquake in Irpinia (southern Italy) in 1982, adopting similar procedures, a cooperative cow barn and a school were built by the ELCI in Caposele and Fisciano.

A new ecumenical awareness has gripped the ELCI. Ecumenical services are regularly held in all places. In lectures and guest courses, Lutherans are seen actively participating in the ecumenical dialog in Florence, Venice, Bologne, Naples, and Milan. For the ELCI and the ecumenical movement itself, the climax here was the visit of Pope John Paul II to the *Christuskirche* in Rome in 1983. It was as bishop of Rome that the pope visited his neighbor Lutheran congregation. His coming for vespers on the first Sunday of Advent signified at the same time the conclusion of the 500th anniversary of the birth of Luther. The pope's attitude was one of great humility. John Paul II did not preach from his throne, seated, as is customary in St. Peter's, but went up into the pulpit. "I have come to visit my neighbors," he said, "who are at the same time citizens of this city and joined by the bond of a special kinship. . . . For we see ourselves . . . as united at the deepest level in solidarity with all Christians in Advent. We long for unity, and we strive for unity, without allowing the difficulties to discourage us." The message continues to be applicable locally and throughout the world, not least by the members of the ELCI.

The 1985 synod was an expression of the church's new understanding of itself. A "congregational academy" was arranged, and for one-and-a-half days 65 participants were familiarized with the basic principles of pastoral counseling. The idea caught on, and regional versions of the "congregational academy" were organized, including some for holidaymakers and young people. The consistory organized ministers' meetings and intensified visiting campaigns. It was no accident that the meeting place chosen for the synod was Assisi, the city of St. Francis. Here, the spirit of Vatican II is still strong. The hosts were the "Pro Civitate Christiana," a lay society that is enthusiastically committed to the cause of personal self-fulfillment, both within and without congregational structures. The bishop of Assisi honored the synod with a visit. The moderator of the Waldensian Church urged the ELCI to increase its cooperation with the Federation of Protestant Churches in Italy. Cooperation with the Waldensians at the local level continues.

• • •

Already at the time of the Reformation, Lutheranism had close connections with Italy.

Luther himself wrote two long letters of encouragement to the Lutherans in Venice, Treviso, and Vicenza. For a century or more, the Lutheran community in Venice met in strict clandestinity. From 1650, the congregations had permanent pastors. Other congregations were founded in the course of the 19th century—in Trieste, Rome, Naples, Genoa, San Remo, Florence, Bozen, and Milan—as Evangelical Lutheran churches for German-speaking people (Austrians, Swiss, Germans). In 1948, these nine congregations united to form the Evangelical Lutheran Church in Italy. In 1957, a constitution was approved by the synod.

In that same year, three Italian-speaking congregations on the Gulf of Naples were welcomed into membership. They were the fruit of labor begun in 1948 by an Italian-American, Antonio Caliandro. He had emigrated from this area after World War I, had become a Protestant, had studied at the Concordia Seminary in St. Louis, and had been received into the *Lutheran Church–Missouri Synod. With LCMS encouragement, Caliandro returned to his native Potici in the district of Portico—one of the most backward areas in Italy and one most neglected by the church. Here, in an old castle, Caliandro opened the *Instituto Evangelico Biblico d'Italia*. Assisting him was a Waldensian professor. Among the students was a priest, Idelmo Poggioli, who through the influence of his teachers and the reading of Luther decided to become a Lutheran pastor. With evangelical fervor he succeeded in founding congregations in Torre del Greco, Torre Annunziata, and Santa Maria la Bruna. These assembled regularly, first in private homes and then in rented halls or barns. Mobile clinics, emergency schools for children from broken homes, and finally government-recognized kindergartens and day schools emerged. Some of the projects were supported by the LWF. When the LCMS was no longer able to finance the venture, Caliandro and his colleagues turned to the ELCI. As a result, the three congregations and their pastors were almost unanimously accepted by the synod in 1957 as members of the ELCI. The pioneer Idelmo Poggioli died in 1983, but his son has since become a pastor of the ELCI.

After repeated applications, the ELCI was recognized by the state in 1961. Its close relations with VELKD (United Evangelical Lutheran Church of Germany) and with the Conference of European Churches (CEC), as well as the constant aid given by the Martin-Luther-Bund (Erlangen) and the Gustav-Adolf-Werk in Germany have not prevented the ELCI from undergoing a radical change in self-understanding in recent years. Thanks above all to its indigenous Italian-speaking congregations, to its renewed recollection of its historical roots (in Venice for example), and to its ecumenical role as a bridge to the German theology of the Reformation, the ELCI no longer regards itself as a "guest church" but as an active and adult member of the Italian Protestant family, within the general church scene.

LIECHTENSTEIN

A constitutional monarchy, the tiny principality of Liechtenstein lies on the right bank of the Upper Rhine between Austria and Switzerland. Area: 160 sq. km. (62 sq. mi.). Pop. (1984): 27,000. Cap.: Vaduz (pop., 4800). Language: German.

History: In Roman times this land was part of the imperial province of Raetia. From 963 to 1806 it was in the Holy Roman Empire of the German Nation, being made a principality in 1719. A member of the German Confederation (1815–1866), it then became independent and has remained so. Amid Europe's wars it has maintained neutrality. After World War I, it terminated its customs union with Austria, and in 1924 took up this arrangement with Switzerland. In the 1880s, Liechtenstein's agricultural economy was augmented by textile and other industries—including electronics in recent decades. The country's flair for special issues of postage stamp is world famous among collectors.

Religion: The country is 90% Roman Catholic, and nearly 9% Protestant. Roman Catholicism is the official religion. The country's 12 parishes form a single deanery within the Swiss diocese of Chur.

The prince's decree of 1881 granted religious liberty to Protestants; a significant act, considering that the 16th-century Reformation bypassed this protected nook. In that year, a Protestant congregation was organized by immigrant textile workers of Lutheran and Reformed background. From this has grown the Evangelical (Protestant) Church in the Principality of Liechtenstein. Its membership is about 1000, and its ties are with the Swiss Reformed Church in the neighboring canton of St. Gall.

In light of the influx of new residents—the country's population has more than doubled since 1950—elements of the original German church were in 1954 organized as a Lutheran congregation. In 1972, it joined in the formation of the United Evangelical Lutheran Churches in *Switzerland and the Principality of Liechtenstein.

THE NETHERLANDS

A constitutional monarchy (1815), the Netherlands is one of the Benelux countries. Facing the North Sea, its neighbor to the south is Belgium, and to the east the Federal Republic of Germany. Area: 41,548 sq. km. (16,042 sq. mi.). Pop. (1985 est.): 14,472,000. Cap. and largest city: Amsterdam (pop., 1985 est., 676,439). Seat of government: The Hague (pop., 1985 est., 445,213). Language: Dutch.

History: The early inhabitants—Frisians, Batavians, and Saxons—came under Roman rule during the first century A.D. as part of the province of Lower Germany. Subsequently, under Frankish rule, the eventual breaking up of the empire of Charlemagne allotted the Low Countries—Holland, Belgium, Flanders—to various rulers, including those of Burgundy. In 1548, the Hapsburg Emperor Charles V united the Dutch into one separate canton in his German empire. Because Charles was also king of Spain, the Dutch came under Spanish domination. In 1581, under William the Silent (William of Orange), allegiance to Spain was repudiated and the Dutch Republic proclaimed. It rose to naval, commercial, and artistic (Rembrandt) eminence in the 17th century. As a seapower, it competed with Spain, Portugal, and Britain, and extended its colonial enterprises to *North America (New York), *Brazil (Recife), the West Indies, Ceylon, and the East Indies (*Indonesia).

After the fall of Napoleon, the Congress of Vienna (1815) formed a kingdom of the Netherlands, the southern (Flemish) part of which became the kingdom of Belgium

(1830). Although under German occupation during World War II, the Netherlands resisted Nazism and protected Jews bravely but not always successfully. In 1949, the Dutch government formally recognized the independence of Indonesia. In 1975, *Suriname (Dutch Guyana) became independent. Without its colonies, the nation has expressed its spirit of enterprise in new ways at home and abroad in cultural as well as economic life.

Religion: About 40% of the population are Roman Catholic, 35% Protestant. The 23% counted as having no religion, include post-Christian Europeans, a group of organized humanists, and also a large number of Indonesians with animist background. Jews comprise a small (0.2%) but long-influential community. Hindus (0.7%) are mainly immigrants from Suriname who arrived in 1975 (12,000 a month) prior to Suriname's independence. Muslims (1%) are to a large extent migrant workers—Turks, Moroccans, Indonesians, and others.

The conversion of the Low Countries to Christianity began in the 7th century. Of the seven Dutch dioceses, the archdiocese of Utrecht traces its beginnings to A.D. 650. On this territory, Roman Catholicism held sway until the 16th-century Reformation. Thereafter, it continued under curtailed form during the Dutch Republic and the ascendancy of the Reformed as the established church (1651–1795). Subsequently, it experienced renewal under the French occupation of the Netherlands (Napoleon, to 1815) and maintained spiritual strength and numerical stability into the present century. Purposeful and aggressive, Dutch Roman Catholics figured prominently in Vatican II. Their largely ecumenical spirit—there were reactionary forces among them, too—found expression in such forms as the much debated Dutch Catechism. A national pastoral council—which the Vatican required—was later reduced to a National Pastoral Committee (1972). Jan Cardinal Willebrands, president of the Vatican Secretariat for Promoting Christian Unity and an outgoing proponent of its aims, served as archbishop of Utrecht until his retirement in 1983. Pressure from the Vatican in recent years has considerably diminished the liberalizing trend in Dutch Roman Catholicism.

About 30% of the population are Dutch Reformed. Calvinism replaced an initial Lutheran stirring among the people (see below)

and created a rugged and resourceful Netherlands Reformed Church (1568). At times, it disciplined insiders who differed doctrinally (among them Jacobus Arminius, 1560–1609, who opposed Calvin's doctrine of predestination; and Hugo Grotius, 1538–1645, called the "Father of International Law"). Nevertheless, toleration and asylum were early granted to religious refugees, Jews as well as Christians.

In the early 19th century, reaction against liberalism created numerous independent Reformed churches. Later, a number of them united to form the (twice) Reformed Churches in the Netherlands (Gereformeerde Kerken, 1892). Today, this strong and second largest of the six Reformed bodies is in the process of reuniting with the mother church, the Netherlands Reformed Church, a body that has been declining in membership.

In the present century, Dutch Reformed participation in the ecumenical movement has included the contribution of such leaders as Hendrik Kraemer (d. 1965), the noted lay theologian and missiologist; and Willem Adolf Visser't Hooft (1900–1985), general secretary of the World Student Christian Federation (1932–1938) and of the World Council of Churches (1938-1948 "in process of formation"; 1948–1966 fully organized) and thereafter honorary president of the WCC.

The Council of Churches in the Netherlands (CCN) was the new name given the Ecumenical Council of Churches of 1946 when the Roman Catholics joined in 1968. The Reformed and Roman Catholic being the two dominant members, the council's other churches include the Lutheran, Mennonite, Old Catholic, Evangelical Brethren, Friends (Quaker), and Salvation Army. Pentecostals—about 12 different groups—are not members. In a way complementary to the CCN, the Netherlands Missionary Council (1929) seeks to advance the outreach of its participating bodies at home as well as overseas.

One of the numerous centers fostering partnership among the churches and concern for issues facing society has been the Kerk en Wereld Institute in Driebergen near Utrecht. Early led by Kraemer, it blazed new trails after 1945. The First Assembly of the WCC, Amsterdam 1948, encouraged a further advance in ecumenism in the Netherlands. Postwar Dutch Lutheranism was then flowering in its own right with Willem Jan Kooiman, the historian and Luther scholar, prominent among those setting the pace.

Many Jewish refugees from Nazi Germany found a haven in the Netherlands, and some survived the German occupation during World War II, thanks especially to Dutch Christians. The plight of Jewish victims, memorably portrayed in works like *The Diary of Anne Frank,* intensified already sturdy attachments to the Old Testament. This Old Testament emphasis continues to be prominent in Lutheran as well as Reformed worship, preaching, and Bible study. It also fosters an ongoing interfaith climate of mutual trust.

EVANGELICAL LUTHERAN CHURCH IN THE KINGDOM OF THE NETHERLANDS (ELCKN)

(Evangelisch-Lutherse Kerk in het Koninkrijk der Nederlanden)
Member: LWF (1952), WCC, CEC, CCN
Membership: 27,600**
President: The Rev. C.F.G.E. Hallewas
Jan de Bakkerstraat 13-15
NL-3441 ED Woerden

The ELCKN—a minority church—today consists of 62 local congregations served by 35 pastors. Two other pastors serve as chaplains in homes for the aged. Overshadowed by strong Reformed and Roman Catholic churches, the once large Lutheran constituency continues to decline: a loss of 16% since 1976. For the diminished congregations a common problem—acute in some of them—is that of financial self-support. For the pastors an analogous problem is that of having to serve more than one parish, which a number of them are doing. Vacant pastorates, where possible, have arranged for part-time pastoral help from sister congregations.

The present constitution of the ELCKN was adopted in 1955. It provides for a presbyterial structure and a semiannual synodical meeting. The presiding officer is the president of the church, assisted by two vice-presidents. Currently, once again, one of them is a woman. The synod consists of 36 members, 12 of whom are clergy and 24 lay. An executive committee of the synod comprises 11 members.

Ministerial education is provided in two places: at the theological faculty of the University of Amsterdam and at the affiliated Evangelical Lutheran Seminary. The latter, like most other religious institutions in the Netherlands, is partly subsidized by the government. Since 1931, women have had the same rights as men in entering the ordained ministry.

Lay participation in the life and work of the ELCKN has been advanced over the past decade or more. In 1973, the church's seminary in Amsterdam initiated a two-year part-time training course for the laity. Biblical studies, theology, and pastoral care are the main subjects. Students pay their own tuition and other expenses for the 20 sessions. Following the first two-year sequence, students are permitted to concentrate on a field or subject of their choice within the program. Successful completion of another two years earns the student a certificate. In that case, he or she may assist the pastor of a congregation in such functions as parish visitation, Bible study, and small group worship. A few, under supervision of the seminary faculty, may also conduct public worship. This program has satisfied some urgent needs.

The ELCKN maintains a large number of diaconal institutions: homes for the elderly in several towns; a Lutheran Deaconess Hospital (1888); a children's home in Amsterdam; and a guardianship agency for Lutheran children in the Netherlands. All these contribute to the common social services in the country. They are supervised by a diaconal board of the church and are supported by special offerings at weekly worship services and by other gifts and bequests of members and friends.

Among Dutch Lutherans there is a great awareness of and supportiveness for the world's poor countries. Members are expected to give 1% of their income for development and mission projects. They have exceeded this goal and have on occasion reached a 4% giving. This is especially significant for a church that has its own financial problems. The mission board of the church channels these gifts through the LWF, the WCC, and the Netherlands Missionary Council for short-term projects.

The ELCKN does not receive state subsidy, and church leaders are well aware of the chronic problem of self-support. Stewardship and evangelism were spurred by North American influence after World War II. Even with a considerable increase in local offerings, supplemental support—through grants and projects of sister churches in the LWF—remains important to the congregations in their attempts to serve.

Interest in church architecture has also been renewed. Typifying the trend is the new Augustana church in Amsterdam, a functional church center accessible by road and canal.

Exciting news on the home mission front was the recent gathering of a new congregation in Lelystad Polder. It is one of the larger cities springing up on this impressive expanse of land reclaimed from the sea. For the members of the ELCKN moving into this area, it is important to have a church in their midst. In 1983, a new pastor (from the USA) arrived and began his ministry the following year, after having completed his study of the Dutch language.

● ● ●

Looking back, the Dutch Lutherans in 1966 celebrated their 400th anniversary and reviewed a rich history. The first Lutheran congregation had fled persecution in Antwerp (now Belgium, then Southern Netherlands), where it had begun in 1566 as a unique free church with a confession and a church order. In Amsterdam, it was organized in 1588 (see Belgium, above). The members worshiped in each other's homes until 1600 when the Netherlands, which had become Reformed and a bulwark of Calvinism, granted toleration to Roman Catholics and Lutherans. The tolerated confessions were permitted to build houses of worship, provided they did not look like churches. The Lutherans in Amsterdam obtained the use of a warehouse, which they transformed into a church, now the famous "Old Church at the Spui." Dedicated in 1633, it is still in use—after more than 350 years.

The Amsterdam Lutherans early developed a congregational polity. By 1605, an association of six congregations functioned as a synod. The church grew. Following lines of commerce with England and the New World, the influence of the Amsterdam congregation spread to Lutherans in London (*United Kingdom) and to settlers in New Amsterdam (New York after 1664) and even to German Lutherans in Pennsylvania (*USA). In

1650—after eight years of repeated requests—the first Lutheran pastor, Johannes Gutwasser, was sent to the colonists in New Amsterdam, but the intolerance of the Dutch Reformed governor, Peter Stuyvesant, caused his deportation. When the English took New Amsterdam and the environing colony of New Netherland in 1664, Dutch Lutherans were granted religious freedom. Along with pastors sent from Amsterdam came also a church order that subsequently helped shape organized Lutheranism in America.

In the Netherlands, during the 18th century, the Dutch Lutheran pastors, educated in Germany, were influenced by the Enlightenment. Their espousal of Rationalism caused a split in the church. The orthodox, confessional Lutherans seceded and in 1793 formed the Restored Evangelical Lutheran Church. The rise of the Dutch Lutheran Missionary Society (1852) gradually freed the church from the domination of Rationalism. A return to the sources of the Reformation and a renaissance of Luther research and study focused attention once again on justification by faith alone. This commitment became a sustained movement.

An extensive literature in various fields of theological study has been developed by Dutch Lutheran scholars since 1945; among them, Professor Kooiman (above). The influence of the theological report of the first LWF Assembly (Lund 1947) helped reunite the two branches of Dutch Lutheranism in 1952. This, coupled with a return to the liturgy of the Reformation and a fresh point of view on the function of sacred music, culminated in a new hymnal and liturgy in 1955.

Likewise, in the field of relations with the Jewish people, Dutch Lutherans have sought to foster reconciliation, understanding, and a shared concern. One indication of this position is the frequency of preaching from Old Testament text and the prominence of the Old Testament in Bible study.

Lutherans in the Netherlands know that their church's survivability is being tested. As intimated above, there is ecumenical and interchurch cooperation among the Dutch churches at all levels, and the ELCKN participates actively in the Council of Churches in the Netherlands. Developments among the Reformed, however, may radically change the interchurch relations. In 1982, the Lutherans thus entered into conversation with both of the merging Reformed churches to explore the possibility and likely consequences of their inclusion in the merger or in the establishment of a more ecumenical unity based on the 1973 Leuenberg Agreement (*Germany).

However, as responses from the laity to a questionnaire circulated among the ELCKN congregations in 1985 indicated, sentiment is strong (70%) for the Lutheran church to continue its separate identity; to be sure, in ecumenical partnership but not absorbed into or federated with some other denomination. For the time being, at least, the Leuenberg Agreement now in effect among Lutherans and Reformed in most of Europe appears to suffice. Meanwhile, the ELCKN—as its semiannual synod meetings take note—is a church of the aging. In recent years its annual membership losses have averaged 3%.

PORTUGAL

A republic (1910) in the southwesternmost part of Europe, Portugal shares the Iberian Peninsula with Spain. Area: 91,985 sq. km. (35,516 sq. mi.), including the Azores (2247 sq. km.) and Madeira (794 sq. km.). Pop. (1985 est.): 10,151,000. Cap. and largest. city: Lisbon (pop., 1985 prelim., 807,167). Language: Portuguese.

History: A part of Spain until the middle of the 12th century, independent Portugal played a pioneer role in the global expansion of Europe. Its seaborne empire emerged in the course of explorations launched under the imaginative direction of Prince Henry the Navigator (1394–1460). Bartholomeu Dias (c.1450–1500) reached the Cape of Good Hope (1488), and Vasco da Gama (c.1469–1524) opened the way to *India (1498). The discovery and acquisition of *Brazil (1500), the brisk trade with India (Goa), China (Macao), and the East Indies (later lost to the Dutch), and the claims along the coasts of Africa—especially Portuguese West Africa (Guinea Bissau), *Angola, and *Mozambique—all grew into a worldwide network by which Lisbon surpassed Venice as a sought-after center of trade. Britain early linked itself by treaty with Portugal (vis-à-vis Spain). From Angola, Portugal drew most of the black slaves for the sugar plantations in Brazil as well as for work in its own country.

Weakness within and corruption overseas made Portugal unable to hold its own amid the contending European powers. The terrifying destruction of Lisbon by earthquake, flood (the River Tagus), and fire in 1755 was read by many as a sign of divine judgment. The expulsion of the Jesuits (1759), for alleged complicity in conspiracy, led the way for other countries to follow Portugal's example and for the pope to dissolve the order (1773). The French conquest of Portugal sent the royal family fleeing for safety in *Brazil (1807). Shortly after the king's return to Portugal (1822), Brazil went independent—a monarchy in its own right.

For Portugal itself, the monarchy continued until 1910, when revolution turned the country into a French-style republic. Despite the immense changes brought globally by the two world wars, Portugal retained its empire a while longer. In 1962, India seized Goa (near Bombay). Mounting unrest eventually gained independence for Guinea-Bissau (1974), Angola (1975), and Mozambique (1975). The seaborne empire had lasted nearly four centuries. Its demise sent thousands of overseas Portuguese back to their ancestral homeland as refugees. The political course of Portugal over the ensuing decade has been difficult. Constitutional government continues.

Religion: An estimated 85% of the Portuguese are Roman Catholic. The church structure comprises three archdioceses and 14 dioceses. The archdiocese of Lisbon (A.D. 360) has patriarchal status. The church in the southern part of the country is the least active; that in the northern part the most traditional and the location of the famed shrine of Fatima. A shortage of priests has been a drawback. Relations between church and state have passed through at least three significant stages during the present century: the anticlerical (1910–1926), after the overthrow of the monarchy by republican forces; the authoritarian (1926–1960), under the dictatorship of Antonio de Oliveira Salazar (1889–1970), which included a concordat with the Vatican (1940) as well as a revival of church life; and the Vatican era, most marked by intensified youth and lay participation, especially in Catholic action. Missionary endeavors overseas—prior to the dissolution of the Portuguese Empire (1975)—claimed a total of 2.5 million Roman Catholics in *Angola and another 1.25 million in *Mozambique.

As in Spain, the number of Protestants in Portugal is proportionately small. Initial contacts with the 16th-century Reformation—including visits to Wittenberg by Damiao de Goes (1501–1573), a humanist—brought no lasting results. The first Bible translation into Portuguese came roundabout via the Dutch East India Company. A former Portuguese Roman Catholic missionary, Joao Ferreira de Almeida (b.1628), who became a Protestant pastor, completed the translation in Batavia (Jakarta), Java, for the benefit of Portuguese settlers and their descendants in the Far East. This translation, revised in 1959—with strong Lutheran participation—is still the standard.

A Protestant presence in Portugal began in Lisbon with the formation of the German Lutheran congregation (1763), joined later by the Anglicans (1843), and the Scottish Presbyterian (1871). These foreign language beginnings were soon paralleled by evangelistic outreach to the Portuguese. Some of it was done by missionaries from Brazil; some by Portuguese returning from the colonies or elsewhere; some by European and North American societies. Mainline Protestants have not become numerous. Pentecostals (Assembly of God), arriving in 1913, are numerically first. Jehovah's Witnesses are a close second.

The Portuguese Council of Christian Churches (PCCC; 1974), based in Coimbra, is foremost among more than a dozen cooperative associations of various types. Like the Evangelical Presbyterian Church of Portugal and the Lusitanian Catholic-Apostolic Evangelical Church—which are members of the World Council of Churches—the PCCC fosters ecumenical endeavors. The Ecumenical Center for Reconciliation (1969) in Lisbon fosters cooperation between the YMCAs as well as the churches in the Iberian Peninsula.

Lutherans in Portugal, until recently, have been a very small number of expatriates. The German Lutheran congregation, although the first Protestant church in the country (1763), has remained a small German community of less than a 100 members. It receives encouragement and support from the *Evangelical Church in Germany (EKD). The embryonic church described below is the only known Lutheran attempt to evangelize the Portuguese.

EVANGELICAL LUTHERAN CHURCH OF PORTUGAL

(Igreja Evangélica Luterana Portuguesa)
Member: CILCE, ILC
Membership: 173**
President: The Rev. Paulo Proske Weirich
Rua André de Gouveia, Lote B, 5:Dto
P—1700 Lisbon

Founded in 1954 by Portuguese lay people, this church consists of three congregations in the areas of Lisbon, Porto, and the Azores. Led by an appointed lay preacher until 1968, the church has since called its ordained pastors from the Portuguese-speaking and *Lutheran Church–Missouri Synod-related *Evangelical Lutheran Church of Brazil (ELCB). At present, the church has two pastors. One also serves as the manager of the "Lutheran Hour," sponsored by the International Lutheran Laymen's League of the LCMS. Since 1970, it has produced weekly 15-minute Portuguese language programs for the national radio network and for local stations. The "Lutheran Hour" conducts a Bible correspondence course, issues a bulletin called the "Lutheran Messenger," and also produces follow-up literature, such as the first biography on Luther ever done in Portugal.

The social ministry program of the church provides services to children, the elderly, and African refugees.The church is working on a seven-year project to provide it with an indigenous public ministry. For the outreach of this small enterprise, both the ELCB and the LCMS provide some financial assistance. Besides, the church has the partnership of the Finnish Evangelical Lutheran Mission, the Conference of Independent Lutheran Churches in Europe, and the International Lutheran Conference. New facilities in Lisbon, opened in 1985 and completed in 1987, have significantly increased the church's capability of outreach.

SPAIN

A constitutional monarchy, Spain occupies most of Suthwestern Europe's Iberian Peninsula, on which its diminutive neighbor is Portugal. Area: 504,750 sq. km. (195,855 sq. mi.), including the Balearic and Canary Islands. Pop. (1985 est.): 38,765,000. Cap. and largest city: Madrid (pop., 1985, 3,271,800). Language: Spanish, the world's third most widely spoken tongue.

History: Geography has made Spain—and neighboring *Portugal—the bridge between Europe and Africa and the base for launching the world's first encircling empire. In Spain, the forces of Greek and Roman culture and the dynamism of Middle East monotheism—Christianity, Islam, and Judaism—interacted creatively. This stimulation helped shape the course of European civilization and of the Western church, not least by presenting an enlarged (Arab) version of Aristotle's thought to Europe's scholars. The ensuing scholasticism of the High Middle Ages—most notable in Thomas Aquinas (1225–1274)—tended to obscure the gospel and later set off the Reformation of Martin Luther.

In early times—around 200 B.C.—Celts, Iberians, and Basques on this peninsula had passed from North African (Carthaginian) to Roman rule. Six centuries later, with the fall of Rome, Spain came under the Germanic West Goths (Visigoths), whose sway continued for three centuries and whose Arian version of Christianity contrasted with the Latin version established there earlier.

Soon after A.D. 700, a new thrust from North Africa brought in the Muslim Berbers and Arabs, commonly called Moors. For the next nearly 800 years Islamic rule covered most of Spain, except for its northern part. A lively Arab civilization flourished, the chief founder of it being the last of the Omayyad princes of Damascus in distant Syria. Jews (Sephardic) in large numbers as well as Christians (called Mozarabs) played active parts in a flowering of culture unequaled elsewhere in Europe. With the resurgence of Christianity and the consolidation of political power leading to a dynamic national consciousness, the Moors were expelled (1492) and also the Jews—providing they had not converted to Christianity. Those who did convert were called Moriscos (former Moors) and Marranos (former Jews). Emigree Sephardic Jews, loyal to their faith, became influential in North Africa and the eastern Mediterranean lands.

The age of discovery and the age of the Reformation—set in the 16th century—included both Charles V emperor of Germany (1519–1558) and King Charles I of Spain (1516–1556). Spain itself welcomed the new (global) space age but rejected the Reformation. From the New World came the wealth of silver and gold wrested from the Aztec and Inca civilizations and also the missionary challenge to make up overseas for whatever losses the Latin church had sustained in Europe. Spain's readiness for this lay in its own experience. Its use of the Inquisition after 1478—to test the authenticity of forced conversions of Jews and Muslims (Moors)—was like a prelude to the founding of the Jesuit order (1534) by Spain's most ardent champion of the church, Ignatius Loyola (1491–1556). A Basque, Ignatius represented ancient roots as well as high expectations.

Religion: Roman Catholicism claims about 92% of Spain's present population. Protestants account for only about 0.5%, or a little over 170,000. Yet these run the spectrum from Spanish Anglican to Jehovah's Witnesses and Pentecostals. Jews are only a few thousand. In 1968, at the dedication of the first synagogue constructed since the 15th century, the minister of justice revoked the 1492 edict, which had banned all Jews and Muslims. There are today some 200,000 Marranos (baptized Catholics), who still observe the Passover and other Jewish rites. Islam, once the ruling power, has been reduced to a small number of adherents living mainly in Madrid and other university cities.

The Roman Catholic hierarchy—which traces its roots to the first century A.D.—comprises 11 archdioceses and 49 dioceses. The archbishop of Toledo, as primate, heads the Episcopal Conference—a post-Vatican II creation that provides guidelines for the dioceses on specific subjects. Roman Catholicism being the religion of the nation, the church enjoys many advantages and receives extensive support. Yet in recent decades, as in previous centuries, the state has not hesitated to interfere in church affairs or to make

the church an instrument of government policy, should clergy or others espouse politically liberal causes, as happened during the 1970s.

The Lutheran Reformation reached Spain early in the 1520s, and some of Luther's writings were translated into Spanish. Calvinist and Waldensian influences likewise appeared, but—like the Lutheran—were of short duration. (An unusual Spanish collection of Reformation-era books today resides in the library of the interdenominational theological seminary, ISEDET, in Buenos Aires, *Argentina.) Under Philip II (1555–1598), successor to Emperor Charles V, Reformation influence was virtually eradicated. Instrumental in this achievement was not only the Spanish Inquisition but also the Spanish Counter-Reformation, led by the Jesuits and their founder, Ignatius Loyola (above). The hard line against Protestants extended to the Spanish colonies in *Latin America and the *Philippines.

A so-called Second Reformation, beginning in the late 1860s, marked the beginning of present-day Spanish Protestantism. Its first ordained pastor, Francisco Ruet (of Waldensian origin), and others formed the Spanish Evangelical Church (1869). Its membership remains under 3500. Calvinist in orientation, this church includes Methodist, Congregational, and Lutheran elements. It has been a member of the World Council of Churches since 1948.

One of the early leaders was the German Evangelical, Fritz Fliedner (1845–1901). Son of Theodor Fliedner (1800–1864), founder of the deaconess work in 19th-century *Germany, Fritz combined Lutheran and Reformed elements—his spiritual legacy—in the manner of the Evangelical Church of the Old Prussian Union (*Germany). His commitment to diaconic service (homes for the orphans and aged, hospitals) and for evangelically-based education (from kindergarten to university preparatory school), as well as his gift for organization and for a comprehension of Spanish culture, made him a central figure in a consolidation of gains made by those engaged in other forms of evangelism. Fritz Fliedner's two grandsons, particularly Theodor, carried the work forward. In 1953, Theodor wrote that, for the future development of Protestantism in Spain, "it would be warmly welcomed if, in addition to other Evangelical churches, Lutheranism would give more attention than hitherto to the work in Spain."

The Spanish Reformed Episcopal Church (SREC; 1880)—counting some 2000—joined the World Council of Churches in 1962. SREC beginnings entered Spain via Gibraltar, and its ecclesial family ties are with the Church of England. In recent times, more conservative Evangelical groups have entered Spain. Their progress, though not impressive, has nevertheless divided Protestants further. Antiecumenical forces (against the WCC, etc.) have tended to confuse the situation. The older churches have grown more slowly or lost members to others. The Spanish Evangelical Alliance brings together representatives mainly of newer groups, while the Spanish Evangelical Council does the same for the two bodies related to the WCC and to the Conference of European Churches.

Besides the Lutheran elements in the Spanish Evangelical Church, Lutherans in Spain are mainly expatriate Europeans. The **Danish Church Abroad** has a congregation in Fuengirola. The **Swedish Church Abroad** has four pastors stationed in different parts of Spain, where their main task is to serve as chaplains to tourists. The **Evangelical Church in Germany** (*EKD), serving Lutherans as well as United and Reformed, supplies pastors to the two oldest congregations in Barcelona (1885) and Madrid (1901) as well as to newer ones in Algorta (on the Bay of Biscay) and La Nucia (near Alicante on the southeast coast). Three other congregations are on the Spanish islands: at Palma, on Majorca in the Mediterranean; at Las Palmas, Grand Canary; and at Puerta de la Cruz, Tenerife (Canaries) in the Atlantic off the coast of Western Sahara (the former Spanish Sahara).

SWITZERLAND

A federal republic (1848) in West Central Europe, bounded by France, the Federal Republic of Germany, Liechtenstein, Austria, and Italy. It is a confederation of 20 cantons and six half-cantons. Area: 41,293 sq. km. (15,943 sq. mi.). Pop. (1985 est.): 6,473,000. Cap.: Bern (metropolitan pop. c.285,000). Largest cities (metropolitan pop.): Zurich, c.720,000; Basel, c.381,000; Geneva, c.320,000. Language (1980): German 65%; French 18.4%; Italian 9.8%; Romansch 1%; other 5.8%.

History: Known as Helvetia in imperial Roman times—an era of which the Romansch dialect is a reminder—modern Switzerland grew out of a defense league formed already in the year 1291 by three German-speaking eastern cantons. More cantons joined, and by 1499 the Helvetic Confederation (denoted CH) was practically independent of the Hapsburg-led Holy Roman Empire of the German Nation. This status was formally reaffirmed in 1648. During the Napoleonic era, the French and Italian cantons drew closer to the German, and all joined in 1848 under a federal constitution.

Switzerland today stands as a durable symbol of neutrality, defended by a civilian army of 650,000 ever on call. In this century, it has become a foremost center for international and worldwide organizations—most of them based in Geneva, home of the League of Nations (1919–1945). Although not a member of the United Nations, Switzerland participates in several UN agencies such as the International Labor Office, the World Health Organization, and the World Intellectual Property Organization, all of which have headquarters in Geneva.

Among the many nongovernmental organizations (NGOs), some of which have long been in Geneva, are the International Committee of the Red Cross, the World YMCA and YWCA, the World Student Christian Federation, the World Council of Churches, the Lutheran World Federation, the World Alliance of Reformed Churches, the Orthodox Center in Chambésy.

Religion: Roman Catholics (1980 est.), about 49% of the population; Protestants, about 47%; Jews, 0.3%; others, about 3%.

From the fourth to the 16th century, Christianity in this country passed through successive stages. Missionary beginnings, led by Celtic and other monks coming off the Helvetian roads across the Alps are today remembered in such places as Romainmôitier, in the west, or St. Gall, in the east. Imperial domination under a Frankish church crested during the time of Charlemagne (d. 814). Local developments involved struggles for power and patronage, often with the diocese of Geneva in the thick of it, deciding clerical appointments. Swiss unification drew the church into the aims of the freedom-minded Helvetic Confederation (after 1291). Church reform, a big issue by the 15th century, culminated in the Council of Basel (1431–1449) and reasserted regional responsibility. This opened the way to the Reformation and a divided church, beginning in the 16th century.

Today, as earlier, each of the six Swiss dioceses—Basel is the far largest among them—relates directly to Rome, for there is no metropolitan archbishopric in the land. Since 1972, however, the Swiss Catholic Synod—a result of Vatican II—has been addressing the needs of the church on a national basis. The visit of Pope John Paul II in 1984 reaffirmed this common effort as well as the ties with Vatican; ties made visible by the colorful Swiss Guards, the papal bodyguard since 1505. The pope's visit to Geneva, which included a history-making meeting in the Ecumenical Center, also recalled an earlier time when the city was the seat of powerful bishops. Since 1536 and the triumph of Calvinism, Geneva has been part of a diocese that includes Lausanne and Fribourg, with the episcopal seat in Fribourg. Swiss Roman Catholicism has proven durable even as it has sought to adapt to changing times. It has produced theologians of note, some of whom have made their mark outside the country, like the ecumenist Hans Küng (b. 1928). His rapport with Karl Barth (1886–1968) on the basic doctrine of justification by faith, and his almost Luther-like courage to criticize the church's failings, have made him a controversial figure as well as a Swiss contribution to the ecumenical movement.

Swiss Protestantism, propounding a church reformed according to God's Word, early became an international influence. The 16th-century Reformation in German-speaking Switzerland, under Huldreich Zwingli (1484–1531), had differentiated itself permanently from the Lutherans (Marburg 1529). In French-speaking Switzerland, John Calvin (1509–1564) carried the day. Better than Zwingli, Calvin learned from Luther—largely through Martin Bucer (1491–1551) in Strasbourg—and then proceeded to develop his own mode of church reform in Geneva.

The 1984 observance of Zwingli's 500th anniversary helped to restore regard for his understanding of church reform; a matter of particular significance to the Reformed churches in Switzerland, in which the ecclesial and theological inheritance of the German-Zwinglian and French-Calvinist constituencies were already coalesced in the *Helvetic Confession* (1536, 1566). Out of Calvin's academy grew today's University of Geneva. While the 450th anniversary of Calvin's birth, observed in 1959, recalled the Reformer's career, a continuing reminder of the spread of Calvinism as a movement is Geneva's famed monument of the Reformation. Even its location is significant; it is spread along the wall where Savoyard invaders—scaling the heights to surprise the city—were repulsed (December 12, 1602, Escalade), thus securing Geneva's enduring independence.

At the monument's center stand four giant, robed figures—Guillaume Farel (1489–1565), Calvin, Theodore Beza (1519–1605), John Knox (c.1513–1572)—flanked by Reformed leaders of various other countries. At the monument's extremes are two vacant pedestals; one is marked Zwingli, the other Luther. The caption over all, *Post Tenebras Lux* (After Darkness, Light), invites that wider range of remembrance which, in the present ecumenical era, seeks to honor pioneers who spread the faith and whom time has obscured.

German-speaking Switzerland provides an example of outreach in the Basel Evangelical Missionary Society (1815). In its rise, German Lutherans, Swiss Reformed, and British Anglicans became partners. Adolf Steinkopf (1773–1859), a Swabian Lutheran pastor, personified the process. In Basel he got his start, serving as secretary of the German Society for Christianity—a joint endeavor of pastors and lay folk to advance spiritual renewal in an Age of Reason. Founded in 1780, the society's base was in Basel, but it had affiliate groups in many cities, including London. Upon his call to London (1801), as pastor of the German Lutheran congregation there (see *United Kingdom), Steinkopf's contacts with the various British societies enabled him to persuade the people in Basel to transform their concerns for church renewal into a missionary enterprise.

The result was the Basel Evangelical Missionary Society, the first on the continent of many others to follow. While an Anglican enterprise like the Church Missionary Society (1799) had the money but lacked missionary personnel, the Basel society provided the personnel during the early decades of the 19th century. German Lutheran or Swiss Reformed ordination, in those years, was fully recognized by the Anglican partners. Only in 1826 did Basel begin to send out missionaries on its own—and some of these, continuing the Anglican connection, became prominent pioneers in the Middle East and *Ethiopia. Today—officially the Evangelical Missionary Society—the Basel Mission is still supported by Lutheran and Reformed churches in Switzerland, *Germany, *Austria, and *France. Several of the churches founded by Basel are today members of the LWF (*Malaysia and *Hong Kong).

Strictly speaking, there is no Swiss Reformed Church. Historic forces have shaped the character of the Reformed legacy variously in each of the 17 cantons where it exists. The range of relationship is from state church in one canton to independent church in another. Likewise, the theological climate varies. Not only is there the aforementioned distinction between the Zwinglian past in German-speaking cantons in the eastern part of the country and the Calvinist past in the French-speaking part; but there are also the inevitable changes in theological climate. An example is that the Reformed Church in Geneva—heir to decisions of 19th-century liberalism—is theologically quite removed from Calvin's legacy. Yet its medieval cathedral, St. Pierre—its restoration started in 1973 and completed in 1986—suggests continuity and catholicity despite change. So also, in the neighboring canton, Lausanne's cathedral—likewise recently restored—is a landmark of modern efforts to manifest Christian unity. The World Conference on Faith and Order was launched there in 1927. Even more so, Geneva's St. Pierre has been the site of many noteworthy ecumenical events.

The Swiss Protestant role in ecumenical theology has been unsurpassed in this century. The dialectical theologians Karl Barth (1886–1968), in Basel, and Emil Brunner (1889–1966), in Zurich, played major roles in guiding theological thought away from a dominant liberalism and into a biblically oriented direction. During the 1930s, Brunner's teaching in America and Barth's in *Germany (Barmen Declaration) proved widely influential.

Within the nation, the visible sign of unity is the Federation of Swiss Protestant Churches (FSPC). Organized in 1920, the federation grew out of a conference of churches (1858). The federation is overwhelmingly Reformed, but it also includes the country's Methodist Church, the Free Evangelical, and the Evangelical Fellowship. Swiss congregations abroad are also members. A major factor in forming the FSPC was the challenge, after World War I, for cooperative action on the part of Swiss Protestants to assist the destitute victims and their churches in various parts of Europe. This relief activity brought the FSPC into close association with counterparts in other countries, especially with the Federal Council of Churches in the USA.

A leading coordinator of these efforts, and later the recognized interpreter of the European church situation to the English-speaking world, was Adolf Keller (1872–1963). In the 1920s, as the FSPC's secretary and also as theological professor, he drew on his extensive experience with the Life and Work movement (the 1925 Universal Christian Conference on Life and Work in Stockholm was called by Nathan Söderblom) and conducted annual international seminars in Geneva on the ecumenical movement and social concern. During and after World War II, the federation was thus in a position to render service to the refugees and to aid in relief and reconstruction projects through its well conducted HEKS agency (Hilfswerk der Evangelischen Kirchen in der Schweiz). Work of this kind by the Swiss helped to get the much larger program of the World Council of Churches—and of the LWF—under way in Geneva. The FSPC continues to cooperate closely with the WCC. Through the Conference of European Churches (CEC) as well as on its own, the FSPC maintains relations with churches in many parts of Europe. Old connections also link it to churches in South Africa and elsewhere.

Churches outside the Protestant federation include the Christian (Old) Catholic, Baptist, Lutheran, and numerous other groups.

● ● ●

The number of Lutherans in Switzerland is estimated at 12,000. They are by no means newcomers, but their composition keeps changing. Although they have nearly two dozen foreign language congregations scattered across the land, it is only the German-speaking congregations in Geneva, Zurich, and Basel that have their own church plants. For the most part, the others worship in rented quarters. Nevertheless, with the placing of Lutheran World Convention (later Lutheran World Federation) headquarters in Geneva in 1945, the presence of Lutheranism, regardless of size in Switzerland, appears in fresh perspective. Its international ties are many and its kinship vast.

Lutheran congregations in Switzerland have two points of origin: Geneva (1706) and Zurich-Basel (1851/1891). From Geneva's German-speaking congregation, affiliated centers sprang up in the cantons of Bern, Fribourg, Thun, and Neuchatel. From Zurich-Basel, affiliated centers formed in eight places: Schaffhausen, Frauenfeld, St. Gall, Baden (Aargau), Wettingen, Biel, Trogen (Appenzell-Ausser-Rhoden). By 1924, St. Gall's congregation had become independent. These developments among the German-speaking Lutherans—as well as the other foreign language ministries in English, Swedish, Danish, and Finnish—have in recent decades taken on the organizational forms described below.

EVANGELICAL LUTHERAN CHURCH OF GENEVA

Membership: 7275**
Place Bourg-de-Four
20 rue Verdaine
CH—1204 Geneva
Pastors: English: The Rev. Stephen
        Larson
        German: The Rev. Volkmar
        Klopfer
        Swedish: The Rev. Anders
        Rydberg

This independent church, of old German origin, evolved in its present form after 1946. Today, it comprises three linguistic congregations—German, English, Swedish—with a number of other language groups related less formally. A council of elected representatives from the three congregations has responsibility for common concerns: the care, upkeep, and use of the historic church building; the encouragement of cooperation among the congregations; and the fostering of joint participation in ecumenical relations. The council sends an observer to the United Evangelical Lutheran Churches (below), in which full membership remains under consideration. Each congregation has its own elected committee to oversee its internal affairs. An annual meeting of all three congregations reviews their reports.

The German congregation maintains a relationship with and receives pastors through the Division for Foreign Relations of the Evangelical Church in Germany (*EKD). The much smaller (c. 275 members) English-speaking congregation has a diversified membership: not only from English-speaking countries like North America and Australia, but also from Africa, Asia, and Europe. A large percent of the membership have English as a second language. At times, the congregation has attracted people of other denominations. Since most employed members have term calls with international organizations, there is a constant change in the constituency. This has influenced the calling of pastors from various synods in the USA and Canada. Both congregations, concerned for children attending Swiss schools, provide religious instruction also in French. The Swedish congregation, less involved since it is also a part of the Regional Association of Swedish Congregations (below), worships in the nearby St. Léger chapel.

The beginnings of the German congregation go back to the time when Protestants in France were hard pressed. In 1701, six German businessmen and their families received permission from the Geneva government to worship in their own Lutheran tradition. They had been evicted from Lyons after the revocation in 1685 of the Edict of Nantes, which had granted toleration to Protestants. By 1707, a congregation had been formed and a pastor received from Germany. The present church building, near the historic urban center of Calvinism and the cathedral of St. Pierre, was erected in 1766. Its appearance is that of a large townhouse, built to conform to regulations of that day, which permitted only the established church—here the Reformed—to have buildings that looked like churches. For a time, Anglicans and Roman Catholics in Geneva also used these Lutheran premises.

The end of World War II brought a large influx of people from other countries to work in the growing number of Geneva-based international agencies and offices. In 1954, the English-speaking congregation, with encouragement and financial assistance from the LWF at the outset, was formed.

By virtue of their international constituency, the Geneva congregations have had members who have gathered and served their own ethnic groups—Hungarians, Finns, Danes, and Norwegians. The most formalized among these efforts is the Danish Lutheran congregation. It now has its own pastor and worships regularly in the chapel of St. Léger.

REGIONAL ASSOCIATION OF SWEDISH CONGREGATIONS
Membership: 6000**
23 rue du Pré du Marché
CH—1004 Lausanne
Chaplain: The Rev. Anders Rydberg

Under the supervision of the archbishop of Uppsala and united by a regional church council are the five Swedish Lutheran congregations in Switzerland: Bern, Geneva, Lausanne, Lugano, and Zurich. Chaplains are appointed by the board of the Church of Sweden. The care of Swedish Lutherans living in Switzerland was begun in 1961 by the Rev. Lennart Söderstrom, who continued in it until 1980.

UNITED EVANGELICAL LUTHERAN CHURCHES IN SWITZERLAND AND THE PRINCIPALITY OF LIECHTENSTEIN (UELCS-L)
(Bund Evangelisch-Lutherischer Kirchen in der Schweiz und im Fürstentum Liechtenstein)
Member: LWF (1979), ACKS
Membership: 6500
President: Otto Diener
Hirschwiesenstrasse 9
CH—8057 Zurich

The UELCS-L, organized on June 17, 1972, associates the Lutheran congregations in German-speaking Switzerland and the neighboring principality of Liechtenstein. Conforming to Swiss usage for church organizations crossing cantonal lines, the UELCS-L carries the designation *Bund* (federation) in its German title. The English term *United* simply indicates that the several participating and self-governing congregations intend to be known together as a church. Behind this unitive achievement lie prolonged efforts of the four German-speaking congregations located in Basel, Zurich, and St. Gall (Switzerland) and in Vaduz, Liechtenstein.

In 1979, the Evangelical Lutheran Church in the cantons of Bern, Fribourg, and Neuchatel—a bilingual area—joined the others. The UELCS-L congregations are served by four pastors, 10 preachers, and two theologians. The UELCS-L remains open to Lutheran churches in other parts of the country, notably in French-speaking Geneva (above).

The polity of this body is congregational. According to the Swiss right of association, each parish has its own constitution. Legislative power resides in the parish (congregational) meeting. The parish council holds the executive powers.

The UELCS-L confession of faith, in the Lutheran tradition, is also the basis for mutual assistance and cooperation in dealing with theological issues, practical problems, ecumenical relations, and the like. The UELCS-L governing body, which meets twice a year, is an assembly of delegates from the local churches. A quarterly, *Lutherische Beiträge,* treats theological and other matters.

The UELCS-L seeks to lend visibility to the Lutheran minority and to enable it to contribute something distinctive from its own confessional heritage to the Reformed and Roman Catholic majorities and to other religious groups as well. The expectation is to receive something in return. Meanwhile, the local churches endeavor to draw upon resources of their own particular background as the following divided history indicates.

Martin Luther Church, Zurich (Kurvenstrasse 39) was organized in 1891 as the Evangelical Lutheran Church in Zurich. Until 1948, it related to the Lutheran Free Church in Breslau (Old Lutheran) in *Germany. Since then, it has had a working relationship with the Bavarian Lutherans through the United Evangelical Lutheran Church in Germany (*VELKD). Two preaching points, long served by Zurich pastors, are now congregations in their own rights: the Evangelical

Lutheran Church in St. Gall was organized in 1924 as an independent church. The Evangelical Lutheran Church in the Principality of Liechtenstein, situated in the capital city of Vaduz, was reorganized in 1954. It has a diversified international membership and a history of more than a century (see Liechtenstein, above).

The Evangelical Lutheran Church in Basel and Environs (Friedensgasse 57) was organized in 1893. Its roots go back to 1864 when a small group of Swiss businessmen, returning from Silesia, decided to continue as Lutherans. For some years, they received assistance from the Old Lutheran Consistory in Breslau, but even prior to World War II this connection had become problematic (see Germany). The congregation dedicated a new parish house in 1967. The following year it received LWF status as a recognized congregation (R).

The Evangelical Lutheran Church in the Canton of Bern, Fribourg, and Neuchatel (Laubeggstrasse 135, Bern), organized in 1951, was served by a pastor of the German-speaking congregation in Geneva until 1962, when it received a pastor of its own. The ensuing decade saw its membership rise to about 1200. At present, it serves some 17,000 in the area. As an independent congregation, its composition is international and its support local. Participation in ecumenical discussions in the Bern area has fostered understanding among Lutherans, Reformed, Christian (Old) Catholics, and others. The congregation maintains a service program, especially to the ill and elderly. For worship services, it meets in the chapel of the Hospital Order of St. Anthony (Antonier-Spital-Orden), an historic edifice built in 1492–1494.

UNITED KINGDOM

A constitutional monarchy and a member of the Commonwealth of Nations, the UK includes the islands of Great Britain (England, Scotland, and Wales) and Northern Ireland, plus many small islands. Area: 244,035 sq. km. (94,222 sq. mi.). Pop. (1985 est.): 56,620,000. Cap. and largest city: London (greater London pop., 1982 est., 6,765,100). Language: English, with some Welsh and Gaelic also used.

History: Insular and apart, Britain has a distinctive history. Over the millennia its insularity had been penetrated periodically. When the Celts, then being pressed by the Germanic tribes, invaded Britain from the continent some time in the 4th century B.C., they found Stonehenge, the quasi-religious monument of an earlier people. Between the Romans in the first century and the Normans in the 11th (1006), Angles, Saxons, Danes, Norse, and others also invaded. But the tide turned. During the ensuing millennium, would-be invaders, including Philip II's Spain, Napoleon's France, and Hitler's Germany, were repulsed. Meanwhile, over centuries, political and social institutions were developed including a constitutional monarchy (Magna Carta, 1215), parliamentary government, and a judicial system that found applicability later among other peoples.

The arts, philosophy, and science accompanied the inventions and technology that helped Britain to launch the modern world's industrial revolution. Given their insularity—an "island of coal surrounded by fish," as it has been called—the British took to the sea, fostered trade, founded colonies of their own people or created colonies by subjugating others, and established a world-circling empire. UK foreign policy hinged on maintaining a balance of power in Europe in order to assure a freer hand in other parts of the globe.

In world affairs, the UK loomed as one of the great powers from the 18th to the 20th century. In the wake of two world wars during this century, however, the force of circumstances has converted the British empire into a self-governing commonwealth, and the commonwealth into independent nations or political units in various parts of the world—as is evident from descriptions of numerous countries throughout this handbook. It is said that one of the greatest imperial experiments in history has thus been changed into a free association of peoples. In 1973, the UK joined the European Community (Common Market). The flow of North Sea oil began in 1975—a boon for a nation dependent on imported raw materials and the sale of manufactures in a competitive world market.

Religion (est.): Anglican 48%; Roman Catholic 9%; Methodist 5%; Presbyterian 4%; other Protestants 2%; Jews 0.7%. About two out of three British people claim some religious affiliation. The Anglo-Saxon invaders who ended Roman rule and extinguished an emerging Christian church were themselves converted to Christianity by Irish and Italian monks and subsequently sent missionaries of their own—Boniface among them—to aid in the conversion of Germans and later also of Scandinavians. The church became firmly established in medieval England and Scotland, a tribute to its earlier flowering in Ireland. Britain's relations with Rome were strained at various times until, in the 16th century, they finally broke under Henry VIII.

While there was a strong political element in the Reformation in England and Scotland, Lutheran and then Reformed influences entered from the continent. Scotland went Presbyterian; England became Anglican and its bishops retained apostolic succession. The rise of Puritanism and other forms of religious dissent, such as Baptists and Quakers, and the periodic threat of a return to Roman Catholicism (via the crown and an underground Catholic elite) marked the British scene, and in the 17th century brought civil war and, finally, religious toleration (1689). Christianity in Britain differed from, but was in many ways related and indebted to, that on the continent. Its distinctive developments included the rise of Methodism (initially a Wesleyan attempt to renew the Church of England), the formation of societies for service at home—like Sunday schools—and missionary work overseas in the colonies and elsewhere.

Interdenominational efforts, like the Evangelical Alliance (1846), fostered international ties as well, especially with kindred spirits in North America. Predominantly English-speaking confessional families began gathering internationally: the Lambeth Conference of Anglican Bishops (1867), what is now the World Alliance of Reformed Churches (1875), the World Methodist Council (1881), and others. Christianity in 19th- and 20th-century Britain has experienced periods of bloom and blight, the latter—like the present depressed state—often summoning forth new creativity, commitment, and quests for unity.

The British Council of Churches (BCC; 1942) has the same basis as the World Council of Churches. Besides the Church of England, it includes nearly two dozen Protestant church bodies, with observers from the Roman Catholic Church, the Society of Friends (Quakers), and others. The Lutheran Council of Great Britain is an active participant.

Lutheran history: Lutheranism's long and varied past in the UK begins with the influx of Martin Luther's writings into England soon after 1517. Some were translated and their theological thrust discussed by German merchants and their English counterparts in London (the Hanseatic Steelyard was one likely place) as well as by students and faculty at Cambridge. Luther's German Bible figured prominently in the translation of William Tyndale (c.1492–1536), who was martyred for his efforts to reform the church. But the effects of his visit to Wittenberg lived on, notably under the later Authorized Version completed under King James I in 1611.

Similarly, Thomas Cranmer (1489–1556), in his pioneering work on the Anglican Book of Common Prayer (1549), embodied Lutheran elements. Many of these endured even in subsequent revisions of the prayerbook. More than three centuries later, when Lutherans in North America were recovering the Lutheran liturgy of the Reformation era and rendering it into English, Cranmer's translations, composition of collects, and other items were embodied into the Common Service Book (1888) of an increasingly English-speaking Lutheranism. Nor should the 450th anniversary of the *Augsburg Confession* (1980) pass without noting its influence on the Church of England's *Thirty-Nine Articles of Religion* (1563, 1571).

The founding of Lutheran congregations in Britain extended from 1669 up to the present time. The Royal Charter (1672) specifically excluded Lutheran worship in the English language so as to prevent the establishment of a Lutheran church. Under Charles II "all companions of the Augustan Profession" in and around London were given a starting point: Holy Trinity Lutheran Church was to serve Lutherans from Scandinavia as well as Germany. Some of them were businessmen and their families; others were artisans who had come to assist with the rebuilding of London after the Great Fire (1666). It was a time when Christopher Wren was making his reputation as an architect of churches, including Holy Trinity. It was dedicated just before Christmas 1673. Gerhard Martens, its pastor, (in London already for five years) had a congregation of many nationalities. Its diversity as well as purpose prefigured the inclusiveness of the 20th-century Lutheran Council of Great Britain (below).

The number of Lutherans in London grew. Relations with the continent and Scandinavia were strengthened by new royal as well as commercial and other ties in an avowedly pro-Protestant climate. The number of Lutheran congregations increased but, as mentioned above, membership in them was limited to foreigners, the Church of England being for the English. Holy Trinity Lutheran Church soon received most of its support from the prime North German trading city of Hamburg and became known as the Hamburg Church. Thanks to the Toleration Act—with the accession of William and Mary in 1689—and the lifting of certain restrictions, the Danish-Norwegian community was authorized to build its own church near the Tower of London in 1692. Conflict in the Hamburg Church led to the formation of a second German congregation in the political heart of London, the city of Westminster (1694). Here, the Lutheran Church of St. Mary-le-Savoy was, by royal favor, granted the use of a chapel in the old Savoy palace. In 1700, Prince George of Denmark, consort to the princess who became Queen Anne (1702–1714), founded the Lutheran Court Chapel of St. James. Its German chaplains were soon to become highly influential in aiding the resettlement of German emigrants in England's North America colonies. A fifth congregation was formed by the Swedish community (1710) in the wake of hostilities with Denmark. Still another Lutheran church, St. George's (1762), was organized on the initiative of the many Germans who had found employment in London.

The Hanoverian line—today's royal House of Windsor—began with George I (1714–1727) and resulted in a near flood of Germans coming to Britain. Among the servants, artisans, tradespeople, as well as those in the arts (George Frideric Handel, 1685–1759), crafts, and learned professions—not to forget courtiers and diplomats—were many Lutherans. Chaplains at the royal court, like Frederick Michael Ziegenhagen, counseled Germans en route to the colonies and, in the case of Henry Melchior Muhlenberg (1711–1787)—en route to Pennsylvania in 1742—

provided credentials that opened the way for a permanent organization of Lutheranism in North America (*USA). Similarly, the London Lutheran church constitution as well as liturgy—influenced by older versions of the Lutheran church in Amsterdam—provided a model for congregational order and worship among the Lutherans in America.

It remained for a congregation like St. George's to become the forerunner of still more German and several more Scandinavian churches, not only in the capital city but also in other parts of Britain. By 1904, an association of German Lutheran churches had been formed, but a decade later it became a casualty of the tragic First World War.

The presence of Lutherans in London during the 18th and early decades of the 19th century facilitated an ecumenical support of overseas mission. An example is the succession of Protestant missionaries in India. They were German Lutherans trained at Halle (or provided by the institution there), sent out—beginning in 1706—by the king of Denmark to Danish-held lands in *India, and supported in part by contributions from the Anglican Society for the Propagation of the Gospel (SPG). German Lutherans, and some Swiss Reformed, also became the first overseas workers—the real pioneers—of the Church Missionary Society (1799). Likewise, the first foreign secretary of the British and Foreign Bible Society (1804) was Carl F.A. Steinkopff (1773–1859), pastor of the German Lutheran church in the Savoy. He proved pivotal in linking the Basel Mission (combining Swabian Lutherans and Swiss Reformed) with corresponding efforts in Britain (see *Switzerland). Unheralded as these background developments remain, they suggest a far-reaching importance achieved in Britain not only by Lutherans but also by that Lutheran offshoot, the Moravians of Zinzendorf's Herrnhut.

Before the confessional lines were drawn more tightly in the mid-19th century—sending Anglicans and Lutherans on separate ways to India and elsewhere—it is worth noting that in Jerusalem (1846) a joint Anglican-Evangelical episcopate was set up. It linked British and German Protestants (Prussian Union) in a common presence among the more ancient churches in the Holy City (*Bible Lands).

The interbellum period was not auspicious for Lutheran unity in Britain. While Swedish, Finnish, and Baltic Lutherans developed agreement with the Church of England, partly because of their mutually recognized apostolic succession and ministry, it was not so with respect to the Germans. During the 1920s, the war guilt question continued to alienate German Lutherans and even to make them suspect the new ecumenical movement as a global form of Anglican triumphalism. During the 1930s, the rise of Hitler and National Socialism proved an embarrassment to the Germans in Britain. Yet, with the church conflict and the emergence of the Confessing Church in Germany, it remained for Anglican leaders like the bishop of Chichester (George K.A. Bell, 1881–1958), to come out boldly in favor of the Confessing side. In various ways, this lead was followed by other churches in other nations as well. As it did to various heads of state, Britain gave asylum to the king of Norway and his entourage. When Norway's primate, Eivind Berggrav (1884–1959), bishop of Oslo, was released at war's end, the Church of England awarded him the Canterbury Cross. A similar high regard was expressed for the bold resistance leaders in the Danish church. Meanwhile, during the war years, the Church of England found the Swedish church indispensable as a meeting place for a select few church leaders from the German resistance like Dietrich Bonhoeffer (1906–1945). For the future of the ecumenical movement such initiative proved salutary far beyond the several national scenes. Against this background, the rise of the Lutheran Council of Great Britain (LCGB, below) in 1948 seemed like a small yet significant sequel, particularly when noting how the participating church bodies in the Lutheran Council reveal a more diversified confessional family in Britain than earlier.

LUTHERAN COUNCIL OF GREAT BRITAIN (LCGB)

Member: (P), CEC, BCC, LFC/GB
Membership: 28,475
Chair: The Very Rev. Robert J. Patkai
8 Collingham Gardens
GB—London SW5 0HW

The LCGB, formed in 1948, is a coordinating agency with certain ecclesial responsibilities that are carried out on behalf of its participating church bodies and foreign language congregations. It fosters a united Lutheran witness and carries out a variety of functions. These include service projects supported financially by its members; programs in theological education; youth and women's work; and the promotion of fellowship and cooperation in other fields. From its inception, the Lutheran Council has had a designated permanent relation to the Lutheran World Federation and serves as the national committee in Britain.

The council's origins lie mainly among the tens of thousand of refugees from the continent who had been granted asylum in Britain. Among them were a high percentage of Lutherans. Help for their immense and diverse needs required concerted action as well as individual motivation and understanding. Less than a year after its organization, the LWF was on the scene in Britain. Its representative, Pastor David Ostergren (*USA), and others met with leaders of the several groups of Lutherans, including Scandinavian representatives, who were already present. After the model of the then National Lutheran Council in the USA they together set up the Lutheran Council of Great Britain. The council was thus envisioned as a service agency for the churches and also as a link with the LWF. The founding date was March 18, 1948.

The LCGB is governed by lay and clerical representatives officially elected by the participating bodies. Representing about a dozen different languages, the LCGB was called the most multilingual Christian family in Britain. The members include: the Estonian Evangelical Lutheran Church in Great Britain, the German-speaking Evangelical Lutheran Synod in Great Britain, the Latvian Evangelical Lutheran Church in Great Britain, the Polish Evangelical Church of the Augsburg Confession Abroad, the Lutheran Church in Great Britain—United Synod, the Hungarian Lutheran Church in England, and congregations of the Evangelical Lutheran Church of Finland, the National Church of Iceland, the Church of Norway, and the Church of Sweden. The council's headquarters, a gift (1953) from funds collected by the National Lutheran Council in the USA, are centrally located in London. The building contains a chapel, conference rooms, offices for some of the member churches, and several residential apartments for staff.

Hothorpe Hall—a small castle some 140 kilometers (90 miles) northeast of London—was acquired by the council in 1955 through the energetic and far-sighted efforts of the council's first youth director, the Rev. Lloyd Swantz of the ALC/USA. At once, it became the focus of a common project of reconstruction as well as a retreat center for countless young people, mainly refugees in England but also youthful volunteers from other lands. Its dedication in August 1956 brought together some 800 people from all over Britain, as well as distinguished guests from LWF churches that had helped finance the project. Over the years, it has served as a study and retreat center for people of all ages. Since the refugee churches have dwindled and the cost of upkeep has increased, it became necessary for the council to close Hothorpe Hall in early 1985. The last service in the beautiful Holy Trinity Chapel was a sad occasion, not only for the Lutherans of Britain but also for the countless people—now living in other parts of the world—who remember its early days of hope.

The International Lutheran Student Center in London is another project of the council. Located near King's Cross and close to the University of London, the five-story hospice and meeting place was dedicated in 1978. It was built on the land of old St. Mary's Lutheran Church, the host. The finances were coordinated by the LWF. The major donation, up to two-thirds of the costs, came from German Lutheran sources. The importance of providing for the physical and spiritual needs of Third World students was brought to the attention of the LWF Commission of World Mission in 1959 by the first secretary of the LCGB's mission committee, Marja-Liisa Swantz of Finland. She had served as a missionary in *Tanzania and knew firsthand the importance of providing a Christian welcome in a foreign land. With LWF assistance, student work has played an important role in the council's program since the early 1960s. A full-time chaplain oversees the center and ministers to a broad cross-section of students, Christians and those of other religions, from Asia, Africa, and other parts of the world.

In the field of professional education, the Lutheran Council has worked with the LWF in sponsoring two ecumenically significant positions. At Mansfield College (Congregational, now United Reformed), Oxford University, a Lutheran theological lectureship was added (1957). Staffed by a succession of choice faculty members from USA seminaries and enjoying the generosity of faculty colleagues as well as university facilities, the arrangement was intended to aid in the preparation of pastors for Lutheran ministry in the UK. Already in the summer of 1958, the first graduate, a Latvian, was ordained for ministry among Latvians and others in Coventry. In 1967, the first Englishman was graduated, given Lutheran ordination and placed in the new St. Mark's Lutheran Church, Birmingham. A modest flow of graduates has continued. Today, the lecturer's main responsibility is to provide Lutheran input, academically and pastorally, to the theological community at Oxford and be a resource person for ecumenical contacts of the Lutheran Council and its member churches and synods.

Similarly, at Selly Oak Colleges, Birmingham, a Lutheran lectureship in missiology, begun in 1970, contributed to the preparation of overseas missionaries, especially those from German and Scandinavian churches appointed to serve in Anglophone countries of Asia and Africa. It also served pastors and lay workers from those continents who have come to Selly Oak for education. Recently, more emphasis has been placed on mission in Europe and the meeting of different religions there—especially with Islam—as well as on development studies. The Lutheran lecturer is part of a theological team of different traditions that should give depth to a program dealing with the theory and practice of mission.

Since its founding in 1948 under postwar conditions, the work of the council has been subsidized by the Lutheran World Federation. In 1972, the Commission on Church Cooperation projected self-support for the council by 1984, but this has not proven feasible. Refugees of the 1940s are now elderly people who need special assistance and care. Most of the young people have emigrated or joined English-speaking churches. The council has also been weakened by the withdrawal of the Evangelical Lutheran Church of England (below), a founding member. Contact with this church and the congregations of the Danish Lutheran church are maintained through the Lutheran Free Conference of Great Britain

(LFC/GB), which was formed in 1957 on their initiative.

Nevertheless, the member churches of the Lutheran Council, after nearly 40 years of service and witness, are realizing that they are facing new realities. It gives them the new and unique opportunity to stand resolutely. They are taking up the challenge. The Lutheran Council is moving toward new horizons.

ESTONIAN EVANGELICAL LUTHERAN CHURCH IN GREAT BRITAIN

Member: LWF (through EELC/Exile)
Membership: 875
Dean: The Rev. A.E. Aaviksaar
34 Pine Tree Avenue
GB—Leicester LE5 IAF

This segment of the Estonian Evangelical Lutheran Church in Exile (headquartered in Sweden) was organized in 1953 by five congregations of displaced Estonians (above, Exile Churches). Most of them had anticipated resettlement elsewhere—*Australia, *Canada, *South America, or the *USA. However, when they found employment in postwar reconstruction and other lines, the Great Britain "way station" became home. Fortunately, these Estonians could latch onto an ongoing ministry from their own country that had been initiated already in 1920 and had close links with Latvian, Finnish, and Scandinavian seamen's mission work. This facilitated the founding of congregations, the first one already in 1946.

The Estonians were also blessed with strong leadership. Dr. Jack Taul, their chosen dean, was formerly lecturer in theology at Tartu (Dorpat) University. The Taul family saga sums up a fuller story of displaced people: flight from Tartu ahead of the Russian advance in 1944; two years in a displaced persons camp in Germany; resettlement in Britain. Initial aid came to the Estonian and other displaced persons in Great Britain from the National Lutheran Council (USA) and then from the LWF. This led to the above-mentioned formation of the Lutheran Council of Great Britain. Dean Taul was one of its founders.

Of the estimated 2000 Estonians in the UK in 1973, pastors were in contact with over 1200. Today, the two old pastors and several assistants serve five small congregations of mainly older people living on small pensions. Home services are increasingly required to attend to their needs. Many of the young people have emigrated, joined English-speaking churches, or have been lost to the church.

EVANGELICAL LUTHERAN CHURCH OF ENGLAND (ELCE)

Member: ELC, ILC, CELFC, LFC/GB
Membership: 1882**
Chair: The Rev. Arnold E. Rakow
Church office: 110 Warwick Way
Victoria
GB—London SWIV 1SD

The ELCE, with 16 congregations served by 14 pastors, has a strong emphasis on confessional Lutheranism. The church has a synodical structure similar to that of the Lutheran Church–Missouri Synod (*LCMS) to which it is related. The congregations, represented each by a pastoral delegate and a lay delegate, meet in synod annually to study a doctrinal theme, to consider resolutions regarding churchwide programs, policies, and missions, and to elect an executive council and the other boards and committees that form the administrative structure of the ELCE. The ELCE publishes *The British Lutheran* magazine quarterly and the *Link* newsletter monthly. Concordia Publishing House provides Lutheran theological publications and education materials for the ELCE and for general distribution.

The ELCE began in an interesting way. Six young German Lutheran bakers, not satisfied with the theological basis of the German churches in London, wrote to Concordia Lutheran Seminary in St. Louis asking for a pastor, each pledging a sixth of their salary to pay the pastor's salary. A pastor came, and in 1896 the Immanuel Lutheran congregation was formed in Kentish Town, London, but its name was later changed to Luther-Tyndale Congregation. Seven years later Holy Trinity congregation was established in Tottenham, London. Although the work began in German, by 1914 English was also used. Since

1930, all services have been in the English language. After 1954, a concerted effort to reach out to people of all backgrounds throughout Britain resulted in establishing 14 more congregations.

With the help of the LCMS, the church has maintained a theological training program (1956) in Westfield House, Cambridge, with a preceptor and a tutor. An agreement with Fitzwilliam House provides opportunity for qualified students to obtain a University of Cambridge degree in theology.

For a few years after World War II, 1948–1956, the ELCE participated in the Lutheran Council of Great Britain and cooperated with the LWF in providing assistance to the large number of Lutheran refugees from the continent. In 1957, shortly after it withdrew from the council, it initiated the formation of the Lutheran Free Conference of Great Britain (LFC/GB). This enabled the ELCE to maintain a loose relationship with the council's member churches as well as with the Danish and Norwegian congregations. A special relationship exists between the ELCE and the Polish Evangelical Lutheran Church of the Augsburg Confession Abroad, both being partners of the LCMS and members of the International Lutheran Conference (ILC) and its counterpart, the European Lutheran Conference (ELC).

GERMAN-SPEAKING EVANGELICAL LUTHERAN SYNOD IN GREAT BRITAIN
(Evangelische Synode Deutscher Sprache in Grossbritannien)
Membership: 3500
Senior: The Very Rev. Eckhard von Rabenau
8 Collingham Gardens
GB—London SW5 0HW

Since 1970, this German synod comprises 30 congregations and a number of preaching points spread throughout Great Britain. Of Lutheran, Reformed, and United heritage, they are served by 10 pastors. The synod is governed by an annual meeting which is presided over by a layperson. A Council for German Church Work, formed in 1950, continues to function as the executive committee of the synod. Pastors and some support are provided by the *EKD Division for Ecumenics and Foreign Relations, FRG. Although mostly German-speaking, much of the work is carried on in English as a large proportion of the members are married to English-speaking people. Their children grow up using English as their primary and often only language. Many of them join English-speaking churches.

Related to the synod are an advisory bureau for German *au pair* girls and the German Mission to Seamen in Great Britain. The latter involves five stations and eight workers. In London there is a German home for the aged and a German YMCA, which runs a modern hotel.

German-speaking congregations have been in existence in London for some 300 years (see Introduction). The 19th century saw the foundation of strong and flourishing congregations in nearly all major cities in Great Britain. World War I led to the collapse or serious weakening of them. Some of them were reopened during the 1920s and 1930s. During the Hitler period, German refugees, many with a Jewish background, brought in a new element. Then, after World War II, the churches had a new set of people needing their service: ex-prisoners of war, soldiers' wives, technicians and their families, *au pair* girls, and business people.

In 1950, representatives of the various German congregations formed the Council for German Church Work (now called Synodalrat) to meet the needs of those Germans who were not being served by existing congregations. This council also coordinated the work of the congregations and served as their common representative. Congregations were formed in Bournemouth, Bristol, Derby, Leicester, Nottingham, Portsmouth, and Sheffield in England; Belfast and Dublin in *Ireland; in Cardiff, Wales, and in west Wales. All of these developed into independent congregations, but some have dwindled to preaching stations.

In 1955, the way was clear for the formation of the German-Speaking Evangelical Lutheran Synod in Great Britain. Some congregations did not join until 1970.

The synod describes itself as an "association" of congregations which, though bound by their confessions, are united in pulpit and altar fellowship. It unites congregations in

Great Britain that are rooted in the Reformation and worship mainly in German. The synod is linked in partnership with the *Evangelical Church in Germany by a contract that stipulates mutual rights and duties and safeguards the personnel and financial support from Germany.

HUNGARIAN LUTHERAN CHURCH IN ENGLAND (HLCE)
Membership: 350
Dean: The Very Rev. Robert J. Patkai
8 Collingham Gardens
GB—London SW5 OHW

After 1945, Hungarian refugees began to come to Britain from camps in Austria and Germany. Their first congregation, organized in London in 1948, became the center from which a ministry was extended to compatriots dispersed in various parts of the UK. Thousands of other refugees, among them Lutherans, came to Britain after the Hungarian revolt of 1956. While most of them moved on to resettle in North America, South America, Australia, and elsewhere, others remained in Britain. Assistance came to them from the LWF and the Lutheran Council. Among the pastors in the 1956 influx was Robert Patkai, who later became the dean of the HLCE and currently chairs the Lutheran Council. Hungarians have contributed significantly to the total Lutheran enterprise in Britain.

LATVIAN EVANGELICAL LUTHERAN CHURCH IN GREAT BRITAIN
Member: LWF (through LELC/Exile)
Membership: 2250
Dean: The Very Rev. Ringolds Muziks
17 Ivanhoe House
Balham
GB—London SW12 8PS

This church reports a membership of 2250, very slightly more than in 1973. The nine congregations, whose membership also includes some Lithuanians, are served by six pastors. This church is a branch of the *Latvian Evangelical Lutheran Church in Exile whose headquarters are in Canada.

The first Latvian refugee congregation was formed in 1945. Three years later, the church was organized under the leadership of Dean Edgar Bergs, who represented Archbishop Teodor Grünbergs (1870–1962) of the LELC/Exile. At that time, there were 15,500 Latvian displaced persons in Britain, scattered in temporary camps and work locations across the country. The church helped to restore their common bonds and to revive hope. Dean Bergs, like his Estonian colleague Taul (above), was one of the founding fathers of the Lutheran Council of Great Britain.

The Latvians in London have shared a church building with the Estonians and St. John's congregation of the Lutheran Church in Great Britain—United Synod since April 23, 1966. On that day, the ancient St. Anne and St. Agnes church was rededicated after being rebuilt with funds provided by the Anglican London Diocese authorities. Since it was situated in a part of London that was no longer residential, it was given to the Latvian and Estonian congregations on the basis of a theological agreement signed in 1938.

LUTHERAN CHURCH IN GREAT BRITAIN—UNITED SYNOD
Membership: 3000
Dean: The Very Rev. Walter Jagucki
8 Collingham Gardens
GB—London SW5 OHW

At present, there are four congregations belonging to the United Synod, which was formed in 1961. At that time, the potential for growth of English-speaking congregations seemed hopeful. Often, with the formation of refugee congregations, the needs of others desiring Lutheran worship in the English language came to light. Thus, when arrangements were made for the Latvians and Estonians in the restored ancient St. Anne and St. Agnes church, the newly formed St. John's was also included. The membership of this congregation then and today consists mainly of short-term residents.

Less transient congregations were formed in Corby, a city growing up around giant steel works; in Birmingham, where the first ordained graduate of Mansfield College was called as pastor; and in Leeds, where the congregation is made up of people of many nationalities. In 1985, the latter celebrated its 21st anniversary with the dedication of a new sanctuary next to its parish house and student hostel.

During its first quarter century, the United Synod has been greatly dependent upon the financial support of the Lutheran Council of Great Britain and the LWF. At present, there are six ordained pastors.

POLISH EVANGELICAL LUTHERAN CHURCH OF THE AUGSBURG CONFESSION ABROAD (PELCACA)
Member: ELC, ILC, LCGB
Membership: 3000
Bishop: The Rt. Rev. Wladyslaw Fierla Ph.D., D.D.
2 Leinster Road
GB—London N10 3AN

From the time of its formation in 1953 as the Polish Evangelical Lutheran Church in Exile, this church has been the focal point of the Polish Lutheran dispersion in the free world. Besides those in Britain, a similar number or more reside in the *Federal Republic of Germany; others in *France, *Argentina, *Brazil, *Venezuela; and still others in *Australia and *New Zealand. Polish Lutherans in North America—many of them in *Canada and the *USA since early in the present century —have long since taken their congregations into the *Lutheran Church–Missouri Synod. The PELCACA thus has formal ties with the LCMS, with its related Evangelical Lutheran Church of England, and with the International Lutheran Conference. However, it is also a member of the Lutheran Council of Great Britain. In 1983, the present name was adopted.

With headquarters in London, the 16 congregations in England, Wales, and Scotland benefit from the leadership of Bishop Fierla, who in 1983 observed his 30th anniversary in office. The church's legislative body is the synod, which meets every three years. The synodical board has 14 members, and there is a five-member consistory or executive board over which the bishop presides. The six pastors are assisted by lay members.

Other important work includes radio ministry. Bishop Fierla has preached in Polish and Slovak on the BBC since 1947; as Polish speaker on the "Lutheran Hour" since 1953; on Radio Free Europe and programs such as "Christ Lives" on Trans World Radio, Monte Carlo, since 1952; and occasionally on Voice of America.

The rise of this Polish church began in the later 19th century with the emigration from a then politically non-existent Poland. The far larger exodus of Roman Catholics overshadowed this egress of Polish Lutherans. The latter came mainly from the Masurian lake region in East Prussia, in the north, and from the Teschen (Cieszyn) region in Silesia, in the south of *Poland. These emigrants were forerunners to the later exiles of 1939. In that summer, the Nazi German occupation of Poland created thousands of Polish exiles and refugees. Later came many who had been prisoners of war or prisoners of the Nazi concentration camps. About two-thirds were military; others included laborers, farmers, professionals, and diplomats.

By 1945, the first of many congregations had been formed in London under the leadership of Dr. Andrzej Wantula, the chief chaplain of the Polish Armed Forces in Great Britain. After the end of the war, he was among the many who returned to Poland, where he became bishop of the Evangelical Lutheran Church of the Augsburg Confession in 1959.

Replacing Wantula as chief chaplain in 1947 was the Rev. Wladyslaw Fierla. Arrested by the Gestapo in 1940, he was subsequently sent to concentration camps at Dachau and Mathausen-Gusen. On achieving freedom in 1944, Fierla joined the Polish Army in Italy and was made chaplain to the Polish Second Corps. In 1945, he became pastor of the first Polish Lutheran congregation in exile in Jerusalem (established in 1942, this congregation ceased to exist in 1953 due to emigration).

With the growth of the Polish church in the United Kingdom, Fierla was elected senior pastor in 1948 and president with the title of bishop in 1953, when the independent autonomous Polish Evangelical Lutheran Church in Exile was organized. The constitution adopted had been authorized by the Polish government in exile in London in 1952 and is the same as the 1936 constitution of the Lutheran church in Poland.

Exiled Poles became redeployed to other fronts. A Polish Lutheran congregation in exile was formed in Paris, and after the war—when slave laborers were freed and others fled Poland—about 60 congregations were formed in West Germany.

Yet, the cohesiveness that has marked Poles generally has kept the church members in touch with their fellow members in many lands. *Posel Ewangelicki* (Evangelical Herald), the church's monthly paper since 1945, has its base in London. In January 1987, the 500th issue was published. Other publishing ventures include Luther's catechism, hymnals, and works of spiritual power, such as the late Bishop Andrzej Wantula's book, *From the Valley of the Shadow of Death,* the tale of his imprisonment. All congregations use the Gdańsk (Danzig) Bible (1632) and the new translation of 1975 published in Warsaw.

As new generations rise, the PELCACA diminishes numerically and some of its descendants find their way into other churches. But its saga of steadfastness remains.

SCANDINAVIAN CONGREGATIONS

The Lutheran church bodies of Scandinavia—*Denmark, *Finland, *Iceland, *Norway, and *Sweden—all have congregations centered in London as well as seamen's missions in the major ports of Great Britain. These congregations are well established—some dating back to the early 18th and early 19th centuries (see Introduction)—and they play an important part in the life of the different national groups. Pastors, supplied by the several national churches, conduct regular worship services in their language. These are supplemented by social activities with special outreach to the hundreds of young people who come to Britain for study or work. Some congregations also provide schools and youth hostels for their constituencies. Members living outside London are kept in touch by monthly bulletins and occasional pastoral visits.

Sometimes the Scandinavian congregations have a united Sunday morning worship service. Joint youth activities are also arranged periodically. In addition, the clergy meet regularly for discussion and consultation. They also alternate in providing worship services in other parts of Britain. The Finnish, Icelandic, Norwegian, and Swedish congregations are members of the Lutheran Council of Great Britain (above).

The Seamen's Church of the *Evangelical Lutheran Church of Finland (33 Albion Street, London) was established already in 1881. Besides the approximately 3500 seamen served annually, it ministers to another 6000 Finns living in Great Britain and has contact with a further 4500 Finnish-British families. The Finnish church has two pastors, and regular events are organized in about 20 places around Great Britain.

The Swedish Ulrika Eleonora Church (6 Harcourt Street, London), established by the Church of Sweden in 1710 (see Introduction), now has two pastors serving the some 25,000 Swedes living in Great Britain. There are also Swedish Seamen's churches in Liverpool, Middlesbrough, and London. Of this number, the pastors have contact with about 4500 households, of whom 1000 are on the electoral role.

The Danish and Norwegian congregations are members of the Lutheran Free Conference of Great Britain, which relates them more closely with the Evangelical Lutheran Church of England (above).

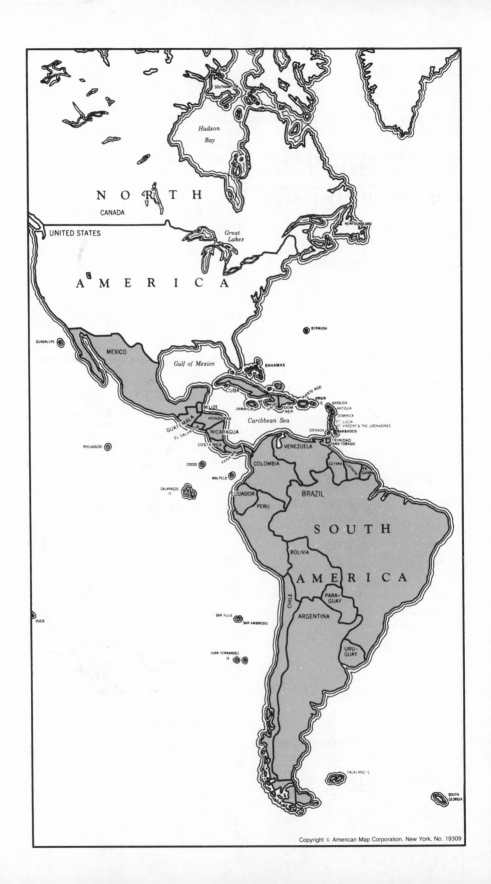

LATIN AMERICA AND
THE CARIBBEAN_____

Ever since the age of discovery, Europeans have spoken of the New World as "the Americas." Collectively, the Spanish and Portuguese and some French acquisitions of the 16th century became known as Latin America. Culture and language continue to give the present independent countries, within this common heritage, natural avenues of communication and cooperation. These have also been used by the churches, including the Lutherans. However, within and around Latin America are countries and islands that have a more Northern European and African heritage. For them, "Caribbean" is a more acceptable designation.

This Latin American and Caribbean region covers 22,988,759 sq. km. (8,875,969 sq. mi.), with a population of 322,543,200. This is 16% more land and 25% more people than in North America (USA and Canada). As the separate country stories relate, this includes Amerindians, as well as people of European, African, and Asian background. Besides the 178 million who speak Spanish, 138.4 million speak Portuguese (Brazil), about six million French, three million English, and 589,000 Dutch.

South America—the fourth largest continent—comprises 77.5% of this area and 82% of the population. Politically it is divided into 12 independent countries and French Guiana, an overseas department of France. The political and religious history of this continent is included in the brief overview (below), and further historical information appears under the 12 countries, all having Lutherans. They number over 1,220,000 and comprise 97.7% of the region's Lutherans.

After a brief introduction to this area as a whole, with special emphasis on the avenues of Lutheran cooperation in the context of the general religious situation, the churches are described in their geographic setting as follows:

Brazil; Intercontinental Area; Non-Latin countries; Northern Andean Zone; and Southern Cone

History

Latin America, as a term, is a cultural as well as a geographic designation. It reflects the Latin origin of the languages spoken by the three major European conquerors and colonizers—the Spanish, the Portuguese, and the French. (Logically, French Canada is part of Latin America by this reasoning, but here geographic separation indicates otherwise.) The main access to the riches of the conquered Aztec and Inca civilizations of Mexico and Peru lay through the Caribbean Sea— the "American Mediterranean" and, as learned later, the warming area for the Gulf

Stream, whose steady flow made Europe's climate temperate. As greed for gold and plundered treasure was veiled by conquest and conversion, the Spaniards in particular fell prey to the self-righteous piracy of English and Dutch Protestants who—later on with the Danes as well—established themselves around the rim of the Caribbean. For Spain, and then Portugal, the course of empire in the New World eventually faltered. The fever of freedom proved contagious, as the British colonies in North America set an example for the viceroyalties in Intercontinental and South America. In place of unity, however, disunity took permanent form. Close-ups of these developments appear in the ensuing accounts of Latin American—and also Caribbean—countries and their churches.

Religion

Latin America, including parts of the Caribbean, has for centuries been synonymous with Roman Catholicism—so much so that the 1910 World Missionary Conference meeting in Edinburgh, Scotland, omitted Latin America from its agenda because the area was deemed Christian. But these Christians often included unwilling and critical heirs to a church establishment that displaced the religions of Aztec, Mayan, and Inca civilizations as well as many other folk religions.

African Traditional religion was brought to the Caribbean islands, Brazil, and elsewhere by the indispensable but enslaved black work force. Baptism was required of slaves serving Christian masters, but its pro forma follow-through left room for giving the names of Christian saints to African deities. Spiritism today manifests the durability of this African legacy in such modes as Umbanda in *Brazil or Vodun (Voodooism) in the *Caribbean.

Roman Catholicism undertook the conversion of Indians and Africans as both a missionary and a political task. In doing so, it shared in the "civilizing" process of the European conquerors. Some of its leaders even contended that God had given the New World to his church in gracious compensation for lands lost to it through the Reformation of Martin Luther. Missioning in America was regarded primarily as a responsibility of the Spanish and Portuguese crowns—with the papacy in the background. By concordat the Iberian monarchs had gained the right of controlling church affairs at home and of spreading the faith in their "possessions" overseas.

The need for education brought schools. Already in the late 16th century universities became partners in mission and bearers of civilization. They also fostered the training of a native priesthood, an example being Santo Toribio Seminary in Lima (1591), long a part of San Marcos University in that city. Church buildings and institutions of various kinds drew on European and indigenous arts and crafts, culminating in colonial baroque or mission-style architecture. Festivals, processions, and observances further enhanced the sights and sounds of a folk-Catholicism, all of which focused finally in the Mass.

European currents of thought over successive generations were not slow in crossing the Atlantic and finding reception among the elite. Eighteenth-century Deism (Rationalism) made its impact, loosening the grip of the church and giving a new rationale to political life. It helped open the way—by the example of North America's War of Independence and then of the French Revolution—for Latin American independence as well.

In the new nations, efforts toward a larger unity, as in the *United States of America, failed—as the career of Simón Bolívar demonstrated. But indigenous political power, in the manner of *Spain and *Portugal, was superior to ecclesial power. The Roman Catholic Church remained established. Catholicism continued as the official religion, but the state was in control.

Protestants gained toleration, then legal recognition, during the late 19th century. But their situation varied from country to country. Their missionary efforts, bound to the Bible and generally anti-Roman Catholic, introduced new modes of education and fresh perspectives on the common life. In effect, since the major Protestant thrust was from North America, the efforts of Methodists, Presbyterians, and Baptists were like an extension of methods developed on the American frontier. Other denominations followed later, intensifying the demand for religious liberty.

Changes in many quarters prompted the papacy, even during World War I, to strengthen its hand via the ecclesiastical hierarchy. In 1916, papal nuncios in the several lands became permanent representatives of the Holy See. In lands like Mexico the church faced opposition from the state. In others, like Colombia, its privileges continued longer. After World War II, in the face of widespread transitions in political and economic life, the Vatican authorized the formation of the Latin American Episcopal Conference (1955). This enabled the bishops of the region to cooperate more effectively in matters of mutual concern.

Developments like these also indicated a Roman Catholic apprehensiveness toward the steady advance of Protestantism. It reminded Rome that the missionary task, begun centuries earlier, was far from done. One instance of pointed significance, the closing of opportunities in China during World War II, caused the Vatican to redirect the (North) American Missionary Society—Maryknoll—to Latin America. A grass roots account in 1946, *Call for Forty Thousand* (John J. Considine), exemplified the widespread challenge for priests and nuns and other missionary workers. But it also showed how the new thrust would side with the poor and endeavor to renew the church from the bottom up.

As Protestant mission personnel came to Latin America in ever greater numbers, small beginnings sometimes led to amazing results. This was especially true among the Pentecostals—the Assemblies of God. First in Brazil (1910), then in Chile, and elsewhere as time passed, they drew ever larger numbers. By a kind of "natural," or spiritual, selection their pastors rose through the ranks of responsibility and provided acceptable as well as imaginative leadership for the ordinary folk. In its Scripture-oriented way, Pentecostalism provided a step forward into the church as people of God, rather than allowing a slip sideways into Spiritism. It has also helped stimulate a missioning outreach among traditional, nonmissionary (German origin) Lutherans.

The Roman Catholics, too, have been affected. The people's quest for liberation from poverty and exploitation, and for the creation of a social order based on a Christian understanding of justice—free from the domination of outside forces (North American and European) allied with overprivileged minorities at home—has brought changes. Some of the church leaders have joined the people in this quest. Expressive of these concerns was the work of the Second General Conference of the Latin American Episcopate at Medellín, near Bogotá, Colombia, in 1968, and of the

Third General Conference in Puebla, near Mexico City, in 1979. These conferences made clear that the masses of poor are to be evangelized by the gospel in action. Supportive of this change in ecclesial climate, and initially also encouraged by it, was Vatican II. The outcome is yet far from clear. But the church is siding increasingly with the poor—not with an imitation of Marxism, but with a gospel-based commitment to human rights and an application of Christian teaching. Strong reservations, in Rome as well as in many parts of the continent, still stand in the way. But the more than 150,000 (estimated) Basic Ecclesial Communities (Comunidades Eclesiais do Base–CEBs) in Brazil and other countries are really house congregations that bring worship, Bible study, and the application of scriptural teaching into the common life.

Events have progressed similarly on the Protestant side. Already in 1916, the Panama Congress—a sequel to Edinburgh 1910—recognized the many Protestant efforts and organized the Committee on Cooperation in Latin America. Fifty years later (1965) came the Movement of Evangelical Unity in Latin America (UNELAM). Akin to the World Council of Churches, its membership included church federations in eight countries (*Argentina, *Brazil, *Chile, *Cuba, Dominica, *Mexico, *Puerto Rico, and *Uruguay). Support for UNELAM's various functions came from the WCC and the National Council of Churches (USA). Late in 1982, this provisional organization convened in Lima, Peru, with 300 delegates and observers from more than 100 demoninations and ecumenical organizations to form the Latin American Council of Churches (CLAI). Joining the council were 16 Lutheran churches from 13 countries. The first executive committee of 14 included three Lutherans.

CLAI continues the earlier concerns of UNELAM, including Bible study, theological issues, the place of women in society, concern for justice, the care of the poor, and education for ministry. Alongside CLAI are other Latin American agencies devoted to church and social renewal: The Latin American Commission on Church and Society (ISAL), the Student Christian Movement (MEC), the Union of Latin America Ecumenical Youth (ULAJE), and the Evangelical Latin American Commission on Christian Education (CELADEC). The activities of these agencies express a Protestantism that not only has become thoroughly indigenous, but also is bringing fresh interpretations of the gospel, relevant and applicable to the needs of modern life both in and beyond Latin American and the Caribbean.

The explosiveness of many social and national situations has called forth an often radical Christian response that involves risks for churches as well as individuals. In the process, a new kind of partnership has emerged in various quarters between Protestants and Roman Catholics. In some instances, Lutherans have been in a mediating position ecumenically, not least because of the Lutheran/Roman Catholic dialog (*France, Strasbourg Institute for Ecumenical Research), which was launched by the LWF in 1963 and included Latin American considerations.

Even so, Protestantism in Latin America continues handicapped by divisions. Some of them cut across denominational lines and set liberal versus conservative, ecumenical versus evangelical, catholic versus anti-Roman Catholic. Much of this stems from earlier times, when Protestant missions were widely anti-Roman; but also from more recent times, when ecumenical has been equated with Marxism— alleged largely because WCC members include Orthodox and other churches in the

Eastern bloc countries of Europe. It remained, however, for the Faith and Order Commission of the WCC, at Lima in early 1982, to reveal in its report on "Baptism, Eucharist, Ministry," a remarkable convergence of understanding in these critical elements of the Christian faith on the part of Catholic, Orthodox, Anglican, and Protestant theologians (see above, General Introduction). For Christianity in Latin America such convergence promises much for the future.

Lutherans in Latin America and the Caribbean

The Lutheran church in Latin America and the Caribbean, like the church in *Australia or *Canada, is predominantly an immigrant church. This fact has often delayed Lutheran cooperation with other Protestants in Latin America who are almost entirely the product of missionary activity by other than Lutheran churches and mission agencies in the *USA and Canada. Lutheran immigrants of both the 19th and 20th centuries have been tempted to remain apart from the surrounding Iberian culture. Moreover, as Protestant Christians with a confessional legacy, they were different from Spanish- or Portuguese-speaking Protestant converts from Roman Catholicism, who tended to be anti-Catholic as well as theologically fundamentalist.

Immigration from Germany brought Lutherans to *Brazil as early as 1824, before the beginning of any Protestant missionary work in that country; to *Argentina, *Uruguay, and *Chile in the 1840s; to *Mexico in the 1860s; and to other parts of Latin America as well. These movements paralleled those to *Southern Africa and *Australia, the much larger ones to the *USA and *Canada, and the eastward flow to *Russia, *Yugoslavia, and *Poland. Missionary societies and emigrant mission agencies were formed in *Germany to help supply pastors. Where possible, these services were coordinated—because diplomatic action was also at times essential—largely through the top administration of the Evangelical Church of the Old Prussian Union in Berlin, which was closely related to the government.

To a lesser extent, the overseas ministry was picked up in adapted form by the German Evangelical Church after World War I, when there was a smaller but also significant German emigration. It took on still another form after World War II. This time the flow of emigrants to Latin America also included large numbers of Hungarians, Slovaks, Estonians, Latvians, and others. Among the latter were many ethnic *Volksdeutsche* from Eastern Europe. The newly organized Lutheran World Federation (1947) created a Committee on Service to Refugees, directed by Stewart W. Herman. He and his staff made valuable contacts with church leaders and other influential residents in *Argentina, *Brazil, *Chile, *Colombia, *Peru, and *Venezuela, laying the basis for a kind of cooperation hitherto unknown in Latin America. This enabled the resettlement of thousands of displaced people.

Along with growth by immigration, there has been growth by mission. Already in 1899, a predecessor body of the *Lutheran Church in America began work in *Puerto Rico, and in 1908 in *Argentina. A predecessor body of the *American Lutheran Church (now ELCA) entered *Mexico in 1947 after 30 years of work with Mexican Americans near the border. In the late 1930s, three faith missions emerged from a prayer group in Minneapolis comprising members of Upper Midwest congregations of various church bodies. The Colombia Evangelical Lutheran Mission (CELMOSA) began work in *Colombia in 1936; the World Mission Prayer League in *Bolivia (1938); and the Latin American Lutheran Mission in *Mexico in 1942. They led still other USA Lutherans to the Andean Amerindians.

A different type of mission activity had been undertaken in 1899, when the *Lutheran Church–Missouri Synod set up activities in *Brazil, and then later in *Argentina and other countries. The initial and sustained purpose was to make Lutherans out of German Evangelicals. Later, the Missourians used their widespread radio ministry via the "Lutheran Hour" to reach out, with some success, to Spanish- and Portuguese-speaking Latin Americans. Today, the result of this mission work is variously estimated at comprising from 2% to 4% of the entire Lutheran constituency.

In 1951, the first All-Latin America Lutheran Conference—including immigrant as well as mission-founded churches—was held in Curitiba, *Brazil, under the auspices of the LWF. The conference proved decisive in the formation of the LWF Committee on Latin America (CLA) at the Hanover Assembly (1952). This committee, also under the direction of Stewart Herman, continued the concern for refugees in cooperation with the Lutheran churches of Latin America and the National Lutheran Council in the USA.

Through this work with refugees, the presence of large numbers of unchurched Germans and Scandinavians became visible. Some had been without pastors for long periods due to the war. Others had never had a pastor and were learning all too well to live without a church. The LWF/CLA worked out a cooperative relationship with the Foreign Office of the *Evangelical Church in Germany (EKD) so that older congregations could be revitalized and integrated with the new congregations of refugees and displaced persons—Latvians, Estonians, Hungarians, and East Germans. In key cities, congregations were formed that provided worship in several languages.

The Scandinavian churches cooperated by providing multilingual pastors for these new efforts. The drama of these congregations unfolds in the stories of the churches below.

In 1956, the time seemed right for the LWF to recognize the new multilingual congregations. The one in Caracas, *Venezuela, was the first to receive the recognized (R) status. This included the right of representation at the Federation's assemblies by an official observer, with voice but no vote. Altogether, 13 congregations in Latin America and the Caribbean have been recognized. Some have or are about to become small church bodies; others have reverted to type.

Besides helping to form congregations, the LWF/CLA was instrumental in the establishment of the Lutheran Theological Seminary (1956) in José C. Paz, a suburb of Buenos Aires. This provided a rallying point for the young mission churches and their USA partners as well as the refugees—among them well-qualified pastors and professors. In an amazingly short period, a recognized school was in operation that was meant to serve all the Spanish-speaking churches of South America (*Argentina). Conditions continued to change, and in 1970 the Lutheran school merged with the much older Union Seminary in Buenos Aires, thus forming the Evangelical Institute of Advanced Theological Study (ISEDET). A more modest undertaking in Mexico City was intended to serve the young churches in Mexico and Colombia. Augsburg House was founded and supported by the American Lutheran Church in 1957 (*Mexico). It later concentrated on theological education by extension (TEE).

The movement toward Lutheran cooperation, which began with the All-Latin America Lutheran Conference (1951) continued with the encouragement of the LWF/CLA. A second conference (1954) met in Petrópolis, Brazil; the third in Buenos Aires (1959). The high point was reached in Lima, Peru (1965), when the conferees (including Missourian-related representatives) voted to create a Latin American Lutheran Council. Sharing the outreaching spirit of UNELAM (above), created the same year, Lutherans gave special urgency to joint efforts in producing materials for Christian education in church schools and other forms of literature and theological works. A draft constitution proposed theological study as an essential part of the projected council's activity. Unfortunately, these hopes did not materialize. Spiraling inflation, political turmoil in several countries, and confessional conflicts stood in the way.

The withdrawal of the LWF Fifth Assembly from Brazil on short notice in 1970 was another setback for Lutheran unity and cooperation. This assembly also re-structured the LWF's organization, eliminating the Committee on Latin America. Instead, the work of assisting and encouraging the churches became the responsibility of the Commission on Church Cooperation.

When the Fifth Latin American Lutheran Congress (the name had been changed) met in José C. Paz, Buenos Aires, in 1971, plans for regional rather than all Latin American coverage were adopted. The four regions were: *Brazil; the Southern Cone—*Argentina, *Chile, *Uruguay, *Paraguay; the Andes—*Bolivia, *Peru, *Ecuador, *Colombia, *Venezuela; and the Caribbean—*Mexico, *Central America, *Panama, *Guyana, *Puerto Rico, and *the Virgin Islands.

Alternate ways of cooperating have been emerging. In 1972, the churches in Colombia, Ecuador, Mexico, Peru, and Venezuela coordinated their theological education by extension (TEE) programs with Augsburg Seminary in Mexico City. The programs—which differ from country to country—have a common coordinator/ pastor. Support comes from the three major Lutheran churches in the USA, the LWF, and local sources. Co-Extension—as it is called—produces literature for the various programs and has its own publication, *El Extensionista*. In some countries, pastoral candidates are trained for ordination. In others it is mainly a lay program for better congregational leadership.

Since 1973, Lutheran church synods, councils, congregations, and missions of different historical background in the Northern Zone, as well as the Spanish-speaking churches in Middle America, have cooperated in the field of Christian education, producing materials and conducting workshops to improve educational standards. The presidents of the various Lutheran churches from all areas, especially those belonging to the LWF, have annual meetings with the LWF secretaries. Workshops on evangelism and mission and area women's conferences have strengthened the understanding of the church.

In deference to the non-Latin churches, the DCC secretary became known as the Secretary for Latin America and the Caribbean. English-language conferences are held to strengthen understanding and mutual helpfulness in the island churches as well as in *Guyana and *Suriname.

The Sixth Latin American Lutheran Congress meeting in Bogotá, Colombia, in August 1980, demonstrated the growth of the churches in strength and self-reliance. The conference, organized mainly by representatives of the LWF-related churches in the region, had "Our Faith and Mission in Latin America" as the theme. Before, during, and after the congress, other groups convened, including Co-Extension (above) and LUC. The latter—Lutherans United in Communication—is a Latin American forum that attempts to share information among Lutheran churches and groups in Latin America and to strengthen the communication work through workshops and seminars. It grew out of an earlier media project known as LAMP (Latin America Media Project).

A recurring concern for most of the churches is the training of their pastors. With the closing of the Augsburg Seminary in Mexico City in 1981 for lack of students, the Faculty of Theology in Brazil is the only LWF-related Lutheran Seminary in all Latin America and the Caribbean. The great distances make it impractical for the northern churches to use the seminary (ISEDET) in Argentina. Many recognized interdenominational seminaries are being used, but the presidents of the churches think that these schools do not adequately train their pastors in Lutheran theology and practice. Co-Extension, which continues, has its limitations. To help meet this urgent need for well-trained pastors, the Brazilian faculty has agreed to receive annually 15 Spanish-speaking students who qualify for LWF scholarships.

The Seventh Latin American Lutheran Congress meeting in Caracas, Venezuela, in April 1986, faced a number of serious issues. One, affecting all, is the rapid urbanization. How can the church more effectively deal with the problems of isolation and unemployment? The delegates also shared their disappointment over the ethnic refugee groups who, after a quarter of a century in their new lands, have yet to become a part of Latin American culture and society. Other concerns included the rapid multiplication of sects and cults—an indication that the older churches, including the Lutherans, are not meeting the longing of people for security and hope. In light of these immense problems, the congress tried to discover methods, means, and possibilities for bringing God's Word and Christ's redemption to a troubled people.

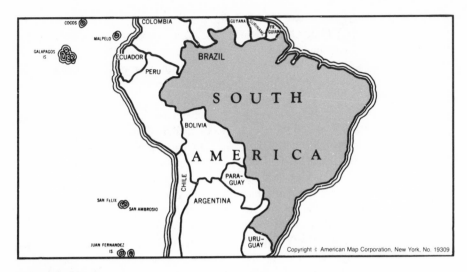

Copyright © American Map Corporation, New York, No. 19309

BRAZIL

Brazil occupies one-half of South America's area and has about one-half of its population. Lutherans number 1,052,750—86.2% of all Lutherans in South America.

A federative republic comprising 23 states, a federal district, and three territories. Area, covering half of the South America continent: 8,511,965 sq. km. (3,286,488 sq. mi.). Pop. (1980 census) 138,403,000. Cap.: Brasília (pop., 1980 census, 411,305). Largest cities: Rio de Janeiro (cap. until 1960), 5,091,000; São Paulo, 7,033,000. Language: Portuguese.

In the Western Hemisphere, Brazil is third in size to Canada and the USA. Its population, concentrated mostly along the coast, doubled between 1960 and 1980. Portuguese and African elements predominate. Amerindians have become a small minority (0.2%). Racial mixing of these three elements began early and continues to this day. Italians, Germans, Lebanese, Japanese, and other nationalities have more or less kept their identity. Yet all are Brazilians first. This is a diverse society, quite free of racial discrimination—except at times toward the completely black as well as toward the Indians in the upper Amazon basin. Blacks are the majority in the north, whites in the southern states. At present, overpopulation is not a problem in this land rich in resources. The problem lies rather in equitable distribution.

History: For three centuries Brazil was a Portuguese colony. Discovered in April 1500 by Pedro Alvarez Cabral—his ships were making a wide westward sweep en route to India—the land was claimed for Portugal and subsequently colonized. During Europe's Napoleonic wars, the Portuguese royal family fled Lisbon and governed from Rio (1808–1822), thus leading to the formation of a Brazilian monarchy (1822–1889). This royal establishment, alone among governments in the Americas, continued through most of the 19th century. A coup d'état in 1889 toppled the monarchy and sent the still personally popular king, Dom Pedro II, into a European exile. Under its new name, the United States of Brazil (1889–1967) found

465

much of its unity generated by two forces: the Roman Catholic Church and the military. Developments in education included the establishment of universities, campaigns against illiteracy, and a nationwide free public school system, compulsory through the eighth year.

A revolution in 1930 ended the era of the Old Republic and opened the door to a period of experimentation in democracy. For the next decades, too, the population increased more rapidly than in any other country in the world. Industrialization and agricultural changes spawned great cities, drawing people not only into urban centers but also into the virgin areas of the west. The leadership in this new era was personified in Getúlio Dornelles Vargas (1883–1954), president and consummate politician from Rio Grande do Sul, Brazil's southernmost state. In the top office for all but six of the years between 1930 and 1954, he also advocated relocating the national capital some 900 kilometers (540 miles) inland from Rio de Janeiro. Opened in 1960, Brasília (built by President Juscelino Kubitschek) stands as a monument to the country's perennial, but periodically tested, confidence in the future.

Inflation and financial crises have caused a progressive centralization of government and involvement of the military. A revolution to the right in 1964 replaced the democratic legislative process with a government by directive. The new constitution of 1967 strengthened the powers of the presidency, reduced those of the congress, and changed the country's name to Federative Republic of Brazil. For two decades (1964–1985), a succession of five generals—by vote of the nation's electoral college—stood at the helm. The third (1974–1978) in this military succession was Brazil's first

Lutheran head of state, Ernesto Geisel. Like Vargas and several other leaders, he hailed from Rio Grande do Sul and was the son of immigrant parents from Stuttgart, Germany. The good education that his father, a teacher in one of the church-related schools, sought for him, paid off. It also demonstrated the upward mobility that a military career promised countless Brazilians in a society that continues efforts to enlarge its middle class. Geisel's reaffirmation of the promise to return the country as soon as feasible to democratic government and popular elections was carried out in part by his successor. In January 1985, for the first time in 21 years, Brazilians elected a civilian president, Tancredo Neves. Sadly, illness and death prevented his inauguration. Elected vice-president, José Sarney became president. Popular elections for many other offices took place in 1985 and 1986.

Inflation, meanwhile, continues to be devastating, more than doubling the cost of living for several years in succession. An enormous national debt, linked to the International Monetary Fund, holds Brazil hostage to the future, weakens its potentially powerful economy, and breeds an ominous unrest.

The peopling of Brazil deserves special notice. The original Tupi and other Amerindian tribes had to recede in face of an ever stronger advance. White Europeans came voluntarily, and black Africans as slaves. The Amerindians did not need the newcomers, but the whites needed the blacks in order to succeed at all. From the 16th century beginnings of the plantation economy, the slave trade went on until 1856. Slavery as an institution continued in Brazil until 1888—when some 700,000 slaves were set free. That number was relatively small inasmuch as the "mulatto escape hatch" had, for generations, enabled those of mixed blood to be manumitted into the free status. This fact stands in sharp contrast to the freeing of slaves in the *USA. In Brazil, anyone with some evidence of white blood is considered white; in the United States, anyone with some black blood is considered black. The antecedents of Brazil's huge influx of slaves came largely from Portugal's African colonies: Angola, Guinea-Bissau, and Mozambique, as well as from Dahomey (today Benin) and other places along the long western coast. No other major country in the New World bears such strong African influences as Brazil. In recent decades, Brazil's anticolonialist stance reflects strong and abiding feeling for Africa on the part of many.

Correspondingly, the eventually heavy immigration of Europeans—especially after the middle of the 19th century—gravitated to the southern and more temperate parts of Brazil. Aside from the pioneering generations from Portugal and the Azores, who had come earlier, the first immigrants from Northern Europe were mainly Germans—and Lutherans. Their story, beginning in 1824, continues below. Meanwhile, the mingling of European and African elements have given Brazil's religious scene a distinctive character.

Religion: Roman Catholic nearly 90%, including an estimated 35 million or more devotees of Spiritism; other Christians about 6%. The Jewish community, with antecedents in colonial times, numbers under 230,000. Among the one million Brazilians of Japanese origin and 20th-century immigration are less than 400,000 Buddhists, while the more than 600,000 Roman Catholic adherents among them exceed the number of Roman Catholics in *Japan.

Brazil has the largest Roman Catholic population of any country in the world. The church's more than 200 jurisdictions—archdioceses, dioceses, prelatures—are grouped into 14 regions. The oldest is the archdiocese of São Salvador de Bahia (1551), followed by that in Rio de Janeiro (1575). Jesuit missionary activity among the Amerindians and the faith brought by the colonists planted the church. Today, the more than 5600 parishes are staffed mainly by diocesan priests; the others by priests of various orders. Since 1952, the country has had a National Conference of Brazilian Bishops. Its tasks include issues involving church-state relations and cooperation in the Conference of Latin American Roman Catholic Bishops (CELAM; 1955). The shortage of priests, deplored for decades, has grown acute in recent years. At the same time, Basic Ecclesial Communities (Comunidades Eclesiais do Base–CEBs)—some 80,000 of them by 1981—have been springing up across the country. Much like house congregations of old, these base communities have become centers of spiritual renewal and scripturally-oriented study of the social situation. Their greatest following is among the poor, and their quest is for social justice and liberation from the bondage of exploitation. Among their most eloquent advocates has been the bishop of Olinda and Recife, Dom Helder Camara, and the Franciscan exponent of liberation theology, Leonardo Boff. The latter, summoned to Rome for colloquy (1985), had the support of Brazil's leading bishops. Boff, they maintained, was theologically sound and not opening a gap between the hierarchy and the popular church of the base communities, as Rome suspected. The Brazilian government, however, had for years allowed repressive measures against Christian demands for social justice and had thus been violating human rights. Already in 1970, when these violations were flagrant, the LWF relocated its assembly from Brazil to France as a sign of protest (above, Latin America Introduction).

Protestantism came to Brazil cautiously. The constitution of 1824 granted Protestants limited rights. Religious liberty came with the separation of church and state in 1890. Protestant beginnings were of two kinds: by immigration after 1824 (German and Swiss Evangelical Lutheran and Reformed), and by missionary work after 1836, mainly by leading North American communions. By the beginning of the present century, Presbyterian, Methodist, Baptist, Episcopal, and other work had laid the basis for an advancing Protestant pluralism. Except for the Lutherans, the Episcopalians, and a few others, most of the Protestant efforts were accompanied by an anti-Roman attitude.

The foremost religious developments in this century have been in the realm of the spirit. On the Roman Catholic side—more recently also among Protestants—Spiritism exploded with astonishing vigor. It had an African lineage lodged in Traditional religion and brought to Brazil by slaves. They, in turn, adapted it to the Roman Catholicism of the plantations and later perpetuated it in towns and cities. Spiritism had also a European lineage, systematized by Alan Kardec and conveyed from France as Kardecism during the 19th century. Its following was among the more educated in the cities. A mingling of these two lines—as well as the absence of any set organization—resulted in a vast proliferation. Umbanda and Kardecism are probably the best known among the many types. Spiritism has a mixed but massive following. Estimates that perhaps 30% of Brazil's Roman Catholics have some relation to Spiritism would place their present number over 40 million.

On the Protestant side, Pentecostalism entered Brazil in 1910 via an Italian Waldensian and two Swedish missionaries, all three from Chicago. Fanned by other influences as well, the small beginnings burst into a movement. Assembly of God and kindred congregations won large followings in big cities as well as in small towns. The biggest single church edifice—that of the "O Brasil para Cristo" (Brazil for Christ) Pentecostal Church in São Paulo—seats 40,000. With a claimed membership of over one million, this body of 200 parishes joined the World Council of Churches in 1969. The Pentecostal movement is seen as an evangelical answer to popular Spiritism and as a 20th-century reformation. All told, it claims over four million adherents in Brazil. In contrast to the older Protestant denominations, the Pentecostal movement has rapidly become indigenous and continues to grow here as elsewhere in Latin America (see Chile).

The interdenominational scene in the world's largest Roman Catholic country merits special notice. Until after World War II, the sharp separation between Roman Catholics and Protestants was accentuated by the missionary activities of the Protestants and their anti-Roman position. Lutherans—and to an extent Episcopalians—were seen as nonmissionary churches. The Lutherans had all they could do to keep up with their own potential members of German origin.

Among the Protestants, mainly of North American connection, cooperation developed slowly after the 1916 Panama Conference—a Latin American sequel to "Edinburgh 1910." The Confederação Evangélica do Brasil (CEB; 1934) became a coordinating agency for

Protestant activities in various fields. The postwar period ushered in new developments. In 1948, the Brazilian Bible Society began its now highly significant work, including translations into contemporary Portuguese. The ecumenical movement attracted some churches and alienated others. During the ensuing years five churches joined the World Council of Churches: Methodist (1948), Lutheran (1950), Episcopal (1966), Pentecostal (1969), and Reformed (1972). Baptists, Presbyterians, and others remained apart. Since 1957—following a pattern set in Germany—Lutherans and Roman Catholics in southern Brazil initiated a bilateral dialog, which subsequently encouraged cooperation on several fronts. In contrast to the other Protestants, the "nonmissionary" position of the Lutherans vis-à-vis the Roman Catholics, and their early membership in the WCC, gave them a growing ecumenical significance.

The mounting social need during the postwar decades of development sparked social action among many Christians, but it created new divisions in the process. Presbyterians, the largest of the missionary communions, became bitterly divided. Among Roman Catholics, bishops like Dom Helder Camara (Olinda and Recife), who were close to the poverty-stricken masses in the country's northeast, and others also, shaped new courses of social action and strivings for human rights. The famed Medellín Conference (1968), near Bogotá, *Colombia—held in light of Vatican II—drew much of its agenda from Brazil. Here, too, arose strong impulses leading to liberation theology, to which Leonardo Boff was to give eloquent expression also in the 1980s.

The human plight in the drought-ridden northeast challenged forth action on the part of Protestants as well as Roman Catholics. Yet the masses (22 million rural folk by 1980) in this vast region were the anonymous actors on Latin America's biggest stage where poverty ruled. For perhaps eight million others, government-sponsored new industry offered some promise. Into this situation—its inhabitants almost entirely Roman Catholic—came not only Catholic but also united Protestant efforts. Assistance from the USA was coordinated by Church World Service, and under its umbrella came Lutheran World Relief with material aid, staff, and experience gained in other parts of the world through LWF programs. Assistance came from Europe, via the WCC, as well as directly from the rising overseas aid of the church in Germany. By 1967, a common Brazilian Protestant agency, named Diaconia, was formed by seven church bodies (in the Confederação Evangélica). Others joined later. Diaconia's function was to help, as needed, in emergencies such as floods or other natural disasters and in chronic situations of poverty. Diaconia's policy was (and is) to help people help themselves and to engage in inclusive development. Criteria for projects financed from outside the country were subsequently developed on the basis of experience.

Migration, meanwhile, proceeded ever deeper into Brazil's interior. A high percentage of those moving out from southern Brazil were Protestants—largely Lutherans. Besides the usual hardships of pioneering came also the hazards of uncertain land claims—of big developers moving in on small homesteaders. Along great rivers in the west, like the Paraná, immense hydroelectric projects (one of them the world's biggest) flooded out thousands of small farms. In other places, the plight of dispossessed Indians demanded redress of injustice done to them. Besides, Amazonia's vast rain forest was being cut down.

Major churches, instead of speaking out singly—or through scattered voices—began to address the government together. For Lutherans, their own statement made in Curitiba (October 1970) on behalf of human rights marked their entry into the public debate (below). In the spirit of Vatican II and of ecumenical dialog, Lutherans, Roman Catholics, and others drew closer together. By 1982, five church bodies— Roman Catholic, Lutheran, Episcopal, Methodist, Reformed—created the National Council of Christian Churches in Brazil (Conselho Nacional de Igrejas Cristás do Brasil—CONIC). The council's task has been to draw other churches into this common venture, and together to strive more effectively in behalf of the poor and the voiceless in the name of the gospel of Christ.

While wide divisions remain among Protestants as well as among Roman Catholics, other cooperative efforts have marked the Brazilian church scene. In education for ministry, institutions of the older denominations formed the Association of Evangelical Theological Schools (ASTE). Begun in the early 1960s, ASTE has from the start been part of the global theological education program encouraged by the WCC. ASTE has aimed to set standards, produce texts, exchange faculty and students, and so on. Other denominations with different requirements in 1968 organized their Evangelical Theological Association for Extension Training (AETTE). In 1973, the Interdenominational Association for Education (ASSINTEC) was founded in Curitiba (Paraná) by representatives of the Roman Catholic, Lutheran, Methodist, and Pentecostal churches. Its outreach has been via radio as well as by tape cassettes through lessons prepared especially for elementary school children in Pôrto Alegre and elsewhere.

Not least important is church growth. Between 1960 and 1980, the population of Brazil grew by 86%. The growth of Pentecostals was reportedly much more.

Meanwhile, the two main Lutheran bodies have grown less rapidly than the general population: the Evangelical Church of the Lutheran Confession in Brazil (ECLCB) by 40% (baptized membership); the Evangelical Lutheran Church of Brazil (ELCB) by 55%. For Lutherans, moreover, these two decades marked an increased rate of transition from rural to urban life as well as a westward movement of population to new frontiers. In both situations, the home missionary task was immense, while the burden of skyrocketing inflation became ever harder to bear. Likewise, between 1960 and 1980—at least for the ECLCB—the transition to Portuguese was virtually completed; and it had happened earlier in the smaller but more media-active (Lutheran Hour) ELCB. In any case, the language transition came later in Brazil than it did to Lutherans in North America. The resources for achieving a successful transition to Portuguese were fewer. For Lutheranism the accommodation to a Latin culture has always proven more difficult than to an Anglo-Saxon culture. In this broad context, the following profiles of Brazil's Lutheran churches come alive.

ASSOCIATION OF FREE LUTHERAN CHURCHES OF BRAZIL (AFLCB)

(Associação de Igrejas Luteranas Livres do Brasil)
Membership: 750
President: The Rev. Oséias Camara
Caixa Postal 641
87.300 Campo Mourão, Paraná

This Association of Free Lutheran Churches was formed in 1967 after four of the present

12 congregations had been gathered and organized by missionaries of the Association of Free Lutheran Congregations in the *USA. The work centers in Campo Mourão, a coffee-growing frontier city in the rolling plateau country of the state of Paraná, west of São Paulo. Here also is the Bible School and Seminary where, among others, the six Brazilian pastors and one evangelist serving the congregations have had their training. A few congregations are in the state of Rondônia (formerly Guaporé territory), bordering *Bolivia, and one in *Paraguay, west of Paraná. Assisting with the evangelistic outreach are four missionaries from the AFLC/USA. A strong spirit of independence prevails, accompanied by a "firm conviction of the inerrancy of the Bible."

The 1964 decision of the AFLC to send two missionary families to Brazil was due in large part to the impassioned appeal of John Abel, who with his wife, Ruby, became the AFLC'S first missionaries. The work began in Camp Mourão, a town not far from where they had served (1954–1958) under the World Mission Prayer League, a Lutheran faith mission pioneering in Latin America. As an ordained pastor of the then Evangelical Lutheran Church (ELC; later ALC, now ELCA), Abel had launched the WMPL work on the westward moving frontier—Brazil's new coffee country. When other WMPL missionaries joined the Abels, work extended to other places.

Meanwhile, the ELC had become persuaded to take up work in Brazil (below, ECLCB). In June 1958, when the WMPL agreed to turn over its Brazilian venture to the ELC, Abel became part—yet himself independent—of the growing team of ELC missioners in Brazil. Moving to the young but more established city of Londrina, his efforts in missioning and education continued, including the organization of a boarding school.

Pioneering had prepared Abel for the new venture of the AFLC. No congregations or church members of this earlier work are in the new church. Nor does the AFLCB have any cooperative ties with other Lutheran churches in Brazil; rather it works with other Evangelical bodies of kindred outlook. Abel continues to serve in Brazil as president of the AFLCB missionary conference. His three sons serve as missionaries, two of his daughters as teachers, and a third as a medical doctor—all in Brazil. The AFLCB story throws light on one aspect of an otherwise manifold missioning process—that of pursuing a strong conviction.

EVANGELICAL CHURCH OF THE LUTHERAN CONFESSION IN BRAZIL (ECLCB)

(Igreja Evangélica de Confissão Luterana no Brasil)
Member: LWF (1952), WCC, CLAI, CONIC, CEB
Membership: 850,000
President: The Rev. Dr. Gottfried Brakemeier
Caixa Postal 2876
90.001 Pôrto Alegre
Rio Grande do Sul

Since 1954, this biggest Lutheran body in Latin America has borne the name Evangelical Church of the Lutheran Confession in Brazil. In early 1990 it is to be host to the LWF Eighth Assembly (Curitiba). Its 850,000 members are gathered into some 1500 congregations, comprising 302 parishes. These, with other institutions and agencies of the church, are served by 420 ordained ministers and many other workers. Geographically, the ECLCB's 32 local districts are divided into five regions—each district having its convener, and each region its full-time administrator or regional pastor. The general assembly, meeting biennially as a synodical convention, is the church's top legislative body. The church council oversees the ongoing work of the ECLCB, and the church president heads the ecclesial administration. Church headquarters are in Pôrto Alegre, capital of the southernmost state, Rio Grande do Sul.

The ECLCB membership resides largely in the southern, more temperate part of the country. Its antecedents are mainly German, dating from immigration as far back as the 1820s to as recently as the resettlement era after World War II. The ECLCB thus has a sprinkling of Baltic, Hungarian, Slovak, Scandinavian, Japanese, and other ethnic elements, as well as a growing number of typically indigenous or Luso-Brazilian adherents. During recent decades, the use of

German in worship and other church activities has rapidly given way to Portuguese. Similarly, a once predominantly rural and small-town membership has increasingly been drawn to the big cities—or outward to the advancing western and northern frontiers. The church's members are engaged in many different occupations. Some are economically well-off, but the large majority—especially amid prolonged inflation—barely make ends meet, and a rising number are unemployed. Stewardship and church finance are under severe pressure. The church's experience with its own members has increasingly raised its concern for justice and for the needs of others in a rapidly growing nation.

Between 1970 and 1985, the ECLCB—as noted more fully below—may be said to have come out of seclusion and joined the common life. The 1970 statement on church-state relations, adopted by the synod in Curitiba, not only spoke out for human rights but also showed how this public concern roots in the uniqueness of Christian worship and grows out of the premises of Christian education. The church was far from agreed as to next steps. But it remained for the then president, Karl Gottschald, and particularly for his successor, Augusto Kunert, to use also their ecumenical experience in helping to reconcile differences and live with them creatively. Kunert's retirement in 1985 was highlighted by a recognition of this achievement.

Among the ECLCB's functions, five are noted here.

Education: The Escola Superior de Teología—the church's theological seminary in São Leopoldo, near Pôrto Alegre—performs the basic task of preparing and maintaining an able company of ministers. Since its founding (1946), this school has symbolized the church's unity. Today, its programs, deployed in part to affiliated institutions, enroll over 300 students—women as well as men, late vocationers as well as those in the usual academic sequence. Scholarships (mainly LWF) enable students from Spanish-speaking countries to receive theological instruction in São Leopoldo and elsewhere in Brazil. Greater enrollment is anticipated, as is also a second theological center in another part of the country.

In a parallel development, the church's ministry to university students, and also to faculty members, has been under way since the 1950s, with Richard H. Wangen (ALC) and Karl Ernst Neisel (EKD) among the pioneers. Much older are its church-related secondary schools (Ginasio-Colegio) and its teacher training college (Escola Normal). The latter, in Ivoti (near São Leopoldo) prepares its graduates to give religious instruction in the public schools. Christian education in the local congregation rounds out the picture of efforts to engraft the gospel ever anew.

Mission: The forming of new congregations continues. During the past decade their number has jumped by about 200, or 15%. Most of these are still small, but they draw attention to the time-honored home mission task, whether in the expanding city or on the advancing frontier. While many congregations are growing, some are declining and others are threatened by new developments. An example of the latter has been in the Paraná River basin, where construction of the world's biggest hydroelectric project has been dispossessing thousands of farmers, among them many Lutherans. Foremost among those leading their protest for more equitable compensation was a young ECLCB pastor. As a student, he had used his fellowship year to study in India and had also acquainted himself with the plight of the poor in Africa. Back in Brazil, negotiations with the government netted the farmers on the Paraná River some measure of justice.

Similarly, missioning among the Indians—not a new venture—has punctuated an ongoing concern with intervention on their behalf. Whether in the Amazon interior or in western Rio Grande do Sul the intrusion of land-hungry developers is seen to violate not only the human rights of Indians but also the ecological balance essential to sustaining life itself. This kind of applied concern is widening the ECLCB's missionary horizon. Domestically alone, the task is enormous.

Emissaries of the Norwegian Missionary Society began coming in 1975. Like their earlier counterparts from the American Lutheran Church they came to strengthen and extend the ministry of the ECLCB. By 1988 some 15 Norse helpers were active in such places as the national capital, Brasília, as well as in cities like Curitiba, Joinville, and elsewhere.

Service: In some ways the current use of the term "diaconia" to denote joint Protestant work among the destitute in Brazil's northeast (above) has roots in the ECLCB's range of diaconal services. The multiple services rendered in the Pella-Bethania institutions (Taquari, RS)—begun in 1894—are indicative of the variety of needs that the church seeks to relieve. The model at Pella has been the famed "Colony of Mercy," Bethel/Bielefeld, in Germany. Likewise, Moinhos de Vento Hospital, Pôrto Alegre, has achieved its top rating and character in association with a deaconess nursing staff. Initially, the sisters came from Germany's famed Kaiserswerth deaconess house, but in recent years nearly all are from Casa Matriz, the motherhouse in São Leopoldo. From there, too, deaconesses are serving in over a dozen small hospitals across the land, as well as in parishes and community centers. Many other workers have been drawn into the never ending diversity of opportunity in this diaconal ministry.

Much of this ministry continues to benefit from overseas support, but community response has grown significantly. Meanwhile, care for the elderly has become a mounting challenge to initiative in such parishes as Joinville (Santa Catarina). Yet the greatest rallying points for community-wide diaconia have been the periodic inundations by devastating floods in the country's southern states, the grim opposite to the chronic drought in the northeast.

Communication: The ECLCB's use of the electronic as well as print media includes some unconventional features. Radio União (Union), a five-station commercial network, became a project of the church's communication foundation in 1982. Over one 50kW AM and one FM station in Blumenau, Santa Catarina, and FM stations in Novo Hamburgo, São Leopoldo, and Joinville come round-the-clock programs offering religious segments as part of the cross section of modern life. It includes ad hoc counsel in tackling everyday problems and dares also to speak up for justice and Christian responsibility. Radio União has built up a lively following. Assistance from overseas helped to initiate the venture. The older production in the studios of the church in Pôrto Alegre continues to supply parishes with recordings for broadcast over local stations.

Church use of the print media runs back to 1877 when the Rio Grande synod's enterprising chief pastor, Wilhelm Rotermund, opened a publishing house and founded a newspaper. What began as the *Deutsche Post* has long since become the biweekly *Jornal Evangélico,* serving the ECLCB as a whole. Through the church editorial office, audio-visual aids as well as printed materials continue to supply the needs of congregations as well as individuals. Theological books have also been coming out for some time. But only in 1985 did the first of a projected 15-volume selection of Luther's works in Portuguese make its appearance, as part of a joint venture with the *Missouri-related Evangelical Lutheran Church of Brazil (below).

Interchurch and ecumenical relations: The way developments, during the 15 years from 1970 to 1985, accelerated from an already existing process has placed the ECLCB in a new situation. It has given fresh importance to an old issue like the transition to the Portuguese language, which today is virtually complete. It has taken old relationships like those with Roman Catholics and has pursued them with the promise of practical partnership. Above all, the ECLCB has not only survived the trauma of disappointment in 1970—when the Fifth Assembly of the LWF was abruptly relocated from Brazil to France over the issue of human rights violations in Brazil—but it has grown into a church body that is increasingly concerned about the social and political context in which its ecclesial task is set. Its role in helping to form the new National Council of Christian Churches in Brazil (CONIC, above) placed it in a mediating position between the other Protestants and the Roman Catholics. None of this has come easily, but all is part of sharing more fully the task of the church in and beyond Brazil.

While the ECLCB has for years done much on its own, it has not stood alone. This is part of its history that follows below. But a crucial turn that appears to have been effected since 1970 is the change—at least in outlook and disposition—from overdependence to independence, and from there to self-assured interdependence. This was stated clearly to the church synod in late 1970 by one of its young theologians, when he took the seeming rebuff of relocation and applied the assembly's motto—"Sent Into the World"—to his own church. In 1985 this man, Gottfried Brakemeier, became the fifth president of the

ECLCB. The following year the church invited the LWF to hold its 1990 assembly in Brazil.

• • •

The name Evangelical Church of the Lutheran Confession combines identity and history. Adopted in 1954, the name covered various antecedent designations. Foremost was the intention to be a manifestation of the church of Jesus Christ in Brazil. Evangelical identified it as Protestant, not only in the Germany of its forebears but also in contemporary Brazil. Although the spectrum of its own membership ranged from conservative Lutheran to conscientious Reformed, the great majority had a broadly Lutheran background best denoted by the term Confession. The present name was adopted five years after the official formation of this ecclesial body. At the time of its organization in 1949, it was a federation, practically speaking, of four synods. Each of them retained its name and structure until 1968, when the present regional pattern was introduced. Those four were: the Synod of Rio Grande do Sul (1886), oldest and largest; the Lutheran Synod (1901); the Synod of Santa Catarina and Paraná (1911); and the Middle Brazilian Synod (1912). They all grew out of earlier settlements as well as out of specific connections with Germany.

In fact, it had for a long time been possible for immigrant German Protestants and their descendants to survive as Protestants because of the periodic interventions of Prussia and the Evangelical *Oberkirchenrat* or Executive Council in Berlin. This, in turn, helps account for the formative role played by policies reflecting the Evangelical Church of the Old Prussian Union and its inclusion of Lutheran and Reformed (see Germany). This, moreover, was precisely the issue that prompted the *Missouri Synod intervention from North America after the year 1900 and the creation of an aggressive, competitive, confessional Lutheran church body (below). Yet, even earlier, the coming of the Jesuits in the 1860s put an end to the hitherto friendly relations—and frequent mixed marriages—among German Protestants and Roman Catholics. In short, if interchurch relations today appear generally good—and better than formerly—they have distant precedents that take us back to the earlier part of the 19th century and the initial influx of settlers.

Hans Staden provides a 16th-century prelude to the Lutheran story in Brazil. A Hessian German adventurer with the Portuguese pioneers and a professed Lutheran (as Protestants were in those days), he was also a writer of the first exact description of Brazil's Indians (1557). The continuous story, however, begins much later. After the wars of Napoleon in Europe, the new constitutional monarchy in Portugal determined to introduce European-style farming into the more temperate southern part of Brazil. This was seen as a potential counterweight to the sugar plantations in the tropics and to the society based on black slave labor. Royal ties led from Lisbon to Vienna and also to the Protestant German courts. Failing to recruit sufficient Swiss Catholic colonists, the crown settled for German Protestants.

In 1823, an initial venture in Nova Friburgo, northeast of Rio de Janeiro, proved the feasibility of this kind of project—including the admission of Protestant colonists to a Roman Catholic domain like Brazil. The following year, a much larger undertaking opened far to the south, in Rio Grande do Sul. In São Leopoldo—inland from Pôrto Alegre and on the navigable Rio dos Sinos—the first German settlers moved into an abandoned hemp plantation formerly worked by black slaves. Most of the colonists were farmers, others represented various trades. Many came as families. Other contingents soon followed. They came from Hanover, Hesse, Hamburg, and elsewhere in western Germany, but most were from the Palatinate—the impoverished middle Rhine Valley. Their Palatine dialect, Hunsrück, prevails among country folk and old timers to this day, being akin to the "Pennsylvania Dutch" perpetuated by other Palatines who had come to North America a century earlier. By the end of the first decade, the settlement in São Leopoldo and the outlying new villages—still called "colonies" by their dwellers—had received nearly 5000 people. At this stage, the newcomers were nearly all Protestants, and among them for spiritual care were a number of pastors. The founding month—July 1824—is still observed as the historic starting point of an eventually vigorous community and its nascent church.

The early stages of this venture benefited from grants made by the Brazilian crown, for the new constitutional monarchy—Brazil had declared itself an empire in 1822—was eager to see projects like that in Rio Grande do Sul succeed.

For the colonists it remained an uphill struggle. They faced not only the hardships normal in pioneering but also the shocks of frontier war. Brazil's southern boundary was at that time not yet firm, and one of the German pastors early fell victim to violence. Although the settlements grew in size and number, they were poorly supplied with pastors. For a time, during the late 1840s, there was only one pastor for all the German Protestants in Rio Grande do Sul. John Haesbert had come to Brazil with his wife from Baltimore, in the USA. It remained for another— Hermann Borchard, likewise a German Lutheran who had served congregations in America before the Civil War—to rally the Rhenish Missionary Society in *Germany prior to setting out for Brazil in 1864. His insistence led also other missionary societies—like the Basel and the Neuendettelsau— to see the needs of settlers in Brazil as akin to those in North America. The challenge of mission, to Borchard and soon to others, was not only to reach out to the so-called heathen but also to retain the neglected emigrants for Germany.

In time, other projects in the neighboring states of Santa Catarina and Paraná drew more immigrants from Germany and elsewhere. Commercial interests attracted still others to Rio de Janeiro and to the states of São Paulo, Minas Gerais, Espírito Santo, and beyond. Congregations were gathered by an ordained ministry always in too short supply. In some regions—Pelotas in southeast Rio Grande do Sul was particularly marked for this—itinerants posed as pastors and exploited their opportunities. "Pseudo-pastors," as others called them, handicapped the growth of the church. Yet other dangers were even more serious.

The larger the German element grew, the more divided it became. Already in the 1850s a considerable group of Free Thinkers established themselves in Pôrto Alegre. Their newspaper and cultural activities set an antichurch attitude, contagious also among those in the outlying "colonies." A decade later came the Jesuits who, as already noted, put an end to friendly relations between Catholics and Protestants and began building up an aggressive Romanism. As the 20th century dawned, the coming of Missouri Lutherans throve on the confessional ambivalence mentioned earlier and on the numerous vacant congregations. In contrast to the Missourian determination to train an indigenous ministry, the several German synods continued to rely on pastors sent from Germany.

The years of World War I proved that dependence on the church in Germany was hazardous, that German as a language could be banned, and that a church-related parish school system was in jeopardy. These schools flowered again in the 1920s and early 1930s, only to succumb to two rival forces. From within, Brazil's public school system improved and became nationwide. From without, Hitler's National Socialism wooed people of German descent living abroad and was especially effective in Latin America. In 1938, the Brazilian government nationalized the foreign language schools, including those maintained by the German-speaking parishes. Synodically related secondary schools (Ginasio-Colegio) fared better and, as we have seen, retained their church connection.

Against this background, the rise of theological education in the ECLCB is noteworthy. To prepare an eventually indigenous ministry, Hermann Dohms in 1922 opened his pretheological school. Four years later, it was relocated from Cachoeira do Sul to São Leopoldo. Its graduates then studied theology in Germany's universities. World War II put an end to that. German pastors in sensitive regions were imprisoned. Pretheological students, some not yet 20 years of age, were sent forth by Dohms as "substitutos." Many a future leader in the ECLCB found his practical training in ministry accelerated in this way. In the parishes, a hasty transition to the use of Portuguese necessitated a speedy translation of worship and other materials. Not surprisingly, the founding of the Faculdade de Teología in 1946 became a unifying event. The subsequent building of seminary facilities, while aided by grants from abroad (via the LWF and other sources), stimulated unprecedented fund raising in Brazil. The Legião Evangélica, an organization of the laity in all synods, blazed a trail to self-support and an eventually wider stewardship (mordomia).

Meanwhile, the four synods mentioned earlier joined in 1949 in founding the Synodical Federation—in effect a church. As such, it joined the World Council of Churches in 1950, and the LWF in 1952. With its name change in 1954, and with its numbers greater than those of any other Protestant body in Brazil at that time, the ECLCB joined the Evangelical Confederation of Brazil (CEB) in 1959. By the end of the 1950s, its ecumenical and interchurch relations were extensive and balanced, but unfinished.

Among the items still on the agenda, four are representative and also interdependent. In the late 1950s, an informal bilateral dialog between Lutherans and Roman Catholics was under way as members of the Lutheran Faculdade de Teología (the seminary) met regularly with Jesuits of the Cristo Rei faculty in São Leopoldo. In 1957, a link began to be fashioned between the ECLCB and the Evangelical Lutheran Church (an antecedent body of the 1960-formed *American Lutheran Church). Over this route, an impressive number of young North American pastors came to Brazil, learned Portuguese, were called to congregations of the ECLCB, and accelerated that body's transition to the language of the land. In 1959, the LWF sent a visiting professor (E. Theodore Bachmann) from North America for a year at the then Faculdade de Teología. One of the results was a narrowing of the gap between that institution and Concordia Seminary of the other Lutheran body. The periodic meetings of that day still continue. Another North American, Richard H. Wangen (above), has become an influential veteran on the Faculdade.

In the 1960s, the time-honored practice of the *Evangelical Church in Germany (EKD), through its Foreign Office, providing also Brazilian-born pastors a year in Germany, began to pay off academically. Brazilian scholars were earning their theological doctorates at German universities. They became successors to the young scholars from Germany who, for two decades or more, had staffed the Faculdade. But some of those scholars on their return to Europe turned their Brazil experience to wider good. One of them, Harding Meyer, heads the LWF-related Institute for Ecumenical Research in Strasbourg, *France. Another, Hans-Jürgen Prien, in his comprehensive study *Die Geschichte des Christentums in Lateinamerika* (Göttingen: 1978), has set a new course and high standard for studying the history of Christianity in Latin America as a whole, and—

in subsequent works—for dealing with issues facing church and society in that part of the world. Anyone familiar with the ECLCB situation in the late 1950s and with the pivotal role of the theological school will welcome also this aspect of the church's indigenization.

The ECLCB has also provided persons for staff positions at key points in Europe, notably in the Foreign Office of the EKD in West Germany and at the LWF/DCC Latin America desk and LWF/DS in Geneva.

EVANGELICAL LUTHERAN CHURCH OF BRAZIL (ELCB)

(Igreja Evangélica Luterana do Brasil)
Member: ILC
Membership: 202,000
President: The Rev. Johannes H. Gedrat
Rua Cel. Lucas de Oliveira 894
Caixa Postal 1076
90.001 Pôrto Alegre, Rio Grande do Sul

The ELCB is the second largest Lutheran church body not only in Brazil but also in Latin America as a whole. Its 269 parishes, subdivided into 954 congregations and mission points, are served by 364 pastors along with many teachers and other nonordained workers. Its constituency reaches into all but two of the nation's 23 states, although the majority is concentrated in the south of Brazil. Its mission outposts extend northward to Boa Vista near the Venezuelan border and westward up the Amazon along the new transcontinental highway. Its predominantly German derivation today includes a growing percentage of Brazilians of Luso (Portuguese) and other backgrounds. This church's distribution corresponds roughly with that of the larger and older Lutheran body, the ECLCB (above). Yet confessionally, it is more conservative and accepts the Lutheran Confessions in the *Book of Concord* (1580) "as the only correct exposition of the Holy Scripture . . . and does not admit any alteration of this norm." Its polity combines congregational and synodical elements and is much like that of the *Lutheran Church–Missouri Synod, of which it was a district from 1904 to 1980.

Church headquarters, located for over a decade in São Leopoldo, were in 1985 returned to Pôrto Alegre—to the former campus of Concordia Seminary and its preparatory school. Increased enrollment on the new Concordia educational complex near São Leopoldo—not far from that of the ECLCB's Escola Superior de Teología—necessitated the headquarters relocation.

A second seminary, also bearing the Concordia name, opened (1983) in São Paulo, closer to the church's needs farther north and west. The two theological seminaries and their preparatory schools in 1984 reported a total enrollment of 884 students. The church's teacher training institutes prepare personnel for the 62 parish schools and other teaching duties as well. In the field of service to the needy, the church maintains a dozen social assistance (ministry) centers.

The Lutheran University of Brazil, located in Canoas, near Pôrto Alegre, was begun in 1972, initiated by St. Paul's congregation of Canoas. In 15 years, the student enrollment in its several departments topped 2700. Branches are being developed in other parts of the country. The university is now owned and operated by the Lutheran Education Foundation, formed by St. Paul's congregation of the ELCB. Substantial grants have come from the Central Evangelical Agency for Development (EZE, West Germany). When completed, the Canoas campus, with its associated colleges, is to have facilities for 20,000 students.

The ELCB has made effective use of the mass media and continues to prime its pastors and lay leaders in their use. Already in 1929, it introduced the "Lutheran Hour," which today is heard over 127 radio stations. The featured preacher recently retired after 20 years of this ministry. This program is said to enroll over 10,000 persons in Bible correspondence courses. On television, "This Is the Life," began its Portuguese run in 1982 over the national network. The church's editorial offices and publication house in Pôrto Alegre have meanwhile enlarged their production of church papers, educational materials, theological works, and the mainstays of common worship and devotional life. Pastors and congregations are thus better equipped to follow through with the task of evangelism.

The history of this church, like that of its counterpart in *Argentina, represents the conservatism as well as the methods and resourcefulness of the Missouri Lutherans in North America. These and other characteristics have made it a sharp competitor of the older and larger body, the ECLCB (above), whose lines ran directly to Germany. In response to pleas from Brazil, the Missouri Synod acted much like the mission societies in Germany when, in 1900, it began sending pastors to work among the German Protestant immigrants and their descendants.

As in *Australia and elsewhere, the Missourians were spurred on by the desire to overcome the "Unionism" they perceived in others. In 1903, they opened what was to become Concordia Seminary and its preparatory school in Pôrto Alegre. Their training of an indigenous ministry was decades ahead of what is now the Escola Superior de Teología of the ECLCB. Early, the Missourians began filling vacancies and forming congregations. At one point their acquisition of already established congregations almost included a dissenting group from Christ Church, São Leopoldo, the mother church of the Rio Grande Synod. The intra-Lutheran North American struggle was painfully replayed in Brazil as well as in other parts of Latin America. Especially during the two world wars, the ELCB's ties with North America rather than Germany proved advantageous both in support and in hastening the transition to Portuguese. The ELCB's rate of growth has consistently been faster than that of the larger body.

In recent years, relations between the two churches have improved considerably. Since 1959, the theological faculties of the ELCB and the ECLCB have engaged in mutually helpful discussions, beginning with the *Augsburg Confession*. Joint projects in translation and publication of Lutheran doctrinal and other writings have been stimulated by similar, but earlier, undertakings in *Argentina (where a 10-volume edition of selected works by Martin Luther has already appeared in Spanish translation). In 1985, the first volume of an eventually 15-volume set of Luther's works in Portuguese appeared in Brazil as part of a joint venture (above).

During this century, the ELCB has been a springboard for Missouri-related work in other Latin countries, notably in *Argentina, *Paraguay, and *Portugal.

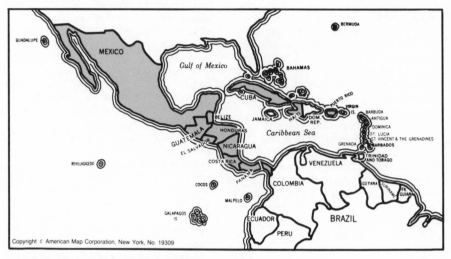

Copyright © American Map Corporation, New York, No. 19309

INTERCONTINENTAL AMERICA

Intercontinental America has a Lutheran population of about 29,000 almost equally divided between three areas: Caribbean islands, Central America and Panama, and Mexico. Included are 22 units—some small church bodies (two LWF members), other single congregations or missions of European or North American churches, and still other isolated believers struggling for identity and recognition. Among them is one of the oldest churches in the Western Hemisphere as well as several of the newest. Intercontinental American Lutherans comprise 2.3% of those in the entire Latin American and Caribbean region.

CARIBBEAN ISLANDS

Lutherans in six Caribbean islands—Antigua, Bahamas, Cuba, Haiti, Puerto Rico, and the Virgin Islands—comprise 37% of Intercontinental American Lutherans. Distant Bermuda is a bonus.

This island world between the Americas is a lure for tourists, a haunt for historians, and a home to some 26 million people in 13 separate political entities. The area is commonly reckoned as extending eastward from Mexico and Central America over 3200 kilometers (2000 miles) to the Bahama islands, off the Florida coast, USA. Varying in composition from big Cuba to the tiny Lesser Antilles; racially mixed, with Europeans, Africans, Asians, and traces of Amerindians in varying combinations; politically complex, with various types of free or dependent status; and

linguistically divided with Dutch, English, French, Spanish, and local languages making communication difficult—the "Mediterranean of the Americas" is an exciting point where forces converge which are shaping the contemporary world scene.

Historically, this has been true since Spain first claimed the region in the time of Columbus. With the discovery of the Pacific (1513), the Spanish "silver fleets"—carrying treasures from Peru and Mexico—soon fell prey to English, Dutch, and French marauders in the Caribbean. The islands themselves became early sites for European sugar plantations and the accompanying slave trade, in which the Danish West Indies (*Virgin Islands) also came to play a key part. During the 19th century, the Caribbean became important to the USA, especially during the California "gold rush" when the isthmuses of Panama and Nicaragua became transfer points. The Panama Canal—begun by the French, finished by the Americans, and opened in 1914—increased the importance of the Caribbean as a route to the Pacific. Puerto Rico (ceded to the USA after the Spanish-American War) and the Virgin Islands (purchased from Denmark in 1917) reflect the USA interests in the area. Cuba's alliance with the East keeps the region vulnerable to the international power struggles of the time.

Religion: Most of the people in the Caribbean are Christian, with members almost equally divided between Roman Catholic and Protestant. Of the latter, Anglicans predominate. The Caribbean Conference of Churches (CCC), formed in 1973, includes Roman Catholics. Its purpose is the renewal of the church and the development of Caribbean peoples. Headquarters, originally in Trinidad, are now located in Bridgetown, Barbados. The Lutheran Church in Guyana, the Evangelical Lutheran Church in Suriname, and the Caribbean Synod of the Evangelical Lutheran Church in America are members. The ELCA (formerly LCA) also supports ecumenical work in Trinidad through the CCC, providing a pastor to help develop a more functional ministry.

The United Theological College of the West Indies, an English-speaking institution located near the University in Kingston, Jamaica, is an ecumenically significant institution providing many of the Protestant churches in the Caribbean with well-trained pastors. From its beginning, the *LCA gave support, first by sending a theological professor and then by supporting a tutor from the Lutheran Church in Guyana. Tragically, the latter was killed in a plane crash while on duty in theological extension work (see Guyana, below). Since then assistance has been through student scholarships. Lutheran students at the institution are from non-Latin countries.

Lutherans in the Caribbean, located in Antigua, the Bahamas, Cuba, Haiti, Puerto Rico, and the Virgin Islands, as well as in the Atlantic islands of Bermuda, number about 10,700. English, French, and Spanish languages are used. All but the youngest church in Haiti have relations of some kind with churches in the *USA. None are completely autonomous. The second oldest Lutheran church in the Americas (the first being in New York) is in the *Virgin Islands. It

traces its beginnings to 1666, when the Danish West India Company established the congregation in Charlotte Amalie.

As indicated in the general introduction to Latin America, an LWF conference for English-speaking churches in the Caribbean is held every three or four years. The purpose is to provide the churches with an opportunity to discuss issues and concerns common to the region. Included are the LWF member churches of *Suriname and *Guyana (South America, below), and the *Virgin Islands (through ELCA), the former ALC (now ELCA) congregations in the Bahamas and Bermuda, and the LCMS congregations in the Bahamas and Panama (Central America and Panama, below).

ANTIGUA

Antigua and Barbuda, two islands in the Leeward Islands of the British West Indies, together form an associated state of Great Britain with full internal self-government. Area: 441.6 sq. km. (170.5 sq. mi.). Pop. (1985): 80,500, of which 94.4% are black, 1.3% white, 4.3% other. Cap.: St. John's (pop., 1982 est., 30,000).

History: Antigua, discovered by Columbus in 1493, was unsuccessfully settled by Spanish and French. In 1632, the British began fruitful settlements. Today, the chief industry is tourism.

Religion (1980): Anglican 44.5%; other Protestant, largely Moravian and Methodist, 41.6%; Roman Catholic 10.2%; other 3.7%. The latter includes a few Muslims and a growing number of Rastafarians—an Afro-American cult from Jamaica—mainly among unemployed blacks. The Moravians, after becoming established in the *Virgin Islands, came to Antigua in 1756, and were immediately successful in converting the blacks working in the sugar plantations. The Antigua Christian Council, formed in 1964, includes the Protestant churches mentioned above, the Salvation Army and the Roman Catholic Church. Concerns include the renewal of the church in the Caribbean as well as social justice and disaster relief.

ST. JOHN'S EVANGELICAL LUTHERAN CHURCH, *WELS
Membership: 225**
PO Box 1248
St. John's
Pastors: The Rev. Richard M. Seeger;
The Rev. Mark Henrich

This congregation of the South Atlantic District of *Wisconsin Evangelical Lutheran Synod (WELS), now served by two pastors and four parochial teachers, was founded in the early 1970s by an Antiguan layman who had been reached by the Lutheran Hour. Membership is a good cross section of Antiguans—poor laborers, shopkeepers, skilled workers, and professionals, as well as expatriates serving at the USA naval base. Members living in the surrounding villages are transported to the attractive church on a hill in St. John's by church vans. The school—through eighth·grade—has recently added preschool care. Gifted students have attended a WELS high school in Michigan and its college in New Ulm, Minnesota. Heavily subsidized by WELS, the congregation assumes its fair share of costs and also participates in local welfare projects.

BAHAMAS

A member of the Commonwealth of Nations, the Bahamas comprise an archipelago of about 700 islands southeast of the USA state of Florida. Area: 13,939 sq. km. (5382 sq. mi.). Pop. (1980 census) 209,506. Cap. and largest urban area: Nassau: (pop., 1982 est., 135,000). Language: English (official).

History: Columbus first set foot in the New World on the Island of San Salvador (also called Watling's Island), October 12, 1492. A British settlement (1647) eventually became a British colony (1783). The Bahamas received internal self-government in 1964 and became independent in 1973. In 1980, 72.4% of the population was black, 14.2% mixed, 12.8% white, and 0.6% other.

Religion: Baptists, Anglicans, Roman Catholics, and Methodists (in that order) account for most of the inhabitants. The Church of God and various other groups have small followings. Lutherans, gathered into two

congregations (below) have a combined membership of about 300. Due to their proximity to the Caribbean islands, these congregations have been included in the LWF-sponsored Caribbean Conference.

LUTHERAN CHURCH OF NASSAU, *LCMS
Membership: 205**
PO Box 4794
Nassau, New Providence
Pastor: The Rev. Paul Zalman

This congregation comprises mainly Bahamians. It is a member of the Florida-Georgia District of the LCMS.

OUR SAVIOUR LUTHERAN CHURCH, ELCA
Membership: 118**
East Sunrise Highway
PO Box F-267
Freeport, Grand Bahama Island
Pastor: The Rev. Winfred Craig Belcher

Organized in 1964 by the American Lutheran Church to serve expatriates and tourists, this congregation is now composed mainly of Bahamians—both black and white. Sunland, the largest Christian dayschool of the former ALC, has 600 pupils (K through 9th) and is served by a staff of 23. It helps meet the shortage of schools on the island. The congregation is a member of the Florida Synod (ELCA).

BERMUDA

A British colony since 1619, located some 900 kilometers (570 miles) east of USA's Cape Hatteras. Area: Several small islands totaling 47.9 sq. km. (18.5 sq. mi.). Pop. (1986 est.): 57,000. Cap.: Hamilton (pop., 1985 est., 1676) Largest city, St. George.

History: Bermuda, settled in 1609 by shipwrecked Englishmen en route to Virginia (see Shakespeare's play *The Tempest*), has remained a colony. Ethnic composition: black

61.3%; white 37.3%: other 1.4%. The island's balmy climate is a perennial tourist attraction, the chief source of income.

Religion: Christian, of which 45% are Anglican, with two-thirds being black. Other Protestants, mainly Methodists, 37.3%. Roman Catholic 18.6%. Lutherans have one congregation (below). A Joint Committee of Churches includes both Protestants and Catholics.

PEACE LUTHERAN CHURCH *ELCA
Membership: 181**
South Shore Road
Box 182
Bermuda
Pastor: The Rev. Thomas W. Andersen

The church of this small but active congregation is located on the South Shore Road across from the Bermuda Botanical Garden—a popular tourist attraction. Founded in 1964 by the former American Lutheran Church (ALC) to serve the then large numbers of U.S. military personnel, it now serves a good cross section of Bermuda's population—half black and half white, as well as tourists. Free of debt (thanks to a nonmember Bermuda family) and self-supporting, the congregation continues to be supplied by pastors from the ELCA. Ecumenically, the congregation is active in relief projects for the Caribbeans. Peace Lutheran Church is a member of the Metropolitan Washington Synod, ELCA.

CUBA

A Socialist republic, the largest island in the Greater Antilles in the Caribbean Sea. Area: 110,922 sq. km. (42,827 sq. mi.) including several thousand small islands and cays. Pop. (1986 est.): 10,194,200, including about 70% white, 15.4% mestizo, 12.4% black. Cap. and largest city: Havana (pop., 1985 est., 1,992,600). Language: Spanish.

History: Initially inhabited by Carib Indians, and discovered by Columbus in 1492, the islands remained a Spanish possession until 1898. First colonized in 1511, this "Pearl of the Antilles" over the next three centuries was an early assembly point for Spain's treasure fleets. Laden with the wealth of *Mexico and *Peru, Cuba later became the haven of Spanish loyalists fleeing the newly independent nations on the mainland. In the later 19th century, the "Faithful Isle" became restive under Spanish rule and revolted. American intervention—the Spanish-American War (1898)—turned Cuba into a republic, though under USA tutelage. In 1933, the republic became a dictatorship under Fulgencio Batista y Zaldívar. His overthrow in 1959 by Fidel Castro soon turned Cuba into the first Communist state in Latin America. With firm ties to the *USSR, Cubans not only seek to eradicate remnants of their own colonial and exploited past but are also ready to participate in distant struggles such as those in *Angola, *Ethiopia, and *Afghanistan.

Religion: Roman Catholic c. 42%; Protestant and Anglican c. 2%. Over half of the population expresses no religious affiliation. The present four Roman Catholic dioceses and two archdioceses (Havana and Santiago) trace their roots to Dominican and Franciscan activities beginning in 1512. After centuries of siding with conservative political forces, the church was ill-prepared to cope with the revolution in 1959—an event in some ways comparable to those earlier in *Mexico. In time, the church has adapted itself to the changed situation, even as Fidel Castro himself has expressed his Christian beliefs in book form, *Fidel and Religion* (1985). For the Catholic church, the road ahead requires the development of an indigenous leadership.

Protestantism's beginnings in Cuba go back to the first Anglican worship in 1741, forefunner of today's Episcopal Church of Cuba. In 1883, Baptist and Methodist missionaries arrived, followed by Presbyterian and Reformed (1890). Early in the present century (up to 1914) other groups came in, with Pentecostals eventually drawing the largest following. The Presbyterian-Reformed and Methodist joined the WCC in 1967 and 1968, respectively.

Cooperative work in Christian education and other areas led in 1941 to the present Ecumenical Council of Cuba, an association of 13 Protestant church bodies. Union Theological Seminary in Matanzas, 95 kilometers (60 miles) east of Havana, has been a leading center of ministerial education interdenominationally and internationally since 1947. Its activities, however, were substantially cut back after 1959. As a 1984 consultation of the Ecumenical Council stated, the preceding 26 years had been filled with tension and frustration but also with spiritual growth and wider social concern. The missionary past, dominated and fragmented by American denominations, was viewed critically. Yet there was also thankfulness, particularly for the heritage of freedom (quoting Luther) to express a divine discontent as seekers of God's kingdom.

A small Lutheran constituency grew out of the missionary work of the *Lutheran Church–Missouri Synod. In 1911, a Missouri Synod pastor, C. Richard Oertel, came to the Isle of Pines for reasons of health. In this pleasant place off the mainland of southwest Cuba, Oertel found fellow Lutherans among residents from North America and Germany. Within three years, three congregations had been gathered. The third one, in Havana, consisted of Germans who had lived there for years without pastoral care. Oertel found open doors among the Cubans themselves, most of them non-practicing Catholics. Even so, growth was slow. The Lutheran Church on the Isle of Pines in 1927 counted a little over 150 baptized members, with many others attending services. The fact that the work had become trilingual held promise.

New growth marked the period from World War II until 1959. That was the era of LCMS's concerted advance into this northern tier of Latin American lands. At its height, the Lutheran church in Cuba consisted of about 540 members, gathered in six congregations. The Spanish-language broadcasts of the International Lutheran Hour widened the outreach. However, in the wake of the revolution drastic changes marked the early 1960s, and most of the members left Cuba. By the mid-1960s, there were no more pastors on the scene, and work had been turned over to local leadership. The remaining 200 or so Lutherans reside in Havana, Pinar del Río, San José, Bocca del Garafre, and the Isle of Pines.

In the mid-1970s the director of the LWF Department of Church Cooperation visited this diminished constituency. In 1981, a staff member of the Norwegian Santal Mission (an agency active in *Ecuador since 1968) visited the Cuban Lutherans on behalf of the Missouri Synod as well as the LWF. He found the members faithful, though they lacked Bibles, hymnals, catechisms, and other Christian literature. Two forces remain supportive: the "Lutheran Hour" Spanish broadcasts and the Santal Mission mediation. Concern and helpfulness has also come from the Episcopal and Methodist churches in Cuba. A new church law (1983) made it possible for the Lutherans to register as a church, provided they were able to establish a responsible leadership. This attainment of church status has remained pending (1988), as well as the return of church buildings now occupied by the government.

HAITI

A republic on the western end of the Caribbean island of Hispaniola, which it shares with the Dominican Republic, Haiti's area: 27,750 sq. km. (10,715 sq. mi.). Pop. (1986 est.): 5,427,000. Cap. and largest city: Port-au-Prince (1986 est.: 457,564). Language: French and Creole.

History: Visited by Columbus (1492); held by Spain until 1697, when it became a French colony; gained independence in 1804 under leadership of former African slaves. In 1844, the predominantly Spanish (eastern) two-thirds of the island broke away from Haiti, creating the Dominican Republic. Political violence brought in USA military occupation (1915–1934). The Duvalier era (1957–1986), a father-son succession in presidency, began with François Duvalier (d.1971) and ended with the banishment of Jean-Claude Duvalier. The wealth of a dictatorial presidency stood in sharp contrast to general poverty of the people. Severe drought in 1975–1977 brought famine, and a 1980 hurricane caused massive devastation and crop loss. Decline in tourism also proved costly. Aid from European communities and OPEC (Organization of the Petroleum Exporting Countries) prodded development via public works. Deep resentments are shaping the post-Duvalier era in the efforts to recover a democratic society.

Religion: Vodun (Voodoo), especially among rural folk, lives on. This blend of African Traditional religion (largely from Benin, Dahomey) and Roman Catholic practice recalls early colonial times. A form of

Spiritism, Vodun relates also to that in *Brazil. In a population claiming 98% Christian, this popular religion thrives where it will.

While Roman Catholicism claims 84% of the people, most of the others are Protestant, the largest proportion in any Latin American country. The archdiocese of Port-au-Prince and four other dioceses comprise the Roman Catholic hierarchy. Among the Protestants, Baptist, Pentecostal, Adventist, and other conservative churches predominate. Eleven of them associate in the Evangelical Council of Churches of Haiti. Since 1968, an Ecumenical Research Group has been bringing together Roman Catholic, Episcopal, Methodist, and other representatives.

In 1985, LWF World Service established a program of assistance to Haitians in Haiti and to Haitian refugees in nearby countries (Dominican Republic, French Guiana, Guadeloupe, *Venezuela, and the USA/Florida). Working with Haitian communities, church and other local groups, the program in Haiti provides agricultural assistance, including aid to small farm cooperatives, advocacy and legal assistance, functional literacy, and appropriate technology. Thus LWF/WS seeks to bring encouragement to Haiti's poorest.

LUTHERAN CHURCH OF HAITI
(Eglise luthérienne de Haïti)
Membership: 1050**
Contact person: Ben Bichotte
PO Box 13147 Delmas
Port-au-Prince

The currently five congregations of this small mission church are located in Fonfrede, Duvalierville, Fond Verrettes, Fond Parisien, and Petite Place Cazeau. The congregation in the latter place is the largest, having about 300 baptized members. These locations extend outward from the capital, Port-au-Prince, from the coastal area eastward to the Dominican Republic border. The membership is mainly rural and impoverished, especially by periodic droughts.

This group of Christians, without benefit of an ordained pastor or other professional leadership, nevertheless maintains a day school of some 350 pupils (in Petite Place Cazeau). It has some connections with *France's Church of the Augsburg Confession of Alsace and Lorraine, and it has also

benefited from the French-language "Lutheran Hour."

The lay leader of this group is Mr. Ben Bichotte, a trained agriculturalist, who, during a period of study in Germany, received instruction in the teachings of the Lutheran church. Capturing a vision of improving the lot of his rural Haitians, upon his return home, he founded a Christian community that comes together for worship and other congregational activities. Since 1985, Bichotte has supervised a dual project of farming and goat raising, a venture aided by a grant from the LWF Community Development Service. In 1986, a staff team from the *Lutheran Church in America (now ELCA) followed up with an exploratory canvassing of possibilities for further ministry in Haiti.

PUERTO RICO

A self-governing commonwealth associated with the USA. Area: 8958 sq. km. (3459 sq. mi.). Pop. (1984 est.): 3,270,000. Cap. and largest city: San Juan (metro. area pop.: 1,535,000). Language: Spanish (official) and English.

History: Arawak Indians were the early inhabitants. Columbus discovered the island on his second voyage (1493) and took possession of it for Spain, naming it San Juan Bautista. Occupation began under Ponce de Léon (1508). By inverse usage, what Columbus called Puerto Rico, the splendid port, became the name of the island; and what he called the island, San Juan, became the name of its capital. Enslaved to dig for gold, the Indians did not survive beyond 1582. West Africans, imported as slaves, continued the quest for gold, but soon worked the sugar plantations on the lowlands and the coffee in the highlands.

The island's exposed position made it vulnerable to attack by the French, Dutch, and British. But El Morro castle, the bastion of San Juan, proved impregnable. Economically and otherwise, Puerto Rico had difficult times, but it remained a Spanish possession until after the Spanish-American War (1898), when it was ceded to the USA. Like Cuba, about the 1820s, it became an asylum for loyalists from liberated Latin American lands, among them church people.

When an independence movement gathered strength, the USA granted citizenship to all Puerto Ricans (1917). USA business created large corporate plantations out of subsistence farms, and, since World War II, it has profited by the tax incentives and cheap labor on the island. In 1952, the Commonwealth of Puerto Rico was proclaimed. Statehood is still not the desire of a majority of the people. Poverty makes many leave the country for USA cities.

Religion: Over 90% Roman Catholic; nearly 5% Protestant; others include Afro-American Spiritists, atheists, Bahais, Jews, and nonreligionists.

Roman Catholicism traces its beginnings from the first diocese (1511), today the archdiocese of San Juan. Over the ensuing centuries Puerto Rican society, with its Spanish, mestizo, and African elements, was solidly Roman Catholic and served by priests mainly from Spain. The church depended heavily on government favor, and the clergy were custodians of conservatism. Spain's declaration of religious tolerance (1868) was a harbinger of change. Agitation for independence, the Spanish-American War (1898), and new ties with the United States seriously weakened the traditional church. Only slowly did it regain strength, as the new diocese of Ponce (1924), in the south, indicated. Under Pope John XXIII, San Juan became an archdiocese, and two new dioceses were added.

Protestantism found Puerto Rico an exceptional challenge. Presbyterians (1860) and Anglicans (1872, subsequently Episcopalians) were first on the scene. The end of the war against Spain (mid-1898) opened the door to a long and diverse succession of missionaries from the north. Preceding them all was a student from Augustana College (Rock Island, Illinois), launching a Lutheran effort (below). Meanwhile, in New York, an interdenominational consultation determined the comity that would guide Protestant work on the island, the several churches and societies being assigned to specific localities. For five denominations 1899 became the year of beginnings, as there arrived Baptists, Disciples, and workers of three bodies now forming the United Church. Methodists came in 1900, as did the Christian and Missionary Alliance, with Seventh Day Adventists entering the following year. In the 1930s, the first of a variety of Pentecostals appeared,

becoming in time the largest and most accessible of the non-Roman communions. Having been granted U.S. citizenship (1917), the ensuing migratory to-and-fro between the island and New York as well as other big cities made Puerto Ricans themselves agents of change in Protestantism.

Interdenominationally, the famed Panama Congress of 1916 (see Latin America Introduction), under USA initiative, endeavored to see Christian work in Latin America as a whole, and conducted one of its four regional follow-up conferences in San Juan. To this day, Puerto Rican Protestantism provides a significant linkage between the Americas. It is also a participant in the Latin American Council of Churches (CLAI). Its own Evangelical Council of Puerto Rico (Concilio Evangélico de Puerto Rico; 1954)—antecedents reach back to 1905—has eight fully participating denominations as well as a number of adjunct bodies, like the Puerto Rico district of the Caribbean Synod of the ELCA. Lutherans are known for La Reforma (Fortress, *LCA), in Rio Piedras, the major religious bookstore on the island.

Efforts to train an indigenous ministry as well as teachers and other Christian workers led to the founding of the Evangelical Seminary (1919) and other schools. The seminary is now supported by 10 denominations, including grants from the LCA, and serves churches in a dozen countries. Its faculty, library, and buildings experienced major gains in the 1960s. It cooperates with the Episcopal Seminary of the Caribbean and also with the Catholic Theological Faculty of the Central University of Bayamón, west of San Juan. It also has a working relationship with the Lutheran Theological Seminary in Philadelphia (below). Poverty in much of the island has motivated Protestant health and welfare services.

EVANGELICAL LUTHERAN CONFESSIONAL CHURCH
(Iglesia Evangélica Luterana Confesional)
Membership: 200**
Pastors: The Rev. Tomás Horner
Apartado 334, Guayama, PR-00655
The Rev. Carlos Flunker
Apartado 1809, Las Piedras, PR-00671

Three congregations and one preaching point, organized by the missionaries of the Wisconsin Evangelical Lutheran Synod (WELS/

USA), have a combined membership of about 200. The aim is to establish an indigenous church that is self-governing, self-propagating, and self-supporting as soon as possible. To aid in these efforts a Bible Institute is maintained in Guayama. The work began in the San Juan area in 1964.

PUERTO RICO DISTRICT, CARIBBEAN SYNOD, *ELCA

Membership: 5222**
Bishop: The Rt. Rev. Rafael Malpica-Padilla
415 Bellavista Street
Monteflores, San Juan, PR 00915
Mail: PO Box 14426
Barrio Obrero Station, Santurce, PR 00916

Over the past decade, the number of Lutherans in Puerto Rico has increased by nearly 50%. The 26 congregations of the Puerto Rico District together with the seven congregations of the Virgin Island District form the Caribbean Synod of the ELCA. Most of the Puerto Rico congregations are situated in or near San Juan. Grace Church dates from the original Spanish and English service, January 1, 1899; St. Paul Temple, near the entrance to the old city, from 1900. St. Paul's neo-Gothic edifice, dedicated in 1916, was recently restored (1981).

The congregations participate fully in the programs and missions of the ELCA. All use the Spanish language, with the exception of one congregation in San Juan that is English-speaking, and meet the needs of Virgin Islanders and other expatriates. Two of the congregations have parish day schools accommodating some 500 pupils through the ninth grade.

Most Puerto Rican pastoral candidates receive their education at the Evangelical Seminary (above), although a few still attend the Lutheran Theological Seminary in Philadelphia. Periodically, members of the Philadelphia faculty visit the Evangelical Seminary to instruct the Lutheran students. Some pastors have come into the Lutheran church from other communions as well as from other Latin American countries. Mainland pastors are required to be proficient in Spanish. To compensate for not having theological education

by extension, a lay training school was established in 1978. Selected Puerto Rican pastors train lay leaders. If, after a period of service, they desire to be ordained, they are encouraged to undertake the necessary university studies. The program has already increased the number of indigenous pastors. In 1984, two men—one a lawyer and one a physician—completed their theological training at the Evangelical Seminary. The physician continues his medical practice and serves a small congregation.

In recent years, the Puerto Rico Conference organized a Lutheran Social Service agency similar to the one in the Virgin Islands. It has awakened social conscience and provides service in several locations, including a church camp, a day-care center for children and the elderly, and a home for battered women.

Lutherans, as noted above, were among the first Protestants to undertake work in Puerto Rico. In 1898, a month after the Spanish-American War ceased, an Augustana Lutheran pretheological student, Gustav Sigfrid Swenson, arrived in Puerto Rico to learn Spanish. Seeing the great need for the gospel, Swenson opened a teaching and preaching center, taught English to support himself, and gathered a bilingual congregation composed of English-speaking blacks from the Danish West Indies and Spanish-speaking Puerto Ricans. The first service was held on January 1, 1899 (above).

The then General Council of the Evangelical Lutheran Church in America responded to Swenson's challenge by sending two young graduates from the Philadelphia Seminary. Their short stay was followed by the longtime service of experienced pastors and other workers, mainly from the Augustana Synod. Among them, and especially noteworthy, was the extensive term (1905–1931) of missionary Albert Ostrom and his wife, Betty. The missionaries began at once to train Puerto Ricans for pastoral service. However, stateside, the Lutheran General Council was reluctant to ordain anyone who had not had complete theological training. When the United Lutheran Church (which included the General Council) was formed in 1918, Puerto Rico won a wider basis of support. However, the well-laid plans of the missionaries for a Spanish-speaking theological seminary in San Juan—including purchased property and contributed funds—were never carried out. Instead, a few pastoral candidates were given scholarships to prepare for the ordained ministry in the USA. As already noted, substitute plans are still being used.

VIRGIN ISLANDS

An unincorporated territory of the USA, this cluster of 68 islands lies some 60 km. (40 mi.) east of Puerto Rico. St. Croix, St. Thomas, and St. John are the three important ones. Area: 433 sq. km. (133 sq. mi.). Pop. (1985 est.): 110,800, about 80% of African descent. Cap.: Charlotte Amalie, St. Thomas (metro. pop., 1984 est., 19,304). Language: English.

History: The Carib nation inhabited these islands initially. Columbus, on November 14, 1492, sent a landing party to the well-cultivated island he then called Santa Cruz (St. Croix, as renamed by the French). He named the cluster in honor of St. Ursula and the Eleven Thousand Virgins, of medieval legend. The skirmish at the Salt River marked the first European encounter with the (Carib) Indians. Later, the Spaniards, having taken possession of all the great prizes, feared that the Virgin Islands might simply pose a threat as a pirates' hangout. As early as 1625, it is said, English and Dutch settled on St. Croix, a convenient way station en route to other Caribbean islands and to South American *Guiana.

Danes, too, had ventured into the region. Authorized by the Danish crown, an initial shipload of colonists, accompanied by their pastor, Kjeld Jensen Slagelse, settled on the island of St. Thomas in 1666. The prospects of trade seemed promising, and in 1671 the Danish West India Company was organized—with white convicts (including women) from Denmark as the first labor force. The harbor settlement bore the name of Charlotte Amalie, Denmark's German-born queen. Before long, Danish installations (called factories) on Africa's west coast were directing Danish slavers to St. Thomas. Eventually, St. Thomas became an important provisioning center for sailing ships and one of the largest markets in the African slave trade. In 1683 Denmark claimed St. John Island; in 1733 it purchased St. Croix from France.

Europeans on the Danish Islands were a motley gathering of Dutch, Germans, English, Scots, French, and Spaniards as well as Danes. Yet Africans far outnumbered them. Responsibilities grew, and in 1755 the crown bought out the trading company, making the islands officially the Danish West Indies, a Royal Colony.

Although slave trade through the West Indies was at its peak in the late 18th and early 19th centuries, it was also a time when the Danish government prepared for emancipation. Already in 1787, it began to provide schools for the slaves. Reforms of 1792 led to the act of 1841, which provided free and compulsory education for all slaves—children and adults. Sentiment against slavery in England and Denmark reached the islands. By the time of emancipation (1848)—declared by Governor von Schloten, the Abraham Lincoln of the Danish West Indies—one-third of all Africans were "Free Colored," the middle class in the West Indies.

Nearly a decade of British occupation during the Napoleonic wars (1801, 1807–1814) and the coming of English planters hastened the process of English becoming the dominant and later official language. Periodic natural disasters made clear how far removed the islands were from Denmark and the sources of help, as in 1867, when plague, the worst of hurricanes, an earthquake, and a tidal wave struck in rapid succession. These and other circumstance dictated that the time had come for Denmark to offer its West Indies for sale to the United States. Only 50 years later (1917) was the Danish offer accepted. Renamed the Virgin Islands, they have remained an unincorporated territory of the USA. As in the case of Puerto Rico, thousands of islanders have emigrated to the mainland. The economic significance of the islands has been eclipsed by their attraction for tourists.

Religion: About 98% Christian. Nearly one-third of the population is Roman Catholic. On the Protestant side, Episcopalians are by far the most numerous, followed by Moravians, Pentecostals, Methodists, Lutherans, Salvation Army, Seventh-Day Adventists, and others. The St. Thomas Interchurch Council includes the Lutherans among its six member bodies.

Christian work among the Africans was begun by German Moravians in 1732. This

West Indies outreach was the first Moravian mission overseas. It grew from an appeal (1730) of a freed slave, who depicted the spiritual plight of his fellow Africans to Count Zinzendorf, the patron of the Moravians, while attending the coronation of the new king in Copenhagen. By agreement with the crown, the Moravian missionaries worked among the responsive rural population, while the Danish church cared for the townspeople. The missionaries, mainly lay, combined their spiritual ministry with instruction in black-smithing, shoemaking, and other trades. In applying the education act of 1841, Governor von Schloten chose the Moravians to provide the teachers for the schools and the Lutheran church to provide the supervision. The Moravians—some were from their British congregations—were quicker to accept the English language in their work. This helps to account for their greater growth than the Lutherans. The Lutheran story, both of settlement and mission, unfolds below.

VIRGIN ISLAND DISTRICT, CARIBBEAN SYNOD, *ELCA
Member: CCC
Membership: 3500**
(see *USA, *Puerto Rico)

Lutherans in the Virgin Islands, together with those in Puerto Rico, have since 1952 been a part of the self-governing bilingual Caribbean Synod of the Lutheran Church in America (now ELCA). Today, the Lutherans in the Virgin Islands number slightly less than 3500. Of the seven English-speaking congregations, four are located on St. Croix, two on St. Thomas, and one on St. John.

Most of the members are of African descent and have acquired and retained elements of Danish culture. Many have done well in business, the professions, and agriculture. However, the majority have been hurt badly by the prolonged depression on the islands. Since the early 1920s, this has induced many young people to emigrate to the USA. Congregations of Virgin Islanders in New York City's Harlem (Transfiguration Church, 1923, today reports over 1200 baptized members) and in other cities have over the years been served by fellow islanders

trained for ministry in the USA. The congregations in the Virgin Islands have preferred white pastors, perpetuating, it is said, the long experience with pastors from Denmark. Some members, however, believe that the well-being of the congregations will improve when Virgin Islanders themselves accept and develop their own indigenous ministry. To provide role models for young people, black pastors from the USA are serving in two congregations.

Besides congregational work, like that of the ELCA elsewhere, there is Lutheran Social Services of the Virgin Islands. Headquartered in Frederiksted, this agency maintains the modern Queen Louise Home for Children and its associated Thrift Shop enterprise as well as the Lutheran Housing Association for the Elderly. In 1981, Lutheran Social Services began a summer program for disabled children and projected plans for their residential care. Counseling service began in 1982. Now a crisis intervention center enables trained teenagers to counsel their peers who have drug or sexual abuse problems. In both St. Croix and St. Thomas new housing for the elderly is under construction with funds supplied by the government. These services carry on the work begun in the early 20th century by the Danish Lutherans (below). Likewise, the Frederik congregation on St. Thomas still maintains it parish elementary school. Recently, this congregation established a preaching point on the west end of the island in cooperation with the Anglican church.

Historically, Frederik congregation in Charlotte Amalie traces its beginnings to 1666, a few years after the first two congregations were begun on the North American mainland. Other Lutheran congregations were founded on St. John (1717) and on St. Croix (1736 and c.1766). Still others followed. The Danish West India Company endeavored to supply the congregations with pastors, but this was difficult. In the words of their church historian, the islands were long known as the "graveyard of pastors" as well as a "horrible place of convicts, pirates, fever, hunger, and death."

When the Danish government took over the West India Company (1754), the spiritual needs of the colonists received more attention, and Danish Lutherans began work among the Africans (1757) to supplement that of the Moravians. For 25 years, Johannes

Christian Kingo, the first of several missionaries, labored among the slaves, teaching, preaching, and serving their needs as well as defending their rights before the government and church. His translation of Christian literature—the New Testament, Luther's *Small Catechism*, hymns, and materials necessary for the schools—into Creole Dutch was monumental. By 1771, the mission adopted a policy of centralized education and evangelistic work, and Creole was substituted for the Africans' worship. The effectiveness of the schools founded after 1787 became the excuse for discontinuing the missionary pastors. In 1798, the Danish government combined the offices of missionary and minister and allotted only one pastor to each of the two largest islands. Even so, the government continued to send out missionary catechists until the middle of the 19th century. About 1800, the mission congregation on St. Thomas numbered 1000—half of them slaves and half free "colored." The Danish and Creole congregations met at separate times in the same churches and were served by the same pastor. In time, the congregations merged, the one on St. John doing so before 1852. The first choir in St. Thomas for the Danish service was a black, boy's choir.

A number of years before emancipation in 1848, the Danish Lutheran congregations had freed their slaves. Language was the big problem. Since Creole had become the language of faith for the Africans, the Lutheran church was the conspicuous loser with the advancing use of English. In 1950, Lutherans numbered 4000; by 1911 they were slightly more than 3000.

During the first part of the 20th century, the first provost (dean) for the Danish West Indies, Laurits Petersen, led the congregations in developing active welfare work. This included the establishment of two Queen Louise homes for sick and neglected children (in Christiansted and in Frederiksted) as well as the Ebenezer Lutheran Orphanage on St. Thomas and the Pleasant Grove Old People's Home. The congregations also provided small homes near the churches for the elderly of the parish. With other denominations, Lutherans helped serve the leper colonies. Deaconesses, sent from Copenhagen, headed this diversified work.

When the Danish West Indies in 1917 became the Virgin Islands of the United States,

the Lutheran church faced a greater change than the other churches on the islands. The visit of the Danish American pastor, A.C. Kildegaard, to St. Thomas opened the way for new ties with the General Council of the Evangelical Lutheran Church in America. Subsequently, three Virgin Island delegates attending the 1917 General Council convention in Philadelphia objected to being placed under a board of foreign missions, insisting that they were neither "foreign nor heathen." Therefore, a West Indies Mission Board was formed. This provided assistance and personnel, including deaconesses for the social service agencies, until 1926, when the United Lutheran Church in America's home mission board assumed responsibility.

CENTRAL AMERICA AND PANAMA

Lutherans in Costa Rica, El Salvador, Guatemala, Honduras, Nicaragua, and Panama comprise 29.5% of Intercontinental American Lutherans.

This mountainous land bridge between North and South America extends 2000 kilometers (1250 miles) from Mexico to Colombia, covers an area of over 330,000 sq. km. (nearly 200,000 sq. mi.), and has a population (1984 est.) of about 25 million. The seven independent countries comprising this region—from north to south, Belize, Guatemala, El Salvador, Honduras, Nicaragua, Costa Rica, and Panama—are described briefly below. Except for Costa Rica, whose population is mainly of Spanish descent, that of the other countries is predominantly mestizo—a mingling of Amerindian and European stock—besides African and some later European elements. The language is Spanish, but various Indian tongues persist. Education, compulsory and free, is not evenly available—especially among the poor.

History: The Mayan civilization occupied a mediating position between that of the Aztecs in *Mexico and the Incas in *Peru. Its superb achievements in architecture and science—its pyramids suggest affinity with Egypt and the Middle East, its sculpted figures seem akin to the religious symbolism in Southeast Asia, its calendar and astronomical observations reveal an accuracy unmatched until modern times—were paralleled by advanced forms of agriculture and were tested in war as well as enjoyed in peace. Spread over Guatemala, Honduras, and Yucatán, as well as beyond, the Mayan civilization—as archaeologists claim—had existed over 2000 years prior to the coming of the Spanish conquistadors in the 1520s. The mystery of the Mayan rise was at last matched by a sudden demise, while traces of this ancient past live on among a present-day troubled and often tormented people.

Independence, led by Mexico, came to the region in 1821 after nearly three centuries of Spanish colonial rule. Costa Rica went its own way. Belize remained a British possession (1678–1973). Panama was part of Colombia until 1903. Guatemala, El Salvador, Honduras, and Nicaragua, after 15 years as the United Provinces of Central America, in 1838/1839 went their respective ways. The shaky Central American Common Market has been a modern effort to reassert the region's potential unity, yet geographic location has made the region's economy as well as its politics subject not only to internal dissension but also to external design. Dependence on export crops—coffee and bananas—has paralleled foreign intervention, especially from the USA, during the 19th and 20th centuries. The 1849 gold rush to California and the ensuing westward lunge to the Pacific coast made Nicaragua a choice route for crossing the isthmus with least effort, while the Panama Canal at last opened the sea route (1914) under USA control.

Export crops encouraged the continuation of large holdings by an elite of landlords and, late in the 19th century, by transnational agribusinesses. For them, dictators proved easier to deal with than democracies. But the chronic postponement of land reform, plus the fluctuation of international markets, spawned ever new situations of poverty and violence. Politically and economically, Central America's condition placed capitalism and Communism on a collision course. With its concern for the poor, the Christian church inevitably became involved. Lutherans, too, became involved in a region where they had been only lightly represented but were now greatly challenged.

Religion: Basic data on this predominantly Roman Catholic region is included under each of the countries treated below. Most of the Lutherans are included in two groupings. One, bearing the title Evangelical Lutheran Church of Costa Rica, El Salvador, Honduras, Nicaragua, and Panama, consists of German-speaking congregations, recognized by the LWF and supplied with pastors by the Foreign Office of the *Evangelical Church in Germany (EKD). It is described under Costa Rica, its headquarters. The other is the Council of Lutheran Churches in Central America and Panama (CONCAP). Its small church bodies are all affiliated with the *Lutheran Church–Missouri Synod (USA). It is described under Guatemala, its headquarters.

COSTA RICA

A Central American republic, Costa Rica has Nicaragua to the north and Panama to the south, with coastlines on the Caribbean and the Pacific. Area: 51,000 sq. km. (19,730 sq. mi.). Pop. (1984 est.): 2,460,200. Cap. and largest city: San José (pop., 1984, metro. area: 652,660). Language: Spanish. The people are of mainly European origin, plus 15% divided among Indian, mestizo, African, Chinese, and others.

History: Guaymi Indians lived here when Columbus first touched these shores in 1502 and called this the Rich Coast. But the gold ornaments of the natives led to no rich mineral troves, and the region did not come into its own until after the Spanish period (1821). Pulling out of the experimental United Provinces of Central America (1838), Costa Rica's leaders promoted agricultural development. Among the Europeans attracted hither were numerous Germans.

Coffee growing and banana plantations as well as other enterprises exploited the agricultural potential at the various climatic levels in this land of mountainous beauty. Its capital, San José, worked like a magnet and served the growing number of settlers coming in to the rolling plateau and a temperate climate. Happily, landholdings were kept generally modest. The dangers of a landed oligarchy, the bane of most other Latin American lands, were thus largely avoided. Except for rare eruptions, the political life of Costa Rica has been far more stable than in its neighbors to the north. In recent years the preservation of neutrality has at times been difficult. Almost like a Switzerland of Central America, Costa Rica has welcomed refugees—while keeping up its own social programs, fighting inflation, and seeking to reduce its big foreign debt. Diversification into light industry has balanced and helped reduce overdependence on coffee and banana export. Meanwhile, the salubrious climate of the high plateaus continues to attract also North Americans—10,000 by recent count.

Religion: Roman Catholic 91%; Protestant around 8%; and others. Missionary friars arrived among the Indians in the 1520s. Ecclesial matters came under the new diocese of León, Nicaragua in 1531. Despite occasional remedial efforts, spiritual life languished. With independence, Roman Catholicism continued as the official religion. The present archdiocese of San José de Costa Rica dates its beginnings from 1850. Three dioceses have been added since the 1920s. Relations between church and state have been better in this country than anywhere else in Central America or Mexico. The Roman Catholic Church has been influential in education as well as in the nation's social programs. There is reasonable liberty for other religious faith and practice.

Protestantism traces its beginnings from the first (not yet public) worship services in 1848. Denominationally, Baptists (1887), Methodists (1891), Episcopalians (1896), Adventists (1903) were in the van of an increasingly diverse array. Lutherans, with tenuous antecedents in the German 19th-century immigration, surfaced officially after 1946. Fastest growing were not the mainline but the marginal denominations like the Pentecostal, Foursquare Gospel, and others. A cross section of the conservative but cooperative groups formed the Costa Rican Evangelical Alliance (1951). Social programs and mobile rural medical services followed later. In the absence of any official ecumenical activity, various interconfessional ventures bring Catholics and Protestants together in youth activities and interseminary programs. Best known outside Costa Rica is the Presbyterian-founded Spanish Language Institute. Begun in Colombia (1942), it was relocated to San José in 1950. Used by some 30 denominations, its annual enrollment is about 300 future missionaries.

EVANGELICAL LUTHERAN CHURCH OF COSTA RICA, EL SALVADOR, HONDURAS, NICARAGUA, AND PANAMA

(Iglesia Evangélica Luterana de Costa Rica, El Salvador, Honduras, Nicaragua y Panamá)
Member: (R), EKD
Membership: 600**
Pastor: The Rev. Ulrich Epperlein
Apartado 2159
1000 San José

This international church serves mainly German-speaking people in five Central American countries as listed in its title. Its small congregations worship in facilities made available by Episcopal and other churches and by the German school in Managua, Nicaragua. The largest congregation and the headquarters for the pastor are in San José, the capital. The pastor reaches congregations of the other countries by plane on a monthly basis. In El Salvador and Honduras his contacts with the national Lutheran pastor and churches are close. Pastors are called through the Foreign Office of the *Evangelical Church in Germany (EKD), and the LWF Department of Church Cooperation provides a subsidy for travel costs. A number of the members of the Costa Rica congregations are in the country permanently; others are on short-term business or diplomatic missions. Only the Costa Rican congregation has government recognition. A similar status for that in El Salvador is pending. In contact with the LWF and EKD, the church council in San José represents all affiliated congregations.

This church resulted from the concern shown for resettled refugees and unchurched Europeans by the LWF Committee on Latin America during the early 1950s. When Pastor Åke Kastlund, the committee's representative, made his first trip through Central America in 1953, he found the German-speaking people in Costa Rica, numbering over 400, to be the most ready to form a congregation and have periodic worship services. Women soon volunteered to instruct the children. Visits by LWF-sent pastors, supplemented by the services of Lutheran pastors studying at the Spanish language school, made possible monthly services held in the

Episcopal church. A permanent pastor came in 1958, and a year later the San José congregation dedicated a house chapel. Services in English and Spanish were added.

The response in El Salvador, where the German colony numbered around 300, was also positive. Mrs. Eugene Klee, wife of the German diplomatic minister, began at once to arrange for Christian education and the formation of a congregation. This took place after the first worship service on December 19, 1954, held in a Baptist church. The elected parish council consisted of six Germans, two Scandinavians, and one Swiss.

In Honduras, the number of prospective members was limited; but for these few, pastoral service would be indeed welcome. In Nicaragua, the response was problematic. The German "colony," numbering around 200, were still recovering from their personal losses during World War II. Nearly all had been interned. While they now placed religious affiliation above nationality, they also habitually went to the mountains on weekends in order to endure the climate. Aware of such problems, many from long periods of neglect, the Committee on Latin America continued its concern until these congregations were well established.

EL SALVADOR

A republic, fronting on the Pacific coast, with Guatemala to the west and Honduras to the north and east, El Salvador is Central America's smallest but most populous nation. Area: 21,041 sq. km. (8124 sq. mi.). Pop. (1984 est.): 5,337,000. Cap. and largest city: San Salvador (metro. pop.: 720,000). Language: Spanish. Ethnic composition: mestizo over 90%; Amerindian 5%; Salvadoran white 1.7%; and others.

History: Pipil and Lenca Indians surrendered their land to the Spanish conquistadors in 1524. El Salvador was thereafter under the viceroyalty of Guatemala until independence (1821). After a turbulent time in the United Provinces of Central America—until 1839—the country's subsequent history has been punctuated by outside intervention and border warfare. The rise of coffee plantations and a landed elite in the 19th century, the sharp increase of population in the 20th, the influence of transnational corporations, and the

struggle of laissez-faire capitalism and Marxist Socialism have been leading contributors to the country's unrest and domestic tragedy.

A 1979 moderate military coup—supported by a Christian Democratic party, opposed to both left and right—passed control to a civilian-military junta. Violence continued. Archbishop Oscar Romero's assassination (March 1980), attributed to extreme rightists, nearly caused civil war. In quick succession, three civilian-military governments formed and dissolved. Subsequently, members of their supporting parties—moderate to leftist—formed the Frente Democratico Revolutionario (FDR), comprising trade unions, professional associations, popular organizations, and student groups. Its military counterpart, Frente Farabundo Martí para la Liberación Nacional (FLMN), united five guerrilla forces. The selection of José Napoleon Duarte as president (1980–1982) precipitated a major leftist offensive.

Oppression has taken two major forms. In the one, death squads openly attack people critical of the government or those accused of being informers. Intimidation is the purpose even more than death. Yet the estimated 50,000 civilians killed express the staggering dimension of this national torment. The other form is that of government attacks on rural civilians living in areas controlled by the FLMN forces. The number of persons thus displaced is estimated to be over one million. But another half-million have fled to the USA; and a quarter-million to other Latin American countries.

While the churches see the refugees as suffering people in need of assistance and protection, the government regards them as subversive. Even the camps of old people, women, and children are classified as rebel centers. Consequently, church workers responsible for the camps and other forms of aid have become major targets of death squads. In 1980, four church women, three of them Catholic nuns, were murdered. In 1983 and 1984, Lutherans, too, paid the price (below). The government's relentless drive against the feared forces of Communism continues while the innocent suffer.

Religion: Roman Catholic over 96%, Protestant about 3%, and others. An estimated three out of five Roman Catholics adhere to a folk- or Mayan-Catholicism, a blend of traditional religion of the Mayans and Christianity. Beginnings of the present archdiocese of San Salvador go back to 1842. Four dioceses have been added between 1913 and 1954. Religious freedom dates from 1886, but on the whole the Roman Church has retained its favored position. Only in recent years—since the 1960s—has its general supportiveness of the government and the vested interest begun to shift from the elite to the poor. Prophetic of this change at the top levels—many priests and lay leaders had already taken the step—was Archbishop Oscar Romero (above).

Protestantism came late to El Salvador. The Central America Mission (1896) preceded Pentecostal, Adventist, and Baptist missions as well as various other denominational ventures. Lutheran work dates from the 1950s (below). There is no national council of churches, but the plight of the poor and the unleashing of terrorism—especially in the late 1970s and thereafter—has attracted outside help and fostered cooperation among the Catholics and Protestants. An ecumenical organization, *Diaconia,* brings Roman Catholics, Baptists, Episcopalians, Lutherans, and a number of other agencies together to coordinate the work of its members in the alleviation of suffering in San Salvador. Relief organizations estimate that 500,000 people—about 10% of the population—have abandoned their villages for refugee camps and squatter settlements near cities due to the armed conflict between the government and rebels.

EVANGELICAL LUTHERAN CHURCH OF COSTA RICA, EL SALVADOR, HONDURAS, NICARAGUA, AND PANAMA (see Costa Rica)

LUTHERAN SALVADORAN SYNOD (LSS)

(Sínodo Luterano Salvadoreño)
Member: LWF (1986), CONCAP, CLAI
Membership: 6000**
President: The Rt. Rev. Dr. Medardo Ernesto Gómez Soto
Calle 5 de Noviembre 242
Apartado (02)
9 Barrio San Miguelito

This synod, the largest member of CONCAP, comprises 20 congregations and 18 preaching

stations. The membership—an eightfold increase since 1977—is served by only two ordained pastors, since one was murdered and two others left the country. These two resident pastors—one also serving as president and director of Socorro (below)—are assisted by 20 lay preachers.

The synod is divided into six stations. Pasquina, the oldest (1954) and largest is in the western part of the country. The next is San Miguel (1963). Work began in San Salvador in 1972, in Santa Ana in 1973, in Ahuachapán in 1976, and in Usulután in 1977. Although legally registered as an independent church in El Salvador, the *Lutheran Church–Missouri Synod—the founder—still considers the LSS as a mission synod. All LCMS missions in Central America are united in CONCAP (below). The president of the Salvadoran Synod serves as its vice-president. Independently, the LSS, at its January 1984 general assembly, voted to apply for membership in the Lutheran World Federation, an action precipitated by emergency events (below).

Socorro Luterano Salvadoreño (Salvadoran Lutheran Relief) is a social service arm of the LSS. Its work among the poor began already in 1972; but during the early 1980s, with the acceleration of civil conflict and the increasing number of displaced persons, the work expanded dramatically. Members of Resurrection congregation in San Salvador organized to assist in the various settlements for the displaced around the city. This included a mobile clinic directed by Dr. Angel Ibarra. In 1983, he and the president of the synod were arrested. The latter was soon released. Dr. Ibarra, tortured and held for six months, was then allowed to leave the country, perhaps due to the pressure of USA and European Lutherans. Ibarra and his mother found sanctuary in Canada.

Like other helping agencies, LSS was drawn further afield. In 1983, several hundred displaced people, hiding in the hills, pleaded for help from LSS. Norwegian Church Aid enabled LSS to acquire some land near the town of Nejapa about 15 kilometers from the capital. Quickly, Lutheran World Relief (USA) provided additional funds. With the people themselves doing much of the construction, "Faith and Hope" soon became a model camp, caring for some 300 refugees.

Careful assessment of need brought LWF assistance in 1983. Besides material aid, a program coordinator was seconded to LSS. This expatriate has the dual role of helping the church's programming and of being an international presence, hopefully shielding the Salvadoran staff amid the riskiness of their service to the needy. Even so, in 1984 two young workers fled to the USA after receiving death threats. David Ernesto Fernández Espino, the young and able pastor of the congregation in San Miguel, was tortured and murdered. Earlier, the accountant of the Lutheran church had been abducted, then imprisoned.

Harassment continues. One sign of hope was the conviction of Espino's murderers in June 1987. The devastating earthquake of 1986 added another burden to the LSS. Together with LWF/WS and *Diaconia* (above) certain slum areas of San Salvador are being rehabilitated.

Meanwhile, the flight of Salvadorans to the *USA and *Canada has made many congregations, including Lutheran, offer sanctuary to the refugees. Some cities, like Los Angeles, have done the same despite U.S. laws to the contrary.

GUATEMALA

A Central American republic, fronting on the Caribbean and the Pacific, with Mexico to the north and Belize, Honduras, and El Salvador to the east and south. Area: 108,889 sq. km. (42,042 sq. mi.). Pop. (1984 est.): 7,599,000. Cap. and largest city: Guatemala City (pop., metro area, 1,100,000). Language: Spanish (official), plus Indian tongues.

Guatemala is the country in Latin America with the highest proportion of Amerindian population (over 42%) and perhaps the greatest diversity of Indian tribal languages (some 200) still in use. Although nominally Roman Catholic, and accepting of Spanish as a common tongue, these Indians are keepers of a past whose roots are in the Mayan civilization, which flourished for over a millennium before the Spanish conquest (1524).

The majority (55%) of Guatemalans are Ladinos (mestizos), blending Spanish and Indian strains and feeling generally superior to the Amerindians. The three centuries of colonial life (1524–1821) fostered such attitudes. Two other groups are important: Africans (2%), and Europeans (mainly Spanish) 1%.

History: In the colonial era, Guatemala was the base of the Spanish viceroyalty governing all Central America. After independence the United Provinces of Central America lasted only until 1839. Like its neighbors, Guatemala went its own way, but interfered at times in the affairs of its former partners or disputed boundaries. Democratic processes of election were formally observed, but most often yielded to political coups and dictatorship. The country's potential for supplying the outside world with coffee, bananas, cotton, rice, and—later on—also forest products, oil, and minerals, attracted investors from abroad. Germans became known for their large coffee plantations; Americans (in the present century, especially the United Fruit Company) for their ever-growing investment in bananas. Guatemala received its share of attention of government intervention from the USA, whose concern for Central American affairs was heightened after the completion of the Panama Canal (1914). When Guatemala declared war on Germany (1941), most of the members of its German population were interned in the USA (below), and the property owned by Germans expropriated.

Historically, of course, the Indians are the ones whose land has been expropriated and whose traditional social fragmentation has left them prone to exploitation. Segregated by villages, separated by language, customs, and attire, Indians have been employed for labor on estates and plantations but—until recent decades—have remained disunited.

Likewise, among the Ladinos, various groups of workers and others—short of a middle class—had little to rally them until a new social consciousness arose after World War II. The decade after 1945 saw unrest mounting in protest against the chronic injustices of an entrenched oligarchy of privilege. Poverty, land reform, and the like were issues that brought laissez-faire capitalism and Soviet Communism on collision course. To expedite land reform, the government of Jacobo Arbenz (1950–1954) expropriated United Fruit of four-fifths of its 300,000 acres. Other USA corporations were also targets of protest. The Washington administration determined to stem this course of events and prevent what it saw as an ominous spread of Communism into Latin America.

After 1954, the civil conflict continued, as government forces on the one hand and guerrillas on the other have struggled for power and the righting of wrongs. In the process, 1.3 million women, children, and men—most of them Guatemalan Indians—were made refugees, victims in large part of search-and-destroy operations. Violence, reportedly, had claimed over 100,000 lives by 1985. Guatemala had become a land of fear to countless citizens. Even nature's violence entered the fray. The enormous earthquake of February 1976 left 23,000 dead, perhaps 77,000 injured, and several hundred thousand homeless. The huge arc of destruction, from near Antigua to the Caribbean, laid bare the poverty of the chief sufferers, the Indians. More than anything else, the disaster drew the attention of the world to Guatemala and rallied help from churches in many lands.

Later, the election of Roberto Ríos Montt (1982) to the presidency made history and raised hopes. For the first time Guatemala had a Protestant (born-again Christian) as head of state, but conditions did not improve—and he was out in less than two years. Taking office early in 1986 after 30 years of military control, Guatemala's new civilian president, Marco Vinicio Cerezo Arévalo, called for great austerity and sacrifice.

Religion: Roman Catholic 90%; Protestant over 5%; and others, including a small Jewish community. Popular Catholicism retains some Mayan and other traditional Indian elements. In light of past waves of missionary effort—Franciscans, Dominicans, Jesuits, and others were deeply involved from the 16th to the 18th century—efforts to re-Christianize the people have increased since the 1940s. To strengthen the woefully inadequate ranks of Guatemalan clergy, large numbers of expatriate priests, nuns, teachers, and others have come. Church structures bear out the change. After four centuries, the present archdiocese of Guatemala City (1534)—in Antigua until the devastating earthquake of 1773 caused a relocation of the capital—has since 1921 been augmented by eight new dioceses.

A basic change in the church's relation to the people is still in progress. Many see it as reviving the advocacy of Bartolomé de Las Casas (1474–1566), famed defender of Indian rights and for a time also missionary in Guatemala. The spirit of the 1960s—Vatican II and the ensuing Medellín conference (1968; see Latin America Introduction)—has spurred Catholic action against injustice and the violation of human rights. Even earlier, the elements of a liberation theology emerged, especially at the local level, as church agencies aided the poor, and priests joined lay leaders in pushing for reform. This has divided the church, for the bishops have traditionally been expected to support government policy. While Pope John Paul II during his Central American visit (1983) counseled caution, expatriate priests and nuns have suffered, even death, at the hands of a rightist military. Roman Catholicism, despite previous experiences of governmental retaliation against privilege, remains the religion of the state, but freedom of religion (1870) was reaffirmed constitutionally in 1966.

Protestantism, diversified and largely North American in its connections, has been in Guatemala for over a century and has grown rapidly over the past 50 years. Its coming anticipated, and perhaps stimulated, Roman Catholic efforts to re-Christianize the people. Protestant work in Guatemala, moreover, gave rise—as from a laboratory—to at least two movements that have achieved worldwide application: the Wycliffe Bible Translators (1934) and theological education by extension (TEE, 1964). What William C. Townsend had discovered among the Guatemalan Cakchiquel people (1917) led to his pioneering a concerted effort to translate the Scriptures into tribal tongues throughout the world. His experience in Guatemala proved that the Bible in the official language, like Spanish, does not suffice to help the Word come alive.

Similarly, training for ministry, as seen by members of the Presbyterian Seminary faculty in Guatemala City (1963), required education within the contexts of daily living and would remain misdirected so long as confined to seminaries apart from the people. In this case, the learning process was deployed into an area of southwestern Guatemala inhabited by Ladinos, Indians, and urban and rural folk of many types. Teachers moved among the students on location, selected students remained employed and self-supporting, and periodically they came to the seminary. Much of their study was self-directed, and the number of ordainable persons—women as well as men—increased greatly. Tested widely, TEE has spread from Latin America to every continent. Not without critics, TEE has been employed in many churches, including Lutheran, especially in the Two-Thirds World (see references throughout this book).

From another angle, a natural disaster like Guatemala's 1976 earthquake and the country's prolonged and bitter struggle for social justice and relief of its victims have brought Catholics and Protestants from Europe and the Americas into cooperative efforts of ecumenical significance in and beyond this country.

Historically, Episcopalians (Anglicans) from Belize (British Honduras) entered early (c.1871), but their numbers have remained small. An invitation of the country's president (Barrios) brought in Presbyterians (1882) in hopes that they might help develop the country educationally and otherwise. Other denominations followed, including the Central American Mission (1899, a society akin to the China Inland Mission), the Friends (Quakers, 1902), Nazarenes (1904), Adventists (1908), Pentecostals (1916, the first of various branches), and numerous others. Among the nonmissionary churches, Lutherans comprised a major part of the German Protestant congregation in Guatemala City and countryside. The membership around 1900 was reportedly over 1000, and its pastors, until 1941, were provided by the Evangelical Foreign Office in Berlin. As already mentioned, Guatemala's entry into World War II and the removal of most Germans ended this chapter but set the stage for a new one six years later (below).

In cooperative work, the Evangelical Alliance of Guatemala (1953), in lieu of a national council, is a meeting ground for some 17 bodies. An EAG-sponsored Committee on Permanent Aid (CEPA), fortunately, had begun shortly before the massive earthquake in 1976. In the prolonged relief and reconstruction programs, aided from abroad and carried out by Guatemalans, CEPA was reorganized into the Evangelical Committee for Integral Development (CEDI; 1977). In the context

of extensive international and ecumenical effort, Lutheran participation became significant. Besides Lutheran World Relief and LWF World Service in the early stages, aid from church agencies in other countries contributed to the reconstruction operations. The fact that the Guatemalan president at the time—Kjell Eugenio Laugerud Garcia—was the son of a Norwegian immigrant farmer and a Guatemalan mother, gave added motivation for a (US) $1.5 million grant from Norwegian Church Relief for the construction of 1000 houses (for 1350 families) in a new settlement, Carolingia, outside Guatemala City. In Antigua, close to the heart of the disaster area, the Lutheran Center (Lutheran Hour, etc.) helped coordinate relief efforts. Efforts were also made to regain the trust of Indians and secure their participation in planning longer term projects.

COUNCIL OF LUTHERAN CHURCHES IN CENTRAL AMERICA AND PANAMA (CONCAP)

(Consejo de Iglesias Luteranas en Centro América y Panamá)
President: The Rev. Felipe Alvarez
Apartado Postal 234
Antigua

Member bodies of CONCAP are related to the *Lutheran Church–Missouri Synod through the Board for Mission Services. They include: Lutheran Christian Church of Honduras, Lutheran Salvadoran Synod (El Salvador), National Council of Lutheran Churches (Guatemala), and Panama Lutheran Mission Association. These bodies are described below under their respective countries.

Interest in Latin America, especially among immigrant German-speaking Lutherans, had been growing in the LCMS since the beginning of the present century (*Brazil, *Argentina, *Cuba). But work among the Spanish-speaking people received a major impetus during the early 1940s. At Concordia Seminary, St. Louis, a number of students responded to the challenge of missioning in Mexico and Central America. Among them was Robert F. Gussick, who pioneered first in Guatemala. The choice of this country was influenced in large part by contact and ministry among the Guatemalan Germans interned in the USA during World War II. Success in Guatemala led to work in the neighboring countries.

NATIONAL COUNCIL OF LUTHERAN CHURCHES (NCLC)

(Consejo Nacional de Iglesias Luteranas)
Member: ILC, CONCAP
Membership: 1410**
President: The Rev. Héctor Arnoldo Canjura Guzmán
Apartado Postal 1111
Guatemala

This oldest of CONCAP members (1948) consists of eight congregations and 21 preaching places. They are served by five national pastors, three lay preachers, and one teacher as well as four expatriate pastors, two vicars, and two other church workers. The congregations span the country and include a cross section of Guatemalans. The NCLC, although legally registered as an independent church, is considered and treated as a mission by the *Lutheran Church–Missouri Synod, its founder.

One of the oldest congregations, Cristo el Salvador in Puerto Barrios on the eastern shore, has developed an evangelism program to reach the Garifuna-speaking people living in its area. Garifuna speakers—a blend of Carib Americans and African slaves of the mid-17th century—live along the Caribbean coast, mainly in Belize and Honduras. Yet there are some 5000 in Guatemala. Recently, the New Testament was translated into Garifuna, and part of the program is to distribute 2000 copies. One-fourth of the congregation is now black Carib. Two of the newest congregations—Quezaltenango (1967) and Chajabal (1975)—are in the high western mountains where the Quiché live. One of the two pastors serving here is a Quiché, and the response is positive. Farther west a Guatemalan pastor serves a rather new group in San Marcos (1980).

In Guatemala City, the congregation (1948) shares its facilities with the Epiphany German Lutheran congregation serving the large German Protestant colony in Guatemala. It receives pastors through the Foreign Office of the *Evangelical Church in Germany (EKD). Halfway between the capital and the port is the largest and oldest of the congregations (1947) in the city of Zacapa; and, still closer to the port, the parish in Gualán (1969).

In the historic city of Antigua, west of Guatemala City, are the headquarters of the National Council as well as of CONCAP. Here also is the studio of the "Lutheran Hour." Programs, using indigenous forms of communication, are broadcast from various cities in all Central America. The director, well trained in theology as well as journalism, also serves the Antigua Resurrection congregation (1950).

The LCMS work in Guatemala grew out of three antecedent groups. The one consisted of German Protestant settlers. One of their number, while being interned in the USA during World War II, received ministry from a Missouri Synod clergyman. This led to a request for help in rehabilitating German church life in Guatemala, realizing that the assistance from Germany would not be available soon. Another was a group of Friends (Quakers) in Zacapa, who were looking for a more biblical theology with less legalism. Their leader, Alfredo Vasquez, acquired a *Small Catechism* and other Lutheran literature, which convinced him that the Lutheran church was the answer to their quest. Still another was a group of English-speaking blacks from Caribbean islands residing in Puerto Barrios.

After an exploratory visit (1947), Robert F. Gussick, a young LCMS pastor, arrived the following year and began work among the Friends in Zacapa and Puerto Barrios, and among expatriates and German-speaking residents in Guatemala City. Assisting him were seminary interns. In the capital, worship services were conducted in English, German, and Spanish. Headquarters were established in Antigua in 1950. Soon a hospital, clinic, and conference center strengthened the outreach. In 1953, the "Lutheran Hour" began its Central American broadcasts.

In time, the German congregation needed less assistance, and more time could be spent on Spanish work. As additional missionaries came from the USA, they joined in the training of evangelists and catechists to produce local leadership among volunteers. When Augsburg Seminary in Mexico City opened, a number of Guatemalans enrolled and became ordained pastors. Theological education by extension has also been used effectively.

After the devastating earthquake of 1976 when 90% of Antigua was damaged (above), the Lutheran Hour staff and the missionaries played a prime role in the relief program. Although "Lutheran Hour" facilities suffered some destruction, they could be used for shelter and the distributing of food and other emergency aid. This diaconal service and the large new housing program in Zacapa opened many doors for spiritual care. There are large school programs in Puerto Barrios (650) and Zacapa (950).

HONDURAS

A Central American republic, fronting on the Caribbean and the Pacific, with Nicaragua and El Salvador to the south and Guatemala to the west. Area: 112,088 sq. km. (43,277 sq. mi.). Pop. (1984 est.): 4,135,000. Cap.: Tegucigalpa (pop., 508,044). Language: Spanish.

History: This land was part of the Mayan civilization for centuries prior to the Spanish conquest. Independence (1821) and separation from the United Provinces of Central America (1838) have been followed by political turbulence and frequent military coups. While Spaniards had promoted mining, Americans in the 19th century developed plantations. Today, bananas make up at least half of the country's export trade, with coffee second. Minerals and hardwoods are also important exports. But the country is economically weak and struggling with social needs. Relations with its neighbors have been tense. A brief war with El Salvador (1969) resulted in Honduras withdrawing from the Central American Common Market. A haven for refugees from Nicaragua as well as El Salvador, Honduras has also harbored "Contras" fighting the Nicaraguan government. The country has been pivotal for USA involvement in Central America.

Religion: Roman Catholic 96%; Protestants nearly 3%; Spiritism, tribal religion, and other forms account for the rest. The course of church history here has been closely linked with that in *Guatemala. The archdiocese of Tegucigalpa (1561) and three dioceses created since 1916, plus two papal nunciatures, comprise the Roman Catholic structure. Next to *Haiti, church adherence in Honduras is said to be the most nominal. Church and state separation has existed since 1880, but relations have been good in recent years.

Expatriates outnumber native priests by a wide margin, and there is but one priest per 9000 or so parishioners. For their siding with the poor and the landless, especially the foreign clergy have fallen into disfavor on occasion. Social action is part of the church's avowed aim of re-Christianization.

Protestantism is represented in fragmented diversity, but only since the 1890s. Besides, a sizable community of Eastern Orthodox—Palestinian Arabs of the Greek Patriarchate of Jerusalem—has been growing since 1910. Among the Protestant entrants, the Methodists (1860) were forerunners to the main succession that included Adventists (1891), Central America Missions (1896), Friends (Quakers, 1902), Evangelicals and Reformed (United, 1920), Moravians (1930), Pentecostals (1937), Mennonites (1950), and many others. Lutherans, among expatriates (1954), began among Hondurans in 1961 (below).

The Honduras Evangelical Alliance (1945) provides a common meeting ground for a dozen or so church bodies on an annual basis.

EVANGELICAL LUTHERAN CHURCH OF COSTA RICA, EL SALVADOR, HONDURAS, NICARAGUA, AND PANAMA (see Costa Rica)

LUTHERAN CHRISTIAN CHURCH OF HONDURAS (LCCH)
(Iglesia Cristiana Luterana de Honduras)
Member: CONCAP
Membership: 175**
President: The Rev. Eduardo A. Cabrera
Colonia "Las Colinas," Bloque N, No. 355
Tegucigalpa

Known formerly as the Lutheran Mission of Juticalpa, this small body was in 1984 granted legal status as the Lutheran Christian Church of Honduras (LCCH). LCCH comprises three congregations and five preaching points, served by two national pastors. It is a partner in CONCAP and a mission of the *Lutheran Church–Missouri Synod.

This Lutheran venture originated among El Salvadorans migrating to Honduras in search of "soil to sow." As there were Lutherans among them, their missionary pastor in El Salvador, Gerhard Kempff, began visiting them in 1960. Some had settled not far from El Salvador in the Honduran states of Valle and Choluteca. Others had crossed the mountains to the eastern state of Cortés, near the Caribbean coast. But the majority settled near Juticalpa, the capital of the Department of Olancho, which lies some distance northeast of Tegucigalpa in the foothills of the Cordillera de Galta. In 1964, Kempff himself relocated to Tegucigalpa and served these scattered enclaves from this central location for the next seven years. Meanwhile, the 1969 border war between El Salvador and Honduras caused the eviction of many Salvadorans and a drastic reduction in the mission's membership. Most of those permitted to remain lived in the Juticalpa district.

There is a second congregation in the beautifully situated village of San Nicolas, some 25 kilometers (15 miles) from Juticalpa in the foothills of Cerro Brujo. The 1500 villagers have during the past 25 years gained some prosperity. Their pastor—a 1970 graduate of the Augsburg Seminary in *Mexico City—found them eager for the gospel. The thriving worship services, Bible study, and Sunday school—under local leadership—are harbingers of a new day, not only in San Nicolas but also in the little LCCH. In 1980, a third congregation was established in the second largest city, San Pedro Sula. Recently, a small chapel was built in the Barrio of La Unión.

PANAMA

A republic (1903), Panama lies between Costa Rica in the north and Colombia in the south and straddles the isthmus separating the Caribbean Sea on the east and the Pacific Ocean on the west. Area: 77,082 sq. km. (29,762 sq. mi.) Pop. (1984 est.): 2,101,000. Cap.

and largest city: Panama City (pop., 1984 est., 388,000). Language: Spanish.

History: Panama declared its independence from Colombia in 1903, and by treaty ceded a 16-kilometer wide band across its narrowest point to the *USA for canal construction. Completed in 1914, the Panama Canal changed the world's maritime routes, even as the Suez Canal had done 45 years earlier. The Canal Zone was ceded back to Panama in 1979. The country's mixed population includes many of African origin, brought in from Jamaica and elsewhere during the 19th century to augment the labor force not only in agriculture but later also in construction.

Religion: Catholic 85%; Protestant 12%; and others. Roman Catholic beginnings date from 1513 (part of the diocese of Antigua, oldest in the Americas); later under Colombian judicature. The archdiocese of Panama (1925) was supplemented by the dioceses of Chitré, David, and Santiago de Veraguas in the 1950s and 1960s, and also by the vicariates of Bocas del Toro, Colón-Darién, and Coclé. Most clergy and nuns are expatriates.

Protestantism entered via the Methodist Jamaican black laborers early in the 19th century. Baptists, Episcopalians, and others came during the second half of the 19th. Adventists, Pentecostals, and Foursquare Gospel preceded still other fringe groups after 1900. Interchurch relations benefit from the Archdiocesan Department of Ecumenism as well as from the Panama Evangelical Alliance. The latter includes Methodists, Baptists, and Pentecostals.

EVANGELICAL LUTHERAN CHURCH OF COSTA RICA, EL SALVADOR, HONDURAS, NICARAGUA, AND PANAMA (see Costa Rica)

LUTHERAN DIOCESE OF COSTA RICA AND PANAMA

(Diocesis Luterana de Costa Rica y Panamá)
Member: CLAI
Membership: 260**
Bishop: The Rt. Rev. Kenneth Mahler
Apartado Postal 445
Panamá 9A

As an ecclesial entity, this is an association of like-minded persons seeking to apply

Christian teaching of Lutheran derivation to recognized needs of the Panamanian and other peoples, especially the poor. Rooted in earlier work of the *Lutheran Church–Missouri Synod in the Canal Zone, largely among the English-speaking people, this association is said to be the product of two significant developments in the 1970s. The one was the critical struggle within the Missouri Synod during the 1970s. The other was the lively political issue resulting in the US returning the Canal Zone to Panama (1979).

The pivotal figure in the rise of this separate Lutheran entity was the veteran Missouri pastor, Kenneth Mahler. As a means of fostering readier understanding in this heavily Roman Catholic setting, the Lutheran association adopted traditional ecclesial terms: diocese for itself, and bishop for its pastor. Its governing unit is a council of elders.

Behind the two changes of the 1970s lies a third. Earlier in his missioning among the Spanish-speaking peasants in the hill country—for which the diocese received LWF Community Development Service (CDS) assistance—it appeared that Mahler's initial success was thwarted by incoming Pentecostals, who claimed to bring the full gospel. However, the rural work has continued and prospered, under Argentine missionary Ernesto Weigandt, and has become a model for similar efforts in the region. Mahler redirected his efforts to the plight mainly of the urban poor and to advocacy on Central American issues among U.S. Lutheran churches.

The main outside support for this organization has come through Partners in Mission, an arm of the Association of Evangelical Lutheran Churches (AELC) in the *USA. Ecumenically, the diocese holds membership in the Latin American Council of Churches (CLAI). Its contacts in *Costa Rica continue those of earlier times, and new ones have been initiated in *Venezuela, Nicaragua, and *Guatemala.

PANAMA LUTHERAN MISSION ASSOCIATION (PLMA)

Member: CONCAP
Membership: 100**
Redeemer Lutheran Church
Overseer: The Rev. Merell Wetzstein
Apartado Postal 5014
Balboa/Ancon

This mission association, known also as Panama Mission Team, has grown out of the work in the former Canal Zone as begun by the *Lutheran Church–Missouri Synod in 1942. Redeemer Church (built in 1947) in Balboa—contiguous to Panama City—is its base and historic landmark; and Redeemer Chapel, Margarita (1960)—adjoining Colón—is its presence on the Atlantic side of the isthmus. With the return of the Canal Zone to Panama (1979), the former concentration on English-speaking people broadened. Today, the far largest work is among the Panamanians, both urban and rural. Newer stations in ministry include Chitré, near the Gulf of Panama; David, inland from the Gulf of Chiriquí—both on the Pacific side; and in the Panama City suburb of Los Andes. Meanwhile, work continues in Colón and along the Transisthmian Highway.

Heading a team of five expatriate missionaries is the experienced Merrell Wetzstein, who entered Panama in 1980 after nine years of work at the mouth of the Amazon in the coastal city of Belém, Brazil. The Spanish "Lutheran Hour" and radio dramas help in surprising ways. Hearers are responsive and often offer their homes for places of Bible study. Statistics are still low, but the Word is being sown for an expected harvest.

PLMA is the newest partner in the Council of Lutheran Churches in Central America and Panama (CONCAP).

MEXICO

Mexico's nearly 10,000 Lutherans comprise 33.5% of those in Intercontinental America. They are grouped into five church bodies—one an LWF member—and four congregations related to European and North American church bodies.

A federal republic of North America (1823), Mexico comprises 31 states and one federal district. It borders the US to the north, and Guatemala and Belize to the south, with coastlines on the Pacific Ocean, the Gulf of Mexico, and the Caribbean Sea. Area: 1,958,201 sq. km. (756,065 sq. mi.). Pop. (1985 est.): 77,938,300, including about 55% mestizo, 29% Indian, 10% white, and others. Cap. and largest city: Mexico City (pop., 1985 est., 8,831,079). Language: Spanish (official).

History: Civilization, perhaps with distant roots in Asia, flowered among the Maya and other peoples of Mexico before its fruition in the wealthy Aztec empire. Yet two treacherous years (1519–1521) saw its monarch, Montezuma, murdered, its gold taken, and its storied capital razed by Spanish conquistadors. On the ruins of Tenochtitlán, Hernán Cortéz founded Mexico City, from 1521–1821 the seat of government of New Spain. Soon Spanish crown claims extended from Florida to California as well as southward. For the Indians, a harsh colonial rule was softened by the work of the Franciscans and other missionary friars. Spaniards, creoles (Mexican-born Spaniards), mestizos, and Indians—plus a few Africans and others—made up the new society. By the 1780s, Mexico City was by far the largest urban center in the Americas.

After three centuries under Spain came independence, won between the years 1810 and 1821. Mexico's subsequent course was stormier than that of most other former Spanish-American colonies. Mineral wealth, arable land, and other resources, including Europe-oriented higher learning, were part of its great potential. The Catholic Church (below) embodied continuity, but acquired about one-third of the land and defended its privileges. Constitutional government, hard to achieve, often gave way to dictatorial tactics. The turbulent era of Antonio López de Santa Anna (1794–1876), for example, saw the war with the USA deprive Mexico of Texas and all its other lands north of the Rio Grande (1846–1848). The "reform" era of the brilliant Indian, Benito Juárez (1806–1872), lessened clergy domination and shifted power from the creoles to the mestizos. But it also witnessed the strange interlude of Maximilian (1864–1867), with its Hapsburgian dream of empire.

The stable but dictatorial rule of Porfirio Díaz (1877–1880, 1884–1911) led to bloody strife as well as to the new constitution of 1917, which provided for social reform and placed the church under the power of the state (below). Since then, Mexico has developed large-scale programs of social security, labor protection, and school improvement. The Institutional Revolutionary Party (PRI) has been dominant since 1929. Under its current president, Miguel de la Madrid Hurtado (elected 1982), the country continues to face massive problems in such areas as land reform, unemployment, foreign debt, and a rapidly growing population. The massive earthquake of September 1985 dealt Mexico City, especially, a disastrous blow.

Religion: Roman Catholicism predominates, still claiming nearly 90% of the population. Protestants (including Evangelicals) are under 4%; Jews, 0.1%. All church real estate—whatever the denomination—is vested in the nation, but the care of church buildings is the responsibility of the congregations. These, and other, provisions of the 1917 constitution express the anticlericalism evident already in the reform constitution of 1857. No foreigners, only Mexican citizens, may serve as clergy or minister to Mexican congregations.

For the Roman Catholic Church a role reversal changed it from a dominant to a controlled political force. A decade after the adoption of the constitution of 1917 the struggle with the state came to a head. For a three-year period (1926–1929) the church refused to celebrate mass anywhere in the land. Reconciliation came eventually. With a church that had become more pastoral than political, it appeared spiritually stronger than in other Latin American countries. Even so, the Christo-paganism of the Amerindians and the synergism of the mestizos (the cult of the Virgin of Guadalupe) continue to challenge the church's own missionary efforts.

Of the church's many dioceses and 11 archdioceses, that of Mexico City is the far largest (over 7 million) and one of the oldest (1530). The constitutional requirement of an indigenous clergy has actually been good for the church.

For Protestants, too, the period since the 1920s has become a time of advance. A century earlier, the independence movement had prepared the ground. Dissident priests and others were receptive to Bibles in Spanish, as made available by the British and Foreign Bible Society agents. In Mexico, as in other parts of Latin America, Free Masonry fostered freedom of religion, particularly in mid-century during the reform era of Juárez. In 1857 a group leaving the Roman Catholic Church formed the present Mexican Episcopal Church. German-speaking Lutherans (1861), Baptists (1862), Presbyterians and Congregationalists (1872), as well as Latter Day Saints (1879), Eastern Orthodox (1890), Church of God, Seventh Day Adventists, Jehovah's Witnesses (1893), and others were early arrivals. A large movement of Mennonite settlers from Canada (1922)—originally from Russia—drew wide attention. Meanwhile, Pentecostal and kindred missioning groups from the USA came on the scene and today have the largest non-Roman Catholic following (350,000 among the Otomí Indians).

Among the mainline denominations, the Presbyterians are the largest, but Methodists are the most active ecumenically. They have been leaders in the Evangelical Federation of Mexico (FEM; Federación Evangélica de México, 1926), an association of over a dozen church bodies. The Methodist Church of Mexico was a charter member of the World Council of Churches, and is still the only Mexican WCC member church. Church cooperation, in fact, reached its high point during the 1960s and early 1970s. Its main achievement was the Theological Community, a cooperative venture of Baptist, Episcopal, Lutheran, Methodist, and Presbyterian churches for the education of their future ministers. Unhappily, by the early 1980s the joint venture had dissolved. Given the conservative bent of Mexican Protestantism, the resident enrollment of the Theological Community was never high.

The Lutheran constituency in Mexico numbers under 10,000 and is highly diversified and geographically dispersed. It lacks an overall cooperative structure. The three bodies related to the LWF account for under one-half of this confessional grouping. With the exception of the German congregation, in Mexico City since the 1860s, nearly all Lutheran work in Mexico has emerged since 1940.

To train an adequate indigenous ministry for Mexico, Central America, and northern South America (the Lutheran seminaries in *Argentina were too far away), two small theological schools were opened during the 1950s. The *American Lutheran Church (now ELCA) sponsored the one in Mexico City; the *Missouri Synod, the one in Monterrey. In 1965, the two schools merged and became Seminario Augsburgo, located soon (1967) in the cluster of cooperating theological schools. Episcopal, Methodist, Baptist, and Lutheran then shared a common campus near the University of Mexico City. It was an era of promise, and support came not only from north of the border but also from the

Scandinavian and German congregations as well as from other sources.

Even so, a resident program did not suffice, and in 1972 a coordinating committee of Lutheran seminaries launched a program of theological education by extension (TEE). Co-Extension, so named, was based at Augsburg Seminary. Support came from the ALC and the LCMS, and also from the *Lutheran Church in America (now ELCA) and the LWF. Even though Augsburg Seminary itself was closed in 1981 for lack of students—and the cooperative venture with the other denominations ended—the extension program continues, based now at the headquarters of the Evangelical Lutheran Church of Colombia in Bogotá. The seminary building, renamed the Mexican Lutheran Center is now used for retreats, short courses, and other events helpful also to USA colleges and seminaries. Co-Extension, meanwhile, reaches theological students in seven countries: *Bolivia, *Colombia, *Ecuador, Mexico, *Peru, *Uruguay, and *Venezuela.

CONFESSIONAL EVANGELICAL LUTHERAN CHURCH IN MEXICO
(Iglesia Evangélica Luterana Confesional en México)
Membership: 320**
Chair: The Rev. David Chichía G.
Monrovia 522
Apartado Postal M-8896
Mexico 13, D.F.

The 10 congregations and preaching places of this young church are in Mexico City, Guadalajara, and in the northern part of the country. They are served by five pastors. The work began in 1968, when two Mexican pastors left their former church body and applied for support from the *Wisconsin Evangelical Lutheran Synod in the USA. Additional pastors have been trained at the Bible Institute and Seminary in Juárez near the USA border. A Spanish church paper, *El Mensajero Luterano,* is published bimonthly and distributed to several thousand addresses throughout Latin America.

EVANGELICAL LUTHERAN CHURCH OF MEXICO (ELCM)

(Iglesia Evangélica Luterana de México)
Membership: 3000**
President: Encarnación Estrada O.
Mina Boniente 5808, Nuevo Laredo
Tamaulipas

ELCM, the largest Lutheran church body in Mexico, is autonomous but has a close working relationship with its founder, the Latin American Lutheran Mission (LALM). The latter has a station in Laredo, Texas, one of the main links into Mexico via two international bridges. Here the LALM receives and distributes food and clothing, maintains a bookstore and guest accommodations as well as homes for the director and other workers who go in and out of Mexico in the interest of the ELCM.

Across the border in Nuevo Laredo are the ELCM headquarters. The president serves the local congregation and oversees the growing church. He is assisted by a church council of seven elected pastors, which meets regularly with the director of the LALM in Laredo. Also in Nuevo Laredo is a small school for the blind, maintained by the LALM and directed by a husband-and-wife team for more than 25 years. Each summer, they tour the Midwest states to raise American interest and support.

Monterrey, a city of three million located about 240 kilometers (150 miles) south of Laredo, is the geographic center of the 23 congregations that comprise the ELCM. Since most of the people are poor, the LALM assists with the cost of church construction as it is able. Some of the congregations have adequate and attractive churches; others are still in rented quarters or meet in members' homes.

The congregations are served by devoted men and women trained by national teachers at the ELCM's Bible School in Saltillo, 80 kilometers (50 miles) west of Monterrey. Selected young people, supported by their congregations, are urged to combine their Bible school education with trade school training so as to be self-supporting when serving the church. Annual pastoral institutes and theological education by extension (TEE) supplement the Bible school training.

The first ELCM pastoral candidate with full theological training graduated in 1985 from the Wartburg Theological Seminary Extension in Austin, Texas (an *ALC/USA, now ELCA, institution that provides Spanish instruction). Ordained, he teaches at the Bible School and also does evangelistic work throughout the church with special concern for young people. With a number of other gifted second generation ELCM-ers, he helps spark a lively youth program among high-school- and college-age students. In 1985, the annual summer camp brought together about 100 Mexican youth and a busload of young people from Midwest USA. Vacation Bible schools, conducted in all the congregations, reach three or four thousand children each year. The ELCM has a bright future.

The inspiration for the Latin American Lutheran Mission (1946) came from the South America Prayer League, a Minneapolis-based group meeting between 1932 and 1939. This group gave rise to the Colombia Evangelical Lutheran Mission (1936; see Colombia) and to the World Mission Prayer League (1939; see LAAM below). Myrtle Nordin, who had started the work in Colombia, moved to Mexico in 1942 and began evangelistic work. Her marriage to Heliodoro Huerta, a Mexican citizen, gave her the right to work freely in Mexico. With support from the LALM, she and her husband served for 30 years in evangelistic and educational work, preparing national workers to advance the work.

The LALM is still an active independent mission agency, drawing its support from Lutherans of various church bodies living in the Upper Midwest. Annual meetings and the quarterly *Clarion,* as well as bus trips to Mexico, keep members interested and their support sustained. Each year, several volunteers assist with the work in Laredo, Texas.

LUTHERAN APOSTOLIC ALLIANCE OF MEXICO (LAAM)

(Alianza Luterana Apostólica de México)
Membership: 250**
Pastor: The Rev. Gabriel Mercado
Salvador Alvarado No. 16
Colonia Adolfo López Mateos
Mazatlán, Sinaloa

The Lutheran Apostolic Alliance of Mexico was formed in 1977 by the congregations founded by the former Lutheran Missionary Conference of Northwestern Mexico, a subsidiary of the World Mission Prayer League (WMPL)—a USA-based Lutheran faith mission. The 11 congregations and 10 missions, located mainly in the states of Sinaloa and Sonora (bordering the Gulf of California) and in the state of Puebla east of Mexico City, have the service of 11 national ministers. Three of these are full-time and serve as pastors and evangelists. The rest are volunteers—tentmaking ministers. The ministers receive their training through the St. Paul TEE (theological education by extension) program.

The LAAM constitution provides for a representative church government. An annual meeting elects the president, secretary, and treasurer plus three other persons, who meet four times a year and serve as the executive committee. Currently, many of the congregations own property and have a worship center in some stage of construction. The remainder either rent a building or meet in the homes of members.

The work began in La Paz, the capital of Baja California, in 1945. Forced to abandon the work there, a new start was made in Sinaloa in 1950. Some of the congregations established in the Mazatlán area were turned over to the Mexican Lutheran Church (below). The work begun in Puebla in 1971 includes congregations among the Nahuatl people in the north and also in the city of Puebla. Nogales is the center of the work in Sonora (1976).

WMPL respects the autonomy of the LAAM, working with it as a partner in mission within the country of Mexico. The workers form the Mexican Field Conference of the WMPL.

LUTHERAN SYNOD OF MEXICO (LSM)

(Sínodo Luterano de México)
Membership: 1775**
President: The Rev. Arnulfo
Domínguez E.
Amado Nervo 320 Sur
6400 Monterrey, N.L.

Formed as an independent church body in 1968, this synod is composed of 13 congregations and 15 preaching points. Four of the congregations are situated in the cities of Juárez, Matamoros, Mexicali, and Reynosa, all near the USA border. They maintain a close relationship with the Spanish-speaking missionaries of their partner church, the *Lutheran Church–Missouri Synod, working in the USA border cities. Others are located in the plateau cities, on the Gulf of California, and in Mexico City. Four of the congregations have Christian day schools.

The polity of the Lutheran Synod is patterned after that of the LCMS, its partner since 1973. The annual conferences review and plan the work of the church. Stewardship and evangelism are high on the agenda. A full-time secretary, trained in the USA, helps the local congregations extend their missions. A master plan for the 1980s expects each pastor—using theological education by extension methods—to train at least one leader for a new congregation and another for an eventual replacement of himself. In 1988 there were 13 national pastor and three lay preacher candidates receiving instruction.

The LCMS began its work in Mexico in 1940 as an expansion of its Spanish work north of the border. The first pastors were trained in an institute in Monterrey. In 1965, the institute merged with the Augsburg Seminary of the American Lutheran Church to form the Augsburg Center of Theological Studies in Mexico City (above). Since the close of the Augsburg Seminary in 1981, ministerial students have been trained in an extension program by their local pastors. Financial aid continues to come from LCMS.

MEXICAN LUTHERAN CHURCH (MLC)

(Iglesia Luterana Mexicana)
Member: LWF (1957), CLAI
Membership: 1500**
President: The Rev. Daniel Trejo C.
Apartado Postal 1-1034
Guadalajara, Jalisco

This autonomous church of 12 congregations and an equal number of national pastors is located in the metropolitan area of Mexico City and in the west central states of Jalisco and Sinaloa. Its members are mainly a cross section of middle class and poor urbanites. An annual church convention determines the work and policies. A president, vice-president, secretary, and treasurer, elected every four years, constitute the executive committee. Received into LWF membership the year of its founding (1957), MLC remains the only full LWF member in Mexico.

Most of the present pastors of MLC had their training at the Augsburg Center of Theological Studies or its predecessor. Its closing, due to a lack of students, now handicaps a church greatly in need of indigenous pastors. Recently, the LWF arranged with the Episcopal seminary—adjacent to the Lutheran center in Mexico—to provide training for an MLC candidate.

The earthquake of 1985 hit the MLC hard, damaging many homes and several churches. Help quickly came from LWF churches.

The "old" American Lutheran Church, after working among Mexican-Americans for nearly 30 years, entered Mexico in 1947. Ordained Mexican pastors, trained at a Lutheran Bible School in San Juan, Texas, plus a few trained in USA seminaries, developed congregations in a dozen Mexican cities. The World Mission Prayer League (above; active in northwestern Mexico) contributed three congregations, all in the state of Sinaloa on the west coast. For 10 years, this endeavor was known as the Mexican ALC Conference.

In 1957, these congregations formed an autonomous church body and elected a pastor, David Orea Luna, president. The same year, the ALC opened a theological seminary in Mexico City. Known as Casa Augsburgo, it was conveniently near Mexico City's remarkable university. Before the Casa could be used for the training of the initial three students (one from Colombia) it, like all other church property, had to be nationalized. Heading the new school was a prominent ALC scholar, Professor William Nehrenz. He prepared the way for the future Augsburg Center (see Introduction).

In 1963, the MLC related to the new American Lutheran Church. Two years later, by mutual agreement, decreasing subsidies of the ALC came to the MLC through the LWF's Department of Church Cooperation. The ELCA continues its interest and, within government regulations, maintains a presence in the Lutheran center in Mexico.

ETHNIC CONGREGATIONS: ALL SAINTS' LUTHERAN CHURCH

Membership: 100**
Pastor: The Rev. David Schneider
Apartado Postal 5-174
Guadalajara 5
Jalisco

This English-speaking congregation has been a mission of the *Lutheran Church–Missouri Synod since 1981 when their first ordained missionary was sent to Guadalajara. The congregation had been started in 1968 as a joint trial project with the American Lutheran Church (now ELCA). The name of the Episcopal church in which they worshiped was St. Mark's, so the young congregation became known as St. Mark's. It was served by theological interns supervised by a pastor of the Mexican Lutheran Church.

During its early years the congregation's opportunites for service were great, particularly among the many paraplegics coming to Guadalajara for care. There were also many expatriate medical students as well as other English-speaking residents. Medical standards in the USA have caused a decline in the number of students. But the paraplegics continue to come. Here they find care less expensive and more understanding than in the USA.

In 1982, when the chapel, educational building, and parsonage were completed, the congregation chose the All Saints' name. Helped by a Mexican pastor, work has begun in Spanish in these same facilities.

GERMAN-SPEAKING CONGREGATION IN MEXICO

(Iglesia Evangélica Luterana de Habla Alemana en México)
Member: (R), CLAI
Membership: 963**
President: Johann Mestern
Botticelli 74
Col. Mexcoac
Deleg. Benito Juárez
03190 Mexico, D.F.

This church, actually a parish, seeks to minister to the spiritual needs of German-speaking people throughout the entire country of

Mexico. The core congregation is in Mexico City. Smaller organized groups are in the large cities of Guadalajara, west of Mexico City, and Monterrey, in the northeast. Puebla, Cuernavaca, León, Queretaro, Torreón, and Chihuahua are preaching points. Two pastors—secured through the Foreign Office of the *Evangelical Church in Germany (EKD)—are in Mexico City. They are involved in an intensive program of pastoral care and Christian education, also to isolated groups of German-speaking people. The pastors travel thousands of kilometers to visit people in various places, from Tijuana in the north, to Tapachula in the south. A third pastor, secured by the LWF Department of Church Cooperation, is located in Monterrey and serves all parishioners in the northern part of the country.

Worship services for German Protestants began as early as 1861. The first formal organization was recorded in 1875. In 1904, the Evangelical Church of the Old Prussian Union established a formal relationship with the congregation. It was without a resident pastor from 1908 until its reorganization in 1927, but since then has had a continuous existence. During World War II, the membership dwindled. New life began in 1954 through the encouragement and assistance of the LWF Committee on Latin America and the *Evangelical Church in Germany. Until 1958, the congregation worshiped in a Methodist church. The 1958 dedication of its own centrally located building, the attractive Holy Spirit Church, enabled it to reciprocate earlier Methodist hospitality. For many years it was host to a Methodist congregation.

LUTHERAN CHURCH OF THE GOOD SHEPHERD

(Iglesia Luterana del Buen Pastor)
Membership: 190**
Pastor: The Rev. Paul S. Collinson-Streng
Paseo de las Palmas 1910
Lomas de Chapultepec, Del. Miguel Hidalgo
CP 11000 Mexico 10, D.F.

Good Shepherd is a 1964 merger of two English-speaking congregations founded by USA Lutherans: Lutheran Church of the Good Shepherd (1946) of the *Lutheran Church–Missouri Synod, and the Ascension Lutheran Church (1959) of the Evangelical Lutheran Church (later *ALC, now ELCA). Good Shepherd's name and attractive modern edifice became the common property. The members—mainly American and European professional families living in Mexico on short-term assignments, longer-term residents, and Mexican-Americans—come from a variety of Christian backgrounds. Already in 1965, a Spanish-language ministry extended the membership to a wide cross section of Mexican-American national families.

Supplemental support continues to come from the founding churches, and pastors can be called from either body. Opportunities for growth are enhanced by a favorable location and the presence of an estimated 50,000 Americans in Mexico City.

SCANDINAVIAN CONGREGATION IN MEXICO

(Congregación Escandinava en México) (P)
Membership: 1600**
Pastor: The Rev. Peter Hellgren
Secretariat: Embajada de Suecia
Plaza Comermex
Blvd. Av. Camacho No. 16 piso
Mexico 11000, D.F.

Most of the members of this congregation live in the metropolitan area of Mexico City. Groups residing in other parts of the country, such as Cuernavaca, depend on the pastor's itinerant ministry. Worship is held in the Lutheran Church of the Good Shepherd (above). The Church of Sweden provides pastors and economic help. The congregation participates in local ecumenical projects and has an extensive service program.

Until 1954, the Scandinavians in Mexico were without the services of a pastor. Stewart Herman, director of the LWF Committee on Latin America, visited Mexico in 1953 and discussed the possibility of an itinerant pastor with a representative group of Scandinavians. Of the then 400–500 Scandinavians in Mexico, many had become quite indifferent to the church. However, the diplomatic representatives of the various countries responded favorably and worked with the LWF in forming a temporary organization and providing monthly services. The first was on December 12, 1954. Held in the Anglican church in Mexico City, it brought together 150 people—including two choirs—and a Swedish pastor stationed in Colombia, Åke Kastlund.

When Hilding Olsson, the first permanent pastor, arrived from Sweden in 1957, the congregation was formally organized. It grew rapidly and soon became largely self-supporting. From the beginning the congregation has issued an annual directory and a monthly bulletin.

Copyright © American Map Corporation, New York, No. 19309

NON-LATIN COUNTRIES

Guyana and Suriname have a combined Lutheran membership of some 18,400 or 1.5% of all Lutherans in South America. These churches, using Dutch and English, relate more readily to the Caribbean than to South America.

History: With neighboring French Guiana, Guyana and Suriname comprise the old Guiana region, "Land of Many Waters" to the Amerindians. Columbus first sighted it in 1498. Spaniards scouted it, but went on to greater prizes. English, Dutch, and French grappled for it as a mainland counterpoise to their Caribbean islands and their larger designs on the New World.

When the Congress of Vienna (1815) tripartitioned Guiana into British, Dutch, and French colonies, it not only set the direction for the present three countries—Guyana, Suriname, French Guiana—but also ended that region's unstable past. Except for the French part, Guiana had been Dutch colonial territory most of the time. Periodically, English action intervened and, in light of later identities, origins are the reverse of what they appear today. Guyana had Dutch beginnings, while Suriname had English. The Dutch settled on Essequibo Island (1616) and later built New Amsterdam, all in present Guyana. The British founded Paramaribo (1630), on the Suriname River, which became the capital of the later Dutch Guiana—the region called Suriname by the Dutch since the 17th century. In fact it was the Treaty of Breda (1667) that gave the Dutch the lion's share of the Guiana region in return for their surrender of New Netherlands (and its New Amsterdam) to the British in North America. During the wars of Napoleon, the British occupied all of Guiana, an action opening the way to the kind of settlement determined at Vienna in 1815.

Even before the Dutch gained control in 1667, a significant pioneer missionary venture began in Suriname, not far from Paramaribo, among the "heathen." Justinian von Weltz (1621–1668) was practicing what he had vigorously been advocating about the missionary obligation of the Protestant churches and of his own Lutheran church in particular. Of Austrian nobility, resettled in Saxony, Weltz's academic career took him to Holland. There he experienced a profound conversion, which grew into a deep commitment to bring the gospel to people far away. His efforts to persuade the Corpus Evangelicorum—representatives of the Protestant territories in Germany who met annually—to accept the challenge were without effect. Nor did his proposal to organize a missionary society succeed. His final act, in 1666, was to go himself as a missionary. Suriname, then under Dutch auspices, was the one opening. His work bore fruits decades later.

A second event was the coming of Moravian missionaries to Guiana in 1735. Based in Saxony, on Zinzendorf's estate, Herrnhut (*Germany), their international outreach included friends in the Netherlands as well as in England and Denmark. At the coronation of Danish King Christian VI (1730), Zinzendorf heard at first hand from a slave accompanying a planter from the Danish West Indies (*Virgin Islands) about the spiritual neglect of the enslaved Africans. Resolved to do something about it, Zinzendorf initiated an overseas missionary enterprise that, four years later, extended also to Guiana. Today, it is by far the largest of the Protestant churches in Suriname (below).

A third event pertains to the two Lutheran congregations that arose in rapid succession: the first (1741) on the Suriname River (*Suriname), the second (1743) on the Berbice River (*Guyana). These are the oldest Lutheran churches in South America and stem from help supplied by the same source, the Lutheran Church in Amsterdam (*the Netherlands). Each of these provides a starting point for the story of Lutheranism in the two countries below.

GUYANA

A republic (1970) and a member of the Commonwealth, Guyana is bordered by Venezuela, Brazil, Suriname, and the Atlantic Ocean. Area: 215,000 sq. km. (83,000 sq. mi.). Pop. (1984): 934,000, including 50% East Indian; 30% African; 10% mixed; 5% Amerindian; 5% others, Chinese and European. Cap. and largest city: Georgetown (pop., 1980 est., 167,839). Language: English (official).

History: As indicated above, the Congress of Vienna (1815) awarded the Berbice, Demerara, and Essequibo settlements to Great Britain, and these later united as British Guiana (1831). Slavery was abolished in 1834. To work the sugar plantations, the British began in 1903 to bring in East Indians, Chinese, and Portuguese as indentured servants.

Following World War II, agitation for independence was accompanied by sharp political strife between the ethnic groups. Through their People's Progressive Party (Communist oriented), the East Indians took power. Britain sent troops and suspended the constitution. The blacks formed their own People's National Congress (1955) under the strong leadership of Forbes Burnham. The introduction of proportionate representation (1964) made possible a coalition government with Burnham as prime minister. Independence came in 1966, with Queen Elizabeth II accepted as head of state. In 1970, Guyana became a republic and a member of the United Nations. Leanings toward Communism increased. Since 1978, Guyana has been an associate member of the Communist bloc's Council for Mutual Economic Assistance (COMECON). As with other countries, Guyana's foreign debt poses an enormous burden. A dictatorial government compounds the pressures.

Religion: Christian 52%; Hindu 34.4%; Muslim 9.2%; Traditional 2.2%; Spiritist 0.8%; Bahai 0.3%; Chinese folk religion 0.1%; nonreligious 0.8%; atheist 0.2%.

The Guyana government guarantees religious freedom. It also makes grants to churches providing social work among the Amerindians. In 1976, all schools, including those of the churches, were nationalized.

No other South American country has such religious diversity as Guyana. The Hindus and Muslims are almost entirely of East Asian origin. Traditional Amerindian religion still prevails among the Taruma in the south and the Arawak in the southwest. Although most Guyanese of African descent are Christian, Afro-American Spiritism or Voodoo flourishes among non-Christian blacks.

Roman Catholic missionaries were in the Guiana area in the 16th century, but their work was almost completely erased during the Dutch occupation. The first priest of the modern period came in 1826. Portuguese settlers became the mainstay of the church. Today, the Catholic church is the largest denomination, with some 110,000 members. Growth is affected by emigration, and most priests are still expatriates.

The Anglican church (1810), with about 100,000 members, is the largest non-Roman body. Baptists are next, with some 17,000 members, all gathered after World War II. Lutherans (1743) are third. Then come Seventh Day Adventists, Presbyterians, and Methodists. Two indigenous bodies are the Jordanists and the Halleluja Church. The latter, over 100 years old, extends into Venezuela and combines elements of Christian and Traditional religion.

Also on the religious front during the 1970s was the transplanted People's Temple commune from San Francisco, California. Some 900 members, mainly black, lived in total subjection to their white leader, the Rev. Jim Jones. An apparent mix of eschatological hope and fear of an impending investigation triggered the horrifying mass suicide of over 900 men, women, and children in Jonestown (November 1978).

The Guyana Council of Churches (GCC) was formed in 1967 by the merger of the Christian Social Council (1937), which included the Catholics, and the Evangelical Council (1960). One of the council's main projects is the Guyana Extension Seminary. Initiated by the Lutherans in 1972, the program is now supported and used by 11 denominations, including the Catholics. Designed for a land where 70% of the Christian congregations are without resident pastors, the resources—including volunteer tutors—of the various denominations are used to enable adult Christians of all ages to become more effective workers within their local churches.

LUTHERAN CHURCH IN GUYANA (LCG)
(Iglesia Luterana en Guyana)
Member: LWF (1950), CCC, GCC
Membership: 14,437
President: The Rev. James Lochan
28-29 North and
Alexander Streets
Lacytown, Georgetown

The members of the LCG reflect the ethnic diversity of Guyana. The church has been notably successful in bridging differences among the East Indians, Africans, Chinese, Amerindians, and others. Most of the members live on the seacoast, including the town of New Amersterdam and the capital city, Georgetown, and along the two main rivers, the Berbice and the Demerera. Agriculture is the main occupation, and many of the members are subsistence farmers.

The LCG's 53 congregations, grouped into 14 parishes, are served by nine ordained pastors, two ordained deacons and several lay workers, some of whom have been trained at the Guyana Extension Seminary (above). An annual convention, composed of the pastors and delegates from the parishes, is the legislative body. An executive council of seven members administers the work between conventions. The present constitution was adopted in 1981. Thereafter its longtime partner, the *Lutheran Church in America (now ELCA), no longer provided subsidy. The LCG since then has been self-reliant on the congregational and administrative levels. Despite its conscientious stewardship, the church, like the country as a whole, has been hit hard by the emigration of members leaving for political, economic, and other reasons.

The ELCA continues to assist with special projects in Christian education, with the Guyana Extension Seminary, and with the training of pastors. At present, training takes place at the United Theological College of the West Indies (UTC-WI) in Kingston, Jamaica. Here, for many years, Lutheran professors supplied by the LCA strengthened the ecumenical faculty and served as advisers to the Lutheran students attending UTC-WI. The last tutor, the Rev. Geoffrey Y. Tannassee, was from the LCG. His death in a plane crash (1979), while en route to an extension class, was a great loss to the LCG. Six LCG students were enrolled in the UTC-WI in 1984. Yet there is an urgent need for more pastors and other workers to meet the challenges facing the church, especially those presented by the rural East Indian population.

• • •

This next-to-the-oldest Lutheran church in South America (1743) was founded by six Dutch settlers. Their petitions to the directors of the colony for permission to band together those professing the *Unaltered Augsburg Confession,* to exercise their religion freely, and to have a pastor of their own were granted. The congregation, named Ebenezer, "stone of help," waited nine years before the first pastor arrived from the Lutheran church in Holland. Over the next 100 years, the congregation was without a pastor about half the time. After the British took over, all the Christian congregations organized in Dutch times died out except the Ebenezer Lutheran Church, and it barely survived.

Ebenezer revived when the first Guyanese pastor, John Robert Mittelholzer (1840–1913) offered his services in 1878. Mittelholzer, a black born in British Guiana, was a mechanical engineer when he was challenged by the London Missionary Society representative to prepare for the Christian ministry. As pastor of Ebenezer, he served not only the Dutch descendants but also those of African, Amerindian, and East Indian origin. He and his helpers gathered five congregations in the Berbice region and organized the Mission Chapel Endeavor Society as a local support system.

In 1890, Mittelholzer secured the admission of himself and the Ebenezer congregation into the East Pennsylvania Synod of the General Synod of the Evangelical Lutheran Church in the United States. After Mittelholzer's death, people in Berbice joined with Ebenezer in giving thanks for a remarkable Christian pastor.

On the urging of Ebenezer members, the Board of Foreign Missions of the General Synod took charge and assumed much of the responsibility that the laypeople in Guyana had carried for so long. In 1918, when the United Lutheran Church in America (ULCA) was formed—with the General Synod one of the components—British Guiana became one of its mission fields. The work was enlarged by missionary personnel; congregations were formed and schools established. Emphasis was placed on ministering to the East Indians and Amerindians. The former included Christians who had been members of the *Gossner Evangelical Lutheran Church in India. This continuous relationship with the church in North America had both strengths and weaknesses. Pastoral candidates were educated in the USA or Canada. After the first one was ordained in 1936, the church experienced growth and vitality from his ministry. However, there were other candidates who remained in the USA or returned there instead of serving their own people. This increased the dependency upon expatriate missionaries.

In observing the Ebenezer bicentennial in 1943, 29 congregations, with a membership of 1615, united. This Evangelical Lutheran Church in British Guinea (ELCBG) elected Pastor Patrick A. Magalee its first president. The next year it became an associate synod of the ULCA. In 1946, the ELCBG ordained a pastor for the first time. A Guyanese pastor represented the church at the Lund assembly (1947), and in 1950 the ELCBG was received into LWF membership.

Despite the political unrest in the 1950s, the church was on the move. In partnership with the ULCA, it sought out the East Indian plantation workers; helped the young people form a churchwide Luther League; opened a school in New Amsterdam for lay leaders; and developed the practice of stewardship. Select high school graduates, sent to ULCA colleges, prepared for teaching positions in the church schools. At its peak, the church maintained—with some government assistance—18 elementary and two high schools.

Urban work grew during the 1960s. In 1964, Ebenezer dedicated a new edifice replacing that of 1743. National independence (1966) had its impact, also in the new name—Lutheran Church in Guyana. A new constitution gave administrative powers to the elected executive council instead of to one appointed by the LCA's mission board. Although 13 young men from the LCG graduated from North American theological seminaries and were ordained during this decade, more than half did not return to Guyana. To stem this loss, LCA scholarships were given to Guyanese students enrolled in the United Theological College of the West Indies in Kingston, Jamaica. Six students were there in 1968 and had the benefit of a Lutheran professor and adviser. In the 1970s, the LCA reduced other grants year by year preparing for self-reliance by 1980.

In 1981, a representative of the LCA visited Guyana. He praised the LCG as a partner church and presented a plaque commemorating the long and warm relationship between the two churches. The Guyana church leaders expressed confidence that national personnel could assume responsibilities currently held by LCA missionaries, the last of whom left in 1983.

SURINAME

This republic (1975) of northern South America borders *Guyana, *Brazil, French Guiana, and the Atlantic Ocean. Area: 163,820 sq. km. (63,251 sq. mi.), not including a 17,635 sq. km. area disputed with *Guyana. Pop. (1980 census): 354,860, including (by 1980 est.) Hindustanis 35%; Creoles 32%; Indonesians 13%: Bush Negroes (descendants of escaped slaves) 10%; Amerindians 3%; Chinese 3%; Europeans 2%. Cap. and largest city: Paramaribo (metro. pop., 1980, 150,000). Language: Dutch (official); English and Sranan (Taki–Taki), a mix of English, Dutch, French, Spanish, and even Hebrew, used in interracial communication. Hindi, Javanese, Chinese, and Amerindian tongues continue in ethnic communities.

History: As indicated above, the Congress of Vienna (1815) fixed the tripartite division of Guiana and reduced the Dutch holding to the present Suriname, so named for its main river. Economically, the colony became more profitable with the exploitation of bauxite deposits.

The 1954 Dutch constitution raised the colony to a level of equality with the Netherlands. In the 1970s, the Dutch government pressured for independence, which came on November 25, 1975, despite objections from East Indians and some Bush Negroes. About 40% of the population emigrated during the months prior to independence. Eventually some 180,000—mostly East Indians— moved to the Netherlands. Relations with the Netherlands were tense, especially over the issue of development aid, but a state visit by Queen Juliana (1978) reaffirmed mutual good will.

Domestically, divergent political and economic forces led, in 1980, to the imposition of a National Military Council. A prolonged strike in the bauxite industry—accounting for nearly 80% of the country's exports—as well as high unemployment underscored the seriousness of the country's problems.

Religion (1980): Christian 41.7% (Protestant 18.8%; Roman Catholic 22.9%); Muslim 19.6%; Hindu 27.4%. Also Tribal religionist 7%; Afro-American Spiritist 3%; Jewish, Bahai, Buddhist, and others, under 1% each.

Roman Catholicism was temporarily on the scene in the 17th century, but became a rapidly growing constituency in the 19th. Its Paramaribo diocese includes people of all ethnic groups but is especially strong among the Amerindians.

Protestantism unfolded during the 18th century. The Moravian Church in Suriname (1735)—now numbering over 52,000—is larger than the other non-Roman churches combined. The Dutch Reformed Church (1750) is next in size, while the Lutheran church (1741) is third.

Relations between church and state are close. The government grants subsidies to registered church bodies, allows religious instruction in the schools, and pays the salaries of Protestant pastors as well as of a given number of Roman Catholic clergy. Teachers of religion are also on the public payroll.

Besides the small Moravian theological seminary (1902), which serves other Protestants as well, the Christian Pedagogical Institute (1970) is an ecumenical undertaking that provides further training for Roman Catholic priests as well as Protestant pastors and teachers.

The Suriname Christian Council of Churches (SCCC; 1960) is more inclusive than most such associations and reflects an ecumenism like that in the Netherlands through its Roman Catholic as well as Protestant—Moravian, Dutch Reformed, and Lutheran—membership. The Moravian church is Suriname's one member body in the World Council of Churches.

EVANGELICAL LUTHERAN CHURCH IN SURINAME (ELCS)

(Evangelisch Lutherse Kerk in Suriname)
Member: LWF (1979), CCC, SCCC
Membership: 4000*
President: Ilse Labadie
Waterkant 102
PO Box 585, Paramaribo

As indicated above, this Dutch-speaking church has the longest Lutheran history in South America (1741). It consists of three congregations in and near Paramaribo, the capital. Two congregations have both Lutheran and Reformed constituency, the third and largest is all Lutheran. The union congregations have modern church buildings; but Martin Luther congregation, in downtown Paramaribo, still worships in an 1834 edifice that replaced the original church built on the same site in 1747. Presently, the ELCS is served by the first and only Surinamese pastor, now in semiretirement, and a missionary pastor from the *Evangelical Lutheran Church in America.

Members of the ELCS, mainly of African descent, are for the most part engaged in business and trades, as were their forebears. In recent years, the extensive emigration of Surinamese people to Holland and the difficulty of securing overseas pastors have posed serious challenges. Increasingly, the church is training lay leadership and encouraging young people to enter full-time ministry. Since 1982, an LCA (now ELCA) missionary pastor-teacher has assisted these efforts. The ELCS has links with the local Moravian seminary and with the United Theological College of the West Indies in Jamaica. In 1986, the first ELCS candidate completed a full theological course at the UTC-WI and received further training through an internship in Holland. She began her service at Martin Luther congregation in 1987. Two other students are in training, one in Jamaica and the other in Holland.

Since 1975, the ELCS has participated in Lutheran World Federation Caribbean consultations, hosting the one in 1982. A Surinamese observer attended the 1977 Dar es Salaam assembly, and two years later the ELCS was received into LWF membership. Ecumenically, the church is a member of the Suriname Christian Council of Churches and the Caribbean Conference of Churches. It participates in a radio and television ministry in cooperation with other Paramaribo churches.

Looking back, the Lutheran congregation formed in 1741 was not the result of mission but of settlement. On November 15 of that year, Lutherans in Suriname received permission from the directors of the Suriname Society to practice their religion according to the teachings and confession of the Lutheran church and to establish a congregation. It remained under the jurisdiction of the Lutheran Consistory in Amsterdam, Holland, until 1819. Then a synod, set up under King William I of the Netherlands, appointed a commission to oversee the affairs of the Protestant churches in both the East and West Indies. This included Suriname. The commission was dissolved only in 1959.

Several attempts by the Suriname church to become more closely allied with either the Lutheran church in Holland or the United Lutheran Church in America proved futile. The church remained isolated from the Lutheran family. The one exception occurred in the 1870s when the Suriname church was able to provide pastoral help to the Evangelical Lutheran Church in British Guiana (*Guyana). For most of its history, the Suriname Lutheran church was served by Reformed pastors from Holland.

In the early 1970s, through the help of a Dutch Army chaplain, the relations between the Lutheran church in the Netherlands and the ELCS grew closer. Since 1980, help has come from a Swedish pastor and the Lutheran Church in America (now ELCA). Over the generations, 29 pastors have served the ELCS.

Copyright © American Map Corporation, New York, No. 19309

NORTHERN ANDEAN ZONE

Included are five countries (Bolivia, Colombia, Ecuador, Peru, and Venezuela) where some 29,900 Lutherans live. The churches described below account for 2.4% of South American Lutherans. Spanish is the dominant language, but Amerindian tongues are also prominent.

BOLIVIA

A republic. Area: 1,098,581 sq. km. (424,165 sq. mi.). Pop. (1986 est.): 6,611,000; mixed 31.2%, Quechua 25.4%, Aymará 16.9%, white 14.5%, other 12%. Administrative cap. and largest city: La Paz (pop., 1985 est., 992,592). Judicial cap.: Sucre (pop., 1985 est., 84,505); located 480 kilometers (300 miles) southeast of La Paz. Official languages: Aymará, Quechua, Spanish.

History: Aymará Indians of Bolivia had been absorbed into the Inca empire long before the Spanish conquest of Bolivia (1538). Spaniards ruled until independence in 1825. A series of dictators and political disturbances culminated in 1952 when the Nationalist Revolutionary Movement won control over the government. Tin mines were nationalized and a program of agrarian reform was launched. A military takeover in 1964 renewed political strife and instability. In 1982, a civilian government assumed leadership.

Religion: Although the official religion is Roman Catholicism, religious liberty is fully accepted. By baptism, the Roman Catholic Church claims over 92% of the population. About half of these are Christo-pagans, combining elements of 16th century Catholicism with indigenous religions of that period. The church today, divided into four metropolitan sees—La Paz, Sucre, Cochabamba, and Santa Cruz—is making serious attempts to increase spiritual services and to bring education and social services to the masses. Married deacons assist the overburdened priests. Missionaries from North America are working among the Aymará Indians, of whom a considerable number have been trained as catechists and some for the diaconate.

Traditional Indian religions continue to hold the allegiance of substantial numbers, especially among the Guaraní, Guayaru, and Quechua. The latter are also nominally Catholic. Bahai, in Bolivia since 1956, now claims 2.6% of the population and is advancing.

513

Protestantism was late in coming to Bolivia: Brethren (1895); Canadian Baptist (1898); Methodist (1901); Andes Evangelical Mission (1903); and Seventh Day Adventist (1907). Today, the latter is the largest Protestant church. It gained rapidly after World War I, when it responded to a request to establish schools in the Lake Titicaca area. Membership is over 50,000. The second largest is the Evangelical Christian Union, the result of a 1959 merger of the Andes Evangelical Mission and the Evangelical Union of South America. Assemblies of God are third, followed by Methodist, Nazarene, Friends, Baptist, Lutheran, Mennonite, and numerous smaller groups.

The National Association of Evangelicals of Bolivia (Asociación Nacional de Evangélicos de Bolivia—ANDEB; 1966) has a large membership but has been weakened by tensions between conservative evangelicals and ecumenical groups. The Ecumenical Association for Cooperation and Coordination of Social Development (ASEC) was formed in 1976 on the initiative of the Conference of Lutheran Pastors of Bolivia (below). Its aim is to improve agricultural production and marketing and to promote the organization of farmers so they can assess and improve their living.

The Conference of Lutheran Pastors of Bolivia is the uniting factor of Lutheran work in Bolivia. It includes both indigenous and expatriate missionary pastors from the three church bodies described below and also those from the two mission agencies working in the nation. The World Mission Prayer League (WMPL) continues to be supportive to one of the two church bodies resulting from its work. It also initiates new work, including some in the city of Santa Cruz de la Sierra and a radio station in the jungle town of Caranavi. Since 1978, the Norwegian Lutheran Mission has cooperated and worked closely with the WMPL among the Quechua around Cochabamba and Potosi. Small congregations (with a total of 141 members) have been formed, and a radio ministry in the Quechua language has been developed.

BOLIVIAN EVANGELICAL LUTHERAN CHURCH (BELC)

(Iglesia Evangélica Luterana Boliviana)
Member: LWF (1975), CLAI
Membership: 18,000**
President: Lic. Zenobio Cordero
Quito
Casilla de Correo 8471
La Paz

This church of 150 congregations is served by 13 ordained pastors and numerous resident preachers and lay associates in ministry. Its members, Aymará Indians, live in the Andean highlands in and around La Paz, its headquarters, and northward into Peru. A few congregations use the Spanish language, but the main work of the church is carried on in Aymará. This accounts for its rapid early growth, as Aymarás themselves shared the gospel in their own tongue. It is the largest indigenous Amerindian Lutheran church in Latin America.

The BELC was formed in 1972 and incorporated under the laws of Bolivia in 1974. Organized on a congregational basis, the church is divided into six districts, each with its presiding officer. A synod, an executive committee, and elected officers provide for self-government. With the generous inheritance of property from the World Mission Prayer League (WMPL), the indigenous church is self-supporting. Seeking wider fellowship, the BELC applied for and was received into LWF membership in 1975. Its doctrinal basis was set early by the WMPL and is in harmony with the requirements of the Federation.

Most BELC ministers—lay and ordained—have attended the church's Bible school in La Paz and have received further theological training by extension. The latter is also provided for catechists and lay workers at Coaba Farm and in more remote places like Apolo, farther north. Since February 1984, the Bible institute in La Paz, upgraded to Lutheran Center of Theological Education (CLET), provides more advanced training for pastors and other church workers.

The BELC is the outcome of work begun near La Paz in 1938 by the WMPL. At that time, the WMPL itself was new, and work in Bolivia was its first foreign venture. The WMPL owes its origin to a student prayer fellowship of the early 1930s in Minneapolis, Minnesota. It is a faith mission supported mainly by Lutherans of Scandinavian descent living in Midwest USA (see Colombia, Mexico).

Through the good offices of the Bolivian consul in Los Angeles and comity arrangements with other mission groups, the WMPL began its work among a hitherto unevangelized people who were nominally Roman Catholic but virtually without spiritual care. The first two missionaries settled on a farm, Coaba, at Sorata in an Andean mountain valley about 144 kilometers (90 miles) north of La Paz. The ensuing Bible school and home for orphans, plus simple medical services and agricultural counseling, turned Coaba Farm into a people-centered base for outreach into the scattered Aymará villages.

Over the decades the work expanded. By the early 1960s, the WMPL had some 30 missionaries in Bolivia. La Paz had become the base of operations. A center—complete with a modernistic Redeemer Church (1957), educational facilities, meeting place for students, bookshop, and WMPL offices—was a visible evidence of progress. In addition, the center served the Spanish-speaking people who were also being reached by the WMPL. As this work grew in strength and importance, two worship services were held simultaneously, one in Aymará and one in Spanish. In time, due to language and cultural differences, tensions evolved that culminated in the separation of part of the Spanish-speaking group, which formed the Latin American Lutheran Church (LALC; below).

Meanwhile, the Aymarás had become missionaries in their own way and had reached the Quechua Indians, dwellers like themselves in the Andean country, thus extending the mission into *Peru. A spirit of confidence animated the Aymarás, and by the early 1970s forces were at work that brought about a self-governing body in 1972. The lack of growth since 1977 is in part due to a number of congregations leaving to join the LALC.

GERMAN-SPEAKING EVANGELICAL LUTHERAN CHURCH IN BOLIVIA
(Iglesia Evangélica Luterana de Habla Alemana en Bolivia)
Member: (R), CLAI
Membership: 600**
Pastor: The Rev. Irene Sievers
Casilla de Correo 2851
La Paz

This recognized congregation of the LWF serves as a small church body for German-speaking Lutherans living in Bolivia. Centered in La Paz, it has branch congregations in Santa Cruz, Cochabamba, Oruro, and elsewhere in the country's lower-lying agricultural regions. The members in La Paz are largely business, technical, and professional people, in Bolivia for longer or shorter periods. The church receives pastors and other aid from the Foreign Office of the *Evangelical Church in Germany (EKD).

The history of this church goes back to the early 1920s when German immigrants came to La Paz after World War I. They were served by a German pastor who also conducted a school. Between 1931 and 1948, pastors came periodically from Buenos Aires (*Argentina) and Fruitilar (*Chile). With new immigration after World War II, the congregation gained members. A young German pastor arrived in 1952, but died tragically within a year. During his short service, he had made an impact on the intellectual circles of La Paz and had provided religious instruction to the 1400 pupils enrolled in the German school.

A missionary of the WMPL (above) then served the congregation until a replacement was found in 1956. Two years later, the new pastor made his first trip into the interior of Bolivia in search of Lutheran families. In Santa Cruz, Cochabamba, Sucre, and Oruro he found groups of neglected Lutherans eager for pastoral care and worship services. It was the first time in eight years that many of these people had been visited. In the meantime, many children had been baptized as Catholics so they would not grow up as pagans.

Until recently, the church has had a friendly working relationship with the BELC. Participation in joint Lutheran and ecumenical work in La Paz has characterized this church.

Good relations with the Roman Catholics have been fostered.

LATIN AMERICAN LUTHERAN CHURCH (LALC)

(Iglesia Luterana Latinoamericana)
Member: (P), CLAI, ANDEB
Membership: 1270**
President: The Rev. Jaime Michel Aguirre
Casilla de Correo 3809
La Paz

This church body was until 1969 part of the La Paz congregation of the BELC (above). It withdrew, reportedly, in order to extend the Lutheran church to Spanish-speaking Bolivians more effectively. With the leadership of a self-educated theologian, a lawyer by training and profession, the church has reached out to the "up and outers" often neglected by the church. Pastor Jaime Michel Aguirre is assisted by some lay preachers and WMPL missionaries. In worship it uses *Culto Cristiano*, the Lutheran liturgical service book and hynmal developed in Latin America for use in Spanish-speaking churches.

The LALC has grown from a membership of 60 in 1977 to over 1200 and has two congregations—in La Paz and Sorata. Encouragement for its work has come from the WMPL, which in 1982 deeded the Redeemer Church building to the LALC. This, however, has been an additional cause of tension with the BELC, which claims to be the only recognized and legally responsible Lutheran church body in Bolivia.

The LALC participates in the National Association of Evangelicals of Bolivia (ANDEB) as well as in other ecumenical efforts in Latin America. Its 1979 application for membership in the LWF remains pending due to the objection of the BELC, a member.

COLOMBIA

A republic. Area: 1,141,748 sq. km. (440,831 sq. mi.). Pop. (1985 census) 28,231,000, mainly mixed Indian and Iberian; small groups of Indians and also some blacks. Cap. and largest city: Bogotá (pop., 1985, 3,982,941). Language: Spanish.

History: During the 1530s, Spaniards overpowered the Chibcha and other Indian tribes and settled the territory as far as Panama. The movement toward independence, led by the Venezuelan patriot, Simón Bolívar (1783–1830), culminated in 1819. The state of Great Colombia included Colombia, Panama, Ecuador (after 1822), and Venezuela. When this union broke up (1830), Colombia and Panama became first the Republic of New Granada and then the Republic of Colombia (1886). Panama withdrew in 1903. Over a century of periodic civic strife preceded an era of stability. However, the situation deteriorated between 1948 and 1958 and again in the 1970s. Unrest continues into the present. Unresolved issues include poverty, anticlericalism, class conflict, expropriation of Indian land. Added to this misery were the two disasters of 1985. On November 6, President Belisario Betancur Cuartas sent army troops against guerrillas who had taken over the Palace of Justice. The ensuing battle left nearly 100 dead. A few days later, one of the deadliest volcanic eruptions on record occurred in Colombia killing some 20,000 people and leaving at least 150,000 homeless.

Religion: Roman Catholic 97% (1983). The Roman Church has had a tighter hold on national and daily life in Colombia than in any other Latin American country. It is largely conservative, though with liberal elements. The concordats of 1887 and 1892 still prevail. A marked increase in the devotional life of Catholics occurred during a period when Protestant groups were openly persecuted (1948–1952). However, since Vatican II, there has been a much improved relationship with Protestant churches. This was evident in 1968 when the Second General Conference of Latin American Roman Catholic Bishops (CELAM), meeting in Medellín, Colombia, officially recognized that Latin America is a mission area, posing an enormous evangelistic task in which all Christians should be engaged. The Medellín conference also declared that the Roman Catholic Church must identify itself with the masses of people who are poor. The Ministerial Association of Bogotá, organized in 1970 for the purpose of dialog and prayer, includes both Catholic and Protestant clergy.

The Protestant minority in Colombia (2%) had a period of rapid growth after the painful period of persecution. Protestantism in Colombia, as in most parts of Roman Catholic Latin America, presents a conservative, fundamentalistic, and fragmented array of 60 organized religious bodies. About half of these, including the Evangelical Lutheran Church of Colombia (below), cooperate in the Evangelical Confederation of Colombia (Confederación Evangélica de Colombia—CEDEC; 1950). Oldest among them is the 20,000-member Presbyterian Church of Colombia (1856); the largest and most numerous are the various Pentecostal groups. Among the most recent are the Episcopalians and Lutherans.

Other religions are also present. In the interior, tribal religions are practiced by lowland and jungle tribes. Judaism has some 10,000 adherents, most of whom arrived in Colombia after World War II. Of the Colombian university students, 2% are Jewish. Bahai has grown rapidly since 1964. Islam and Hinduism are also present in the large cities.

Besides the small organized church bodies (below), about 500 Lutherans are members of two independent congregations recognized by the LWF: the 150-member **St. Martin's Congregation Cali** (c/o The Pastor, Diagonal 26A, No. 27-31, Barrio San Fernando) and the 350-member **St. Matthew's Congregation, Bogotá** (Rev. Ferdinand Schubert, Carrera 7, No. 128-96, Bogotá 10). These two, comprising mainly expatriates living in Colombia for longer or shorter periods, are largely self-supporting. They receive pastors, and subsidy if necessary, from the Foreign Office of the *Evangelical Church in Germany (EKD). The Cali congregation has outposts in Medellín (1952) and Pasto (1953) and participates in ecumenical projects among the poor. The Bogotá congregation has a mission in Barranquilla (1952) on the Atlantic coast, and sponsors a day-care center in a slum area near the church.

The above constituency is a remnant of a short-lived federation of seven growing congregations formed in 1952 under the sponsorship of the LWF Committee on Latin America (LWF/CLA) whose director was the Rev. Stewart W. Herman. Already in 1949, a German theological student living in Colombia, Hermann Müller, had been appointed by the LWF Service to Refugees to work among the newly displaced Europeans in Colombia. He found very few because Colombia limited visas almost entirely to Roman Catholics. However, he did discover hundreds of neglected Lutherans—mainly Germans and Scandinavians—some of whom had been in Colombia for decades, others who were there for a short period. He gathered groups in Bogotá and Cali and conducted worship services.

In 1952, the LWF/CLA granted Müller leave to complete in Germany and the USA the theological studies that he had begun in Colombia. In his place came the energetic and experienced Pastor Åke Kastlund from Sweden. Within a year he had organized congregations in Bogotá, Cali, Medellín, Barranquilla, and Pasto near the Ecuador border. Altogether he, his wife, and other helpers found between 2000 and 3000 Lutherans in Colombia during the year 1952. Many of them became grateful and enthusiastic members of German-speaking and Scandinavian groups. Children—some older than 10 years—were baptized and instructed. Young people were gathered into study and social groups. Councils were organized, and funds were collected for the construction of church buildings in Bogotá and Cali.

Hermann Müller returned to Colombia in January 1953. After finishing his theological studies at Luther Theological Seminary in St. Paul, Minnesota, he was ordained by the president of the Evangelical Lutheran Church, Dr. J. A. Aasgaard. Müller was assigned the three congregations in the western part of the country. This permitted Kastlund to concentrate on the Scandinavians and to seek out other Lutheran groups.

During 1953, a constitution was adopted by all the congregations. It was "large enough to accommodate a countrywide church, and deep enough to provide for all Lutherans regardless of their origin." This set the stage for the federation that was formed in November 1954. Delegates gathered in Bogotá from all five congregations. They represented many national origins: Danish, Finnish, German, Lithuanian, North American, Swedish, Swiss. The federation was to be a permanent link between widely separated parishes, including a request for legal recognition as a corporation, a joint treasury to which each congregation would contribute 5% of its income, a youth paper, and a youth camp program on a national basis. A representative of the Colombian mission (see ELCC, below) was also present and shared information about the work and the hardships of its members. The Europeans lent a sympathetic ear. Soon, two new congregations, Bucaramanga and Cucuta, joined the five.

Unfortunately, enthusiasm for a federation could not be sustained. Instead, two separate congregations—the one in Bogotá and the other in Cali, each with satellite groups—in time gained legal recognition and their own church facilities. This was not easy during a period when Colombia was extremely intolerant of Protestants and was suffering severely from inflation. Nor did the congregations have the benefit of refugees, who made stronger church members than the other Europeans who had lived without the church for many years and had prospered during the war.

Although the LWF/CLA kept sending pastors and vicars, most of them could stay for only short terms. Efforts to train Colombian residents continued. The LWF/CLA further aided the congregations by sending Dr. Arne Bentz for an extended visit in 1958. A Swedish-American theologian with missionary experience in China and Indonesia, he was quick to analyze the situation in Colombia. He helped to secure the legal recognition necessary for security; and also convinced the LWF that more pastoral service, especially for the Swedish groups, was essential. Within a year, a Swedish pastor, P.O. Wahlberg, arrived in Colombia after a period of Spanish language study in Costa Rica.

After the LWF assembly in Helsinki (1963), the LWF/CLA office was moved from New York to Bogotá, and Dr. Stewart Herman was succeeded by a Brazilian, the Rev. Guido Tornquist, who continued to encourage the young congregations in addition to his other work in Latin America until his transfer to Geneva. In 1970, responsibility shifted to the Department of Church Cooperation of the LWF.

CONFESSIONAL EVANGELICAL LUTHERAN CHURCH OF COLOMBIA (WISCONSIN SYNOD)

(Iglesia Evangélica Luterana Confesional de Colombia (Sínodo de Wisconsin)

Membership: 195**
President: The Rev. Philipe Strackbein
Apartado Aéreo 5277
Calle 128 A No. 52A-47
Bogotá

This mission of the *Wisconsin Evangelical Lutheran Synod (USA) was organized as a national church body after a decade of preparatory work. In the early 1970s, a Bible institute and seminary program were established. The first Colombian graduate of the seminary was ordained and installed in January 1983. The same year, work was extended to Bogotá. The church has committees serving in the areas of theological education, mission, and congregational education.

EVANGELICAL LUTHERAN CHURCH OF COLOMBIA (ELCC)

(Iglesia Evangélica Luterana de Colombia)
Member: LWF (1966), CEDEC
Membership: 2000**
President: The Rev. José Hernán Ariza
Calle 75 Nr. 20-54
Apartado Aéreo 51538
Bogotá 2

The 10 congregations and eight mission points of this church are served by eight Colombian pastors and one expatriate missionary. Geographically, the major part of the constituency extends from Bogotá, the church headquarters, northward among the mountains in an arc that includes the old city of Tunja and the towns of Sogamoso, Socota, El Cocuy, and Bucaramanga. To the east, congregations are in the lower-lying plateaus in the towns of Paz de Ariporo and El Banco.

Organized as a church in 1958, the ELCC has a synodical form of polity with a strong accent on congregational responsibility. Executive power is vested in a church council headed by the president. Five of the congregations maintain elementary schools. Under government license, the Lutheran secondary school in Sogamoso offers the country's official curriculum. As many of the students are not members of the church, the school is a means of evangelism. Efforts continue to strengthen congregational worship through a program of liturgical and hymnody renewal.

During the 1960s and early 1970s, pastoral candidates had their training at the Lutheran theological seminaries in *Argentina and *Mexico, and in the late 1970s and early 1980s at the international Baptist Theological Seminary in Cali. Recently, LWF scholarships for study at the Theological Faculty in São Leopoldo, Brazil, have been available to Colombian students. Increased use is being made of theological education by extension (TEE) for pastors and also for lay workers. TEE in Colombia is part of a coordinated program of six Latin American and some Central American countries, Co-Extension, with headquarters in Bogotá.

Since becoming an LWF member in 1966, the ELCC has taken an active part in Latin American Lutheran interests and has been host to various events of broad concern, including theological education. It has taken a lead in the Lutheran Literature and Christian Education Committee of the Northern Zone, which prepares educational material for local and regional churches. In turn, the LWF has assisted the church with its media communication project of radio programs and audiovisual aids to congregations. Recently, a five-story building was completed with assistance from its partner, the *American Lutheran Church (now ELCA), and three departments of the LWF—DOC, DCC, and CDS. It provides space for the church headquarters, a library, Co-Extension, community development, literature publication (editor's office), and communication. The building also provides a residence for the church president.

In the field of development, LWF/CDS has aided the church in providing loans for simple basic housing for 207 families in the slum areas of La Esperanza and El Panuelito near Bogotá. Here, the church provides medical and social services, including an outpatient clinic, a day nursery for 35 children of working mothers, and classes in literacy and vocational training. Extensive relief work has been carried out for the victims of the volcanic eruption in November 1985. The world Lutheran community provided the means, and the ELCC the coordination and services, concentrating in the Manizales and Ibagué areas.

● ● ●

This Lutheran work was begun in 1936 by an independent group that registered its mission undertakings under the name CEL-MOSA. This Colombia Evangelical Lutheran Mission of South America was the first of three that grew out of the USA South American Prayer League, which met in Minneapolis 1932–1939. Myrtle Nordin and Marie Thompson, the first missionaries, settled in Soata, a little town hidden away in the Andes, where no evangelical missionaries had been. Other volunteers followed, and small Bible schools opened. In 1944, these were consolidated in Duitama, and the work was reinforced by personnel and funds from two antecedent bodies of the former *American Lutheran Church. A mission station was opened in Tunja, the historic capital of the state of Boyacá, north of Bogotá, and in 1946 the USA church bodies assumed responsibility for the entire mission. Two years later, the mission was incorporated under Colombian law just as the persecution (above) was accelerating.

This period of testing became solid gain. Evangelical commitment was engrafted firmly, especially in younger persons and potential leaders. Until its closing in 1964, the Bible Institute in Bogotá trained teachers and evangelists and prepared others for theological study and an indigenous ordained ministry. Two young Colombians were ordained pastors in 1954 and two more in 1958. The persecution also led directly to the establishment of El Redentor congregation in Bogotá, which was formed mainly by refugees from the rural areas. With help from the supporting USA churches, a beautiful church building was erected.

Five congregations with some 500 members in 1958 formed the Evangelical Lutheran Church–Colombia Synod. Missionary A.C. Morck (Canada) became its first president. The name "Synod" was deliberately chosen in the hope that the five Lutheran congregations of German and Scandinavian background (above) would likewise form a synod under the same title. During the preceding years, a warm relationship had developed between the two groups, encouraged by Stewart Herman, director of the Committee on Latin America of the LWF. Unfortunately, this hope did not materialize, and the present name was adopted in 1983.

When Protestant schools were again permitted, a fine, large school was established in the town of Sogamoso, northeast of Bogotá. Half of the children enrolled in 1959 were from the rural areas where the schools were still not allowed. Although the church was honored, it also felt the loss of the lay leadership of Gustavo Rodriguez, the director of the Bible Institute and the elementary schools, when he was chosen in 1962 to head the American Bible Society in Colombia. A decade later, he became the LWF Community Development Service's secretary for Latin America (until 1988).

Lacking leadership and students, the Bible Institute closed in 1964. However, in 1968, the church demonstrated its strength as an indigenous body by electing one of its own pastors, Pausanias Wilches, as president (1968–1977). He was succeeded by the Rev. Gerardo Wilches (1977–1983) and the Rev. Viesturs Pavasars (1983–1989).

ECUADOR

A republic, straddling the equator, on the northwest coast of South America. Area: 283,561 sq. km. (109,483 sq. mi.), including the Galápagos Islands (7992 sq. km. or 3086 sq. mi.), an insular province of Ecuador 960 kilometers (600 miles) offshore. Pop. (1984 est.): 9,114,900. Ethnic composition (1981): Quechua 41.3%; mestizo 40%; white 10%; black 5%; Amerindian 1%; other 2.7%. Cap.: Quito (pop., 1986, 1,093,278). Largest city and port: Guayaquil (pop., 1986, 1,509,108). Language: Spanish (official); Indians speak Quechua and Jivaroan.

History: The present Ecuador—once part of the Inca empire—was conquered by Spain in 1533. It gained independence in 1822 but remained a part of the state of Greater Colombia until 1830. Attempts to create a diversified economy have paralleled a prolonged political instability. In 1925, the army replaced the banking interests as the ultimate power. A new constitution (1979) inaugurated democratic presidential and legislative elections. A trans-Andean pipeline (1972) has enabled Ecuador to become one of the largest oil producers and exporters in Latin America. Yet its national debt is huge and poverty rampant.

Religion (1984): Roman Catholics 92.1%; Protestants 6.2%; other (including followers of Traditional religions, mainly Amazon jungle tribes) 1.7%.

Roman Catholicism is an outgrowth of Franciscan missions that began shortly after the Spanish conquest. Quito and other places are famed for their 17th-century churches and convents. Tensions, developed in the 19th century between "liberals" and the Roman Church, have continued. Roman Catholic bishops of German origin have tried to raise the level of Christian observance by the people. For several years, attention has been focused on the bishop of Riobamba, who is an avowed defender of Indian rights and an initiator of pastoral reforms.

The first Protestant missionaries were those of the Gospel Missionary Union (USA) in 1896. Today, the Evangelical Missionary Union Church is the largest Protestant body in Ecuador. It is active among the Jivaro Indians in the Amazon area, the mestizos on the coastal lowlands, and the Quechuas in the Andes. The Christian Missionary Alliance (1897) and the Seventh Day Adventists (1905) were other early arrivals. In 1945, four major USA churches—Evangelical and Reformed, Presbyterian, United Presbyterian, and Evangelical United Brethren—formed the United Andean Indian Mission with the intention of evangelizing the Indians in Ecuador, Peru, and Bolivia. However, the work has remained limited to Ecuador, and the resulting church is still small. Two of the larger churches are the Foursquare Gospel (1953) and the United Pentecostal (1959). Altogether, 35 Protestant churches and missions divide 160,000 adherents between them. Among the smallest are the Lutherans (below). In the 1970s, ecumenical dialogs began between Ecuador's Roman Catholics and Protestants.

Most of these missions and churches take part in the Ecuador Evangelical Fellowship (CEE; Confraternidad Evangélica Ecuatoriana), which replaced the Inter-Mission Fellowship in 1965.

The "Voice of the Andes," begun in 1931, has grown from an ambitious dream into one of the largest radio stations in the world. It broadcasts in 14 languages for a total of 1300 hours each week, and its 500-kilowatt transmitter is the largest in Latin America. Its USA multidenominational sponsor, the World Radio Missionary Fellowship, has a broad statement of faith and has been able to avoid political clashes with a succession of governments. This was not true of the widely active Summer Institute of Linguistics, which was expelled from Ecuador amid controversy over its work of translation among Indian tribes. Tragically, in 1956, five young American missionaries were killed by Auca Indians in the Amazon jungle. Later, the wife and sister of two of those killed returned to serve. Since then some 30 Aucas have been baptized, including the assassins.

Lutheran work in Ecuador began in 1951 with the World Mission Prayer League (a USA faith mission) taking responsibility for evangelical witness among the Quechua Indians in the provinces of Azuay and Cañar. This area had been abandoned by another agency after 28 years of labor (see below). Lutherans in recent years have also been involved in development.

The *Lutheran Church in America (now *ELCA) subsidized the Community Development Center at Banco de Arena, a few miles east of Milagro, in the flood plain between the Pacific Ocean and the Andes. The founder and director is a Lutheran laywoman whose Peace Corps experiences prompted her to continue serving the Ecuadorean Indians. The center is supported by the sale of her paintings and by contributions of Lutherans and Roman Catholics in Australia and Lutherans in the USA. The LCA gave a large subsidy for the purchase of the land (1973) and in 1982 sent a woman pastor from Canada to serve the community as counselor and chaplain. The standard of living among the Indians has been raised and a community spirit generated. Organic gardening, the introduction of milk cows and chickens, and a mobile clinic have improved the people's health. A trade school is providing new skills for the young people.

Lutheran World Relief (USA) supplements the United Brethren Foundation's work in Otavalo, a Quechua village in the Quito area. Here a four-member team has helped to establish a center for women to learn weaving and also experimental farms to increase food production.

FEDERATION OF EVANGELICAL LUTHERAN CHURCHES IN ECUADOR (FIEL)
(Federación de Iglesias Evangélicas) Luteranas en el Ecuador
Member: CEE
Membership: 721
President: The Rev. Martin Samaniego
Casilla 1334, Cuenca

FIEL, founded in 1963 as the Consejo Evangélico Luterano de Ecuador (CELE) by the congregations that had been formed by the World Mission Prayer League and the Lutheran World Federation, was reorganized in 1974 when it took its present name. It now also includes the congregations formed by the Norwegian Santal Mission. In 1988 there were altogether 16 congregations.

FIEL attempts to coordinate the development of the widely scattered and diverse work of the member congregations. Its main success has been in providing a legal entity for the registration of property. However, with the growing strength and independence of the members, it serves more and more as a church agency with active participation of local leaders. A common project is the radio station in Cañar, north of Cuenca. Short descriptions of the three groupings, beginning with the largest and oldest, follow.

ASSOCIATED NATIONAL CHURCH/ WMPL
Member: FIEL
Membership: 900**
Field Director: Mr. Lowell Quam
Bilingual School
Casilla 1334, Cuenca

The World Mission Prayer League has organized 11 of the 16 member congregations of the FIEL. Although, as noted above, the WMPL came to Ecuador in 1951 for the purpose of evangelization among the Quecha, by 1958 efforts had switched to the Spanish-speaking people in and around the mountain town of Cuenca.

Today they are served by 15 WMPL missionaries, aided by Ecuadorean evangelists and other church workers trained by missionaries through TEE. Recently the congregations have been encouraged to select young persons who qualify for LWF scholarships for study at the theological faculty in São Leopoldo, *Brazil.

The WMPL's largest project in Ecuador is its Bilingual School in Cuenca, founded in 1959. Instruction in both primary and secondary departments is in Spanish with only a remnant of English in the secretarial classes. The student body of 1225 includes a section for retarded children. The school has a bookstore and programs for training church workers. Its high standards have given it an excellent reputation throughout Ecuador. Scholarships for over 200 students are provided by Swedish and Norwegian churches.

EVANGELICAL LUTHERAN CHURCH IN ECUADOR (ELCE)

(Iglesia Evangélica Luterana en el Ecuador)
Member: (R), CLAI, FIEL
Pastor: The Rev. Uwe Mundt
Isabel La Católica 1431
Casilla 415-A, Quito

Together the two LWF-recognized congregations—Advent in Quito and Our Saviour's in Guayaquil—comprise the ELCE. Their pastor is supplied by the Foreign Office of the *Evangelical Church in Germany (EKD).

Only in 1953, when Stewart W. Herman visited Quito, did the LWF become aware of Lutherans in Ecuador. He found a small group of Lutherans and Reformed who had been worshiping in a Swiss home on high festivals. An American missionary of the Evangelical and Reformed Church had come into the city to serve them, but he soon left Ecuador. Since the group desired more frequent worship, Herman arranged to have Pastor Hermann Müller of Cali, *Colombia, come periodically. This he did until February 1955, when Pastor Odd Knävelsrud and his family arrived from Norway.

As in Venezuela, language groups in Ecuador—German, Scandinavian, and English—unitedly formed congregations in both lofty Quito and coastal Guayaquil. By 1958, with LWF assistance, a grateful Quito (Advent) congregation could dedicate a parsonage and church in a beautiful section of the city. Five years later, the Guayaquil congregation (Our Savior's) had a practical church

center in the suburb of Urdesa. Besides the congregational work, Knävelsrud began a mission to Scandinavian seamen, for almost every day there was a ship in port. He also arranged broadcasts to vessels at sea over the "Voice of the Andes" (above).

These congregations also attracted some Ecuadoreans, one of whom studied theology at the Lutheran seminary in *Argentina. Through their membership in FIEL, the congregations are increasingly abandoning their ethnic roots and assuming more responsibilities toward Ecuadorean society, not only in social but also in missionary terms.

LUTHERAN SOUTH AMERICAN MISSION OF NORWAY

Member: FIEL
Director: Mr. Berge Tope
Casilla 175
Cuenca

Three of the congregations belonging to FIEL were founded by the Norwegian Santal Mission. The NMS came to Ecuador in 1968, upon invitation of the WMPL, to supplement the ministry in Cuenca. Known in Latin America as the Lutheran South American Mission of Norway, its activities have extended into the mountainous and isolated areas where there are few roads or schools. Most of the people, Quechua-speaking Indians, although baptized Roman Catholics, are totally ignorant of the Christian faith. Some of the ancient Inca rites still prevail. A mobile health unit as well as radio and agricultural guidance programs are proving helpful to these rural people. The NSM provides the Bilingual School (WMPL) with a dormitory for students from the mountains.

The NSM, with assistance from the LWF/ DOC, has updated the FIEL radio station in Cañar. With increased wattage, the "Voice of the Inca Castle" broadcasts 15 hours a day (six in Quechua) and is an integral part of the educational and evangelical activities of both missions. Music supplements the development and religious programs as well as the news. NSM also provides social services in the slums of Quito and Guayaquil, and in Ambato it publishes and distributes Christian literature in both Spanish and Quechua.

PERU

A republic on the Pacific coast of South America. Area: 1,285,215 sq. km. (496,224 sq. mi.). Pop. (1986 est.): 20,207,100. European and mestizo 52%; Indian 46%; African, Chinese, Japanese, and other minorities. Cap. and largest city: Lima (metro. area pop., 1985 est., 5,523,600). Language: Spanish and Quechua, both official; plus Aymará, and many other Indian tongues.

History: Peru is famed as the home of the advanced Inca civilization, whose language was Quechua, and whose capital, Cuzco—high in the Andes—was the seat of the empire that at its peak dominated the entire Andean region. Just as Atahualpa, son of the last great Inca emperor, was regaining the unity of the realm, the Spanish invasion began. Francisco Pizarro, arriving in 1532, via a previously explored searoute from Panama, completed the conquest in less than six years. The audacious achievement of his small force was marred by his treachery—a course that cost him his life in 1541. Before that, however, he had founded the city of Lima (1535), capital of Spain's empire in the New World until the 19th century. The Inca culture was relentlessly hispanicized, but remnants of it in Lima's archaeological museum attest to a departed glory, even as the massive ruins at Cuzco recall its grandeur and final fortress. The Spaniards never discovered Machu Picchu, the last fortified stand of Inca civilization. It now draws awed visitors to its lonely heights.

From Lima, the viceroyalty of Peru in time included all Spanish lands on the continent except Venezuela. Spanish rule, in contrast to Incaic rule, appears to have been more oppressive, exploitive, and money-oriented. The great Inca rebellion ended an era.

Colonial Peru achieved independence from Spain in 1824 through the efforts of José de San Martín and Simón Bolívar leading the forces of a growing Creole (native-born Spanish) population. This did not improve the situation of the Indians. They withdrew more and more into the mountains as their fertile and once well-cultivated lands were taken over by owners of large estates. Peruvian society was sharply divided between the privileged rich and the masses of poor. The political situation alternated between revolts and dictatorships. A radical reform movement—the American Popular Revolutionary Alliance (APRA), launched in 1924—has kept up a continuing pressure for social justice and an equitable economic system. A moderate reformer, Fernando Belaúnde Terry, elected in 1963 and deposed five years later, was reelected in 1980. His successor, Alan García Peréz, in 1985 became the first president of Peru from the APRA party. Throughout the present century, Peru's struggle with reform has wavered between legislation recognizing the rights of Indians and other minorities, on the one hand, and the necessity of land reform and overcoming political bossism, on the other.

Religion: Roman Catholicism claims over 90% of the population; Protestantism, about 4%; disaffiliated and others, 6%.

For the Roman Catholic Church, Peru was long its stronghold in Spanish America. In contrast to *Mexico, the relationship in Peru was one of interdependence and spanned the centuries from 1536 to 1915. Even after the enactment of religious toleration, Roman Catholicism has continued to be favored. But whereas it long upheld the claims of the elite and wealthy minority, it has in recent decades given increasing support to the rights of the poor. An early precedent for this change occurred in the 16th and 17th centuries, when the church defended the Indians against their new rulers. Later on, however, the clergy often shared in taxing the masses for the benefit of the church.

Peru is not alone as a priest-poor country. Gone are the days when the sons of the well-to-do entered the priesthood and provided superior leadership in religion. The country's long history of higher education began in 1551 with the founding of San Marcos University in Lima. Much later, after toleration, a separate Catholic University was set up (1917). The Seminario Santo Toribio (1591) continues as Peru's major seminary, but its decline in enrollment is also a measure of the change faced by the church.

While an advancing secularism, often linked with Marxism, has created difficulties for the church, a much older problem is the persistence of a semi-pagan Catholicism among the Indians. The response to this situation by the Peruvian bishops, entitled, "On Justice in the World," is seen by some as the central pronouncement of the Latin American episcopate during the 1970s.

Protestantism is fragmented and accounts for only a small percentage of the population. Private worship by non-Roman Catholics was permitted after 1839, but public worship only after 1915. As in *Argentina and *Chile, Protestant beginnings go back to the early 1820s, when the British and Foreign Bible Society's agent, James Thomson, distributed the Scriptures and also introduced elementary schools. British and North American commercial connections facilitated an eventually broad diversity of Protestants to enter Peru. Anglicans (1849) were followed by Methodists (1877), German and Swiss Protestants (1897), and Seventh Day Adventists (1898). The latter, along with the Assemblies of God (1911), are today the two biggest Protestant church bodies. Baptists, Nazarenes, Plymouth Brethren, and many other groups round out the list. Mission work, both Protestant and Roman Catholic (Maryknoll), accelerated during World War I, when access to other parts of the world was difficult. During World War II, under similar circumstances, Wycliffe Bible translators entered Pucallpa in eastern Peru. There, on a tributary of the Amazon, they have painstakingly approached the highly diversified and isolated Indian tribes.

The Evangelical (Protestant) Council of Peru (ECP), formed in 1940, seeks to foster cooperation in common concerns. In 1966, the Methodists withdrew, charging that mission societies dominated the council. In 1972, they joined the World Council of Churches, becoming its only member in Peru. Most other Protestant groups look on the ecumenical movement with suspicion. A helpful impulse for cooperation was the initial meeting in Lima (1982) of the new Latin American Council of Churches (CLAI, see Latin American Introduction, above).

The Association of Theological Schools, organized in 1965 with a membership of 10, struggles to find a balance between groups requiring a professional ministry (like the Lutherans) and those fostering a lay ministry (like the Pentecostals). Overarching such concerns is the challenge to relate the gospel to social justice and an amelioration of the poverty burdening much of the population.

The Asociación Misionera Evangélica à las Naciones (AMEN; Evangelical Missionary Association to the Nations), begun in 1946 in a Methodist context, got new life in 1979 when a group of young people, led by Obed Alvarez, gave it an international vision. Today, AMEN emissaries, supported by Peruvians, are active in Latin American countries and in Spanish-speaking communities of Europe and North Africa. The youthful Alvarez also heads a modest school of missiology in Lima.

Lutherans gained an identity in Peru after World War II, when representatives of the LWF sought out neglected expatriate and refugee Lutherans and helped them form a multilingual congregation (below). This precipitated an outreach to Peruvians. Besides the churches and the work of their partners in mission, described below, there are now other Lutherans at work in Peru.

The **Norwegian Lutheran Mission** has been active in Peru since the late 1970s. Known in Peru as Centro Biblico, it is directed by the Dr. Arno Espegren (Apartado 1387, Arequipa). Several small Spanish-speaking congregations have been formed in Arequipa, the second largest city in Peru with a population of some 500,000. They are the result of social work and evangelism aided by an extensive mass media program—radio and TV. High in the Andes around Lake Titicaca, medical, agricultural social service, and literacy programs reach the Quechua and Aymará people. Here, too, small congregations have been formed and a Bible School established in Juliaca, north of Puno.

In this same area, where some of the poorest of the poor live, Lutheran World Relief of the USA unites with other relief agencies in meeting survival needs and promoting self-help organizational structures, with special attention to the needs of women.

Lutherans have also led the way in developing a nationwide ecumenical media program. Until 1983, this Lima-centered outreach was known as Liga de Amigos Cristianos (The League of Christian Friends). Initiated in 1976 by the "Lutheran Hour" in Venezuela, it became a joint program with the *Lutheran Church in America (now ELCA) in 1978, when imported programs were prohibited. Under the direction of an LCA missionary, 250 Peruvian-produced programs a week—in Spanish and Quechua—were broadcast on local stations. Some were geared to the general public, others to young people. The Bible correspondence courses enrolled thousands. In Arequipa, a coastal city farther south, TV programs were offered.

A 1982 evaluation indicated the need for more indigenous control and program production. With a board of selected individuals within the Protestant community in Peru, the program was reorganized in 1983 as the "Servico Ecuménico de Pastoral y Estudios de la Comunicación" (SEPEC). Its purpose is to promote the understanding and use of media within Protestant churches and organizations for evangelization, social work, and development. The ELCA continues its support through the LWF/DOC, which adopted the project.

CHRISTIAN CENTER—MISSION OF THE EVANGELICAL LUTHERAN SYNOD IN PERU

(Centro Cristiano—Misión del Sínodo Evangélico Luterano en el Perú)
Member: ECP
Membership: 486**
Coordinator: The Rev. Timothy E. Erickson
Mariano Carranza 826
Santa Beatriz, Lima 1

This independent national church consists of five small Spanish-speaking congregations situated in Lima, Chimbote (on the coast north of Lima), and in the surrounding mountain villages. They are served by nine pastors. A church council oversees the work.

Pastors are trained by the Mission of the Evangelical Lutheran Synod in Peru (MELSP) in its extension seminary. The MELSP, which began the work in 1968, continues its mission outreach in the slums of Peru and in the mountain regions to the north in close cooperation with the Christian Center church it founded. The MELSP is supported by the *Evangelical Lutheran Synod/USA, a church that places great stress on confessional Lutheranism.

EVANGELICAL LUTHERAN CHURCH IN PERU (ELCP)

(Iglesia Evangélica Luterana en el Perú)
Member: (R), CLAI
Membership: 550**
President: Dr. Franz R. Sennhauser
Ricardo Rivera Navarrete 495
San Isidro, Lima 27

This small church body has developed within and around a congregation formed in 1950 under the auspices of the Lutheran World Federation. The intention was to embrace Lutherans of all languages, nationalities, and cultures. At present, the ELCP consists of four congregations. Two of these—one German-speaking and one Spanish-speaking—share a beautiful church edifice in the attractive San Isidro district of Lima. Their members are mainly business and professional people and include expatriates. Pastors for these congregations come from Germany, supplied by the *Evangelical Church in Germany (EKD) and the Evangelical Lutheran (Hermannsburg) Mission. Two small Peruvian congregations are located in the poorer district of Breña and in the squatter town of Julio C. Tello, 24 kilometers (15 miles) south of Lima. Several other embryo congregations are in slum areas. The Peruvian congregations have indigenous leaders trained by missionaries of the *Lutheran Church in America (now *ELCA) in a theological education by extension (TEE) program. All four congregations are self-supporting.

A church council, elected by the San Isidro congregations, is the decision-making body between their annual meetings. The ELCP generously supports its social service institution, Casa Belén, in the urban area of Lima. Its longtime program of day care for poor children is now augmented by other needed services, including medical care for children and mothers (below).

In 1983, the ELCP formed a legally recognized development branch known as *Diaconia*. A separate board of church members, with interest and expertise, now reviews and plans the work together with a representative of LWF World Service, the agency providing the service. This cooperative relationship with LWF/WS began after the devastating earthquake of May 1970, when the ELCP requested emergency aid to assist the church in meeting the needs of the survivors. This led to a continuing development program in the areas of Ancash, north of Lima, and Ayacucho, between Lima and Arequipa. The success of the self-help programs brought further requests for help from neighboring areas. A 1985 evaluation indicated that much has been done to improve the life of the highland Indians. Self-confidence and village morale have gained strength. In a few villages, evangelism has been introduced. This good news is accompanied by the fact that the highland

Indians still face the uncertainties of terror attacks by Maoist guerrillas, natural disasters of drought and flood, high inflation, and unemployment. The flow to the cities, curbed for a time by the project, has again increased.

● ● ●

The German-speaking congregation of the ELCP has a long but disrupted history. It dates from 1899 when Pastor Buegner arrived from Germany. This was two years after a group of Swiss Reformed and German Evangelicals (Lutheran, Reformed, and United) had formed a congregation. A school and church building in Callao soon followed, and the congregation affiliated with the Evangelical Church of the Old Prussian Union (*Germany). Pastor Buegner served with notable success for 25 years despite the general hostility of Catholicism. Two other pastors followed for brief periods. More often, the parish had to depend on annual or biennial visits from pastors located in Chile or Bolivia. In 1939, the church building was destroyed by an earthquake, and the following year the pastor had to leave. World War II caused the congregation's demise.

After World War II, LWF concern for European refugees and ethnic German communities focused on Latin America, including Peru. With interest and financial assistance from the USA National Lutheran Council, a German pastor began work in 1950 to "gather up the fragments." Already that year about 800 prospective members were located, some of whom formed a Lutheran congregation. Among them were 15 refugee families who had dared to start life anew in a financially depressed land. The needs of these families as well as the increasing awareness of other expatriates, especially the Scandinavians, persuaded the congregation to drop "German" from its name and to become a multilanguage parish, as urged by the LWF Committee on Latin America. To provide for the pastoral needs of the Germans, an agreement was made between the LWF and the Foreign Office of the *Evangelical Church in Germany (EKD). A modern building with facilities for worship and other congregational activities was dedicated in 1954. Since then, the congregation has been self-supporting and has contributed strong lay leadership for the numerous and varied programs of the ELCP.

From Casa Belén has come the most unifying of various outreach programs. It began in the early 1950s, when the German women's organization of the church extended welfare services to the children of the very poor. Soon members of the newly gathered (1953) Scandinavian congregation (below) lent a hand. A decade later, the purchase of a site and further funding—the Church of Sweden's Lutherhjälpen assisted via the LWF—culminated in new facilities. The festive dedication of the modern building included local officials and foreign guests from German, Norwegian, Swedish, and American churches.

In 1964, the ELCP requested *Lutheran Church in America (now ELCA) help in developing English and Spanish work. In 1965, a pastor arrived to serve the ELCP's English congregations. A year later, an LCA social worker joined the ELCP staff as director of Casa Belén. There followed ordained pastors, who worked among the poor. Around Casa Belén in Breña, the first congregation arose. Another developed 24 kilometers (15 miles) south of Lima in the squatter town of Julio C. Tello.

Many of the urban poor seeking employment in the big city or on the nearby plantations were Amerindians from the high mountains. Naturally the missionaries were attracted to the areas from which they had come. In the Andes, the Quechua "Lutheran Hour" broadcasts were heard, and some of the people were eager to hear more, including the charismatic Jesus Cuyo. Under his leadership and with the encouragement of occasional visits from a missionary, work began in the Yurimaguas area around Cuzco in 1970. This developed into a theological extension program (TEE) in the Quechua language with LCA missionaries as teachers (1972). This program was later discontinued.

After a thorough study to determine the best means of communicating the gospel to the people of the high Andean culture, the LCA worked out an agreement with the ELCP granting more flexibility for a holistic outreach and a team approach. In 1985, by friendly agreement, this work—launched under the auspices of the ELCP—became the autonomous mission of the Lutheran Church in America. As indicated, the ELCA missionaries continue to be supportive to the ELCP Peruvian congregations and missions, and the ELCA contributes to the Evangelical Lutheran Mission (Hermannsburg) work in Isidro. At two sites in the hinterland of the Andean region, the ELCP has started mission work in conjunction with the Hermannsburg Mission.

Since the ELCP has not been able to meet the needs of all Lutherans in Peru, as originally expected by idealistic founders, new avenues for uniting or federating the Lutherans in Peru are being studied.

NATIONAL EVANGELICAL LUTHERAN CHURCH OF THE ANDES

(Iglesia Evangélica Luterana Nacional Andina)
Member: CLAI
Membership: 120**
President: The Rev. Antero Espinoza V.
Apartado 4500, Lima 100

This legally registered and independent church is an offshoot of the ELCP (above). Congregations are located in the department of Lima and in the village of Victor Andrés Belaunde near Arequipa. The latter is a new settlement of very poor people. A woman pastor, Jenny Zavala Ames, began social work and evangelism here in 1979 after her ordination in Lima. In the urban area of Lima, there is a small congregation that meets in private homes to worship and to plan church and social work. It is mainly composed of young and middle-class people. There is also new outreach work in Chanchamayo and Puerto Bermúdez.

When the ELCP in the mid-1950s was beginning Spanish work, the young Peruvian, Antero Espinoza, was attracted to the congregation. After a period of demonstrated interest and commitment, he was received into membership through confirmation. His positive influence on the young people of the congregation singled him out as a prospective pastor. In 1964, he was enrolled in the Lutheran Theological Seminary in José C. Paz in Argentina. When he returned to Lima in 1970, he served within the ELCP. In 1972, language and cultural differences with the largely expatriate ELCP prompted him to begin an independent indigenous church.

SCANDINAVIAN CHURCH

(Iglesia Escandinava)
Membership: 400**
Pastor: The Rev. Bjørn Westlund
Juan Pezet 1965
San Isidro, Lima 27

This congregation ministers to all Scandinavians living in Peru as well as to the increasing number of Scandinavian tourists coming to Lima. The Swedish pastor also serves the Scandinavian Seamen's Mission in the port of Callao. The congregation's responsibility is to coordinate and administer the health education and human rights projects funded by the Church of Sweden.

The first Scandinavian worship service in Lima was in September 1953. Sponsored by the LWF Committee on Latin America, Pastor Åke Kastlund of Sweden officiated. For two decades or more, the Scandinavian congregation was affiliated with the multilingual Evangelical Lutheran Church in Peru (above), using its edifice for worship and other activities. In time it became independent. Every three or four months Pastor Odd Knävelsrud, a Norwegian, came to Lima from Quito, Ecuador, to serve the congregation. Transferred to Lima in 1961, he became the multilingual pastor to various groups (English, Spanish, Norwegian). In time, he gathered and served the Scandinavian community of about 400 souls. The same year (1961), Pastor Norgaard of Denmark opened the Seamen's Center in Callao (with LWF help), thus reviving work carried out before World War II.

Within the ELCP, the Scandinavian congregation actively participated in the development and support of Casa Belén (ELCP). At its dedication in 1965, both Kastlund and Knävelsrud as well as a representative of the Norwegian government participated. Through Lutherhjälpen, the Swedish Church provided $50,000 for the new social center.

VENEZUELA

A republic. Area: 912,050 sq. km. (352,144 sq. mi.). Pop. (1986 est.): 17,791,000, of whom mestizo 69%, European 20%, African

9%, Indian 2%. Cap. and largest city: Caracas (1987 est., 2,661,088). Language: Spanish.

History: The mouth of the River Orinoco was discovered by Columbus in 1498. In 1499, the coast was traced by Spanish navigators Ojeda and de la Cosa, and the country named "Little Venice." During a short-lived agreement (1528–1546) with the Welser merchant family of Augsburg, German explorers—notably Nikolaus Federmann—accomplished most of the Indian conquest while searching the Orinoco valley for the mythical El Dorado. Dominicans and Franciscans were the first missionaries (1513). In an effort to overcome the Indians' semi-nomadic lifestyle, they combined evangelization with development, introducing the Indians to cocoa, coffee, and sugar plantations as well as to stock raising. Spanish settlements—"reductions"—began on the coast, an adjunct area of New Granada, in 1520. Between 1658 and 1758, Capuchins founded about 100 missions around Caracas, and Jesuits opened stations along the Orinoco River.

The war of independence from Spain, begun in 1810 under Francisco de Miranda, was completed in 1821 by Simón Bolívar. During this struggle, many of the missions were destroyed. Between 1821 and 1830, when Venezuela was a part of the state of Greater Colombia, the church was further weakened, although ties between church and state continued. By dictatorial power, religious foundations, parish schools, and even theological seminaries were abolished. Priests were educated by the theological faculty of the state university. Except for a few centers, the Roman Catholic Church lost its intellectual influence with the upper classes, and also became an object of contempt among the masses. Independent Venezuela (1830) fairly early made attempts to restore the destroyed missions and to encourage the church's work among the Indians.

Dominated by military dictators from the landholding class for much of its history, the country has, since 1945, experienced periods of democracy and social reform. A revolt in 1958 ushered in free elections. Oil wealth has given Venezuela the highest per capita income in Latin America. Yet poverty grips the masses.

Religion: With this historical background, it is understandable that Roman Catholicism is not as strong in Venezuela as in other Latin American countries. While the number of claimed adherents exceeds 90%, the vast majority are nominal Catholics. A pastoral letter of 1967 deplored the spreading "practical atheism." An estimated 400,000 are Afro-American Spiritists, combining elements of Traditional African, Caribbean, and Amerindian religions with those of Roman Catholicism. The church has had a hard time recruiting candidates for the priesthood; thus most priests are Spanish. National sisters (nuns) are more numerous, and some of them have been given special training for service among the slum dwellers in Caracas. Among the young people, concern for the oppressed indicates an awakened spiritual life.

Although British and Foreign Bible Society representatives visited Venezuela in 1819 and the Anglicans began work among British nationals in 1832, it was not until 1883 that the first Protestant congregation was formed by the Canadian Brethren. Today, the Brethren church is one of the largest with a membership of over 20,000. USA Presbyterians arrived in 1897. Their growth has been slow in spite of their extensive institutional ministry. The largest churches are those of the Pentecostals (1916). Southern Baptists are active. In addition, there are a significant number of indigenous churches, the largest commonly known as Bethel Church. The first Lutheran congregation, formed in 1893, is now a part of a small body organized in 1985 (below). The Venezuela Council of Churches (Consejo Evangélico de Venezuela; 1967) includes most of the Protestant churches and missions. It has no external affiliations.

Traditional religions (1%) remain influential among people of the Chibcha, Arawak, and Carib families in the southern part of the country.

EVANGELICAL LUTHERAN CHURCH IN VENEZUELA (ELCV)

(Iglesia Evangélica Luterana en Venezuela)
Member: LWF (1986), CLAI
Membership: 4023**
President: The Rev. Georg Metzger
Apartado 68.738
YV—Caracas 1062-A

In 1985, nine of the 10 independent congregations that had been partners since 1959 in the Lutheran Council of Venezuela formed one church body. The Evangelical Lutheran Church in Venezuela (ELCV) was received into LWF membership a few months later. Most of the members are transplanted Europeans and their descendants as well as some expatriate Americans and Europeans living in Venezuela for shorter periods of time. The mother tongues are used in worship, but Spanish is the common denominator. Four of the congregations are a part of a five-component international parish in Caracas: German, Hungarian, Latvian, Scandinavian, and Spanish. Others are located in the interior: Valencia, Barquisimeto, Turen, Maracaibo, and San Cristobal.

The congregations of this new church, plus the Latvian—which opted to continue its membership in the Latvian Evangelical Lutheran Church in Exile (see Exile Churches)—have been individually recognized by the LWF since the 1950s and all have been members of the above-mentioned council. Although this council had no authority over its members, it served as a uniting force and a common voice. Since it lacked authority to ordain pastors, resolve conflicts, or initiate evangelism, the formation of a church body was essential. The goal was achieved through the dedicated efforts of Pastor Hanns-Henning Krull, president of the Lutheran Council in Venezuela, who could rely on the assistance of the LWF, especially through the Rev. Karl Gottschald, a former LWF Executive Committee member and former president of the Evangelical Church of the Lutheran Confession in Brazil.

One of the first responsibilities of the new church was to provide pastoral care and leadership for all the congregations. The one in the fast-growing industrial city of Valencia—its parish school enrolls over 600 students—has often been without a pastor. This also affects the congregation in Barquisimeto, which depends upon Valencia for pastoral care. Maracaibo, the oil center, has been served from Caracas for several years. The small German and Hungarian congregation in San Cristobal depends mainly on lay services, with only occasional pastoral visits from Caracas.

Among the internal problems of the ELCV are those created by small numbers, especially in the outlying congregations. Likewise, the fact of a still divided Lutheranism

in Venezuela (below) weighs heavily on the ELCV agenda. The difficulty of providing an indigenous ordained ministry for the congregations is intensified by the great distance to the Lutheran seminaries in Argentina and southern Brazil. Meanwhile, the largest of the components, the German-speaking St. Michael congregation, has ties with the *Evangelical Church in Germany (EKD) and receives pastors through its Foreign Office. Yet the ELCV's own diversity gives it an ecumenical potential of more than ordinary significance.

The ELCV continues to carry out the LWF/CDS projects of the former council. In Caracas, these include a primary and vocational training school and a child creativity center in the Santa Ana slum area. Other projects are with the Venezuelan Evangelical Committee for Justice (CEVEJ) and with the Latin American Federation of Farmworkers in its attempt to assess the ways of food production in Latin America.

In 1985, LWF World Service, in cooperation with the ELCV, established a program of assistance to Haitians and Haitian refugees living in Venezuela. During the early 1980s, the ELCV developed contacts with them. They were members of the largest labor union in Haiti, CATH, and its local committee, ACODESHA (Association for Cooperation and the Development of the Haitian Community). ACODESHA also coordinates other regional work of CATH from its Venezuela offices. The LWS Caribbean-Haitian program, which also has its regional field office in Venezuela, works with ACODESHA in providing assistance to grass-roots groups, with community organization, advocacy and legal assistance, vocational and leadership training, communication, and self-help projects (see Haiti, above).

• • •

This new church has a unique history. Already in the 1870s, Protestant Christians living in Roman Catholic Venezuela envisioned an international church that would include Danish, Dutch, English, and German Christians. Unfortunately this plan failed. Thereupon, the Prussian Union Church assisted the Germans in forming their own congregations. As pastoral services were not always available, there were extended periods when the congregation had to rely on ships' captains for services, baptisms, and weddings. During World War II, Venezuela suspended German activities and seized German property, including that of the congregation. This was a great handicap just when a large influx of postwar immigrants needed a church. After the normalization of relations between Germany and Venezuela, the congregation held a last general assembly, dissolved the German congregation and formed its successor—the German-speaking San Miguel (St. Michael) congregation.

The flow of displaced persons—proportionately heavy to Venezuela—included Hungarians. While still in a refugee camp and without a pastor, they held their first worship service in 1948. By 1950, a "Provisional Presbyterium" was formed and held monthly services in a borrowed church, mainly under lay leadership. For two years, the congregation sought a pastor, a difficult task due to the reduced financial circumstances of the members.

The Latvian refugees in Caracas fortunately had among them Pastor Teabald Aviks, who early established contact with Dr. Stewart Herman, then director of the LWF Service to Refugees and in 1952 director of the LWF Committee on Latin America. Herman encouraged Aviks to hold German and Latvian services and employed him as the local LWF representative.

Earlier, in 1951, the USA National Lutheran Council's Division of Cooperation in Latin America had sent Pastor and Mrs. Fred Kern to locate and serve the Lutherans in Venezuela. In early 1952, as a result of these preliminary surveys, the LWF/CLA sent three pastors: a German, Dr. Heinrich Falk; a Hungarian-American, Pastor George Posfay; and a Latvian, Pastor Alfred Gulbis. Each of these pastors spoke three languages and all began to study Spanish. Their work prospered: Monthly attendance at worship averaged over 1000, and a Lutheran school was established with an enrollment of 156.

By October 1952, the three distinct language groups, having a common faith, formed one congregation, the Evangelical Church of the Resurrection. Its unique constitution provided opportunity for additional groups (or chapters) to be included. In 1954, a Scandinavian group—comprising Danish, Norwegian, Swedish, and Finnish expatriates—was formed after preparatory visits of Bishop Elis Malmeström from Sweden and Pastor Åke Kastlund, then serving in *Colombia. The first Swedish pastor, Hilding Hasselmyr, arrived in May 1956. A year of language study in Costa Rica prepared him for his second task of coordinating the youth program in Spanish among the four linguistic groups.

With the aid of the LWF, which had established a revolving fund for Venezuela, a church center was begun in 1955 and dedicated in 1957 with Bishop Hanns Lilje, then president of the LWF, presiding. The strikingly modern and beautifully situated Church of the Resurrection was complete with facilities allowing for two worship services at the same time, rooms for education and fellowship, church offices, quarters for pastors' families and others—all made possible by local gifts plus help from many lands channeled through the LWF. In 1958, an American pastor, William H. Balkan, arrived to explore the whole field of further work in English.

Meanwhile, in 1953, congregations were being formed under similar circumstances in Valencia, Barquisimeto, and Turen. After 1956, they too were granted recognition by the LWF. By 1960, all three had church facilities and parsonages. Dutch Lutherans and others, many of them oil company personnel, formed congregations in Maracaibo (1956) and San Cristobal (1957).

These developments reflected the new self-awareness among Lutherans in other parts of Latin America as well. The succession of All-Latin America Lutheran conferences that began in 1951 (see Latin America Introduction), with their joy over unity amid a freshly gathered diversity, made special note of developments in Venezuela. The multilingual parish plan, as in Caracas, grew in large part out of the far-sighted leadership of Dr. Paul C. Empie (at that time director of the USA national committee/LWF). Through others who shared his vision for Latin America, the Caracas multiparish in 1956 became the first of its kind to receive LWF status as a recognized congregation. Not surprisingly, tensions and discord occasionally marred the basic unity. Nevertheless, the creation of a permanent church body in 1985 reaffirmed the courage of the pioneers three decades earlier.

LUTHERAN CHURCH OF VENEZUELA (LCV)

(Iglesia Luterana de Venezuela)
Member: ILC
Membership: 890**
President: The Rev. Alcides Franco
Apartado 60387
YV—Caracas 1060A

Organized as a legal entity in 1956, this church body today consists of 13 congregations and is served by seven national pastors, 18 expatriate missionaries of the *Lutheran Church–Missouri Synod, and two expatriate missionaries of the *Evangelical Lutheran Church of Brazil.

The LCMS sent its first missionaries to work in Caracas in 1951. Later, work was begun in the rural areas of Monagas state through the efforts of a German lay worker. In order to strengthen an urban evangelism emphasis, the number of missionaries increased greatly between 1984 and 1986.

The "Lutheran Hour"—in Venezuela since 1954—is another asset for evangelization. With offices and studio in Caracas, programs are prepared in Spanish for Venezuela, Colombia, Peru, Ecuador, Bolivia, Panama, Chile, the Dominican Republic, Spain, and the USA. A branch office in Peru coordinates the production in Quechua and Aymará to reach the 12 million persons using these tongues in Ecuador, Peru, and Bolivia. About 2500 students are enrolled in the five Bible courses given in these three languages. In Venezuela, special emphasis has been placed on reaching young people.

The LCV has gained from the usual Missouri Lutheran accent on education. A primary and high school in Caracas has 600 students. Preschool education is offered in the barrios. One congregation operates a medical and dental clinic. An active program of theological education by extension (TEE) operates in most congregations.

The church participates in Lutherans United in Communication (LUC) and is a member of the International Lutheran Conference.

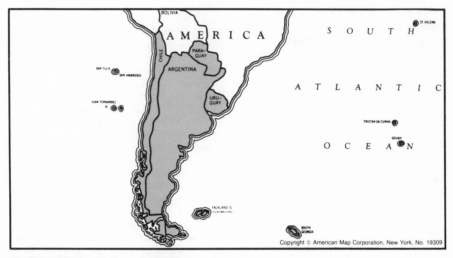

Copyright © American Map Corporation, New York, No. 19309

SOUTHERN CONE

Southern Cone, including Argentina, Chile, Paraguay, and Uruguay, has some 119,762 Lutherans—9.8% of all Lutherans in South America. Spanish is the dominant language.

ARGENTINA

A federal republic with a liberal constitution (1853, 1956). Area: 2,780,092 sq. km. (1,073,399 sq. mi.). Pop. (1985 est.): 30,564,000, almost entirely of European descent, mainly Spanish and Italian, but also French, German, Swiss, British, and many other nationalities, including Hungarian, Latvian, Slav, and other post-World War II refugees. Cap. and largest city: Buenos Aires (pop., 1980, 2,924,829). Language: Spanish, official.

History: Between the discovery of the Rio de la Plata estuary (1516) and the proclamation of independence (1816), Argentina—the land of silver, as named by early explorers—was claimed by Spain. During this period, the primitive and scattered Indian tribes were pushed farther into the interior and Spanish colonists took over. Buenos Aires became the capital of a Spanish viceroyalty in 1776.

Independence was followed by periodic unrest in the region, including armed conflict with Brazil, Uruguay, and Paraguay. Despite

the constitution of 1853, in effect until 1949, the country continued to suffer political instability. In 1944, Colonel Juan Perón seized power and established a popular dictatorship with the support of his second wife, Eva, the army, and the Roman Catholic Church. Eva's death in 1952 and the following economic depression led to Perón's ousting (1955) by the military. Eighteen years later, he returned from exile and won the election with his third wife, Isabel Martínez, his running mate. With her succession, following his death in 1974, terrorism and inflation increased. A military coup took over in 1976, and the "dirty war" followed. Some 9000 people disappeared during the campaign against leftist urban guerrillas as well as people working for social justice.

With General Galtieri as president, Argentina in 1982 occupied the Malvina (Falkland) Islands, long coveted from the British. Military defeat caused Galtieri's resignation and strong public criticism of the military government. A democratically elected President, Raúl Alfonsín (1983), revoked the law giving amnesty to military personnel accused of violating human rights. The ensuing civil trial of military leaders in 1985 convicted and sentenced two to life imprisonment and gave three others less severe sentences. The trial, in which military leaders were held responsible for actions committed under their government (30,000 people disappeared), was the first of its kind in Latin America. It was expected to warn other countries where human rights are ignored.

President Alfonsín's other serious problems included his country's immense international debt, spiraling inflation, and mounting labor unrest. An agreement (1984) between leaders in government and labor—negotiated during Isabel Perón's brief return from Spain—pointed out ways to social justice, economic growth, national unity, and a democratic system. The same year, Argentina and Chile signed a treaty at the Vatican, settling their long-standing dispute in the far south over the Beagle Channel. This country, weary of conflict and war, continues to reorder its life.

Religion: Although freedom of religion is guaranteed by law, Roman Catholicism has been the official and publicly maintained religion since independence in 1816. Some 90% of the people are nominal adherents, but this number continues to decrease and practicing Catholics are around 10%. Protestantism is increasing at a faster rate than the population. The strong Jewish community of half a million—the largest in Latin America and the fifth largest in the world—is mainly in the Buenos Aires area. Traditional Indian religions have largely disappeared, except among the Chiriguano. The Guaraní- and Quechua-speaking Indians, emigrating from Paraguay (and, to a lesser extent, Bolivia) to work in the sugar plantations, are also Traditionalists. Islamic communities, founded by Arab immigrants, are increasing and to a lesser degree Bahai is spreading. Many intellectuals and labor leaders profess no religion. Spiritism and oriental cults have large followings in the urban areas.

Roman Catholic structure includes 12 archdioceses and 39 dioceses. The priests and other church vocations as well as the lay apostolic workers are mainly middle-class Argentinians. This has developed from the time of independence, when a strong anti-Spanish feeling drove Spanish priests out of the country. The four million immigrants who arrived between 1857 and 1950—from Italy (46%),

Spain (31%), Ireland, Germany, Poland, and other European countries—have greatly enlarged and strengthened the Catholic church. Immigration from the Ukraine after 1897 accounts for the present 100,000-member Ukrainian-rite Catholic Church, which is in communion with Rome. During the "dirty war," as it was called, the Roman Catholic hierarchy upheld the military government even though 100 priests were imprisoned and some 20 had disappeared. Several bishops spoke out boldly against the system. Among them was Bishop Jorge Novak, a strong advocate of "the church of the poor" as stressed at the Medellín (1968) and Puebla (1979) conferences (see Latin America Introduction). In 1976 and 1977, the church issued two documents critical of the government, but both concentrated on the workers' right to work, health care, and education, and made little mention of human rights violations.

Beginnings of an evangelical witness in Argentina date from 1818, when James Thomson, a Baptist lay-reader, came to Argentina with a supply of Bibles. Connected with the British and Foreign Bible Society and also the English and Foreign School Society, he sold the Bibles widely, often with the enthusiastic help of priests and bishops. He opened dozens of schools based on the Lancastrian System of Education, a 19th-century literacy campaign for children. When Roman Catholic reaction set in, he had to leave (1821).

English (1824) and Scottish immigrants were the first to establish congregations, and they were helpful to the German and Swiss Protestants in establishing theirs. The English took interest in the Mataco Indians. Missioning Methodists from North America (1836) drew their membership mainly from the immigrants of Northern Europe. The Methodist church remains small but influential. Several Baptist groups—some from Russia—were united in the Argentine Baptist Convention (1908), one of the largest denominations. Pentecostals, including some Scandinavians, are not as strong as in most Latin American countries.

The Argentina Federation of Evangelical Churches (Federación Argentina de Iglesias Evangélicas; AFEC), formed in 1958, unites 28 of the approximately 70 church bodies in the country, including most of the Lutheran.

A Peace and Justice Movement, headed by the 1981 Nobel peace prize winner, Adolph Perez Esquivel, won the support of Bishop Novak (above) as well as some of the Protestant churches. Statements supporting human rights were issued by the United Evangelical Lutheran Church (below) in 1982 and by the Evangelical Methodist Church and the AFEC in 1983.

The Instituto Superior Evangélico de Estudios Teologicos (ISEDET), situated in Buenos Aires, was formed in 1970 by a merger of the Union Theological Seminary and the Lutheran Theological Seminary (below). Union, founded in 1884, had been in Buenos Aires since 1916 and was long considered the strongest Protestant theological school in Latin America. First supported by Methodists and Waldensians, it was later joined by Presbyterians and Disciples.

The Lutheran Seminary, founded in 1955, not only served the Evangelical Church of the River Plate and the United Evangelical Lutheran Church, but also the other Spanish-speaking churches in South America affiliated with the Lutheran World Federation. It was largely supported by the *Lutheran Church in America (now ELCA) and the LWF. Lutheran participation in ISEDET was welcomed as an important ecumenical element. Although the Lutheran faculty quickly became respected colleagues, integration also brought problems. Confessional identity, the give-and-take between students and faculty, and the relation of church and academia posed ever new challenges. For a while, it was not easy to discover how these could best be overcome, and they were compounded by financial problems and the general disruption caused by political upheaval. During the 1980s, the problems have been largely overcome, and there is renewed confidence in this large and important institution for the training of pastors and teachers. ISEDET is the one theological school in Argentina authorized to confer a doctor's degree. For Lutherans, the school remains ready to serve all Spanish-speaking churches in South America. Lutheran financial support continues to come mainly from the ELCA and the LWF.

Lutheranism came to Argentina during the 19th century. First German and then Danish and Swedish immigrants formed their separate communities. Pastors sent from Europe gathered congregations, most of which are incorporated into the three church bodies described below. Those still independent require some recognition.

Danish, Finnish, and Swedish congregations in Buenos Aires were initially set up to serve seamen. They reflect the importance of that port in world trade. Pastors from Finland and Norway continue to serve these missions. The **Danish Church in Buenos Aires** (Carlos Calvo 257) has a membership of 284. Its use of the Spanish language attracts some of non-Danish background, especially young people.

The many Danes who settled in the rural region 300 to 450 kilometers (190 to 280 miles) south of Buenos Aires in the late 19th century formed three communities. The congregation in the coastal town of Necochea, known as the **Protestant Society of the South-East,** (Pastor: The Rev. Steen Lerfeldt, Calle 5 No. 2966, 7630 Necochea, Pcia. de Buenos Aires) is affiliated with the Danish Church Abroad and receives pastors from the Evangelical Lutheran Church in Denmark. With a membership around 700, its mission is to provide occasional Danish services to other congregations in Argentina as well as to a Scandinavian congregation in São Paulo, Brazil. Inland from Necochea, the **Protestant Society in Southern Argentina,** centered in the town of Tres Arroyos (9 de Julio 392, 7500 Pcia. de Buenos Aires), has a pastor, Aldo Raúl Bidán, who is not of Danish descent. He serves some 4000 Danish-Argentinians. The congregation has a lay president Poul Dam.

The **Danish Congregation, Tandil,** considerably south of Buenos Aires, is the oldest (1866). Its 100th anniversary observance drew special guests, including Denmark's Princess Benedikte, Bishop Fugalsang-Damgaard (Copenhagen), and the then president of Argentina, Arturo Illia.

The independent **German Evangelical Lutheran Church,** Buenos Aires (1000 Correo Central) reports a membership of 7500. When it was formed after 1945, its membership was mainly recent emigrants from Germany. In the last 10 years, its membership has increased. The first and present pastor, Wilhelm Schön, formerly served in the Evangelical Church of the River Plate and then in the UELC.

The **Swedish Congregation in Buenos Aires** (President: The Rev. Paul Lundell,

Azopardo 1428, 1107 Buenos Aires) continues to serve seamen, but it also reaches out to short-term Swedish residents and to descendants of Swedish immigrants in Argentina and Uruguay. Under the jurisdiction of the archbishop of Uppsala, it maintains working relations with the Church of Sweden Abroad. For some time the congregation was served by Dr. Béla Lesko (1922–1988), a Hungarian refugee who had his theological education in Sweden and later was received on the pastoral roll of the Church of Sweden. He had served the Argentine Evangelical Lutheran Church (UELC, below) as president of the Lutheran seminary and then as professor at the ISEDET (above).

The **Lutheran Council of the River Plate** was formed in 1972—after a UELC overture for a merged church was rejected. Its membership includes the Argentine Evangelical Lutheran Church, the Evangelical Church of the River Plate, the United Evangelical Lutheran Church, and the independent Scandinavian congregations described above.

The council members have a history of working together since the late 1940s and 1950s, when they helped settle European refugees sponsored by the LWF Refugee Service. Strengthened by the Committee on Latin America, under the direction of Stewart Herman, this interest continued and was mutually helpful. For example, at the suggestion of the LWF member church, the UELC, the Argentine LWF national committee, formed in 1953, included representatives of Latvian, Hungarian, German, and Slovak congregations, as well as representatives from the two nonmember church bodies. Besides sponsoring fellowship activities to break down the barriers of language and culture, this committee carried out a stiff program of work in the areas of theology, world service, stewardship, and evangelism. In 1954, it published a directory of all Lutheran congregations and institutions in Argentina.

This committee's role was most helpful in preparing the way for establishing the Lutheran Theological Seminary in Buenos Aires. The preliminary proposal, drawn up by a Hungarian refugee pastor, Béla Lesko, was accepted by the then United Lutheran Church in America and the Committee on Latin America of the LWF. It appeared to solve the pastoral training needs of all Spanish-speaking Lutheran churches in South America.

With financial assistance from the ULCA and the LWF, the seminary opened in the pre-theological school of the UELC in 1955. Its board of directors included representation from the Lutheran churches in *Colombia, *Peru, *Uruguay, and *Venezuela as well as Argentina.

In 1956, the seminary moved into an adequate new structure in the suburb of José C. Paz. Within a few years, it had a full, well-trained faculty, a good library, and adequate housing facilities for faculty and for the growing student body. By 1958, the school was received into membership of the American Association of Theological Schools. A 1963 survey revealed that of the 24 graduates, 18 were serving as pastors, two were doing graduate work abroad (seven had already done so), and two were ready to teach at the seminary. Even though its positive influence on the churches in Argentina as well as on other countries cannot be overestimated, it had a short life. By the late 1960s, a troubled nation brought changes, including a drastic drop in students for the ministry. Protestant Christians were drawn together, and most of the Lutherans were ready for fuller ecumenical partnership. In 1970, the Lutheran Seminary merged with Union Theological Seminary to form ISEDET (above).

During the 1970s, when neighboring Chileans were suffering after the change of government, many Lutherans—remembering the help once received—joined with Methodists and others in tiding over Chilean refugees. This was at the cost of frequent misunderstandings and even threats of violence. However, a period of growth in self-reliance and of transition to Argentine culture ensued, as the following church descriptions attest.

ARGENTINE EVANGELICAL LUTHERAN CHURCH (AELC)

(Iglesia Evangélica Luterana Argentina)
Member: LCRP
Membership: 28,770**
President: The Rev. Roberto Kroeger
Ing. Silveyra 1639/41
1607 Villa Adelina
Prov. Buenos Aires

This church—earlier a district of the Lutheran Church–Missouri Synod—by the mid-1980s attained partnership status with that body. Congregations of the LCMS in Chile, Uruguay, and Paraguay are satellites of the AELC. Altogether, the 150 congregations and 71 preaching points are served by 68 pastors. The 132 Argentina congregations are widely scattered. There are nine congregations and seven preaching points in the Buenos Aires area. Others are in the interior, including the cities of Rosario and Bahia Blanca. Other city churches are in Montevideo, the Uruguayan capital, and in Valparaiso, Chile. Convention action (1987) approved new mission sites in northern and central Argentina. Membership is mainly middle class, including farmers, merchants, carpenters, and school teachers.

The congregations maintain 13 Christian day schools, enrolling 2836 pupils. Even in a period of high inflation, inactive church members are willing to pay tuition for good Christian education for their children. The government helps by providing salaries for full-time teachers with 30 or more students. A mission congregation in Córdoba, the nation's second largest city, began with a kindergarten in 1971 and now has a full elementary school with 530 children. Parents are asking for a high school.

As in the LCMS, emphasis has been placed on secondary and professional education. A pre-theological school in Crespo—not far from Paraná, the capital of the province of Entre Ríos—operated from 1926 to 1950. Future pastors attended Concordia Seminary in Pôrto Alegre (*Brazil) until 1942, when Seminario Concordia opened in Argentina. In 1948, this seminary found its permanent location, also for a Colegio, some 18 kilometers (10 miles) northwest of midtown Buenos Aires in Villa Ballester (called José Léon Suárez since 1970). A preparatory school, Colegio Concordia, far to the northwest from the national capital, has functioned in Obera, Misiones, since 1956.

A valuable educational and evangelism tool is the Argentine "Lutheran Hour." It reaches into many homes, also beyond the Andes. In Chile, the congregations in Viña del Mar and Valparaiso have sprung from these Lutheran Hour broadcasts.

LCMS mission work in Argentina was an offshoot of the work in *Brazil. Beginning in 1905 in the Entre Ríos province among the German and German Russian immigrant farmers, the work spread into the Misiones province and from there into Paraguay.

Most of the AELC membership derives from those twice-removed German Lutherans whose forebears originally settled in southern Russia's Ukraine and Volga regions (*USSR) during the 18th and 19th centuries. Periodic famine and other pressures brought them to South as well as North America during the late 19th century. Still other Russian Germans emigrated to Argentina after World War I.

Among ready-made Lutherans, education and stewardship were two prime demands of a basically pastoral ministry. Henry Wittrock, the first pastor, years later recounted harrowing tales of pioneering in San Juan, then a small settlement among others around Urdinarrain, Entre Ríos. His three years in Brazil (1902–1905) had already taken their toll, and two additional years in Argentina brought him and his family back to the USA exhausted. Yet he was the first Missourian on the Argentine field, and the 1400-member San Juan congregation remains the mother church of today's AELC. Spanish work, begun in 1924 in Buenos Aires, expanded gradually.

The AELC has cooperated with the other Lutheran churches in various undertakings. The LWF-coordinated refugee resettlement projects after World War II opened doors to other ventures. In publications, Concordia Seminary professors for more than two decades worked closely with colleagues in the other bodies to produce the now completed 10-volume Spanish edition of Luther's works. In confessional unity there have been gains, even though the AELC could not accept the overture from the UELC to form a merged Lutheran church.

It was not possible for a district of the Missouri Synod outside the USA to join a national move toward Lutheran Union. It did not work in Argentina, nor a little later in Canada. However, already in 1972, the AELC had worked with the UELC and the ECRP (below) to form the Lutheran Council of the River Plate (above).

EVANGELICAL CHURCH OF THE RIVER PLATE (ECRP)
(Iglesia Evangélica del Río de la Plata)
Member: WCC, CLAI, AFEC, LCRP
Membership: 47,000**
President: The Rev. Rodolfo Reinich
Sucre 2855, piso 3
1428 Buenos Aires

At least three features lend distinction to this body: First, it is international, having three congregations in *Uruguay and eight in *Paraguay. Second, it is a United (*Germany) church, with 90% of its members Lutheran and others Reformed. And third, it is the oldest (1843) Lutheran-related church in Argentina and over the past four decades has played a pivotal part in ecumenical endeavors as well as in furthering cooperation among Lutherans.

Headquarters of the Evangelical Church of the River Plate are in Buenos Aires near the city center. For well over a century, its base has been the point of contact for the many congregations gathered among German and Swiss Protestants and their descendants. Twenty-four of today's 35 ECRP parishes are in Argentina. Most of them are rural, and each has one or more congregations and a number of preaching points. The ECRP as a whole has the services of 36 ordained pastors and 17 vicars, six of the latter being women. While in the past all pastors came from Germany, at present only 14 have been supplied through the *Evangelical Church in Germany's (EKD) Foreign Office, and only five of the vicars are from abroad. Increasing numbers of ECRP pastors are Argentine-educated graduates of ISEDET (above)—or, earlier, of the former Lutheran Theological Seminary in José C. Paz, which merged with ISEDET in 1970.

In Argentina, the ECRP has congregations in major cities such as Buenos Aires, Rosario, and Córdoba and in the provinces of Buenos Aires, Córdoba, Chaco, Entre Ríos, Mendoza, Misiones, Río Negro, and Santa Fe. Worship services are conducted in Spanish as well as in German. Various diaconic agencies, supported by congregations, include children's homes, retirement centers, and residences for students.

Ecclesially, the ECRP has come into its own since World War II. Organized as the German Evangelical La Plata Synod in 1899, it only slowly disengaged itself from its German ties. A negotiated agreement in 1956 made the River Plate Synod independent of the Evangelical Church in Germany, but it retained a close working relationship. The ECRP adopted its present name in 1965, dropping the word German from its title. Its independence coincided with its joining the World Council of Churches in 1956. Having overcome earlier tendencies toward a cultural Protestantism, the ECRP became increasingly active ecumenically as a member of the Argentine Federation of Evangelical Churches (AFEC) and also of the more recently formed Latin American Council of Churches (CLAI). ECRP helped form and continues as a member of the Lutheran Council of the River Plate. Although not a member, the ECRP has cooperated closely with the LWF since the late 1940s.

ECRP also participates in the Christian Communication Center (Centro Evangélico Cristiano—CEC), the Protestant publishing firm, "La Aurora"; the Argentine Bible Society (Sociedad Bíblica Argentina); the Argentine Commission on Refugees (Comisión Argentina para los Refugiados—CAREF); and the United Mission Federation (Junta Unida de Misiones—JUM).

● ● ●

Historically, the roots of the ECRP run back to the early 19th century. Not long after Argentine independence, young businessmen and others from Germany settled in Buenos Aires. For a time, as Hermann Schmidt's centennial history (1845–1943) relates, their spiritual needs were attended by the newly-formed Anglican church (1825) and by the Scottish Presbyterian. After the British and the French, the Germans were the third largest foreign colony in Buenos Aires, and the records of the Anglican church (1825–1842) show 58 baptisms of children born to parents with German names. The Protestants among the Germans were unitedly determined to have a church of their own. With enterprising businessmen at the helm, they began raising funds. The obliging minister of the Scottish church—he had been in Argentina for 15 years—in 1842 drafted a letter fully descriptive of the kind of pastor required by an ethnic congregation in a foreign land. This letter accompanied the request sent by the Germans in Buenos Aires to the Evangelical Mission Society in Bremen, Germany, and in September 1843 August Ludwig Siegel began an 11-year ministry in Buenos Aires.

For nearly a decade, the Germans worshiped in their mother tongue every Sunday afternoon in the Anglican church. Siegel's leadership in various fields pointed up the will to unity in the ever-growing group. An evangelical school provided the desired alternative to a Roman Catholic education. Confirmation prepared the young for informed commitment to the Christian faith and life. Music uplifted the community. Already in 1844, a benefit concert for the church building fund attracted wide attention when the German congregation, using the facilities of the new North American Methodist church, presented Haydn's oratorio, "The Creation."

In 1847, a church site on Esmeralda was secured, and in 1853 the completed edifice, designed by an English architect, was dedicated, an occasion marked by guests from other Protestant churches as well as from top ranks of the government. Only a Roman Catholic greeting was missing. After Europe's "Year of Revolution"—as 1848 was called—immigration picked up. As the German Protestant community grew, it also became more scattered. A visionary Argentine merchant, Aaron Castellano, promoted the recruiting of settlers from Germany, Switzerland, and northern France for colonizing the interior. In 1855, the Esperanza settlement up the Paraná River in Santa Fe province led the way. More colonies followed in that province as well as to the east, in Entre Ríos. The Protestants among these German and Swiss settlers presented the Buenos Aires congregation with a lively home missionary challenge. By 1857, a congregation was formed in Montevideo, *Uruguay, and served semiannually from Buenos Aires. Soon after Siegel's return to Germany (1854), other pastors were sent. By 1863, the first pastors' conference showed the makings of a synod. An international note sounded from two sides in 1868 when Hermann Borchard and his colleagues in *Brazil launched the proposal for a German Evangelical synod. A decade of periodic visits and exchanges of information ensued. Similarly, from *Chile came an overture from two German pastors and an expressed desire for continuing fellowship in

ministry. After 1880, these occasional pastoral meetings and exchanges seem to have ceased, but only for a while.

More settlers continued to arrive. In 1893 at Asunción, where the Paraguay and Pilcomayo Rivers join, the first German congregation in *Paraguay was formed. It, too, had ties with the mother church in Buenos Aires. When the pastor of the mother church became overburdened, the executive office of the Evangelical Church in Berlin sent a pastor to serve as itinerant among the mushrooming rural communities. By 1899, at the urging of Wilhelm Bussmann, pastor of the mother church, plans were adopted for an organizational convention, and in 1900 the German Evangelical La Plata Synod held its first regular meeting.

Until 1932, the pastor of the Buenos Aires church also served as president of the synod. The purpose of that body was twofold: to draw the congregations into an ever-stronger fellowship of mutual supportiveness; and to cultivate ties with the mother country in Europe. When the mounting duties of the synodical presidency became too much for the Buenos Aires pastor, the EKD Foreign Office in Berlin responded by sending its own appointee. From 1933, the synod was headed by a dean (Propst), a title that continued until the mid-1960s.

One of those who helped most to make the ECRP ecumenically active and confessionally attuned to its basically Lutheran legacy was its president during the late 1960s and early 1970s, Heinz Joachim Held. Like Siegel more than a century earlier, Held became a pivotal figure. Son of a well-known leader in Germany's Confessing Church, Held identified with the Argentinians and encouraged the ECRP to become fully at home in Latin America. Other church leaders continued this emphasis, and many changes occurred during the difficult years of the late 1970s. In 1980, the synodical assembly, meeting in Asunción, Paraguay, elected for the first time an Argentinian-born pastor, Rodolfo Reinich, to be its president.

UNITED EVANGELICAL LUTHERAN CHURCH (UELC)

(Iglesia Evangélica Luterana Unida)
Member: LWF (1951), CLAI, AFEC, LCRP
Membership: 7653**
President: The Rev. Raúl E. Denuncio
Simbrón 4661
1417 Buenos Aires

This smallest of the Lutheran church bodies in Argentina—usually referred to as "Unida"—has served as host for the many strands of Lutheranism that have converged in Argentina since World War II. Today, its 23 congregations are served by 22 ordained pastors. All but two of the congregations have regular Spanish services, but worship is also conducted in Estonian, German, Hungarian, Latvian, and, occasionally, Swedish and Slovak. Despite the political unrest of the 1960s and 1970s and the present rampant inflation, the church is self-supporting on the congregational and administrative levels. Church polity combines congregational, district, and synodical interest. A biennial convention, with delegates from all congregations, is the highest authority.

Five of the congregations maintain parish schools, and this helps alleviate a general shortage of public schools and also provides Christian education for children of nonpracticing and unchurched parents. A youth program, strengthened by summer camping and leadership training, exerts a strong unifying force within the church. The women's support of the UELC's Armbruster home for the aged in José C. Paz is especially helpful, and this home is increasingly becoming a haven for aged people coming from all walks of life and various religious backgrounds. The addition of a 44-bed pavilion in 1982 was in large part made possible by a gift of US $500,000 from a family in the Hungarian congregation of Buenos Aires. Supplemental grants came from the LWF and the *Lutheran Church in America (now ELCA).

Church headquarters are in the capital city, and about half of the congregations are in greater Buenos Aires, an area with a population of over nine million. These include the oldest of the UELC's parishes and most of the congregations founded by the refugees in the early 1950s. One of the largest of the latter is the Cross of Christ parish in Belgrano, an older residential suburb that today has many inner city problems. A growing Spanish-speaking congregation is fast replacing an aging Hungarian one. Both groups still have equal representation in the church council, but all business is conducted in Spanish. The pastors serve two outlying congregations that still have need of Hungarian, and the senior pastor regularly visits the isolated Hungarian groups in Asunción (*Paraguay) and Montevideo (*Uruguay). This is facilitated by assistance from a number of lay people qualified to lead worship in Hungarian and Spanish. Other UELC congregations have similar programs.

The next largest group of congregations are in the subtropical state of Misiones in the far northeast, an area almost surrounded by Brazil and Paraguay. Here, new congregations have been planted and old German and Swedish congregations revived. One of these is in the capital city of Posadas, where strong lay leadership helped a congregation—long clinging to the German language—to relate more vigorously to the Argentine nation. In 1960, this congregation opened a hostel to provide wholesome living quarters for country girls attending the public high school.

A Swedish congregation, centered in the city of Obera, Misiones, has been a member of the UELC since the 1960s. This largest Swedish farm colony in the interior of Argentina began in 1891, when Swedish immigrants settled there after a period in Brazil. During most of its life, the Church of Sweden, through its seamen's mission, has provided pastors and assistance. In 1956, a new church edifice was constructed with generous help from Sweden, and in 1963 an elementary school was opened. Two years later, it was enlarged to accommodate a hostel for rural young people attending the city high school.

Other congregations are in the southern part of the province of Buenos Aires: One is in the resort town of Mar del Plata; another in Tandil. Evangelism and the planting of new congregations have high priority in the 1980s. To accomplish this, the UELC requested the assistance of pastors of the Lutheran Church in America (now ELCA), its longtime partner and founder.

In 1981, the UELC voted to ordain qualified women. ISEDET (above) is the theological training school for ministerial candidates. In addition to the four Lutheran professors and one instructor on the general faculty, the Lutheran students benefit from the services of a UELC pastor who serves as their chaplain and director of studies.

• • •

Historically, North American Lutheran interest in Argentina was awakened by the exploratory visit by Dr. W.D. Dougherty (1908–1912) and the following pioneer work of the Pan Lutheran Society (1917–1920). One of the missionaries was the Rev. Emil Ceder of the Augustana Lutheran Church. While serving the Swedish congregation in Buenos Aires, he began Spanish work, including the translation of Christian literature. In 1919, the newly formed United Lutheran Church in America (later part of the LCA) assumed responsibility for the mission and sent an experienced India missionary, Edward H. Mueller. He promoted an active laity, a well-prepared clergy, liturgy and literature in the Spanish language, and solid stewardship. Within four years, he had founded three schools (two elementary and one secondary), four congregations, and a seminary. Before his untimely death in 1923, he had also laid the cornerstone for the Redeemer Church in Villa del Parque in Buenos Aires, the first church building in Argentina for a Spanish-speaking Lutheran congregation.

In spite of the faithful work of members and missionaries, the embryonic church took long to recover from its early loss of strong leadership. Only in 1948 was a synod of 11 small congregations formed. Pastor Jonas Villaverde—a student of the short-lived seminary in 1923—became the first president. That same year, the ULCA received the church as an associate synod. In 1951, the UELC was accepted into LWF membership.

Meanwhile, during this postwar period, the UELC grew increasingly aware of the European Lutherans in their midst. Refugees and displaced persons—Estonians, Germans, Hungarians, Latvians, and Slovaks—were arriving in great numbers. Helped by the LWF Service to Refugees and then the Committee on Latin America, the refugees formed their own congregations, affiliated with the UELC, and brought strength of numbers, talent, and leadership. But the Spanish-speaking members did not always appreciate this fact. They thought the immigrants should be quicker to adopt the language and ways of their new country. The newcomers thought the Argentinians were too nationalistic and set in their ways. Although the use of many languages brought frequent misunderstandings, a common Christian faith overcame the discord. The new constitution (1953) for an autonomous church, adopted by all, enabled the UELC to apply for government recognition. This was granted on June 15, 1955.

During the next decade, the church prospered as the various strains learned to work together. With Perón's downfall, the long-closed Posadas congregation could reopen, and visas were granted to missionaries. Generous support from the ULCA and the LWF encouraged the founding of congregations and schools as well as the construction of new buildings. To mark the 50th anniversary of Lutheran work in Argentina the ULCA sent an evangelism promoter, who gave the church publicity and confidence. The number of students entering the seminary increased, and a new generation of Argentinian-trained pastors assumed leadership roles. In 1959, the church hosted the LWF-sponsored All-Latin America Lutheran Conference.

Toward the end of the 1960s, when the economic situation worsened and governmental controls increased, church growth was slow and the number of young men and women preparing for Christian service decreased. The new pre-seminary was closed, women studying in the Parish Workers' Institute were transferred to Union Theological Seminary, and later the prized Lutheran Seminary merged with interdenominational Union to form ISEDET (1970). The 1970s were hard years. Missionaries were not welcome. The depression, fear, and distrust overshadowing the nation affected all churches, not least the UELC.

The 1980s brought hopeful changes. The UELC led the Protestant churches in speaking out for human rights (1982). When democratic elections were achieved in 1983, members of the UELC cast their ballots with the help of guidelines offered in a pastoral letter from their president, Raúl Denuncio. He urged them to show their responsibility in voting and their evangelical commitment in helping to rebuild a nation.

CHILE

A republic, independent since 1818. Area: 756,845 sq. km. (292,258 sq. mi.). Pop.

(1985 est.): 11,976,000. About 65% are of mixed Indian and Spanish descent; the rest include Spanish, Italian, French, German, and other European nationalities as well as a small Indian remainder. Cap and largest city: Santiago (metro. pop., 1985 est., 4,271,500). Language: Spanish, and some Araucanian Indian tongues.

History: Among the numerous Indian tribes inhabiting the length of Chile, the Araucanian group occupied the central region. An agricultural people, they lived in villages and bravely defended their tribal turf. By the 15th century, however, invasions of other Indians from northeast Argentina and then from southern Peru—notably the Chinchas and the Quechua—brought much of Chile under the civilizing influence of the Inca empire and its capital, Cuzco.

In due time, the Spaniards, having conquered the Incas, pushed southward from Peru into Chile. After an initial victory over the Araucanians in 1540, the Spanish force under Pedro de Valdivia founded the city of Santiago (1541). Chile proved to be a difficult land for Spanish rule due to the continuing resistance of the Araucanians. From the outset, the Roman Catholic Church, especially through its missionary orders, was an integral part of the new Chilean scene. Conversion of the Indians proceeded apace.

Chile's colonial period spanned over 250 years and ended with independence in 1818. Bernardo O'Higgins (1778–1842), son of an Irish-born official in the Spanish government of Chile and Peru, led the successful revolt. However, his nation-making measures went too far too fast, and by 1823 he was deposed. In 1826, Chileans completed the independence movement by evicting Spanish forces from their last stronghold, the island of Chiloé, southwest of today's city of Puerto Montt.

From early times into the present, a landed and proprietary oligarchy has frustrated the attempted reforms by a growing middle and lower class. Even so, Chile has long had one of the best school and social welfare systems in Latin America and has been a relatively stable democracy.

International disputes have punctuated its relations with neighboring countries: a four-year war with Bolivia and Peru over mineral deposits, which Chile won in 1883; and the bitter border disputes with *Argentina, concluded in 1902. The latter is symbolized by the giant statue "Christ of the Andes" on the highest peak of the Andes on the international boundary. More recently, the rival territorial claims between Argentina and Chile at the southernmost tip of South America—the Beagle Channel—were settled in 1984 by Vatican arbitration.

In higher education, several institutes begun by the Jesuits during the 18th century lasted until the order was expelled (1767). The University of San Filipe (1756) was replaced in 1842 by a national institution, the University of Chile, in Santiago. The Catholic University (1888), was founded to provide a religious basis for professional studies.

As Chile's intellectual elite joined others in grappling with the social problems of the 20th century, the influence of Marxism grew. In the 1960s, the Chileans tackled their problems in earnest. Unemployment was high; the average diet, poor; inflation, persistent; bureaucracy, overloaded; wealth, monopolized. With Eduardo Frei Montalva as president and the slogan, "Revolution in Freedom," they attempted agrarian reforms. Their ineffectiveness made way for the election in 1970 of Socialist Salvador Allende Gossens, who proceeded with more drastic reforms. By 1972, his Marxist-oriented regime was troubled by mounting inflation and widespread middle-class resistance. Meanwhile, the Roman Catholic Church was gradually distancing itself from the proprietary upper class and associating itself increasingly with the poor. On the whole, the church saw itself as Socialistic but not Marxist.

A military junta seized power in September 1973 and installed General Augusto Pinochet Ugarte as president. His military dictatorship was often ruthless. The detention of some 7000 suspected Marxists—in retaliation to an alleged Communist plot—resulted in torture, executions, banishment, or the sheer disappearance of many. Periodic waves of protest appear to have had little effect. The sharpest moral judgment upon the political scene has come from the Roman Catholic Church. In 1988 Chileans voted against Pinochet continuing for another term.

Religion (estimates): Roman Catholic 80%; Protestant 14%; atheists and nonreligious 2%; Traditional 1%; other 3%.

The roots of Chilean Roman Catholic hierarchy go back to the founding of Santiago (1541). Today, the country's Episcopal Conference includes five archdioceses, 14 dioceses, and other judicatories. The church dates its significant reorientation from the old social order to the new as occurring on the eve of Vatican II. In 1962, five changes could be noted: a coordination of the various apostolates working for church renewal; a fresh involvement of women in the concerns of the church and society; the holding of diocesan synods for updating the clergy; the conducting of socioreligious surveys to assess the contemporary situation; and the recognition that social concern on the part of the church in Chile was already a half-century in the making, going back to 1910.

For church people supporting the Christian Democrats, the election of President Frei Montalva was the answer to Fidel Castro's Cuba. But when the Christian Democrats failed and—for the first time in a Latin American country—a Marxist was elected president, the Roman Catholic Church found a way to adapt, by being supportively "neutral." Since the 1973 coup, conservative elements in the church have reasserted themselves, while other elements continue to be sustained by the position the Latin American bishops took in Medellín and Puebla (see Latin America Introduction).

Protestant influences in Chile derive mainly from small beginnings in the 19th century. Besides the German Lutherans (below), these included the Anglican entry (1830) and later a temple (church) in Valparaiso, which became (1858) San Andres Cathedral for all the South Pacific. A missionary outreach from North America brought Presbyterians (1845), Methodists (1877), Seventh Day Adventists (1890), and Baptists (1892)—representative of still other groups. Eastern Orthodox—Russian and especially Greek—came directly from Europe. Like the Lutherans, they tended to be nonmissionary. The various missioning denominations grew moderately during the present century. Yet their growth dwarfs in comparison to the explosion of Pentecostalism. Although the exact number is unknown, the adherents of Pentecostal groups in Chile are said to outnumber the other Protestants anywhere from 7:1 to 14:1. Their beginning in 1910—as an offshoot from the local Methodist venture—has proliferated, and today there are perhaps 1.5 million Pentecostals in Chile. The two largest bodies—the Methodist Pentecostal (1909) and the Evangelical Pentecostal (1933), an offshoot, each claim nearly half a million. The biggest congregation—the Jotabeche, in Santiago—drew a crowd of 100,000 at the dedication of its new church (1974). The amazing fact is that all this growth has been possible without a creative rapport between the masses and an indigenous ministry of proven leadership. Two small Pentecostal bodies have been members of the World Council of Churches since 1961.

Church cooperation has taken various forms. The Evangelical Council of Chile (Concilio Evangélico de Chile, CECH), formed in 1941, includes a number of the older denominations. More recently, the Confederation of Evangelical Fundamentalist Churches of Chile has been active. Differences between the two groups have arisen over the ecumenical issue, including membership in the WCC, as well as action on behalf of social justice and human rights. Cooperative work has been fostered by specific needs. The resettlement of refugees and displaced persons from Europe after World War II and assistance to earthquake victims (1960) are examples. Fortunately, Chilean Protestants were somewhat prepared for the quakes of May 1960: For two years, they had been developing a relief program for the poor with the help of Theo Tschuy (Swiss Reformed), who was engaged by Church World Service and Lutheran World Relief (USA). Just a few weeks before the quake, 100 representatives from all parts of Chile had conferred in Santiago on Christian work and social problems.

There has also been cooperation in theological education. Since the mid-1960s—and with help from the WCC Theological Education Fund—Anglicans, Lutherans, Methodists, and Pentecostals have worked together in the Theological Community, centered in Santiago. In 1974, an extension program (TEE) was added, which, by 1979, had well over 4000 participants—mainly members of the many independent churches.

For all the Chilean churches the road has been rough since 1973, and especially so for those who have chosen to respond to ethical challenges involving human rights and service to victims of inhumanity and injustice. In this complex setting, the split occurring in the Lutheran church (1975) is a revealing case study.

Lutheran historical background: The present two Lutheran church bodies and the two independent congregations grew out of the periodic inflow of German Protestant immigration during the 19th and 20th centuries. As elsewhere in Latin America, the term German includes Austrian, Swiss, and ethnic elements; even as Protestant denotes Lutheran, United, and Reformed. The periods of inflow were strongest after major events in Europe, notably the Year of Revolution (1848), the Franco-Prussian War (1871), World War I (1918), the Nazi takeover (1933), and World War II (1945). The common bond, especially in Chile, has been that of language, nationality, and the Bible. Ever since the failure of the first attempts to bring Roman Catholic settlers from Germany in the late 1840s, Protestants have been in the majority. In the 1920s, they still comprised 80% of Chile's then 25,000 German-speaking population. Until the end of the 1950s, there was no designation other than German and Evangelical for the congregations or the church body, but there was over a century of history that requires notice.

In a Roman Catholic land like Chile, cultural Protestantism was a badge of identity and a mode of survival. In the coastal town of Valparaiso, the first German colony, or enclave, gathered in 1822. By 1845, Santiago had its German society. Both cities soon had a German school, but only in 1867 was there a German congregation in Valparaiso; only in 1887, one in the national capital. For those engaged mainly in business and the professions, the felt need for a pastor was mainly for baptisms, weddings, and funerals. For such occasional services, the good offices of a North American or British clergyman often sufficed, even as they had at first in *Argentina.

It was a different story further south where German and Swiss farmers, handworkers, and others began pioneering. They were Protestants recruited by a young German officer in the Chilean army, Bernard Eunom Philippi, who settled them on arable land between the towns of Valdivia and Osorno some 800 kilometers (500 miles) south of Santiago. Within a decade, about 700 families had settled there as well as in other towns, including Puerto Montt. As early as 1852 two pastors

arrived on their own from Electoral Hesse, *Germany. Friedrich Geiss (who had earned his doctorate) and H.C. Manns were young pastors who were apparently dislodged by reactionary forces following the 1848 revolution and were evidently ready to make a bold new beginning in Chile.

In Santiago, a brother of the navy officer, Rudolfo Amando Philippi, took up his professorship in botany at the University of Chile in 1851. He, too, came from Electoral Hesse, where he had taught in the capital, Kassel. Over the ensuing years, no one labored more effectively than Philippi to obtain pastors, to assist in the organization of congregations (by his counsel), and to obtain funding for church buildings—particularly from the Gustav-Adolf-Werk (*Germany), which specialized in aiding Protestant congregations in Roman Catholic countries.

As non-Roman Catholics, the Germans were permitted to worship only in private. Over the decades, this perpetuated in them a certain cultural and religious ghetto mentality, staunchly defending its Germanism. Hard work, economic success, and determination to perpetuate their inherited faith, marked many a congregation. Between 1863 and 1908, congregations were formally founded in ten places, from Puerto Montt and Osorno (1863) to Santiago (1887) to Punta Arenas (1908), each of the congregations having a variety of preaching points. Pastors were sent from Germany for specified terms of service through the headquarters of the Evangelical Church of the Old Prussian Union in Berlin. In fact, a church law in 1900 provided that congregations thus supplied were officially part of the church in Germany, either of the Prussian Union or the *Evangelical Lutheran Church of Saxony. This South American connection ran via *Argentina.

A synod of congregations, formed in 1904, long remained loosely organized. In 1937, it became the German Evangelical Church in Chile. German immigrants after World War I, and then German as well as Hungarian, Baltic, and other refugees after World War II were added to the church's membership. Largely through the farsighted and long leadership of Friedrich Karle, pastor in Santiago from 1930 and provost (dean) after 1937, the church survived trying times and gained new ecclesial stature in the 1950s.

In place of the close ties with Germany came the far wider connections offered by membership in the LWF (1955). The adoption of a new constitution (1959) also opened the way for changing the name to Evangelical Lutheran Church in Chile (ELCC). Later on, the title of president was replaced by that of bishop. The synod (as legislative body) and the church council (as executive unit) provided the structures of self-government. But the ELCC remained essentially a gathering of congregations for whom local independence had long been a prized possession.

The Lutheran congregations were drawn together by the disastrous earthquake of 1960. The congregations in the south, especially the one in Valdivia, suffered great loss of property, and the parishes of Santiago and Valparaiso were quick to provide relief and shelter. Their efforts were followed by generous assistance from Lutherans in other countries for the replacement of lost churches, parsonages, and homes.

During the 1960s, the changing political tides affected the fortunes of the ELCC as they did everything else. Distant were the days when a "foreign" and Protestant church constituency could stay aloof. The ELCC Chileanization—including an increasing use of Spanish—was accelerated in various ways. While the *American Lutheran Church had struck a partnership in that direction with the Evangelical Church of the Lutheran Confession in *Brazil, the *Lutheran Church in America entered upon a similar arrangement with the ELCC. Missioning pastors from North America, as well as from Germany, were helping the Chilean Lutherans reach out to the indigenous Spanish-speaking community. New congregations were organized and the ELCC, like other Protestant bodies, endeavored to be a missioning church.

This included service among the poor. In 1969, three Santiago congregations began providing school and medical assistance for families in La Faena, a shantytown on the edge of the capital. By 1974, the people had formed Good Shepherd congregation. This paralleled efforts elsewhere, but it also involved the church more deeply in the context of human need. Consequences were predictable. Successive changes in government, from Christian Democrat to Socialist coalition, and the lack of success in grappling with the nation's massive needs, created turbulence also in the churches—including the ELCC.

Troubles in the church came to a head with the downfall of the Allende regime in September 1973. Tensions between pastors and laity were not new. The pastors, most of them supplied on a limited term basis by the Foreign Office of the *Evangelical Church in Germany (EKD), and some of the laity tended to have a broader understanding of human rights than the rank-and-file members of the congregations. The latter, as self-made "haves," tended to be conservative in politics and against a social application of the gospel, especially if this aided people on the political left.

The mediating efforts of Helmut Frenz, the duly elected head of the ELCC and widely known as bishop, sprang from his Christian faith and his own experience as a World War II German refugee. His heading of an ecumenical effort to aid Chilean political refugees and their families, along lines authorized by the Pinochet government, triggered reaction in his church. Although awarded the Nansen Medal by the United Nations High Commissioner for Refugees, Frenz was eventually expelled by the Chilean government in September 1975 on charges of being too far left. The break in the ELCC was complete. Most of the pastors remained with the remnant church and elected a new president. Of the church's 12 parishes, eight seceded, taking with them church properties and all but 2000 of the 25,000 members. Some observers saw this as a victory for an older cultural Protestantism over the more socially concerned Lutheranism that had marked the LWF Fifth Assembly (Evian, 1970).

The traumatic events of 1975 and the ensuing burdens of separateness eventually yielded to overtures of reconciliation. First impulses came from the south in 1980. Others followed the lead of the independent congregation in Puerto Montt, and in 1981 representatives of the two church bodies and the two independent congregations (below) met for three days to study the meaning of discipleship. They pledged to work for reconciliation and to cooperate in matters of common concern, and for that purpose they formed a council.

The **Council of Lutheran Churches in Chile**—Consejo de las Iglesias Luteranas en

Chile (CILCH)—has been active since 1982. It aims to facilitate interaction among all Lutherans in Chile without pressure or mutual misgivings: to allow the will to unity among Chile's Lutherans to express itself; to take up matters of common interest; and to study and develop proposals for the creation of a permanent common organization. Translating resolve into action, the council focused on the distant tip of Chile. Although a German congregation had been formed there already in 1908 (above), Punta Arenas—the world's southernmost city—presented a new missionary challenge. The old-new congregation in Punta Arenas is now an affiliated member of the CILCH, giving substance to the vision of reunion. Meanwhile, in line with the worldwide ecumenical discussion of the 1980s—the noted "Lima Document" of Faith and Order—the CILCH has also been engaged in theological study, taking up baptism, holy communion, and related subjects.

The 750-member **German Evangelical Congregation of Valparaiso** (Corporación Iglesia Evangélica Alemana de Valparaiso) and the 350-member **German Evangelical Church, Puerto Montt** (Iglesia Evangélica Alemana de Puerto Montt) are two parishes that seceded from the ELCC in 1975 and went independent. They are situated in coastal cities about 1000 kilometers (620 miles) apart, Valparaiso being Chile's oldest port (1544) and international center, and Puerto Montt (1853) serving as the terminus of the southern railway and departure point for coastal shipping further south. Both cities have long had enclaves of German descent. The independent congregations support themselves, and over the past two decades have been served by able pastors from Brazil and elsewhere. Their membership has remained fairly constant. Both are members of the CILCH (above). In addition, the *Argentine Evangelical Lutheran Church reports one congregation in Chile, the 139-member Evangelical Lutheran Congregation "Espíritu Santo" in Valparaiso.

EVANGELICAL LUTHERAN CHURCH IN CHILE (ELCC)
(Iglesia Evangélica Luterana en Chile)
Member: LWF (1955), WCC, CLAI, CILCH

Membership: 2500**
President: The Rev. William Gorski
Av. Ricardo Lyon 1483
Casilla 15167
Santiago

This body is a continuation of the ELCC (above), but its membership is only about one-twelfth of what it was before the breakup in 1975. It comprises two German-speaking and three Spanish-speaking congregations and is served by eight pastors. It retains the name, legal entity, and ecumenical memberships of former times. Its headquarters, most of its congregations, and a new mission are in metropolitan Santiago. For ministerial education, it relies on the interdenominational Theological Community, where one of its pastors is at present dean and two of its pastors are part-time teachers. Its ties with confessional kindred bodies in *Argentina and *Brazil continue to be supportive, even as are those with the *Evangelical Church in Germany (EKD) and the *Lutheran Church in America (now ELCA).

In cooperation with the ELCA, the ELCC continues the Spanish work begun in 1962 (above) extending it southward from Santiago and locating it in San Bernando, La Bandera, Coronel, Concepción, and Osorno. A missioning spirit, quite different from any in earlier times, appears to animate the ELCC today. Spiritual growth comes with an improved life-style. In Coronel, a depressed congregation took on new life when its members were helped by a pastor and others to organize a community and establish an association of artisan fishermen. In Santiago, the new congregation provides a diagnostic facility and a school for children with learning difficulties. The present president, an ELCA pastor, was elected in 1986. He succeeds the Rev. Stefan Schaller.

LUTHERAN CHURCH IN CHILE (LCC)
(Iglesia Luterana en Chile)
Membership: 12,000**
President: Dr. Julio Lajtonyi Gruber
Bishop: The Rev. Richard Wagner
Casilla 16067
Santiago 9

Having seceded from the Evangelical Lutheran Church in Chile (above) in 1975, this new church body took with it most of the members and church property. Its congregations and preaching points stretch southward from Santiago to Temuco, Valdivia, La Union, Osorno, Frutillar, and Rhamiza. Its membership includes about 80% of Chile's Lutherans.

By its own recent statement, the Lutheran Church in Chile (LCC) relies upon the Holy Scriptures as its sole and supreme guide, and it recognizes the three Ecumenical Creeds as well as Luther's *Small Catechism* and the *Augsburg Confession* as norms derived from Scripture. The LCC is expressly a church of the laity, taking that term in its original sense as being part of the people of God.

The LCC dissociates itself clearly and consistently from every manner of clericalism. It seeks positively to keep its members aware of the general priesthood of all believers and to actualize this awareness responsibly. In this way, the LCC encourages its members in diaconic service, while remaining sharply on guard against any politicization of such service. For a while, the LCC was short on pastors. But in recent years it has been receiving them mainly from Europe, especially from Hermannsburg, *Germany, and from Basel, *Switzerland—two historic mission centers. The present bishop is a Chilean pastor (born in Transylvania, *Romania), and the president is a layman of Hungarian background.

In its own words, the LCC's secession in 1975 was for the sake of its two essential concerns: for diaconic service without politics, and for an activated priesthood of all believers. The goal of the LCC is to work for a reunited Lutheran church in which these inalienable concerns may again come into their own (see above).

PARAGUAY

A republic. Area: 406,752 sq. km. (157,048 sq. mi.). Pop. (1985 est.): 3,404,000. Cap. and largest city: Asunción (pop., 1983 est., 479,547). Language: Spanish (official); Guaraní is the language of the majority of mestizos, who comprise 90.8% of the population.

History: Spaniards founded Asunción about 1536 after 20 years of exploration in the La Plata River area. By 1609, Jesuit missionaries, on the scene since 1558, had established flourishing Indian missions. Patterned after those in other Spanish and Portuguese colonies, the "reductions," as they were called, gathered the Indians—mainly Guaranís—into villages. Protected from the vices of European colonists, they received religious instruction, learned occupational skills, and conformed to a closely regulated community life centered in the church. Cattle raising, agriculture, and handicrafts produced wealth. The Jesuits, with authorized civil as well as religious supervision, armed Indians to ward off slave hunters and to guard the country's borders. This authoritarian system did not prepare the Indians for leadership. Hence, the royal expulsion of the Jesuits in 1767 brought disaster. Efforts of the Franciscans to save the "reductions" failed. Indians were killed, carried off, or scattered. Today, the isolated Indian groups on the Chaco plains have little part in national life.

Paraguay's independence from the Spanish viceroyalty of Rio de la Plata in 1811 prepared the way for an eventual immigration of settlers from Germany, Italy, and France as well as a few from Ireland and Scotland. Politically, three dictators influenced the 19th century: José Gaspar Rodriguez Francia (1814–1840); Carlos Antonio López (1844–1862); and Francisco Solano López (1865–1870). The latter involved Paraguay in a disastrous war with Argentina, Brazil, and Uruguay (1865–1870), which brought death to more than half of the nation's population. Recovery was painfully slow and not complete before the Chaco War (1932–1935) with Bolivia. Although victorious, Paraguay was exhausted. Again dictators took control: Higinio Morínigo (1940–1948) and, 1954–1989, General Alfredo Stroessner. By suppressing opposition and changing the constitution (in 1967), he continued to be reelected until ousted by General Andres Rodriguez in early 1989.

Religion: The 1967 constitution guarantees religious freedom. It also recognizes Roman Catholicism as the official religion and requires the president to be of this faith. For centuries, the Roman Catholic Church was subject to tyrannical political powers, and this left it weaker in leadership and membership than in any other South American country.

Only in recent years did the church take a firm stand against the state's abuse of power and even excommunicate offending officials. The change is largely due to the impact of Vatican II and the 1968 Medellín conference (see Latin America Introduction).

The small Protestant churches are the result of both mission and immigration. Mission, mainly from the USA, first came through the American Bible Society (1856), followed by Methodists (1886), Seventh Day Adventists (1900), the New Testament Missionary Union (1902), and the Disciples of Christ (1916), the latter taking over the Methodist work. Although the first Baptists (1920) were from Argentina, they have been aided since 1945 by Southern Baptist missionaries from the USA. The Anglican South American Mission Society has worked among the Indians in the Chaco area since 1888.

The pioneer Protestant immigrants were Lutherans from Germany, who formed their first congregation in 1893 (see ECRP, below). In 1909, the government passed a law giving the president power to grant large tracts of land to Protestant immigrants who worked among the Indians in the manner of the Jesuit "reductions." The first to respond were Mennonite refugees from Russia after the Bolshevik revolution of 1917. Their concern for the Indians encouraged the resettlement of 5000 Canadian Mennonites to the center of the Chaco Plains—Lengua Indian territory. More Russian Mennonites came in the early 1930s and others after World War II. By 1966, there were some 10,000 Mennonites living among the Indians. With an ever-increasing awareness of the rights of the Indians and their need for self-development, the Mennonites established 36 Indian villages, each with a school, some with a church, and all having access to medical care. Today, the Mennonite church is the largest in Paraguay, 2000 of the some 12,000 members being Indian. After World War II, Pentecostal immigrants from eastern Slavic countries were assisted by Assemblies of God (USA). Orthodox Ukraine refugees have a 3000-member church.

The Evangelical Coordinating Committee of Paraguay (Comisión Coordinadora Evangélica de Paraguay, CCEP) composed of five churches, includes the Evangelical Church of the River Plate (below). Lutherans in Paraguay are almost as numerous as the Mennonites.

The **Association of Free Lutheran Churches of Brazil** (see Brazil) reports one congregation in Paraguay, not far from the border with the Brazilian state of Paraná.

The **Evangelical Church of the River Plate** (ECRP—see Argentina) has eight congregations in Paraguay, each with several preaching points. The membership, of German and ethnic German descent, is mainly engaged in agriculture except for those in Asunción. Worship is conducted in both Spanish and German. For the past three decades, an Argentine pastor of the UELC (above) has made occasional visits to the Hungarian-Paraguayans and conducted services in the ECRP Asunción church. Presently, the concern is mainly for the elderly, a group of about 40 persons.

This regional part of the ECRP is active in the Evangelical Coordinating Committee of Paraguay (CCEP, above). It also participates in various kinds of diaconic service such as the Christian Assistance Program in the areas of new settlement and the Integrated Guaraní Project among the Indians. The congregation in Asunción (1893) maintains a student hostel, as also does the one in Alto Paraná in the "Hohenau Colony." In Katuete, the church recently opened an agricultural school.

In Paraguay, the ECRP has grown by stages. In the late 19th century, German-speaking settlers came via Argentina; still more after World War I. These immigrants, and especially those in the rural areas, were extremely isolated and only had occasional pastoral service from Asunción. Change came with the improvement of roads and the interest of partner churches as well as of the LWF in the 1950s. The first resident pastor came to the Hohenau area in 1954. Within a few years, several church buildings were erected. In recent years, more settlers have moved in from Brazil.

EVANGELICAL LUTHERAN CHURCH OF PARAGUAY (ELCP)

(Iglesia Evangélica Luterana del Paraguay)
Membership: 3800**
President: The Rev. Eugenio Wagner
Hohenau II

This church body, formed March 12, 1983, combined the Paraguayan congregations of the *Argentine Evangelical Lutheran Church (AELC) and the *Evangelical Lutheran Church of Brazil (ELCB), both being partners of the *Lutheran Church–Missouri Synod (USA). A convention of delegates from 47 congregations (representing some 3000 members) adopted a constitution and elected Pastor Egon Hamann Wachholz as first president. The new church is served by two pastors and one vicar from the AELC and four pastors from the ELCB.

Already in 1925, the then Argentine District of the LCMS began work in Paraguay, ministering to German-speaking Lutherans in and around Hohenau, a town north of Posadas, Argentina. The Hohenau parish, served by one pastor, comprises several congregations. German is still the preferred language in this area. Beginning in 1971, ELCB pastors began traveling back and forth across the border, serving the Brazilian immigrants who had accepted the Paraguayan government's offer of cheap land and other incentives in return for clearing and developing the jungle.

Mission work has been carried on mainly by the laity. When a few Lutheran families move to an area without a church, they are expected to arrange a house-service, inviting their neighbors at a time when a Brazilian pastor is expected. Pioneering, with its dangers and difficulties, it is said, has turned many lukewarm Christians to God and the church.

Portuguese-speaking Brazilian pastors are learning the Paraguayan variety of Spanish, and many of the congregations have initiated adult instruction and Sunday school in Spanish. They also have the benefit of hearing the "Lutheran Hour" broadcasts. Thus, the new church intends to identify with the nation and the people.

URUGUAY

A republic (1830). Area: 176,215 sq. km. (68,037 sq. mi.). Pop. (1984 est.): 3,013,000. Cap. and largest city: Montevideo (pop., 1980 est., 1,260,573). Language: Spanish.

History: Most of the few original inhabitants of Uruguay, the Charrua Indians, were absorbed by the Spanish and Portuguese settlers who began colonization in the early 17th century. By 1825, the country declared itself independent from the Rio de la Plata viceroyalty of Spain, and in 1830 the Oriental Republic of Uruguay became the smallest of all South American republics. Long in danger of being submerged by its larger neighbors, it also struggled through decades of civil strife between two traditional parties, the Colorados and the Blancos. Only in the first decades of the 20th century, under the leadership of José Batlle y Ordóñez, was anarchism replaced with an orderly government, and Uruguay became one of the most stable and prosperous nations of Latin America (although prosperity has slowed down recently). Laws providing for eight-hour workdays, national insurance, university education for women, state control of monopolies and divorce, and the general furthering of education, were some of the measures taken.

Economic problems and the social unrest of the 1960s and 1970s, coupled with the threats of an urban guerrilla movement, resulted in a repressive military regime in 1973 and a complete takeover in 1976. During the 1980s, encouraged by the happenings in Argentina and Brazil, the Uruguayans strongly expressed their objection to the repression of human rights. After 11 years of a military regime, the country returned to civilian rule in November 1984.

Religion (1980): Christian 62.9% (59.5% Roman Catholic); nonreligious 35.1%; Jewish 1.7%; other 0.3%.

Uruguay's first constitution (1830) established freedom of religion and that of 1916 separated church and state. Nonreligion and atheism have had a longer history and larger following than in any other South American country. The government avoids religious recognition and attempts to "de-Christianize" public life. Christmas and Holy Week have become "Family Day" and "Tourist Week." No religious instruction is given in public schools, but this is compensated by an emphasis on the moral and civic character of the students. Uruguay is known as the most "secularized" nation in Latin America.

The Roman Catholic Church lost its status as a state church in 1916, but it gained more than it lost: title to church property; freedom from governmental control and interference; and unimpeded communication with the Vatican. The Catholic Church maintains its own school system, in which Christian education plays an important part, and this has resulted in a marked revival of loyalty to the faith. Since anticlericalism has been strong, and the diocese of Montevideo was only created in 1878, Roman Catholic organization is not prominent. The Medellín conference (see Latin America Introduction) somewhat influenced the church to social action and the involvement of the laity. The church suffers from a lack of priests, especially for the interior villages.

Although Protestantism has been quite vigorous in Uruguay, it has not filled the void left by a decreasing Catholic membership. However, through education and social work, Protestant influence has been greater than its numbers. The USA Methodists were the first to send missionaries to Uruguay (1838). The resulting Methodist church has remained small (some 6000 members), but it has produced able leaders not only for Uruguay but also for the Christian church at large. The present general secretary of the World Council of Churches, Emilio Castro, is one of its members.

The Salvation Army and the Seventh Day Adventists also came in the 19th century, and the latter is now one of the larger churches. Through immigration, the Italians established their Waldensian church (1856) and the Germans the Evangelical (Lutheran and Reformed) in 1860. Numerous other denominations are present, many of them begun after World War II. The largest of these, the New Apostolic Church—an offshoot of the Catholic Apostolic Church (Irvingites), founded in England in the 19th century—has a membership of some 20,000, mainly German-speaking immigrants. Assemblies of God and Jehovah's Witnesses are growing. Russian Orthodoxy is strong.

The Federation of Evangelical Churches of Uruguay (Federación de Iglesias Evangélicas del Uruguay, FIEU), formed in 1956, is the successor to the Uruguay Committee of the Confederation of Evangelical Churches of the River Plate (1939), which also included Argentinian and Paraguayan churches. The federation is affiliated with the WCC. Its membership includes eight churches and three associated members: the Bible Society, the Evangelical Hospital, and the Ecumenical Institute.

The Evangelical Hospital, built in 1957 by several Protestant bodies, including the Lutherans, had the leadership of the *Lutheran Church in America's pioneer missionary, Pastor Herman Hammer.

The Ecumenical Institute was founded in 1966 by the LCA/USA as a center for training Christian laity. Since then, it has developed into an institute sponsored and supported by four national Protestant churches as well as by the Roman Catholic Church, all having members on the board of directors. Through lectures, workshops, seminars, retreats, encounters, and dialog, the institute reaches people who have been alienated from the Christian faith and churches. The federation and the institute share the same director. The LCA (now ELCA) continued to provide suitable quarters for the Ecumenical Institute and also for the FIEU and other groups offering Christian service.

The institute's building at Avenue 8 de Octubre 3324, Montevideo, was also intended for a Lutheran congregation, the fruit of a quarter-century of mission work. After a beginning in 1948 by Augustana (later LCA; now ELCA) missionaries serving in Argentina, the first missionary to Montevideo was sent in 1952 by the Latin American Division of the Lutheran Council in the USA. This work in Spanish was encouraged by the pastor of the German congregation (see ECRP below). Congregational growth was slow but steady. In 1957, the work was transferred back to Augustana (LCA), and the work was extended. However, during the repressive regime of the early 1970s, the supporting church (then LCA) was not able to provide sufficient pastoral care to sustain the fragile parish. Along with the satellite congregations in the suburbs of Santo Teresito and Delo el Tigre it was disbanded. Only the Rivera congregation remained (ELCU below).

The **Argentine Evangelical Lutheran Church** (AELC—see Argentina) has only one congregation, San Pablo in Montevideo. It has a membership of 282 and maintains both an elementary and a high school. The 386 pupils are mainly from Roman Catholic or unchurched homes. All receive Christian education, and many are confirmed after the sixth grade. Young people, well trained in evangelism skills and helped by the Spanish Lutheran Hour, are aids to church growth. The AELC also has preaching stations in the western border cities of Paysandu and Salto and points between. These are served from Concordia Seminary in greater Buenos Aires.

The Evangelical congregations (Lutheran, United, and Reformed) in Uruguay are a part of the **Evangelical Church of the River Plate** (ECRP—see Argentina), whose headquarters are in Buenos Aires. The three congregations—each with several preaching stations—are located in Montevideo; in Nueva Helvecia, west and a little north of Montevideo; and in Paysandu on the western border. The combined membership is about 3000. Worship is conducted in both German and Spanish. The Montevideo congregation supports social work in the city's Borro district, and the Nueva Helvecia parish maintains a retirement center. As a unit of the ECRP, these congregations are members of the Federation of Evangelical Churches of Uruguay (FIEU, above) and participate actively in ecumenical work.

Not long after the first German settlers arrived in 1857, the congregation in Montevideo was formed. For some time, it served the large German community in eastern Uruguay. After World War II, this congregation cooperated with the LWF in the resettlement of European refugees, and during the 1950s its German pastor greatly encouraged the pioneer American missionaries who began work in the Spanish language (above).

The congregation in Nueva Helvecia was formed in 1874 by Swiss immigrants. The Paysandu congregation developed from German colonists, some of whom had come from Russia and had been helped to emigrate by the USA National Lutheran Council during the late 1920s. For many years, they had only occasional services from the ECRP.

EVANGELICAL LUTHERAN CHURCH OF URUGUAY (ELCU)

(Iglesia Evangélica Luterana del Uruguay)
(P)
Membership: 94**
Pastor: The Rev. Huberto Willrich
Calle Dr. Anollés No. 322
Casilla 64039
Rivera

This nascent church body, autonomous since 1978, is situated 492 kilometers (308 miles) north of Montevideo in the capital of the province of Rivera. Spanish and Portuguese are both understood in this area bordering Brazil. Besides the original central congregation, the ELCU has two mission stations in the barrios of Quintas al Norte and Pueblo Nuevo, all served by one pastor and trained volunteers. Three times a week, the church provides religious programs for the local radio station. From 1982 to 1985, an ordained woman pastor of the *Lutheran Church in America accepted the call to be director of its adult leadership training program (TEE) and its youth ministry. Thus its longtime partner continued its interest and support. Otherwise, the ELCU is economically and juridically independent.

Lutheran mission work began in Rivera in 1955 when the Latin American Division of the National Lutheran Council in the USA expanded the work begun in Montevideo to Rivera. Most responsive were the people in the economically poorer sections of the city, where outside help provided schools and social services.

In 1957, the Augustana Evangelical Lutheran Church (LCA in 1962) assumed responsibility for the mission, and by 1960 it had constructed a beautiful church complex that overlooked the international park. It includes a large chapel, a parish center, and a parsonage. In the 1970s, missionaries introduced radio and television programs as well as theological education by extension (TEE). Through these avenues, a Pentecostal and his congregation were drawn to Lutheranism and requested to be received by the congregation in 1974. This brought two legally registered congregations and their preaching points together, and they formed an independent church body in 1978. By the authority of this church, a Uruguayan pastor, José da Motta, was ordained in 1979 and served as its pastor for six years. He received the "laying on of hands" by representatives of the LCA, the ECRP (above), the AELC (above) and the *Evangelical Church of the Lutheran Confession in Brazil. In 1981, the LCA transferred the mission property to the ELCU. After 1985, the ELCU again had the pastoral services of an LCA missionary.

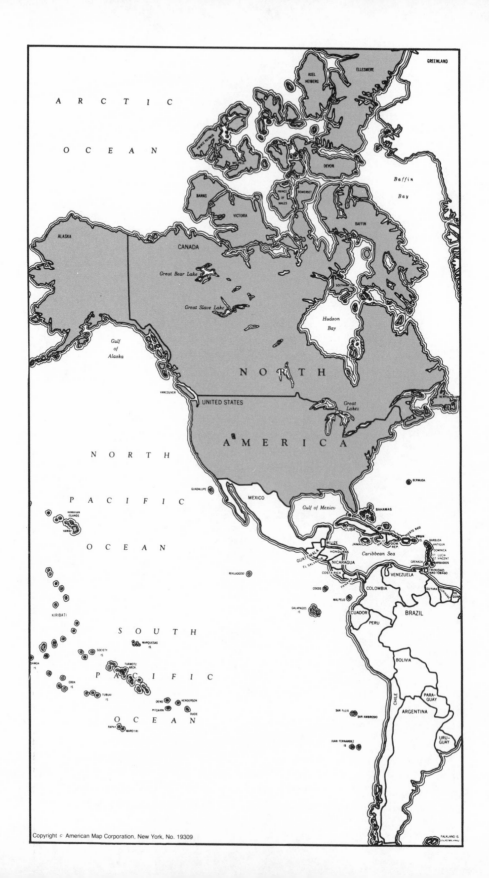

NORTH AMERICA_____

Canada and the United States of America comprise North America in its narrower designation, one that relates it to Northern Europe and makes sense particularly when dealing with churches of Lutheran confession. There is, however, also the larger—the geographer's—designation which sees North America not simply as the landmass lying north of the Rio Grande River but as the entire complex of mainland and islands (see Central America and the Caribbean, above) extending from Panama to Alaska and from the islands of the Caribbean to Greenland. For the historically minded, there is always October 12, 1492, the European discovery of America, when Christopher Columbus and his crew landed on a small island on the edge of the Bahama group and, thankful for land after so much sea, called the place El Salvador—The Savior. From there the drama of the New World unfolds.

The treatment of Lutheranism in this section of the book attempts to strike a balance between the inclusive geographic designation and the narrower one that here focuses on Canada and the United States. It is thus important to bear the Caribbean region (see Latin America) in mind as well as those parts of the continent where French (Quebec) and Hispanic adaptations of European culture abound.

Area (Canada and the United States): 19,355,331 sq. km. (7,473,136 sq. mi.). Pop. (1986 est.): 267,129,000. Compared with 1960, this total figure represents an increase of about 30% in 25 years. (During that same period, neighboring Mexico's population more than doubled.)

History

A prehistoric past links America's early inhabitants to peoples of Asia and North Africa as well as Europe. Increasingly, archaeological finds point to the settlement of Celts, Basques, Lybians, and even Egyptians on the east coast of North America as early as 2500 years ago. But the indigenous inhabitants, the American Indians, were a highly diversified array of peoples, whose ancestors are thought to have been of Asian origin a number of millennia ago, making their way down the Pacific coast from Alaska and in time spreading across the continent. Much more recent was the influx of Africans from the 17th to the early 19th century. Increasingly, the presence and the rights of minority peoples—Indians, Blacks, French, Hispanic, Asians—living in the USA and Canada are being asserted and recognized.

The descendants of successive waves of immigrants from Europe eventually took over the North American continent. They developed their own version of Western civilization and transformed an immense wilderness into a pair of interdependent nations. For its part, following the War of Independence, the USA found its unity tested especially by civil war and the emancipation of the slaves, and later by participation in two world wars which overcame its isolation, raised it to a world power, and made it in some ways successor to the global interests of Europe, with all the hazards of such a position. For its part, Canada, granted Dominion status (1867) and an active member of the Commonwealth of Nations, complements USA involvements by its own composition (French minority, Anglo-Saxon majority, plus a growing proportion of others) and bilingual culture as well as types of international outreach. The location of the United Nations headquarters in New York City (since 1946) asserts the global significance given by people in the mid-20th century to this once unknown continent.

Religion

In contrast to Latin America, once almost completely dominated by the Roman Catholic Church, North America (here seen minus Mexico and Central America as well as the Caribbean) has long been the breeding ground of ecclesial pluralism. This has combined an inclusive civil religion (e.g., "this nation under God") at one end of the scale with a growing number of sects at the other. North America thus has a climate of religious liberty quite different from that traditionally found in Europe and in the other continents. The majority of North Americans still claim adherence to some form of Christianity. The Jewish community, numerically larger in North America than elsewhere in the world, is influential beyond its numbers in the common life but is not much inclined to make converts. Islam, on the contrary, as well as Zen Buddhism, forms of Hinduism, Bahai, and other religions are enlarging their following. Among young people, these and other religious movements, some of them with a strong impact on European youth as well, have been gaining adherents, many of them ardent and committed. New Age syncretistic cults are growing rapidly.

Traditional Christianity, as embodied in Roman Catholicism, Eastern Orthodoxy, and the churches of Reformation heritage—together they may be called the "old line" churches—thus finds itself challenged on many fronts. However, in longer retrospect, the opportunities offered European Lutherans by the North American setting as early as the 17th century stimulated a response and a struggle to make Lutheranism viable among English-speaking peoples.

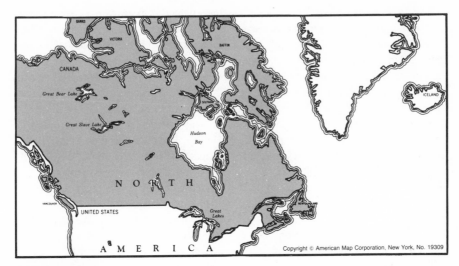

CANADA

The 300,622 baptized members of Canada's Lutheran churches comprise about 1.2% of the nation's population and account for some 3.4% of the total Lutheran church membership in North America. Many Canadians of Lutheran background, it is said, are still unreached by the churches of their own confessional heritage.

A federal parliamentary state and member of the Commonwealth of Nations, Canada covers North America north of the conterminous United States and east of Alaska.

Area: 9,970,610 sq. km. (3,849,672 sq. mi.). Pop. (1986 est.): 25,640,000. Ethnic composition by language (est. 1981): English 61.2%; French 25.6%; Italian 2.2%; German 2.1%; Ukranian 1.2%; other European 4.6%; Asian 2.3%; native Indians and Inuit (Eskimo) 0.8%. Cap. Ottawa (metro. pop., 1984 est., 717,978). Major metropolitan areas (1983 est.): Toronto, 3,067,700; Montreal, 2,862,300; Vancouver, 1,310,600; Ottawa-Hull, 737,600. Language: English and French (official).

History: Like the rest of North America (above), Canada's prehistoric past lies in the mists of obscurity and the realms of archaeological anthropology. The Asian origin of the native Indians and Inuit (Eskimos) is virtually certain, but the essential details are elusive. Likewise, from the European shores came early ventures in a sequence that emerged in the Greenland based expedition of Leif Ericsson in about the year 1000 to "Vinland" (the later Newfoundland?) and periodic returns there by other Norse. Later the discoveries by John Cabot (1497) and Jacques Cartier (1534–1535) initiated a process that drew the land that is now Canada into the orbit of Europe's expansion and made it a modern nation. The prolonged quest for a Northwest Passage by sea from Europe to Asia played an important part in placing Canada in global perspective.

Some quick reminders suggest Canada's stages of growth: French colony (1534–1763); a British colony (beginning with Nova Scotia, 1713, and then including the

555

whole of Canada, 1763–1867); a self-governing dominion, internally until 1931, and also externally thereafter. In 1982, Canada's constitution was repatriated from Great Britain. Others also had early eyed Canada, like the ill-fated Danish expedition seeking a Northwest Passage (1619–1620). Its chaplain, Rasmus Jensen, the first Lutheran pastor in North America, lies buried in Churchill, Hudson Bay. Over 150 years later, 40,000 or more Loyalists leaving the newly independent United States found refuge in Nova Scotia and Ontario.

Receptive to change, Canada has always had to struggle for its own identity: at home, with its bilingual cultural composition; across the border, with its far more populous neighbor; and overseas, with a mother country managing a world empire. Not least demanding was its coping with climate and size.

Its enormous expanse has been a boon for settlement but also a problem for unity. For one country to have most of its population in a 320-kilometer wide band, stretching for a distance as far as from England to the Persian Gulf, presents a giant challenge in nation making. The saga of settlement unfolds in the east, jumps to the Pacific coast, and then fills in the midwestern Prairie Provinces. The latter—Manitoba, Saskatchewan, Alberta—received a substantial part of their immigrant population via the upper Midwest of the *United States, among whom Scandinavian rural folk were prominent. The initial federation of the eastern provinces (1867), accelerated by the reunification of the United States after the Civil War, drew in the western provinces as they were formed. The transcontinental rail network built up the economy and helped develop a national sense of unity. Politically, Canada's adaptation of inherited political institutions

has enabled it to grow and, while growing, to absorb successive waves of immigrants, mainly from Europe, but more recently also from Asia and the Caribbean. After World War II, about 2,000,000 Europeans and others found a fresh start in Canada. About three out of every five of these were resettled in Ontario. This feat was due at least in part to the active participation of the churches. Similar opportunities have been extended to Chinese and other Asians.

Fair treatment of the native population, Indian and Inuit, remains unfinished business. Shared concern and legal action have been helping to mitigate chronic injustices.

Internationally, Canada's distinctive place has often enabled it to mediate understanding between nations. Where doors were sometimes closed to other English-speaking nations, Canada has had entry, whether in the case of *China (after the 1949 revolution) or other parts of the politically polarized world.

Religion: Roman Catholic (1981) 47.3%; Anglican and Protestant 41.7%; Orthodox 1.5%; Jewish 1.5%; adherents of other religions 1.2%; and others, including those claiming no religious connection.

Traditional religion among native Indian and Inuit (Eskimo) people shows evidence of resurgent ancient beliefs, especially in support of the quest for identity and the assertion of minority rights. Historically, Indians in French Canada and westward proved more resistant to conversion than those in Spanish America.

Christianity in Canada has developed somewhat differently than in the USA, due in some measure to the longer (until 1852) presence of established churches, Anglican and Roman. Since the days of the vicar apostolic, François Xavier de

Laval, the first and highly influential bishop of Quebec (1674), the Roman Catholic Church has been a power in public as well as religious affairs. Its attachment to Rome has remained strong, and its majority has continued to be French despite the later influx of Irish, German, Italian, and other believers. The current 68 dioceses (18 are archdioceses) are relatively high in number because of the vast spread across the continent. The church's extensive involvement in education and in many fields of social welfare is visible in the institutions dotting the landscape, especially in Quebec. The Canadian Catholic Conference of Bishops is on good terms with its Anglican-Protestant counterpart, the Canadian Council of Churches (below), in which it now has associate membership. The Catholic Ecumenical Center in Montreal, and a new one in Saskatoon, serve clergy and laity in the several dioceses and also promote the aims of Christian unity. The numerous French Canadian missionaries, active in many parts of the world, translate the devotions of a martyr (like the work of Jesuit Jean de Brebeuf [1649] among the Huron Indians) into contemporary terms.

Parallel developments gave Canada its heavily Anglo-Saxon Protestant array of church bodies. The present Anglican Church of Canada began in the 18th century as the Church of England in Canada. Today, it is the country's third largest church body, claiming between 5% and 10% of the population. A general synod embraces its 30 dioceses (grouped in four ecclesial provinces, each under an archbishop), and the presiding head (called the primate) oversees the church from the headquarters in Toronto.

The United Church of Canada (1925), the country's second largest church body, was a consolidation of Presbyterian, Methodist, and Congregational churches—communions having their Canadian origin in the early 19th century. Their growth was considerable, and their contacts with Britain and the USA also conveyed impulses of the ecumenical movement at an early stage. Even as before World War I the movement toward an eventual Church of South *India got under way, so in Canada those same churches, of Anglo-Saxon rootage, united, with this major exception: the Anglicans went their own way. As in India, the Baptists in Canada also remained separate.

In terms of chronology, these developments were flanked by others. In the 18th century, German Lutheran colonists under British sponsorship had settled in Nova Scotia about 1750 (below); Moravian missionaries had begun work in Labrador (1770); and Mennonites (Loyalists from Pennsylvania) came after 1783. At the other end, in time, various groups of Eastern Orthodox arrived in the late 19th and early 20th centuries, settling especially in the Prairie Provinces. After World War I, numerous newer religious groups from the USA extended their influence into Canada.

The Canadian Council of Churches (CCC), organized in 1944, includes Anglican, United, Baptist, Presbyterian (those not joining the United Church), Lutheran, Armenian, Greek Orthodox, and other bodies. The council is concerned for the mission and unity of the churches, and to that end promotes ecumenical study as well as common action and service in situations involving justice, human rights, peace, and nuclear disarmament. It assists the churches, upon request, in dealing with specific problems and projects, such as resettlement, and helps them coordinate their efforts. Council headquarters are in Toronto. Its member churches have long been supportive of the World Council of Churches. The WCC statement on "The Church, the Churches, and the World Council of Churches" (1950) early defined the ecclesiology of the world body and was fittingly adopted by the WCC Central Committee in Toronto. Over three decades later, the CCC was host to the Sixth Assembly of the WCC, held in Vancouver, British Columbia (1983), which gave particular attention to the churches in Asia and the Pacific.

• • •

Lutherans in Canada number slightly over 300,000. Serving about 1050 congregations are 719 parish pastors as well as many other ordained ministers in various fields. The number of clergy, including retirees, is over 1100. Teaching, administration, mission work, campus ministry to students and faculty, welfare services, and related activities include many other workers as well.

Despite their mid-18th and early 19th century antecedents in the Maritimes (the provinces of New Brunswick, Nova Scotia, and Prince Edward Island) and Ontario, Lutherans have until recent years been looked upon as "foreign" and as relative outsiders to the largely Anglo-Saxon Protestant church scene. The repeated influx of newcomers from continental Europe has kept this impression alive as all their use of English had to be acquired. This imported ethnic diversity at times also made for strife among Lutherans themselves. Not only the hard life of pioneering but also the lack of pastors aggravated the situation, as did the occasional inability of fellow Lutherans stateside to render effective assistance. In the process of Canadianization, many younger Lutherans

went over to other communions. Others, by way of reaction, cultivated confessional conservatism. This tended to make Lutherans in Canada more homogeneous, despite their divisions, than their counterparts in the USA. However, as the ecumenical movement welcomed diversity within unity, and as Vatican II and Luther's 500th anniversary revealed the importance of positive Lutheran-Roman Catholic relations, Lutherans were drawn out of their relative obscurity. Becoming active participants, they have been able to add valuable ingredients to theological discussion and various kinds of interchurch enterprises.

Their own experience has tended to give Canada's Lutherans a feel for churches in Asia, Africa, and Latin America. They reflect a kind of theology and style of piety brought to peoples of the Two-Thirds World by missionaries and maintained by their own churches in Canada. Being so much smaller than their counterparts south of the border, Canada's Lutherans can, and often do, see themselves as occupying a mediating position between those in the USA and those in other parts of the world.

Canadian Lutherans divide into the two main bodies described below. The pattern of consolidation was similar to that in the USA. Until the end of 1985, there were three Lutheran general bodies: the Evangelical Lutheran Church of Canada, the Lutheran Church in America-Canada Section, and the Lutheran Church-Canada. Forerunners of these three bodies entered into various forms of cooperation during World War II. In 1940, a Commission on War Service was organized to represent the Lutheran churches in the appointment of chaplains in the armed forces and to help congregations keep in touch with their members and others in the military. After the war, this commission was authorized by the federal government to organize **Canadian Lutheran World Relief** (1946), an agency that has long served all Lutherans in the field of immigration and material aid. Today, this agency channels assistance to development projects in Africa, Asia, and Latin America.

With the formation of the Lutheran World Federation (1947), Canadian participation gained recognition in its own right, particularly in the resettlement of European refugees. Within a year, the Canada Committee of the LWF was operative. In 1952, the LWF-related bodies organized the Canadian Lutheran Council, encouraging broad Lutheran cooperation in Canada. Regrettably, the Canadian districts of the Missouri Synod did not join at that time. But 15 years later they all joined in forming the **Lutheran Council in Canada** (1967). This paralleled the creation of the Lutheran Council in the USA (below) and marked the high point of Lutheran unity in North America. On the Canadian scene, the new council's functions included theological studies, mission, chaplaincies, work among university students and faculty, social service, public relations, information, and the like. All these were functions done better together than separately.

Lutheran unity rode high on the churches' agenda. One of its best signs was the institutional merger that created the Lutheran Theological Seminary on the University of Saskatchewan campus in Saskatoon. The location on a public university campus realized a long-held hope, and the proximity to other theological colleges was ecumenically stimulating. Its facilities were dedicated in 1968. The seminary is a merger (1965) of two Saskatoon institutions: Lutheran College and Seminary (1915) of the Lutheran Church in America-Canada Section and Luther Seminary (1930) of the Evangelical Lutheran Church of Canada (below). For a time, the merged seminary faculty included a Missouri Canadian (see Lutheran Church-Canada).

Hopes were running high when, in 1972, the Evangelical Lutheran Church of Canada (formerly part of the American Lutheran Church, now ELCA, *USA) issued an invitation to its sister churches in Canada to enter into official merger negotiations. But a major problem suddenly developed. The change of leadership (1969) in the Lutheran Church–Missouri Synod and the ensuing bitter controversy within that body (*USA), affected the Canadian situation as well. Merger negotiations ground to a halt in 1977 over the issue of the interpretation of Scripture and the ordination of women. But a new round of negotiations commenced between the two LWF-related bodies, the ELCC and the LCA-CS in 1978. These efforts reached a successful conclusion in 1985, creating the Evangelical Lutheran Church in Canada (ELCIC, below).

Meanwhile, the ELCIC and the LC-C continue as partners in the Lutheran Council in Canada. The council remains the bearer of promise for a full union of Lutherans in Canada. The council's headquarters were relocated in 1986 from Winnipeg, long the center of cooperative Lutheranism, to Toronto. With its role still further delimited, the council's chief concern centers in relationships: governmental in Ottawa, and ecumenical in Toronto. The president of the Lutheran Council in Canada is the Rev. Dr. William D. Huras (50 Queen Street N., Kitchener, Ontario N2H 6 P4); the executive director is the Rev. Lawrence R. Likness (25 Old York Mills Road, Willowdale (Toronto), Ontario, M2P 1B5).

ESTONIAN EVANGELICAL LUTHERAN CHURCH
(EELC; in North America)
Membership: 14,601**
Bishop in North America: The Rev. Karl Raudsepp
30 Sunrise Avenue
Apt. 216
Toronto, Ontario M4A 2R6

This North American section of the church dispersed outside Estonia (see Exile Churches, above) has a baptized membership of about 14,600, almost evenly divided numerically between the United States and Canada. Of its 37 congregations, 24 are in the USA. The Canadian membership is strongest in the Toronto area. Of the currently 39 pastors, 33 are serving congregations (22 in the USA, 11 in Canada). The EELC, like its Latvian counterpart (LELCA, *USA) finds that maintaining separate identity is still an asset at this point in time, and is preferable to being dispersed among the major Lutheran bodies in North America. The EELC maintained a liaison relationship with the Lutheran Council in Canada and with the Lutheran Council in the USA, both of which were active during the years after World War II in resettling Displaced Persons from Europe, including Estonians. (See also Europe and USA.)

EVANGELICAL LUTHERAN CHURCH IN CANADA (ELCIC)

Member: LWF (1986), WCC, CCC, LCIC
Membership: 208,403
Presiding Bishop: The Rev. Dr. Donald W. Sjoberg
1512 St. James Street
Winnipeg, Manitoba R3H 0L2

The press release from Winnipeg exulted, "A new Lutheran church of nearly 210,000 baptized members was born here May 16-19, 1985, becoming Canada's fourth largest denomination. The 524 delegates . . . approved documents permitting the merger of the Evangelical Lutheran Church of Canada [ELCC, below] and the Lutheran Church in America–Canada Section [LCA–CS, below] into a new church, to be known as the Evangelical Lutheran Church in Canada (ELCIC)."

Following the adoption of a constitution and the election of officers, important next steps included interchurch relations. "The ecumenical commitment of the ELCIC was evident in the unanimous vote for membership in the Lutheran Council in Canada (above), the Lutheran World Federation (LWF), the Canadian Council of Churches, and the World Council of Churches." Visiting LWF president, Bishop Dr. Zoltán Káldy (Hungary), affirming that "we are called to unity," placed the event and its decisions in broad perspective.

The ELCIC officially began functioning January 1, 1986. Headquartered in Winnipeg, the new church could build on patterns of inter-Lutheran cooperation fashioned over five decades. The church's five synods or territorial jurisdictions, from west to east, are: British Columbia, Alberta, Saskatchewan,

Manitoba/Northwestern Ontario, and Eastern. The Eastern Synod stretches from the Great Lakes to Nova Scotia and covers not only most of Ontario but also contains nearly 40% of the ELCIC membership.

The biennial convention is the ELCIC's top legislative authority, and the 19-member church council its governing body. The chief elected officer—initially president—bears the title of presiding bishop; the synod heads are bishops. In order to respond effectively to its challenges, the six operational divisions deal with Canadian missions, church and society, college and university services, parish life, theological education and leadership, and world mission. The areas of communication, finance, and resource development (stewardship) each have their own office. There is also a Committee on Pensions. Evangelical Lutheran Women, as an organization, continues to uphold the significant place of women in the life of the church.

Of the ELCIC's over 730 pastors, 452 are in parish ministry. Of the 654 congregations, 314 have roots in the former ELCC, and 340 in the former LCA–CS. The church's two theological seminaries—Waterloo in the east and Saskatoon in the west—are institutional reminders of a diversified past as well as centers of ministerial education in ecumenical contexts. Similarly, its three colleges—in Camrose, Alberta, and in Regina and Outlook, Saskatchewan—carry a pioneering tradition into the new era. The church's synods maintain camps for youth and conference centers, and its social services include a number of retirement homes as well as other agencies.

By 1987 the ELCIC had seven Chinese Lutheran pastors serving recent immigrants from Hong Kong and the Chinese dispersion in Southeast Asia. Congregations have been formed from Montreal to Vancouver.

The ELCIC chief officer—the 1987 convention action favored the title of presiding bishop (if reaffirmed in 1989)—is Donald W. Sjoberg. Formerly bishop of the Western Canada Synod (LCA), he has rural roots in Manitoba. Higher education in Saskatoon at the University of Saskatchewan and the Lutheran Seminary led him to eight years in an Edmonton parish, a decade as regional home mission supervisor, and 15 years as bishop. His churchly duties, from the Maritimes to the Pacific, stretch farther than in any other

Lutheran church. They suggest the earlier career of another pastor of Swedish origin, Nils Willison (below), whose teaching ministry in both eastern and western Canada was illuminated by a vision of Lutheran unity across the enormous land.

Some 900 delegates and visitors gathered in Ottawa, on the university campus, in late July 1987 for the ELCIC's first regular convention. The opening eucharist in neighboring St. Joseph's Roman Catholic Church struck an ecumenical and international tone that has its place among Canadian Lutherans. A reaffirmed commitment to social justice (Dean T. Simon Farisani [ELC/Southern Africa], assailed *apartheid*) proved to be a convention highlight. The Canadian Lutheran-Anglican dialog report revealed progress, and interim eucharistic hospitality is a possibility after the 1989 convention. In many ways Canada's Lutherans, despite economic stringency (or perhaps because of it), showed themselves to be a dynamic new church body.

Now, as then, the foward look, especially for the ELCIC, presupposes some familiarity with the past. Brief accounts of this church's predecessor bodies follow, as well as a description of the third body (Missourian) that had initially expressed willingness to join the merger.

EVANGELICAL LUTHERAN CHURCH OF CANADA (ELCC)
(1967–1985)

On the eve of its consolidation with the LCA-CS to form the Evangelical Lutheran Church in Canada (ELCIC), the ELCC's 314 congregations had a baptized membership of nearly 85,000. These were served by 214 parish pastors and 118 other ordained clergy, counting the retired. Most of the members of the church are of Norwegian, German, and Danish origin, though many other backgrounds are also represented. The ELCC became operational as an autonomous Canadian church in 1967. Prior to that time it was the Canada District of the American Lutheran Church (ALC), and its three antecedent bodies of basically Norse, German, and Danish descent. A sketch of this background follows

below. It was fitting that in Canada's centennial year (1967) the ELCC became autonomous under a charter of the Canadian parliament. As the first Lutheran body fully independent of governance from south of the border, the ELCC gained distinction among its ecclesial peers.

Though comparatively small numerically, the ELCC contributed significantly to the development of Canadian society. Through its educational institutions, thousands of graduates entered the mainstream of Canadian life, lending Christian perspective to various facets of Canadian culture. In addition, Bible schools contributed a significant number of missionaries who took their skills to various parts of the globe, sharing the gospel and helping people cope in a changing world. In earlier years and up to the decade after World War II, the ELCC's antecedent bodies not only provided a meaningful cultural link for immigrants but also assisted in their integration into the country's cultural mosaic.

The 1970s also saw the beginnings of evangelical outreach to the people scattered across the Northwest Territories. An airborne ministry, in collaboration with the Lutheran Association of Missionaries and Pilots (a free movement), reached many isolated communities in the far north all the way to Inuvik, Northwest Territories, near the Arctic Ocean. New congregations gathered in recent years are maturing, also in the support of still further outreach, while others, in their decline or demise, have affirmed the need for adaptability and confident change.

Central to this task was the education of a capable and committed ministry. The already mentioned Lutheran Theological Seminary at Saskatoon came into its own when the ELCC's Luther Seminary and the LCA-CS seminary (below) merged in 1960 and, seven years later, moved into its new facilities on the University of Saskatchewan campus. In 1984, it reported slightly over 100 students in its first professional degree program, a record for this church.

In collaboration with others, the ELCC carried forward a diversified social ministry. Its retirement centers cared for the elderly. Its "caring community courses" for clergy and laity dealt with the problems of the contemporary family. Linked to evangelism, worship, and witness, ELCC efforts sought to sensitize the members on issues of social justice, peace, and the threat of nuclear catastrophe. Concretely, the church worked for understanding and participation in the large task of securing justice for Indian, Metis (mixed race), Dene (far northern), and other native people.

In global terms, the ELCC was an active member in the World Council of Churches as well as in the LWF. It supported Canadian Lutheran World Relief in helping people in distant lands even as it continued to assist Asian and other newcomers to Canada. In these and many other ways, it endeavored to link a theologically sound faith to personal, corporate, and community life. In this spirit, it initiated the invitation in 1972, as already described, to the two other general bodies to unite in one Lutheran church in Canada. From its own experience the ELCC knew the way to union as a slow process. Its history is here briefly recalled.

The year 1960 marks the beginning of the ELCC as a unified constituency, but at that time it was the Canada District of the *American Lutheran Church (now ELCA), which itself was a consolidation of congregations of the Norse, German, and Danish origins already mentioned. They were part of the great surge into the Prairie Provinces in the late 19th and early 20th centuries. Most of them followed the northward routes from Minnesota, the Dakotas, and Montana, crossing over into Manitoba and Saskatchewan and moving westward into Alberta. Winnipeg was the major Canadian center for expansion westward in the years of heavy immigration, having been raised to that role by the completion of the transcontinental railway (1885) and the earlier rail link to Minnesota. The lure of the far west drew newcomers also to British Columbia, where many, especially from Scandinavia, entered Canada via Vancouver. In short, the settlement of these provinces was part of the great westward movement in North American history.

Among the Prairie Provinces, Saskatchewan—north of western North Dakota and eastern Montana, and the last to become a province—attracted the highest percentage (12% in 1940) of Lutherans, particularly those of German and Norwegian stock. A large proportion of the German Lutherans were gathered up after 1905 by the mission work of the Joint Synod of Ohio (later part of the ALC). A seminary of this synod in St.

Paul (Phalen Park, 1892) aimed to supply pastors also for western Canada. A ministerial preparatory school, Luther Academy, set up in Melville, Saskatchewan (1913), branched into other fields as well, was relocated to Regina (1925), and became the present Luther College. All of these developments paralleled, up to a point, the creation of Lutheran College and Seminary, Saskatoon, by the mainly German-language antecedent of the LCA–CS Central Canada Synod (below).

Among the Scandinavian newcomers, the Danes were far outnumbered by the Norwegians. Although the latter were divided, as in the States, into at least four groups—Synod, Hauge, United, and Free—the United Norwegian Lutherans were a majority. Matching their Germanic counterparts, and outdoing their fellow Norse in neighboring Saskatchewan, the Alberta Norwegian Lutheran College Association (1911) pooled the efforts of the United and the Hauge constituencies and, two years later, had the present Camrose College in operation. A similar association in Saskatchewan founded a Lutheran academy in Outlook, some 50 miles (80 kilometers) south of Saskatoon. It has survived as the Lutheran Collegiate Bible Institute and, in recent years, has been especially helpful to Chinese and other students entering higher education in Canada.

For decades, the ELCC's antecedent bodies (the mother churches) had relied on the stateside education of their ministers. In 1939, however, Luther Seminary was launched by the Canada District of the then Norwegian Lutheran Church of America (NLCA; after 1946 Evangelical Lutheran Church of America, and after 1960 the major component of the former ALC). A departure from the single seminary policy of the NLCA, Luther Seminary in Saskatoon developed a working relationship with the already operative Lutheran College and Seminary of the then Western Canada Synod (ULCA, below). Wartime pressures of the 1940s and the ensuing postwar challenges on many fronts affirmed the importance of an indigenous ministry in western Canada and, as already noted (ELCIC), made the two seminaries, by their very separateness, contribute powerfully to the forces

of confessional unity and ecumenical wholeness.

LUTHERAN CHURCH IN AMERICA–CANADA SECTION (LCA–CS)
(1962–1985)

Prior to the ELCIC merger this largest and
oldest of the three major Lutheran church
bodies in Canada comprised 340 congregations. They were spread across the continent,
from the Maritime Provinces in the east to
British Columbia in the west. Serving them
were 217 parish pastors and 156 other ordained ministers as well as other workers in
various fields. The largest concentration still
today is in Ontario, mostly in the environs
of Toronto and westward. Clusters of congregations remain in Nova Scotia and various
parts of the Prairie Provinces—Manitoba
(Winnipeg), Saskatchewan (Saskatoon), and
Alberta (Edmonton), and in more isolated
areas. The members of LCA–CS range from
recent Canadians to those descended from
settlers arriving over two centuries earlier.
The largest number are of German origin, the
next largest of Swedish. Others are of Icelandic, Danish, Finnish, Estonian, Latvian,
Lithuanian, Hungarian, Slovak, Volga (Russian) German, Transylvanian (Romanian)
German, and (by intermarriage) Anglo-Saxon lineage. This kind of ethnic mixture, perhaps more diverse in the LCA–CS than in the
other two Canadian Lutheran bodies, is typical of a country that has been open to all
comers, including those from Asia in recent
years.

The LCA–CS met all the legal requirements of a recognized Canadian church in
dealing with the government and in participating with other churches in common causes. As such, it was the only Lutheran body
(prior to the ELCIC) to hold membership in
the Canadian Council of Churches. In doing
so, it was parelleling in Canada what the rest
of the LCA had done in the *USA. Although
formed in 1962, the constituting year of the
LCA, it was only in 1973 that the Canada
Section received its first full-time staff official, an executive secretary.

The Canada Section, as a church body, was
made up of three synods: Eastern Canada (as

presently in the ELCIC), comprising congregations in the provinces of Ontario, Quebec, Nova Scotia, New Brunswick, and Newfoundland and including 64% of the total
Canada Section baptized membership; Central Canada, including westernmost Ontario,
Manitoba, Saskatchewan, with nearly 18%;
Western Canada, including Alberta and British Columbia, with over 18%. For the education of its ministry, the Canada Section supported two seminaries, Waterloo, Ontario
(1911), and Saskatoon (1913), the latter becoming a joint venture with the ELCC
(above) during the 1940s. Both seminaries
included preparatory colleges. Whereas the
college in Saskatoon folded during the
depression of the 1930s, the one in Waterloo
gave rise to two universities: the University
of Waterloo (1957), which separated from the
church, and Waterloo Lutheran University
(WLU; 1958), which was acquired by the
Province of Ontario in 1973 and renamed
Wilfred Laurier University after the nation's
first premier, a native of French Canada.
While still a church institution, WLU prepared hundreds of young people for ministerial and other professions. It also developed
the first professional school of social work
in a then still church-related Canadian university.

● ● ●

The origins of the former LCA–CS are
highly diverse in time and place. In Nova
Scotia, for instance, German colonists from
Hanover, mainly, in the 1750s were among
the pioneer settlers in Halifax and Lunenburg.
They were getting established when the defeat of the French turned Canada into a British
possession (1763). While Hanoverian George
III was king of England, Hanoverians formed
Canada's earliest Lutheran congregations:
Halifax in 1752, and Lunenburg in 1761. The
Halifax congregation was the first of many
to turn Anglican. The Lunenburg congregation persevered through many difficulties
to remain Lutheran. Its first pastor, "little"
Friedrich Schultz, as Henry Melchior Muhlenberg called him, was sent there in 1772,
and remained a decade. After the War of
Independence, the Lunenburgers received
pastors from the famed mission center in
Halle, Germany, but apparently lost contact
with fellow Lutherans in the *USA. Thus
they were "discovered" by the young American pastor, William Alfred Passavant, in

1846, while he was en route to London, to the constituting meeting of the Evangelical Alliance. An unexpected stopover in Halifax turned his brief stay into a discovery. Ensuing connections with the mission-minded Lutheran Pittsburgh Synod in the USA led to the eventual organization of the Nova Scotia Synod (1903) and to partnership with other synods in forming the United Lutheran Church in America (ULCA; 1918)—a predecessor body of the LCA.

In Ontario, Loyalist Lutherans had moved in from New York State and Pennsylvania after the revolution and settled along the St. Lawrence near Morrisburg and Williamsburg. Some of the congregations they founded later became Anglican. Others remained Lutheran and grew in number as immigration from Germany began during the second quarter of the 19th century. In 1850 the Pittsburgh Synod again responded to a layman, Adam Keffer, who, having hiked 320 kilometers, pleaded for pastors. In 1861, the Canada Synod was formed. It became a charter member of the confessionally solid Evangelical Lutheran General Council (1867), a predecessor body of the ULCA (below). In 1962, the Canada and Nova Scotia Synods became the Eastern Canada Synod of the LCA.

To meet the long-felt need for an indigenous ministry in eastern Canada, Waterloo Lutheran College and Seminary, as already noted, was founded in 1911. Today, the seminary is associated with the two neighboring universities and also with the interdenominational Toronto School of Theology.

The story of the LCA–CS in Canada's western half is shorter but equally complex, filled with struggle, and peopled with newcomers from the USA and European lands. The Canada Synod itself, with modest help from the General Council, undertook missionary activity that led to the formation of the Manitoba Synod in 1897. Its primary constituency was in Winnipeg, the city from which most arrivals deployed westward. There were many Swedes among them, as well as Germans, Norwegians, and others. More unusual was the large number of Icelanders. Early to arrive, they had already in 1885 formed their own Icelandic Evangelical Lutheran Synod in America. Based in the Winnipeg area but extending, along with Icelandic immigration, from Nova Scotia to the

State of Nebraska (USA), this was an international association of congregations. As a nongeographic synod, it became a member of the ULCA. In 1962, it was absorbed into the territorial synods of the LCA.

The LCA Synods of Central Canada and Western Canada grew out of successive expansions of the original Manitoba Synod. On their turf, the need for an indigenously trained ministry had led already in 1913 to the chartering of the Lutheran College and Seminary at Saskatoon, mentioned earlier. This venture became a major partner in the advancement of Lutheran unity in the west (see ELCC, above). This fact becomes more striking as the perspective widens. Among western Canada's total Lutheran population, the Central and Western Synods are a numerical minority, but they provide the chief link with Lutherans in eastern Canada, a pivotal factor in achieving the consolidation embodied in the ELCIC today.

To sum up, the LCA–CS was the most heavily involved ecumenically among the Canadian Lutheran bodies. It was a member of the Canadian Council of Churches as well as a participant in various coalitions organized for specific purposes and peculiar to the Canadian scene, such as advocacy in matters of economic justice, native rights, and political refugee rescue work.

LATVIAN EVANGELICAL LUTHERAN CHURCH (see USA)

LUTHERAN CHURCH–CANADA (LC-C)

Member: ILC, LCIC

Membership: 82,733

President: The Rev. Dr. Edwin G. Lehmann

PO Box 55, Station A,

2727 Portage Avenue, Unit 203

Winnipeg, Manitoba R3K 1Z9

Until 1987, when it became autonomous, this church was a federation of the Canadian districts of the Lutheran Church–Missouri Synod (LCMS). It included the Alberta-British Columbia, Manitoba and Saskatchewan, and

Ontario Districts, as well as the Canada Conference of the English District and the Canadian congregations in the Minnesota North District and in the (formerly Slovak) Synod of Evangelical Lutheran Churches District.

The 353 congregations of the LC–C are served by 211 parish pastors as well as by others among the remaining 95 ordained men, some of whom are retirees. Nearly 42% of the more than 94,000 baptized members reside in Ontario. Another 20% are in Alberta, and 17% are in Saskatchewan. British Columbia has nearly 13%, and Manitoba almost 7%. Quebec has under 500 members and the Maritime Provinces have none.

The LC–C, as a Canadian entity, was organized in Winnipeg in 1958. The name, Lutheran Church–Canada, was an important change in a country where the designation "Missouri" was meaningless. Six years later, when the question of relation to the stateside LCMS came to vote, the two western districts voted for an independent church, but the larger Ontario District was deadlocked on the issue. In the late 1970s and early 1980s, another initiative advocated that this church became autonomous in Canada. In 1985, a majority of congregations voted to form an autonomous LC–C. This was granted by the July 1986 LCMS convention and came into effect on July 1, 1987.

Behind the LC–C name lies over a century of history. The Ontario District (1879) was followed by the formation of the two western districts in 1920. But these coalitions of congregations point to earlier events. Ontario's first Missouri-related congregation—the first in Canada—was formed in 1854. In Ontario, as later in the west, Missouri's ability to supply pastors for German-speaking Lutheran immigrants enabled it to build on the work begun by others. Of the 25 congregations initially comprising the Ontario District, nine had been started by Missourians, two by the Buffalo Synod, and one had been independent; but 13 were of the former Canada Synod (General Council; above). Inter-Lutheran competition, here as elsewhere, was intense,

at times bitter. Missouri's growth was steady, concentrating in the attractive region between Toronto and London, to the west.

Success in Ontario stimulated similar efforts later in the Prairie Provinces and British Columbia. The spirit in the west was different. Clashes with other Lutherans of German origin occurred, but here the presence of many Scandinavian Lutherans created a different confessional milieu than in Ontario, a fact of growing importance later, when English became the common tongue also of Lutherans. The Manitoba and Saskatchewan District as well as the Alberta-British Columbia District were offshoots of the Minnesota and Dakota District (1881). Again, it was Missouri's ability to supply pastors speaking the language of the settlers that gave them the edge among those of German origin. This advantage was evident even after World War II in the resettlement of ethnic Germans from Europe.

For generations, the Missouri Synod sent pastors to Canada who had been educated in St. Louis or Springfield, Illinois (see *USA). But with the formation of the LC–C, and especially after Missouri's internal strife in the 1970s, the stage seemed set for an indigenously trained ministry. A first step was an LCMS-approved professorship (1971) in Saskatoon, at the joint ELCC and LCA–CS seminary. But soon thereafter two seminaries were founded expressly for the LC–C; one in St. Catharines, near Niagara Falls, for Ontario; the other in Edmonton, Alberta, for the west. The founding of these two seminaries, intended to strengthen the LC–C, also marked the end of Missouri participation in fashioning a united Lutheran church in Canada (above). But the two seminaries also recalled the fact that already in 1921 the Missouri Synod had opened Concordia College (Junior), in Edmonton in the hope of providing an indigenous Canadian ministry for its congregations.

WISCONSIN EVANGELICAL LUTHERAN SYNOD (see USA)

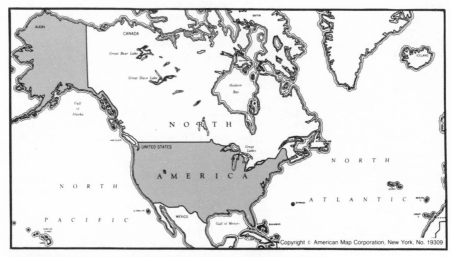

Copyright © American Map Corporation, New York, No. 19309

UNITED STATES OF AMERICA

The 8,520,419 (1987) baptized members of Lutheran churches in the USA comprise about 3.5% of the nation's population. In the 1920s it was estimated that over 14 million Americans (about 14%), by virtue of their Central or Northern European background, were of Lutheran "preference." Such estimates have fallen into disuse, even as memories of immigration have faded. Many people of Lutheran antecedents have long since become active in other communions or dissociated from any church. Still others have joined, and become active Lutherans—adding Black, Indian, Hispanic, and Asian as well as Anglo-Saxon and other elements to an essentially diversified Lutheranism. In 1986, the ALC, LCA, and the small AELC—all three member churches in the LWF—accounted for about 11.7% of the Federation's numerical composition. A merger of these three bodies took effect in 1988.

The USA is a federal republic composed of 50 states, 49 of which are in North America. The other state is comprised of the Hawaiian Islands. Area: 9,384,721 sq. km. (3,623,461 sq. mi.). Pop. (1986 est.): 241,077,000, including 85.1% white, 12.1% black, and 2.8% other races. Cap.: Washington, District of Columbia (pop., 1986 est., 626,000). Largest city: New York (pop., 1986 est., 7,183,984). Language: English; Spanish is recognized in areas heavily populated by Cubans, Puerto Ricans, Mexicans, and other Spanish-speaking people.

History: The renovated Statue of Liberty in New York Harbor—rededicated July 4, 1986, with great pageantry—stands as a 100-year reminder, since 1886, that the United States is a nation of immigrants and their descendants; of the Afro-Americans, whose forebears came as slaves and who are now the nation's largest minority (12%); and of the native Americans, whose distant antecedents are said to have been in Asia and whose present number represents a contested retreat before the advancing tide of settlers sprung from the global outreach of Europe.

The statue itself—the robed and crowned female figure holding high a torch— was originally known as "Liberty enlightening the world." A gift of France to the

American people, it recalls French assistance to the 13 original colonies in their struggle for independence from Britain. The statue's artist, Frédéric Auguste Bartholdi (1834–1904), born in Colmar (Alsace), was of Lutheran heritage. The poet Emma Lazarus (1849–1887) of New York (whose lines "Give me your tired, your poor" are inscribed on the pedestal) was Jewish and a fiery protester against injustice, especially as shown in the Russian pogroms. Near the statue is Ellis Island, widely known as the immigrant point of entry for over 50 years (1892–1943) and now part of the Statue of Liberty National Monument.

In magnitude, the immigration to America is unmatched in human history. From the first settlement in Jamestown (Virginia) in 1607, more than 45 million people arrived in America from other countries; three out of four remained. The presence of resources, the vastness of space, the magnetism of a free society, and other attractions overshadowed the inevitable hardships and made this an extraordinary land of promise. Skills and labor were the common sign language; the learning of English followed.

Americanization was and continues to be a process drawing perennially on three ideas: liberty, equality, and government by consent of the governed. In this setting, cultural pluralism has often been in jeopardy, but it has survived.

The basic patterns of American society are broadly derived from Europe, but from Britain in particular. While Britain won Canada from France in 1763, it soon thereafter lost its 13 more populous and English-speaking colonies along the Atlantic coast. The War of Independence (1776–1783) opened the way for the rise of the USA. Although English stock predominated, the American mix already included Welsh, Scots, Irish, Germans, Dutch, Swedes, French, and others, as well as the thousands of African slaves working on southern plantations and elsewhere. Native Americans were mainly outside the mix and were pushed ever farther west.

Today, Americans descended from English-speaking forebears—English, Scots, Welsh, and Irish—comprise a little over 40% of the population. An almost equal number have roots in other European countries, with the largest number (20%) from Germany, and significant numbers from France, Italy, and the Scandinavian countries. More recent immigrants and refugees have come from the Spanish-speaking lands south of the border as well as from Asian countries—including Chinese, Japanese, Koreans, Indians, Vietnamese, and Kampucheans. The largest minority have African roots. Already in 1619, the first African slaves were brought to Jamestown. All but the native Americans are people "from somewhere else."

When white colonists settled in North America in the 17th century, it is estimated that the present area of continental USA was inhabited by about 1,000,000 native Americans grouped into some 200 "nations" (a European term) or tribes. Dispossessed, placed in reservations, and left with a "trail of broken treaties," most American Indians today live on land west of the Mississippi, with the largest number in the states of Oklahoma, Arizona, and California. Significant numbers also are in Wisconsin, Minnesota, and the Dakotas.

Wounded Knee (South Dakota), site of the last major battle of the Indian wars (1890), came into fresh prominence in the struggle of the American Indian Movement during the early 1970s—a struggle that has also challenged Lutherans to reassess their general indifference to Indian concerns (below).

American Indians remain a highly diverse people. Since 1924 they have full USA citizenship.

The federal constitution, adopted in Philadelphia in 1787, and ratified by the states (the former colonies), expressed the will of the people "to form a more perfect union." A concise instrument of government, its initial nine amendments comprised a Bill of Rights, and their number (now grown to 26) suggests how the amending process has applied the meaning of the original document to changing needs over two centuries. Constitutionally, the exercise of the legislative, executive, and judicial functions of government has been kept on course by interrelated checks and balances. States rights, vis-à-vis the federal government, have played a prominent part from the beginning, but have steadily been diminished as national considerations took precedence over territorial practice.

The treatment of the nation's largest minority exemplifies the process. During the Civil War era, Abraham Lincoln's presidential Emancipation Proclamation (January 1, 1863), declared the slaves in the southern states free. The 14th and 15th amendments (1868) extended the results of emancipation nationwide, including citizenship. Yet it remained for the Supreme Court decision (1954) to declare public school segregation unconstitutional, and for the Civil Rights Act (1964), and subsequent legislation by Congress, to ban discrimination and provide for the full integration of African-Americans into the national community.

Where white churches, from the standpoint of Christian ethics, might well have been expected to take the lead in desegregation, it remained for other agencies—including the National Association for the Advancement of Colored People (NAACP), the Southern Christian Leadership Conference (SCLC), and others—to mobilize public opinion and induce government action. The outstanding leader in this process was Martin Luther King Jr., a Baptist minister in the South. A moving orator, his vision of a racially reconciled society is best remembered in "I have a dream," his address to the thousands assembled before the Lincoln Memorial during the massive march on Washington (1963). Felled by an assassin's bullet (1968), King's own policy of nonviolence had already then begun to yield to demands of "black power," and to the violence that exploded after his death. January 16—the birthday of Martin Luther King Jr.—today stands as the first national holiday honoring one who was not a president of the United States but the personification of an ongoing struggle for human rights and mutual respect in America.

The 19th-century westward movement of American-born white settlers created an ever-changing frontier. The role of women in frontier society was fully as heroic as that of men. Although clashes with Indians were often violent, the initial disposition of Indians (as with most of the world's peoples) was that of friendliness toward strangers—a fact that a frontier mother was more likely to ascertain than her husband. As new territories were opened, future Midwestern states—like Illinois, Wisconsin, Iowa, Minnesota, and the Dakotas—engaged agents to recruit settlers in Europe and send them directly to frontier lands. Germans and Scandinavians, mostly from rural villages, came in large numbers to a burgeoning rural life in America (a fact of much significance to the rise of Lutheranism in the Midwest and beyond). In any case, these newcomers had been preceded by the westward-moving streams of Anglo-Americans who laid out the towns, chose the place names, and ran the government. Other leading minorities, notably the Irish—and later the Italians—came as laborers, digging canals or building railroads, and then settling mainly in cities and remaining close to their church.

For countless Europeans, America continued to be a "land of unlimited opportunity," a latter day promised land. For Europe's Jews this was especially pertinent. Today numbering about 6,000,000, they came to America in three major stages: prior to 1880, mainly from German lands (180,000); then to 1924, from Eastern Europe and the Russian regions of Jewish settlement (2.3 million); thereafter, from pre- and post-World War II Europe (about 275,000 refugees and others, as well as some 300,000 immigrants from Israel). Those of the early stage filled an essential function in commercial life, with connections in business and finance spanning the continent and peddlers reaching the smallest hamlets. They identified mainly with the larger German community.

While Eastern European Jews comprised only about one-sixth of the total Jewish community in the America of 1880, they comprised five-sixths of it by 1924. The enormous change was evident in the cities, especially New York, but also elsewhere. For many, the garment industry was a starting point. Other business enterprises soon beckoned. Education aided acculturation and occupational mobility; many entered the legal profession. Music, the arts, and the ever-expanding entertainment industry were in many ways shaped by Jewish interest and participation. Being perhaps America's most influential minority, they have many times given decisive encouragement to the country's largest minority

(the blacks) and the movement of civil rights.

Geographically, the expansion of the United States followed an age-old process of the stronger overcoming the weaker. Not only were American Indians displaced, but vast lands once claimed by Europe's leading powers—Britain, France, Spain—were embodied into the expanding USA: the Mississippi Valley, by purchase from France (1803); Texas and the Southwest as far as California, by defeating Mexico (1846–1848); the Pacific Northwest, by compromise with Britain (1846); Alaska, by purchase from Russia (1867); Puerto Rico, by the defeat of Spain (1898); American Samoa, by treaty with Britain and Germany (1899); Hawaii, by following up an overthrown monarchy (1900); the Virgin Islands (Danish West Indies), by purchase from Denmark (1917); Panama Canal Zone, by acquisition from Colombia, and U.S.-administered, 1903–1979.

The location of the United States, between two great oceans, has fostered political isolationism, but the process by which the country grew supplied unlimited international ties. America's power as a nation became evident only via its reluctant participation in this century's two world wars—engagements in which idealism ("make the world safe for democracy") was the catchword in World War I, and realism (to combat militant totalitarianism and its violation of human rights) was the challenge in World War II (or so it can be oversimplified in retrospect). Similarly, a prolongation of resolves made during the conflicts evoked characteristic responses: America helped to inspire a League of Nations, but then failed to join it (isolationism won out); America loomed large in founding the United Nations, provided the headquarters location in New York, played an active role for years, but—as the membership of Third World nations has leaped in numbers, and as programs have multiplied and problems intensified—American interest has diminished and aspects of isolationism have reappeared.

Meanwhile, one of the big changes in American foreign policy emerged with the disclosures of the Nazi-perpetrated Holocaust (see *Germany). A once evenhanded relationship to the nations of the Middle East had, by the 1980s, brought the United States strongly to the side of the new state of Israel, while also trying to keep its oil supply from Arab nations secure. All of this is part of the prolonged and deepened postwar tension between the United States and Russia, countries often referred to in the 19th century as the sleeping giants among the nations and today the so-called superpowers of the nuclear age.

American involvement in the Far East became increasingly complicated, not only with respect to postwar Japan and postwar revolutionary China, but also in terms of the Korean War (1950–1953) and the prolonged conflict in Vietnam (1954–1975). The latter triggered widespread protest at home, left its mark politically, and revealed a nation divided between those supporting a strong military and those working for peace. The resettlement of refugees from Vietnam and Kampuchea during the past decade, especially on the Pacific coast, brought still another Asian element into American life. The Reagan presidency endeavored to make up for the nation's no-win experience in Vietnam and to reassert power internationally. The ominously spiraling national debt and the continuing nuclear buildup (also in the USSR) carried forebodings of deep troubles ahead—for other nations as well.

Religion (1980 est.): Protestant 40%; Roman Catholic 30%; Eastern Orthodox 2.1%; Jewish 3.2%; Muslim 0.8%; Hindu 0.2%; nonreligious and atheist 6.9%; other 16.8%.

The religious traditions of the American Indians, alone indigenous to this country, are not only incalculably old but also gifted with powers of survival that, in the absence of a written language, convey a living spiritual legacy from one generation to the next. Among many native Americans there is a reviving interest in the wholeness of their traditional religion, which encompasses all of life within the creation of the Great Spirit. For America's indigenous people—as for those of other primal religions—there is no separating religion from life or compartmentalizing the faith. Essential values have persisted, among them rites of purification, the annual tribal Sun Dance, and the individual spiritual retreat. Despite generations of Christian missions among them, American Indians have clung to their spiritual inheritance. They have done so in ways capable of enriching the religious life—or filling the spiritual void—of those who have long since taken possession of their land. The tragic note in Indian religious tradition, observers have found, lies not in the internecine warfare among their nations but in the white conqueror's practice to stereotype the Indian and thus to break the promise of partnership. Ironically, the tobacco American Indians cultivated (long before its discovery by Europeans) was intended for the peace pipe they used in their rituals of reconciliation.

Christian missions among the Indians in what is now continental USA began in the 17th century—Protestant in the northeast and Roman Catholic in the southwest—and have continued under various auspices into other parts of the country and on to the Indian reservations. The 18th-century Franciscan missions in California, with their restored church buildings (as in Santa Barbara), are visible reminders of the Spanish colonial era. For their conversion to Christianity, the "praying Indians," as they were called, at times paid the price of being caught in the crossfire between the advancing white settlers and the Indians defending their lands. The Native American Church of North America, founded in 1870, now has adherents in nearly all tribes. With its inclusion of numerous Indian religious traditions, it is considered marginally Christian. Meanwhile, white Christians who would rally support for the rights of Indians have often found members of their churches, especially those living near reservations, reluctant to change old attitudes.

Basic to American religious history is the separation of church and state guaranteed by the First Amendment to the Constitution (1787). For the first time since Emperor Constantine espoused Christianity in the fourth century, the principle of separation was adopted as a governmental policy and subsequently carried out with considerable consistency. Although the authors thought in terms of the religious situation of their day, they provided a basis for the religious pluralism of present-day America.

The rise and practice of a so-called civil religion—the matrix of religious pluralism—already finds reference in the Declaration of Independence (1776): "All men are created equal, and are endowed by their Creator with certain inalienable rights." The founding fathers relied on the "protection of divine Providence." While these are expressions of Deism, in the manner of John Locke (1632–1704), they later on are the assumptions of a variously held democratic

faith: that there is a fundamental law underlying all laws, applying to all nations, and upholding a moral order. This frank supernaturalism, derived from the Judeo-Christian faith, found endless application: from the New England Puritan notion of Massachusetts Bay Colony being "like a city set on a hill" for all the world to take note, to the current moralistic pronouncement claiming "America as the world's last best hope." The national motto, "In God We Trust," the practice of invocation at political conventions or in the Congress or in many another setting, are among the symbols of civil religion. Paradoxically, however, the strict adherence to separation has banned religious instruction from the public schools, and has (except for treatment of the colonial era) virtually omitted reference to religious life and the churches from the history textbooks. By the 1980s, however, a backlash to this kind of omission has found expression in a resurgence of fundamentalism and its use of television (often through its own networks) to draw uncounted numbers into its "electronic churches."

• • •

Continental American church history begins with a prelude of struggle (see Lutherans, below), when Spaniards exterminated a colony of French Huguenots in 1564 ("Lutherans," as they were then called) near the site of the oldest of American cities, St. Augustine, Florida. Later, the dual motif of European-style established (state) church, on the one hand, and European-advocated separate (free) church, on the other, determined the religious history of the colonial period. By the early 1770s, the Anglican Church had become established in six of the (southern) British colonies and part of a seventh (New York); the Congregational Church was established in three colonies (all in Puritan New England). Religious liberty (separation of church and state) was practiced in three (Pennsylvania, Rhode Island, and New Jersey), as well as in parts of New York.

With the coming of independence, all churches were eventually disestablished, last of all (1833) in Massachusetts. They were henceforth on their own, dependent on support contributed voluntarily by their members and on an evangelistic outreach (home mission) to the indifferent and the unchurched. Also involved was the necessity of churches to govern themselves. In an individualistically oriented society, this three-self situation—self-government, self-support, self-propagation—led to periodic revival movements as well as to the multiplication of religious bodies of all kinds.

Under these circumstances, older concepts of the unity of the church, especially in a given territory—as long practiced in Europe—were seriously altered. Once marginal groups, like the Baptists and the Methodists, had the least to lose and the most to gain from the new situation. Eventually, these became the two most numerous Protestant communions in America: the Methodists, following an episcopal polity; and the Baptists, a congregational. Today the largest of the Methodist denominations (self-governing church bodies), the United Methodist Church, has over 14.3 million (baptized) members; the largest Baptist, the Southern Baptist Convention, claims about 15 million adherents.

Churches of the Reformation heritage—Episcopalians (the Anglican name was dropped after the revolution), Presbyterians, Congregationalists, Lutherans, and Reformed—also grew, but were rapidly outdistanced in the course of the 19th century. One reason for this lay in their continued requirement of a theologically educated ministry and the frequent lack of ministers. Having no such requirement, Baptists relied on farmer-preachers selected from among members of the congregation, and Methodists used quasi-lay circuit riders responsible to a superintendent. In either case, the supply of preachers was always adequate and the overhead cost low.

The major demoninations of the Reformation churches today are: United Presbyterian Church (3.5 million); Episcopal Church (3.2 million); United Church of Christ (Congregational and the Evangelical and Reformed Church [German origin], 2.7 million); and Lutheran (two chief bodies [see below] together over 8 million).

● ● ●

Roman Catholicism, beginning with Lord Baltimore's initially Catholic colony of Maryland (1632), was lightly represented in the colonial period; but it became America's single largest and most powerful church. Today, it claims about 50 million baptized members. These are mainly descendants of massive immigration during the 19th and early 20th centuries, first from Ireland, then also from Germany, and subsequently from Italy, Poland, France, and the Hapsburg lands of the Danube basin. Settling in the cities more than in rural areas, Catholics roused the fears of Protestants, including the specter of a papal takeover of "Protestant America." The anti-Catholic riots in New York, Philadelphia, and other cities during the 1840s and 1850s (dubbed later as the "Protestant Crusade") availed little, except to strengthen the Catholic resolve to retain and nurture their identity in America. Parish churches, parochial schools, high schools, colleges, universities, and theological seminaries were visible signs of the Roman Catholic presence. Through welfare services for the poor, including hospitals, orphanages, convents, and other institutions, a sense of cohesiveness was fostered.

With respect to European origins, Catholics, like the Lutherans, had to contend with ethnic differences and rivalries in their midst. Yet their governance under a strong hierarchy, which included bishops and lay people with political acumen, enabled them to adapt to the conditions of a free society. Usually belonging to the biggest ecclesial body in urban settings, Roman Catholics in time have become influential at all levels of political life. The election of John F. Kennedy as president of the United States in 1960 marked the apex of a long upward climb. In the process, those of Irish extraction—both lay and clergy—have played a leading role. The current 32 archdioceses and over 130 dioceses are spread throughout the nation. The U.S. Catholic Conference (successor in 1967 to the National Catholic Welfare Conference, begun in 1917) serves as a general agency for the church. The U.S. Conference of Catholic Bishops (CCB; 1967) provides a platform for coping with major issues. The CCB pastoral letter on nuclear weapons (1983) brought the US Roman Catholic hierarchy closer to the so-called "peace churches" than ever before. Since Vatican II, relations between Catholics and Protestants have improved greatly. Yet tensions within the communion, heightened by social change and a questioning of traditional authority and practices, have taken their toll among the faithful.

Eastern and Oriental Orthodoxy in the United States are separated into factions and ethnic traditions. The largest of these, the Greek Orthodox (1864), lists some 1.9 million baptized members. The formerly Russian, now Orthodox, Church of America (1792), counts 960,000 members. Romanian, Ukranian, and other ecclesial bodies—some 20 all together—present a complex picture, rich in historical diversity. Generations of life in America and participation in the ecumenical movement have brought the Eastern Orthodox closer together. An experience like this is true also of the Oriental Orthodox, those small Middle Eastern bodies of Christians outside the bounds of the old Roman Empire. While not receiving the Christological formulation of the Council of Chalcedon (A.D. 451), they nevertheless do not deny its substance.

Black churches in the USA present an array of some 140 separate denominations. Some are offshoots of white churches; some have broken away from other black churches. While most white denominations also have black members, the formation of separate black churches began early. The two largest black churches, the National Baptist Convention of America (3.3 million) and the National Baptist Convention, USA (6.4 million), trace their beginnings to 1773. On the Methodist side, the African Methodist Episcopal Church (1.5 million) grew out of a dissident group in Philadelphia (1787); the African Methodist Episcopal Zion Church (1.3 million) emerged in New York (1796). These were small beginnings among freed slaves and came to mean a great deal later on, after the emancipation.

Pentecostalism, as a movement, took its rise early in the present century as a revival among blacks and whites. The usual reference is to the Azusa Street Mission, under Charles Seymour, in Los Angeles (1906). Among the movement's many white antecedents, it suffices to name the Wesleyan tradition of Holiness, or the many American revivals on the frontier and in the cities. The accent fell on "speaking in tongues," and "baptism of the Spirit." In its history and present world outreach, Pentecostalism knows no racial or linguistic boundaries, but it has benefited from the ability of Americans to understand and communicate beyond "the Book" and the written word. Among black people, the largest Pentecostal body is the Church of God in Christ, which claims 1.6 million members. By way of the charismatic movement, Pentecostalism has also found expression in the Reformation churches and in the Roman Catholic Church.

• • •

Unity among Protestants in America has come slowly and has grown out of the dual conviction that God wills unity, and that among churches—regardless of doctrinal differences—some things are done better together than separately. Many specific functions, in mission or education or charitable services, had led to the formation of societies during the 19th century. By the early 20th century, the Social Gospel Movement—to assist the needy and to strive for justice—had touched large segments of Protestantism. The abolition of slavery, in the mid-19th century, had called forth the greatest efforts.

The Federal Council of Churches (1908), as a common Protestant agency, had its counterparts at the state and city levels. Functioning for over four decades, the Federal Council was succeeded in 1950 by the National Council of Churches of Christ in the USA. With functions more inclusive than those of its predecessor agency, the NCCC/USA currently serves more than 30 church bodies whose total membership exceeds 40 million. Most of the Protestant communions and Eastern Orthodox bodies

take part. The Lutheran Church in America (below) was the only Lutheran participant. The ELCA (below), pending action of its biennial convention in 1989, participates in the NCCC on the basis of the former LCA. Southern Baptists are the largest among the nonparticipating churches. In recent times, there have been sustained attacks on the NCCC from the side of conservative and fundamentalist-minded Evangelicals. Major criticism has focused on such issues as the alleged abandonment of biblical Christianity, the engagement in political activity in the furtherance of human rights, peace and the abolition of nuclear arms, and the combating of racism, notably in the churches. NCCC policies have often paralleled those of the WCC, but the two agencies are quite separate.

Outside the NCCC/USA—in addition to those bodies already mentioned—are many other independent or nonconciliar churches. In part, they represent earlier divergences like the Unitarian and Universalist Association (1778), whose membership is small (265,000) but whose influence on American Protestantism has been extensive. The above-mentioned Church of Jesus Christ of Latter Day Saints (1830, Mormons), whose American membership is said to comprise about one-half of a more than 5,000,000 worldwide constituency, is reportedly growing at some 5% per year.

Another array of believers is Jehovah's Witnesses (1872). Begun in America, where its membership well exceeds 1,000,000, it, too, has been internationally active (and, in some countries, persecuted). The Seventh Day Adventist Church (1844), currently with over 700,000 members in America, is known internationally for its hospitals and medical missionary emphasis. The list is almost endless. In addition, the mobility of adherents across organizational lines has been vastly increased by such factors as the coalescing of religious and political conservatism, and the already noted rise of "electronic churches" via television's more charismatic preachers.

Conservatism, meanwhile, has crossed denominational lines, drawn countless members of "mainline" church bodies into its ranks, pursued an ecclesially independent course, and defended the Bible's literal inerrancy. It has been known by various names. Fundamentalism became a movement decades ago, when *The Fundamentals* (12 small volumes by a combination of American and British authors) were published (1910–1913) and circulated widely. As diverse as Anglican and Baptist, they opposed theological liberalism and the gathering force of the Social Gospel Movement. Evangelicalism is another and more recent collective term, often used to denote a conservative Protestantism. Since World War II, Evangelicals have generally surpassed the major denominations in missionary zeal, and their personnel overseas now considerably outnumbers those of the mainline churches. Many Evangelicals have also become politically active.

● ● ●

The role of Jews in American religious life complements their presence in other areas that have already been mentioned. The three major branches of American Judaism go by the names of Reform, Conservative, and Orthodox. Except for some Sephardic Jews (whose unusual odyssey, as 17th-century refugees from Spain, had taken them from Holland to *Brazil to New York), the vast majority of arrivals in 19th- and 20th-century America were Ashkenazi Jews first from Germany and then from Eastern Europe.

Yet the Ashkenazim were nowhere more differentiated from each other than in religion. Those from Germany, prior to 1880, brought with them the ingredients of Reform Judaism and the readiness to adapt. This was not far from the mood of liberal Protestantism nor from "American Lutheranism" (below, Lutherans). They called their synagogues temples, modified their traditional worship, trained the first American rabbis at their Hebrew Union College and Seminary (1875) in Cincinnati, and for a time—as they covered the country and had their conference of rabbis—they seemed to be American Judaism. They identified with the great poets and thinkers of romantic Germany. A brilliant Chicago rabbi (Bernard Felsenthal) seemed to speak for many when he declared himself racially a Jew, politically an American, and spiritually a German. Now, over a century later, Reform Judaism claims perhaps 30% of what is collectively known as the American Synagogue.

As we have seen, the great influx of Jews from Eastern Europe concentrated not only in New York City but gathered in other major cities also. Many of them had experienced persecution, and for most of them, if religion was to mark their identity, the choice lay between a moderate Judaism (the Conservative branch) and a strong traditional Judaism (the Orthodox branch). For the Conservative branch, the Jewish Theological Seminary in New York, from the 1890s, rose to prominence in shaping thought as well as future leaders. Its ultimate goal was to unify Judaism by combining the openness of Reform Judaism and the commitment of Orthodox Judaism. For its part, the Orthodox branch created its own center of influence by founding Yeshiva College (now University) in New York. Again, in terms of numbers,

perhaps 40% of the American Synagogue are Conservative, and under 30%
Orthodox. The several branches have
lost considerable numbers of their descendants to secular Judaism. In general
terms, this is no different from the losses
experienced in Catholicism and Protestantism and even in Eastern Orthodoxy.
Yet there is this difference: the Holocaust. That incredible event has changed
the perspective of how Jews relate to
each other as well as to Christians, and
vice versa.

• • •

Beyond the Europeanized Judeo-
Christian tradition, American life has
progressively been touched by Asian religions. While the Chicago Fair's Parliament of World Religions (1893) remains
a landmark in public awareness of other
religions, the 1960s, with the Vietnam
War and protests against it, mark a turning away by many Americans from the
religious traditions of the West. Among
blacks, the Nation of Islam (Black Muslims, 1946) drew on an earlier movement
and gained a new identity for black people. Through immigration from the Middle East, the nearly half-million Sunni
Muslims (spread nationwide, but concentrated in the Detroit area) are giving
Islam a visible presence, as in the Washington, D.C., mosque. The Sunni regard
the Black Muslims as heretics.

Hinduism likewise found response in
America. Trade with India in the 19th century
found New England thinkers, like Ralph Wal-
do Emerson, Henry David Thoreau, and the
so-called Transcendentalists, receptive to the
all-embracing Over-Soul. In the present century, Swami Vivekananda and others introduced Vedanta as a means of sharing the mysticism of Indian religious leaders—
Ramakrishna, Tagore, and Gandhi. Martin
Luther King, Jr., and the American Quakers
before him, found in Gandhi's nonviolence
a power to be applied for racial justice.

Buddhism, particularly in its Zen (Japanese) form has found considerable response
among intellectuals beginning in the 1950s,
although the first Buddhist priest arrived in
1898. By 1970, there were about 400,000
adherents, gathered mainly in churches in
California and Hawaii, and including many
nonorientals as well as Japanese, Chinese,
and others.

Meanwhile, Bahaism (Iran) made its initial
impact in the 1890s. In less than a half-century, its largest nine-sided temple stood on
rising ground in Willmette, a Chicago suburb, while its world headquarters are in Haifa, Israel. The Bahai bid for inclusiveness in
religion has roots in its Shiite Muslim past,
and in eschatological hope it sees the convergence of the great world religions.

Theosophy, linking European, American,
and Asian (Indian) elements, emphasized es-
oteric knowledge and occultism. It engaged
the interests of many Americans who, for the
most part, remained in their traditional
churches.

In this vaster setting of religious pluralism,
the great majority of Americans—biblically
ignorant as most have become—still regard
themselves in the Judeo-Christian tradition.

LUTHERANS IN THE USA: IDENTITY AND CONTINUITY

For Lutheranism immense signficance at-
taches to its extension into the American
scene. Of the 45 million immigrants arriving
between the years 1820 and 1970, a magnitude unmatched, European Lutherans comprised a substantial minority. By virtue of
ethnic backgrounds and rates of Americanization, they were the most diversified Protestant communion in the rising nation. But
the *Augsburg Confession* of faith and Luther's
Small Catechism were their symbols of mutual recognition as well as a stimulus to unity
and organic union. Maturing into the English
language, whose worldwide spread was in
progress, America's Lutherans gained a common tongue for their common confession. An
awakening interest in their confessional kin
in other continents—marked by reminders
like John N. Lenker's book, *Lutherans in All
Lands* (1893; 5th edition 1896)—was an overture to mutual caring worldwide.

The rise of America as a world power, following its part in World War I, was epoch-making for Lutheranism, not least for the subsequent tasks of America's Lutherans. Their transition to English was greatly accelerated by the war experience. This ecumenical language, English, helped open up opportunities for timely service overseas as well as at home. The experiences of World War II extended and intensified these developments. By 1986, if a Gallup religious poll is reliable, Lutherans—of all communions—were shown to be the "most American." This "fitting in," whether an asset or a liability, invites attention to the course and identity of Lutheranism in America over generations.

As a continuous account, the Lutheran story begins about 350 years ago on Manhattan Island (New Amsterdam then, New York after 1664). In the unfolding life of the nation, Lutherans have accounted for 3% to 4% of the American population: an estimated 122,000 by the end of the colonial period and attainment of national independence (1783); over 3.6 million by the end of America's participation in World War I (1917–1918); and 8.5 million near the bicentennial of the American Constitution (1987). Had Lutherans remained closer to the church of their forebears, as most Roman Catholics had, one wonders how many times larger their numbers would be today. But two factors are revealing in this regard.

First, in the wake of the Atlantic migration, according to careful estimates, under 30% of the Norwegians joined any church, not over 20% of the Swedes, only about 15% of the Germans, perhaps 12% of the Finns, and 7% of the Danes. Second, American Protestants tended to regard European Lutherans like Roman Catholics: as mere formalists in religion and therefore ripe for conversion. Methodists, Baptists, Congregationalists, and Presbyterians maintained so-called linguistic missionaries to seek out Swedes, Norwegians, Germans, and others, while Episcopalians (as in the case of the descendants of New Sweden on the Delaware River) could offer their communion as the English equivalent to Lutheranism on the European continent.

Under circumstances like these, the faithful minority among the Lutherans learned to survive by applying principles of the later so-called three-self movement: self-governing, self-propagating, self-supporting. Like the pictures of a triptych, three successive stages in time tell the unfolding story.

Colonial Era to 1783

Roman Catholic Spaniards (above) killed the pioneer French garrison on the St. Johns River (1565), in northeast Florida, not because they were French but because they were hated "Lutherans." Bitter cold and hunger killed most of the Danes and Norwegians, who were wintering on Hudson Bay (1619–1620) at the present town of Churchill, not because they wished to settle there but because their Danish expedition was in search of a Northwest Passage to India. Among the dead was Rasmus Jensen, their chaplain (see above, Canada).

In New Amsterdam the Dutch tolerated no Lutheran "domine," and sent Johannes Gutwasser, pastor to the Lutheran settlers, back to the Netherlands (1657), because only the Reformed faith was allowed. The Indians on the Delaware (eastern Pennsylvania) peacefully shared their land with the Swedes and Finns, founders of New Sweden (1638). The Swedish pastor, Johannes Campanius, learned their language, endeavored to share the faith, and translated Luther's *Small Catechism* into the Indian dialect—the earliest missionary attempt of its kind by a Protestant in America.

When hard winters, poor harvests, and a campaigning French king (Louis XIV) turned thousands of peasants into refugees, many of them left the Palatinate and the Rhine valley and came via London to New York's Hudson valley. The resettlement project, sponsored by Britain's Queen Anne and her Danish consort, began in 1708. It eventually brought some 2000 "Pfälzer," about one-third of them Lutheran. Indenture, a form of delayed payment of travel costs and keep, was paid off by servant-labor over an average seven-year period. The pattern was widely applied. The lack of pastors among the immigrant Germans was chronic.

When Firmian, archbishop of Salzburg, *Austria, exercised his rights and expelled 22,000 Lutherans from his territory, a train of refugees moved across Germany. Most were resettled in East Prussia, but some, accompanied by two pastors, came to the new British colony of Georgia (1734).

When William Penn toured Germany in the 1670s to attract additional settlers for his colony in North America, the first to respond were oppressed sectarians—Mennonites, Schwenkfelders, and others. Their leader, Francis Daniel Pastorius, a Lutheran who became a Quaker, laid out Germantown (1683), their initial settlement adjacent to Philadelphia. But these settlers were eventually followed by ever larger numbers from Germany, Lutheran mostly, but also Reformed.

Pennsylvania, Penn's "Holy Experiment" in religious liberty, was a proprietary colony under Quaker governance. English, Welsh, Scots, and Irish comprised the English-speaking majority, while Germans soon became the second largest group, with Swedish, Dutch, and other minorities. Among the Germans, sectarian diversity ran rampant, leading some to call it "Pennsylvania religion." The Halle-trained Count Zinzendorf, patron of the Moravians, crossed the Atlantic and tried but failed to unite all the Germans into a Church of God in the Spirit (1741–1742). His followers thereupon set up their own settlements.

After some years of importuning the directors of the Halle mission center in *Germany, the three United congregations in the Philadelphia area received a pastor: Henry Melchior Muhlenberg (1711–1787), of Einbeck, Hanover. Intended initially for missionary service in *India (the Danish-Halle Mission), he was sent to North America to unite the Lutherans on a confessional basis and prevent their being absorbed into the ethnic amalgam Zinzendorf had wished. Muhlenberg was not the first Lutheran pastor among the Germans, but the first one with authority to unite them—if possible. Arriving in 1742, he had come via London (and its Lutheran royal chaplain) with credentials and via Georgia's Salzburgers with valuable orientation. At his coming, Zinzendorf departed. Muhlenberg's association with the Swedish pastors, serving among the descendants of New Sweden, proved supportive.

Serving congregations in the Philadelphia area, supplying in New York, and visiting in many settlements, also in the South, Muhlenberg by 1748 was able to organize the first permanent synod, later called the Ministerium of North America. The agenda of that first meeting, held in Philadelphia after Easter, was itself memorable: to examine and ordain a candidate for the ministry (from Halle); to dedicate a new church building (St.

Michael); and to adopt a common liturgy for congregational worship. This meeting prefigured so many things to come that it has been called the most important of its kind in American Lutheran history. By 1762, Muhlenberg and the elders had completed a congregational constitution. Adopted by St. Michael's, it soon became a model for congregations in many parts of the country. Its provisions included maintenance of a school, a matter of particular importance in the years ahead.

Equally important was the fact that, with few exceptions, pastors from Germany came to stay. This was in contrast to those from Sweden, who came for terms of six years. They eventually lost rapport with the rapidly Americanized descendants of New Sweden, whose main churches—Gloria Dei (Philadelphia, 1700) and Holy Trinity (Wilmington, Delaware, 1699)—have been in Episcopalian hands since the early 1800s.

Muhlenberg married Anna Maria, daughter of Conrad Weiser (of the early Palatine immigration). As a lad on the frontier, Weiser had grown up among Indians, spoke their language, kept their trust, and was respected as an agent mediating between the Indians and the Pennsylvania government. His daughter and Muhlenberg became the parents of a distinguished line of clergy and scholars. For his part, Muhlenberg's conscientiously kept journals, besides voluminous correspondence, remain among the richest records of colonial life (a three-volume English translation, 1942–1955).

Lutheranism in this colonial period is obviously not compressed into the story of one leader and his family. During the 18th century the Halle directors sent a succession of 24 young pastors. Others came from a variety of places, including Hamburg and Hanover. Still others, "tramps," and impostors showed up from nowhere. As congregations multiplied—also into Maryland, Virginia, and the Carolinas—so did the schools, and good teachers (schoolmasters in those days) were as hard to find as good pastors.

The beginning of an indigenous ministry therefore remains especially noteworthy. Justus Falckner, a former theological student at Halle (who with his brother, Daniel, had become a promoter of German settlement in Pennsylvania) was ordained in 1703, in Philadelphia. The service in Gloria Dei church was led by Andrew Rudman, dean of the three Swedish pastors in the colony, while a company of German mystics (many of them Lutheran) had come from their wilderness watch outside the city to provide music and lead the congregation in song. From this event, Falckner went on to New York, there to relieve Rudman from his increasingly arduous duties in that city's lone Lutheran congregation—a gathering of many nationalities all using the Dutch language. From New York, Falckner served the Hudson Valley congregations as far north as Albany. He also founded the first one (1714) in New Jersey—near the present Oldwick—in the home of a freed black slave, Aree van Guinee, and his family.

By the time of the War of Independence (1776–1783) the far largest number of Lutheran congregations—spread from New England to Georgia—were in Pennsylvania. Muhlenberg's three sons had become Lutheran ministers, and had even received part of their education at Halle. Like others of the second generation, they were bilingual and proficient in English. Amid the spreading war, Henry Melchior's eldest son, Peter, left his Woodstock, Virginia, parish and became a general in George Washington's army. For the father, this was hard to take, for he was a Loyalist at heart. Another son, Frederick Augustus—still prior to his father's death—presided over the Pennsylvania convention that adopted the new federal constitution for this state (1787). Meanwhile, John Christopher Kunze, Muhlenberg's son-in-law, had become a pastor and professor in New York. In 1786 he led in the founding of the New York Ministerium—the first such Lutheran body to be created since 1748, when the Ministerium of North America (Pennsylvania) was organized by Muhlenberg.

National Era: 1787-1918

Mission, mission, and more mission! This was the relentless challenge to the churches amid the rising ride of population. Newcomers and natural increase powered the westward-moving settlement. The native-born or American-educated supply of Lutheran pastors was woefully inadequate. Europe's mission institutes, which trained men (and some women) for service in Asia, Africa, or Latin America, were persuaded to prepare them for North America too. Their training, often superimposed on some previously learned trade

or rural work, fell short of a university education in theology but was more practical. In this way, hundreds of future pastors came to the United States from Germany and even from Scandinavia and Switzerland. The Basel Mission Institute—heavily supported from South Germany—sent over a total of 276 men to Lutheran, Reformed, and United churches between the years 1830 and 1914. Often American seminaries completed the training and applied the synodical label in ordination.

Mission challenges might arise from a thousand places, but mission was one—in Christ. The outreach was to the spiritually neglected in towns and cities as well as in villages or the scattered rural expanse. In a modest way, it also approached American Indians—as in the case of German farm families from Franconia (Bavaria) in the 1840s who settled on lands near the Indians in Michigan—in hopes for a people-to-people spread of the gospel, accompanied by the ringing of churchbells in the forest. This was one among many ventures in various places. At times, the efforts throbbed with devotion, but the results were usually meager, for the Indians realized that their land was being taken by the advancing tide of newcomers. Ministry among the Apaches in Arizona, begun in the 1890s, has become the most noteworthy (see Wisconsin Synod).

Among American blacks, Lutherans had limited associations. Few of them, in the South, were slave holders. But from the days of the Salzburgers in colonial times, pastoral acts for blacks (such as baptisms) were entered in the church records along with all others. Church attendance was segregated in the European village manner: men on one side, women on the other; young people in the balcony—and blacks. An occasional freed African slave, like Daniel A. Payne, might come north. The Lutheran pastor in New York, seeing Payne as a young man of promise, sent him to Gettysburg Seminary. Students helped support him. Ready for ordination, there was no prospect for him in a Lutheran congregation. Therefore he joined the African Methodist Episcopal Church in 1839, becoming one of its leading educators and the founder of the present Wilberforce University in Ohio. In the South, ministry by the Missouri Synod, begun in 1877, resulted in the largest black constituency among Lutherans. Concordia College, in Selma, Alabama, remains the institutional landmark of a variety of previous ventures. This work among black Americans eventually brought also the Missouri-led Synodical Conference (below) to Africa itself (*Nigeria, 1935). Meanwhile, at the close of this national era, the American acquisition (1917) of the Danish West Indies (*Virgin Islands) added another dimension to the linkage of Lutheranism with people of African descent.

Similarly, the American Lutheran entry into the Hispanic realm came on the heels of the Spanish-American War (1898), when an adventurous theological student of Swedish descent single-handedly undertook mission in *Puerto Rico. This has endured and provided a springboard to other parts of Latin America (*Argentina).

Overseas missions on the part of America's Lutherans began in 1842, the centennial year of Muhlenberg's arrival. Already in 1810, the Congregationalists, with their American Board, had set the pace. Other denominations followed. The Ministerium of Pennsylvania's John Christian Frederick Heyer (1793–1873), the first American Lutheran overseas missionary, at age 50 commenced work in Guntur, *India (Andhra Evangelical Lutheran Church). An immigrant lad from Germany, a pastor and proven home missionary in America, he blazed a trail others would follow. He personified, at home and abroad, that Christ's mission is one.

The Lutheran General Synod (LCA, below) followed other American Protestants to *Liberia (1860). Norse Lutherans from the Midwest joined fellow Norwegians in *Madagascar (1887). Later, others of Norse descent went to *Cameroon, and also to *South Africa. Asia was a powerful magnet, and in 1890 Daniel Nelson (Hauge Synod, see ALC) led the way that many others eventually followed to *China. Not far behind was the Lutheran entrance into *Japan (1892), by two pastors from the United Synod in the South (LCA). Via its own connections, the Missouri Synod developed ties with *Australia (1881); through an offshoot of the Leipzig Mission, with South *India (1895); through German immigrants, with *Brazil (1901) and *Argentina (1905); and through individual pioneering, notably that of Eduard Louis Arndt, in China (1913).

This listing, though only partial, suggests how widespread the missionary ties became.

In virtually all cases there was some connection with missionary societies in Europe. This fact became enormously significant in the wake of World War I and the need of the German missions overseas for assistance from America.

The accent on the oneness of mission echoed from many quarters. In student groups, but especially in women's missionary societies, the endless task at home and overseas was interpreted, drew support, and recruited personnel. No one conveyed this unitive task better than William Alfred Passavant (1823–1893). His monthly, *The Missionary*, was subtitled, "devoted to the work of Home, Inner and Foreign Missions of the American Lutheran Church." From his base in Pittsburgh (Pennsylvania), he operated across synodical lines and ethnic groups, initially with the General Synod, and then with the General Council (LCA, below). In word and deed he supported congregations, colleges, seminaries, hospitals, social agencies; fostered interchurch relations and community projects; publicized national issues, the reports of missionaries, and the needs of newcomers—Swedes, Danes, Norwegians, Germans, and others. His attendance at the first meeting of the Evangelical Alliance, London (1846) led to his visiting Inner Mission pioneers in *Germany, especially Theodor Fliedner in Kaiserswerth. Three years later, Fliedner brought four deaconesses to Pittsburgh, there to staff the first Protestant hospital in America. The Institution of Protestant Deaconesses, so named, was recognized as a restoration of an office, that of deaconess, from the primitive church. Despite this promising beginning, the deaconess work was interrupted by service during the Civil War and other factors.

Later, the deaconess work was resumed when John D. Lankenau, an affluent merchant (see Germany, Bremen), secured seven deaconesses from Germany as administration and nursing staff for the German (later Lankenau) Hospital in Philadelphia (1884). The Philadelphia deaconess community was the first, and remained the largest, of the subsequently formed Lutheran Deaconess Motherhouse Conference in America (1896). The houses in Omaha (Swedish), Brooklyn, Chicago, Minneapolis (Norwegian), Milwaukee (German—a continuation of Pittsburgh),

Baltimore (American), and Philadelphia exemplified a new role of women in the life of the church as well as the place of *diakonia,* Christian unity, and an ecumenical perspective.

Of all tasks, home missions remained the largest, the most competitive, and resulted in real growth as well as in a proliferation of synods. But this theme, like that of higher education and ministerial training, is subsumed under the profiles of the separate churches presented below. Here it is enough to note that the one synod of the colonial era, the Ministerium of North America (1748), emerges early but stands like a fleeting preview of a distant future.

International Era, since 1918

A "calamity theory" of progress (this author used the term in *Lutheran Churches of the World,* 1952) fits the process by which Lutherans have been brought into partnership with each other and others. Two world wars, and much else, have altered relationships and driven home the necessity of unity and mutually recognized interdependence. No readier example exists, in terms of time, than the 70-year span between the formation of the National Lutheran Council (1918) and the realization of the Evangelical Lutheran Church in America (1988). By virtue of their respective backgrounds, virtually the same ecclesial components that first learned to cooperate in the NLC have progressively moved through consolidations and mergers and seen their autonomous organizations reduced from 10 or 12 to two—the American Lutheran Church (1960) and the Lutheran Church in America (1962)—and, at last, to one.

At the same time, however, as the disparate sizes of the churches described below reveal, the move toward greater unity has left remnants. This fact, painful in its choices, is sobering and perhaps salutary. Remainders are reminders—of previously held positions among other things. The Lutheran Church–Missouri Synod comes to mind; it has never merged with anyone. But it has absorbed, and it has dismissed.

Each of the two large bodies, the ALC and the LCA, represents a "confessional continuum" of a particular kind. This became evident at the outset of the National Lutheran Council, with a polarization of theological

positions by 1920. The mainly midwestern bodies (later ALC) took a position akin to that of the Missouri Synod on the Scriptures, doctrine, and practice. The mainly eastern body (see LCA history—United Lutheran Church in America) took a position no less confessionally sound but also historically more ready to let an acceptance of the Confessions suffice, without the requirement of additional agreed statements. In 1940, this kind of internal polarization was still widely evident, and was perpetuated in the several theological seminaries.

Later in the 1940s, postwar conditions—including intensified partnership in the National Lutheran Council as well as in the newly formed Lutheran World Federation and participation in the rising ecumenical movement (World Council of Churches)—fostered extensive changes in traditionally held positions. Lutheran seminaries, increasingly staffed with professors who had done graduate studies in leading universities at home and abroad, turned out future pastors more likely to see Lutheranism as a movement of the gospel within the church catholic than simply as a custodian of pure doctrine. Differences among the various Lutheran bodies diminished as understanding among them grew. Among the helps in this direction was the consultation of younger theologians who gathered at least annually at the Dekoven Foundation (Racine, Wisconsin) over a period of two decades (1945–1965). They came from the major Lutheran church bodies. Among them was Fredrik A. Schiotz, at that time a leader in the ministry to university students, then active in LWF affairs, and later the first president of the ALC (below).

In the latter capacity, Schiotz also strengthened ties with the Lutheran Church–Missouri Synod. By 1969, the ALC and the LCMS had pulpit and altar fellowship. However, that same year a growing uneasiness among the rank-and-file of Missouri members brought a change in leadership that reversed the trend toward Lutheran fellowship. It also brought about the painful withdrawal of some 100,000 members who formed the Association of Evangelical Lutheran Churches (see ELCA, below). In turn, this body of dissenters became the catalyst for bringing together the ALC and the LCA.

With nothing to lose, the AELC promoted Lutheran union with an ecumenical orientation and a social conscience. The 1982 conventions of the three prospective partners marked a turning point. The ALC, AELC, and LCA all voted by wide margins to merge and form what is now the Evangelical Lutheran Church in America (ELCA, below). By action reciprocated on the Episcopalian side, the three Lutheran bodies also voted for "interim eucharistic hospitality" with the Episcopal Church and adopted appropriate guidelines. The 70-member Commission on a New Lutheran Church (CNLC) completed its work in June 1986.

A second look at the "calamity theory" shows an unexpected propulsion into partnership among Luther's ecclesial heirs, as occasioned by two world wars. The National Lutheran Council, as already mentioned, was formed as World War I was ending and helped to rally America's diversified Lutherans to common action—with the exception of the Missouri Synod and several other bodies. The NLC played a major role in postwar aid to Europe's churches, especially to hard-pressed Lutheran minorities in the Eastern countries and in the revolution-born Soviet Union. The NLC, as we have seen in *Europe, cosponsored, with the General Evangelical Lutheran Conference in *Germany, the founding of the Lutheran World Convention.

Today, it is hard to imagine the effort and patience required in those days to build mutual trust among America's Lutherans. Care for others in distant lands helped to advance a feeling of unity at home. As tasks overseas diminished, the NLC was given to new ones at home in welfare services, public relations, and other functions done better in concert than separately by the participating bodies.

Extraordinary responsibilties during and after World War II gave the NLC new stature and an improved structure. Its work at home was balanced by services overseas. Where support from German missions was cut off, the NLC was often able to arrange alternate help. So-called orphaned missions in Tanzania, Southern Africa, India, China, Indonesia, Papua New Guinea, and elsewhere were aided by American funds and personnel. Between 1939 and 1947, contributed funds totaled about $2.5 million. Later, when the postwar period called for greatly expanded services, the council and its related agencies

helped to resettle refugees. By 1969, those resettled totaled about 110,000; and beyond this figure were the host of sponsoring families and welcoming congregations. Lutheran Refugee Service in recent years has been rendering comparable assistance to Asian refugees, as well as to those from Central America and the Caribbean.

The greatest and most sustained fund-raising effort by the churches in the NLC was Lutheran World Action. During its 37 years (1940–1977), LWA—often interpreted as "Love's Working Arm"—raised a total of $227 million. Paralleling this effort, and still continuing as the agency for emergency material aid, is Lutheran World Relief (1945–).

The transformation of the NLC into the Lutheran Council in the United States of America (LCUSA) took place in 1966. LCUSA became operative in January the following year. It was more inclusive than the NLC in that the Lutheran Church–Missouri Synod was a prominently participating member. At Missouri's insistence, shared by the LCA, LCUSA's structure had a division of theological studies in which all member churches were to participate. Other divisions and departments included mission, welfare services, immigration and refugee services, service to military personnel as well as to students and faculty in academic institutions, specialized pastoral care and clinical education programs, research and planning, the archives of cooperative Lutheranism, information services, and public relations—including those with federal govenment and other agencies.

With the merger of the ALC and LCA, and the diminished participation of the Missouri Lutherans since the mid-1970s, LCUSA's functions were gradually distributed among the major church bodies. In the words of LCUSA's last director, John Houck, the council's activities entered a process of "countdown to completion."

The Archives of Cooperative Lutheranism, relocated to Chicago in 1987 from New York, have proven a mine of information on the worldwide outreach of Lutherans working together. They are all the more important in light of the destruction of much archival material of this sort in Europe during World War II. In these records, the personal dimension emerges as a unifying force under the guidance of the Holy Spirit. Among the hundreds of names, those of the succession of directors stand out: Lauritz Larsen, John A. Morehead, Ralph H. Long, Paul C. Empie of the National Lutheran Council; C. Thomas Spitz, Arnold R. Mickelson (interim), George F. Harkins, and John R. Houck of LCUSA.

Until 1966, the National Lutheran Council had served as the USA national committee of the LWF. When the NLC's successor agency, LCUSA, took over in 1967, the U.S. National Committee required a separate structural unit, inasmuch as the Lutheran Church–Missouri Synod was not a member of the LWF. The general secretaries of the U.S. committee since that time have been: Paul C. Empie, Carl H. Mau Jr., Paul A.

Wee, and Harold T. Hanson. Known as Lutheran World Ministries, since its 1977 reorganization, the U.S. national committee became a unit in the new Evangelical Lutheran Church in America (below). The location of this unit, like that of the Archives, in late 1987 changed to Chicago. The familiar address of LCUSA and of Lutheran World Ministries—360 Park Avenue South, 16th floor, New York, NY 10010—became history.

Before describing the several Lutheran church bodies, including a few very small ones, a glance at the accompanying chart should help to simplify an otherwise confusing array as it was in earlier decades and as it is now.

COOPERATION AND CONSOLIDATION AMONG LUTHERANS IN 20TH-CENTURY USA

THEN
National Lutheran Council (NLC, 1918–1966)
Evangelical Lutheran Church (1917)
American Lutheran Church (1930)
United Evangelical Lutheran Church (1896)
Lutheran Free Church (1897)
→ **The American Lutheran Church** (ALC, 1960)
United Lutheran Church in America (1918)
Augustana Lutheran Church (1860)
American Evangelical Lutheran Church (1872)
Suomi Synod (Finnish ELCA, 1890)
→ **Lutheran Church in America** (LCA, 1962)

American Section, Lutheran World Convention, 1923–1947, became USA national committee, Lutheran World Federation, 1947–1977

LATER
Lutheran Council in the USA (LCUSA, 1966–1987)
The American Lutheran Church (ALC, 1960–1987)
Lutheran Church in America (LCA, 1962–1987)
Association of Evangelical Lutheran Churches (AELC, 1976–1987)
→ **Evangelical Lutheran Church in America (ELCA, 1988–)**
Latvian Evangelical Lutheran Church (LELC, 1975)
Lutheran Church—Missouri Synod (LCMS, 1847)

became
Lutheran World Ministries, USA national committee/ LWF, 1977–1987

NOW
Committee (bilateral) on Lutheran Cooperation (1988–)
Evangelical Lutheran Church in America (includes) USA national committee/ LWF
Lutheran Church—Missouri Synod

Continuing Inter-Lutheran Agencies
Lutheran World Relief (LWR, 1945–)
Lutheran Immigration and Refugee Service (LIRS, 1948–)
Lutheran Educational Conference in North America (LECNA, 1910–)
Lutheran Resources Commission (LRC, 1970–)
Lutheran Film Associates (LFA, 1948–)
Social Ministry Organizations (regional cooperation)

FORMER PARTNERSHIP

Evangelical Lutheran Synodical Conference (1872–1964)

Lutheran Church—Missouri Synod (1847–)

(Slovak) Synod of Evangelical Lutheran Churches (1902, joined the LCMS in 1971)

Wisconsin Evangelical Lutheran Synod (1892)

(Norwegian) Evangelical Lutheran Synod (1918)

Other Independent Lutheran Church Bodies

(Comprise about 6% of the USA Lutheran total)

Currently 17 in number, these bodies appear in the alphabetical sequence of this section.

THE AMERICAN ASSOCIATION OF LUTHERAN CHURCHES (TAALC)

Membership: 15,150
Presiding Pastor: The Rev. Dr. Duane R. Lindberg
Headquarters: 1120 SE Fifth Street
PO Box 17097
Minneapolis, Minnesota 55417

Congregations opposed to the newly formed ELCA (below) in November 1987 officially constituted TAALC. Dissenting from the alleged universalism of the large church body, they reaffirmed their stand on the Scriptures as the "inerrant Word of God." Their emphasis is on congregational autonomy and democratic procedures. Foremost among their objectives are evangelism and missions. A few other conservative Lutheran bodies of TAALC-like leanings have offered the facilities of their respective seminaries, such as Concordia, Fort Wayne, Indiana (LCMS), and Faith, Tacoma, Washington (WCLA). In time, there may be a TAALC house of studies near one or more of the conservative and academically strong Lutheran seminaries.

The roots of TAALC are varied, but in large part run back to the former Lutheran Free Church (Norwegian), whose other current embodiment is the Association of the Free Lutheran Congregations (AFLC, below). Already in 1986 the first steps toward the eventual formation of TAALC got under way. TAALC's 68 affiliated congregations, and over 50 others in the wider fellowship, were mainly in the upper Midwest. They are a reminder of the 863 congregations opposed to the ALC joining the nationwide ELCA.

Emmaus Lutheran Church, Bloomington, Minnesota, host to TAALC meetings and conventions, is not a member of that body, but, having quit the ALC, joined the Association of Free Lutheran Congregations (below). Some others, like that of the presiding pastor (Ascension, Waterloo, Iowa), are offshoots of congregations that have remained in the ELCA.

APOSTOLIC LUTHERAN CHURCH OF AMERICA (ALCA)

Membership: 6353**
President: The Rev. George Wilson
New York Mills, Minnesota 56567

Comprising 49 congregations, this Apostolic Lutheran Church is served by 33 ordained pastors and a number of part-time lay preachers. A few of the pastors have had seminary training, but the majority are "self-educated, experienced and seasoned veterans who have a testimony of faith among many believers." Worship services are informal but orderly with emphasis on "inspired congregational singing and the preaching of the Word, enlightened by the Holy Spirit." The imposition of hands in the pronouncement of the absolution marks the traditional accent on renewal in this community's basically simple and spiritual life.

The polity of the ALCA is congregational. The three-day annual conventions, with delegates from all the congregations, combine inspirational services with business meetings. A central board of nine members plans and directs the convention. This board is also responsible for the examination and ordination of pastoral candidates. The congregations are divided into two mission districts, Eastern and Western, with the Rocky Mountains as the dividing point. These districts have their own bylaws and boards of trustees with authority to select their pastors.

Most of the ALCA congregations have Sunday schools, and these have the benefit of a national Sunday school committee. Foreign missions are handled on a "Macedonian Call" basis. At present, the ALCA is active in Guatemala and Nigeria.

The ALCA was formed in 1929 in Pendleton, Oregon, by a group of Finnish-Americans who broke away from the Apostolic Lutheran Congregation (the Old Laestadians) because it "allowed pulpit privileges only to a favored few." Thirty years later, with a membership of 10,000 and 45 pastors, the ALCA was considerably larger than the mother church. Since then, its membership has gradually decreased.

Apostolic Lutherans are followers of the 19th-century Swedish revivalist, Lars Levi Laestadius. Both a botanist and a theologian, he served in Sweden's northernmost parish where Lapps and Finns resided. After the death of his three-year-old son, Laestadius began attacking the sins of people, especially drunkenness, and preaching the gospel with deep emotion. The greatest response was in northern *Finland. Some of his followers came to America and settled in upper Michigan, Minnesota, Oregon, and Washington. The first congregation, served by a lay preacher, was formed in 1871 in Calumet, Michigan, and was registered accordingly as the "Salomon Korteniemi Lutheran Society." The name was changed to the "Apostolic Lutheran Congregation" in 1879, and since then the Apostolic name has characterized the Laestadians in America. A number of Apostolic groups have been formed, but the ALCA remains the largest and most active.

ASSOCIATION OF FREE LUTHERAN CONGREGATIONS (AFLC)
Membership: 26,510
President: The Rev. Richard Snipstead
3110 East Medicine Lake Boulevard
Minneapolis, Minnesota 55441

The AFLC comprises those congregations that did not go along when their body, the former Lutheran Free Church (LFC; 1897), joined the ALC in 1963. The congregations of this association endeavor to carry on the tradition of the LFC, seeking to maintain a soundly biblical theology, a firm commitment to the Scriptures, a strict adherence to the Lutheran Confessions, an evangelistic piety, and Christian fellowship nurtured in congregational autonomy as well as in solid Christian education.

AFLC members—over 26,000—are gathered into 155 congregations. Its clergy roster includes 130 ordained ministers, of whom 86 are pastors of congregations; a number teach or are in other church occupations (including overseas missions), and some are retired. The main strength of the church is in the upper Midwest, and from there out to the Pacific coast.

The pioneers of what later became the LFC already in 1872 founded Augsburg College and Seminary in Minneapolis, later part of the ALC (now ELCA) enterprise in higher education. In their place, the AFLC maintains its own Association Free Lutheran Theological Seminary (1964) and Bible School (1966) at the above address. These institutions seek to continue the old LFC emphasis on education as brought initially from Norway by theologians. Prominent among them was George Sverdrup (1848–1907), one of the foremost theological scholars of his time in America.

AFLC's missionary endeavors outside the country include Central Mexican Lutheran Church, Association of Free Lutheran Churches of *Brazil, and the diminutive Bible Faith Lutheran Church of India—including a child-care agency.

The major part of the LFC agency, such as its early venture into deaconess work, overseas mission, ecumenical interest, and the promotion of Lutheran unity (personified in the LFC's president T.O. Burntvedt [in office 1930–1958]) lived on in the ALC (below). But the AFLC, mindful of this legacy, is trying to shape its own identity.

CHURCH OF THE LUTHERAN BRETHREN (CLB)

Membership: 4830
President: The Rev. Robert M. Overgaard
PO Box 655
1007 Westside Drive
Fergus Falls, Minnesota 56537

The Church of the Lutheran Brethren consists of 104 congregations. These, plus 17 independent congregations that work closely with the CLB are served by 139 Lutheran Brethren pastors. The denomination's organizational structure combines elements of congregational polity on the synodical level and presbyterial on the local level. Its college and seminary as well as its headquarters are located in Fergus Falls, Minnesota. Although originally the major concentration of strength was in the Midwest, in recent years the CLB has penetrated other areas of the United States and Canada through its church planting mission, which has increased the number of congregations by 42%.

The CLB characterizes itself as a "fellowship of believers, organized into congregations for the purpose of worship, edification, fellowship, and ministry in harmony with the Lutheran Confessions with the purpose of bringing the gospel to all the world." It is committed to "the authority of the Scriptures, the teaching and practice of the Lutheran understanding of the Sacraments, and imminent return of our Lord." Its worship services are nonliturgical but involve all participants. To facilitate the maximum use of spiritual gifts, education in the local congregation as well as in the schools it sponsors receives strong support.

From its inception, the CLB has emphasized evangelism and mission. Believing that the local congregation should be composed of confessing Christians, it challenges its members "to a living and vital walk with God through a personal appropriation of the atonement," and to an involvement in world evangelization. Thus, lay participation in missionary activity is at a high point. The CLB has 49 missionaries serving in the countries of *Cameroon, *Chad, *Taiwan, and *Japan. In these countries, too, evangelism is the work of all members.

The CLB was organized in 1900 in Milwaukee, Wisconsin, by a group of several independent Lutheran congregations who adopted a constitution patterned closely after that of the Evangelical Lutheran Free Church of Norway (1877).

CHURCH OF THE LUTHERAN CONFESSION (CLC)

Membership: 8717
President: The Rev. Daniel Fleischer
460 75th Avenue, NE
Minneapolis, Minnesota 55432

Founded in 1960, the CLC comprises 70 congregations served by 74 ordained pastors and 34 teachers. Although most of the congregations are in the upper Midwest, others are located in such distant states as Florida, California, Virginia, Washington, Alaska, and Texas. A combination high school, college, and seminary is located in Eau Claire, Wisconsin. CLC supports mission undertakings in Nigeria and India.

The original congregations, pastors, and teachers were at one time members of three synods of the Synodical Conference: Evangelical Lutheran Synod, Lutheran Church–Missouri Synod, and the Wisconsin Evangelical Lutheran Synod. They left in order to preserve "the Gospel witness and the Scripture principles of fellowship" and "complete agreement [in the doctrines of Scripture] before such fellowship is exercised."

CONCORDIA LUTHERAN CONFERENCE (CLC)

Membership: 343
President: The Rev. David T. Mensing
Office: Central Avenue at 171st Place
Tinley Park, Illinois 60477

Protesting the "unionistic" trend they saw in the Missouri Synod's Common Confession with the ALC (1949–1953), some pastors and congregations withdrew from the LCMS and other Synodical Conference bodies. In 1956 they formed the Concordia Lutheran Conference. Today this is a small church body of six pastors and six congregations, located in six states (Illinois, Michigan, South Dakota, Texas, Oregon, and Washington). The

CLC maintains a theological education program and a publishing house. Despite its wide dispersion, the CLC's sense of purpose and mission as well as its annual conventions enliven its fellowship. All its congregations are self-supporting, although the largest (Seattle) has only 85 baptized members. Its paper, *The Concordia Lutheran*, a bimonthly, upholds the CLC's conservatism in doctrine and practice—a position seen as "original Missouri" and as reflecting C.F.W. Walther's position in his book *Church and Ministry*.

ESTONIAN EVANGELICAL LUTHERAN CHURCH (EELC)

(see EXILE CHURCHES, above)
Membership: 7418
Bishop in North America: The Rev. Karl Raudsepp
30 Sunrise Avenue, Apt. 216
Toronto, Ontario M4A 2R3, Canada
District Dean/USA: The Rev. Rudolph Reinaru
607 East 7th Street
Lakewood, New Jersey 08701

The 24 congregations of the EELC's USA District report a baptized membership of over 7000. Almost an equal number are in Canada (above). Of the church's 25 ordained ministers in the USA, 22 serve congregations. Pastors and lay delegates from the congregations gather annually (as in Lakewood, New Jersey, in 1986) for a synodical meeting of the district, led by the bishop and the lay president. Unlike its Latvian counterpart (see LELCA, below), the EELC was not a member of the Lutheran Council in the USA. However, its pastors and many of its members remain in close touch with their former host churches—the ALC, LCA (both now part of the ELCA), and LCMS. The far largest number of EELC in Exile members reside in *Sweden, as described above (Europe).

EVANGELICAL LUTHERAN CHURCH IN AMERICA (ELCA)

Member: LWF (1988), WCC, NCCC/USA
Membership: 5,288,230
Bishop: The Rev. Dr. Herbert W. Chilstrom
8765 W. Higgins Road (at River Road and Kennedy Expressway)
Chicago, Illinois 60631

Constituted at its first churchwide convention—April 30–May 3, 1987, in Columbus,

Ohio—the Evangelical Lutheran Church in America (ELCA) became the largest Lutheran body in the United States and, through its antecedents, also the oldest. Among Lutheran churches worldwide, the ELCA is exceeded in numbers only by the Church of Sweden. Its almost 5.3 million baptized members account for over three-fifths (62%) of the total Lutherans reported in the USA. (In the American context, the Lutheran Church–Missouri Synod, below, claims 32%; the many smaller church bodies, 6%.)

A highlight of Bishop Chilstrom's installation in Chicago (October 10, 1987) was the presence of church dignitaries from Europe, Africa, Asia, and Latin America, including LWF President Johannes Hanselmann (Bavaria), Archbishop Bertil Werkström (Upsala), Bishop Kleopas Dumeni (Namibia), and many others. The installation into office was performed by the bishops of the three consolidating churches, Drs. James Crumley, Will Herzfeld, and David Preus. Meanwhile, the process of organizational transition exceeded anticipation in complexity as well as costliness, testing the will to ecclesial continuity and evangelical purpose at all levels.

ELCA membership is gathered into nearly 11,000 congregations, served by an ordained ministry (in various fields besides the parochial) of over 16,000. The congregations are scattered across the nation's 50 states as well as in Puerto Rico and the Virgin Islands (see Caribbean, above). They are oldest and most numerous in Pennsylvania but reach a higher proportion of the population in Minnesota and other parts of the upper Midwest. The number of members per congregation ranges from under 100 to over 12,000, the average size being close to 490.

The ELCA confession of faith, like that of its predecessor church bodies, upholds a traditional Lutheran position. Summarized, "This church confesses the Gospel, recorded in the Holy Scriptures and confessed in the ecumenical creeds and Lutheran confessional writings, as the power of God to create and sustain the Church for God's mission in the world" (Constitution, ch. 2). In corporate worship the ELCA continues a liturgical life (*Lutheran Book of Worship*, 1978) that links it historically to the Reformation era and, via the Mass, to roots in the early church, and that associates it contemporaneously with fellow Christians worldwide.

Bishop Chilstrom, elected by the Columbus convention, came to this position from the Minnesota Synod, largest in the LCA (below). There he had served as bishop for over a decade (1976–1987). A descendant of Swedish forebears, his prior experience as parish pastor and college teacher as well as his forthrightness and spirit of conciliation were important gifts in fostering church unity. His wife, Corinne, of Danish background, was an ordained pastor in the ALC (below).

The other elective offices are held by persons from the merging churches. The vice-president—Christine Grumm (AELC), San Francisco, an agency administrator—chairs the ELCA church council. The secretary—Lowell G. Almen (ALC), Minneapolis, former editor of *The Lutheran Standard*—is responsible for the minutes, records management, and archives of the general church. The editor of *The Lutheran*—Edgar R. Trexler (LCA), Philadelphia, edited his church body's paper for the preceding 18 years—provides the church with its official periodical. The treasurer, George E. Aker, is appointed by the church council and directs the office of finance.

Of the ELCA's ordained ministers, about 10,000 serve in congregations. Others work in a wide variety of fields. A significant number are in the category of temporarily awaiting a call. A normal proportion are pensioned. The ELCA's ordained women in ministry number close to 1000. Also in service are consecrated deaconesses, deacons, commissioned teachers, and commissioned lay professional workers.

Organizationally, the congregations are grouped into 65 synods, all but the Slovak Zion Synod being assigned a geographic area. In seven states—New Jersey, Virginia, North Carolina, South Carolina, Florida, Montana, and Oregon—synod and state boundaries coincide. In all others, the synodical lines are new. The synods, in turn, are grouped into nine regions. Each has its designated regional center for mission to coordinate various churchwide functions.

In some ways the most obvious change—the recognition of the church's center of gravity—has been the placing of ELCA headquarters in Chicago. An 11-story office building, conveniently near the city's giant O'Hare International Airport and ground transportation, was acquired in March 1987. Amid the change, time-honored centers of Lutheranism—New York and Philadelphia, especially—have been given up. The church's main archives are housed separately, near the headquarters; and the nine regional archives are linked to the national.

With many changes introduced simultaneously, the ELCA requires time to mature. Its heritage represents more riches than most of its members realize. To its blend of American and older European backgrounds—largely but by no means exclusively of Germanic and Nordic origin—have been added American Indian, African, Latin American, and Asian strains.

Determined to continue the tradition of cultural diversity within Lutheranism in a new way, the planners of the ELCA have sought to capture a vision of inclusiveness for a church both catholic and evangelical. For the first time, the official documents of a Lutheran church specify not only an equitable balance between clergy and laity but also equality of participation by women as well as men. To ensure this, ELCA units (conventions, councils, committees, boards, commissions, etc.) are given a decade (1989–1999) to meet a sociological membership requirement: a minimum percentage (10%) "shall be persons of color and/or persons whose primary language is other than English." This reflects the outreach goal set for the ELCA as a whole (below, missions).

For its governance and function, the ELCA continues on a grander scale—and with adaptations—what has long since become familiar in a denomination. The top legislative authority is the churchwide convention. It meets biennially and is made up of over 1000 delegates elected by the several synods on an allocated basis. The church council, with 33 members, is the ELCA's board of directors and its "interim legislative authority." The three elected officers—the bishop, vice-president, and secretary—and the appointed treasurer have complementary duties. Only the bishop is required to be an ordained minister, and all four of these positions, like others in the ELCA, are open to women as well as men.

Churchwide functions—many of them necessarily decentralized—are assigned to variously designated units. Divisions attend to congregational life, education, global mission, ministry, home mission (Outreach

USA), and social ministry. Commissions deal with issues confronting the church in society, communication, financial support, the contribution and participation of women in the life of the church, and multicultural ministries at home and abroad. Other churchwide units include: a women's organization, a publishing house, a church periodical, a pension board, and a conference of bishops. The latter, in effect, reflects the work of the churchwide units in policy and practice locally. The long-standing ecumenical commitment in American Lutheranism finds its focus in an Office for Ecumenical Affairs, whose executive director serves as an assistant to the bishop.

To serve and challenge the rising generation, a youth organization (established by the Division for Congregational Life) continues the aims of the long-operative Luther League. A parallel function (Division of Education) carries out the church's concern for the educational process from preschool to university, with special attention to the 29 ELCA-related colleges (below) and to campus ministry, as described earlier.

Through its Division for Ministry, the ELCA commits itself to guide and assist not only its eight theological seminaries (below) but also the cognate training of lay professionals as well as various aspects of ministry by the laity. The ongoing (continuing) education of pastors and lay persons, now more than ever, is to help a Christian ministry adapt to change while remaining committed to the high calling of God in Christ.

Mission in the ELCA has its main thrust in two churchwide units, one domestic, the other global. Here the church places itself on a critical frontier. The already-mentioned membership goal of "10% persons of color and/or persons whose primary language is other than English"—if achieved in the selected decade (1989–1999)—would mean, it is said, an increase in this category of about 500,000 persons. For each of the 11,000 ELCA congregations this would average five persons per year in this category, or 50 over the decade. This may not seem an unreasonable figure. But, as noted below, the declining growth rate among the old-line communions like the Lutheran, makes this goal a stiff challenge. The quest of its attainment requires a complementary effort in missionary partnership with churches overseas.

Concerning the ELCA and the media, there are highlights. *The Lutheran,* the church's biweekly periodical—its antecedents extend back well over a century—has a circulation of 1,250,000, making it the largest of any Protestant denomination. The publishing house of the ELCA, combining the well-known Augsburg (ALC) and Fortress (LCA) enterprises, is based in Minneapolis. It is third largest among the denominational publishing houses in the USA.

Television on a national scale involves the ELCA in the complexities of sharing network facilities, such as those of the interreligious venture, VISN (Vision Interfaith Satellite Network), on cable TV. The radio ministry "Lutheran Vespers," begun in 1946, is currently aired by 138 stations. It reaches most age groups, draws a wide response, and is 90% listener-supported. The ELCA also continues "Scan," the 400-station program on social issues begun by the ALC (below). It also participates, on a one-fourth time basis, in the nationwide "Protestant Hour," long an LCA venture.

In the closing stages of the ELCA merger, many issues were widely debated. The doctrine of the ministry, the nature of the church, the role of the congregation, the adequacy of the pension plan, the place and participation of women and of the laity generally, the introduction of quotas (like 10%) to guarantee minority membership in the organizational units, and a multitude of cognate concerns clamored for attention. The Commission for a New Lutheran Church (CNLC)—its 70 members and many consultants having labored four years—published its plan in the spring of 1986. Thereupon, in church conventions and in many groups the CNLC proposals were studied, debated, amended, and finally approved. The decisive outcome was reached in two stages. First, by the requirement of a two-thirds approving vote of the delegates to the three respective church conventions in August 1986. For the AELC one action sufficed. Second, for the two larger bodies, their 1986 action required substantiation, in the ALC by a two-thirds majority of its congregations voting directly, and in the LCA by a two-thirds majority vote of the delegates at the church's special (closing) convention, April 28-29, 1987, in Columbus, Ohio.

The formation of the ELCA calls to mind the course its merging church bodies had come. Consolidation was indeed achieved, but the years of church growth—for Lutherans as well as for most other "old line" communions—were in the past. The ALC (below) peaked in 1966, but since then has seen its membership drop by about 13.2%. The LCA (below) peaked in 1967, but has since then declined by 12.9%. The AELC remained fairly constant during its short existence (below); while its parent body, the Lutheran Church–Missouri Synod, peaked in 1972, and over the next dozen years (including those of internal conflict) declined by 9%. In recent years, Lutheran church membership statistics appear to have leveled off. Yet the nation's growth rate continues upward, and the only ones matching or even exceeding it are the conservative evangelical and formerly marginal groups (above). Nevertheless, the ELCA has aimed high. Its uniting churches have achievements to be remembered.

THE AMERICAN LUTHERAN CHURCH (ALC)
(1960–1987)

One of the three major Lutheran bodies in the USA, the ALC was constituted in 1960—a merger of the (old) American Lutheran Church, the Evangelical Lutheran Church, and the United Evangelical Lutheran Church. In 1963, the Lutheran Free Church became a part of the ALC. This new body brought together Lutherans of three ethnic backgrounds: Danish, German, and Norwegian (see history, below). In 1988, the ALC became part of the new Evangelical Lutheran Church in America (above). Over its 27 years the ALC was headed by: Fredrik A. Schiotz (1960–1969), Kent S. Knutson (1969–1973), and David W. Preus (1973–1987). The title change from president to presiding bishop occurred in 1982.

The more than 2.3 million-member ALC was the ninth largest Protestant body in the USA. Of its 7443 ordained pastors, 4626 served the 4940 congregations, located in all but three of the 50 states. Its main concentration (56%) lay in the five states of Minnesota, Wisconsin, Iowa, and North and South Dakota. Another six states—Ohio,

California, Texas, Illinois, Washington, and Michigan—accounted for 28% of the members. The average size of the congregations was 479 baptized members.

The ALC had a synodical form of church organization, with the congregation as basic. Functionally, it was more centralized than either the LCA or the Lutheran Church–Missouri Synod (below). The biennial convention exercised the legislative authority and elected the general officers of the church—the president (presiding bishop), vice-president, and general secretary, as well as the Board of Trustees. It determined the policy of the church body. The president gave ongoing direction within these policies. The general secretary maintained the church's records, gathered congregational and personnel data, published the yearbook and the ALC minutes, managed the conventions, supervised the archives, provided information, etc. The church council, a 64-member (including advisory members) executive body, guided the church's work between conventions. Its members included the three elected officers, two members of the Board of Trustees, two youth representatives, and three members of each of the church's 19 districts. Each district had a full-time bishop and several additional staff. Districts held annual conventions with delegates from all congregations. Within the districts, the congregations were grouped into small conferences. These elected the delegates to the national biennial convention. Only pastors serving congregations had a vote at the district convention or could be elected delegates to the national convention.

The Division for Life and Mission in the Congregation (DLMC) worked with the church's Augsburg Publishing House (Minneapolis) in providing educational resources for all ages. In the autumn of 1986, a new Witness Sunday school series—preschool through 12th grade—was introduced. Like many other Augsburg publications, it is widely used by other demonitions.

"Search," the title of a five-year intensive and systematic Bible study program for adults, has been used by a large number of ALC groups and others. Introduced in 1983, it is designed to equip participants for and to be a part of the congregations' outreach to their communities. The Search program features study material for four eight-week units per year. Pastors and laity compose each leadership team. Participants renew their commitment for each unit.

These resources strengthened the ALC's Christian education programs within the congregations: Sunday schools, weekday schools, and vacation church schools. The latter reached nearly 300,000 pupils, one-fourth of them not members of the ALC. Camps, retreats, and outdoor ministries numbered nearly 100 and served both youth and adults.

The two auxiliaries of the church—the Luther League and the American Lutheran Church Women (ALCW)—were under the auspices of the DLMC. The ALCW, active in almost all congregations, had a national organization with units at the conference and district levels. Women's involvement in parish life, including Bible study and education in mission and contemporary issues, advanced their opportunity for growth and influence. The initiatives of the ALCW in the South Pacific District led to the production of the Search series. The election in 1982 of Kathryn E. Baerwald as ALC general secretary placed her in the highest elective office so far held by a woman in any Lutheran body in the USA.

Although youth auxiliaries have waned in many denominations in recent years, the ALC's Luther League retained its strength. With units in some 3000 parishes, the league offered teenagers opportunities for growth through caring and sharing. Conference, district, and national events supplemented the local activities. ALC youth gatherings have drawn as many as 15,000 youth and their sponsors for inspiration, study, and fellowship on a grand scale.

Higher education, a long-standing priority in the ALC, included 11 colleges and universities and one junior college in close relationship to the church. The Division of College and University Services contributed to the operating budgets of the colleges. Individual congregations often provided scholarships, enabling students to attend one of the following institutions.

California Lutheran University (1959), founded and supported in cooperation with the LCA, is the youngest of the schools. The others came from the bodies that merged in 1960. The old ALC brought its Capital University (1850), Wartburg College (1852), and

Texas Lutheran College (1891); the UELC its Dana College (1884); the ELC its Augustana, Sioux Falls (1860), Luther (1861), St. Olaf (1874), Concordia, Moorhead (1891) colleges, Pacific Lutheran University (1891), and Waldorf Junior College (1907); and the LFC its Augsburg College (1869). Besides these church colleges, all of which have departments of religion, the ALC participated with the LCA and the AELC in the National Lutheran Campus Ministry. Pastoral service and programs of study and fellowship reached students and faculty on some 300 campuses of private and state-supported institutions.

Most of the ALC pastors were educated at three seminaries jointly owned and operated with the LCA before the ELCA was formed: Trinity at Columbus, Ohio; Luther Northwestern in St. Paul, Minnesota; and Pacific Lutheran Theological Seminary in Berkeley, California. The latter is a participating institution in the Graduate Theological Union, composed of seminaries adjacent to the University of California. A fourth seminary, Wartburg, in Dubuque, Iowa, also maintains a house of studies in Denver, Colorado, and a branch in Austin, Texas. The Austin operation provides for Spanish-speaking pastors in the USA as well as in Latin America. The ALC's Board of Theological Education and Ministry shaped policy, set admission standards, and oversaw and supported the work of the seminaries. The board executive kept in touch with ALC pastoral candidates attending non-Lutheran institutions. In 1981, the ALC reaffirmed its endorsement of a well-educated clergy by raising U.S. $45 million to strengthen its four theological schools. In 1986, 741 ALC students (26.6% of them women) attended these institutions. Ordination of women was approved by the 1970 church convention. By April 2, 1986, there were 249 ordained women on the ALC roster.

The Division for Service and Mission in America (DSMA) held a wide range of responsibilities. The gathering of new congregations continued with ever-renewed commitment. In choosing sights for new congregations, the DSMA sought to remedy the very low percentage of minority groups in the ALC. In 1984, 20% of its missions reached into communities where minorities (blacks, Hispanics, Asians, and native Americans) dominate. During the years 1983–

1985, 30 new congregations and another 20 outreach ministries were initiated. To curb the decline and discouragement among older congregations in changing communities—both rural and urban—the DSMA offered financial aid as well as assistance in program and renewed outreach. Consequently, over five years the number of minority-race members increased significantly (from 16,982 in 1981 to 19,683 in 1986).

The DSMA also had responsibility for the approximately 200 social service agencies related to the ALC. These included institutions for the care of the aging, for disturbed or mentally handicapped children and hospitals, as well as agencies for family counseling, child placement, chemical dependency, and other needs as they arose. Some of these were statewide and inter-Lutheran agencies. The DSMA's identification with native Americans helped them form the National Lutheran Indian Board, an inter-Lutheran agency through which assistance and advocacy can be channeled.

The ALC had a long history of overseas involvement that built on the work of its predecessor bodies. A 1976 United Mission Appeal, an ingathering of US $35 million enabled the ALC greatly to extend this work. In 1986, there were some 300 missionaries working in partnership with and under the direction of churches in 21 countries outside the United States. The largest numbers were in *Japan, *Madagascar, and *Papua New Guinea. About half of the overseas missionaries were lay people who served in a variety of positions: agriculturalists, accountants, linguists, physicians, nurses, houseparents, hospital administrators, communication specialists, teachers, and others. The pastors included seven serving in Germany and Australia to alleviate the shortage of pastors there. New work was coordinated with other churches through the LWF Department of Church Cooperation. An example is the work begun in Senegal in cooperation with the Finnish Evangelical Lutheran Mission and the Evangelical Lutheran Church in Namibia (ELCIN). The Division for World Mission and Inter-Church Cooperation oversaw this work in close touch with the Division for World Mission and Ecumenism of the LCA. Together, these divisions published *Encounter* to keep the churches informed on mission activities and opportunities.

In recent years, the ALC combined its traditional cultivation of piety with a greater commitment to social action and justice. It placed emphasis on peace-making, and demonstrated a concern for alleviating hunger throughout the world, raising more than U.S. $16 million above the regular budget during a nine-year period. Both spiritual growth and Christian responsibilities have been brought to the attention of ALC members through the bimonthly *The Lutheran Standard,* the official magazine with a circulation of 500,000. The electronic media were also used to channel a variety of radio and television programs. "Lutheran Vespers," a weekly half-hour devotional program, came over more than 100 radio stations (see ELCA, above). "Scan," a half-hour weekly radio program featuring contemporary music and discussions of social issues, was aired over 400 stations. Several pilot television programs and films won national awards for their excellence.

"Commitment to Mission" (CTM), begun in 1985, became a churchwide program to foster in members of all congregations a renewed dedication to mission and a deepened understanding of stewardship. The program brought together the ongoing mission support needs with a special appeal for designated gifts. It trained approximately 1200 mission interpreters—clergy and laity—to visit all congregations of the ALC. The CTM goal was to raise US $130 million in ongoing mission support as well as U.S. $40 million in extrabudgetary gifts to expand the church's mission and to provide ALC's share in the cost of the new Evangelical Lutheran Church in America.

Antecedents: The American Lutheran Church (ALC) history is indeed a mixture of backgrounds. The earliest forerunners of the old ALC came from Pennsylvania and Virginia to Ohio in the early 19th century and for a time (1812) remained a conference of the Pennsylvania Ministerium. In 1818, the Lutheran Synod of Ohio was formed, followed by the Buffalo Synod (1845) and the Iowa Synod (1854). The latter included (1896) the semi-independent Texas Synod (1851). In 1930, these synods, all of German heritage, joined to form the first ALC. As a charter member of both the LWF and the WCC, this body became a strong supporter of confessional unity within the worldwide ecumenical movement. This was manifested in the service of its leaders: Sylvester C. Michelfelder (1889–1951), postwar coordinator of relief programs in Europe and first general secretary of the LWF (1947–1951); Ralph H. Long (1882–1948), director of the National Lutheran Council and coordinator of Lutheran efforts in America for aid in other lands; Julius Bodensieck (1894–1986), theologian, a leading American Lutheran enabler in Europe after World War II, and editor of the monumental three-volume *Encyclopedia of the Lutheran Church* (1965).

The Evangelical Lutheran Church (ELC) formed in 1917 as the Norwegian Lutheran Church of America, was a merger of the Hauge Synod (1876), the Norwegian Synod (1853), and the United Norwegian Church (1890). The latter and largest—a merger of several Danish and Norwegian groups—helped bridge the gap between the Pietism of the Haugeans and the strong confessionalism of the synod. The name change from Norwegian to Evangelical took place in 1946. The ELC also contributed to Lutheran world service and unity: H.G. Stub (1849–1931), first president of the National Lutheran Council (NLC); Lauritz Larsen (1880–1923), first executive director of the NLC and leader in channeling American help to fellow Lutherans in Eastern Europe; Lars Wilhelm Boe (1875–1942), president of St. Olaf College and early advocate of Lutheran cooperation at home and overseas through the Lutheran World Convention; Howard V. Hong (1912–), Kierkegaard scholar and, in the critical years 1947–1950, field director of the largely student-staffed LWF Service to Refugees team, which prepared thousands of Baltic and other homeless people for resettlement; and Fredrik A. Schiotz (1901–1989), director of the NLC-based Commission on Service to Younger Churches and Orphaned Missions, and promoter of cooperation between the churches and mission agencies in Europe and North America on the one hand, and the rising church in Asia, Africa, and Latin America on the other. At the time of the 1960 merger, the ELC had been a member of the WCC for four years and was a charter member of the LWF. Fredrik Schiotz became the LWF's fourth president at the Helsinki assembly in 1963.

The United Evangelical Lutheran Church in America (UELCA), the third and smallest partner in the merger, actually initiated the consolidation. This was first proposed in 1948 by the UELC's president, N.C. Carlsen. The UELC itself was a merger in 1896 of the Danish Lutheran Church Association (1884) and the Danish Lutheran Church of North America (1894), both with Inner Mission background (see Denmark).

The Lutheran Free Church (1897) joined the ALC in 1963, bringing a crisp Norse spirit of independence and a strong espousal of congregational sovereignty. Though small in numbers, the LFC produced several outstanding theologians: George Sverdrup (1848–1907) and his son George (1879–1937); Thorvald Olson Burntvedt, the statesmanly president (1930–1958); and Bernhard M. Christensen (1901–1984), long-time faculty member at Augsburg College and its president from 1938–1962. Christensen's accent on spirit, intellect, and service made a lasting impression on students at Augsburg and beyond, one of whom was Warren Quanbeck (below).

Under President John Stensvaag the majority of the LFC congregations joined the ALC. A minority remained separate, constituting themselves as the Association of Free Lutheran Congregations (above). Dr. Stensvaag, formerly professor (Old Testament) at Augsburg Seminary, joined the faculty of Luther Northwestern Seminary, where he served until 1981.

Elected to lead the new ALC was Fredrik Schiotz. His long experience in patiently letting diverse participants have their say created a spirit of harmony. During his decade in office (1960–1970), and greatly to his credit, the ALC declared pulpit and altar fellowship with the Lutheran Church–Missouri Synod (withdrawn by LCMS in 1981) and affirmed it with the Lutheran Church in America; joined the WCC; and participated in Roman Catholic and Reformed dialogs. Serving the ALC in these ecumenical responsibilities was the remarkably gifted theologian, Warren Quanbeck (1917–1979).

Kent S. Knutson (1924–1973), another able scholar and leader, filled his brief presidency of the ALC (1969–1973) with promise, advancing a soundly inter-Lutheran and ecumenical policy. His early death brought the vice-president, David W. Preus, to leadership. Re-elected as president, Preus continued a strong commitment to mission at home and abroad; an active participation in peace efforts; and an expansion of interdenominational partnership. Not least significant was his firm support for the new Evangelical Lutheran Church in America.

ASSOCIATION OF EVANGELICAL LUTHERAN CHURCHES (AELC)
(1976–1987)

The 279 congregations (112,169 members in all) in the AELC were served by 298 pastors. The inclusive number of ordained clergy in this body was 680. Organized in December 1976 in Chicago, the AELC constitution combined congregational and synodical elements. Its congregations formed four regional synods, each under a bishop: East Coast (office in New York); English (Detroit); Pacific (San Francisco); Southwest (Great Bend, Kansas). AELC headquarters were in St. Louis, including the offices of the executive secretary as well as of mission and other functions. Over its 11 years the AELC was headed by William H. Kohn (1976–1984) and Will L. Herzfeld (1984–1987). The title change from president to presiding bishop was in 1982.

The AELC's major institutional concern was Christ Seminary/Seminex (1974–). Located in St. Louis until mid-1983, it was then deployed. The majority of its faculty were added to the Lutheran School of Theology at Chicago and to Pacific Lutheran Theological Seminary in Berkeley, California. Christ Seminary has continued as a separate entity, even with its faculty and students integrated into these two schools.

A strong missionary motivation marked the AELC from the time of its formation. Partners in Mission, at first an independent agency, served the AELC from 1982 as its Division of Mission. Its work included ministries with partner churches in other countries—Papua New Guinea, Costa Rica, Panama, India, Lebanon—as well as developing ministries in the United States.

Currents in Theology and Mission, the quarterly journal of the AELC, has been produced by the Christ Seminary faculty. The AELC published *Perspectives* in cooperation with ELIM (Evangelical Lutherans in Mission, forerunner of the AELC).

The AELC memberships included the LWF (1977), the Lutheran Council in the USA (1978), National Lutheran Campus Ministries (1978), Lutheran World Ministries (1978), and Lutheran World Relief (1977). Although not a member, the AELC participated in a number of programs of the National Council of Churches of Christ in the USA and the World Council of Churches.

During its brief history, the AELC exerted considerable influence on the process of Lutheran union. As the smallest among the three consolidating bodies, the AELC's advocacy, for example, of adequate representation for women and minorities in the new Evangelical Lutheran Church in America (1988) was pivotal. The AELC background helps explain an influence far beyond its small numbers.

Antecedents: Historically, the AELC is a product of creative change in the Lutheran Church–Missouri Synod. Over the past decades, diverse developments required Missouri's response. As noted earlier (introduction to ELCA), in the 1940s came the movement toward closer partnership among Lutherans at home and worldwide. It also challenged the LCMS to participate in the ecumenical movement. In the 1950s, increasing numbers of future faculty members in Concordia Seminary, St. Louis, and in other synodical schools were earning their graduate degrees in institutions outside the Lutheran fold and were learning to express their confessional position in new ways. In the 1960s, the LCMS itself was ready for unprecedented steps. Its 1962 synodical convention, a turning point, placed world mission and church unity in broadened perspective. It joined the new Lutheran Council in the USA (1966) and voted pulpit and altar fellowship with the American Lutheran Church (1969). These were high points of departure from the past. But the 1969 convention changed that. It elected a new and conservative president, Jacob A.O. Preus of Norwegian descent, and placed tradition in the driver's seat. In the 1970s, the forces of advance and return clashed on such key points as biblical interpretation, mission policy (overseas and ecumenical), and theological education.

Concordia Seminary, St. Louis, became the main battleground. A new "mind of Missouri" contended with the old. Backed by a synodical majority, the old won out. Most students and faculty made a dramatic exodus from the Concordia campus on February 19, 1974. The ways parted. A seminary in exile, Seminex, had begun. The pastors and congregations supporting this move eventually formed a new church body, the AELC. Gains intended for the LCMS thus became available to the two other major Lutheran bodies—the ALC and the LCA—which had already been talking merger. The climax came in September 1982, when three church conventions— ALC, LCA, AELC—were held simultaneously and voted overwhelmingly for union. In a real sense, the AELC was the winner. Its own existence presupposed moving ahead to greater challenges in mission and unity.

LUTHERAN CHURCH IN AMERICA (LCA)
(1962–1987)

This largest—nearly 29 million baptized members in 1986—and, by its antecedents, oldest Lutheran church body in America was constituted in June 1962 in Detroit, Michigan. A consolidation of four churches (described below), the LCA blended many American backgrounds and origins, including Danish, Finnish, German, and Swedish. Over its 25 years the LCA's chief officers were: Franklin Clark Fry (1962–1968), Robert J. Marshall (1968–1978), and James R. Crumley (1978–1987).

The LCA's more than 5800 congregations extended into all 50 states as well as to *Puerto Rico and the *Virgin Islands. Of the more than 8400 ordained ministers, over 5100 served in congregations, while others were in teaching positions, chaplaincies, and other specialized ministries. About 1700 (past age 65) are pensioned. By mid-1986, the number of women in the ordained ministry exceeded 450, a striking contrast to only 30 a decade earlier. The large number of other workers— most of them women—in allied fields of service included the deaconess community (in Gladwyne, near Philadelphia), whose pioneering role in the 19th century has been noted above.

Numerically, the LCA (baptized) membership was at its height in 1967, but its decline by over 12% since then parallels the experience of most other North American mainline communions. Although continental in spread, about one-half of the LCA members resided in the eastern states, roughly from Florida to New England, with 25% of the church's total concentrated in Pennsylvania (Colonial Period, above). Another 20% were in the upper Midwest, in the contiguous states of Illinois, Wisconsin, and Minnesota. Other areas of significant numbers ranged from Ohio to the Pacific Coast, with rapid accessions into Arizona and other parts of the increasingly popular "Sun Belt."

In organization, the LCA combined presbyterial and congregational elements, with bishops (formerly called presidents) heading its 29 geographic synods and one nongeographic—the Slovak Zion Synod. Its special interest conferences—the Danish, Finnish, German, and Hungarian—were reminiscent of earlier times, when Swedish, Icelandic, and other groupings maintained their ethnic identity. Today, as noted elsewhere, this kind of recognition seeks to build up black, Hispanic, Asian, and other groups as bearers of diversity within Christian unity. Yet this part of the task is slow.

The biennial convention was the LCA's top legislative authority, to which the synods elected their allocated number of clerical and lay delegates. The convention elected the church's presiding officer (the title was changed from president to bishop in 1980) as well as other officers, the members of the executive council, and those of its boards and management committees. The latter were advisory to the respective divisions responsible for mission in North America, parish service, professional leadership (ministry, ordained, and lay), and world mission and ecumenism. Two boards governed publications and pensions. Organizationally, the LCA sought to balance churchwide, synodical, and local elements as part of an ecclesial whole.

LCA pastors, with some exceptions, were educated in the church's seven theological seminaries: Gettysburg (1826) and Philadelphia (1864), both in Pennsylvania; Columbia, South Carolina (1830); and Chicago (1860)— a consolidation of five schools in the 1960s; as well as in three seminaries owned jointly with the ALC—in Columbus, Ohio (1830), St. Paul, Minnesota (1869), and Berkeley, California (1950). A number of LCA students attended university divinity schools like those at Harvard, Yale, or Chicago; still others

Union Seminary in New York or Princeton (Presbyterian) in New Jersey. In its assigned synods, each LCA seminary had its own support system, supplemented where necessary and guided by the church's Division for Professional Leadership. In cooperation with the seminaries and synods, the division provided opportunities for the continuing education as well as career guidance of pastors.

The LCA's 18 church-related colleges—the type of relationship varying with each one—in 1984 enrolled over 23,000 full-time students (down about 14% from a decade earlier), with a total full-time faculty of 1500 teaching in the arts and sciences and including religious studies. The majority of faculty as well as students were not Lutheran, but the greater number of LCA pastors and church workers still came from these schools. Among them, Gettysburg College (1832) is the oldest, and all of them represent the historic effort of American denominations to provide for an educated ministry and a leading Christian laity in the community at large.

Health and welfare services were offered by a wide variety of church-related institutions and agencies. These were founded earlier by antecedent bodies of the LCA to meet specific needs locally and regionally. Yet here, as with the colleges, the outreach—by law—was nondiscriminatory as to race or religion. Major support came from public and community funds, with most of the staff being non-Lutheran. As in other denominations, the church's many youth camps and other programs expressed its concern for the future.

In this respect, heavy responsibility was seen to rest on the nurture of a Christian laity. The Division of Parish Services—often in close cooperation with its ALC counterpart—provided materials and training opportunities for parish education and other activities. Early participation in the Lord's Supper (before age 10, usually) and confirmation instruction a few years later—as in most other Lutheran churches—proved a valued sequence in Christian growth.

While all denominations, at some point, include Bible study opportunities for the laity, the LCA "Word and Witness" program won particular distinction. Launched in 1976, W-W had 65,000 participants over the decade 1975–1985. Its intensive 54-session exercise promoted the dual aims of Bible study and education for witness. Program leaders—numbering over 3000 in 1986—were paced through a 12-day preparatory course. The interdisciplinary character of W-W linked past and present in practical hermeneutics, placing the gospel in the settings of what it meant and what it means. About 40% of the LCA congregations joined in this program. Basic materials of W-W, including the 582-page leader guide, have been translated into German, Swedish, Finnish, and Spanish and were being done in Mandarin for the Chinese dispersion in Malaysia and beyond.

Among church publishing houses, Fortress Press (formerly Muhlenberg and Augustana) became a leader. Its production especially of scholarly works, original and in translation, helped account for its ready reception in the academic world as well as in the church at large. Like other major church houses, its international and ecumenical connections resulted in a publication of titles of interest to those of the Lutheran tradition in the wider sense and to many others as well. With the 1986 publication of Volume 55 (the elaborate index), the long project of bringing *Luther's Works* to the English-speaking world ended. Replacing the earlier six-volume Philadelphia Edition, the first volume of this massive undertaking of many scholars appeared in 1955. This was a joint venture of Concordia Publishing House (LCMS, below), which brought out a selection of the Reformer's biblical writings in 30 volumes, and of the LCA's Fortress Press (Philadelphia), whose 25 additional volumes offered a wide range of Luther's works in other fields. A companion volume (1959), by Jaroslav Pelikan has served as an invaluable introduction. This English-language edition is closely linked to the long standard and still unfinished *Weimarer Ausgabe* (WA) of now more than 100 volumes, published in Germany and in progress for over a century.

Over recent years, the Division for Mission in North America (DMNA) engaged in the frequently uphill struggle to gather and assist congregations in new housing areas, and to aid older congregations caught amid the forces of urban change or deterioration. The demands of this many-sided ministry, as intimated earlier in many other contexts, were part of a worldwide process of transition. The DMNA thus continued the work of one of its predecessor units (Social Ministry) in providing studies and guidelines for the LCA membership in grappling with issues of social justice, the needs of minorities, the struggle against racism, the role of women in church and society, the needs of the elderly, the challenge of disarmament and the waging of peace, and other vital issues.

Similarly, the Division for World Mission and Ecumenism sought to apply its resources in ways conducive both to the spread of the gospel and to the furthering of Christian unity. The LCA continued its ties with the nine churches it helped to establish and with whom it has a shared history: *India, *Liberia, *Guyana, *Argentina, *Japan, *Taiwan, *Hong Kong, *Malaysia/Singapore, and *Tanzania. From 1977, financial agreements were made with them for specific activities and definite periods of time. The projects might be on the territory of the overseas church, on LCA territory, or in a third country. In recent years, the LCA spread its involvement to other countries in Africa (*Egypt, *Ethiopia, *Ghana, *Kenya); in Asia (*Burma, *Indonesia, *Israel, *Korea, *Nepal, *Philippines, *Thailand); and in Intercontinental and South America (*Chile, *Haiti, Jamaica, *Suriname, Trinidad, *Uruguay). In these countries, it works with Lutherans or other Christians in a variety of bilateral and multilateral arrangements. In Europe, the LCA helped supply pastors for expatriate ecumenical congregations in key cities as well as for Lutheran churches in the *Netherlands and *Germany.

Ecumenically, the LCA became particularly close to the more liturgical communions—the Anglican (Episcopalian), Roman Catholic, and Eastern Orthodox—which was not to minimize the importance of the Lutheran-Reformed relationship. The LCA participated actively in the National Council of Churches of Christ in the USA (NCCC/USA), being the only Lutheran body to do so. Besides, through its predecessor bodies, the LCA was a charter member of the World Council of Churches (see LCA history, ULCA, below).

Antecedents: The current concern that minorities be duly represented in the new Evangelical Lutheran Church in America (ELCA, above), recalls the "minority power" of the two small bodies in the formation of the LCA.

The four ecclesial traditions that ultimately formed the LCA were quite evenly balanced in representation on the Joint Commission on Lutheran Unity (JCLU, 1956–1962). Numerically, however, the imbalance could hardly have been more extreme. Of then nearly 3.2 million, the American Evangelical Lutheran Church (AELC, Danish origin) accounted for 0.7%; the Finnish Evangelical Lutheran Church (Suomi), 1.1%; the Augustana Lutheran Church (Swedish origin), 19.8%; and the United Lutheran Church in America (ULCA—see also Colonial Era, above), 78.4%.

The small Danish element played a large historical role. Formed in 1872 as the Danish Evangelical Lutheran Church in America, it divided in 1896. One branch, the United Evangelical Lutheran Church in America (UELCA, above) became a part of the American Lutheran Church in 1960. The other, the American Evangelical Lutheran Church, became a part of the LCA (1962), but retained its identity in the Danish Special Interest Conference. Prior to 1962, the AELC counted nearly 24,000 baptized members. Its 76 congregations were divided into nine districts that spanned the country from New England to the Pacific Coast. Church headquarters and Grand View College, keeper of the Grundtvigian tradition (*Denmark), were in Des Moines, Iowa. Already in the 1950s the theological department had joined the Chicago Lutheran Seminary, then in Maywood, Illinois. Folk High Schools, as in Tyler, Minnesota, or Solvang, California, for some decades perpetuated the faith-and-life passion of Grundtvig.

Suomi's contribution to the LCA was characteristically different. Diversity within the church in Finland became disunity in America. Of the 300,000 Finns who immigrated between 1880 and 1914, the largest number formed the Suomi Synod in 1890. (Another group, the National Evangelical Church, joined the LCMS in 1964. The rest are in the many subdivisions of Laestadian piety [*Finland], of which the Apostolic Lutheran Church of America [above] is the largest.) A free Finland after World War I marked a turning point in Suomi's relations: closer ties with the church in Finland, whose archbishop visited America for the first time in 1921; as well as a supportive arrangement with ULCA in home missions. Events surrounding World

War II gave America's Lutherans and other Christians a new appreciation of Finland, its people, and the role of its spiritual heritage active in daily life.

Before becoming part of the LCA in 1962, the Suomi Synod counted about 36,000 baptized members, gathered in 153 congregations, and served by 103 pastors. The synod's seven districts extended from New England to the Pacific, with heaviest concentration in Michigan and Minnesota. Suomi College (Hancock, Michigan) even today remains a focal point of the Finnish heritage, but in the 1950s its theological department also relocated to the ULCA's Chicago Lutheran Seminary. Like the Danes, the Finns had a Special Interest Conference within the LCA.

Surrendering its 102-year existence as a separate body, the Augustana Lutheran Church in 1962 entered the LCA with a baptized membership of nearly 630,000. Its 1268 congregations were served by over 1350 ordained ministers. Its order of worship followed that of the Church of Sweden, though its accents on piety made it low church and its clergy did not continue in apostolic succession. Its colleges—Augustana (Rock Island, Illinois, 1860), Gustavus Adolphus (St. Peter, Minnesota, 1861), Bethany (Lindsborg, Kansas, 1881), Upsala (East Orange, New Jersey, 1893)—upheld Swedish culture, prepared an American-oriented Christian laity, and sent successive generations of ministerial students to the theological seminary in Rock Island.

Unlike the larger but more divided Norwegian constituency, Augustana retained its ecclesial unity, even at the expense of losing possibilities for greater growth through fellowships on the margin of Lutheranism, like the Swedish Mission Covenant (*Sweden). Augustana's own mission endeavors overseas—in Asia, Africa, and Latin America—as well as at home were early coordinated with those of other synods in the General Council over a 50-year span (1868–1918, see ULCA, below). Augustana's mediating role in the National Lutheran Council from 1918 onward has already been noted. Its withdrawal from midwestern church unity efforts that bypassed the ULCA, actually expedited the formation of the LCA as a counterpart to the ALC. A kinship of spirit found Augustana and the ULCA making common cause already in the 1920s in the rising ecumenical

movement. This direction was highlighted in 1923 by Archbishop Nathan Söderblom's visit to America, and subsequently given substance by such leaders as Conrad Bergendoff during his long (1931–1962) presidency of Augustana College, Rock Island. Likewise, the full transition to the use of English in the Augustana Synod owes much to the leadership of Gustav Albert Brandelle, its president from 1918-1935. Nor can one imagine the inner strength and missionary outreach of Augustana without the dynamic contributions of countless women, personified in the organizational genius and devout leader, Emmy Carlsson Evald, daughter of one of synod's founders (Erland Carlsson).

● ● ●

The United Lutheran Church in America, comprising nearly four-fifths of the new LCA, entered the 1962 consolidation with a baptized membership of almost 2.5 million. Its 4677 congregations were served by 3736 pastors out of a total clergy roster of 5125. Its 31 synods—three of them in Canada and one (Slovak Zion) nongeographic—spanned the continent, including Alaska, Hawaii, and the Caribbean (*Puerto Rico and the *Virgin Islands). Its headquarters in New York—a reminder that the ULCA's constituting convention had taken place in Manhattan in 1918—were linked closely with other operations in Philadelphia and Minneapolis. Among its 12 colleges (one in Canada), Gettysburg (1832) was the oldest. Its pastors were trained in nine theological seminaries (two in Canada), of which Gettysburg (1826) was the oldest and that in Berkeley (California, 1950) the youngest. In these and many other configurations, the ULCA manifested itself as a product of many previous mergers.

Contrasted with a church body like Augustana—whose unity could be seen in its single seminary, its ordination of new pastors at successive conventions of the church, and its sense of solidarity—the ULCA was a federation. But it was also more than a federation, and during its 44-year history its two presidents—Frederick H. Knubel (1918–1944) and Franklin Clark Fry (1944–1962)—personified continuity, wisdom, and persuasiveness. Besides, the ULCA's understanding of the wholeness of the church (the "Washington Declaration of Principles" of the 1920 convention, as noted above) anticipated greater unity ahead and marked ways already come. In this anticipation the ULCA was not alone, but its gathered experience provided momentum for unity.

Rooted in colonial times, the ULCA was the product of efforts to integrate the three major lines into which the Muhlenberg tradition of colonial origin had become divided. As we have seen, the intention to have but a single synod for North America did not survive. With the formation of the New York Ministerium (1786), the Ministerium of North America became the Ministerium of Pennsylvania and Adjacent States (1792), and so continued for the next 170 years, as the "mother of synods," or "grandmother."

Once the break had occurred in New York, the proliferation of synods, southward and westward especially, kept pace with the movement of American-born Lutherans and successive waves of ready-made Lutheran immigrants from Germany and elsewhere. Confessionally akin, this was still by no means a like-minded constituency, either in theological stance or political allegiance. The three main lines of the Muhlenberg tradition thus reflected this complex, and often painful, historical process, as follows.

First came the *General Synod* (1820). Seeking to unite the growing number of regional synods, it also aimed to adapt Lutheranism to the American scene where Anglo-Protestantism (largely the Calvinist tradition) held sway. The General Synod's attempt to promote an "American Lutheranism," compatible with the prevailing Reformed tenets as well as fully at home in the English language, did not succeed. Its often eloquent architect was Samuel Simon Schmucker (1799–1873), a second-generation American, a graduate of Princeton Seminary (Presbyterian), and founder of Gettysburg Seminary and College. In time, the General Synod became more confessionally Lutheran and upheld its part of the Muhlenberg tradition.

With the American Civil War, Lutheran synods in the slave-holding states formed their *United Synod in the South* (1863–1918). Least affected by the European immigration, their own colonial background and confessional steadfastness made them the most thoroughly Americanized Lutherans. Among their leaders, John Bachman (1790–1874), of Charleston, South Carolina, stands out as pastor, synod president, theologian, and also naturalist. Other Southerners carried forward the advocacy of liturgical worship and thus contributed to the *Common Service* (1888) for Lutheran worship in America, as mentioned earlier. In this field and others, too, the Muhlenberg tradition had its keepers in the South. Its Southern Seminary (1830), and its colleges—Roanoke (Virginia, 1842), Newberry (South Carolina, 1856), Lenoir-Rhyne (Hickory, North Carolina, 1891)— gave this heritage institutional continuity.

The third group, the *General Council* (1867), was soon the strongest and most important in its prefiguring the further place of the Lutheran church in American society. The council was born of a painful and massive breakaway from the General Synod. In this it followed the founding of the Philadelphia Seminary (1864) as a separation from Gettysburg. The council was bilingual, with deference to Swedish (Augustana Synod) and various other groups. But it became the bearer of a new English-language Lutheran leadership, in whose ranks Charles Porterfield Krauth (1823–1883) was the foremost theologian.

With the Ministerium of Pennsylvania as its base, the General Council comprised a coalition of synods from coast to coast and into Canada, with centers of strength in the Midwest. The Augustana Synod—a charter member—proved a balancing influence between those of German and multigenerational American background. The polity on whose basis synods had joined the council—and others, like Iowa, remained observers—designated congregations the "primary bodies" and saw them, represented in synods, as committed to a larger ecclesial unity.

The General Council's hopes to rally all conservative Lutheran synods were foiled in 1872 by the Missouri-led formation of the Synodical Conference (see below, LCMS). The council's position was determined by history but its place delimited by the times. Confessionally, it stood between the evangelicalism of the General Synod and the rigid orthodoxy of the Synodical Conference. Practically, the General Council upheld the conservative Reformation, meaning (in Krauth's terms) a place of witness between Roman Catholicism, on the one side, and American Protestantism, on the other, with the inference that much of the latter derived from the radical wing of the 16th-century Reformation. The Evangelical Protestant (the Lutheran) Church was seen by the council as the "mother church" of Protestantism. It was committed to a historical and not only doctrinal grasp of the *Augsburg Confession*—a commitment of later ecumenical potential. But in the late 19th century, conservative Lutherans shunned the risks of "unionism," which they understood as syncretism. To cultivate their identity, they adopted the rule: "Lutheran pulpits are for Lutheran ministers only. Lutheran altars are for Lutheran communicants only. The exceptions to the rule belong to the sphere of privilege, not of right." (The famed "Galesburg Rule" was adopted by the General Council convention in the Illinois town of that name, 1875.)

In mission at home and overseas and in welfare services, the council supported extensive work. Leader in this farflung field was William Alfred Passavant (above). Like many others, he had earlier been prominent in the General Synod. In higher education and ministerial training, the council's seminaries in Philadelphia and later in Chicago (1891) emphasized the importance of a Lutheran clergy thoroughly at home in the American scene as well as capable of service to immigrants of many nationalities. Krauth's successor at the Philadelphia Seminary was Henry Eyster Jacobs (1844–1931). His teaching career began at Gettysburg College. He became widely influential with his translations (*Book of Concord*, with notes and historical background, 1882–1883), his reference works (*The Lutheran Cyclopedia*, with J.A.W. Haas, 1899), and his original works on Luther, the 16th-century Lutheran movement in England, the history of the Lutheran Church in the United States (in the American Church History Series), his textbook *Summary of the Christian Faith* (1905), and other writings.

Responsive to the General Synod's invitation, the General Council and the United Synod in the South joined in trilateral dialogs after 1877. Called Lutheran Free Diets, these were succeeded in the 1890s by General Conferences. Other activities by lay folk—women's and men's organizations as well as the Luther League of America for Young People (1895)—were educational and acquainted members with a church far larger than they imagined. Similarly, the 400th anniversary of Luther's birth (1883) made American Protestants as well as Lutherans ponder the Reformer's career and his far-reaching influence.

As ways opened for reuniting the separated parts of the Muhlenberg tradition, the partners came increasingly to share the General Council's commitment to retain doctrinal and liturgical elements of the past, provided they did not contradict but furthered a response to the gospel. We have already seen how the United Synod in the South took up interest in the historic liturgy. This had its parallel in the General Synod and received its strongest impulse from the General Council. *The Common Service for Lutheran Congregations* (1888) resulted, and was adopted, eventually also by other Lutheran bodies. Drawn from the authentic Lutheran church orders (liturgies) of the Reformation era, Wilhelm Loehe (Neuendettelsau) and others in *Germany led the way. The Service, along with Matins and Vespers, revealed a kinship with the Roman Mass as well as the early church, while in language it reflected the Anglican *Book of Common Prayer*, which had Lutheran links to the Continent. Discovery by recovery—also with hymns of many times and places, chorales from Germany and beyond, songs of praise from Britain and America—lent depth and buoyancy to worship. The publication of *The Common Service with Hymnal* (1917) coincided with the 400th anniversary of the Reformation.

The formation of the United Lutheran Church in America (ULCA, 1918) followed by a year the creation of the Norwegian Lutheran Church of America in Minnesota. This impressive development on the Scandinavian side gave added reason for the Augustana Synod to close its 50-year partnership in the General Council by going it alone and not joining the ULCA. The Swedish church heritage required further cultivation before being shared on a wider scale, as in the LCA 44 years later.

• • •

With its doctrinal basis planted in the canonical Scriptures, confessed in the ecumenical creeds, and interpreted in the Unaltered Augsburg Confession and other confessional writings contained in the *Book of Concord*, and with its worship expressing an ongoing Trinitarian faith, the ULCA saw itself as a way station to greater unity. The preamble of its constitution invited all Evangelical Lutheran congregations and synods in America who agree with this doctrinal basis to unite with the ULCA on the terms of its constitution.

The ULCA began with well over a million baptized members (nearly 800,000 of them confirmed). Its congregations numbered almost 4000, and its ordained ministry about 2800. It soon surpassed the Missouri Synod in size, and for its duration remained the largest Lutheran body in America. Its 45 synods—some of them bitterly split over the forming of the General Council decades earlier—were reunited or reduced in number. The synods all surrendered some of their accustomed powers, but the representative character of the ULCA polity accentuated the inclusiveness of the new church. Its biennial convention legislated and shaped policy. Its executive board governed and reviewed the work of interest boards guiding the work in specific fields. To keep all this on course much depended on the president of the church.

The ULCA's first president, Frederick Herman Knubel (1870–1945), held office 26 years. A native New Yorker, he was a graduate of Gettysburg Seminary, with further study at Leipzig University. As parish pastor, encourager of young people, and then as executive of the National Lutheran Commission for Soldiers' and Sailors' Welfare during World War I, he was a man of proven leadership. His theological adviser was Charles M. Jacobs (Philadelphia Seminary, the son of Henry Eyster Jacobs).

Together, Knubel and Jacobs prepared the statement of ULCA policy (Washington Declaration, above) on language, relations with other Lutheran bodies, cooperation among Protestants, and, by implication, on pulpit and altar fellowship—as well as a cautioning of pastors against membership in secret societies. Underlying and transcending these practical matters was the declaration's accent on the "Catholic Spirit in the Church," by whose means the doctrines already contained in the Confessions become applicable to present conditions. The ULCA thus recognized no doctrinal reasons against complete cooperation and organic union with other Lutheran bodies. Besides, on this basis the ULCA saw conditions set for its participation in cooperative movements with other Protestants. These conditions were equivalent, doctrinally, to what has since become known ecumenically as bilateral and multilateral dialogs—fostering fuller Christian unity.

A prior testing of this position was the formation of the Slovak Zion Synod (1919) and its joining the ULCA—in contrast to the larger Slovak Synod in the Missouri-led Synodical Conference. For the ULCA this led to several parallel developments: a working relationship, as already mentioned, with the Suomi Synod (1921), as well as a mutual recognition between the ULCA and the newly autonomous Lutheran churches in Hungary and Slovakia. The long cordial relations with the Icelandic Synod (1885) brought that body into the ULCA in 1940.

As noted earlier, the ULCA's role in the concurrently formed National Lutheran Council was crucial from the outset, and its part in forming the Lutheran World Convention (1923) was decisive. The Southern churchman and educator, John Alfred Morehead (1867–1935), was the convention's leading proponent and later president. Ecumenically, the ULCA—already through one of its predecessor bodies, the General Synod in 1910—became involved in the Faith and Order movement. It sent delegates to Lausanne (1927) and Edinburgh (1937), as well as to Life and Work at Oxford (1937). Through its representatives on the Continuation Committee (1938–), ULCA initiative led to the adoption of proportionate confessional representation—as well as a basic national representation—in the assembly and central committee of the World Council of Churches.

The ULCA's second and last president, Franklin Clark Fry (1900–1968), became a world figure ecumenically and, for some time, was America's best-known Protestant leader. Holding office for 18 years, he continued for his last six years as first president of the new Lutheran Church in America, of which he was one of the prime planners. Coming from a parish ministry (Akron, Ohio), his gifts of leadership grew rapidly amid the challenges of the postwar era. Internationally, he helped set the stage for the rise of the LWF and the terms for American Lutheran participation in the World Council of Churches. At home, he led the ULCA—

accompanied by Augustana—into membership in the newly formed (1950) National Council of Churches of Christ in the USA, but only after a prior change in that body's constitution provided for an "evangelical and representative principle" as the standard for participation. In this case, evangelical meant Trinitarian theology, and representative meant governance of the NCCC by persons officially representing their church bodies. Fry's extended role on the world scene personified a rare combination of the ecumenical and the confessional; on the WCC Central Committee 20 years, first as vice-chair (1948–1954), then as chair; on the LWF Executive Committee from 1947 onward; and Federation president for six years (1957–1963). The ULCA itself had meanwhile benefited from the postwar boom in religion, its baptized membership having grown by nearly 40% between 1945 and 1961.

EVANGELICAL LUTHERAN CHURCH IN AMERICA (Eielsen Synod)
Membership: 50**
President: Mr. Truman Larson
Route 1
Jackson, Minnesota 56143

This minuscule church body with the inclusive name and a trail-blazing past has been reduced to two congregations in southwestern Minnesota—Jackson and French Lake (some 200 kilometers or 130 miles apart)—and an active adult membership of 50. The ELCA president, Truman Larson, a layman, preaches nearly every Sunday and is assisted by another lay preacher. Larson's father, Thore, who died in 1982, was the church's last ordained pastor. The son, like his father, has had no formal theological education. But he, too, is steeped in the tradition of Hans Nielsen Hauge, the great revivalist of Norway in the early 19th century and protagonist of a low church Lutheranism of the laity.

Among Norwegian immigrants in Wisconsin, Elling Eielsen (1804–1883)—an ardent Haugean and congregationally oriented critic of the organized church—reluctantly formed a body called the Evangelical Lutheran Church in North America. The original body, commonly known by its founder's name, was governed by a constitution that

Eielsen himself had dictated. While other Haugeans eventually found their way into the larger Norse Lutheran church, and so into the ALC, the Eielsen Synod remained independent. Its adherents disparaged an academically trained ministry and avoided liturgical worship and other aspects of generally accepted Lutheran church life. But they have held fast to Luther's Catechism, specifically in the form elaborated by the 18th-century theologian and bishop in Norway, Erik Pontopiddan. In 1936, the Eielsen Synod published 3000 copies of the famed "Epitomes of Rev. Dr. Erik Pontopiddan's Explanation of Martin Luther's *Small Catechism*."

During its long history, the Eielsen Synod has carried on mission work among the American Indians in northern Wisconsin and also supported the work of the Santal Mission of Northern Churches in *India. As a church body, however, its story is a succession of departures as its members have joined other churches, leaving a dwindling constituency of elderly. The word North has long since disappeared from the synod's official title, and the ultimate compliment—unwittingly made—is that the three-way consolidation of the ALC, LCA, and AELC has chosen to be known as the Evangelical Lutheran Church in America. "No," said the widow of Pastor Thore Larson in 1986, "we've not given away our name. They've taken it." More than ever, history is likely to remember this little body not by its official name but as the Eielsen Synod.

EVANGELICAL LUTHERAN FEDERATION (ELF)
Membership: 501
President: The Rev. Ervin C. Dobberstein
PO Box 477
Kingston, Washington 98346

The Evangelical Lutheran Federation's five congregations—in New York, Ohio, Michigan, Indiana, and Washington—report a total baptized membership of 501 and are served by four pastors. This body was organized in 1977, of then independent Lutheran congregations "who wanted to get on with the Great Commission." The autonomy of the local congregation is deemed a basic doctrine.

ELF, by providing advice and support, seeks to be, "a true servant of the local congregations." Subscription to the Confessions of the Evangelical Lutheran Church as set forth in ELF's constitution binds the congregations together.

EVANGELICAL LUTHERAN SYNOD (ELS)

Membership: 20,000
President: The Rev. George M. Orvick
447 North Division Street
Mankato, Minnesota 56001

This body of 118 congregations and 126 pastors is of Norse origin. Its reported baptized membership grew by 16% between 1975 and 1985. Championing scriptural inerrancy, the ELS is also intensely confessional. It requires full agreement in doctrine and practice as prerequisite to union among Lutherans. Congregational in polity, the annual ELS convention of pastors and lay delegates pursues the way of consensus in maintaining its own unity.

Pastors and teachers, formerly educated in institutions of the LCMS and the Wisconsin Synod, are now trained in Bethany College and Seminary (Mankato, Minnesota), founded by the ELS in 1926. Congregations of this body are concentrated in the upper Midwest of the USA, but others are located in the Northeast, and in Florida, Texas, Arizona, and California. Besides gathering new congregations at home, the ELS supports a small mission in *Peru.

Roots of the ELS lie in the churchly oriented old Norwegian Synod (1853). When that body joined with two others in 1917 to form the Norwegian Lutheran Church of America (see ALC), a dissenting remnant of 13 pastors (out of 351), plus a small number of congregations, remained separate. In 1918, they organized and took the name Norwegian Synod of the American Evangelical Lutheran Church—soon popularly known as the "little Norwegian Synod." The intense debate at that time—especially over justification and how election and conversion relate to this central doctrine—extends into the present. This recalls the prominent role of controversy in the life of the Norwegian Synod over many generations. From the 1850s

onward, the synod sought to uphold a churchly tradition and a soundly evangelical Lutheran theology. In the process, disputes were inevitable, whether with other Norse of low-church Pietist (Haugean) persuasion, or with German synods embroiled in doctrinal debate over issues like the church and the ministry. Links with Missouri Lutherans—especially with Concordia Seminary and the training of an indigenous Norse ministry—began in the 1850s but at times were strained. Orthodox Lutheran in commitment, the Norwegian Synod in 1872 joined in founding the Synodical Conference, but withdrew in 1883. In 1920, the Norwegian Synod returned, but left again in 1963—contributing, along with the Wisconsin Synod's withdrawal, to the demise of the Conference. Meanwhile, in 1957, the ELS adopted its present name, dropping "Norwegian" from its title. With the return of the LCMS to its traditional conservatism, persons of ELS origin, who had joined Missouri, contributed significantly. Jacob A.O. Preus, LCMS president (1969–1981), and Robert D. Preus (his brother), head of Concordia Seminary, Fort Wayne, Indiana, are prominent examples (see LCMS below).

FELLOWSHIP OF LUTHERAN CONGREGATIONS (FLC)

Membership: 600
President: The Rev. Robert J. Lietz
320 Erie Street
Oak Park, Illinois 60302

Organized in 1979, the FLC's six congregations—located mainly in the states of Illinois, Missouri, and Minnesota—report a baptized membership of 600. Five of its eight pastors are serving congregations. This body has roots in the LCMS (below) and is one of several formed by members objecting to what they saw as liberal trends in Missouri. The FLC paper, *The Voice,* is a guardian of rigorous confessionalism.

INTERNATIONAL LUTHERAN FELLOWSHIP (ILF)

Membership: 350
President: The Rev. E. Edward Tornow
387 East Brandon Drive
Bismarck, North Dakota 58501

The ILF is an association of four independent Lutheran congregations: two in North Dakota, one in Minnesota, and one in Chicago.

According to its president, the ILF contends that each congregation be allowed "a personality of its own so long as it is grounded on the biblical and historical foundations of our Lutheran confessions of faith." The ILF is not separatist but open to fellowship "with all Lutherans and other evangelicals as well." The International in its name reminds this small group of the Lord's Great Commission to "go into all the world."

LATVIAN EVANGELICAL LUTHERAN CHURCH IN AMERICA (LELCA)

(Latviešu Evangeliski Luteriská Bazníca Ameriká)
(see Europe, Exile Churches)
Member: LWF (1947), WCC
Membership: 13,323
President: The Rev. Vilis Varsbergs
6551 West Montrose Avenue
Chicago, Illinois 60634

The LELCA is part of the Latvian Evangelical Lutheran Church in Exile (*Europe, above). For practical purpose the Latvian congregations in the USA and Canada in 1975 gave themselves an administrative structure and most of them withdrew from their host church bodies—the ALC, LCA, and LCMS. The total number of Latvian Lutherans in the USA and Canada is reckoned at 15,533. About 86% of these are in the 68 congregations of the LELCA. These are served by 38 ordained pastors, assisted by volunteer and full-time workers. The LELCA's first president, the Rev. Arturs Voitkus, retired in 1984, but continued to work as editor of the church's monthly, *Cela Biedrs* (The Companion).

To reaffirm partnership with their former host churches, the 61 LELCA congregations in the United States in 1982 collectively joined the Lutheran Council in the USA. Pastors of the LELCA continue to be educated in North American Lutheran seminaries, the present president being a graduate of the Lutheran School of Theology at Chicago. Meanwhile, ties with fellow Latvian Lutherans in other parts of the world continue to be cultivated, also through their yearbook, *Baznícas Gada Grámata*. The head of the Latvian Church in Exile, Archbishop Arnolds Lusis, resides in Toronto, Canada (above).

LITHUANIAN EVANGELICAL LUTHERAN CHURCH
(see Europe, Exile Churches)

There are currently three Lithuanian Lutheran congregations in North America, each with a number of preaching stations. One is located in Toronto, Canada, the other two in Chicago. Their baptized membership is relatively small, and their need of pastors presents problems. Unlike the larger Estonian and Latvian constituencies, these three Lithuanian congregations have no common association other than with the Lithuanian Evangelical Lutheran Church in Exile (above). Of the two congregations in Chicago, one has for many years been a member of the Lutheran Church–Missouri Synod, while the other is independent. The one in Toronto is a member of the Evangelical Lutheran Church in Canada, and is at present being served by a pastor of the Presbyterian Church in Canada, himself of Lithuanian Reformed background.

LUTHERAN CHURCH–MISSOURI SYNOD (LCMS)

Member: ILC
Membership: 2,707,134
President: The Rev. Dr. Ralph A. Bohlmann
1333 Kirkwood Road
St. Louis, Missouri 63122

The Lutheran Church–Missouri Synod is North America's second largest Lutheran church body and the oldest (1847) in continuous organization. Its 35 districts are spread across the country with the heaviest concentration in the Midwest, Texas, and California. An English District, named for the late 19th-century transition from German, and the Slovak Evangelical Lutheran Church, which joined the LCMS during the past decade, are nongeographic in composition. In organization, the LCMS is basically congregational. The triennial church convention is the legislative authority and elects the officers. All voting delegates are congregationally based, with their members equally divided between lay and clergy. Recent presidents of the LCMS have been: John W. Behnken (1935–

1962), Oliver R. Harms (1963–1969), Jacob A.O. Preus (1969–1981), and Ralph A. Bohlmann (1981–).

The LCMS is well known for its emphasis on biblical doctrine and faithful adherence to the historic Lutheran Confession. This stance is maintained by a strong educational system, the largest of any Protestant church in the USA. Some 1600 of its congregations maintain elementary schools, while groups of congregations support 70 secondary (high) schools. Spread throughout the country are 12 junior and senior colleges. All the congregations and the schools are served by more than 6000 ordained parish pastors, 5952 parochial school teachers, and numerous other full-time workers such as deaconesses and directors of Christian education. Heading the LCMS enterprise in educating its pastors are its two theological seminaries: Concordia in St. Louis and Concordia in Fort Wayne.

In their worship and congregational life, generations of Missourians have been kept aware of their confessional legacy and Christian responsibility. More than most Lutherans, they cultivate their identity. In their understanding of fidelity to scriptural precept, they have required of others full agreement in doctrine and practice as prerequisite to pulpit and altar fellowship. At the same time, the LCMS has a long history of working together with other Lutherans in areas not directly related to Word and sacrament ministry—such as Lutheran World Relief, immigration and refugee work—and it has led in areas of media and missions. The LCMS helped form and maintained membership in the Lutheran Council in the USA until its closing (1987). It continues cooperation in "external matters" with the new Evangelical Lutheran Church in America on a limited basis. A Committee on Lutheran Cooperation—six members from each body—maintains liaison.

In the print media, Concordia Publishing House has become the fourth largest Protestant publisher in America. What began over 125 years ago as an entirely German-language enterprise has long since become English and multilingual. Its Arch Series for children has sold about 35 million copies. For the 55-volume joint edition of *Luther's Works* in English, Concordia published the first 30 on the Reformer's biblical writings,

while the LCA's Fortress Press brought out the other 25 (above).

More than any other Lutheran body, LCMS has a long history of using the electronic media effectively. The "Lutheran Hour," begun in 1929, is heard in more than 100 countries each week and in many languages. Its dramatic series, "This is the Life," completed its 30th year in 1983, the longest such series in television history; and this, too, is being aired in a growing number of countries. Meanwhile, Hispanic language broadcasts are reaching out to the fastest growing American constituency.

Most American blacks who are Lutheran are members of the LCMS. Ministry among them has been a part of the LCMS's work for over 100 years. The LCMS has a leadership role in encouraging other churches to assume community responsibility. For example, in 1982, the LCMS worked with other denominations on Project Nehemiah, which is turning a burned-out area in Brooklyn, New York, into 5000 single-family homes. Other disadvantaged groups also have the LCMS's concern. A library for the blind produces sermons and devotional literature. Of the 90 congregations for the deaf maintained by all religious bodies, nearly 50 are members of the LCMS.

In 1980, the LCMS became the first denomination in the USA to urge its members to will body organs for transplants. The LCMS also has a strong pro-life position. It supports efforts calling for constitutional protection for all human life including the unborn.

Missouri's worldwide outreach, combined today under one Board for Mission Services, extends to 32 countries and involves churches and gospel-oriented activities in all continents. Starting points were home missions in the 19th century among European immigrants as well as American Indians and Southern blacks. German settlers in *Australia, *Brazil, and *Argentina appealing for pastors—the supply from Germany proved insufficient—opened new intercontinental ties in the 1890s. Mission work overseas among the non-Christian people developed—via German and other connections—in *India (1894) and then in *China (1912). Work in Africa—linked to that among blacks in America—began in *Nigeria (1935) and spread to other continents. The 1940s, in the wake of World

War II, saw Missourians coming to *Guatemala, *Mexico, the *Philippines, *Japan, *Korea, *Hong Kong, *Taiwan, *Papua New Guinea, *Lebanon, *Venezuela, and *Paraguay. Earlier they had come to England (*UK) and to the aid of small Free churches on the European continent.

Various influences caused the Missouri Synod to become more involved outside its own circles, e.g., postwar conferences in Germany (at Bad Boll after 1948); the progress toward Lutheran union in North America; and the rise of Missouri's new scholars through graduate study in foremost European and American universities. An enlarged understanding of the church as the church universal—seen especially in light of the LCMS commitment in world mission—was affirmed by the Cleveland convention (1962) and hailed as a turning point. In 1966, Missouri joined the other major Lutheran bodies—ALC and LCA—in forming the Lutheran Council in the USA. Pulpit and altar fellowship with the ALC was adopted in 1969.

For many people long-accustomed to their own confessional continuum, troublesome questions arose. The rank-and-file in Missouri Synod congregations inevitably asked: What has changed? By what authority had the new generation of synod leaders and seminary professors charted another course? A countermovement gathered strength. A new administration came to power in 1969. Dr. Jacob A.O. Preus replaced the irenic and farsighted Dr. Oliver Harms (d. 1980). A decade of soul-searching and controversy resulted. The aim was to reaffirm Missouri's traditional position. The world-spanning mission board became an early target. Then came the assault on the alleged liberalism of Concordia Seminary, St. Louis—the synod's revered heartland. The dramatic egress of most faculty and students, early in 1974, led to the creation of a seminary in exile, Seminex—later, Christ Seminary. Eventually, about 100,000 members and over 200 congregations withdrew (see ELCA, above). The LCMS-ALC pulpit and altar fellowship ended in 1981. Thus the synod, so it was said, "reclaimed its historic confessional stance on the doctrine of the authority of Scripture" and reaffirmed its ban on the ordination of women to the pastoral office.

When Dr. Ralph Bohlmann, a former Fulbright scholar with a doctorate from Yale became president (1981), there was little evidence of controversy. By the 1982–1983 academic year, Concordia Seminary had regained its pre-walk-out enrollment level: 753 students. In 1982, the LCMS published a new hymnal, *Lutheran Worship*. A special ingathering of US $75 million, together with a strong Church Extension Fund, assisted the LCMS in establishing 102 new ministries in one year (1982). In May 1983, new headquarters were dedicated in the St. Louis suburb of Kirkwood, Missouri. Meanwhile, the far right has again become openly critical but not regained synodical control.

Missouri's relations to other Lutherans—not to overlook other Christians—remain a concern to outsiders. While the ALC, LCA, and AELC were merger-bound (1988), the LCMS remained alone in North America. Nevertheless, the continued participation of the LCMS in Lutheran World Relief, Lutheran Educational Conference of North America, and other task-oriented groups keeps the theme of Lutheran unity alive (above).

Worldwide, however, the LCMS is not alone. Under its leadership, the International Lutheran Conference was organized at Uelzen, Federal Republic of Germany, in 1952. It aims to provide a sustained confessional fellowship and to exercise a mutual supportiveness. Triennial conferences bring together representatives of some 25 churches for discussion on common theological interests and mission concerns. The LCMS is the leading and far largest member. Antecedents of the ILC relate it, among others, to the free theological conferences held after 1948 in Bad Boll (Württemberg). Participants at that time saw these meetings with German and other theologians and church leaders as contributing significantly to a broadening of Missouri's perspective. In 1975, the word "theological," initially in the ILC title, was dropped. The ninth meeting of the ILC, in Papua New Guinea (1978), reaffirmed its continuing purpose to be "a forum to which member churches may bring their theological and practical needs and challenges to mutual consideration." In 1987, the 12th meeting was in the Federal Republic of Germany.

Whether alone or in association, yet ever "firmly committed to continuing the Synod's traditional emphasis on the centrality of the Gospel of Jesus Christ as taught in the divinely authoritative Scriptures and confessed in the historic Lutheran Confessions," the LCMS looks forward with renewed zeal and enthusiasm to carrying out the Great Commission in the years ahead. Indeed, it has entered 18 new countries and has begun more than 400 new congregations in North America in the last five years.

• • •

The LCMS's history goes back to 1839 when over 600 Saxon immigrants—under the Dresden pastor, Martin Stephan—came to the state of Missouri seeking freedom from religious Rationalism in Germany. They settled in St. Louis and Perry County. With Carl Ferdinand Wilhelm Walther (1811–1887) as their astute champion of confessional Lutheranism, a congregational polity as their basis of expansion, and a seminary (at first a log cabin, some 170 kilometers [110 miles] downriver from St. Louis) as their training center for pastors and teachers, the Saxons found fellowship with like-minded Lutherans. Most of the latter were young Franconian (Bavarian) pastors sent to North America after 1844 by Wilhelm Loehe of Neuendettelsau (see Germany). Together they founded the (German) Evangelical Lutheran Synod of Missouri, Ohio, and Other States in 1847. In 1850, Concordia Seminary was moved to St. Louis. Subsequently, Missourians broke with Loehe and with other Loehe pastors. The latter in 1854 organized the German Evangelical Lutheran Synod of Iowa and Other States (see ALC). A prolonged colloquy with the so-called Buffalo Synod of Johannes Grabau-led Lutheran emigrees from Prussia (see ALC) brought many conservative Lutherans into Missouri ranks after 1856, largely from around Buffalo, New York, and Milwaukee, Wisconsin.

With other confessional Lutherans in the Midwest, including the Wisconsin Synod (below) and the Norwegian Synod (now Evangelical Lutheran Synod, above), the Missourians in 1872 were instrumental in forming the Evangelical Lutheran Synodical Conference.

The Synodical Conference, a Missourian reply to the recently formed General Council (see ELCA/ULCA, above), was an advisory association fostering a strict confessional position. Its mission among freed American blacks, begun in 1877, was its only major activity. This was strengthened when former black congregations of Lutherans in the North Carolina Synod (above, ELCA/LCA history) joined the Synodical Conference. Growth was slow, but in 1903 the Conference opened Immanuel College and Seminary, in Greensboro, North Carolina. During the presidency of a German-born pastor, Henry Nau—he had served as a missionary in India—Immanuel became the launching point for extending the Synodical Conference mission to *Nigeria. The Synodical Conference itself, troubled by tensions, continued until 1964, when the Wisconsin Synod (below) withdrew and Missouri stood alone.

LUTHERAN CHURCHES OF THE REFORMATION (LCR)

Membership: 500**
General Secretary: Herbert C. Gade
3125 26th Avenue N.
Minneapolis, Minnesota 55422

This small group comprises eight core congregations and another seven that are counted in fellowship. The LCR's eight ordained ministers and their congregations are of Missouri Synod origin. They left the LCMS in protest to that body's alleged "unionism" and failure to practice its avowed teachings as set forth in the Brief Statement adopted in 1932. Various dissenting groups united in 1964 and formed the LCR. The congregations are scattered across the upper Midwest. Future pastors are tutored by the Rev. Sheldon Twenge, at the Martin Luther Institute of Sacred Studies in North Sioux City, South Dakota.

THE PROTES'TANT CONFERENCE (LUTHERAN)

Membership: 979
Chair: Albert Meier
728 North Ninth Street
Manitowoc, Wisconsin 54220

This group of 10 congregations and 10 ordained ministers in and near the state of Wisconsin is purposely not organized as a synod or church body in the strict sense. Instead, it exists as a permanently protesting (witnessing) free theological conference. Although its reported baptized membership has declined by 20% over the 10 years after 1975, the Protes'tant Conference remains an embodiment of the so-called Wauwatosa Theology. Historical-exegetical in nature, this theology was largely the result of efforts to rescue Lutheranism from its confinement to the 17th-century orthodoxism prevailing among Wisconsin, Missouri, and other synodical bodies during the 19th and early 20th centuries.

Chief proponent of this theological renewal was John Philipp Koehler (1859–1951), professor of New Testament exegesis and church history at the Wisconsin Synod's theological seminary in Wauwatosa (adjoining Milwaukee). His three decades of teaching there were abruptly terminated in 1930. For six years prior to that time unrest had been developing over the possible effect of his theology on the traditions of the synod. By 1927, between 30 and 40 pastors and a number of congregations had been suspended from the Wisconsin Synod. Under the leadership of Karl Koehler, Paul Hensel, and W.F. Beitz, they charged the synod with spiritual tyranny and sterile orthodoxy. The Protes'tants' journal, *Faith-Life,* summing up the aims of the ousted in its title, begun in 1928, still appears on a bimonthly basis. J.P. Koehler was for years an important contributor and published in it a penetrating history of the Wisconsin Synod's remarkably varied course (see below).

As a renewal movement, the Wauwatosa Theology failed. Yet its emphases on scriptural hermeneutics and church history, as aids to understanding and renewal, remain relevant. The former moderator of the Protes'tant Conference, Marcus Albrecht, represented its second generation of participants. Future pastors of the conference receive their theological education in various seminaries other than the Wisconsin Synod's.

WISCONSIN EVANGELICAL LUTHERAN SYNOD (WELS)

Membership: 419,806
President: The Rev. Carl H. Mischke
2929 North Mayfair Road
Milwaukee, Wisconsin 53222

Between the three large Lutheran bodies in the USA and the several minor bodies stands this unusual and highly conservative synod. Its 1200 congregations are served by 1130 ordained pastors and a large number of teachers, professors, and other church workers. Wisconsin Synod congregations are found in all 50 states. The synod has a congregational polity and is divided into twelve geographic districts. The synod and districts have advisory powers only.

Consensus in Lutheran doctrine rather than reliance on structure holds this body together. A network of 375 elementary schools, 19 area high schools, three synodical preparatory schools, three colleges, and a theological seminary (Mequon, Wisconsin) cultivate the confessional consensus at all levels. Basic is its method of teaching the Bible in terms of wholeness—God's dealings with sinful human beings—and church history as an extension of the account of how the gospel has fared among people. The synod's confessional position is held with a rigidity that virtually excludes fellowship with church bodies other than those with which it is in full agreement in doctrine and practice. Even the Missouri synod was charged with "unionism," and fellowship broke off in 1961. This terminated the Synodical Conference (see LCMS).

The synod's overseas mission ventures include *Mexico, *Puerto Rico, *Colombia, *Zambia, *Malawi, Japan, Taiwan, Indonesia, and *Hong Kong. Brazil was added in 1986. The synod's oldest mission is among the Apache Indians in Arizona. It also supports work in Nigeria, Cameroon, and India and has close ties with the Lutheran Confessional Church in Scandinavia (Sweden, Norway, and Finland).

The present Wisconsin Synod is the union of three synods. The original Wisconsin Synod was broadly Lutheran. Formed in 1850, it was the product of several German and Swiss mission societies—Barmen (Langenberg), Berlin, Basel, St. Chrischona—whose emissaries were serving German immigrants in the then American Northwest. These broadly confessional beginnings by John Mühlhäuser (1803–1867) and others did not prevail. Subsequently, leadership turned the synod toward Missouri Lutheranism.

A second synod, that of Minnesota, was formed in 1860, largely through the efforts of Christian Fredrick Heyer (1793–1873) of

Pennsylvania and the first Lutheran missionary from America to India (1842) and of Eric Norelius (1833–1916), the Swedish Augustana pioneer in Minnesota (see ELCA, LCA, above). Subsequent developments also brought this synod into the Synodical Conference.

A third and smaller synod in Michigan, also organized in 1860, at first joined the General Council in 1868 (see LCA), but by 1888 had withdrawn and turned to the Wisconsin Synod. A federation of the Wisconsin, Minnesota, and Michigan Synods occurred in 1892. They merged in 1917. The present name was adopted in 1959. Over the years, this synod has had influential teachers and theologians. Some of them, like Franz Pieper (1852–1931), have gained international reputation. He became the leading dogmatician of the Missouri Synod in the early 20th century.

Wisconsin's rigid confessionalism has held it aloof from the ecumenical movement and all recent efforts at Lutheran union.

WORLD CONFESSIONAL LUTHERAN ASSOCIATION (WCLA)
Membership: 343
President: The Rev. Dr. Reuben H. Redal
PO Box 7186
35th and N. Pearl St.
Tacoma, Washington 98407

Formed in 1980 as the Conservative Lutheran Association (CLA), the name was changed in 1984 so as to avoid the impression that Conservative meant political rather than confessional commitment. Of the WCLA's 24 ordained pastors, 17 serve congregations. Its president, a graduate of Luther (Northwestern) Theological Seminary, St. Paul, Minnesota, states that the WCLA represents the "true American Lutheran Church (ALC) since it adheres to that church body's *Statement of Faith* of 1960."

In that year the founders of the present WCLA opposed what they saw as dangerous trends in the then new ALC (above, ELCA) in such matters as the interpretation of Scripture, liberal ecumenical participation, and the like. *Lutherans Alert-National* began at that time to sound the warning, and has continued to do so.

Gathering strength led to the founding of Faith Evangelical Lutheran Seminary (1969) in Tacoma. Headed by the WCLA president, the seminary trains pastoral candidates not only for its own supporting congregations but also for others.

The WCLA's areas of concern include: social service, education, apologetics, congregations, mission outreach (Lutheran World Concerns), media (Words of Faith programs), and support services.

At its 21st annual convention (June 1987), the WCLA offered its own fellowship as an alternative to congregations and individuals not desiring to join the new ELCA or the equally new American Association of Lutheran Churches (above).

Overseas the WCLA has links with Nigeria (a congregation near Lagos), as well as in South Korea, the People's Republic of China, and Hong Kong. Its School of Missions opened in September 1987 with some 20 students.

THE CONSTITUTION OF THE LUTHERAN WORLD FEDERATION

First adopted in 1947 by the Lund assembly, the Federation's constitution has remained basically unchanged over the past four decades. The following is the full text of the constitution as amended by the Seventh Assembly (Budapest 1984). (Significant modifications are expected from the Eighth Assembly, Curitiba, Brazil, 1990.)

I. NAME

The name and title of the body organized under this Constitution shall be The Lutheran World Federation.

II. DOCTRINAL BASIS

The Lutheran World Federation acknowledges the Holy Scriptures of the Old and New Testaments as the only source and the infallible norm of all church doctrine and practice, and sees in the three Ecumenical Creeds and in the Confessions of the Lutheran church, especially in the Unaltered Augsburg Confession and Luther's Small Catechism, a pure exposition of the Word of God.

III. NATURE, FUNCTIONS, AND SCOPE

1. Nature
The Lutheran World Federation shall be a free association of Lutheran churches. It shall act as their agent in such matters as they assign to it. It shall not exercise churchly functions on its own authority nor shall it have power to legislate for the churches belonging to it or to limit the autonomy of any member church.

The member churches of the Lutheran World Federation understand themselves to be in pulpit and altar fellowship with each other.

2. Functions
In accord with the preceding paragraphs, the Lutheran World Federation shall:
  a) Further a united witness before the world to the gospel of Jesus Christ as the power of God for salvation.
  b) Cultivate unity of faith and confession among the Lutheran churches of the world.
  c) Develop community and cooperation in study among Lutherans.
  d) Foster Lutheran interest in, concern for, and participation in the ecumenical movement.

e) Support Lutheran churches and groups as they endeavor to extend the gospel and carry out the mission given to the church.

f) Help Lutheran churches and groups, as a sharing community, to serve human need and to promote social and economic justice and human rights.

3. Scope of authority

In accordance with its nature, function, and structure, the Lutheran World Federation may take action on behalf of one or more member churches in such matters as they may commit to it.

IV. MEMBERSHIP AND OTHER FORMS OF AFFILIATION

1. Member churches

The Lutheran World Federation consists of churches which accept the doctrinal basis set forth in Article II of this Constitution. Each church which applies for membership in the Federation shall declare its acceptance of this Constitution. Its reception into membership shall be decided by the Lutheran World Federation in Assembly, or in the interim, if not more than one-third of the member churches raise an objection within one year, by the Executive Committee.

Membership in the Federation may be terminated by vote of the Assembly or by withdrawal.

2. Recognized churches, councils, and congregations

The Lutheran World Federation may recognize as eligible to participate in the work of the Federation non-member churches, councils, or congregations which accept the doctrinal basis set forth in Article II of this Constitution. The granting, conditions, and continuation of such recognition shall be governed by the bylaws.

V. ORGANIZATION

The Lutheran World Federation shall exercise its functions through the following: 1. the Assembly; 2. the Executive Committee; 3. commissions; 4. relevant instrumentalities of member churches, such as national committees. In all the functions of the Federation, both clerical and laypersons shall be eligible to participate.

VI. THE ASSEMBLY

1. An Assembly of the Federation shall normally be held every six years at the call of the President. The time and place and program of each Assembly shall be determined by the Executive Committee. Special meetings of the Assembly may be called by the Executive Committee.

2. The Assembly shall consist of representatives of the member churches of the Federation. The representatives in the Assembly shall be chosen by the member churches themselves. The number of the representatives shall be determined by the Executive Committee.

The allocation of the representatives in the Assembly shall be made to the member churches by the Executive Committee with the advice of the national committees, and due regard shall be given to such factors as numerical size of churches, geo-graphical distribution by continents and countries, representation of all churches, and the right of each completely independent member church to have at least one representative in the Assembly. Suggestions for readjustments in the apportionment of representatives in the Assembly may be made to the Executive Committee by member churches or groups of member churches, national or regional, and these readjustments shall become effective if approved by the Executive Committee and by the member churches concerned.

Whenever Lutheran congregations in union church bodies combine to ask for representation in the Assembly, the Executive Committee may invite them to send representatives to the Assembly in a consultative capacity. Lutheran associations and organizations designated by the Executive Committee may be invited to send representatives to the Assembly in a consultative capacity in such numbers as the Executive Committee may determine.

3. The Assembly shall be the principal authority in the Federation. It shall elect the President of the Federation and the other members of the Executive Committee, shall receive reports from national committees, may establish commissions, and shall determine the fundamental lines of the Federation's work.

VII. EXECUTIVE COMMITTEE

1. Each Assembly shall elect 29 persons who with the President shall constitute the Executive Committee of the Federation. A person eligible for election to the Executive Committee shall belong to a member church of the Lutheran World Federation. A person shall not be nominated without prior consultation with the respective member church. At least seven persons so elected shall be lay persons. Membership in the Executive Committee shall be allocated with due regard to such factors as numerical size of churches and geographical distribution by continents and countries. An effort shall be made to effect such changes at each Assembly as will facilitate an appropriate rotation of representatives on the Executive Committee.

2. The Executive Committee shall meet at least once annually. It shall choose from its own membership five Vice-Presidents as Officers of the Federation. It shall also elect a Treasurer of the Federation. The duties of these Officers shall be those usually assigned to those offices.

3. The Executive Committee shall conduct the business of the Lutheran World Federation in the interim between Assemblies, shall encourage the formation and work of national committees and receive annual reports from them, and shall elect a General Secretary and prescribe the duties of that office. The Executive Committee may terminate the services of the General Secretary by a two-thirds vote. It shall make a full annual report (including complete financial statements) to all member churches, may establish commissions and/or committees not otherwise provided for, shall appoint the membership for the commissions and such committees, and shall represent the Federation in all external relations.

4. Vacancies in the Executive Committee ad interim shall be filled by the Committee.

5. The chairpersons of commissions shall attend the regular meetings of the Executive Committee as consultants.

VIII. COMMISSIONS

Commissions shall be established under the authority of the Federation either by the Assembly or by the Executive Committee. It shall be the purpose of these commissions to discharge designated functions of the Federation. They shall report annually to the Executive Committee, which shall exercise general supervision over them.

IX. NATIONAL COMMITTEES

The member church(es) in each country shall be encouraged to elect a group of persons or provide for some other instrumentality which, together with the member or members of the Executive Committee in that country, may constitute an LWF national committee and as such be given delegated responsibility for the relationship between the member church(es) and the Lutheran World Federation, except that each member church shall always retain the right of direct communication with the Lutheran World Federation.

Each national committee shall be asked to present to the Executive Committee an annual report.

X. OFFICERS

The President of the Federation shall be chosen by ballot of the Assembly, and a majority of the votes cast shall be necessary for an election. The President shall assume office immediately after the close of the Assembly at which the election was held and before the organization of the new Executive Committee. The President shall be the chief official representative of the Federation. The President shall hold office until the close of the following Assembly and shall not be eligible for a second term. Other Officers shall be the Vice-Presidents and the Treasurer, who shall be elected by the Executive Committee.

XI. GENERAL SECRETARY

Immediately following the close of each Assembly the Executive Committee shall elect a General Secretary who shall devote full time to this office and who shall serve until the close of the next Assembly. The General Secretary shall be responsible to the Executive Committee. It shall be the General Secretary's duty to carry out the decisions of the Assembly and of the Executive Committee in consultation with the President and to report through the Executive Committee to the Assembly of the Federation.

XII. FINANCE

The Executive Committee shall receive submissions from commissions and committees as compiled in a Composite Statement of Needs by the General Secretariat and shall authorize annually the transmission of the Composite Statement of Needs to member churches, national committees, and other agencies commending it for support through designated and undesignated contributions.

The Executive Committee shall allocate membership contributions to be paid by member churches and shall apply these funds to specific areas of the Federation's work.

The Treasurer shall authorize depositories in various countries.

XIII. AMENDMENTS AND BYLAWS

1. Amendments
Amendments to this Constitution may be made by a two-thirds vote of those present at any regularly called Assembly, provided notice of intention to amend shall have been given the preceding day. Amendments so made shall become effective one year after their adoption by the Assembly unless objection has been filed with the Executive Committee by one-third of the member churches of the Federation.

2. Bylaws
The Executive Committee may adopt bylaws not inconsistent with this Constitution for the conduct of the business of the Lutheran World Federation. Such bylaws adopted or amended by the Executive Committee shall become effective one year after their adoption unless objection has been filed with the Executive Committee by one-third of the member churches of the Federation. The Assembly may adopt, amend, or suspend bylaws by a simple majority.

Basically, the present Constitution of the Lutheran World Federation is that which was adopted by the Constituting Assembly at Lund, Sweden, on July 1, 1947. Amendments were made in that first and subsequent Assemblies.

The incorporation of the LWF as a legal entity according to Article 60 of the Swiss Civil Code enables it to own or take over as trustee such property as member churches or their agencies (such as missionary societies) may want to entrust to it. In case of an international conflict, such property would be placed under the protection of the neutral Swiss consular authorities.

LWF PRESIDENTS AND GENERAL SECRETARIES

PRESIDENTS

Anders Nygren Born November 15, 1890 in Sweden. First LWF president, 1947–1952. Theologian, University of Lund, 1924–1949. Bishop of Lund, 1949–1958. Helped unify Lutherans after World War II, and showed how a confessional heritage can be shared ecumenically. Author: *Agape and Eros* (1937–1939), and other works. Died October 20, 1978. Details: *Lutheran World* 4/75.

Hanns Lilje Born August 20, 1899 in Germany. Second LWF president, 1952–1957. General secretary, Lutheran World Convention, 1935–1946. Bishop, Evangelical Lutheran Church of Hanover, 1941–1971. Active in student work, Evangelical Academies, and publications. Outstanding preacher, lecturer, writer. Ecumenically active; a WCC president 1968–1975. Author: *The Valley of the Shadow* (1950, 1977), and other works. Died January 6, 1977. Details: *Lutheran World* 4/74.

Franklin Clark Fry Born August 30, 1900 in USA. Third in succession of LWF presidents, 1957–1963. Initially a parish pastor in New York and Ohio, he was president of United Lutheran Church in America (1944–1962) and of LCA (1962–1968). Strengthened Lutheran role ecumenically (vice-chair, 1948–1954; chair, WCC Central Committee, 1954–1968) and helped unify Lutherans confessionally. Died June 6, 1968. Details: *Lutheran World* 3/75.

Fredrik Axel Schiotz Born June 15, 1901 in USA. Fourth LWF president, 1963–1970. Parish pastor, leader in student work, pioneer in LWF cooperation in worldwide mission (1948–1954). President: Evangelical Lutheran Church, 1954–1960; ALC, 1961–1971. Died February 25, 1989. Details: *Lutheran World* 4/76.

Mikko Juva Born November 22, 1918 in Finland. Fifth LWF president, 1970–1977. Chancellor, University of Helsinki. Archbishop of Turku. Theologian, historian, author, also active politically. Leader in Finnish Church Assembly and Mission Society. Details: *Lutheran World* 1/77.

Josiah Mutabuuzi Kibira Born August 28, 1925 in then Tanganyika. The Dar es Salaam assembly elected him sixth LWF president, 1977–1984. Bishop (1964–1985), ELCT northwestern diocese, based in Bukoba, Lake Victoria, near Ugandan border. Retired 1985. Parents were first-generation Christians (Anglican). He became Lutheran and moved from teaching career to ordained ministry. Preparation included theological study in Germany (Bethel/Bielefeld), USA (Boston University), and Sweden (Uppsala). Became successor to Bengt Sundkler, the Swedish missiologist and first bishop in Bukoba. Kibira active in East Africa revival movement and in promoting Swahili as national language. Served internationally on WCC Faith and Order Commission and later on the WCC Central Committee and on LWF Commission on Church Cooperation (chair). Died July 18, 1988. Details: *LW Information* 21/88.

Zoltán Káldy   Born March 29, 1919 in Hungary. Budapest assembly (1984) elected him seventh president—the first East European in that post. Presiding bishop of the Lutheran Church in Hungary since 1967 and bishop of the southern district since 1958, he began as assistant pastor in Pécs and had risen to superintendent of Tolna Baranya district by 1954. His early focus on evangelization grew into a theology of diakonia (Hungary, above), which shaped his concept of church–state relations. With other leading bishops, he sat in the Hungarian parliament. As LWF president he hoped to foster better East–West relations. Incapacitated by a stroke in late 1985, Bishop Káldy died on May 17, 1987—the first LWF president not to complete his term. Details: *LW Information* 19, 20, 21/87.

Johannes Hanselmann   Born March 9, 1927 in Ehingen (on the Danube southwest of Ulm), Germany. Eighth LWF president, he was elected by the Executive Committee at Viborg, Denmark, in July 1987. He filled the unexpired term (until 1990) of the late Bishop Káldy. As bishop of the 2.6 million-member Evangelical Lutheran Church in Bavaria since 1975, he followed prominent leaders in the LWF—Hermann Dietzfelbinger and, before that, Hans Meiser. Hanselmann's theological education at the University of Erlangen was supplemented by further study in America, at the former Hamma School of Theology (now part of Trinity Theological Seminary, Capital University, Columbus, Ohio) 1949–1950, and at the then Hartford Theological Seminary Foundation (Connecticut). His doctoral dissertation was on the German philosopher, Martin Heidegger. Parish ministry in Coburg, diaconic service in Berlin, including journalistic duties, preceded his election (1974) as church executive for the Bayreuth district of the Bavarian church.

GENERAL SECRETARIES

(For more information on the first four, see *Lutheran World* 2/74)

Sylvester C. Michelfelder   Born October 27, 1889 in USA. First LWF executive (general) secretary, 1947–1951; represented NLC member churches in Geneva, Switzerland, beginning July 1945. Coordinated Lutheran relief, reconstruction, and refugee services with those of WCC, whose Material Aid Division he also headed. Michelfelder set the style and pace of this office. Prepared first LWF assembly (Lund 1947). Died September 30, 1951 while preparing the Second Assembly. Earlier career in parish ministry (Pennsylvania and Ohio) and church welfare work (Pittsburgh).

Carl E. Lund-Quist   Born September 19, 1908 in USA. Second LWF executive (general) secretary, 1951–1960. Responsible for preparation of two assemblies: Hanover 1952, Minneapolis 1957. Traveled widely, administered wisely, fostered ongoing unity. Earlier career in parish ministry, service to university students, public relations of NLC (1946–1951). Resigned LWF post for health reasons. Died August 26, 1965.

Kurt Schmidt-Clausen   Born October 1, 1920 in Germany. Served as Federation's third general secretary, 1961–1965, after beginning in Geneva in 1959. Responsible for preparation of Fourth Assembly, Helsinki 1963. Events during his term included opening Radio Voice of the Gospel (Addis Ababa, Ethiopia) and the Institute for Ecumenical Research (Strasbourg, France). Schmidt-Clausen was (district) Landessuperintendent of Osnabrück, Evangelical Lutheran Church of Hanover (1970–1982) and a member of the LWF Executive Committee from 1970–1977. By training and avocation a church historian, in 1976 he published *Die Lutherische Kirche in Geschichte und Gestalt, 1923–1947.*

André Appel   Born December 20, 1921 in Alsace, France. As the Federation's fourth general secretary, 1965—1974, he was the first to come from a minority church. Led the preparations for the Fifth Assembly—planned for Pôrto Alegre, Brazil, but switched (by action of the officers) to Evian-les-Bains, 1970. The LWF was restructured after 1970, its staff and program expanded. Appel's career began in ministry to students, and continued in the Protestant Federation of France (1957–1964). Appel, now retired, was president of the Church of the Augsburg Confession of Alsace and Lorraine (1975–1988). He also headed the Conference of European Churches for over a decade.

Carl Henning Mau Jr.   Born June 22, 1922 in Seattle, Washington, USA. The fifth LWF general secretary, Mau held this position 1974–1985. His overseas career began in Germany, 1950–1957, as stewardship and evangelism counselor in the Evangelical Lutheran Church of Hanover—in close association with Bishop Lilje. Parish ministry in the USA and work among university students (Madison, Wisconsin), plus a brief period as general secretary of the USA National Committee of the LWF in New York rounded out his American activities. From 1964 to 1972 he was LWF associate general secretary. After 1985, he was an associate pastor, Church of the Reformation, in Washington, D.C.

Gunnar Staalsett   Born February 10, 1935 in Nordkapp, northernmost Norway, he became the sixth LWF general secretary in 1985. A 1961 graduate of the Church of Norway Free Faculty of Theology, Oslo, his career has included a variety of posts in church and society: youth work, parish ministry (diocese of Hamar); lecturer (Stavanger School of Mission and Theology); general secretary, Norwegian Bible Society. Ecumenically, he has served on the WCC Central Committee and its executive committee. He has held offices as member of the Norwegian government and deputy to parliament and served on government commissions on disarmament and peace issues. He is a member of the Nobel Peace Prize Committee. Previous work on LWF commissions (Church Cooperation, Communication) has been good preparation for the task of general secretary.

LUTHERAN WORLD STATISTICS

The following figures were in most cases gathered in 1988. They give the baptized, or inclusive, membership of Lutheran churches, missions, and recognized congregations as reported to the LWF in Geneva. These figures appeared in *LW Information* 1/89.

General Summary		*1988*
Members of 105 LWF member churches and		
LWF recognized congregations		54,938,614
Lutherans outside LWF constituency		4,064,587
	Total	59,003,201

Continental Lutheran Membership	*All Lutherans*	*LWF Membership*
Europe	39,346,430	39,239,289
USA and Canada	8,790,907	5,496,633
Asia (inc. Middle East)	4,072,364	3,981,011
Africa	4,688,689	4,557,134
Latin America	1,240,133	914,047
Australia and Pacific	754,678	640,500
(Exile Churches)	110,000	110,000

Countries with more than 500,000 Lutherans

Fed. Rep. of Germany	12,221,400	Tanzania	1,301,013
USA	8,520,419	India	1,097,897
Sweden	7,700,000	Brazil	1,052,750
Denmark	4,624,155	Madagascar	840,000
Finland	4,617,672	Ethiopia	792,905
German Democratic		South Africa	711,160
Republic	3,960,550	Papua New Guinea	640,000
Norway	3,819,700	Namibia	577,154
Indonesia	2,780,582		

Lutheran Churches with more than 500,000 members

Church of Sweden	7,700,000
Evangelical Lutheran Church in America	5,288,230
Evangelical Lutheran Church in Denmark	4,624,000
Evangelical Lutheran Church of Finland	4,616,691
Church of Norway	3,800,000
Evangelical Lutheran Church of Hanover (FRG)	3,453,000
Lutheran Church–Missouri Synod (USA and Canada)	2,789,867

North Elbian Evangelical Lutheran Church (FRG)	2,656,000
Evangelical Lutheran Church in Bavaria (FRG)	2,561,000
Evangelical Lutheran Church in Württemberg (FRG)	2,392,000
Protestant Christian Batak Church (Indonesia)	2,000,000
Evangelical Lutheran Church of Saxony (GDR)	1,800,000
Evangelical Lutheran Church in Tanzania	1,301,013
Evangelical Lutheran Church in Thuringia (GDR)	1,000,000
Evangelical Church of the Lutheran Confession in Brazil	850,000
Malagasy Lutheran Church (Madagascar)	840,000
Ethiopian Evangelical Church Mekane Yesus	776,673
Evangelical Lutheran Church of Mecklenburg (GDR)	700,000
Evangelical Lutheran Church in Southern Africa (RSA)	552,000
Evangelical Lutheran Church of Papua New Guinea	545,500
Evangelical Lutheran Church in Brunswick (FRG)	505,000
Evangelical Lutheran Church in Oldenburg (FRG)	502,000

SELECTED BIBLIOGRAPHY—
An Informal Orientation

Besides the works already mentioned in the Preface, the following focus directly on the Lutheran theme. Titles in German, Swedish, and other languages collectively outnumber those in English. For ready orientation, those in English cover the Lutheran story from various angles.

The most complete, but now dated, account of Lutheran churches in the world is in *The Encyclopedia of the Lutheran Church* (Minneapolis: Augsburg, 1963, 3 vols.), edited by Julius Bodensieck. Turn here for individual accounts of churches in Europe and North America. Africa, Asia, and Latin America are treated in separate articles, with no comparable accounts of churches.

Two books present an overall Lutheran picture. Conrad Bergendoff's *The Church of the Lutheran Reformation* (St. Louis: Concordia, 1967) presents a popular and penetrating historical survey. *The Lutheran Church Past and Present* (Minneapolis: Augsburg, 1977), edited by Vilmos Vajta (long at the Institute for Ecumenical Research, Strasbourg), is a symposium of 17 international scholars. It takes the subject from the Reformation era to the present, with theological, confessional, and ecumenical considerations complementing the historical continuity.

Two other works recount the gathering together of the confessional family. Foremost is E. Clifford Nelson, *The Rise of World Lutheranism: An American Perspective* (Philadelphia: Fortress, 1982), a thoroughly researched and informative study of the Lutheran World Convention up to its transition in 1947 into the present Federation. Individual treatment of the churches in relation to the Federation appeared in: the *Lutheran Directory, 1963*, Part I: *Lutheran Churches of the World;* Part II: *The Lutheran World Federation* (Berlin: Lutherisches Verlagshaus, 1963)—in German and English editions, but now out of print. Annually, however, a short form of the *Lutheran Directory* has been published by the LWF in Geneva, bringing updated particulars about the member churches and the Federation, and appearing alternately in English and German editions. A statistical summary of Lutheran churches worldwide comes out each year in *LW Information* releases (the first or last number of a given year). See above for the latest (1988 release) summary.

Other works of value on this global subject have appeared in connection with periodic gatherings of the Convention or the Federation. These include: *The Lutheran Churches of the World* (Minneapolis: Augsburg, 1929), edited by Alfred Th. Jørgensen, Paul Fleisch, and Abdel Ross Wentz; a book by the same title, edited by Wentz (Geneva: LWF, 1952), which included early postwar reports from various countries and churches; and again, *Lutheran Churches of the World* (Minneapolis: Augsburg, 1957), edited by Carl E. Lund-Quist, with essays by specialists covering seven world areas. E. Theodore Bachmann's *Epic of Faith: The Background of the Second Assembly* (New York: National Lutheran Council, 1952) was the first post-World War II summary of Lutherans the world over and the way they were drawing together.

The inclusive reference work, *Lutheran Mission Directory*, by Mercia Brenne Bachmann (Geneva: LWF, 2nd ed., 1982, 421 pp.) is the single most helpful resource for showing the interrelatedness of Lutheran endeavors worldwide, including those ecumenically linked.

LCW—Bibliography

Monographs on Lutherans working together include a variety of informative and well researched volumes. *Mission and Unity in Lutheranism* (Philadelphia: Fortress, 1969), by

James A. Scherer, is a perceptive account by a recognized missiologist. *As Between Brothers: The Story of Lutheran Response to World Need* (Minneapolis: Augsburg, 1957), by Richard W. Solberg, recounts the way concern for people drew Lutherans into global patterns of service from the 1920s onward. Compare this with a later and quite differently oriented account, *The Politics of Altruism* (Geneva: LWF Department of Studies, 1977), by Jørgen Lissner. Kurt Schmidt-Clausen's recent history of the Lutheran World Convention (Volume II in *Die Lutherische Kirche in Geschichte und Gestalt,* 1976, below) is a factual coverage by a theologically interested historian. The work by the Swedish scholar, Bengt Wadensjö, *Toward a World Lutheran Communion* (Uppsala: Verbum, 1976) takes the LWC story to 1929 and depicts some inter-Lutheran struggles in the process. In German, Siegfried Grundmann's *Der Lutherische Weltbund* (Köln/Graz: Böhlau, 1957), is a thorough, standard work. In Swedish, Lars Österlin's edition of *Nordisk Lutherdom Över Gränserna* (Stockholm: 1972) supplies the often overlooked efforts by Lutherans in Northern Europe to coordinate their own efforts and to reach out.

A quite different account, mainly historical, is volume one of the two-volume work, *Die Lutherische Kirche in Geschichte und Gestalt* (Gütersloher Velagshaus Gerd Mohn, 1976), which recounts many of the efforts toward unity among Lutherans, from the Reformation to the 1920s. A concluding section by Gottfried Klapper treats Lutheran churches throughout the world individually (much like the Lutheran Directory 1963, above).

Recent accounts of the churches in the USA and Canada include the basic work, *Lutherans in North America* (Philadelphia: Fortress, 1975), edited by E. Clifford Nelson. *Lutherans in Concert* (Minneapolis: Augsburg, 1968), by Frederick K. Wentz, tells the story of the National Lutheran Council, 1918–1966, including its international role. Many other works could be cited, especially those dealing with the churches in other lands. *An African Church Is Born* (Viby, Denmark: c/o Danish Missionary Society, 1968), by Margaret Nissen, depicts in detail the beginnings of the Lutheran Church of Christ in Nigeria. Similarly, *Batak Blood and Protestant Spirit* (Grand Rapids: Eerdmans, 1970), by Paul B. Pedersen, penetrates ground unfamiliar to most Westerners.

The centennial volume, *The Lutheran Church in Papua New Guinea* (Adelaide: Lutheran Publishing House, 1986, 677 pp.), edited by Herwig Wagner and Hermann Reiner—in English and German editions—is a model of comprehensive coverage by a team including the ELC/PNG's first bishop, John Kuder.

However, the need for the churches to tell their own story is especially urgent in Asia, Africa, and Latin America. (See H. W. Gensichen's article on this subject in LW 4/76.) Steps toward this end are already under way. In Indonesia, for example, self-studies by the churches have been published (LW 1/77). The ecclesiology study, sponsored by the LWF Department of Studies has published 35 reports of self-studies in 46 churches, plus a summary and interpretation in *The Identity of the Church and Its Service to the Whole Human Being* (Geneva: LWF/Studies, Final Vols. I and II, 1977).

Other source materials—too numerous to be named here—include such varied items as the *Proceedings* of the several LWF assemblies, the pre-assembly reports by commissions/departments, the church description drawn up by staff members in connection with projects of the Department of Church Cooperation, by Community Development Service, and the like. In addition each LWF member church is annually expected to turn in a report on recent developments in its own life and work. Reports of All-Africa, All-Asia, and other regional conferences provide valuable input. Finally, the *Lutheran World,* 1954–1977, was an important source on churches in the world and the issues they face.

INDEX OF LUTHERAN CHURCHES/ORGANIZATIONS (BY ENGLISH NAME)

INDEX OF COUNTRIES